Fodor's 98

Mexico

The complete guide, thoroughly up-to-date

Packed with details that will make your trip

The must-see sights, off and on the beaten path

What to see, what to skip

Mix-and-match vacation itineraries

City strolls, countryside adventures

Smart lodging and dining options

Essential local do's and taboos

Transportation tips, distances and directions

Key contacts, savvy travel tips

When to go, what to pack

Clear, accurate, easy-to-use maps

Fodor's Travel Publications, Inc.
New York • Toronto • London • Sydney • Auckland
www.fodors.com/

Fodor's Mexico

EDITOR: Deborah Field Washburn

Editorial Contributors: Patricia Alisau, Robert Andrews, Trudy Balch, David Brown, Christina Knight, Wendy Luft, Maribeth Mellin, Dan Millington, Jane Onstott, Kate Rice, Heidi Sarna, Helayne Schiff, M. T. Schwartzman (Gold Guide editor), Susana Sedgwick, Dinah A. Spritzer, Melanie Young

Editorial Production: Janet Foley

Maps: David Lindroth, *cartographer;* Steven K. Amsterdam, *map editor*

Design: Fabrizio La Rocca, *creative director;* Guido Caroti, *associate art director;* Jolie Novak, *photo editor*

Production/Manufacturing: Rebecca Zeiler

Cover Photograph: Joan Iaconetti

Copyright

ISBN 0-679-03496-X

Special Sales

Fodor's Travel Publications are available at special discounts for bulk purchases for sales promotions or premiums. Special editions, including personalized covers, excerpts of existing guides, and corporate imprints, can be created in large quantities for special needs. For more information, contact your local bookseller or write to Special Markets, Fodor's Travel Publications, 201 East 50th Street, New York, NY 10022. Inquiries from Canada should be directed to your local Canadian bookseller or sent to Random House of Canada, Ltd., Marketing Department, 1265 Aerowood Drive, Mississaugua, Ontario L4W 1B9. Inquiries from the United Kingdom should be sent to Fodor's Travel Publications, 20 Vauxhall Bridge Road, London SW1 2SA, England.

PRINTED IN THE UNITED STATES OF AMERICA

10 9 8 7 6 5 4 3 2 1

CONTENTS

ON THE ROAD WITH FODOR'S

WE'RE ALWAYS THRILLED to get letters from readers, especially one like this:

It took us an hour to decide what book to buy and we now know we picked the best one. Your book was wonderful, easy to follow, very accurate, and good on pointing out eating places, informal as well as formal. When we saw other people using your book, we would look at each other and smile.

Our editors and writers are deeply committed to making every Fodor's guide "the best one"—not only accurate but always charming, brimming with sound recommendations and solid ideas, right on the mark in describing restaurants and hotels, and full of fascinating facts that make you view what you've traveled to see in a rich new light.

About Our Writers

Our success in achieving our goals—and in helping to make your trip the best of all possible vacations—is a credit to the hard work of our extraordinary writers.

A psychologist-turned-journalist and archaeology buff, **Patricia Alisau** updated the Chiapas and Tabasco, Northeastern Mexico and Veracruz, and Mexico City chapters of this book. She was so drawn to the surrealism of Mexico City—"Where in the U.S. can you find pyramids?" she asks—that she moved to the capital; what began as a one-week vacation became a 20-year sojourn. She was restaurant-and-nightclub columnist for the *News,* Mexico's English-language daily, and has written for Mexico's *Vogue* magazine.

Guadalajara updater **Trudy Balch** has been a Tapatía (as residents of the city are called) *in absentia* since the early 1990s, when a stint as a newspaper reporter there sent her scouring Guadalajara for stories. Now based in New York City, she writes about travel and business in Mexico and other Latin American countries and spends her spare time searching for good birria and mariachi music.

When she was fresh out of college, our Acapulco and Pacific Coast Resorts correspondent, **Wendy Luft,** jumped at the chance to take a job with the Mexican tourist office—for a year or two at most, she figured. Some 25 years later, she and her Mexican husband and their adolescent sons, inveterate travelers all, traverse the country together from their home base in Mexico City. As a writer, editor, and public relations representative, Wendy has written and collaborated on many travel books and articles about her adopted country. In 1997 she won the *Pluma de Plata,* an award from the Mexican government, for an article on Oaxaca that appeared in *Journeys.*

Maribeth Mellin, our longtime Baja California updater, covers Mexico for *San Diego Magazine.* She writes in an office filled with photos and artifacts from Mexico's two isolated peninsulas, including a snapshot of the 140-pound marlin she caught in the Sea of Cortés. She refused to marry her husband (who'd been traveling to Baja for over 20 years) until he rambled through her beloved Yucatán with her in a rented VW bug. She finally said "yes" en route to Chichén Itzá while humming the Mexican ballad "Amor," which became their wedding song.

A freelance writer and photographer based in Laguna Beach, California, **Dan Millington** has worked extensively in Mexico and is familiar with many regions of the country. This past year he traveled to Cancún, Cozumel, and Isla Mujeres for Fodor's.

Jane Onstott was primed for adventure travel in her late teens, when she wandered Honduras for six months after being stood up at the airport by an inattentive suitor. A stoic if inefficient traveler, she has since survived a near plunge into a gorge in the highlands of Mexico, a knife-wielding robber in Madrid, and a financial shipwreck on one of the more remote Galápagos islands. In between trips all over Latin America, she lives in Oaxaca, where she studies painting. She updated the Oaxaca and Heartland chapters.

It was the silver jewelry her aunt brought back from Mazatlán that hooked **Kate Rice,** who wrote the introduction to this book, on Mexico. During a summer spent in the country in a vain attempt to improve her Spanish, she fell hard for its art and cuisine—especially the mangoes dipped in hot sauce sold on the street corners of Guadalajara. For the past few years, Kate has been covering Mexico for publications including *Tour & Travel News* and *Business Traveler International.*

Susana Sedgwick, who updated the Sonora chapter, grew up with the sounds of Sonora echoing just over the fence from where she lived with her family in Nogales, Arizona. It wasn't long before the land of fiesta and siesta drew her ever deeper into Mexico's regional history, mysteries, and cultural traditions. She's an elected member of the Explorer's Club in New York and a fellow of the Royal Geographical Society in London.

A writer and travel photographer based in San Antonio, **Melanie Young** has been reporting on Mexico for more than 10 years. In 1995 she won the prestigious *Pluma de Plata* for a story on the Copper Canyon that appeared in *Tour & Travel News*. She also contributes regularly to *Modern Bride* and the *San Antonio Express-News*. To update the Copper Canyon chapter, she took the fabled train ride and marveled once again at the spectacular scenery.

We'd also like to acknowledge Burson-Marsteller and Aeromexico for their assistance with travel arrangements.

New This Year

This year, Fodor's joins Rand McNally, the world's largest commercial mapmaker, to bring you a detailed color map of Mexico. Just detach it along the perforation and drop it in your tote bag.

On the Web, check out Fodor's site (http://www.fodors.com/) for information on major destinations around the world and travel-savvy interactive features. The Web site also lists the 80-plus radio stations nationwide that carry the Fodor's Travel Show, a live call-in program that airs every weekend. Tune in to hear guests discuss their wonderful adventures—or call in to get answers for your most pressing travel questions.

How to Use This Book

Organization

Up front is the **Gold Guide,** an easy-to-use section divided alphabetically by topic. Under each listing you'll find tips and information that will help you accomplish what you need to in Mexico. You'll also find addresses and telephone numbers of organizations and companies that offer destination-related services and detailed information and publications.

The first chapter in the book—Destination: Mexico—helps get you in the mood for your trip. New and Noteworthy cues you in on trends and happenings, What's Where gets you oriented, Pleasures and Pastimes describes the activities and sights that make Mexico unique, Fodor's Choice showcases our top picks, and Festivals and Seasonal Events alerts you to special events you'll want to seek out.

Chapters in Fodor's *Mexico '98* are arranged geographically. We take you first to Mexico City, the capital and main transportation hub, and then move from the northwest (Baja California) to the southeast (the Yucatán Peninsula), heading roughly north to south along the two coasts. Each city chapter begins with an Exploring section subdivided by neighborhood; each subsection recommends a walking or driving tour and lists sights in alphabetical order. Each regional chapter is divided by geographical area; within each area, towns are covered in logical geographical order, and attractive stretches of road and minor points of interest between them are indicated by the designation *En Route*. Throughout, Off the Beaten Path sights appear after the places from which they are most easily accessible. And within town sections, all restaurants and lodgings are grouped together.

To help you decide what to visit in the time you have, most chapters begin with recommended itineraries; you can mix and match those from several chapters to create a complete vacation. The A to Z section that ends all chapters covers getting there and getting around. It also provides helpful contacts and resources.

In the last chapter you'll find a detailed list of important events in Mexico's history, followed by suggestions for any pretrip reading you want to do. At the end of the book there's a Spanish Vocabulary to help you learn a few basics.

Icons and Symbols

- ★ Our special recommendations
- ✕ Restaurant
- 🏨 Lodging establishment
- ✕🏨 Lodging establishment whose restaurant warrants a special trip
- 🦆 Good for kids (rubber duckie)
- ☞ Sends you to another section of the guide for more information
- ✉ Address
- ☎ Telephone number
- ⏲ Opening and closing times
- 🎟 Admission prices (those we give apply to adults; substantially reduced fees are almost always available for children, students, and senior citizens)

Numbers in white and black circles that appear on the maps, in the margins, and within the tours correspond to one another.

Dining and Lodging

The restaurants and lodgings we list are the cream of the crop in each price range. Price charts appear in the Pleasures and Pastimes section that follows each chapter introduction.

Hotel Facilities

We always list the facilities that are available—but we don't specify whether they cost extra: When pricing accommodations, always ask what's included. In addition, assume that all rooms have private baths unless otherwise noted.

Assume that hotels operate on the **European Plan** (EP, with no meals) unless we note that they use the **Continental Plan** (CP, with a Continental breakfast daily), **Modified American Plan** (MAP, with breakfast and dinner daily), or are **all-inclusive** (all meals and most activities).

Reservations are always a good idea; we note only when they're essential or when they are not accepted. Book as far ahead as you can, and reconfirm when you get to town. Unless otherwise noted, the restaurants listed are open daily for lunch and dinner. We mention dress only when men are required to wear a jacket or a jacket and tie. Look for an overview of local habits in the Gold Guide and in the Pleasures and Pastimes section that follows each chapter introduction.

Credit Cards

The following abbreviations are used: **AE,** American Express; **DC,** Diners Club; **MC,** MasterCard; and **V,** Visa.

Please Write to Us

You can use this book in the confidence that all prices and opening times are based on information supplied to us at press time; Fodor's cannot accept responsibility for any errors. Time inevitably brings changes, so always confirm information when it matters—especially if you're making a detour to visit a specific place. In addition, when making reservations be sure to mention if you have a disability or are traveling with children, if you prefer a private bath or a certain type of bed, or if you have specific dietary needs or other concerns.

Were the restaurants we recommended as described? Did our hotel picks exceed your expectations? Did you find a museum we recommended a waste of time? If you have complaints, we'll look into them and revise our entries when the facts warrant it. If you've discovered a special place that we haven't included, we'll pass the information along to our correspondents and have them check it out. So send us your feedback, positive *and* negative: e-mail us at editors@fodors.com (specifying the name of the book on the subject line) or write the *Mexico '98* editor at Fodor's, 201 East 50th Street, New York, New York 10022. Have a wonderful trip!

Karen Cure
Editorial Director

Mexico

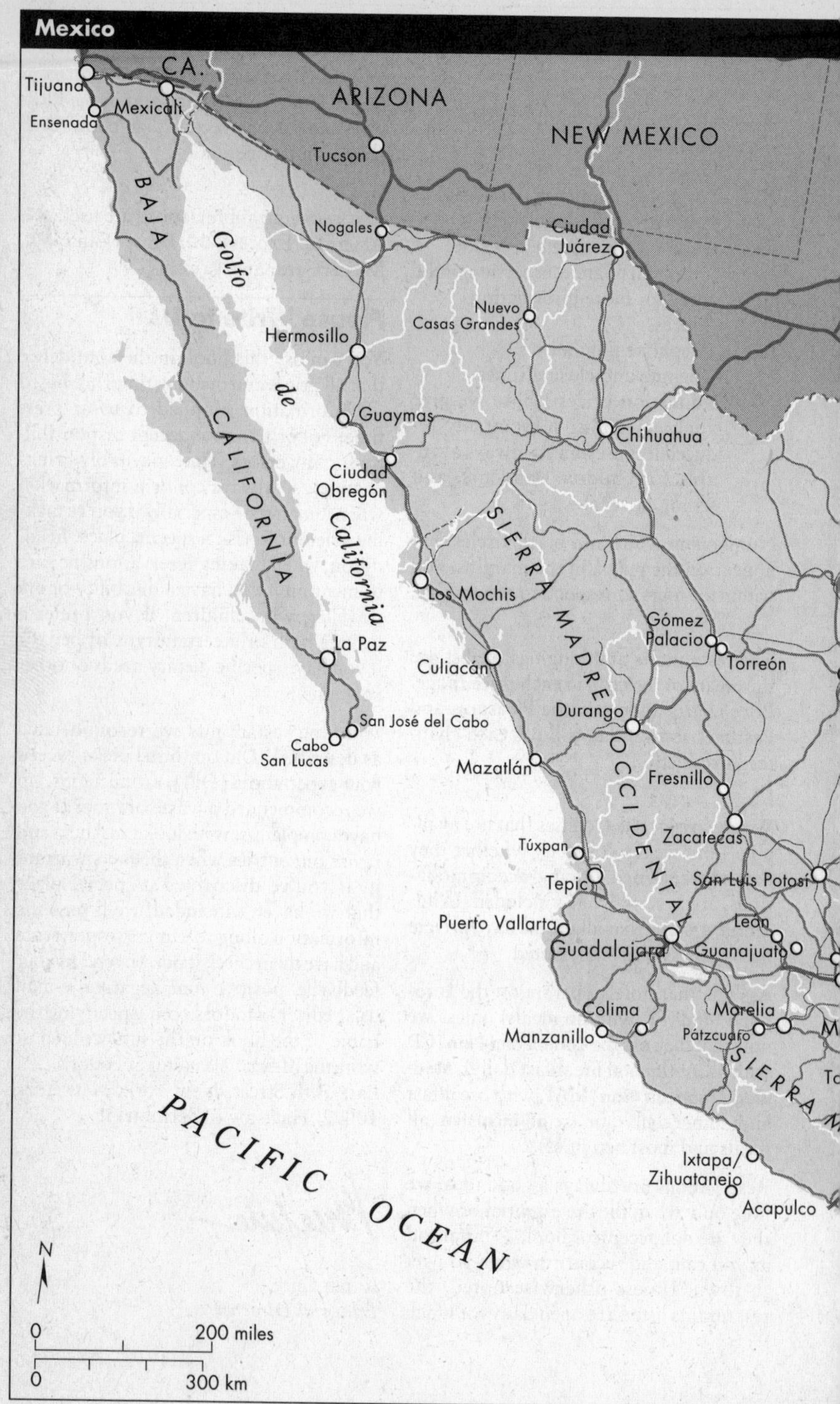

CA.
Tijuana
Mexicali
Ensenada
ARIZONA
NEW MEXICO
Tucson
BAJA
Golfo
de
CALIFORNIA
California
Nogales
Ciudad Juárez
Nuevo Casas Grandes
Hermosillo
Guaymas
Chihuahua
Ciudad Obregón
SIERRA MADRE OCCIDENTAL
Los Mochis
La Paz
Culiacán
Gómez Palacio
Torreón
San José del Cabo
Cabo San Lucas
Durango
Mazatlán
Fresnillo
Zacatecas
Túxpan
Tepic
San Luis Potosí
Puerto Vallarta
León
Guadalajara
Guanajuato
Colima
Morelia
Manzanillo
Pátzcuaro
SIERRA
Ixtapa/ Zihuatanejo
Acapulco
PACIFIC OCEAN
N
0
200 miles
0
300 km

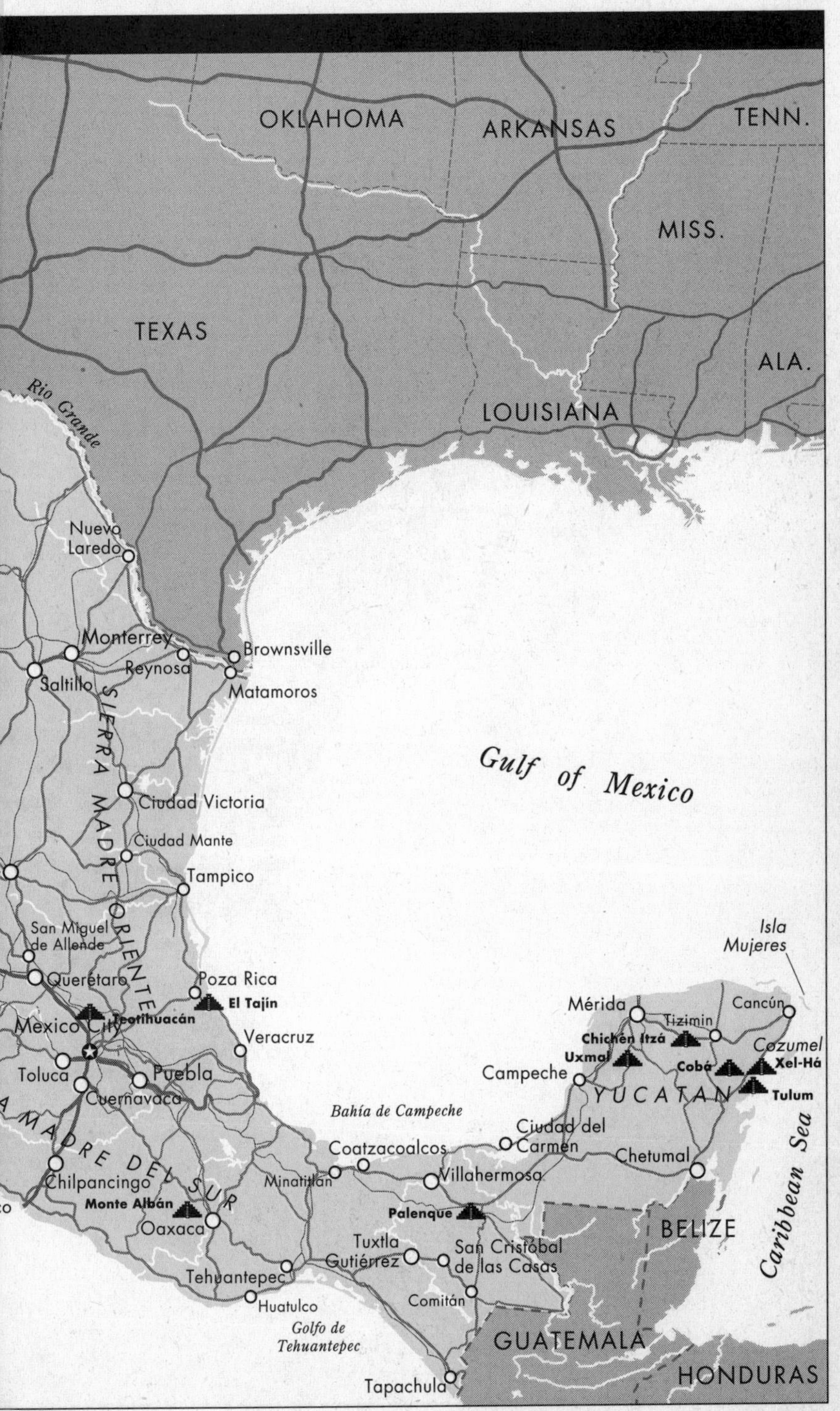
OKLAHOMA
ARKANSAS
TENN.
MISS.
TEXAS
ALA.
LOUISIANA
Rio Grande
Nuevo Laredo
Monterrey
Brownsville
Reynosa
Saltillo
Matamoros
SIERRA MADRE ORIENTE
Gulf of Mexico
Ciudad Victoria
Ciudad Mante
Tampico
San Miguel de Allende
Querétaro
Poza Rica
El Tajín
Teotihuacán
Mexico City
Veracruz
Toluca
Puebla
Cuernavaca
Isla Mujeres
Mérida
Cancún
Tizimin
Chichén Itzá
Cozumel
Uxmal
Cobá
Xel-Há
Campeche
YUCATAN
Tulum
Bahía de Campeche
Ciudad del Carmen
Coatzacoalcos
Chetumal
Minatitlán
Villahermosa
Chilpancingo
SIERRA MADRE DEL SUR
Monte Albán
Palenque
BELIZE
Caribbean Sea
Oaxaca
Tuxtla Gutiérrez
San Cristóbal de las Casas
Tehuantepec
Huatulco
Comitán
Golfo de Tehuantepec
GUATEMALA
HONDURAS
Tapachula

Mexican States and Capitals

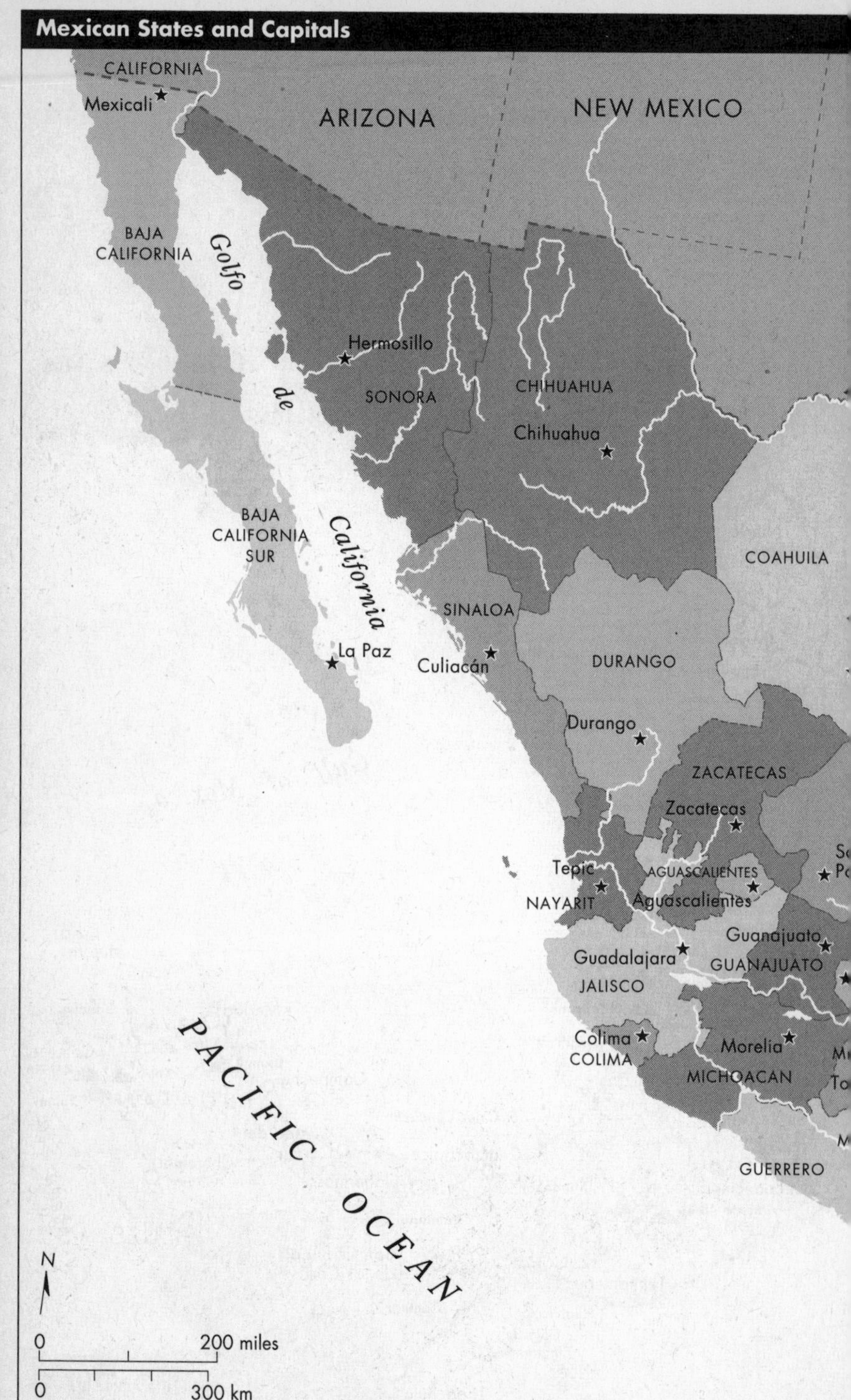

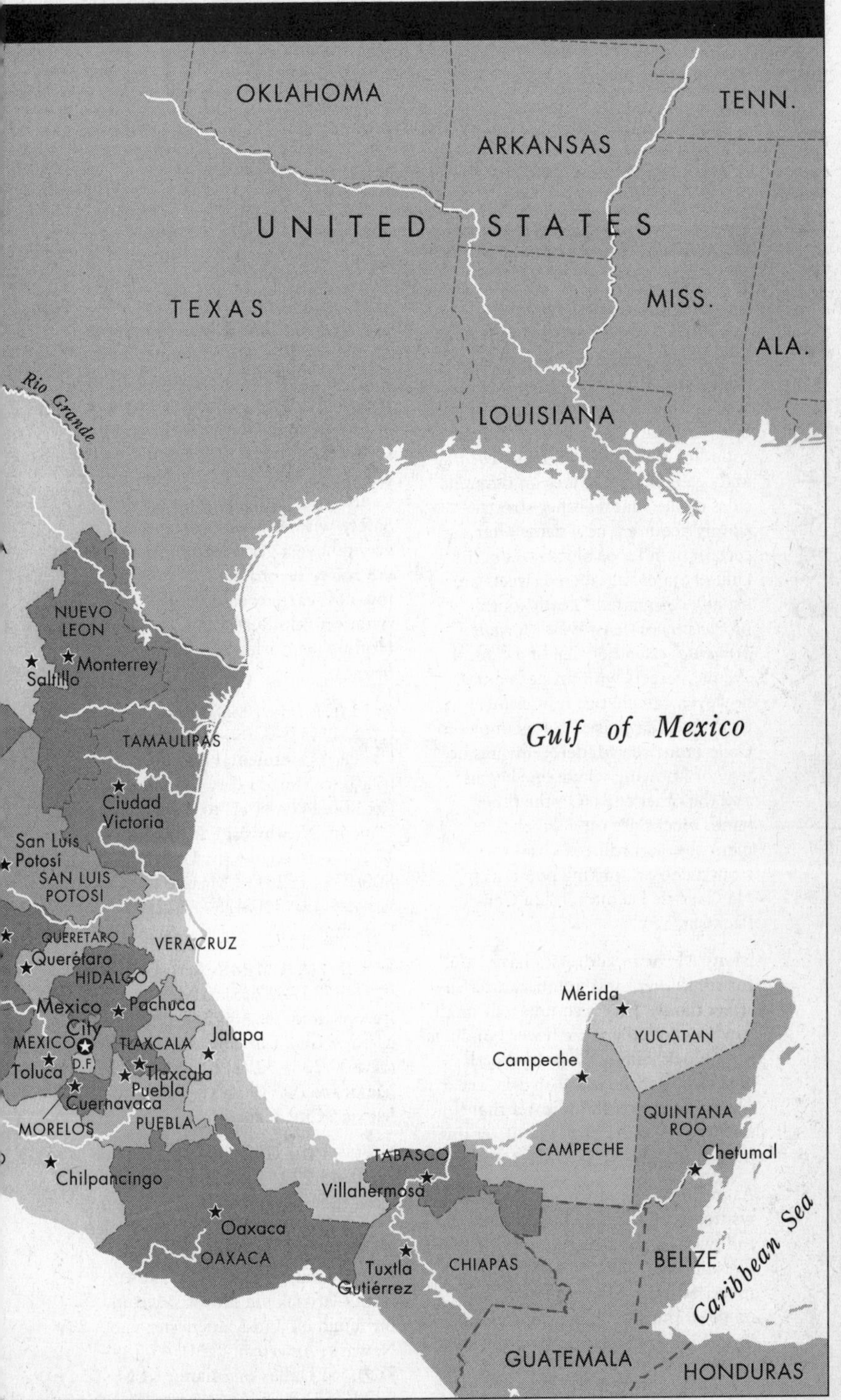
OKLAHOMA
TENN.
ARKANSAS
UNITED STATES
TEXAS
MISS.
ALA.
Rio Grande
LOUISIANA
NUEVO LEON
Monterrey
Saltillo
TAMAULIPAS
Gulf of Mexico
Ciudad Victoria
San Luis Potosí
SAN LUIS POTOSI
QUERETARO
VERACRUZ
Querétaro
HIDALGO
Mérida
Mexico City
Pachuca
YUCATAN
MEXICO
TLAXCALA
Jalapa
D.F.
Campeche
Toluca
Tlaxcala
Puebla
Cuernavaca
QUINTANA ROO
MORELOS
PUEBLA
TABASCO
CAMPECHE
Chetumal
Chilpancingo
Villahermosa
Oaxaca
Caribbean Sea
OAXACA
Tuxtla Gutiérrez
CHIAPAS
BELIZE
GUATEMALA
HONDURAS

SMART TRAVEL TIPS A TO Z

Basic Information on Traveling in Mexico, Savvy Tips to Make Your Trip a Breeze, and Companies and Organizations to Contact

A

ADDRESSES

The Mexican method of naming streets is exasperatingly arbitrary, so **be patient when searching for street addresses.** Streets in the centers of many colonial cities (those built by the Spaniards) are laid out in a grid surrounding the main square, or *zócalo,* and often change names on different sides of the square; other streets simply acquire a new name after a certain number of blocks. As in the United States, numbered streets are usually designated "north/south" (*norte/sur*) or "east/west" (*oriente/poniente*) on either side of a central avenue. Streets with proper names, however, can change mysteriously from Avenida Juárez, for example, to Calle Francisco Madero; one has no way of knowing where one begins and the other ends. On the other hand, blocks are often labeled numerically, according to distance from a chosen starting point, as in "la Calle de Pachuca," "2a Calle de Pachuca," etc.

Many Mexican addresses have "s/n" for *sin número* (no number) after the street name. This is common in small towns where there are fewer buildings on a block. Similarly, many hotels give their address as "Km 30 Carr. a Querétaro," which indicates that the property is at the 30th kilometer on the main highway to Querétaro.

As in Europe, addresses in Mexico are written with the street name first, followed by the street number. The five-digit zip code (*código postal*) precedes, rather than follows, the name of the city. Apdo. (*apartado*) Postal, or A.P., means post office box number.

AIR TRAVEL

MAJOR AIRLINE OR LOW-COST CARRIER?

Most people choose a flight based on price. Yet there are other issues to consider. Major airlines offer the greatest number of departures; smaller airlines—including regional, low-cost, and no-frills carriers—usually have a more limited number of flights daily. Major airlines have frequent-flyer partners, which allows you to credit mileage earned on one airline to your account with another. Low-cost airlines offer a definite price advantage and fewer restrictions, such as advance-purchase requirements. Safety-wise, low-cost carriers as a group have a good history, but **check the safety record** before booking any low-cost carrier; call the Federal Aviation Administration's Consumer Hotline (☞ Airline Complaints, *below*).

➤ MAJOR AIRLINES: **American** (☎ 800/433–7300) to Mexico City, Cancún. **Continental** (☎ 800/525–0280) to Mexico City, Cancún. **Delta** (☎ 800/241–4141) to Mexico City, Cancún. **Northwest** (☎ 800/447–4747) to Mexico City. **United** (☎ 800/538–2929) to Mexico City. **US Airways** (☎ 800/428–4322) to Cancún.

➤ SMALLER AIRLINES: **Aero California** (☎ 800/237–6225) to Mexico City. **Aeromexico** (☎ 800/237–6639) to Mexico City, Cancún. **America West** (☎ 800/235–9292) to Mexico City. **Mexicana** (☎ 800/531–7921) to Mexico City, Cancún.

➤ FROM THE U.K.: **British Airways** (☎ 0345/222–111) has a direct flight from the United Kingdom to Mexico City. Other airlines flying to Mexico, with brief stops en route, include **Continental** (☎ 0800/776–464), from Gatwick via Houston, from Birmingham and Manchester via Newark; **American** (☎ 0345/789–789), via Dallas or Miami; **KLM** (☎ 0990/750–900), via Amsterdam; **Air France** (☎ 0181/742–6600), via Paris; **Delta** (☎ 0800/414–767), via Atlanta; **United** (☎ 0800/888–555), via Chicago or Washington, Dulles;

Lufthansa (☎ 0345/737–747), via Frankfurt; and **Iberia** (☎ 0171/830–0011), via Madrid.

GET THE LOWEST FARE

The least-expensive airfares to Mexico are priced for round-trip travel. Major airlines usually require that you book far in advance and stay at least seven days and no more than 30 to get the lowest fares. Always **ask about "ultrasaver" fares,** which are the cheapest; they must be booked 90 days in advance and are nonrefundable. A little more expensive are "supersaver" fares, which require only a 30-day advance purchase. Remember that penalties for refunds or scheduling changes are stiffer for international tickets, usually about $150. International flights are also sensitive to the season: **plan to fly in the off season** for the cheapest fares. If your destination or home city has more than one gateway, **compare prices to and from different airports.** Also price flights scheduled for off-peak hours, which may be significantly less expensive.

To save money on flights from the United Kingdom and back, **look into an APEX or Super-PEX ticket.** Both should be booked in advance and have certain restrictions, though they can sometimes be purchased right at the airport.

DON'T STOP UNLESS YOU MUST

When you book, **look for nonstop flights** and **remember that "direct" flights stop at least once.** International flights on a country's flag carrier are almost always nonstop; U.S. airlines often fly direct. Try to **avoid connecting flights,** which require a change of plane. Two airlines may jointly operate a connecting flight, so ask if your airline operates every segment—you may find that your preferred carrier flies you only part of the way.

USE AN AGENT

Travel agents, especially those who specialize in finding the lowest fares (☞ Discounts & Deals, *below*), can be especially helpful when booking a plane ticket. When you're quoted a price, **ask your agent if the price is likely to get any lower.** Good agents know the seasonal fluctuations of airfares and can usually anticipate a sale or fare war. However, waiting can be risky: The fare could go *up* as seats become scarce, and you may wait so long that your preferred flight sells out. A wait-and-see strategy works best if your plans are flexible, but if you must arrive and depart on certain dates, don't delay.

CHECK WITH CONSOLIDATORS

Consolidators buy tickets for scheduled flights at reduced rates from the airlines then sell them at prices that beat the best fare available directly from the airlines, usually without advance restrictions. Sometimes you can even get your money back if you need to return the ticket. Carefully read the fine print detailing penalties for changes and cancellations, and **confirm your consolidator reservation with the airline.**

➤ CONSOLIDATORS: **United States Air Consolidators Association** (✉ 925 L St., Suite 220, Sacramento, CA 95814, ☎ 916/441–4166, FAX 916/441–3520).

CONSIDER A CHARTER

Charters usually have the lowest fares but are not dependable. Departures are infrequent and seldom on time, flights can be delayed for up to 48 hours or can be canceled for any reason up to 10 days before you're scheduled to leave. Itineraries and prices can change after you've booked your flight, so you must **be very careful to choose a legitimate charter carrier.** Don't commit to a charter operator that doesn't follow proper booking procedures. Be especially careful when buying a charter ticket. Read the fine print regarding refund policies. If you can't pay with a credit card, **make your check payable to a charter carrier's escrow account** (unless you're dealing with a travel agent, in which case his or her check should be made payable to the escrow account). The name of the bank should be in the charter contract.

AVOID GETTING BUMPED

Airlines routinely overbook planes, knowing that not everyone with a ticket will show up, but sometimes everyone does. When that happens, airlines ask for volunteers to give up their seats. In return these volunteers usually get a certificate for a free flight and are rebooked on the next flight out. If there are not enough volunteers the airline must choose who will be denied boarding. The first to get bumped are passengers who checked in late and those flying on discounted tickets, so **get to the gate and check in as early as possible,** especially during peak periods.

Always **bring a photo ID to the airport.** You may be asked to show it before you are allowed to check in.

ENJOY THE FLIGHT

For better service, **fly smaller or regional carriers,** which often have higher passenger-satisfaction ratings. Sometimes you'll find leather seats, more legroom, and better food.

For more legroom, **request an emergency-aisle seat**; don't however, sit in the row in front of the emergency aisle or in front of a bulkhead, where seats may not recline.

If you don't like airline food, **ask for special meals when booking.** These can be vegetarian, low-cholesterol, or kosher, for example.

Some carriers have prohibited smoking throughout their systems; others allow smoking only on certain routes or even certain departures from that route, so **contact your carrier regarding its smoking policy.**

➤ FLYING TIME: Mexico City is 4½ hours from New York, 4 hours from Chicago, and 3½ hours from Los Angeles. Cancún is 3½ hours from New York and from Chicago, 4½ hours from Los Angeles. Acapulco is 6 hours from New York, 4 hours from Chicago, and 3½ hours from Los Angeles.

COMPLAIN IF NECESSARY

If your baggage goes astray or your flight goes awry, complain right away. Most carriers require that you file a claim immediately.

➤ AIRLINE COMPLAINTS: U.S. Department of Transportation **Aviation Consumer Protection Division** (✉ C-75, Washington, DC 20590, ☎ 202/366–2220). **Federal Aviation Administration (FAA) Consumer Hotline** (☎ 800/322–7873).

WITHIN MEXICO

Mexicana and Aeromexico provide the bulk of air service within Mexico, and regional airlines have filled in most of the gaps.

➤ DOMESTIC AIRLINES: **Aerocaribe** (reserve through Mexicana) serves the Yucatán and the Southeast. **Aeromar** (reserve through Mexicana or Aeromexico) serves central Mexico. **Aerolitoral** (reserve through Aeromexico or Mexicana) serves northeastern Mexico. **Aeroponiente** (reserve through Aeromexico) serves southwestern Mexico. **Aviacsa** (☎ 961/2–80–81 in Chiapas; 5/559–1955 in Mexico City) serves Cancún, Chetumal, and Mérida. **AeroCalifornia** (☎ 800/237–6225) serves Colima, Guadalajara, Loreto, Los Mochis, Puebla, Tepic, Tijuana, and several other gateways.

➤ MAJOR AIRPORTS: Acapulco (**General Juan Alvarez airport,** ☎ 748/40887). Cancún (**Cancún airport,** ☎ 981/42239). Cozumel (**Cozumel airport,** ☎ 987/20485). Guadalajara (**Don Miguel Hidalgo airport,** ☎ 36/89–00–24). Ixtapa (**Ixtapa/Zihuatanejo airport,** ☎ 473/42070). Mazatlán (**General Rafael Buena airport,** ☎ 678/24–87–42). Mérida (**Licenciado Manuel Crescencio Rejon airport,** ☎ 99/24–87–42). Mexico City (**Benito Juarez airport,** ☎ 5/571–3600). **Puerto Vallarta** (☎ 322/21298). San José (**Los Cabos airport,** ☎ 684/30341).

B

BUS TRAVEL

Gateway cities such as El Paso, Del Rio, Laredo, McAllen, Brownsville, and San Antonio, Texas, along with Tijuana, are served by several small private bus lines as well as by **Greyhound Lines** (☎ 800/231–2222). If you'll be leaving Mexico by bus, you can buy tickets for the U.S. leg of your trip from the Greyhound representative in Mexico City (✉ Amores 707, Suite 102, ☎ 5/669–12–87 or 5/669–09–86).

WITHIN MEXICO

Getting to Mexico by bus is no longer for just the adventurous or budget-conscious. In the past, bus travelers were required to change to Mexican vehicles at the border, and vice versa. Now, however, in an effort to bring more American visitors and their tourist dollars to off-the-beaten-track markets and attractions, the Mexican government has removed this obstacle and a growing number of trans-border bus tours are available.

For travel within Mexico, buses run the gamut from comfortable air-conditioned coaches with bathrooms, televisions, and hostess service (premier, deluxe, or first class) to dilapidated "vintage" buses (second and third class) on which pigs and chickens travel and stops are made in the middle of nowhere. While a lower-class bus ride can be interesting if you are not in a hurry and want to see the sights and experience the local culture, these fares are only about 10% to 20% lower than those in the premium categories. Therefore, travelers planning a long-distance haul are well advised to **buy tickets for first class or better when traveling by bus within Mexico**; unlike tickets for the other classes, these can be reserved in advance.

The Mexican bus network is extensive, far more so than that of the railroads. Buses go where trains do not, service is more frequent, tickets can be purchased on the spot (except during holidays and on long weekends, when advance purchase is crucial), and first-class buses are faster and much more comfortable than trains. On all overnight bus rides, **bring something to eat** in case you don't like the restaurant where the bus stops, and **carry toilet tissue,** as rest rooms vary in cleanliness. Smoking is prohibited on a growing number of Mexican buses, though the rule is occasionally ignored.

In large cities, bus stations are a good distance from the center of town. Though there's a trend toward consolidation, some towns have different stations for each bus line. Bus service in Mexico City is well organized, operating out of four terminals.

➤ BEST FIRST-CLASS BUS LINES: ADO (☎ 5/542–7192 or 5/542–7193) serves Yucatán, Cancún, Villahermosa, and Veracruz from the Eastern Bus Terminal (known by its Spanish acronym, TAPO), and Oaxaca and Tampico from the Northern Bus Terminal (*Terminal Central Autobuses del Norte*) (☎ 5/567–6247). **ADO GL** (☎ 5/719–9600) leaves from the same terminals and offers deluxe service to the same destinations. **Cristóbal Colón** (☎ 5/756–9926) goes to Chiapas, Oaxaca, Puebla, and the Guatemala border from the Eastern Bus Terminal. **Estrella Blanca** (☎ 5/729–0707) goes to Manzanillo, Mazatlan, Monterrey, and Nuevo Laredo from the Western Bus Terminal (*Terminal Central Poniente*). **ETN** (☎ 5/273–0251) goes to Acapulco, Mazatlán, and Morelia from the Western Bus Terminal. **Estrella de Oro** (☎ 5/689–3955) goes to Acapulco, Cuernavaca, Taxco, and Ixtapa from the Western Bus Terminal.

BUSINESS HOURS

Banks are generally open weekdays 9 to 1:30. In larger cities, most are open until 5:30 or 6. Many of the larger banks keep a few branches open Saturday 9 to 2:30 and Sunday 10 to 1:30; however, the extended hours are often for deposits or check cashing only. Banks will give you cash advances in pesos (for a fee) if you have a major credit card.

Government offices are usually open to the public 8 to 3; along with banks and most private offices, they are closed on national holidays.

Along with **theaters** and most **archaeological zones, museums** close on Monday, with few exceptions.

Stores are generally open weekdays and Saturday from 9 or 10 AM to 7 or 8 PM; in resort areas, shops may also be open on Sunday. Business hours are 9 to 7, with a two-hour lunch break (siesta) from about 2 to 4.

C

CAMERAS, CAMCORDERS, & COMPUTERS

Always **keep your film, tape, or computer disks out of the sun.** Carry an extra supply of batteries, and **be prepared to turn on your camera, camcorder, or laptop** to prove to security personnel that the device is real. Always **ask for hand inspection of film,** which becomes clouded after successive exposure to airport x-ray machines, and **keep videotapes and**

computer disks away from metal detectors.

➤ PHOTO HELP: **Kodak Information Center** (☎ 800/242–2424). *Kodak Guide to Shooting Great Travel Pictures,* available in bookstores or from **Fodor's Travel Publications** (☎ 800/533–6478; $16.50 plus $4 shipping).

CUSTOMS

Before departing, **register your foreign-made camera or laptop with U.S. Customs** (☞ Customs & Duties, *below*).

CAR INSURANCE

Experienced and reliable sources for Mexican car insurance are **Sanborn's Mexican Insurance** (✉ 2009 S. 10th St., McAllen, TX 78505, ☎ 210/686–0711) and **Instant Mexico Auto Insurance** (✉ 223 Via de San Ysidro, San Ysidro, CA 92173, ☎ 619/428–3583).

CAR RENTAL

When considering this option, bear in mind that you may be sharing the road with some less-than-ideal drivers (sometimes acquiring a driver's license in Mexico is more a question of paying someone off than of having tested skill). In addition, the highway system is very uneven: In some regions, modern, well-paved superhighways prevail; in others, particularly the mountains, potholes, untethered livestock, and dangerous, unrailed curves are the rule.

Rates in Mexico City begin at $35 a day and $189 a week for an economy car with air-conditioning, a manual transmission, and unlimited mileage. Rates in Acapulco begin at $35 a day and $189 a week. This does not include tax on car rentals, which is 15%.

➤ MAJOR AGENCIES: **Alamo** (☎ 800/522–9696, 0800/272–2000 in the U.K.). **Avis** (☎ 800/331–1084, 800/879–2847 in Canada). **Budget** (☎ 800/527–0700, 0800/181181 in the U.K.). **Dollar** (☎ 800/800–4000; 0990/565656 in the U.K., where it is known as Eurodollar). **Hertz** (☎ 800/654–3001, 800/263–0600 in Canada, 0345/555888 in the U.K.). **National InterRent** (☎ 800/227–3876; 0345/222525 in the U.K., where it is known as Europcar InterRent).

CUT COSTS

To get the best deal, **book through a travel agent who is willing to shop around.**

Also **ask your travel agent about a company's customer-service record.** How has it responded to late plane arrivals and vehicle mishaps? Are there often lines at the rental counter, and, if you're traveling during a holiday period, does a confirmed reservation guarantee you a car?

Be sure to **look into wholesalers,** companies that do not own fleets but rent in bulk from those that do and often offer better rates than traditional car-rental operations. Prices are best during off-peak periods. Rentals booked through wholesalers must be paid for before you leave the United States.

➤ RENTAL WHOLESALERS: **Auto Europe** (☎ 207/842–2000 or 800/223–5555, FAX 800/235–6321). **DER Travel Services** (✉ 9501 W. Devon Ave., Rosemont, IL 60018, ☎ 800/782–2424, FAX 800/282–7474 for information or 800/860–9944 for brochures). The **Kemwel Group** (☎ 914/835–5555 or 800/678–0678, FAX 914/835–5126).

NEED INSURANCE?

When driving a rented car you are generally responsible for any damage to or loss of the vehicle. You also are liable for any property damage or personal injury that you may cause while driving. Before you rent, **see what coverage you already have** under the terms of your personal auto-insurance policy and credit cards.

BEWARE SURCHARGES

Before you pick up a car in one city and leave it in another, **ask about drop-off charges or one-way service fees,** which can be substantial. Note, too, that some rental agencies charge extra if you return the car before the time specified on your contract. To avoid a hefty refueling fee, **fill the tank just before you turn in the car,** but be aware that gas stations near the rental outlet may overcharge.

MEET THE REQUIREMENTS

In Mexico your own driver's license is acceptable. An International Driver's Permit is a good idea; it's available from the American or Canadian automobile association, or, in the United Kingdom, from the Automobile Association or Royal Automobile Club.

CHILDREN & TRAVEL

CHILDREN IN MEXICO

All children, including infants, must have proof of citizenship for travel to Mexico. Children traveling with a single parent must also have a notarized letter from the other parent stating that the child has his or her permission to leave their home country. In addition, parents must now fill out a tourist card for each child over the age of 10 traveling with them.

Be sure to plan ahead and **involve your youngsters** as you outline your trip. When packing, include things to keep them busy en route. On sightseeing days try to schedule activities of special interest to your children. If you are renting a car don't forget to **arrange for a car seat** when you reserve. Most hotels in Mexico allow children under a certain age to stay in their parents' room at no extra charge, but others charge them as extra adults; be sure to **ask about the cutoff age for children's discounts.**

FLYING

As a general rule, infants under two not occupying a seat fly at greatly reduced fares and occasionally for free. If your children are two or older **ask about children's airfares.**

In general the adult baggage allowance applies to children paying half or more of the adult fare. When booking, **ask about carry-on allowances for those traveling with infants.** In general, for babies charged 10% of the adult fare you are allowed one carry-on bag and a collapsible stroller, which may have to be checked; you may be limited to less if the flight is full.

According to the FAA, it's a good idea to use safety seats aloft for children weighing less than 40 pounds. Airlines, however, can set their own policies: U.S. carriers allow FAA-approved models but usually require that you buy a ticket, even if your child would otherwise ride free, since the seats must be strapped into regular seats. Airline rules vary regarding their use, so it's important to **check your airline's policy about using safety seats during takeoff and landing.** Safety seats cannot obstruct any of the other passengers in the row, so get an appropriate seat assignment as early as possible.

When making your reservation, **request children's meals or a free-standing bassinet** if you need them; the latter are available only to those seated at the bulkhead, where there's enough legroom. Remember, however, that bulkhead seats may not have their own overhead bins, and there's no storage space in front of you—a major inconvenience.

GROUP TRAVEL

If you're planning to take your kids on a tour, look for companies that specialize in family travel.

➤ FAMILY-FRIENDLY TOUR OPERATORS: **Families Welcome!** (✉ 92 N. Main St., Ashland, OR 97520, ☎ 541/482–6121 or 800/326–0724, FAX 541/482–0660). **Rascals in Paradise** (✉ 650 5th St., Suite 505, San Francisco, CA 94107, ☎ 415/978–9800 or 800/872–7225, FAX 415/442–0289).

CONSUMER PROTECTION

Whenever possible, **pay with a major credit card** so you can cancel payment if there's a problem, provided that you can supply documentation. This is a good practice whether you're buying travel arrangements before your trip or shopping at your destination.

If you're doing business with a particular company for the first time, **contact your local Better Business Bureau and the attorney general's offices** in your state and the company's home state, as well. Have any complaints been filed?

Finally, if you're buying a package or tour, **consider travel insurance** that includes default coverage (☞ Insurance, *below*).

➤ LOCAL BBBS: **Council of Better Business Bureaus** (✉ 4200 Wilson Blvd., Suite 800, Arlington, VA 22203, ☎ 703/276–0100, FAX 703/525–8277).

CRUISING

Cruises that call at ports on the Caribbean coast and Mexican Riviera are available from Miami, Tampa, and Los Angeles. Some ships also call in Mexico as part of a Panama Canal transit. To get the best deal on a cruise, **consult a cruise-only travel agency.**

➤ CRUISE LINES: Among the many cruise lines that ply Mexican waters are **Cunard** (☎ 800/5–CUNARD), **Holland America** (☎ 800/426–0327), **Carnival** (☎ 800/327–9501), **Celebrity** (☎ 800/437–3111), **Costa** (☎ 800/462–6782), **Dolphin** (☎ 800/222–1003), **Majesty** (☎ 800/532–7788), **Norwegian** (☎ 800/327–7030), **Princess** (☎ 800/421–0522), **Regal** (☎ 800/270–SAIL), **Regency** (☎ 800/388–5500), **Royal Caribbean** (☎ 800/327–6700), **Silversea** (☎ 800/722–9955), and **Sun** (☎ 800/872–6400).

Usually, the best deals on cruise bookings can be found by consulting a cruise-only travel agency. Contact the **National Association of Cruise Only Travel Agencies (NACOA)** (✉ 3191 Coral Way, Suite 622, Miami, FL 33145, ☎ 305/446–7732 or 305/446–9732) for a listing of such agencies in your area.

➤ SPECIAL-INTEREST CRUISES: For whale-watching and educational cruises, contact the **Oceanic Society Expeditions** (✉ Fort Mason Center, Bldg. E, San Francisco, CA 94123, ☎ 415/441–1106 or 800/326–7491), **Classical Cruises** (✉ 8132 E. 70th St., New York, NY 10021, ☎ 800/367–6766, FAX 212/249–6896), or the **Smithsonian Institution's Study Tours and Seminars** (✉ 1100 Jefferson Dr. SW, Room 3045, Washington, DC 20560, ☎ 202/357–4700).

CUSTOMS & DUTIES

When shopping, **keep receipts** for all of your purchases. Upon reentering the country, **be ready to show customs officials what you've bought.** If you feel a duty is incorrect, appeal the assessment. If you object to the way your clearance was handled, get the inspector's badge number. In either case, first ask to see a supervisor, then write to the port director at the address listed on your receipt. Send a copy of the receipt and other appropriate documentation. If you still don't get satisfaction you can take your case to customs headquarters in Washington.

ENTERING MEXICO

Upon entering Mexico, you will be given a baggage declaration form and asked to itemize what you're bringing into the country. You are allowed to bring in 2 liters of spirits or wine for personal use; 400 cigarettes, 50 cigars, or 250 grams of tobacco; a reasonable amount of perfume for personal use; one movie camera and one regular camera and 12 rolls of film for each; and gift items not to exceed a total of $300. You are not allowed to bring meat, vegetables, plants, fruit, or flowers into the country.

ENTERING THE U.S.

You may bring home $400 worth of foreign goods duty-free if you've been out of the country for at least 48 hours and haven't already used the $400 allowance or any part of it in the past 30 days.

Travelers 21 and older may bring back 1 liter of alcohol duty-free. In addition, regardless of your age, you are allowed 200 cigarettes and 100 non-Cuban cigars. (At press time, a federal rule restricting tobacco access to persons 18 years and older did not apply to importation.) Antiques, which the U.S. Customs Service defines as objects more than 100 years old, enter duty-free, as do original works of art done entirely by hand, including paintings, drawings, and sculptures.

You may also send packages home duty-free: up to $200 worth of goods for personal use, with a limit of one parcel per addressee per day (and no alcohol or tobacco products or perfume worth more than $5); **label the package PERSONAL USE, and attach a list of its contents and their retail value.** Do not label the package UNSOLICITED GIFT, or your duty-free exemption will drop to $100. Mailed items do not affect your duty-free allowance on your return.

➤ INFORMATION: **U.S. Customs Service** (Inquiries, ✉ Box 7407, Washington, DC 20044, ☎ 202/927–6724; complaints, ✉ Commissioner's Office, 1301 Constitution Ave. NW, Washington, DC 20229; registration of equipment, ✉ Resource Management, 1301 Constitution Ave. NW, Washington DC, 20229, ☎ 202/927–0540).

ENTERING CANADA

If you've been out of Canada for at least seven days you may bring in C$500 worth of goods duty-free. If you've been away for fewer than seven days but more than 48 hours, the duty-free allowance drops to C$200; if your trip lasts 24–48 hours, the allowance is C$50. You may not pool allowances with family members. Goods claimed under the C$500 exemption may follow you by mail; those claimed under the lesser exemptions must accompany you.

Alcohol and tobacco products may be included in the seven-day and 48-hour exemptions but not in the 24-hour exemption. If you meet the age requirements of the province or territory through which you reenter Canada you may bring in, duty-free, 1.14 liters (40 imperial ounces) of wine or liquor *or* 24 12-ounce cans or bottles of beer or ale. If you are 16 or older you may bring in, duty-free, 200 cigarettes and 50 cigars; these items must accompany you.

You may send an unlimited number of gifts worth up to C$60 each duty-free to Canada. Label the package UNSOLICITED GIFT—VALUE UNDER $60. Alcohol and tobacco are excluded.

➤ INFORMATION: **Revenue Canada** (✉ 2265 St. Laurent Blvd. S, Ottawa, Ontario K1G 4K3, ☎ 613/993–0534, 800/461–9999 in Canada).

ENTERING THE U.K.

From countries outside the European Union, including Mexico, you may import, duty-free, 200 cigarettes or 50 cigars; 1 liter of spirits or 2 liters of fortified or sparkling wine or liqueurs; 2 liters of still table wine; 60 milliliters of perfume; 250 milliliters of toilet water; plus £136 worth of other goods, including gifts and souvenirs.

➤ INFORMATION: **HM Customs and Excise** (✉ Dorset House, Stamford St., London SE1 9NG, ☎ 0171/202–4227).

D

DINING

Mexican restaurants run the gamut from humble hole-in-the-wall shacks, street stands, *taquerías,* and American-style fast-food joints to internationally acclaimed gourmet restaurants. Prices, naturally, follow suit. To save money, **look for the fixed-menu lunch** known as *comida corrida* or *menú del día,* which is served between 1 and 4 PM almost everywhere in Mexico.

Lunch is the big meal; dinner is rarely served before 8 PM. There is no government rating of restaurants, but you'll know which ones cater to tourists simply by looking at the clientele and the menu (bilingual menus usually mean slightly higher prices than at nontourist restaurants). Credit cards—especially American Express, MasterCard, and Visa—are widely accepted.

DISABILITIES & ACCESSIBILITY

ACCESS IN MEXICO

When discussing accessibility with an operator or reservationist, **ask hard questions.** Are there any stairs, inside *or* out? Are there grab bars next to the toilet *and* in the shower/tub? How wide is the doorway to the room? To the bathroom? For the most extensive facilities meeting the latest legal specifications, **opt for newer accommodations,** which are more likely to have been designed with access in mind. Older buildings or ships may offer more limited facilities. Be sure to **discuss your needs before booking.**

➤ COMPLAINTS: **Disability Rights Section** (✉ U.S. Dept. of Justice, Box 66738, Washington, DC 20035-6738, ☎ 202/514–0301 or 800/514–0301, FAX 202/307–1198, TTY 202/514–0383 or 800/514–0383) for general complaints. **Aviation Consumer Protection Division** (☞ Air Travel, *above*) for airline-related problems. **Civil Rights Office** (✉ U.S. Dept. of Transportation, Departmental Office of Civil Rights, S-30, 400 7th St. SW, Room 10215, Washington, DC 20590, ☎ 202/366–4648) for problems with surface transportation.

TRAVEL AGENCIES & TOUR OPERATORS

The Americans with Disabilities Act requires that travel firms serve the needs of all travelers. That said, you should note that some agencies and operators specialize in making travel arrangements for individuals and groups with disabilities.

➤ TRAVELERS WITH MOBILITY PROBLEMS: **Access Adventures** (✉ 206 Chestnut Ridge Rd., Rochester, NY 14624, ☎ 716/889–9096), run by a former physical-rehabilitation counselor. **Accessible Journeys** (✉ 35 W. Sellers Ave., Ridley Park, PA 19078, ☎ 610/521–0339 or 800/846–4537, FAX 610/521–6959), for escorted tours exclusively for travelers with mobility impairments. **CareVacations** (✉ 5019 49th Ave., Suite 102, Leduc, Alberta T9E 6T5, ☎ 403/986–6404, 800/648–1116 in Canada) has group tours and is especially helpful with cruise vacations. **Hinsdale Travel Service** (✉ 201 E. Ogden Ave., Suite 100, Hinsdale, IL 60521, ☎ 630/325–1335), a travel agency that benefits from the advice of wheelchair traveler Janice Perkins. **Wheelchair Journeys** (✉ 16979 Redmond Way, Redmond, WA 98052, ☎ 206/885–2210 or 800/313–4751), for general travel arrangements.

➤ TRAVELERS WITH DEVELOPMENTAL DISABILITIES: **New Directions** (✉ 5276 Hollister Ave., Suite 207, Santa Barbara, CA 93111, ☎ 805/967–2841, FAX 805/964–7344). **Sprout** (✉ 893 Amsterdam Ave., New York, NY 10025, ☎ 212/222–9575 or 888/222–9575, FAX 212/222–9768).

DISCOUNTS & DEALS

Be a smart shopper and **compare all your options before making a choice.** A plane ticket bought with a promotional coupon may not be cheaper than the least expensive fare from a discount ticket agency. For high-price travel purchases, such as packages or tours, keep in mind that what you get is just as important as what you save. Just because something is cheap doesn't mean it's a bargain.

LOOK IN YOUR WALLET

When you use your credit card to make travel purchases you may get free travel-accident insurance, collision-damage insurance, and medical or legal assistance, depending on the card and the bank that issued it. American Express, MasterCard, and Visa provide one or more of these services, so **get a copy of your credit card's travel-benefits policy.** If you are a member of the American Automobile Association (AAA) or an oil-company-sponsored road-assistance plan, always **ask hotel or car-rental reservationists about auto-club discounts.** Some clubs offer additional discounts on tours, cruises, or admission to attractions. And don't forget that auto-club membership entitles you to free maps and trip-planning services.

DIAL FOR DOLLARS

To save money, **look into "1-800" discount reservations services,** which use their buying power to get a better price on hotels, airline tickets, even car rentals. When booking a room, always **call the hotel's local toll-free number** (if one is available) rather than the central reservations number—you'll often get a better price. Always ask about special packages or corporate rates.

When shopping for the best deal on hotels and car rentals **look for guaranteed exchange rates,** which protect you against a falling dollar. With your rate locked in you won't pay more even if the price goes up in the local currency.

➤ AIRLINE TICKETS: ☎ **800/FLY–4–LESS.** ☎ **800/FLY–ASAP.**

➤ HOTEL ROOMS: **Players Express Vacations** (☎ 800/458–6161). **Room Finders USA** (☎ 800/473–7829). **Steigenberger Reservation Service** (☎ 800/223–5652).

SAVE ON COMBOS

Packages and guided tours can both save you money, but don't confuse the two. When you buy a package your travel remains independent, just as though you had planned and booked the trip yourself. Fly-drive packages, which combine airfare and car rental, are often a good deal.

JOIN A CLUB?

Many companies sell discounts in the form of travel clubs and coupon books, but these cost money. You must use participating advertisers to get a deal, and only after you recoup the initial membership cost or book price do you begin to save. If you plan to use the club or coupons frequently you may save considerably. Before signing up, find out what discounts you get for free.

➤ DISCOUNT CLUBS: **Entertainment Travel Editions** (✉ Box 1068, Trumbull, CT 06611, ☎ 800/445–4137; $28–$53, depending on destination).

Great American Traveler (✉ Box 27965, Salt Lake City, UT 84127, ☎ 800/548–2812; $49.95 per yr). **Moment's Notice Discount Travel Club** (✉ 7301 New Utrecht Ave., Brooklyn, NY 11204, ☎ 718/234–6295; $25 per yr, single or family). **Privilege Card International** (✉ 201 E. Commerce St., Suite 198, Youngstown, OH 44503, ☎ 330/746–5211 or 800/236–9732; $74.95 per yr). **Sears's Mature Outlook** (✉ Box 9390, Des Moines, IA 50306, ☎ 800/336–6330; $14.95 per yr). **Travelers Advantage** (✉ CUC Travel Service, 3033 S. Parker Rd., Suite 1000, Aurora, CO 80014, ☎ 800/548–1116 or 800/648–4037; $49 per yr, single or family). **Worldwide Discount Travel Club** (✉ 1674 Meridian Ave., Miami Beach, FL 33139, ☎ 305/534–2082; $50 per yr family, $40 single).

DRIVING

There are two absolutely essential things to remember about driving in Mexico. First and foremost is to **carry Mexican auto insurance,** which can be purchased near border crossings on either the U.S. or Mexican side. If you injure anyone in an accident, you could well be jailed—whether it was your fault or not—unless you have insurance. Guilty until proven innocent is part of the country's Code Napoléon. Purchase enough Mexican automobile insurance at the border to cover your estimated trip. It's sold by the day, and if your trip is shorter than your original estimate, some companies may issue a pro-rated refund for the unused time upon application after you exit the country. (☞ Car Insurance, *above.*)

The second item is that **if you enter Mexico with a car, you must leave with it.** In recent years, the high rate of U.S. vehicles being sold illegally in Mexico has caused the Mexican government to enact stringent regulations for bringing a car into the country—at great inconvenience to motoring American tourists. In order to drive into the country, you must cross the border with the following documents: title or registration for your vehicle; a birth certificate or passport; a credit card (AE, DC, MC, or V); a valid driver's license with a photo. The title holder, driver, and credit card owner must be one and the same—that is, if your spouse's name is on the title of the car and yours isn't, you cannot be the one to bring the car into the country. For financed cars, leased cars, rental cars, or company cars, a notarized letter of permission from the bank, lien holder, rental agency, or company is required.

When you submit your paperwork at the border and pay a $12 charge on your credit card, you will receive a tourist visa, a car permit, and a sticker to put on your vehicle, all valid for six months. Be sure to turn in the permit and the sticker at the border prior to their expiration date; otherwise you could incur high fines.

One alternative to going through this hassle when you cross is to **have your paperwork done in advance** at a branch of Sanborn's Mexican Insurance; look in the Yellow Pages for an office in almost every town on the U.S.–Mexico border. You'll still have to go through some of the procedures at the border, but all your paperwork will be in order and Sanborn's express window will ensure that you get through relatively quickly. There is a $10 charge for this service. The fact that you drove in with a car is stamped on your tourist card, which you must give to immigration authorities at departure. If an emergency arises and you must fly home, there are complicated customs procedures to face.

For day trips and local sightseeing, engaging a car and driver (who often acts as a guide) for a day can be a hassle-free, more economical way to travel than renting a car and driving yourself. Hotel desks will know which taxi companies to call, and you can negotiate a price with the driver.

ROAD & TRAFFIC CONDITIONS

There are several well-kept toll roads in Mexico—primarily of the two-lane variety—covering mostly the last stretches of major highways (*carreteras*) leading to the capital. (*Cuota* means toll road; *libre* means no toll, and such roads are usually not as smooth.) Some excellent new roads have recently opened, making car travel safer and faster. These include highways connecting Acapulco and Mexico City; Cancún and Mérida;

Nogales and Mazatlán; León and Aguascalientes; Guadalajara and Tepic; Mexico City, Morelia, and Guadalajara; Mexico City, Puebla, Tehuacán, and Oaxaca; and Nuevo Laredo and Monterrey. However, tolls as high as $30 one-way can make using these thoroughfares prohibitively expensive. Approaches to most of the large cities are also in good condition, and the government-sponsored Northern Border Program has encouraged the border states to keep their roads in good repair.

In rural areas, roads are quite poor: **use caution, especially during the rainy season,** when rock slides are a problem. Driving in Mexico's central highlands may also necessitate adjustments to your carburetor. Generally, driving times are longer than for comparable distances in the United States. *Topes* (road cops, or bumps) are also common; it's best to slow down when approaching a village.

Driving at night is not recommended and should be avoided especially in remote and rural areas because of free-roaming livestock, the difficulty of getting assistance, and the risk of banditry. The last can occur anywhere, and it is best to use toll roads whenever possible. Although costly, they are much safer. Common sense goes a long way: If you have a long distance to cover, **start early and fill up on gas**; don't let your tank get below half-full. Allow extra time for unforeseen occurrences as well as for the trucks that seem to be everywhere. By day, **be alert to animals,** especially cattle and dogs. (The number of dead dogs lying beside—and in the middle of—Mexican highways is appalling.)

Traffic can be horrendous in the cities, particularly in Mexico City. As you would in metropolitan areas anywhere, **avoid rush hour** (7–9 AM and 5–7 PM) and lunchtime (1–3 PM). Signage is not always adequate in Mexico, so if you are not sure where you are going, **travel with a companion and a good map.** Always lock your car, and never leave valuable items in the body of the car (the trunk will suffice for daytime outings).

The Mexican Tourism Ministry distributes free road maps from its tourism offices outside the country. *Guía Roji* and PEMEX (the government petroleum monopoly) publish current city, regional, and national road maps, which are available in bookstores; gas stations generally do not carry maps.

RULES & SAFETY REGULATIONS

Illegally parked cars are either towed, locked, or their license plates removed, which can require a trip to the traffic police headquarters for payment of a fine. When in doubt, **park in a lot instead of on the street;** your car will probably be safer there, anyway.

If an oncoming vehicle flicks its lights at you in daytime, slow down: It could mean trouble ahead. When approaching a narrow bridge, the first vehicle to flash its lights has right of way. One-way streets are common. One-way traffic is indicated by an arrow; two-way, by a two-pointed arrow. A circle with a diagonal line superimposed on the letter *E* (for *estacionamiento*) means "no parking." Other road signs follow the now widespread system of international symbols, a copy of which will usually be provided when you rent a car in Mexico.

In Mexico City, **watch out for *"Hoy no Circula"* notices.** Because of pollution, all cars in the city are prohibited from driving one day a week. Posted signs show certain letters or numbers paired with each day of the week, indicating that vehicles with those letters or numbers in their license plates are not allowed to drive on the corresponding day. Foreigners are not exempt.

➤ AUTO CLUBS: In the United States, **American Automobile Association** (☎ 800/564–6222). In the United Kingdom, **Automobile Association (AA,** ☎ 0990/500600), **Royal Automobile Club** (RAC, ☎ 0990/722722 for membership inquiries, 0345/121345 for insurance).

➤ SPEED LIMITS: Mileage and speed limits are given in kilometers: 100 kph and 80 kph (62 and 50 mph, respectively) are the most common maximums. A few of the newer toll roads allow 110 kph (68.4 mph). In cities and small towns, **observe the**

posted speed limits, which can be as low as 20 kph (12 mph).

NATIONAL ROAD EMERGENCY SERVICES

To help motorists on major highways, the Mexican Tourism Ministry operates a fleet of more than 275 pickup trucks, known as the *Angeles Verdes,* or Green Angels. The bilingual drivers provide mechanical help, first aid, radio-telephone communication, basic supplies and small parts, towing, tourist information, and protection. Services are free, and spare parts, fuel, and lubricants are provided at cost. Tips are always appreciated (figure $5 to $10 for big jobs, $1 to $2 for minor repairs). The Green Angels patrol fixed sections of the major highways twice daily from 8 AM to 8 PM (later on holiday weekends). If you break down, **pull off the road as far as possible,** lift the hood of your car, hail a passing vehicle, and ask the driver to **notify the patrol.** Most bus and truck drivers will be quite helpful. If you witness an accident, do not stop to help but instead locate the nearest official.

➤ GREEN ANGELS: ☎ 5/250–8221 in Mexico City.

FUEL AVAILABILITY & COSTS

PEMEX franchises all the gas stations in Mexico. Stations are located at most road junctions, cities, and towns but generally do not accept U.S. credit cards or dollars. Fuel prices are the same at all stations (except near the U.S. border, where they are a bit lower) and run slightly higher than in the United States. Premium unleaded gas—called Magna Premio—and regular unleaded gas—called Magna Sin—is now available nationwide, but it's still a good idea to fill up whenever you can. Fuel quality is generally lower than that in the United States and Europe. Vehicles with fuel-injected engines are likely to have problems after extended driving.

At gas stations, keep a close eye on the attendants; and, even though standards of cleanliness have improved considerably in most gas stations in cities and on the major highways, especially franchised (franquicia) stations, there are still some that are filthy.

E

ELECTRICITY

Electrical converters are not necessary because Mexico operates on the 60-cycle, 120-volt system; however, many Mexican outlets have not been updated to accommodate three-prong and polarized plugs (those with one larger prong), so you may need an adapter. Hotels sometimes have 110-volt outlets for low-wattage appliances marked FOR SHAVERS ONLY near the sink; don't use them for high-wattage appliances like blow-dryers.

G

GAY & LESBIAN TRAVEL

Same-sex couples keep a low profile in Mexico, and two people of the same gender can often have a hard time getting a *cama matrimonial* (double bed), especially in smaller hotels. This could be attributed to the influence of the Catholic Church—Mexico is a devoutly Catholic country and the Church has historically exerted a powerful influence on both Mexican politics and the mores and attitudes of the Mexican people. However, the same rule that applies all over the world holds in Mexico as well: Alternative lifestyles (whether they be homosexuality or any other bending of conventional roles) are more easily accepted in the more cosmopolitan destinations such as Acapulco, Cancún, Puerto Vallarta, San Miguel de Allende, Ajijic, Cuernavaca, Guadalajara, and Mexico City.

➤ TOUR OPERATORS: **R.S.V.P. Travel Productions** (✉ 2800 University Ave. SE, Minneapolis, MN 55414, ☎ 612/379–4697 or 800/328–7787), for cruises and resort vacations for gays. **Olivia** (✉ 4400 Market St., Oakland, CA 94608, ☎ 510/655–0364 or 800/631–6277), for cruises and resort vacations for lesbians. **Atlantis Events** (✉ 9060 Santa Monica Blvd., Suite 310, West Hollywood, CA 90069, ☎ 310/281–5450 or 800/628–5268), for mixed gay and lesbian travel. **Toto Tours** (✉ 1326 W. Albion Ave., Suite 3W, Chicago, IL 60626, ☎ 773/274–8686 or 800/565–1241, FAX 773/274–8695), for groups.

➤ GAY- AND LESBIAN-FRIENDLY TRAVEL AGENCIES: **Advance Damron** (✉ 1 Greenway Plaza, Suite 800, Houston,

TX 77046, ☎ 713/682–2002 or 800/695–0880, FAX 713/888–1010). **Club Travel** (✉ 8739 Santa Monica Blvd., West Hollywood, CA 90069, ☎ 310/358–2200 or 800/429–8747, FAX 310/358–2222). **Islanders/Kennedy Travel** (✉ 183 W. 10th St., New York, NY 10014, ☎ 212/242–3222 or 800/988–1181, FAX 212/929–8530). **Now Voyager** (✉ 4406 18th St., San Francisco, CA 94114, ☎ 415/626–1169 or 800/255–6951, FAX 415/626–8626). **Yellowbrick Road** (✉ 1500 W. Balmoral Ave., Chicago, IL 60640, ☎ 773/561–1800 or 800/642–2488, FAX 773/561–4497). **Skylink Women's Travel** (✉ 3577 Moorland Ave., Santa Rosa, CA 95407, ☎ 707/585–8355 or 800/225–5759, FAX 707/584–5637), serving lesbian travelers.

H

HEALTH

AIR POLLUTION

The air pollution in Mexico City can pose a health risk. The sheer number of people in the capital, thermal inversions, and the inability to process sewage have all contributed to the high levels of lead, carbon monoxide, and other pollutants in the atmosphere in Mexico City. Though the long-term effects are not known, children, the elderly, and those with respiratory problems are advised to avoid jogging, participating in outdoor sports, and being outdoors more than necessary.

SHOTS & MEDICATIONS

According to the Centers for Disease Control and Prevention (CDC), there is a limited risk of malaria and dengue fever in certain rural areas of Mexico. Travelers in most urban or easily accessible areas need not worry. However, if you plan to visit remote regions or stay for more than six weeks, check with the CDC's International Travelers Hotline (☎ 404/332–4559). In areas with malaria and dengue, which are both carried by mosquitoes, take mosquito nets, wear clothing that covers the body, apply repellent containing DEET, and use a spray against flying insects in living and sleeping areas. The hot line recommends chloroquine (analen) as an antimalarial agent; no vaccine exists against dengue.

The major health risk in Mexico is posed by the contamination of drinking water, fresh fruit, and vegetables by fecal matter, which causes the intestinal ailment known as traveler's diarrhea. To prevent it, **watch what you eat and drink.** Stay away from uncooked food and unpasteurized milk and milk products, and **drink only bottled water or water that has been boiled** for at least 20 minutes. When ordering cold drinks at untouristed establishments, skip the ice: *sin hielo.* (You can usually identify ice made commercially from purified water by its uniform shape and the hole in the center.) Hotels with water purification systems will post signs to that effect in the rooms. *Tacos al pastor*—thin pork slices grilled on a spit and garnished with the usual cilantro, onions, and chili peppers—are delicious but dangerous. Be wary of Mexican hamburgers, because you can never be certain what meat they are made with (horsemeat is very common).

If these measures fail, try paregoric, a good antidiarrheal agent that dulls or eliminates abdominal cramps, which requires a doctor's prescription in Mexico; or in mild cases, Pepto-Bismol or Imodium (loperamide), which can be purchased over the counter. Get plenty of purified water or tea—chamomile is a good folk remedy for diarrhea. In severe cases, rehydrate yourself with a salt-sugar solution (½ tsp. salt and 4 Tbsp. sugar per quart/liter of water).

➤ HEALTH WARNINGS: **National Centers for Disease Control** (✉ CDC, National Center for Infectious Diseases, Division of Quarantine, Traveler's Health Section, 1600 Clifton Rd., M/S E-03, Atlanta, GA 30333, ☎ 404/332–4559, FAX 404/332–4565).

SUNBURN

Caution is advised when venturing out in the Mexican sun. Sunbathers lulled by a slightly overcast sky or the sea breezes can be burned badly in just 20 minutes. To avoid overexposure, **use strong sunscreens and avoid the peak sun hours** of noon to 2 PM.

MEDICAL PLANS

No one plans to get sick while traveling, but it happens, so **consider sign-**

ing up with a medical-assistance company. Members get doctor referrals, emergency evacuation or repatriation, 24-hour telephone hot lines for medical consultation, cash for emergencies, and other personal and legal assistance. Coverage varies by plan, so **review the benefits carefully.**

➤ MEDICAL-ASSISTANCE COMPANIES: **International SOS Assistance** (✉ Box 11568, Philadelphia, PA 19116, ☎ 215/244–1500 or 800/523–8930; ✉ Box 466, pl. Bonaventure, Montréal, Québec H5A 1C1, ☎ 514/874–7674 or 800/363–0263; ✉ 7 Old Lodge Pl., St. Margarets, Twickenham TW1 1RQ, England, ☎ 0181/744–0033). **MEDEX Assistance Corporation** (✉ Box 5375, Timonium, MD 21094, ☎ 410/453–6300 or 800/537–2029). **Traveler's Emergency Network** (✉ 3100 Tower Blvd., Suite 1000B, Durham, NC 27707, ☎ 919/490–6055 or 800/275–4836, FAX 919/493–8262). **TravMed** (✉ Box 5375, Timonium, MD 21094, ☎ 410/453–6380 or 800/732–5309). **Worldwide Assistance Services** (✉ 1133 15th St. NW, Suite 400, Washington, DC 20005, ☎ 202/331–1609 or 800/821–2828, FAX 202/828–5896).

DIVERS' ALERT

Do not fly within 24 hours of scuba diving.

I

INSURANCE

Travel insurance is the best way to protect yourself against financial loss. The most useful policies are trip-cancellation-and-interruption, default, medical, and comprehensive insurance.

Without insurance you will lose all or most of your money if you cancel your trip, regardless of the reason. You are strongly advised to **buy trip-cancellation-and-interruption insurance,** particularly if your airline ticket, cruise, or package tour is nonrefundable and cannot be changed. When considering how much coverage you need, look for a policy that will cover the cost of your trip plus the nondiscounted price of a one-way airline ticket, should you need to return home early. Also **consider default or bankruptcy insurance,** which protects you against a supplier's failure to deliver.

Medicare generally does not cover health-care costs outside the United States, nor do many privately issued policies. If your own policy does not cover you outside the United States, **consider buying supplemental medical coverage.** Remember that travel health insurance is different from a medical-assistance plan (☞ Health, *above*).

Citizens of the United Kingdom can buy an annual travel-insurance policy valid for most vacations during the year in which it's purchased. If you are pregnant or have a preexisting medical condition, make sure you're covered.

If you have purchased an expensive vacation, particularly one that involves travel abroad, comprehensive insurance is a must. Always **look for comprehensive policies that include trip-delay insurance,** which will protect you in the event that weather problems cause you to miss your flight, tour, or cruise. A few insurers sell waivers for preexisting medical conditions. Companies that offer both features include Access America, Carefree Travel, Travel Guard International, and Travel Insured International (☞ *below*).

Always **buy travel insurance directly from the insurance company**; if you buy it from a travel agency or tour operator that goes out of business you probably will not be covered for the agency or operator's default—a major risk. Before you make any purchase, **review your existing health and home-owner's policies** to find out whether they cover expenses incurred while traveling.

➤ TRAVEL INSURERS: In the United States, **Access America** (✉ 6600 W. Broad St., Richmond, VA 23230, ☎ 804/285–3300 or 800/284–8300), **Carefree Travel Insurance** (✉ Box 9366, 100 Garden City Plaza, Garden City, NY 11530, ☎ 516/294–0220 or 800/323–3149), **Near Travel Services** (✉ Box 1339, Calumet City, IL 60409, ☎ 708/868–6700 or 800/654–6700), **Travel Guard International** (✉ 1145 Clark St., Stevens Point, WI 54481, ☎ 715/345–0505 or 800/826–1300), **Travel Insured International** (✉ Box 280568, East Hartford, CT 06128-0568, ☎ 860/528–7663 or 800/243–3174), **Trav-**

elex Insurance Services (✉ 11717 Burt St., Suite 202, Omaha, NE 68154-1500, ☎ 402/445–8637 or 800/228–9792, FAX 800/867–9531), **Wallach & Company** (✉ 107 W. Federal St., Box 480, Middleburg, VA 20118, ☎ 540/687–3166 or 800/237–6615). In Canada, **Mutual of Omaha** (✉ Travel Division, 500 University Ave., Toronto, Ontario M5G 1V8, ☎ 416/598–4083, 800/268–8825 in Canada). In the United Kingdom, **Association of British Insurers** (✉ 51 Gresham St., London EC2V 7HQ, ☎ 0171/600–3333).

L

LANGUAGE

Spanish is the official language of Mexico, although Indian languages are spoken by approximately 20% of the population, many of whom speak no Spanish at all. Basic English is widely understood by most people employed in tourism, less so in the less developed areas. At the very least, shopkeepers will know the numbers for bargaining purposes.

As in most other foreign countries, knowing the mother tongue has a way of opening doors, so **learn some Spanish words and phrases.** Mexicans are not scornful of visitors' mispronunciations and grammatical errors; on the contrary, they welcome even the most halting attempts to use their language.

The Spanish most Americans learn in high school is based on Castilian Spanish, which is different from Latin American Spanish. Not only are there differences in pronunciation and grammar but also in vocabulary: Words or phrases that are harmless or everyday in one country can take on offensive meanings in another. Unless you are lucky enough to be briefed on these nuances by a native coach, the only way to learn is by trial and error.

LANGUAGE PROGRAMS

Attending a language institute is an ideal way not only to learn Mexican Spanish but also to acquaint yourself with the customs and the people of the country. For total immersion, most language schools offer boarding with a Mexican family, but your choice of lodgings and of length of stay is generally flexible.

➤ LANGUAGE INSTITUTES: Recommended places to learn Spanish and live with a Mexican family include **Cetlalic** (✉ Apdo. 1-201 Cuernavaca, Morelos, CP 62000, ☎ 73/13–35–79), with an emphasis on social justice as well as language acquisition; the **SLI–Spanish Language Institute** (✉ Apdo. Postal 2–3, Cuernavaca, Morelos 62191, ☎ FAX 73/17–52–94; in the U.S., contact Language Link Inc., ✉ Box 3006, Peoria, IL 61612, ☎ 800/552–2051); **Centro Internacional de Estudios para Estranjeros** (✉ Tomás V. Gómez 125, Guadalajara, Jalisco 44000, ☎ 3/616–43–99; ✉ Libertad 42, Local 1, Puerto Vallarta, Jalisco 48360, ☎ 322/3–20–82, FAX 322/3–29–82); **Instituto Falcón** (✉ Mora 158, Guanajuato 36000, ☎ FAX 473/2–36 –94); **Instituto Allende** (✉ Apdo. Postal 85-A, San Miguel de Allende, Guanajuato 37700, ☎ 465/2–01–90, FAX 465/2–45–38; ✉ Apdo. Postal 201-B, Puerto Vallarta, Jalisco 48350, ☎ 322/90–329–2–18–44 cellular, FAX 322/3–08–01); **National Autonomous University of Mexico (UNAM) School for Foreign Students** (✉ Apdo. Postal 70, Taxco, Gro. 40200, ☎ FAX 762/2–01–24); **Centro de Idiomas de la Universidad Autónoma Benito Juárez** (✉ Burgoa, at Armenta y López, Oaxaca 68000, ☎ 951/659–22, FAX 951/91–95–1), which offers classes in Mixtec and Zapotec as well as in Spanish; and **Instituto Jovel, A.C.** (✉ Apdo. Postal 62, Ma. Adelina Flores 21, San Cristóbal de las Casas, Chiapas 29200, ☎ FAX 967/8–40–69). **AmeriSpan Unlimited** (✉ Box 40513, Philadelphia, PA 19106, ☎ 800/879–6640, FAX 215/985–4524) can arrange for language study and homestay in a number of Mexican cities.

LODGING

The price and quality of accommodations in Mexico vary about as much as the country's restaurants, from superluxurious, international-class hotels and all-inclusive resorts to modest budget properties, seedy places with shared bathrooms, *casas de huéspedes* (guest houses), youth hostels, and *cabañas* (beach huts). You may find appealing bargains while you're on the road, but if your comfort level is high, **look for an English-speaking staff, guaranteed**

dollar rates, and toll-free reservation numbers in the United States.

Hotel rates are subject to the 15% value-added tax (the tax in the states of Quintana Roo, Baja California, and Baja California Sur is 10%), and many states are charging a 2% hotel tax, the revenues from which are being used for tourism promotion. Service charges and meals are generally not included. The Mexican government categorizes hotels, based on qualitative evaluations, into *gran turismo* (superdeluxe hotels, of which there are only about 50 nationwide); five-star down to one-star; and economy class. Keep in mind that many hotels that might otherwise be rated higher have opted for a lower category to avoid higher interest rates on loans and financing.

High- versus low-season rates can vary significantly (☞ When to Go, *below*). Hotels in this guide have air-conditioning and private bathrooms with showers, unless stated otherwise, but bathtubs are not common in inexpensive hotels and properties in smaller towns.

Mexican hotels—particularly those owned or managed by the international chains—are always being expanded. In older properties, travelers may often have to choose between newer annexes with modern amenities and rooms in the original buildings with possibly fewer amenities and—equally possible, but not certain—greater charm.

It's essential to **reserve in advance** if you are traveling during high season or holiday periods. Overbooking is a common practice in some parts of Mexico, such as Cancún. Travelers to remote areas will encounter little difficulty in obtaining rooms on a "walk-in" basis.

One last note of advice: If you are particularly sensitive to noise, you should **call ahead to learn if your hotel of choice is located on a busy street.** Many of the most engaging accommodations in Mexico are on downtown intersections that experience heavy automobile and pedestrian traffic. And large hotels are known to have lobby bars with live music in the middle of an open-air atrium leading directly to rooms. When you book, **request a room far from the bar.**

APARTMENT & VILLA RENTALS

If you want a home base that's roomy enough for a family and comes with cooking facilities, **consider a furnished rental.** Though these can save you money, some rentals are luxury properties—economical only when your party is large. Home-exchange directories list rentals (often second homes owned by prospective house swappers), and some services search for a house or apartment for you (even a castle if that's your fancy) and handle the paperwork. Some send an illustrated catalog; others send photographs only of specific properties, sometimes at a charge. Up-front registration fees may apply.

➤ RENTAL AGENTS: **At Home Abroad** (✉ 405 E. 56th St., Suite 6H, New York, NY 10022, ☎ 212/421–9165, FAX 212/752–1591). **Europa-Let/Tropical Inn-Let** (✉ 92 N. Main St., Ashland, OR 97520, ☎ 541/482–5806 or 800/462–4486, FAX 541/482–0660). **Property Rentals International** (✉ 1008 Mansfield Crossing Rd., Richmond, VA 23236, ☎ 804/378–6054 or 800/220–3332, FAX 804/379–2073). **Rental Directories International** (✉ 2044 Rittenhouse Sq., Philadelphia, PA 19103, ☎ 215/985–4001, FAX 215/985–0323). **Rent-a-Home International** (✉ 7200 34th Ave. NW, Seattle, WA 98117, ☎ 206/789–9377 or 800/488–7368, FAX 206/789–9379). **Vacation Home Rentals Worldwide** (✉ 235 Kensington Ave., Norwood, NJ 07648, ☎ 201/767–9393 or 800/633–3284, FAX 201/767–5510). **Villas and Apartments Abroad** (✉ 420 Madison Ave., Suite 1003, New York, NY 10017, ☎ 212/759–1025 or 800/433–3020, FAX 212/755–8316). **Villas International** (✉ 605 Market St., Suite 510, San Francisco, CA 94105, ☎ 415/281–0910 or 800/221–2260, FAX 415/281–0919). **Hideaways International** (✉ 767 Islington St., Portsmouth, NH 03801, ☎ 603/430–4433 or 800/843–4433, FAX 603/430–4444) is a travel club whose members arrange rentals among themselves; yearly membership is $99.

HOME EXCHANGES

If you would like to exchange your home for someone else's, **join a home-exchange organization,** which will send you its updated listings of available exchanges for a year and will include your own listing in at least one of them. Making the arrangements is up to you.

➤ EXCHANGE CLUBS: **HomeLink International** (✉ Box 650, Key West, FL 33041, ☎ 305/294–7766 or 800/638–3841, FAX 305/294–1148) charges $83 per year.

HOTELS

After choosing your hotel, it's best to **reserve ahead,** especially for the high season (December–February).

➤ INTERNATIONAL CHAINS: **Best Western** (☎ 800/528–1234). **Choice/Calinda** (☎ 800/424–6423). **Club Med** (☎ 800/258–2633). **Hyatt International** (☎ 800/233–1234). **Marriott** (☎ 800/223–6388). **Holiday Inn** (☎ 800/465–4329). **Omni (800/843–6664). Princess** (☎ 800/442–8418, 800/223–1818 in NY). **Radisson** (☎ 800/333–3333). **Sheraton** (☎ 800/325–3535). **Presidente** (☎ 800/327–0200). **Westin Regina Hotels** (☎ 800/228–3000). **Grupo Sol's Melía Hotels** (☎ 800/336–3542) are part of a reliable Spanish-owned chain.

➤ MEXICAN-OWNED CHAINS: **Camino Real** (☎ 800/722–6466). **Krystal** (☎ 800/231–9860). **Posadas de México** (Crowne Plaza, Fiesta Americana, and Fiesta Inn hotels, ☎ 800/343–7821). **Quinta Real** (☎ 800/445–4565). **Sidektur** (Sierra and Continental Plaza hotels, ☎ 800/882–6684).

➤ RESERVATION ASSISTANCE: If you arrive in Mexico City without a reservation, the **Mexican Hotel and Motel Association** (☎ 5/571–3268 or 5/571–3262) operates a booth at the airport that will assist you.

M

MAIL

The Mexican postal system is notoriously slow and unreliable; **never send packages** or expect to receive them, as they may be stolen (for emergencies, use a courier service or the new express-mail service, with insurance). There are post offices (*oficinas de correos*) even in the smallest villages and numerous branches in the larger cities. International postal service is all airmail, but even so your letter will take anywhere from 10 days to three weeks to arrive. Service within Mexico can be equally slow. It costs $2.70 pesos to send a postcard or letter weighing under 20 grams to the United States or Canada, and $3.40 pesos to Great Britain.

RECEIVING MAIL

To receive mail in Mexico, you can have it sent to your hotel or use *poste restante* at the post office. In the latter case, include the words "a/c Lista de Correos" (general delivery), followed by the city, state, postal code, and country. To use this service, you must first register with the local post office in which you wish to receive your mail. A list of names for whom mail has been received is posted and updated daily by the post office. American Express card- or traveler's-check holders can have mail sent to them at the local American Express office. For a list of the offices worldwide, write for the *Traveler's Companion* from **American Express** (✉ Box 678, Canal Street Station, New York, NY 10013).

MONEY

At press time, the peso was still "floating" after the devaluation enacted by the Zedillo administration in late 1994. While exchange rates were as favorable as one U.S. dollar to $7.9 Mexican pesos, one Canadian dollar to $5.7 pesos, and a pound sterling to $13 pesos, the market and prices are likely to continue to adjust. **Check with your bank or the financial pages of your local newspaper for current exchange rates.**

Mexican currency comes in denominations of 10-, 20-, 50-, 100-, 200-, and 500-peso bills. Coins come in denominations of 20, 10, and 5 pesos and 50, 20, 10, and 5 centavos. Many of the coins and bills are very similar, so check carefully. To avoid fraud, it's wise to **make sure that "pesos" is clearly marked on all credit-card receipts.**

Dollar bills but not coins are widely accepted in many parts of the Yucatán, particularly in Cancún and Cozumel. Many tourist shops and market vendors, as well as virtually all hotel service personnel, take them, too.

Traveler's checks and all major U.S. credit cards are accepted in most tourist areas of Mexico. The large hotels, restaurants, and department stores accept cards readily. Most of the smaller, less expensive restaurants and shops, however, will only take cash. Credit cards are generally not accepted in small towns and villages, except in tourist-oriented hotels. When shopping, you can usually get better prices if you **pay with cash.**

ATMS

Before leaving home, **make sure that your credit cards have been programmed for ATM use in Mexico.** Note that Discover is accepted mostly in the United States. Local bank cards often do not work overseas or may access only your checking account; **ask your bank about a MasterCard/Cirrus or Visa debit card,** which works like a bank card but can be used at any ATM displaying a MasterCard/Cirrus or Visa logo. These cards, too, may tap only your checking account; check with your bank about its policy.

➤ ATM LOCATIONS: **Cirrus** (☎ 800/424–7787). A list of **Plus** locations is available at your local bank.

COSTS

Mexico has a reputation for being inexpensive, particularly compared with other North American vacation spots such as the Caribbean; the devaluation of the peso, started in late 1994, has made this particularly true, though prices of the large chain hotels, calculated in dollars, have not gone down, and some restaurant owners and merchants have raised their prices to compensate for the devaluation. In general, costs will vary with the when, where, and how of your travel in Mexico. "When" is discussed in When to Go, *below.* As to "how," tourists seeking a destination as much as possible like home, who travel only by air or package tour, stay at international hotel chain properties, eat at restaurants catering to tourists, and shop at fixed-price tourist-oriented malls, may not find Mexico such a bargain. Anyone who wants a closer look at the country and is not wedded to standardized creature comforts can spend as little as $25 a day on room, board, and local transportation. Speaking Spanish is also helpful in bargaining situations and when asking for dining recommendations. As a rule, the less English is spoken in a region, the cheaper things will be.

Cancún, Puerto Vallarta, Mexico City, Monterrey, Acapulco, Ixtapa, Los Cabos, Manzanillo, and to a lesser extent Mazatlán and Huatulco are the most expensive places to visit in Mexico. Taxis are supposed to charge fixed rates to and from the airport and between hotels and beaches or downtown, but be sure to **agree upon a price before hiring a cab.** Water sports can cost as much as they do in the Caribbean islands. All the beach towns, however, offer budget accommodations, and the smaller, less accessible ones are often more moderately priced, examples being the Gulf coast and northern Yucatán, parts of Quintana Roo, Puerto Escondido, and the smaller Oaxacan coastal towns as well as those of Chiapas.

Average costs in the major cities vary, although less than in the past because of the increase in business travelers. A stay in one of Mexico City's top hotels can cost more than $200 (as much or more than at the coastal resorts), but meal prices have gone down with the devaluation of the peso; you can get away with a tab of $40 for two at what was once an expensive restaurant.

Probably the best value for your travel dollar is found in the smaller inland towns, such as San Cristóbal de las Casas, Mérida, Morelia, Guanajuato, and Oaxaca, where tourism is less developed. Although Oaxaca lodging can run more than $150 a night, simple colonial-style hotels with adequate accommodations for under $40 can be found, and tasty, filling meals are rarely more than $15.

CURRENCY EXCHANGE

For the most favorable rates, **change money at banks or a money exchange (casa de cambio).** The difference from one place to another is usually only a few centavos. Although fees charged for ATM transactions may be higher abroad than at home, Cirrus and Plus exchange rates are excellent because they are based on wholesale rates offered only by major banks. You won't do as well at exchange booths in airports or rail and bus stations, in hotels, in restaurants, or in stores, although you may find their hours more convenient. To avoid lines at airport exchange booths, **get a small amount of local currency before you leave home.**

➤ EXCHANGE SERVICES: **International Currency Express** (☎ 888/842–0880 on the East Coast or 888/278–6628 on the West Coast for telephone orders). **Ruesch International** (☎ 800/424–2923 for locations). **Thomas Cook Currency Services** (☎ 800/287–7362 for telephone orders and retail locations).

TRAVELER'S CHECKS

Whether or not to buy traveler's checks depends on where you are headed. Traveler's checks are easier to use in cities than in small towns or rural areas, where they may not be accepted. If your checks are lost or stolen, they can usually be replaced within 24 hours. To ensure a speedy refund, **buy your checks yourself.** When making a claim for stolen or lost checks, the person who bought the checks should make the call.

P

PACKING FOR MEXICO

It's not easy, but **pack light:** Though baggage carts are available now at airports, luggage restrictions on international flights are tight, and you'll want to save space for purchases. Mexico is filled with bargains on textiles, leather goods, arts and crafts, and silver jewelry.

What clothing you bring depends on your destination. For the resorts, bring lightweight sports clothes, bathing suits, and cover-ups for the beach. Bathing suits and immodest clothing are inappropriate for shopping and sightseeing, both in cities and beach resorts. Mexico City is a bit more formal than the resorts and, because of its high elevation, cooler. Men will want to bring lightweight suits or slacks and blazers for fancier restaurants; and women should pack tailored dresses. Many restaurants require jacket and tie. Jeans are acceptable for shopping and sightseeing, but shorts are frowned upon for men and women. You'll need a lightweight topcoat for winter and an all-weather coat and umbrella in case of sudden summer rainstorms.

Resorts, such as Cancún and Acapulco, are both casual and elegant; you'll see high-style designer sportswear, tie-dyed T-shirts, cotton slacks and walking shorts, and plenty of colorful sundresses. The sun can be fierce; **bring a sun hat (or buy one locally) and sunscreen** for the beach and for sightseeing. You'll need a sweater or jacket to cope with hotel and restaurant air-conditioning, which can be glacial, and for occasional cool spells. Few restaurants require a jacket and tie.

Bring an extra pair of eyeglasses or contact lenses in your carry-on luggage, and if you have a health problem, **pack enough medication** to last the entire trip or have your doctor write you a prescription using the drug's generic name, because brand names vary from country to country. It's important that you **don't put prescription drugs or valuables in luggage to be checked**: it might go astray. To avoid problems with customs officials, carry medications in the original packaging. Also, don't forget the addresses of offices that handle refunds of lost traveler's checks.

LUGGAGE

In general, you are entitled to check two bags on flights within the United States and on international flights leaving the United States. A third piece may be brought on board, but it must fit easily under the seat in front of you or in the overhead compartment.

If you are flying between two foreign destinations, note that baggage allowances may be determined not by piece but by weight—generally 88 pounds (40 kilograms) in first class, 66 pounds (30 kilograms) in business class, and 44 pounds (20 kilograms) in economy. If your flight between two cities abroad *connects* with your transatlantic or transpacific flight, the piece method still applies.

Airline liability for baggage is limited to $1,250 per person on flights within the United States. On international flights it amounts to $9.07 per pound or $20 per kilogram for checked baggage (roughly $640 per 70-pound bag) and $400 per passenger for unchecked baggage. Insurance for losses exceeding these amounts can be bought from the airline at check-in for about $10 per $1,000 of coverage; note that this coverage excludes a rather extensive list of items, which is shown on your airline ticket.

Before departure, **itemize your bags' contents** and their worth, and label the bags with your name, address, and phone number. (If you use your home address, cover it so that potential thieves can't see it readily.) Inside each bag, **pack a copy of your itinerary.** At check-in, **make sure that each bag is correctly tagged** with the destination airport's three-letter code. If your bags arrive damaged or fail to arrive at all, file a written report with the airline before leaving the airport.

PASSPORTS & VISAS

Once your travel plans are confirmed, **get a passport even if you don't need one to enter Mexico**—it's always the best form of ID. It's also a good idea to **make photocopies of the data page**; leave one copy with someone at home and keep another with you, separated from your passport. If you lose your passport, promptly call the nearest embassy or consulate and the local police; having a copy of the data page can speed replacement.

U.S. CITIZENS

For stays of up to 180 days, any proof of citizenship is sufficient for entry into Mexico. Minors also need parental permission.

CANADIANS

You need only proof of citizenship to enter Mexico for stays of up to six months.

U.K. CITIZENS

Citizens of the United Kingdom need only a valid passport to enter Mexico for stays of up to three months.

➤ INFORMATION: **London Passport Office** (☎ 0990/21010) for fees and documentation requirements and to request an emergency passport.

S

SAFETY

Many Americans are aware of Mexico's reputation for corruption. The patronage system is a well-entrenched part of Mexican politics and industry, and workers in the public sector—notably policemen and customs officials—are notoriously underpaid. Everyone has heard, at least secondhand, a horror story about highway assaults, pickpocketing, bribes, or foreigners (not to mention the Mexicans themselves) languishing in Mexican jails.

Just as you would anywhere, **use common sense.** Wear a money belt; put valuables in hotel safes; avoid driving on untraveled streets and roads at night; and carry your own baggage whenever possible. Also, **be especially careful when traveling in remote areas.** Reporting a crime to the police is often a frustrating experience unless you speak excellent Spanish and have a great deal of patience. If you are the victim of an assault, contact your local consular agent or the consular section of your country's embassy in Mexico City, especially if you need medical attention (☞ Mexico City A to Z *in* Chapter 2).

Women traveling alone are likely to be subjected to *piropos* (catcalls). To avoid this, try not to wear tight clothes or enter street bars or cantinas alone. Your best strategy is always to try and ignore the offender and go on about your business. If the situation seems to be getting out of hand, do not hesitate to ask someone for help. *Piropos* are one thing, but outright harassment of women is not considered acceptable behavior. If you express outrage, you should find no shortage of willing defenders.

SENIOR-CITIZEN TRAVEL

To qualify for age-related discounts, **mention your senior-citizen status up front** when booking hotel reservations (not when checking out) and before you're seated in restaurants (not when paying the bill). Note that discounts may be limited to certain menus, days, or hours. When renting a car, **ask about promotional car-rental discounts,** which can be cheaper than senior-citizen rates.

➤ EDUCATIONAL TRAVEL PROGRAMS: **Elderhostel** (✉ 75 Federal St., 3rd floor, Boston, MA 02110, ☎ 617/426–7788). **Interhostel** (✉ University of New Hampshire, 6 Garrison Ave., Durham, NH 03824, ☎ 603/862–1147 or 800/733–9753, FAX 603/862–1113).

SHOPPING

At least three varieties of outlets sell Mexican crafts: indoor and outdoor municipal markets; shops run by Fonart (a government agency to promote Mexican crafts); and tourist boutiques in towns, shopping malls, and hotels. If you buy in the municipal shops or markets, you can avoid the VAT and you'll be able to pay in pesos or dollars. Be sure to **take your time and inspect the merchandise closely**: Bargains are to be had, but quality may be inconsistent. Fonart shops are a good reference for quality and price (the latter are fixed). Boutiques usually accept credit cards if not dollars; although their prices may be higher, they are convenient, and sometimes carry one-of-a-kind items you won't find anywhere else. (You may be asked to pay up to 7% more on credit-card purchases; savvy shoppers with cash have greater bargaining clout.) The 15% tax (I.V.A.; 10% in the states of Quintana Roo, Baja California, and Baja California Sur) is charged on most purchases but is often included in the price or disregarded by eager or desperate vendors.

It is not always true that the closer you are to the source of an article, the better the selection and price are likely to be. Mexico City, Oaxaca, Puerto Vallarta, and San Miguel de Allende have some of the best selections of crafts from around the country, and if you know where to go, you will find bargains. Prices are usually higher at beach resorts.

Bargaining is widely accepted in the markets, but you should understand that not all vendors will start out with outrageous prices. If you feel the price quoted is too high, start off by offering no more than half the asking price and then slowly go up, usually to about 70% of the original price. Always **shop around.** In major shopping areas like San Miguel, shops will wrap and send purchases back to the United States via a package delivery company. In some areas you will be able to have items such as huaraches (leather sandals), clothing, and blankets tailor-made. If you buy woolens or wood items, it's wise to freeze or microwave them when you return to destroy possible insect infestation. Keep in mind that buying items made from tortoiseshell and black coral contributes to ecological destruction. Furthermore, such items are not allowed into the United States.

SPORTS

TENNIS & GOLF

Most resorts either offer tennis and golf or can arrange access to clubs that do.

➤ TOURNAMENT INFORMATION: **Federación Mexicana de Tenis** (✉ Miguel Angel de Quevedo 953, Colonia Rosedal, Coyoacán, Mexico D.F. 04330, ☎ 5/689–9733). **Federación Mexicana de Golf** (✉ Av. Lomas de Sotelo 1112, Despacho 103, Col. Lomas de Sotelo, Mexico, D.F. 11200, ☎ 5/395–8642).

STUDENTS

To save money, **look into deals available through student-oriented travel agencies.** To qualify you'll need a bona fide student ID card. Members of international student groups are also eligible.

➤ STUDENT IDS AND SERVICES: **Council on International Educational Exchange** (✉ CIEE, 205 E. 42nd St., 14th floor, New York, NY 10017, ☎ 212/822–2600 or 888/268–6245, FAX 212/822–2699), for mail orders only, in the United States. **Travel Cuts** (✉ 187 College St., Toronto, Ontario M5T 1P7, ☎ 416/979–2406 or 800/667–2887) in Canada.

➤ HOSTELING: **Hostelling International—American Youth Hostels** (✉ 733 15th St. NW, Suite 840, Washington, DC 20005, ☎ 202/783–6161, FAX 202/783–6171). **Hostelling International—Canada** (✉ 400-205 Catherine St., Ottawa, Ontario K2P 1C3, ☎ 613/237–7884, FAX 613/237–7868). **Youth Hostel Association of England and Wales** (✉ Trevelyan House, 8 St. Stephen's Hill, St. Albans, Hertfordshire AL1 2DY, ☎ 01727/855215 or 01727/845047, FAX 01727/844126). Membership in the United States, $25; in Canada, C$26.75; in the United Kingdom, £9.30.

➤ STUDENT TOURS: **Contiki Holidays** (✉ 300 Plaza Alicante, Suite 900, Garden Grove, CA 92840, ☎ 714/740–0808 or 800/266–8454, FAX 714/740–0818).

T

TAXES

AIRPORT

An airport departure tax of US$13.37 or the peso equivalent must be paid at the airport for international flights from Mexico, and there is a domestic air departure tax of around US$10. Traveler's checks and credit cards are not accepted.

VAT

Mexico has a value-added tax of 15% (10% in the states of Quintana Roo, Baja California, and Baja California Sur) called I.V.A. (*impuesto de valor agregado*), which is occasionally (and illegally) waived for cash purchases. Other taxes and charges apply for phone calls, dining, and lodging.

HOTEL

Many states are charging a 2% tax on accommodations, the funds from which are being used for tourism promotion.

TAXIS

Government-certified taxis have a license with a photo of the driver and a taxi number prominently displayed, as well as a meter. However, in many cities, taxis charge by zones. In this case, be sure to agree on a fare before setting off. For reasons of security, especially in Mexico City, it is always best to call a *sitio* cab rather than to flag one on the street. Tipping is not necessary unless the driver helps you with your bags, in which case a few pesos are appropriate.

AT THE AIRPORT

From the airport, **take the authorized taxi service.** Purchase the taxi vouchers sold at stands inside or just outside the terminal, which ensure that your fare is established beforehand. However, before you purchase your ticket, it's wise to locate the taxi originating and destination zones on a map and make sure your ticket is properly zoned; if you only need a ticket to zone three, don't pay for a ticket to zone four or five.

IN CITIES & BEACH RESORTS

In Mexican cities, **take a taxi rather than public transportation,** which, though inexpensive, is frequently slow and sometimes patrolled by pickpockets. Always **establish the fare beforehand,** and **always count your change.** In most of the beach resorts, there are inexpensive fixed-route fares, but if you don't ask, or your Spanish isn't great, you may get taken. In the cities, and especially the capital, meters do not always run, and if they do, their rates have usually been updated by a chart posted somewhere in the cab. For distances more than several kilometers, negotiate a rate in advance; many drivers will start by asking how much you want to pay to get a sense of how street-smart you are. In all cases, if you are unsure of what a fare should be, ask your hotel's front desk personnel or bell captain.

Taxis are available on the street, at taxi stands (*sitios*), and by phone. Street taxis—usually yellow or green Volkswagen Beetles—are always the cheapest; sedans standing in front of hotels will charge far more. Never leave luggage unattended in a taxi.

In addition to private taxis, many cities operate a bargain-price collective taxi service using VW minibuses (called *combis*) and sedans, both downtown and at the airports. The service is called *colectivo* or, in Mexico City, *pesero*. Peseros run along fixed routes, and you hail them on the street and tell the driver where you are going. The fare—which you pay before you get out—is based on distance traveled. (For information on taxis in Mexico City, *see* Chapter 2.)

TELEPHONES

The country code for Mexico is 52.

Thanks to the privatization of Telefónos de México in 1991, Mexico's phone service, long exasperatingly inefficient, is gradually being overhauled. In the meantime, the variety of public phones that exist in the country can be confusing at best. Occasionally you'll see traditional black, square phones with push buttons or dials; although they have a coin slot on top, you may make local calls on them for free. Then there are the new blue or ivory push-button phones with digital screens. Other new phones have both a coin slot and an unmarked slot; the latter are for LADATEL (Spanish acronym for "long-distance direct dialing") cards, handy magnetic-strip debit cards that can be purchased at tourist offices as well as at newsstands and stores with a LADATEL logo. They come in denominations of up to $50 pesos and can be used for both local and long-distance calls. Still other phones have two unmarked slots, one for a LADATEL card and the other for a credit card. These are primarily for Mexican bank cards, but some accept U.S. Visa or MasterCard, though *not* U.S. telephone credit cards. U.S. calling cards can be used from LADATEL phones with the appropriate access code.

As of January 1997, Teléfonos de México's monopoly ended, enabling competition from several long-distance services, including Avantel and AT&T. Many phones, especially in the better city hotels, have Touch-Tone (digital) circuitry. If you think you'll need to access an automated phone system or voice mail in the United States and you don't know what phone service will be available, it's a good idea to take along a Touch-Tone simulator (you can buy them for about $17 at most electronics stores). With the increased installation of new phone and fax lines in major Mexican cities, many phone numbers are in the process of being changed; a recording may offer the new number, so it's useful to learn the Spanish words for numbers 1 through 9.

LONG-DISTANCE

To make a call to the United States or Canada, **dial 001 before the area code and number**; to call Europe, Latin America, or Japan, **dial 00** before the country and city codes.

Before you travel, **find out the local access codes** for your destinations. AT&T, MCI, and Sprint long-distance services make calling home relatively convenient, but you may find the local access number blocked in many hotel rooms. First ask the hotel operator to connect you. If the hotel operator balks, ask for an international operator, or dial the international operator yourself. One way to improve your odds of getting connected to your long-distance carrier is to travel with more than one company's calling card (a hotel may block Sprint, for example, but not MCI). If all else fails, call your phone company collect in the United States or call from a pay phone in the hotel lobby.

➤ ACCESS CODES: **AT&T USA Direct** may be accessed from within Mexico by dialing 95–800/462–4240 from any private or hotel phone or any public phone marked LADATEL. From the same phones, dial 95–800/674–7000 for **MCI WorldPhone,** or 95–800/877–8000 for **Sprint.**

TIPPING

When tipping in Mexico, remember that the minimum wage is the equivalent of $8 a day and that the vast majority of workers in the tourist industry live barely above the poverty line. However, there are Mexicans who think in dollars and know, for example, that in the United States porters are tipped about $1 a bag; many of them expect the peso equivalent from foreigners but are happy to accept 5 pesos a bag from Mexicans. They will complain either verbally or with a facial expression if they feel they deserve more—you and your conscience must decide. Following are some general guidelines. Naturally, larger tips are always welcome.

Porters and bellboys at airports and at moderate and inexpensive hotels: $1 per person.

Porters at expensive hotels: $2 per person.

Maids: $1 per night (all hotels).

Waiters: 10%–15% of the bill, depending on service (make sure a 10%–15% service charge has not already been added to the bill, although this practice is not common in Mexico).

Taxi drivers: Tipping necessary only if the driver helps with your bags—5 to 10 pesos should be sufficient, depending on the extent of the help.

Gas station attendants: 2–3 pesos.

Parking attendants and theater ushers: 2–5 pesos; some theaters have set rates.

TOUR OPERATORS

Buying a prepackaged tour or independent vacation can make your trip to Mexico less expensive and more hassle-free. Because everything is prearranged you'll spend less time planning.

Operators that handle several hundred thousand travelers per year can use their purchasing power to give you a good price. Their high volume may also indicate financial stability. But some small companies provide more personalized service; because they tend to specialize, they may also be more knowledgeable about a given area.

A GOOD DEAL?

The more your package or tour includes, the better you can predict the ultimate cost of your vacation. Make sure you know exactly what is covered, and **beware of hidden costs.** Are taxes, tips, and service charges included? Transfers and baggage handling? Entertainment and excursions? These can add up.

If the package or tour you are considering is priced lower than in your wildest dreams, **be skeptical.** Also, **make sure your travel agent knows the accommodations** and other services. Ask about the hotel's location, room size, beds, and whether it has a pool, room service, or programs for children, if you care about these. Has your agent been there in person or sent others you can contact?

BUYER BEWARE

Each year consumers are stranded or lose their money when tour operators—even very large ones with excellent reputations—go out of business. So **check out the operator.** Find out how long the company has been in business, and ask several agents about its reputation. Then **don't book unless the firm has a consumer-protection program.**

Members of the National Tour Association and United States Tour Operators Association are required to set aside funds to cover your payments and travel arrangements in case the company defaults. Nonmembers may carry insurance instead. Look for the details, and for the name of an underwriter with a solid reputation, in the operator's brochure. Note: When it comes to tour operators, **don't trust escrow accounts.** Although there are laws governing charter-flight operators, no governmental body prevents tour operators from raiding the till. For more information, *see* Consumer Protection, *above*.

➤ TOUR-OPERATOR RECOMMENDATIONS: **National Tour Association** (✉ NTA, 546 E. Main St., Lexington, KY 40508, ☎ 606/226–4444 or 800/755–8687). **United States Tour Operators Association** (✉ USTOA, 342 Madison Ave., Suite 1522, New York, NY 10173, ☎ 212/599–6599, FAX 212/599–6744).

USING AN AGENT

Travel agents are excellent resources. When shopping for an agent, however, you should **collect brochures from several sources**; some agents' suggestions may be skewed by promotional relationships with tour and package firms that reward them for volume sales. If you have a special interest, **find an agent with expertise in that area** (☞ Travel Agencies, *below*). Don't rely solely on your agent, who may be unaware of small-niche operators. Note that some special-interest travel companies only sell directly to the public and that some large operators only accept bookings made through travel agents.

SINGLE TRAVELERS

Prices for packages and tours are usually quoted per person, based on two sharing a room. If traveling solo, you may be required to pay the full double-occupancy rate. Some operators eliminate this surcharge if you agree to be matched with a roommate of the same sex, even if one is not found by departure time.

GROUP TOURS

Among companies that sell tours to Mexico, the following are nationally known, have a proven reputation, and offer plenty of options. The classifications used below represent different price categories, and you'll probably encounter these terms when talking to a travel agent or tour operator. The key difference is usually in accommodations, which run from budget to better, and better-yet to best.

➤ SUPER-DELUXE: **Abercrombie & Kent** (✉ 1520 Kensington Rd., Oak Brook, IL 60521-2141, ☎ 630/954–2944 or 800/323–7308, FAX 630/954–3324). **Travcoa** (✉ Box 2630, 2350 S.E. Bristol St., Newport Beach,

CA 92660, ☎ 714/476–2800 or 800/992–2003, FAX 714/476–2538).

➤ DELUXE: **Globus** (✉ 5301 S. Federal Circle, Littleton, CO 80123-2980, ☎ 303/797–2800 or 800/221–0090, FAX 303/347–2080).

➤ BUDGET: **Cosmos** (☞ Globus, *above*).

➤ ALL DESTINATIONS: **Gadabout Tours** (✉ 700 E. Tahquitz Canyon Way, Palm Springs, CA 92262, ☎ 619/325–5556 or 800/952–5068). **Go With Jo** (✉ 910 Dixieland Rd., Harlingen, TX 78552, ☎ 210/423–1446 or 800/999–1446, FAX 210/421–5787).

➤ COPPER CANYON: **American Wilderness Experience** (✉ 2820-A Wilderness Pl., Boulder, CO 80301-5454, ☎ 303/444–2622 or 800/444–0099, FAX 303/444–3999). **Brendan Tours** (✉ 15137 Califa St., Van Nuys, CA 91411, ☎ 818/785–9696 or 800/421–8446, FAX 818/902–9876). **Brennan Tours** (✉ 1402 3rd Ave., #717, Seattle, WA 98101, ☎ 206/622–9155 or 800/237–7249). **Frontier Tour and Travel** (✉ 1923 N. Carson St., Carson City, NV 89706, ☎ 702/882–2100 or 800/647–0800). **Gadabout Tours** (☞ All Destinations, *above*). **Globus/Cosmos** (☞ *above*). **Maupintour** (✉ 1515 St. Andrews Dr., Lawrence, KS 66047, ☎ 913/843–1211 or 800/255–4266, FAX 913/843–8351). **Mayflower Tours** (✉ Box 490, 1225 Warren Ave., Downers Grove, IL 60515, ☎ 708/960–3793 or 800/323–7604). **Questers** (✉ 381 Park Ave. S, New York, NY 10016, ☎ 212/251–0444 or 800/468–8668, FAX 212/251–0890). **Remarkable Journeys** (✉ Box 31855, Houston, TX 77231-1855, ☎ 713/721–2517 or 800/856–1993). **Smithsonian Study Tours and Seminars** (✉ 1100 Jefferson Dr. SW, Room 3045, MRC 702, Washington, DC 20560, ☎ 202/357–4700, FAX 202/633–9250). **Tauck Tours** (✉ Box 5027, 276 Post Rd. W, Westport, CT 06881-5027, ☎ 203/226–6911 or 800/468–2825, FAX 203/221–6828).

PACKAGES

Like group tours, independent vacation packages are available from major tour operators and airlines. The companies listed below offer vacation packages in a broad price range.

➤ AIR/HOTEL: **Aeromexico Vacation** (☎ 800/245–8585). **American Airlines Fly AAway Vacations** (☎ 800/321–2121). **Certified Vacations** (✉ 110 E. Broward Blvd., Fort Lauderdale, FL 33302, ☎ 954/522–1440 or 800/233–7260). **Continental Vacations** (☎ 800/634–5555). **Delta Dream Vacations** (☎ 800/872–7786, FAX 954/357–4687). **United Vacations** (☎ 800/328–6877). **US Airways Vacations** (☎ 800/455–0123).

➤ FROM THE U.K.: **Bales Tours** (✉ Bales House, Junction Rd., Dorking, Surrey RH4 3HL, ☎ 01306/876–881 or 01306/885–991, FAX 01306/740–048). **British Airways Holidays** (✉ Astral Towers, Betts Way, London Rd., Crawley, West Sussex RH10 2XA, ☎ 01293/723–181, FAX 01293/722–624). **Journey Latin America** (✉ 14–16 Devonshire Rd., Chiswick, London W4 2HD, ☎ 0181/747–8315, FAX 0181/742–1312). **Kuoni Travel** (✉ Kuoni House, Dorking, Surrey RH5 4AZ, ☎ 01306/742–222, FAX 01306/744-222).

For a custom-designed holiday, contact **Steamond Travel** (✉ 23 Eccleston St., London SW1 9LX, ☎ 0171/286–4449, FAX 0171/730–3024) or **Trailfinders** (✉ 42–50 Earls Court Rd., London W8 6FT, ☎ 0171/937–5400, FAX 0171/938–3305).

THEME TRIPS

➤ ADVENTURE: **Adventure Center** (✉ 1311 63rd St., #200, Emeryville, CA 94608, ☎ 510/654–1879 or 800/227–8747, FAX 510/654–4200). **American Wilderness Experience** (☞ Copper Canyon, *above*). **Baja Expeditions** (✉ 2625 Garnet Ave., San Diego, CA 92109, ☎ 619/581–3311 or 800/843–6967, FAX 619/581–6542). **Himalayan Travel** (✉ 110 Prospect St., Stamford, CT 06901, ☎ 203/359–3711 or 800/225–2380, FAX 203/359–3669). **Mountain Travel-Sobek** (✉ 6420 Fairmount Ave., El Cerrito, CA 94530, ☎ 510/527–8100 or 800/227–2384, FAX 510/525–7710). **OARS** (✉ Box 67, Angels Camp, CA 95222, ☎ 209/736–4677 or 800/346–6277, FAX 209/736–2902). **Remarkable**

Journeys (☞ Copper Canyon, *above*). **Trek America** (✉ Box 189, Rockaway, NJ 07866, ☎ 201/983–1144 or 800/221–0596, FAX 201/983–8551).

➤ ART & ARCHAEOLOGY: **Archaeological Conservancy** (✉ 5301 Central Ave. NE, #1218, Albuquerque, NM 87108-1517, ☎ 505/266–1540). **Far Horizons Archaeological & Cultural Trips** (✉ Box 91900, Albuquerque, NM 87199-1900, ☎ 505/343–9400 or 800/552–4575, FAX 505/343–8076). **Maya-Carib Travel** (✉ 7 Davenport Ave., #3F, New Rochelle, NY 10805, ☎ 914/354–9824 or 800/223–4084, FAX 914/353–7539). **M.I.L.A.** (✉ 100 S. Greenleaf Ave., Gurnee, IL 60031-3378, ☎ 847/249–2111 or 800/367–7378, FAX 847/249–2772). **Sanborn's Viva Tours** (✉ 2015 S. 10th St., Box 519, McAllen, TX 78505-0519, ☎ 210/682–9872 or 800/395–8482, FAX 210/682–0016). **Smithsonian Study Tours and Seminars** (☞ Copper Canyon, *above*).

➤ BICYCLING: **Backroads** (✉ 801 Cedar St., Berkeley, CA 94710-1800, ☎ 510/527–1555 or 800/462–2848, FAX 510/527–1444.

➤ FISHING: **Anglers Travel** (✉ 3100 Mill St., #206, Reno, NV 89502, ☎ FAX 702/853–9132). **Cutting Loose Expeditions** (✉ Box 447, Winter Park, FL 32790, ☎ 407/629–4700 or 800/533–4746). **Fishing International** (✉ Box 2132, Santa Rosa, CA 95405, ☎ 707/539–3366 or 800/950–4242, FAX 707/539–1320). **Mexico Sportsman** (✉ 100–115 Travis St., San Antonio, TX 78205, ☎ 210/212–4566 or 800/633–3085, FAX 210/212–4568). **Rod and Reel Adventures** (✉ 3507 Tully Rd., #B6, Modesto, CA 95356-1052, ☎ 209/524–7775 or 800/356–6982, FAX 209/524–1220).

➤ GOLF: **Stine's Golftrips** (✉ Box 2314, Winter Haven, FL 33883-2314, ☎ 941/324–1300 or 800/428–1940, FAX 941/325–0384).

➤ NATURAL HISTORY: **Earthwatch** (✉ Box 9104, 680 Mount Auburn St., Watertown, MA 02272, ☎ 617/926–8200 or 800/776–0188, FAX 617/926–8532) for research expeditions. **Forum Travel International** (✉ 91 Gregory La., #21, Pleasant Hill, CA 94523, ☎ 510/671–2900, FAX 510/671–2993). **National Audubon Society** (✉ 700 Broadway, New York, NY 10003, ☎ 212/979–3066, FAX 212/353–0190). **Natural Habitat Adventures** (✉ 2945 Center Green Ct., Boulder, CO 80301, ☎ 303/449–3711 or 800/543–8917, FAX 303/449–3712). **Oceanic Society Expeditions** (✉ Fort Mason Center, Bldg. E, San Francisco, CA 94123-1394, ☎ 415/441–1106 or 800/326–7491, FAX 415/474–3395). **Pacific Sea-Fari Tours** (✉ 2803 Emerson St., San Diego, CA 92106, ☎ 619/226–8224).

➤ RIVER RAFTING: **Far Flung Adventures** (✉ Box 377, Terlingua, TX 79852, ☎ 915/371–2489 or 800/359–4138, FAX 915/371–2325).

➤ SCUBA DIVING: **Rothschild Dive Safaris** (✉ 900 West End Ave., #1B, New York, NY 10025-3525, ☎ 800/359–0747, FAX 212/749–6172). **Tropical Adventures** (✉ 111 2nd Ave. N, Seattle, WA 98109, ☎ 206/441–3483 or 800/247–3483, FAX 206/441–5431).

➤ SPAS: **Spa-Finders** (✉ 91 5th Ave., #301, New York, NY 10003-3039, ☎ 212/924–6800 or 800/255–7727).

➤ TRAIN TOURS: **Mexico by Train** (✉ Box 2782, Laredo, TX 78044-2782, ☎ FAX 210/725–3659 or 800/321–1699).

➤ VILLA RENTALS: **Villas International** (✉ 605 Market St., San Francisco, CA 94105, ☎ 415/281–0910 or 800/221–2260, FAX 415/281–0919).

➤ WALKING: **Backroads** (☞ Bicycling, *above*).

➤ YACHT CHARTERS: **Ocean Voyages** (✉ 1709 Bridgeway, Sausalito, CA 94965, ☎ 415/332–4681 or 800/299–4444, FAX 415/332–7460). **The Moorings** (✉ 19345 U.S. Hwy. 19 N, 4th floor, Clearwater, FL 34624-3193, ☎ 813/530–5424 or 800/535–7289, FAX 813/530–9474).

TRAIN TRAVEL

In recent years, train schedules and first-class service from the U.S.–Mexico border have been cut significantly, in part because of the introduction of good trans-border bus transport (☞ Bus Travel, *above*). Although Ferrocarriles Nacionales de México began upgrading service in 1987 with air-conditioning and dining, club, and sleeping cars, the effort lost its steam. The Mexican government officially announced in 1994 that it was slowly moving out of the luxury rail business and would be looking to privatize this segment of the industry over the next several years. As first-class bus service proliferates throughout the country, first-class rail cars and schedules are being cut, often with little or no advance notice.

Primera especial (special first-class) tickets on overnight trains entitle passengers to reserved, spacious seats. *Primera regular* (regular first-class) service, also available on many trains, gets you the same seat, but no reservation. Second-class tickets are not available from U.S. agents, but first-class seats are not expensive and, in terms of comfort, are well worth the few extra pesos.

Sleeping accommodations consist of *camarines* (private rooms with bath and a single lower berth), *alcobas* (same as *camarines,* but with an upper and a lower berth), and couchettes, also called *camarotes.*

Train tickets must be purchased at least one day in advance, from Mexico City's Buenavista Station, local stations, or local Mexican travel agents, who will, of course, charge you extra. You can also reserve first-class tickets and rail-hotel packages in advance (10 to 15 days is recommended) from the United States by calling Mexico by Train (☞ *below*).

In general, rail travel in Mexico is slower than and not as comfortable as bus travel, which is recommended for most journeys; the slight savings in price are not worth the extra hassle. The exception is the spectacular train ride through the Copper Canyon (☞ Chapter 5).

➤ INFORMATION: **Ferrocarriles Nacionales de México** (Mexican National Railways, ☎ 5/547–6593) has information on trains throughout Mexico. From the United States, you can get information on trains and rail-hotel packages by contacting **Mexico by Train** (☎ FAX 210/725–3659 or 800/321–1699). *See also* Train Tours *under* Tour Operators, *above.* On the U.S. side, **Amtrak** (☎ 800/872–7245) will get you only as far as San Antonio; **Greyhound** (☎ 800/231–2222) offers bus service from there to Nuevo Laredo, where you can change for the coach to Monterrey.

TRAVEL AGENCIES

A good travel agent puts your needs first. Always **look for an agency that specializes in your destination, has been in business at least five years, and emphasizes customer service.** If you're looking for an agency-organized package or tour, your best bet is to choose an agency that's a member of the **National Tour Association** or the **United States Tour Operator's Association** (☞ Tour Operators, *above*).

➤ LOCAL AGENT REFERRALS: **American Society of Travel Agents** (✉ ASTA, 1101 King St., Suite 200, Alexandria, VA 22314, ☎ 703/739–2782, FAX 703/684–8319). **Alliance of Canadian Travel Associations** (✉ 1729 Bank St., Suite 201, Ottawa, Ontario K1V 7Z5, ☎ 613/521–0474, FAX 613/521–0805). **Association of British Travel Agents** (✉ 55–57 Newman St., London W1P 4AH, ☎ 0171/637–2444, FAX 0171/637–0713).

TRAVEL GEAR

Travel catalogs specialize in useful items, such as compact alarm clocks and travel irons, that can save space when packing. They also offer dual-voltage appliances, currency converters, and foreign-language phrase books.

➤ MAIL-ORDER CATALOGS: **Magellan's** (☎ 800/962–4943, FAX 805/568–5406). **Orvis Travel** (☎ 800/541–3541, FAX 540/343–7053). **TravelSmith** (☎ 800/950–1600, FAX 800/950–1656).

U

U.S. GOVERNMENT

The U.S. government can be an excellent source of inexpensive travel information. When planning your trip, **find out what government materials are available.**

➤ ADVISORIES: **U.S. Department of State American Citizens Services**

Office (✉ Room 4811, Washington, DC 20520); enclose a self-addressed, stamped envelope. Interactive hot line (☎ 202/647–5225, FAX 202/647–3000). Computer bulletin board (☎ 202/647–9225).

➤ PAMPHLETS: **Consumer Information Center** (✉ Consumer Information Catalogue, Pueblo, CO 81009, ☎ 719/948–3334) for a free catalog that includes travel titles.

V

VISITOR INFORMATION

For general information or if you want to drive into Mexico, contact the government tourist offices below.

➤ MEXICAN GOVERNMENT TOURIST OFFICES (MGTO): **United States:** (☎ 800/446–3942 nationwide; ✉ 405 Park Ave., Suite 1402, New York, NY 10022, ☎ 212/838–2949 or 212/421–6655, FAX 212/753–2874; ✉ 70 E. Lake St., Suite 1413, Chicago, IL 60601, ☎ 312/606–9252, FAX 312/606–9012; ✉ 1801 Century Pk. E, Suite 1080, Los Angeles, CA 90067, ☎ 310/203–8191, FAX 310/203–8316; ✉ 5075 Westheimer, Suite 975W, Houston, TX 77056, ☎ 713/629–1611, FAX 713/629–1837; ✉ 2333 Ponce de Leon Blvd., Suite 710, Coral Gables, FL 33134, ☎ 305/443–9160, FAX 305/443–1186). **Canada:** (✉ 1 Place Ville Marie, Suite 1626, Montréal, Québec H3B 2B5, ☎ 514/871–1052, FAX 514/871–3825; ✉ 2 Bloor St. W, Suite 1801, Toronto, Ontario M4W 3E2, ☎ 416/925–0704, FAX 416/925–6061; ✉ 999 W. Hastings St., Suite 1610, Vancouver, British Columbia V6C 2WC, ☎ 604/669–2845, FAX 604/669–3498). **United Kingdom:** (✉ 60 Trafalgar Sq., London WC2N 5DS, ☎ 0171/734–1058, FAX 0171/930–9202).

➤ DRIVING INTO MEXICO: **Mexican Government Tourist Board** (✉ 5075 Westheimer, Suite 975W, Houston, TX 77056, ☎ 713/629–1611, FAX 713/629–1837).

W

WHEN TO GO

Mexico is sufficiently large and geographically diverse enough that you can find a place to visit any time of year. October through May are generally the driest months; during the peak of the rainy season (June–September), it may rain for a few hours every day. But the sun often shines for the rest of the day, and the reduced off-season rates may well compensate for the reduced tanning time.

From December through February, the Mexican resorts—where the vast majority of tourists go—are the most crowded and therefore the most expensive. To avoid the masses, the highest prices, and the worst rains, **consider visiting Mexico during October, April, or May.** Hotel rates at the beach resorts can be cut by as much as 30% in the shoulder season, 50% in the off-season.

Mexicans travel during traditional holiday periods—Christmas through New Year's, Semana Santa (Holy Week, the week before Easter), and school vacations in the summertime—as well as over extended national holiday weekends, called *puentes* (bridges). Festivals play a big role in Mexican national life. If you plan to travel during a major national event, reserve both lodgings and transportation well in advance (☞ Festivals and Seasonal Events *in* Chapter 1).

CLIMATE

The variations in Mexico's climate are not surprising considering the size of the country. The coasts and low-lying sections of the interior are often very hot if not actually tropical, with temperatures ranging from 17°C to 31°C (63°F to 88°F) in winter and well above 32°C (90°F) in summer. A more temperate area ranging from 16°C to 21°C (60°F to 70°F) is found at altitudes of 1,220–1,830 meters (4,000–6,000 feet). In general, the high central plateau on which Mexico City, Guadalajara, and many of the country's colonial cities are located is springlike year-round.

➤ FORECASTS: **Weather Channel Connection** (☎ 900/932–8437), 95¢ per minute from a Touch-Tone phone.

Climate in Mexico

ACAPULCO

Jan.	88F	31C	May	90F	32C	Sept.	90F	32C
	72	22		75	24		75	24
Feb.	88F	31C	June	90F	32C	Oct.	90F	32C
	72	22		77	25		75	24
Mar.	88F	31C	July	90F	32C	Nov.	90F	32C
	72	22		77	25		73	23
Apr.	90F	32C	Aug.	91F	33C	Dec.	88F	31C
	73	23		77	25		71	22

COZUMEL

Jan.	84F	29C	May	91F	33C	Sept.	89F	32C
	66	19		73	23		75	24
Feb.	84F	29C	June	89F	32C	Oct.	87F	31C
	66	19		75	24		73	23
Mar.	88F	31C	July	91F	33C	Nov.	86F	30C
	69	21		73	23		71	22
Apr.	89F	32C	Aug.	91F	33C	Dec.	84F	29C
	71	22		73	23		68	20

ENSENADA

Jan.	66F	19C	May	70F	21C	Sept.	79F	26C
	45	7		52	11		59	15
Feb.	68F	20C	June	73F	23C	Oct.	75F	24C
	45	7		54	12		54	12
Mar.	68F	20C	July	77F	25C	Nov.	72F	22C
	46	8		61	16		48	9
Apr.	69F	21C	Aug.	79F	26C	Dec.	68F	20C
	48	9		61	16		45	7

GUADALAJARA

Jan.	75F	24C	May	90F	32C	Sept.	79F	26C
	45	7		57	14		59	15
Feb.	79F	26C	June	84F	29C	Oct.	79F	26C
	46	8		61	16		55	13
Mar.	82F	28C	July	79F	26C	Nov.	77F	25C
	48	9		59	15		48	9
Apr.	86F	30C	Aug.	79F	26C	Dec.	75F	24C
	52	11		59	15		46	8

LA PAZ

Jan.	73F	23C	May	91F	33C	Sept.	95F	35C
	54	12		59	15		73	23
Feb.	77F	25C	June	95F	35C	Oct.	91F	33C
	54	12		64	18		66	19
Mar.	80F	27C	July	97F	36C	Nov.	84F	29C
	54	12		71	22		661	16
Apr.	86F	30C	Aug.	97F	36C	Dec.	77F	25C
	55	13		73	23		54	12

MEXICO CITY

Jan.	70F	21C	May	79F	26C	Sept.	72F	22C
	44	6		54	12		52	11
Feb.	73F	23C	June	77F	25C	Oct.	72F	22C
	45	7		54	12		50	10
Mar.	79F	26C	July	73F	23C	Nov.	72F	22C
	48	9		52	11		46	8
Apr.	81F	27C	Aug.	73F	23C	Dec.	70F	21C
	50	10		54	12		45	7

MONTERREY

Jan.	68F	20C	May	88F	31C	Sept.	88F	31C
	48	9		68	20		70	21
Feb.	73F	23F	June	91F	33C	Oct.	81F	27C
	52	11		72	22		63	17
Mar.	79F	26C	July	91F	34C	Nov.	73F	23C
	57	14		72	22		55	13
Apr.	86F	30C	Aug.	93F	34C	Dec.	70F	21C
	64	18		72	22		50	10

PUERTO VALLARTA

Jan.	84F	29C	May	90F	32C	Sept.	93F	34C
	63	17		69	21		75	24
Feb.	84F	29C	June	91F	33C	Oct.	93F	34C
	63	17		75	24		73	23
Mar.	84F	29C	July	91F	33C	Nov.	90F	32C
	64	18		75	24		68	20
Apr.	86F	30C	Aug.	93F	34C	Dec.	86F	30C
	66	19		75	24		66	19

SAN MIGUEL DE ALLENDE

Jan.	75F	24C	May	88F	31C	Sept.	79F	26C
	45	9		59	15		59	15
Feb.	79F	26C	June	88F	30C	Oct.	79F	26C
	48	9		59	15		54	12
Mar.	86F	30C	July	82F	28C	Nov.	75F	24C
	54	12		59	15		50	10
Apr.	88F	31C	Aug.	82F	28C	Dec.	75F	24C
	57	14		59	15		46	8

1 Destination: Mexico

MEXICO: WHERE PAST AND PRESENT MEET

MEXICO IS LIKE *mole,* the complex and uniquely Mexican sauce whose myriad variations appeal to many tastes at once.

It is a nation so diverse that most Americans have only a vague inkling of what it's about. It's a place of ethereal cloud forests and regions so barren they were the setting for *Dune,* the science fiction film about a desert planet; of chill mountain heights and tropical jungles filled with shrill monkeys and a verdant growth of mango, papaya, and avocado. Its dimensions can be mind-boggling: Sections of the Copper Canyon are half again as deep as the Grand Canyon in Arizona.

It is a land of powerful muralists whose works chronicle the struggles of its people, while at the same time its musicians and dancers celebrate their survival.

Worlds collide in Mexico. It can be a bastion of Spanish formality or an enclave of California casualness, with businesspeople dressed in flip-flops and shorts, their cellular telephones poking out of their shirt pockets.

It is a vacation mecca of computer-designed resorts—sites chosen for their perfect confluence of white beach and crystal sea, where hotels have sprouted shoulder-to-shoulder as high-glitz destinations for sand, sun, and fun.

Yet much of it remains unchanged since the days of the conquistadors. In Chiapas, Maya Indians still work their fields with little more than machetes, smiling with benign amusement at the mountains of gear that adventure-travel outfitters use for rafting the rivers that have served as Maya highways for a millennium.

A past that is still very much a part of the present is central to Mexico's allure. In Mexico City's *Zócalo*—as the main square of any Mexican town or city is called—the pre-Hispanic Templo Mayor sits in the corner created by the juxtaposition of the 16th-century Cathedral and the 17th-century National Palace. Nearby, the ruins of another Aztec temple have been incorporated into a subway stop.

Some contrasts verge on the comic. Even as Jack Nicklaus declares an oceanfront hole in one of his courses in Cabo San Lucas his favorite, drivers on the four-lane highway nearby must beware of the area's greatest traffic hazard in the cool desert night: cows drawn to the pavement, which retains the sun's warmth hours after sunset. Fences remain a relatively new concept in Cabo, but cows are beginning to sport Day-Glo collars.

And halfway up the Baja Peninsula from Los Cabos, where bulldozers and construction crews are busily erecting condos for golfers, 1,000-year-old polychrome paintings of men and women, sea turtles, and whales lie hidden in the Sierra San Francisco, mountainous terrain so rough that only adventure travelers willing to travel by burro can see them.

Passengers on private trains crossing Mexico's Copper Canyon in cruise ship–style luxury wander through tiny gems of colonial villages and watch the dances of the Tarahumara, indigenous people who live in caves or stone huts, just one step removed from hunter-gatherers.

An air-conditioned bus ride from the beaches of ultramodern Cancún stand Maya temples, built with such cunning that on spring and autumn equinoxes the sun's shadows make it appear as though a giant serpent were descending a pyramid's steps, melding with a carved serpent's head at the base. Tent cities of vendors hawking T-shirts and other souvenirs have sprouted outside some temples; yet others remain entwined in the vines of the jungles that surround them, looking much as they did when another era of tourists sought them out a century ago.

In the Pacific resort of Mazatlán, the old city center is a mix of Spanish and French-style buildings carefully restored, while a string of modern, beachfront hotels lines the water's edge. Beyond the city limits lie the Sierra Madres and the mountain villages where the veins of gold that first attracted the fortune-seeking, empire-building conquistadors are still mined.

Cities such as Querétaro, San Miguel de Allende, and Morelia were also of major importance in the days of colonial Mexico—at one point, a third of the world's silver came from the mines of Guanajuato. Their architecture—European baroque facades and French doors opening onto wrought-iron balconies—has the feel of a Parisian neighborhood suddenly relocated to the American West.

The colorful colonial capital of Oaxaca is itself a babe compared to the Zapotec pyramids outside the city, which date back to 500 BC. Villagers living in the ring of settlements that surround Oaxaca like moons still practice crafts honed and perfected by their ancestors centuries before the arrival of the first Europeans.

Mexico, in short, is a land that has blended the legacies and traditions of both conqueror and vanquished and made them so uniquely Mexican that it is hard to see where one ends and the other begins.

IT IS A BLEND so distinct that visitors can quite literally taste the difference in seemingly familiar foods. A simple cup of American hot chocolate is pale and insipid next to Mexican hot chocolate, a virile, lusty drink sweetened by honey or sugar, thickened with cornmeal, and spiced to perfection.

Certainly, much of Mexico is familiar to many Americans—17 million visit annually. With the advent of the wide-bodied jet and cheap charters, resorts such as Acapulco and Puerto Vallarta, once getaways for movie stars and the super-rich, opened to the masses. More recently, isolated enclaves like Cabo San Lucas, whose private airstrips had kept it accessible only to fanatical and idiosyncratic fishermen and their celebrity cronies, opened international airports. The result: a desert-by-the-sea golf mecca.

But although Mexico is America's next-door neighbor, it can also seem remote. Only recently has Mexico's Ministry of Tourism sought to deal with the red tape that made it almost impossible for American motor coaches to drive across the border. Now passengers no longer need to switch to a Mexican bus when continuing into Mexico. However, driving a car into Mexico has become extremely complicated, with requirements that include obtaining a temporary importation permit for the vehicle.

An airline system centered on Mexico City can make domestic travel roundabout—often the only way to get from one resort to another is via Mexico City. And despite repeated efforts to privatize and improve Ferrocarriles Nacionales de Mexico (FNM), the federal rail system, Mexican trains make Amtrak look like the Concorde.

Communication with home can be tough, too—even in major resorts. Anyone who has actually tried to use Mexican phones can do nothing but marvel at the popularity of Telmex, the Mexican phone company, on the stock market. Cellular phones abound because they are easier to get and often more reliable.

Still, privatization has greatly improved the quality of the nation's buses. Brazilian-built Mercedes motor coaches and American imports have replaced smoke-belching recycled intercity buses used in the past for tours. Moreover, with deluxe service between many cities—plush reclining seats, hostesses dispensing drinks and snacks, and current movies playing overhead—Mexican bus travel has entered what was once the exclusive realm of the airlines.

And more than 11,260 km (7,000 mi) of roads were built under the Salinas administration. They link major tourist centers, such as the megaresort of Cancún and the colonial city of Mérida, which has been a major center in the Yucatán since the days the Maya flourished. The Green Angels, a highway patrol whose mechanics aid motorists in distress, patrol these roads. The Zedillo administration is continuing to improve land transportation systems.

Indeed, tying it all together is the common denominator of Mexico: It is a land of great courtesy. That could be one reason that tourist crime is relatively low. Mexico's vacation destinations are as safe as—if not safer than—major U.S. destinations. A fundamentally Mexican security springs from the innate graciousness of a friendly and hospitable people.

–Kate Rice

NEW AND NOTEWORTHY

The **economic crisis** triggered by the late-1994 peso devaluation has begun to turn around, thanks to a massive bailout of the economy led by the United States. The recovery is as yet fragile, however, and many Mexicans are still feeling economically pinched. Travelers should be sensitive to local hardship and avoid wearing expensive jewelry or displaying large sums of cash. The exchange rates for foreign currency remain extremely favorable for visitors, although prices at chain hotels, generally calculated in dollars, have not been much affected by the devaluation. Many tourist developments are still on hold until the dust from the economic bombshell clears further.

At the same time, new types of tourism ventures continue to be developed. The opening of the first of several planned environmentally friendly jungle lodges in the Xpujil area of the state of **Campeche** (☞ Chapter 13) has made possible extended visits to the ruins at Bécan, Xpujil, Hormiguero, Río Bec, and Calakmul, all of which are undergoing continued restoration. In the state of **Veracruz,** the Ruta de Cortés (Route of Cortés) allows visitors to follow the conquistador's footsteps. The tour starts at the beaches in the port of Veracruz, where the Spaniards first landed on what is now Mexican soil, and continues through the ruins, colonial cities, and battle sites that mark the conquistador's path to Mexico City. The states of Tlaxacala, Puebla, and Mexico play a large part in this route (☞ Chapter 11).

A more usual tourist activity, golf has become a major attraction in **Los Cabos,** where three 18-hole courses designed by pros draw devotees of the sport; more golf courses are planned (☞ Chapter 3).

It's rare for scenery to change for the better as a result of technological improvements, but in the **Copper Canyon** a new river dam has added lovely, mountain-reflecting "lake" views on the railway route between Los Mochis and Divisadero.

WHAT'S WHERE

Mexico City

Two volcanoes and a pyramid complex flank Mexico's capital, once the center of Aztec civilization and now the country's cosmopolitan business, art, and culinary hub. From the Alameda, a leafy center of activity since Aztec times, to the Zona Rosa, a chic shopping neighborhood, and the marvelous Chapultepec Park, with its many museums, gardens, and walking paths, Mexico City offers endless options to urban adventurers.

Baja California

Separated from mainland Mexico by the Gulf of California, Baja has a 3,218-km-long (2,000-mi-long) coast that stretches from Tijuana to Los Cabos. The earliest of the south-of-the-border retreats for the rich, reclusive, or rebellious against Prohibition, Baja still hosts isolated fishing enclaves and raucous watering holes; nature lovers come to watch the whales migrate in winter.

Sonora

Rancheros continue to ride the range in Mexican cowboy country, but beef has been upstaged by beaches in this northwestern state's economy. Along with relatively unspoiled (and inexpensive) coastal towns such as Kino Bay and Guaymas, Sonora's lures include colonial Alamos, an immaculate former silver-mining center, and a sprinkling of Spanish missions.

The Copper Canyon: From Los Mochis to Chihuahua City

The Copper Canyon is actually a series of gorges, some of them deeper than the United States' Grand Canyon; they are home to the Tarahumara Indians, renowned for their running ability. A train trip through this magnificent, largely uncharted region usually begins or ends in Chihuahua, a lively midsize city with a museum devoted to Pancho Villa.

Pacific Coast Resorts

Hollywood introduced us to two of the Mexican Riviera's most popular towns: sleepy, steamy Puerta Vallarta in *Night of the Iguana* and the sparkling Manzanillo coast in *10.* These days both places are prime cruise-ship destinations, as is

Mazatlán, a bustling port that attracts sportfishing enthusiasts and surfers. Ixtapa/Zihuatenejo is a two-for-one attraction, a laid-back fishing village adjoined by a glitzy resort.

Guadalajara

The colonial architecture that dates to Guadalajara's heyday as a silver lode for the Spanish is among the lures of Mexico's second-largest city; Guadalajara also introduced the world to mariachis and tequila. Some of the best arts and crafts in the country can be found at Tlaquepaque, on the outskirts of town, and Tonalá, about 10 minutes away.

The Heartland of Mexico

Rich with the history of Mexico's revolution, the heartland is a treasure of colonial towns—Zacatecas, Guanajuato, Querétaro, Morelia, and Pátzcuaro—whose residents now lead quiet, largely traditional lives. Even in San Miguel de Allende, an American art colony, women wash their clothes and gossip at the *lavandería* as they have for hundreds of years.

Acapulco

If Acapulco no longer tops the glitterati top-10 list, it remains both a sentimental favorite and a party-hearty resort town, with some of the glitziest discos this side of the Pacific. The cobblestone streets of nearby Taxco, the silver city, are lined with master jewelers.

Oaxaca

The geographic, ethnic, and culinary diversity of Oaxaca has made the state a favorite of Mexico aficionados. Descendants of the Mixtec and Zapotec Indians, who built the Monte Albán and Mitla complexes near Oaxaca City, compose the majority of residents. Although less exotic, the state's coastal developments of Puerto Escondido and Bahías de Huatulco are beloved by surfers and beach bums.

Northeastern Mexico and Veracruz

Many Texans get their first taste of Mexico in the northeastern border towns of Nueva Laredo, Reynosa, and Matamoros; those who venture farther down to Monterrey are rewarded with the more sophisticated dining and shopping of the country's third-largest city. The little-explored pyramids of El Tajín and the raffish charm of Veracruz, the first European city established on the North American mainland, are among the many reasons to continue south.

Chiapas and Tabasco

Much in the news in recent years because of the rebellion of its indigenous people, who have now reached limited agreement with the central authorities, the state of Chiapas has always been an off-the-beaten-path destination, a gateway to Guatemala best known for the colonial town of San Cristóbal and the jungle-covered ruins of Palenque, considered by many to be the most interesting in Mexico. Neighboring Tabasco is flat, humid, and tropical. Best known as the gateway to Palenque, it has its own Maya site, Comalcalco.

The Yucatán Peninsula

Mexico's most visited region, the Yucatán has something for everyone: the high-profile sparkle of Cancún; the spectacular snorkeling of Cozumel; the laid-back beachcombing of Isla Mujeres; the fascinating Spanish-Maya mix of Mérida; and the evocative Maya ruins of Tulum, Chichén Itzá, and Uxmal. The region is an ecotourist's dream, too, from the Sian Ka'an Biosphere Reserve on the Caribbean coast to Río Lagartos National Park on the Gulf of Mexico, migration ground for thousands of flamingos and other birds.

PLEASURES AND PASTIMES

Beaches

Beaches are the reason most tourists visit Mexico. Generally speaking, the Pacific is rougher and the waters less clear than the Caribbean, which is a better choice for snorkeling and scuba diving. Cancún, Cozumel, and Isla Mujeres, as well as what has come to be called the Cancún–Tulum Corridor, are among the best and most popular beach destinations on the Caribbean coast. Beaches on the Gulf of Mexico are often covered with tar. The Acapulco waters, though much improved by a cleanup effort, are still somewhat polluted, but there is no such problem at the other Pacific resorts. All beach resorts offer a variety of water sports, including waterskiing, windsurfing, parasailing, and if the water is clear enough, snorkeling and scuba diving. Surfers favor Puerto Escondido, near Huatulco, and Santa Cruz, near San Blas.

Bullfighting

An import of the Spanish conquistadores, bullfighting was refined and popularized over the centuries, until every major city and most small towns had a bullring or some semblance of an arena. As in Spain, the last few decades have seen some decline of the popularity of the sport in Mexico, where it has been superseded by such modern games as soccer and has been the object of negative publicity by animal-rights activists. It remains a strong part of the Latin American culture, however, and can be thrilling to watch when performed by a skilled toreador. Ask at your hotel about arenas and schedules; most fights are held on Sunday afternoon, and the most prestigious toreadors perform during the fall season.

Charreada

This Mexican rodeo is a colorful event involving elegant flourishes and maneuvers, handsome costumes, mariachi music, and much fanfare. There are charreadas most Sunday mornings at Mexico City's Rancho del Charro; inquire at your hotel or at a travel agency.

Dining

Mexico's food is as diverse and abundant as its geography. Distinct regional specialties typify each of the republic's 32 states and even the different provinces within the states. Fresh ingredients are bountiful, recipes are passed down through generations, and preparation requires much patience and loving care. (Mexican gastronomes are dismayed by foreigners' glaring misconceptions of Mexican food as essentially tacos, enchiladas, and burritos; they are bewildered by Tex-Mex and appalled by Taco Bell.)

The staples of rice, beans, and tortillas on which the poor subsist form the basis for creative variations of sophisticated national dishes but are by no means the only ingredients commonly used. As Mexican cooking continues to develop an international reputation, more people are recognizing its versatility.

Seafood is abundant, not just on the coasts but also in the lake regions around Guadalajara and in the state of Michoacán. Seviche—raw fish and shellfish (*mariscos*) marinated in lime juice and topped with cilantro (coriander), onion, and chili—is almost a national dish, though it originated in Acapulco. It is worth trying, but make sure it's fresh. Shrimp, lobster, and oysters can be huge and succulent; bear in mind the folk adage about eating oysters only in months with names that contain the letter *r,* and be sure to avoid raw shellfish in any area where cholera or water pollution may be a risk. Other popular seafood includes *huachinango* (red snapper), abalone, crab, and swordfish.

Mexicans consume lots of beef, pork, and barbecued lamb (*barbacoa*), with a variety of sauces. Chicken and other poultry tend to be dry and stringy, but when drenched in sauces or disguised in enchiladas, tacos, or burritos, they are quite palatable. Mole, a complex, spicy sauce with more than 100 ingredients, including many kinds of chilies and even a bit of chocolate, is one of Mexico's proudest culinary inventions. It is usually served over chicken or lamb. Regional variations are described in the appropriate chapters.

Maize was sacred to the Indians, who invented innumerable ways of preparing cornmeal, from the faithful tortilla to the tamale (cornmeal wrapped in banana leaves or corn husks), tostada (lightly fried, open tortilla heaped with meat, lettuce, and the like) and simple taco (a tortilla briefly heated, filled, and wrapped into a slim cylinder). *Atole* (a sweet, corn-based drink similar in consistency to hot chocolate) is a favorite breakfast or before-bed treat.

Fresh fruits and vegetables are another Mexican pleasure. Jicama, papaya, mamey, avocado, mango, guayaba, peanuts, squash, and tomatoes are just some of the produce native to Mexico. (All fresh produce should be washed in water with a commercial disinfectant, however, because bacteria exist in Mexico to which foreigners may not have been exposed.)

Other Mexican specialties less common abroad are any number of local *antojitos* or *botanas* (appetizers), *chilaquiles* (a rich breakfast dish made with eggs and tortilla strips scrambled with chili, tomatoes, onions, cream, and cheese), and *chiles en nogada* (a large poblano chili stuffed with beef or cheese, raisins, onion, olives, and almonds and topped with a creamy walnut sauce and pomegranate seeds). Soups are hearty—particularly the corn-and-pork-based *pozole, sopa azteca* (avocado and tortilla in a broth) and *sopa de flor de calabaza* (squash-flower soup).

But this barely touches on the plenitude and diversity of Mexican cuisine, which also encompasses an astonishing assortment of breads, sweets, beers, wines (which are fast improving), and cactus-based liquors. Freshly squeezed fruit juices and fruit shakes (*licuados*) are safe to drink—if ordered in a restaurant with hygienic practices—and taste heavenly. Coffee varies from standard American-style and Nescafé to espresso to the newer organic varieties to *café de olla,* which is laced with spices and served in a coarse clay mug. Imported liquor is very expensive; middle-class Mexicans stick with the local rum and tequila.

Handicrafts

Mexico is one of the best countries in the world to purchase *artesanías* (handicrafts), and many items are exempt from duty. The work is varied, original, colorful, and inexpensive, and it supports millions of families who are carrying on ancient traditions. Though cheap, shoddy merchandise masquerading as "native handicraft" is increasingly common, careful shoppers who take their time can come away with real works of art.

Mexican craftspeople excel in ceramics, weaving and textiles, silver, gold, and semiprecious stone jewelry, leather, woodwork, and lacquerware; each region has its specialty.

CERAMICS➢ Blue majolica (Talavera-style) tiles and other ceramic ware are at their best in Puebla. Oaxaca state is known for the burnished black pots hand-produced by its craftspeople. Inventive masks and figurines come from Michoacán, Jalisco, Taxco, Valle de Bravo, Tlaquepaque, and Chiapas.

JEWELRY➢ Silver is best bought in Taxco, San Miguel de Allende, and Oaxaca; be sure purchases are stamped "925," which means 92.5% pure silver. Gold filigree is sold in Oaxaca and Guanajuato. Oaxaca and Chiapas are also known for their amber, but beware, because much of what is sold as amber is in fact glass or plastic. (Good rules of thumb: Don't buy amber off the street, and if it seems like a great bargain, it's probably fake.) For semiprecious stones, try the jewelers of Puebla and Querétaro. Coral jewelry is sold in the Yucatán and other coastal areas, but buying it is discouraged, because of the massive ecological damage caused by coral harvesting.

LEATHER➢ The Yucatán, Chiapas, Oaxaca, and Jalisco are key destinations.

METALWORK➢ Look for copper in Santa Clara del Cobre in Michoacán, tin in San Miguel de Allende.

WEAVINGS AND TEXTILES➢ Options are many and varied: shawls (*rebozos*) and blankets around Oaxaca, Guadalajara, Jalapa, and Pátzcuaro; *huipiles* (heavily embroidered tunics worn by Indian women) and other embroidered clothing in Oaxaca state, the Yucatán, and Michoacán; masterfully woven rugs, some colored with natural dyes, in Oaxaca; hammocks and baskets in Oaxaca and the Yucatán; lace in the colonial cities of the heartland area; *guayaberas* (comfortable, embroidered tunic-style shirts, now usually mass-produced) along the Gulf coast; and reed mats in Oaxaca and Valle de Bravo. The Mezquital region east of Querétaro can also be rewarding, as can shopping for Huichol Indian yarn paintings and embroidery near Puerta Vallarta.

WOODWORK➢ Best bets include masks (Guerrero, Mexico City), *alebrijes* (painted wooden animals, Oaxaca), furniture (Guadalajara, Michoacán, San Miguel de Allende, and Cuernavaca), lacquerware (Uruapan and Michoacán, as well as Chiapa de Corzo in Chiapas and Olinalá in Guerrero), and guitars (Paracho, Michoacán).

Horseback Riding

Horseback riding is a sport the Mexicans love. The dry ranch lands of northern Mexico have countless stables and dude ranches, as do San Miguel de Allende and Querétaro in the heartland. Horses can be rented by the hour at most beaches, and horseback expeditions can be arranged to the Copper Canyon in Chihuahua and the forest near San Cristóbal, Chiapas.

Hot Springs

Mexico is renowned for its *balnearios* (mineral bath springs), which today are surrounded by a cluster of spa resorts and hacienda-type hotels. Most of the spas are concentrated in the center of the country, in the states of Aguascalientes, Guanajuato, México, Morelos, Puebla, and Querétaro.

Ruins

Amateur archaeologists will find heaven in Mexico, where some of the greatest ancient civilizations—among them, the Aztecs, the Olmecs, and the Maya—left their mark. Pick your period and your preference, whether for well-excavated sites or overgrown, out-of-the-way ruins barely touched by a scholar's shovel. The Yucatán is, hands down, the greatest source of ancient treasure, with such heavy hitters as Chichén Itzá and Uxmal, but you're unlikely to find any region in the country that doesn't have some interesting vestige of Mexico's pre-Columbian past. A visit to Mexico City's archaeological museum, arguably the best in the world, could ignite the imagination of even those who thought they had no interest in antiquity, and help others focus on the places they'd most like to explore further.

Soccer

As in Europe, this is Mexico's national sport (known as *futból*). It is played almost year-round at the *Estadio Azteca* in Mexico City as well as in other large cities.

Tennis and Golf

Most major resorts have lighted tennis courts, and there is an abundance of 18-hole golf courses, many designed by such noteworthies as Percy Clifford, Joe Finger, and Robert Trent Jones. At private golf and tennis clubs, you must be accompanied by a member to gain admission. Hotels that do not have their own facilities will often secure you access to ones in the vicinity.

FODOR'S CHOICE

Archaeological Sites

★**Chichén Itzá.** The best known Maya ruin, Chichén Itzá was the most important city in the Yucatán from the 11th to 13th centuries. Its eclectic architecture is evidence of a complex intermingling of ancient cultures.

★**Palenque.** Nestled in a rain forest in Chiapas, these Maya ruins have a magical quality, perhaps because of their intimacy. The most magnificent royal tomb in the Maya empire was uncovered here.

★**Teotihuacan.** Predating the Aztecs and believed by them to be the birthplace of the gods, this pyramid complex outside Mexico City was one of the largest cities in the ancient world.

★**Tulum.** The spectacular backdrop of the Caribbean and proximity to Cancún explain why Tulum is the most visited archaeological site in the Yucatán.

★**Uxmal.** Arguably the most beautiful of Mexico's ruins, Uxmal represents Maya style at its purest, including ornate stone friezes, intricate cornices, and soaring arches.

Beaches

★**Barra Vieja, near Acapulco.** Those tired of fighting for space on the Acapulco beaches often retreat to Barra Vieja, a long stretch of uncrowded beach with several equally uncrowded seafood restaurants, where *pescado a la talla* is served by the kilo.

★**Lo de Marcos, Sayulita,** and **San Francisco.** These are just a few of the dozens of beautiful, unspoiled beaches north of Puerto Vallarta, across the state line in Nayarit. Sayulita is often described as Puerto Vallarta some 40 years ago.

★**Playa de Amor, Cabo San Lucas.** From this secluded cove at the very tip of Baja California you can see the Sea of Cortés on one side, the Pacific Ocean on the other.

★**Playa Norte** and **Playa Cocoteros, Isla Mujeres.** These adjoining beaches on sleepy Isla Mujeres are ideal for water sports and *palapa* lounging alike.

★**Zicatela, Oaxaca Coast.** A long stretch of cream-color sand, Zicatela is one of the top 10 surfing beaches in the world.

Special Moments

★**Sunsets, Puerto Vallarta.** The setting sun is bigger and more fiery here than any place else in the world and spreads like orange mercury over Banderas Bay before disappearing behind the horizon.

★ **The divers at La Quebrada, Acapulco.** It's heart-stopping to see these swimmers take the plunge off 130-ft-high cliffs—after praying at a small cliff-side chapel.

★ **Whale-watching at Scammon's and San Ignacio lagoons, Baja.** Go out on a boat for the best views of the great gray mammals, who pass here en route from Alaska each winter.

★ ***Los voladores,* Papantla.** A precursor of bungee jumping, this ancient ceremony involves five "flyers" who hurl themselves from a tiny platform set atop a 100-ft pole.

★ **A *calesa* (horse-drawn carriage) ride through Mérida.** Discover old-world graciousness by trotting slowly through the wide streets and French-style neighborhoods of Yucatán's capital.

★ **Overlooking the Copper Canyon from Divisadero.** Whether you just get off the train briefly or stop overnight, you'll be astounded by the vista of the grand abyss.

Museums

★ **La Venta Museum Park, Villahermosa.** Giant Olmec heads placed along a jungle pathway are among the most fascinating exhibits of the pre-Hispanic jaguar cult on which this park complex focuses.

★ **Museo de Frida Kahlo, Mexico City.** The former home of the now-fashionable Kahlo is filled with her disturbing, surrealistic paintings and those of friends such as Klee and Duchamp.

★ **Museo Nacional de Antropología, Mexico City.** There are 100,000 square ft of displays at the greatest museum in the country, which hosts archaeological treasures from all of Mesoamerica.

★ **Museum of Contemporary Art, Monterrey.** The best of postmodern Latin American art is gathered at this gallery, where a chic coffeehouse attracts the city's intellectuals.

★ **Na-Bolom, San Cristobal de las Casas.** Franz and Gertrude Blom lived in a lovely garden-filled setting; their former residence contains displays reflecting their extensive archaeological, ethnological, and ecological interests.

Shopping

★ **Tlaquepaque, outside Guadalajara.** Crafts seekers throng to this village where some of the most talented glassblowers, potters, and jewelers in Mexico gather.

★ **Saturday market, Oaxaca.** At the largest Indian market in Mexico you'll find a wealth of colorful wares, including native huipiles, hand-carved wooden animals, and black regional pottery.

★ **Zona Rosa, Mexico City.** Antiques, crafts, and the latest fashions are abundant in this tony neighborhood, chock-full of galleries, boutiques, and cafés.

★ **Casa de las Artesanías** and **San Jolobil, San Cristóbal de Las Casas.** Some of Mexico's most striking Indian weavings, hand-embroidered blouses and tunics, multicolored *fajas* (sashes), and beribboned hats can be found in these two outlets.

★ **El Centro (downtown), Puerto Vallarta.** Few Mexican cities have a collection of native crafts, among them clothing and household goods, as representative as that of Puerta Vallarta.

Restaurants

★ **Coyuca 22, Acapulco.** Some diners book a year in advance to ensure a table at this Continental restaurant for high season; it's one of the most expensive dining rooms in town, and one of the most beautiful. *$$$$*

★ **Cicero Centenario, Mexico City.** The setting, in a restored 17th-century mansion, is superb, and the menu is enticing, featuring inventive versions of authentic Colonial dishes. *$$$$*

★ **La Belle Epoque, Mérida.** Middle Eastern, French, and Yucatecan specialties star in the former ballroom of an elegant mansion, overlooking a pretty urban park. *$$$$*

★ **Nuu-luu, Oaxaca.** Excellent Oaxacan cooking is the draw at this open-air restaurant, which lives up to its Mixtec name, "picturesque place." *$$*

★ **Rincón Maya, Cozumel.** This friendly downtown restaurant, decorated with folk art, serves good versions of traditional Maya fare. *$$*

Hotels

★**La Casa Que Canta, Zihuatanejo.** Perched on a cliff overlooking Zihuatanejo Bay, this thatched-roof complex features individualized suites with handcrafted furnishings. $$$$

★**Las Brisas, Acapulco.** Jeeps transport guests around this secluded hillside haven, set on 110 acres that offer every imaginable activity and amenity. $$$$

★**Quinta Real, Guadalajara.** Classical Mexican architecture and Spanish-style furnishings distinguish this luxury hotel in a quiet residential neighborhood. $$$$

★**Chan Kah, Palenque.** A resident monkey is among the charms of this jungle retreat near the Maya ruins; accommodations are in comfortable bungalows. $$$

★**La Mansión del Bosque, San Miguel de Allende.** This renovated hacienda across the street from a park rents moderately priced rooms on a short- or long-term basis. $$

After Hours

★**Fantasy** and **Extravaganzza discos, Acapulco.** Two standouts in a city where Saturday-night fever still rages, Fantasy attracts an older crowd, while Extravaganzza boasts a great light-and-sound show as well as a drop-dead view of Acapulco Bay.

★**Plaza de los Mariachis, Guadalajara.** A personal serenade is expensive, but the price of a beer will let you listen in on the heart-rending songs in the city where they originated.

★**Gran Café del Portal, Veracruz.** People-watch into the wee hours over a cup of *café con leche* at this classic coffeehouse, renowned all over Mexico.

★**Zona Rosa, Mexico City.** Niza and Florencia streets in the capital's Pink Zone are lined with lively nightclubs, bars, and discos that don't get hopping until after midnight.

★**Plaza Garibaldi, Mexico City.** The most musical square in Mexico, this picturesque place is filled with roving mariachis and bars that stay open till dawn; all locals come here at least once in their lives to celebrate something.

FESTIVALS AND SEASONAL EVENTS

Mexico has a full calendar of national holidays, saints' days, and special events; below are some of the most important or unusual ones. For further information and dates, contact the Mexican Government Tourism Office hot line at 800/446–3942.

WINTER

The month of January is full of long, regional festivals. Notable are the celebrations of the **Fiesta de la Inmaculada Concepción** (Feast of the Immaculate Conception), which transforms the city of Morelia into a sea of lights and flowers for much of the month; and a series of folkloric dances held in Chiapa de Corzo, Chiapas, and culminating in the **Feast of San Sebastian,** held there the third week in January.

JAN. 1➢ **New Year's Day** is a major celebration throughout the country. Agricultural and livestock fairs are held in the provinces; in Oaxaca, women display traditional *tehuana* costumes.

JAN. 6➢ **Feast of Epiphany** is the day the Three Kings bring gifts to Mexican children and the day the founding of Mérida is celebrated.

JAN. 17➢ **Feast of San Antonio Abad** honors animals all over Mexico. Household pets and livestock alike are decked out with flowers and ribbons and taken to a nearby church for a blessing.

FEB. 2➢ **Día de la Candelaria,** or Candlemas Day, means fiestas, parades, bullfights, and lantern-decorated streets. Festivities include a running of the bulls through the streets of Tlacotalpan, Veracruz.

FEB.–MAR.➢ **Carnaval** is celebrated throughout Mexico but most notably in Mazatlán and Veracruz, where there are parades with floats and bands.

SPRING

MAR. 21➢ **Benito Juárez's Birthday,** a national holiday, is most popular in Guelatao, Oaxaca, where Juárez, the beloved 19th-century president of Mexico and champion of the people, was born. This is also the day that Fiesta de la Primavera, held in Cuernavaca near Mexico City, marks the beginning of spring with carnivals and agricultural fairs.

MAR.–APR.➢ **Semana Santa** (Holy Week) is observed throughout the country with special passion plays during this week leading up to Easter Sunday.

APR.–MAY➢ **San Marcos National Fair,** held in Aguascalientes, is one of the country's best fairs. It features lively casino gambling, Indian *matachnes* (dances performed by grotesque figures), mariachi bands, and bullfights. Also during this time, the **Feria de la Primavera** (Spring Fair) in Cuernavaca celebrates the local flower industry with flower shows and open-air concerts, and the 10-day **Festival de las Artes** (Arts Festival) brings music, theater, and dance troupes from all over Latin America to San Luis Potosí.

MAY 1➢ **Labor Day** is a day for workers to parade through the streets.

MAY 5➢ **Cinco de Mayo** marks the anniversary of the French defeat by Mexican troops in Puebla in 1862 with great fanfare throughout the country.

MAY 15➢ **Feast of San Isidro Labrador** is noted nationwide by the blessing of new seeds and animals. In Cuernavaca, a parade of oxen wreathed in flowers is followed by street parties and feasting.

SUMMER

JUNE 1➢ **Navy Day** is commemorated in all Mexican seaports and is especially colorful in Acapulco, Mazatlán, and Veracruz. The **Feast of Corpus Christi** is celebrated in different ways. In Mexico City, children are dressed in native costumes and taken to the cathedral on the zócalo for a blessing. In Papantla, Veracruz, the Dance of the Flying Birdmen, a pre-Hispanic ritual to the sun, is held throughout the day.

JUNE 24➢ **Saint John the Baptist Day,** a popular national holiday, sees many Mexicans observing a tradition of tossing a "blessing" of water on most anyone within reach.

EARLY JULY➢ The **Feria Nacional** (National Fair) in Durango runs from the Day of Our Lady of Refuge (July 4) to the anniversary of the founding of Durango in 1563 (July 22). The celebration, which has the feel of an old-time agricultural fair, has taken on national renown for its carnival rides, livestock shows, and music.

JULY 16➢ **Our Lady of Mt. Carmel Day** is celebrated with fairs, bullfights, fireworks, sporting competitions, even a major fishing tournament.

JULY 24–31➢ **Guelaguetza Dance Festival,** a Oaxacan affair, dates back to pre-Columbian times.

LATE JULY➢ **Feast of Santiago,** a national holiday, features *charreadas,* Mexican-style rodeos.

AUG.➢ The **Festival de San Agustín** brings a month of music, dance, and fireworks to Puebla. On August 26 (Saint Augustine's feast day) it is customary to prepare the famous *chiles en nogada* (☞ Dining *in* Pleasures and Pastimes, *above*).

AUG. 15➢ **Feast of the Assumption of the Blessed Virgin Mary** is celebrated nationwide with religious processions. In Huamantla, Tlaxcala, the festivities include a running of the bulls down flower-strewn streets.

AUG. 25➢ **San Luis Potosí Patron Saint Fiesta** is the day the town honors its patron, San Luis Rey, with traditional dance, music, and foods.

AUTUMN

SEPT. 15–16➢ **Independence Day** is marked throughout Mexico with fireworks and parties that outblast those on New Year's Eve. The biggest celebrations take place in Mexico City.

SEPT. 29➢ **San Miguel Day** honors St. Michael, the patron saint of all towns with San Miguel in their names—especially San Miguel de Allende—with bullfights, folk dances, concerts, and fireworks.

OCT.➢ **October Festivals** mean a month of cultural and sporting events in Guadalajara.

OCT. 4➢ **Feast of St. Francis of Assisi** is a day for processions dedicated to St. Francis in various parts of the country.

OCT. 12➢ **Columbus Day** is a national holiday in Mexico.

OCT.–NOV.➢ **International Cervantes Festival,** in Guanajuato, is a top cultural event that attracts dancers, singers, and actors from a number of different countries.

NOV. 1–3➢ **All Souls' Day,** or **Day of the Dead,** the Mexican version of Halloween, commemorates the departed in a merry way, with candy skulls sold on street corners and picnickers spreading blankets in cemeteries.

NOV. 20➢ **Anniversary of the Mexican Revolution** is a national holiday.

NOV.–DEC.➢ **National Silver Fair,** an annual Taxco event, is an occasion for even more silver selling than usual, the crowning of a Silver Queen, jewelry and silver exhibitions, and various cultural events.

DEC. 12➢ **Feast Day of the Virgin of Guadalupe** is the day on which Mexico's patron saint is feted with processions and native folk dances, particularly at her shrine in Mexico City.

DEC. 16–25➢ **The Posadas** and **Christmas** are candlelight processions that lead to Christmas parties and to piñatas (suspended paper animals or figurines) that are broken open to yield gifts. Mexico City is brightly decorated, but don't expect any snow.

DEC. 23➢ **Feast of the Radishes,** a pre-Christmas tradition in Oaxaca, is one of the most colorful in Mexico: Farmers carve prize radishes into amusing shapes and display them in the city's main plaza, while celebrants devour fritterlike *buñuelos* and smash their ceramic plates in the streets.

2 Mexico City

Two volcanoes and a pyramid complex flank Mexico's capital, once the center of Aztec civilization and now the country's cosmopolitan business, art, and culinary hub. From the Alameda, a leafy center of activity since Aztec times, to the Zona Rosa, a chic shopping neighborhood, Mexico City offers endless options to urban adventurers. Day trips might include the legendary Pyramids of Teotihuacán, colonial Puebla, where mole sauce and Talavera tiles originated, or the floating gardens of Xochimilco.

By Frank "Pancho" Shiell

Updated by Patricia Alisau

MEXICO CITY IS A CITY OF SUPERLATIVES: It is both the oldest (670 years) and the highest (7,349 ft) city on the North American continent, and with nearly 24 million inhabitants, it is the most populous city in the world. It is Mexico's cultural, political, and financial core—on the verge of the 21st century but clinging to its deeply entrenched Aztec heritage.

As the gargantuan pyramids of Teotihuacán attest, the area around Mexico City was occupied from early times by a great civilization, whose name is as yet unknown (they were precursors of the Toltecs). The founding of the Aztec capital nearby did not occur until more than 500 years after Teotihuacán was abandoned. As the annals have it, the nomadic Aztecs were searching for a promised land in which to settle. Their prophesies said they would recognize the spot when they encountered an eagle, perched on a prickly-pear cactus, holding a snake in its beak. In 1325, the disputed date given for the founding of the city of Tenochtitlán, the Aztecs discovered this eagle in the valley of Mexico. They built Tenochtitlán on what was then an island in shallow Lake Texcoco and connected it to lakeshore satellite towns by a network of *calzadas* (canals and causeways, now freeways). Even then it was the largest city in the Western hemisphere and, according to historians, one of the three largest cities on earth. When he first laid eyes on the city in the 16th century, Spanish conquistador Hernán Cortés was dazzled by the glistening metropolis, which reminded him of Venice.

A combination of factors made the conquest possible. The superstitious Aztec emperor Moctezuma II believed the white, bearded Cortés on horseback to be the mighty plumed serpent-god Quetzalcóatl, who, according to a tragically ironic prophesy, was supposed to arrive from the east in the year 1519 to rule the land. Moctezuma therefore welcomed the foreigner with gifts of gold and palatial accommodations.

But in return, Cortés initiated the bloody massacre of Tenochtitlán, which lasted almost two years. Joining forces with him was a massive army of Indian "allies," gathered from other settlements like Cholula and Tlaxcala, who were fed up with the Aztec empire's domination and with paying tribute, especially sending warriors and maidens to be sacrificed. With the strength of their numbers and the European tactical advantages of brigantines built to cross the lake, imported horses, firearms, armor, and, inadvertently, smallpox and the common cold, Cortés succeeded in devastating Tenochtitlán. Only two centuries after it was founded, the young Aztec capital lay in ruins, about half of its population dead from battle, starvation, and contagious European diseases against which they had no immunity.

Cortés began building the capital of what he patriotically dubbed New Spain, the Spanish empire's colony that would spread north to cover what is now the United States southwest, and south to Panama. Mexico comes from the word Mexica (Meh-she-ka), which is the original name of the Aztecs. (The Spaniards were the ones who dubbed the Mexica Indians "Aztecs.") At the site of the demolished Aztec ceremonial center—now the 10-acre Zócalo—he started building a church (the precursor of the gigantic Metropolitan Cathedral), mansions, and government buildings. He utilized the slave labor—and artistry—of the vanquished native Mexicans. On top of the ruins of their city, and using rubble from it, they were forced to build what became the most European-style city in North America; but instead of having the random layout of contemporary medieval European cities, it followed the sophisticated grid pattern of the Aztecs. The Spaniards also drained and filled in Lake Texcoco, preferring wheels and horses (which they introduced to Mexico) over canals and canoes for transport. (The filled-in lake bed turned out to be a soggy support for the immense buildings that have been slowly sinking into it ever since they were built.) For much of the construction material they quarried local volcanic porous stone called *tezontle,* which is the color of dried blood and forms the thick walls of many historic downtown buildings.

During the colonial period the city grew, and the Franciscans and Dominicans converted the Aztecs to Christianity. In 1571 the Spaniards established the Inquisition in New Spain and burned heretics at its palace headquarters, which still stands in Plaza de Santo Domingo.

More than 200 years later, Mexicans rose up against Spain. The historic downtown street 16 de Septiembre commemorates the "declaration" of the War of Independence. On that date in 1810, Father Miguel Hidalgo rang a church bell and cried out his history-making *grito* (shout): "Viva Ferdinand VII [king of Spain at the time]! Death to bad government!" Some historians conclude that Hidalgo's call to arms in the name of the Spanish monarch was just a facade to start an independence movement, which Hidalgo successfully accomplished. That "liberty bell," which now hangs above the main entrance to the National Palace, is rung on every eve of September 16 by the president of the republic, who then shouts a revised version of the patriot's cry: "Viva Mexico! Viva Mexico! Viva Mexico!"

Today, travelers flying into or out of Mexico City get an aerial view of the still-remaining portion of Lake Texcoco on the eastern outskirts of the city; at night the vast expanse of city lights abruptly ends at a black void that appears to be an ocean. In-flight views also provide a panorama of the vast, flat 1,482-square-km (572-square-mi) Valley of Mexico, the Meseta de Anáhuac, completely surrounded by mountains—including, on its south side, two supposedly extinct and usually snow-capped volcanoes, Popocatépetl and Iztaccíhuatl, both well over 17,000 ft high. The volcanoes are separated by the 4-km-high (2½-mi-high) Cortés Pass, from where the arriving conquistador, after a nine-month trek from Veracruz, gazed down for his first astonishing glimpse of Tenochtitlán.

Unfortunately, the single most widely known fact about Mexico City is that its air is polluted. Many foreigners envision the city as being wrapped in black smog every day; they picture gray skies and streets packed with vehicles. But in reality, although the capital does have a serious pollution problem, it also has some of the clearest, bluest skies anywhere. At 7,349 ft, it often has mild daytime weather perfect for sightseeing and cool evenings comfortable for sleeping. Mornings can be glorious—chilly, but bright with the promise of the warming sun.

Smog is not the only thing Mexico City has in common with Los Angeles: The city lies on a fault similar to the San Andreas in California. In 1957 a major earthquake took a tragic toll, and scars are still visible from the devastating 1985 earthquake (8.1 on the Richter scale); the government reported 10,000 deaths, but according to vox populi, the death toll reached 50,000.

Growing nonstop, Mexico City covers about a 1,000-square-km (386-square-mi) area of the valley. The city is surrounded on three sides by the state of Mexico and bordered on the south by the state of Morelos. Advertising campaigns and tour packages usually tout Mexico's paradisiacal beach resorts and ancient ruins, but cosmopolitan, historic Mexico City is an important destination in itself—more foreign and fascinating than many major capitals on faraway continents.

Pleasures and Pastimes

Dining

Mexico City has been a culinary capital ever since the time of Moctezuma. Chronicles tell of the daily banquet extravaganzas prepared for the slender Aztec emperor by his palace chefs. More than 300 different dishes were served for every meal, comprising vast assortments of meat and fowl seasoned in dozens of ways; limitless fruit, vegetables, and herbs; freshwater fish; and fresh seafood that was rushed to Tenochtitlán from both seacoasts by sprinting relay runners.

Until the 15th century, Europeans had never seen indigenous Mexican edibles such as corn, chilies of all varieties, tomatoes, potatoes, pumpkin, squash, avocado, turkey, cacao (chocolate), and vanilla. In turn, the colonization brought European gastronomic influence and ingredients—wheat, onion, garlic, olives, citrus fruit, cattle, sheep, goats, chickens, domesticated pigs (and lard for frying)—and ended up broadening the already complex pre-Hispanic cuisine into one of the most multifaceted and exquisite in the world: traditional Mexican.

Today's cosmopolitan Mexico City, with some 15,000 restaurants, is a gastronomic melting pot. Here you can find establishments ranging from simple family-style eateries to five-star world-class restaurants. In addition, there are fine international restaurants specializing in cuisines of practically every foreign culture. Among them, the most prevalent are Spanish and haute-cuisine French—France also invaded Mexico and influenced its eating traditions.

In the past decade a renaissance of Mexican cooking has brought about a new wave known as *cocina mexicana moderna* (modern Mexican cuisine), which is served in many Mexico City restaurants. Emphasis is on the delicate tastes of traditional regional dishes gleaned from colonial cookbooks; portions are smaller and aesthetically presented. Also significant in this modern trend is the revival of ancient indigenous cooking techniques like steaming and baking, which used a lot less fat—remember there were no pigs for lard—plus items such as crunchy fried grasshoppers and cooked *maguey* (cactus) worms, which now grace the menus of the best restaurants in town.

Lodging

As might be expected of a megalopolis, Mexico City has 25,000 hotel rooms—enough to accommodate every taste and budget. You can lodge in the quaint or the colonial, the smoked-glass-and-steel high-rise, or the elegant replica of an Italianate palace. Wherever you decide to unpack your bags, you're in for a special experience.

Museums

Mexico City is the cultural as well as political capital of the country, as evidenced by its 85 museums—some of the finest in Latin America. In buildings often notable for their architecture, you can see the sweeping murals of native sons like Diego Rivera, Clemente Orozco, and Juan O'Gorman; the gripping surrealism of Frida Kahlo; stunning pre-Hispanic ceremonial pieces, and outstanding collections of religious art.

Nightlife and the Arts

Mexico City is the cultural capital of Latin America and, with the exception of Río de Janiero, has the liveliest nightlife of the region. There's something for every taste, from classical opera to symphony concerts, from a deservedly renowned folklore ballet to a lively square where *mariachi* (musicians) play, and from discos to offbeat places where salsa and *danzon* (Cuban dance music) are headliners.

Shopping

Native crafts and specialties from all regions of Mexico—some already big export items—are available in the capital, as are designer clothes. You'll also find modern art by some of the best young painters on the contemporary art circuit, many of whom are already making a name for themselves in the United States, but you might come across some undiscovered talent, too. You can pick up quality goods at big savings if you buy here instead of at overseas outlets of Mexican goods.

Sports and the Outdoors

Latin sports like jai alai and the *fiesta brava* (bullfighting)—both brought to Mexico by the Spanish conquerors—have enjoyed popularity for more than four centuries in the capital, which attracts the best athletes the country has to offer in these fields. The racetrack at the swank *hipódromo* offers live thoroughbred races daily. (These are getting harder to find in the country, as horses are being swapped for foreign off-track betting operations, which receive major U.S. derbies via satellite.) Tennis, golf, jogging—even rowing a boat in a park—are other sporting options for visitors.

EXPLORING MEXICO CITY

Most of Mexico City is aligned around two major intersecting thoroughfares: Paseo de la Reforma and Avenida Insurgentes. Administratively, the city is divided into 16 *delegaciones* (districts) and about 400 *colonias* (neighborhoods), each with street names fitting a given theme, such as river, philosopher, doctor, or revolutionary hero. The same street can change names as it goes through different colonias. Hence, most street addresses include the colonia they are in, and, unless you're going to an obvious place, it is important to tell your taxi driver the name of the colonia.

The principal sights of Mexico City are organized into three areas. You need a full day to cover each thoroughly, though each can be done at breakneck speed in four or five hours. The first two areas—Alameda Central and the Zócalo, and Chapultepec Park and the Zona Rosa—can be covered on foot; exploring Coyoacán and San Angel in southern Mexico City will require a taxi ride or two.

Numbers in the text correspond to numbers in the margin and on the Alameda Central and the Zócalo, Chapultepec Park and Zona Rosa, and Coyoacán and San Angel maps.

Great Itineraries

You can spend a month in Mexico City and hardly touch the tip of the iceberg of its sights and attractions. But for stays shorter than this, here are some highlights.

IF YOU HAVE 3 DAYS

Start with the **Zócalo** ① with its exotic ruins, museums, and public buildings; then stroll to the **Palacio de Bellas Artes** ⑮ and surroundings (don't forget a stop at the **Casa de los Azulejos** ⑬ for a Mexican lunch), and end the day at **Alameda Central** ⑱. Day 2, head for the **Museo Nacional de Antropología** ㉖ in the morning and the **Zona Rosa** in the afternoon, when it starts to come alive; visit the **Mercado Insurgentes** (☞ Shopping, *below*) for some fun shopping, or any other of the stores on our list. Day 3, go to **Bosque de Chapultepec** ㉑ to stroll the green pathways past the rowing lake and visit the **Castillo de Chapultepec** ㉒, the **Museo de Arte Moderno** ㉔, **Museo Rufino Tamayo** ㉕, and, of course, the **Zoológica** ㉗ to see the pandas. Visit downtown's **Plaza Garibaldi**

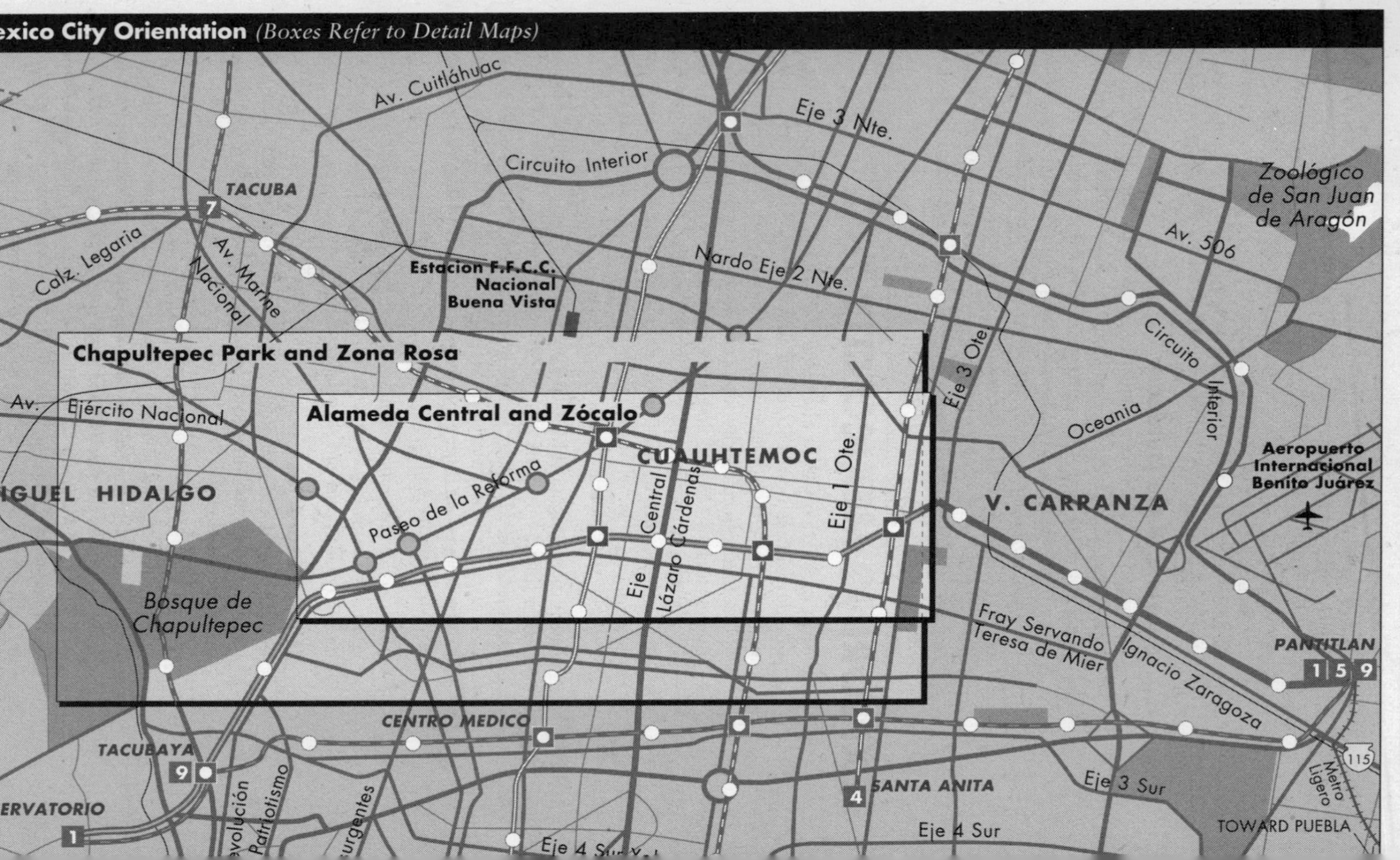
Mexico City Orientation (Boxes Refer to Detail Maps)
Av. Cuitláhuac
Eje 3 Nte.
Circuito Interior
TACUBA
7
Calz. Legaria
Av. Marina Nacional
Estacion F.F.C.C. Nacional Buena Vista
Nardo Eje 2 Nte.
Zoológico de San Juan de Aragón
Av. 506
Circuito Interior
Chapultepec Park and Zona Rosa
Alameda Central and Zócalo
Av. Ejército Nacional
Eje 3 Ote.
Oceania
Aeropuerto Internacional Benito Juárez
CUAUHTEMOC
Eje 1 Ote.
MIGUEL HIDALGO
Paseo de la Reforma
Eje Central Lázaro Cárdenas
V. CARRANZA
Bosque de Chapultepec
Fray Servando Teresa de Mier
Ignacio Zaragoza
PANTITLAN
1 5 9
CENTRO MEDICO
TACUBAYA
9
Eje 3 Sur
115
Metro Ligero
SANTA ANITA
4
OBSERVATORIO
1
Eje 4 Sur
TOWARD PUEBLA
Patriotismo
urgentes

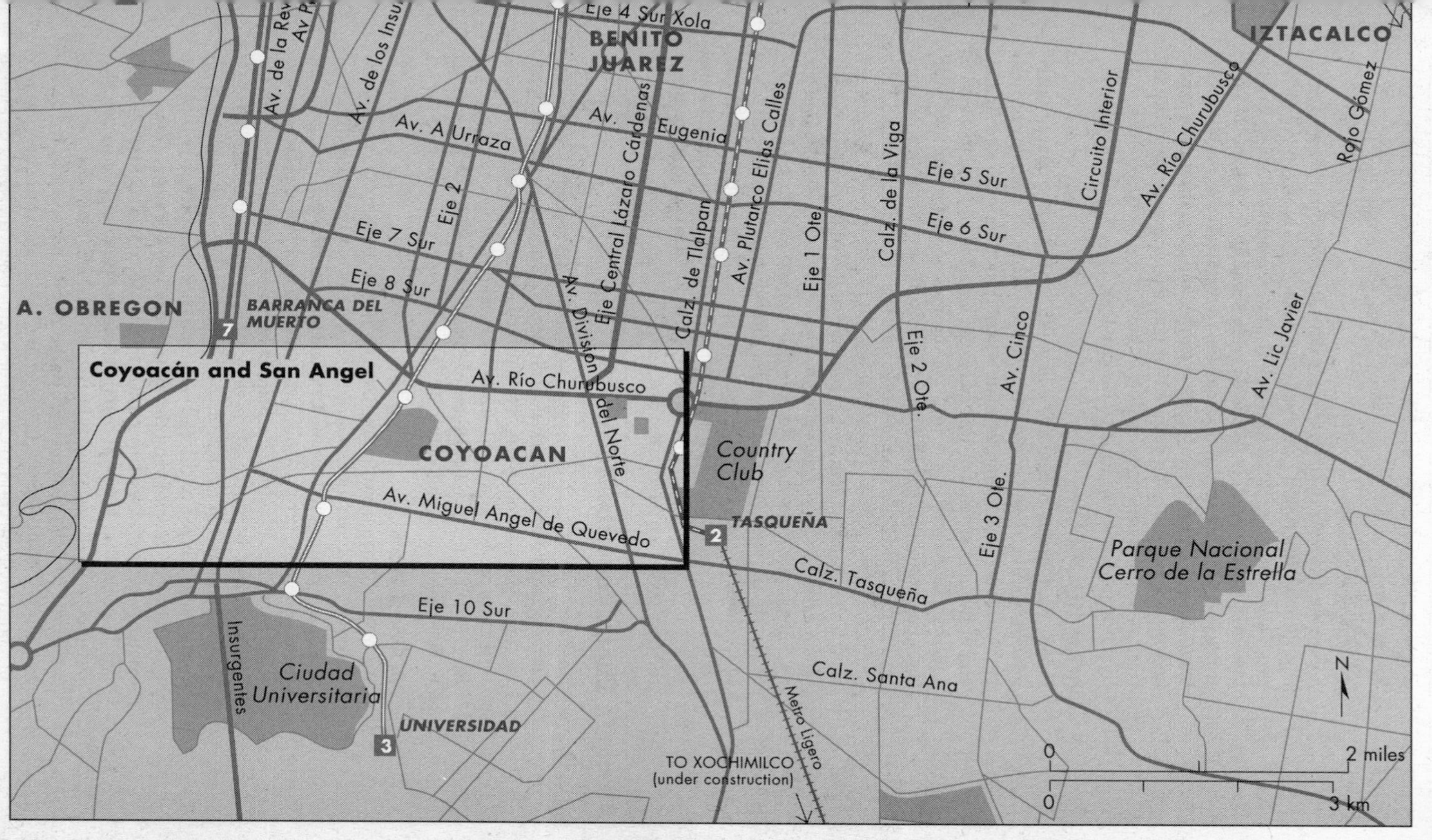
IZTACALCO
Rojo Gómez
Av. Río Churubusco
Circuito Interior
Eje 5 Sur
Eje 6 Sur
Calz. de la Viga
Eje 1 Ote.
Av. Plutarco Elías Calles
Calz. de Tlalpan
Eje 4 Sur Xola
BENITO
JUAREZ
Av. Eugenia
Eje Central Lázaro Cárdenas
Av. División del Norte
Av. A Urraza
Eje 2
Eje 7 Sur
Eje 8 Sur
Av. de los Insu
Av. de la Rev
A. OBREGON
BARRANCA DEL
MUERTO
Coyoacán and San Angel
Av. Río Churubusco
COYOACAN
Av. Miguel Angel de Quevedo
Country
Club
TASQUEÑA
Eje 2 Ote.
Av. Cinco
Av. Lic Javier
Eje 3 Ote.
Parque Nacional
Cerro de la Estrella
Calz. Tasqueña
Eje 10 Sur
Insurgentes
Ciudad
Universitaria
UNIVERSIDAD
Calz. Santa Ana
Metro Ligero
TO XOCHIMILCO
(under construction)
N
0
2 miles
0
3 km

(☞ Nightlife, *below*) on your last night in town for a rousing mariachi send-off.

IF YOU HAVE 5 DAYS

Follow the itinerary of the first three days (☞ *above*); on Day 4 spend your time in **San Angel** (start with the Bazar Sábado if you are lucky enough to hit this area on a Saturday) and **Coyoacán** with its lovely casa-museums, especially **Museo de Frida Kahlo** ㊲ and **Museo de Leon Trotsky** ㊳. On Day 5 take an excursion to the **Basílica of the Virgin of Guadalupe,** Latin America's holiest shrine, and the **pyramids of Teotihuacán,** the holy site of a culture that reached its zenith before the arrival of the Spanish conquistadors. Climb at least one pyramid, visit the museum, and head back to Mexico City.

IF YOU HAVE 10 DAYS

Follow the five-day option and add a visit to the resort town of **Cuernavaca,** about an hour's drive from Mexico City; spend the day browsing in its museums and pretty main square, and then stay overnight at one of the converted mansions here. On Day 7 head back to Mexico City by Highway 95 and stop in **Xochimilco,** where you can ride through the floating gardens on a gondola-like boat and view an outstanding private collection of works by Diego Rivera and Frida Kahlo at the Dolores Olmedo Patino Museum. On Day 8 go to see the ancient Toltec ruins at **Tula** and then drive to the village of **Tepozotlán,** which has a beautiful Jesuit church. The next day, head to **Puebla** for a couple hours' tour, including the main square and the fine Amparo Museum, and then continue on for a short distance to the small town of **Cholula,** once a sacred ceremonial site. Climb to the top of the church built over a pyramid, and return to Puebla to overnight. En route back to Mexico City on this last day, drive to **Cacaxtla** to see some of the best-preserved Mesoamerican murals in Mexico.

Alameda Central and the Zócalo

This area is historical in focus: The Zócalo, its surrounding Centro Histórico, and Alameda Park were the heart of both the Aztec and Spanish cities. Many of the streets in downtown Mexico City have been converted into pedestrian-only thoroughfares, adding to the ease of strolling here. In 1996, the city affixed bronze nameplates with historic legends to 500 buildings in this district.

A Good Walk

An excellent departure point for any tour of the city's center is the **Zócalo** ①, the heart and soul of old downtown. On the north side of this huge square you'll see the **Catedral Metropolitana** ② and, adjacent to it, the comparatively small 18th-century Sagrario Chapel, even more tilted than the cathedral. The **Templo Mayor** ③, temple ruins from the Aztec capital, is northeast of the cathedral on Calle Seminario. If you're interested in modern art, walk south about half a block from the Templo Mayor to the end of Seminario; then detour two blocks east to Calle Academia and the **Museo José Luis Cuevas** ④. Take Academia two blocks west to return to the Zócalo. The first building you'll see on your left is the massive **Palacio Nacional** ⑤, covering two city blocks. Walk south past the palacio to the corner, cross the street, and turn right to reach the part of the Zócalo occupied by the **Ayuntamiento** ⑥; then recross the street and walk across the open square in a northwest direction to Calle 5 de Mayo, where the **Monte de Piedad** ⑦ stands. Now head north 3½ blocks to the **Plaza de Santo Domingo** ⑧; then walk one block east along Calle Republica de Cuba and one block south to Calle Justo Sierra and the **Conjunto de San Idelfonso** ⑨. Continue 3½ blocks west along Calle Justo Sierra (which

Alameda Central and the Zócalo

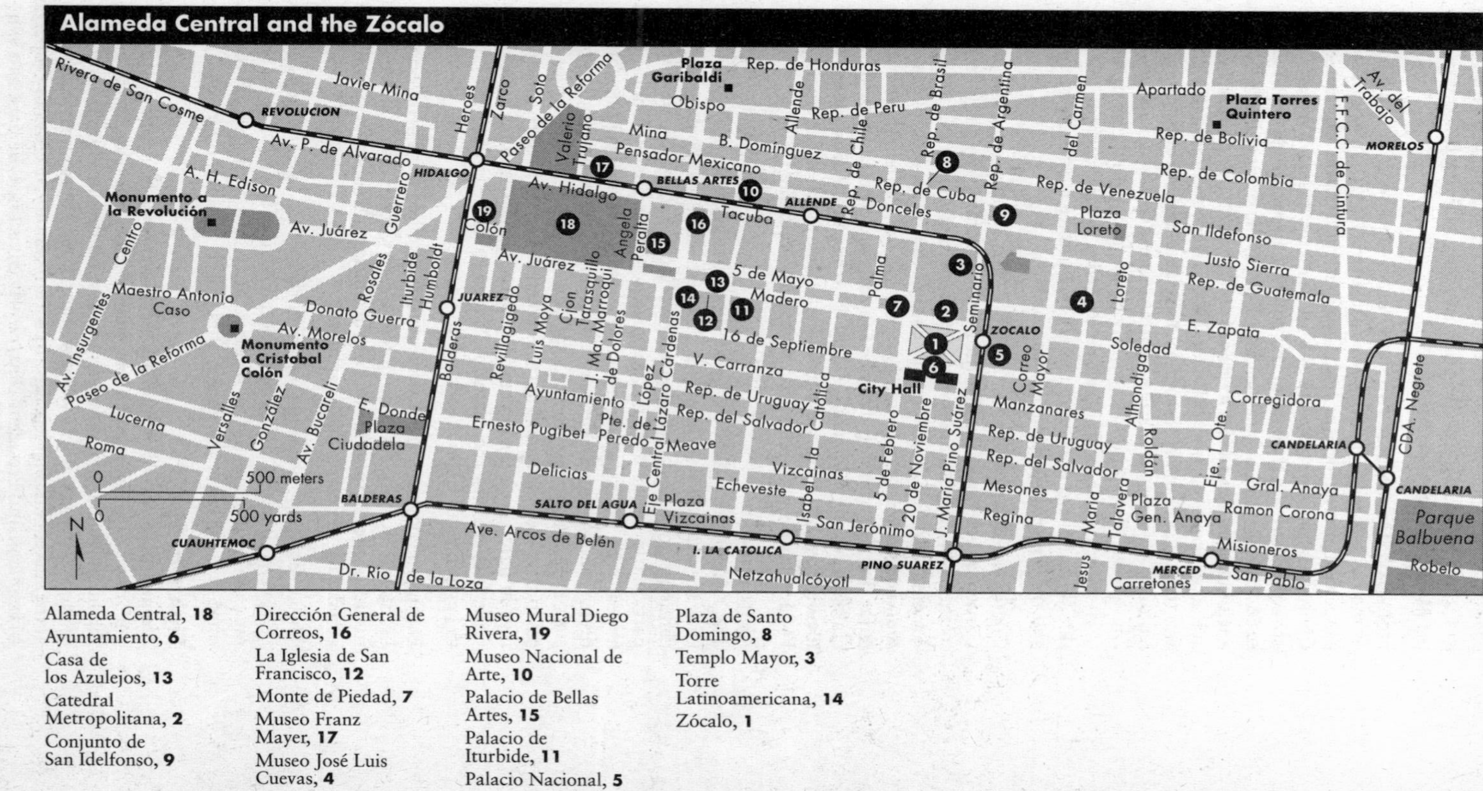

Alameda Central, **18**
Ayuntamiento, **6**
Casa de los Azulejos, **13**
Catedral Metropolitana, **2**
Conjunto de San Idelfonso, **9**
Dirección General de Correos, **16**
La Iglesia de San Francisco, **12**
Monte de Piedad, **7**
Museo Franz Mayer, **17**
Museo José Luis Cuevas, **4**
Museo Mural Diego Rivera, **19**
Museo Nacional de Arte, **10**
Palacio de Bellas Artes, **15**
Palacio de Iturbide, **11**
Palacio Nacional, **5**
Plaza de Santo Domingo, **8**
Templo Mayor, **3**
Torre Latinoamericana, **14**
Zócalo, **1**

changes into Calle Donceles) to Calle Allende, then walk a block south to Calle Tacuba; here, at the colonial Plaza Manuel Tolsa, you'll see the **Museo Nacional de Arte** ⑩.

From Calle Tacuba, head two short blocks south to Calle Madero, one of the city's most architecturally varied streets. On the south side of Madero, between Bolivar and Gante, is the **Palacio de Iturbide** ⑪. Continue along on the south side of Madero; less than a block west of the palacio you'll come to the colonial **La Iglesia de San Francisco** ⑫. An eye-catching blue facade just across the street will attract your attention to the **Casa de los Azulejos** ⑬ on the north side of Calle Madero at the corner of Callejón de la Condesa. In stark contrast to the church and the house is the 20th-century **Torre Latinoamericana** ⑭, less than half a block west on the Eje Central Lázaro Cárdenas, a wide four-lane avenue. Two other noteworthy buildings are on the same avenue to the north: the beautiful **Palacio de Bellas Artes** ⑮, whose one long side skirts Lázaro Cárdenas, though its entrance is actually on Juárez; and the **Dirección General de Correos** ⑯.

Continue north past the post office to Calle Tacuba and cross Lázaro Cárdenas; here Calle Tacuba turns into Avenida Hidalgo. One block to the west, you'll come to the **Museo Franz Mayer** ⑰, and across Avenida Hidalgo from the museum is the north side of the leafy **Alameda Central** ⑱. Avenida Juárez forms the southern border of the park; on this street you'll notice **Fonart,** a government-owned handicrafts store (☞ Shopping, *below*). To reach the **Museo Mural Diego Rivera** ⑲, take Juárez west to Calle Balderes (about 3½ blocks from Fonart); turn right and walk a short block to Calle Colon.

TIMING

The Zócalo area will be the quietest on Sunday, when the bureaucrats have their day of rest. However, Alameda Park will be jumping with children and their parents enjoying a Sunday outing. The park will be particularly festive during Christmas, when dozens of "Santas" will appear with plastic reindeer to take wish lists from long lines of children. The traditional Mexican Christmas kicks in on January 5, the eve of the Day of the Three Kings, and the Three Wise Men of biblical lore replace the Santas in the Alameda. Gorgeous Christmas paintings in lights deck the entire Zócalo from end to end and stream up Calle Madero past the Alameda Park to Paseo de la Reforma beyond the museums in Chapultepec Park.

During the daytime, the downtown area is filled with people and vibrant with activity. As in any other big city, travelers should be alert to pickpockets, especially on crowded buses and subways, and should avoid dark, deserted streets at night.

The streets in the walking tour are fairly close to one another and can be covered in half a day. The National Palace, Templo Mayor and its museum, and Franz Mayer Museum are worth an hour each of your time; you can cover the Palace of Fine Arts in a half hour.

Sights to See

⓲ **Alameda Central** (Alameda Park). This park has been one of the capital's oases of greenery and a center for activities since Aztec times, when the Indians held their *tianguis* (market) on the site. In the early days of the Viceroyalty, it was where victims of the Inquisition were burned at the stake. National leaders, from 18th-century viceroys to Emperor Maximilian and President Díaz, clearly envisioned the park as a symbol of civic pride and prosperity: Over the centuries, it has been endowed with fountains, railings, a Moorish kiosk imported from Paris, and ash, willow, and poplar trees. Its most conspicuous man-made structure is the white marble semicircular **Hemiciclo a Benito Juárez** (monument to Juárez) on the Avenida Juárez side of the park. It is a fine place for strolling (and resting) and listening to live music on Sundays and holidays.

6 **Ayuntamiento** (City Hall). Mexico's city hall comprises twin buildings on the south side of the Zócalo. The one on the west is decorated with colonial tiles of arms of Cortés and other conquistadores; it was originally built in 1532, destroyed by fire in 1692, and rebuilt in 1722. In 1935 the Distrito Federal needed more office space; to maintain architectural symmetry in the Zócalo, the "matching" structure across the street (20 de Noviembre) was built.

13 **Casa de los Azulejos** (House of Tiles). Built as the palace of the counts of the Valle de Orizaba, an aristocratic family from early Spanish rule, this 17th-century masterpiece acquired its name from the tilework installed by a later descendant, a ne'er-do-well scion who married a rich woman. In addition to its well-preserved white, blue, and yellow tiles, the facade also features iron grillwork balconies and gray stonework. One of the prettiest baroque structures in the country, it is currently occupied by Sanborns, a chain store–restaurant. The dazzling interior, which includes a Moorish patio, a monumental staircase, and a mural by Orozco, is worth seeing. If you have plenty of time, this is a good place to stop for breakfast, lunch, or dinner—service is slow. ✉ *Calle Madero 4,* ☎ *5/512–9820.* ⏲ *Daily 7 AM–1 PM.*

2 **Catedral Metropolitana** (Metropolitan Cathedral). Construction on this oldest and largest cathedral in Latin America began in 1573 on the north side of the Zócalo and continued intermittently throughout the next three centuries. The result is a medley of baroque and neoclassical touches. Inside are four identical domes, their airiness made earthbound by rows of supportive columns. There are five altars and 14 chapels, mostly in the fussy churrigueresque style, an extremely decorative form of Spanish baroque from the mid-17th century. Like most other Mexican churches, the cathedral itself is all but overshadowed by the innumerable paintings, altarpieces, and statues—in graphic color—of Christ and the saints. Over the centuries, this cathedral has sunk noticeably into the spongy subsoil. Its lopsidedness is evident when it is viewed from across the square, but engineering projects to stabilize the structure are always being undertaken.

9 **Conjunto de San Idelfonso** (San Idelfonso Complex). This colonial building with lovely patios started out as Jesuit school for the sons of wealthy Mexicans in the 18th century, then took life as a medical college, and finally became a public preparatory school. After a complete renovation, it reopened with the "Splendors of Mexico: 30 Centuries of Art" in 1992 and has been showcasing outstanding traveling Mexican exhibits ever since. The interior contains extraordinary works by the big three of mural painting—Diego Rivera, David Alfaro Siquieros, and Clemente Orozco. ✉ *Justo Sierra 16, almost at corner of República de Argentina, 2 blocks north of Zócalo,* ☎ *5/789–2505.* 🎟 *$2.* ⏲ *Sun.–Fri. 10–5.*

16 **Dirección General de Correos** (General Post Office). Mexico City's main post-office building is a lovely example of neo-Renaissance architecture. Constructed of cream-color sandstone in 1908, it epitomizes the grand imitations of European architecture common in Mexico during the Porfiriato, or dictatorship of Porfirio Díaz (1876–1910). On the upper floor, the **Museo de la Filatelia** exhibits the postal history of Mexico. The post office looks brand new since the facade underwent cleaning in 1996. ✉ *Calle Tacuba and Eje Central Lázaro Cardenas,* ☎ *5/564–*

3133 or 5/510–2999 for museum. 🎟 *Free.* ⏲ *Museum weekdays 9–7; post office Mon.–Sat. 8* AM*–midnight, Sun. 8–4.*

12 **La Iglesia de San Francisco.** Built on the site of Mexico's first convent (1524), this church supposedly was once the site of Moctezuma's zoo. The present 18th-century French Gothic church is one of the newest buildings on the street. The beautiful ceiling paintings have been restored. ✉ *Calles Madero and 16 de Septiembre.* ⏲ *Daily 9–5.*

7 **Monte de Piedad** (Mountain of Pity). Now housing the National Pawn Shop—which sells jewelry, antiques, and other goods not reclaimed by their owners—this structure was built to help the poor in the late 18th century. It's on the far northwest corner of the Zócalo, on what was once the site of an Aztec palace. ⏲ *Mon.–Sat. about 10–7.*

17 **Museo Franz Mayer.** Opened in 1986 in the 16th-century Hospital de San Juan de Dios, this museum has exhibits that include 16th- and 17th-century antiques, such as wooden chests inlaid with ivory, tortoiseshell, and ebony; tapestries, paintings, and lacquerware; rococo clocks, glassware, and architectural ornamentation; and an unusually large assortment of Talavera ceramics and tiles. Wall plaques explain in detail the history of the production of tiles (*azulejos*), a technique carried from Mesopotamia and Egypt to the Persians, Arabs, and Spaniards, who brought it to Mexico. The museum also has an impressive collection of more than 700 different editions of the book *Don Quixote*. The old hospital building is faithfully restored, with pieces of the original frescoes peeking through; classical music plays in the background. ✉ *Av. Hidalgo 45 at Plaza Santa Veracruz,* ☎ *5/518–2267.* 🎟 *$1.25.* ⏲ *Tues.–Sun. 10–5. Call ahead for English-speaking guide.*

4 **Museo José Luis Cuevas.** One of the newest museums in the downtown area, installed in a refurbished ex-convent, it offers a superb collection of modern art, as well as works by Mexico's enfant terrible, José Luis Cuevas, who is ranked as one of the country's best contemporary artists. The sensational **Sala Picasso** contains more than 30 original works by the Spanish master. Up-and-coming Latin American artists may be seen at rotating temporary exhibits. ✉ *Academia 13,* ☎ *5/542–8959.* 🎟 *Small fee.* ⏲ *Tues.–Sun. 10–6.*

19 **Museo Mural Diego Rivera.** The museum was built to display Diego Rivera's controversial mural *Sunday Afternoon Dream in the Alameda Park,* originally painted on a lobby wall of the Hotel Del Prado in 1947–48. The controversy was due to the Marxist Rivera's inscription, "God does not exist," which the artist later replaced with the bland "Conference of San Juan de Letrán" to placate Mexico's dominant Catholic population. Following the hotel's destruction in the 1985 earthquake, this gentle and poetic mural, which survived undamaged, was moved in its entirety across the street to the museum built to house it. ✉ *Calles Balderas and Colón,* ☎ *5/510–2329.* 🎟 *$2.* ⏲ *Tues.–Sun. 10–6.*

10 **Museo Nacional de Arte** (National Art Museum). This neoclassical building contains a superb collection of religious and contemporary artwork, both on permanent display and in temporary exhibitions. ✉ *Calle Tacuba 8,* ☎ *5/521–7320.* 🎟 *$1.25.* ⏲ *Tues.–Sun. 10–5.*

★ 15 **Palacio de Bellas Artes** (Fine Arts Palace). Construction on this colossal white-marble opera house was begun in 1904 by Porfirio Díaz, who wanted to add yet another ornamental building to his accomplishments. He was ousted during the same revolution that he bred and never got to see the building's completion (1934). Today the theater serves as a handsome venue for international and national artists, including such groups as the Ballet Folklórico de México. The palace is renowned for its architecture, by the Italian Adamo Boari, who also designed the post office; it includes an art-nouveau facade trimmed in pre-Hispanic motifs. Inside are a Tiffany stained-glass curtain (depicting the two volcanoes outside Mexico City) and paintings by several celebrated Mexican artists, including Rufino Tamayo and Mexico's trio of muralists: Rivera, Orozco, and Siqueiros. It was here that Rivera reconstructed his mural *Man at the Crossroads,* which was commissioned for and then torn down from Rockefeller Center in New York City because of its political message (epitomized by the face of Lenin). Temporary art exhibits are also held at the palace museum. ✉ *Eje Central Lázero Cardenas and Av. Juárez,* ☎ *5/709–3111.* 🎫 *$1.25.* ⏲ *Tues.–Sun. 10:30–6:30.*

OFF THE BEATEN PATH

TLATELOLCO – At Avenida Reforma's northern end, about 2 km (1 mi) north of the Palacio de Bellas Artes, the area known as Tlatelolco (Tla-tel-*ohl*-coh) was the domain of Cuauhtémoc—the last Aztec emperor before the conquest—and the sister city of Tenochtitlán. In modern times its name makes residents shudder, because it was here that several hundred protesting students were massacred by the Mexican army in 1968. The 1985 earthquake destroyed several high-rise apartments in Tlatelolco, killing hundreds.

The center of Tlatelolco is the Plaza de las Tres Culturas, so named because Mexico's three cultural eras—pre-Hispanic, colonial, and modern—are represented on the plaza in the form of the small ruins of a pre-Hispanic ceremonial center (visible from the roadway); the Iglesia de Santiago Tlatelolco (1609) and Colegio de la Santa Cruz de Tlatelolco (1535–36); and the ultracontemporary Ministry of Foreign Affairs (1970). The church contains the baptismal font of Juan Diego, the Indian to whom the Virgin of Guadalupe appeared in 1531. The Colegio (college), founded by the Franciscans after the conquest, was once attended by the sons of the Aztec nobility. ✉ *Plaza is bounded on north by Manuel González, on west by Av. San Juan de Letrán Norte, and on east by Paseo de la Reforma, between Glorieta de Peralvillo and Glorieta Cuitláhuac.*

11 **Palacio de Iturbide** (Emperor Iturbide's Palace). Built in 1780, this handsome baroque structure—note the imposing door and its carved-stone trimmings—became the residence of Iturbide in 1822. One of the heroes of the independence movement, the misguided Iturbide proclaimed himself emperor of a country that had thrown off the imperial yoke of the Hapsburgs only a year before; his own empire, needless to say, was short-lived. Now his home is owned by Banamex (Banco Nacional de México) and sponsors major cultural exhibitions in the atrium. ✉ *Calle Madero 17,* ☎ *5/518–2187.* 🎫 *Free.* ⏲ *Inner atrium weekdays 9–6 and weekends during exhibitions.*

★ 5 **Palacio Nacional** (National Palace). This grand government building was initiated by Cortés on the site of Moctezuma's home and remodeled by the viceroys; its current form dates from 1693, although a third floor was added in 1926. Now the seat of government, it has always served as a public-function site. In fact, during colonial times, the first bullfight in New Spain took place in the inner courtyard.

Diego Rivera's sweeping, epic murals on the second floor of the main courtyard have the power to mesmerize. For more than 16 years (1929–45), he and his assistants mounted the scaffolds day and night, perfecting techniques adapted from Renaissance Italian frescoes. The result, nearly 1,200 square ft of vividly painted wall space, is grandiosely entitled *Epic of the Mexican People in Their Struggle for Freedom and*

Independence. The larger-than-life paintings represent two millennia of Mexican history, as seen through the artist's vivid imagination. The innocence of pre-Hispanic times is portrayed by idyllic, almost sugary scenes of Tenochtitlán. Only a few vignettes—a lascivious woman baring her leg in the marketplace, a man offering a human arm for sale, and the carnage of warriors—acknowledge other aspects of ancient life. As you walk around the floor, you'll pass images depicting the savagery of the conquest and the hypocrisy of the Spanish priests, the noble independence movement, and the bloody revolution. Marx appears amid scenes of class struggles, toiling workers, industrialization (which Rivera idealized), the decadence of the bourgeoisie, and nuclear holocaust. The murals are among Rivera's finest works. They are also the most accessible and probably the most visited of the artist's paintings. The palace also houses two minor museums—dealing with 19th-century president Benito Juárez and the Mexican Congress—and the liberty bell rung by Padre Hidalgo to proclaim independence in 1810 hangs high on the central facade. It chimes every eve of September 16, while from the balcony below, the president repeats *el grito,* the historic shout of independence. ✉ *East side of the Zócalo.* 🎫 *Free.* ⏲ *Daily 9–5.*

8 **Plaza de Santo Domingo** (Santo Domingo Plaza). According to legend, here is where the nomadic Aztecs spied an eagle sitting on a cactus with a snake clutched in its beak, an omen indicating they should settle here; later the Aztec emperor Cuauhtémoc built a palace here and during the colonial era it served as the intellectual hub of the city. Today, its most colorful feature is the **Portal de los Evangelistas** (Portal of the Evangelists), filled with scribes at old-fashioned typewriters who are most likely composing letters for love-stricken swains. This age-old custom, which originated when quill pens were in vogue, has successfully launched quite a few of Cupid's arrows. The gloomy-looking **Palace of the Inquisition,** founded by the Catholic Church 50 years after the Conquest in 1571 and closed by government decree in 1820, is catercorner to the lively portal and now functions as a nursing school. The 18th-century baroque **Santo Domingo church** slightly north of the portal is all that remains of the first Dominican convent in New Spain. The convent building was demolished in 1861 under the Reform laws that forced clerics to turn over all religious buildings not used for worship to the government. Today, you can still see white-robed Dominican nuns visiting the church. ✉ *Between República de Cuba, República de Brasil, Republica de Venezuela, and Palma.*

9 **Templo Mayor** (Great Temple). The ruins of the ancient hub of the Aztec empire were unearthed accidentally in 1978 by telephone repairmen and have since been turned into a vast and historically significant archaeological site and museum. At this temple, dedicated to the Aztec cult of death, captives from rival tribes—as many as 10,000 at a time—were sacrificed to the bloodthirsty god of war, Huitzilopochtli. Seven rows of leering stone skulls adorn one side of the structure.

The adjacent **Museo del Templo Mayor** contains 3,000 pieces unearthed from the site and from other ruins in central Mexico; they include ceramic warriors, stone carvings and knives, skulls of sacrificial victims, a rare gold ingot, models and scale reproductions, and a room on the destruction of Tenochtitlán by the Spaniards. The centerpiece is an 8-ton disk discovered at the Templo Mayor; it depicts the moon goddess Coyolxauhqui, who, according to myth, was decapitated and dismembered by her brother Huitzilopochtli for trying to persuade her 400 other brothers to murder their mother. ✉ *Guatemala and Argentina,* ☎ *5/542–4784, 5/542–4785, or 5/542–4786.* 🎫 *$2.25.* ⏲ *Tues.–Sun. 9–5. Call to schedule English-language tours.*

14 **Torre Latinoamericana** (Latin American Tower). Touted as the tallest building in the capital before the Hotel de Mexico was built in the 1980s, this 47-story skyscraper was completed in 1956, and on clear days the observation deck and restaurant on the top floors afford fine views of the city. ✉ *Calle Madero and Eje Central Lázaro Cárdenas.* 🎫 *$1.50.* ⏲ *Observation deck daily 9 AM–11 PM.*

1 **Zócalo** (formal name: Plaza de la Constitución). Mexico City's historical plaza was built by the Spaniards, using Indian slave labor. This enormous paved square, the largest in the Western Hemisphere, occupies the site of the ceremonial center of Tenochtitlán, the capital of the Aztec empire, which once comprised 78 buildings. Throughout the 16th, 17th, and 18th centuries, the Spaniards and their descendants constructed elaborate churches and convents, elegant mansions, and stately public edifices, many of which have long since been converted to other uses. There is an air of Old Europe to this section of the city, which, in its entirety (the Centro Histórico), is a national monument that has been undergoing a major refurbishing; at press time, much had already been accomplished and even more was under way. Imposing buildings are constructed with the ubiquitous blood-red volcanic tezontle stone and the quarry stones that the Spaniards recycled from the rubble of the Aztec temples they razed. Throngs of small shops, eateries, cantinas, street vendors, and women dressed in native Indian dress contribute to an inimitably Mexican flavor, even an exuberance.

Zócalo means "pedestal" or "base": In the mid-19th century an independence monument was planned for the square, but it was never built. The term stuck, however, and now the word "zócalo" is applied to the main plazas of most Mexican cities. Mexico City's Zócalo (because it's the original, it is always capitalized) is used for government rallies, protest marches, sit-ins, and festive events. It is the focal point for Independence Day celebrations on the eve of September 16 and is spectacularly festooned during the Christmas holiday season. Flag-raising and -lowering ceremonies take place here in the early morning and late afternoon. ✉ *Bounded by 16 de Septiembre to south, 5 de Mayo to north, Piño Suarez to east, and Monte de Piedad to west.*

Chapultepec Park and Zona Rosa

A Good Walk

The Paseo de la Reforma, modeled after the Champs-Elysées in Paris, was built by Emperor Maximilian in 1865 to connect the Palacio Nacional (☞ Alameda Central and the Zócalo, *above*) with his residence, the Castillo de Chapultepec. At the northern end of Reforma are Tlatelolco (☞ Alameda Central and the Zócalo, *above*), the Lagunilla Market, and Plaza Garibaldi, where the mariachis gather; to the south, Reforma wends its leisurely way west into the wealthy neighborhoods of Lomas de Chapultepec, where most of the houses and estates are behind stone walls.

Two areas along Reforma of particular interest are the Zona Rosa (Pink Zone) and Chapultepec Park. Start your exploration of these sections at the junction of Reforma, Avenida Juárez, and Bucareli, just west of the Alameda Central. Along the stretch of Reforma west of this intersection are a number of statues erected at the request of Porfirio Díaz to honor illustrious men, including Simón Bolívar, Columbus, Pasteur, and Cuauhtémoc. The best known, the **Monumento a la Independencia** 20, also known as Angel Monument, marks the western edge of the Zona Rosa.

For years the Zona Rosa has been a favorite part of the city for tourists and residents because of the plethora of restaurants, cafés, art and antiques galleries, hotels, discos, and shops. With the mushrooming of fast-food places and some tacky bars and stores, the Zona—as it is affectionately called—has lost some of its former gloss but nonetheless still draws the faithful. Most of the buildings in the Zona Rosa are two or three stories high; they were originally private homes built in the 1920s for the wealthy. All the streets are wistfully named after European cities; some, such as Genova, are garden-lined pedestrian malls accented with contemporary bronze statuary.

To enjoy the Pink Zone, just walk the lengths of Hamburgo and Londres and some of the side streets, especially Copenhague—a veritable restaurant row. The large handicrafts market on Londres is officially Mercado Insurgentes, though most people call it either Mercado Zona Rosa or Mercado Londres. Just opposite the market's Londres entrance is Plaza del Angel, a small shopping mall that has a *minitianguis* (native market) on weekends. Contrasting with the mercado is the sleek Plaza La Rosa shopping mall.

Four blocks southwest of the Zona Rosa, at Avenida Chapultepec, you'll come to the main entrance to **Bosque de Chapultepec** ㉑, or Chapultepec Park.

TIMING

You can easily spend an hour each at the museums (☞ Sights to See, *below*), with the exception of the National Museum of Anthropology, which is gigantic compared to its sister cultural centers. You can have a quick go-through in two hours, but to really appreciate the fine exhibits, anywhere from a half-day to two full days would be more appropriate. Tuesday to Saturday are good days to visit the museums and stroll around the park. On Sunday and Mexican holidays, when museum entry is free, the park and museums are packed with families with lots of small children.

Sights to See

㉑ **Bosque de Chapultepec** (Chapultepec Park). This 1,600-acre green space, divided into three sections, draws families on weekend outings, cyclists, joggers, and museum goers. It is one of the oldest parts of Mexico City, having been inhabited by the Mexica (Aztec) tribe as early as the 13th century. The Mexica poet-king Nezahualcoyotl had his palace here and ordered construction of the aqueduct that brought water to Tenochtitlán. Ahuehuete trees (Moctezuma cypress) still stand from that era, when the woods were used as hunting preserves.

At the park's principal entrance, one block west of the Chapultepec metro station, you'll see the **Monumento a los Niños Héroes** (Monument to the Boy Heroes), consisting of six marble columns adorned with eaglets. In the monument are supposedly buried the six young cadets who wrapped themselves in the Mexican flag and then jumped to their deaths from the ramparts during the U.S. invasion of 1847. (That war may not take up much space in American textbooks, but to the Mexicans it is still a troubling symbol of their neighbor's aggressive dominance: The war cost Mexico almost half of its national territory—the present states of Texas, California, Arizona, New Mexico, and Nevada.)

Uphill from the entrance is the ☞ **Castillo de Chapultepec** and its National History Museum. Heading downhill again after leaving the Castillo, you'll go past the much smaller ☞ **Museo del Caracol.** North of the Castillo on the south side of Paseo de la Reforma is the ☞ **Museo de Arte Moderno**; almost directly across Paseo de La Reforma on its

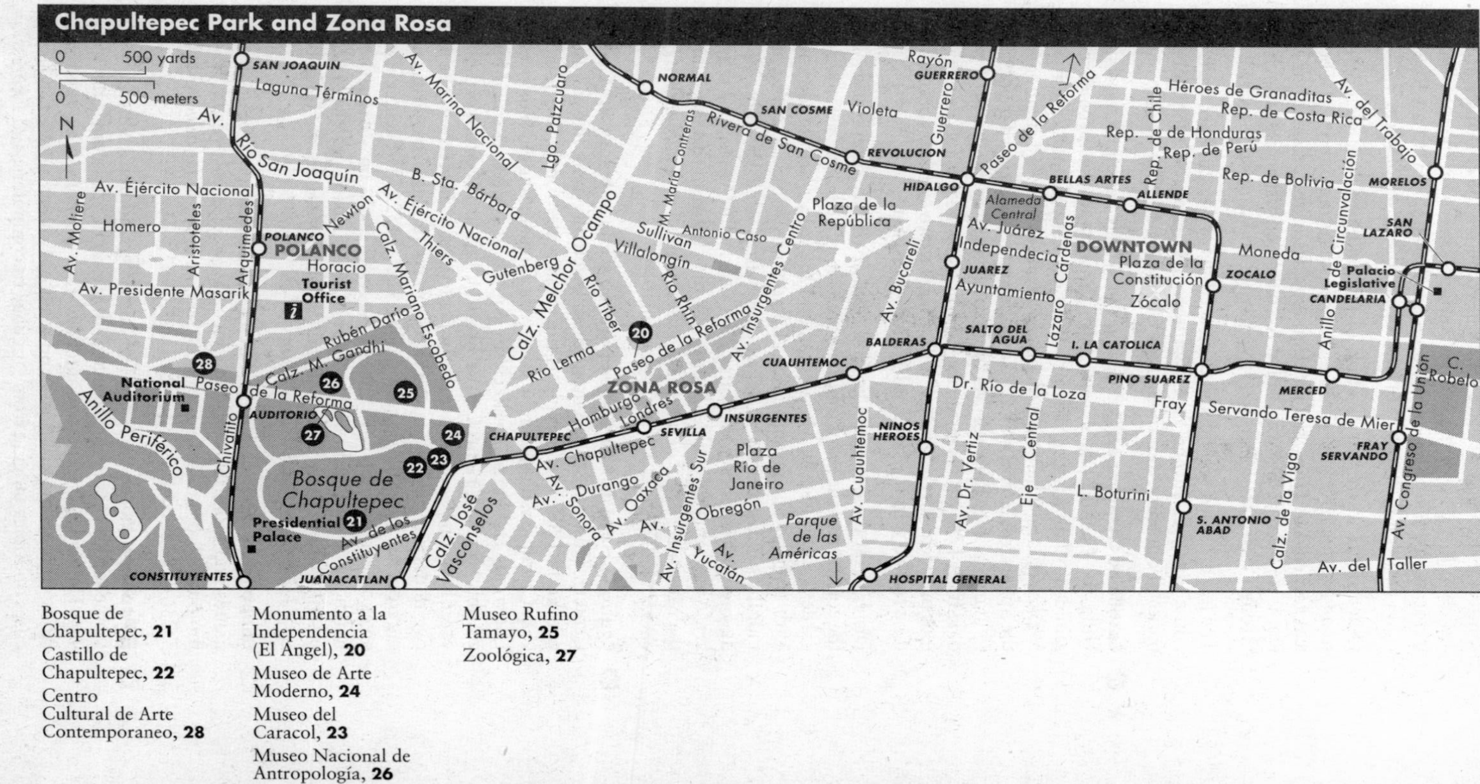

Bosque de Chapultepec, **21**

Castillo de Chapultepec, **22**

Centro Cultural de Arte Contemporaneo, **28**

Monumento a la Independencia (El Angel), **20**

Museo de Arte Moderno, **24**

Museo del Caracol, **23**

Museo Nacional de Antropología, **26**

Museo Rufino Tamayo, **25**

Zoológica, **27**

south side and west of Calle Gandhi, you'll see the ☞ **Museo Rufino Tamayo.** Just west of the Museo Rufino Tamayo on the same side of Reforma is the ☞ **Museo Nacional de Antropología.** Cross Reforma again and you'll come to the entrance to the ☞ **Zoológica.**

Other sights in the first section of Chapultepec Park include three small boating lakes; the Casa del Lago, a cultural center; and a botanical garden. **Los Pinos,** the residential palace of the president of Mexico, is on a small highway called Avenida Constituyentes, which cuts through the park. This is heavily guarded and cannot be visited.

The less crowded second and third sections of Chapultepec Park contain a fancy restaurant; ☞ **Chapultepec Mágico;** ☞ **El Papalote;** the national cemetery; and the **Lienzo Charro,** or Mexican rodeo.

★ 22 **Castillo de Chapultepec.** Located on Cerro del Chapulín (Grasshopper Hill), the Castillo (Castle) has borne witness to the turbulence and grandeur of all Mexican history. In its earliest permutations, it was a Mexica palace, where the Indians made one of their last stands against the Spaniards; later it was a Spanish hermitage, gunpowder plant, and military college. Emperor Maximilian used the castle (parts of which date from 1783) as his residence, and his example was followed by various presidents from 1872 to 1940, when Lázaro Cárdenas decreed that it be turned into the **National History Museum.**

Displays on the museum's ground floor cover Mexican history from the conquest to the revolution; the bathroom, bedroom, tea salon, and gardens were used by Maximilian and his wife, Carlotta, during the 19th century. The ground floor also contains works by 20th-century muralists O'Gorman, Orozco, and Siqueiros, while the upper floor is devoted to temporary exhibits, Díaz's malachite vases, and religious art. A free, but unreliable, shuttle bus runs between this museum and the Museo del Caracol (☞ *below*). ✉ *Section 1 of Chapultepec Park,* ☎ *5/286–0700.* 🎟 *$2.* ⏲ *Tues.–Sun. 9–5.*

28 **Centro Cultural de Arte Contemporaneo** (Contemporary Art Cultural Center). This four-story center, which is actually more like a museum, opened in 1985 after serving as the press center for the World Soccer Cup Championships held the same year. Outstanding exhibits from the Louvre or Del Prado are likely to pop up as well as exciting photographic works of Henri Cartier Bresson, Edward Weston, or Lola Alvarez Bravo in the center's excellent Photographic Art section. The upper two floors feature a permanent exposition of pre-Hispanic artifacts dating from the Post-Classic period of AD 1000–1521. The center also has an excellent gift shop with English-language books on Mexican artists, handicrafts, postcards, and replicas of pre-Hispanic jewelry. ✉ *Campos Eliseos and Jorge Elliot next to J.W. Marriott hotel,* ☎ *5/282–0355.* 🎟 *$1.25; free Wed.* ⏲ *Tues.–Sun. 10–6, Wed. 10–9.*

Chapultepec Mágico. This children's amusement park offers various games and more than 50 rides, including a *montaña rusa* ("Russian mountain," or roller coaster). ✉ *Section 2 of Chapultepec Park,* ☎ *5/230–2112.* 🎟 *Under $3.* ⏲ *Tues.–Sun. 9–7.*

El Papalote, Museo del Niño (The Butterfly, Children's Museum). Five theme sections compose this excellent interactive museum: *Our World; The Human Body*; the pun-intended *Con-Sciencia,* with exhibits relating to both consciousness and science; *Communication,* which focuses on topics ranging from language to computers; and *Expression,* which includes art, music, theater, and literature. There are also temporary exhibits, workshops, an IMAX theater, store, and restaurant.

⊠ *Av. Constituyentes 268, Section 2 of Chapultepec Park,* ☎ *5/237-1781.* 🎟 *$5.* ⏲ *Fri.–Wed. 9–1 and 2–6; Thurs. 9–1, 2–6, and 7–11.*

20 **Monumento a la Independencia** (Independence Monument). A Corinthian column topped by a gold-covered angel is the city's most beautiful monument, built to celebrate the 100th anniversary of Mexico's War of Independence. Beneath the pedestal lie the remains of the principal heroes of the independence movement; an eternal flame burns in their honor. ⊠ *Traffic circle between Calle Río Tiber, Paseo de la Reforma, and Calle Florencia, 1 block west of U.S. embassy.*

24 **Museo de Arte Moderno** (Museum of Modern Art). Two rooms are devoted to plastic arts from the 1930s to the 1960s; a third focuses on the past 20 years; and a fourth room and annex house temporary exhibits of contemporary Mexican painting, lithography, sculpture, and photography. ⊠ *Reforma and Gandhi, Section 1 of Chapultepec Park,* ☎ *5/553-6233.* 🎟 *$2.50.* ⏲ *Tues.–Sun. 10–6.*

23 **Museo del Caracol.** Officially, it's the Galeria de la Lucha del Pueblo Mexicano por su Libertad, but most people refer to it by the more fanciful name "Museum of the Snail," because of its spiral shape. The gallery concentrates on the 400 years from the establishment of the Viceroyalty to the Constitution of 1917, using dioramas and light-and-sound displays that children can appreciate. ⊠ *Section 1 of Chapultepec Park,* ☎ *5/553-6285.* 🎟 *$1.25.* ⏲ *Tues.–Sun. 9–5.*

★ 26 **Museo Nacional de Antropología** (National Museum of Anthropology). This is the greatest museum in the country—and arguably one of the finest archaeological museums anywhere. Even its architectural design (by Pedro Ramírez Vázquez) is distinguished. The collection is so extensive—covering some 100,000 square ft—that you could easily spend a full day, and that in itself might be barely adequate. However, bilingual guides take you through the highlights in two-hour tours. English-language guidebooks are available in the bookshop.

Begin in the Orientation Room, which traces the course of Mexican prehistory and the pre-Hispanic cultures of Mesoamerica. The 12 rooms on the ground floor include preclassical cultures, Teotihuacán, the Toltecs, Huastecs, Olmecs, Totonacs, Mixtec, the Maya, and the north and west of Mexico. The so-called Aztec calendar stone, profusely feathered Aztec headdresses, and vivid reproductions of Maya murals in a reconstructed temple are just some of the highlights. These, however, are dwarfed by the magnificence of the tomb of the 8th-century Maya ruler Pacal, which was discovered in the ruins of Palenque. A soft light plays on the perfectly preserved skeletal remains lying in state in an immense stone chamber; light reflecting off his rich green jade necklaces is truly mesmerizing. The walls of the stairwell leading to the chamber are beautifully decorated with scenes of the underworld done in bas-relief; Pacal's jade death mask is on display nearby. The Maya section was updated in 1996 to include pieces from digs in remote places like Calakmul in Campeche and Tonina and Yaxchílan in Chiapas. Otherwise the ground floor is filled with statuary, jewelry, weapons, clay figurines, and pottery that evoke the brilliant, quirky, and frequently bloodthirsty civilizations that peopled Middle America during Europe's Dark Ages. The nine rooms on the upper floor contain faithful ethnographic displays of current indigenous peoples, using maps, photographs, household objects, folk art, clothing, and religious articles. ⊠ *Section 1 of Chapultepec Park,* ☎ *5/553-1902.* 🎟 *$2.50.* ⏲ *Tues.–Sat. 9–7, Sun. 10–6.*

25 **Museo Rufino Tamayo.** Within its modernistic trappings, this sleek museum contains the private collection of the noted Mexican mural-

ist as well as many of his own paintings. Tamayo's unerring eye for great art is evidenced by paintings and sculptures by such contemporary masters as Picasso, Miró, Warhol, and Henry Moore. ✉ *Av. Reforma west of Gandhi, Section 1 of Chapultepec Park,* ☎ *5/286–6519.* *$1.25.* ⏲ *Tues.–Sun. 10–6.*

Ripley's Museo de lo Increíble (Museum of the Incredible). Fun for children of all ages, it has 14 exhibit rooms chockablock with believe-it-or-not items. ✉ *Londres 4 (east of Zona Rosa),* ☎ *5/546–3784 or 5/546–7670.* *$5.* ⏲ *Weekdays 11–7, weekends 10–7.*

27 **Zoológica.** In the early 16th century, Mexico City's zoo housed a small private collection of animals belonging to Moctezuma II; it became quasi-public when he allowed favored subjects to visit it. The current zoo opened on this site in the 1920s and features the usual suspects as well as some superstar pandas: A gift from China, the original pair produced the world's first panda baby born in captivity (much to competitive China's chagrin). The zoo is surrounded by a miniature train depot, botanical gardens, and lakes where you can go rowing. You'll see the entrance on Reforma, across the street from the Museum of Anthropology. ✉ *Section 1 of Chapultepec Park,* ☎ *5/553–6229.* *Free.* ⏲ *Tues.–Sun. 9–4:15.*

Coyoacán and San Angel

Originally separate colonial towns, Coyoacán and San Angel were both absorbed by the ever-growing capital, yet they retain their original pueblo charm and tranquillity.

Coyoacán means "Place of the Coyotes"—according to local legend, a coyote used to bring chickens to a friar who had saved the coyote from being strangled by a snake. Coyoacán was founded by Toltecs in the 10th century and later settled by the Aztecs, or Mexica. Bernal Díaz Castillo, a Spanish chronicler, wrote that there were 6,000 houses at the time of the conquest. Cortés set up headquarters in Coyoacán during his siege of Tenochtitlán and at one point considered making it his capital. He changed his mind for political reasons, but many of the Spanish buildings left from the two-year period during which Mexico City was built still stand.

Today, Coyoacán still exudes its charm as an old pueblo. The neighborhood has had many illustrious residents from Mexico's rich and intellectual elite, including Miguel de la Madrid, president of Mexico from 1982 to 1988; Orozco, the muralist; Gabriel Figueroa, cinematographer for Luis Buñuel and John Huston; the film star Dolores del Río; El Indio Fernández, a film director; and writers Carlos Monsiváis, Elena Poniatowska, and Jorge Ibargüengoitia. Although superficially it resembles San Angel, Coyoacán has a more animated street life. Most of the houses and other buildings honor the traditions of colonial Mexican architecture, and the neighborhood is well kept by residents, many of whose families have lived here for generations.

San Angel is a little colonial enclave of cobblestone streets, gardens drenched in bougainvillea, stone walls, and pastel houses. It became an enclave of wealthy Spaniards during the Viceroyalty period, around the time of the construction of the **Ex-Convento del Carmen** (☞ *below*). Drawn to the area because of its rivers, pleasant climate, and rural ambience, the elite class proceeded to build haciendas and mansions that, for many, were country homes. Like neighboring Coyoacán, San Angel was known only as a suburb of Mexico City until the government decided to incorporate it into the capital.

A Good Tour

To explore the southern part of the city—which until 50 years ago comprised separate pueblos—take a taxi or *pesero* (minibus) down Avenida Insurgentes and get off at Avenida La Paz. (The longest avenue in the city, at 34 km [21 mi], Insurgentes did not exist as such before the 1920s.) On the east side of Insurgentes is the bizarre **Monumento al General Alvaro Obregón** ㉙. Cross Insurgentes on Avenida La Paz, and take the southern fork off Avenida La Paz (Calle Madero) until you come to the **Plaza San Jacinto** ㉚. You are now in San Angel. Stroll to the **Casa del Risco** ㉛ on the south side of the plaza and, if it's a Saturday, visit the **Bazar Sábado** (☞ Shopping, *below*) on the northern end. Return to Avenida Revolución and Plaza del Carmen, which lies at the corner of Calle Monasterio; inside is the colonial **Ex-Convento del Carmen** ㉜. Now take Avenida Revolución one long block north to the **Museo Alvar y Carmen T. de Carrillo Gil** ㉝.

The next part of the tour is set in Coyoacán, which extends east of Avenida Insurgentes about 1 km (½ mi) from San Angel. Consider taking a taxi to the Plaza de Santa Catarina on Avenida Francisco Sosa, about halfway into the center of Coyoacán, because the tour involves a lot of walking.

If you decide to hoof it, go south on Avenida Universidad past the Viveros de Coyoacán—an expansive, tree-filled park. A long block past the end of the Viveros, you'll come to Avenida Francisco Sosa. Head east on this major thoroughfare until you come to the pretty 16th-century Iglesia de Santa Catarina, which dominates the tiny Plaza de Santa Catarina; the plaza also contains a bust of Mexican historian Francisco Sosa, who lived here and wrote passionately about Coyoacán. Continue east along Avenida Francisco Sosa until you come to No. 202, the Casa de Jesús Reyes Heroles; the former home of the ex–minister of education is a fine example of 20th-century architecture on the colonial model (it's now used as a cultural center). If you keep going in the same direction, you'll pass Casa de Diego de Ordaz at the corner of Tres Cruces. This *mudéjar* (Spanish-Arabic) structure, adorned with inlaid mortar, was home to a former captain in Cortés's army.

Now you're standing at the entrance of the **Jardin Centenario** ㉞. The Templo de San Juan Bautista and the **Casa de Cortés** ㉟ sit in the small Plaza Hidalgo adjacent to and north of the Jardin. Walk two blocks southeast of Plaza Hidalgo on Calle Higuera to the corner of Calle Vallarta where the **Casa de la Malinche** ㊱ is. The house, darkened with age, faces an attractive park called Plaza de la Conchita, in the center of which lies an 18th-century church.

Return to Plaza Hidalgo and walk five blocks north on Calle Allende to the corner of Calle Londres and the **Museo de Frida Kahlo** ㊲. It's linked historically with the fortresslike **Museo de Leon Trotsky** ㊳; to reach it, go three blocks east on Londres and two long blocks north on Morelos to Calle Viena.

TIMING

You're likely to want to linger in these elegant and beautiful sections of town, especially in Coyoacán. The Frida Kahlo and Leon Trotsky museums give you an intense and intimate look at the lives of two famous people who were friends and lovers and who breathed their personalities into the places where they lived; you should spend at least an hour at each one. The other museums are much smaller and merit less time. The weekends are the liveliest at the Plaza Hidalgo and its neighboring Jardin Centenario, where the street life explodes into a fiesta.

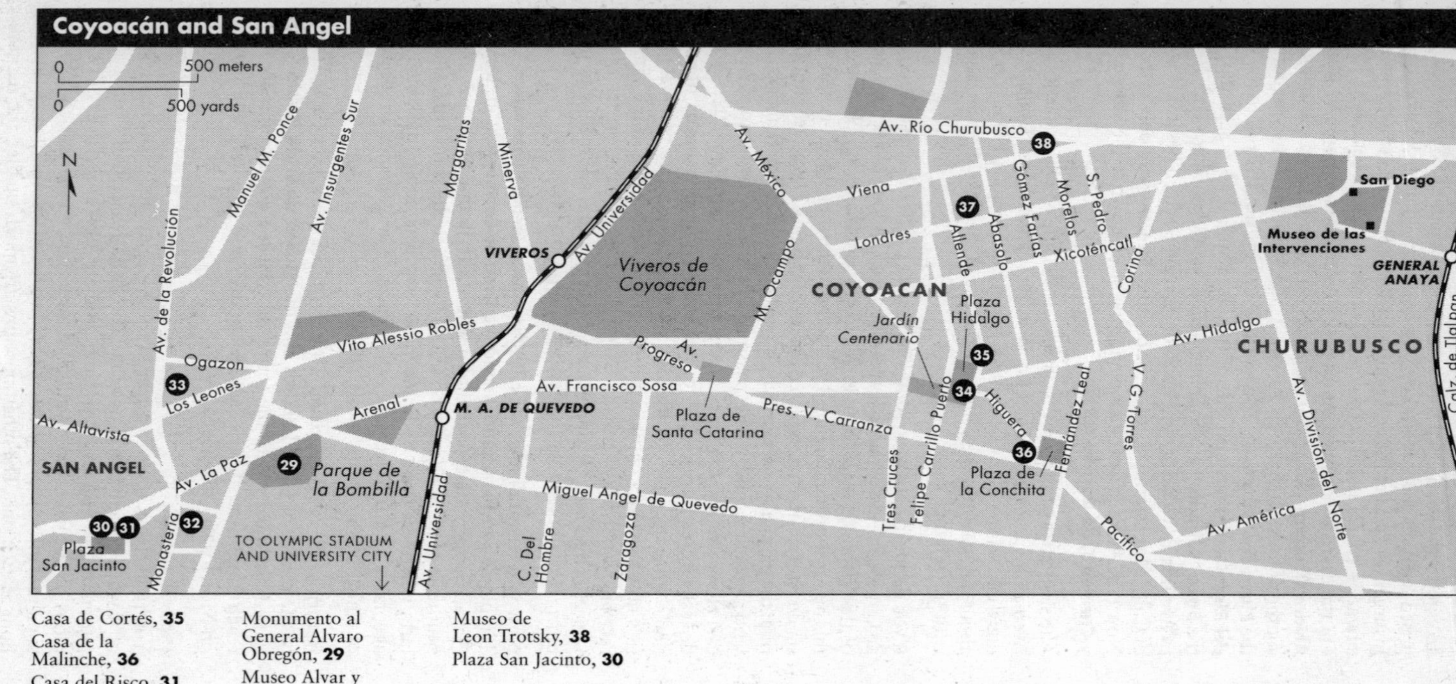

Casa de Cortés, **35**
Casa de la Malinche, **36**
Casa del Risco, **31**
Ex-Convento del Carmen, **32**
Jardin Centenario, **34**
Monumento al General Alvaro Obregón, **29**
Museo Alvar y Carmen T. de Carrillo Gil, **33**
Museo de Frida Kahlo, **37**
Museo de Leon Trotsky, **38**
Plaza San Jacinto, **30**

Sights to See

35 **Casa de Cortés.** The place where the Aztec emperor Cuauhtémoc was held prisoner by the conquistador Cortés is reputed to have been rebuilt in the 18th century from the stones of his original house by one of Cortés's descendants; the municipal government now has offices here. Dominating the little square on which it sits, this was almost the city's first city hall, but Cortés decided to rebuild Tenochtitlán instead. The two-story, salmon-color structure is gorgeous, with its wide arches and tiled patio. ⊠ *Plaza Hidalgo off Avs. Hidalgo and Francisco Sosa.*

36 **Casa de la Malinche.** One of the most powerful symbols of the conquest is located in Coyoacán but, significantly perhaps, is not even marked. It's the somber-looking, fortresslike residence of Malinche, Cortés's Indian mistress and interpreter, whom the Spaniards called Doña María and the Indians called Malintzín. Malinche aided the conquest by enabling Cortés to communicate with the Nahuatl-speaking tribes he met en route to Tenochtitlán. Today she is a much-reviled Mexican symbol of a traitorous xenophile—hence the term *malinchista,* used to describe a Mexican who prefers things foreign. The legends say that Cortés's wife died in this house, poisoned by the conquistador. ⊠ *2 blocks east of Plaza Hidalgo on Calle Higuera at Vallarta.*

31 **Casa del Risco.** If you visit this 1681 mansion, you'll see one of the prettiest houses facing the Plaza de San Jacinto. A huge free-form sculpture—exploding with colorful porcelain, tiles, shells, and mosaics—covers the entire eastern wall of its patio. Although it's not ranked among the city's top museums, the **Museo de la Casa del Risco** houses a splendid collection of 14th- to 18th-century European and colonial Mexican paintings as well as period furnishings. ⊠ *Plaza de San Jacinto 5 and 15,* ☎ *5/616–2711.* 🎫 *Free.* ⏲ *Tues.–Sun. 10–5.*

32 **Ex-Convento del Carmen** (Carmelite Convent and Church). Erected by Carmelite friars with the help of an Indian chieftain between 1615 and 1628, this cloister with its tile-covered domes, fountains, and gardens is one of the most interesting examples of colonial religious architecture in this part of the city. The church still operates, but the convent is now the **Museo Regional del Carmen,** with a fine collection of 18th-century religious paintings, icons, and mummified corpses. ⊠ *Av. Revolución 4 at Monasterio 10,* ☎ *5/616–2816 or 5/616–1177.* 🎫 *$2; free Sun.* ⏲ *Tues.–Sun. 10–5.*

34 **Jardín Centenario.** Small fairs, amateur musical performances, poetry readings, and palm readings are frequent occurrences in this large park surrounded by outdoor cafés. At the far end of the Jardin you'll see **Templo San Juan Bautista,** one of the first churches to be built in New Spain. It was completed in 1582, and its door has a baroque arch. ⊠ *Between Calles Centenario, Hidalgo, and Caballo Calco.*

29 **Monumento al General Alvaro Obregón.** This somber gray granite monument marks the spot where the national hero Obregón was gunned down in a restaurant in 1928. ⊠ *Parque de la Bombilla, east of Av. La Paz at Av. Insurgentes.*

33 **Museo Alvar y Carmen T. de Carrillo Gil.** This private collection contains early murals by Orozco, Rivera, and Siqueiros; works by modern European artists such as Klee and Picasso; and temporary expositions of young Mexican artists. ⊠ *Av. Revolución 1608 at Desierto de los Leones,* ☎ *5/550–3983.* 🎫 *$1.25.* ⏲ *Tues.–Sun. 10–5:50.*

★ 37 **Museo de Frida Kahlo.** The house where the painter Frida Kahlo was born—and lived with Diego Rivera almost continuously from 1929 until her death in 1954—is fascinating. Kahlo has become a cult figure, not only because of her paintings—mostly self-portraits in the surrealist tradition—but also because of her bohemian lifestyle and flamboyant individualism. As a child Kahlo was crippled by polio, and several years later she was impaled on a tramway rail. She had countless operations, including the amputation of a leg; was addicted to painkillers; had affairs with Leon Trotsky and several women; and married Rivera twice. Kahlo's astounding vitality and originality are reflected in this house, from the giant papier-mâché skeletons outside and the painted tin *retablos* (ex-votos) on the staircase to the gloriously decorated kitchen and the bric-a-brac in her bedroom. Even if you know nothing about Kahlo, a visit to the museum—also filled with letters, diaries, clothes, and paintings by Kahlo and other great moderns, including Klee and Duchamp—will leave you with a strong, visceral impression of this early feminist artist. ✉ *Londres 127,* ☎ *5/554–5999.* 🎫 *$1.25.* 🕑 *Tues.–Sun. 10–5:45.*

38 **Museo de Leon Trotsky.** Resembling an anonymous and forbidding fortress, with turrets for armed guards, this is where Leon Trotsky lived and was murdered. It is difficult to believe that it's the final resting place for the ashes of one of the most important figures of the Russian Revolution, but that only adds to the allure of the house, which is owned by Trotsky's grandson.

This is a modest, austere dwelling—anyone taller than 5 ft must stoop to pass through doorways to Trotsky's bedroom (with bullet holes in the walls from the first assassination attempt, in which the muralist Siqueiros was implicated), his wife's study, the dining room, and the study where Ramón Mercader finally drove an ice pick into Trotsky's head. (On his desk, cluttered with writing paraphernalia and an article he was revising in Russian, the calendar is open to that fateful day, August 20, 1940.) The volunteers will tell you how Trotsky's teeth left a permanent scar on Mercader's hand; how he clung to life for 26 hours; what his last words were; and how his death was sponsored by the United States. Not all of the volunteers, however, speak English. ✉ *Viena 45,* ☎ *5/658–8732.* 🎫 *$1.25.* 🕑 *Tues.–Sun. 10–5.*

Nuevo Reino Aventura. This 100-acre theme park on the southern edge of the city comprises six "villages": Mexican, French, Swiss, Polynesian, American, and Children's World. Shows include performances by trained dolphins. The most famous of the playful swimmers was an orca whale named Keiko, star of the film *Free Willy,* who was sent to an aquarium in Oregon to recover his health prior to being released into the wild again. ✉ *Southwest of Coyoacán on Carretera Picacho a Ajusco, Km 1.5,* ☎ *5/645–5434 or 5/654–6232.* 🎫 *$10, includes entrance and all rides.* 🕑 *Fri.–Sun. 10–6:30.*

★ 30 **Plaza San Jacinto.** This cozy plaza with a grisly history is the center of San Angel. In 1847 about 50 Irish soldiers of St. Patrick's Battalion—who had sided with the Mexicans in the Mexican-American War—had their foreheads branded here with the letter *D* (for deserters) and were then hanged by the Americans. These men had been enticed to swim the Rio Grande and desert the ranks of U.S. General Zachary Taylor by pleas to the historic and religious ties between Spain and Ireland; as settlers in Mexican Texas, they felt their allegiance lay with Catholic Mexico, and they were among the bravest fighters in the war. They met their end when the American flag flew over Castillo de Chapultepec (☞ *above*) after the death of the *niños héroes.* A memorial plaque at No. 23 listing their names and expressing Mexico's gratitude for their help in the "unjust North American invasion" now stands in the plaza, where each September a ceremony is conducted in their honor. Off to one side of the plaza, the excellent handicrafts market, **Bazar Sábado,** is held on Saturday (☞ Shopping, *below*). ✉ *Between Miramon, Cda. Santisima, Dr. Galvez, and Madero.*

DINING

Mexico City mealtime hours are 7–11 AM for breakfast (*desayuno*), 1–4 PM for lunch (*comida*), and 9 PM–midnight for dinner (*cena*). At deluxe restaurants, dress is generally formal (jacket and tie), and reservations are almost always required; see reviews for details. (Even if a deluxe restaurant doesn't *require* a jacket and tie, diners are likely to feel out-of-place if they're not well dressed.) For tourists on the run there are American-style coffee shops (VIPS, Denny's, Shirley's, and Sanborns) all over the city; some are open 24 hours.

Zona Rosa restaurants get filled pretty quickly on Saturday nights, especially the Saturday coinciding with the *quincena,* or payday, for nearly everyone in the city, which falls on the 1st and 15th of each month.

CATEGORY	COST*
$$$$	over $40
$$$	$25–$40
$$	$15–$25
$	under $15

**per person for a three-course meal, excluding drinks and service*

French

$$$$ ★ ✕ **Fouquet's de Paris.** Located in the Camino Real hotel, this is a branch of the renowned Parisian restaurant and an elegant haven of peace and tranquillity. The best pâtés in Mexico and tender, juicy lamb chops are part of the diverse and stylish menu. The desserts are in a class all their own. The sorbets, such as the delicately flavored passion fruit, are outstanding, and the cakes, mousses, and pastries are light and delicious. Monthlong gastronomic festivals are held here throughout the year, and each October or November, chefs from the original Fouquet's de Paris take over the kitchen. ✉ *Hotel Camino Real, Mariano Escobedo 700,* ☎ *5/203–2121. Reservations essential. Jacket and tie. AE, DC, MC, V. Closed Sun. No lunch Sat.*

$$$ ★ ✕ **Champs Elysées.** On the corner of Amberes and Reforma, commanding an impressive view of the Independence (Angel) Monument, is one of the bastions of haute cuisine in Mexico City. The variety of sauces served with both meat and fish dishes is impressive, with the hollandaise sauce over sea bass or red snapper probably taking top honors. Regulars find either the roast duck (carved at your table) or the pepper steak hard to resist. Of particular note is the generous cheese board. ✉ *Paseo de la Reforma 316, Zona Rosa,* ☎ *5/514–0450. AE, DC, MC, V. Closed Sun.*

$$ ✕ **La Petite France.** This restaurant in the Pasaje de Polanco has a very Mediterranean feel, with tables spilling out onto the street, hanging plants, and white wrought-iron furniture. The imaginative menu includes such specialties as fish soup with Pernod and roast lobster with basil, along with such typically Mediterranean dishes as stuffed mushrooms and *moules Provençales* (mussels Provençal). Fish dishes are popular, with *truite meunière* (trout, lightly fried and served with lemon), a giant prawn brochette, and deep-fried sea bass claiming most of the attention. Beautifully garnished and presented, the dishes come with a colorful, good selection of steamed vegetables. Soft piano music is played nightly from 9 to 11:30. ✉ *Av. Presidente Masaryk 360, Col. Polanco,* ☎ *5/280–8851 or 5/280–9335. AE, DC, MC, V. No dinner Sun.*

Mexico City Dining

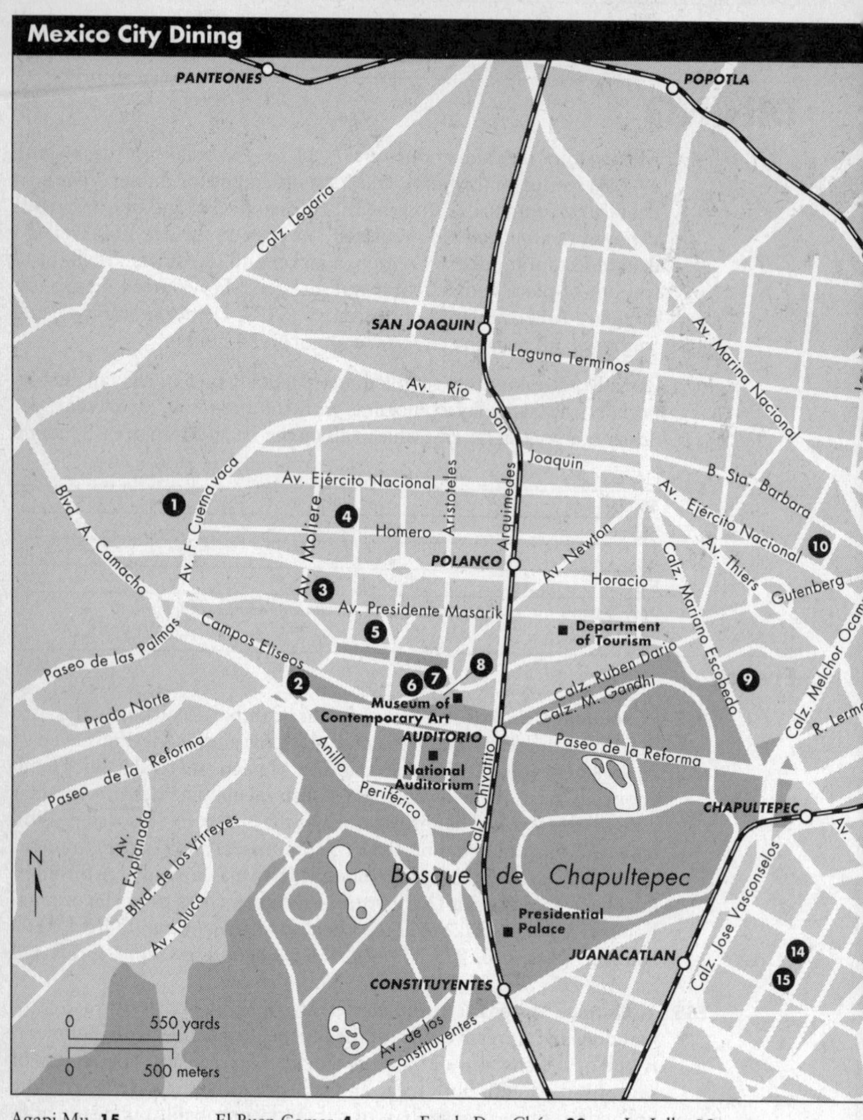

Agapi Mu, **15**
Bellinghausen, **19**
Bellini, **32**
Café de Tacuba, **27**
Champs Elysées, **17**
Cicero Centenario, **29**
El Arroyo, **22**
El Buen Comer, **4**
El Jug, **16**
El Parador de Manolo, **3**
El Tajin, **33**
Estoril, **6**
Fonda del Recuerdo, **10**
Fonda Don Chón, **30**
Fonda El Refugio, **18**
Fouquet's de Paris, **9**
Hacienda de los Morales, **1**
Hosteria de Santo Domingo, **28**
Isadora, **2**
La Jolla, **12**
La Lanterna, **11**
La Petite France, **5**
Las Cazuelas, **21**
Las Fuentes, **13**
Les Célébrités, **8**
Los Arroces, **14**

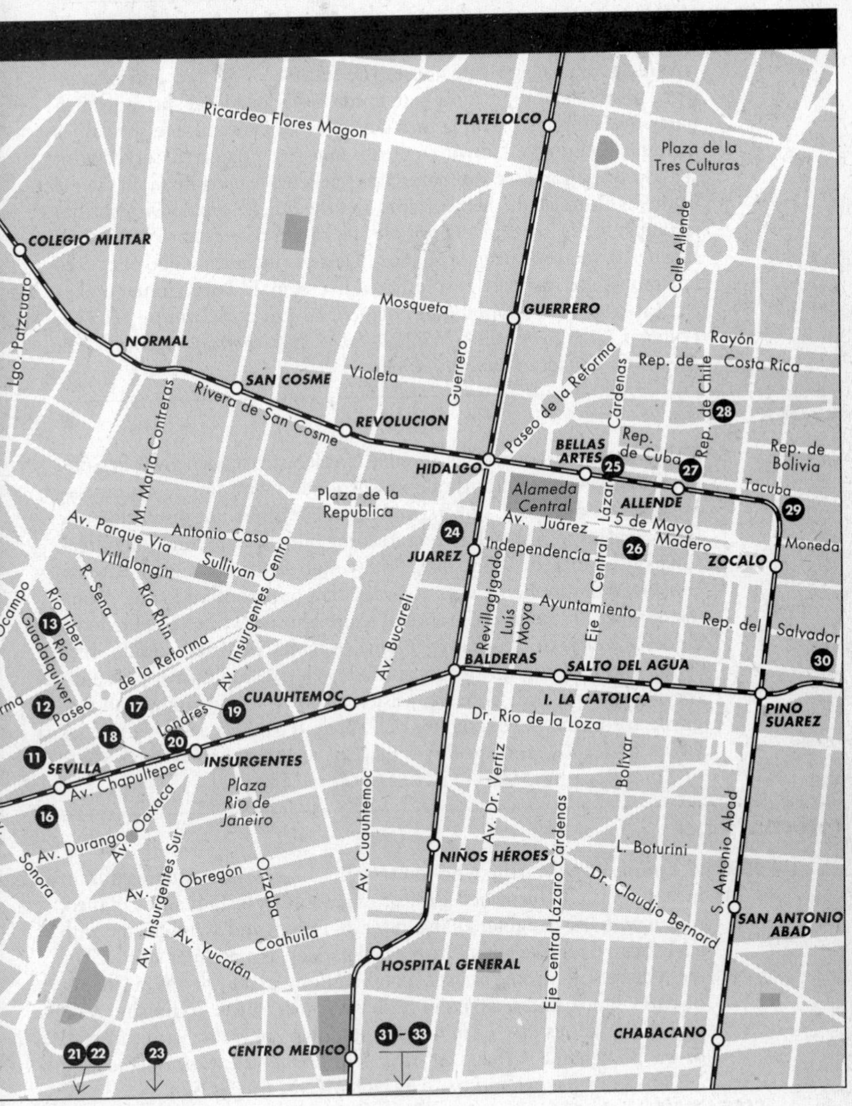

Los Girasoles, **25**
Los Irabien, **33**
Maxim's de Paris, **7**
Meson El Cid, **24**
Prendes, **26**
San Angel Inn, **31**
Suntory, **23**
Tezka, **20**

$ ✕ **El Buen Comer.** One of the more original Polanco eating spots, El Buen Comer (Eating Well) consists of not more than 20 tables in the covered garage of a private house. The entrance is discreet and can easily be missed, and the atmosphere inside is that of a large, private lunch party. The emphasis is on French cuisine from Lyon. House specialties include an endive salad with a cream-and-nut vinaigrette served with scallops. The fondues and pâtés are excellent. A favorite main course of the habitués is quiche Lorraine, and the quiche royale with shrimp is a must for seafood lovers. Whole steaks can be served to order with fine herbs, pepper, tartar, or shallots. Desserts include mango or chocolate mousse or raspberries smothered in cream. El Buen Comer makes a great stop after shopping in Polanco. ✉ *Edgar Allan Poe 50, Col. Polanco,* ☎ *5/281–1094 or 5/282–0325. Reservations essential. AE, DC, MC, V. Closed Sun. No dinner.*

Greek

$ ✕ **Agapi Mu (My Love).** This 16-table Greek bistro hidden away in Colonia Condesa—a neighborhood mushrooming with fine restaurants—attracts lots of actors, singers, and artists. It offers not only authentic Greek cuisine in a casual, intimate setting but also rambunctious Greek song and dance on Thursday, Friday, and Saturday nights. The reconverted family home with a Greek flag out front and snug rooms inside is decorated in cool tones of azure blue on white. The menu includes *Paputsáka* (stuffed eggplant), *Kalamárea* (fried squid Greek style), *Dalmádes* (grape leaves stuffed with rice and meat), plus daily specials such as lamb fricassee; wash it all down with a Hungarian Sangre de Toro wine. Save room for rich honeyed baklava dessert and thick Greek coffee. ✉ *Alfonso Reyes 98, Col. Condesa, a few mins south of Zona Rosa,* ☎ *5/286–1384. AE. Closed Sun.*

International

$$$$ ★ ✕ **Estoril.** Rosa Martin, who founded this highly successful restaurant in an exquisitely furnished 1930s town house in fashionable Polanco, runs it with her daughter Diana. It serves French and Swiss cuisine with a Mexican flair. The *perejil frito* (fried parsley) is a popular starter. The main dishes offer some unusual combinations: giant prawns in Chablis or curry sauce, and sea bass in fresh coriander sauce. To finish, try either the delicious *tart Tatin* (an upside-down apple tart with caramel) or the homemade sorbets. ✉ *Alejandro Dumas 24, Col. Polanco,* ☎ *5/280–9828. Jacket and tie. AE, DC, MC, V. Closed Sun.*

$$$$ ✕ **Hacienda de los Morales.** This Mexican institution, set in a former hacienda that dates back to the 16th century, is grandly colonial in style, with dark wood beams and huge terra-cotta expanses. The menu combines both international and Mexican cuisines, with some imaginative variations on both. The walnut soup, served either hot or cold, is a delicate and unusual specialty. Fish is seemingly unlimited, with a rainbow trout meunière (lightly sautéed in butter, served with lemon juice and parsley), sea bass *marinière* (in a white-wine sauce), and a mixed seafood gratin. The charcoal-broiled grain-fed chicken has a distinct flavor, and the paillard is always of the highest quality. ✉ *Vázquez de Mella 525, Col. Chapultepec Morales,* ☎ *5/281–4554 or 5/281–4703. AE, DC, MC, V.*

$$$$ ✕ **La Jolla.** This chic, intimate restaurant in the Marquis Reforma is the first in the country to specialize in Belgian cuisine. The menu, which also includes fine Mexican fare, is supervised by French executive-chef Marc Brault, who has won many awards for his creative cookery. Some of the most popular entrées are rib-eye steak in 10-chile sauce and *chile poblano* (stuffed green pepper) filled with salmon mousse. La Jolla is especially romantic at night, with its candlelit tables, soft piano music, and splendid view of Paseo de la Reforma, the city's grand avenue. Well-heeled Mexican executives pack the place at breakfast. ✉ *Paseo de la Reforma 465,* ☎ *5/211–3600. Jacket and tie. AE, DC, MC, V. Closed weekends.*

$$$$ ★ ✕ **Les Célébrités.** In addition to offering superb French fare, this elegant restaurant also serves good Mexican cuisine. When the Nikko México hotel opened in 1987, chef Joël Robouchon, one of the creators of nouvelle cuisine in France, came to Mexico to set up this restaurant off the hotel lobby. With him came the ultimate in restaurant technology and a policy of using only the very finest ingredients. The menu, which changes every three months, features such one-of-a-kind entrées as medallions of lobster in guayaba sauce or smoked salmon with spinach crepes; for dessert you might find pomegranate or prickly-pear sherbet. ✉ *Nikko México, Campos Elíseos 204, Col. Polanco,* ☎ *5/280–1111. Reservations essential. Jacket and tie. AE, DC, MC, V. Closed Sun. No lunch Sat.*

$$$$ ✕ **Maxim's de Paris.** This restaurant—which became famous under the tutelage of Yves Ferrer, one of the city's finest French chefs—serves classic Gallic cuisine spiced up with the best of Mexican ingredients. Among the offerings are tongue in a delicate vermouth sauce, duck à l'orange, and abalone dressed in zesty chipotle chilies. Some of the irresistible desserts whipped up by the pastry chef include mouthwatering Grand Marnier or hazelnut soufflés and extra-rich chocolate *turrón* (Spanish nougat). Operated under the auspices of the original Maxim's in Paris, this spacious but intimate restaurant is Parisian art deco under a stained-glass ceiling; the wine cellar is nonpareil and the service impeccable. ✉ *Hotel Presidente Inter-Continental México, Campos Elíseos 218, Col. Polanco,* ☎ *5/327–7700. Reservations essential. Jacket and tie. AE, DC, MC, V. Closed Sun. No lunch Sat.*

$$$ ✕ **Bellini.** This new revolving restaurant on the 45th floor of the World Trade Center is packed with executives from surrounding offices at lunch and the romantically inclined at night, when the view of the city by lamplight is fantastic. Bellini first operated in the now defunct Clarion Hotel, and its faithful clientele has followed it here. Although the new Bellini kept the Italian name, it serves very few Italian dishes—the majority are Mexican and international. The house special is lobster prepared to your taste; you can choose your dinner from a tank of the live creatures brought tableside. Or try the filet mignon or homemade pastas prepared with classic Italian sauces; finish off with a flambéed dessert such as strawberries jubilee or crêpes suzette. After dinner, work off the extra calories at the disco one floor above the restaurant. ✉ *Av. de las Naciones 1, World Trade Center Tower, Col. Napoles, 10 mins by car south of Zona Rosa,* ☎ *5/628–8325. Jacket and tie. AE, DC, MC, V. No dinner Sun.*

$$–$$$ ✕ **Bellinghausen.** This is one of the pleasantest lunch spots in the Zona Rosa. The partially covered hacienda-style courtyard at the back, set off by an ivy-laden wall, is a magnet midday for executives and tourists. A veritable army of waiters scurries back and forth serving such tried-and-true favorites as *sopa de hongos* (mushroom soup) and *filete chemita* (broiled steak with mashed potatoes). The *higaditos de pollo* (chicken livers) with a side order of sautéed spinach is another winning dish. Other specials include *cabrito* (baby goat), roast lamb, and Spanish paella; the fish and seafood are also superb. ✉ *Londres 95, Zona Rosa,* ☎ *5/525–8738 or 5/207–4978. AE, DC, MC, V. Closed Sun.*

Italian

$–$$ ✕ **La Lanterna.** The Petterino family has run this two-story restaurant for more than 20 years. The downstairs has the rustic feel of a northern Italian trattoria, with the cramped seating adding to the intimacy. Upstairs is more spacious. All the pastas are made on the premises, and the Bolognese sauce, in particular, is a local favorite. Try the raw artichoke salad, *conejo al Salmi* (rabbit in a wine sauce), *filete al burro nero* (steak in black butter), and *saltimbocca à la Romana* (veal and ham in Marsala sauce). ✉ *Paseo de la Reforma 458, Col. Juárez,* ☎ *5/207–9969. Reservations not accepted. MC, V. Closed Sun.*

$ ✕ **Los Arroces.** The name means "rices" and that's exactly what you'll get. Located in a pale orange stucco building in Colonia Condesa, the city's hot new neighborhood for restaurants, this trendy spot offers 50 different rices from around the world in soups, salads, and main dishes—everywhere but desserts. There's *pastel de arroz,* for example—white Mexican rice prepared with *rajas* (green pepper strips), *flor de calabaza* (squash flower), corn, and bacon; Maya rice—rice with squid, chopped red onion, sour oranges, and beans; and Spanish paella with rice from Valencia. There are a few noteworthy nonrice dishes like chicken with raspberry mole (spicy chocolate sauce) and blue tortilla quesadillas stuffed with cheese, spinach, and chili. ✉ *Michóacan 126, corner of Mázatlan,* ☎ *5/286–4287. AE, MC, V.*

Japanese

$$$ ✕ **Suntory.** Suntory restaurants in Boston, Singapore, Paris, and São Paulo have made the name synonymous with the best in Japanese dining. As you enter this one, by way of three rocks in a bed of well-raked sand, you are transported into a dense green garden. In this enchanted world you are not absolved of the difficulty of choice. Will it be the teppanyaki room to watch your fresh meat or fish prepared with a variety of vegetables? Or perhaps the shabu-shabu room with its wafer-thin sashimi and a copper pot of steaming vegetable broth in which elegant slices of beef are cooked? If you are a raw-fish enthusiast, perhaps the sushi bar? Prices are high, but the ingredients are of the best quality. ✉ *Torres Adalid 14, Col. del Valle,* ☎ *5/536–9432;* ✉ *Montes Urales 555, Lomas Chapultepec,* ☎ *5/202–4711. AE, DC, MC, V.*

Mexican

$$$ ★ ✕ **Cicero Centenario.** The talk of the town since its inauguration in 1993, this thoroughly Mexican restaurant occupies a restored 17th-century mansion in the heart of the downtown historic center. Elegant colonial antiques are strikingly posed against folk art and pastel walls; the bar has an outstanding collection of tin ex-votos and other religious memorabilia, and the gift shop is full of old apothecary bottles from the restaurant's days as a pharmacy. The enticing menu includes excellent versions of authentic colonial dishes such as *pollo en pipián verde* (chicken in green-pumpkin-seed sauce). Try the *chicharrón* (crispy pork rind)/guacamole appetizer, but be sure to leave room for desserts such as rose-petal ice cream. An ebullient street-level cantina features drinks, *botanas* (appetizers), and afternoon serenades by a folk trio. ✉ *República de Cuba 79,* ☎ *5/518–4447 or 5/521–7866. Reservations essential. AE, DC, MC, V.*

$$$ ★ ✕ **San Angel Inn.** In the south of the city, this magnificent old hacienda and ex-convent, with its elegant grounds and immaculately tended gardens, is both a joy to the eye and an inspiration to the palate. The dark mahogany furniture, crisp white table linens, and beautiful blue-and-white Talavera place settings all combine to strike the right note of restrained opulence. Many dishes are to be recommended, especially the *crepas de huitlacoche* (corn-fungus crepes) and the *sopa de tortilla* (tortilla soup). The *puntas de filete* (sirloin tips) are liberally laced with chili, and the *huachinango* (red snapper) is offered in a variety of ways. Desserts—from light and crunchy meringues to pastries bulging with cream—can be rich to the point of decadence. ✉ *Calle Diego Rivera 50 at Altavista, Col. San Angel Inn,* ☎ *5/516–1527 or 5/516–1402. Jacket required. AE, DC, MC, V.*

$$ ✕ **El Arroyo.** More than just a restaurant, this dining complex is a famous attraction in itself, complete with its own bullring. Located at the south end of town near the beginning of the highway to Cuernavaca, it was founded more than 50 years ago by the Arroyo family and is now run by jovial Jesús ("Chucho") Arroyo. His loyal following includes celebrities, dignitaries, and bullfighters, along with local families, groups, and tourists: More than 2,600 people can dine simultaneously in a labyrinth of 11 picturesque dining areas. Typical Mexican specialties—roast baby lamb wrapped in maguey leaves, chicken mole, a dozen types of tacos, and much more—are prepared in open kitchens. There's mariachi music and the full gamut of Mexican drinks, including *pulque* (an alcoholic beverage made from cactus). The small bullring is the forum for *novilleros,* or young bullfighters just beginning their careers, during the season (from about April through October), as well as for special banquets and lively fiestas. Breakfast starts at 8 AM and lunch is served until 7 PM. ✉ *Insurgentes Sur 4003, Col. Tlalpán,* ☎ *5/573–4344. AE, MC, V. No dinner.*

$$ ✕ **El Tajín.** Named after a magnificent pre-Columbian pyramid in Veracruz, this restaurant is a good example of the innovative Mexican cooking that is taking the metropolis by storm. Opened in 1993 by Alicia De'Angeli, El Tajín adds zest and style to many well-known dishes—and makes them low in fat to boot. Dazzling main dishes include soft-shell crab accented by sesame seeds and a tad of chipotle chili. This lovely restaurant is hidden behind the functional facade of the Veracruz Cultural Center in Col. Coyoacán; ancient Huastecan faces grinning from a splashing fountain add a bit of levity to the dining experience. ✉ *Miguel Angel de Queveda 687 in Coyoacán,* ☎ *5/659–4447 or 5/659–5759. AE, MC, V. Closed Sun.–Wed.*

$$ ★ ✕ **Fonda del Recuerdo.** A popular family restaurant, the *fonda* (inn) also has a solid reputation among tourists. Every day from 2 to 10, five different marimba groups from Veracruz provide festive music. The place made its name with its fish and seafood platters from the gulf state of Veracruz, and the house special is huachinango *à la Veracruzano* (a whole red snapper swimming in a succulent sauce made of tomato, chopped onion, olives, and mild spices). Sharing its fame is the *torito,* a drink made from tequila and exotic tropical fruit juices (be careful—it really packs a punch). The rest of the traditional Mexican menu features meat and *antojitos* (appetizers). Meat from the kitchen's own *parillas* (grills) is always first-rate. The portions here are huge, but if you have room for dessert, the *crepas de cajeta al tequila* (milk-caramel crepes with tequila) are worth trying. ✉ *Bahía de las Palmas 39, Col. Anzures,* ☎ *5/260–1290. AE, DC, MC, V.*

$$ ✕ **Fonda Don Chón.** This simple family-style restaurant, deep in downtown, is famed for its indigenous Mexican dishes. Fonda Don Chón is for the adventurous. A knowledge of zoology, Spanish, and Nahuatl helps in deciphering the menu, which changes daily. A gamut of products from throughout the republic is prepared fresh every day, and no processed foods are used. *Escamoles de hormiga* (red-ant roe), 97% protein, is known as the "caviar of Mexico" for both its deliciousness and its costliness. Among the exotic entrées are armadillo in sesame mole sauce, iguana soup, and snake (boa or rattle) steak. More traditional specialties include *mixiote de carnero* (barbecued lamb in maguey leaves). The coconut cake is excellent, and live music adds to the atmosphere. ✉ *Misionarios 213 near La Merced market, Col. Centro,* ☎ *5/522–2160. Reservations not accepted. AE, MC, V.*

$$ ✕ **Fonda El Refugio.** Since it opened in 1954, this Zona Rosa restaurant in a converted two-story town house has featured the best dishes from each major region of the country—for example, Guerrero, Michoacán, Sonora, and Veracruz. Atmosphere is casual but elegant in the intimate colonial-decor dining rooms (the one downstairs is the prettiest). Along with the varied regular menu, there is a daily selection of appetizers and entrées; you might find a mole sauce made with pumpkin seeds or *albóndigas en chile chipotle* (meatballs in chipotle chili sauce). Try the refreshing *aguas* (fresh-fruit and seed juices) with your meal and the *café de olla* (cinnamon-flavored coffee sweetened with brown sugar) after dessert. ✉ *Liverpool 166, Zona Rosa,* ☎ *5/207–2732 or 5/525–8128. AE, DC, MC, V. Closed Sun.*

$$ ✕ **Isadora.** Some of Mexico City's most inventive cooking takes place in this converted private house in Polanco. The three smallish dining rooms have a 1920s feel but are uncharacteristically ascetic—pale walls dabbed with modern-art squiggles. The management sponsors "cooking festivals," and every three months the kitchen produces dishes from a different country. The basic menu changes six times a year, and over that same period it will include three Mexican food fests. The set menu features duck pâté and excellent seafood pasta, with juicy prawns, shellfish, and squid. Ice creams, meringues, and chocolate cake for dessert benefit from the addition of the chef's delicate, pale green mint sauce. ✉ *Molière 50, Col. Polanco,* ☎ *5/280–1586. Jacket and tie. AE, DC, MC, V. Closed Sun.*

$$ ✕ **Los Girasoles.** This downtown "in" spot, which has been staked out by the local yuppies and trendsetters, is owned by two prominent Mexico City society columnists who know how to get their names in print. Los Girasoles (Sunflowers) is on a lovely old square in a restored three-story colonial home and serves nouvelle Mexican cuisine—light, tasty, and innovative. For example, the traditional Mexican bean soup is dressed up with a pinch of chili and noodles. Meat, fish, and seafood dishes are blended with exotic herbs and spices. There are also pre-Hispanic delicacies such as *escamoles* (ant roe), *gusanos de maguey* (chilied worms), and *chapulines* (crispy fried grasshoppers). The desserts pay homage to the fine fruits found in the country with such creations as *guanabana* and *zapote* mousse. One of the nicest places for dining is the covered terrace outdoors on the street level. A branch of the restaurant has opened in Miami. ✉ *Plaza Manuel Tolsa on Calle Tacuba,* ☎ *5/510–0630 or 5/510–3281. AE, MC, V.*

$$ ✕ **Los Irabien.** This beautiful dining area filled with plants and the owner's impressive art collection is a worthwhile stop for gourmets and culture hounds alike. Chef Arturo Fuentes turns out nouvelle cuisine à la Mexicaine along with traditional Mexican dishes. His *ensalada Irabien* triumphs as a mixture of smoked salmon, abalone, prawn, quail eggs, and watercress. Two outstanding entrées include nopal cactus stuffed with fish fillet in garlic and fillet steak in strawberry sauce *à la pimienta.* Less exotic dishes, such as juicy porterhouse and rib-eye steaks, are also available, and lavish care in preparation and presentation is evident in all courses. Los Irabien is one of the city's breakfast spots par excellence. Where else could one be tempted by *huevos de codorniz huitzilopochtli* (quail eggs with tortilla on a bed of corn fungus in a squash-blossom sauce)? ✉ *Av. de la Paz 45, Col. San Angel,* ☎ *5/616–0014. Jacket and tie. AE, DC, MC, V. No dinner Sun.*

$$ ✕ **Prendes.** This downtown institution, first opened in 1892, has an air of history and legend—the president of Mexico comes here, as did his predecessors. Trotsky ate here with Ramón Mercader, who axed him to death two days later. The decor is minimal but is highlighted by the famous Prendes murals, which depict such celebrities as Gary Cooper and Walt Disney, who also dined here. Some traditional Mexican dishes remain on the menu, but the emphasis is now on delicate and decorative nouvelle Mexican cuisine. Oysters, seviche, or a cream of maize soup are typical starters. The filete chemita and the fillet of fish meunière with nuts are two popular main courses. ✉ *16 de Septiembre 10, Col. Centro,* ☎ *5/512–7517. Reservations essential. Jacket and tie. AE, DC, MC, V. No dinner.*

$ ✕ **Café de Tacuba.** This classic Mexican restaurant is an essential breakfast, lunch, dinner, or snack stop for those exploring the city's downtown historic district. Since it opened in 1912, in a section of an old convent, it has charmed locals and visitors with its warm colonial decor and traditional Mexican fare. In the rear dining room, huge 18th-century oil paintings depict the historic invention of *mole poblano,* a complex sauce including a variety of chilies and chocolate, created by the nuns in the Santa Rosa Convent of Puebla. Of course, mole poblano is on the menu here, as are delicious tamales made fresh every morning—Oaxaca style with black mole and wrapped in banana leaf, or a fluffy Mexico City version. Enjoy pastries galore. ✉ *Tacuba 28, Col. Centro,* ☎ *5/518–4950. Reservations not accepted. AE, DC, MC, V.*

$ ✕ **Hosteria de Santo Domingo.** This dining institution near downtown's Plaza Santo Domingo has been serving *authentico* colonial dishes for more than a century in an atmospheric turn-of-the-century town house. Genteel waiters are schooled to provide good service and old-fashioned courtesy. Feast on tried-and-true favorites such as stuffed cactus paddles, thousand-flower soup, pot roast, and a stunning array of quesadillas filled with meat or the delicious *flor de calabaza* (pumpkin flower). Among what may be the best homemade Mexican desserts in town are the comforting flan, *arroz con leche* (rice pudding), and the rich milk-based *natilla* (another type of pudding). The place is open for breakfast and always full at lunch. Get there early so you don't have to stand in line. ✉ *Belisario Dominguez 72, Col. Centro,* ☎ *5/510–1434 or 5/526–5276. AE, MC, V. No dinner Sun.*

$ ★ ✕ **Las Cazuelas.** Traditional Mexican cooking at its best is on tap at one of the most famous of the capital's fondas. The open-view kitchens are kept immaculately clean, and diners often take a peek at the bubbling mole and *pipián* sauces (the latter a piquante sesame-flavored Yucatecan specialty) before being seated. The large dining area is brightened by hand-painted chairs from Michoacán and by the crisp green-and-white table linen. Ideal Mexican appetizers to share are *ranchero de carnitas* (pork morsels in red sauce). The tortilla soup, with its dash of *chili pasilla* and bits of cheese, makes another excellent starter. Main courses center on various moles or pipián sauces with pork or chicken. Finish with a *café de olla* (cinnamon coffee in a clay mug) and a domestic brandy. ✉ *San Antonio 143 at Illinois, Col. Napoles,* ☎ *5/563–4118. Reservations not accepted. AE, MC, V.*

Spanish

$$ ✕ **El Parador de Manolo.** A period two-story house was remodeled into this Spanish restaurant in fashionable Polanco. The Bar Porrón on the ground floor serves a variety of Spanish tapas, including an excellent prawn mix in a spicy sauce. In the brasserie-style dining room upstairs, choose from a Spanish menu or from the list of the chef's recommendations. The specially cured Serrano ham is possibly the best in the city, while the *calamares fritos* (fried squid) or the *crepas de flor de calabaza al gratin* (squash-blossom crepes) make other fine starters. Fish dishes are the most appealing for a main course, although the chateaubriand Parador for two (in a black corn-fungus sauce) is truly original. Desserts cater to the Spanish sweet tooth and are less notable. Wines are on display downstairs, as are the fresh fish of the day. ✉ *Presidente Masaryk 433, Polanco,* ☎ *5/281–4918 or 5/281–1118. AE, MC, V. No dinner Sun.*

$$ ✕ **Meson El Cid.** The Meson (tavern), which exudes Old Spain atmosphere, was founded about 15 years ago by a Spanish emigré. During the week, classic dishes like paella, spring lamb, suckling baby pig, and Cornish hens with truffles keep customers happy, but on Saturday night this place really comes into its own with a unique dining experience: a medieval banquet. The fun unfolds with a procession of costumed waiters carrying huge trays of steaming hot viands. A caged cat (the grandson of the first feline to play this role, the waiters will tell you) heads the parade as in olden days, when a king's food was tested for poisoning by letting a cat nose around in it first. (The cat was always smart enough not to touch the stuff if it had been tampered with.) Entertainment is provided by a student singing group dressed in Spanish medieval capes and hats. ✉ *Humboldt 61, Col. Centro,* ☎ *5/521–1940 or 5/521–1661. AE, DC, MC, V. No dinner Sun.*

$$ ✕ **Tezka.** This Pink Zone restaurant is Mexico's first and only with nouvelle Basque cuisine created by famous Basque chef Arzac, who transposed many of his best dishes to Mexico from his restaurant in San Sebastíen, Spain. It's always packed with Spanish clientele. The menu is composed of regenerated recipes with lots of creative touches and bigger portions than standard nouvelle fare. Feast your palate on baked fish in parsley sauce and sweet garlic cream or pheasant prepared with dates, pine nuts, and apple puree. Arzac disdains appetizers, which he believes ruin appreciation of the entrée; consequently you will find none here. There are tempting and original desserts, however, like cheese tart with blueberries and clotted English cream plus pears in toffee sauce. There's a decent list of Spanish wines such as Cune, Vina Ardanza, and Reserva 904. ✉ *Amberes 78 and Liverpool in the Royal Hotel,* ☎ *5/525–4850. AE, DC, MC, V. Closed Sun.*

Vegetarian

$ ✕ **El Jug.** For a respite from the madding crowd, head for this small, tidy retreat near the Pink Zone. You'll enjoy delicious vegetarian fare to the accompaniment of soothing New Age music. Heaping salads, homemade soups, and entrées such as *chiles rellenos* (green pepper stuffed with cheese or meat) are accompanied by chunks of whole-grain bread. You can choose the filling daily *comida corrida* (fixed-price menu) or order à la carte. After lunch, you might want to browse through the store on the premises and absorb the vibes of crystals, incense holders, aromatherapy pillows, and the like. ✉ *Puebla 326-A (entrance on Calle Cozumel), Col. Roma,* ☎ *5/553–3872. Reservations not accepted. No credit cards. Closed Sun.*

$ ✕ **Las Fuentes.** About three blocks from the U.S. Embassy, Las Fuentes is run by Philipe Culbert, a lifelong vegetarian who ascribes to the time-honored dietary dictates of ancient Persia in balancing the nutrients of his menu. A sample meal might be tacos stuffed with carrots and potatoes accompanied by apple salad and followed by whole-grain cookies made with honey. Don't be put off by the sterile Formica tables; most of the suit-and-tie professionals who pack the place at lunchtime come for the food rather than the ambience. ✉ *Rio Panuco*

27, at Río Tiber, Col. Cuauhtémoc, ☎ 5/525–7095. Reservations not accepted. MC, V.

LODGING

Though the city is huge and spread out, most hotels are located within the districts listed below, which are not far from one another. Chapultepec Park and the swank Polanco neighborhood are on the west side of the city. Paseo de la Reforma runs from Chapultepec, northeast through "midtown," and intersects with Avenida Juárez at the beginning of the downtown area. Juárez becomes Avenida Madero, which continues east to the downtown historic district and its very core, the Zócalo. The Zona Rosa, replete with boutiques, cafés, restaurants, and nightspots, is just south of Reforma in the western midtown area. Huge numbers of business travelers tend to fill up deluxe hotels during the week; some major hotels discount their weekend rates. You can expect hotels in the $$$ and $$$$ categories to have purified water, air-conditioning, cable TV, radio, minibars, and extended (often 24-hour) room service. The pretty Colonial Plaza Hotel, set in an 18th-century edifice facing the Zócalo, at press time was scheduled to open in summer 1997.

The following selection is organized by the major areas of the city and then by price.

CATEGORY	COST*
$$$$	over $160
$$$	$90–$160
$$	$40–$90
$	under $40

**All prices are for a standard double room, excluding service charge and 15% sales tax. An extra 2% room tax went into effect in 1996.*

Airport

$$$ **Marriott Aeropuerto.** Formerly the Continental Plaza, this deluxe hotel was remodeled from top to bottom when Marriott took over in 1996. The hotel is located over a short covered footbridge from the airport terminal, making it convenient for those who arrive late and have an early morning flight. For this convenience you pay a price. Discounted corporate rates are available. ✉ *Benito Juárez International Airport, 15520, ☎ 5/230–0505 or 800/228–9290, FAX 5/230–0134. 600 rooms and suites. Restaurant, bar, coffee shop, pool, sauna, health club, meeting rooms, car rental, free parking. AE, DC, MC, V.*

Chapultepec Park and Polanco

$$$$ ★ **Camino Real.** Super luxurious and immense—about the size of the Pyramid of the Sun in Teotihuacán—this 8-acre city within a city executed in a sleek Mexican minimalist style hosts heads of state and celebrities as well as business and pleasure travelers. Impressive works of art embellishing the endless corridors and lounges include Rufino Tamayo's mural of *Man Facing Infinity* and an imposing sculpture by Calder. The fifth-floor executive level features 100 extra-large guest rooms with special amenities. **Fouquet's de Paris** restaurant (☞ Dining, *above*) holds frequent culinary festivals, and the airy **Azulejos** offers Mexican cuisine and special Sunday buffet brunches. The hotel finished a complete refurbishing of all its rooms and public areas in June 1996. A nightclub features top Latin American artists who perform Thursday–Saturday starting at 11 PM; there's dancing after the show. ✉ *Mariano Escobedo 700, 11590, ☎ 5/203–2121 or 800/722–6466, FAX 5/250–*

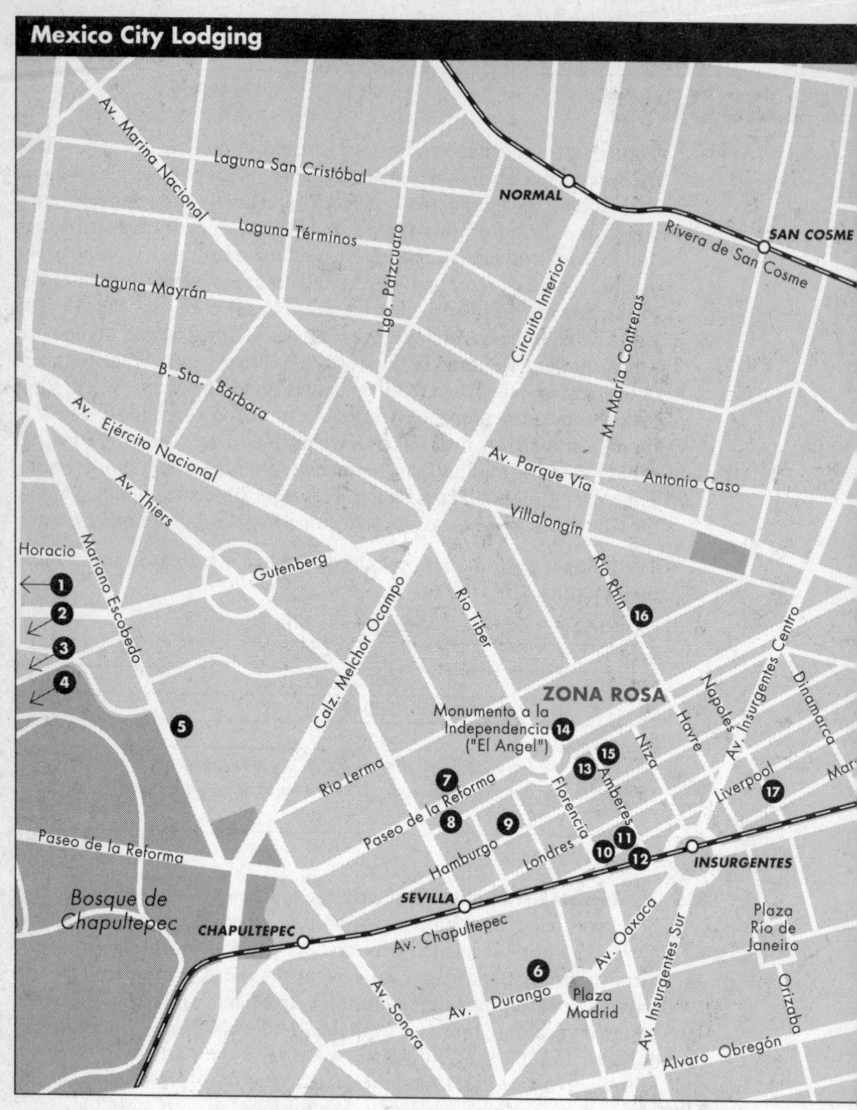

Aristos, **15**
Calinda Geneve, **12**
Camino Real, **5**
Casa Vieja, **3**
Catedral, **23**
Crowne Plaza Reforma 1, **21**
Fiesta Americana Reforma, **19**
Four Seasons Mexico City, **8**
Galería Plaza, **9**
Gran Hotel de la Ciudad de México, **25**
Hotel de Cortés, **22**
Imperial, **20**
J.W. Marriott, **4**
Krystal Rosa, **11**
La Casona, **6**
Majestic, **24**
Marco Polo, **13**
María Cristina, **16**
María Isabel Sheraton, **14**
Marquis Reforma, **7**
Marriott Aeropuerto, **26**
Misión Park Plaza México, **17**
Nikko México, **1**

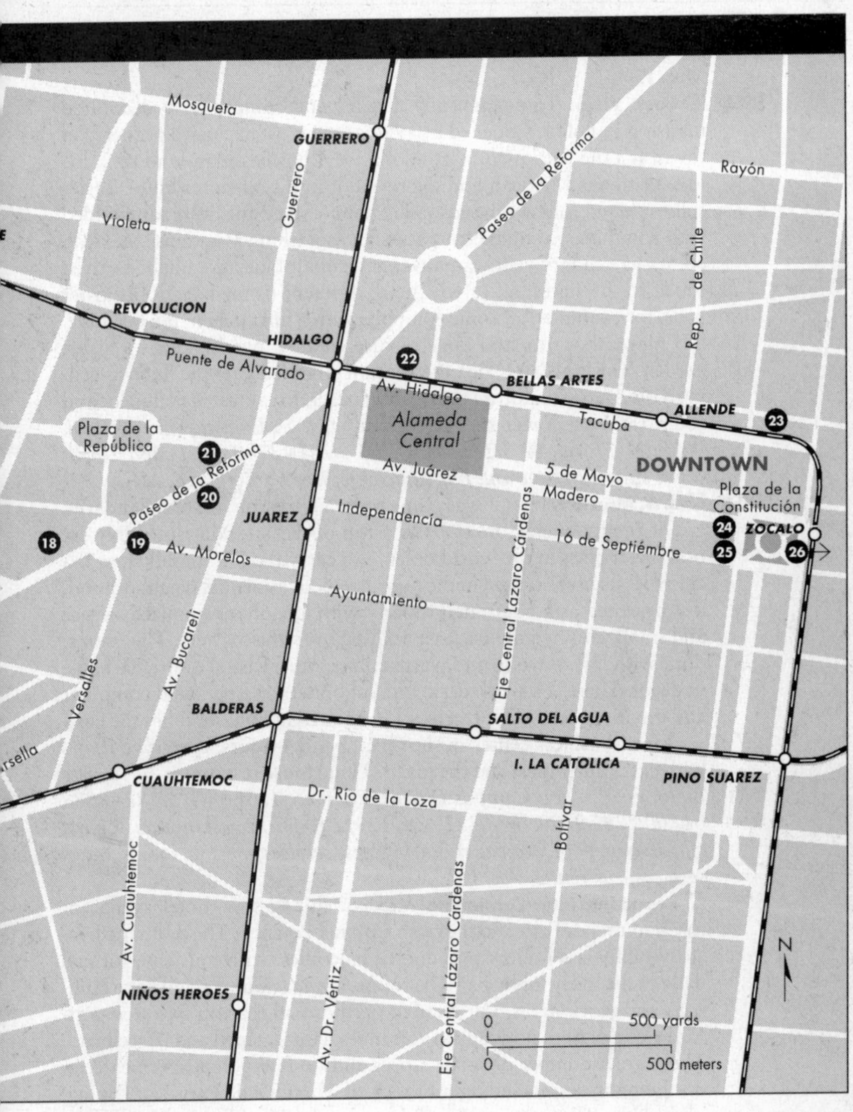

Plaza Florencia, **10**
Presidente Inter-Continental México, **2**
Sevilla Palace, **18**

6897 or 5/250–6723. 713 rooms and suites. 10 restaurants and bars, pool, 4 tennis courts, health club, nightclub, business services. AE, DC, MC, V.

$$$$ **Casa Vieja.** This classically elegant and sumptuously decorated mansion in Polanco opened in 1994 as the most exclusive property in town. It's the dream-come-true of a local businessman who took his love of things Mexican and expressed it in his all-suites hotel. Tastefully selected folk art, handsomely hand-carved furniture, and gilded wall trimmings complement patios and splashing fountains. Mexican colors like canary yellow, mauve, and cobalt blue add a light-hearted touch to the suites, all of which are different (some have four-poster beds, for example); all come equipped with a full kitchen, fax machine, CD player, hot tub, and huge picture window overlooking an inside garden. The hotel's Mexican restaurant is named after the floor-to-ceiling *Tree of Life* sculpture that dominates it. Breakfast is included, and room rates are lower the longer you stay. ✉ *Eugenio Sue 45, Col. Polanco, 11560,* ☎ *5/282–0067,* FAX *5/281–3780. 10 1- and 2-bedroom suites. Restaurant, bar, concierge, free parking. AE, MC, V.*

$$$$ **J.W. Marriott.** First it was going to be a Radisson, than a Mandarin, and it finally opened in 1996 as a top-of-the-line Marriott; only six other Marriotts in the world deserve to carry the J.W. moniker, so exclusive is its use. Located in the posh Polanco residential neighborhood, it is designed as a boutique property with lots of personalized service and small, clubby public areas; nothing overwhelms here. The rooms, done with lots of wood and warm colors, otherwise are unremarkable in decor. There is a work desk with an outlet for a personal computer and modem, and the TV receives 11 channels in English. It has the best-equipped business center in the city, open 24 hours; executive floors with extra amenities; and the pretty **Thai House** restaurant. ✉ *Andrés Bello, no. 29, and Campos Eliseos, Polanco, 11560,* ☎ *5/282–8888 or 800/228–9290,* FAX *5/282–8811. 312 rooms. 2 restaurants, 2 bars, coffee shop, pool, exercise room, business services, meeting rooms, travel services, car rental. AE, DC, MC, V.*

$$$$ **Presidente Inter-Continental México.** This 42-story hotel is adjacent to Chapultepec Park and the posh Colonia Polanco. The dramatic five-story lobby is a hollow pyramid of balconies, with music performed daily at the lively lobby bar. The rooms are spacious, and all have minibars and work areas. On clear days, those on the top two floors afford views of two snowcapped volcanoes, Popocatépetl and Iztaccíhuatl. There are a number of smart stores and no fewer than seven eateries on the premises, including a branch of **Maxim's de Paris** (☞ Dining, *above*), the **Palm,** a franchise of the venerable Washington, DC, eatery, and a new **Tony Di Roma** restaurant. ✉ *Campos Elíseos 218, 11560,* ☎ *5/327–7700 or 800/327–0200,* FAX *5/327–7730. 659 rooms and suites. 5 restaurants, coffee shop, lobby lounge, exercise room, babysitting, parking. AE, DC, MC, V.*

Zona Rosa

$$$$ ★ **Galería Plaza.** Part of the Westin Hotel deluxe chain, this ultramodern property is conveniently located on a quiet street in the elegant Zona Rosa, ideal for shopping, enjoying the nightlife, and dining out. Standard rooms are relatively small, but service and facilities are faultless. Rooms on the executive floor, where a special concierge desk provides personalized service and easy checkout, are larger. Other advantages include the 24-hour restaurant, which has a popular buffet breakfast; voice mail in all rooms; a rooftop heated pool with sundeck; and a secure underground parking lot. ✉ *Hamburgo 195 at Varsovia, 06600,* ☎ *5/230–*

1717 or 800/228–3000, FAX *5/207–5867. 450 rooms and suites. Restaurant, lobby lounge, room service, concierge. AE, DC, MC, V.*

$$$ **Aristos.** This 15-story hotel is on the busy Paseo de la Reforma, on the edge of the Zona Rosa, in front of the U.S. Embassy, and near the Mexican Stock Exchange. The rooms are well supplied with all the amenities and are attractively decorated in shades of peach and mauve, with brass and wood accents. The business center has a bilingual staff and a message service. ✉ *Paseo de la Reforma 276, 06600,* ☎ *5/211–0112,* FAX *5/514–4573. 360 rooms and suites. Restaurant, beauty salon, sauna, exercise room, travel services. AE, DC, MC, V.*

$$$ **Calinda Geneve.** A Quality Inn, referred to locally as El Génova, this is an older but continually refurbished five-story hotel. Traditional colonial-style carved wood chairs and tables furnish the pleasant lobby, and guest rooms are smallish but comfortable. The hotel's attraction as a gathering place has always been the **Salón Jardín,** a striking Belle Epoque gallery with a profusion of plants and a high stained-glass ceiling. It's a popular place for both guests and nonguests for meals and cocktails. The hotel's informal street-front **Café Jardín** serves until 11 PM, and a branch of Sanborns, which sells sundries and has a restaurant, opens off the lobby. A gym was added to the hotel in 1996. ✉ *Londres 130, 06600,* ☎ *5/211–0071 or 800/228–5151,* FAX *5/208–7422. 318 rooms. Restaurant, bar, café, room service, exercise room, coin laundry, travel services. AE, DC, MC, V.*

$$$ **Krystal Rosa.** Part of the Mexican Krystal Hotel chain, this superbly run high-rise hotel is centrally located in the heart of the Zona Rosa and has an excellent view of the city from the rooftop pool terrace. There is a chic lobby cocktail lounge; a bar with local entertainers; and a restaurant, **Kama Kura,** that serves excellent Japanese cuisine. Three club floors offer VIP check-in and service, complimentary Continental buffet breakfast, and rooms with extra amenities. ✉ *Liverpool 155, 06600,* ☎ *5/228–9928 or 800/231–9860. 300 rooms and suites. 2 restaurants, 2 bars, pool, business services. AE, DC, MC, V.*

$$$ **La Casona.** This elegant yet understated turn-of-the-century mansion registered as an artistic monument by Mexico's Institute of Fine Arts has been turned into a charming 30-room hotel. Filled with sunny patios and sitting rooms, the hotel, which opened in 1996, is exquisitely decorated with antiques, expensive rugs, hardwood floors, and Art Deco accessories, mirroring the days of the *Porfiriato* (presidency of Porfirio Díaz) when the home was built. Although no two rooms are alike, they come with modern hair dyer, fluffy bathrobes and slippers, soaps and shampoos, good-size bathtubs, and color TV with satellite hookup; room service orders are discreetly delivered through a tiny two-way cupboard near the door. There's a small restaurant serving old-style country cooking. The two-story building with the demure salmon facade looks out on a tree-lined street in Colonia Condesa about a 10-minute walk south of the Pink Zone and in easy reach of museums, restaurants, and Reforma Avenue. ✉ *Durango 280, at Cozumel,* ☎ *5/286–3001 or 800/223–5652,* FAX *5/211–0871. 30 rooms. Restaurant, bar, exercise room. AE, DC, MC, V.*

$$$ ★ **Marco Polo.** Posh and right in the center of the Zona Rosa, this intimate yet ultramodern all-suites hotel offers the amenities and outstanding personalized service often associated with a small European property. All rooms feature climate control, color cable TV, FM radio, minibar, and kitchenette; some suites have hot tubs, too. Rooms on the top floor facing north have excellent views of Paseo de la Reforma (the four penthouse suites have terraces), and the U.S. Embassy is close by. In the street-level **El Bistro de Marco Polo,** you can listen to sophisticated jazz at lunch, over cocktails, and at dinner. ✉ *Amberes*

27, 06600, ☎ 5/207–1893, FAX 5/533–3727. 60 suites. Restaurant, bar, business services. AE, DC, MC, V.

$$$ 🏨 **Nikko México.** Part of the Japanese Nikko chain, this glistening, 42-floor high-rise occupies a prime position: It's in Polanco and adjacent to Chapultepec Park, just a five-minute walk to the Anthropology Museum. The executive floor has better rooms and extra facilities. The standard rooms are a little claustrophobic. Three top restaurants excel in their gastronomic specialties: **Les Célébrités** (French) (☞ Dining, *above*), **Teppan Grill** (Japanese), and **El Jardín** (Mexican). The elegant, cozy **Shelty's Pub** is also a big hit with locals and serves a fancy high tea (⏲ Weekdays 5–7). ✉ *Campos Elíseos 204, 11560, ☎ 5/280–1111 or 800/645–5687, FAX 5/280–9191. 771 rooms and suites. 3 restaurants, 2 bars, indoor pool, 3 tennis courts, health club, jogging, dance club, meeting rooms, travel services, car rental. AE, DC, MC, V.*

$$ 🏨 **Misión Park Plaza México.** A part of the Misión chain, this very comfortable hotel is well placed for shopping and sightseeing. All rooms are air-conditioned and have a color TV with U.S. channels. A conference room for 100 persons and free shoe shines were added in 1996. ✉ *Nápoles 62, 06600, ☎ 5/533–0535, FAX 5/533–1589. 50 rooms. Coffee shop, lobby lounge, meeting room. AE, MC, V.*

$$ 🏨 **Plaza Florencia.** This is a modern hotel on a busy avenue that borders the Zona Rosa. Rooms are well furnished, cheerfully decorated, and soundproofed against the location's heavy traffic noise; the higher floors have views of the Angel monument. Some large family suites are available. All rooms have air-conditioning, heat, a color TV, and a phone. ✉ *Florencia 61, 06600, ☎ 5/211–0064, FAX 5/511–1542. 130 rooms, 10 suites. Restaurant, bar, coffee shop. AE, DC, MC, V.*

Midtown and along the Reforma

$$$$ 🏨 **Four Seasons Mexico City.** Inaugurated in 1994, this is one of the newest and—perhaps by definition—one of the most luxurious hotels in the capital. Surrounding a traditional courtyard with a fountain, the stately eight-story building was modeled after the 18th-century Iturbide Palace downtown. A spacious marble lobby is filled with huge bowls of fresh flowers and lovely European furnishings. Definitely geared to the business traveler, rooms have outlets for PCs; there's also a boardroom on the premises and a business center with computer and cellular phone rentals. Dining and drinking areas have original names: **El Restaurant** (for breakfast, lunch, and dinner), **El Bar, El Café,** and **El Lobby Bar.** All Four Seasons amenities are offered. ✉ *Paseo de la Reforma 500, 06600, ☎ 5/230–1818 or 800/332–3442, FAX 5/230–1808. 240 rooms and suites. 2 restaurants, bar, pool, exercise room, health club, business services. AE, DC, MC, V.*

$$$$ 🏨 **María Isabel Sheraton.** Don Antenor Patiño, the Bolivian "Tin King," inaugurated this Mexico City classic in 1969 and named it after his granddaughter, socialite Isabel Goldsmith. The entire hotel was remodeled in 1992, but the glistening brown marble and art deco details in the lobby and other public areas remain. All guest and public rooms are impeccably maintained, but penthouse suites in the 22-story Tower section are extra-spacious and exceptionally luxurious. The location—across from the Angel and the Zona Rosa, with Sanborns next door and the U.S. Embassy a half block away—is prime. ✉ *Paseo de la Reforma 325, 06500, ☎ 5/207–3933 or 800/334–8484, FAX 5/207–0684. 751 rooms and suites. 3 restaurants, bar, room service, pool, massage, sauna, health club, concierge floor, business services. AE, DC, MC, V.*

$$$$ ★ 🏨 **Marquis Reforma.** Opened in 1991, this privately owned hotel is not only plush but also within walking distance of the Zona Rosa. It has a striking pink stone and curved glass facade, and its seventh-floor suites afford picture-perfect views of Chapultepec Castle. The elegant lobby is done up in classic European style, with paintings, sculpture, and palatial furniture. Guest-room furniture and decor are Art Deco–inspired. The award-winning **La Jolla** restaurant specializes in Belgian cuisine (☞ Dining, *above*). The fully staffed Corporate Center offers state-of-the-art computer services, and guest-room phones feature a second plug for computers with fax modem. The health club offers hard-to-find holistic, stress-busting massages. ✉ *Paseo de la Reforma 465, 06500,* ☎ *5/211–3600 or 800/525–4800,* FAX *5/211–5561. 209 rooms, including 84 suites. 2 restaurants, bar, tennis court, exercise room, business services, meeting room. AE, DC, MC, V.*

$$$ **Crowne Plaza Reforma 1.** Perched at the junction of Reforma, Juárez, and Bucareli—convenient to downtown, the Pink Zone, and the Stock Exchange—this flashy 22-story smoked-glass behemoth looks quite spectacular in its otherwise nondescript surroundings. Opened in September 1995, it touts the ultimate in high-tech amenities for the business traveler: stock market indicator; computers; secretarial, translation, messenger, and shipping services; and cellular phones. All rooms have PC and fax-modem outlets, coffeemakers, and three telephone lines. Public areas include a coffee bar with 20 different java concoctions, an oyster-jazz bar, and a French restaurant. Other amenities include limousine rental, pharmacy, and boutiques. ✉ *Reforma 1, Col. Tabacalera, 06030,* ☎ *5/128–5000 or 800/227–6963,* FAX *5/128–5050. 500 rooms and suites. 2 restaurants, 2 bars, room service, beauty salon, shops, business services, travel services, car rental. AE, DC, MC, V.*

$$$ **Fiesta Americana Reforma.** This immense hotel is well organized for business travelers and large groups. It has an ample selection of bars, restaurants, and entertainment, including a popular nightclub, the **Barbarella.** There is not much Mexican atmosphere, but you can get a good tan on the sundeck, work out in the gym, listen to live Mexican music in the lobby bar, or eat in one of the three restaurants. All rooms are equipped with minibars. ✉ *Paseo de la Reforma 80, 06600,* ☎ *5/705–1515 or 800/343–7821,* FAX *5/705–1313. 610 rooms. 3 restaurants, 2 bars, exercise room. AE, DC, MC, V.*

$$$ **Sevilla Palace.** This is a glistening modern showplace with five panoramic elevators to its 23 floors, a covered rooftop pool with hot tub, health club, terraced rooftop lounge with a city view, restaurants, a top-floor supper club with entertainment, and convention halls with capacities of up to 1,000. It's well located near the Columbus traffic circle and attracts lots of tourists from Spain. ✉ *Paseo de la Reforma 105, 06030,* ☎ *5/705–2800 or 800/732–9488,* FAX *5/703–2115 or 5/703–1521. 413 rooms. 2 restaurants, 3 bars, pool, health club, nightclub, meeting rooms. AE, DC, MC, V.*

$$ **Imperial.** Opened in 1990, the Imperial occupies a stately turn-of-the-century European-style building right on the Reforma alongside the Columbus Monument. Quiet elegance and personal service are keynotes of this privately owned property. The hotel's **Restaurant Gaudí** has an understated, tony atmosphere and serves fine Continental cuisine with some Spanish selections. All rooms have safes, minibars, cable TV, and air-conditioning. ✉ *Paseo de la Reforma 64, 06600,* ☎ *5/705–4011,* FAX *5/703–3122. 60 rooms, junior and master suites. Restaurant, bar, café, business services, meeting rooms, travel services. AE, DC, MC, V.*

$ ★ **María Cristina.** Full of old-world charm, this Spanish colonial–style gem is a Mexico City classic. Impeccably maintained since it was built in 1937 (it was last refurbished in January 1995), the peach-color building surrounds a delightful garden courtyard, which is the setting for its **El Retiro** bar. Three tastefully decorated apartment-style master suites, complete with hot tubs, were added in the early '90s. All rooms have color cable TV, a minibar, and a safe. Located in a quiet residential setting near Sullivan Park, the hotel is just a block from the Paseo de la Reforma and close to the Zona Rosa. ✉ *Río Lerma 31, 06500,* ☎ *5/703–1787,* FAX *5/566–9194. 156 rooms and suites. Room service, beauty salon, travel services. DC, MC, V.*

Downtown

$$ **Gran Hotel de la Ciudad de México.** Ensconced in what was formerly a 19th-century department store, this older, more traditional hotel has contemporary rooms with all the amenities. Its central location—adjacent to the Zócalo and near the Templo Mayor—makes it the choice of serious sightseers. And its distinctive belle epoque lobby is worth a visit in its own right, with a striking stained-glass Tiffany dome, chandeliers, gilded birdcages, and 19th-century wrought-iron elevators. The fourth-floor **Mirador** breakfast restaurant overlooks the Zócalo. The **Del Centro** restaurant-bar run by Delmónicos is one of Mexico City's best. The hotel has been undergoing a long-term, gradual refurbishing; be sure to request a renovated room and one that does not look out onto a brick wall. ✉ *16 de Septiembre 82, 06000,* ☎ *5/510–4040,* FAX *5/512–2085. 125 rooms. 2 restaurants, bar, concierge, travel services, parking (fee). AE, MC, V.*

$$ **Hotel de Cortés.** This delightful small hotel, operated by Best Western, is housed in a colonial building (1780) that has been designated a national monument. A major renovation in 1990 improved the colonial-decor rooms, which are small and simply furnished and open onto the enclosed central courtyard. Two comfortable soundproofed suites overlook Alameda Park across the busy street. A restaurant also views the park, and a friendly bar opens to the tree-shaded central courtyard and fountain, a lovely setting for tea or cocktails. The Franz Mayer Museum is just a block away, and it's an easy walk to Bellas Artes. Loyal guests make reservations many months in advance. ✉ *Av. Hidalgo 85, 06000,* ☎ *5/518–2184 or 800/334–7234,* FAX *5/512–1863. 29 rooms and suites. Restaurant, bar. AE, DC, MC, V.*

$$ **Majestic.** The atmospheric, colonial-style Majestic, built in 1937, is a Best Western hotel and perfectly located for anyone interested in exploring the downtown historic district: It is right on the Zócalo at the corner of Madero. It's also perfect for viewing the Independence Day (September 16) celebrations, which draw hundreds of thousands of people to this square. In fact, many tourists book a room a year in advance of the festivities. Decorated in the style of the 1940s with modern touches, rooms have air-conditioning and king-size beds, remote-control color TVs, and minibars; although the front units have balconies and a charming view of the plaza, they can be noisy with car traffic until about 11 at night. The service is efficient and courteous. The seventh-floor **La Terraza** dining room and terrace—which feature international and Mexican specialties—have marvelous panoramas of the entire Zócalo. The Sunday buffet (⏲ 1–5 PM) features live Mexican music. The fun **El Campanario** piano bar welcomes anyone who wants to make his first singing debut and has become a favorite with locals. The pretty lobby is decorated with lots of stone, wood, bronze, etched glass, and colorful hand-painted Talavera tile from Puebla. ✉ *Madero 73, 06000,* ☎ *5/521–8600 or 800/528–1234,* FAX *5/512–6262. 85 rooms. Restaurant, bar, coffee shop, travel services. AE, DC, MC, V.*

$ ★ **Catedral.** Located in the heart of the downtown historic district, this older but refurbished hotel is a great bargain, offering many of the amenities of the more upscale hotels at less than half the price. Public areas sparkle with marble and glass. The guest rooms are done in a cheerful contemporary fashion, and all offer color TVs (local channels only) and phones. You can get one with a view of the namesake Catedral, but keep in mind that its bells chime every 15 minutes late into the night. Service is friendly, the hotel restaurant is excellent, and the **El Retiro** bar attracts a largely Mexican clientele to hear live Latin music. ✉ *Donceles 95, 06000,* ☎ *5/512–8581,* FAX *5/512–4344. 116 rooms. Bar, coffee shop, room service, nightclub, dry cleaning, laundry service, travel services. AE, MC, V.*

NIGHTLIFE AND THE ARTS

Good places to check for current events are the Friday edition of *The News,* a daily English-language newspaper, and *Tiempo Libre,* a weekly magazine listing activities and events in Spanish. Both are available at newsstands.

Summer city-wide cultural festivals with free music, dance, and theater performances by local groups take place in July and August. A three-week spring cultural festival with lots of international headliners, for which tickets are available, takes place in the Historic Center between March and April. Check with the Mexico City Tourist Office (☞ Visitor Information *in* Mexico City A to Z, *below*) for dates and details.

The Arts

Dance

The world-renowned **Ballet Folklórico de México,** directed by Amalia Hernández, offers a stylized presentation of Mexican regional folk dances and is one of the most popular shows in Mexico. Performances are given Sunday at 9:30 AM and at 8 PM at the beautiful Palacio de Bellas Artes (Palace of Fine Arts), at Avenue Juárez and Eje Central Lazaro Cardenas; it's a treat to see the Tiffany glass curtain lowered. Call the Palace of Fine Arts box office (☎ 5/512–3633), or TicketMaster (☎ 5/325–9000), for information on prices and for reservations. Hotels and travel agencies can also secure tickets.

Not to be confused with the above is the **Ballet Folklórico Nacional de México,** directed and choreographed by Silvia Lozano. The company performs authentic regional folk dances Sunday at 9:30 AM and Tuesday at 8:30 PM at the Teatro Jimenez Ruedo next to the Crowne Plaza Hotel, at Avenida de la República 154 while the Teatro de la Ciudad, their usual auditorium, is undergoing remodeling.

The **National Dance Theater,** a component of the National Auditorium complex in Chapultepec Park (☎ 5/202–3502), and the **Dance Center** (✉ Campos Elíseos 480, ☎ 5/520–2271) frequently sponsor modern-dance performances.

Music

The primary venue for classical music is the **Palace of Fine Arts** (✉ Av. Juárez and Eje Central Lázaro Cárdenas, ☎ 5/709–3111), which has a main auditorium and the smaller Manuel Ponce concert hall. The National Opera has two seasons at the Palace: January–March and August–October. The National Symphony Orchestra stages classic and modern pieces at the palace in the spring and fall.

The top concert hall, often touted as the best in Latin America, is **Ollin Yolitzli** (✉ Periférico Sur 1541, ☎ 5/606–7573), which hosts the Mexico City Philharmonic several times a year. The State of Mexico Symphony performs at **Nezahualcoyotl Hall** in University City (☏ 5/622–7112).

For top pop music recording stars like Michael Jackson, Luis Miguel, Yanni, Bon Jovi, Elton John, and Juan Gabriel check the newspapers for attractions at the **Auditorio Nacional** (✉ Reforma 50 across the street from the Nikko Hotel, ☏ 5/280–9234 or 5/280–9979), **Teatro Metropolitano** (✉ Independencia 90 downtown, ☏ 5/510–1035 or 5/510–1045), or the **Palacio de los Deportes** (✉ Av. Río Churubusco and Calle Añil, ☏ 5/237–9999).

Theater

An amateur theater group called the **Theater Workshop** puts on plays in English at various times of the year at the Universidad de las Americas (University of the Americas), Puebla 223 (no phone), within walking distance of the Zona Rosa; check *The News* for listings. Visitors with a grasp of Spanish will find a much wider choice of theatrical entertainment, including recent Broadway hits. Prices are reasonable compared with those for stage productions of similar caliber in the United States. Though Mexico City has no central theater district, most theaters are within a 15- to 30-minute taxi ride from the major hotels. The top theaters include **Hidalgo** (✉ Av. Hidalgo 23, ☏ 5/521–3859), **Insurgentes** (✉ Av. Insurgentes Sur 1587, ☏ 5/595–2117), and **Virginia Fabregas** (✉ Velasquez de Leon 29, ☏ 5/592–0577). Theater tickets are available through TicketMaster (☏ 5/325–9000).

Nightlife

Night is the key word to understanding the timing of going out in Mexico City. People generally have cocktails at 7 or 8 PM, take in dinner and a show at 10 or 11, head to the discos at midnight, and then find a spot for a nightcap somewhere around 3 AM. The easiest way for the non–Spanish-speaking visitor to do this is on a nightlife tour (☞ Guided Tours *in* Mexico City A to Z, *below*). However, those who set off on their own should have no trouble getting around. For starters, Niza and Florencia streets in the Zona Rosa are practically lined with nightclubs, bars, and discos that are especially lively on Friday and Saturday nights. The big hotels offer both bars and places to dance or be entertained, and they are frequented by locals. Outside of the Zona Rosa, Paseo de la Reforma and Insurgentes Sur have the greatest concentration of nightspots. Remember that the capital's high altitude makes liquor extremely potent, even jolting. Imported booze is very expensive, so you may want to stick with what the Mexicans order: tequila, rum, and *cerveza* (beer).

Dancing

Dance emporiums in the capital run the gamut from cheek-to-cheek romantic to throbbing strobe lights and ear-splitting music. Most places have a cover charge, but it is rarely more than $10. **Dinasty** at the Hotel Nikko (✉ Campos Elíseos 204, ☏ 5/280–1111) is a popular disco that opens for dancing Thursday through Saturday at 9 PM. **Antillanos** (✉ Francisco Pimentel 78, ☏ 5/592–0439), a short cab ride from the Zona Rosa, is *the* place to go for hot salsa music and dancing to well-known local bands. One of the capital's best-kept secrets is **Mamá Rumba** (✉ Medillín and Querétaro in Col. Roma, 10-min cab ride from the Zona Rosa, ☏ 5/564–6920). A nondescript Cuban restaurant during the day, it turns on the hot salsa, danzón, cha-cha-cha, and conga beat Thursday, Friday, and Saturday nights, when a lineup of Cuban bands take the stand. The habitués not only pack the tiny dance floor but take to the tables as well. Reservations for these nights are definitely encouraged by the management.

Dinner Shows

The splashiest shows are found in the big hotels and in Zona Rosa clubs. **La Bohemia** (✉ Camino Real Hotel, ☎ 5/203–2121) is the newest venue for well-known singers from Mexico and the rest of Latin America, including Armando Manzanero and Tania Libertad. Show time is Thursday through Saturday starting at 11 PM; the dance music starts around 12:30 AM after the show. In the Fiesta Americana Reforma, **Barbarella** (✉ Paseo de la Reforma 80, ☎ 5/705–1515) features top international entertainers Thursday through Saturday nights. **La Veranda** (✉ María Isabel Sheraton, Paseo de la Reforma 325, ☎ 5/207–3933, ext. 3718) serves dinner while international-caliber stars perform; afterward the dance floor is open.

Hotel Bars

The lobby bars in the **María Isabel Sheraton** (✉ Reforma 325, ☎ 5/207–3933), **Presidente Inter-Continental México** (✉ Campos Elíseos 218, Polanco, ☎ 5/327–7700), **Camino Real** (✉ Mariano Escobedo 700, ☎ 5/203–2121), and **Galería Plaza** (✉ Hamburgo 195, Zona Rosa, ☎ 5/211–0014) are all good bets for a sophisticated crowd and lively music, usually until long after midnight.

After Midnight

Gitanerías (✉ Oaxaca 15, Col. Roma, ☎ 5/208–9066) continues to be an authentic Spanish flamenco nightclub (*tablao*). Now, in addition to a fiery flamenco there is also disco dancing to flamenco and Latin rhythms. Only light supper and drinks are served, and the first show starts at 12:30 Tuesday to Saturday. There is a $6.50 cover for men; free admission for women.

The traditional last stop for nocturnal Mexicans is **Plaza Garibaldi** (✉ East of Eje Central Lázaro Cárdenas, between República de Honduras and República de Perú), where exuberant mariachis gather to unwind after evening performances—by performing even more. The mariachis play in the square—well-to-do Mexicans usually park along the west side to enjoy some "drive-up" serenading—and inside the cantinas and clubs surrounding it; the better ones are **Guadalajara de Noche** (☎ 5/526–5521) and **Tenampa** (☎ 5/526–6176). Choose a cantina and order a tequila; the musicians will be around shortly to serenade you (tipping is essential). These places stay open Sunday through Thursday until 4 AM, and even later on Friday and Saturday. Note: The square was spruced up in 1993 to rid it of its seedy image, but things can still get a bit raucous late at night.

OUTDOOR ACTIVITIES AND SPORTS

Bullfights

The main season is the dry season, around November through March, when celebrated *matadores* appear at **Plaza México** (✉ Calle A. Rodín and Holbein, Col. Nápoles, ☎ 5/563–3961), the world's largest bullring, which seats 40,000. Gray Line Tours offers bullfight tour packages (☞ Guided Tours *in* Mexico City A to Z, *below*); or tickets, which range from about $3 to $25, can be purchased at hotel travel desks. Try the bullring ticket booths on Saturday between 11 AM and 2 PM or Sunday between 11 AM and 3:30 PM for tickets as well. The ring is located next to the Ciudad de Deportes sports complex, and the show goes on at 4:30 PM.

Golf

All golf courses are private in Mexico City, but you can play if you are a guest of a member. Travelers staying at the Sheraton Maria Isabel and the Camino Real hotels can have the hotel arrange admittance to the Bella Vista Golf Club, located off the Querétaro Highway (☎ 5/360–3501). Green fees Tuesday through Friday are $38; weekends, $75.

Horse Racing

The season at the beautiful **Hipódromo de las Américas** (✉ Av. Industria Militar, Lomas de Sotelo, ☎ 5/557–4100) lasts from mid-January through December, when thoroughbreds run daily. Betting is pari-mutuel. The races are especially enjoyable to watch from the swank Derby or Jockey Club restaurant. Tickets cost about 1 peso and can be purchased at the track, which is located in the northwest section of the city near the Querétaro Highway.

Jai Alai

You can watch and bet on men playing this lightning-fast Basque-style handball game at the remodeled **Frontón México** (✉ Plaza de la Republica 17, across the street from Monument to the Revolution, ☎ 5/546–3240 or 5/591–0098) Tuesday through Saturday at 7 PM, Sunday at 5 PM. Women's matches are played at **Frontón Metropolitano** (✉ Bahía de Todos los Santos 190) Monday–Saturday 4–10 PM. Betting, which goes on while the games are being played, is a fascinating skill in itself; instructions on the betting sheets are in Spanish and English. Dress up if you attend a game; jacket and tie for men are obligatory.

Jogging

There are jogging tracks in Chapultepec Park and at the Villa Olímpica (Olympic Village). Another joggers' favorite is along the pastoral paths of the Coyoacán Nurseries by the Viveros Station of the No. 3 metro line. Early-morning runners will probably see young novice bullfighters there going through their training maneuvers. Keep in mind, by the way, that air quality is often poor and this is the highest city in North America—7,349 ft above sea level—so take it easy until your heart and lungs become accustomed to the altitude.

Tennis

Tennis clubs are private in Mexico, so tennis buffs should consider staying at one of the hotels (☞ Lodging, *above*) that have courts on site.

Water Sports

The best place for swimming is your hotel pool. The vast **Cuemanco** sports park (✉ Canal de Cuemanco, on the way to Xochimilco) has an artificial lake for canoeing. Rowers can also ply their sport in the lakes of Chapultepec Park. Rentals are nearby.

SHOPPING

The best, most concentrated shopping area is the **Zona Rosa,** a 29-square-block area bounded by Reforma on the north, Niza on the east, Avenida Chapultepec on the south, and Varsovia on the west. The neighborhood is chock-full of boutiques, jewelry stores, leather-goods shops, antiques stores, and art galleries, as well as dozens of great little restaurants and coffee shops. Day or night, the Zona Rosa is always lively.

Polanco, a choice residential neighborhood along the northeast perimeter of Chapultepec Park, is blossoming with fine shops and boutiques, many of which are branches of Zona Rosa or downtown establishments. Many are located in malls like the huge ultramodern **Plaza Polanco** (⊠ Jaime Balmes 11) and the **Plaza Mazaryk** (⊠ Mazaryk and Anatole France).

There are hundreds of shops with more modest trappings and better prices spread out along the length of Avenida Insurgentes, as well as along Avenida Juárez and in the old downtown area.

Department Stores, Malls, and Shopping Arcades

The major department-store **chains** are **Liverpool** (⊠ Av. Insurgentes Sur 1310, Mariano Escobedo 425, and in the Plaza Satélite and Perisur shopping centers), **Suburbia** (⊠ Horacio 203, Sonora 180, Av. Insurgentes Sur 1235, and also in Plaza Satélite and Perisur), and **El Palacio de Hierro** (⊠ Durango and Salamanca), which is noted for fashions by well-known designers at prices now on par with those found in the United States. The posh and pricey shopping mall **Perisur** is out on the southern edge of the city near where the Periférico Expressway meets Avenida Insurgentes. **Plaza Satélite** mall is in a northern suburb called Satellite on the Anillo Periférico. Department stores are generally open Monday, Tuesday, Thursday, and Friday from 10 to 7, and on Wednesday and Saturday from 10 to 8.

Sanborns is a mini-department-store chain with 20 branches in Mexico City alone. Those most convenient for tourists are at Madero 4 (its original store in the House of Tiles, downtown); on the Reforma at La Fragua (one at the Angel monument and another 4 blocks west of the Diana Fountain); and in the Zona Rosa (one at the corner of Niza and Hamburgo and another at Londres 130 in the Hotel Calinda Geneve). They feature a good selection of quality ceramics and handicrafts (they can ship anywhere), and most have restaurants or coffee shops, a pharmacy, ATM machines, and periodical and book departments carrying English-language publications.

Plaza La Rosa, a sparkling modern shopping arcade (⊠ Between Amberes and Génova in Zona Rosa), houses 72 prestigious shops and boutiques. It spans the entire depth of the block from Londres to Hamburgo, with entrances on both streets.

Bazar del Centro (⊠ Downtown, at Isabel la Católica 30, just below Madero) is a restored late-17th-century noble mansion built around a garden courtyard that houses several chic boutiques, top-quality handicraft shops, and prestigious jewelers such as **Aplijsa** (☎ 5/521–1923 or 5/510–1800), known for its fine gold, silver, pearls, and gemstones; **TFS** (☎ 5/521–1679) for superb French writing pens; and **Ginza** (☎ 5/518–6453) for Japanese pearls including the highly prized cultured variety. Other shops sell Taxco silver, Tonalá stoneware, and Mexican tequilas and liqueurs. This complex is elegant and also has a congenial bar.

Portales de los Mercaderes (Merchants' Arcade; extending along the entire west side of the Zócalo between Avs. Madero and 16 de Septiembre) has attracted merchants since 1524. Today it is lined with jewelry shops selling gold (sometimes by the gram) and authentic Taxco silver at prices lower than those in Taxco itself, where the overhead is higher. In the middle of the arcade is **Tardán** (⊠ Plaza de la Constitución 17, ☎ 5/512–2459), an unusual shop specializing in fine-quality fashionable men's and women's hats of every imaginable type and style.

Markets

A Saturday "must" for shoppers and browsers is a visit to the **Bazar Sábado** (Saturday Bazaar) at Plaza San Jacinto in the southern San Angel district. It's been specializing in unique high-quality handicrafts at excellent prices for more than three decades. Outside, vendors sell embroidered clothing, leather goods, wooden masks, beads, *amates* (bark paintings), and trinkets. Inside the bazaar building, a renovated two-story colonial mansion, are the better-quality—and higher-priced—goods, including *alebrijes* (painted wooden animals from Oaxaca), glassware, pottery, jewelry, and papier-mâché flowers. There is an indoor restaurant as well. Market and restaurant are open 10–7.

On Sunday, more than 100 artists exhibit and sell their paintings and sculptures at the **Jardín del Arte** (Garden of Art) in Parque Sullivan, just northeast of the Reforma–Insurgentes intersection. Along the west side of the park, a colorful weekend mercado with scores of food stands is also worth a visit.

The **Mercado Insurgentes** (also called **Mercado Zona Rosa**) is an entire block deep, with entrances on both Londres and Liverpool (☒ Between Florencia and Amberes). This is a typical neighborhood public market with one big difference: Most of the stalls (222 of them) sell crafts. You can find all kinds of handmade items—including serapes and ponchos, baskets, pottery, silver, pewter, fossils, and onyx, as well as regional Mexican dresses and costumes.

Also in the Zona Rosa, the pink neocolonial Plaza del Angel (☒ Londres 161) has a **Centro de Antigüedades** (antiques center) with several fine shops. On Saturday, together with other vendors, the antiques dealers set up a flea market in the arcades and patios. On Sunday, bibliophiles gather here to sell, peruse, and buy collectors' books and periodicals.

The Zócalo and Alameda Park areas have interesting markets for browsing and buying handicrafts and curios; polite bargaining is customary. The biggest is the **Centro Artesanal Buenavista** (☒ Aldama 187, by Buenavista Train Station, about 1½ km [1 mi] northwest of downtown). **La Lagunilla** market (☒ Libertad, between República de Chile and Calle Allende) attracts antiques hunters who know how to determine authenticity, and also coin collectors. The best day is Sunday, when flea-market stands are set up outside, with everything from collectibles to interesting knickknacks to junk. This market is known affectionately as the Thieves' Market: Local lore says you can buy back on Sunday what was stolen from your home on Saturday. Within the colonial walls of **La Ciudadela** market (☒ Balderas and Ayuntamiento, about 4 blocks south of Av. Juárez) are 344 artisans' stalls selling a variety of good handicrafts from all over the country, at better prices than you can find at the rest of the markets.

Specialty Shops

Antiques

Antigues Coloniart (☒ Estocolmo 367, Zona Rosa, ☎ 5/514–4799) has good-quality antique paintings, furniture, and sculpture. The store is open by appointment only.

Art

The **Juan Martín Gallery** (☒ Dickens 33-B, Polanco, ☎ 5/280–0277) is an avant-garde studio. The store and gallery of the renowned **Sergio Bustamante** (☒ Amberes 13, Zona Rosa, ☎ 5/525–5029; ☒ Campos Eliseos 204–6, Polanco, ☎ 5/282–2638) displays and sells the artist's wildly surrealistic sculptures and interior-design pieces. The **Oscar Roman Gallery** (✉ Anatole France 26, Polanco, ☎ 5/281–4939) is packed with work by good Mexican painters with a contemporary edge. The **Nina Menocal de Rocha Gallery** (✉ Zacatecas 93, Col. Roma, ☎ 5/564–7209) specializes in up-and-coming Cuban painters. **Misrachi** (✉ Presidete Masaryk 523, Polanco, ☎ 5/280–2967), a veteran among galleries, promotes well-known Mexican and international artists.

Candy

Celaya (✉ Cinco de Mayo 13, ☎ 5/521–1787), in the downtown historic section, is a decades-old haven for those with a sweet tooth. It specializes in candied pineapple, papaya, guava, and other exotic fruit, almond-paste, candied walnut rolls, and *cajeta,* a typical Mexican dessert of thick caramelized milk.

Clothing

Acapulco Joe's (✉ Amberes 19, Zona Rosa, ☎ 5/533–4774; ✉ Mazaryk 318, Polanco, ☎ 5/581–3044) has great T-shirts, beachwear, and hip unisex sports clothes. **Guess** (✉ Amberes 17, Zona Rosa, ☎ 5/207–2891) features chic denim sportswear for guys and gals.

Designer Items

Cartier (✉ Amberes 9, Zona Rosa, ☎ 5/207–6104; ✉ Masaryk 438, Polanco, ☎ 5/545–8064) sells genuine designer jewelry and clothes, under the auspices of the French Cartier. However, **Gucci** (✉ Hamburgo 136, Zona Rosa, ☎ 5/207–9997) has no connection with the European store of the same name; nevertheless, it has a fine selection of shoes, gloves, and handbags. **Ralph Lauren** (✉ Amberes 21, Zona Rosa, ☎ 5/514–1563) is the home of Polo sportswear made in Mexico under license and sold at Mexican prices.

Jewelry

The owner of **Los Castillo** (✉ Amberes 41, Zona Rosa, ☎ 5/511–8396) developed a unique method of melding silver, copper, and brass and is considered by many to be Taxco's top silversmith. Taxco silver of exceptional style is sold at **Arte en Plata** (✉ Londres 162, Zona Rosa, ☎ 5/511–1422), with many designs inspired by pre-Hispanic art. **Pelletier** (✉ Torcuato Caso 237, Polanco, ☎ 5/250–8600) sells fine jewelry and watches. **Tane** (✉ Amberes 70, Zona Rosa, ☎ 5/511–9429; ✉ Edgar Allan Poe 68, Polanco, ☎ 5/281–4775; and other locations) is a treasure trove of superb silver works—jewelry, flatware, candelabra, museum-quality reproductions of antique pieces, and bold new designs by young Mexican silversmiths. The **Mexican Opal Company** (✉ Hamburgo 203, Zona Rosa, ☎ 5/528–9263) is run by Japanese who sell set and loose opals as well as jewelry in silver and gold. It's open by appointment only.

Leather

For leather goods, you have more than a few choices in Mexico City. **Gaitán** (✉ Hamburgo 97, Zona Rosa, ☎ 5/203–9061) carries an extensive array of leather coats, luggage, golf bags, and saddles. **Aries** (✉ Florencia 14, Zona Rosa, ☎ 5/533–2509; ✉ Santa Catarina 207, San Angel, ☎ 5/616–2248) is Mexico's finest purveyor of leather goods, with a superb selection of clothes, shoes, and accessories for both men and women; the prices are high. **Antil** (✉ Florencia 22, Zona Rosa, ☎ 5/525–1573) also specializes in high-quality leather goods.

Mexican Handicrafts

Browse for fine works of folk art, sculpture, and handicraft, from silver to ceramics, in the two-story gallery **Manos Mexicanas** (✉ Amberes 57, Zona Rosa, ☎ 5/514–7455). Handwoven wool rugs, tapestries, and fabrics with original and unusual designs can be found at **Tamacani**

(✉ Varsovia 51, Zona Rosa, ☏ 5/207–3696). **Arte Popular en Miniatura,** with two Zona Rosa locations (✉ Hamburgo 85, ☏ 5/525–8145; ✉ In the Plaza del Angel at Londres 161, ☏ 5/208–2222), are tiny shops filled with tiny things, from dollhouse furniture and lead soldiers to miniature Nativity scenes. **Flamma** (✉ Hamburgo 167, Zona Rosa, ☏ 5/511–8499 or 5/511–0266) is a town house that sells a beautiful array of handmade candles. **Javi** (✉ Humboldt 44-3, downtown, no phone) sells exceptional handmade guitars and has a thriving export business.

Under the auspices of the National Council for Culture and Arts, **Fonart** (National Fund for Promoting Handicrafts) operates four stores in Mexico City and others around the country. The most convenient locations are at Londres 136, 2nd floor, Zona Rosa (☏ 5/525–2026), and at Juárez 89 (☏ 5/521–0171), downtown just west of Alameda Park. Prices are fixed, and the diverse, top-quality folk art and handcrafted furnishings from all over Mexico represent the best artisans. Major sales at near wholesale prices are held at the main store-warehouse (✉ Av. Patriotismo 691, Col. Mixcoac) year-round.

Museo de Artes Populares (Museum of Arts and Crafts) could well be a museum but is in fact a large store displaying and selling an array of folk art and handicrafts—pottery, ceramics, glassware, textiles, and more—from practically every region of the country. Housed in an early 18th-century convent (✉ Across from Alameda Park and Juárez Monument, Juárez 44, ☏ 5/518–3058), it is open Monday–Saturday.

Feders (✉ Bufon 25 in Colonia Nueva Anzures, ☏ 5/260–2958 factory; ✉ Bazar Sábado, Plaza San Jacinto 11, San Angel, booth) has great handblown glass, Tiffany-style lamps, and artistic wrought iron.

SIDE TRIPS

North of Mexico City

Hugging the roads to the north of Mexico City are several of the country's most celebrated pre-Columbian and colonial monuments. The Basílica de Guadalupe, a church dedicated to Mexico's patron saint, and the pyramids of Teotihuacán make an easy day tour, as does the combination of the ex-convent (now a magnificent museum of the viceregal period) at Tepotzotlán and the ruins at Tula, also to the north but in a slightly different direction.

La Villa de Guadalupe

"La Villa"—more formally known as La Villa de Guadalupe, the site of the two Basilicas of the Virgin of Guadalupe—is Mexico's holiest shrine. Its importance derives from the miracle that the devout believe transpired here on December 12, 1531, when an Indian named Juan Diego received from the Virgin a cloak permanently imprinted with her image so he could prove to the priests that he had indeed had a holy vision. On that date each year, millions of pilgrims arrive, many crawling on their knees for the last few hundred yards, and praying for cures and other divine favors. The **Antigua Basílica** (Old Basilica) dates from 1536, although various additions were made during the intervening centuries; the altar was executed by sculptor Manuel Tolsá. The basilica now houses a museum of ex-votos. (hand-painted tin retablos and popular religious art, painting, sculpture, and decorative and applied arts from the 15th to the 18th century.

Because the structure of the old church had weakened over the years and the building was no longer large enough, or safe enough, to accommodate all the worshipers, Pedro Ramírez Vázquez, the architect

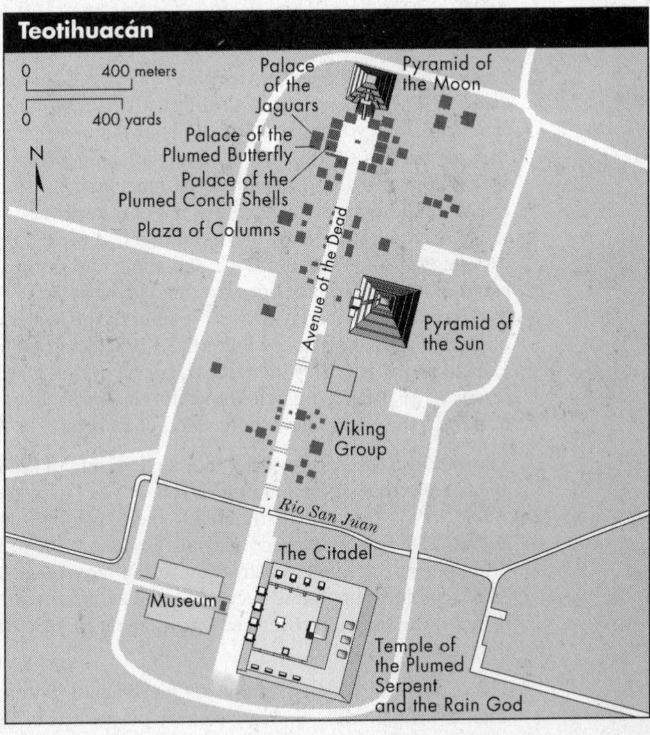

responsible for Mexico City's splendid National Museum of Anthropology, was commissioned to design a new shrine. In this case the architect's inspiration failed him, however: The **Nueva Basílica,** completed in 1976, is a grotesque and most unspiritual mass of steel, wood, resinous fibers, and polyethylene designs. It holds 10,000 people; the famous cloak is enshrined in its own altar and can be viewed from a moving sidewalk that passes below it.

Teotihuacán

Most tour buses to the ruins stop briefly in **San Agustín Acolmán** to see the outstanding plateresque church and ex-convent, now a museum. The original Augustinian church (1539) is noteworthy for its vaulted roof and pointed towers; the ornate cloister and plateresque facade, set off with candelabra-like columns, were added a century later by the monks.

Teotihuacán occupies a monumental place in early Mexican history that is easily matched by the physical grandeur and scale of the site itself. It was, most likely, already a small town around 100 BC and reached its zenith about four centuries later. At the time of its decline in the 8th century, it was one of the largest cities in the world, with possibly as many as 200,000 people. The sacred city lay in the midst of rich obsidian mines, which provided the means for its rise as a major trading power in the region; the glasslike obsidian is still being fashioned into animal figures, which are sold in the market stalls on the site. Teotihuacán was set on fire and destroyed around AD 750 and over the years was completely buried. Its history and even its original name were lost.

Centuries later, the Aztecs arrived in the Valley of Mexico. Because the memory of the grandeur of the city in this area survived the passage of time, these new settlers named the site Teotihuacán, which meant "place where the gods were born." It was here, the Aztecs believed, that the gods created the universe.

The most impressive sight in Teotihuacán is the 4-km-long (2½-mi-long) **Calzada de los Muertos** (Avenue of the Dead), the main axis of the ancient city along which have been built six major structures. The Aztecs named the avenue thus because of the stepped platforms lining it, which they mistook for tombs. The graceful 126-ft-high **Pyramid of the Moon** dominates the northern end of the avenue and the compact, square **Ciudadela** (Citadel) the opposite end; more than 4,000 one-story dwellings constructed of adobe and stone and occupied by artisans, warriors, and tradesmen once surrounded the avenue. On the west side of the spacious plaza facing the Pyramid of the Moon are the **palaces of Quetzalpápalotl** (Plumed Butterfly), **Caracoles Emplumados** (Plumed Conch Shells), and **Los Jaguares** (Jaguars), which is where the priests resided. The palaces are best known for the spectacular bird and jaguar murals in their winding underground chambers.

The oldest structure—the solid-looking **Pyramid of the Sun** with a base as broad as that of the pyramid of Cheops in Egypt—is farther south along the avenue and is estimated to have been built between AD 100 and AD 250. Scientists even today are amazed at the precise placement of its planes and angles in relation to the movement of the sun. The 242 steps of the pyramid face west, the cardinal point where it was believed the sun is transformed into a jaguar in order to pass through the darkness of death.

The Ciudadela, with its **Temple of Quetzalcóatl** (Plumed Serpent) and **Tlaloc** (Rain God) is expressive of the plastic arts of the time with its sculptures of toothy serpent heads stuck into a temple facade. Quetzalcón and Tlaloc together represent the fusion of earth and sky.

Climbing one pyramid is probably enough for most people. The Pyramid of the Sun is the larger, standing 210 ft high, and affords a spectacular view of the entire area. Wear comfortable clothes (especially shoes) and bring sunscreen or a visored hat when you visit.

Many of the artifacts uncovered at Teotihuacán are on display at the Museum of Anthropology in Mexico City. The **on-site museum,** opened in 1994 near the Pyramid of the Sun, contains fabulous pieces from the archaeological zone such as stone sculptures of Tlaloc, the goggle-eyed god of rain; black and green obsidian arrowheads; and simulated burial sites of exalted personages of the empire, their skeletons arranged as they were upon discovery. *$3; free Sun. ⌚ Archaeological site daily 8–5, on-site museum Tues.–Sun. 8–5.*

Seeing the ruins will take two to four hours, depending on how taken you are with the place (or when your tour bus leaves).

DINING AND LODGING

If you would like to overnight at the pyramids, there's a **Villa Arqueológica** hotel (☎ 595/60909 in Teotihuacán; 5/203–3086 in Mexico City; 800/258–2633 in the U.S.) across the road from the fenced-off site with 20 snug rooms and a huge garden and patio restaurant-bar surrounding a pool. This Club Med is the only hotel that has permission to be in the area. Nonguests can dine in the restaurant.

Tepotzotlán

The **Jesuit church** and **school of San Francisco Javier** at Tepotzotlán rank among the masterpieces of Mexican churrigueresque (baroque) architecture. The unmitigated baroque facade of the church (1682) is the first thing to catch the eye, but inside and out, every square inch has been worked over, like an overdressed Christmas tree. Note especially the gilded, bemirrored Chapel of the Virgin of Loreto.

In pre-Hispanic times, the village was an important stop along the salt route (salt was used as money) between Toluca and Texcoco near Teotihuacán and had a prestigious school of dance and the plastic arts. When Corté arrived, sadly he massacred the whole town on the pretense of asking for help for his wounded soldiers. In 1580, four Jesuit priests arrived, learned the native language, and turned the village into a center of evangelization by setting up a school for the young nobles of the conquered nation. The church, of course, was built with Indian slave labor, but as a concession to the slaves, many of the angels decorating the chambers have been painted with dark-skinned indigenous faces; this is probably the only church in Mexico where you will find this. There's also a museum of religious art in the complex. There are two notable restaurants for taking a light snack or lunch after viewing the Jesuit complex. One is the museum's coffee shop and the other is **Casa Mago,** directly across the square from the church. Casa Mago's owners will proudly recount how Liz Taylor dropped in in 1963 to have a beer.

This village is also famous for its traditional Christmas *pastorela,* a charming and humorous morality play that has been taking place for more than 30 years and tells the story of the birth of Jesus Christ. Staged every year from December 15 to 23 in the patio of the church at night, the cast includes a few professionals and loads of extras from the town who portray shepherds, angels, and, of course, the Devil. Tickets are available through TicketMaster (☎ 5/325–9000 in Mexico City; 5/876–0243 in Tepotzolán).

Tula

Tula, capital of the Toltecs (its original name was Tollán), was founded in about AD 1000 and abandoned two centuries later. Quetzalcóatl was born in Tula and became its priest-king; under his rule, the Toltecs reached the pinnacle of their civilization, with art, science, and philosophy flourishing. According to myth, Quetzalcóatl went into exile in Yucatán but vowed to return—on a date (1519) that unfortunately coincided with the arrival of Hernán Cortés, whom the Aztecs therefore welcomed. The 15-ft **warrior statues** (called *atlantes*), rather than the ruins themselves, give Tula its fame. These basalt figures tower over Pyramid B, their harsh geometric lines looking vaguely like totem poles. Crocodiles, jaguars, coyotes, and eagles are also depicted in the carvings and represent the various warrior orders of the Toltecs. *$2; free Sun. Tues.–Sun. 8–5.*

North of Mexico City A to Z

GETTING THERE

To reach La Villa de Guadalupe by car, take Paseo de la Reforma Norte until it forks into Calzada de Guadalupe, which leads directly to the shrine. Alternatively, you can take the No. 3 metro from downtown to the Basílica stop. Buses run every half hour from the Central de Autobuses del Norte to Teotihuacán, and the trip takes about one hour. In addition, many tour companies offer combination visits to the two sights.

To get to Tepotzotlán from Mexico City, follow Periférico Norte. After 41 km (25 mi), you'll come to the exit for Tepotzotlán. Tula is about 8 km (5 mi) north of Tepotzotlán. Buses to Tula/Tepotzotlán leave Mexico City every 20 minutes.

VISITOR INFORMATION

There are no tourist offices in the area, but a good English-language guidebook to Teotihuacán is sold at the site.

South and Southwest of Mexico City

This excursion to the south and southwest of Mexico City begins in Xochimilco (So-chee-*meel*-co), famous for its floating gardens, where visitors can take rides in gondola-like boats and get a fleeting sense of pre-Hispanic Mexico City. Beyond Xochimilco, in the neighboring state of Morelos, lies Cuernavaca, a weekend retreat for wealthy *chilangos* (residents of Mexico City) and foreigners. From Cuernavaca we suggest a detour to the town of Tepoztlán, which has a 16th-century Dominican convent, a lively Sunday market, its own little pyramid, and lots of New Age devotees.

Xochimilco

When the first nomadic settlers arrived in the Valley of Mexico, they found an enormous lake. As the years went by and their population grew, the land was not sufficient to satisfy their agricultural needs. They solved the problem by devising a system of *chinampas* (floating gardens), rectangular structures something like barges, which they filled with reeds, branches, and mud. They planted them with willows, whose roots anchored the floating gardens to the lake bed, making a labyrinth of small islands and canals on which they carried the flowers and produce grown on the chinampas to market.

Today Xochimilco is the only place in Mexico where the gardens still exist. Go on a Saturday, when the *tianguis* (market) is most active, or on a Sunday. (Note that Xochimilco is a popular destination for families on Sunday.) On weekdays the place is practically deserted, so it loses much of its charm. Hire a *trajinera* (flower-painted launch); an arch over each launch spells out its name—usually a diminutive for a woman's name—in flowers. As you sail through the canals, you'll pass mariachis and women selling tacos from other launches.

Folks are also flocking to Xochimilco for the **Museo Dolores Olmedo Patino,** which carries the largest private collection of works by the flamboyant Mexican muralist Diego Rivera; it was put together by Olmedo, his lifelong model, patron, and onetime mistress (although she denies it). The lavish display of works, housed in a magnificently restored 18th-century hacienda, includes nearly 140 pieces from his cubist, post-cubist, and mural periods. The museum also has works by Rivera's legal wife, Frida Kahlo, and his common-law wife, Angelina Beloff; a bust of Rivera holds the ashes of his Russian lover, Marinka. ✉ *Av. México 5843,* ☎ *5/555–1016.* 🎫 *$2.* ⏲ *Tues.–Sun. 10–6.*

Cuernavaca

The climate in Cuernavaca, just 85 km (53 mi) from Mexico City, changes dramatically to lush semitropical as the altitude descends almost 2,500 ft. In fact, it was this balmy springlike temperature that first attracted the rich and famous to the resort—starting with Hernán Cortés, who built a summer palace here in the 16th century. The city is also known for its many Spanish-language schools, some spectacular hotels and restaurants, the beautiful Borda Gardens, and Diego Rivera murals in the Palacio de Cortés. An overnight stay is recommended.

Cuernavaca is built on a series of small hills whose streets intertwine at a maddening pace. If you're not used to driving in San Francisco, say, it's better to take a cab to get around, especially on the weekends, when the number of cars swells to disproportionate numbers.

Most of the attractions are concentrated around the main plaza called **Plaza de la Constitución,** which is surrounded by handicraft shops, sidewalk cafés, and government buildings. The square itself is filled with sidewalk vendors from neighboring villages hawking local arts and crafts throughout the week. On weekends, one side of the square is taken over by stalls selling leather as well as silver and gold jewelry from other regions of the country. A smaller square called **Jardín Juárez** lies just across the street from the Plaza de la Constitución and has the charming tradition of putting on free band concerts every Sunday afternoon under the archways of the colonial kiosk. Either of these two squares is the perfect place for whiling away a pleasant afternoon after a visit to the tourist sights.

The major attractions include the **Palacio de Cortés** (Cortés's palace-cum-fortress), which now houses the **Museo de Cuauhnáhuac** (Museum of Cuauhnáhuac, the Indian name for Cuernavaca), which focuses on Mexican history before and after the conquest. On permanent exhibit is a collection of some of Diego Rivera's finest murals, which, like those of Mexico City's National Palace, dramatize the history and the horrors of the conquest, colonialism, and the revolution. The murals were donated to the museum by former U.S. Ambassador to Mexico Dwight Morrow. ✉ *Av. Juárez,* ☎ *73/12–81–71.* 🎫 *$2.* ⏲ *Tues.–Sun. 10–5.*

The beautiful and spacious **Jardín Borda** (Borda Gardens) is the most visited attraction in Cuernavaca. They were designed in the late 18th century by a member of the Borda family (rich miners of French extraction) for one of his relatives; Maximilian and Carlotta visited the gardens frequently. This is where Maximilian had a dalliance with the gardener's wife, La India Maria. She was immortalized in a portrait by a noted painter of the time. In this century novelist Malcolm Lowry turned the gardens into a sinister symbol in *Under the Volcano.* ✉ *Av. Morelos, no. 103, 3 blocks west of Cortés's Palace, no phone.* 🎫 *Less than $1; free Wed.* ⏲ *Tues.–Sun. 10–5:30.*

The **Catedral de la Asunción,** an architecturally eclectic structure begun in 1529 by Hernán Cortés is noteworthy for its 17th-century Japanese wall paintings. It's also famous for its mariachi Masses each Sunday morning. Diagonally opposite the cathedral is the **Palacio Municipal;** the paintings inside depict life in the city before the Spaniards. ✉ *(Cathedral) Hidalgo and Av. Morelos opposite Borda gardens.*

Also near the main square is the **Robert Brady Museum,** a delightful restored colonial mansion housing a diverse collection of art and artifacts assembled by the late Brady, an artist, antiquarian, and decorator who hailed from Fort Dodge, Iowa. You can see ceramics, antique furniture, sculptures, paintings, and tapestries—all beautifully arranged in rooms painted with bright Mexican colors. ✉ *Netzahuacóyotl 4, between Hidalgo and Abasolo,* ☎ *73/18–85–54.* 🎫 *$2.* ⏲ *Tues.–Sun. 10–6.*

The small ruins of **Zochicalco,** which means "place of flowers," have a pyramid and ball court. Showing Maya, Toltec, and Zapotec influences, the site—which researchers now say was a fortress/city—reached its heyday between AD 700 and AD 900. A solar-powered museum opened in 1996 and displays six rooms of artifacts, including beautiful sculptures of Zochicalco deities and symbols for fertility and drought, found on the site in 1993 and 1994. ✉ *23 mi southwest of Cuernavaca (take Hwy. 95D south; look for sign for turnoff).* 🎫 *$1.25; free Sun.* ⏲ *Tues.–Sun. 9–5.*

DINING AND LODGING

If you've not been invited to one of the mansions of the wealthy weekenders set in the hills on the edge of town, not to worry: There are a number of spectacular hotels and restaurants with equally spectacular gardens—several of them housed in restored colonial mansions and even haciendas—where visitors can get a sampling of life behind the high stone walls. Indeed, many people come here just for a sumptuous meal in a glorious garden setting. Many Cuernavaca hostelries began as restaurants and added on rooms to satisfy clients who felt too relaxed to drive back to Mexico City after a heavy meal.

$ ✕ **La Strada.** Those who want a change from Mexican food can enjoy a good Italian meal on a colonial candlelit patio at this establishment, which is one of the old-timers of good dining in town. You can't go wrong with the fish dishes, pizzas, or *filete de Estrada* served with homemade pasta. There's a guitarist at lunchtime to soothe the digestion, and every Friday the chef whips up a special-of-the-day. ✉ *Salazar 3, just around the corner from Palace of Cortés,* ☎ *73/18–60–85. AE, MC, V. Closed Mon.*

$ ✕ **Vienes.** Founded by an Austrian several generations ago, this restaurant, which has grown up with the town, serves excellent Austrian and Hungarian dishes such as Wiener schnitzel and goulash and irresistible pastries like Sacher torte and apple strudel. ✉ *Lerdo de Tejada, 302, at Comonfort, 1 block west of main square,* ☎ *73/18–40–44. AE, MC, V.*

$$$–$$$$ ✕🏨 **Las Mañanitas.** Among the most spectacular—and priciest—places, both for dining and lodging, is this hostel near the center of town; opened 41 years ago by an American ex-pat, it offers rooms and suites exquisitely decorated in traditional Mexican furnishings like beds with hand-carved headboards, fireplaces, hand-painted tiles in the bathrooms, and gilded handicrafts. Mexico City residents journey an hour by road to Cuernavaca on weekends just to dine at the restaurant. La Mañanitas' most spectacular dining areas are the open-air terraces and the garden inhabited by flamingos, peacocks, and African cranes. It looks like something out of a lavish movie set. Portions are ample, and a tried-and-true favorite is the Mexican Plate—enchilada, chile relleno, *carne asada* (thinly sliced oven-grilled beef), and tamale, served with side dishes of guacamole and refried beans. Desserts, which are changed daily, include chocolate pie and diced fruit over grapefruit, lemon, and strawberry sherbet. ✉ *Ricardo Linares 107, Cuernavaca 62550,* ☎ *73/14–14–66. 23 rooms and suites. Restaurant, bar. AE.*

$$$ 🏨 **Camino Real Sumiya.** The romantic hideaway, built by Woolworth heiress Barbara Hutton, was converted into a restaurant after she died. In 1993 new owners took over and turned it into a posh hotel. It's set amid formal Japanese gardens (including a rock garden for contemplation) and features an original Kabuki theater that was brought over from Kyoto. A concierge takes care of every need. The rooms, which are equipped with modern furniture, two queen-size beds, and color satellite TVs, are set in the far part of the garden for privacy. Nonguests can dine in the restaurant. ✉ *About 15 mins south of town at Interior del Fracc. Sumiya, Col. José Parres, Juitepec, Moreles 62550. (To get here, take Civac exit on Acapulco Hwy.),* ☎ *73/20–91–99 or 800/722–6466,* FAX *73/20–91–55. 163 rooms. Restaurant, 2 bars, coffee shop, pool, 8 tennis courts, travel services. AE, DC, MC, V.*

$$ 🏨 **Clarion Cuernavaca Racquet Club.** Although this hotel started out as a posh tennis club, Choice Hotels International turned it into an all-purpose hotel as well. Less expensive than the above-mentioned hotels, the

Clarion attracts many guests who come for the beautiful gardens and extra-spacious two-room suites equipped with a romantic fireplace. Families converge here on the weekends. The restaurant admits nonguests. ✉ *Francisco Villa 100, Rancho de Cortés, Cuernavaca 62120,* ☎ *73/11–24–00 or 800/228–5151,* FAX *73/11–54–93. 52 suites. 2 restaurants, bar, pool, 9 tennis courts, travel services. AE, MC, V.*

$–$$ **Hacienda de Cortés.** This old hacienda dates from the 16th century and actually once belonged to *El Conquistador* himself. The rooms are beautifully decorated in traditional old Mexican furnishings—the absence of TV is more than compensated for by the lovely patios and gardens that beckon one outdoors. There's a TV room off the lobby for addicts. ✉ *Plaza Kennedy 90, Atlacomulco, Moreles 62250,* ☎ *73/15–88–44. 22 rooms. Restaurant, bar, pool. MC, V.*

Tepoztlán

Some say Tepoztlán, surrounded by beautiful sandstone monoliths that throw off a russet glow at sunset, is a magical place—Mexico's answer to Sedona, Arizona. It attracts the esoteric, which means you can find practitioners of hatha yoga, meditation, crystal healing, herbal cures, astrology, and native sorcery, among others. This town of 13,000, with a village atmosphere and cobblestone streets, is primarily known for its tiny **Tepozteco pyramid,** probably of Aztec origin, perched on top of a hill; hundreds of people come each weekend to climb it. Other attractions include the lively **Sunday market** filled with fruits, vegetables, and handicrafts, and the **dances** held during the pre-Lenten Carnival, when celebrants don bright masks depicting birds, animals, and Christian figures. Anthropologists Robert Redfield and Oscar Lewis both did fieldwork here in the 1950s. The town's landmark is the multi-buttressed **Templo y Ex-Convento de la Natividad de la Virgen María** (1559), its fine paneled doors adorned with Indian motifs. Each September 8th, the faithful assemble here to celebrate the birth of the Virgin Mary, the town's patron saint. The date also commemorates the baptism of the legendary ruler Tepoztecatl for whom the pyramid is named.

Tepoztlán drew national attention in September 1995, when townspeople stormed City Hall with sticks and stones and took government officials hostage to protest the proposed building of a mega–golf resort on their revered Tepozteco terrain. They eventually ousted the mayor and town police and were still protesting at press time because the developers had not abandoned the project.

South and Southwest of Mexico City A to Z

GETTING THERE

To reach Xochimilco by car, take Periférico Sur to the extension of División del Norte; an alternate route is from Calzada de Tlalpán to Calzada México Xochimilco and then Calzada Guadalupe Ramírez. Xochimilco is 21 km (13 mi) from the Zócalo in Mexico City; the trip should take between 45 minutes and 1 hour, depending on traffic. If Xochimilco is your final destination, you are probably best off taking a taxi. By public transportation, take metro line No. 2 to Taxqueña and then any bus marked Xochimilco.

To continue south by car, return to Periférico Sur, turn left (south) on Viaducto Tlalpán, and watch for signs to Cuernavaca in about a half hour. The *cuota,* or toll road (Rte. 95D), costs about $7 but is much faster than the *carretera libre,* or free road (Rte. 95). On Route 95D, it will take you about 1½ hours to cover 85 km (53 mi).

Tepoztlán is 26 km (16 mi) east of Cuernavaca via Route 95D. Buses also run every 20 minutes.

VISITOR INFORMATION

The **Morelos State Tourist Office** (✉ Morelos Sur 802, ☎ 73/14–38–72) in Cuernavaca is located in Colonia Las Palmas; it's open weekdays 8–9, Saturday 8–3.

Southeast of Mexico City

Southeast of Mexico City lies Puebla, a well-preserved colonial city and once the center of the Spanish tile industry. Nearby Cholula is a sacred spot in ancient Mexico and home to an important pyramid and scores of churches. You can detour along the way to see the volcanoes, Popocatépetl (Poh-poh-kah-*teh*-petal) and Iztaccíhuatl (Eez-tah-*see*-waddle). On your return to the capital, leave time—an entire day would be best—to visit the city of Tlaxcala, with its rare church and former convent, and an amazing archaeological site nearby.

The Volcanoes

As you leave Mexico City—if the smog is not too thick—Popocatépetl and Iztaccíhuatl will be visible to the south. "Popo," 17,887 ft high, last erupted in 1802, but rumblings and bubblings in late 1994 were sufficiently strong to cause nearby villages to be evacuated temporarily. It continued to burp and belch during 1995 and caused a bit of alarm when it sent forth large clouds of smoke in 1996 and 1997, though most seismologists found no cause for alarm. In any case, check with the U.S. State Department for the latest developments if you plan to climb it or "Itza"—a feat for serious mountaineers; the Parque Nacional, a verdant pine forest, makes a good spot for a picnic.

The legend states that Popocate, an Aztec warrior, had been sent by the emperor—father of his beloved Iztaccíhuatl—to bring back the head of a feared enemy in order to win Iztaccíhuatl's hand. He returned triumphantly only to find that Iztaccíhuatl had killed herself, believing him dead. The grief-stricken Popo laid out her body on a small knoll and lit an eternal torch that he watches over, kneeling. Each of the four peaks composing the volcano is named after different parts of her body, and the silhouette of the volcano resembles the figure of a reclining woman—hence its nickname, "The Sleeping Lady."

LODGING

At the 12,000-ft marker on Popo, there's a park shelter with spartan (cement slab beds) dormitory accommodations, for which you pay a few dollars a night; you must bring your own sleeping bag. You can drive here from the main highway, but this is the end of the road; if you want to go higher, you'll have to hoof it. For lodging in town, try the venerable **Los Volcanes** (✉ Blvd. Los Volcanes, Popo Park, ☎ 597/60294) at the foot of the volcano which has 40 rustic rooms, all with potbellied stoves.

Cholula

The town fathers claim that Cholula has 365 church cupolas, one for every day in the year. Most of the 40 colonial churches in Cholula are in poor condition, but 6½ km (4 mi) south of town, in **San Francisco Acatepec**, is one of the two most stunning and well-preserved churches in the country. Completely covered with Puebla tiles, it has been called the most ornate Poblano rococo facade in Mexico. Equally unusual is the interior of the church in **Santa María Tonantzintla**, 3 km (2 mi) toward Cholula. Its polychrome wood-and-stucco carvings—inset columns, altarpieces, and the main archway—are the epitome of churrigueresque. Set off by ornate gold-leaf figures of vegetal forms, angels, and saints, the carvings were done by native craftsmen.

Closer to town, the **Gran Piramide** (Great Pyramid) was the centerpiece of a Toltec and then Aztec religious center and consists of seven superimposed structures connected by tunnels and stairways. The Spaniards, as they often did, built a chapel to **Nuestra Señora de los Remedios** (Our Lady of the Remedies) on top of it. Behind the pyramid is a vast temple complex of 43 acres, once dedicated to Quetzalcóatl. *About $3.* *Daily 10–5.*

Puebla

Maize was first cultivated in the Tehuacán Valley; later, the region was a crossroads for many ancient Mesoamerican cultures, including the Olmecs and Totonacs. The town of Puebla is notable for its idiosyncratic baroque structures, which are built of red brick, gray stone, white stucco, and the beautiful Talavera tiles produced from local clay. The Battle of May 5, 1862—resulting in a short-lived victory against French invaders—took place just north of town. The national holiday, Cinco de Mayo, is celebrated yearly on that date in its honor. The city's early importance to the Spanish Crown can be summed up in the fact that it had the first glass factory, first textile mill, and second hospital in the young colony.

Puebla today retains a strong conservative religious element and was one of the cities chosen by Pope John Paul II to visit during his 1978 Mexican tour. Overrun with religious structures, this city probably has more ex-convents and monasteries, chapels, and churches per square mile than anywhere else in the country. In fact, the valley of Puebla, which takes in Cholula, was said to have 224 churches and 10 convents and monasteries in its heyday. It's no wonder, as its founding in 1531 was undertaken by the Franciscan and Dominican fathers. Determined to show off the city to its best advantage, there's now a massive restoration and cleanup campaign going on downtown that includes the placement of more signs with historic legends. Don't miss the **cathedral,** partially financed by Puebla's most famous son, Bishop Juan de Palafox y Mendoza—who donated his personal fortune to build its famous tower, the second-largest church tower in the country. Palafox was the illegitimate son of a Spanish nobleman who grew up poor but inherited his father's wealth upon his death. Onyx, marble, and gold adorn the cathedral's high altar, designed by Mexico's most illustrious colonial architect, Manuel Tolsá; the facade is gray and cheerless, however. In addition, the **Iglesia de Santo Domingo** (Santo Domingo Church) is especially famous for its Rosary Chapel, where almost every centimeter of the walls, ceilings, and altar is covered with gilded carvings and sculptures. The **Amparo Museum,** filled with the private collection of pre-Hispanic and colonial art of Mexican banker and philanthropist Manuel Espinoza Yglesias, is one of the most beautiful in Mexico. Puebla is one of the few cities in Mexico declared a Patrimony of Humanities site by the United Nations because of the splendor of its colonial architecture.

The colonial **Convento de Santa Rosa,** now a museum of native crafts, contains the intricately tiled kitchen where Puebla's renowned mole sauce was believed to have been invented by the nuns as a surprise for their demanding gourmet bishop. Puebla is also famous for *camote,* a popular candy made from sweet potatoes and fruit. **La Calle de las Dulces** (Sweets Street) is lined with shops competing to sell a wide variety of freshly made camote.

DINING AND LODGING

Puebla is noted for its cuisine, considered by some to be the best in the country; two of Mexico's most popular dishes were created here to celebrate special occasions. Already noted above, mole is a type of spicy sauce made with about 15 different ingredients; the best-known mole includes bitter chocolate. Another Puebla specialty believed to have been initiated by the town's nuns is *chiles en nogada,* a green poblano chili filled with ground meats, fruits, and nuts, then covered with a sauce of chopped walnuts and cream, and topped with red pomegranate seeds; the colors represent the red, green, and white of the Mexican flag.

Las Bodegas del Molino is set in a 16th-century hacienda at the edge of town (✉ Molino de San José del Puente, ☎ 22/49–03–99), this restaurant is truly remarkable, both for its setting and its cuisine. A traditional favorite is **Fonda Santa Clara** (✉ 307 Calle 3 Poniente, ☎ 22/42–26–59), just a few blocks from the Zócalo. For a folksy touch, venture over to **La Pasita** (✉ 5 Oriente 602, across the street from Plazuela de los Sapos [Plaza of the Frogs], ☎ 22/55555), a funky bar with two tables, a congenial host, and dozens of homemade fruit liquors. This cozy hole-in-the-wall has been a favorite watering hole of the locals for well over eight decades.

Fine hotels in Puebla include the 83-room **Camino Real** (✉ 7 Poniente 105, ☎ 22/32–89–83 or 800/722–6466), in a converted 16th-century convent two blocks from the Zócalo, the new 12-room **Meson Sacristia de la Companía** (✉ 6 Sur, no. 304, at Callejón de los Sapos, ☎ 22/32–45–13), a reconverted town house where every room is outfitted in priceless antiques that can be purchased right out of the room, and the 192-room **El Meson del Angel,** at the entrance to the city (✉ Hermanos Serdan 807, ☎ 22/24–30–00). The 47-room **Royalty** on the main square (☎ 22/42–47–40) is small, well maintained, and considerably less expensive.

Cantona

Puebla state is home to fascinating Cantona—opened to the public in 1995—which has 24 ball courts where a precursor to soccer was played. It's built into a hillock that looks like a massive military fortress from afar. Larger than Teotihuacán (its archenemy) outside Mexico City, it supposedly reached its pinnacle after AD 600, and we can judge its importance from the fact that around 500 cobblestone streets and lanes crisscross its 13-square-km (5-square-mi) area. ✉ *125 km (75 mi) northeast of the city of Puebla following Hwy. 129 to Oriental on Hwy. 125; turn off highway here and take dirt road to site. In rainy season, you can only navigate it with a 4-wheel drive.* 🎫 *$1.25.* ⏲ *Tues.–Sun. 9–5.*

Tlaxcala

The warriors of the state of Tlaxcala (Tlas-*ca*-la) played a pivotal role in the Spanish Conquest by aligning themselves with Cortés against the army of the hated Aztecs, thus swelling the military ranks of the conqueror by 5,000 men. The state capital, seat of the ancient nation with the same name, will interest both archaeology buffs and church lovers. The former Franciscan church, now called the **Catedral de Nuestro Señora de la Asunción** (Our Lady of the Assumption Cathedral), with its adjoining monastery (1537–40), standing atop a hill one block from the handsome main square, was the first permanent Catholic edifice in the New World. The most unusual feature of the church is its wooden ceiling beams, carved and gilded with gold studs after the Moorish fashion. There are only three churches of this kind in Mexico. (Moorish, or mudéjar, architecture appeared in Mexico only during the very early years after the conquest, when Spain was still close enough in time to the Moorish occupation to be greatly influenced by Arabic architectural styles.) The austere monastery, now a museum of history, displays 18th-century religious paintings and a small collection of pre-Columbian pieces. Near the monastery is a beautiful outdoor **chapel** whose symmetrical rear arches show Moorish and Gothic traces.

The **Palacio de Gobierno** (Government Palace), which occupies the north side of the Zócalo, was built in about 1550. Inside are vivid epic murals of Tlaxcala before the conquest, painted in the 1960s by local artist Desiderio Hernández Xochitiotzin.

About 1 km (½ mi) west of Tlaxcala is the large, ornate **Basilica of Our Lady of Ocotlán.** The legend of the Virgin dates from 1541, when, during a severe epidemic, she appeared to a poor Indian and told him to take the water from a steam that had miraculously appeared to his people to cure them. The villagers recovered. The Virgin then asked for the Franciscan monks from a nearby monastery. When they arrived in Her forest, they were blinded by the raging flames of a fire that didn't harm the trees. They returned the next day with an axe to cut open one particular pine (*ocotlán*) tree that had caught their attention. When they split it open, they discovered the wooden image of the Virgin, which they installed in the present basilica. Many miracles have been attributed to the Virgin since then. Noteworthy sights of the church here are the churrigueresque white-plaster facade, which conjures up images of a wedding cake; the two Poblano (red-tile) towers; and, inside, the brilliantly painted and gilded **Camarín de la Virgen** (the Virgin's Dressing Room).

Cacaxtla

This archaeological site, accidentally discovered in 1975 by a grave robber, contains a breathtaking series of **murals,** they date back to between AD 650 and AD 700 and depict scenes of a fierce battle between Maya and Central Mexican warriors; it is considered a major breakthrough in tracing the immigration and trade patterns of pre-Hispanic Mexico. The site was settled around 2000 BC by the Olmeca-Xicalancas, a transition culture lying between the Olmecs and the peoples of central Mexico, researchers say. However, it reached its height between AD 600 and AD 900 and was abandoned by AD 1000. The vividly portrayed battle scenes with life-size figures show warriors in lofty bird headdresses and plumage being vanquished by victors wearing jaguar skins and wielding spears, obsidian knives, and lances. The murals are painted on the walls of a series of palaces built one on top of one another. A huge roof now protects the precious murals from the ravages of rain and wind and sunlight. The site is some 22 km (13 mi) southwest of Tlaxcala. *$1.25. Tues.–Sun. 10–5; Tues.–Sun. 10–1 for viewing frescoes.*

Xochitécatl

While Cantona in neighboring Puebla is all military ambience (☞ *above*), little Xochitécatl is decidedly soft and feminine, having been dedicated to a bevy of important goddesses. Four Classic period **pyramids** are built on a hill that affords a spectacular view of the valleys of Tlaxcala and Puebla. A small on-site **museum** has a good collection of sculpted stone heads and pregnant women. ✉ *Less than 1½ km (1 mi) north of Cacaxtla. $1.25. Tues.–Sun. 9–5.*

Southeast of Mexico City A to Z

GETTING THERE

From Mexico City, head east toward the airport and turn onto Calzada Zaragoza, the last wide boulevard before arriving at the airport; it becomes the Puebla Highway at the tollbooth. Route 190D is the toll road straight to Puebla; Route 150 is the more scenic free road (the trip on the former takes about 1½ hrs, on the latter approximately 3 hrs). To go directly to Cholula, take the exit at San Martín Texmelucan and follow the signs. From Puebla, Cholula is 8 km (5 mi) west. To stop at the volcanoes, take the free road 33 km (20 mi) to Chalco. From there it is 4 km (2½ mi) to the Amecameca-Chalco sign, from which you continue 22 km (13½ mi) on Route 115 to Amecameca. You'll need to go to Puebla to get to Tlaxcala; from there, take Highway 119 north.

VISITOR INFORMATION

Puebla Tourist Office (✉ 5 Oriente 3, ☎ 22/46–12–85); open Monday–Saturday 9:30–8:30, Sunday 9:30–2.

West of Mexico City

A good excursion west of Mexico City would encompass a stop at Toluca, renowned for its Friday market, and a longer stay at Valle de Bravo, a lovely lakeside village popular with vacationing *chilangos*; it's often called Mexico's Switzerland because of its green, hilly setting. We suggest a brief stop en route at Desierto de los Leones, a forested national park whose centerpiece is an intriguing Carmelite monastery, and a detour from Toluca for a picnic at Nevado de Toluca Park.

Desierto de los Leones

There are several walking trails throughout the pine forest of this 5,000-acre national park. Its focal point is the ruined 17th-century **ex-monastery of the Carmelites**, strangely isolated amid an abundance of greenery. The park played a significant role during the War of Independence: At a spot called **Las Cruces**, the troops of Father Hidalgo trounced the Spaniards but resolved not to go on and attack Mexico City, an error that cost the insurgents 10 more years of fighting.

Toluca

The capital of the state of Mexico, Toluca is an industrial town. Once famous only for its Friday market, Toluca now has much more to offer. Indians still come in from the surrounding villages on Friday to sell their produce and handicrafts at the huge municipal market, but it's hard to find any indigenous goods among the radios and CDs from Asia and the denim jackets and jeans from the United States. For local crafts, your best bet is the **Casa de Artesanías** on Paseo Tolloca. Two sights that shouldn't be missed are the **Jardín Botánico Cosmovitral** (Cosmovitral Botanical Garden), in a remodeled, turn-of-the-century Art Nouveau structure that once housed the public market, and the **Museo de Artes Populares** (Museum of Popular Arts) in the Centro Cultural (Cultural Center).

Nevado de Toluca Park

At 15,390 ft, the Nevado de Toluca, a now-extinct volcano, is Mexico's fourth-largest mountain; on clear days its crater affords wonderful views of the valley. You can hire a guide at the entrance to go with your car to the top of the crater and lead you down to its sandy floor, which surrounds two lakes. There are also self-guided hiking trails throughout the park.

Valle de Bravo

Valle de Bravo is colonial, with white-stucco houses trimmed with wrought-iron balconies and red-tile roofs, and red-potted succulents cluttering the doorways. A hilly town that rises from the shores of Lake Avandaro and is surrounded by pines and mountains, Valle was founded in 1530 but has no historical monuments to speak of other than the town church, which has a famous figure of a rare black Christ. It does, however, offer plenty of diversions: boating, waterskiing, and swimming in the lake and its waterfalls, and the more sociable pleasures of the Sunday market, where exceptionally good pottery is the draw. Although Valle and its suburb of Avandaro are enclaves for artists and the wealthy, it attracts inhabitants who prefer a low profile.

LODGING

For a weekend stay, head for the posh **Avandaro Golf & Spa Resort** (✉ Vega del Río s/n, Fracción Avandaro, Valle de Bravo, 52100, ☎ 726/6–03–66 in Mexico; 800/525–4800 in the U.S.; FAX 726/6–01–22), a former country club. All 110 junior suites have romantic fireplaces. In addition to its 18-hole golf course, the resort also has one of the best high-tech spas in Mexico, equipped with hot tubs and offering massage, facial, body toning, and aerobic classes.

West of Mexico City A to Z

GETTING THERE

By car from Mexico City, follow Paseo de la Reforma all the way west. It eventually merges with the Carretera Libre at Toluca, and after 20 km (12 mi), you'll see signs for the turnoff to the Desierto de los Leones; it's another 10 km (6 mi) to the park. To go straight to Toluca, take the toll highway (expensive, but worth it); alternatively, buses depart Terminal Poniente every 20 minutes. To reach Nevado de Toluca Park, make a 44-km (27-mi) detour south of Toluca on Route 130. There are two choices for getting to Valle de Bravo: the winding but scenic route, which you pick up 3 km (2 mi) west of Zincantepec, or Route 15. The former takes twice as much time but is worth it if you have the leisure and enjoy unspoiled mountain scenery.

VISITOR INFORMATION

Mexico State Tourist Office (✉ Edificio Plaza Toluca, Av. 5 Lerdo de Tejada Pte. 101, Toluca, ☎ 721/4–10–99); open weekdays 9–3 and 5–8.

MEXICO CITY A TO Z

Arriving and Departing

By Bus

Greyhound (☎ 800/231–2222) buses make connections to major U.S. border cities, from which Mexican bus lines depart throughout the day. Reserved seating is available on first-class coaches, which are comfortable but not nearly as plush as the intercity buses. If you plan stopovers en route, make sure in advance that your ticket is written up accordingly. In Mexico, platform announcements are in Spanish only.

Within Mexico, buses are becoming the most popular way to travel: You can board ultramodern, superdeluxe motor coaches that show U.S. movies and serve soft drinks and coffee. ETN (Enlaces Terrestres Nacionales, ☎ 5/567–9466, 5/576–9654, or 5/567–9634) serves cities to the west and northwest, such as Guadalajara, Morelia, Querétaro, Guanajuato, and Toluca. ADO (☎ 5/785–9659, 5/542–7192, or 91-800/70362 within Mexico) buses depart southeast to such destinations as Puebla, Oaxaca, Veracruz, Mérida, and Cancún. Reserved-seat tickets can be purchased at Mexico City travel agencies.

Various other classes of intercity bus tickets can be purchased at **Mexicorama** (☎ 5/525–2050) in the Plaza del Angel arcade in Zona Rosa. Buses depart from four outlying stations (*terminales de autobuses*), where tickets can also be purchased: Central de Autobuses del Norte, going north (✉ Cién Metros 4907, ☎ 5/587–5973); Central de Autobuses del Sur, going south (✉ Taxqueña 1320, ☎ 5/689–9795); Central de Autobuses del Oriente, known as TAPO, going east (✉ Ignacio Zaragoza 200, ☎ 5/762–5977); and Terminal de Autobuses del Poniente, going west (✉ Río Tacubaya and Sur 122, ☎ 5/271–4519).

By Car

Major arteries into Mexico City include Highway 57 to the north, which starts at Laredo, Texas, and goes through Monterrey and Querétaro. Highway 95 comes in from Cuernavaca to the south, and Highway 190D from Puebla to the east. Highway 15 via Toluca and Valle de Bravo is the main western route.

By Plane

AIRPORTS AND AIRLINES

All roads (and flights) lead to Mexico City. **Mexicana** (☎ 5/325–0990) has scheduled service from Chicago, Denver, Dallas, Los Angeles, Miami, New York, Philadelphia, San Antonio, San Francisco, and San Jose. It has direct or connecting service at 30 locations throughout the country. **Aeromexico** (☎ 5/228–9910) serves Mexico City daily from Atlanta, Houston, Los Angeles, Miami, New Orleans, New York, Ontario (California), Phoenix, San Antonio, San Diego, and Tucson (as well as Tijuana). Aeromexico serves some 35 cities within Mexico. **Aerolitoral,** a subsidiary of Aeromexico based in Monterrey, serves north-central cities as well as San Antonio and McAllen, Texas, via Monterrey from Mexico City. **Taesa** (☎ 5/227–0700), a fast-growing Mexican airline, has direct flights (but not nonstop) to Mexico City from Chicago and Oakland; directs and nonstops from Tijuana; and nonstops from Laredo, Texas.

U.S. carriers serving Mexico City include **Air Canada, Alaska, American, America West, Canadian, Continental, Delta, Trans World Airlines, United,** and **US Airways. Air France** flies nonstop between Houston and Mexico City.

BETWEEN THE AIRPORT AND CENTER CITY

The newest wing of Mexico City's *Aeropuerto Internacional Benito Juárez,* inaugurated in February 1994, is a high-tech, state-of-the-art elongation of the east end of the existing airport. It is occupied by American, Delta, and United airlines, as well as by all the major car-rental agencies; four banks and seven currency exchanges (*casas de cambio*); Cirrus and Plus ATMs that disburse pesos to Visa and MasterCard holders; places to rent cellular phones; and a food court, pharmacy, bookstore, and pricey shops. A multilevel parking garage for 2,500 cars has also been added (short-term parking: about $1.25 per hr).

Porters and free carts are available in the baggage-retrieval areas. Banks and currency exchanges rotate their schedules to provide around-the-clock service. Though dollar bills (not coins!) are acceptable at the airport, for convenience—and especially if you prefer a rapid departure from the airport—bring $100 in pesos with you. The Mexico City Tourist Office, Mexican Ministry of Tourism (SECTUR), and the Hotel Association have stands in the arrival areas that can provide information and find visitors a room for the night.

If you're taking a taxi, be sure to purchase your ticket at one of the official airport taxi counters marked **Transportación Terrestre** (ground transportation), located in the baggage carousel areas as well as in the concourse area and curbside; avoid *pirata* (taxi drivers offering their services). Government-controlled fares are based on which colonia you are going to and are usually about $7 (per car, not per person) to most hotels. A 10% tip is customary for airport drivers if they help with baggage. All major car-rental agencies have booths at both arrival areas, but renting a car is not recommended unless you are heading out of town or know Mexico City *very* well.

By Train

The train system in Mexico is currently in a state of flux and badly in need of refurbishing. At press time there was no nonstop train service from the U.S. border to Mexico City; bus service from Nuevo Laredo, across from Laredo, Texas, departed to Monterrey, where passengers could pick up the *Regiomontano* to Mexico City. We don't recommend train travel, but if you're determined to go by rail, you can get up-to-date information about schedules and prices in the United States from **Mexico by Train** (☏ FAX 210/725–3659 or ☏ 800/321–1699).

Getting Around

By Bus

The Mexico City bus system is used by millions of commuters daily because it's cheap and goes everywhere. Buses are packed during rush hours, so as in all big cities, you should be wary of pickpockets. One of the principal bus routes runs along Paseo de la Reforma, Avenida Juárez, and Calle Madero. This west–east route connects Chapultepec Park with the Zócalo. A southbound bus also may be taken along Avenida Insurgentes Sur to San Angel and University City, or northbound along Avenida Insurgentes Norte to the Guadalupe Basilica. Mexico City Tourism offices provide free bus-route maps. The price was raised at the end of 1996 from 1 to 2 pesos—still a bargain, especially for foreigners.

By Car

Millions of intrepid drivers brave Mexico City's streets every day and survive, but for out-of-towners the experience can be frazzling. One-way streets are confusing, rush-hour traffic is nightmarish, and parking places can be hard to come by. Police tow trucks haul away illegally parked vehicles, and the owner is heavily fined. As in any large city, getting your car back here is a byzantine process. LOCATEL (☏ 5/658–1111) is an efficient 24-hour service for tracing vehicles that are towed, stolen, or lost (in case you forgot where you parked). There's a chance an operator on duty may speak English, but the service is primarily in Spanish. Visitors can hire a chauffeur for their cars through a hotel concierge or travel service such as American Express.

Also keep in mind that the *strictly enforced* law *Un Día Sin Auto* (One Day Without a Car) applies to all private vehicles, including your own. One of several efforts to reduce smog and traffic congestion, this law prohibits every privately owned vehicle (including out-of-state, foreign, and even rental cars) from being used on one designated weekday. During emergency smog-alert months, mainly December and January, cars are prohibited from circulating on two days of the week. Cars in violation are inevitably impounded by the police. Expect a hefty fine as well. The weekday is specified by the last number or letter of the license plate. To find out which is your day (or days) to be without a car, contact the Mexican Government Tourism Office nearest you, and by all means plan your schedule accordingly.

By Pesero

Originally six-passenger sedans, then vans, and now minibuses, peseros operate on a number of fixed routes and charge a flat rate (a peso once upon a time, hence the name). Peseros offer a good alternative to buses and taxis; however, be prepared for a jolting ride because many drivers like to turn their buses into bucking broncos. Likely routes for tourists are along the city's major west–east axis (Chapultepec Park–Reforma–Avenida Juárez–Zócalo) and north–south along Insurgentes, between the Guadalupe Basilica and San Angel–University City. Peseros pick up passengers at bus stops and outside almost all metro stations these days. Just stand on the curb, check the route sign on the oncoming pesero's windshield, and hold out your hand. Tell the driver where to stop, or press the button by the back door; if it's really crowded and you can't reach the back door in time, just bang on the ceiling and yell, "Baja," which means "Getting off" in Spanish. Base fares are 2 pesos with the price going up the farther you travel. Exact change is appreciated by drivers.

By Subway

Transporting 5 million passengers daily, Mexico City's metro is one of the world's best, busiest, safest, and cheapest transportation systems—the fare is the same as for buses, 2 pesos. The impeccably clean marble-and-onyx stations are brightly lit, and modern French-designed trains run quietly on rubber tires. Some stations, such as Insurgentes, are shopping centers. Even if you don't take a ride, visit the Zócalo station, which has large models of central Mexico City during three historic periods. The Bellas Artes station has replicas of archaeological treasures on exhibit, and inside the Pino Suárez station is a small Aztec pyramid, a surprise discovery during construction.

There are 10 intersecting metro lines covering more than 160 km (100 mi). It's a bit confusing: The number 8 had been previously assigned to a line whose construction was canceled because it would have destroyed unearthed Aztec ruins. Line 9 was subsequently built. Now number 8 designates a newer (9th) line. The newest lines are A (10th) and B (11th), and plans to build 12 have been already been announced. In 1996 the government pledged $2 million to build 29 more km (18 more mi) of subway. Segments of lines 1 and 2 cover most points of interest to tourists, including the Zona Rosa, Bellas Artes, and the Centro Histórico. At the southern edge of the city, the Taxqueña station (line 2) connects with the electric train (*tren eléctrico*) that continues south to Xochimilco. To the southeast, the *Metro Ligero* from the Pantitlán station (lines 1, 5, and 9) heads east to Chalco in the state of Mexico. "A" runs to outlying southern suburbs from line 9 and "B" heads west to east from the Buenavista train station to beyond the airport. The various lines also serve all four bus stations, the Buenavista train station, and the airport; however, only light baggage is allowed on board during rush hours. User-friendly, color-coded maps are available free at metro-station information desks (if there's an attendant) and Mexico City tourism offices, and color-keyed signs and maps are posted all around.

Trains run frequently (about a minute apart) and are least crowded at night and between 10 AM and 4 PM. To reduce discomfort during crowded rush hours, regulations require men to ride separate cars from women and children. Hours vary somewhat according to the line, but service is essentially from 5 or 6 AM to 12:30 AM on weekdays; 6 AM to 1:30 AM on Saturday; 7 AM to 12:30 AM on Sunday and holidays.

By Taxi

The Mexico City variety comes in several colors, types, and sizes. Unmarked *turismo* sedans with hooded meters are usually stationed outside major hotels and in tourist areas; however, they are uneconomical for short trips. Their drivers are almost always English-speaking guides and can be hired for sightseeing on a daily or hourly basis (always negotiate the price in advance). *Sitio* (stationed) taxis operate out of stands, take radio calls, and are authorized to charge a small premium. Among these, **Servi-Taxis** (☎ 5/271–2560) and **Taxi-Mex** (☎ 5/538–0912 and 5/538–0573) offer 24-hour service. Taxis that cruise the streets range from sedans to Volkswagen Beetles—the latter with the front pas-

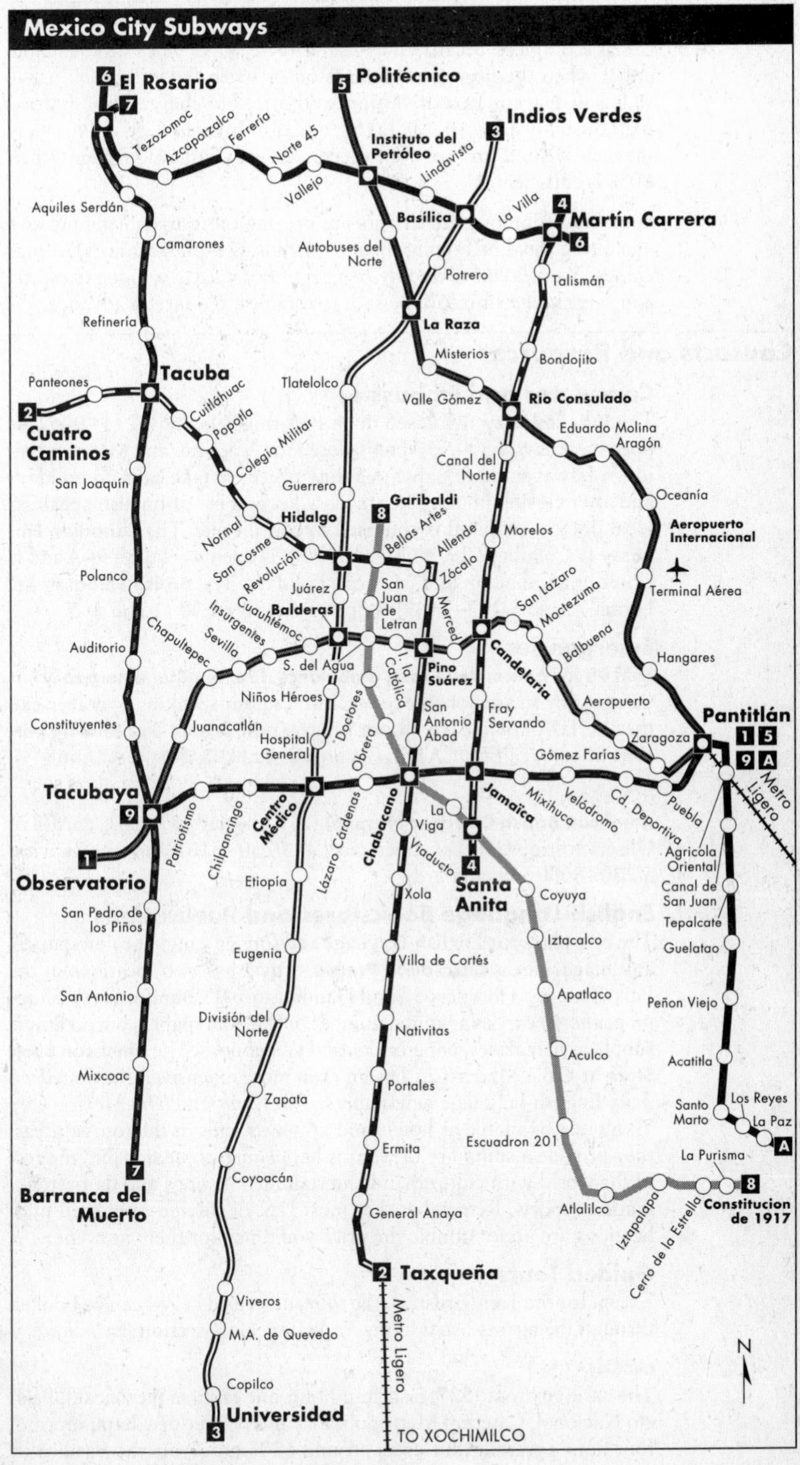
Mexico City Subways
6 El Rosario
7
5 Politécnico
3 Indios Verdes
Tezozomoc
Azcapotzalco
Ferreria
Norte 45
Vallejo
Instituto del Petróleo
Lindavista
Basílica
La Villa
4 Martín Carrera 6
Aquiles Serdán
Camarones
Autobuses del Norte
Potrero
Talismán
Refinería
La Raza
Misterios
Bondojito
Panteones
Tacuba
Tlatelolco
Valle Gómez
Rio Consulado
2 Cuatro Caminos
Cuitláhuac
Popotla
Colegio Militar
Eduardo Molina
Aragón
Canal del Norte
San Joaquín
Guerrero
Oceanía
Normal
Hidalgo
Garibaldi 8
Bellas Artes
Allende
Morelos
Aeropuerto Internacional
San Cosme
Revolución
Zócalo
Polanco
Juárez
San Juan de Letran
San Lázaro
Terminal Aérea
Cuauhtémoc
Balderas
Merced
Moctezuma
Insurgentes
Chapultepec
Sevilla
Auditorio
S. del Agua
I. la Católica
Pino Suárez
Candelaria
Balbuena
Hangares
Niños Héroes
Doctores
San Antonio Abad
Fray Servando
Aeropuerto
Constituyentes
Juanacatlán
Hospital General
Obrera
Zaragoza
Pantitlán 1 5 9 A
Gómez Farías
Tacubaya 9
Centro Médico
Chabacano
Jamaica
Mixihuca
Velódromo
Cd. Deportiva
Puebla
Metro Ligero
Patriotismo
Chilpancingo
Lázaro Cárdenas
La Viga
Viaducto
1 Observatorio
Etiopía
Xola
4 Santa Anita
Coyuya
Agricola Oriental
Canal de San Juan
Tepalcate
San Pedro de los Piños
Iztacalco
Guelatao
Eugenia
Villa de Cortés
San Antonio
Apatlaco
Peñon Viejo
División del Norte
Nativitas
Aculco
Acatitla
Mixcoac
Zapata
Portales
Los Reyes
Santo Marto
La Paz A
Escuadron 201
Ermita
La Purisma
7 Barranca del Muerto
Coyoacán
Atlalilco
8 Constitucion de 1917
General Anaya
Iztapalapa
Cerro de la Estrella
2 Taxqueña
Metro Ligero
Viveros
M.A. de Quevedo
Copilco
N
Universidad 3
TO XOCHIMILCO

senger seat removed for more legroom. (Some Beetles are green and called *ecologicos* because they use lead-free gas.) They are available either when the *libre* (free) light is on or when the windshield LIBRE sign is displayed. Taxi drivers are authorized to charge 10% more at night, usually after 10 PM. Taking a taxi in Mexico City is extremely inexpensive and tips are not expected unless you have luggage—then 10% is sufficient.

Some unscrupulous cab drivers are preying on tourists, robbing and assaulting them or forcing them to withdraw money from ATM machines. *You should take only registered hotel taxis or have the hotel concierge call a* sitio *cab.* Be sure to establish the fare in advance.

Contacts and Resources

Consulates and Embassies

The **U.S. Embassy** (✉ Paseo de la Reforma 305, ☎ 5/211–0042) is open weekdays 8:30–5:30 but is closed for American and Mexican holidays; however, there's always a duty officer to take calls on holidays and after closing hours. The embassy keeps a list of English-speaking local doctors on hand if you need to consult one. The **Canadian Embassy** (✉ Schiller 529, ☎ 5/724–7900) is open weekdays 9–4 and is closed for Canadian and Mexican holidays. The **British Embassy** (✉ Lerma 71, ☎ 5/207–2449) is open weekdays 9:30–1 and 4–7.

Emergencies

Dial **08** for **police, Red Cross, ambulance, fire,** or **other emergency** situations. If you are not able to reach an English-speaking operator, call the SECTUR hot line (☞ Visitor Information, *below*). For **missing persons or cars,** call LOCATEL (☎ 5/658–1111).

HOSPITAL

American British Cowdray Hospital (✉ Calle Sur 137–201, corner of Observatorio, Col. las Américas, ☎ 5/230–8161 for emergencies, 5/230–8000 switchboard).

English-Language Bookstores and Publications

The best place for English-language and foreign-language newspapers and magazines is **Casa de la Prensa,** which has two locations in the Pink Zone (✉ Florencia 57 and Hamburgo 141). **Sanborns** (☞ Shopping, *above*) carries a limited number of U.S. newspapers but an ample supply of magazines, paperbacks, and guidebooks. The **American Book Store** at Calle Madero 25 has an even more extensive selection. Two daily English-language newspapers, *The News* and *The Mexico City Times,* are available at hotels and at newsstands in the tourist areas; they provide a summary of what is happening in Mexico and the rest of the world with cultural and entertainment listings and daily stock-market reports. Remember that most U.S. or foreign-published publications are about double the price you'd pay for them at home.

Guided Tours

Except for the Tren Turístico, the tours described below can be booked through the agents listed in the Travel Agencies section (☞ *below*).

ORIENTATION

The basic city tour ($27) lasts four hours and takes in the Zócalo, Palacio Nacional, Catedral Metropolitana, and Bosque de Chapultepec. A four-hour pyramid tour costs around $30 and covers the Basílica de Nuestra Señora de Guadalupe and the major ruins at Teotihuacán.

A wonderful way to see the downtown historic center is via the **Tren Turístico** (☎ 5/709–5589), which runs charming replicas of 1920s 20-passenger trolleys. The 30-minute narrated tour covers sights including the Zócalo, Colegio de San Idelfonso, Plaza de Santo Domingo, Plaza Manuel Tolsá (location of the Palacio de Minería and Museo Nacional de Arte), Plaza de la Santa Veracruz (Museo Franz Mayer), and the Palacio de Iturbide. The trolleys depart from and return to Pino Suárez 30 (⊠ 3 blocks south of the Zócalo at the corner of República de Salvador). You can get off at any stop you wish and board a subsequent trolley. Departures are every half hour from 10 AM to 5 PM, Tuesday–Sunday; English-language tours depart Tuesday and Sunday at 11 AM. The price is $3.

SPECIAL-INTEREST

Cultural: The seven-hour tour ($55) is run on Sunday mornings only and includes a performance of the folkloric dances at the Palacio de Bellas Artes, a gondola ride in the canals of Xochimilco's floating gardens, and a visit to the modern campus of the National University.

Bullfights: Also on Sunday only are trips to the bullring with a guide who will explain the finer points of this spectacle. This four-hour afternoon tour (🎫 $41) can usually be combined with the Ballet Folklórico–Xochimilco trip.

Nightlife: These tours are among the most popular tours of Mexico City. The best are scheduled to last five hours and include transfers by private car rather than bus; dinner at an elegant restaurant (frequently Del Lago); a drink and a show at the Plaza Garibaldi, where mariachis play; and a nightcap at Gitanerías, which features Spanish flamenco performances. Nightlife tours begin at $78.

Travel Agencies

American Express (⊠ Paseo de la Reforma 234, ☎ 5/207–7132), **Mexico Travel Advisors (MTA)** (⊠ Génova 30, ☎ 5/525–7520), and **Gray Line** (⊠ Londres 166, ☎ 5/208–1163; 5/208–2833 night phone 8 PM–7 AM).

Visitor Information

The **Mexico City Tourist Office** (Departamento de Turismo del Distrito Federal, or DDF) maintains information booths at both the international and domestic arrivals areas at the airport, at the Buenavista train station, and inside the Fonart handicraft store at Avenida Juárez 89. In town visit the lobby of its main office at Amberes 54 at the corner of Londres in the Zona Rosa. This office also provides information by phone with its INFOTUR service (☎ 5/525–9380) from 9 to 9 daily. Operators are multilingual and have access to an extensive data bank. The **Secretariat of Tourism (SECTUR)** operates a 24-hour multilingual hot line that provides information on both Mexico City and the entire country (☎ 5/250–0123, 5/250–0493, 5/250–0027, 5/250–0589, 5/250–0151, 5/250–0292, or 5/250–0741). If the lines are busy, keep trying. You can also call toll-free from anywhere in Mexico other than Mexico City (☎ 91–800/9–03–92; 800/482–9832 from the U.S.). These numbers reach SECTUR's Tourist Information Center at Presidente Masaryk 172 (in Polanco), open weekdays 8–8.

3 Baja California

Separated from mainland Mexico by the Sea of Cortés, the Baja California peninsula stretches 1,625 km (1,000 mi) from Tijuana to Los Cabos. The desert landscape harbors isolated fishing retreats, Prohibition-era gambling palaces, state-of-the-art golf courses, and one of the busiest international borders in the world. Adventurers delight in kayaking alongside migrating gray whales, diving with hammerhead sharks, and hiking to hidden cave paintings.

By Maribeth Mellin

BAJA (LOWER) CALIFORNIA is a moonscaped finger of land dipping southward from the international boundary that divides California and Mexico. Separated from the Mexican mainland by the 240-km-wide (150-mi-wide) Sea of Cortés—also called the Gulf of California—Baja extends about 1,625 km (1,000 mi) into the Pacific. Despite their names, both Baja California and the Gulf of California are part of Mexico.

Although only 21 km (13 mi) across at one point and 193 km (120 mi) at its widest, Baja has one of the most varied and beautiful terrains on the planet. The peninsula's two coasts are separated by soaring mountain ranges, with one peak more than 10,000 ft high. Countless bays and coves with pristine beaches indent both shores, and islands big and small—many inhabited only by sea lions—dot the 3,364 km (2,000 mi) of coastline. You'll find stretches of desert as empty as the Sahara where only cacti thrive and, in contrast, you'll see cultivated farmlands and vineyards.

Varied, too, is the demographic makeup of Baja. The border strip of northern Baja is densely populated. Tijuana, Mexico's fourth-largest city, is home to nearly 2 million people, making it more populous than the entire remainder of the peninsula. La Paz, with about 170,000 residents, is the only city of any size south of Ensenada. The two towns at Los Cabos (The Capes) have yet to reach city status.

Baja is divided politically into two states—Baja California (also referred to as Baja Norte, or North Baja) and Baja California Sur (South)—at the 25th parallel, about 710 km (440 mi) south of the border. Near the tip of the peninsula, a monument marks the spot where the Tropic of Cancer crosses the Transpeninsular Highway (Mexico Highway 1).

Native Baja Californians will tell you in no uncertain terms that they live in the first California, discovered by pirates, missionaries, and explorers long before the California of the United States. Most of Baja's visitors have that same sense of adventure, and the peninsula has become a cult destination. Long before the rich and famous stumbled upon the resorts of mainland Mexico, they found Baja. Back in the days of Prohibition, when Hollywood was new, the movie crowd learned the joy of having an international border so near. John Steinbeck brought attention to La Paz when he made it a setting for his novella *The Pearl.* Erle Stanley Gardner took a break from writing to battle marlin off Los Cabos. Bing Crosby put up some of the money for the first resort hotel in San José del Cabo, when the only way to get there was aboard a yacht or private plane.

Today's visitors fly in on commercial jets and check into thoroughly modern hotels. The rich and famous still find Baja (particularly the southern tip) an ideal escape and can be spotted in secluded hotels along the Los Cabos Corridor. But Baja is no longer the exclusive turf of adventurers and the owners of private yachts and planes. Caravans of motor homes and pickups occasionally clog the Transpeninsular Highway, and flights into Loreto, La Paz, and Los Cabos are often packed with regular folks on their first forays into Mexico. Baja's resort towns have become mainstream, but adventure and sublime solitude can still be found at the peninsula's hidden beaches and bays.

Pleasures and Pastimes

Dining

Baja's cuisine reflects its natural setting, highlighting food from the sea. Fresh fish, lobster, and shrimp are the dining draws here, along with abalone and quail. Throughout Baja, scores of restaurants and kitchens serve great, authentically Mexican seafood dishes. Beef and pork are also excellent, both grilled and marinated. Imported steaks, quail, lamb, and duck are popular in the more expensive places. Mexicali, the capital of Baja, offers several good Chinese restaurants (the construction of the Imperial Canal in 1902 brought an influx of Chinese residents to the region). And although very few restaurants serve regional Mexican cuisine, plenty of spots throughout the peninsula combine U.S. and Mexican flavors in tacos, burritos, burgers, and pizza.

Two special dishes that originated in Baja have become standard fare in southern California. Lobster Puerto Nuevo–style (the shellfish grilled or boiled in oil and served with beans, rice, and tortillas) comes from the fishing settlement of the same name near Tijuana. Fish tacos (chunks of deep-fried fish wrapped with condiments in a corn tortilla) are said to have originated in the northern Baja town of San Felipe. Mexico's best domestic wines are nurtured in the vineyards and wineries in the Santo Tomás and Guadalupe valleys outside Ensenada, and one of the country's most popular beers, Tecate, comes from the Baja Norte town of the same name.

Restaurants as a rule are low-key, except in Tijuana, Ensenada, and Los Cabos, where dining options range from *taquerías* (taco stands) to upscale Continental palaces. Dress is accordingly casual at nearly all Baja restaurants, and reservations are not required unless otherwise noted. Moderate prices prevail even in city restaurants—except in Los Cabos, where the tariffs as well as the selections reflect a distinct California influence. Some restaurants add a 15% service charge to the bill.

CATEGORY	COST*
$$$	over $20
$$	$10–$20
$	under $10

**per person for a three-course meal, excluding drinks and service*

Fishing

Sportfishing is one of Baja's greatest attractions. The fishing is best in the south, with large fishing fleets in Loreto, La Paz, and Los Cabos. Though the summer months bring the most fish, anglers are sure to catch something year-round. Fishing from Ensenada and San Quintín is best in the late summer and early fall.

Golf

Baja is becoming a prime destination for golfers, with championship-level courses in Tijuana, Rosarito Beach, and Ensenada. Los Cabos is experiencing a particular golfing boom; several excellent courses have opened in the past few years.

Kayaking

Both the Pacific Ocean and the Sea of Cortés have isolated bays and coves ideal for kayaking. Some hotels and outfitters in Loreto, La Paz, and Los Cabos offer kayak rentals and excursions, and some U.S. companies offer kayaking trips to the Sea of Cortés.

Lodging

Lodgings throughout Baja are mostly low-key, except in Los Cabos, which has evolved into a world-class coastal destination. Until the 1980s,

Los Cabos's hotels were mostly fishing lodges where die-hard sportsmen took refuge. Today, Los Cabos draws golfers, too, and deluxe hotels front championship courses. Rates are much higher here than in the rest of Baja, where some great deals be can found at small one-of-a-kind hostelries.

Reservations are a must on holiday weekends for most of Baja's coastal towns; some hotels require a minimum two-night stay for a confirmed reservation. Several hotels in Baja have toll-free 800 numbers that connect directly to the hotel; though the operator may answer in Spanish there is usually someone who speaks English in the reservations office. Many hotels have fax numbers (a good way to confirm reservations), though you may have to ask them to turn on the fax machine when you call. A few of the out-of-the-way and budget-priced hotels do not accept credit cards; some of the more lavish places add a 10%–20% service charge to your bill. Most properties also raise their rates for the December–April high season. Rates here are based on high-season standards. Expect to pay 25% less during the off-season. Many hotels offer midweek discounts of 30%–50% off the weekend rates; always ask about special promotions.

Several agencies in the United States book reservations at Baja hotels, condos, and time-share resorts, which may actually cost less than hotel rooms if you are traveling with a group of four or more (☞ Contacts and Resources *in* Baja Norte A to Z, *below*).

CATEGORY	COST*
$$$$	over $160
$$$	$90–$160
$$	$40–$90
$	under $40

**All prices are for a standard double room, excluding service charge and 10% sales tax.*

Whale-Watching

Gray whales migrate to the Pacific coast of Baja from January through March. Whale-watching expeditions are available in Ensenada, Guerrero Negro, Loreto, La Paz, and Los Cabos.

Exploring Baja California

The Baja California Peninsula is made up of two states: Baja California (Norte), at the border with the United States, and Baja California Sur.

The northern half of the peninsula contains the largest cities and highest population. Tijuana, Tecate, and Mexicali—the peninsula's border cities—are U.S. suburbs in a sense. San Felipe, the northernmost town on the Sea of Cortés, is a popular weekend escape for travelers from Arizona and southern California. Similarly, Rosarito Beach and Ensenada, on Baja Norte's Pacific coast, are practically extensions of southern California's coast, offering an experience both familiar and foreign. South of Ensenada the natural side of Baja begins to appear in desolate mountain ranges and fields of cacti and boulders.

Baja California Sur is a more remote region, though strongly steeped in American influences. The most populated areas lie along the coast bordering the Sea of Cortés. The Pacific side is more popular with migrating gray whales, who travel by the thousands every winter from the Bering Strait to isolated coves and lagoons along this coast. For those few months, travelers come from all over the world to Guerrero Negro and a few bays and lagoons farther south. Loreto, on the Sea of Cortés, is beloved by sportfishing enthusiasts who find seclusion in this small, largely undiscovered town. La Paz, capital of Baja Sur, is the region's major port and a busy center of commerce and government. Los Cabos, made up of the two towns of Cabo San Lucas and San José del Cabo, has become one of the fastest-growing resort areas in Mexico. Despite all the development that has taken place there and the steep prices, it remains a mysteriously natural hideaway.

Numbers in the text correspond to numbers in the margin and on the Tijuana, Ensenada, La Paz, Los Cabos Coast, San José del Cabo, and Cabo San Lucas maps.

Great Itineraries

Baja aficionados will tell you that you haven't really explored the peninsula unless you've driven its entire length, stopping at small towns and secluded beaches along the way. Such a journey is a major undertaking, however, requiring at least 10 days of travel time. If you plan to drive the peninsula certain precautions are in order. You must have Mexican auto insurance, available by the day, for the length of your drive. Always carry water, and make sure your vehicle is in good condition. Keep your gas tank at least half full at all times—some remote gas stations may be out of gas just when you need it. For the most part, the Transpeninsular Highway is well maintained, though you may come across areas filled with potholes or gravel and rocks.

Those with less time can still see plenty of the peninsula's attractions by limiting their explorations to the region around their point of entry. A full week would allow a quick rush through the peninsula or a more leisurely exploration of Baja Norte or Baja Sur. If you have five days, you can see the most interesting towns and still be able to linger a bit. With three days you're best off staying within the immediate vicinity of your entry point.

IF YOU HAVE 3 DAYS

In Baja Norte, you can explore Tijuana, Rosarito Beach, and Ensenada. Start in **Tijuana** at the **Centro Cultural** ⑨, then stroll down **Avenida Revolución** ③. Head south before nightfall to a hotel in **Rosarito Beach** or **Puerto Nuevo.** Tour **Ensenada** the next day, taking in the **Fish Market** ⑭, the **Riviera del Pacífico** ⑱, and the shops on **Avenida López Mateos** ⑲. Devote your third day to the coast and Rosarito Beach.

In Baja Sur, you're best off staying in **Los Cabos,** allowing time for golf, sportfishing, and snorkeling at **Playa de Amor** or **Bahía Chileno.**

IF YOU HAVE 5 DAYS

You can do a thorough tour of Baja Norte, starting with a full day and overnight in **Tijuana.** From there head to the small town of **Tecate,** then on to **Mexicali** and **San Felipe.** Overnight in San Felipe; then spend Day 3 checking out the beaches before driving the backcountry to **Ensenada.** Devote Day 4 to exploring **La Bufadora** and downtown Ensenada; then head up the coast for a lobster feast at **Puerto Nuevo.** On Day 5 head back to Tijuana and the border.

In Baja Sur, start your tour in **Los Cabos,** spending the night there and starting out early the next day for **La Paz.** Spend Day 2 exploring downtown La Paz; don't miss the **Museum of Anthropology** ㉚ and the **Plaza Constitución** ㉗. On Day 3, head up the coast to the small mission town of **Loreto.** Spend Days 4 and 5 making your way back to Los Cabos at a leisurely pace, stopping to explore the desert and coast along the way.

IF YOU HAVE 7 DAYS

It's possible to drive the entire peninsula in a week, especially if you arrange to begin your tour in the north and drop off your car in the south. Start in **Tijuana** on Day 1, touring the Centro Cultural and Avenida Revolución. Head south before nightfall to a hotel in **Rosarito Beach** or **Puerto Nuevo.** On Day 2, move on to **Ensenada** for a brief tour of the city; then head south to **San Quintín** and **Guerrero Negro.** If you're traveling between January and March, arrange for a whale-watching tour for the next day and spend Nights 2 and 3 in Guerrero Negro. If not, overnight in Guerrero Negro and then move on for a full day's trip to **Mulege** on the Sea of Cortés. The drive between the two coasts, through stark desert scenery, is one of the most beautiful and desolate in Baja. Spend Night 3 or 4 in Mulege, allowing plenty of relaxation time after the long drive. Move on to **Loreto,** stopping off for a swim at **Bahia Concepción,** and spend the next night there. If you didn't stay in Guerrero Negro for whale-watching, spend an extra night in Loreto and arrange a boat tour of the Sea of Cortés. Devote Day 6 to the drive to **La Paz,** spending the evening strolling the waterfront *malecón* (boardwalk). On Day 7, continue on to **Los Cabos.**

When to Tour Baja

Baja's climate is one of extremes, thanks to its desert locale. Temperatures are less drastic in the northern regions; the climate in Tijuana, Ensenada, and Rosarito Beach is similar to that in southern California. Mexicali, on the other hand, gets extremely hot in the summer months. Baja Norte's resort cities are very crowded on holiday weekends, and advance reservations are a must. Tijuana's attractions are rarely overcrowded, and you should be able to tour them easily at any time of day.

Baja Sur's winters are mild, but not warm; Loreto, La Paz, and Los Cabos can get downright chilly in the evening. Sportfishing aficionados prefer the summer months: Though the temperatures are high, the fish are abundant. Again, the towns only tend to be crowded on holiday weekends.

BAJA NORTE

The most densely populated area of the Baja California peninsula, Baja Norte begins at the U.S. border and extends 699 km (437 mi) to the border with Baja California Sur. Tijuana, just 29 km (18 mi) south of San Diego, is Baja's largest city; in fact, with a population that has now surpassed 2 million, it is the fourth-largest city in Mexico. Tijuana's promoters like to call it "the most visited city in the world," and certainly the border crossing to Tijuana is the busiest in the United States.

By comparison, the state's capital, Mexicali, has a population of only 800,000 residents. Though it also sits on the U.S. border, Mexicali attracts few tourists. Tecate, located between Tijuana and Mexicali, is a typical village whose main claim to fame is the Tecate brewery, where one of Mexico's most popular beers originates. Those travelers who do pass through Tecate and Mexicali are usually en route to San Felipe, the northernmost town on the Sea of Cortés.

On Baja's Pacific coast, travelers stream down the Transpeninsular Highway (Highway 1) to Rosarito Beach and Ensenada. These beach communities are like Mexican suburbs of southern California, where English is spoken as freely as Spanish and the dollar is as readily accepted as the peso. Between Baja Norte's towns, the landscape is unlike any other, with cacti growing beside the sea, and stark mountains and plateaus rising against clear blue skies.

Highway 3 runs east from Ensenada to San Felipe through the foothills of the Sierra Pedro San Martir. The same highway runs north from En-

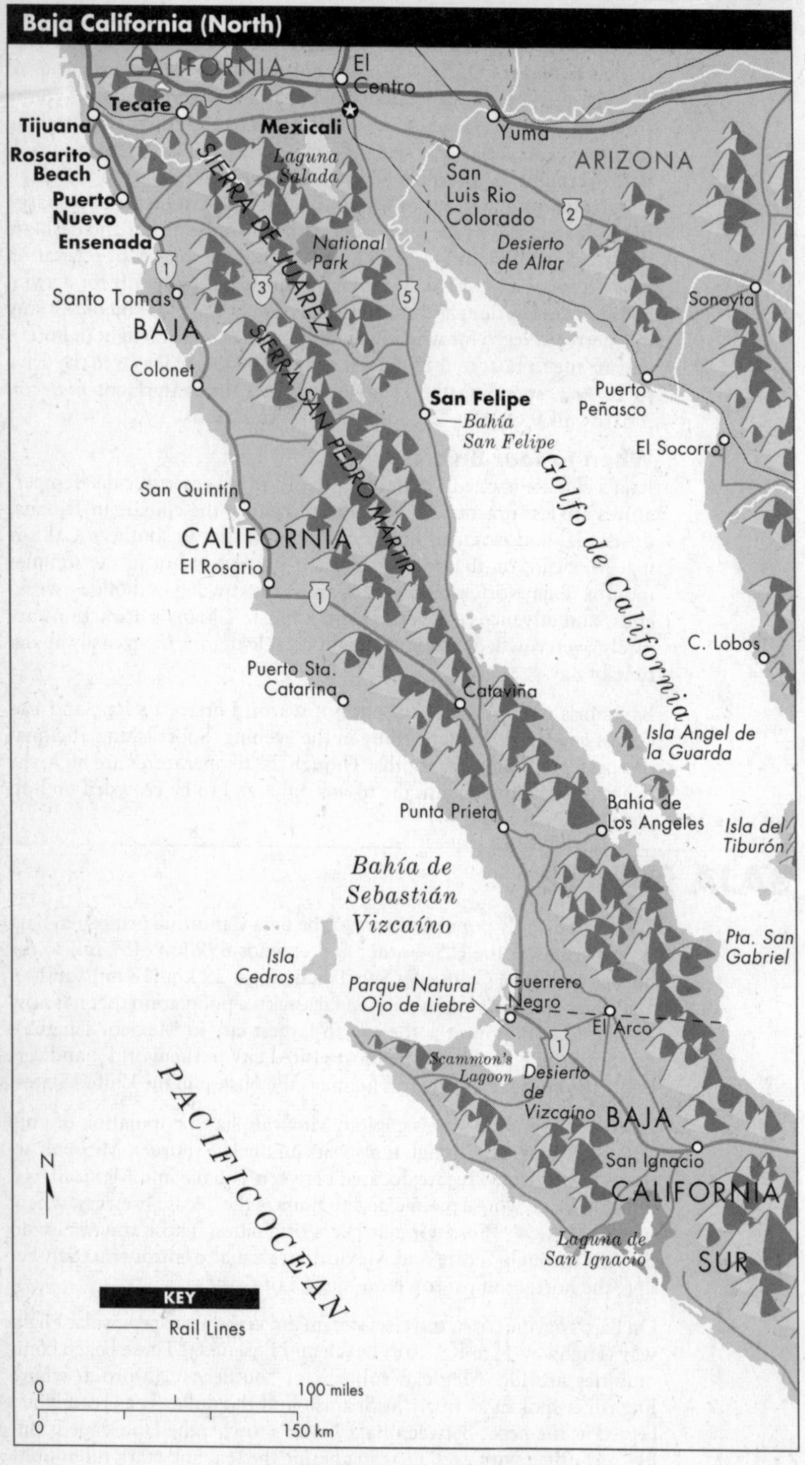
Baja California (North)
CALIFORNIA
El Centro
Tecate
Tijuana
Mexicali
Yuma
Rosarito Beach
Laguna Salada
San Luis Rio Colorado
ARIZONA
Puerto Nuevo
Ensenada
SIERRA DE JUAREZ
National Park
Desierto de Altar
Santo Tomas
BAJA
Sonoyta
SIERRA SAN PEDRO MÁRTIR
Colonet
Puerto Peñasco
San Felipe
Bahía San Felipe
El Socorro
San Quintín
Golfo de California
CALIFORNIA
El Rosario
C. Lobos
Puerto Sta. Catarina
Cataviña
Isla Angel de la Guarda
Bahía de Los Angeles
Punta Prieta
Isla del Tiburón
Bahía de Sebastián Vizcaíno
Pta. San Gabriel
Isla Cedros
Parque Natural Ojo de Liebre
Guerrero Negro
El Arco
Scammon's Lagoon
Desierto de Vizcaíno
BAJA
PACIFIC OCEAN
San Ignacio
CALIFORNIA
Laguna de San Ignacio
SUR
N
KEY
Rail Lines
0
100 miles
0
150 km

senada to Tecate through the Guadalupe Valley, where many of the area's vineyards and wineries are located. If you are traveling south, Ensenada is the last major city you'll see for hundreds of miles on Mexico Highway 1. San Quintín, 184 km (115 mi) south of Ensenada, is an agricultural community said to be the windiest spot in Baja. Sportfishing is particularly good here, and tourism is increasing. Farther south are turnoffs for a dirt road to San Felipe and a paved road to Bahía de los Angeles, a formerly remote bay beloved by fishermen and naturalists.

At the end of the northern section of Baja, 595 km (372 mi) from Ensenada, stands a steel monument in the form of an eagle, 138 ft high. It marks the border between the states of Baja Norte and Baja Sur. The time changes from Pacific to Mountain as you cross the 28th parallel. Guerrero Negro, Baja Sur's northernmost town, with hotels and gas stations, is 2 km (1½ mi) south.

Tijuana

29 km (18 mi) south of San Diego.

Tijuana is the only part of Mexico many people see, and it gives both a distorted and an accurate view of the country's many cultures. Before the city became a gigantic recreation center for southern Californians, it was a ranch populated by a few hundred Mexicans. In 1911 a group of Americans invaded the area and attempted to set up an independent republic; they were quickly driven out by Mexican soldiers. When Prohibition hit the United States in the 1920s and the Agua Caliente Racetrack and Casino opened (1929), Tijuana boomed. Americans seeking alcohol, gambling, and more fun than they could find back home flocked across the border, spending freely and fueling the region's growth. Tijuana became the entry port for what some termed a "sinful, steamy playground" frequented by Hollywood stars and the idle rich.

Then Prohibition was repealed, Mexico outlawed gambling, and Tijuana's fortunes declined. However, although the flow of travelers from the north slowed to a trickle for a while, Tijuana still captivated those in search of the sort of fun that was illegal or just frowned upon at home. The ever-growing numbers of servicemen stationed in San Diego kept Tijuana's sordid reputation alive, while southern Californians continued to cross the border to explore the foreign culture and landscape. Drivers heading into Baja's wilderness drove through downtown Tijuana, stopping along Avenida Revolución and its side streets for supplies and souvenirs.

When the toll highway to Ensenada was finished in 1967, travelers bypassed the city and tourism dropped again. But Tijuana began attracting residents from throughout Latin America. The city's population mushroomed from a mere 300,000 in 1970 to over 2 million today. The city has spread into canyons and dry riverbeds, over hillsides, and onto ocean cliffs. As the government struggles to keep up with the growth and demand for services, thousands live without electricity, running water, or adequate housing in squatters' villages along the border. Crime has become a significant problem in Tijuana in the 1990s. The fall of the peso caused many Mexicans from the interior to move to the border in search of work at all levels of industry. Poverty is vast and petty crime is on the rise. Moreover, the area has become headquarters for serious drug cartels, and violent crime—reaching the highest levels of law enforcement and business—is booming. Average tourists are unlikely to witness a shooting or other frightening situation, but should be mindful of their surroundings and guard their belongings.

City leaders, realizing that tourism creates jobs and bolsters Tijuana's fragile economy, are working hard to attract visitors. Avenida Revolución, the main street that was once lined with brothels and bars, now has a lineup of shopping arcades and pseudo-Mexican restaurants and bars that cater to (often rowdy) tourists. The city has an international airport; a fine cultural center that presents professional music, dance, and theater groups from throughout the world; and deluxe high-rise hotels. The demand for high-end accommodations has increased with the growth of *maquiladoras* (foreign manufacturing plants). Casual tourists tend to visit for the day or one night. Although it's no longer considered just a bawdy border town, the city remains best known as a place for an intense, somewhat exotic daylong adventure.

Tijuana's tourist attractions have remained much the same throughout the century. The impressive El Palacio Frontón (Jai Alai Palace), where betting is allowed, draws crowds of cheering fans to its fast-paced matches. Some of Mexico's greatest bullfighters appear at the oceanfront and downtown bullrings, and there are an extraordinary number of places in town that provide good food and drink.

And then, of course, there's shopping. From the moment you cross the border, people will approach you or call out and insist that you look at their wares. If you drive, workers will run out from auto-body shops to place bids on new paint or upholstery for your car. All along Avenida Revolución and its side streets, shops sell everything from tequila to Tiffany-style lamps; serious shoppers can spend a full day searching and bargaining for their items of choice. If you intend to buy food in Mexico, get the U.S. customs list of articles that are illegal to bring back so that your purchases won't be confiscated.

❶ At the **San Ysidro Border Crossing,** locals and tourists jostle each other along the pedestrian walkway through the Viva Tijuana dining and shopping center and into the center of town. Artisans' stands line the walkway and adjoining streets, offering a quick overview of the wares to be found all over town.

❷ An unusual perspective on Mexico's culture can be found at **Mexitlán,** a fascinating combination of museum and entertainment-shopping center. Designed by architect Pedro Ramírez Vásquez, the complex has scale models of all the major architectural and cultural landmarks throughout Mexico; unfortunately, the place has not been well maintained and has lost its festive air. ✉ *Av. Ocampo between Calles 2 and 3,* ☎ *66/38–41–01.* 🎟 *$2.50.* ⏲ *Wed.–Sun. 9–5.*

❸ Tijuana's main tourism zone has long been the raffish **Avenida Revolución,** lined with a cacophonous array of shops and restaurants, all catering to uninhibited tourists. Shopkeepers call out from their doorways, offering low prices for an odd assortment of garish souvenirs. Many shopping arcades open onto Avenida Revolución; inside the front doors are mazes of small stands with low-priced pottery and other handicrafts.

❹ The Moorish-style **El Palacio Frontón** (Jai Alai Palace) is a magnificent building and an exciting place for watching and betting on fast-paced jai alai games. Next door, at a large branch of the Caliente Race Book, bettors can wager on horse races and sports events broadcast from California via satellite TV (☞ Outdoor Activities and Sports, *below*).

Most of Baja's legendary wineries are located in the Ensenada region,
❺ but Tijuana now has a branch of the **L.A. Cetto Winery.** Visitors are in-

Avenida Revolución, **3**
Centro Cultural, **9**
El Palacio Frontón (Jai Alai Palace), **4**
L.A. Cetto Winery, **5**
Mexitlán, **2**
Mundo Divertido, **6**
Playas Tijuana, **11**
Plaza de Toros Monumental, **12**
Plaza Río Tijuana, **10**
Pueblo Amigo, **7**
Río Tijuana, **8**
San Ysidro Border Crossing, **1**

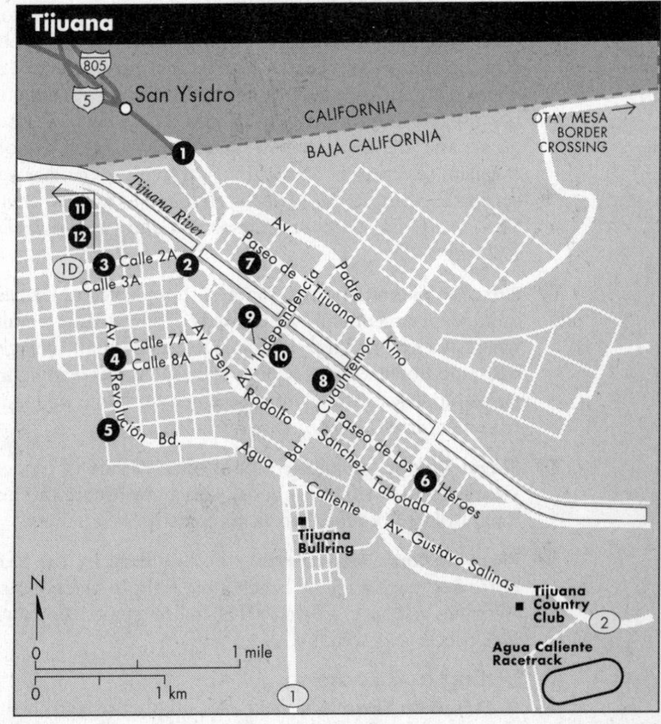

vited to tour the bottling plant, sample the wines, and spend as long as they'd like in the gift and wine shop. ✉ *Cañon Johnson 8151, at Av. Constitución,* ☎ *66/85–30–31.* *$1; $2 with wine tasting.* ⏲ *Tues.–Sun. 10–5.*

6 **Mundo Divertido** is a popular family attraction in the Río zone. The amusement park includes a miniature golf course, batting cages, an exciting roller coaster, and a video-game parlor with more than 130 games. The park has a food court with hot dogs and burgers along with tacos and corn on the cob. Admission is free, and the rides cost just a few pesos. ✉ *Paseo de los Héroes at Calle Velasco, no phone.* ⏲ *Weekdays noon–9, weekends 11–10.*

7 **Pueblo Amigo** contains enough distractions to be a destination unto itself. This entertainment center is built to resemble a colonial Mexican village, with stuccoed buildings painted soft yellow, blue, and rose and tree-lined pathways leading to a gazebo with a brick dome. The complex includes the fanciest hotel near downtown, several restaurants and clubs, a huge grocery store, and a large branch of the Caliente Race Book, where gambling on televised races and sporting events is legal. ✉ *Paseo Tijuana between Puente Mexico and Av. Independencia.*

8 The **Río Tijuana** area—as the section that runs along Avenida Paseo de los Héroes parallel to the dry Tia Juana River is called—is one of the city's main thoroughfares, with large statues of historical figures, including one of Abraham Lincoln, in the center of the *glorietas* (traffic circles). With its impressive Cultural Center, several shopping complexes, fine restaurants, and fashionable discos, this part of town rivals Avenida Revolución for the tourists' and locals' attention. ✉ *Between Blvd. Agua Caliente and border.*

9 The **Centro Cultural** was designed by architects Manuel Rosen and Pedro Ramírez Vásquez, who also created Mexico City's famous Museum

of Anthropology. The center's exhibits of Mexican history are a good introduction for those visitors whose first taste of Mexico is at the border. The Omnimax Theater, with its curving 180-degree screen, shows films on a rotating schedule, often coinciding with temporary exhibits. Usually one English-language film is shown daily. Temporary exhibits on art and culture change frequently. The center's bookstore has an excellent selection of Mexican history, culture, and arts in both Spanish and English. ✉ *Paseo de los Héroes and Av. Independencia,* ☎ *66/84–11–11.* *Museum $2, museum and Omnimax Theater $3.50.* ⏲ *Daily 9–8.*

10 **Plaza Río Tijuana,** the area's largest shopping complex has good restaurants, department stores, hundreds of shops, and a multiplex theater where at least one English-language film is usually being shown. Shade trees and flowers line the long, wide sidewalks leading from the shopping complex to the Cultural Center. ✉ *Paseo de los Héroes across from Cultural Center.*

11 **Playas Tijuana,** along the oceanfront, is a mix of modest and expensive residential neighborhoods, with a few restaurants and hotels. The long, isolated beaches are visited mostly by residents.

12 **Plaza de Toros Monumental,** the "Bullring by the Sea," sits at the northwest corner of the beach area, right by the border (☞ Outdoor Activities and Sports, *below*). The bullring is occasionally used for summer concerts as well.

Dining and Lodging

$$ ✕ **El Faro de Mazatlán.** Fresh fish simply prepared is the hallmark of one of Tijuana's best seafood restaurants. This is the place to try seviche, abalone, squid, and lobster without spending a fortune. Meals start with a savory soup and crusty rolls. The dining room, frequented by professionals from nearby offices, is a peaceful spot for a long, leisurely lunch. Appetizers and soup are included in the price of the meal. ✉ *Blvd. Sanchez Taboada 9542,* ☎ *66/84–88–82. MC, V.*

$$ ✕ **La Fonda de Roberto.** Roberto's is by far the best restaurant in Tijuana for traditional cuisine from the many culinary regions of Mexico. Try the *chiles en nogada* (chilies stuffed with raisins and meat and topped with cream and pomegranate seeds), meats with spicy *achiote* (a blend of spices) sauce, and many varieties of *mole* (a blend of spices and bitter chocolate). Portions are small, so order liberally and share samples of many dishes. ✉ *La Siesta Motel, Old Ensenada Hwy. (also called Calle 16 de Septiembre) near Blvd. Agua Caliente,* ☎ *66/86–16–01. MC, V.*

$$ ✕ **La Taberna Española.** The mainstay of Plaza Fiesta's multiethnic cafés, this Spanish tapas (appetizers) bar attracts a youthful, sophisticated crowd. The tapa menu is printed only in Spanish, but with a bit of imagination you should be able to select a representative sampling, such as octopus in its own ink, spicy sausages, Spanish tortilla with potatoes and eggs, and fava beans. Inside the café, it's smoky, fragrant, and invariably crowded; sit at the outdoor tables for a view of the folks waiting in line. ✉ *Plaza Fiesta, Paseo de los Héroes 10001,* ☎ *66/84–94–01. No credit cards.*

$$ ✕ **Tia Juana Tilly's.** Popular with both tourists and locals looking for revelry and generous portions of Mexican specialties, this is one of the few places where you can get *cochinita píbil* (a Yucatecan dish made of roast pig, red onions, and bitter oranges) or the traditionally bitter and savory chicken mole. Part of the same chain is Tilly's Fifth Ave., catercorner to the original on Avenida Revolución. ✉ *Av. Revolución at Calle 7,* ☎ *66/85–60–24. AE, MC, V.*

$ ✕ **Carnitas Uruapan.** You'll need to take a cab to this large, noisy restaurant, where patrons mingle at long wood tables, toasting one another with chilled *cervezas* (beer). The main attraction here is *carnitas* (marinated pork roasted over an open pit), sold by weight and served with homemade tortillas, salsa, cilantro, guacamole, and onions. ✉ *Blvd. Díaz Ordaz 550,* ☎ *66/81–61–81;* ✉ *Paseo de los Héroes at Av. Rodríguez, no phone. No credit cards.*

$ ★ ✕ **La Especial.** Located at the foot of the stairs leading to an underground shopping arcade, this restaurant attracts diners in search of home-style Mexican cooking at low prices. The gruff, efficient waiters, decked out in black slacks and vests, shuttle platters of *carne asada* (grilled strips of marinated meat), enchiladas, and burritos, all with a distinctive flavor found nowhere but in this busy, cavernous basement dining room. ✉ *Av. Revolución 718,* ☎ *66/85–66–54. No credit cards.*

$ ✕ **Señor Frog's.** Heaping plates of barbecued chicken and ribs and buckets of ice-cold bottles of cerveza are the mainstay at this fun and festive formula eatery, one of many in the Carlos Anderson chain. The loud music and laughter make for a raucous atmosphere, and the food is consistently good. ✉ *In Pueblo Amigo Center, Paseo Tijuana,* ☎ *66/82–49–58. AE, MC, V.*

$$$ **Camino Real.** Elegant and fashionable, this branch of one of Mexico's best hotel chains opened in 1996 near the Cultural Center. The location is ideal for walking to most attractions, and the rooms are plushly decorated in browns and gold. The **Fouquet's de Paris** restaurant specializes in French haute cuisine, and has a garden café; **Azulejos** is more informal. ✉ *Paseo de los Héroes 10305, 22320,* ☎ *66/33–40–00 or 800/722–6466,* FAX *66/33–40–01. 250 rooms and suites. 2 restaurants, 2 bars, room service, laundry service, in-room fax lines and direct-dial phones. AE, MC, V.*

$$$ **Holiday Inn Pueblo Amigo.** The only thoroughly modern hotel in the center of Tijuana's tourist zone, the bright, white Holiday Inn has several sizes of rooms decorated in green, beige, and peach, with cable TV, minibars, and direct-dial long-distance telephones. The indoor pool, sauna, and gym are popular with business travelers, who also have use of meeting facilities and a business center. The hotel's **Café Alcazar** is a favorite luncheon meeting spot. Ask about special rates. ✉ *Via Oriente 9211, at Pueblo Amigo, 22450,* ☎ *66/83–50–30 or 800/465–4329,* FAX *66/83–50–32. 108 rooms and suites. Restaurant, indoor pool, beauty salon, sauna, exercise room. AE, MC, V.*

$$ ★ **Gran Hotel.** The two mirrored towers of the hotel are Tijuana's most ostentatious landmarks. The atrium restaurant is a favorite lunch and Sunday brunch spot. The rooms used to be the nicest in town, but new hotels have upped the standards. Still, it's a good spot for golfers, business travelers, and those who want moderately priced luxury. ✉ *Blvd. Agua Caliente 4558, 22420,* ☎ *66/81–70–00 or 800/472–6385,* FAX *66/81–70–16. 422 rooms. Restaurant, pool, 2 tennis courts, exercise room, nightclub, travel services. AE, MC, V.*

$$ **Lucerna.** Once one of the most charming hotels in Tijuana, the Lucerna shows its age. Still, the lovely gardens, large swimming pool surrounded by palms, touches of tile work, and folk art lend Mexican character to the hotel. ✉ *Paseo de los Héroes 10902, and Av. Rodríguez, 22320,* ☎ *66/34–20–00 or 800/582–3762,* FAX *66/34–24–00. 170 rooms, 9 suites. Restaurant, coffee shop, pool, nightclub, travel services. MC, V.*

$$ **Otay Bugambilias.** Proximity to the Tijuana airport and the Otay Mesa manufacturing plants makes this modest hotel a great find. The pink three-story building has motel-like rooms; suites have kitchenettes. The hotel offers free transportation to and from the Tijuana

airport. ✉ *Blvd. Industrial at Carretera Aeropuerto, 22450,* ☎ FAX *66/23–76–00 or 800/472–1153. 129 rooms. Restaurant, bar, pool, exercise room, meeting rooms. AE, MC, V.*

$ **La Villa de Zaragoza.** This brown stucco motel is such a success that the management keeps adding rooms—the newest have kitchenettes, and all offer air-conditioning and cable TV. The location, near the Jai Alai Palace and one block from Revolución, is ideal. The neighborhood can be noisy, however, and it's best to choose a room at the back. The guarded parking lot is a major plus, though you won't need a car if you stay here. The motel is used by tour groups, so book ahead for holidays and weekends. Discounts are available for extended stays. ✉ *Av. Madero 1120, 22000,* ☎ *66/85–18–32,* FAX *66/85–18–37. 66 rooms. Restaurant. MC, V.*

Nightlife and the Arts

Tijuana has toned down its Sin City image; much of the nighttime action now takes place at the **El Palacio Frontón** and the racetrack. Several hotels, especially the **Holiday Inn Pueblo Amigo** and **Gran Hotel,** have live entertainment.

The **Hard Rock Cafe** (✉ Av. Revolución 520, between Calles 1 and 2, ☎ 66/85–02–06) has the same menu and decor as other branches of the famous London club and is popular with both families and singles. **Como Que No** (✉ Av. Sanchez Taboada 95, ☎ 66/84–27–91) is popular with the sophisticated disco set, while the adjacent **Dime Que Si** (☎ 66/84–27–91) is a romantic piano bar. **Baby Rock** (✉ Calle Diego Rivera 1482, ☎ 66/88–04–40), an offshoot of a popular Acapulco disco, attracts a young, hip crowd. Tijuana's discos usually have strict dress codes, with no T-shirts, jeans, or sandals allowed.

Outdoor Activities and Sports

BULLFIGHTS

Bullfights feature skilled matadors from throughout Mexico and Spain. They are held at **El Toreo de Tijuana** (✉ Av. Agua Caliente outside downtown, ☎ 66/85–22–10) on Sunday at 4, May through October. In July and August you can also see fights at the **Plaza de Toros Monumental** (✉ Playas Tijuana area, Ensenada Hwy., ☎ 66/85–22–10) on Sunday at 4. Admission to bullfights varies, depending on the fame of the matador and the location of your seat.

GOLF

The **Tijuana Country Club** (✉ Blvd. Agua Caliente, east of downtown, ☎ 66/81–78–55) is open to Gran Hotel guests; other hotels can set up golf for their guests, too. It provides rental clubs, electric and hand carts, and caddies for the 18-hole course.

GREYHOUND RACES

At the **Hipódromo de Agua Caliente,** horse racing was phased out in 1993, but greyhounds race nightly at 7:45 and afternoons at 2 on Saturday and Sunday. In the Foreign Book area, gamblers can bet on races taking place in California and shown at Caliente on TV monitors. ✉ *Blvd. Agua Caliente at Salinas,* ☎ *66/81–78–11; 619/231–1919 in San Diego, CA.*

JAI ALAI

This ancient Basque sport, in some ways similar to handball but using a large, scooped-out paddle called a *frontón,* is played in the Moorish-style **El Palacio Frontón,** or Jai Alai Palace. Matinee games start at noon on Monday and Friday; night games start at 8 PM from Tuesday through Saturday. General admission is $5; box seats in the Concha Club are $5. ✉ *Av. Revolución and Calle 8,* ☎ *66/85–25–24; 619/231–1919 in San Diego, CA.*

Shopping

The Avenida Revolución shopping area spreads down Calle 1 to the pedestrian walkway leading from the border. Begin by checking out the stands along the border-crossing walkway, comparing prices as you travel toward Avenida Revolución. You may find that the best bargains are closer to the border; you can pick up your piñatas and serapes on your way out of town. The traditional shopping strip is Avenida Revolución, between Calles 1 and 8; it's lined with shops and arcades that display a wide range of crafts and curios. Bargaining is expected on the streets and in the arcades, but not in the finer shops.

The shops in **Plaza Revolución,** at the corner of Calle 1 and Avenida Revolución, stock quality crafts. **La Piel** (☒ Av. Revolución between Calles 4 and 5, ☎ 66/87–23–98) offers dependable quality in leather jackets, backpacks, and luggage. **Ralph Lauren Polo Outlet** (☒ Viva Tijuana Center, ☎ 66/88–76–98) is a licensed outlet for the designer's sportswear. **Sanborns** (☒ Av. Revolución at Calle 8, ☎ 66/88–14–62) has beautiful crafts from throughout Mexico, an excellent bakery, and chocolates from Mexico City. **Sara's** (☒ Av. Revolución at Calle 4, ☎ 66/88–29–32), one of the best department stores in Tijuana, sells imported perfumes and fine clothing. The finest folk-art store, **Tolan** (☒ Av. Revolución between Calles 7 and 8, ☎ 66/88–36–37), carries everything from antique carved wooden doors to tiny ceramic miniature village scenes.

MARKET

The **Mercado Hidalgo** (☒ Av. Independencia at Av. Sanchez Taboada, 2 blocks south of Paseo de los Héroes) is Tijuana's municipal market, with rows of fresh produce, grains, herbs, some souvenirs, and the best selection of piñatas in Baja.

SHOPPING CENTERS

Plaza Fiesta, on Paseo de los Héroes across from Plaza Río Tijuana, has a collection of boutiques, jewelry stores, and stained-glass shops. You can find great buys on fashionable clothing and shoes at **Plaza Río Tijuana** on Paseo de los Héroes. **Pueblo Amigo,** also on Paseo de los Héroes, has a few small folk-art shops and Ley, a gourmet grocery that sells salad by the pint and hard-to-find Mexican delicacies such as fresh mole sauce and pickled carrots and cauliflower.

Rosarito Beach

29 km (18 mi) south of Tijuana.

Not so very long ago, Playas de Rosarito (Rosarito Beach) was a small seaside community with virtually no tourist trade. It was part of the municipality of Tijuana, an overlooked suburb on the way to the port city of Ensenada. But as the roads improved, and particularly after Baja's Transpeninsular Highway was completed in 1973, Rosarito Beach began to flower. In 1995 it became its own municipality, with a government separate from that of Tijuana. Rosarito's population, about 110,000, is growing steadily.

Rosarito's main street, alternately known as the Old Ensenada Highway and Boulevard Benito Juárez, reflects the unrestrained growth and speculation that have both helped and harmed the city. The street is packed with restaurants, bars, and shops in a jarring juxtaposition of architectural styles, with some of the largest developments halted midway for lack of investors.

It nevertheless remains a relaxing place to visit. Southern Californians have practically made Rosarito a weekend suburb. Surfers, swimmers, and sunbathers come here to enjoy the beach, one of the longest in northern Baja: It's an uninterrupted stretch of sand from the power plant at the far north end of town to below the Rosarito Beach Hotel, about 8 km (5 mi) south. Horseback riding, jogging, and strolling are popular along this strand. Whales pass not far from shore on their winter migration; dolphins and sea lions sun on rocks jutting out from the sea. Rosarito has always attracted a varied crowd, and today's group is no exception—an assemblage of prosperous young Californians building villas in vacation developments, retired Americans and Canadians homesteading in trailer parks, and travelers of all ages from all over the world.

Hedonism and health get equal billing in Rosarito. One of the area's major draws is its seafood, especially lobster, shrimp, and abalone. The visiting Americans act as if they've been dry for months—margaritas and beer are the favored thirst quenchers. People throw off their inhibitions here, at least to the degree permitted by the local constables. A typical Rosarito day might begin with a breakfast of eggs, refried beans, and tortillas, followed by a few hours of horseback riding on the beach. Lying in the sun or strolling through the shops takes care of midday. Siestas are imperative and are usually followed by more shopping, strolling, or sunbathing before dinner, dancing, and sleep.

Rosarito Beach has few historic or cultural attractions, beaches and bars being the main draws. Sightseeing consists of strolling along the beach or down **Boulevard Benito Juárez,** which runs parallel to it.

An immense PEMEX gasoline installation and electric plant anchor the northern end of Boulevard Juárez, which then runs along a collection of shopping arcades, restaurants, and motels. The eight-story **Quinta Del Mar** condo and hotel complex is the first major landmark, followed by the **Quinta Plaza** shopping center, which hosts a car wash, pharmacy, bakery, specialty shops, and restaurants, as well as the tourism office and the Centro de Convenciones, a 1,000-seat convention center. The **Festival Plaza** hotel and shopping center, with its distinctive roller coaster–like facade, sits a bit farther south on Boulevard Juárez, just before the **Rosarito Beach Hotel,** which marks the end of the strip.

Dining and Lodging

$$ ✕ **Azteca.** The enormous dining room at the Rosarito Beach Hotel has a view of the pool and beach area. Many visitors come here exclusively for the Sunday brunch; expect to wait in line on holiday weekends. Both Mexican and American dishes are offered, and the size of the portions makes up for the erratic quality of the food. The hotel offers a Mexican buffet and fiesta here on Friday nights. ✉ *Rosarito Beach Hotel, Blvd. Juárez,* ☎ *661/2–01–44. MC, V.*

$$ ✕ **Calafia.** Though not in Rosarito proper, this unusual restaurant and trailer park are worth a visit (it's a 10-minute car or cab ride south). The owners have added a historic element to their property by filling the public spaces with photos and artifacts from Baja's early days. But most visitors are drawn to Calafia's dining room, where tables are scattered on small terraces down the cliffside to the crashing sea. The food is standard Mexican fare, but it all tastes great when combined with the fresh salt air and sea breezes. Calafia has an outdoor dance floor at the base of the cliffs, where live bands sometimes perform. ✉ *Km 35.5 Old Ensenada Hwy., 22710,* ☎ *661/2–15–81 or 800/225–2342,* FAX *661/2–15–80. MC, V.*

$$ ✕ **Dragon del Mar.** A miniature waterfall greets guests in the marble foyer of this elegant Chinese restaurant, where a pianist plays relaxing music. Carved wooden partitions in the expansive dining room help

create an intimate dining experience. The food is well prepared and appealing to the eye as well as the palate. ✉ *Blvd. Juárez 283,* ☎ *661/2–06–04. MC, V.*

$$ ✕ **El Nido.** A dark, wood-paneled restaurant with leather booths and a large central fireplace, this is one of the oldest eateries in Rosarito. Diners unimpressed with the newer, fancier establishments come here for the good mesquite-grilled steaks and for grilled quail from the owner's farm in the Baja wine country. ✉ *Blvd. Juárez 67,* ☎ *661/2–14–30. MC, V.*

$$ ★ ✕ **La Leña.** The cornerstone restaurant of the Quinta Plaza shopping center, La Leña is spacious and impeccably clean, with the tables spread far enough apart for privacy. Try any of the beef dishes, especially the tender carne asada with tortillas and guacamole. ✉ *Quinta Plaza,* ☎ *661/2–08–26. MC, V.*

$$ ✕ **Ortega's Place.** Music blares from this two-story restaurant-bar where tourists flock to inexpensive buffets. The breakfast and lunch spreads include scrambled eggs, lots of beans and rice, and basic Mexican dishes. The à la carte entrées are much more expensive, and though Ortega's is known for its lobster, you'll get a better deal elsewhere. ✉ *Blvd. Juárez 200,* ☎ *661/2–27–91. MC, V.*

$$ ✕ **René's.** One of the oldest restaurants in Rosarito (1924), René's features chorizo (Mexican sausage), quail, frogs' legs, and lobster. There's an ocean view from the dining room, a lively bar, and mariachi music. ✉ *Blvd. Juárez south of Rosarito Beach Hotel,* ☎ *661/2–10–20. MC, V.*

$ ✕ **La Flor de Michoacán.** Carnitas Michoacán-style, served with homemade tortillas, guacamole, and salsa, are the house specialty at this Rosarito landmark, established in 1950. The tacos, *tortas* (sandwiches), and tostadas are great. The surroundings are simple but clean. Takeout is available. ✉ *Blvd. Juárez 291,* ☎ *661/2–18–58. No credit cards. Closed Wed.*

$$$ ★ 🏨 **Marriott Real Del Mar Residence Inn.** Golfers and escapists relish their privacy at this all-suites hotel set on a cliff with faraway views of the sea north of Rosarito. The standard accommodations have living rooms with vaulted-brick ceilings, fireplaces, kitchens, and two double beds; larger units offer one or two bedrooms. Greens fees at the on-site golf course are included in packages. The hotel, 19 km (12 mi) south of the border and 10 km (6 mi) north of Rosarito, is completely removed from the action. An on-site branch of Tijuana's **Pedrin's** restaurant offers good seafood meals and Mexican dishes. ✉ *Km 19.5 Ensenada toll road, 22710,* ☎ *66/31–36–70 or 800/331–3131,* FAX *66/31–36–77. 66 suites. Restaurant, bar, snack bar, pool, 18-hole golf course, pro shop. AE, MC, V.*

$$$ 🏨 **Oasis Resort.** This full-scale resort on a long, perfect beach north of Rosarito is incredibly popular with families. The hotel section has one-bedroom, ocean-view suites with heat, air-conditioning, cable TVs, minibars, and fold-out couches; two children under the age of 12 stay free with two adults. Deluxe recreational vehicles (RVs) with full kitchens, cable TV, and maid service are the most costly accommodations. Full hookups for private mobile homes are the least expensive, though the rates are far higher than in other campgrounds. The Oasis is a fun spot where guests quickly become friends and end up booking return visits together. The resort is 30 km (18 mi) south of the border. ✉ *Old Ensenada Hwy., 22710,* ☎ *661/3–32–55,* FAX *661/3–32–52. 100 suites, 22 RVs, 55 RV spaces. Restaurant, bar, 2 pools, wading pool, 2 hot tubs, sauna, miniature golf, tennis court, exercise room, recreation room, laundry service. MC, V.*

$$ **Brisas del Mar.** A modern motel (built in 1992), the Brisas del Mar is especially good for families, since the large pastel rooms comfortably accommodate four persons. A few of the suites on the second story have hot tubs and views of the ocean; all have air-conditioning and TV. The motel is located on the inland side of Boulevard Juárez, and traffic noise can be a problem. ✉ *Blvd. Juárez 22, 22710,* ☎ FAX *661/2–25–47; reservations in the U.S.:* ✉ *Box 1867, Chula Vista, CA 91912,* ☎ *800/697–5223. 66 rooms. Bar, coffee shop, heated pool. MC, V.*

$$ **Festival Plaza.** Designed with unrestrained fun in mind, Festival Plaza is geared toward a youthful crowd. The motel-like rooms are in an eight-story building with a facade resembling a roller coaster. The casitas (in the $$$ range) close to the beach are the quietest accommodations and have small hot tubs, separate living rooms with fold-out couches, and private garages, but no kitchen facilities. The hotel also operates a complex of 14 villas just south of Rosarito; these have full kitchens. Within the hotel complex are several bars and good restaurants (try the traditional Mexican dishes at **El Patio,**) and the central courtyard serves as a concert stage, children's playground, and party headquarters. Discounted room rates are often available, especially in winter. ✉ *Blvd. Juárez 11, 22710,* ☎ *661/2–08–42, 661/2–29–50, or 800/453–8606,* FAX *661/2–01–24. 114 rooms and suites. 2 restaurants, 3 bars, pool, dance club, playground. AE, MC, V.*

$$ **Hotel Quinta Terranova.** Pretty and peaceful, this small hotel sits at the edge of the Quinta del Mar development facing a relatively quiet section of Boulevard Juárez. The green and beige rooms in a two-story, motel-like building have coffeemakers mounted on the wall, hair dryers, carpeting, and small bathrooms. The pool is set back from the street with enough plants to offer a sense of seclusion. ✉ *Blvd. Juárez 25500, 22710,* ☎ *661/2–16–44,* FAX *661/2–16–42. 84 rooms and suites. Restaurant, pool. MC, V.*

$$ **Los Pelicanos Hotel.** One of the few hotels situated directly on the beach, the Pelicanos is a favorite with Americans and Canadians who stay for weeks on end in the winter. The best rooms have oceanfront balconies, though the others—with white walls, light-wood furnishings, and large bathrooms—are nice as well. The lack of a pool is a drawback, though the sea is just a few steps away. The second-story restaurant and bar, popular sunset-watching spots, tend to attract an older, more subdued clientele feasting on steak and lobster. ✉ *Calle Cedros 115, at Calle Ebano, 22710,* ☎ *661/2–04–45,* FAX *661/2–17–57; U.S. mailing address:* ✉ *Box 433871, San Ysidro, CA 92143. 39 rooms. Restaurant, bar. AE, MC, V.*

$$ **Rosarito Beach Hotel.** Dating from the Prohibition era, this venerable hotel is Rosarito's centerpiece. It's a charmer, with huge ballrooms, tiled public rest rooms, and a glassed-in pool deck overlooking a long beach. The very plain rooms and suites in the tower are air-conditioned; some units in the original building have fans only and are very rundown. Keep in mind the noise factor when looking at rooms near the pools, playground, and side lawn where live bands play on summer afternoons. Midweek reduced rates and special packages are often available; ocean-view rooms are in the $$$ category. A refurbished 1930s mansion next door hosts the Casa Playa Spa, with massage, beauty treatments, exercise equipment, saunas, and hot tubs. ✉ *Blvd. Juárez, south end of town, 22710,* ☎ *661/2–01–44, 661/2–11–26, or 800/343–8582,* FAX *661/2–11–76; reservations in the U.S.:* ✉ *Box 430145, San Diego, CA 92143. 275 rooms and suites. 2 restaurants, bar, 2 pools, spa, tennis court, health club, beach. MC, V.*

$ **Cupalas del Mar.** This small hotel between Boulevard Juárez and the beach is quieter than most, with sunny, clean rooms and satellite

TV. ✉ *Calle Guadalupe Victoria 9, 22710,* ☎ *661/2-24-90. 39 rooms. Pool, hot tub. AE, MC, V.*

Nightlife and the Arts

The many restaurants in Rosarito Beach keep customers entertained with live music, piano bars, or *folklórico* (folk music and dance) shows; the bar scene is also active. Drinking-and-driving laws are stiff—the police will fine you no matter how little you've had. If you plan to drink, take a cab or assign a designated driver.

There's a lot going on at night at the **Rosarito Beach Hotel** (✉ Blvd. Juárez, ☎ 661/2-01-44): live music at the ocean-view **Beachcomber Bar** and **Hugo's**; a Mexican Fiesta on Friday nights; and a live band at the cavernous disco. **Papas and Beer** (✉ Blvd. Juárez near Rosarito Beach Hotel, ☎ 661/2-03-43) draws a young, energetic crowd. The **Festival Plaza** (✉ Blvd. Juárez 11, ☎ 661/2-08-42) has become party central for Rosarito's youthful crowd and presents live concerts on the hotel's courtyard stage most weekends; in the hotel complex are **El Museo Cantina Tequila,** dedicated to the art of imbibing tequila and offering more than 130 brands of the fiery drink, and **Rock & Roll Taco**—as its name suggests, a taco stand and boisterous bar all in one.

Outdoor Activities and Sports

GOLF

The **Real del Mar Golf Club** (✉ 18 km [12 mi] south of the border on Ensenada toll road, ☎ 66/31-34-01) has 18 holes overlooking the ocean. Golf packages are available at some Rosarito Beach hotels.

HORSEBACK RIDING

Horses can be rented at the north and south ends of Juárez and on the beach south of the Rosarito Beach Hotel for $6 per hour. In the past, some of the animals were pathetically thin and misused. Their number is now restricted and the horses are better cared for. If you're a dedicated equestrian, ask about tours into the countryside, which can be arranged with the individual owners.

SURFING

The waves are particularly good at **Popotla,** Kilometer 33; **Calafia,** Kilometer 35.5; and **Costa Baja,** Kilometer 36, on the Old Ensenada Highway. **Tony's Surf Shop** (✉ Blvd. Juárez 312, ☎ 661/2-11-92) offers surfing gear for sale or rent.

Shopping

Rosarito is a great place to shop for pottery and wood furniture. Curio stands and open-air artisans' markets line Boulevard Juárez both north and south of town, with the best pottery stands on the highway to the south. The major hotels have shopping arcades with restaurants, taco stands, and some decent crafts stores.

Interios del Rio Casa del Arte y La Madera (✉ Quinta del Mar Plaza, ☎ 661/2-13-00) always features an irresistible selection of Mexican folk art with a fish and sea theme, and creatively painted furnishings. **Casa la Carreta** (✉ Km 29 Old Ensenada Hwy., ☎ 661/2-05-02), one of Rosarito's best furniture shops, is worth a visit just to see the wood-carvers create elaborate desks, dining tables, and armoires. **Casa Torres** (✉ Rosarito Beach Hotel Shopping Center, ☎ 661/2-10-08) carries a wide array of imported perfumes. **Margarita's** (✉ Rosarito Beach Hotel Shopping Center, no phone) has a great selection of Guatemalan textiles and clothing. The shelves of **Taxco Curios** (✉ Quinta del Mar Plaza, ☎ 661/2-18-77) are filled with handblown glassware.

The **Calimax** grocery store on Boulevard Juárez is a good place to stock up on necessities.

Puerto Nuevo

Km 44 Old Ensenada Hwy., 12 km (7½ mi) south of Rosarito Beach.

Not that many years ago, the only way you could tell you'd reached this fishing community at Kilometer 44 on the old highway from Rosarito Beach was by the huge painting of a 7UP bottle on the side of a building. You'd drive down the rutted dirt road to a row of restaurants where you were served the classic Newport meal: grilled lobster, refried beans, rice, homemade tortillas, butter, salsa, and lime. The meal became a legend, and now at least 30 restaurants in the same area have the identical menu. An artisans' market sits at the entrance to the restaurant row; other stands selling pottery, serapes, and T-shirts line the nearby highway. Several hotels have opened in the area, making Puerto Nuevo a self-contained destination where diners can party all day and night and not have to drive to hotels in Rosarito or Ensenada. Several longtime favorite small inns and restaurants line the road south of Puerto Nuevo to Ensenada.

Dining and Lodging

Don't expect there to be much variety in the food at any of the Puerto Nuevo restaurants: Diners come here for the classic lobster meal, and they're not about to be disappointed. Some places have full bars; others serve only wine and beer. **Ortega's,** with four branches in Newport and two in Rosarito, is the most crowded; **Ponderosa** is smaller and quieter and is run by a gracious family; **Costa Brava** is the most elegant, with tablecloths and an ocean view; and **La Casa de la Langosta** serves grilled fish along with lobster and shrimp. Lobsters in most places are priced as small, medium, and large—medium is about $15. Some of the lobster served in Newport comes from local waters during lobster season (October through March), though the supply can hardly keep up with the demand and most of the lobster is imported the rest of the year. There is some concern that the waters close to shore have become polluted, but the fishermen say they trap the lobsters 1½ km (1 mi) or so offshore, where the waters are safe. Most places are open for lunch and dinner on a first-come, first-served basis. Some take credit cards.

$$ ★ ✕🏨 **La Fonda.** A longtime favorite with beachgoers, La Fonda has a few well-worn rooms decorated with carved-wood furniture, old bullfighting posters, and folk art; most have great views of the ocean. There are no phones or televisions, just the sound of the surf and miles of empty beach to keep you entertained. Even the hotel doesn't have a phone; reservations can only be made by mail (allow two weeks to receive your confirmation) or in person. At the restaurant, you can sit on an outdoor patio and sip potent margaritas served with fresh lobster, grilled steaks, prime rib, suckling pig, and traditional Mexican dishes. The Saturday and Sunday brunch is a feast well worth a few hours of your time. The bar is packed on weekend nights, and the patrons boisterous. If you plan on getting any sleep, ask for a room as close to the sounds of the surf as possible. ✉ *Km 59 Old Ensenada Hwy., 22710, no phone; reservations in the U.S.:* ✉ *Box 430268, San Ysidro, CA 92143. 26 rooms. Restaurant, bar, beach. MC, V at restaurant; no credit cards at hotel.*

$$ 🏨 **Hacienda Las Glorias.** Located on the grounds of the Bajamar golf resort, about halfway between Rosarito and Ensenada, the Hacienda Las Glorias surrounds a central courtyard. Rooms have hand-carved

furnishings and French doors leading to landscaped patios. Staying here can be peaceful except when golfers neglect to remove their shoes and clomp around the brick hallways like herds of goats. Maintenance has been a problem, and some rooms need renovation. Private homes and condos (some for rent) edge the golf course and the cliffs overlooking the ocean. ✉ *Km 77.5 Old Ensenada Hwy., Ensenada 22800,* ☎ *615/5–01–51; 619/299–1112 or 800/225–2418 for reservations in the U.S;* FAX *615/5–01–50. 80 rooms. Restaurant, bar, pool, golf course, 2 tennis courts. AE, MC, V.*

$$ **Hotel New Port Baja.** The closest accommodations to the lobster restaurants are in this sand-color complex with ocean views. The rooms don't have air-conditioning, but they do have heaters for chilly winter nights, along with cable TV, small balconies, and simple blue-gray and white furnishings. ✉ *Km 45 Old Ensenada Hwy., 22712,* ☎ *661/4–11–66; 619/298–4105 or 800/582–1018 for reservations in the U.S.;* FAX *661/4–11–74. 150 rooms. Restaurant, bar, pool, 2 tennis courts, exercise room. MC, V.*

$$ **Las Rocas.** This white hotel with blue-tile domes is still the prettiest in the area, but it is beginning to show its age. The building is terraced up a hillside, giving all the rooms ocean views, but the accommodations are not otherwise equal. The least expensive ones are small, with dripping faucets and worn furnishings. The most expensive are much larger and offer fireplaces, coffeemakers, and microwaves. The pool and whirlpool seem to spill over the cliffs into the ocean. ✉ *Km 37 Old Ensenada Hwy., 22710,* ☎ FAX *661/2–21–40; reservations in the U.S.:* ✉ *Box 8851, Chula Vista, CA 91912,* ☎ *619/425–2682; 800/733–6394 outside CA. 74 rooms and suites. Restaurant, bar, hot tub, beach. AE, MC, V.*

Outdoor Activities and Sports

GOLF

Bajamar (✉ Km 77.5 Old Ensenada Hwy., ☎ 615/5–01–51; 615/5–01–61 tee times), a 1976 course revamped and reopened in late 1993, offers 18 holes of challenging championship golf on the cliffs above the ocean, and another nine holes near the beach.

En Route Vast vistas of pounding surf and solitary cliffs are interspersed with one-of-a-kind hotels and restaurants along the coastline between Rosarito Beach and Ensenada. The paved highway (Mexico Route 1) between the two cities often cuts a path between low mountains and high oceanside cliffs; exits lead to rural roads, oceanfront campgrounds, and an ever-increasing number of resort communities. The small fishing communities of **San Miguel** and **El Sauzal** sit off the highway to the north of Ensenada, and the **Coronado Islands** can be clearly seen off the coast.

Ensenada

104 km (65 mi) south of Tijuana, 75 km (47 mi) south of Rosarito.

In 1542 Juan Rodríguez Cabrillo first discovered the seaport that Sebastián Vizcaino named Ensenada-Bahía de Todos Santos (All Saints' Bay) in 1602. Since then the town has drawn a steady stream of "discoverers" and developers. First ranchers made their homes on large spreads along the coast and up into the mountains. Gold miners followed, turning the area into a boomtown during the late 1800s. After the mines were depleted, the area settled back into a pastoral state for a while, but the harbor gradually grew into a major port for shipping agricultural goods from the surrounding ranches and farms. Now, with a population of some 300,000, it is one of Mexico's largest seaports and has a thriving fishing fleet and fish-processing industry. The smell of fish from the canneries lining the north and south sides of the city can be overpowering at times.

There are no beaches in Ensenada proper, but beaches north and south of town are satisfactory for swimming, sunning, surfing, and camping. On summer and holiday weekends the population swells, but the town rarely gets overly crowded. While the hotels and resorts along the coast, especially around Rosarito Beach, attract many of the travelers seeking weekend escapes, Ensenada tends to draw those who want to explore a more traditional Mexican city.

In a concerted effort to attract vacationers, conventioneers, and business travelers, the waterfront area has been razed and rebuilt, with taco stands replaced by shopping centers, hotels, and the massive Plaza Marina, a large shopping complex with few tenants. Several strip malls have opened in town, but many of the storefronts remain empty. Cruise ships occasionally anchor in the port, bringing day-trippers for shopping and dining.

Ensenada, the third-largest city in Baja, hugs the harbor of Bahía de Todos Santos. As Alternate Highway 1 leads into town from the north, it becomes Boulevard Costero, running past shipyards filled with massive freighters.

13 **Parque Revolución** (Revolution Park) is the most traditional plaza in Ensenada, with a bandstand, playground, and plenty of benches in the shade. The plaza takes on a festive feeling on Saturday and Sunday evenings, when neighbors congregate on the benches and children chase seagulls down the pathways. ✉ *Av. Juárez at Av. Obregón.*

At the northernmost point of Boulevard Costero, the main street along
14 the waterfront, sits an indoor-outdoor **Fish Market,** where row after row of counters display piles of shrimp as well as tuna, dorado, marlin, snapper, and dozens of other species of fish caught off Baja's coasts. Outside, stands sell grilled or smoked fish, seafood cocktails, and fish tacos. Browsers can pick up some standard souvenirs, eat well for very little money, and take some great photographs. The original fish taco stands line the dirt path to the fish market; those with delicate stomachs might want to sample fish tacos at the cleaner, quieter **Plaza de Mariscos** in the shadow of the giant beige **Plaza de Marina** that blocks the view of the traditional fish market from the street.

15 Fishing and whale-watching tours depart from the **Sportfishing Pier** (✉ Blvd. Costero at Av. Alvarado).

16 **Plaza Cívica** (✉ Blvd. Costero at Av. Riveroll) is a block-long concrete park with sculptures of Mexican heroes Benito Juárez, Miguel Hidalgo, and Venustiano Carranza. A now-defunct cruise-ship pier sits south
17 of the plaza by the **Centro Artesenal de Ensenada** shopping center. The ships now dock amid ship repair yards at the north end of the port; taxis and tour buses carry passengers from the port to the main attractions and the center has lost many of its tenants.

18 The **Riviera del Pacífico** is a rambling, white, hacienda-style mansion built in the 1920s with money raised on both sides of the border. An enormous gambling palace, hotel, restaurant, and bar, the glamorous Riviera was frequented by wealthy U.S. citizens and Mexicans, particularly during Prohibition. When gambling was outlawed in Mexico and Prohibition ended in the United States, the palace lost its raison d'être. During daylight, visitors can tour some of the elegant ballrooms and halls, which host occasional art shows and civic events. Many of the rooms are locked; check at the main office to see if there is someone available to show you around. The gardens alone are worth vis-

Avenida López Mateos, **19**
Avenida Juárez, **20**
Centro Artesenal de Ensenada, **17**
Fish Market, **14**
La Bufadora, **23**
Las Bodegas de Santo Tomás, **21**
Our Lady of Guadalupe, **22**
Parque Revolucíon, **13**
Plaza Cívica, **16**
Riviera del Pacífico, **18**
Sportfishing Pier, **15**

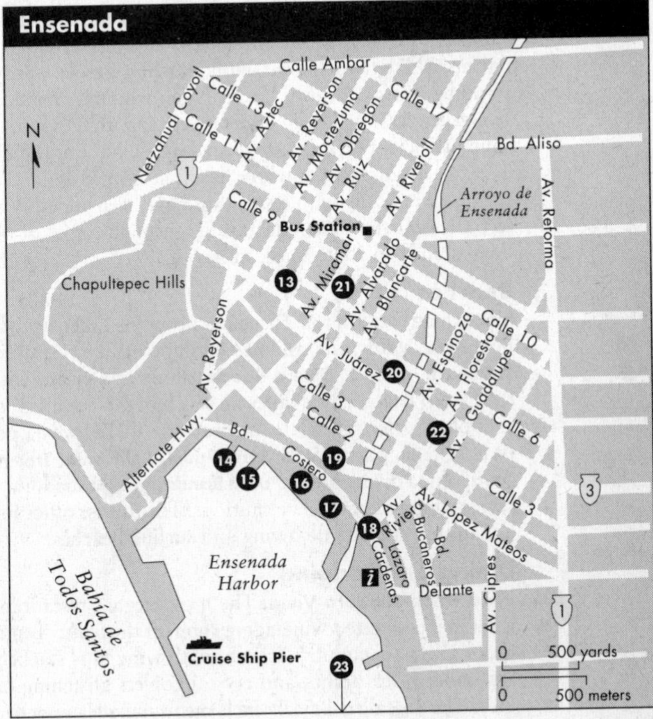

iting, and the building now houses the **Museo de Historia de Ensenada,** a museum on Baja's history. The Riviera del Pacífico is officially called the Centro Social, Cívico y Cultural de Ensenada (Social, Civic and Cultural Center of Ensenada). ✉ *Blvd. Costero and Av. Riviera,* ☎ *61/76–43–10; 61/76–05–94 museum.* *Building and gardens free, museum $1.* ⏲ *Daily 9–5.*

19 Ensenada's traditional tourist zone is centered along **Avenida López Mateos.** High-rise hotels, souvenir shops, restaurants, and bars line the avenue from its beginning at the foot of the Chapultepec Hills for eight blocks south to the dry channel of tne Arroyo de Ensenada. Locals shop for furniture, clothing, and other necessities a few blocks inland on
20 **Avenida Juárez** in Ensenada's downtown area.

21 **Las Bodegas de Santo Tomás,** Baja's oldest winery, gives tours and tastings of its downtown winery and bottling plant. The restaurant in the winery is one of Baja's finest. The winery also operates **La Esquina de Bodegas,** a café, shop, and gallery in a bright blue building across Avenida Miramar. ✉ *Av. Miramar 666,* ☎ *61/78–33–33; 619/454–7166 in the U.S.* *$1.* ⏲ *Tours Mon.–Sat. 11 AM, 1 PM, and 3 PM; Sun. 11 AM and 1 PM.*

22 The city's largest cathedral, **Our Lady of Guadalupe** (✉ Av. Floresta at Av. Juárez) is the center of processions and celebrations during religious holidays.

23 **La Bufadora** (✉ Hwy. 23, 31 km [20 mi] south of Ensenada) is an impressive blowhole ("la bufadora" means the buffalo snort) in the coastal cliffs at **Punta Banda,** an isolated, mountainous point jutting into the sea. The road along Punta Banda to La Bufadora is lined with stands where growers sell locally grown olives, homemade tamales, strands of chilies and garlic, and terra-cotta planters. The drive gives

short-term visitors a sampling of Baja's wilderness and is well worth a half-day excursion. The blowhole is impressive, with seawater splashing up to 75 ft in the air with startling power, spraying sightseers standing nearby. Legend has it the blowhole is created by a whale or sea serpent trapped in an undersea cave; both these stories and the less romantic scientific facts are posted on a plaque at the side of the road. The area around the blowhole has been cleaned up, and a viewing platform and building with rest rooms have been added. Visitors now pay to park near the blowhole and file through a row of permanent vendors' stands en route to the cliff.

Beaches

Since the waterfront in Ensenada proper is taken up by fishing boats, boat repair yards, and commercial shipping, the best swimming beaches are south of town. **Estero Beach** is long and clean, with mild waves; the Estero Beach Hotel takes up much of the oceanfront but the beach is public. Surfers populate the beaches off Highway 1 north and south of Ensenada, particularly **San Miguel, California, Tres Marías,** and **La Joya**; scuba divers prefer **Punta Banda,** by La Bufadora. Lifeguards are rare; swimmers should be cautious. The tourist office in Ensenada has a map that shows safe diving and surfing beaches.

Dining and Lodging

$$$ ★ ✕ **La Embotelladora Vieja.** The most elegant restaurant in Ensenada is set in a converted wine-aging room at the Santo Tomás winery. The decor is classic country French, with wine bins stacked floor-to-ceiling under brick arches and crystal goblets glistening on candlelit tables. The so-called Baja French menu includes appetizers of smoked tuna and French pâté; among the most sublime entrées are the grilled lobster in cabernet sauvignon sauce, beef Montpellier with green peppercorns, and quail with sauvignon blanc sauce. Teetotalers, note: Nearly every dish is prepared with wine, though you can order some without alcohol-laden sauces. All of Baja's wineries are represented on the impressive wine list. ✉ *Av. Miramar 666,* ☎ *61/74-08-07. MC, V. Closed Sun.*

$$ ✕ **Bronco's Steak House.** A great find near the San Nicolas Hotel, Bronco's serves exceptional steaks and Mexican specialties. Try the Boca del Rio, a New York steak stuffed with grilled onions and fiery serrano chilies. Tripe appears frequently on the menu, satisfying the cravings of local diners gathered at many of the wood tables. Brick walls, wood plank floors, and hanging spurs and chaps give the place a Wild West feel, but the mood is subdued and relaxed. ✉ *Av. López Mateos 1525,* ☎ *61/76-49-00. MC, V.*

$$ ✕ **Casamar.** A long-standing, dependable restaurant, Casamar is known for its wide variety of excellent seafood. Lobster and shrimp are prepared in several ways but seem freshest when grilled *con mojo y ajo* (with butter and garlic). When choosing a fish dish, always ask about the catch of the day; you may luck out and get a thick steak of fresh yellowfin tuna. ✉ *Blvd. Lázaro Cárdenas 987,* ☎ *61/74-04-17. MC, V.*

$$ ★ ✕ **El Rey Sol.** A family-owned French restaurant more than 40 years old, El Rey Sol is in a charming building with stained-glass windows and is decorated with wrought-iron chandeliers and heavy oak tables and chairs. Specialties include French and Mexican presentations of fresh fish, poultry, and vegetables grown at the owner's farm in the Santo Tomás Valley. Appetizers come with the meal; the excellent pastries are baked on the premises. A side room at the front of the restaurant has been turned into a patisserie with a few small lace-covered tables and a pastry case displaying delectable strudels and tarts. It's a lovely spot for an afternoon espresso and sweets, or you can choose a

few tasty items to go. ✉ *Av. López Mateos 1000,* ☎ *61/78–17–33. AE, MC, V.*

$ ★ ✕ **El Charro.** You can find less (and more) expensive rotisserie chicken, beans, rice, and tortillas at other places in downtown, but El Charro still attracts a steady stream of locals and tourists. Part of the draw is the location—not far from popular bars—and the consistently good food. Hungry patrons hover over platters of *chiles rellenos* (chilies stuffed with cheese and deep-fried in batter), enchiladas, and fresh chips and guacamole at heavy wooden picnic tables under a ceiling of charred wooden beams. Plump chickens slowly circle over a wood fire by the front window, and the aroma of grilled beef and simmering beans fills the air. Other restaurants with similar names have opened on the same block; stick with the original and you won't be disappointed. ✉ *Av. López Mateos 475,* ☎ *61/78–38–81. MC, V.*

$ ★ ✕ **Mariscos de Bahía de Ensenada.** Red lights flicker around the front door, making this popular seafood house just off the main drag easy to spot. On weekends the upstairs and downstairs dining rooms are packed for both lunch and dinner; tables are easier to come by on weeknights. Clams, shrimp, lobster, red snapper, squid, and any other sea creatures in season appear on the menu fried, baked, broiled, or grilled, and served with a basic iceberg lettuce salad, white rice, and tortillas made fresh at the window-front tortilleria. ✉ *Av. Riveroll 109,* ☎ *61/78–10–15. MC, V.*

$$$ ★ **Hotel Coral & Marina.** This ambitious project is the largest resort on the Baja Norte coast. A marina, long needed in Ensenada, has slips for 600 boats and facilities for clearing customs. The rooms in two eight-story towers are decorated in burgundy and dark green, with waterfront balconies, seating areas, cable TV, and in-room international phone service (still a novelty in this area). The hotel opened in 1995 and unlike other projects in the area it appears to be built to survive and thrive. Conventions, fishing and golf tournaments, and boat races fill the hotel on weekends; rates are often 30%–50% lower on winter weekdays. ✉ *Mexico Hwy. 1 north of town, 22800,* ☎ *61/75–00–00 or 800/862–9029; 800/94–627–462 for reservations in the U.S.;* FAX *61/75–00–05. 147 rooms and suites. Restaurant, 3 pools (1 indoor), 2 hot tubs, spa, 2 tennis courts, exercise room, dive shop, boating, fishing. MC, V.*

$$$ ★ **Las Rosas.** This elegant pink palace just north of town is both intimate and upscale; the atrium lobby features marble floors, mint green–and–pink upholstered couches facing the sea, and a green-glass ceiling that glows at night. All rooms face the ocean and pool; some have fireplaces and hot tubs, and even the least expensive accommodations are lovely. The hotel is booked solid most weekends; make reservations far in advance. ✉ *Mexico Hwy. 1 north of town, 22800,* ☎ *61/74–43–20,* FAX *61/74–45–95. 32 rooms and suites. Restaurant, bar, pool, hot tub. AE, MC, V.*

$$$ ★ **Punta Morro.** For seclusion and the sound of crashing surf, you can't beat this all-suites hotel. The three-story tan building faces the north end of the bay. The lovely restaurant sits on rock pilings above the waves; you won't find a more romantic spot than at a window seat here. Enjoy eggs Benedict or French toast in the morning, or toast the sunset with champagne while feasting on lobster, steak, or quail. All accommodations have terraces facing the ocean, kitchenettes, and seating areas; some have fireplaces. Stairs lead down to a rocky beach, but the surf is usually too rough for swimming. Rates are significantly lower on weekdays. ✉ *Mexico Hwy. 1, 3 km (2 mi) north of town, Box 2891, 22800,* ☎ *61/78–35–07 or 800/526–6676,* FAX *61/74–44–90; reservations*

in the U.S.: ✉ *Box 43-4263, San Ysidro, CA 92143. 30 suites. Restaurant, bar, pool, hot tub, beach. MC, V.*

$$ 🏨 **Estero Beach Resort.** Families settle in for a week or more at this long-standing resort on Ensenada's best beach. The rooms (some with kitchenettes) are housed in several mint-green buildings. The best are those right by the sand; the worst (and cheapest) are in the oldest section by the parking lot. No one expects anything fancy here, and at times it seems all the guests are attending huge wedding or birthday celebrations or family reunions. Guests spend their days swimming in the ocean (a pool was under construction at press time), fishing, riding horses, playing volleyball, and generally hanging out with friends. Nights are spent at the casual restaurant and bar. The resort is 10 km (6 mi) south of town. Midweek winter rates are a real bargain, and the resort feels almost deserted and peaceful at this time. Nonguests can use the hotel's facilities for a low daily fee. ✉ *Mexico Hwy. 1 between Ensenada and Maneadero, 22810,* ☎ *61/76–62–35,* FAX *61/76–69–25; reservations in the U.S.:* ✉ *482 San Ysidro Blvd., Suite 1186, San Ysidro, CA 92173. 106 rooms, 2 suites. Restaurant, bar, kitchenettes, 4 tennis courts, horseback riding, volleyball, shops, playground. MC, V.*

$$ 🏨 **Hotel Mision Santa Ysabel.** The most authentically Mexican hotel right in the tourist zone, this two-story charmer has a peaceful courtyard and pool area, heavy colonial-style wood furnishings in the rooms, and lots of tile and folk art in the decor. ✉ *Av. López Mateos (also called Calle 1) and Av. Castillo, Box 76, 22800,* ☎ *61/78–36–16,* FAX *61/78–33–45. 58 rooms and suites. Restaurants, pool. MC, V.*

$$ 🏨 **San Nicolás.** Hidden behind cement walls painted with Indian murals, this massive resort doesn't look like much from the street. The San Nicolás was built in the early 1970s, but much of it has been refurbished. The suites have tiled hot tubs; living rooms with deep-green carpeting, mauve furnishings, and beveled-glass doors; and bedrooms with mirrored ceilings. The less extravagant rooms are comfortable and decorated with folk art. A waterfall cascades into the pool, and a good restaurant overlooks the gardens. Special rates are often available on weekdays and in the winter. ✉ *Av. López Mateos (also called Calle 1) and Av. Guadalupe, Box 19, 22800,* ☎ *61/76–19–01,* FAX *61/76–49–30; reservations in the U.S.:* ✉ *Box 43706, San Diego, CA 92143,* ☎ *619/491–0682. 150 rooms and suites. 2 restaurants, bar, 2 pools (1 indoor), hot tub, dance club. AE, MC, V.*

$$ 🏨 **Travelodge Ensenada.** Dependable, clean, and secure, this three-story hotel just off the main shopping street offers such comforts as in-room coffeemakers and safes and electronic door locks. The rooms, with brick ceilings and walls, feel old and dark, but carpeting and firm mattresses add warmth and comfort. ✉ *Av. Blancarte 130, Box 1467, 22800,* ☎ *61/78–16–01; 800/578–7878 for reservations in the U.S.;* FAX *61/74–00–05. 52 rooms and suites. Restaurant, pool, hot tub, parking. MC, V.*

$ 🏨 **Corona Hotel.** One of the few in-town hotels right by the water, the Corona is a favorite for bus-tour groups. Few rooms actually have a view of the water and most suffer a bit from lack of maintenance. But there is plenty of parking, the room rates are low, and most sights are within easy walking distance. ✉ *Blvd. Costero 1442, 22800,* ☎ *61/76–09–01,* FAX *61/76–40–23; reservations in the U.S.:* ✉ *482 San Ysidro Blvd., Suite 303, San Ysidro, CA 92173. 90 rooms. Restaurant, pool. MC, V.*

$ 🏨 **Hotel del Valle.** Fishermen and budget travelers frequent the clean, basic rooms in this small hotel on a relatively quiet side street. Though the rooms lack air-conditioning they do have fans, phones, and televisions (with local stations only). Guests have use of a coffeemaker in the lobby and parking spaces in front of the rooms. Ask about rate discounts; the rates posted behind the front desk are about 40% higher than guests in the know normally pay. ✉ *Av. Riveroll 367, 22800,* ☎ *61/78–22–24,* FAX *61/74–04–66. 20 rooms. AE, MC, V.*

$ **Joker Hotel.** A bizarre, brightly colored mishmash of styles makes it hard to miss this hotel, conveniently located for those traveling south of Ensenada. Spacious rooms have private balconies, satellite TV, and phones. ✉ *Km 12.5 Mexico Hwy. 1, 22800,* ☎ FAX *61/76–72–01. 40 rooms. Pool, hot tub. MC, V.*

Nightlife and the Arts

Ensenada is a party town for college students, surfers, and other young tourists. **Hussong's Cantina** (✉ Av. Ruíz 113, ☎ 61/78–32–10) has been an Ensenada landmark since 1892 and has changed little since then. A security guard stands by the front door to handle the often-rowdy crowd—a mix of locals and tourists of all ages over 18. The noise is usually deafening, pierced by mariachi and ranchera musicians and the whoops and hollers of the inebriated. **Papas and Beer** (✉ Av. Ruíz at López Mateos, ☎ 61/78–42–31) is oriented toward the college set, who hang out the second-story windows shouting at their friends.

Outdoor Activities and Sports

FISHING

Boats leave the **Ensenada Sportfishing Pier** regularly. The best angling is from April through November, with bottom fishing good in the winter. Charter vessels and party boats are available from several outfitters along Avenida López Mateos, Boulevard Costero, and off the sportfishing pier. Trips on group boats cost about $35 for a half day or $100 for a full day. You can book sportfishing packages including transportation, accommodations, and fishing through **Baja California Tours** (☎ 619/454–7166 in the U.S.). Licenses are available at the tourist office or from charter companies. **Ensenada Clipper Fleet** (✉ Sportfishing Pier, ☎ 61/78–21–85) has charter and group boats. **Gordo's Sportfishing** (✉ Sportfishing Pier, ☎ 61/78–35–15, FAX 61/78–23–77), one of the oldest sportfishing companies in Ensenada, has charter boats, group boats, and a smokehouse. Gordo's also operates whale-watching trips from December through February.

GOLF

The **Baja Country Club** (✉ Hwy. 1 south of Ensenada at Maneadero, ☎ 61/73–03–03) has a secluded 18-hole course in a resort development.

Shopping

Most of the tourist shops are located along Avenida López Mateos beside the hotels and restaurants. There are several two-story shopping arcades, many with empty shops. Dozens of curio shops line the street, all selling similar selections of pottery, woven blankets and serapes, embroidered dresses, and onyx chess sets.

Artes Don Quijote (✉ Av. López Mateos 503, ☎ 61/76–94–76) has an impressive array of carved-wood doors, huge terra-cotta pots, crafts from Oaxaca, and large brass fish and birds. **Artesanías Castillo** (✉ Av. López Mateos 656, ☎ 61/76–11–87) and **Los Castillo** (✉ Av. López Mateos 815, ☎ 61/76–11–87) both have extensive displays of silver jewelry from Taxco. **Girasoles** (✉ Av. López Mateos, no phone) stocks a great selection of dolls, pine-needle baskets, and pottery made by the Tarahumara Indians from the Copper Canyon. **La Mina de Salomón** (✉ Av. López Mateos 1000, ☎ 61/78–28–36) carries elaborate jewelry in a tiny gallery next to El Rey Sol restaurant. **Carlos Importer** (✉ Av. López Mateos at Alvarado, ☎ 61/78–24–63) is one of the largest shops in town with high-quality pottery, tile, blown glassware, and iron furniture.

Centro Artesenal de Ensenada has a smattering of galleries and shops. The best by far is the **Galería de Pérez Meillón** (✉ Blvd. Costera 1094–39, ☎ 61/74–03–94), which carries museum-quality pottery and varied folk art by the indigenous peoples of northern Mexico. **La Esquina de Bodegas** (✉ Av. Miramar at Calle 6, ☎ 61/78–35–57) is an innovative gallery, shop, and café in a century-old winery building. Baja's finest wines are sold here at reasonable prices, and an upstairs gallery features some fine glassware, pottery, and books. The small café at the back of the building serves coffees, wines, and a small menu of soups and entrées.

Tecate

32 km (20 mi) east of Tijuana, 112 km (70 mi) northeast of Ensenada.

Tecate is a quiet community, a typical small Mexican town (population about 100,000) that happens to be on the border. So incidental is the border to local life that its gates are closed from 10 PM until 6 AM. Tecate beer, one of the most popular brands in Mexico, is brewed here. Maquiladoras and agriculture are the other main industries. Tecate's primary tourist draw is Rancho la Puerta, a fitness resort that caters to well-heeled southern Californians. A bit farther south, the valleys of Guadalupe and Calafía boast some of Mexico's lushest vineyards. Olives and grain are also grown in profusion here.

If you allocate an hour for exploring Tecate, you'll be hard put to fill your time. **Parque Hidalgo,** in the center of town, is a typical Mexican village plaza, with a small gazebo and a few wrought-iron benches. On summer evenings, dance and band concerts are held in **Parque López Mateos,** on Highway 3 south of town.

Dining and Lodging

$$ ✕ **El Passetto.** The best Italian restaurant in Tecate, El Passetto has superb garlic bread and homemade pasta. The proprietor makes his own wines, and they're pretty good. There's live music on weekends. ✉ *Callejón Libertad 200,* ☎ *665/4–13–61. MC, V.*

$ ✕ **Plaza Jardin.** The setting is plain and the food simple Mexican fare, but the café tables outside offer a gratifying view of the plaza. ✉ *Callejón Libertad 274,* ☎ *665/4–34–53. No credit cards.*

$$$$ **Rancho la Puerta.** This peaceful, isolated health spa and resort, just west of Tecate, is nice—for those who can afford $1,600 or more a week. Spanish-style buildings with red-tile roofs and modern glass-and-wood structures are spread throughout the sprawling ranch. Hiking trails lead off into scrub-pine hills surrounding the resort, and a large bright-blue pool is a central gathering spot. Guests stay in luxurious private cottages and usually check in for a week or more, taking advantage of the special diet and exercise regimen to lose weight and shape up. Transportation is available to and from the San Diego airport. ✉ *Hwy. 2, 5 km (3 mi) west of Tecate, 21275,* ☎ *665/4–11–55 or 800/443–7565; 619/744–4222 in CA;* FAX *665/4–11–08. 80 rooms. Restaurant, pool, beauty salon, massage, 4 tennis courts, health club. AE, MC, V.*

$$ **Hacienda Santa Veronica.** Billed as an off-road and dirt-racing country club, the Hacienda is a pretty countryside resort whose rooms are furnished with Mexican colonial beds, bureaus, and fireplaces. The off-road raceway is sufficiently far away from the rooms to keep the noise of revving engines from disturbing the guests, and a number of trails for horseback riding traverse the property. ✉ *Hwy. 2, 3 km (2*

mi) east of Tecate, 21275, no phone; ☎ *619/298–4105 or 800/522–1516 reservations in the U.S. 87 rooms. Restaurant, bar, pool, 2 tennis courts, horseback riding. MC, V.*

Mexicali

136 km (85 mi) east of Tijuana.

Mexicali, with a current population estimated at 850,000, shares the Imperial Valley farmland and the border crossing with Calexico, a small California city. The capital of Baja California, Mexicali sees a great deal of government activity and a steady growth of maquiladoras. Though water is scarce in these largely desert lands, the Mexicali area is blessed with some of the world's richest topsoil, and agriculture is a primary source of income in this section of Mexico. Mexicali is not a tourist destination but rather a place where politicians and bureaucrats meet.

Most visitors come to town on business, and the city's sights are few and far between. A tourist-oriented strip of curio shops and sleazy bars is located along Avenida Francisco Madero, one block south of the border. The **Museo del Estado** (State Museum), administered by the Autonomous University of Baja California (UABC), provides a comprehensive introduction to the natural and cultural history of Baja. ⊠ *Av. Reforma 1998, near Calle L,* ☎ *65/52–57–17.* 🎫 *Free.* ⏲ *Tues.–Sat. 9–6, Sun. 10–2.*

Parque Obregón at Avenida Reforma and Calle Irigoyen and **Parque Constitución** at Avenida México and Zuazua are the only two parks in downtown Mexicali. The **Mexicali Zoo** is in the City Park, Bosque de la Ciudad, south of town; the entrance is at the south end of Calle Victoria, between Cárdenas and Avenida Independencia.

Dining and Lodging

$$ ✕🏨 **La Lucerna.** The prettiest hotel in Mexicali, the colonial-style La Lucerna has lots of palms and fountains around the pool and carved wood furnishings in the dark, somber rooms. A newer section offers suites with separate seating areas and more modern furnishings. The restaurant is pleasant and serene, with Mexican decor and good Mexican meals. ⊠ *Av. Benito Juárez 2151, 21270,* ☎ *65/66–10–00 or 800/582–3762,* FAX *65/66–47–06. 175 rooms, 28 suites. Restaurant, bar, coffee shop, pool. MC, V.*

$$$ 🏨 **Crowne Plaza.** This is the perennial favorite of those doing business in the city, with standard rooms and services and no surprises.The coffee shop and restaurant serve decent American and Mexican meals. ⊠ *Blvd. López Mathéos and Av. de los Heroes 201, 21270,* ☎ *65/57–3600; 800/227–6963 for reservations in the U.S.;* FAX *65/57–05–55. 158 rooms. Restaurant, bar, coffee shop, pool. AE, MC, V.*

Outdoor Activities and Sports

GOLF

You can tee off at the 18-hole **Mexicali Campestre Golf Course** (Km 11.5 Hwy. 5 south of town, ☎ 65/61–71–30).

San Felipe

198 km (124 mi) south of Mexicali, 244 km (151 mi) southeast of Ensenada.

San Felipe (population 18,000) is the quintessential dusty fishing village with one main street (two if you count the highway into town). The malecón runs along a broad beach facing the Sea of Cortés and

San Felipe Bay, with a swimming area in the middle and public changing rooms at the north end. Taco stands, bars, and restaurants line the sidewalk across the street from the beach. The only landmark in town is the **shrine of the Cerro de la Virgen** (Virgin of Guadalupe), at the north end of the malecón on a hill overlooking the sea.

Not until 1948, when the first paved road from the northern capital was completed, did San Felipe become a significant town; until then only a few fishermen and their families lived along the coast. Now it is home to an impressive fishing and shrimping fleet. **Bahía San Felipe** has dramatic changes in its tides. They crest at 20 ft, and because the beach is so shallow, the waterline can move in and out up to 1 km (about ½ mi). The local fishermen are well aware of the peculiarities of this section of the Sea of Cortés. Many of them visit the shrine of Guadalupe before setting sail.

A getaway spot for years, San Felipe used to be a place where hardy travelers in RVs and campers hid out for weeks on end. Now there are at least two dozen campgrounds and a dozen hotels in town and on the coastline both north and south of town, which fill up quickly during the winter and spring holidays. Dune buggies, motorcycles, and off-road vehicles abound. On holiday weekends San Felipe can be boisterous, but most of the time it's a quiet, relaxing place. The town also draws many sportfishermen, especially in the spring; launches, bait, and supplies are readily available.

Dining and Lodging

$$ ✕ **George's.** A favorite with resident Americans, George's has comfy padded red Naugahyde booths, powerful margaritas, and very good chiles rellenos, carne asada, and seafood. ✉ *Av. Mar de Cortés 336,* ☎ *657/7–10–57. MC, V.*

$ ✕ **El Toro.** Open only for breakfast, El Toro is renowned among locals and San Felipe regulars for its chorizo, *machaca* (marinated shredded beef), *huevos rancheros* (fried eggs served on a corn tortilla and covered with a tomato, onion, and green-pepper sauce), and American-style breakfasts. The parking lot fills with trailers hauling dune buggies and motorcycles as large groups gather to fuel up before a long day on the dunes. ✉ *Hwy. 5 north of town,* ☎ *657/7–10–32. No credit cards.*

$ ✕ **Tony's Tacos.** The most popular of the many taco stands along the waterfront, Tony's is a simple spot with sidewalk picnic tables and a counter lined with condiments for the house specialty—cheap, delicious fish tacos. ✉ *Malecón at Av. Chetumal, no phone. No credit cards.*

$ ✕ **Viva Mexico.** This family-run operation (formerly called Juan's Place) two blocks east of the waterfront offers consistently excellent home-style cooking at reasonable prices. The catch of the day and grilled meats come with boiled vegetables—ask for beans, rice, and the delicious homemade tortillas instead. ✉ *Calle de Ensenada, no phone. No credit cards.*

$$$ **San Felipe Marina Resort.** This full-scale resort will eventually include a 100-slip marina along with resort homes and hotels, though construction has been delayed. At present, the low-slung terra-cotta building facing the sea has 60 units available as hotel rooms, time-share units, or private condos. Most rooms have kitchens with microwaves, coffeemakers, and refrigerators; woven rugs on white-tile floors and folk art decorations; and balconies or patios with sea views. The least expensive rooms lack kitchens and ocean views. The pool sits above the beach next to a palapa bar; a second indoor pool is a delight on cold winter days. The resort is a five-minute drive south of town and has an

RV campground with 1,434 spaces next door. ✉ *Km 4.5 Carretera San Felipe Aeropuerto, 21850,* ☎ *657/7–15–68 or 619/558–0295; 800/291–5397 in the U.S.;* FAX *657/7–14–55. 60 rooms. Restaurant, bar, 2 pools, 2 tennis courts, exercise room, shops. AE, MC, V.*

$$ **Costa Azul.** The Costa Azul is the largest hotel right in town, at the south end of the malecón. Several three-story buildings frame a parking lot and pool area, and the restaurant and bar are in a two-story building on the beach. The rooms are far from spectacular, but the location can't be beat. Monday through Wednesday, room rates are almost 20% lower. ✉ *Av. Mar de Cortés at Calle Ensenada, 21850,* ☎ *657/1–15–49; reservations in the U.S.:* ✉ *233 Pauline Ave., No. 6252, Calexico, CA 92231. 140 rooms. Restaurant, bar, pool. MC, V.*

$$ **Las Misiones.** A pretty oasis of blue pools and green palms by the beach, this resort is big with group tours. It's also a good choice for travelers who want to get away from it all—but you'll need a car or cab to get to town. A building just down the street from the hotel contains suites with kitchens. ✉ *Av. Misión de Loreto 130, 21850,* ☎ *657/7–12–80 or 800/464–4270; 800/664–7466 or 800/336–5454 for reservations in the U.S.;* FAX *657/7–12–83. 185 rooms, 32 suites. Restaurant, bar, 2 pools, 2 tennis courts. AE, MC, V.*

$ **El Cortez.** Easily the most popular hotel in San Felipe, the El Cortez has several types of accommodations, including moderately priced bungalows and modern hotel rooms with white walls, pastel bedspreads and drapes, and white-tile floors; some have two bedrooms. The hotel's beachfront and second-story bars are both enduringly beloved, and the restaurant is the nicest water-view dining spot in town. The hotel is a five-minute walk from the malecón. ✉ *Av. Mar de Cortez s/n, 21850,* ☎ *657/7–10–56,* FAX *657/7–10–55; reservations in the U.S.:* ✉ *Box 1227, Calexico, CA 92232. 102 rooms. Restaurant, bar, pool. MC, V.*

Outdoor Activities and Sports

FISHING

The Sea of Cortés offers plentiful sea bass, snapper, corbina, halibut, and other game fish. Clamming is good here as well. Several companies offer sportfishing trips; among the most established are **Alex Sportfishing** (☎ 657/7–10–52), **Pelicanos** (☎ 657/7–11–88), and **San Felipe Sportfishing** (☎ 657/7–10–55). **Del Mar Cortés Charters** (✉ Box 9, San Felipe 21850, ☎ 657/7–13–03) conducts fishing trips, full- and half-day trimaran tours of the Sea of Cortés, and boat charters. It can also arrange kayak and Hobie Cat rentals through the El Dorado private community north of town. **Enchanted Island Excursions** (✉ 233 Paulin 8512, Calexico, CA 92231, ☎ 657/7–14–31, FAX 657/7–11–38) offers off-road, dune-buggy tours in addition to boat excursions.

San Quintín

191 km (118 mi) south of Ensenada.

Agricultural fields line the highway as you enter San Quintín, the largest producer of tomatoes in Baja. The Oaxacan migrant workers who plant and pick the fertile valley's produce live in squalid camps out of the view of travelers, many of whom are towing boats behind their Suburbans. The **Bahía de San Quintín** is one of northern Baja's best fishing grounds, and the area's few hostelries have been steadily improving their facilities. Travelers en route farther south typically stop at the roadside markets for ice and other essentials and to lunch on clams from nearby mudflats. Explorers turn down sandy side roads to windswept coves and isolated hideaways.

Lodging

$$ **Rancho Sereno.** A real find for the escapist traveler, this three-bedroom bed-and-breakfast has the feeling of a comfy home inhabited by Baja experts. The bedrooms have individual patio entrances and adjacent bathrooms; some have kitchens and fireplaces. Guests gather in the large rec room, where a fireplace, kitchen, books, and games offer simple, countrified diversions. The ranch runs on a private generator, ensuring uninterrupted electricity. Trails lead through the trees and chaparral; the bay is 3 km (2 mi) east. Breakfast is included in the rate, and San Quintín has many good cafés for seafood and down-home Mexican cooking. ✉ *2 km (1 mi) west of Hwy. 1 on north side of town,* ☎ *617/1–44–75; reservations in the U.S.:* ✉ *1442 Hildita Ct., Upland, CA 91786,* ☎ *909/982–7087. 33 rooms. No credit cards.*

$ **Old Mill.** Anglers ease their boats into the sheltered bay at this longtime favorite hideaway and set up housekeeping in a variety of rooms, some with kitchens and fireplaces. Others arrive in RVs. The lodge-style bar with its huge fireplace is filled with locals and travelers on weekend nights, and the restaurant serves hearty meals including thick steaks and generous Mexican combo plates. ✉ *South of town on a dirt road leading to the bay, no local phone;* ☎ *619/428–2779 or 800/479–7962,* FAX *619/428–6269 for reservations in the U.S. 28 rooms. Restaurant, bar, camping, fishing. No credit cards at resort, but MC and V accepted with advance reservations.*

BAJA NORTE A TO Z

Arriving and Departing

By Bus

Greyhound (☎ 619/239–1288 or 800/231–2222) serves Tijuana from San Diego several times daily; the Greyhound terminal in Tijuana is at Avenida Mexico at Calle 11 (☎ 66/86–06–95). **Five Star Tours/Mexicoach** (☎ 619/232–5049) runs buses from the trolley depot on the U.S. side of the border to their depot on Avenida Revolución in Tijuana. **ABC–US** (☎ 66/26–11–46) runs buses from the San Ysidro trolley stop to downtown Tijuana, Pueblo Amigo, Plaza Rio Tijuana, and the Agua Caliente racetrack.

Buses connect all the towns in Baja Norte and are easy to use. Buses traveling to Rosarito no longer stop in town, but instead stop at the Rosarito exit on the toll road where taxis are waiting to transport passengers to town. There is no official bus station here; check at the hotels for bus schedule information.

Autotransportes de Baja California covers the entire Baja route and connects in Mexicali with buses to Guadalajara and Mexico City. **Elite** has first-class service to mainland Mexico. **Transportes del Pacífico** goes to Mexico City and other points on the mainland from Mexicali; **Transportes Norte de Sonora** frequents border towns in Baja and on mainland Mexico.

Bus stations in Baja Norte are **Ensenada** (✉ Av. Riveroll between Calles 10 and 11, ☎ 61/78–67–70 or 61/78–66–80), **Mexicali** (✉ Centro Cívico, Av. Independencia, ☎ 65/57–24–22), **San Felipe** (✉ Av. Mar Caribe at Av. Manzanillo, ☎ 657/7–15–16), **Tecate** (✉ Av. Benito Juárez and Calle Abelardo Rodríguez, ☎ 665/4–12–21), and **Tijuana** (✉ Calzada Lázaro Cárdenas and Blvd. Arroyo Alamar, ☎ 66/21–29–82).

By Car

From San Diego, U.S. 5 and I–805 end at the border crossing into Tijuana at San Ysidro; Highway 905 leads from I–5 and I–805 to the Tijuana border crossing at Otay Mesa, near the Tijuana airport. U.S. 94 from San Diego connects with U.S. 188 to the border at Tecate, 57 km (35 mi) east of San Diego. I–8 from San Diego connects with U.S. 111 at Calexico—203 km (126 mi) east—and the border crossing to Mexicali. San Felipe lies on the coast, 200 km (125 mi) south of Mexicali via Highway 5.

To head south into Baja from Tijuana, follow the signs for Ensenada Cuota, the toll road (also called Highway 1 and on newer signs the Scenic Highway) that runs south along the coast. There are two clearly marked exits for Rosarito Beach, and one for Puerto Nuevo, Bajamar, and Ensenada. The road is excellent, though it has some hair-raising curves atop the cliffs and is best driven in daylight (the stretch from Rosarito Beach to Ensenada is one of the most scenic drives in Baja). Tollbooths accept U.S. and Mexican currency; tolls are usually about $1.60. Rest rooms are available near the booths. The alternate free road—Highway 1D or Ensenada Libre—has been vastly improved, but it is difficult for the first-timer to navigate. Highway 1 continues south of Ensenada through San Quintín to Guerrero Negro at the border between Baja California and Baja Sur and on to the southernmost tip of Baja; it is no longer a toll road past Ensenada, however.

Mexico Highway 2 runs from Tijuana to Tecate and Mexicali. A toll road between Tijuana and Tecate opened in 1994, and another was completed between Tecate and Mexicali in 1995. The 134-km (84-mi) journey from Tecate east to Mexicali on La Rumorosa, as the road is known, is as exciting as a roller-coaster ride, with the highway twisting and turning down steep mountain grades and over flat, barren desert.

Visitors traveling only as far as Ensenada or San Felipe do not need tourist cards unless they are staying longer than 72 hours. If you know you'll be traveling south of Ensenada, you can get the form at the **Tijuana Convention and Tourism Bureau** (✉ Inside San Ysidro border crossing, ☎ 66/83–1405 or 66/84–7790). You must have Mexican auto insurance, available at agencies near the border.

Many car-rental companies do not allow their cars to be driven into Mexico (☞ Car Rentals, *below*).

By Plane

Tijuana's Aeropuerto Alberado Rodriguez is located on the eastern edge of the city, near the Otay Mesa border crossing, and is served from cities in Baja and mainland Mexico by **Mexicana** (☎ 66/83–28–50), **Aeromexico** (☎ 66/85–44–01), **AeroCalifornia** (☎ 66/84–21–00 or 66/84–28–76), and **Taesa** (☎ 66/84–84–84). Mexicali's international airport is served by **Mexicana** (☎ 65/52–93–91) and **Aeromexico** (☎ 65/57–25–51).

By Trolley

The **San Diego Trolley** (☎ 619/233–3004) travels from the Santa Fe Depot, at Kettner Boulevard and Broadway, to within 100 ft of the border every 15 minutes from 5 AM to midnight. The 45-minute trip costs $1.75.

Getting Around

By Bus

In **Tijuana,** the downtown station for buses within the city is at Calle 1a and Avenida Madero (☎ 66/86–95–15). Most city buses at the border will take you downtown; look for the ones marked CENTRO CAMIONERA. To catch the bus back to the border from downtown, go to Calle Benito Juárez (also called Calle 2a) between Avenidas Revolución and Constitución. **Five Star Tours/Mexicoach** (☎ 619/232–5049) runs buses from the trolley depot on the U.S. side of the border to their depot on Avenida Revolución in Tijuana. *Colectivos* (small vans usually painted white with colored stripes) cover neighborhood routes in most Baja cities and towns. The destination is usually painted on the windshield; look for them on main streets.

By Car

The best way to tour Baja Norte is by car, though the driving can be difficult and confusing at times. If you're just visiting Tijuana, Tecate, or Mexicali, it's easiest to park on the U.S. side of the border and walk across.

The combination of overpopulation, lack of infrastructure, and heavy winter rains makes many of **Tijuana**'s streets difficult to navigate by automobile. It's always best to stick to the main thoroughfares. There are parking lots along Avenida Revolución and at most major attractions. Most of **Rosarito Beach** proper can be explored on foot, which is a good idea on weekends, when Boulevard Juárez has bumper-to-bumper traffic. To reach **Puerto Nuevo** and other points south, continue on Boulevard Juárez (also called Old Ensenada Highway and Ensenada Libre) through town. Most of **Ensenada**'s attractions are situated within five blocks of the waterfront; it is easy to take a long walking tour of the city. A car is necessary to reach La Bufadora and most of the beaches. When driving farther south to **San Quintín, Guerrero Negro,** and **Baja Sur,** be sure to fill up your gas tank when it's half full. Few towns appear on the highway, and you quickly have the feeling you are headed into the unknown (unless you're following a caravan of RVs). Don't drive at night, and watch your speed. You never know when a pothole or *arroyo* (riverbed) will challenge your driving skills.

By Train

Although there is no train service available through Baja, **El Tren del Pacífico** (✉ Estación de Ferrocarril, Box 3-182, Mexicali, Baja California, Mexico, ☎ 65/57–23–86) runs rather uncomfortable trains (no private compartments) from Mexicali to points south in the mainland interior. The station is located at the south end of Calle Ulises Irigoyen, a few blocks north of the intersection of Avenida López Mateos and Avenida Independencia.

Contacts and Resources

Car Rental

Avis (☎ 800/331–1212) permits its cars to go from San Diego into Baja as far as 724 km (450 mi) south of the border. Cars must be returned by the renter to San Diego, and Mexican auto insurance is mandatory. Cars leased from **Courtesy Rentals** (✉ 2975 Pacific Hwy., San Diego, CA 92101, ☎ 619/497–4800 or 800/252–9756) may be taken as far as Ensenada. **M&M Jeeps** (✉ 2200 El Cajon Blvd., San Diego, CA 92104, ☎ 619/297–1615, FAX 619/297–1617) rents two- and four-wheel-drive vehicles with packages covering tours of the entire Baja California peninsula.

ENSENADA

Fiesta Rent-a-Car (☎ 61/76–33–44) has an office in the Hotel Corona at Boulevard Costero; **Hertz** (☎ 61/78–29–82) is on Avenida Blancarte between Calles 1 and 2.

TIJUANA

The larger U.S. rental agencies have offices at the Tijuana International Airport. Offices in town include **Avis** (✉ Av. Agua Caliente 3310, ☎ 66/86-40-04 or 66/86-37-18), and **Budget** (✉ Paseo de los Héroes 77, ☎ 66/34-33-03).

Emergencies

THROUGHOUT BAJA NORTE

Police (☎ 134), **Red Cross** (☎ 132), and **Fire** (☎ 136).

TIJUANA

U.S. Consulate (☎ 66/81-74-00). The **Attorney General for the Protection of Tourists Hot Line** (☎ 66/88-05-55) takes calls weekdays to help with tourist complaints and problems.

Guided Tours

Baja California Tours (✉ 7734 Herschel Ave., Suite O, La Jolla, CA 92037, ☎ 619/454-7166, FAX 619/454-2703) offers comfortable, informative bus trips throughout Baja and can arrange special-interest tours, including shopping, culture, whale-watching and fishing trips, and tours to the wineries and La Bufadora. They also offer adventure tours to Meling Ranch, a working ranch in the San Pedro Martir mountains about 240 km (150 mi) south of the border. **San Diego Mini-Tours** (✉ 1726 Wilson Ave., National City, CA 91950, ☎ 619/477-8687 or 800/235-5393, FAX 619/477-0705) has frequent departures throughout the day from San Diego hotels to Avenida Revolución in Tijuana and back.

Language Classes

A great way to get to know Ensenada and simultaneously improve your Spanish is to attend weekend or weeklong classes at the **International Spanish Institute of Ensenada** (☎ 61/76-01-09; 619/755-7044 in CA).

Reservation Agencies

Several companies specialize in arranging hotel reservations in Baja Norte. Contact **Baja Information** (✉ 7860 Mission Center Ct., Suite 202, San Diego, CA 92108, ☎ 619/298-4105; 800/225-2786 in the U.S., Canada, Puerto Rico; 800/522-1516 in CA, NV, AZ; FAX 619/294-7366); **Baja California Tours** (✉ 7734 Herschel Ave., Suite O, La Jolla, CA 92037, ☎ 619/454-7166, FAX 619/454-2703); **Baja Lodging** (☎ 619/491-0682); and **Mexico Resorts International** (✉ 4126 Bonita Rd., Bonita, CA 91902, ☎ 619/422-6900 or 800/336-5454, FAX 619/472-6778).

Travel Club

A monthly newsletter, Mexican auto insurance, Baja tours, and workshops are available through **Discover Baja Travel Club** (✉ 3089 Clairemont Dr., San Diego, CA 92117, ☎ 619/275-4225 or 800/727-2252, FAX 619/275-1836).

Visitor Information

Regional tourist offices are usually open Monday through Friday from 9 to 7 (though some may close in early afternoon for lunch), and Saturday and Sunday from 9 to 1: **Ensenada** (✉ Blvd. Costera 1477, ☎ 61/72-30-22, FAX 61/72-30-81; ✉ Blvd. Costera at entrance to town, ☎ 61/78-24-11), **Mexicali** (✉ Convention and Tourism Bureau, Calz. López Mateos at Calle Compresora, ☎ 65/52-23-76; ✉ State Secretary of Tourism Office, Calle Calafia at Calz. Independencia, ☎ 65/56-10-72), **Rosarito Beach** (✉ Blvd. Juárez, 2nd floor of Quinta Plaza shopping center, ☎ 661/2-03-96 or 661/2-30-78), **San Felipe** (✉ Av. Mar de Cortés, ☎ 657/7-11-55 or 657/7-18-65), **Tecate** (✉ Callejón Libertad, ☎ 665/4-10-95), **Tijuana Chamber of Commerce**

(✉ Av. Revolución and Calle 1, ☎ 66/88–16–85), and the **Tijuana Convention and Tourism Bureau** (✉ Inside San Ysidro border crossing, ☎ 66/83–14–05 or 66/84–77–90; ✉ Av. Revolución between Calles 3 and 4, ☎ 66/83–05–30).

BAJA SUR

Baja Sur was nearly inaccessible by land until the 1,708-km-long (1,059-mi-long) Transpeninsular Highway, also called Mexico Highway 1, was completed in 1973. Until then, commerce was conducted via boats from mainland Mexico, across the Sea of Cortés. After the paved, four-lane road was completed, travelers gradually found their way south, drawn by the wild terrain and the pristine beaches along the Pacific Ocean and Sea of Cortés coastlines. In 1974, Baja California Sur became Mexico's 30th state, and the population and tourism began to increase. Still, Baja Sur remains a mysterious and largely undeveloped land. Highway 1, which travels through some of the most desolate desert and mountains imaginable, could hardly be called a freeway. Most travelers still make their way here via plane.

Whale-watching draws winter visitors to Guerrero Negro, Scammon's Lagoon, San Ignacio Lagoon, and Magdalena Bay. History buffs enjoy Loreto, where Padre Eusebio Kino established the first mission in the Californias. La Paz, today a busy governmental center and sportfishing city, was the Spaniard's first settlement in Baja. At the southernmost tip of the peninsula, where the Pacific Ocean and the Sea of Cortés merge, fishing aficionados, golfers, and sun worshippers flock to Los Cabos, one of Mexico's most popular coastal resorts.

Guerrero Negro and Scammon's Lagoon

720 km (450 mi) south of Tijuana, 771 km (479 mi) northwest of La Paz.

Humans aren't the only travelers who migrate below the border in the winter months. Every January through March, thousands of great gray whales swim 8,000 km (6,000 mi) south from the Bering Strait, off Alaska, to the tip of the Baja Peninsula. For those few months, travelers come from all over the world to Guerrero Negro and a few bays and lagoons farther south. Up to 6,000 whales stop close to the shore at several spots along the Baja coast, including Scammon's Lagoon—at the 28th parallel, just over the state line between Baja California and Baja Sur—to give birth to their calves. Far from diminutive, the newborns weigh about half a ton and drink nearly 50 gallons of milk each day.

If it weren't for the whales and the Transpeninsular Highway, which runs near town, few travelers would venture to **Guerrero Negro** (☞ Baja California [North] map), a town of 10,000. Those traveling south can easily bypass the town. The name Guerrero Negro, which means Black Warrior, was derived from a whaling ship that ran aground in nearby Scammon's Lagoon in 1858. Near the Vizcaíno desert, on the Pacific Ocean, the area is best known for its salt mines, which provide work for much of the town's population and produce one-third of the world's salt supply. Saltwater collects in more than 780 square km (300 square mi) of sea-level ponds and evaporates quickly in the desert heat, leaving huge blocks of pure white salt. The town is dusty, windy, and generally unpleasant, though it is a favored destination for the osprey, a hawklike bird of prey that can be found building huge nests on power poles around town.

Baja California (South)

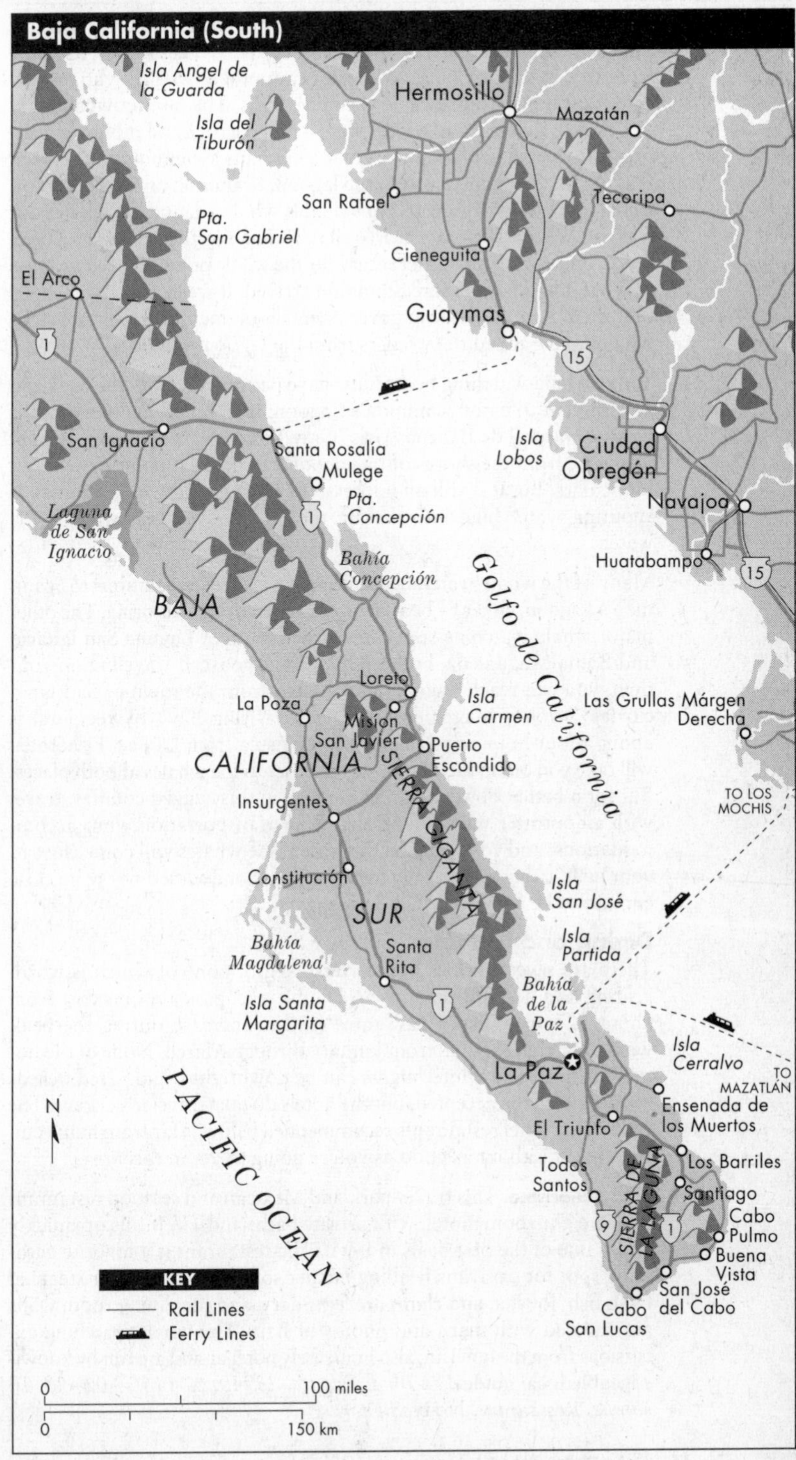
Isla Angel de la Guarda
Isla del Tiburón
Hermosillo
Mazatán
San Rafael
Tecoripa
Pta. San Gabriel
Cieneguita
El Arco
Guaymas
1
15
San Ignacio
Santa Rosalía
Mulege
Isla Lobos
Ciudad Obregón
Navajoa
Laguna de San Ignacio
Pta. Concepción
1
Bahía Concepción
Golfo de California
Huatabampo
15
BAJA
Loreto
La Poza
Misión San Javier
Isla Carmen
Las Grullas Márgen Derecha
Puerto Escondido
CALIFORNIA
SIERRA GIGANTA
TO LOS MOCHIS
Insurgentes
Constitución
Isla San José
SUR
Bahía Magdalena
Santa Rita
Isla Partida
Bahía de la Paz
Isla Santa Margarita
1
Isla Cerralvo
TO MAZATLÁN
La Paz
PACIFIC OCEAN
N
Ensenada de los Muertos
El Triunfo
Los Barriles
Todos Santos
Santiago
SIERRA DE LA LAGUNA
9
1
Cabo Pulmo
Buena Vista
KEY
Rail Lines
Ferry Lines
San José del Cabo
Cabo San Lucas
0
100 miles
0
150 km

Scammon's Lagoon is about 27 km (17 mi) south, down a passable but rough sand road that crosses the salt flats. The lagoon got its name from U.S. explorer Charles Melville Scammon of Maine, who discovered it off the coast of Baja in the mid-1800s. The mother whales and calves that visited these waters were a much easier and more plentiful prey for the whalers than the great leviathans swimming in the open sea. On his first expedition to the lagoon, Scammon and his crew collected more than 700 barrels of valuable whale oil, and the whale rush was on. Within 10 years, nearly all the whales in the lagoon had been killed, and it took almost a century for the whale population to increase to what it had been before Scammon arrived. It wasn't until the 1940s that the U.S. and Mexican governments took measures to protect the whales and banned the whalers from the lagoon.

Today whale-watching boats must have permission from the Mexican government to enter Scammon's Lagoon, now a national park called **Parque Natural de Ballenas Gris** (Gray Whale Natural Park). Whale-watching from the shores of the lagoon can be disappointing without binoculars. But it is still an impressive sight to see the huge mammals spouting water high into the air, their 12-ft-wide tails striking the water.

Many of the whale-watching tour operators offer expeditions to Scammon's Lagoon, either by boat or motor coach from California. The other major whale-watching spots are farther south at **Laguna San Ignacio** and **Bahía Magdalena,** both on the Pacific coast. If traveling on your own, you can reach Laguna San Ignacio from the town of San Ignacio (☞ *below*); Magdalena Bay (called "Mag Bay" by regulars) is about a four-hour drive across the peninsula from La Paz. Fishermen will take you out in their boats to get closer to the whales at both places. But for a better view, and an easier stay in this rugged country, travel with an outfitter who will arrange your transportation, your accommodations, and your time on the water. The whales will come close to your boat, rising majestically from the water, and sometimes swim close enough to be petted on their backs.

Dining and Lodging

There are several hotels in Guerrero Negro, none of which is worth visiting as a destination in itself. Double-occupancy rooms cost from about $25 to $70 per day; rates tend to increase during the peak whale-watching season from January through March. None of the hotels has heat, and winter nights can be downright frigid. Credit cards are not normally accepted, but the hotels do take traveler's checks. The food in the hotel restaurants recommended below is far from haute cuisine, but it's about as good as you're going to get in this area.

$ ✕ **Malarrimo.** This trailer park and Mexican and seafood restaurant has an eight-room motel, with private baths and TV. It fills up quickly and is one of the best deals in town. The restaurant is a favorite gathering spot for caravans heading farther south. The grilled or steamed fresh fish, lobster, and clams are legendary, and the dining room walls are covered with maps and photos of Baja. The whale-watching excursions from the hotel are also immensely popular and are run by knowledgeable local guides. ✉ *Blvd. Zapata, 23940,* ☎ *115/7–02–50. 10 rooms. Restaurant. No credit cards.*

$$ **La Pinta.** A few kilometers outside of town and looking like an oasis of palms in the desert, La Pinta is the largest hotel in the area. The clean, functional rooms are dependable, the setting more attractive than that of other local lodgings, and the American-Mexican restaurant decent, but the rates are high for the area. Package deals are sometimes avail-

able for travelers using the La Pinta hotels throughout the peninsula. Whale-watching excursions can be arranged here. ✉ *La Pinta Hwy. 1 at 28th parallel, Domicilio Conocido, 23940,* ☎ *115/7–13–01 or 800/542–3283; 800/336–5454 for reservations in the U.S.;* FAX *115/7–13–06. 26 rooms. Restaurant. MC, V.*

San Ignacio

227 km (142 mi) southeast of Guerrero Negro.

This small town is set in an oasis by a lovely river. The **Spanish mission** on the town square is one of the best preserved on the peninsula. Some groups use the hotels in town as a base for whale-watching trips to Laguna San Ignacio and Magdalena Bay.

Lodging

$$ **La Pinta.** If the room rates weren't so high, this small hotel would be a wonderful Baja hideaway. White arches frame the courtyard and pool, and the rooms are decorated with folk art and wood furnishings. Both the river and town are within walking distance. The hotel staff can set up whale-watching trips with local guides. ✉ *2 km (1 mi) west of Hwy. 1 on unnamed road into town, Apdo. 37, 23943, no phone;* ☎ *800/336–5454 or 800/542–3283 for reservations in the U.S. 28 rooms. Restaurant, bar, pool. No credit cards.*

Santa Rosalia

77 km (48 mi) southeast of San Ignacio.

You'll find a fascinating mix of French, Mexican, and American Old West–style architecture in the dusty mining town of Santa Rosalia. It's known for its **Iglesia Santa Barbara,** a prefabricated iron church designed by Alexandre-Gustave Eiffel, creator of the Eiffel Tower. Be sure to stop by **El Boleo** (✉ Av. Obregón at Calle 4), the best-known bakery in Baja, where fresh breads bring a lineup of eager customers weekday mornings at 10.

Mulege

64 km (40 mi) south of Santa Rosalia.

Once a mission settlement and now a charming tropical town set beside a river flowing into the Sea of Cortés, Mulege has become a popular destination for travelers who are interested in exploring the nearby mountains and for kayakers drawn to **Bahía Concepción,** the largest protected bay in Baja. The village of some 5,000 residents swells in the winter months, when Americans and Canadians escaping the winter cold arrive in their motor homes. There are several campgrounds outside town, and a few good hotels and restaurants both in town and along the coast.

Lodging

$ **Hacienda.** Guests read and lounge in rocking chairs by the pool or at stools along the bar at this small, comfortable hotel. Special festivities include paella nights, pig roasts, and trips to the nearby cave paintings in the mountains. Even when other hotels in the area are nearly empty, the Hacienda is filled with European travelers attracted by the ambience and incredibly low (by Baja standards) room rates. ✉ *Calle Madero, 23900,* ☎ FAX *115/3–00–21. 18 rooms. Restaurant, bar, pool, travel services. No credit cards.*

Outdoor Activities and Sports

KAYAKING

Baja Tropicales (✉ Box 60, Mulege, BCS 23900, ☎ 115/3–04–09, FAX 115/3–01–90) offers kayaks, wet suits, and other gear and several types of kayaking tours, including day trips and overnighters in the area of Mulege; whale-watching trips on the Pacific coast are also available.

Loreto

134 km (84 mi) south of Mulege.

On the Sea of Cortés, Loreto's setting is truly spectacular. The gold and green hills of the Sierra Gigante seem to tumble into the cobalt sea. Rain is rare. According to the local promoters, the skies are clear 360 days of the year. There are few bugs to plague vacationers. The dry, desert climate is not one in which insects thrive.

Loreto was the site of the first California mission, founded in 1697 by Jesuit Father Juan María Salvatierra. In 1769 Father Junípero Serra, a Franciscan monk from Mallorca, Spain, set out from Loreto to establish a chain of missions from San Diego to San Francisco, in the land then known as Alta California. Four Indian tribes—the Kikiwa, Cochimi, Cucapa, and Kumyaii—inhabited the barren lands of Baja when Father Salvatierra arrived; it didn't take long for war and European diseases to nearly obliterate them.

Mexico won its independence from Spain in 1821, and the missions were gradually abandoned. The priests, who often were from Spain, were ordered to return home. Loreto had been the administrative as well as the religious center of the Californias, but with the withering of the mission and the 1829 hurricane that virtually destroyed the settlement, the capital of the Californias was moved to La Paz. A severe earthquake struck the Loreto area in 1877, further demolishing the town.

For a century the village languished. The U.S. fishermen who rediscovered Loreto were a hearty breed who flew down in their own aircraft and went after marlin and sailfish in open launches. Loreto's several small hotels were built to serve this rough-and-ready set; most of the properties were built before 1960, when no highway came down this far and there was no airport worthy of the name.

In 1976, when the coffers were filled with oil revenue, the government tapped the Loreto area for development. Streets were paved in the dusty little village, and telephone service, electricity, potable water, and sewage systems were installed in both the town and the surrounding area; even an international airport was built. A luxury hotel and championship tennis center were opened in Nopoló, about 8 km (5 mi) south of town. Then the money dried up, investors could no longer be found, and everything came to a halt. A second surge of development occurred in the early 1990s, when the government invested in an 18-hole golf course at the edge of the sea in Nopoló.

Today Loreto, with a population of 15,000, is a good place to escape the crowds, relax, and go fishing. The fears of sports enthusiasts that the town would be spoiled have thus far been largely unfounded, though the residential trailer parks are filling up and private homes are clustered in secluded enclaves. Loreto is much the way it was decades ago, except that now it is more accessible.

One could allocate 15 minutes for a tour of downtown Loreto and still have time left over. The renovated **malecón,** built in 1991, has turned the waterfront into a pleasant place for a stroll: A marina houses the *panga* (small skiff) fleet and private yachts; the adjoining beach is a popular gathering spot for locals, especially on Sunday afternoons; and the beach playground has a great assortment of play equipment for children. The small plaza and town center is one block west of the waterfront, on Calle Salvatierra.

Loreto's only historic sight is **La Misión de Nuestra Señora de Loreto,** the first of the California missions. The carved stone walls, wood-beam ceilings, gilded altar, and primitive-style portraits of the priests who have served there are worth seeing. The **Museum of Anthropology and History,** also called El Museo de los Misiones (☎ 113/5–05–41), contains religious relics, tooled leather saddles used in the 19th century, and displays of Baja's history; it's next door to the mission; hours are erratic.

Nopoló, an area being developed for luxury resorts, is about 8 km (5 mi) south of Loreto. The nine-court tennis complex and 18-hole golf course are ready for play, and private homes are appearing in the neighborhood.

In **Puerto Escondido,** 16 km (10 mi) down the road from Nopoló, the marina contains more than 100 boat slips. An RV park, Tripui, has a good restaurant, a few motel rooms, a snack shop, a bar, stores, showers, a laundry, a pool, and tennis courts. A boat ramp has been completed at the marina; to pay the fee required to launch here, go to the port captain's offices (☎ 113/5–06–56, FAX 113/5–04–65), just south of the ramp; the offices are open weekdays 8–3. **Isla Danzante,** 5 km (3 mi) southeast of Puerto Escondido, has good diving and reefs.

Picnic trips to nearby **Coronado Island,** inhabited only by sea lions, may be arranged in Loreto at Nopoló or in Puerto Escondido. The snorkeling and scuba diving on the island are excellent.

Dining and Lodging

$$ ✕ **El Super Burro.** This large, palapa-covered restaurant a half block from the waterfront is as popular with locals as tourists. Meats are grilled at the front of the dining room, where cooks juggle take-out and dine-in orders. The Mexican combination plate isn't outstanding, but it is plentiful; a better choice is the fresh fish. Those on a budget can fill up on tacos or baked potatoes stuffed with cheese and meat. ✉ *Paseo Hidalgo between Madero and malecón, no phone. No credit cards.*

$$ ✕ **Embarcadero.** This restaurant's open-air deck looking out at the marina and beach is the perfect spot for catching up on the local fishing news. Alfredo's Sportfishing is next door, and anglers with their own boats in the marina often stop by for lunch. Fish tacos and grilled-fish dinners are the best choices. ✉ *Blvd. Mateos at Juárez,* ☎ *113/5–01–65. No credit cards.*

$ ✕ **Café Olé.** The best taquería in town also offers good burgers, ice-cream cones, chocolate shakes, and french fries. ✉ *Calle Francisco Madero,* ☎ *113/5–04–96. No credit cards.*

$$$$ 🏨 **Diamond Eden.** The former Presidente hotel in Nopoló has been remodeled and turned into an all-inclusive, adults-only resort. Part of a chain of Latin American and Caribbean resorts, the Diamond has the biggest pool in Loreto, a hot tub for 30, large rooms with ocean or garden views, and plenty of activities and buffet meals to keep guests happy. Part of the beach is clothing-optional (a novel concept in these parts), and the resort has been wildly popular; the chain uses charter flights and bargain packages to bring in large groups. The town of Loreto is a 10-minute drive away; taxis are available at the hotel. Ask about the all-inclusive package with air from Los Angeles—a real bargain. ✉ *Blvd. Mision, Nopoló 23880,* ☎ *113/3–07–00 or 800/858–2258,*

FAX 113/3-03-77. 245 rooms and suites. Restaurant, bar, pool, fishing, water sports. MC, V.

$$ **La Pinta.** Part of a chain of Baja California hotels, La Pinta is a collection of plain brick buildings housing spacious, air-conditioned rooms with satellite TVs. ✉ *Blvd. Misión de Loreto, 23880,* ☎ *113/5-00-25 or 800/542-3283; 800/336-5454 for reservations in the U.S.; FAX 113/5-00-26. 48 rooms. Restaurant, bar, pool, tennis court, fishing. MC, V.*

$$ **Oasis.** One of the original fishing camps, Oasis remains a favorite with those who want to spend as much time as possible on the water. Many of the rooms, set amid an oasis of palms, have a view of the water. The hotel has its own fleet of skiffs. ✉ *Calle de la Playa at Zaragoza, Box 17, 23880,* ☎ *113/5-01-12 or 800/662-7476, FAX 113/5-07-95. 35 rooms. Pool, tennis court, boating, fishing. MC, V.*

$$ ★ **Plaza Loreto.** Since its opening in 1992, the Plaza Loreto has garnered a loyal following of Loreto regulars who appreciate the comfortable rooms and prime downtown location near the old mission. The two-story hotel has an upstairs bar overlooking the street. The rooms are by far the best in town, with TVs, coffeemakers, and huge showers. Construction on the swimming pool has stopped, and although breakfast is served on the terrace, there is no full restaurant yet. ✉ *Paseo Hidalgo, 23880,* ☎ *FAX 113/5-08-55. 20 rooms. Bar. MC, V.*

$$ **Villas de Loreto.** New owners took over this long-defunct property in 1992 and created one of Loreto's nicest hideaways just south of town. There are 10 large rooms with refrigerators and front porches, along with a large swimming pool. An RV campground is behind the hotel buildings. Bikes are available for guests' use free of charge, and horseback riding, kayaks (for experienced paddlers), and fishing tours can be arranged. Continental breakfast is included in the room rate. To get here, turn right off Salvatierra onto Madero and drive across the dry riverbed to signs for the hotel. ✉ *Antonio Mijares at beach, 23880,* ☎ *FAX 113/5-05-86. 10 rooms. Pool, laundry service. MC, V.*

Outdoor Activities and Sports

FISHING

Fishing put Loreto on the map, especially for American sports enthusiasts. Cabrillo and snapper are caught year-round; yellowtail in the spring; and dorado, marlin, and sailfish in the summer. Visitors who plan to fish should bring tackle with them because top-notch gear can be difficult to find, though some sportfishing fleets do update their equipment regularly. All Loreto-area hotels can arrange fishing, and many own skiffs; the local fishermen congregate with their small boats on the beach at the north and south ends of town. **Alfredo's Sportfishing** (✉ Blvd. Mateos at Juárez, across from marina, ☎ 113/5-01-65, FAX 113/5-05-90) has good guides for anglers. **Arturo's Fishing Fleet** (✉ Calle Juárez and Callejón 2, 1 block from marina, ☎ 113/5-04-09) has several types of boats and fishing packages. **Sportsman's Tours** (☎ 800/234-0618) in the United States arranges bus and air tours to Loreto with fishing included.

GOLF

The first nine holes of the 18-hole **Loreto Campo de Golf** (☎ 113/5-07-88), located along Nopoló Bay at the south side of Fonatur's resort development, opened in 1991. Several hotels in Loreto offer golf packages and reduced or free greens fees.

TENNIS

The **Loreto Tennis Center** (☎ 113/5-07-00), 8 km (5 mi) south of Loreto, has nine courts open to the public.

Shopping

There are few opportunities for shopping in Loreto. Curios and T-shirts are available at shops at the hotels and downtown. **El Alacran,** which is in the small complex behind the church on Calle Salvatierra, has a remarkable selection of folk art, jewelry, and sportswear. You can also find some nice silver shops in this complex. Groceries and ice are available on Calle Salvatierra at **El Pescador,** the town's only supermarket.

La Paz

354 km (220 mi) south of Loreto.

La Paz is one of those cities that make you wish you'd been here 20 years ago. In the slowest of times, in late summer when the heat is oppressive, you can easily see how it must have been when it was a quiet place, living up to its name: "Peace." Today the city has a population of 170,000, with a large contingent of retirees from the United States and Canada. Travelers use La Paz as both a destination in itself and a stopping-off point en route to Los Cabos. Sportfishing is a major lure, though some enjoy La Paz as the most Mexican city on the peninsula, with the feel of a mainland community that has adapted to tourism while retaining its character.

Hernán Cortés and his soldiers were drawn to La Paz in 1535 by stories of the magnificent pearls and beautiful women. In 1720 the Jesuits arrived to civilize and convert the Indians. Instead, the missionaries inadvertently decimated the local populace by introducing smallpox. Within 30 years, there was no one left to convert.

While the rest of Mexico was being torn apart by revolution, a permanent settlement was established in 1811. La Paz became a refuge for those who wished to escape the mainland wars. In 1829, after Loreto was leveled by a hurricane, La Paz became the capital of the Californias. Troops from the United States occasionally invaded but sent word to Washington that the Baja Peninsula was not worth fighting for. In 1853 a different group of invaders arrived from the United States. Led by William Walker, these southerners were intent on making La Paz a slave state but were quickly banished by the Mexicans. Peace reigned for the next century. In 1940, disease wiped out the oyster beds, and with the pearls gone, La Paz no longer attracted prospectors and was left tranquil.

La Paz officially became the capital of Baja California Sur in 1974 and is now the state's largest settlement. It is the site of the power plant for all the state, the ferry to Mazatlán, the state bureaucracy, the governor's home, and the state jail. It is the stop off for fishermen and divers headed for **Cerralvo, La Partida,** and **Espíritu Santo** islands, where parrot fish, manta rays, neons, and angels blur the clear waters by the shore, and marlin, dorado, and yellowtail leap out of the deep, dark sea.

24 The **malecón** is La Paz's seawall, tourist zone, and main drag rolled into one. As you enter town from the southwest, Paseo Alvaro Obregón turns into the malecón at a cluster of high-rise condos. Construction continues at the west entrance to town, where a marina and hotel have
25 opened at the 500-acre **Fidepaz Marina.**

26 A two-story white gazebo is the focus of the **Malecón Plaza,** a small cement square where musicians sometimes appear on weekend nights. The tourist information center sits beside the gazebo. Across the street, Calle 16 de Septiembre leads inland to the city center. Around the plaza and all along the malecón, a steady stream of teens cruise through town,

Biblioteca de las Californias, **29**
Ferry Terminal, **32**
Fidepaz Marina, **25**
Government House, **31**
La Catedral de Nuestra Señora de La Paz, **28**
Malecón, **24**
Malecón Plaza, **26**
Museum of Anthropology, **30**
Pichilingue, **33**
Plaza Constitución, **27**

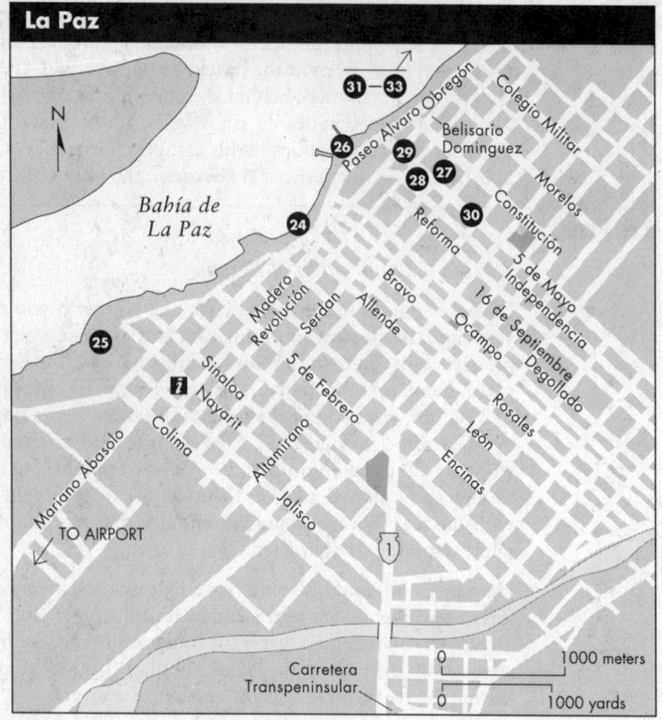

red and yellow car lights twinkling around their license plates and the latest U.S. hits blaring on their radios.

La Paz's downtown district is the busiest in all Baja Sur, with shops crammed together on narrow crowded streets. The central plaza, or
27 zócalo, also goes by the names **Plaza Constitución** and Jardín Velazco.
28 **La Catedral de Nuestra Señora de La Paz** (Our Lady of La Paz Cathedral) is downtown's big attraction. It was built in 1860 near the site of La Paz's first mission, which was established in 1860 by Jesuit Jaime Bravo. You'll see it just across from the zócalo.

29 The **Biblioteca de las Californias,** a library specializing in the history of Baja California, has reproductions of the local prehistoric cave paintings, oil paintings of the missions, and the best collection of historical documents on the peninsula. Films and lectures are sometimes presented in the evening. Check the bulletin board outside the library or ask the librarian for information. ✉ *Madero at Cinco de Mayo,* ☎ *112/2–01–62.* ⏲ *Weekdays 8–6.*

30 One gets an excellent sense of La Paz's culture and heritage at the **Museum of Anthropology,** constructed in 1983. Exhibits include re-creations of Comondo and Las Palmas Indian villages, photos of cave paintings found in Baja, and copies of Cortés's writings on first sighting La Paz. Many of the exhibit descriptions are written only in Spanish, but the museum's staff will help translate for you. ✉ *Altamirano and Cinco de Mayo,* ☎ *112/2–01–62.* 🎫 *Donation.* ⏲ *Weekdays 8–6, Sat. 9–2.*

South of town, Paseo Alvaro Obregón, or the malecón, becomes what is commonly known as the **Pichilingue Road,** which curves north along the bay about 16 km (10 mi) to the terminals where the ferries from Mazatlán and Topolobampo arrive and many of the sportfishing boats depart. Just outside town the road divides, with outgoing traffic climbing up a steep cliff overlooking deserted beaches.

31 The **Government House,** surrounded by guards and gates, is a few kilometers south of the spot where the road divides. Home of the governor of Baja California Sur, the house has an impressive view of the curving
32 bay and city lights. At the **Ferry Terminal,** south of Government House, warehouses serve as waiting rooms. Roadside stands serving oysters and grilled fish line the highway across the street.

33 Since the time of pirate ships and Spanish invaders, **Pichilingue** was known for its preponderance of oysters bearing black pearls. In 1940 an unknown disease killed off all of them, leaving the beach deserted. Now Pichilingue is a pleasant place for sunbathing and watching the sportfishing boats bring in their haul. Palapa-covered restaurants on the beach serve cold beer and oysters *diablo* (raw oysters steeped in a fiery-hot sauce), as well as some of the freshest and least expensive grilled fish in town.

Beaches

Paved roads to La Paz's most beautiful beaches were completed in 1992. Off a dirt road just past Pichilingue, **Playa Tecolote** is a small, crystal-blue cove with a clean beach and no facilities. The larger **Playa Coyote** has a restaurant, water-sports equipment rentals, and palapas for shade; the facilities are only open when tourism is high. Overnight camping is currently allowed at both beaches.

Dining and Lodging

$$$ ★ ✕ **El Bismark.** You've got to wander a bit out of your way to reach this down-home restaurant, where locals go for good, home-style Mexican food. Specialties include the carne asada, served with beans, guacamole, and homemade tortillas; and enormous grilled lobsters. The seafood cocktails are huge, too, and the fish fillets are always fresh from the sea. You'll see families settle down for hours at long wood tables, while waitresses divide their attention between the patrons and the soap operas on the TV above the bar. ✉ *Santos Degollado and Av. Altamirano,* ☎ *112/2–48–54. MC, V.*

$$$ ✕ **Restaurant Bermejo.** The most upscale, elegant restaurant in town has a faithful following of locals and tourists in search of comfortable booths, candles, and courteous waiters. The menu is primarily Italian these days. There are a few moderately priced dishes here, and the steaks are worth splurging on. ✉ *Paseo Obregón 498,* ☎ *112/2–27–44. AE, MC, V.*

$$ ✕ **La Paz-Lapa.** The noise level here is deafening, but this is a fun place, with a wide-screen TV in the bar and waiters so jolly you expect them to break into song. The food—your basic beef, chicken, fish, and Mexican selections—is tasty and plentiful. Also referred to as Carlos 'n' Charlie's, La Paz-Lapa is a member of the popular Carlos Anderson restaurant chain. Live bands appear on weekend evenings on the back patio. ✉ *Paseo Obregón at Calle 16 de Septiembre,* ☎ *112/5–92–90. MC, V.*

$$ ✕ **La Terraza.** The open-air restaurant at the Hotel Perla is the best people-watching spot in town, with sidewalk-level tables facing the malecón. The menu includes everything from French toast to pasta—with decent enchiladas, huevos rancheros, and fresh fish. La Terraza is a good hangout for morning coffee and afternoon and evening snacks. ✉ *Paseo Obregón,* ☎ *112/2–07–77. MC, V.*

$ ✕ **El Quinto Sol Restaurante Vegetariano.** El Quinto's bright green exterior walls are painted with Indian snake symbols and smiling suns. The back room is a natural-foods store stocked with grains, soaps, lotions, oils, and books. The restaurant serves yogurt with bananas and wheat germ, seviche tostadas, and a nonmeat version of machaca. ✉

Belisario Domínguez and Independencia, ☎ *112/2–16–92. No credit cards.*

$ ✕ **Taco Hermanos Gonzalez.** La Paz has many great taco stands, but the Gonzalez brothers still corner the market with their hunks of fresh fish wrapped in corn tortillas. Bowls of condiments line the small stand, and customers jam the sidewalk while munching on the best fast food in town. ✉ *Mutualismo and Esquerro, no phone. No credit cards.*

$$$ **Club El Moro.** A vacation-ownership resort with suite rentals on a nightly and weekly basis, El Moro boasts a garden of lush palms and a densely landscaped pool area with one of the few hot tubs in town. You can recognize the building by its stark-white turrets and domes; rooms are Mediterranean in style and decor, with arched windows, Mexican tiles, and private balconies. Some rooms have kitchens and can sleep up to five persons. The restaurant is excellent and elegant. ✉ *Km 2 Carretera a Pichilingue, Box 357, 23010,* ☎ FAX *112/2–40–84 or 112/2–70–10. 17 suites. Restaurant, bar, pool, travel services. AE, MC, V.*

$$$ ★ **Mar y Sol.** Those planning to stay a week or more will be delighted with these lovely apartments. Each is furnished with folk art, colorful serapes, leather *equipale* (pigskin) chairs, and full kitchens. Fountains and a square swimming pool are set amid palms and flowering plants. It's a two-block walk to the beach, and the owners can arrange fishing, diving, and whale-watching tours. ✉ *Calle Insurgentes at Margaritas, Box 438, 23000,* ☎ *112/5–24–67,* FAX *112/2–01–80. 10 apartments. Pool. No credit cards.*

$$ **La Concha Beach Resort.** Come to La Concha for its clean, curving beach; modern, well-maintained rooms; complete water-sports center; and very good restaurant. The rooms have been remodeled with tiled floors, TVs, phones, and small refrigerators. Guests gather at the second-story sports bar, the pool, and the **Cortez Club,** where scuba, snorkeling, kayaking, and sportfishing tours can be arranged. Its whale-watching trips are extremely popular in winter; those not staying here can still arrange tours and rentals through the club. Condos ($$$) on the property and downtown are available for nightly rental as well, and there is a shuttle to town and back. ✉ *Km 5 Carretera a Pichilingue, 23010,* ☎ *112/1–63–44; 800/999–2252 for reservations in the U.S.;* FAX *112/1–62–18. 107 rooms. Restaurant, 3 bars, pool, water sports, shop, travel services, car rental. AE, MC, V.*

$$ **La Perla.** This brown low-rise hotel has a long-standing reputation as one of the best places to stay in La Paz. The rooms have white walls and light-wood furnishings; some have king-size beds. The pool is located on a second-story sundeck away from the traffic on the main street. Noise is a factor in the oceanfront rooms; the trade-off is a wonderful view of the malecón and the sunset. ✉ *Paseo Obregón 1570, 23010,* ☎ *112/2–07–77,* FAX *112/5–53–63. 101 rooms. Restaurant, bar, pool, shop. MC, V.*

$$ **Los Arcos.** Los Arcos is the only true colonial Mexican lodging in town. Resist the waterfront view and request a room in the central courtyard, where the rush of water in the fountain drowns out the music from the street and the noise from the pool area. All rooms have balconies and TVs. The self-service coffee shop opens early so those headed out on fishing boats can have breakfast and pick up a box lunch; it's also a cool escape from the midday heat at lunchtime. The Cabañas de Los Arcos next door offers several small brick cottages surrounded by gardens and a small hotel with a swimming pool. ✉ *Paseo Obregón 498, between Rosales and Allende, 23000,* ☎ *112/2–27–44,* FAX *112/5–43–13; reservations in the U.S.:* ✉ *6 Jenner St., No. 120, Irvine, CA 92618,* ☎ *714/450–9000 or 800/347–2252,* FAX *714/450–9010.*

180 rooms at main hotel, 30 bungalows and rooms at Cabañas. Restaurant, bar, coffee shop, 2 pools, sauna, fishing. MC, V.

$ 🏨 **Hotel Revolucion.** The former Maria Cristina Hotel, this is a long-time favorite of budget travelers. The building is now a bright orange, and the rooms were repainted and refurbished in 1996; all offer private bathrooms and TVs. There is a small, economical restaurant on the property. ✉ *Av. Revolución 86 at Dego-llado, 23000,* ☎ *112/5–80–22. 20 rooms. Restaurant. MC, V.*

$ 🏨 **Pension California.** This run-down hacienda, offering clean blue-and-white rooms with baths and a courtyard with picnic tables and a TV, draws backpackers and low-budget travelers. A laid-back, friendly camaraderie prevails. ✉ *Av. Degollado 209, 23000,* ☎ *112/2–28–96. 25 rooms. No credit cards.*

Nightlife and the Arts

El Teatro de la Ciudad (✉ Av. Navarro 700, ☎ 112/5–00–04) is La Paz's cultural center. The theater seats 1,500 and is used for stage shows by visiting performers as well as local ensembles.

Outdoor Activities and Sports

BOATING AND FISHING

The considerable fleet of private boats in La Paz now has room for docking at three marinas: the **Fidepaz** at the north end of town, and the **Marina Palmira** and **Marina La Paz** south of town. Most hotels can arrange sportfishing trips. The **Dorado Velez Fleet** (✉ Box 402, 23000, ☎ 112/2–27–44, ext. 608), operated by Jack Velez in the Los Arcos hotel, has cabin cruisers that can be chartered starting at about $240 per day. Fishing tournaments are held in August and November. **Sportsman's Tours** (☎ 800/234–0618) in the United States arranges bus and air tours to Loreto with fishing included.

DIVING

Popular diving spots include the white coral banks off Isla Espíritu Santo, the sea-lion colony off Isla Partida, and the seamount 14 km (9 mi) farther north. **Scuba Aguilar** (✉ Independencia 107, ☎ 112/2–18–26, FAX 112/2–86–44) gives windsurfing and sailing lessons, rents equipment, and operates dives and excursion tours to Espíritu Santo and the wreck of the *Salvatierra,* a sunken ferryboat. Two-tank dive trips run about $65. Dive trips can also be set up through the Cortez water-sports center at the La Concha Beach Resort (☞ Dining and Lodging, *above*).

Shopping

Shops carrying a predictable assortment of sombreros, onyx chess sets, and painted plaster curios are scattered along Avenida Obregón across from the malecón. **Artesanías la Antigua California** (✉ Av. Obregón 220, ☎ 112/5–52–30) has the nicest selection of Mexican folk art in La Paz, including wooden masks and lacquered boxes from Guerrero, along with a good supply of English-language books on Baja. **La Tiendita** (✉ Los Arcos Hotel, Av. Obregón 498, ☎ 114/2–27–44) has embroidered guayabera shirts and dresses, tin ornaments and picture frames, and some black pottery from Oaxaca.

The East Cape

105 km (65 mi) south of La Paz, 81 km (50 mi) north of San José del Cabo.

The Sea of Cortés coast north of Los Cabos has long been a favored hideaway for anglers and adventurers; now it's growing with housing developments and hotels. The attractions? A curvaceous, sometimes craggy coastline with great bays for fishing, diving, kayaking, and windsurfing, plus a sense of really getting away. The nearest airport is at San José del Cabo, about a two-hour drive from the East Cape hotels. Rental cars come in handy for exploring the coast; otherwise you'll need to rely on expensive shuttle services from the hotels.

Lodging

$$ **Hotel Buena Vista Beach Resort.** The most pleasant surroundings on the coast are at this old-time resort built around a 1940s private mansion. The hotel has gone through several transitions, and now has 60 tiled-roof bungalows set along flower-lined pathways, next to swimming pools and lawns. The rooms all have private terraces with hammocks. The fishing fleet is one of the best in the area, and there are plenty of other diversions including scuba diving, snorkeling, trips to natural springs and caves, and tours into Los Cabos and La Paz. Airport shuttle service can be arranged in advance. ✉ *Buena Vista, 32 km (20 mi) north of San José,* ☎ *114/1-00-33 or 800/752-3555,* FAX *114/1-01-33; 619/425-1832 for reservations in the U.S. 60 rooms. Restaurant, 2 pools, 2 hot tubs, massage, beach, dive shop, fishing. AE, MC, V.*

Los Cabos

195 km (122 mi) south of La Paz.

At the southern tip of the 1,625-km (1,000-mi) Baja California peninsula, the land ends in a rocky point called El Arco (The Arch), a place of stark and mysterious beauty. The warm waters of the Sea of Cortés swirl into the Pacific Ocean's rugged surf as marlin and sailfish leap above the waves. The desert ends in sand coves, with cactus standing at their entrances like sentries under the soaring palm trees.

Pirates found the capes at the tip of the peninsula an ideal lookout for spotting Spanish galleons traveling from the Philippines to Spain's empire in central Mexico. Missionaries soon followed, seeking to save the souls of the few thousand local Indians who lived off the sea. The good fathers established the missions of **San José del Cabo** and **Cabo San Lucas** in the mid-1700s, but their colonies did not last long. The missionaries (and other Europeans) had brought syphilis and smallpox along with their preachings, and by the end of the century the indigenous population had been nearly wiped out.

A different sort of native, the mighty game fish that appeared to be trapped in the swirl of surf where the ocean meets the sea, brought the explorers back. In the 1940s and 1950s the capes became a haven for wealthy adventurers who built lodges on rocky gray cliffs overlooking secluded coves and bays. By the 1960s lavish resorts had begun to rise in the barren landscape.

Connected by a 32-km (20-mi) stretch of highway called the **Corridor,** the two towns that grew around the Spanish missions, Cabo San Lucas and San José del Cabo, were distinct until the late 1970s, when the Mexican government's office of tourism development (Fonatur) targeted the southern tip of Baja as a major resort and dubbed the area Los Cabos. The destination now consists of three major areas: San José del Cabo, Cabo San Lucas, and the 32-km-long (20-mi-long) Corridor separating the two towns.

The region has become one of Mexico's most popular and most expensive coastal getaways, with deluxe hotels, championship golf courses, and some of the finest sportfishing in the world. Despite all the development that has taken place there, and its steep prices, Los Cabos remains a mysteriously natural hideaway.

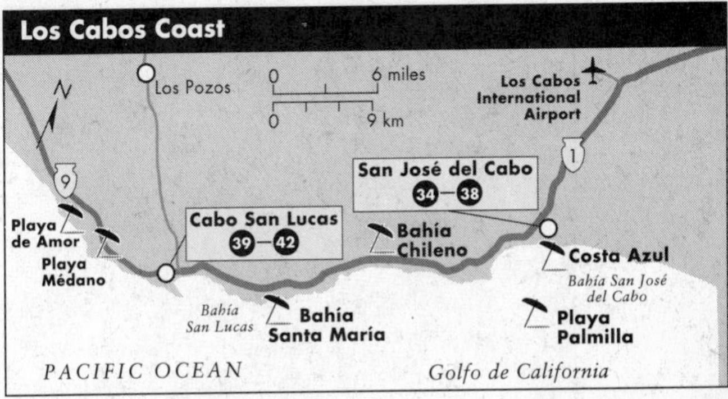

San José del Cabo

San José del Cabo is the municipal headquarters for the two Los Cabos towns and has a population of about 25,000. The hotel zone faces a long stretch of waterfront on the Sea of Cortés; a nine-hole golf course and private residential community have become established south of the town center. The picturesque downtown, with colored lights in the fountains along the main street, still maintains the languid pace of a Mexican village. Despite the development, San José remains the more peaceful of the two towns and is the one that travelers seeking a quiet escape prefer.

34 The main street in San José del Cabo is **Boulevard Mijares.** The south end of the boulevard has been designated the tourist zone, with the Los Cabos Club de Golf as its centerpiece. A few reasonably priced hotels are situated along this strip, on a beautiful long beach where the surf, unfortunately, is too dangerous for swimming.

35 The **Estero de San José,** where the freshwater Río San José flows into the sea, is at the end of the tourist strip, on Paseo San José by the Hotel Presidente Forum. The estuary is now a natural preserve closed to boats. Wildlife is gradually reappearing; more than 200 species of birds can be spotted here. A building at the edge of the estuary serves as a cultural center with exhibits on Baja's indigenous people.

Within town, Boulevard Mijares is lined with restaurants and shops.
36 The modest yellow **City Hall** is near Avenida Zaragoza, where Boulevard Mijares ends—a spot marked by a long fountain illuminated at night by colored lights. There is a small, shaded plaza here with a few café tables in front of small restaurants.

37 Locals and travelers mingle at the large central **plaza,** with a white wrought-iron gazebo and green benches set in the shade. The town's
38 church, the **Iglesia San José,** looms above the plaza. Be sure to walk up to the front and see the tile mural of a captured priest being dragged toward a fire by Indians.

BEACHES

Playa Hotelera is the stretch of beach that most of the finer hotels use. It's beautiful, but the current is dangerously rough, and swimming is not advised. At the east end of the beach, near the Hotel Presidente, there is a freshwater lagoon filled with tropical birds and plants. If you plan to spend time here, be sure to douse yourself with insect repellent. The best swimming beach near San José is **Playa Palmilla,** which is protected by a rocky point just south of town. The northern part of the beach is cluttered with boats and shacks, but if you walk south you'll reach the Hotel Palmilla beach, a long stretch of white sand and calm sea.

Boulevard Mijares, **34**
City Hall, **36**
Estero de San José, **35**
Iglesia San José, **38**
Plaza, **37**

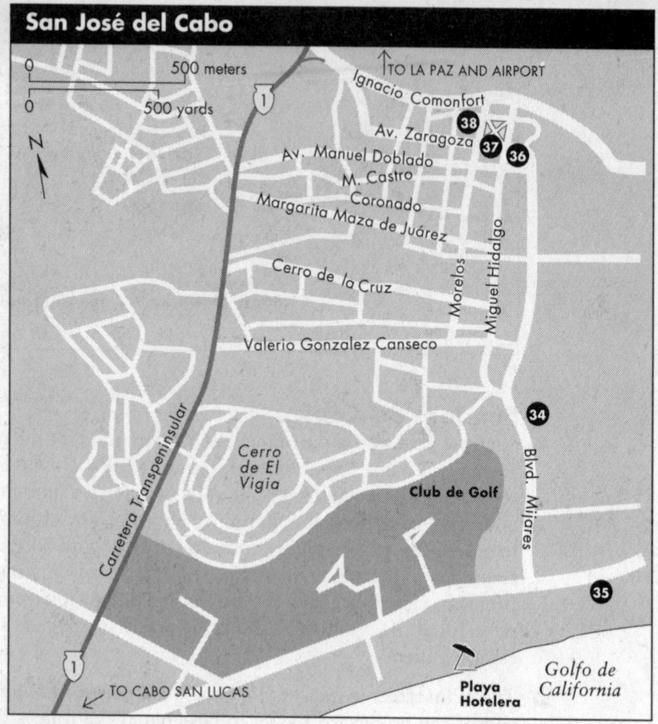

DINING AND LODGING

$$$ ★ ✕ **Damiana.** For a special night out, visit this small hacienda tucked beside the plaza, past the center of town. The lounge area has overstuffed couches where you can unwind before claiming your table on the patio. Fuchsia bougainvillea wraps around the tall pines shading the wrought-iron tables, and the pink adobe walls glow in the candlelight. Start with fiery oysters diablo; then move on to the tender chateaubriand, charbroiled lobster, or the restaurant's signature imperial shrimp steak, made with ground shrimp. You'll find the setting so relaxing and charming that you will want to linger well into the night. ⊠ *Blvd. Mijares 8,* ☎ *114/2–04–99. AE, MC, V. No lunch.*

$$ ✕ **Tropicana Bar and Grill.** Start the day with coffee and French toast at the sidewalk tables in front of this enduringly popular restaurant. Later, as the temperature rises, it's more comfortable to sit inside the large, air-conditioned bar over an ice-cold lemonade, watching sporting events and music videos on TV. In the evening, the back patio quickly fills with a loyal clientele who enjoy the garden setting and reliable cooking. The menu has grown over the years to include U.S. cuts of beef and imported seafood along with fajitas, chiles rellenos, and lobster, always in demand. The nightly dinner special is usually a good deal. ⊠ *Blvd. Mijares 30,* ☎ *114/2–09–07. AE, MC, V.*

$ ✕ **Las Hornillas.** Chicken roasted on a spit over an open fire is the specialty at this casual eatery, more popular with locals than tourists. The half chicken with rice, beans, and tortillas is more than sufficient for a ravenous diner, and the chicken fajitas come on a platter loaded with grilled onions, green peppers, and white meat. ⊠ *Calle Manuel Doblado 610,* ☎ *114/2–23–24. No credit cards.*

$ ✕ **Pescaderia del Mar.** Seafood doesn't get any better than at this small fish market and café on the highway just outside downtown San José. A brick smoker stoked with mesquite sits in one corner of the patio restaurant, and the aroma of smoking dorado, marlin, and wahoo fills the air. Budget diners can fill up on fish tacos or chilies stuffed with smoked fish but may find themselves splurging on giant shrimp cocktails followed by grilled lobster or a whole fried fish. ✉ *Blvd. Mauricio Castro 1110,* ☎ *114/2–32–66. No credit cards.*

$ ✕ **Restaurant La Playita.** A longtime local secret, this small, out-of-the-way restaurant has a great chef and draws crowds of locals and tourists. The main attraction is the seafood brought in daily by fishermen who beach their boats just a few yards away. The food is some of the freshest you'll find in the area. Try the shrimp *playita* (giant shrimp stuffed with crab and wrapped with bacon), or the imported filet mignon. The full bar serves more than 50 brands of tequila. Live Brazilian jazz bands play most nights. Lunch here is a nice midday outing, especially when followed by a long walk down the largely deserted beach. ✉ *Pueblo la Playa, 2 km (1 mi) south of San José,* ☎ *114/2–37–74. MC, V.*

$$$ 🏨 **Hotel Presidente Los Cabos Forum.** By far the nicest hotel in San José, this property sits at the end of the hotel zone amid cactus gardens, next to the estuary. The buildings curve around an enormous blue pool; the rooms have shaded patios, king-size beds, and a sitting area facing the sliding glass doors. The hotel operates on an all-inclusive basis, with all meals and some activities included in the room rate. As there are few other restaurants in the immediate vicinity, you'll save on taxis by eating here, and the rate is quite reasonable. ✉ *Paseo San José, at end of hotel zone, 23400,* ☎ *114/2–02–11; 800/327–0200 in the U.S.;* FAX *114/2–02–32. 244 rooms, 6 suites. 2 restaurants, bar, pool, 2 tennis courts, horseback riding, beach, fishing, dance club. AE, MC, V.*

$$ 🏨 **Fiesta Inn.** The nicest moderately priced hotel on San José's long beach, the Fiesta has buildings that frame a garden of cactus and palms. The rooms have two double or one king-size bed, satellite TV, carpeting (which can tend to smell musty) or tiled floors, and ocean-front balconies. Horses are available for rides along the beach to the nearby estuary. ✉ *Blvd. Malecón s/n 30, 23400,* ☎ *114/2–07–01; 800/343–7821 in the U.S.;* FAX *114/2–04–80. 152 rooms. Restaurant, bar, pool. MC, V.*

$$ 🏨 **Huerta Verde.** Set amid mango and citrus groves just north of San José, this eight-room B&B is one of the most picturesque properties in Los Cabos. Some rooms are in the main house, others in adjoining buildings. All have domed ceilings, brick archways, gorgeous handcrafted furnishings, and private baths. Breakfast is included in the room rate; other meals can be ordered in advance. The heated pool is surrounded by tropical gardens. Hikers enjoy the trails leading to hilltops with views of the sea. ✉ *Las Animas Altas, 2 km (1 mi) off Hwy. 1, 23400,* ☎ FAX *114/8–85–11;* ☎ *303/431–5162,* FAX *303/431–4455 for reservations in the U.S. 8 rooms. Restaurant, bar, pool. No credit cards.*

$$ 🏨 **La Playita.** The small community of Pueblo la Playa just outside San José has long been a favorite day-trip escape for those in the know. A small hotel opened on the beach in 1995, and it's the perfect hideaway if you're not interested in shopping or bar-hopping. The rooms in the two-story building are painted stark white and have air-conditioning, tiled bathrooms, ceiling fans, and satellite TVs; phone service is available at the front desk. The restaurant is a two-minute walk away. Rates go down about 20% in summer. ✉ *Pueblo la Playa, 2 km (1 mi) south of San José, 23400,* ☎ FAX *114/2–41–66;* ☎ FAX *818/962–2805,* ☎ *888/242–4166 for reservations in the U.S. 24 rooms, 2 penthouses (1 with 2 bedrooms, 1 with 1 bedroom). Restaurant, bar, pool, beach, fishing. MC, V.*

$$ 🏨 **Tropicana Inn.** This small hotel is a great option for those who aren't desperate to be on a beach. The stucco buildings decorated with tiled murals of Diego Rivera paintings frame a pool and palapa bar in a quiet enclave behind San José's main boulevard. The rooms are air-conditioned, have satellite TV, and are maintained to look brand new. Book in advance in high season. ✉ *Blvd. Mijares 30, 23400,* ☎ *114/2–09–07,* FAX *114/2–15–90; 510/939–2725 for reservations in the U.S. 39 rooms, 1 suite. Restaurant, bar, room service, pool. AE, MC, V.*

$ **Posada Terranova.** San José's best budget hotel is a friendly place where guests return so frequently they're almost part of the family. The large, air-conditioned rooms are painted bright white and have two double beds and tiled bathrooms. The hotel has expanded in recent years, but when guests congregate at the front patio tables or in the restaurant it still feels like a private home. ✉ *Calle Degollado at Zaragoza, 23400,* ☎ *114/2–05–34,* FAX *114/2–09–02. 25 rooms. Restaurant, bar. AE, MC, V.*

NIGHTLIFE AND THE ARTS

The hottest nightspot in town is **Bones Disco** at the Hotel Presidente Forum (✉ Paseo San José, ☎ 114/2–00–38). **Iguana Bar** (✉ Blvd. Mijares 24, ☎ 114/2–02–66) is a local hangout, with live rock and roll on weekend nights during the high season.

OUTDOOR ACTIVITIES AND SPORTS

Fishing. Most hotels in San José can arrange fishing trips. As there is no marina in town, you'll have to board your boat at the marina in Cabo San Lucas. Hotels typically can set up the excursions and provide transportation to the marina and box lunches. There is a fleet of pangas at Pueblo la Playa, about 1½ km (1 mi) south of San José and another at Playa Palmilla.

Golf. The public, nine-hole **Los Cabos Campo de Golf** (✉ Blvd. Mijares, ☎ 114/2–09–05) in San José was built in 1988 and for many years was the only golf course in Los Cabos. It now has plenty of competition from the lavish courses in the Corridor. The green fees are much lower here, however.

Surfing. Killer Hook Surf Shop (✉ Av. Hidalgo, ☎ 114/2–24–30) sells and rents snorkeling gear, along with surfboards and boogie boards.

Tennis. The **Los Cabos Campo de Golf** (☞ Golf, *above*) has two lighted tennis courts that are open to the public; fees are $8 per hour during the day and $12 per hour at night.

SHOPPING

Shopping opportunities in San José del Cabo occur in the few streets around the main plaza and City Hall. Across from City Hall is **Almacenes Goncanseco** (✉ Blvd. Mijares 18, ☎ 114/2–09–12), where you can get film, postcards, groceries, and liquor. **ADD** (✉ Av. Zaragoza at Hidalgo, ☎ 114/2–27–27), an interior design shop, sells gorgeous hand-painted dishes from Guanajuato and carved-wood furniture from Michoacán. **Copal** (✉ Zaragoza 20, ☎ 114/2–30–70) has a nice array of carved animals from Oaxaca, masks from Guerrero, and heavy wooden furnishings. For fresh produce, flowers, meat, fish, and a sampling of local life in San José, visit the **Mercado Municipal** off Calle Doblado.

The Corridor

Many of the legendary fishing lodges and exclusive resorts built before the government stepped in were located along the wild cliffs between San José del Cabo and Cabo San Lucas. Since the mid-1980s, the area has developed as a destination unto itself. It now has several private communities and large-scale resorts, and three championship golf courses. The highway along the Corridor has been widened to four lanes. The road is in good shape most of the time, but tends to flood during heavy rains, especially between August and November.

Two bays, **Bahía Chileno** and **Bahía Santa María,** offer terrific diving and snorkeling (☞ Outdoor Activities and Sports, *below*).

BEACHES

Costa Azul is the most popular surfing beach in Los Cabos. A few small campgrounds and casual restaurants line the beach facing the waves. **Playa Palmilla** is one of the Corridor's best swimming beaches.

DINING AND LODGING

$$$ ✕ **Pitahayas.** Now that the Corridor resorts are firmly established, smaller businesses are cropping up to take advantage of the upscale clientele. This elegant restaurant has found its niche in a lovely setting just above the beach at Cabo del Sol. The wide-ranging menu features Pacific Rim cuisine, blending touches of Thai, Polynesian, and Chinese cooking in unusual recipes. Lobster appears in the form of gourmet hash, duckling is served with a plum tangerine sauce, and fresh organic vegetables are lightly stir-fried and served while still crisp. Soft jazz plays in the background, and the setting is decidedly romantic. The breakfast buffet is a great way to start the day, especially when whales are spouting just offshore. ✉ *Km 10 on Hwy. 1,* ☎ *114/3–21–57. MC, V.*

$$ ✕ **Da Giorgio.** The best sunset watching in all of Los Cabos may be enjoyed at the cliffside tables outside this restaurant. The tables, staggered along the cliffs and poised beside a small pond with a waterfall, have a great view of the arch at land's end. The menu focuses on pastas and pizza, and the salad bar has an abundance of fresh veggies. ✉ *Km 5 on Hwy. 1,* ☎ *114/3–29–88. MC, V.*

$$$$ 🏨 **Las Ventanas al Paraíso.** New on the corridor scene in early 1997, Las Ventanas sets the standard for luxury, privacy, and amenities. The all-suite accommodations have individual hot tubs, wood-burning fireplaces, and even telescopes for viewing whales in the sea and stars at night. ✉ *Km 19.5 Carretera Transpeninsular, Cabo San Lucas 23400,* ☎ *114/4–0257,* FAX *114/4–0255;* ☎ *888/525–0483,* FAX *310/824–1218 for reservations in the U.S. 60 suites. Restaurant, pool, spa, golf course, tennis courts, beach, fishing. AE, MC, V.*

$$$$ ★ 🏨 **Palmilla.** Just outside San José, the Palmilla is a gracious, sprawling, hacienda-style resort with a small white adobe chapel. Established in 1956, the Palmilla underwent a $12 million renovation in 1996, resulting in more lavish accommodations set amid palm groves and lush gardens. Tiled stairways lead up from flower-lined paths to large apartments with hand-carved furniture, French doors opening onto private patios, tiled baths, and, for the first time in the hotel's history, TVs and phones in all rooms. The buildings are spread along a hillside overlooking the beach, the service is delightfully personalized, and the hotel's **La Paloma** restaurant is excellent. Construction is under way on a large-scale resort development surrounding the hotel; an 18-hole Jack Nicklaus–designed golf course was completed in 1993. The Palmilla's excellent fishing and diving fleet is anchored just offshore. ✉ *Km 1 Carretera Transpeninsular (about 8 km [5 mi] from San José), 23400,* ☎ *114/2–05–82,* FAX *114/2–05–83; reservations in the U.S.:* ✉ *4343 Von Karman Ave., Newport Beach, CA 92660,* ☎ *800/637–2226. 114 rooms, suites, and villas. Restaurant, bar, pool, golf privileges, 2 tennis courts, beach. AE, MC, V.*

$$$$ 🏨 **Twin Dolphin.** Sleek and Japanese-modernistic, with an austere air, the Twin Dolphin has been a hideaway for the rich and famous since 1977. The guest rooms, remodeled in 1996, are in low-lying casitas along a seaside cliff and are furnished in minimalist style, without TVs and phones. The hotel is worth a visit if only for the reproductions of Baja's cave paintings on the lobby wall. ✉ *Km 11.5 Carretera Transpeninsular, Cabo San Lucas 23410,* ☎ *114/3–25–90,* FAX *114/3–48–11; reservations in the U.S.:* ✉ *1625 W. Olympic Blvd., Suite 1005, Los Angeles, CA 90015,* ☎ *800/421–8925,* FAX *213/380–1302. 44 rooms, 6 suites. Restaurant, bar, pool, massage, 2 tennis courts, beach, fishing. MC, V.*

$$$$ **Westin Regina Resort.** The Westin is architecturally astounding, if a bit intimidating in size. It's a long walk from the parking lot and lobby to the rooms and pool, set above a man-made beach. The luxurious rooms are among the best in Los Cabos, with satellite TV, in-room safes, hair dryers, bathtubs and separate walk-in showers, and both air-conditioning and ceiling fans—a boon to those who prefer open windows and sea breezes. The **Royal Beach Club Villas** are decorated with gorgeous pottery and have full kitchens and whirlpool tubs facing the sea view. Two of Los Cabos's best golf courses are nearby, and the hotel is designed to keep its guests happy without their ever having to leave the grounds. ✉ *Km 22.5 Carretera Transpeninsular, Box 145, San José del Cabo 23400,* ☎ *114/2–90–00 or 800/937–8461,* FAX *114/2–90–10. 243 rooms, 60 villas. 3 restaurants, 5 pools, 2 tennis courts, exercise room, beach. AE, MC, V.*

$$$ **Meliá Cabo Real.** This Meliá sprawls over a hilltop with a crystal-blue pool, fountains, waterfalls, white canopies shading rest areas, and a private beach created by a small jetty jutting from the rocky hillside. Maya carvings and bas-reliefs adorn the walls in the rooms, which all have landscaped terraces. The Cabo Real resort development around the hotel is ongoing, with an 18-hole golf course now open. Meliá guests can use it for a fee. The hotel operates a shuttle service to its sister property in Cabo San Lucas. ✉ *Km 19.5 Carretera Transpeninsular, Cabo San Lucas 23400,* ☎ *114/3–09–67,* FAX *114/3–10–03;* ☎ *800/336–3542,* FAX *305/854–0660 for reservations in the U.S. 300 rooms. 2 restaurants, café, pool, 2 tennis courts, exercise room, beach, dive shop, fishing. AE, MC, V.*

$$ **Hotel Cabo San Lucas.** Looking like a mountain lodge nearly buried in palms, this long-standing Corridor hotel is a favorite of Baja devotees. The rooms are furnished with sturdy, dark-wood pieces; suites and villas are more luxurious. The hacienda-style buildings are located right above **Chileno Beach,** one of the best diving spots in Los Cabos. ✉ *Km 14.5 Carretera Transpeninsular, Cabo San Lucas 23410,* ☎ *114/3–34–57; 800/733–2226,* FAX *213/655–3243 in the U.S. 89 rooms. Restaurant, pool, beach, dive shop, fishing. AE, MC, V.*

OUTDOOR ACTIVITIES AND SPORTS

Diving and Snorkeling. Bahía Chileno, an underwater preserve, teems with marine life and is a wonderful place for snorkeling and diving. You'll need to bring your own equipment. **Bahía Santa María,** a picture-perfect white-sand cove protected by towering brown cliffs, also has superb snorkeling, with hundreds of colorful fish swarming through chunks of white coral. There is a concession stand on the beach with snorkeling gear rental, but its hours are erratic.

Fishing. Most Corridor hotels have excellent fishing fleets, with the boats anchored at the marina in Cabo San Lucas. Hotels typically can set up the trips and provide transportation to the marina and box lunches. **Victor's Aquatics** (☎ 114/2–10–92, FAX 114/2–10–93) has a fleet of pangas on the Palmilla beach. **Jig Stop Tours** (☎ 800/521–2281 in the U.S.) books fishing trips for several Los Cabos fleets.

Golf. In just the past few years, Los Cabos has become a major golf destination, hosting tournaments including the PGA Senior Grand Slam. The courses that have brought so much attention this way are all located in the Corridor and serve as the centerpieces for megaresort developments. Among the most spectacular is the 18-hole Jack Nicklaus–designed course at the **Palmilla Golf Club** (⊠ Palmilla Resort, ☎ 114/2–17–01, 114/2–17–08, or 800/637–2226). A second 18-hole Nicklaus course is open at **Cabo del Sol** (☎ 114/3–39–90 or 800/386–2465), a resort development in the Corridor that will eventually include three 18-hole courses (a second 18-hole course is being designed by Tom Weiskopf). The Robert Trent Jones–designed **Cabo Real Golf Club** (⊠ Melia Cabo Real Hotel, ☎ 114/2–90–00, ext. 9205) has 18 of its 36 holes open for play.

Cabo San Lucas

Cabo San Lucas, once an unsightly fishing town with dusty streets and smelly canneries, has become the center of tourism activity for Los Cabos. The sportfishing fleet is headquartered here, and cruise ships anchored off the marina disperse passengers into town. Trendy restaurants and bars line the streets, and massive hotels have risen on every available plot of waterfront turf; a five-story condo-hotel complex along the bay blocks the view from the town's older hotels. Cabo San Lucas has become an in spot for travelers seeking fun, rowdy nightlife and extensive dining and shopping options.

Highway 1 leads into the center of Cabo San Lucas, ending at Kilometer 1 on the Transpeninsular Highway. The main downtown street,
39 Avenida Lázaro Cárdenas, passes the pretty **Plaza San Lucas** with its
white wrought-iron gazebo. Buildings around the plaza house galleries and restaurants. Most of the shops, services, and restaurants are
located between Avenida Cárdenas and the waterfront.

Boulevard Marina has been transformed from a dusty main drag into
a busy thoroughfare lined with hotels and cafés. Paved walkways now
run from here to the hotels and beaches on the east end of town and
40 west to the **Handicrafts Market** at the Cabo San Lucas marina (☞ Shop-
41 ping, *below*). The sportfishing fleet is docked in the **Bahía de Cabo San
Lucas,** and there are glass-bottom boats available at the water's edge.

42 The most spectacular sight in Cabo San Lucas is **El Arco.** The natural
rock arch is visible from the marina and from some of the hotels but
is more impressive from the water. **El Faro de Cabo Falso** (Lighthouse
of the False Cape), built in 1890 and set amid sand dunes, is a little
bit farther on from El Arco. You need a four-wheel-drive vehicle to reach
the lighthouse by land. If you don't take at least a short boat ride out
to the arch and Playa de Amor, the beach underneath, you haven't fully
appreciated Cabo.

BEACHES

Playa de Amor consists of a secluded cove at the very end of the peninsula, with the Sea of Cortés on one side and the Pacific Ocean on the other. The contrast between the peaceful azure cove on the Sea of Cortés and the pounding white surf of the Pacific is dramatic.

Playa Hacienda, in the inner harbor by the Hacienda Hotel, has the calmest waters of any beach in town and good snorkeling around the rocky point.

Playa Médano, just north of Cabo San Lucas, is the most popular stretch in Los Cabos (and possibly in all Baja) for sunbathing and people-watching. The 3-km (2-mi) span of white sand is always crowded, especially on weekends.

Bahía de Cabo San Lucas, **41**
El Arco, **42**
Handicrafts Market, **40**
Plaza San Lucas, **39**

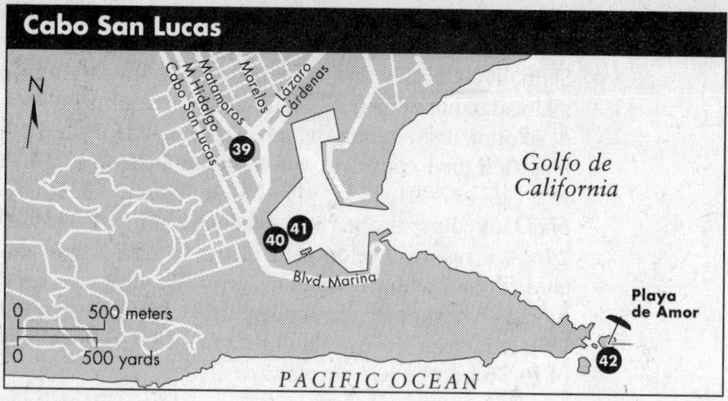

Playa Solmar, fringing the Solmar Hotel, is a beautiful wide beach at the base of the mountains leading into the Pacific, but it has dangerous surf with a swift undertow. Stick to sunbathing here.

DINING AND LODGING

$$$ ✕ **Casa Rafael's.** European antiques and a pair of tropical toucans in a glass-fronted cage provide the visual distractions in this intimate, elegant restaurant. The chef, a transplant from Maui, has created an exciting Pacific Rim menu featuring lamb, lobster medallions in black bean sauce, imported steaks, and smoked local dorado, all with Asian touches. A pianist plays romantic ballads during dinner, and couples sip champagne in cozy upholstered booths that allow ample privacy. ✉ *Calle Medano at Camino Pescador,* ☏ *114/3–07–39. AE, MC, V.*

$$$ ✕ **El Galeón.** Considered the most distinguished dining room in town, El Galeón is across from the marina. The choice seats are on the outside terraces facing the water; the inside is decorated with lots of heavy wood furniture. Traditional Italian, Mexican, and American dishes are prepared expertly, with an emphasis on thick, tender cuts of beef. The piano bar is a nice setting for a late-night brandy. ✉ *Across from marina by road to Finesterra Hotel,* ☏ *114/3–04–43. AE, MC, V.*

$$$ ★ ✕ **Mi Casa.** One of Cabo's best restaurants is in an eye-catching, cobalt-blue building painted with a mural of a burro, just across the street from the main plaza. Mexican cuisine reaches gourmet status here with fresh tuna and dorado (sea bass) served with tomatillo salsa or Yucatecan achiote, or with sophisticated dishes such as *chili en nogada* (a meat-stuffed pepper topped with walnut sauce and pomegranate seeds). The restaurant quickly outgrew its small dining room and has spread into a large back courtyard. It's especially nice at night, illuminated by candlelight and the moon. ✉ *Av. Cabo San Lucas,* ☏ *114/3–19–33. MC, V.*

$$$ ★ ✕ **Peacocks.** The ubiquitous fresh-fish dinner achieves gustatory eminence when prepared by chef Bernard Voll. His dorado is coated with a crust of chopped pecans, and his shrimp masterfully tossed with spinach fettuccine. This chef is known for his incredible desserts—if you miss dinner, be sure to stop by for a cappuccino and tequila mousse. The candlelit two-level dining room has an open kitchen and is topped by an enormous palapa; you can also dine on an outdoor patio. ✉ *Paseo Pescador near Playa Médano,* ☏ *114/3–18–58. AE, MC, V.*

$$ ✕ **El Shrimp Bucket.** This is the calmest of the three Carlos Anderson restaurants in Cabo San Lucas. A few tables are set out on the walkway that runs along the marina in front of the Marina Fiesta Hotel, a good spot to relax and watch the boats rock on the water. The indoor dining room has the chain's typical mishmash decor with quirky adornments hanging about. The food—barbecued ribs and chicken, burg-

ers, piles of fried shrimp—is dependable and abundant. ✉ *Blvd. Marina in Marina Fiesta complex,* ☎ *114/3–25–98. AE, MC, V.*

$ ✕ **Fish Company.** It's easy to overlook this small seafood restaurant surrounded by flashier establishments, but the owner has perfected the art of preparing flavorful meals for reasonable prices. Nine tables covered with blue-and-white cloths sit just in from the sidewalk in the narrow dining room, and the aroma of fresh grilled fish fills the air. Breakfast specialties include a great chorizo-and-cheese omelette; among the lunch and dinner choices are shrimp with oyster sauce and fresh fish smothered in garlic. You can bring your catch here and have it prepared in a low-cost feast. ✉ *Av. Guerrero between Blvd. Marina and Zapata,* ☎ *114/3–14–05. No credit cards.*

$ ✕ **Tacos Chidos.** Taco stands appear all over Cabo San Lucas. Chidos has been around for a long time and serves one of the cheapest breakfasts in town: Egg dishes served with beans, rice, tortillas, and coffee run well under $5. Tostados, tamales, and tortas fill out the menu, along with the requisite fish, beef, and pork tacos. ✉ *Av. Zapata at Guerrero,* ☎ *114/3–05–51. No credit cards.*

$$$$ **Hotel Hacienda.** Set on the tip of a tree-filled point jutting into San Lucas Bay, the Hacienda resembles a Spanish colonial inn with its white arches and bell towers, stone fountains, and statues of Indian gods set amid scarlet hibiscus and bougainvillea. The white rooms have red-tile floors, tile baths, and folk art on the walls; the bar is a veritable museum of Indian artifacts. The water-sports center, located on the calmest beach in town, has kayaks, Jet Skis, snorkeling equipment, and any other gear you might need. The hotel has a three-night minimum stay on weekdays, and a four-night minimum on weekends in the high season. ✉ *Playa Medano, 23410,* ☎ *114/3–01–22; 800/733–2226;* FAX *213/655–3243 for reservations in the U.S. 112 rooms, suites, and beachfront cabanas. Restaurant, bar, pool, beach, dive shop. MC, V.*

$$$$ ★ **Meliá San Lucas.** From the moment you enter the Meliá and spot El Arco framed by the lobby's arches, you know you're at a hotel where details are important. The blue walls and linens in the rooms complement the views of the aquamarine sea; the outer adobe walls of the terraced hotel buildings glow orange and gold with the changing sunlight. The Meliá has a long beach with calm waters, a spacious hot tub under the palms, and all the equipment you could need for playing on and in the water. ✉ *Playa Medano, 23410,* ☎ *114/3–10–00 or 114/3–10–60; 800/336–3542 in the U.S.;* FAX *114/3–04–18. 161 rooms and suites. 3 restaurants, 2 pools, hot tub, beach, meeting rooms. AE, MC, V.*

$$$ **Casa Rafael's.** An intimate boutique hotel, this is the perfect spot for those seeking privacy rather than abundant diversions. The rooms are individually decorated with an eclectic collection of antiques and modern furnishings; all have air-conditioning and private baths. A lap pool on the terrace behind the house is surrounded by plants, and there's a small exercise room and hot tub. ✉ *Calle Medano at Camino Pescador, 23410,* ☎ FAX *114/3–07–39,* FAX *114/3–16–79. 12 rooms. Restaurant, pool, hot tub, exercise room. AE, MC, V.*

$$$ **Finisterra.** One of the oldest hotels in Cabo, the Finisterra is now also one of the most modern, thanks to the eight-story tower rising directly from the beach. A second tower was completed in 1997, adding 40 rooms and new shops to the property. An eight-story-high palapa covers the restaurant and bar on the beach next to two free-form swimming pools. The rooms in the new buildings, with oceanfront balconies, are by far the nicest; some have king-size beds. The older section of the hotel (with the least expensive rooms) is favored by longtime guests who like the fishing-lodge feel of the stone buildings. The restaurant is only fair, but the **Whale Watcher** bar atop a high cliff has the

best view in town. ✉ *Blvd. Marina, 23410,* ☎ *114/3–33–33,* FAX *114/3–05–90; reservations in the U.S.:* ✉ *6 Jenner St., No. 120, Irvine, CA 92618,* ☎ *714/450–9000 or 800/347–2252,* FAX *714/450–9010. 237 rooms. 2 restaurants, 2 bars, 3 pools, travel services. AE, MC, V.*

$$$ ★ **Solmar Suites.** From afar, the Solmar looks like a space colony, set against granite cliffs at the tip of Land's End, facing the wild Pacific. The rooms, decorated in Mexico–Santa Fe style, have separate sitting areas and tile baths; the best ones are set up against the rocks right over the beach. The adjacent time-share and condo units have kitchenettes and a private pool area. The surf here is far too dangerous for swimming, but don't miss a stroll along the wide strip of beach. Most visitors hang out around the two additional pools and swim-up bars, joining in with the ever-present musicians. The Solmar's sportfishing fleet is first-rate. The good restaurant hosts a Saturday night Mexican fiesta and buffet dinner. ✉ *Blvd. Marina, Box 8, 23410,* ☎ *114/3–35–35,* FAX *114/3–04–10; reservations in the U.S.:* ✉ *Box 383, Pacific Palisades, CA 90272,* ☎ *310/459–9861 or 800/344–3349,* FAX *310/454–1686. 86 rooms, 4 suites, 68 condos. Restaurant, bar, 3 pools, beach, dive shop. AE, MC, V.*

$ **Las Villas Turismo Juvenil.** Cabo's youth hostel is about 10 blocks from the waterfront in a quiet neighborhood. Two dormitory rooms have bunk beds and shelves, and there are several private rooms with shared baths. In the courtyard, guests can use sinks and counters to wash their clothes and fix meals. ✉ *Av. de la Juventud, 23410,* ☎ *114/3–01–48. 2 dorms, 11 private rooms. No credit cards.*

$ **Siesta Suites.** You'll have to forgo air-conditioning to remain in the inexpensive range, but you'll get a large, immaculate room with kitchenette. The three-story hotel, opened in 1994, sits on a fairly quiet side street just two blocks from the marina, and the proprietors are the friendliest in town. ✉ *Calle Zapata, Box 310, 23410,* ☎ FAX *114/3–27–73;* ☎ FAX *909/945–5940 for reservations in the U.S. 15 suites. Kitchenettes. No credit cards.*

NIGHTLIFE AND THE ARTS

Some travelers choose Cabo San Lucas for its nightlife, which consists mainly of rowdy bars where the music blares, the customers dance, flirt, and drink, and a general no-holds-barred sense of frivolity reigns. Members of the rock band Van Halen own **Cabo Wabo** (✉ Calle Guerrero, ☎ 114/3–11–88). The latest U.S. bands play over an excellent sound system, but the real highlight is the impromptu jam sessions with appearances by Van Halen's many friends in the music business. **Squid Roe** (✉ Av. Cárdenas, ☎ 114/3–06–55) is the rowdiest spot in town, packed with young foreigners who work in the local tourist industry and know how to party. **Giggling Marlin** (✉ Blvd. Marina, ☎ 114/3–06–06) seems to have been around forever as the favorite watering hole for fishermen and their girlfriends. **Río Grill** (✉ Blvd. Marina, ☎ 114/3–13–35) absolutely booms with rock and roll and reggae, except when the live bands give way to the karaoke contingent. The **Hard Rock Cafe** (✉ Blvd. Marina, ☎ 114/3–37–79) is packed with families in the early evening and revelers later at night. **El Galeón** (✉ Blvd. Marina, ☎ 114/3–04–43) is about the only refuge for the quieter crowd, who sip brandy by the piano bar.

OUTDOOR ACTIVITIES AND SPORTS

Diving. El Arco is a prime diving and snorkeling area, as are several rocky points off the coast. Most hotels offer diving trips and equipment rental. The oldest and most complete dive shop in the area is **Amigos del Mar** (✉ Near sportfishing docks at harbor, ☎ 114/3–05–05 or 800/344–3349, FAX 114/3–08–87). The ***Solmar V*** (✉ At Solmar Hotel and marina, ☏ 114/3-00-22 or 800/344-3349, FAX 310/454-1686), a live-aboard dive boat, takes weeklong trips to the islands of Socorro, San Benedicto, and Clarion, and the coral reefs at Cabo Pulmo. It has 12 cabins with private baths (maximum: 24 passengers).

Fishing. There are more than 800 species of fish in the waters off Los Cabos. Most of the hotels will arrange fishing charters, which include a captain and mate, tackle, bait, licenses, and drinks. Prices start at $250 per day for a 25-ft cruiser. Some charters provide lunch, and most can arrange to have your catch mounted, frozen, or smoked. Most of the boats leave from the sportfishing docks in the Cabo San Lucas marina. Usually there are a fair number of pangas for rent at about $25 per hour with a five-hour minimum. Dependable companies include the **Gaviota Fleet** (✉ At marina, ☏ 114/3-04-30 or 800/521-2281), **Minerva's** (✉ At marina and on Madero between Blvd. Marina and Guerrero, ☏ 114/3-12-82, FAX 114/3-04-40), **Pisces Sportfishing Fleet** (✉ At marina, ☏ 114/3-12-88), and **Solmar Fleet** (✉ At Solmar Hotel and Marina, ☏ 114/3-00-22, 800/344-3349; FAX 310/454-1686 in the U.S.).

SHOPPING

Some of the nicest shops in Cabo San Lucas are located in **Plaza Bonita** on the waterfront at the beginning of Boulevard Marina. **Cartes** (✉ Plaza Bonita, ☏ 114/2-17-70) is the best of the many interior-design stores in Los Cabos, with an irresistible array of hand-painted pottery and tableware, pewter frames, hand-blown glass, and carved furniture. **Libros** (✉ Plaza Bonita, ☏ 114/3-17-70) carries a vast number of English-language novels and magazines. **Dos Lunas** (✉ Plaza Bonita, ☏ 114/3-19-69) offers a trendy selection of colorful sportswear. **Francisco's Café del Mundo** (✉ Plaza Bonita, no phone) is the place to take a break for an espresso or cappuccino.

Boulevard Marina and the side streets between the waterfront and the main plaza are filled with an ever-changing parade of small shops. **Necri** (✉ Blvd. Marina between Madero and Ocampo, ☏ 114/3-02-83) has an excellent selection of folk art and furnishings. **Casa Mexicanas** (✉ Av. San Lucas, ☏ 114/3-19-33) handles special-order furnishings and fabrics along with pottery, wall hangings, and folk art. **Cuca's Blanket Factory** (✉ Cardenas at Matamoros, ☏ 114/3-19-13) sells the typical array of serapes and cotton blankets with a twist—you can design your own and have it ready the next day. **Mama Eli's** (✉ Av. San Lucas, ☏ 114/3-16-16) is a three-story gallery with fine furnishings, ceramics, appliquéd clothing, and children's toys. **Galeria Gatemelatta** (✉ On dirt road to Hotel Hacienda, ☏ 114/3-11-66) specializes in colonial furniture and antiques.

At the **Handicrafts Market** in the marina you can pose for a photo with an iguana, plan a ride in a glass-bottomed boat, or browse to your heart's content through stalls packed with blankets, sombreros, and pottery.

Todos Santos

30 km (50 mi) north of Cabo San Lucas.

The Pacific Ocean side of the tip of Baja has remained largely undeveloped. The exception is the small agricultural town of Todos Santos, which has become a haven for artists, architects, and dropouts. The town sits a bit inland from the rugged coast and is classically charming with its 19th-century brick-and-stucco buildings and small central plaza. Tour buses sometimes clog the streets around the plaza; when they're gone the town is pleasantly peaceful. Entrepreneurs have turned some of the plaza-front buildings into galleries and cafés; time will tell if they can survive in low season. If you drive to Todos Santos on your own be sure to head back to Cabo before dark; Highway 19, the route between the two towns, is not lit and is prone to high winds and flooding.

Dining and Lodging

$$ ✕ **Cafe Santa Fe.** Owners Paula and Ezio Colombo have created an Italian restaurant that's become a destination in its own right; many Cabo residents lunch here weekly. The setting, with tables amid herb gardens in an overgrown courtyard, is one of the attractions. But the real reason you can't get a table on weekends is the food—salads and soups made from organic, homegrown vegetables and herbs, homemade pastas and calzone, and fresh fish with light herbal sauces. It's tempting to linger for hours over a bottle of imported Chianti, but make sure you've got an alert designated driver to get you home. ✉ *Calle Centenario,* ☎ *114/4–03–40. No credit cards.*

$$ 🏨 **Hotel California.** The biggest hotel in town is the 15-room California, a simple establishment with a pool and restaurant. ✉ *Calle Juárez, 23300,* ☎ FAX *114/5–00–02. 15 rooms. Restaurant, pool. No credit cards.*

BAJA SUR A TO Z

Arriving and Departing

By Boat

Several cruise lines—including **Carnival** (☎ 800/327–9501), **Princess** (☎ 800/421–0522), and **Royal Caribbean** (☎ 800/327–0271)—use Cabo San Lucas as a port of call.

By Bus

Tres Estrellas de Oro and **Autotransportes de Baja California** bus lines run the length of the peninsula from Tijuana to Los Cabos, stopping at towns en route; the peninsula-long trip takes 22 hours. The **Aguila** bus line runs from Santa Rosalia to Los Cabos.

GUERRERO NEGRO

Tres Estrellas de Oro (☎ 112/2–64–76) runs buses from La Paz to Guerrero Negro; the bus stops at the highway entrance to town.

LA PAZ

Tres Estrellas de Oro and **Autotransportes de Baja California** (☎ 112/2–64–76 for both) and **Aguila** (☎ 112/2–70–94) operate buses along the Transpeninsular Highway to the border and to Los Cabos.

LORETO

Loreto is serviced by **Tres Estrellas de Oro, Autotransportes de Baja California,** and **Aguila.** The bus terminal (✉ Salvatierra and Tamaral, ☎ 113/5–07–67) sits at the entrance to town.

LOS CABOS

Tres Estrellas de Oro (☎ 114/2–02–00) travels from Tijuana to Los Cabos and between Cabo San Lucas and San José daily.

By Car

Mexico Highway 1, also known as the Transpeninsular Highway, runs the entire 1,600 km (1,000 mi) from Tijuana to Cabo San Lucas. The highway's condition varies depending on the weather and intervals between road repairs. It should not be driven at high speed or at night (the road is not lit). There are exits for all the principal towns in Baja Sur.

The city of La Paz curves along the bay of La Paz and faces the sea in a northwesterly, rather than an easterly, direction. When you approach the city on Highway 1 from the north, you'll enter from the southwest.

The road between San José del Cabo and Cabo San Lucas was widened to four lanes and is in good condition, though dips and bridges become flooded in heavy rains.

By Ferry

LA PAZ

The ferry system connecting Baja to mainland Mexico has been privatized and is constantly undergoing changes in rates and schedules. Currently there are Sematur ferries from La Paz to Mazatlán five days a week. Tickets are available at the ferry office at the dock on the road to Pichilingue (☎ 112/2–94–85, FAX 112/5–65–88) and at the downtown Sematur office (✉ Av. 5 de Mayo 502, ☎ 112/5–38–33, FAX 112/5–46–66). Purchase your ticket personally in advance of your trip—and expect confusion. Travelers planning to take cars and motor homes on the ferry to the mainland must obtain a vehicle permit before boarding the ferry. Tourism officials in La Paz strongly suggest that you obtain the permit when crossing the border into Baja; though permits are not needed in Baja, offices at the border are better equipped to handle the paperwork than those in La Paz. Everyone crossing to the mainland needs a tourist card, also available at the border.

SANTA ROSALIA

The ferry travels from Santa Rosalia to Guaymas on the mainland Pacific coast. Currently, the ferry departs for the 12-hour trip to the mainland at 8 AM on Wednesday and Sunday and arrives in Santa Rosalia on Tuesday and Friday at 3 PM. Advance tickets are available at the Santa Rosalia ferry terminal (☎ 115/2–00–14, FAX 115/2–00–13), just south of town on Highway 1, but schedules are often erratic.

By Plane

LA PAZ

The La Paz airport, about 16 km (10 mi) north of town, is served by **AeroCalifornia** (☎ 112/5–10–23) from Tijuana and Loreto and **Aeromexico** (☎ 112/2–00–91) from Los Angeles, Tucson, Tijuana, Mexico City, and other cities within Mexico.

LORETO

AeroCalifornia (☎ 113/5–00–50 or 113/5–05–66) has daily flights from Los Angeles and La Paz to Loreto's airport, which is 7 km (4 mi) southwest of town.

LOS CABOS

The **Los Cabos International Airport** (☎ 114/2–03–41) is about 11 km (7 mi) north of San José del Cabo and about 48 km (30 mi) from Cabo San Lucas. **AeroCalifornia** (☎ 114/2–09–43) flies to Los Cabos from Los Angeles and Tijuana; **Mexicana** (☎ 114/2–09–60) from Guadalajara, Mexico City, and Los Angeles; **Aeromexico** from San Diego and Mexico City; **Alaska Airlines** (☎ 114/2–09–59) from Anchorage, Fairbanks, Portland, Phoenix, San Francisco, San Diego, Los Angeles, and Seattle; **American** (☎ 114/2–27–17) flies in from Dallas; **America West** from Phoenix; **Continental** from Houston.

Getting Around

La Paz

A car isn't necessary if you plan to stay in town; taxis are readily available and inexpensive. It's also fairly easy to get around by bus in La Paz: City buses run along the malecón and into downtown. If you'd like to explore the remote beaches, a car is necessary (☞ Car and Jeep Rental, *below*).

Loreto

Taxis are in good supply and fares are inexpensive. There are two gas stations in Loreto; be sure to fill your tank before heading out on any long jaunts.

Los Cabos

The best way to see the sights is on foot. The downtown areas of San José and Cabo San Lucas are compact, with the plaza, church, shops, and restaurants within a few blocks of one another. There is bus service between the two towns, although buses may not stop along the Corridor.

Contacts and Resources

Car and Jeep Rental

LA PAZ

Avis (✉ At airport, ☎ 112/2–26–51), **Budget** (✉ Paseo Obregón at Hidalgo, ☎ 112/2–10–97), **Hertz** (✉ At airport, ☎ 112/2–09–19), and **Servitur Autorento** (✉ 5 de Febrero at Abasolo, ☎ 112/2–14–48). **AMCA** (✉ Calle Madero 1715, 112/3–03–35).

LORETO

M&M Jeeps (✉ Madero 78, ☎ 113/5–09–71 or 113/5–09–72, FAX 113/5–09–81; 619/297–1615, FAX 619/297–1617 in San Diego, CA), rents two- and four-wheel-drive vehicles that can be taken throughout Baja. Advance reservations are strongly recommended.

LOS CABOS

The following car-rental agencies all have desks at the airport and in one or both towns: **Amca** (☎ 114/2–13–14), **Avis** (☎ 114/2–06–80), **Budget** (☎ 114/3–02–41), **Dollar** (☎ 114/2–06–71), **Hertz** (☎ 114/3–02–11), **National** (☎ 114/3–60–00), and **Thrifty** (☎ 114/2–16–71). **M&M Jeeps** (✉ At Hotel Presidente Forum, ☎ 114/2–11–81; ☎ 619/297–1615, FAX 619/297–1617 in San Diego, CA), which rents two- and four-wheel-drive vehicles, offers a package option: Travelers can rent the vehicles for a one-way trip from San Diego to Los Cabos without a drop-off fee and arrange their own accommodations or they can purchase an all-inclusive self-guided tour package. Reservations must be arranged through the San Diego office; cars are not available in Los Cabos unless you have advance reservations.

Emergencies

LA PAZ

Police (☎ 112/2–66–10), **Fire** (☎ 112/2–00–54), and **Red Cross** (☎ 112/2–11–11).

LOS CABOS

Police: Cabo San Lucas (☎ 114/3–39–77) and San José del Cabo (☎ 114/2–03–61). **Hospital:** Cabo San Lucas (☎ 114/3–01–02) and San José del Cabo (☎ 114/2–00–13).

Guided Tours

GUERRERO NEGRO

The best way to see the whales is with a tour company that's familiar with Baja California. **Baja Expeditions** (✉ 2625 Garnet Ave., San Diego, CA 92109, ☎ 619/581–3311; 800/843–6967 in the U.S. and Canada), the premier Baja adventure operator in the United States, has whale-watching trips on boats and kayaks. The company can also arrange trips to Mulege and Bahía Concepción, especially popular for paddling. **Baja California Tours** (✉ 7734 Herschel Ave., Suite O, La

Jolla, CA 92037, ☎ 619/454–7166, FAX 619/454–2703) has information and makes reservations with several companies offering whale-watching tours. **Discover Baja** (✉ 3089 Clairemont Dr., San Diego, CA 92117, ☎ 619/275–4225 or 800/727–2252, FAX 619/275–1836) offers whale-watching trips to San Ignacio Lagoon. **Eco-Tours Malarrimo** (✉ Blvd. Zapata at entrance to Guerrero Negro, ☎ 115/7–02–50) conducts guided tours from Guerrero Negro to Scammon's Lagoon; two hours in a small boat watching the whales runs $40 per person.

LA PAZ

Travel agencies in the hotels and along Paseo Obregón offer tours of the city, daylong trips to Los Cabos, sportfishing, and boating excursions. **Baja Expeditions** (☞ Guerrero Negro, *above*) offers hotel and diving packages and live-aboard dive-boat trips to the islands, seamount, and wrecks. The **Cortez Club** at the La Concha Beach Resort (☞ Dining and Lodging, *above*) offers diving, fishing, whale-watching, and cruising tours and is the most complete tour facility in La Paz.

LORETO

Picnic cruises to Isla Coronado, excursions into the mountains to visit the San Javier Mission and view prehistoric rock paintings, and day trips to Mulege can be arranged through hotels. **Alfredo's Sportfishing** (✉ On malecón, Box 39, Loreto BCS 23880, ☎ 113/5–01–65, FAX 113/5–05–90) can arrange tours as well as fishing excursions and is a good source of general information on the area.

LOS CABOS

With the water as the main attraction, most tours involve getting into a boat and diving or fishing. It's a must to take a ride to El Arco, the natural rock arches at Land's End, and Playa de Amor (Lover's Beach), where the Sea of Cortés blends into the Pacific. Nearly all hotels have frequent boat trips there; the fare depends on how far your hotel is from the point. Tour boats dock by the arts-and-crafts market in the Cabo San Lucas marina, and the sidewalk along the water is lined with salesmen offering boat rides. Check out the boat before you pay, and make sure there are life jackets on board.

Contactours (✉ Hotel Finisterra, ☎ 114/3–33–33; also at several other hotels) and **TourCabos** (✉ Plaza los Cabos, Paseo San José, ☎ 114/2–09–82, FAX 114/2–20–50) offer tours of the region, boat trips, horseback riding, and information on water sports. **Baja Travel Adventures** (☎ 114/3–19–34) runs trips to Todos Santos and La Paz and individually designed tours; ask at the hotel tour desks if there's no answer when you phone.

Pez Gato (✉ On marina near Plaza Las Glorias hotel, ☎ 114/3–37–97) has sailing and sunset cruises on a 46-ft catamaran, with live music ($50 per person, including drinks), as well as snorkeling and sailing tours ($30 per person). All trips depart from the marina in Cabo San Lucas; call or stop by the booth at the marina for further information.

Visitor Information

Cabo San Lucas (✉ Av. Hidalgo at Guerrero, ☎ 114/3–41–80, FAX 114/3–22–110). **La Paz** (✉ Mariano Abasolo s/n, ☎ 112/4–01–00, FAX 112/4–07–22; on malecón near Calle 16 de Septiembre, ☎ 112/2–59–39). **San José del Cabo** (✉ Zaragoza at Mijares, ☎ 114/2–29–60).

4 Sonora

Cowboys continue to ride the range in Mexican ranch country, but beef has been upstaged by beaches in this northwestern state's economy. Along with relatively unspoiled (and inexpensive) coastal towns such as Bahía Kino and Guaymas, Sonora's lures include colonial Alamos, an immaculate former silver-mining center, and a sprinkling of Spanish missions.

Updated by Susana Sedgwick

SONORA, Mexico's second-largest, second-richest state, is a vacationland with its own band of devoted followers. Many are from Arizona, for whom the beaches of Sonora, its sister state, are closer, cheaper, and more interesting than those of southern California. This stretch of the Mexican northwest is reminiscent of the old Wild West in the United States. *Rancheras,* ballads not unlike country-and-western songs, blare from saloons and radios. Irrigated ranch lands feed Mexico's finest beef cattle, and rivers flowing westward from the Sierra Madre are diverted by giant dams to irrigate the once-barren land that now produces cotton, sugarcane, and vegetables. Hermosillo, Sonora's capital, bustles with agricultural commerce in the midst of the fertile lands that turn barren again toward the coast.

Mexico Highway 15 begins at the border town of Nogales, Sonora, adjacent to the U.S. town of Nogales, Arizona. It passes southward through Hermosillo and reaches the Gulf of California (also called the Sea of Cortés) at Guaymas, 418 km (261 mi) from the Arizona border. The Sonoran desert dominates the landscape through northern Sonora, as it does in southern Arizona. Long stretches of flat scrub are punctuated by brown hills and mountains, towering saguaros, and organ-pipe cacti. Highway 15 continues southward after Guaymas, as the landscape gradually takes on a more tropical aspect, and finally enters the state of Sinoloa just north of the city of Los Mochis. Except in the mountains, the entire region is uncomfortably warm between May and late September, with afternoon temperatures sometimes exceeding 120°F.

In 1540 Francisco Vázquez de Coronado, governor of the provinces to the south, became the first Spanish leader to walk the plains of Sonora. More than a century later, Father Eusebio Francisco Kino led a missionary expedition to Sonora and what is now southern Arizona (an area referred to historically as the Pimeria Alta), founding several towns and missions there. Although Alamos, in the south of Sonora, boomed with silver-mining wealth in the late 17th century, no one paid much attention to the northern part of the region for the next three centuries; it was not part of the Mexican territory ceded to the American flag after the War of 1847. Sonora became a haven for Arizona outlaws, and international squabbles bloomed and faded over the next decades as officials argued over issues such as the right to pursue criminals across the border. During the last quarter of the 19th century, Porfirio Díaz, dictator of Mexico for three decades, finally moved to secure the state by settling it.

For Don Porfirio, however, developing Sonora may have been a mistake: The revolutionaries who later overthrew him came from here. In fact, Mexico was ruled by the Sonora dynasty for nearly a quarter of a century and, until the tragic 1994 assassination of Sonora native son Luis Donaldo Colosio, the ruling party candidate for president, it appeared likely that a Sonoran would soon control the destiny of the country again. The Mexican Revolution brought prosperity to the state, and it continues to thrive. Its inhabitants have adopted modern farming techniques that allow them to grow enough wheat not only for Mexico but for export as well.

Pleasures and Pastimes

Beaches

There are lively hotels and restaurants by the shores of San Carlos, Guaymas, Puerto Peñasco, and Bahía Kino, but those willing to take the time to get there and forgo facilities will also find miles and miles of more secluded beaches that run along the Sea of Cortés. All the main beaches of the state have paved access roads.

Dining

Sonoran cuisine is distinguished by the excellent quality of its steaks as well as the freshness of its fish. Sonora is also the home of the giant flour tortilla and bean burros. There are no five-star restaurants in the state, but shrimp aficionados will find plenty to like in Sonora (especially in Guaymas), as will those drawn to traditional Mexican dishes such as enchiladas, burritos, tamales, and *carne asada* (grilled meat); indeed, the style of Mexican cooking with which most Americans are familiar derives from this region. Casual dress (but not beachwear) is always acceptable, and reservations are rarely needed.

CATEGORY	COST*
$$$$	over $35
$$$	$25–$35
$$	$15–$25
$	under $15

**per person for a three-course meal, excluding drinks, service, and tax*

Lodging

In Sonora you may find yourself sleeping in a converted convent in fashionable Alamos, growing a Hemingway beard in a beach bungalow at Bahía Kino, or luxuriating in a five-star resort in San Carlos. Lodging in Sonora is no longer the bargain it once was, but prices are still lower here than for comparable accommodations in the better-known vacation spots in other parts of Mexico.

CATEGORY	COST*
$$$$	over $90
$$$	$60–$90
$$	$25–$60
$	under $25

**All prices are for a standard double room, excluding tax.*

Missions

Nestled among the hills and river valleys of Sonora are a handful of almost forgotten missions founded by Jesuit fathers in the 17th and early 18th centuries, and completed by the Franciscans in the late-18th and 19th centuries. Some of the churches, such as San Ignacio, still service the small agricultural communities around them, whereas others, like Cocospera, are no more than a vestige of a remarkable past.

Exploring Sonora

The landscape of Sonora is as vast and varied as the state itself. From the seemingly endless tracks of Sonoran desert that finally tumble into the Sea of Cortés to the mountains of the Sierra Madre and the agricultural fields and valleys that produce its livestock, Sonora is a place of dramatic contrasts.

Mexico Highway 2 enters Sonora's far northwest from Baja California, paralleling the U.S. border. There are several crossing points, but most people entering from the United States do so at Nogales, which is also a point of entry for winter fruit and vegetables exported to the United States.

Numbers in the text correspond to numbers in the margin and on the Sonora map.

Great Itineraries

Because it is so diverse, the state of Sonora requires a visit of eight days or more to really do it justice. Those who have less time must decide whether seashore, mountains, or missions are most important.

IF YOU HAVE 3 DAYS

Take Highway 15 south from Nogales to **Magdalena** ⑤; stop off to see the plaza and the church where the bones of missionary explorer Eusebio Francisco Kino are displayed. If you're interested in churches, you might spend the night in this area; nine missions founded by Father Kino are accessible from here by car. Then continue south on the same highway to the state capital, **Hermosillo** ⑥, where a variety of good hotels and restaurants is available. Overnight here and spend the next morning touring the city or browsing through the Centro Ecologico (of special interest to children.) After lunch, drive west on Highway 16 to **Bahía Kino** ⑦, a perfect beach retreat, for a one- or two-night stay. It's about six hours from Kino Bay back to the Arizona border.

An alternative three-day itinerary would be to cross the U.S. border at Lukeville-Sonoyta, explore the lunarlike regions of the **Sierra del Pinacate** ②, and then cool off on the beaches of **Puerto Peñasco** ③ for the rest of that day and the next one. Then take Highway 2 to **Magdalena** ⑤, a drive of about 2¾ hours, and stop for lunch and a visit to the Kino shrine before heading north on Highway 15 to **Nogales** ①. Spend an afternoon shopping there before you cross the U.S. border.

IF YOU HAVE 5 DAYS

Take Highway 15 from Nogales to **Guaymas** ⑨; the drive will take about six or seven hours. Exploring the town of Guaymas and the adjacent resort area of **San Carlos** ⑩ will give you plenty to do for two days and nights. Continue south and then east for 3½ hours to charming colonial **Alamos** ⑪, in the foothills of the Sierra Madre. After one or two nights in Alamos, head back north; you might overnight in Bahía Kino on your way home.

IF YOU HAVE 8 DAYS

Combine the second of the three-day itineraries with the five-day itinerary, but stop off at Hermosillo on the way down to Guaymas. Those with additional time might want to take a short side trip from Alamos to **Aduana** ⑫, where a very wealthy silver mine once thrived.

When to Tour

The temperatures in Sonora in the summer months are as high as they are in southern Arizona, so unless you are prepared to broil, plan your trip around the months between September and May.

Nogales

❶ *100 km (60 mi) south of Tucson via Highway 19, on the Arizona-Mexico border.*

Bustling Nogales can become fairly rowdy on weekend evenings, when underage Tucsonans head south of the border to drink. It has some good restaurants, however, and visitors can find fine-quality crafts and furnishings in addition to the usual made-for-tourists souvenirs. If you're just coming for the day, it's best to park on the Arizona side of the border (you'll see many guarded lots that cost about $4 for the day) and walk across. Practically all the good shopping is within easy strolling distance of the border.

The shopping area centers mainly on **Avenida Obregón,** which begins a few blocks west of the border entrance and runs north–south; just

Sonora

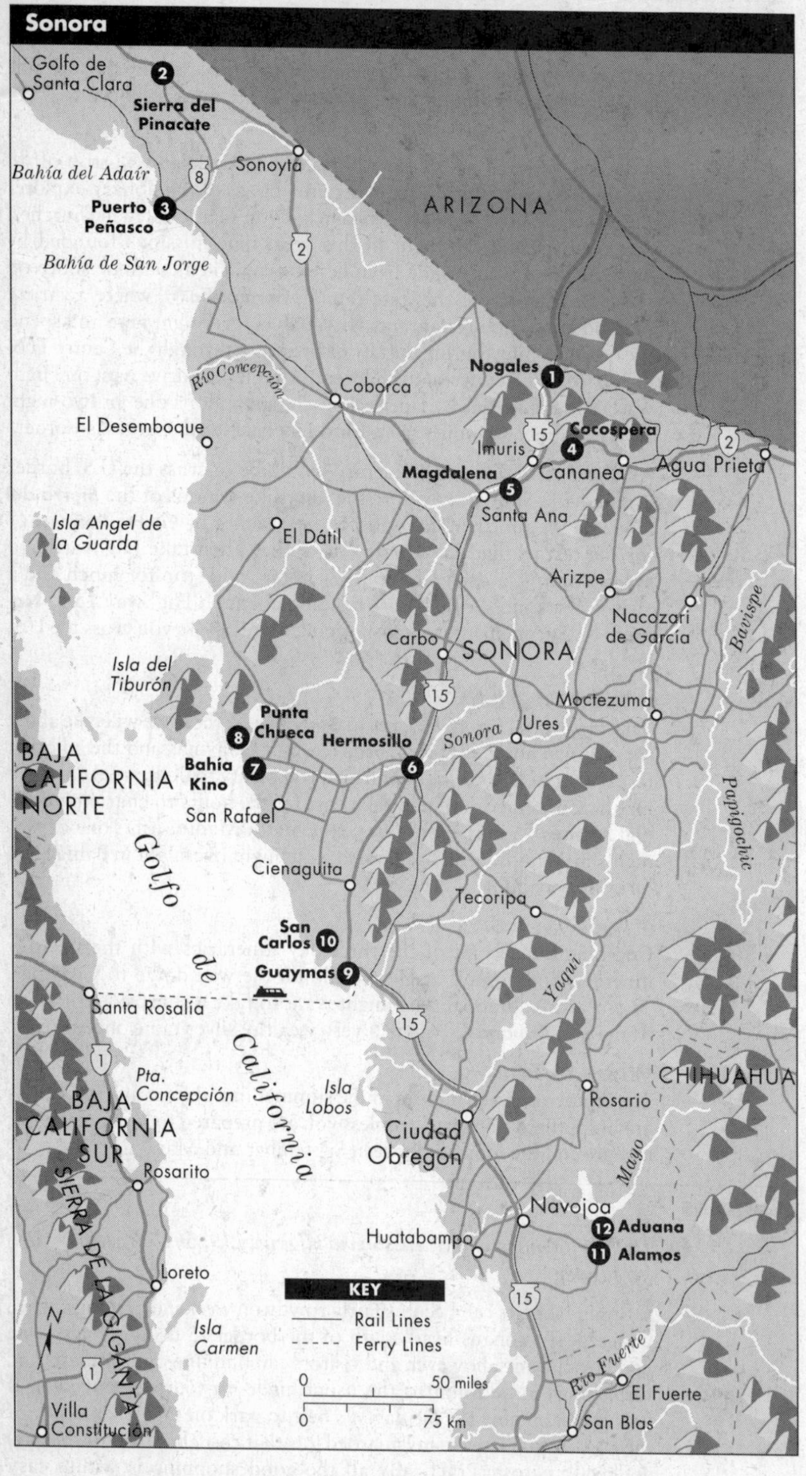
Golfo de Santa Clara
Sierra del Pinacate
Bahía del Adaír
Sonoyta
Puerto Peñasco
Bahía de San Jorge
ARIZONA
Nogales
Río Concepción
Coborca
El Desemboque
Cocospera
Imuris
Cananea
Agua Prieta
Magdalena
Santa Ana
Isla Angel de la Guarda
El Dátil
Arizpe
Nacozari de García
Bavispe
Carbo
SONORA
Isla del Tiburón
Moctezuma
Punta Chueca
Hermosillo
Ures
Sonora
BAJA CALIFORNIA NORTE
Bahía Kino
San Rafael
Papigochic
Golfo de California
Cienaguita
Tecoripa
San Carlos
Guaymas
Yaqui
Santa Rosalía
CHIHUAHUA
Pta. Concepción
Isla Lobos
Rosario
BAJA CALIFORNIA SUR
Ciudad Obregón
Mayo
Rosarito
SIERRA DE LA GIGANTA
Navojoa
Aduana
Huatabampo
Alamos
Loreto
KEY
Rail Lines
Ferry Lines
Isla Carmen
0
50 miles
0
75 km
Río Fuerte
El Fuerte
Villa Constitución
San Blas

follow the crowds. Most of the good restaurants near the border are also on Obregón. Take Obregón as far south as you like; you'll know you have entered workaday Mexico when the shops are no longer fronted by smiling, English-speaking hucksters trying to hustle you in the door ("Take a look! Good prices!").

Dining

$$ ★ ✕ **El Balcon de la Roca.** This elegant restaurant on the sprawling second floor of a stately old stone house has huge beamed ceilings, fireplaces, and a variety of dining rooms to choose from. The best place for a margarita is on the balcony overlooking a charming patio with magnolia trees and a gurgling fountain. Among the excellent variety of meat and seafood dishes is *carne tampiqueña,* an assortment of grilled meats that comes with a *chile relleno* (chili pepper stuffed with cheese and fried in batter) and an enchilada. The *queso la Roca* (seasoned potato slices covered with melted cheese) makes a fine starter. ✉ *Calle Elias 91,* ☎ *631/2–07–60,* FAX *631/2–08–91. AE, DC, MC, V.*

$$ ✕ **El Cid.** The menu here offers a wide selection—everything from sandwiches and burgers to fresh seafood. There is candlelight dining and dancing with live music on Friday and Saturday nights and mariachi music on Sunday evenings. ✉ *Av. Obregón 124,* ☎ *631/2–64–00. AE, MC, V.*

$$ ✕ **El Greco.** As its name suggests, this place has a distinctly Mediterranean ambience, but with a Mexican colonial twist. You can choose from excellent Greek salads, Alaskan king crab, or typical American and Mexican fare. Free margaritas come with lunch and dinner. ✉ *Av. Obregón 152,* ☎ *631/2–42–59 or 631/2–43–58. AE, MC, V.*

$ ✕ **Elvira.** The free shot of tequila that comes with each meal will whet your appetite for Elvira's fine fish dishes, chicken *mole* (chicken in a spicy chocolate sauce), or chiles rellenos. This large, friendly restaurant (divided into more intimate dining areas) is at the very end of Avenida Obregón next to the border and popular with frequent visitors to Nogales. ✉ *Av. Obregón 1,* ☎ *631/2–47–73. Reservations not accepted. DC, MC, V.*

Shopping

Nogales is one of Sonora's best shopping areas, with a wide selection of handicrafts, furnishings, and jewelry. At the more informal shops, bargaining is not only acceptable but expected. The following shops, however, tend to have fixed prices: **El Sarape** (✉ Av. Obregón 161, ☎ 631/2–03–09) specializes in sterling-silver jewelry from Taxco and designer clothing for women. **Mickey & CIA** (✉ Av. Obregón 128–130, ☎ 631/2–22–99) has two floors of handcrafted Mexican treasures, *equipale* (pigskin) furniture, Talavera ceramic dishes, pottery, glassware, and liquors. **Firenze** (✉ Av. Obregón 111, ☎ 631/2–22–52) features gifts, fine perfumes and beauty products, and crafts. East of the railroad tracks and off the beaten tourist path, **El Changarro** (✉ Calle Elias 93, ☎ 631/2–05–45), in the same building as El Balcon de la Roca Restaurant, carries high-quality furniture, antiques, pottery, and handwoven rugs.

Sierra del Pinacate

❷ *50 km (31 mi) west of Lukeville-Sonoyta.*

Midway between the Arizona border and the beach town of Puerto Peñasco is Sierra del Pinacate, a Biosphere Reserve International Park most notable for its rock formations and craters so moonlike that they were used for training the Apollo astronauts. The diversity of the lava flows makes Pinacate unique, as does the striking combination of Sonoran desert and volcanic field. Highlights of the area include **Santa**

Clara peak, a little more than 4,000 ft high and 2.5 million years old, and **El Elegante crater,** 1½ km (1 mi) across and 750 ft deep, created by a giant steam eruption 150,000 years ago. There are no facilities of any kind at Pinacate; you'll need to bring your own water (take plenty of it), food, and extra gasoline, as well as a good map; you can get one in Arizona at Si Como No bookstore in Ajo or at Tucson's Map and Flag Center, or in Mexico at CEDO (☞ Puerto Peñasco, *below*). A high-clearance vehicle is strongly advised, and four-wheel drive is recommended. Camping is allowed with a permit obtainable from the Oficina Sierra del Pinacate in Sonoyta, a block south of the border crossing on the west side of the street. Visitors must register at the park entrance.

Summer temperatures can be blistering; the best time to visit is between November and March, when daytime temperatures hover between 60 and 90°F. Tours can be arranged through the tourism office in Puerto Peñasco; an excellent naturalist-led tour in English is also available from **Ajo Stage Lines** (✉ 1041 Solana St., Ajo, AZ 85321, ☎ 520/387–6559 or 800/942–1981). As with protected wilderness areas in the United States, no animals, plants, or archaeological artifacts may be removed.

Puerto Peñasco

❸ *104 km (65 mi) south of the Arizona border at Lukeville on Mexico Highway 8.*

Set at the northern end of the Sea of Cortés, this is a popular wintering spot for American RVers and retirees, and a favorite weekend getaway for beach-seeking Arizonans—especially college kids during spring break. It was dubbed Rocky Point by British explorers in the 18th century, and that's the name most Americans know it by today. The Mexican immigration laws are relaxed for tourists crossing in this so-called free zone; simply drive through (but don't neglect to get Mexican auto insurance—crucial in case of an accident).

The town was established about 1927, when Mexican fishermen found abundant shrimp beds in the area and American John Stone built the first hotel; Al Capone was a frequent visitor during the Prohibition era, when he was hiding from U.S. law. Puerto Peñasco is rather faceless, but the "old town" area has a number of interesting shopping stalls, fish markets, and restaurants. The real draw, however, is the miles of sandy beaches, often punctuated by stretches of black, volcanic rock that get inundated at high tide. Rocky Point boasts one of the largest tide changes in the world—as much as 23 ft, depending on the season. At low tide the rocky stretches of coastline are great for poking among countless shallow tidal pools inhabited by such local marine life as octopus, shrimp, and starfish. This coastline will probably change very soon, however; the construction of the $150 million Marina Peñasco—a complex that will eventually include a shopping center, luxury hotel, condos and villas, a yacht club, and a 200-slip marina—is designed to attract a more upscale U.S. clientele, and other developers are waiting in the wings.

The northern Gulf area forms a desert-coast ecosystem unmatched in the Western Hemisphere, and scientists from both the United States and Mexico conduct active research programs at the **Desert and Ocean Studies Center** (known as CEDO, its acronym in Spanish), about 3 km (2 mi) east of town on Fremont Boulevard. You can tour the facility to learn about its history and current projects, or come by to pick up a tide calendar—useful if you're planning beach activities. Don't forget to step in at the small **CETMAR Aquarium** next door, which is an especially kid-friendly, hands-on experience. ✉ *Turn east at munici-*

pal building and follow signs for Caborca Rd., where there will be signs for Las Conchas Beach and CEDO. ☎ *638/3–54–03.* ⏲ *Tour hrs posted on door.*

Dining and Lodging

$$$ ★ ✕ **Puesta del Sol.** As the name implies, this is a perfect place to see the sun set, with plenty of outdoor seating on a patio overlooking the beach. Puesta del Sol offers many seafood dishes and soups, with appetizers for the American palate. The fish Mornay (with a creamy cheese sauce) is good, as is the grilled lobster—and the margaritas are to die for. ✉ *Hotel Playa Bonita, Paseo Balboa,* ☎ *638/3–25–86. MC, V.*

$$–$$$ ✕ **Costa Brava.** In town, this small, split-level restaurant has excellent service and a great view overlooking the Gulf. For four, try the excellent *marinera de la casa,* a combination of octopus, shrimp, sea snails, and clams. The Shrimp Carlos V—broiled fish and shrimp stuffed with cheese and wrapped in bacon—is also good. Hundreds of business cards on the wall testify to this place's popularity with Americans. ✉ *Blvd. Kino and 1° de Junio,* ☎ *638/3–31–30. MC, V.*

$$ ✕ **Friendly Dolphin.** You'll recognize this charming downtown spot by the bright blue dolphins decorating its doorway. Inside, the place feels like a wealthy Mexican family's home, with ornately stuccoed ceilings, wood-paneled windows, and exquisite hand-painted tiles; interesting old photographs, including some of Emiliano Zapata and Pancho Villa, line the hallways. Gaston, the owner, can often be found on the premises singing in an operatic baritone as rich and robust as the food he serves. Unique family recipes include foil-wrapped shrimp or fish prepared *estilo delfin*—steamed in orange juice, herbs, and spices. An upstairs porch overlooks the harbor. ✉ *Av. Alcantar 44,* ☎ *638/3–26–08. AE, DC, MC, V.*

$$ ✕ **La Casa del Capitan.** Perched atop Rocky Point's tallest "rock," this restaurant has the best views over the bay and the town below. There's inside dining, but the long outdoor porch overlooking the sea is the place to be. A wide-ranging menu includes everything from nachos and quesadillas to flaming brandied jumbo shrimp. ✉ *Follow Blvd. Benito Juárez to* LA CASA DEL CAPITAN *sign and head up the steep hill,* ☎ *638/3–60–27. Reservations not accepted. AE, MC, V.*

$ ✕ **Cocodrilos Restaurant, Bar, and Grill** is a lively spot, distinctively painted in bright green. Open from 7 AM to midnight, this is a quick food and drink spot anytime. ✉ *Calle 13, Paseo Balboa,* ☎ *638/3–63–76. AE, MC, V.*

$ ✕ **La Curva.** This friendly family restaurant with great Mexican food is easy to spot if you look for the mermaid on the sign. Turn east where the railroad tracks cross the main road into town. ✉ *Blvd. Kino and Comonfort,* ☎ *638/3–34–70. MC, V.*

$$$–$$$$ 🏨 **Plaza Las Glorias.** One of a chain of hotels in Mexico, Plaza Las Glorias is the first lodging of its kind at Puerto Peñasco. Changing the face of the town, this soaring monument to Mexico's desire to promote tourism at any cost sits like a sand-colored fortress overlooking the beach. The open, marble-floored lobby with its towering quadrangular ceiling and bamboo-covered skylights draws gasps of admiration from the busloads of tourists who have started to flock to the hotel after its inauguration in 1995. Rooms are well appointed, many of them with kitchenettes; all offer ocean views. The hotel sells condominiums and time shares and is in the process of putting in a marina and shopping center. ✉ *Paseo Las Glorias, Las Explanadas 83550,* ☎ *638/3–60–10, 638/3–60–27, or 800/544–4686. 210 rooms. Restaurant, pool. AE, MC, V.*

$$$ **Playa Bonita.** One of the first three hotels in Rocky Point, Playa Bonita offers clean, comfortable rooms; ask for one facing the hotel's broad, sandy beach. This place is very popular with Americans, who also enjoy the **Puesta del Sol** restaurant (☞ *above*). An RV park offers 200 hookups at $16 a day. ✉ *Paseo Balboa 100, 83550,* ☎ *638/3–25–86; 520/994–4475 or 800/569–1797 in the U.S. 76 rooms, 2 suites. Restaurant, bar, beach. MC, V.*

$$ **Costa Brava.** All the rooms in this small, clean, and economical downtown hotel overlook the Gulf. Right down the street are the fish markets, popular with those who like to bring the catch of the day back across the border. ✉ *Malecón Kino and 1° de Julio, 83550,* ☎ *638/3–41–00 or 638/3–41–01,* FAX *638/3–36–21. 25 rooms. Bar. MC, V.*

Nightlife and the Arts

Nightlife tends to be spontaneous and informal in Puerto Peñasco. A favorite dance spot is the **Pitahya Bar.** All ages tend to congregate along the beaches near **Manny's Beach Club** (☞ Water Sports, *below*), where recorded music is always blaring. Manny's is the place for those who don't want to put too much distance between the water's edge and their next margarita; it's right on the beach, with signs like NO SHOES, NO SHIRT, NO PROBLEM. The food is nothing special, but as the quintessential beach hangout for all ages, Manny's is not to be missed.

Outdoor Activities and Sports

WATER SPORTS

Manny's Beach Club (✉ Av. Coahuila and Blvd. Matamoros, ☎ 638/3–36–05) offers an all-day fishing trip in the Gulf for $40, as well as day and sunset cruises. At **China Sea Sailing and Diving** (✉ Paseo Victor Estrella, ☎ 638/3–54–50; 520/566–7614 in AZ) you can rent diving equipment or receive snorkeling and scuba instruction.

Cocospera

❹ *104 km (65 mi) southeast of Nogales, between Imuris and Cananea.*

Cocospera is one of the two dozen churches established in the state of Sonora and Arizona by Father Eusebio Francisco Kino between 1687 and 1711; the crumbling adobe mission sits on a bluff above an oak forest and farmlands in a mountain pass in the Sierra Madre Occidental. To get here, take Highway 15 Libre to Highway 2.

Magdalena

❺ *25 km (13 mi) south of Imuris, 96 km (60 mi) from Nogales.*

The grave of Father Eusebio Francisco Kino was discovered in Magdalena in 1966. His remains are in a mausoleum across the plaza from Santa Maria Magdalena de Buquivaba, the cathedral that stands on one of the missions he founded. A $1 million monument to the memory of this pioneer priest also stands here. A number of shops surround the plaza, selling curios, blankets, and religious artifacts; stop in at the bakery for some excellent sweet rolls and bread. Magdalena is now also known as the final resting place of its beloved native son, slain presidential candidate Luis Donaldo Colosio, whose statue also presides over the plaza.

If you're really interested in Spanish missions and in rural Mexican life as it has been lived for centuries, drive just a few kilometers north of Magdalena on a clearly marked dirt road to **San Ignacio,** another of Father Kino's churches, still in use in a tiny Mexican farming village.

Hermosillo

❻ *185 km (115 mi) south of Magdalena on Highway 15.*

Hermosillo (population about 600,000) is the capital of Sonora, a status it has held on and off since 1831. It is the seat of the state university and benefits from that institution's cultural activities. Although those who know a bit of Spanish might think the city's name means "little beauty," it actually honors José Mariá González Hermosillo, one of the leaders in Mexico's War of Independence. Settled in 1742 by Captain Augustín de Vildosola and a contingent of 50 soldiers, Hermosillo was originally called Pitic, the Pima Indian name for "the place where two rivers meet." The city's most prestigious neighborhood—home to the governor and U.S. consul, among other prominent citizens—still bears the name Pitic. Located immediately north of the highway into town and just behind the Hotel Bugambilia, the area is worth an hour's stroll to view the creative handling of concrete, tile, and other materials in the homes of Hermosillo's more affluent residents.

A business center for the state of Sonora, Hermosillo is largely modern, but some lovely plazas and parks hark back to a more graceful postcolonial past. Although Hermosillo is usually just considered a jumping-off point for Bahía Kino or Guaymas, it has a number of attractions in its own right, as well as the best accommodations and restaurants until you reach Guaymas. The city's main boulevard is lined with monuments to Sonora's famous sons: Adolfo de la Huerta, Alvaro Obregón, Plutarco Elías Calles, and Abelardo Rodríguez (after whom the boulevard is named), all presidents of the country after the revolution (Rodríguez also served as governor of Sonora). At the center of town, the **Plaza Zaragoza** boasts the impressive **Catedral de San Agustín** (1878), regilded at great expense. Across from the cathedral is the **Palacio de Gobierno del Estado,** its graceful courtyard surrounded by somewhat disjunctive modern murals depicting Sonoran history, and between the two buildings sits an ornate Victorian gazebo. On the south edge of town, the **Plaza de los Tres Pueblos** marks the original settlement.

Two of Hermosillo's **museums** are worth a visit. Overlooking the city, on the Cerro la Campana (Hill of Bells), the **Museo de Sonora,** a former penitentiary, now hosts a variety of regional history displays; you can also tour the tiny, dark prison cells. Admission is $1.50 (free Sunday); hours are Tuesday–Saturday 10–5 and Sunday 9–4. The **Museo de la Universidad de Sonora** (on Blvds. Luis Encinas and Rosales) has interesting exhibits of pre-Columbian artifacts. Admission is free; hours are weekdays 9–1 and 4–6, Saturday 9–1. On the highway south of town, stop at the **Centro Ecologico,** an environmental and ecological park where over 300 species of plants and animals native to Sonora can be found. It is modeled after the Arizona-Sonora Desert Museum in Tucson (best visited November through March because of summer heat). If you don't feel like walking through the entire park, which is rather spread out, consider arranging for a golf cart by calling the office of tourism. ⏲ *Wed.–Sun. 9–3.*

Dining and Lodging

$$$ ✕ **Xochimilco.** This large and friendly place, which offers indoor and outdoor dining, is deeply shaded by large fiddle-leaf figs and yucateca trees on a narrow side street in the southern part of town (from Rosales, follow the sign near the Oxxo store). Popular with locals and regulars from across the border, Xochimilco serves well-prepared typical Sonoran dishes. ✉ *Av. Obregón 5,* ☎ *62/50–40–89. AE, MC, V.*

$$ ✕ **Don Simon.** Here in grand old Hermosillo style you can enjoy the finest cuts of the famous Sonoran beef. ✉ *Calle Monroy y Concepcion de Soria 102,* ☎ *621/13–61–26. AE, MC, V.*

$$ ✕ **Hotel Bugambilia Restaurant.** A small dining room with beamed ceilings and red-checked tablecloths and curtains, this cheerful place serves excellent tortilla soup and Mexican-style veal cutlets. For breakfast, try the *chilaquiles con huevos* (chopped tortillas, cooked in a red chili sauce, topped with scrambled or fried eggs), a specialty of the house. ✉ *Blvd. Kino 712,* ☎ *62/14–50–50. Reservations not accepted. AE, MC, V.*

$$$ **Fiesta Americana.** Hermosillo's only five-star hotel, this full-service property is the largest in town and popular among business travelers. The decor is predictable, but some rooms have excellent views, and the beds are large and firm. ✉ *Blvd. Kino 369, 83010,* ☎ *62/59–60–60; 800/343–7821 for U.S. reservations;* FAX *62/59–60–60 or 62/59–60–62. 222 rooms. Restaurant, cafeteria, lobby lounge, pool, hot tub, tennis courts, dance club, travel services. AE, MC, V.*

$$$ **Holiday Inn Hermosillo.** Two-thirds of the attractive rooms in this contemporary Spanish-style hotel look out on extensive, well-kept gardens and a good-size pool. The staff is geared toward accommodating the many Mexican business travelers who stay here. ✉ *Blvd. Kino and Ramon Corral, 83010,* ☎ *62/14–45–70,* FAX *62/14–64–73. 144 rooms with shower. Restaurant, bar, pool, nightclub, travel services, free airport shuttle. AE, MC, V.*

$$$ **Hotel Bugambilia,** one of the first motels in Hermosillo, is a green oasis on the boulevard into town. Here you will find a more personal atmosphere than at some of the faceless chain hotels around it. ✉ *Blvd. Kino 712, 83010,* ☎ *62/14–50–50,* FAX *62/14–52–52. 107 rooms. Restaurant, pool. AE, DC, MC, V.*

$$ **Hotel Gandara.** One of the old traditional spots in Hermosillo, this hotel, with its palm trees, gardens, and colonnades, has the charm of Old Spain. You can stay in bungalows or in conventional-style hotel rooms; all offer cable TV and coffeemakers. ✉ *Blvd. E. Kino 1000, 83010,* ☎ *62/14–44–14 or 62/15–64–24,* FAX *62/14–99–26. 154 rooms. Restaurant, bar, coffee shop, pool. AE, DC, MC, V.*

Nightlife and the Arts

Hermosillo is home to several lively night spots: **Bar Ali Baba** at the Plaza Pitic (✉ Blvds. Kino and Roman Yocupicio, ☎ 62/14–43–87) and, for the younger set, **Blocky'O Disco** (✉ Blvd. Rodríguez at Aguascalientes, no phone).

Shopping

In the downtown markets of Hermosillo, particularly along Avenidas Serdán and Monterrey, you can buy anything from blankets and candles to wedding attire, as well as a variety of *charro* (Mexican cowboy) items; the variety of goods concentrated in this area equals what you'll find in Nogales, and the prices are better.

En Route Drive from Hermosillo through flat agricultural land and dusty vineyards to where the desert finally meets the sea and the monochrome landscape gives way to a refreshing palette of colors.

Bahía Kino

7 *104 km (65 mi) west of Hermosillo on Highway 16.*

On the shore of the Sea of Cortés lies Bahía Kino (Kino Bay), home to the prettiest beaches in northwest Mexico. For many years, Bahía Kino was undiscovered except by RV owners and other aficionados of the unspoiled; but a great change has taken place in the last decade as Arizonans have begun to build condos here. Bahía Kino itself is divided into **Kino Viejo** (Old Kino), the Mexican village, and **Kino Nuevo** (New Kino), where the beaches, condos, RV sites, and other typical tourist facilities are.

Consider taking a run across the narrow channel to **Isla del Tiburón** (Shark Island), which is being developed into one of the finest wildlife and game refuges in North America. Permission to visit Tiburón may be obtained from the Port Captain, at the end of the main street in Kino Viejo. Ask at any of the area hotels or RV parks where to find a reliable guide. Only the Seri Indians, for whom Isla del Tiburón is a traditional fishing ground, need no permit. You might see some of these Indians at Bahía Kino selling their fine ironwood carvings of animals (☞ Punta Chueca, *below*). Turtle hunting used to be an integral part of the Seri culture, and the capture of a turtle was once the subject of a ritual observance, but these creatures are now protected by law. (Note: The Seris are sensitive about having their picture taken. The polite thing to do is to ask their permission before snapping.)

Dining and Lodging

$$ ✕ **El Pargo Rojo.** The best-known restaurant in town has fish and fishnets decorating its two rooms (with a small bandstand for musicians). The catch of the day varies, but you can depend on excellent dishes, including such classics as a brimming shrimp cocktail for starters and fresh lobster any way you want it. Fine cuts of meat are available and Mexican musicians serenade nightly. ✉ *Blvd. Mar de Cortés 1426, Kino Nuevo,* ☎ *624/2–02–05. MC, V.*

$ ✕ **La Palapa.** This thatch-roof restaurant, with a casual interior and a small balcony overlooking the beach, attracts seafood enthusiasts. The shrimp brochette with green chilies is memorable, especially when accompanied by some very palatable Mexican wines. ✉ *Mar de Cortés and Wellington on the way into Kino Nuevo, no phone. No credit cards.*

$ ✕ **Restaurant Kino Bay.** Owned by an American, this clean, comfortable family restaurant overlooks the bay. One of the few places serving breakfast, lunch, and dinner, it's a perfect spot for coffee, morning pancakes, and pelican viewing. ✉ *Blvd. Mar de Cortés, Kino Nuevo,* ☎ *624/2–00–49. Reservations not accepted. No credit cards.*

$ ✕ **Restaurant Marlin.** This restaurant in Kino Viejo is only hard to find the first time; after that, you will return frequently, drawn by the clean, unpretentious atmosphere and congenial service—not to mention margaritas as big as fishbowls. After serving you superb seafood dishes such as *sopa de siete mares* (soup of the seven seas) or *jaiba a la diabla* (deviled crab), your waiter might produce a guitar and serenade you free of charge. ✉ *Calle Tastiota and Calle Guaymas,* ☎ *624/2–01–11. Reservations not accepted. No credit cards.*

$$$ 🏨 **Anchor House.** Opened in June '96, this bed-and-breakfast, the first in town, is a spacious, beachfront home away from home for travelers who want a warm American welcome. The owners have lived in Kino for years and are knowledgeable about every facet of life in this growing community. Coffee is always brewing, and the breakfasts, included in the rate, are hearty. Children and pets are not allowed, and there is a two-night minimum. ✉ *Blvd. Mar de Cortés 3525, 83340,* ☎ *624/2–01–41. 4 rooms. No credit cards.*

$$$ 🏨 **Posada Santa Gemma.** On a beautiful strip of beach, these eclectically furnished two-story bungalows with kitchenettes, fireplaces, and spectacular views of the sea are ideal for families. Each has two bedrooms and sleeps four or five comfortably. Bring your own cooking utensils and settle in. ✉ *Blvd. Mar de Cortés, 83340,* ☎ *624/2-00-26. 14 bungalows. Beach. MC, V.*

$$ **Posada del Mar.** Across the street from the beach and set back from a rambling garden with a small swimming pool and winding walkways hewn from rock, this mission-style hotel was one of the first in Kino Nuevo. Antiques and Mexican art lend the place an old-world charm. ✉ *Blvd. Mar de Cortés and Creta, Box 132, 83340,* ☎ *624/2-01-55; 62/18-12-17 in Hermosillo. 42 rooms, 2 suites, 4 bungalows. Restaurant, bar, pool. MC, V.*

$ **Kino Bay RV Park and Motel.** Your best buy for the money, this small, friendly motel across from the beach offers rooms with two double beds, microwaves, refrigerators, and sinks; in addition it has 180 RV spaces with full hookups ($14). A barbecue area sits under huge rubber trees. ✉ *At end of main road (reservations:* ✉ *Box 857, Hermosillo 83000),* ☎ *624/2-02-16,* FAX *624/531-97. 8 rooms. Grocery, 5-hole golf course. MC, V.*

Punta Chueca

❽ *27 km (15 mi) north of Bahía Kino.*

This rustic Seri fishing village perches at the end of a bumpy, winding dirt road. You'll pass exquisite vistas of the bay, distant empty beaches, and rolling mountains. The inhabitants of this community eke out a meager living from sea and desert, much as they have for hundreds of years.

With fewer than 1,000 Seris left in existence, this tribe represents an ancient culture on the verge of extinction. The Seris' love for their natural surroundings is evident in the necklaces that they have traditionally worn and now create to sell. Pretty little shells are wound into the shape of flowers and strung with wild desert seeds and tiny bleached snake vertebrae to result in delicate necklaces. Seri women weave elaborate *canastas* (baskets) of torote grass, which have become highly prized and expensive.

As you get out of your car and head toward the only "store" in town for a soda, be prepared to encounter a growing entourage of Seri women dressed in colorful ankle-length skirts, their heads covered with scarves and their eager outstretched arms laden with necklaces for sale. The Seri are also famous for carving figures from ironwood that represent the animal world around them, including dolphins, turtles, and pelicans. (Note: In recent years, many Mexican merchants have taken to machine-making large figures out of ironwood for the tourist trade, thereby seriously depleting the supply of the unique tree that grows only in the Sonoran desert. Make sure the ones you buy are made by the Seris.)

Guaymas

❾ *128 km (83 mi) south of Hermosillo.*

Long considered a quiet fishing town that drew only the most hardy, adventuresome travelers, in the past 20 years Guaymas has begun to emerge as a major commercial port and tourist destination. In many parts of Mexico, it can be said that the mountains come down to meet the sea; but at Guaymas, both the mountains and the desert abut the water. The clear air and the sun shining on the mountains provide panoramas of striking, ever-changing beauty.

The Spanish arrived in this "port of ports" as early as the mid-16th century. In 1701, two Jesuit priests, Father Francisco Eusebio Kino and his colleague Juan María Salvatierra, erected a mission base here intended to convert the native Guaimas, Seri, and Yaqui Indians.

Guaymas was officially declared a port in 1814 and became an important center of trade with Europe as well as within Mexico. In 1847, during the Mexican War, the town was attacked by naval forces from the United States and occupied for a year. In 1866, during Maximilian's brief reign, the harbor was taken over by the French. The waters of Guaymas Bay have been raided by pirates and plumbed by the once-legendary pearl divers.

Downtown, take a walk on the **malecón,** and look out over the bay at fishing boats loaded down with heavy black nets and the giant shrimp Guaymas is famous for. Fishing boats are only allowed to go out to sea between September and May so that the shrimp have time to replenish themselves. A small plaza along the port has a handsome bronze statue commemorating the local fishermen. After pushing your way through the throngs at the *mercado,* a daily municipal market, the 19th-century **Cathedral of San Fernando** offers a quiet respite. Or you might relax in the typical Mexican park across the street from the church, **Plaza 13 de Julio,** with its white, Moorish-style, lacy wrought-iron bandstand and time-worn, tree-shaded benches. Within walking distance is the **Plaza de los Tres Presidentes,** where, in front of the 1899 Palacio Municipal (City Hall), loom imposing statues of the three presidents of Mexico born in Sonora: Plutarco Elías Calles, Adolfo de la Huerta, and Abelardo Rodríguez.

The original **mission of San José de Guaymas** no longer stands, but another church was erected in its place at the end of the last century. During the past decade, it has been somewhat remodeled by a group of American Franciscan monks. The small church is located about 16 km (10 mi) north of the center of the city, near a field of giant saguaro cactus (some measuring taller than 40 ft).

After you get too much history and downtown dust in your head, the only thing left is to soak up some sea at the various beaches in the area. Guaymas has not one but two bays: Bacochibampo Bay and Guaymas Bay. The beaches most of the people flock to are at San Carlos and beyond (☞ San Carlos, *below*).

Dining and Lodging

$$ ✕ **Los Barcos.** Across the street from the harbor, Los Barcos offers a predictable seafood-and-steak menu. The main room is large and pseudo–beach casual, with picnic tables and overhead palm fronds and nets; there are also two smaller, more traditional dining rooms. Especially good is the house special seafood plate, which includes calamari, octopus, and shrimp in a white wine sauce. ✉ *Malecón Malpica between Calles 21 and 22,* ☎ *622/2–76–50. Reservations not accepted. MC, V.*

$ ✕ **Los Delfines.** At the end of the harbor, this spacious restaurant offers a variety of no-frills fresh seafood and a postcard-perfect view of the water. Popular with the locals, who enjoy the *ambiente familiar* (family atmosphere), Los Delfines has a festive air; on weekends, a band plays in the afternoon. ✉ *At end of Blvd. Sanchez Taboada,* ☎ *622/2–92–30. Reservations not accepted. No credit cards.*

$$$ 🏨 **Playa de Cortés.** This fine, sprawling old hotel overlooking the Bacochibampo Bay is built and decorated like a Spanish colonial hacienda, with towering wooden beamed ceilings and a lavish fireplace in the reception room. With tropical landscaping and a sweeping view of the bay, this hotel evokes its genteel past before condos and time-shares.

The rooms are furnished with hand-carved antiques; many have fireplaces and balconies. Some private casitas are available, each with the name of a small Sonoran town. To reach this hotel from the highway, take the turnoff for Colonia Miramar. ✉ *Bahía Bacochibampo, San Carlos 85506,* ☎ *622/1–12–24 or 622/1–10–48,* FAX *622/1–01–35. 120 rooms. Restaurant, bar, pool, tennis, beach. AE, DC, MC, V.*

$$–$$$ **Hotel Armida.** Close to the shops and restaurants of downtown Guaymas, this sand-colored hotel has a large, well-kept pool; a good coffee shop where locals gather for power breakfasts; and an excellent steak house, El Oeste. Rooms in the hotel's old section are dark, with ill-matched furnishings. The larger, brighter accommodations in the newest section, done in light wood, are worth the higher rates; many have balconies overlooking the pool. ✉ *Carretera Internacional, Box 296, 85420,* ☎ *622/4–30–35; 800/732–0780 for U.S. reservations;* FAX *622/2–04–48. 80 rooms, 45 suites. 2 restaurants, bar, coffee shop, room service, pool, dance club, laundry service, airport shuttle, car rental. AE, MC, V.*

$$ ★ **Las Playitas.** The best deal in town, this combination trailer park–motel on Guaymas Bay has plain but appealing rooms—with tinwork mirrors and beamed ceilings—opening out onto a cobblestoned, bougainvillea-lined path. Even if you don't sleep here, come for the lively, eclectically decorated restaurant and bar. The food is good and inexpensive, but if you'd rather eat what you caught that day, you can get it cooked up, with trimmings added, for a small price. ✉ *Carretera al Varadero Nacional, 85420,* ☎ *622/2–27–27 or 622/2–27–53. 29 bungalows with shower, 93 RV spaces. Restaurant, bar, pool. MC, V.*

Nightlife and the Arts

Gathering spots in the area include the disco **Xanadu** (✉ Malecón Malpica, ☎ 622/2–83–88) and, for the younger set, **Charles Baby** (✉ Av. Serdán and Malecón, no phone).

Shopping

Plaza el Vigía, a huge shopping center on the main road from the north into Guaymas, has everything from groceries, film, toiletries, and clothes to household wares. In Guaymas itself, the **Mercado Publico** is the best place for *artesanías* such as baskets, hats, necklaces, and other trinkets. Visit the **Casa de las Conchas** (✉ Calle 23 and Av. Serdán, across from Plaza de los Tres Presidentes, ☎ 622/2–01–99) and admire beautiful seashell handicrafts, as well as 400 to 500 types of seashells; right next door is a great little ice-cream parlor.

San Carlos

❿ *32 km (20 mi) northwest of Guaymas.*

Long considered an extension of Guaymas, this resort town—on the other side of the rocky peninsula that separates Bacochibampo Bay from San Carlos Bay—has a personality of its own. Whitewashed, red tile–roof houses snuggle together along the water where countless yachts and motorboats are docked. The town is a laid-back favorite among professional anglers, North American tourists, and the time-share crowd, as well as wealthy Mexican families from Guaymas. There is a growing assortment of hotels, motels, and condominiums, as well as a country club with an 18-hole golf course.

The overlapping of desert and tropical flora and fauna has created a fascinating diversity of species along this coast. Among marine life, more than 650 species of fish exist here; red snapper, marlin, corbina, yellowtail, sea bass, and flounder are commonly caught. Whales have been spotted in San Carlos Bay, and there is an abundance of dolphins and pelicans. The water is calm and warm enough through October for the whole family to enjoy excellent swimming. Scuba, snorkeling, fishing, and boat excursions are popular, too.

The quiet 5-km (3-mi) stretch of sandy beach at **Los Algodones,** where the Plaza San Carlos and Club Med are now, was in the 1960s a location site for the film *Catch 22.* Mexico's first man-made marina lies in the shadow of the jagged twin-peaked **Tetakawi mountain,** once a sacred site where Indian warriors gathered to gain spiritual strength. An interesting day trip can be made by boat out to the pristine **San Pedro Island,** where sea lions frolic on the rocks.

To reach San Carlos, take the road north of Guaymas for about 8 km (5 mi), past the signs to your left for the turnoff to Bocachibampo Bay and the residential area of Miramar. Continue along for 24 km (15 mi) on the four-lane **Corredor Escenico** (Scenic Corridor), completed in 1995 to replace an infamously bumpy road.

Dining and Lodging

$$ ✕ **Bananas.** American food (BLTs, burgers, fries) and Mexican fare—try the "shrimp bananas," wrapped in bacon with barbecue sauce—are served in a single large room with a peaked ceiling lined with palm fronds; there are a few seats in the entrance patio as well. A copy of Charlie Chaplin's 1924 marriage license hangs on the wall by the rest rooms. ✉ *On main road through San Carlos, no phone. Reservations not accepted. MC, V.*

$–$$ ✕ **Rosa's Cantina.** In this cozy, pink, laid-back restaurant, picnic tables fill two large dining rooms where diners feast on ample breakfasts of *huevos rancheros* (eggs with chorizo). The tortilla soup is great for lunch or dinner. ✉ *Carretera San Carlos,* ☎ *622/6–03–07. Reservations not accepted. MC, V.*

$ ✕ **Jax Snax.** Located on the main thoroughfare of San Carlos, this little place, which could be missed in the blink of an eye, tastes better than it looks. Open for breakfast, lunch, and dinner, it offers something quick and easy for all appetites. From pizza any way you request it (even cheeseless with veggies—vegan style), grilled shrimp with garlic, hamburgers, guacamole, and pancakes to hot coffee or cold Tecate, this is Mexican-American fast food. ✉ *Carretera San Carlos,* ☎ *622/6–02–70. Reservations not accepted. MC, V.*

$$$$ **Club Med Sonora Bay.** Although San Carlos is expanding rapidly in its direction, this Club Med is still secluded from the main tourist area, its verdant 42-acre complex spread fortresslike behind a large gate fronted by saguaro cactus. Accommodations are characteristically tasteful but plain, and the range of available activities is as great as one would expect from the chain. All meals, soft drinks, and tips—and many sports, such as sailing and scuba diving—are included. It's worth paying extra for the dawn horseback ride to the foothills of the nearby Sierra Madre. ✉ *Playa de los Algodones, 85400,* ☎ *622/6–01–66; 800/258–2633 for U.S. reservations;* FAX *622/6–00–70. 375 rooms. Restaurant, bar, pool, 2 saunas, golf course, 31 tennis courts, horseback riding, beach, windsurfing, boating. AE, MC, V. Closed Oct. 27–Mar. 12.*

$$$$ **San Carlos Plaza Hotel and Resort.** Formerly a Howard Johnson's, this huge structure, rising from San Carlos Bay en route to Club Med, is thoroughly, strikingly, pink. This is the most luxurious hotel in Sonora, with an impressive marble-floor atrium lobby that opens onto a large pool and beach. Rooms are done in an attractive contemporary style. All have safes and minibars, and rooms on the first two floors have balconies overlooking the sea. Children love the swimming-pool slide and horseback riding on the beautiful beach. ✉ *Mar Barmejo 4, Los Algodones, Box 441, 85506,* ☎ *622/6–07–94; 800/654–2000 for U.S. reservations;* FAX *622/6–07–77. 148 rooms, 25 suites. 2 restaurants, 2 bars, snack bar, 2 pools, hot tub, 2 tennis courts, exercise room, horseback riding, volleyball, beach, travel services, car rental. AE, MC, V.*

$$$ **Plaza Las Glorias.** This condo-hotel complex, opened in 1994, overlooks the San Carlos marina. It's smaller than the San Carlos Plaza but nearly as impressive. Subtle pastels set a tasteful tone in the comfortable modern rooms. Most accommodations have a tiny kitchenette; a few have private hot tubs. ✉ *Plaza Comercial San Carlos 10, Planta Baja, 85006,* ☎ *622/6–10–21 through 34,* FAX *622/6–10–35. 87 rooms, 18 suites. Restaurant, snack bar, 3 pools, golf, baby-sitting, travel services, car rental. AE, MC, V.*

$$ **Fiesta San Carlos.** One of the first in San Carlos, this small hotel on the bay has a lot of charm and is clean and comfortable. Accommodations with kitchens are available. Breakfast is included in the room rate. ✉ *San Carlos Bay, 85006,* ☎ *622/6–02–29,* FAX *622/6–37–33. 33 rooms. Restaurant, bar, pool. MC, V.*

$$ **Hacienda Tetakawi.** This hotel and trailer park across from the beach on the main street of town is a Best Western. The rooms are generic but clean, and each has a balcony with a view of the sea. ✉ *Carretera San Carlos, Km 10,* ☎ *622/60–24–8 or 622/60–22–0. 22 rooms. Restaurant, bar. AE, MC, V.*

Nightlife and the Arts

Gathering spots in the area include **Pappas Tappas** (✉ Sector Creston, Lot 37, ☎ 622/6–07–07), a bar and grill; and **Ranas Ranas** (✉ Carretera San Carlos, Km 9.5, ☎ 622/6–07–27), from which you can enjoy a view of the beach. For a feast of artwork by a variety of Mexican and foreign artists, stop by the two floors at the **Galería Bellas Artes** (✉ Villa Hermosa 111, ☎ 622/60–07–3), where art is for sale. It's open Monday–Saturday 9:30–5.

Outdoor Activities and Sports

DIVING

Gary's Boat Trips (✉ Main street of San Carlos, Apdo. 655, ☎ 622/6–00–49; 622/6–00–24 after hrs) runs fishing and diving excursions.

FISHING

Cortez Explorers (✉ Carreterra Bahía, across from Marina San Carlos, ☎ 622/6–08–09; 520/577–4982 in Tucson, AZ; FAX 622/6–08–08; ✉ San Carlos Plaza, ☎ 622/6–07–94) runs deep-sea fishing trips as well as sunset cruises and diving charters. The company also rents Jet Skis and ski boats. Other smaller outfitters have boats for rent in the bay.

GOLF

Most hotels in the Guaymas–San Carlos area can arrange for temporary membership at the **San Carlos Country Club,** which has an 18-hole golf course.

HORSEBACK RIDING

Inquire at the San Carlos Plaza (formerly the Howard Johnson's) about the few small *ranchitos* next door that have horses for hire.

Shopping

Lourdes Gift Shop (✉ Plaza Comercial San Carlos 16, ☎ 622/6–00–22), next to the Plaza Las Glorias Hotel, offers an extensive selection of folk art, glassware, and clothing. **Sagitario's Gift Shop** (✉ Carretera San Carlos 132, ☎ 622/6–00–90), across from the entrance to the San Carlos Country Club, features clothing and a variety of crafts, including wood carvings, baskets, and Talavera tile. **Kiamy's Gift Shop** (✉ Carretera San Carlos, Km 10, ☎ 622/6–04–00) is like a bazaar, with something for everyone, at a reasonable price; silver jewelry, earrings, leather bags, Yaqui Indian masks, T-shirts, and caps, as well as a variety of ceramics can be found here.

Alamos

11 *53 km (32 mi) east of Navojoa, 257 km (160 mi) southeast of Guaymas.*

A Mexican national monument, Alamos is the most authentic colonial-style town in Sonora. It's set at the spot where the lower Sonoran desert meets the dry tropical forest in the foothills of the Sierra Madre Occidental, an area marked by rivers, cottonwoods (for which the town of Alamos is named), and evergreens.

Coronado camped here in 1540, and a Jesuit mission was established in 1630, but the town really boomed when silver was discovered in the area during the 1680s. Wealth from the mines financed Spanish expeditions to the north—as far as Los Angeles and San Francisco during the 1770s and 1780s—and the town became the capital of the state of Occidente, which combined the provinces of Sinaloa and Sonora, from 1827 to 1832. A government mint was established here in 1864. The mines closed by the end of the 19th century, and the town went into decline; but today Alamos, with many houses beautifully restored by Americans who have settled here, serves as a showcase of its glorious past. A British visitor to the town in the early 19th century remarked on its cleanliness, and Alamos remains spotless today, with streets swept by local residents early every morning.

Points of interest include the imposing **cathedral** in the central Plaza las Armas, begun in 1787 on the site of a 17th-century Jesuit adobe church and completed in 1894. It is fronted by an ornate Moorish-style wrought-iron gazebo, brought from Mazatlán in 1904. To the west of the square, on Guadalupe Hill, is the Alamos **jail**, built around the turn of the century; visitors may tour the structure on certain days, and the shop by the prison entrance sells items such as bolo ties, belts, and key chains made by the inmates. Tours of the many beautiful **restored colonial homes** in town are also offered; the tourist office and all the local hotels have listings of the times and rates.

Not to be missed, the **Museo Costumbrista de Sonora** gives an excellent overview of the cultural history of the entire state of Sonora. The numerous well-marked (but only in Spanish) displays include artifacts from the nearby silver mines and coins from the mints of Alamos and Hermosillo, as well as typical examples of the clothing and furnishings of prominent local families. ✉ *Calle Guadalupe Victoria 1 (on Plaza las Armas),* ☎ *642/8–00–53.* *Free; donation suggested.* *Wed.–Sat. 9–1 and 3–6, Sun. 9–6.*

Dining and Lodging

$$ ✕ **Mariscos 7 Mares.** This seafood restaurant gives the illusion that you're dining in an Italian palazzo under the open sky. Although the food may not be as impressive as the atmosphere, this is probably the only place for miles where you can be served frogs' legs. ✉ *Calle Obregon 4, no phone. Reservations not accepted. No credit cards.*

$ ✕ **Asadero Los Sabinos.** This small, unpretentious café, with indoor and outdoor seating, offers house specials of beef tips and ranch-style shrimp, along with several types of tacos and hamburgers. It's two blocks west of the Hotel Casa de los Tesoros, across the arroyo. ✉ *2 de Abríl No. 5, no phone. Reservations not accepted. No credit cards.*

$ ✕ **Las Palmas.** This Mexican family restaurant is crammed onto the sidewalk across the street from the Museo Costumbrista and right on the main square. Here you might get homemade "Rosca" bread with your coffee and an assortment of daily specials. ✉ *Lazaro Cardenas 9,* ☎ *642/8–00–65. Reservations not accepted. No credit cards.*

$$$ **Casa de los Tesoros.** This hotel, the House of Treasures, is a picturesque and romantic converted 18th-century convent. The rooms are former nuns' cells and have fireplaces, tiled baths, antique furnishings, and high-quality handicrafts on the walls. Room rates include breakfast, and there is an excellent restaurant. ✉ *Av. Obregón 10, Box 12, 85760,* ☎ *642/8–00–10,* FAX *642/8–04–00. 14 rooms. Restaurant, bar, pool. MC, V.*

$$$ **Casa Encantada.** Set just off the main square, this lovely B&B owned by a California couple is the converted 250-year-old mansion of one of Alamos's former Spanish mine owners. Rooms retain a colonial character, with high-beamed ceilings, fireplaces, and carved-wood furnishings; all have tiled private baths and good lighting, Andalusian-style. The copious breakfast, served on a plant-filled patio overlooking a small pool, might include frittatas, fresh fruit, and home-baked breads. ✉ *Calle Juárez 20, 85760,* ☎ *642/8–04–82 or 800/422–5485,* FAX *642/8–02–21. 9 rooms. Pool, bicycles, meeting room. MC, V.*

$$$ **Casa Obregón Dieciocho.** It would be hard to find more charming accommodations at a better price ($48 a night) than those in this sprawling 275-year-old casa owned by artist and chef Roberto Bloor. Each of the inn's three suites has a bedroom, sitting room, fireplace, coffeemaker, bath, and private patio. Guests can sit out in a lovely, lush garden; colorful crafts and paintings abound throughout the house. Write away for reservations or (at a slightly extra expense) book through Fraser & Pratt Real Estate in Alamos (☎ 642/8–07–90 or 642/8–01–18). ✉ *Av. Obregón 18, 85760, no phone. 3 suites. No credit cards.*

$$$ **Hacienda del Perico.** Formerly called La Posada, this refurbished adobe building sits on a hill overlooking the trees and cathedral dome of Alamos. The ruins of a 19th-century hospital have been left as part of the hotel's dramatic backdrop. Sonoran-style barbecues and folkloric dancing are often on the evening's agenda. Rates include breakfast. ✉ *Barrio el Perico 45, 85760,* ☎ *642/8–00–45. 8 rooms. Kitchenettes. No credit cards.*

$$$ **Hotel la Mansion.** With its stately rooms centered on a flowering courtyard, this pretty 17th-century mansion and well-run hotel holds the honor of having hosted several of Mexico's presidents. ✉ *Calle Obregón 2, 85760,* ☎ *642/8–02–21. 12 rooms. Restaurant, tapas bar. No credit cards.*

Shopping

It's worth a peek into the three small rooms of **El Nicho Curios** (✉ Calle Commercio 4, no phone), filled with treasures from Mexican *retablos* (religious paintings) to old jewelry and regional pottery. In addition, small stores lining the **Alameda** (northwest of the central plaza) sell Mexican sweets, fabrics, belts, and hats, among other items.

Aduana

⓬ *8 km (5 mi) west of Alamos, along the road from Navajoa.*

Aduana was formerly the site of one of the richest mines in the district. There's not much to see here now except the **church of Nuestra Señora de Balvanere.** A cactus that grows out from one of its walls is said to mark the spot where the Virgin appeared to the Yaqui Indians in the late 17th century, an event that is celebrated by a procession every November 21.

SONORA A TO Z

Arriving and Departing

By Bus

In Mexico, **Elite** runs a deluxe air-conditioned coach from Nogales to Hermosillo for around $12. Frequent buses travel to Hermosillo and Guaymas from Nogales, Tijuana, and Mexicali via **Tres Estrellas de Oro** and **Transportes de Sonora.** Try the comfortable **TUFESA** buses, which travel all the way to Ciudads Obregón and Navajoa.

By Car

Many visitors to Sonora travel by car from Tucson via I–19 to the border in Nogales, Arizona, and then pick up Mexico 15, which begins in Nogales, Sonora. Highway 15 is now a divided four-lane highway, making the ride much quicker and easier than it used to be. This convenience, however, doesn't come cheap: Drivers heading down to Alamos can expect to pay approximately $35 in fees. The alternative "Libre" (Free) routes are much slower and often poorly maintained.

There are two points of entry into Nogales. Most drivers take U.S. I–19 all the way to the end and then follow the signs to the border crossing. This route, however, will take you through the busiest streets of Nogales. It's better to take the Mariposa exit west from I–19, which leads to the international truck crossing and joins a small periphery highway that connects with Highway 15 after skirting the worst of Nogales traffic.

The official checkpoint for entering Mexico is 21 km (13 mi) south of Nogales. It is here that you have to buy insurance and complete the paperwork to bring in your car if you haven't already done so in Tucson at either **Sanborn's Mexico Insurance** (✉ 2900 E. Broadway, ☎ 520/327–1255) or the **Arizona Automobile Association** (✉ 8204 E. Broadway, ☎ 520/296–7461; ✉ 6950 N. Oracle Rd., ☎ 520/885–0694). *See* Driving *in* the Gold Guide regarding the requirements for driving into Mexico.

As a result of the **Sonora Only** program, started in September 1995, if you are not planning to go farther into Mexico, you do not have to leave a credit-card imprint or pay an $11 deposit (though insurance is still required). Stop at the "Sonora Only" booth at the Kilometer 21 checkpoint.

By Ferry

Ferries from Guaymas to Santa Rosalia on the Baja coast leave on Tuesday and Friday at 11 AM and arrive at 6 PM. You can buy tickets on the day you plan to travel unless you have a car, for which you must make reservations three weeks in advance. Fares are about $15 for a reclining seat and $27 for a cabin. Car transportation is priced by car size, with the smallest cars costing at least $100. Purchase tickets at the Sematur ferry terminal on Avenue Serdan, just east of the center of Guaymas (☎ 622/2–23–24). Check with the Guaymas tourist office (☞ Visitor Information, *below*) for the latest information and schedules.

By Plane

AeroCalifornia offers a daily nonstop jet service from Los Angeles and Tucson to Hermosillo (☎ 62/60–25–55 or 800/237–6225). **Aeromexico** and its subsidiary **Aero Litoral** has daily flights to Hermosillo (☎ 62/16–82–06) and Guaymas (☎ 622/1–11–22) from Tucson and flights from Los Angeles to Hermosillo via Tijuana (☎ 800/237–6639; 91–800/80–999 in Mexico). Aeromexico has direct flights to Hermosillo from many cities in Mexico—including Mexico City, Chihuahua, and Guadalajara—and from La Paz and Mexico City to Guaymas; connections to other U.S. cities can be made from these points. **Great Lakes Airlines** has daily nonstop service from Phoenix and Tucson to Hermosillo, Guaymas, and Ciudad Obregon (☎ 800/274–0662).

By Train

As we went to press, Mexican first-class train service from the U.S. border into Sonora was nonexistent. For the most current information, contact **Mexico by Train** (☎ FAX 210/725–3659 or 800/321–1699).

Getting Around

By far the easiest way to get around is by automobile; Guaymas and San Carlos are particularly spread out. Most hotels have car-rental agencies. Buses between towns are frequent and inexpensive.

Contacts and Resources

Car Rental

In **Guaymas,** the agencies to contact are **Budget** (☎ 622/2–14–50) and **Hertz** (☎ 622/2–10–00), both on the main highway.

Rental agencies in **Hermosillo** include **Hertz** (✉ Blvds. Rodríguez and Tamaulipas, ☎ 62/14–81–00) and, across the street, **Budget** (☎ 62/14–08–85).

Consulate

There is a U.S. consulate in Hermosillo (✉ Calle Monterrey, in back of Hotel Calinda near downtown, ☎ 62/17–26–13; 62/17–23–75 for emergencies).

Emergencies

Red Cross/Sonora (☎ 638/3–22–66).

Guaymas: Police (☎ 622/2–00–30), **Red Cross** (☎ 622/2–08–79), **hospital** (☎ 622/2–01–22).

Hermosillo: Police (☎ 62/16–15–64), **Red Cross** (☎ 62/14–07–69), **hospital** (☎ 62/12–18–70). The **Green Angels** (☎ 62/14–63–04) is a very helpful state-run road service for travelers.

Kino Bay: Rescue One (☎ 624/2–03–21), a volunteer search-and-rescue unit, can help with both land and sea emergencies. Notify the group if you're planning a trip over water or into isolated desert regions; if you're very late in returning, Rescue One will go looking for you. Headquarters are at the Club Deportivo in Kino Nuevo, one block before Motel Kino Bay.

Guided Tours

Arizona Coach Tours (✉ 5865 E. 2nd St., Tucson, AZ 85711, ☎ 520/748–0369) runs mostly senior citizen package tours to Alamos, San Carlos, and Puerto Peñasco. **Mexico Tours** (✉ 2780 N. Campbell, Tucson, AZ 85719, ☎ 520/323–6054) offers package tours to San Carlos and Puerto Peñasco. **Apex Mexi Trips** offers group and individual trips to the area (✉ Box 32368, ☎ 520/770–9304 or 800/863–8785).

Visitor Information

Note: In addition to the tourism offices listed below—which are better to visit than to try to reach by phone—the Sonora Department of Tourism has an excellent Travel Fax line that operates out of Arizona.

If you dial 602/930–4815 from a fax phone, a recorded menu will allow you to receive information about Puerto Peñasco, Hermosillo, Guaymas, or Kino Bay. Those who don't have a fax can phone 602/930–4871 to receive an information packet by mail. From the United States and Canada, dial the Sonoran Secretary of Tourism toll-free at 800/476–6672.

Alamos (✉ Main Plaza, Calle Juárez 6, ☎ 642/8–04–50).

Guaymas (✉ Av. Serdán 441, between Calles 12 and 13, 2nd floor, ☎ 622/2–56–67 or 622/4–29–32).

Hermosillo (✉ Palacio Administrativo, Calles Tehuántapec and Comonfort, ☎ 62/14–63–04, FAX 62/17–00–60; 800/476–6662 from the U.S.).

Puerto Peñasco (✉ Blvds. Juárez and V. Estrella, ☎ 638/3–41–29 or 638/3–25–55).

5 The Copper Canyon: From Los Mochis to Chihuahua City

The Copper Canyon is actually a series of gorges, some of them deeper than the Grand Canyon in the United States; they are home to the Tarahumara Indians, renowned for their running ability. A train trip through this magnificent, largely uncharted region usually begins or ends in Chihuahua, a lively midsize city with a museum devoted to Pancho Villa.

By Edie Jarolim

Updated by Melanie Young

THE MAGNIFICENT series of gorges known collectively as the Copper Canyon (in Spanish, *Barranca del Cobre*) is the real hidden treasure of the Sierra Madre. Inaccessible to the casual visitor until the early 1960s and still largely uncharted, the canyons may now be explored by taking one of the most breathtaking rides in North America: The *Chihuahua al Pacífico* railroad whistles down 661 km (410 mi) of track, passing through 87 tunnels and crossing 35 bridges through rugged country as rich in history and culture as in physical beauty.

The *barrancas* (canyons) of the Sierra Tarahumara, as this portion of the Sierra Madre Occidental is known, are on the western edge of the Pacific "Ring of Fire." Formed by seismic and volcanic activity, which at the same time hurled a good quantity of the earth's buried mineral wealth to the surface, the canyons were carved throughout the millennia by the Urique, Septentrión, Batopilas, and Chínipas rivers and further defined by wind erosion. Totaling more than 1,452 km (900 mi) in length and capable of enveloping four times the area of the Arizona Grand Canyon, the gorges are nearly a mile deep and wide in places; the average height of the peaks is 8,000 ft, and some rise to more than 12,000 ft. Four of the major barrancas—Copper, Urique, Sinforosa, and Batopilas—descend deeper than the Grand Canyon, Urique by nearly 1,500 ft.

The idea of building a rail line to cross this region was first conceived in 1872 by Albert Kinsey Owen, an idealistic American socialist. Owen met with some success initially. More than 1,500 people came from the states to join him in Topolobampo, his utopian colony on the Mexican west coast, and in 1881 he obtained a concession from Mexican president General Manuel Gonzáles to build the railroad. Construction on the flat stretches near Los Mochis and Chihuahua presented no difficulties, but eventually the huge Sierra Madre mountains got in the way of Owen's dream, along with the scourge of typhoid and disillusionment within the community.

After Owen abandoned the project in 1893, it was taken up in 1900 by American railroad magnate and spiritualist Edward Arthur Stilwell. One of Stilwell's contractors in western Chihuahua was Pancho Villa, who ended up tearing up his own work during the Mexican Revolution in order to impede the movement of government troops. By 1910, when the Mexican Revolution started, the Mexican government had taken charge of building the railroad line; but progress was very slow until 1940, when surveying of the difficult Sierra Madre stretch finally began in earnest. Some 90 years and more than $100 million after it started, the Ferrocarril Chihuahua al Pacífico was dedicated on November 23, 1961.

The rail line no longer starts at Topolobambo but at nearby Los Mochis. Chihuahua City, at the other end of the line, was established in 1709. Today Chihuahua, the capital of the state of that name and a prosperous economic center, derives its wealth from mining—the Spanish discovered silver in the region as early as 1649—as well as from ranching, agriculture, and lumber.

The Tarahumara Indians, who once occupied the entire state of Chihuahua, were not unaffected by the foreign activity in the area: They were forced to serve in the mines by the Spanish and on the railroad by the Mexicans and the Americans. The threat of slavery and the series of wars that began in the 1600s and continued until the 20th century forced them to retreat deeper and deeper into the canyons, where they are still subject to having their lands taken over by loggers or drug lords. Many are seminomadic, roaming the high plateaus of the Sierra Madre in summer and moving down to the canyon floor in winter to live in stone cliff dwellings or hidden wooden houses. The Tarahumara population, ravaged by disease and poverty, is now estimated at approximately 50,000.

Pleasures and Pastimes

Dining

Along the Copper Canyon trail you'll encounter rustic areas where there are few eateries besides those connected with lodges. In Los Mochis and Topolobampo your best bet is seafood. At the hotels in Cerocahui, Divisadero, and Posada Barrancas, food is included in the price of the room. Don't even think about dieting here: You'll get three freshly cooked, hearty meals a day. There are a few more dining options in Creel, where, in addition to the hotel dining rooms, you'll find a number of small cafés along the town's main street, Avenida López Mateos.

You'll have the greatest choice of restaurants in Chihuahua City. The state is a large producer of beef, so upscale steak houses and places serving *carne asada* (charbroiled strips of marinated beef) abound, but a variety of Mexican specialties and seafood flown in from the coast is also available. Many of Chihuahua's well-appointed international restaurants are located in the Zona Dorada, on Calle Juárez starting from its intersection with Calle Colón.

Dress is casual everywhere except at a few of the more upscale restaurants in Chihuahua. Unless otherwise indicated, reservations are not necessary.

CATEGORY	COST*
$$$$	over $20
$$$	$15–$20
$$	$8–$15
$	under $8

**per person for a three-course meal, excluding drinks, service, and 10% sales tax*

Hiking

Hiking in the Copper Canyon can be an unforgettable experience, if the proper precautions are taken; *Mexico's Copper Canyon Country,* by M. John Fayhee, is a good source of information. But even the most experienced trekkers should enlist the help of local guides, who can be contacted through all the hotels in the area or through travel agents in Los Mochis and Chihuahua. Few adequate maps are available for even the so-called marked trails, and many of the better-worn routes into the canyon are made by the Tarahumara, whose prime concern is getting from one habitable area to the next rather than getting to the bottom.

Urique Canyon is most easily reached from Cerocahui (Bahuichivo stop). The Copper Canyon is most accessible from Divisadero; trails range from easy rim walks to a 27-km (17-mi) descent to the bottom, which takes seven or eight hours. If you're in Creel, a gentle and rewarding hike is the 5-km (3-mi) walk from the Copper Canyon Lodge to the Cusárare Falls. More difficult but equally scenic are the treks down to Recohauta Hot Springs and to the base of Basaseachi Falls; both are full-day outings. The descent into Batopilas Canyon from Creel requires an overnight stay.

Horseback Riding

All hotels in the canyon area can arrange for local guides with gentle horses. Most trips are not for couch potatoes, however. The trails into the canyon are badly defined and can be rocky as well as slippery if the weather is icy or wet; at rough spots you might be asked to dismount and walk part of the way. A fairly easy and inexpensive ride is to Wicochic Falls at Cerocahui, about two hours round-trip, including a half-hour hike at the end, where the trail is too narrow for the horses. From Divisadero, the four-hour round-trip to Bacajipare, a Tarahumara village in the Copper Canyon, affords stunning vistas, but it's not for the fainthearted.

Lodging

Accommodations in this area tend to fall into two categories: comfortable but characterless in the cities, and charming but rustic in the villages. In Cerocahui, Divisadero–Posada Barrancas, and Creel, all the hotels send buses or cars to meet the train; if you don't have a reservation, you'll have to make a quick decision and then hop on the hotel vehicle of your choice. During the summer, October, and around Christmas and Easter, it's important to book in advance. Where indicated, rates for hotels include meals.

CATEGORY	COST*
$$$$	over $90
$$$	$60–$90
$$	$25–$60
$	under $25

**All prices are for a standard double room, excluding 10% tax.*

Nightlife

Sitting around and chatting with fellow guests in your lodge is about the extent of nighttime activity in the heart of Sierra country, though occasionally one of the hotels in Divisadero or Posada Barrancas will have performances in the evening by Tarahumara dancers or Mexican musicians. Nights are a bit more lively in Los Mochis, and Chihuahua is a typical late-night Mexico city.

Shopping

Tarahumara crafts, which provide the Indians with their only cash income, include lovely handwoven baskets made from *sotol* (a claw-like plant) or pine needles; carved wooden dolls; rustic pottery; brightly colored woven belts and sashes made on back-strap looms; primitive wooden masks; and wooden fiddles decorated with faces, from which the men produce haunting music. The Tarahumara women, who are generally shy about talking with tourists, sell their wares throughout the Copper Canyon area; their prices are fair, so bargaining is unnecessary. Tarahumara wares are sold at the market outside the train station at Divisadero and at shops in Creel and Chihuahua.

Exploring the Copper Canyon

Imagine visiting the Grand Canyon in the days before it was tamed by tourist facilities, and you'll have some sense of what a trip through the Copper Canyon will be like—for better and for worse. That is, with the opportunity to encounter a relatively untouched natural site come some of the discomforts of the rustic experience. But if you are careful in your choice of time to visit and are properly prepared, the trip's myriad rewards should far outstrip any temporary inconveniences.

Numbers in the text correspond to numbers in the margin and on the Copper Canyon map.

Great Itineraries

You'll see some beautiful scenery if you just ride the railroad, including a panoramic look at Copper Canyon during a 15-minute stop at Divisadero, but you'll experience only a fraction of what the canyons have to offer if you don't get off the train. If possible, plan on a night in Cerocahui (Bahuichivo stop), one at Posada Barrancas or Divisadero (the train stations are five minutes apart), and one or two at Creel.

About 60% of visitors to the Copper Canyon come via Los Mochis, which is the easiest route if you're traveling from California or Arizona. It's also by far the most desirable route because some of the best scenery is at the western end of the ride, and you're likely to miss it if you approach Los Mochis in the evening. Train delays of three hours or more are not unusual, so even during the extended daylight hours of summer, you can't count on reaching the scenic end of the route before dark. A dam finished in 1996 has added lovely mountain-reflecting "lake" views between Los Mochis and Divisadero.

Even if you drive down to either Los Mochis or Chihuahua, your itinerary will be largely dependent on the schedule of the *Chihuahua al Pacífico* train: It runs in each direction only once a day, so you must plan the time spent in each stop accordingly. The following itineraries assume you will add on a day's train ride to return to your starting point—unless you catch one of the Aerolitoral flights between Los Mochis and Chihuahua. The small turboprops fly low over the mountains and canyons, providing magnificent views.

Note: Los Mochis and El Fuerte are on Mountain Time (called Pacific Time in Mexico); from Bahuichivo east is Central Time.

IF YOU HAVE 3 DAYS

Departing from **Los Mochis** ①, take the 6 AM *Chihuahua al Pacífico* train and get off at Bahuichivo, where you can explore the mission at **Cerocahui** ③ and the overlook into Urique Canyon. The next day, continue on to **Divisadero** ④, where it's practically impossible not to get a room with a view. Spend your last day exploring **Creel** ⑤ and taking a short hike to the falls near Cusárare. Those starting out from **Chihuahua City** ⑧ should make Cerocahui their final stop.

IF YOU HAVE 5 DAYS

Starting out in the west, consider spending a day in the old colonial town of **El Fuerte** ② and then catching the train through the canyons at 7:30 the next morning. Follow the three-day itinerary, *above*, and then for your last day and night, extend your time in **Creel** ⑤ with a visit to the Tarahumara community of San Ignacio or a drive to Basaseachi Falls. Those departing from the east might take the extra day to explore Chihuahua City; be sure to stop in at Pancho Villa's home, now a museum.

IF YOU HAVE 8 OR MORE DAYS

Spend a day each in El Fuerte, Cerocahui, and Divisadero, and then extend your stay in Creel to include a trip down to the former silver mining town of **Batopilas** ⑥; it's six to eight hours each way by car (preferably four-wheel drive) or bus, so you'll want to spend at least two nights. You'll be ready for the modern world after that, so plan to enjoy the restaurants and museums of Chihuahua City for an additional day; another option might be a day trip from Chihuahua to the Mennonite community near **Cuauhtémoc** ⑦.

When to Tour

Unless you are planning to head down deep into the barrancas, winter—December through February—is not the best time to come; many of the

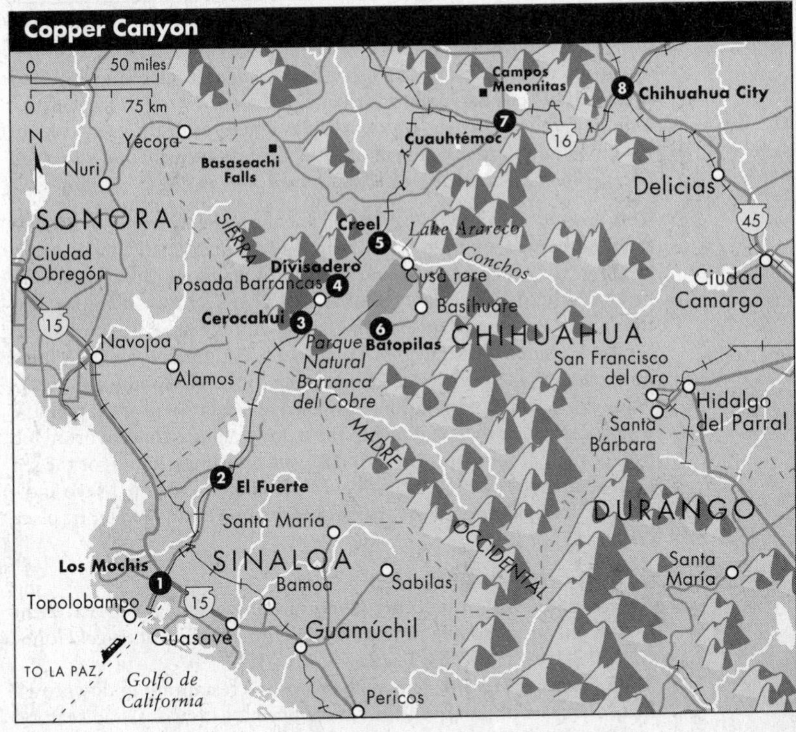

hotels in the region are inadequately prepared for the cold, and the minor rainy season in January renders some of the roads for side excursions impassable. The warm months are May through September; the rainy season, June through September, brings precipitation for a short period every day, but this shouldn't interfere with your enjoyment in any way. It's temperate in the highlands during the summer; if you're planning to hike down into the canyons, however, remember that the deeper you go, the hotter it will get. The best months to visit are October and November, when the weather is still warm and rains have brought out all the colors in the Sierra Tarahumara.

Many people visit during Christmas and Easter, specifically to see the Tarahumara celebrations of those holidays. Closely related to the Pima Indians of southern Arizona, the Tarahumara are renowned for their running ability. (*Tarahumara* is a Spanish corruption of *Rarámuri,* which means "running people" in their language; it is said that in earlier times they survived as hunters by chasing deer to the point of collapse.) Around Christmas, Easter, and other religious feast days, the Tarahumara compete in races that can last up to three days. The men run in small groups, kicking a wooden ball for a distance of 161 km (100 mi) or more. On these and other feast days, tribal elders consume peyote or *tesguino,* a sacred fermented corn liquor.

Los Mochis

❶ *763 km (474 mi) south of Nogales on the Arizona-Mexico border.*

The first stop on the western end of the rail line, Los Mochis (population about 303,500) is an agricultural boomtown; the rail terminus and the city's location about 19 km (12 mi) from the harbor at Topolobampo make it the export center of the state of Sinaloa, which produces many of Mexico's basic crops. Visitors can tour Benjamin

Johnston's sugar refinery, the **Ingenio Azucarero,** around which the town grew. Near Johnston's estate you can still see the American colony—the group of brick bungalows that housed his associates. The **Museo Regional del Valle del Fuerte** has rotating exhibits of work by local artists, and the public library next door displays pictures of the early days of the city. Labels are in Spanish only. ✉ *Calles Obregón and Mina,* ☎ *68/12–46–92.* *$1.60.* ⏲ *Tues.–Sun. 10–1 and 4–7.*

Cottonwood trees and bougainvillea line the highway from Los Mochis to **Topolobampo**; on both sides of the road are fields planted with crops ranging from sugarcane to marigolds and mangoes (36 varieties are produced here). Once the site of Albert Owen's utopian colony and the center of the railroad-building activity in the area, Topolobampo is now considered a suburb of Los Mochis, 15 minutes away. A huge tuna-packing factory sits at the entrance to the bay, and local fisherman—90% of the population—ply the harbor in small shrimp boats; they compete for their catch with the many dolphins that cavort in the bay. **Isla El Farallón,** just off the coast, is a breeding ground for the sea lions that gave the town its name: In the language of the Mayo Indians who once dominated the area, Topolobampo means "watering place of the sea lions."

Dining and Lodging

$$ ✕ **El Farallón.** Nautical decor and murals set the tone for the excellent fish served at this simple restaurant. ✉ *Obregón 593, at Angel Flores,* ☎ *68/12–14–28 or 68/12–12–73. MC, V.*

$$ ✕ **Restaurante España.** This slightly upscale restaurant in downtown Los Mochis is popular with the local business crowd. Good seafood and Spanish dishes are served around an indoor fountain. ✉ *Obregón 526,* ☎ *68/12–22–21 or 68/12–23–35. AE, MC, V.*

$ ✕ **El Taquito.** Located in the very center of Los Mochis, this diner-style restaurant offers well-prepared and reasonably priced Mexican standards 24 hours a day, every day. For a hearty meal try the *carne tampiqueña*—a tasty steak with enchiladas, guacamole, and *frijoles* (beans) on the side. ✉ *Calle Leyva between Hidalgo and Independencia,* ☎ *68/12–81–19. MC, V.*

$$$ ✕ **Hotel Santa Anita.** The central reservations link of the Balderrama chain, this downtown hotel is also an informal information center for what's happening along the *Chihuahua al Pacífico* route, as well as the place to book tours. The restaurant is one of the best in town, too. Built in 1959, the property has medium-size rooms tastefully furnished in muted pastels, with comfortable modern furniture. All have cable TVs, and many have hair dryers and scalloped onyx sinks. ✉ *Leyva and Hidalgo, Box 159, 81200,* ☎ *68/18–70–46; 800/896–8196 for reservations in U.S.;* FAX *68/12–00–46. 133 rooms. Restaurant, bar, travel services. AE, DC, MC, V.*

$$ **El Dorado.** On the main street of town and, as a result, noisy as well as convenient to restaurants and shops, this modest but clean motel-hotel is a good value. Rooms are light-filled and have TVs; a small pool is set among palm trees in the back. ✉ *525 N. Leyva, corner Valdez, 82000,* ☎ *68/15–11–11,* FAX *68/12–01–79. 93 rooms. Bar, coffee shop, pool, travel services. AE, MC, V.*

Nightlife

Locals kick up their heels at **Fantasy Laser Club** (✉ Hotel Plaza Inn, Leyva and Cardenas, ☎ 68/15–80–20) and **Morocco** (✉ Leyva and Rendon, ☎ 68/12–13–88), two downtown discos. The newer **Yesterday** (✉ Obregón and Guerrero, ☎ 68/15–38–10) has live bands.

El Fuerte

❷ *80 km (50 mi) northeast of Los Mochis.*

The small colonial town of El Fuerte was named after the 17th-century fort built by the Spaniards to protect against attacks by the local Mayo, Sinaloa, Zuaque, and Tehueco Indians. Originally called San Juan de Carapoa, it was founded in 1564 by Spanish conquistador Don Francisco de Ibarra and a small group of soldiers. Located on the central El Camino Real route, El Fuerte was at one time the frontier outpost from which the Spanish set out to explore and settle New Mexico and California. For three centuries, it was also a major trading post for gold and silver miners from the nearby Sierras and the most important commercial and farming center of the area; it was chosen as Sinaloa's capital in 1824 and remained so for several years. There are intact colonial mansions in what is now a rather sleepy town of 25,000; one of the best is the Hotel Posada Hidalgo (☞ Dining and Lodging, *below*). Most of El Fuerte's historic houses are set off the cobblestone streets leading from the central plaza; a number of them have been converted into government offices.

Dining and Lodging

$$$ ★ ✕🏨 **Hotel Posada Hidalgo.** You'll be transported back to a more gracious era at this lovely restored hacienda, with its lush tropical gardens and cobblestone paths. Designated a Historic Landmark in 1913, it was built in 1895 by Rafael Almada, a rancher and the richest man in nearby Alamos; he had furniture shipped from as far as San Francisco for his lavish home, where he entertained the local elite. It's difficult to choose between the larger rooms with balconies, set off of a lobby filled with period artifacts, and the ones that open out onto the gardens; all are decorated with rough-hewn handcrafted furniture in Spanish colonial style. *Langostino* (crayfish) is a specialty of the hotel dining room. ✉ *Hidalgo 101,* ☎ *68/93–02–42; reservations:* ✉ *Hotel Santa Anita, Levya and Hidalgo, Box 159, Los Mochis, Sin. 81200,* ☎ *68/18–70–46; 800/896–8196 in U.S.;* FAX *68/12–00–46. 40 rooms. Bar, dining room, pool, dance club. AE, DC, MC, V.*

En Route As the train ascends almost 5,906 ft from El Fuerte to Bahuichivo, it passes through 87 tunnels and over 24 bridges, including the longest and highest ones of the rail system. The scenery shifts from Sinaloan thorn forest, with cactus and scrublike vegetation, to the pools, cascades, and tropical trees of the Río Septentrión canyon, to the oak and pine forest that begins to take over past Temoris, where a plaque marks the dedication of the railroad by President López Mateos in 1961. A new dam adds lakelike pools that reflect the mountains.

Cerocahui

❸ *160 km (100 mi) northeast of El Fuerte.*

From the train station at Bahuichivo, two hotels have buses that make the 45-minute ride up the bumpy, unpaved road to the quiet mountain village of Cerocahui. This is a good place to get a sense of how people live in the canyon area. Next door to the Hotel Misión is a **Jesuit mission,** established around 1690 by Juan María de Salvatierra, who proselytized widely in the region; it is said that because the Tarahumara were the most difficult Indians to convert, he considered this mission his favorite among the many he founded. Nearby, the church operates a boarding school for Tarahumara children. Visitors can hike or ride horses to two nearby **waterfalls** and to a **silver mine** (closed since 1988), but the prime reason to come to Cerocahui is its accessibility to Urique Canyon. It's a kidney-crunching ride to the **Cerro del Gal-**

lego lookout point, where amid mountains spread against the horizon, you can make out the Urique River and the old mining town of **Urique,** a slim thread and a dot on the distant canyon bottom. On the way up you'll pass a Tarahumara cave where Indian women sell baskets; nearby, a shrine to the Virgin is strikingly set against a spring in the mountainside surrounded by tropical foliage. From Cerro del Gallego the road continues down the canyon into Urique, which has a few basic hotels and restaurants. A public bus makes the trip from Cerocahui a few times a week, but many visitors opt for the round-trip, full-day tours offered by the local hotels (☞ Dining and Lodging, *below*).

Dining and Lodging

$$$$ ✕🏨 **Hotel Misión.** Part of the Balderrama chain—the Copper Canyon's equivalent of the Grand Canyon's Fred Harvey hotel empire—this is the only tourist accommodation in Cerocahui itself. The main house, which looks like a combination ski lodge and hacienda, contains the hotel's office, small shops, dining room, bar, and lounge. In winter guests huddle for warmth around two large fireplaces: Cerocahui isn't wired for electricity, and the hotel uses its generator for only a few hours, generally from 7 to 9 in the morning and 7 to 11 in the evening. The plain rooms come with beamed ceilings, Spanish colonial–style furnishings, and wood-burning stoves and kerosene lamps. ✉ *Cerocahui; reservations:* ✉ *Hotel Santa Anita, Leyva and Hidalgo, Box 159, Los Mochis, Sin. 81200,* ☎ *68/18–70–46, ext. 432; 800/896–8196 in U.S.;* FAX *68/12–00–46. 30 rooms. Restaurant, bar. AE, DC, MC, V.*

$$$$ ✕🏨 **Paraíso del Oso Lodge.** This lodge near Cerocahui has plain rooms with simple handmade wooden furniture. Guests must stoke the stove for heat at night, since there is no electricity here. A huge window-filled lobby affords excellent views of the cliffs above the lodge, and a gift shop carries local crafts as well as wares from other parts of Mexico. ✉ *5 km (3 mi) outside of Cerocahui; reservations:* ✉ *Box 31089, El Paso, TX 79931,* ☎ FAX *14/21–33–72 in Chihuahua City. 16 rooms. Dining room. MC, V in U.S.; no credit cards on premises.*

Divisadero

❹ *80 km (50 mi) northeast of Cerocahui.*

There's little to do in Divisadero, a postage stamp of a place on the Continental Divide, but it's impossible to remain unastounded by the vistas of the Copper Canyon, said to have derived its name from both the copper that used to be mined in the area and the color the canyon turns at sunset. You can also glimpse a bit of the distant Urique and Tararecua canyons from here. A popular excursion that takes about four hours round-trip, whether you're traveling on two feet or on horseback, is a visit to Bacajipare, a Tarahumara village. Divisadero and Posada Barrancas offer the greatest comfort in the most spectacular setting on the route.

Dining and Lodging

$$$$ ✕🏨 **Hotel Cabañas Divisadero-Barrancas.** This property sits right on the edge of the Copper Canyon; the dining room and rooms 1 through 10 in the old section and 35 through 52 in the newer section all have panoramic views. The old rooms, with dark furnishings, have decks; the newer ones, lighter in decor, have balconies. Food and service get mixed reviews from the international visitors who sign the guest log, but you're not likely to notice what you're eating when you look out of the dining-room window. ✉ *Divisadero; reservations:* ✉ *Av. Mirador 4516, Box 661, Colonia Residencial Campestre, Chihuahua, Chih. 31000* ☎ *14/10–33–30,* FAX *14/15–65–75. 52 rooms with shower. Restaurant, bar. AE, MC, V.*

$$$$ ★ ✕🏨 **Hotel Posada Barrancas Mirador.** This beautiful pink hotel—the latest link in the Balderrama chain—is perched on the edge of the Copper Canyon. The dining room and all the guest rooms have spectacular views; balconies seem to hang right over the abyss. Accommodations are light and bright, with custom-made furniture, hand-loomed textiles, and heat from fireplaces. The copious meals are good. The hotel can organize day trips to Creel and the surrounding area. ✉ *Posada Barrancas; reservations:* ✉ *Hotel Santa Anita, Leyva and Hidalgo, Box 159, Los Mochis, Sin. 81200,* ☎ *68/18–70–46; 800/896–8196 in U.S.;* FAX *68/12–00–46. 32 rooms. Restaurant, bar, meeting room. AE, DC, MC, V.*

$$$$ ✕🏨 **Rancho Posada Hotel.** This is a good base from which to explore the Barranca del Cobre. The 14 remodeled rooms have ocher stucco walls, ceramic tile floors, and colonial-style, hand-painted furniture; all but six have cozy kiva fireplaces. The older accommodations, also slated for remodeling, have plain, contemporary-style furnishings of dark wood. The redecorated lobby–dining room has a massive stone fireplace, beamed ceiling, and new wood furniture. ✉ *Posada Barrancas; reservations:* ✉ *Hotel Santa Anita, Leyva and Hidalgo, Box 159, Los Mochis, Sin. 81200,* ☎ *68/18–70–46; 800/896–8196 in U.S.;* FAX *68/12–00–46. 34 rooms, 1 suite. Restaurant, bar. AE, DC, MC, V.*

$$$ ✕🏨 **Hotel Mansion Tarahumara.** It's a bit disconcerting to come across a red-turreted, medieval-style "castle" out here in barranca country, but somehow this whimsical property works. All the rooms (15 in separate cabins) have light-pine furniture Spanish contemporary style, plus fireplaces and individual heaters. The newest units have pine-log walls; the older rooms have gray cobblestone walls that match the lodge's exterior. The large dining hall, with its high-vaulted ceiling, is hard to keep warm in winter but has wonderful views of the Sierra Madre. ✉ *Posada Barrancas; reservations:* ✉ *Av. Juárez 1602–A, Colonia Centro, Chihuahua, Chih. 31000,* ☎ *14/15–47–21,* FAX *14/16–54–44. 47 rooms. Restaurant, bar, dance club. AE, MC, V.*

Creel

❺ *60 km (37 mi) northeast of Divisadero.*

Nestled in pine-covered mountains, Creel is a rugged mining, ranching, and logging town that grew up around the railroad station. The largest settlement in the area, it's also a gathering place for Tarahumara Indians seeking supplies and markets for their crafts. It's easy to imagine American frontier towns at the turn of the century looking like Creel—without, of course, the backpacking contingent that makes this town its base. A cluster of small hotels and tour agencies, most of them along the main street, Avenida Lóez Mateos, offer day trips to the many points of interest in the region.

It's 19 km (12 mi) from Creel to **Cusárare,** a Tarahumara village with a 300-year-old Jesuit mission. En route you'll pass limpid-blue Lake Arareco and the strange volcanic-rock formations of the Valley of the Mushrooms. An impressive waterfall can be reached by an easy 4-km (2½-mi) hike from Cusárare through a lovely piñon forest.

If the unpaved roads are passable, consider taking the longer trips to the **Recohuata Hot Springs,** a fairly strenuous hike down from the rim of the Tararecua Canyon, and to **El Tejaban,** a spectacular overlook at the Copper Canyon. Among several worthwhile day trips along the way to the colonial city of Batopilas (☞ *below*) are **Basihuare,** where huge vertical outcroppings of rock are crossed with wide horizontal bands of color; the **Urique Canyon overlook,** a perspective that differs from the one at Cerocahui; and **La Bufa,** site of a former Spanish silver mine. Seventy-three kilometers (45 miles) northeast of Creel but reached via an unpaved, winding road, the 806-ft **Basaseachi Falls** are among the highest cascades in North America.

Dining and Lodging

$ ✕ **Tío Molcas.** Furnished with chunky wooden tables and chairs, this small, cheerful restaurant dishes up delicious Mexican food, especially the cheese enchiladas topped with a zesty red pepper sauce. ✉ *Av. López Mateos 35,* ☎ *145/6–00–33. No credit cards.*

$ ✕ **Veronica's.** This clean, simple eatery on the main street is popular with locals and tourists alike for its wide selection of tasty Mexican standards at very reasonable prices. *Comidas corridas*—set meals with soup, main course, and dessert—are available, or you can order à la carte. Try the excellent *sopa de verduras* (vegetable soup). ✉ *Av. López Mateos 34, no phone. No credit cards.*

$$$$ ★ ✕🏨 **Copper Canyon Sierra Lodge.** About 24 km (15 mi) from the train station, near Cusárare Falls and overlooking a piñon forest, this rustic hotel couldn't have a nicer setting. The pine-wall rooms, with their light-wood, Spanish-style furnishings and small tiled baths, are attractive, and the lodge where hearty meals are served family style is cozy and appealing. The only catch is no electricity: kerosene lamps, wood-burning stoves, and fireplaces provide light and heat. ✉ *Creel, Chih., no phone; reservations in the U.S.:* ✉ *Copper Canyon Lodges, 2741 Paldan, Auburn Hills, MI 48326,* ☎ *810/340–7230 or 800/776–3942. 17 rooms. Restaurant, bar. AE, D, MC, V.*

$$$ 🏨 **Best Western: The Lodge at Creel.** At the other end of town from the plaza, this lodge is actually several log buildings with four rooms each. The spacious, well-lighted quarters exude rustic-chic charm with their pine floors and walls, high double beds with thick coverlets, Tarahumara artifacts, and old-fashioned "woodstove" that's really a gas-log heater controlled by the wall thermostat. A few even have a porch swing. The main lodge building has a small bar/dining area with leather-and-wood furniture. Rates include Continental breakfast; dinner (around $7) must be arranged earlier the same day. ✉ *Av. López Mateos 61, Creel, Chih. 33200,* ☎ *145/6–00–71,* FAX *145/6–00–82 or 145/6–02–00. 15 rooms (27 by 1998). Restaurant, bar. AE, D, MC, V.*

$$$ 🏨 **Parador de la Montaña Motel.** Built in the 1970s, the Parador was once the fanciest hotel in Creel, but it's showing its age. The furniture is dark, the lighting a bit gloomy, and the decor dull. But the hotel is frequently booked up by tour operators, so its restaurant/bar can be lively in the evening. ✉ *Av. López Mateos 44,* ☎ *145/6–00–75,* FAX *145/6–00–85; reservations:* ✉ *Allende 114, Chihuahua, Chih. 31000,* ☎ *14/10–45–80,* FAX *14/15–34–68. 50 rooms with shower. Restaurant, bar. AE, MC, V.*

$$ 🏨 **Margarita's Plaza Mexicana.** This pretty hotel with two floors of rooms around a private courtyard was built to accommodate the demand for more of the hospitality, solid meals, and low prices found at Margarita's (☞ *below*). The rooms, with private baths, individual heat, and plenty of hot water, are decorated with locally crafted pine furniture and charming murals depicting Tarahumara activities. Room prices include breakfast and dinner. ✉ *Calle E. Batista Caro, Creel, Chih. 33200 (a block off Lopez Mateos),* ☎ FAX *145/6–02–45. 26 rooms. Restaurant, bar. AE, MC, V.*

$ ★ 🏨 **Margarita's.** If a small boy at the train station offers to take you to Margarita's, go with him for one of the best deals in town: There's no sign on the door, and even if you follow directions (it's between the two churches facing the plaza), you may think you're walking into a private kitchen when you enter. At this gathering spot for backpackers, you can get anything from a bunk bed in a dorm room (under $5) to a double room with two beds (around $8 per person); prices include breakfast and dinner. The rooms—with wrought-iron lamps, light-wood furnishings, and clean, modern baths—are as pleasant as anything you'll find for three times the price. ✉ *Av. López Mateos y Parroquia 11, Creel, Chih. 33200,* ☎ *145/6–00–45 or 145/6–02–45 (☞ Margarita's Plaza Mexicana,* above*). 21 rooms, most with private bath. Restaurant. No credit cards.*

Nightlife and the Arts

When the sun goes down in Creel, head to the **Parador de la Montaña Motel** (☞ Dining and Lodging, *above*) for an after-dinner drink; local cowboys sometimes hitch their horses in front of **Laylo's Lounge** next to **El Caballo Bayo** restaurant (✉ Av. Lopez Mateos, at the west end of town, no phone). For Tarahumara dolls and handiwork, check out **Artesanías Misíon** and the new **Casa de las Artesanías,** a museum showcasing the crafts of the state of Chihuahua, both on the plaza. At the west end of López Mateos, **Artesanías Victoria** sells huge Tarahumara pots and handmade wood furniture.

Batopilas

6 *110 km (80 mi) southeast of Creel.*

A remote village of about 600 people, Batopilas was once one of the wealthiest towns in Mexico because of the nearby veins of silver mined on and off from the time of the conquistadores; at one time it was the only place in the country besides Mexico City that had electricity. The 80-km (48-mi) ride down dusty, unpaved roads to the now-sleepy town at the bottom of Batopilas Canyon takes about 6½ hours by car from Creel (closer to eight hours on the local bus, which runs about three times a week). Sights in this lush, flower-filled oasis include the ruined **hacienda of Alexander Shepherd,** built in the late 1800s by one of the town's wealthiest mine owners; the original **aqueduct,** which still services the town (it's set along the Camino Real); and a triple-domed 17th-century **cathedral,** mysteriously isolated in the Satevo Valley and reached via a scenic 6½-km (4-mi) hike from town. You'll need to stay overnight at one of Batopilas's modest posadas or at the Copper Canyon Riverside Lodge (☞ Lodging, *below*).

Lodging

$$$$ **Copper Canyon Riverside Lodge.** A restored late-19th-century hacienda, this lodging is quirkily charming. Each of the high-ceilinged rooms is individually decorated—for example, one with a prayer niche, another with vintage Elizabeth Taylor posters—but all have spacious private baths and huge, soft feather duvets. Only partially wired for electricity, the accommodations have an odd mix of kerosene reading lamps and electrical outlets for hair dryers. The home-cooked meals are excellent, and guests are free to raid the refrigerator and liquor cabinet (just sign the book; you'll be billed later). ✉ *Batopilas; reservations in the U.S.:* ✉ *Copper Canyon Lodges, 2741 Paldan, Auburn Hills, MI 48326,* ☎ *810/340–7230 or 800/776–3942. 14 rooms. Restaurant, hiking, library. AE, D, MC, V.*

Cuauhtémoc

7 *128 km (94 mi) northeast of Creel, 105 km (65 mi) southwest of Chihuahua.*

A rather anomalous experience in Mexico is a visit to the large **Mennonite community** (Campos Menonitas) in the town of Cuauhtémoc.

Approximately 20,000 Mennonites came to the San Antonio Valley in 1922 at the invitation of President Alvaro Obregón, who gave them the right to live freely and autonomously in return for farming the 247,000 acres of land they purchased. Tours can be arranged in Chihuahua (☞ Guided Tours *in* The Copper Canyon and Chihuahua City A to Z, *below*), or in Cuauhtémoc at the Tarahumara Inn (✉ Av. Allende and Calle 5A, ☎ 158/1–19–19) or the travel agency Cumbres Friesen, owned by Mennonite David Friesen (✉ Calle 3A No. 466, ☎ 158/2–54–57, FAX 158/2–40–60).

Chihuahua City

8 *375 km (233 mi) south of the El Paso–Ciudad Juárez border, 1,440 km (895 mi) northwest of Mexico City.*

If you're arriving from the peaceful Copper Canyon, the sprawling city of Chihuahua, with nearly 1 million inhabitants, may come as a bit of a jolt. But, then, the city is known for its jolting nature: Two of the most famous figures in Mexico's revolutionary wars are closely tied to Chihuahua. Father Miguel Hidalgo, the father of Mexican independence, and his coconspirators were executed by the Spanish here in 1811. And Chihuahua was home to General Pancho Villa, whose revolutionary army, the División del Norte (Army of the North), was decisive in overthrowing dictator Porfirio Díaz in 1910 and securing victory in the ensuing civil war. In addition, Benito Juárez, known as the Abraham Lincoln of Mexico, made Chihuahua his base in 1865 during the French invasion of the country.

Whatever you do, don't miss a visit to the Museo Histórico de la Revolución en el Estado de Chihuahua, better known as **Pancho Villa's House.** Villa lived in this 1909 mansion, also called the "Quinta Luz" (*quinta* can mean "mansion"), with his second wife, Luz Corral (he had three wives, none of whom he divorced). She stayed here until her death on June 6, 1981, willing the residence to the government, which restored it as a national museum. The 50 small rooms that used to board Villa's bodyguards have been converted into exhibition rooms displaying artifacts of Chihuahua's cultural and revolutionary history. Parked in the museum's courtyard is the bullet-ridden 1919 Dodge in which Villa was assassinated in 1923 at the age of 45. ✉ *Calle Décima 3014,* ☎ *14/16–29–58.* 🎟 *75¢.* ⏲ *Daily 9–1 and 3–7.*

The **Catedral,** on the town's central square, is well worth a visit. Construction on this beautiful baroque structure was started by the Jesuits in 1726 but not completed until 1825 because of Indian uprisings in the area. The exterior is made of the pinkish limestone quarried in this region; inside, the opulent church has altars made of Carrara marble, a 24-karat solid-gold ceiling, a beautiful cedar-and-brass carved depiction of Saint Peter and Saint Paul, and a huge German-made organ. In the back of the cathedral, the **Museum of Sacred Art** displays the work of seven local artists of the 18th-century Mexican baroque tradition, as well as commemorations of the 1990 visit of Pope John Paul II. ✉ *Plaza de la Constitución, no phone.* 🎟 *75¢.* ⏲ *Weekdays 10–2 and 4–6.*

The **Palacio de Gobierno** (State Capitol) was built by the Jesuits as a convent in 1882. Converted into government offices in 1891, it was destroyed by a fire in the early 1940s and rebuilt in 1947. Murals around the patio by artist Pino Mora depict famous episodes from the history of the state of Chihuahua; a plaque commemorates the spot where Father Hidalgo was executed on the morning of July 30, 1811. ✉ *Plaza Hidalgo,* ☎ *14/10–63–24.* ⏲ *Daily 8–8.*

The **Palacio Federal** (Federal Building) houses the city's main post office and telegraph office, as well as the dungeon where Hidalgo was imprisoned before he was executed by the Spanish; his pistols, traveler's trunk, crucifix, and reproductions of his letters are on display here. ✉ *Calle Libertad, around the corner from Plaza Hidalgo,* ☎ *14/15–14–17 or 14/10–35–95.* ⏲ *Daily 9–7.*

The **Iglesia de San Francisco** (San Francisco Church) is the oldest (1721) church built in Chihuahua that is still standing. Father Hidalgo's decapitated body was interred in the chapel of this simple church from 1811 to 1827, when it was sent to Mexico City; his head was publicly displayed for 10 years by Spanish Royalists in Guanajuato on the Alhóndiga de Granaditas (☞ Guanajuato *in* Chapter 8). ✉ *Av. Libertad at Calle 15, no phone.* ⏲ *Daily 7–7.*

Slightly outside the center of town but well worth a visit is the Cultural Center of the University of Chihuahua, known as **Quinta Gameros.** This hybrid French Second Empire/Art Nouveau mansion—with stained-glass windows, ornate wooden staircases, rococo plaster wall panels, and lavish ironwork—was built in 1910 by Julio Latorre, a Columbian architect, for Manuel Gameros, a wealthy mining engineer. Here you'll see European art of the last two centuries as well as changing exhibitions ranging from Mennonite crafts to contemporary art. Concerts and lectures are also held here. ✉ *Calle Bolívar 401,* ☎ *14/16–66–84.* 🎫 *$2.* ⏲ *Tues.–Sun. 10–2 and 4–7.*

Not to be confused with the University Cultural Center, the **Chihuahua Cultural Center** displays exquisite ceramics from the pre-Columbian settlement of Casas Grandes northwest of Chihuahua. Around the turn of the century, this downtown mansion belonged to the state governor. ✉ *Aldama and Ocampo,* ☎ *14/16–13–36.* ⏲ *Tues.–Sun. 10–2 and 4–7.*

A restoration project has made the site of the town's original settlement, **Santa Eulalia,** particularly appealing. The 30-minute drive southeast of town, about $10 one-way by taxi (less by bus), is repaid by the colonial architecture and cobblestone streets of this village founded in 1652. The religious artwork in the 18th-century cathedral is noteworthy, and the **Mesón de Santa Eulalia** restaurant (☎ 14/11–14–27) has a lovely open-air courtyard, open weekends 1:30–7 PM (people start arriving around 3).

Dining and Lodging

$$$ ✕ **La Casona.** Formerly known as La Mansión del Gourmet, this stately 1950s mansion, just across the canal from downtown, serves a variety of international fare. ✉ *Av. Universidad 507,* ☎ *14/14–30–53. AE, DC, MC, V.*

$$ ★ ✕ **Club de Los Parados.** Almost four decades of Chihuahua's history have passed through the doors of this landmark restaurant in an adobe-style house. It was started by Tony Vega, a wealthy cattle rancher who died in 1991, as a place to socialize with his fellow ranchers. The story goes that when they went out drinking, the one who sat (or fell) down first had to pick up the tab; Los Parados means "the standing ones." Excellently grilled steaks and chicken as well as tasty Mexican specialties are served in a large room with a wood-burning kiva fireplace; the carne asada with guacamole is particularly good. A private dining room displays photographs of Tony Vega and important Chihuahuans, including Anthony Quinn, while saddles serve as stools and metal brands line the walls in the bar. ✉ *Av. Juárez 3901,* ☎ *14/15–35–04 or 14/10–35–59. AE, MC, V.*

$$ ✕ **La Calesa.** A large, dimly lit room with wood paneling and red tablecloths and curtains, this looks like the classic steak house it is. The onion soup and chilies with *aserdo* (a local cheese) make good appetizers. The filet mignon and rib-eye steaks from the area are particularly recommended as entrées; try the former cooked in garlic with shrimp and mushrooms. The clubby bar has a good selection of wines and liquors. ✉ *Av. Juárez 3300,* ☎ *14/10–10–38 or 14/16–02–22. AE, MC, V.*

$$ ✕ **Rincon Mexicano.** The folks who run the Mesón de Santa Eulalia restaurant in Santa Eulalia also serve some of the best Mexican food in Chihuahua. ✉ *Av. Cuauhtémoc 224,* ☎ *14/11–14–27 or 14/11–15–10. AE, MC, V.*

$–$$ ✕ **La Casa de Los Milagros.** According to locals, this blue house with frilly white trim was once the favorite "Casa de Muñecas" ("dollhouse") of Pancho Villa and his compañeros. Today it's the happening place for light Mexican snacks, drinks, and music after 9 PM, when the courtyard and rooms of this rambling abode start to fill with well-heeled, twentysomething Chihuahuans. ✉ *Victoria 812 near Ocampo,* ☎ *14/37–06–93. MC, V.*

$ ✕ **El Taquito.** Three blocks south of the Palacio de Gobierno, this modest restaurant specializes in tacos and other typical Mexican dishes. The *chiles rellenos* (stuffed peppers fried in batter), enchiladas suizas, and chicken burritos with *mole* (spicy chocolate) sauce are all good choices; you can get a bottle of sangria to accompany your meal for about $6. ✉ *Venustiano Carranza 1818,* ☎ *14/10–21–44. No credit cards.*

$$$$ 🏨 **Camino Real Chihuahua.** Atop a rise at edge of town with magnificent views of the city and surrounding mountains, Chihuahua's first *gran turismo* hotel sparkles with fountains and marble. Designed around an atrium with a several-story waterfall cascading down one wall, the hotel is a contemporary palace at the end of the road after the rustic accommodations in the Copper Canyon. Rooms are plush with richly patterned textiles, comfortable furniture, TV in a tall chest, and bath with both tub and shower. ✉ *Barranca del Cobre 3211, Frac. Barrancas, 31125,* ☎ *14/29–29–29,* FAX *14/29–29–00. 204 rooms. 2 restaurants, bar, pool, business services, meeting rooms, travel services. AE, MC, V.*

$$$ ★ 🏨 **Holiday Inn Hotel & Suites.** This appealing property combines comfort, style, and convenience: Ten minutes from the downtown sights, Chihuahua's first all-suites hotel is decorated in contemporary style with a green or blue-and-beige color scheme. Each room has a kitchenette with stove, dishwasher, and coffeemaker, as well as a VCR and an exercycle. A complimentary Continental breakfast buffet is served at the Clubhouse, which also houses the hotel's indoor pool, hot tub, and exercise equipment. Eager to accommodate American business travelers, the English-speaking staff is friendly and helpful. ✉ *Escudero 702, 31000,* ☎ *14/14–33–50; 91–800/0–09–99 toll-free in Mexico;* FAX *14/14–33–13. 72 suites. Restaurant, room service, indoor and outdoor pools, spa, basketball, health club, Ping-Pong. AE, DC, MC, V.*

$$ 🏨 **Hotel San Francisco.** A favorite of Mexican business travelers, this modern four-story hotel has a prime location right next to the Catedral and Plaza de Armas. Its clean and comfortable if somewhat bland rooms are equipped with color TVs and telephones. The lobby, somewhat gloomy during the day, can be lively at night. ✉ *Victoria 409, 31000,* ☎ *14/16–75–50; 91–800/1–41–07 toll-free in Mexico; 800/847–2546 in the U.S.;* FAX *14/15–35–38. 111 rooms, 20 suites. Restaurant, bar, travel services. AE, MC, V.*

$$ 🏨 **Posada Tierra Blanca.** Across the street from the Palacio del Sol but considerably less expensive, this modern motel-style property is con-

venient to the downtown sights. Rooms, decorated in red and black with pseudo-antique furnishings, are large and well heated in winter; all have TVs. The striking *Stages of Man* mural in the lobby was painted by Pina Mora, the same artist who decorated the courtyard of the Palacio de Gobierno. ✉ *Niños Heroes 102,* ☎ *14/15–00–00,* FAX *14/16–00–63. 103 rooms. Restaurant, piano bar, pool. AE, MC, V.*

Nightlife and the Arts

Chihuahua has the most nightlife options in the Copper Canyon area. **La Reggae** (✉ Blvd. Ortiz Mena and Bosque de la Reina, ☎ 14/15–47–55) draws a dancing crowd with its rock-and-roll bands. At **Chihuahua Charlie** (✉ Av. Juárez 3329, ☎ 14/15–70–65), DJs spin discs nightly, and the food is as good as the music. **Taberna La Cerveceria** (✉ Av. Juárez 3333, ☎ 14/15–83–80) is a glass-encased, neon-laced restaurant and bar in a four-story former brewery where you can play pool on the first floor or dance on the fourth. The bar at the **Hotel San Francisco** (☞ Dining and Lodging, *above*) features Mexican trios or a singer at the piano. The **Hotel Sicomoro** (✉ Blvd. Ortiz Mena 411, ☎ 14/13–54–45) has live entertainment nightly in its lobby bar.

Shopping

Mercado de Artesanías (✉ Calle Victoria 506, across from cathedral, ☎ 14/15–34–62) sells everything from jewelry, candy, and T-shirts to crafts from all over the region. Across the street from the *calabozo* (calaboose) where Padre Miguel Hidalgo was jailed, the **Casa de las Artesanías del Estado de Chihuahua** (✉ Av. Juarez 705, ☎ 14/37–12–92) carries the best selection of Tarahumara and regional crafts in the state. In addition to selling gems and geodes from the area, the **Rock Shop** (✉ Calle Décima, directly across from Pancho Villa's home, ☎ 14/15–28–82) offers a wide variety of crafts.

THE COPPER CANYON AND CHIHUAHUA CITY A TO Z

Arriving and Departing

By Boat

The Baja Express catamaran from La Paz to Topolobampo is no longer running; the only service provided for passengers is via the Sematur **car ferry,** which takes eight to nine hours and is not always available. In Los Mochis, contact Sematur (☎ 68/15–82–62), or the travel agency Viajes Paotan (✉ Serapio Rendon 517 Pte. [West], ☎ 68/15–19–14) for information and reservations. In Topolobampo, contact Sematur (☎ 68/62–01–41, FAX 68/62–00–35).

By Bus

CHIHUAHUA

The **Chihuahuenses** (☎ 14/29–02–42 or 14/29–02–40) and **Omnibus de México** (☎ 14/10–30–90) lines run clean, air-conditioned buses from Ciudad Juárez to Chihuahua; these leave approximately every 15 minutes from 7 AM to 8 PM. The cost of the trip, which takes about 4½ hours, is approximately $17 for first class, $22 for the Ejectivo luxury coaches. Buses shuttle between El Paso and Ciudad Juárez every two hours; the price is $5.

LOS MOCHIS

The **Elite** (☎ 63/13–54–01 in Nogales; 68/12–17–57 in Los Mochis), **Transportes del Pacífico** (☎ 63/13–16–06 in Nogales; 68/12–03–41 in Los Mochis), **Transport Norte de Sonora** (☎ 63/12–54–54 in Nogales; 68/12–04–11 in Los Mochis), and **TUFESA** (☎ 63/13–38–62 in Nogales) bus lines all leave every hour from Nogales, Sonora, to Los Mochis; with luck, the trip should take about 12 hours. The cost is approximately $30.

By Car

Most U.S. visitors drive to **Chihuahua** via Mexico Highway 45 from the El Paso–Ciudad Juárez border, a distance of 375 km (233 mi), or up from Mexico City, 1,440 km (895 mi). The drive down to **Los Mochis** from Nogales on the Arizona border via Mexico Highway 15, four lanes much of the way, is a distance of 763 km (474 mi).

Paved roads now connect Chihuahua to **Creel**: Take Mexico Highway 16 west to San Pedro, then State Highway 127 south to Creel. The 300-km (186-mi) trip takes 3½ to four hours if the weather is good. This drive, through the pine forests of the Sierra Madre foothills, is more scenic than the railroad route via the plains area. Driving is a good option if you have a four-wheel-drive vehicle, because there are many worthwhile, if difficult, excursions into the canyons from Creel. The road from Creel to **Divisadero** has recently been paved. But from Divisadero to **Bahuichivo,** the road is full of potholes and especially dangerous during rain or snow, even with a four-wheel-drive vehicle. A route to Urique Canyon is also planned.

By Plane

CHIHUAHUA

Aeromexico and its feeder airline, **Aerolitoral** (✉ Paseo Bolivar 405, next to Quinta Gameros, ☎ 14/15–63–03 in Chihuahua; 91–800/9–09–99 toll-free in Mexico), have daily flights to Chihuahua from Los Angeles, Phoenix, and Tucson (with a change at Hermosillo), and from San Antonio (with a change in Monterrey) and El Paso. Within Mexico, the airlines have daily flights to Chihuahua from Mexico City, Monterrey, Guadalajara, and Tijuana. **AeroCalifornia** (☎ 14/37–10–22 in Chihuahua) has flights from Mexico City and Tijuana to Chihuahua. The new **Lone Star Airlines** (☎ 14/20–91–54 in Chihuahua; 95–800/817–1932 toll-free in Mexico), flies nonstop to Chihuahua from El Paso and Dallas.

LOS MOCHIS

AeroCalifornia (☎ 68/18–16–16 in Los Mochis) has daily flights to Los Mochis from Los Angeles, Tucson, Tijuana, Mexico City, and Guadalajara. On **Aeromexico** and **Aerolitoral** (☎ 68/15–29–50 in Los Mochis) you can get to Los Mochis from Los Angeles, Phoenix, Tucson, San Antonio, El Paso, Mexico City, La Paz, and Chihuahua. On clear days, Aerolitoral's flights between Chihuahua and Los Mochis offer spectacular views of the Sierras and canyons, since the smaller planes fly lower than jets.

By Train

At present, there is no first-class service from any U.S. border city to either Los Mochis or Chihuahua. Some luxury trains go directly from the United States to the Copper Canyon (☞ Train Tours *in* Guided Tours, *below*).

Getting Around

By Taxi

In **Chihuahua** and **Los Mochis,** taxis are easy to find and can be engaged at hotels or hailed on the street. From the airport into town costs about $10 in Chihuahua and $17 in Los Mochis. Always agree on a price before entering the cab.

By Train

The *Ferrocarril Chihuahua al Pacífico* line (or *Che'Pa'*, as it is affectionately called by locals) runs a first-class and a second-class train daily in each direction from Chihuahua and Los Mochis through the Copper Canyon. But by November 1997, all of Mexico's trains are expected to be sold to private investors, and no one knows how this will affect the current service. Your best bet is to stay in touch with one of the private train companies or tour operators (☞ Guided Tours, *below*).

The first-class train departs from Los Mochis at 6 AM (be sure to sit on the right side of the train for the best views) and arrives in Chihuahua 12 hours later; westbound, it departs from Chihuahua at 7 AM and arrives in Los Mochis around 7 PM (most of the time, but delays of three hours or more are not unusual). Tickets can be purchased through almost any hotel in Los Mochis or Chihuahua or directly at the train station. The price is about $40 each way, plus a 15% charge for any stopovers en route, which should be arranged at the time of ticket purchase. Reservations (☎ 14/15–77–56, FAX 14/10–90–59 in Chihuahua; ☎ 68/15–77–75 in Los Mochis) should be made at least a week in advance during the busy months of July, August, and October, and around Christmas and Easter. It's best to book through a hotel, tour company, or travel agency, as the phones in the local train stations are rarely answered. Note: Once the pride of the Mexican rail system, the first-class train, called *El Nuevo Chihuahua al Pacifico,* has become run-down in recent years. It's the scenery, not the vehicle, that continues to draw passengers. Guards armed with automatic weapons often patrol the passenger cars, discouraging robberies. Exercise caution by carrying passports and cash in a money belt and leaving your jewelry at home.

The second-class train, referred to as *El Pollero,* leaves an hour later from each terminus but makes many stops and is scheduled to arrive 3½ hours later in both directions than the first-class train. Though it is less comfortable, this train is a good way to meet local residents. No reservations are needed; prices are approximately $12 each way. There are no dining cars on either train; it's best to bring your own food and water. Soda, beer, snacks, and ham-and-cheese sandwiches are available on the first-class train.

It's possible to ship your car on the train, but it's not worth the expense or the bother. If you're driving down to Los Mochis, you're better off leaving your car there and taking the train round-trip. If you're coming via Chihuahua, however, you should consider driving to Creel or Divisadero and doing a round-trip from there (☞ Arriving and Departing by Car, *above*).

Contacts and Resources

Car Rental

CHIHUAHUA

Avis (✉ Av. Universidad 1703, ☎ 14/14–19–99), **Hertz** (✉ Av. Revolución 514, ☎ 14/16–64–73), and **Dollar** (✉ Hotel Sicomoro, Ortiz Mena 405, ☎ 14/14–21–71) all have offices at the airport also.

LOS MOCHIS

Car companies at the airport and in town include **Budget** (✉ G. Prieto 850 Nte. [North], ☎ 68/15–83–00, FAX 68/15–84–00), **Hertz** (✉ Leyva 171 Nte., ☎ 68/15–19–29), and **AGA** (✉ Leyva and Callejón Municipal, ☎ 68/12–53–60).

Emergencies

CHIHUAHUA

Police (☎ 14/81–19–00), **Cruz Roja** (Red Cross; ☎ 14/11–14–84 or 14/11–22–11), and **Bomberos** (Fire Dept.; ☎ 14/10–07–70). Two facilities for handling the injured or sick are **Clínica del Parque** (✉ Calle de la Llave and Leal Rodriguez, ☎ 14/15–74–11 or 14/15–90–87) and **Hospital del Centro del Estado** (✉ Calle 33 and Rosales, ☎ 14/15–47–20).

LOS MOCHIS

Police (☎ 68/12–00–33); **Cruz Roja** (✉ Guillermo Prieto and Tenochtitlan, ☎ 68/15–08–08 or 68/18–64–64).

Guided Tours

Almost all the large hotels in Los Mochis and Chihuahua have in-house travel agencies that can arrange both city tours and tours of the Copper Canyon area, as well as hiking, hunting, and fishing expeditions. In Los Mochis, the Santa Anita and La Colinas hotels offer city tours for about $17 per person; these take approximately 3½ to four hours and include a boat trip around Topolobampo Bay. In Chihuahua, independent travel agencies include **Viajes Dorados** (✉ Calle Periodismo 501, ☎ 14/14–64–38; 800/206–8132 toll-free from the U.S.; FAX 14/14–64–90), the American Express agent **Rojo y Casavantes** (✉ Calle Vincent Guerrero 1207, ☎ 14/15–58–58 or 14/15–74–70, FAX 14/15–53–80), and, particularly recommended, **Turismo Al Mar** (✉ Av. Reforma 400, ☎ 14/16–65–89 or 14/16–59–50, FAX 14/16–65–89). Half-day city tours average $16 per person; full-day van trips into Mennonite country run about $40 per person. In Cuauhtémoc, Cumbres Friesen, owned by Mennonite David Friesen (✉ Calle 3A, No. 466, ☎ 158/2–54–57, FAX 158/2–40–60), can arrange Mennonite or Copper Canyon tours.

From the United States, the oldest operator in the area is **Pan American Tours** (✉ Box 9401, El Paso, TX 79984, ☎ 915/778–5395 or 800/876–3942). Prices for tailor-made tours between Los Mochis and Chihuahua range from about $300 to $700 per person, depending on length of stay and number of stops made. **ATI** (✉ 4301 Westbank Dr., Suite B-360, Austin, TX 78746, ☎ 800/284–5678) specializes in customized itineraries year-round, starting at $379 per person for three nights. **Synergy Tours** (✉ 7336 E. Shoeman La., Suite 120, Scottsdale, AZ 85251, ☎ 800/569–1797, FAX 602/994–4439) runs individual and group trips about 10 times a year, including off-the-beaten-path treks. **Columbus Travel** (✉ 900 Ridge Creek La., Bulverde, TX 78163, ☎ 210/885–2000 or 800/843–1060, FAX 210/885–2010) offers daily departures to the Copper Canyon from Presidio, Tijuana, Los Angeles, Phoenix, Tucson, and El Paso. Trips range from $759 for five nights to $1,799 for a 13-day excursion that includes Batopilas. **California Native** (✉ 6701 W. 87th Pl., Los Angeles, CA 90045, ☎ 800/926–1140) runs a seven-day escorted trip through the Copper Canyon every month for $1,540, and also offers custom backpacking, mountain biking, and deluxe excursions.

TRAIN TOURS

Sierra Madre Express of Tucson (✉ Box 26381, Tucson, AZ 85726, ☎ 520/747–0346 or 800/666–0346) runs its own deluxe trains (with dome/dining and Pullman cars) to the Copper Canyon from Tucson, offering eight-day, seven-night trips approximately four times a year; its trips combine the charm of sleeping on the train with first-class accommodations. Another tour operator, **Tauck Tours** (✉ Box 5027, 276 Post Rd., Westport, CT 06880, ☎ 800/468–2825) charters the Sierra Madre Express for similar excursions the rest of the time. The luxury train **South Orient Express** (✉ 16800 Greenspoint Park Dr., Suite 245 N, Houston, TX 77060, ☎ 800/659–7602) offers all-inclusive "rail cruises" (with dome, dining/lounge, and Pullman cars) from Chihuahua and Los Mochis in the spring and fall (and from Fort Worth twice a year) starting at $1,549 per person for a five-day trip. The company can also book individual trips year-round on its slightly less luxurious "VSP" train, ranging from transportation only ($198 one-way between Chihuahua and Los Mochis with unlimited stops) to packages with lodging, meals, and sightseeing.

Late-Night Pharmacies

CHIHUAHUA

Chihuahua has an abundance of pharmacies in the center of the city that provide late-night service. **Farmacia Mendoza** (✉ Calle Aldama 1901, ☎ 14/16–44–14 or 14/10–27–96) is open 24 hours a day.

LOS MOCHIS

Farmacia San Jorge (✉ Av. Independencia and Angel Flores, ☎ 68/15–74–74) in Los Mochis is open 24 hours a day.

Money Exchange

Be sure to change money before you get into real barranca country: There are no banks in Cerocahui, Divisadero, or Posada Barrancas, and no guarantee that the hotels in those places will have enough cash to accommodate you. A bank in the main plaza at Creel transacts foreign exchanges only from 10:30 to noon. Even in Los Mochis, banking hours are, for the most part, limited to weekdays between 9 and 1; some banks reopen at 3 and a few are open on Saturday morning. In Chihuahua, most banks are open weekdays from 9 to 1:30 and from 3:30 to 7:30, and Saturday from 9 to 1:30; Banco Bital downtown (✉ Libertad 1922, ☎ 14/16–08–80) stays open from 8 until 7 weekdays and 8 to 2 Saturday. The **Casa de Cambio Rachasa** (✉ Av. Ocampo and Niños Heroes, ☎ 14/10–03–33), open Monday–Saturday 9–9, Sunday 9–2, offers good exchange rates and quick service. Hotels have slightly lower exchange rates but charge no commission, and you normally won't have to wait in line.

Visitor Information

CHIHUAHUA

Government Tourist Office (✉ Av. Libertad and Calle 13, 1st floor, ☎ 14/29–34–21 or 14/29–33–00, ext. 4511 or 4512) is open weekdays 8–1:30 and 3:30–6. **Oficina de Información** (✉ Central patio of Palacio de Gobierno in Plaza Hidalgo, ☎ 14/29–33–00, ext. 1061, or 14/10–10–77) is open weekdays 9–7, weekends 10–2. Sonia Estrada, who speaks fluent English, will answer questions and help visitors (in person or over the phone) make travel arrangements all over the state.

LOS MOCHIS

Oficina de Turismo (✉ Allende and Ordoñez, inside the Unidad Administrativa del Gobierno del Estado building, 1st floor in back, ☎ 68/12–66–40 or 68/12–76–10, ext. 131).

6 Pacific Coast Resorts

Hollywood introduced us to two of the Mexican Riviera's most popular towns: Liz Taylor and Richard Burton's sleepy, steamy Puerta Vallarta in The Night of the Iguana *and the sparkling Manzanillo coast that served as the backdrop to Bo Derek in* 10. *These days both places are prime cruise-ship destinations, as is Mazatlán, a bustling port that attracts sportfishing enthusiasts and surfers. Ixtapa/Zihuatanejo is a two-for-one attraction, a laid-back fishing village adjoining a glitzy resort.*

Updated by Wendy Luft

ACROSS THE GULF OF CALIFORNIA from the Baja California Peninsula lies Mazatlán, Mexico's largest Pacific port and the major Mexican resort closest to the United States, some 1,200 km (750 mi) south of the Arizona border. This is the beginning of what cruise-ship operators now call the Mexican Riviera, or the Gold Coast. The coastline for the next 1,400 km (900 mi) is Mexico's tropical paradise. The Gulf of California, or the Sea of Cortés, as it is also called, ends just below the Tropic of Cancer, leaving the Pacific coastline open to fresh sea breezes. The Mexican Riviera resorts—Mazatlán, Puerto Vallarta, Manzanillo, Ixtapa/Zihuatanejo, and Acapulco—are therefore less muggy than gulf towns to the north. The temperature of the water is a bit lower, however, and waves can get very rough.

The Pacific coast doesn't have the rich cultural heritage of Mexico's inland colonial villages and silver cities, and the history is sketchy at best. This is not an area for touring ruins, museums, and cathedrals but rather a gathering spot for sun worshipers, sportfishing enthusiasts, surfers, and swimmers. Not far from the resort regions are jungle streams and ocean coves, but the majority of visitors never venture to these isolated sites, preferring instead to immerse themselves in the simultaneously bustling and restful resort lifestyle, where great dining, shopping, and sunbathing are the major draws.

Mazatlán is first and foremost a busy commercial center, thanks to an excellent port and the fertility of the surrounding countryside. More than 600,000 acres of farmland near Mazatlán produce tomatoes, melons, cantaloupes, wheat, and cotton, much of which is shipped to the United States. And nearly all the 150,000 tons of shrimp that are hauled in annually are processed and frozen for the American and Japanese markets.

Sportfishing accounts for Mazatlán's resort status. The port sits at the juncture of the Pacific and the Sea of Cortés, forming what has been called the world's greatest natural fish trap. But fishing is not the only attraction. Hunters are drawn to the quail, duck, and dove that thrive in the hillsides, and surfers find great waves on nearby beaches. Another draw is the relatively low price of accommodations—about half the going rate of accommodations in Cancún.

Tepic, capital of the state of Nayarit, lies between Mazatlán and Puerto Vallarta. It's the jumping-off point to these destinations for train travelers, who can catch public buses to the coast. Budget travelers and those who eschew the bustle of the megaresorts often head straight for **San Blas,** a small seaside village some 37 km (23 mi) northwest of Tepic through the jungle.

Some 323 km (200 mi) south of Mazatlán is **Puerto Vallarta,** by far the best-known resort on the upper Pacific coast. The late film director (and sometime resident) John Huston put the town on the map when he filmed Tennessee Williams's *The Night of the Iguana* on the outskirts of the village in 1964. Elizabeth Taylor came to keep Richard Burton company during the filming, and the gossip about their romance—both were married at the time, but not to each other—brought this quaint Mexican fishing village with its cobblestone lanes and whitewashed, tile-roofed houses to the public's attention. Before long, travel agents were deluged with queries about Puerto Vallarta, a place many had never heard of before.

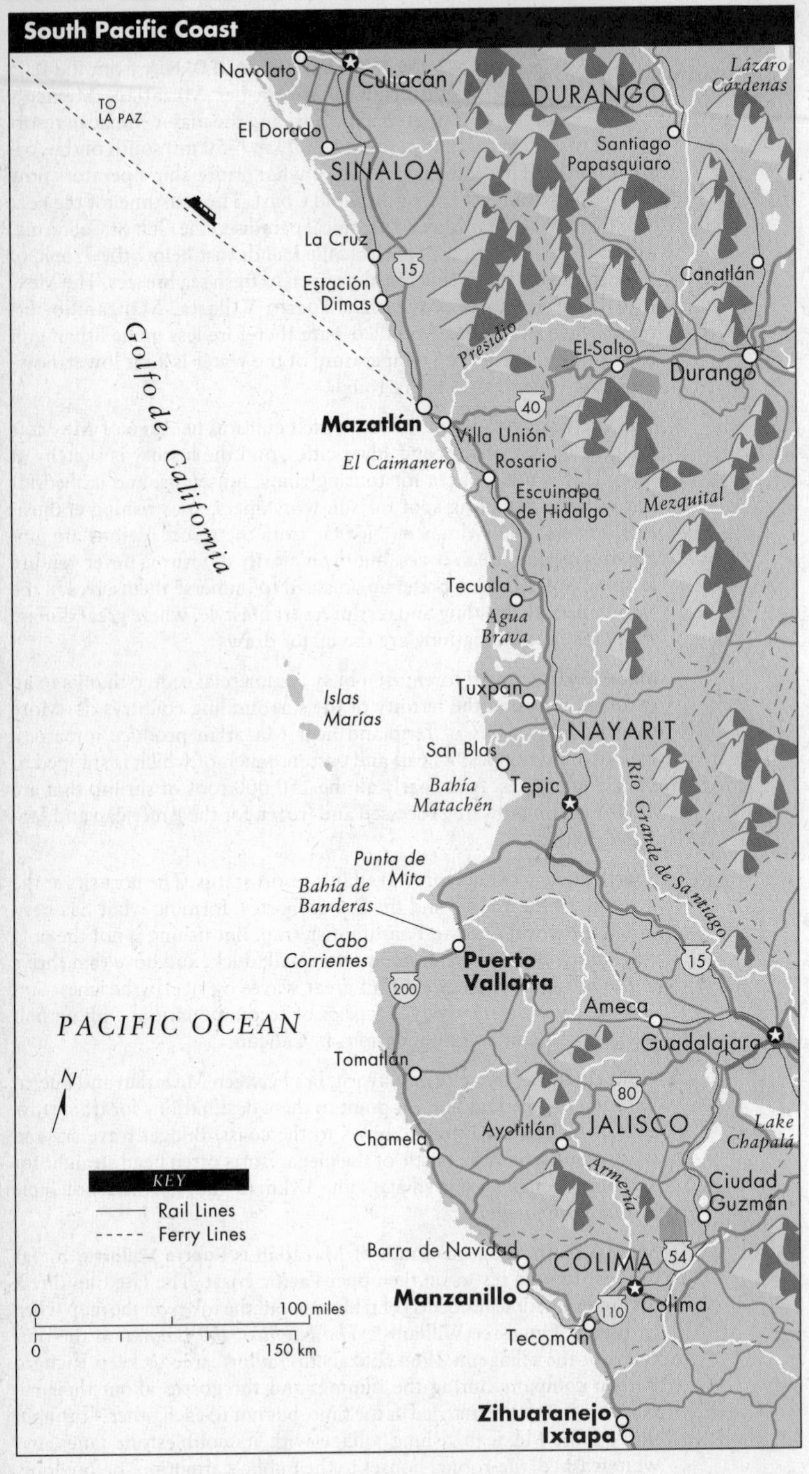
South Pacific Coast
Navolato
Culiacán
DURANGO
Lázaro Cárdenas
TO LA PAZ
El Dorado
Santiago Papasquiaro
SINALOA
La Cruz
15
Canatlán
Estación Dimas
Golfo de California
Presidio
El Salto
Durango
40
Mazatlán
Villa Unión
El Caimanero
Rosario
Escuinapa de Hidalgo
Mezquital
Tecuala
Agua Brava
Tuxpan
Islas Marías
NAYARIT
San Blas
Bahía Matachén
Tepic
Río Grande de Santiago
Punta de Mita
Bahía de Banderas
Cabo Corrientes
Puerto Vallarta
15
200
PACIFIC OCEAN
Ameca
Guadalajara
Tomatlán
N
80
Ayotitlán
JALISCO
Lake Chapalá
Chamela
Armería
KEY
Rail Lines
Ferry Lines
Ciudad Guzmán
Barra de Navidad
COLIMA
54
Manzanillo
Colima
110
0
100 miles
0
150 km
Tecomán
Zihuatanejo
Ixtapa

More than 250,000 people live in Puerto Vallarta today, and about 1 million foreign tourists arrive each year. The fabled cobblestone streets are clogged with bumper-to-bumper traffic during the holiday season, and the sounds of construction often drown out the pounding surf. Elizabeth Taylor's and Richard Burton's adjoining homes are now a bed-and-breakfast. Despite its resort status, parts of Puerto Vallarta are still picturesque. For a sense of the Eden that once was, travel out of town to the lush green mountains where the Río Tomatlán tumbles over boulders into the sea.

Manzanillo, marking the southern end of the central Pacific coast, had more of a storybook start than did Puerto Vallarta. Conquistador Hernán Cortés envisioned the area as a gateway to the Orient: From these shores, Spanish galleons would bring in the riches of Cathay to be trekked across the continent to Veracruz, where they would be off-loaded to vessels headed for Spain. But Acapulco, not Manzanillo, became the port of call for the Manila galleons that arrived each year with riches from beyond the seas. Pirates are said to have staked out Manzanillo during the colonial era, and chests of loot are rumored to be buried beneath the sands.

With the coming of the railroads, Manzanillo became a major port of entry, albeit not a pretty one. Forty or 50 years ago, a few seaside hotels opened up on the outskirts of town, which vacationers reached by train. The jet age, however, seemed to doom the port as a sunny vacation spot. Then Bolivian tin magnate Antenor Patiño built **Las Hadas** (The Fairies), a lavish Moorish-style resort complex inaugurated in 1974. It attracted the beautiful people, and for a while Las Hadas was better known than Manzanillo itself. The film *10* made a star of the resort as well as household names of its stars, Bo Derek and Dudley Moore.

In recent years, there's been a push to turn Manzanillo and coastal villages to the north, such as **Barra de Navidad, Melaque, Tenacatita,** and **Costa de Careyes,** into a tourist zone. A four-lane toll road now cuts the driving time between Manzanillo and Guadalajara, Mexico's second-largest city, to three hours. Older hotels have been spruced up and all-inclusive resorts constructed. January 1997 marked the inauguration of the posh **Grand Bay hotel,** in Isla Navidad, a deluxe residential–tourist–golf complex that spreads over some 1,200 acres on a peninsula between the Pacific Ocean and the Navidad Lagoon, 20 minutes west of the Manzanillo airport.

The southernmost of the Pacific Coast resorts and the newest kid on the scene—like Cancún, it was developed by the Mexican government in the early 1970s—**Ixtapa/Zihuatanejo** lies in the northwestern part of the State of Guerrero coastline, some 500 km (300 mi) south of Manzanillo. It's unique among Mexican beach getaways in that it comprises two distinct destinations only 7 km (4 mi) from each other. Ixtapa is the glitzier of the two, with international chain hotels lining its hotel zone, but it's far smaller and more low key than older resorts like Puerto Vallarta and newer ones such as Cancún. Its development put neighbor Zihuatanejo, a sleepy fishing village virtually unknown even among Mexicans, on the tourist map.

Pleasures and Pastimes

Beaches

This area boasts some of North America's most inviting beaches, with deliciously warm waters and spectacular sunsets. There are beaches for every taste: long stretches of creamy sand, crescents of soft gold and black volcanic grains, secluded coves, and pristine shores accessible only by boat.

Dining

The emphasis in **Mazatlán** is on casual, bountiful dining, and the prices are reasonable. Shrimp and fresh fish are the highlights; be sure to have a seafood cocktail along the beach. **Puerto Vallarta** has the widest array of restaurants, some with spectacular views, others hidden in the small, romantic patios of former homes, and still others—especially those on the *malecón* (seaside walkway)—as popular for people-watching as they are for their great seafood. Several **Manzanillo** dining spots offer scenic views of the jungle and water that compensate for their lack of culinary excitement. In **Ixtapa/Zihuatanejo,** restaurants range from simple beach eateries to deluxe establishments with international chefs.

Dress in all the resorts is usually casual but not sloppy (no bathing suits or bare feet); chic resortwear is appropriate in the more expensive spots. Reservations are almost never necessary, but we have indicated those places that require them. Most menu prices include the 15% VAT tax, but a few places, particularly some hotel restaurants, add a 10%–15% service charge to your tab, as well as the tax.

CATEGORY	COST*
$$$$	over $35
$$$	$25–$35
$$	$15–$25
$	under $15

**per person for a three-course meal, excluding drinks, service, and 15% sales tax*

Fishing

Mazatlán is considered to be the top billfish port on the Mexican Pacific. The sailfish run from May to November and the marlin from November to May, and there is also plenty of swordfish, tuna, shark, bonito, and red snapper, year-round. Nine fishing fleets operate some 80 cruisers. Light tackle fishing in the lagoons is also popular.

Sportfishing is good off **Puerto Vallarta** most of the year, particularly for billfish, rooster fish, dorado, yellowtail, and bonito. The marlin season begins in November.

Manzanillo claims to be the sailfish capital of the world; the season runs from mid-October through March. Blue marlin and dorado are also abundant.

Ixtapa/Zihuatanejo is just being discovered as Mexico's new sportfishing destination. Anglers revel in the profusion of sailfish, black and blue marlin (the record is over 1,000 pounds), as well as yellowfin tuna and dorado. Aeromexico Vacations (☎ 800/245–8585), the airline's in-house tour program, offers comprehensive sportfishing packages including air, hotel, and sportfishing on specialized cruisers with expert bilingual skippers.

In November, Mazatlán, Puerto Vallarta, and Manzanillo host international fishing tournaments.

Horseback Riding

In most of the Pacific Coast resorts, horseback riding along the shore is popular and horses can be rented by the hour at major beaches. In **Puerto Vallarta,** several stables offer three-hour trips into the mountains, sunset rides, and longer excursions to charming colonial villages in the Sierra Madre.

Lodging

Although not known for its upscale resorts, **Mazatlán** now offers travelers a fair dose of luxury properties, along with comfortable beachfront hotels; it also has one of the highest concentrations of trailer parks in the country. In **Puerto Vallarta,** accommodations range from tiny inns to luxury waterfront hotels and spectacular resorts tucked away on hidden coves. Even today, **Manzanillo** is still best known for Las Hadas, the spectacular hotel built in 1974 by Bolivian tin magnate Antenor Patiño. **Ixtapa/Zihuatanejo** runs the lodging gamut—big beachfront properties are the norm in Ixtapa, whereas Zihuatanejo offers downtown budget hotels along with two of the most exclusive small hotels in Mexico.

Most hotels raise their rates for the high season (December 15 through Easter Week); rates are lowest in the summer, during the rainy season. Price categories are based on high-season rates—expect to pay 25% less during the off-season.

CATEGORY	COST*
$$$$	over $200
$$$	$100 to $200
$$	$50–$100
$	under $50

**All prices are for a standard double room, excluding 15% VAT tax (17% in the state of Jalisco).*

Shopping

You can spend as much time shopping in **Puerto Vallarta** as you can lazing in the sun; shops selling excellent crafts from around the country vie with upscale art galleries and clothing boutiques for buyers' attention, especially in the downtown area. The selection of Mexican crafts in **Mazatlán** is almost as good. **Zihuatanejo** has some extremely colorful crafts markets; the unique ceramics and masks from the state of Guerrero, where the little fishing town is located, are especially plentiful.

Water Sports

Parasailing, swimming, windsurfing, sailing, and waterskiing are all popular activities in the warm waters of the Pacific Coast resorts. Manzanillo and Mazatlán offer some of the finest surfing in Mexico, while the best diving spots in this area are found off Puerto Vallarta.

Exploring the Pacific Coast Resorts

The winter season (December through April) is when the Pacific Coast resorts are at their best, with temperatures generally in the 70s and 80s (they're a bit higher in Ixtapa/Zihuatanejo, which is the farthest south). The off-season brings humidity and mosquitoes along with temperatures in the 80s and 90s (here northernmost Mazatlán is the cooler exception), but at this time of year you'll also enjoy emptier beaches, warmer water (well into the 70s), and less-crowded streets—as well as a 25% to 35% reduction in room rates and the opportunity to do a little bargaining on rental-car costs. Toward the end of the rainy season (June through September), which generally involves only brief daily showers, the countryside and the mountainous backdrop of the Sierra Madre del Sur turn brilliantly green with multicolored blossoms of trees and flowers.

Mazatlán holds an especially colorful Carnival during the week preceding Ash Wednesday, with parades, *charreadas* (Mexican-style rodeos), floats, fancy dress balls, and lots of eating and dancing. During the entire month of May, Puerto Vallarta celebrates the incorporation of its city with various festive activities, including bullfights and fireworks.

MAZATLÁN

Mazatlán is the Aztec word for "place of the deer," and long ago its islands and shores sheltered far more deer than humans. Today it is a city of some 400,000 residents and draws about 1.5 million tourists a year. Sunning, surfing, and sailing have caught on here, and in the winter months visitors from inland Mexico, the United States, and Canada flock to Mazatlán for a break in the sun. Hotel and restaurant prices are lower than elsewhere on the coast, and the ambience is more that of a fishing town than a tourist haven.

Upscale resorts and ritzy restaurants are not part of Mazatlán's repertoire, though there is a fair dose of luxury at El Cid, Royal Villas, and Pueblo Bonito resorts. Work is under way on two adjacent marinas on the estuary that stretches north from the El Cid golf course. The El Cid Resort complex is being expanded, and the Mexican development company, Grupo Situr, is building a residential resort community that calls for an 18-hole golf course, a large marina, villas, condos, and a Bel-Air hotel.

Hunting and fishing were the original draw for visitors. At one time, duck, quail, pheasant, and other wildfowl fed in the lagoons; and jaguars, mountain lions, rabbits, and coyotes roamed the surrounding hills. Hunters have to search a little harder and farther for their prey these days, but there's still plenty of wildlife near Mazatlán. The city is the base for Mexico's largest sportfishing fleet; fishermen haul the biggest catches (in size and number) on the coast. The average annual haul is 10,000 sailfish and 5,000 marlin; a record 988-pound marlin and 203-pound sailfish were pulled from these waters.

The Spaniards settled in the Mazatlán region in 1531 and used the indigenous people as a labor force to create the port and village. The center of Mazatlán gradually moved north, so that the original site is now 32 km (20 mi) southeast of the harbor.

The port has a history of blockades. In 1847 during the Mexican War, U.S. forces marched down from the border through northeast Mexico and closed the port. In 1864, the French bombarded the city and then controlled it for several years. Mexico's own internal warring factions took over from time to time. And after the Civil War in the United States, a group of southerners tried to turn Mazatlán into a slave city.

Today Mazatlán has the largest shrimping fleet in Mexico. Sinaloa, one of Mexico's richest states, uses Mazatlán's port to ship its agricultural products.

Exploring Mazatlán

Mazatlán's highlights are spread far and wide, and walking from one section of town to the other can take hours. The best way to travel is via *pulmonías,* (open-air jitneys, literally "pneumonias") so you can sunbathe and take pictures as you cruise along, although you won't be able to roll up any windows to protect yourself from automobile fumes. If you choose to rent a car and drive, you can tour at your own pace. There are no traffic jams in Mazatlán, except near the market in downtown, where parking can also be a major problem. Downtown is virtually the only area of Mazatlán that can be walked; many visitors never see it, but it's worth spending a morning here.

Numbers in the text correspond to numbers in the margin and on the Mazatlán map.

A Good Tour

Most visitors set out to tour the city from the **Zona Dorada** ①, Mazatlán's tourist region, which begins at Punta Camarón. If you travel north from here along the coast on Avenida Sábalo, you'll pass some of the city's most luxurious and priciest hotels; opposite the beach are many of the better low-cost motels. This route affords a good view of Mazatlán's three Pacific islands—Isla de los Pájaros, Isla de los Venados, and Isla de los Chivos. Just past the Camino Real resort, Avenida Camarón Sábalo becomes Avenida Sábalo Cerritos and crosses over the Estero del Sábalo, a long lagoon popular with bird-watchers. The area north of here will someday be an exclusive touring and resort area; towering condos are already being built.

South of the Zona Dorado, the main road changes names frequently. The 16-km (10-mi) malecón, Mazatlán's version of a main highway and beachfront boardwalk, begins at Punta Camarón and is here called Avenida del Mar. In a few blocks, you'll come to the city's aquarium, **Acuario Mazatlán** ②, down Avenida de los Deportes. Avenida del Mar continues past beaches popular with residents and travelers staying at the budget hotels across the street. You're sure to notice the avenue's main landmark, the Monumento al Pescador: An enormous, voluptuous, nude woman reclines on an anchor, her hand extended toward a nude fisherman dragging his nets.

Calle Juárez and Calle Cinco de Mayo intersect with Avenida del Mar and lead to Mazatlán's real downtown, where the streets are filled with buses and people rushing to and from work and the market. The heart of the city is the **Plaza Revolución** ③ or *zócalo*; just across the street you'll see the spires of the **Mazatlán Catedral** ④. On the streets facing the zócalo are the City Hall, banks, post office, and telegraph office. About three blocks southeast of the zócalo, the Teatro Angela Peralta, built in 1860 and now beautifully restored, was declared a historic monument in 1990. Three blocks to the east is the **Museo Arqueológico** ⑤.

Back along the waterfront, Avenida del Mar turns into Paseo Claussen as it heads south. If you continue along the malecón, you'll pass El Fuerte Carranza, an old Spanish fort built to defend the city against the French; Casa del Marino, a shelter for sailors; Playa Olas Altas (☞ Beaches, *below*); High-Divers Park, where young men climb to a white platform and plunge into the sea—spectacular at night, when the divers leap carrying flaming torches; and La Mazatleca, a bronze nymph rising from a giant wave. Across the street is a small bronze deer, Mazatlán's mascot. Paseo Claussen leads to Olas Altas, site of Old Mazatlán, the center for tourism in the 1940s. Olas Altas (which means high waves) ends at a small traffic circle. A plaque at the circle bears the state symbol of Sinaloa. Above Olas Altas is **Cerro de Vigía** ⑥.

Sights to See

❷ **Acuario Mazatlán.** A perfect child-pleaser, Mazatlán's aquarium features tanks of sharks, sea horses, eels, lobsters, and multicolored salt- and freshwater fish. A fanciful bronze fountain and sculpture of two boys feeding a dolphin marks the aquarium's entrance, and an aviary sits amid the trees in the adjacent botanical garden. ✉ *Av. de los Deportes 111,* ☏ *69/81–78–15.* *About $3.50.* ⏲ *Daily 9:30–6:30.*

❻ **Cerro de Vigía** (Lookout Hill). The view from this windy hill above Olas Altas is fantastic: You can see both sides of Mazatlán, the harbor, and the Pacific. It's a steep climb up, better done by taxi than on foot. At the top of the hill you'll see a weather station, along with a

Acuario Mazatlán, **2**
Cerro de Vigía, **6**
Mazatlán Catedral, **4**
Museo Arqueológico, **5**
Zócalo (Plaza Revolución), **3**
Zona Dorada, **1**

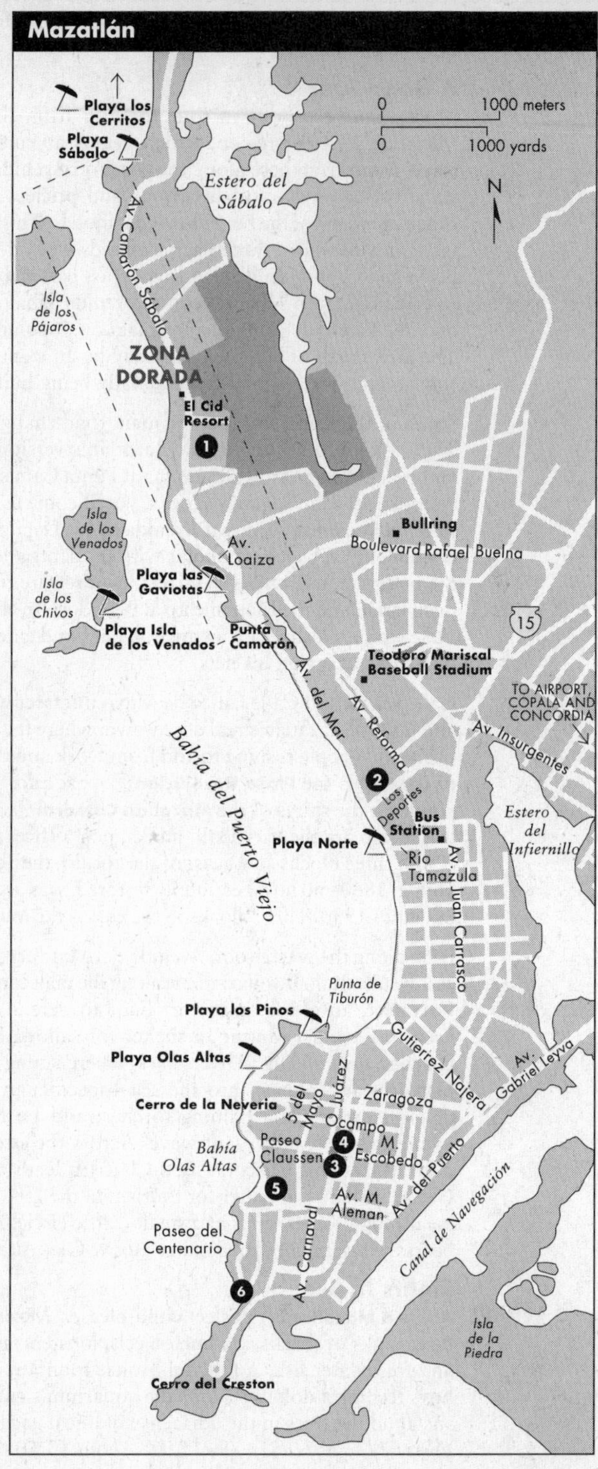

rusty cannon and the **Centenario Pérgola,** used by the Spaniards as a place to watch for pirates.

4 **Mazatlán Catedral.** The blue-and-gold spires of the downtown cathedral are a city landmark. Built in 1890 and made a basilica in 1935, this church has a gilded and ornate triple altar, with murals of angels overhead and many small altars along the sides. A sign at the entrance requests that visitors be appropriately attired (no shorts or tank tops inside). ✉ *Calles Juárez and Plazuela República.*

5 **Museo Arqueológico.** The town's archaeological museum houses a small but fairly interesting collection of artifacts from the region. ✉ *Sixto Osuna 76, off Paseo Olas Altas,* ☎ *69/85–35–02.* *About $1; free Sun.* ⏲ *Tues.–Sun. 10–1 and 4–7.*

3 **Plaza Revolución.** This city square at the center of downtown hosts one of the most fascinating gazebos in Mexico—what looks like a '50s diner inside the lower level and a wrought-iron bandstand on top. The green-and-orange tile on the walls, ancient jukebox, and soda fountain serving shakes, burgers, and hot dogs couldn't make a more surprising sight. ✉ *Bounded by 21 de Marzo to the north, Flores to the south, Benito Juaréz to the east, and Nelson to the west.*

1 **Zona Dorada.** Marking the beginning of Mazatlán's tourist zone is **Punta Camarón** (Shrimp Point), the rocky outcropping on which Valentino's Disco sits, resembling a Moorish palace perched above the sea. To the north, Avenida Camarón Sábalo forms the eastern border of the zone, while Avenida Loaiza runs closer to the beach. In this four-block pocket are most of the hotels, shops, and restaurants, and the majority of nonresidents intent on having a good time sunning, shopping, and partying. This is the place to souvenir-shop, hit the discos, and check out the hotel bars.

NEED A BREAK? **No Name Café** (✉ Av. Rodolfo T. Loaiza 417, ☎ 69/13–20–31), in the Mazatlán Arts and Crafts Center, is a good spot for a beer or *agua mineral* (mineral water) and lime. Mexico's version of Baskin-Robbins, **Helados Bing** (✉ Avs. Camarón Sábalo and Gaviotas, ☎ 69/13–55–10) has good hot-fudge sundaes and ice-cream cones. At the **Panadería Panamá** (✉ Camerón Sábalo across from Las Palmas hotel, ☎ 69/13–69–77), you can sit at a table and enjoy fragrant cinnamon-flavored coffee with fresh-baked pastries.

Beaches

Playa Isla de la Piedra

On weekends, local families bearing toys, rafts, and picnic lunches ride over to the island on *pangas* (small, motor-powered skiffs) from the dock near the train tracks. Sixteen kilometers (10 miles) of unspoiled beaches here allow enough room for all visitors to spread out and claim their own space. On Sunday, the island looks like a small village, with lots of music and fun. Many of the small *palapas* (thatched-roof huts) set up along the sportfishing docks serve a tasty smoked marlin. The palapas near the launches to Isla de la Piedra sell sugarcane sticks, which look like bamboo and are good for quenching your thirst.

Playa Isla de los Venados

Boats make frequent departures from the Zona Dorada hotels for this beach on Deer Island. It's only a 10-minute ride, but the difference in ambience is striking; the beach is pretty, uncluttered, and clean, and you can hike around the southern point of the island to small, secluded coves covered with shells.

Playa Los Cerritos

The northernmost beach on the outskirts of town, which runs from Camino Real Resort to Punta Cerritos, is also the cleanest and least populated. The waves can be too rough for swimming, but they're great for surfing.

Playa Norte

This strand begins at Punta Camarón (Valentino's is a landmark) along Avenida del Mar and the malecón and runs to the Fisherman's Monument. The dark brown sand is dirty and rocky at some points, but clean at others, and is popular with those staying at hotels without beach access. Palapas selling cold drinks, tacos, and fresh fish line the beach; be sure to try the fresh coconut milk.

Playa Olas Altas

This beach, whose name means "high waves," was the first tourist beach in Mazatlán, running south along the malecón from the Fisherman's Monument. Surfers congregate here during the summer months, when the waves are at their highest.

Playa Sábalo and Playa las Gaviotas

Mazatlán's two most popular beaches are at either end of the Zona Dorada. There are as many vendors selling blankets, pottery, lace tablecloths, and silver jewelry as there are sunbathers. Boats, Windsurfers, and parasailers line the shores. The beach is protected from heavy surf by the three islands—Venados, Pájaros, and Chivas. You can safely stroll these beaches until midnight and eavesdrop on the social action in the hotels while enjoying a few solitary, romantic moments without vendors and crowds.

Dining

$$–$$$ ★ ✕ **Angelo's.** With its fresh flowers, cream-and-beige decor, and soft candlelight, this is by far the most attractive restaurant in Mazatlán. The Italian and Continental cuisine is outstanding—try the veal scallopini with mushrooms or shrimp marinara on pasta—and the service impeccable. ✉ *Pueblo Bonito hotel, Av. Camarón Sábalo 2121,* ☎ *69/14–37–00. AE, DC, MC, V. No lunch.*

$$–$$$ ★ ✕ **La Concha.** One of the prettiest waterside dining spots, La Concha is a large enclosed palapa with three levels of seating, including a spacious dance floor decked with twinkling lights and outdoor tables by the sand. Adventurous types might attempt the stingray with black butter or calamari in its ink, while the more conservative can try a thick filet mignon cooked to perfection. During the winter season, a singer croons Las Vegas–style ballads as couples dance. La Concha is also open for breakfast. ✉ *El Cid Resort, Av. Camarón Sábalo,* ☎ *69/13–33–33. AE, DC, MC, V.*

$$ ✕ **Casa Loma.** An out-of-the-way, elegant restaurant in a converted villa, Casa Loma serves international specialties such as chateaubriand, duck à l'orange, and osso buco. Lunch on the patio is less formal. Have a martini made by an expert, and save room for the fine pastries. ✉ *Av. Gaviotas 104,* ☎ *69/13–53–98. MC, V. Closed May–Oct.*

$$ ★ ✕ **El Paraíso Tres Islas.** A wonderful palapa on the beach, across from Sea Shell City (☞ Shopping, *below*), Tres Islas is a favorite with families who spend all Sunday afternoon feasting on fresh fish. Try smoked marlin, oysters diablo, octopus, or the seafood platter. The setting is the nicest in town, close to the water with a good view of the three islands. The waiters are friendly and eager to help. ✉ *Av. Rodolfo T. Loaiza 404,* ☎ *69/14–28–12. MC, V.*

$$ ✕ **El Shrimp Bucket.** In Old Mazatlán, under forest-green awnings, is an establishment that was the original Carlos 'n' Charlie's. The gar-

den patio restaurant is much quieter than its successors—some would call it respectable. Best bets are fried shrimp served in clay buckets and barbecued ribs. Portions are plentiful. Early breakfast (from 6 AM) is also served. It's the place to see where all the action of the wildly popular Carlos Anderson chain began. ✉ *Olas Altas 11–126,* ☎ *69/81–63–50. AE, MC, V.*

$$ ✕ **Señor Frog.** Another member of the Carlos Anderson chain, Señor Frog is as noisy and entertaining as the rest. Bandidos carry tequila bottles and shot glasses in their bandoliers, leather belts that held ammunition in the old westerns. Barbecued ribs and chicken, served with corn on the cob, and heaping portions of standard Mexican dishes are the specialty, and the drinking, dancing, and carousing go on well into the night. The tortilla soup is excellent. ✉ *Av. del Mar,* ☎ *69/82–19–25. AE, MC, V.*

$$ ★ ✕ **Shrimp Factory.** This plain, open-sided restaurant, with white plastic tables and chairs, offers no soups, desserts, or views, just top-quality shrimp and lobster, by the kilo (boiled) or the plate (virtually any style). ✉ *Avs. de las Garzas 14 and Rodolfo T. Loaiza, across from Playa Mazatlán hotel,* ☎ *69/16–53–18. MC, V.*

$$ ✕ **Sr. Peppers.** Elegant yet unpretentious, with ceiling fans, lush foliage, and candlelit tables, Sr. Peppers serves choice steaks and lobsters cooked over a mesquite grill. Enjoy the dance floor and live music. ✉ *Av. Camarón Sábalo across from Camino Real hotel,* ☎ *69/14–01–20. AE, MC, V. No lunch.*

$ ✕ **Club Natural.** Inviting fresh fruit cocktails, with or without yogurt or cream, granola and honey, as well as fruit and vegetable drinks, hearty breakfasts, and tasty sandwiches make this a popular spot for breakfast or a late-night snack. ✉ *Av. Camarón Sábalo 204–1,* ☎ *69/16–51–09. No credit cards.*

$ ★ ✕ **Doney.** This big downtown hacienda has been serving great Mexican meals since 1959. The large dining room has old photos of Mazatlán, a high brick ceiling, and embroidered tablecloths, all of which give you the feeling that you're sitting in someone's home. The Doney is named after a restaurant in Rome, though there is nothing Italian about the menu. Try the *chilaquiles* (casserole of tortillas and chili sauce), chicken *mole* (in spicy chocolate sauce), or fried chicken. The meringue and fruit pies are excellent. ✉ *Mariano Escobedo at Calle Cinco de Mayo,* ☎ *69/81–26–51. AE, MC, V.*

$ ★ ✕ **Karnes en Su Jugo.** A small family-run café on the malecón, with a few outdoor tables and a large indoor restaurant, this establishment specializes in *karnes en su jugo,* literally, "beef in its juice," a Mexican stew with chopped beef, onions, beans, and bacon. It's a satisfying meal, especially when eaten with a basket of homemade tortillas. ✉ *Av. del Mar 550,* ☎ *69/82–13–22. No credit cards.*

$ ★ ✕ **Pepe & Joe's.** This restaurant in the Fiesta Land complex (☞ Nightlife, *below*) is Nirvana for beer lovers; there's never any chance that they'll run out of this liquid refreshment because it's made on the premises. For hungry customers, there are good hamburgers, hot dogs, club sandwiches, and the like. ✉ *Punta Camarón,* ☎ *69/84–16–66. AE, MC, V.*

Lodging

Most of Mazatlán's hotels are in the Zona Dorada, along the beaches. Less expensive places are in Old Mazatlán, the original tourist zone along the malecón on the south side of downtown.

$$$$ ★ **Rancho Las Moras.** Ideal for riders and nonriders alike, this abandoned 19th-century tequila ranch, tucked away at the foot of the Sierra Madre mountains about 30 minutes from Mazatlán, has been

renovated with the finest authentic Mexican furnishings and art. There are more than 3,000 acres to explore either by horseback, wagon, or foot. Exotic animals roam the grounds, along with horses. Accommodations are in six villa-suites or in five individual casitas. There are no televisions, clocks, or even telephones. Communication is by radio with the ranch office in Mazatlán. The rate includes three meals and transportation to and from the airport. ✉ *Mailing address: Av. Camarón Sábalo 204–6, Mazatlán, 82110,* ☎ FAX *69/16–50–45. 12 units. Restaurant, bar, pool, tennis, horseback riding. AE, MC, V.*

$$$ **Camino Real.** Location is the big plus at this property, which is far from the frenzy of the Golden Zone, past a rocky point at the northernmost edge of town. The beach is a bit of a hike from the hotel rooms, through the densely landscaped grounds and down a small hill. The hotel, one of the first in Mazatlán, is still comfortable, if a bit worn. A pink color scheme now prevails. If you're more interested in relaxing in peace than in carousing, this is one of your best bets. ✉ *Av. Camarón Sábalo, 82110,* ☎ *69/13–11–11; 800/722–6466 in the U.S.;* FAX *69/14–03–11. 169 rooms. 2 restaurants, 2 bars, pool, 2 tennis courts, beach. AE, DC, MC, V.*

$$$ ★ **Pueblo Bonito.** By far the most beautiful property in Mazatlán, this all-suites hotel and time-share resort has an enormous lobby with chandeliers, beveled glass doors, and gleaming red-and-white tile floors. The pink terra-cotta rooms have domed ceilings. An arched doorway leads from the tiled kitchen into the elegant seating area, which is furnished with pale pink and beige couches and glass tables. Pink flamingos stroll on the manicured lawns, golden koi swim in small ponds, and bronzed sunbathers repose on padded white lounge chairs by the crystal-blue pool. **Angelo's** (☞ Dining, *above*) is a dining must. This is as elegant as Mazatlán gets. ✉ *Av. Camarón Sábalo 2121, 82110,* ☎ *69/14–37–00; 800/442–5300 in the U.S.;* FAX *69/14–13–76. 250 suites. 3 restaurants, bar, 2 pools, exercise room, beach. AE, MC, V.*

$$$ ★ **Royal Villas Resort.** This startling 12-story structure, shaped like a pyramid, is decidedly more attractive on the inside. Panoramic elevators transport guests from the cool marble atrium lobby to the upper floors. The large guest rooms with tile floors are decorated in cool colors; all have remote-control TVs, balconies, and kitchenettes. Access to the inviting pool is by a bridge that crosses over a tropical fish–filled pond. ✉ *Av. Camarón Sábalo 500, 82110,* ☎ *69/16–61–61; 800/898-3564 in the U.S.;* FAX *69/14–07–77. 130 rooms. 2 restaurants, bar, pool, hot tub, exercise room, beach. AE, MC, V.*

$$ ★ **Casa Contenta.** A small surprise on the beach one block north of Las Flores, this property offers seven one-bedroom apartments in a colonial-style building as well as a large beachfront house with three bedrooms, three baths, living and dining room, and even servants' quarters that can accommodate eight people. Casa Contenta has many long-time repeat clients who book years in advance. ✉ *Av. Rodolfo T. Loaiza 224, 82110,* ☎ *69/13–49–76,* FAX *69/13–99–86. 8 units. Pool. MC, V.*

$$ ★ **El Cid.** The largest resort in Mazatlán, and perhaps in Mexico, El Cid has 1,310 rooms spread over 900 acres. A 100-slip marina began operating in 1994, and the Marina El Cid and Yacht Club, with 210 suites, opened in 1995. A mega–travel service, with its own deep-sea fishing fleet, sightseeing and cultural tours, sailing, snorkeling, sunset cruises, bass fishing, and hunting, is also planned, as is an additional 18-hole golf course. The spacious hotel rooms overlook the pool and beach (one of the longest and cleanest in the area), and the hotel is popular with convention groups as well as individual travelers. The glass-enclosed arcade has nice boutiques, and **La Concha** (☞ Dining, *above*) is one of the most romantic spots on the beach. ✉ *Av. Camarón Sábalo, 82110,*

☎ *69/13–33–33; 800/525–1925 in the U.S.;* FAX *69/14–13–11. 1,310 rooms, suites, and villas. 5 restaurants, 4 bars, 8 pools, 18-hole golf course, 17 tennis courts, shops, dance club. AE, DC, MC, V.*

$$ **El Quijote Inn.** On the beach, in the midst of the hotel zone, the five-story El Quijote Inn is a tranquil alternative to some of the more frenzied facilities. Accommodations include studios and one- or two-bedroom suites (the suites have full kitchens); all the units offer tile floors, rattan furnishings, and patios or balconies. ✉ *Avs. Camarón Sábalo and Tiburón, 82110,* ☎ *69/14–11–34,* FAX *69/14–33–44. 67 suites. Restaurant, bar, pool, hot tub. AE, MC, V.*

$$ **Fiesta Inn.** One of Mazatlán's newest hotels, the Fiesta Inn is operated by Posadas, a large Mexican hotel chain. The sleek nine-story tower is situated on the beach between the Holiday Inn and the Caravelle hotels. All the guest rooms are nicely decorated with marble floors, light-wood furniture, and pleasing pastels. ✉ *Av. Camarón Sábalo 1927, 82110,* ☎ *69/89–01–00; 800/343–7821 in the U.S.;* FAX *69/89–01–30. 117 rooms. 2 restaurants, bar, air-conditioning, pool, exercise room. AE, DC, MC, V.*

$$ **Holiday Inn Sunspree Resort.** A consistently good hotel, the Holiday Inn has been much improved by a drastic renovation in 1994. It's a long walk from here to the Zona Dorada, and little traffic runs by. Tour and convention groups fill the rooms and keep the party mood going by the pool and on the beach. Children have a small play area with swings and a wading pool, and there is live, upbeat music in the lobby. All of the rooms are done in whites and pastels, with large sliding doors that open to pretty views of the islands. Standard amenities now include remote-control cable TV, hair dryer, refrigerator, safe, and coffeemaker. ✉ *Av. Camarón Sábalo 696, 82110,* ☎ *69/13–22–22; 800/465–4329 in the U.S.;* FAX *69/14–12–87. 183 rooms. 2 restaurants, 2 bars, air-conditioning, pool, tennis court, exercise room, volleyball, beach. AE, MC, V.*

$$ **Los Sábalos.** A white high-rise in the center of the Zona Dorada, Los Sábalos has a great location, a long clean beach, and lots of action. You feel as though you're a part of things, amid the flight attendants who lay over here, and it's only a short walk to Valentino's, the best disco in town. ✉ *Av. Rodolfo T. Loaiza 100, 82110,* ☎ *69/83–53–33; 800/528–8760 in the U.S.;* FAX *69/83–81–56. 185 rooms. 2 restaurants, 3 bars, pool, 2 tennis courts, health club, beach. AE, DC, MC, V.*

$$ ★ **Playa Mazatlán.** Palapas are set up on the patios by the rooms in this casual hotel, which is popular with Mexican families and laid-back singles more concerned with comfort than style. The bright, sunny rooms have tiled headboards over the beds and tiled tables by the windows. There's a volleyball net on the beach, and two small stands sell good, inexpensive snacks. ✉ *Av. Rodolfo T. Loaiza 202, 82110,* ☎ *69/13–44–44; 800/762–5816 in the U.S.;* FAX *69/14–03–66. 425 rooms. 2 restaurants, bar, air-conditioning, 3 pools, beach. AE, MC, V.*

$ **Azteca Inn.** This hotel across the street from the Playa Mazatlán hotel is a great find for budget travelers who like to be in the center of things. The brown-and-white exterior color scheme isn't carried over into the rooms, which are decorated in reds and yellows. Most of the accommodations have two double beds, and all have cable TV. The staff couldn't be friendlier. ✉ *Av. Loaiza 307, 82110,* ☎ *69/13–44–77,* FAX *69/13–74–76. 74 rooms. Restaurant, bar, pool, hot tub. AE, DC, MC, V.*

$ **Plaza Gaviotas.** Most of the salmon-color rooms in this clean, colonial-style budget hotel, located across the street from Playa Mazatlán, have balconies and all have showers. ✉ *Av. Rodolfo T. Loaiza, 82110,*

☎ 69/13–43–22, FAX 69/13–60–85. 66 rooms. Restaurant, bar, pool. MC, V.

Nightlife

Caracol Tango Palace (☎ 69/13–33–33) at El Cid is Mazatlán's premier nightspot. Valentino's, Bora Bora, and Sheik are all part of the complex known as **Fiesta Land** (☎ 69/84–17–22, 69/84–16–66, or 69/84–17–77). **Valentino's**, with its stark white towers rising on Punta Camarón at the beginning of the Zona Dorada, still draws a glitzy crowd. Enjoy easy listening or romantic music here. Other options include karaoke, or rocking around the clock on the dance floor. **Bora Bora** is a casual palapa bar on the beach that stays alive with music and dancing from 8 PM to 4 AM. **Sheik** is a restaurant extravaganza, but it needs a lot of improvement in the food and service departments. Still, don't miss it—stop in during early evening for a drink at least.

The **Mexican Fiesta,** held Tuesday, Thursday, and Saturday from 7 to 10:30 PM, at the Playa Mazatlán, is a good entertainment bet. The $20 entrance fee includes a lavish Mexican buffet, folk dances, a cockfight, and live music for dancing. Almost all hotel travel desks can provide you with information on days and times.

Outdoor Activities and Sports

Participant Sports

FISHING

More than a dozen sportfishing fleets operate from the docks south of the lighthouse. Hotels can arrange charters, or you can contact the companies directly. Charters include a full day of fishing, bait, and tackle. Prices range from $60–$70 per person on a party boat, to $150–$300 to charter an entire boat. Charter companies to contact include **Bill Heimpel's Star Fleet** (☎ 69/82–26–65), **Flota Faro** (☎ 69/81–28–24), **Estrella** (☎ 69/82–38–78), **Flota Bibi** (☎ 69/81–36–40), and **De Oro** (☎ 69/82–31–30).

GOLF

The spectacular 18-hole course at **El Cid** (☎ 69/13–33–33), designed by Robert Trent Jones, is reserved for members of the resort, hotel guests, and their guests, so you'll need to make friends with someone who's staying there if you want to play. Another 18-hole course, next door at **Marina Mazatlán** (☎ 69/16–46–72), should be playable by 1998.

HORSEBACK RIDING

You don't have to stay at Rancho Las Moras (☞ Lodging, *above*) to mount one of their steeds; day-trippers are welcome at this huge, converted tequila ranch.

TENNIS

Many of the hotels have courts, some of which are open to the public, and there are a few public courts not connected to the hotels. Call in advance for reservations at **El Cid Resort** (☎ 69/13–33–33), 17 courts; the **Racket Club** (☎ 69/13–59–39), 6 courts; **Costa de Oro** (☎ 69/13–53–44), 3 courts; and **Camino Real** (☎ 69/13–11–11), 2 courts.

WATER SPORTS

Jet Skis, Hobie Cats, and Windsurfers are available for rent at most hotels, and parasailing is very popular along the Zona Dorada. Scuba diving and snorkeling are catching on, but there are no really great diving spots. The best is around Isla de los Venados. For rentals and trips, contact the following operators: **Caravelle Beach Club** (✉ Av. Camarón Sábalo, ☎ 69/13–02–00), **El Cid Resort Aqua Sport Center** (✉

Av. Camarón Sábalo, ☏ 69/13–33–33), **Los Sábalos** (✉ Av. Camarón Sábalo, ☏ 69/83–53–33), and **Camino Real Sports Center** (✉ Punta de Sábalo, ☏ 69/13–11–11).

Parque Acuático Mazaguas (✉ Av. Sábalo Cerritos and Entronque Habal Cerritos, ☏ 69/88–00–41) has water slides, wading pools, and a pool with man-made waves—a total of 20 water activities on 4 acres.

Spectator Sports

BASEBALL

The people of Mazatlán loyally support their team, Los Venados, a Pacific League Triple A team. Games are played at the Teodoro Mariscal Stadium (✉ Av. Deportes) from October through April.

BULLFIGHTS AND CHARREADAS

Bullfights are held most Sunday afternoons between December and Easter at the bullring on Calzada Rafael Buelna. Charreadas take place year-round. Tickets are available at the bullring, through most hotels, and from Valentino's (☏ 69/84–17–22).

Shopping

Zona Dorada

In the Zona Dorada, particularly along Avenida Camarón Sábalo and Avenida Rodolfo T. Loaiza, you can buy everything from piñatas to designer clothing. Leather shops are clustered along the southern end of the Zona Dorada.

CLOTHING

For sportswear, visit **Aca Joe** (✉ Avs. Camarón Sábalo and Gaviotas, ☏ 69/13–33–00), whose line of well-designed casual clothes for men is popular throughout Mexico and the United States.

Designer's Bazaar (✉ Av. Rodolfo T. Loaiza 217, ☏ 69/83–60–39), a two-story shop near Los Sábalos Hotel, has a nice selection of folk art, leather wallets and belts, and hand-embroidered clothing.

Señor Frog's Official Store (✉ Av. Rodolfo T. Loaiza 4B, ☏ 69/82–19–25) carries its own fun line of souvenirs, sports, and beachwear.

CRAFTS

The best place for browsing is the **Mazatlán Arts and Crafts Center** (✉ Av. Rodolfo T. Loaiza 417, ☏ 69/13–50–22), originally designed as a place to view artisans at work and buy their wares. The center offers a good sampling of the city's souvenir selection—onyx chess sets, straw sombreros, leather jackets, sandals, coconut masks, and Mickey Mouse piñatas. The shops are open 9–6. Thursday at 11 AM and 2:30 PM there's a show for cruise-ship passengers (other spectators are welcome, but should check in first with the Public Relations office) featuring the *voladores de Papantla* (a traditional Indian ritual dance performed atop a tall pole) and folk dancing.

Madonna (✉ Av. Las Garzas, ☏ 69/14–23–89) displays an extensive collection of silver and gold jewelry as well as masks and handicrafts.

Dealers Ron and Teresa Tammekand represent a number of top artists at **Mazatlán Art Gallery** (✉ Plaza Balboa on Av. Camarón Sábalo, ☏ 69/14–36–12) and hold one-person shows during the winter season.

La Carreta (✉ Playa Mazatlán, ☏ 69/13–83–20) has the finest selection of high-quality Mexican folk art in town.

Decorative Maya reproductions, as well as an excellent selection of crafts and leather goods, are found at **Casa Maya** (✉ Rodolfo T. Loiaza 411, ☏ 69/14–00–36).

Sea Shell City (✉ Av. Rodolfo T. Loaiza 407, ☎ 69/13–13–01) is a must-see; it has two floors packed with shells from around the world that have been glued, strung, and molded into every imaginable shape from lamps to necklaces. Check out the enormous fountain upstairs, covered with thousands of shells.

Downtown

The **Mercado Central,** between Calles Juárez and Serdán, is a gigantic place filled with produce, meat, fish, and handicrafts that are sold at the lowest prices in town. It takes more searching to find good-quality handicrafts, but that's part of the fun. Browse through the stalls along the street outside the market for the best crafts.

Side Trips

Concordia

48 km (29 mi) northeast of Mazatlán.

Concordia is known for its furniture makers (a huge wood chair marks the entrance to the small town), its 18th-century church, and its brown clay pottery. The trip, over a spectacular road, makes a nice change of pace from Mazatlán.

Copala

25 km (15 mi) east of Concordia.

A scenic colonial mining town at the foot of the Sierra Madre Occidental, Copala features a charming zócalo, cobblestone streets, colorful facades, and beautiful ironwork balconies and windows.

San Blas

211 km (127 mi) southeast of Mazatlán.

Known as the "budget travelers resort," San Blas is neither pretty nor especially interesting, but it's worth a trip here for the boat ride that takes you upriver through mangrove jungle for a swim in a small spring-fed pond.

Mazatlán A to Z

Arriving and Departing

BY BUS

Transportes Norte de Sonora, Estrella Blanca, Elite, and Trans-Pacífico (☎ 69/81–36–84 or 69/81–53–08) have service to Mazatlán from Nogales and Sonora and connect the coast with inland Mexico. The bus terminal is on Carretera Internacional 1203.

BY CAR

Mazatlán is 1,212 km (751 mi) from the border city of Nogales, Arizona, via Mexico Route 15, either on the excellent, but quite expensive, toll road or on the federal highway. An overnight stop is recommended, as driving at night in Mexico can be hazardous.

BY FERRY

Ferry service between La Paz and Mazatlán was privatized a few years back and the service is now fairly reliable. The ferry departs daily from Mazatlán's Playa Sur terminal at 3 PM and takes about 18 hours to reach La Paz. The fare is about $20 for regular passage and $60 per person for a private cabin for two with bed and bath (☎ 69/81–70–20).

BY PLANE

Airport and Airlines. Mazatlán's Rafael Buelna International Airport (☎ 69/82–23–99) is serviced by several airlines. **Aeromexico** (☎ 69/14–11–11) has flights from Tucson and several cities in Mexico.

Alaska Airlines (☎ 69/85–27–30) flies in from San Francisco and Los Angeles. **Delta** (☎ 69/14–41–56) and **AeroCalifornia** (☎ 69/13–20–42) have flights from Los Angeles, and **Mexicana** (☎ 69/82–77–22) flies in from Denver, Los Angeles, and several Mexican cities. **America West** (☎ 800/235–9292, no local phone) links Mazatlán with Phoenix.

Between the Airport and Hotels. The airport is a good 40-minute drive from town. **Autotransportes Aeropuerto** (☎ 69/82–70–08) provides shuttles using Volkswagen vans. The cost is $4 per person for *colectivo* service, $15 for a private car.

BY SHIP

Carnival Cruise Line, Celebrity Cruises, Cunard, Holland American Line, and **Krystal P&O,** among other cruise lines, include Mazatlán on their winter itineraries.

BY TRAIN

The Mexican train system is in a state of flux, with schedules changing constantly. Contact **Mexico by Train** (☎ FAX 210/725–3659 or ☎ 800/321–1699) for the most current information about trains to Mazatlán. The train depot is located south of town. Tickets may be purchased at the train station in the neighborhood of Col. Esperanza (☎ 69/84–66–27).

Getting Around

BY BUS

There are several bus lines, which run frequently along all major avenues. Routes are clearly marked. Fares start at about 10¢ and increase slightly depending on the destination.

BY CAR

A car is not necessary in town since public transportation is good, but you might want one for a self-guided tour of the area. Rentals usually include free mileage. A Volkswagen Beetle costs about $50 per day with insurance; a sedan with air-conditioning and automatic transmission is about $75 per day.

BY TAXI AND JITNEY

Most tourist hotels are located in the Zona Dorada, about 3 km (2 mi) north of downtown, but taxis cruise the strip regularly. Fares start at $1.50. A fun way to get around is on the pulmonías. The fare, for up to three passengers, starts at about $1 and increases according to the length of the trip. Complaints have been registered, however, about one's susceptibility to fumes from other vehicles.

Contacts and Resources

CAR RENTAL

The following rental firms have desks at the airport: **Hertz** (✉ Av. Camarón Sábalo 314, ☎ 69/13–60–60), **Budget** (✉ Av. Camarón Sábalo 402, ☎ 69/13–20–00), and **National** (✉ Av. Camarón Sábalo in Plaza el Camarón, ☎ 69/86–45–61).

EMBASSIES AND CONSULATES

United States (✉ Av. Rodolfo T. Loaiza 202, ☎ 69/85–22–05), **Canada** (✉ Av. Rodolfo T. Loaiza 202, ☎ 69/13–73–20).

EMERGENCIES

The **Public Tourism Ministry** (☎ 69/14–32–22) is an agency of the police department instituted specifically for tourists. **Red Cross** (☎ 69/81–36–90); **IMSS Hospital** (☎ 69/84–22–44).

GUIDED TOURS

Marlin Tours and **Viajes el Sábalo** (☞ Travel Agencies, *below*) offer a full range of tours with pickup service. Note: Formerly ubiquitous sidewalk stands staffed by persuasive individuals offering free tours of the area along with free drinks and meals—whose true goal is to sell timeshares and condos—have been limited to areas in front of these properties.

The three-hour **city tour,** which should cost around $10, is a good way to get the lay of the land, particularly downtown, which can be a bit confusing.

Cruises aboard the *Yate Fiesta* (☎ 69/85–22–37) cost about $8 and navigate the bay and the harbor, past the islands and sportfishing fleet; these and other harbor cruises generally last about three hours and feature music and dancing. Viajes El Sábalo runs a five-hour tour to see the seals at Isla de la Piedra (Stone Island), with time for lunch and a swim. The cost is about $20.

Also available are all-day **country tours,** which go to Concordia and Copala (about $35). Marlin Tours runs a trip to Teacapan, an ecological reserve. The eight-hour excursion costs $35 and includes Continental breakfast served on the bus, a stop at Rosario, and a seafood lunch at the almost deserted La Tambora beach. The **jungle tours** to San Blas and the Río Tovara (in the state of Nayarit) had been canceled because of the deplorable state of the road, but will resume if conditions improve. The tour companies also offer **individual guided tours** and **sportfishing outings.**

TRAVEL AGENCIES

American Express (✉ Plaza Balboa, Locale 4/16, ☎ 69/13–04–66), **Marlin Tours** (✉ Calle Laguna 300, ☎ 69/13–53–01), **Viajes el Sábalo** (✉ Los Sábalos hotel, ☎ 69/83–19–33, ✉ Camino Real hotel [☞ Lodging, *above*]). Agencies are open weekdays 10–2 and 4–7, Saturday 10–2.

VISITOR INFORMATION

City Tourism Bureau (✉ Av. Camaron Sabalo, Banrural Bldg., ☎ 69/16–51–60 to 65). The office is open weekdays 8:30–2 and 5–7.

PUERTO VALLARTA

On the edge of the Sierra Madre range sits one of the most popular vacation spots in Mexico. When Puerto Vallarta first entered the public's consciousness, with John Huston's 1964 movie *The Night of the Iguana,* it seemed an almost mythical tropical paradise. Indeed, at the time it was a quiet fishing and farming community in an exquisite setting.

Puerto Vallarta's Bahía de Banderas (Bay of Flags) attracted pirates and explorers as early as the 1500s; it was used as a stopover on long sailings, as a place for the crew to relax (or maybe plunder and pillage). Sir Francis Drake apparently stopped here. In the mid-1850s, Don Guadalupe Sánchez Carrillo developed the bay as a port for the silver mines by the Río Cuale. Then it was known as Puerto de Peñas and had about 1,500 inhabitants. It remained a village until 1918, when it was made a municipality by the state of Jalisco and named after Ignacio L. Vallarta, a governor of Jalisco.

In the 1950s, Puerto Vallarta was essentially a pretty hideaway for those in the know—the wealthy and some hardy escapists. After the publicity brought on by *The Night of the Iguana,* tourism began to boom.

PV—as the former fishing village is called these days—is now a city with more than 250,000 residents. Airports, hotels, and highways have supplanted palm groves and fishing shacks. About 1.5 million tourists visit each year, and from November through April cobblestone streets are clogged with pedestrians and cars. There are now more than 9,000 hotel rooms in Puerto Vallarta.

Despite the transformation, every attempt has been made to keep the town's character and image intact. Even the parking lot at the local Gigante supermarket is cobblestone, and by law any house built in town must be painted white. Visitors still see houses with red-tile roofs on palm-covered hills overlooking glistening blue water. Pack mules clomp down the steep cobblestone streets. Within 16 km (10 mi) of town are peaceful coves, rivers rushing to the sea, and steep mountain roads that curve and twist through jungles of pines and palms.

Exploring Puerto Vallarta

Central Puerto Vallarta has three major parts: the northern hotel and resort region, the downtown area (also called Old Town), and the Río Cuale and Playa de los Muertos. A rental car or cab is necessary to explore the hotel zone, which is basically a long stretch of shopping centers, restaurants, and hotels, but you don't want to have a car downtown and in the Río Cuale area. Most of the interesting sights can be covered on foot—just be sure you wear comfortable shoes for the cobblestone streets.

Numbers in the text correspond to numbers in the margin and on the Puerto Vallarta map.

A Good Walk

When you start seeing cobblestone streets, you're in the downtown area also known as Old Town. This is the heart of PV, a vestige of old Puerto Vallarta. Start your walk at the northern end of the **malecón** ⑦, which runs parallel to Díaz Ordáz beginning at 31 de Octubre. Two and a half blocks south on Díaz Ordáz, which merges with Morelos at the old lighthouse tower, is the town's main zócalo, Plaza de Armas. On the north side of the plaza you'll see the **City Hall** ⑧. Dominating the square from a block east is **La Iglesia de Nuestra Señora de Guadalupe** ⑨. Head south a few blocks and you'll come to the **Mercado Municipal** (☞ Shopping, *below*); it's at the foot of the upper bridge over the Río Cuale, which runs into the bay just past Plaza Serdán. The steep hillside above, dotted with charming villas, is called **Gringo Gulch** ⑩. In the middle of the river lies **Río Cuale Island** ⑪, reachable via steps leading under the two bridges.

Sights to See

8 **City Hall.** This building is home to a colorful mural, painted in 1981 by Puerto Vallarta's most famous artist, Mañuel Lepe. The mural (above the stairs on the second floor) depicts Puerto Vallarta as a fanciful seaside fishing and farming village. The tourism office is on the first floor. ⊠ *Av. Juárez by zócalo.*

10 **Gringo Gulch.** Named after the thousands of expatriates from the United States who settled here in the 1950s, this neighborhood's most famous attraction is Elizabeth Taylor's home, **Casa Kimberly.** The house was sold in 1990 and has been converted into a B&B (☞ Lodging, *below*), but nonguests need not despair. Tours, which include the Liz and Dick museum, are offered daily 9–6 in season and Monday–Saturday 10–2 off-season. ⊠ *Calle Zaragoza 445,* ☎ FAX *322/2-13-36.*

City Hall, **8**
Gringo Gulch, **10**
La Iglesia de Nuestra Señora de Guadalupe, **9**
Malecón, **7**
Río Cuale Island, **11**

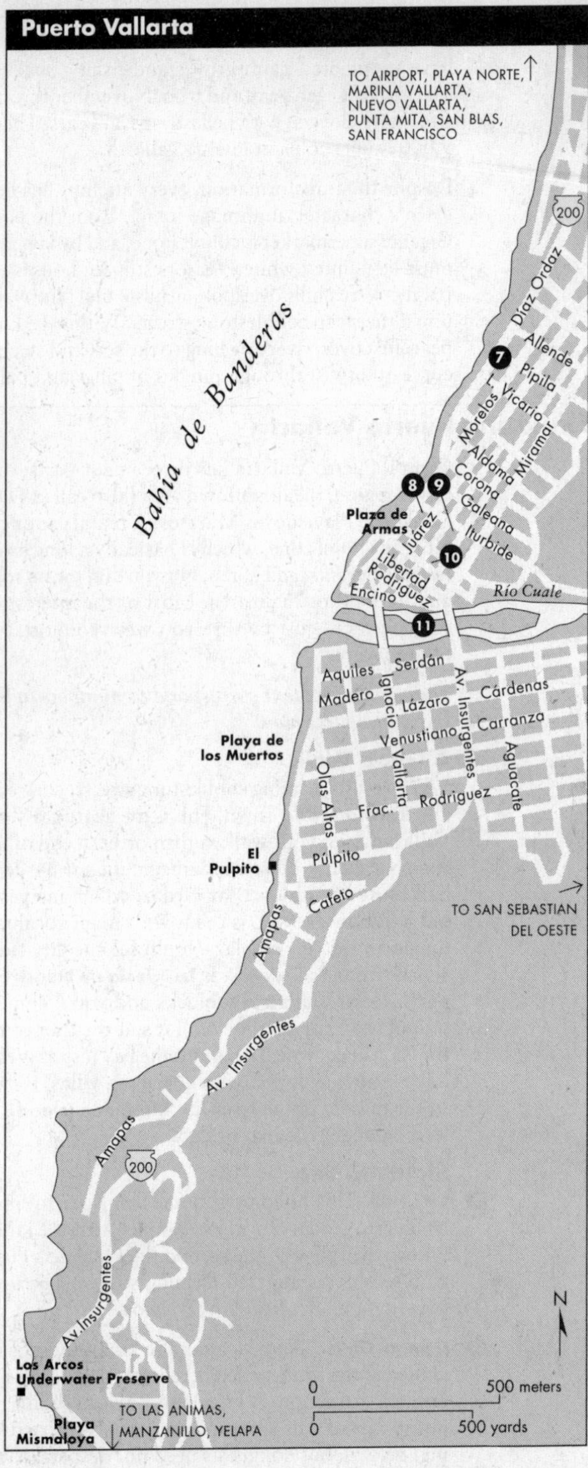

9 **La Iglesia de Nuestra Señora de Guadalupe** (Church of Our Lady of Guadalupe). The town's main church is topped by an ornate crown that replicates the one worn by Carlota, the empress of Mexico in the late 1860s. The crown toppled during the earthquake that shook this area of the Pacific Coast in October 1995, and was quickly replaced with a fiberglass version in time for the celebration of the Feast of the Virgin of Guadalupe (December 12). Most of the townsfolk are still up in arms about the new crown, claiming that it is distorted and that the choice of material is not sufficiently dignified for their beloved church. Signs posted at the entrances to the church ask that you not visit wearing shorts or sleeveless T-shirts. ✉ *Calle Hidalgo, 1 block east of zócalo.*

7 **Malecón.** The malecón is downtown's main drag, a nice place to rest on a white wrought-iron bench. A seawall and sidewalk run along the bay, and restaurants, cafés, and shops are across the street. There are some interesting sculptures along the walkway, including the bronze sea horse that has become Puerto Vallarta's trademark. ✉ *The malecón runs parallel to Díaz Ordáz approximately 16 blocks, extending from Río Cuale northeast to 31 de Octubre.*

NEED A BREAK? Dining and drinking are the malecón's big attractions, from early morning till just before dawn. For a quick picker-upper, sample great fresh squeezed juices at **Tutifruti** (✉ Morelos 552 and Corona, ☎ 322/2-10-68); choose your desired combination of mango, papaya, melon, and pineapple. Filling *tortas* (sandwiches on baguettes) cost about $1.75.

11 **Río Cuale Island.** The island has an outdoor marketplace with boutiques, souvenir stands, trendy restaurants, and inexpensive cafés; a bronze statue of film director John Huston dominates the main square. The **Museo Arqueológico** (western tip of the island, no phone) hosts a nice collection of pre-Columbian figures and Indian artifacts. The museum is open daily 10–2 and 4–6. Also on the Island is a branch of San Miguel de Allende's famed **Instituto Allende** (✉ Isla Río Cuale 36, ☎ 322/2-00-76), which offers classes in Spanish and Art. ✉ *To reach Río Cuale Island from north end of town, cross bridge at Encino and Juárez or at Libertad and Miramar. If you're coming from the south, cross over at Ignacio Vallarta and Aquiles Serdán, or at Insurgentes and Aquiles Serdán.*

Beaches

Puerto Vallarta's stellar attraction is its amazing beaches: crescents of golden sand, fringed with palms, along the hotel zone; endless stretches of gloriously unpopulated beaches to the north; and soft creamy beaches on craggy coves to the south.

Nayarit

North of Puerto Vallarta on the coast of Nayarit is a string of beautiful, unpopulated beach areas. **Lo de Marcos,** about 40 km (25 mi) away, is one of the most attractive. **Sayulita,** about 30 minutes from Puerto Vallarta, with a great beach, excellent surfing, and some good eating spots, has been described as Puerto Vallarta 40 years ago. Fifteen minutes beyond Sayulita is the interesting town of **San Francisco,** unofficially known as San Pancho, with modest rental bungalows and eateries and a 1½-km-long (1-mi-long), barely developed stretch of beach. On the north end of the beach, the **Costa Azul Adventure Resort** (☞ Lodging, *below*) sponsors a turtle-conservation program.

Playa de los Muertos

Playa de los Muertos, the beach on the south side of the Río Cuale, has long been the budget traveler's domain, though it has some of the more expensive restaurants and shops; it's by far the most popular and most crowded beach in Puerto Vallarta. Long ago, the beach was the site of a battle between pirates and Indians. The town's boosters tried for years to change the name Playa de los Muertos (Beach of the Dead) to Playa del Sol (Beach of the Sun), but they weren't successful; if you see an address for the latter, head for the former. Vendors selling lace tablecloths, wooden statues, kites, and jewelry stroll the beach, almost as abundant as sunbathers. Beach toys for rent include everything from rubber inner tubes to Windsurfers. **Plaza Lázaro Cárdenas** is a pretty spot at the north end of the beach; to the south, Playa de los Muertos ends at a rocky point called **El Púlpito.**

NEED A BREAK? Eating grilled fish on a stick at Playa de los Muertos is like having a hot dog at Coney Island: It's what you *do.* Buy it from one of the stands at the south end of the beach, then stroll along and watch the show. For a sit-down break, try the dorado-style fish, broiled with a thick layer of melted cheese at **El Dorado** (✉ Amapas and Púlpito, ☏ 322/2–15–11), on the north end of the beach.

Playa Las Animas and Yelapa

Playa Las Animas and Yelapa are secluded fishing villages accessible only by boat; the former is about 25 minutes from Puerto Vallarta, the latter approximately an hour away. Both villages have small communities of hardy isolationists; of late, Yelapa has attracted more and more foreigners who settle in for good. At Yelapa, take a 20-minute hike from the beach into the jungle to see the waterfalls. Tour groups arriving on cruise ships visit the beaches daily and motor launches leave from Boca de Tomatlán (☞ *below*) for Las Animas, Quimixto—another beautiful beach with calm clear waters to the south of Mismaloya—and Yelapa; the cost is from $3 to $6 per person.

Playa Mismaloya and Boca de Tomatlán

A visit to Puerto Vallarta without a side trip to Playa Mismaloya is nearly unthinkable, since this is where "the movie" was made. The 13-km (8-mi) drive south from the center of town on Route 200 passes by spectacular houses, some of PV's oldest and quietest resorts, and a slew of condo and time-sharing developments. A pretty cove, somewhat spoiled by La Jolla de Mismaloya, a huge hotel complex built on its shores, Mismaloya is backed by rugged, rocky hills and affords a good view of **Los Arcos,** a rock formation in the water. **Iguana Park** has been created to preserve the historic site where *Night of the Iguana* was made, and visitors can enjoy a meal or a drink in the house (restored) where John Huston lived during the filming.

Boca de Tomatlán is a small village at the mouth of the Tomatlán River, about 4 km (2½ mi) south of Mismaloya and 15 km (9½ mi) south of Puerto Vallarta. It's a beautiful spot where you can wade in freshwater pools. Just before you reach the dirt road to the beach, there are several large palapa restaurants. Chee Chee's, a massive restaurant, shopping, and swimming-pool complex, spreads down a steep hillside like a small village. Farther along the main road, through Boca, is Chico's Paradise (☞ Dining, *below*). Tour boats leave from here to Los Arcos and the more secluded beaches of Playa Las Animas and Yelapa (☞ *above*).

Playa Norte

Also known as Playa de Oro, this is Puerto Vallarta's northernmost beach, stretching from the marina and cruise-ship terminal to downtown. The beach changes a bit with the character of each hotel it fronts; it is particularly nice by the Fiesta Americana and the Krystal hotels.

Punta Mita

Twelve kilometers (7 miles) north of Nuevo Vallarta, on yet another beautiful beach, is the town of Bucerias. From there, you follow the bend of Banderas Bay past several small and pristine beaches—including Cruz de Huanacaxtle and Anclote—to Punta Mita, on the northern tip of the Bahía de Banderas. Punta Mita has blue bay water that's perfect for swimming and, around the bend, waves for surfing. Here, the views of the bay and of the Sierra Madre mountains are fantastic; this is definitely a prime spot to view a sunset and, during the winter months, the whales that come here to mate in the warm waters of the Mexican Pacific. Scuba divers like the fairly clear waters around the **Isla Marietas,** offshore.

Dining

$$$ ✕ **Café des Artistes.** Quite breathtaking and exquisitely romantic, this is Puerto Vallarta's most sophisticated dining spot (critics feel that it may be a tad pretentious). Owner/chef Thierry Blouet combines Mexican ingredients with European techniques to produce such interesting combinations as cream of prawn and pumpkin soup and smoked salmon salad in puff pastry served with a blend of avocado and pine nuts. A piano/flute duo provides the musical accompaniment. The menu changes every three months. On Sunday, a spectacular buffet is served in the garden. ✉ *Guadalupe Sánchez 740,* ☎ *322/2–32–28. Reservations essential. AE, DC, MC, V. No lunch.*

$$$ ★ ✕ **Chef Roger.** The cozy patio of a typical Puerto Vallarta house is the unpretentious setting for one of the best restaurants in town. Roger Dreier, the Swiss owner and chef, combines his European training with Mexican ingredients, and the results are superb. Don't leave town without trying the red snapper fillet with banana and almonds and, for dessert, the fried apples with vanilla sauce. ✉ *Augustín Rodríguez 267,* ☎ *322/2–59–00. Reservations essential. AE, DC, MC, V. No lunch.*

$$$ ★ ✕ **La Perla.** This restaurant and its chef are famous for their sublime Mexican haute cuisine, service, and ambience. The best dish by far is the veal stuffed with squash flowers, though the chicken in red wine and the beef fillet with stuffed chili, rice, and beans are also superb. The chef really shows his worth with the pastries, which are renowned throughout PV—and by all means try his flaming crepes. There is a separate lounge in the restaurant for after-dinner drinks, coffee, and dessert. The dining room is lovely, with neoclassical columns, an arched ceiling, and stained-glass murals. ✉ *Hotel Camino Real, Playa Las Estacas,* ☎ *322/3–01–23. AE, DC, MC, V. No lunch.*

$$$ ✕ **Señor Chico's.** On the Alta Vista hill overlooking all of Puerto Vallarta, this spot is magnificent from sunset into nighttime. The Caesar salad is good, as is any seafood choice, but it's the view that really makes the place. Enjoy live music from 7:30 to 10:30 PM. ✉ *Púlpito 377,* ☎ *322/2–35–70. MC, V. No lunch.*

$$–$$$ ✕ **Adobe Café.** Shades of white and earth tones, stark trees, fresh flowers, and an interesting menu make for a delightful dining experience. Specialties include cream of coriander soup, red snapper fillet with mango, and one of the best desserts in town, a sinfully rich chocolate mousse. ✉ *Basilio Badillo 252,* ☎ *322/2–67–20. AE, MC, V. No lunch.*

$$–$$$ ✕ **Bombo's.** This place is elegant and romantic, with a serene orchid and white decor, flickering candles, and a sweeping view of Puerto Vallarta. An exceptionally creative international menu includes smoked salmon mousse, kiwi margaritas, and cream of artichoke soup with pis-

tachio nuts. ✉ *Corona 327 and Matamoros,* ☎ *322/2-51-64. AE, MC, V. No lunch.*

$$ ✕ **Andale.** A Playa de los Muertos hangout and a good spot for an afternoon beer with the locals, this restaurant serves giant shrimp, great herb garlic bread, and an unusual chicken *mestizo* with white wine, pineapple juice, and jalapeño peppers. ✉ *Paseo de Velasco 425,* ☎ *322/2-10-54. AE, DC, MC, V.*

$$ ★ ✕ **Chez Elena.** This restaurant is among the town's best. Located up a steep street behind the church, Chez Elena is especially agreeable for an early dinner after enjoying the sunset and a drink on the rooftop **El Nido** bar. The menu features a few Indonesian dishes as well as some Mexican specialties, including *cochinta pibil* (pork prepared in a spicy pumpkin seed–based Yucatecan sauce), mole, and chicken bathed in a zesty mango sauce. ✉ *Matamoros 520,* ☎ *322/2-01-61. AE, MC, V. No lunch.*

$$ ★ ✕ **Don Pedro's.** Everything is a treat at this giant beachfront palapa in Sayulita, half an hour north of the airport, where European-trained chef and co-owner Nicholas Parrillo offers an array of fish, seafood, and poultry sprinkled with herbs and grilled over mesquite. Everything is fresh as can be and made on the premises, from the crusty herbed breads and pizzas to the rich mango ice cream. ✉ *Midway on Sayulita town beach, 35 km (22 mi) north of Puerto Vallarta airport,* ☎ *327/5-02-29. MC, V. Closed July–Oct.*

$$ ✕ **La Fuente del Puente.** Just across from the market, above the riverbank, this outdoor café is popular with budget travelers. The bright pink-and-blue neon along the ceiling is an unusual touch for PV. The prices are low, the food good, and the crowd amiable. ✉ *Av. Miramar at old bridge,* ☎ *322/2-11-41. MC, V.*

$$ ✕ **Las Palomas.** Better known as a prime spot for people-watching than for its cuisine, breakfast, lunch, or dinner at this malecón café has become a daily ritual for many and a place for the reunion of Puerto Vallarta regulars upon their return to town. The people in the mural on one of the walls are all well-known characters in Puerto Vallarta. Stick around town long enough and you'll probably run into a few of them. ✉ *Díaz Ordáz at Aldama,* ☎ *322/2-36-75. Reservations not accepted. AE, MC, V.*

$$ ✕ **Red Cabbage Café.** The decor of this cozy place is eclectic, the ambience Mexican chic, the food top quality, and the prices exceptionally reasonable. The thoughtfully conceived menu includes light soups, salads, and sandwiches as well as more substantial entrées like *chiles en nogada* (stuffed chilies in a sauce prepared with nuts and cream) and shrimp cooked in tequila. Special reservations-only dinners feature menus from *Frida and Diego's Fiestas* and *Like Water for Chocolate.* There's a piano player on the weekends. ✉ *Rivera Del Río 204-A,* ☎ *322/3-04-11. No credit cards.*

$–$$ ★ ✕ **Chico's Paradise.** It's easy to while away hours—or even spend the day—under the huge palapa, enjoying the sound of the waterfall, taking a dip in the river, or watching tortillas being made by hand. Two parrots will keep you occupied with their antics. Seafood, including fresh jumbo shrimp or stuffed crab, is a specialty, but *chiles rellenos* (stuffed chili peppers) and chicken burritos are also popular. If you think you might want to go for some of the huge tropical drinks, take the bus here (they run about every half hour or so). ✉ *Carretera a Manzanillo, Km 20,* ☎ *322/2-07-47. No credit cards.*

$ ✕ **Rito Baci's.** This popular deli and pizza parlor delivers to homes and hotels. All the pastas are made on the premises. The crispy-crusted pizza is excellent, and the sausage is spicy and flavorful. Try the sausage sandwich as well. ✉ *Calle Ortiz de Domínguez 181,* ☎ *322/2-64-48. MC, V.*

Lodging

Most of PV's deluxe resorts are located to the north of downtown. Many are concentrated in the Marina Vallarta complex, practically a town unto itself with a marina, hundreds of condominiums, shopping centers, an 18-hole golf course, and the Royal Pacific Yacht Club. Farther north is Nuevo Vallarta, just over the Jalisco state line in Nayarit, at the mouth of the Río Ameca. This beautiful community with beachfront houses and condos on canals with direct access to the bay is home to several all-inclusive resorts, including Jack Tar Village, the Plaza Sierra Radisson, and the Diamond Resort Puerta Vallarta. South of downtown and the Río Cuale, in the Playa de los Muertos and Olas Altas areas, the rates are lower. If you head farther south still, the prices go up again: Some spectacular properties are tucked away on hidden coves on the road to Manzanillo.

Budget hotels maintain the same rates year-round, but rates at the pricier places usually go down 25% to 30% just after Easter week through December 15. Reservations are a must at Christmas, New Year's, and Easter. Hotels in the state of Jalisco now charge a 2% room tax in addition to the 15% VAT tax.

$$$$ ★ **La Jolla de Mismaloya.** Despite the fact that the overpowering design of this hotel has ruined the view of beautiful Mismaloya Bay, the lucky guests here literally have half of the bay to themselves, as well as a fabulous view of Puerto Vallarta's famous arches (rock formations jutting out of the sea). The southern half of the bay is crowded with beachfront restaurants and motor launches that go to even more remote beaches. The hotel's huge one- and two-bedroom suites have kitchenettes as well as terraces; this fact, together with the many on-site activities for kids, makes it an ideal family getaway. This hotel consistently gets high marks from its guests. ✉ *Off Hwy. 200 at Mismaloya Bay, 48300,* ☎ *322/8–06–60; 800/322–2344 in the U.S.;* FAX *322/8–05–00. 303 suites. 5 restaurants, bar, 4 pools, 2 tennis courts, exercise room, beach. AE, DC, MC, V.*

$$$$ **Marriott Casa Magna.** Located in Marina Vallarta, with El Salado beach to the front and the Marina's 18-hole, Joe Finger–designed golf course to the rear, the Marriott Casa Magna is one of Vallarta's newest, largest, and most glamorous hotels. The vast, plant-filled marble lobbies that open onto the huge pool area are hung with chandeliers. The rooms are decorated with light woods and soft colors. All have at least a partial view of the bay. And if the water sports, tennis, restaurants, nightclubs, and other amenities of the hotel aren't enough, guests have access to the facilities of the Marina Vallarta complex, including a huge shopping center, a yacht club, and yet more restaurants. Rates include a gigantic buffet breakfast. ✉ *Marina Vallarta, 48354,* ☎ *322/1–00–04 or 800/223–6388,* FAX *322/1–07–60. 433 rooms and suites. 3 restaurants, 2 bars, pool, 3 tennis courts, exercise room, beach, dance club. AE, DC, MC, V.*

$$$$ ★ **Paradisus Puerto Vallarta.** On the beach in Marina Vallarta, this Sol Meliá hotel is a top-of-the-line all-inclusive resort. The exterior is an off-putting institutional style, but the lobby is a delicious blend of textures and colors, with marble and tile floors contrasting with colorful Mexican crafts and cozy wicker furniture. The large rooms are decorated in soft natural tones of cream and sand, with colorful accents. Amenities include hair dryers and safes in the rooms, the largest pool in the area—shaped like Picasso's *Peace Dove*, the Kids' Club, an outdoor theater, and nightly shows. Two children under the age of seven can stay free of charge (including meals and activities) if they share a room with their parents. Extensive refurbishing throughout the re-

sort should conclude at the end of 1997. ✉ *Paseo de la Marina Sur, 48354,* ☎ *322/1–02–00 or 800/336–3542,* FAX *322/1–01–18. 380 rooms. 3 restaurants, 2 bars, pool, 2 tennis courts, beach, water sports, shops, children's program (4–12), meeting rooms. AE, DC, MC, V.*

$$$$ **Sierra Hotel Nuevo Vallarta.** Situated on a long, wide expanse of creamy sand beach in Nuevo Vallarta, the Sierra is another deluxe all-inclusive property. The rooms are light and airy, with tile floors, light-wood and wicker furniture, and the ubiquitous pastel bedspreads. Activities are nonstop: There are cookouts, beach parties, Mexican fiestas, disco blasts, theme nights, musicals, karaoke, restaurants, and bars. Daytime activities include aerobics, beach and pool volleyball, tennis, minigolf, windsurfing, kayaking, water biking, and hot-air ballooning, as well as jungle and city tours. A golf course is minutes away. ✉ *Paseo de los Cocoteros 19, Nuevo Vallarta, 63732,* ☎ *329/7–13–00 or 800/882–6684,* FAX *329/7–08–00. 350 rooms and suites. 3 restaurants, 3 bars, 3 pools, tennis court, aerobics, volleyball, beach, windsurfing, dance club. AE, DC, MC, V.*

$$$ **Bel-Air.** Reminiscent of a grand hacienda, this pale pink mansion with white columns is simply but elegantly decorated. Fresh flowers and plants, antiques, and folk-art furnishings grace the rooms and corridors of this spacious property. There are 50 suites in the main building and freestanding villas. This property's location between the first and 18th holes of the Marina Vallarta Golf Course makes it ideal for golfers. Transportation is provided to and from the airport and within the Marina complex. The pool is lovely and the amenities are many, but the fact that the hotel is not directly on the beach is a drawback. ✉ *Marina Vallarta, Pelicanos 311, 48300,* ☎ *322/1–08–00 or 800/457–7676,* FAX *322/1–08–01. 50 suites, 25 1- to 3-bedroom villas. Restaurant, bar, room service, pool, spa, golf course. AE, MC, V.*

$$$ ★ **Camino Real.** One of PV's first hotels, this property sits on a lovely small bay south of town. The rooms have cool marble floors with white furniture and bright pink, yellow, and purple highlights against stark white walls. The hotel has all the five-star touches—from plush robes in the rooms and the feel of an established, comfortable resort to the palapas on the beach and the fragrant white jasmine blooming along the natural waterfall. The **La Perla** restaurant (☞ Dining, *above*) is one of the best in town. **La Brisa,** on the northern end of the beach, serves superb seafood lunches. A newer 11-story tower houses the Royal Beach Club, which also has a convention-banquet center. The club's upper floors have whirlpool baths. ✉ *Playa Las Estacas, 48300,* ☎ *322/1–50–00; 800/722–6466 in the U.S.;* FAX *322/1–60–00. 337 rooms. 5 restaurants, 3 bars, 2 pools, wading pool, 2 tennis courts, health club, beach. AE, DC, MC, V.*

$$$ **Continental Plaza Puerto Vallarta.** Ideal for tennis buffs, this Mediterranean-style complex has a tennis club with eight courts and daily tennis clinics. The resort has a shopping plaza, several restaurants and bars, a large swimming pool, and a nice beach. ✉ *Carretera Aeropuerto, 48300,* ☎ *322/4–01–23; 800/882–6684 in the U.S. 424 rooms. Restaurants, bars, pool, 8 tennis courts, beach. AE, DC, MC, V.*

$$$ **Fiesta Americana.** A seven-story palapa covers the lobby and a large round bar. The dramatically designed terra-cotta building rises above a deep blue pool that flows under bridges, palm oases, and palapa restaurants set on platforms over the water. The rooms have a modern pink and terra-cotta color scheme; each has white marble floors, tiled bath with powerful shower, and balcony. The beach bustles with activity—parasailing, windsurfing, boat touring, snorkeling, and, of course, sunbathing. The restaurants are excellent, especially the breakfast buffet by the pool. ✉ *Blvd. Francisco M. Ascencio, Km 2.5, 48300,* ☎ *322/4–20–10 or 800/343–7821,* FAX *322/4–21–08. 291*

rooms. 3 restaurants, 4 bars, pool, beauty salon, beach, dance club, travel services. AE, DC, MC, V.

$$$ ★ **Krystal Vallarta.** A full-service resort that sprawls over acreage equivalent to that of a small town, the Krystal offers hotel rooms and villas with private pools. Many of the accommodations have lots of Mexican character, with tiled floors and Spanish colonial–style furnishings. There are five restaurants, including **Tango,** which serves Argentine *churrasco* (barbecue); **Kamakura,** which serves Japanese food; and **Bogart's,** the signature restaurant of the Krystal chain, with a Casablanca theme. Not all rooms are by the ocean, but the secluded beach can accommodate all sunseekers. Christine's disco has a knock-'em-dead light show. ✉ *Carretera Aeropuerto, 48300,* ☎ *322/4–02–02 or 800/231–9860,* FAX *322/4–02–22. 421 rooms, 33 villas. 5 restaurants, 3 bars, 4 pools, 2 tennis courts, beach, dance club, travel services. AE, DC, MC, V.*

$$$ **Qualton Club & Spa.** The Qualton hotel is a spa, with a fitness center and state-of-the-art exercise machines, beauty treatments from hydromassage to herbal wraps, nutritional analysis, and computerized exercise and diet regimes. You don't have to be a fitness freak to stay here, though. The rooms in the two wings and main 14-story tower are done in peaceful mauves and blues; deluxe rooms have ocean-view balconies. Meals, drinks, most sports activities, and general spa facilities and services are included in the room rate. There's an additional charge for massages, facials, and the like. ✉ *Carretera Aeropuerto, 48300,* ☎ *322/4–44–46; 800/446–2727 in the U.S.;* FAX *322/4–44–47. 218 rooms, 3 restaurants, bar, pool, hot tub, spa, beach. AE, DC, MC, V.*

$$$ **Westin Regina.** This attractive hotel is situated on a choice 21-acre site in Marina Vallarta. In addition to four pools, a long stretch of beach, and a full range of facilities and activities (including an excellent kids' club), the Westin offers guests spacious balconied rooms with brightly colored, handwoven spreads and drapes. Each of the rooms has at least a partial view of the bay. ✉ *Paseo de la Marina Sur 205, 48321,* ☎ *322/1–11–00 or 800/892–4580,* FAX *322/1–11–41. 280 rooms. 2 restaurants, 3 bars, 4 pools, exercise room, beach. AE, DC, MC, V.*

$$ ★ **Buenaventura.** This hotel's location is ideal, on the edge of downtown, within walking distance (10 blocks or so) of the Río Cuale and, in the opposite direction, of the shops, hotels, and restaurants on the airport highway. From the street it looks rather austere, but just inside the door is an enormous five-story open lobby and bar. The bright, cheerful rooms, decorated in white and green, have beamed ceilings and pale-wood furnishings. ✉ *Av. México 1301, 48350,* ☎ *322/2–37–37; 800/223–6764 in the U.S.;* FAX *322/2–35–46. 206 rooms, 4 suites. 2 restaurants, 2 bars, pool, hot tub, exercise room, beach. AE, DC, MC, V.*

$$ **Casa Kimberly.** The former homes of Elizabeth Taylor and Richard Burton, located on opposite sides of the street but joined by a footbridge (in a part of town now called Gringo Gulch), have been converted into a B&B. Both houses are surprisingly unpretentious; only Liz's had a pool. The current owner, naturally enough, exploits the Liz and Dick legend and has added on a museum devoted to them. Lavender (supposedly Elizabeth's favorite color, at least during her Puerto Vallarta days) prevails, and tables and walls are adorned with photos of the famous lovers. The rate includes a full breakfast. ✉ *Calle Zaragoza 445, 48300,* ☎ FAX *322/2–13–36. 8 suites. Pool. No credit cards.*

$$ **Costa Azul Adventure Resort.** This environment-friendly resort, some 48 km (30 mi) north of Puerto Vallarta, was designed by a group of southern Californians, and predictably, surfing is big here. But that's not all: The adventure trips, led by enthusiastic and knowledgeable guides, range from kayaking and snorkeling to deep-sea fishing and whale-watching. Horseback riding and mountain biking through an ecological preserve are also offered. The sweeping, palm-fringed beach is as yet unspoiled. Rooms in this intimate, friendly place are simply but attractively decorated, and the adventure package, including all meals and most activities, is very reasonably priced. There is a minimum two-night stay. ✉ *San Francisco, Nayarit,* ☎ FAX *327/5–00–99;* ☎ *800/365–7613 in the U.S. 28 units. Restaurant, pool, bar, horseback riding, snorkeling, surfing, boating. MC, V.*

$$ **Hacienda Buenaventura.** This consistently good, Mexican colonial-style hotel isn't on the beach, but there is a huge pool with a swim-up bar, and guests have access to the beach at the neighboring Vallarta Torre. The comfortable rooms are decorated in soft pastels, with marble floors. ✉ *Blvd. Francisco M. Ascencio 2699, 48310,* ☎ *322/4–66–67,* FAX *322/2–08–70. 155 rooms. 2 restaurants, 2 bars, pool. AE, DC, MC, V.*

$$ ★ **Las Palmas.** The palapa entrance to Las Palmas is unique—four bamboo bridges suspended from the ceiling and parrots screeching under the palms. The rooms have balconies and flowered spreads and draperies. The accommodations are first-rate for this price category. ✉ *Cerrada las Palmas 50, 48380,* ☎ *322/4–06–50,* FAX *322/4–05–43. 114 rooms. Restaurant, bar, pool. AE, DC, MC, V.*

$$ **Molino de Agua.** This hotel's bungalows are spread out along the riverbed amid lush trees and flowers. Stone pathways wind under willows, past caged parrots and monkeys, and lead to cottages with wood shutters and redbrick walls. However, the din emanating from the bar area after 5 PM can be disturbing, and while all the rooms have air-conditioning, none have telephones or TVs. ✉ *Vallarta 130, 48300,* ☎ *322/2–19–07. 53 rooms. Restaurant, snack bar, 2 pools, hot tub, beach. AE, MC, V.*

$$ **Playa Los Arcos.** By far the most popular hotel on the beach by the Río Cuale, Los Arcos has a pretty central courtyard and pool and a friendly air. A glass elevator rises by the pool to the rooms, which have been redone in light-wood and pastel furnishings and offer small balconies. ✉ *Olas Altas 380, 48380,* ☎ *322/2–05–83,* FAX *322/2–24–18. 180 rooms. Restaurant, bar, pool, beach. AE, DC, MC, V.*

$ **Los Cuatro Vientos.** The most charming small hotel in PV, Cuatro Vientos (meaning Four Winds) is located up a steep hill behind town, tucked among the red-tile-roofed cottages. Its 16 rooms are often booked a year in advance by repeat guests. The simple rooms with arched brick ceilings have colorful flowers stenciled on the walls and folk-art knickknacks. The **Chez Elena** restaurant (☞ Dining, *above*) is delightful, and there's a pleasant rooftop bar open in high season. ✉ *Matamoros 520, 48300,* ☎ *322/2–01–61,* FAX *322/2–28–31. 16 rooms. Restaurant, bar. MC, V.*

$ ★ **Posada de Roger.** One of PV's least expensive hotels, the Posada de Roger is in many ways the most enjoyable, if you like the company of Europeans and Canadians who are savvy about budget traveling. The rooms have telephones and air-conditioning, the showers are hot, the beds comfortable, and the pool is an international meeting spot. You can have your mail held there, and the desk clerks are knowledgeable about other budget hotels and restaurants. ✉ *Basilio Badillo 237, 48380,* ☎ *322/2–08–36,* FAX *322/3–04–82. 50 rooms. Restaurant, bar, pool. AE, MC, V.*

$ ★ **Posada Río Cuale.** This small, friendly inn on the south side of Río Cuale has one of the best gourmet restaurants in town (aptly named Le Gourmet) and a nice sense of serenity. The beds are big and comfortable; flowers are placed on each nightstand; and with only 21 rooms, the place rarely becomes noisy. ✉ *Calle Aquiles Serdán 242,*

48380, ☎ 322/2-04-50, FAX 322/2-09-14. 21 rooms. Restaurant, bar, pool. AE, MC, V.

En Route to Manzanillo

The coastline south of Puerto Vallarta is sprinkled with some of the Mexican Riviera's most exclusive and secluded one-of-a-kind resorts. But you'll never see them from the highway when you take Highway 200 south—a rugged, twisting road through a tropical forest of pines and palms. Most of the resorts are reached by unpaved roads (though the coast is only a short distance from Highway 200). Guests usually fly to Puerto Vallarta or Manzanillo (one hour south) and take a taxi or hotel van to their resort. Once there, they stay put for a week or more, leaving only for the requisite shopping spree in PV. As you travel south, the best resorts are in Quemaro, Tecuán, Careyes, and Tenacatita.

Lodging

$$$ **Blue Bay Village Los Angeles Locos.** Canadians come here by the charter-jet load, drawn to the amiable surroundings, the all-inclusive drinks and meals, and the chance to relax with friends. The large, comfortable rooms are clustered in a horseshoe-shape terra-cotta building around the bay. Tours to Puerto Vallarta and Manzanillo are available through the Hectours Travel Agency on the premises. ✉ *Hwy. 200, Km 20, in Tenacatita, 48989, ☎ 335/1-50-05, FAX 322/1-50-50. 201 rooms and suites. Restaurant, bar, pool, horseback riding, beach, dance club, travel services. AE, DC, MC, V.*

$$$$ ★ **Las Alamandas.** One of Mexico's most exclusive—and expensive—resorts, Las Alamandas is low key rather than glitzy. Surrounded by a natural preserve that hosts abundant wildlife, the property's villas and casitas are decorated with folk art and traditional Mexican furnishings (some offer TVs and VCRs). Among the various outdoor activities are horseback riding, fishing, hot-air balloon rides, and boat rides along the San Nicolás River. Many guests fly into the hotel's private helipad; others take the hotel's air-conditioned limo from either the Puerto Vallarta (1¾ hrs) or Manzanillo (1½ hrs) airport. There's a two-night-stay minimum; meal packages are available. ✉ *Apdo. Postal 201, San Patricio Melaque, Jalisco 48980, ☎ 328/5-55-00, FAX 328/5-50-27. Reservations in the U.S.: ✉ 3525 Sage Rd., Houston, TX 77056, ☎ 713/961-3117 or 800/223-6510, FAX 713/961-3411. Casita, 4 villas. Restaurant, in-room VCRs, pool, tennis court, croquet, exercise room, Ping-Pong, volleyball, 5 beaches, mountain bikes. AE, MC, V.*

$$$ **Playa Blanca.** This Club Med has all the services the pioneer all-inclusive chain is known for—diving, fishing, pool bars, horseback riding, and even a trapeze and circus school. The food, usually served buffet style, is ample and good, and there are two restaurants where you can be served by waiters. The guests tend to be young and frenetic, and the resort is far from having a feeling of isolation: With 300 rooms, a disco, and aerobics classes, the ambience is more celebratory than somnolent. ✉ *Off Hwy. 200, ☎ 335/1-00-01; 800/258-2633 in the U.S. 300 rooms. 2 restaurants, bar, dining rooms, pool, tennis court, horseback riding, beach. AE, DC, MC, V.*

Nightlife and the Arts

Puerto Vallarta is a party town, where the discos open at 10 PM and stay open until 3 or 4 AM. A minimum $10 cover charge is common in the popular discos, many of which are at the hotels. The Krystal has **Christine's,** which features a spectacular light show set to music from disco to classic rock nightly at 11:30. **Sixties,** at the Marriott, has music for almost all ages, and **Friday López,** at the Fiesta Americana, has karaoke and dancing. **Ta'izz** (✉ Marina Vallarta, ☎ 322/1–09–68) and **Cactus Club** (✉ Ignacio Vallarta 399, ☎ 322/2–60–37) attract a young crowd. Tables start to disappear from the lower level of the **Hard Rock Cafe** (✉ Díaz Ordáz 652 at Absolo, ☎ 322/2–22–30), downtown on the malecón, at about 10 PM, and by 11 PM the live music starts and there is dancing everywhere. **La Pachanga** (✉ Av. México 918, ☎ 322/3–10–95) is a popular place with live entertainment, mariachis, and a folk ballet. Everything its name implies and more, **Collage** (☎ 322/1–05–05), on the highway at the Marina Vallarta complex, hosts several restaurants, a bowling alley, a large-screen video-golf game, billiards, two bars, shuffleboard, a video arcade, and a disco. If a quiet drink and a stupendous view are what you crave, **El Faro** (✉ Royal Pacific Yacht Club, Marina Vallarta, ☎ 322/1–02–33) is the place to go.

Mexican **fiestas** are popular at the hotels and can be lavish affairs with buffet dinners, folk dances, and fireworks. Reservations may be made with the hotels or travel agencies. Some of the more spectacular shows are at La Iguana Tourist Center (☎ 322/2–01–05), the Krystal, and the Westin Regina.

Outdoor Activities and Sports

Swimming, sailing, windsurfing, and parasailing are popular sports at the beachfront hotels. The hotels have stands on the beach offering boat trips and equipment, and you need not be a guest to buy these services.

Biking

Bike Mexico (✉ Guerrero 361, ☎ 335/3–16–80) provides the gear (21-speed mountain bikes, helmets, lunch, and refreshments) for four- to six-hour bike tours that are tailored to each rider's experience and fitness level.

Fishing

The Progreso Fishermen's Cooperative has a shack on the north end of the malecón and offers a variety of options for fishing trips; most hotels can arrange your reservations. Large group boats cost about $60 per person for a day's fishing; other cruisers may be chartered for prices ranging from $150 to $350 a day, depending on the size of the boat and the length of the trip. Charters include a skipper, license, bait, and tackle; some also include lunch.

Golf

There is a Joe Finger–designed, 18-hole course at the **Marina Vallarta** complex (☎ 322/1–01–71). The 18-hole course at **Los Flamingos Country Club** (✉ 12 km [8 mi] north of airport, ☎ 329/8–02–80) was designed by Percy Clifford. Reservations should be made through your hotel a day in advance.

Horseback Riding

Horseback riding along the shore is popular, and horses can be rented by the hour at major beaches. Several stables, including **Rancho Charro** (✉ Francisco Villa 895, ☎ 322/4–01–14) and **Rancho El Ojo de Agua** (✉ Francisco Villa s/n, ☎ 322/4–82–40), offer three-hour trips into the mountains, sunset rides, and longer excursions to charming colonial villages in the Sierra Madre; time is allotted for lunch and a swim in a mountain stream or lake.

Tennis

Most of the larger hotels have tennis courts. Nonmembers may also play at the **Continental Plaza Tennis Club** (☎ 322/4–01–23), **Los Tules** (☎ 322/4–45–60), and the **Iguana Tennis Club** (☎ 322/1–06–83).

Water Sports

Snorkeling and diving are best at Los Arcos, a natural underwater preserve on the way to Mismaloya. Punta Mita, about 80 km (50 mi) north of Puerto Vallarta, has some good diving spots, as does Quimixto Bay, about 32 km (20 mi) south and accessible only by boat. Experienced divers prefer Las Marietas, a group of three islands off the coast.

Some of the hotels have snorkeling and diving equipment for rent and offer short courses on diving at their pools. For dive trips and rentals, contact **Chico's Dive Shop** (✉ Díaz Ordáz 772, ☎ 322/2–18–95) or **Silent World Diving Center** (✉ Hotel Las Palmas, ☎ 322/4–06–64, ext. 626).

Shopping

Puerto Vallarta has been described as being one huge shopping mall interspersed with hotels and beaches. This is undoubtedly an exaggeration, but PV can definitely get into a shopper's blood. There are dozens of excellent shops stocked with some of the best crafts from all around Mexico, as well as several fine art galleries. Prices in the shops are fixed, and American dollars and credit cards are accepted. Bargaining is expected in the markets and by the vendors on the beach, who also freely accept American money. Most stores are open 10–8. A few close for siesta at 1 or 2, then reopen at 4.

Art

The late Mañuel Lepe is perhaps Puerto Vallarta's most famous artist. His primitive style can be seen in the prints and posters that are still available at several of the galleries and shops around town. Sergio Bustamante, the creator of life-size brass, copper, and papier-mâché animals, has his own galleries: **Sergio Bustamente** (✉ Av. Juárez 275, ☎ 322/2–11–29; ✉ Paseo Díaz Ordaz 700 A, ☎ 322/3–14–07; ✉ Paseo Díaz Ordaz 542, ☎ 322/2–54–80). **Galería Uno** (✉ Morelos 561, ☎ 322/2–09–08) specializes in art from all over Mexico, but owner Jan Lavender is especially enthusiastic about promoting local talent. Contemporary art and sculpture are displayed in one of Mexico's finest galleries, **Galería Pacífico** (✉ Insurgentes 109, ☎ 322/2–19–82). On the promenade in Marina Vallarta, **Arte de las Américas** (✉ Marina las Palmas 11–16, ☎ 322/1–19–85) displays the work of celebrated and emerging contemporary artists.

Clothing

Most of the brand-name sportswear shops are located along the malecón and down its side streets. Many of these stores also have branches in the shopping centers or along Carretera Aeropuerto. **Aca Joe** (✉ Díaz Ordáz 588, ☎ 322/3–04–24) offers excellent quality pants, T-shirts, shorts, jackets, and sweats in smashing colors, all neatly displayed. **Express–Guess** (✉ Paseo Díaz Ordaz 660, ☎ 322/2–64–70) carries its own line of well-designed quality sportswear.

More elegant, dressier clothes, made of soft flowing fabrics in tropical prints, can be found at **Sucesos Boutique** (✉ Libertad and Hidalgo, ☎ 322/2–10–02), which features hand-painted fabrics and fashionable gauze resortwear that is sold in exclusive boutiques throughout Mexico. Just behind the John Huston statue on Río Cuale island is **Tabu Artwear** (✉ Río Cuale-28, ☎ 322/2–35–28), displaying hand-painted clothing created by owner Patti Callardo, accessories for the home, metal sculptures, and wall hangings. **Valenciana** (✉ Corona 160, ☎ 322/3–04–18) offers hand-painted straw hats; cotton fashions for women by Tipicano, Opus I, and Dunas; and some imaginative accessories. **María de Guadalajara** (✉ Puesta del Sol condominiums in Marina Vallarta,

☎ 322/1–02–62, ext. 1015; ✉ Morelos 550, ☎ 322/2–23–87; ✉ Plaza Malecón and Paseo Díaz Ordaz, ☎ 322/2–47–35) carries easy-to-wear clothing for women in gauzy cotton fabrics dyed in luscious colors. **Nina & June** (✉ Hidalgo 227–8, ☎ 322/2–30–99) specializes in Nina's handwoven originally designed fashions, fanciful accessories, and June's silver jewelry. **Con Juntos** (✉ Olas Altas 392, Hotel Playa Los Arcos, ☎ 322/2–15–83) sells outfits created by owner-designer Toody Walton and some of Vallarta's artists.

Folk Art

Few cities in Mexico have a collection of the country's fine folk art that is as representative as the one in Puerto Vallarta. Masks, pottery, lacquerware, clothing, mirrors, glass dishes, windows and lamps, carved-wood animals and doors, antiques and modern art, hand-dyed woven rugs, and embroidered clothing are all available in the markets and from vendors. **Alfarería Tlaquepaque** (✉ Av. México 1100, ☎ 322/3–21–21) stocks a varied selection of baked earthenware suns, carved wood figures, blown glass, baskets, ceramics, and painted animals from all over Mexico. **Attica** (✉ Plaza Marina A–39, ☎ 322/1–01–20) carries items for the home, including handwoven materials, quilted bedspreads, and custom-made hand-painted furniture. **Mundo de Azulejos** (✉ Carranza 374, ☎ 322/2–26–75) offers a line of Talavera tiles and will create tile replicas of your favorite scene or work of art in 24 to 48 hours. **Olinalá** (✉ Lázaro Cárdenas 274, ☎ 322/2–49–95) is a two-story gallery and shop filled with masks from all over Mexico, as well as colonial-inspired carvings, lacquered boxes, and trays from Michoacán. Original hand-loomed rugs, fabrics, and hand-painted furniture are on display at **Tamacani** (✉ Plaza Marina D-2, ☎ 322/1–09–82). **La Rosa de Cristal** (✉ Insurgentes 272, ☎ 322/2–56–98) carries a full line of blown-glass items made in its Tlaquepaque workshop.

Jewelry

There is a good selection of Mexican silver in Puerto Vallarta, but watch out for fake silver made with alloys. Real silver carries the 925 silver stamp required by the government. It is best to visit a reputable jeweler, such as **Ric Taxco** (✉ Pueblo Viejo shopping center, ☎ 322/3–01–43; ✉ Villa Vallarta shopping center, ☎ 322/4–45–98), where much of the sterling silver and gold jewelry was inspired by pre-Hispanic designs. **Joyas Finas Suneson** (✉ Morelos 593, ☎ 322/2–57–15) specializes in fine silver jewelry and objets d'art by some of Mexico's finest designers.

Markets

The **Mercado Municipal,** at Avenida Miramar and Libertad, is a typical market plopped down in the busiest part of town. Flowers, piñatas, produce, and plastics are all shoved together in indoor and outdoor stands that cover a full city block. The strip of **shops along Río Cuale Island** is an outdoor market of sorts, with souvenir stands and exclusive boutiques interspersed with restaurants and cafés. Bargaining at the stalls in the market and on the island is expected.

Shopping Centers

The highway on the north side of town is lined with small arcades and large shopping centers that are occupied by handicrafts and sportswear shops. The best selections are at **Plaza Malecón,** at the beginning of Díaz Ordáz; **Plaza Marina,** on the highway at Marina Vallarta; the **Gigante Plaza,** by the Fiesta Americana hotel; and **Villa Vallarta,** by the Plaza las Glorias hotel.

Puerto Vallarta A to Z

Arriving and Departing

BY BUS

There is no central bus station in Puerto Vallarta, but most of the carriers are located on Avenida Insurgentes between the Río Cuale and Calle Serdán: **Transportes del Pacífico** (⊠ Av. Insurgentes 282, ☎ 322/2–10–15) and **Elite** (⊠ Basilio Badillo 11, ☎ 322/3–11–17), which incorporates three lines (Estrella Blanca, Tres Estrellas de Oro, and Norte de Sonora). Elite offers excellent first-class service (reclining seats, air-conditioning, refreshment service, functioning bathroom) to Guadalajara, Aguascalientes, and Mexico City.

BY CAR

Puerto Vallarta is about 1,900 km (1,200 mi) from Nogales, Arizona, at the United States–Mexico border, 354 km (220 mi) from Guadalajara, and 167 km (104 mi) from Tepic. Driving to Puerto Vallarta is not difficult, but driving in the city can be horrid. From December through April—peak tourist season—traffic clogs the small cobblestone streets; during the rainy season, from July through October, the streets become flooded and the hills are muddy and slippery.

BY PLANE

Airport and Airlines. Puerto Vallarta's **Gustavo Díaz Ordáz International Airport** (☎ 322/1–12–98) is 6½ km (4 mi) north of town, not far from the major resorts. The Mexican airlines have daily flights from Mexico City, Guadalajara, Monterrey, Manzanillo, Tampico, and Tepic. **Mexicana** (☎ 322/4–89–00) has service from Chicago, Los Angeles, and Denver. **Aeromexico** (☎ 322/4–27–77) flies from Los Angeles, New York, Dallas, and San Diego. Several American carriers also serve Puerto Vallarta, including **Alaska Airlines** (☎ 322/1–13–53), **American** (☎ 322/1–17–99), **Continental** (☎ 322/1–10–25), and **Delta** (☎ 322/1–19–86). **America West** (☎ 800/235–9292, no local phone) flies in from Phoenix.

Between the Airport and Hotels. Volkswagen vans provide economical transportation from the airport to hotels, and all the car-rental agencies have desks in the airport.

BY SHIP

Several cruise lines, including **Carnival, Celebrity, Crystal P&O, Cunard, Holland American Line, Krystal, Princess Cruises, Royal Caribbean Cruises,** and **Royal Cruise Line,** sail to Puerto Vallarta from Los Angeles during the winter months.

BY TRAIN

Trains run daily from Mexicali, Nogales, and Guadalajara to Tepic; from Tepic, it is a three-hour bus ride to Puerto Vallarta. The train is unreliable, crowded, and slow and is best left to those with plenty of time and patience.

Getting Around

BY BUS

City buses and *combis* (Volkswagen vans) serve downtown, the northern hotel zone, and the southern beaches. Bus stops—marked by a blue-and-white sign with a drawing of a bus—are located every two or three blocks along the highway (Carretera Aeropuerto) and in town. To take a combi to Mismaloya or other points south, go to the Combi Terminal on Calle Piño Suárez or the bus stop at Plaza Lázaro Cárdenas just south of Los Arcos Hotel.

BY RENTAL CAR

There are several agencies in Puerto Vallarta that rent Jeeps, open-air Volkswagen Beetles, and automatic-transmission sedans (☞ Car Rentals, *below*). During the high season, rentals start at $60 per day, including insurance and mileage; off-season, they start at $45 per day. Be certain to ask about special promotions, even during the high season. All the car-rental agencies below have desks at the airport; some have offices along the highway, but they are spread out, so compare prices at the airport or call from your hotel.

BY TAXI

Many hotels post fares to common destinations; be sure to agree on a fare before the cab takes off. The ride from the north-side hotels to downtown costs about $2.50, plus 50¢ to cross the bridge.

Contacts and Resources

CAR RENTAL

Agencies to contact include **Avis** (✉ Airport, ☎ 322/1–11–12), **Budget** (✉ Carretera Aeropuerto, Km 7.5, ☎ 322/1–18–88), **Dollar** (✉ Paseo de las Palmas 1728, ☎ 322/3–13–54), **Hertz** (✉ Paseo de las Palmas 1602, ☎ 322/2–00–24), and **National** (✉ Carretera Aeropuerto, Km 1.5, ☎ 322/2–11–07).

CONSULATES

U.S. Consul (✉ Calle Zaragoza 160, ☎ 322/2–00–69), **Canadian Consul** (✉ Calle Zaragoza 160, ☎ 322/2–53–98).

EMERGENCIES

Police (✉ City Hall on Calles Morelos and Iturbide, ☎ 322/2–01–23); **Red Cross** (✉ Río de la Plata and Río Balsas, ☎ 322/2–15–33); **Hospital** (✉ Basilio Badillo 365, ☎ 322/2–35–72).

GUIDED TOURS

The three-hour **city tour** is a good way to get the lay of the land, from Gringo Gulch and the Río Cuale to Mismaloya Beach. Almost everyone goes on at least one daytime or sunset cruise around the bay, sighting pretty isolated coves and barren beaches from the deck of a sailboat or yacht. A full-day excursion to Yelapa or Las Animas, seaside communities that can be reached only by boat, gives you a feeling of what life is like in a secluded tropical paradise.

Tropical tours visit mango and banana plantations in Nayarit and include stops in Nayarit's capital, Tepic, and the small seaside town of San Blas for a boat ride on the Río Tovara, through jungle thick with tropical plants and birds, with a stop for a refreshing swim in a natural spring. Other trips head south to Boca de Tomatlán, the mouth of the river that flows from the mountains into the sea.

Charter **airline tours** fly to San Sebastián del Oeste, an interesting old mining town in the Sierra Madre, 62 km (37 mi) from Puerto Vallarta.

Tours may be arranged through your hotel or one of the many tour operators with offices at hotels and in town. City tours run about $16; tours to Yelapa run about $25; and tours to Las Animas and Quimixto cost from $30 to $35. It's worth the few extra dollars to go on a private tour (small groups) in a van rather than with a large group on a tour bus.

TRAVEL AGENCIES

American Express (✉ Morelos 660, ☎ 322/3–29–55). **Intermar Vallarta** (✉ Paseo de la Marina s/n, Condominio Via Golf, ☎ 322/1–07–34).

VISITOR INFORMATION

State Tourism Office (✉ City Hall on Av. Juárez by zócalo, ☎ 322/2-02-42). The office is open weekdays 9–7, Saturday 9–1.

MANZANILLO

Nature is undoubtedly Manzanillo's best attraction. Its twin *bahías* (bays), Manzanillo and Santiago, where crystal blue waters lap the black and gold volcanic sand, have caught outsiders' eyes since Cortés conquered Mexico. In the July–September rainy season, rivers and lagoons swell, forming waterfalls and ponds. White herons and pink flamingos flock to the fertile waters, and white butterflies flutter above the flowers in the chamomile fields (*manzanillo* is Spanish for chamomile).

Santiago Peninsula, which divides Bahía Santiago and Bahía Manzanillo, is the site of **Las Hadas** (The Fairies) resort. From the water or points above the beach, the resort seems a mirage, a sea of white domes and peaks that radiate in the midday heat. When Bolivian tin magnate Antenor Patiño conceived of this white palace in the early 1960s, Manzanillo was easier to reach by sea than land, a rugged, primitive port that attracted the hardy who didn't mind creating their own tropical paradise. In 1974, when Señor Patiño's retreat was complete, the international social set began to visit Manzanillo, thus putting the city in magazines and on television screens around the world. Even then, Manzanillo remained essentially a port city with only a few tourist attractions.

The October 1995 earthquake did considerable damage to the area. It leveled one of the hotels as well as the headquarters of the state attorney general and caused a great deal of damage to the golf courses. With typical Mexican resilience in the face of adversity, however, most everything was back in shape by the start of the winter season.

Manzanillo is still relatively undeveloped, a sleeper compared with other Pacific Coast resorts. Investors have plenty of land to divvy up for their financially rewarding havens, and existing resorts are spread out. The latest of these, **Isla Navidad,** is going up on 1,230 acres on a peninsula about 20 minutes north of the Manzanillo airport. Robert Von Hagge designed the 27-hole golf course, and other amenities include a full-service marina. The luxury 158-room Grand Bay hotel opened in January 1997. Many shops and hotel desks close for afternoon siesta, and on Sunday most businesses (including restaurants) shut down and everyone heads for the beach.

Exploring Manzanillo

A vacation in Manzanillo is not spent shopping and sightseeing. You stay put, relax on the beach, and maybe take a few hours' break from the sun and sand to survey the local scene casually.

A Good Tour

The **Santiago** area, on Santiago Bay between the Santiago and Juluapan peninsulas, is tourist-oriented, with clusters of shops and restaurants by the beach. The next area to the east, **Salahua,** is residential, with a baseball field and restaurants. Farther southeast on Manzanillo Bay, past the traffic circle and Avenida Morelos, you'll see **Las Brisas** beach, where some of the more reasonably priced hotels are located.

Downtown is busy and jam-packed, but of little tourist interest, except for the bustling seaport. At the beginning of the harbor, Route 200 jogs around downtown and intersects with Highway 110 to Colima. Avenida

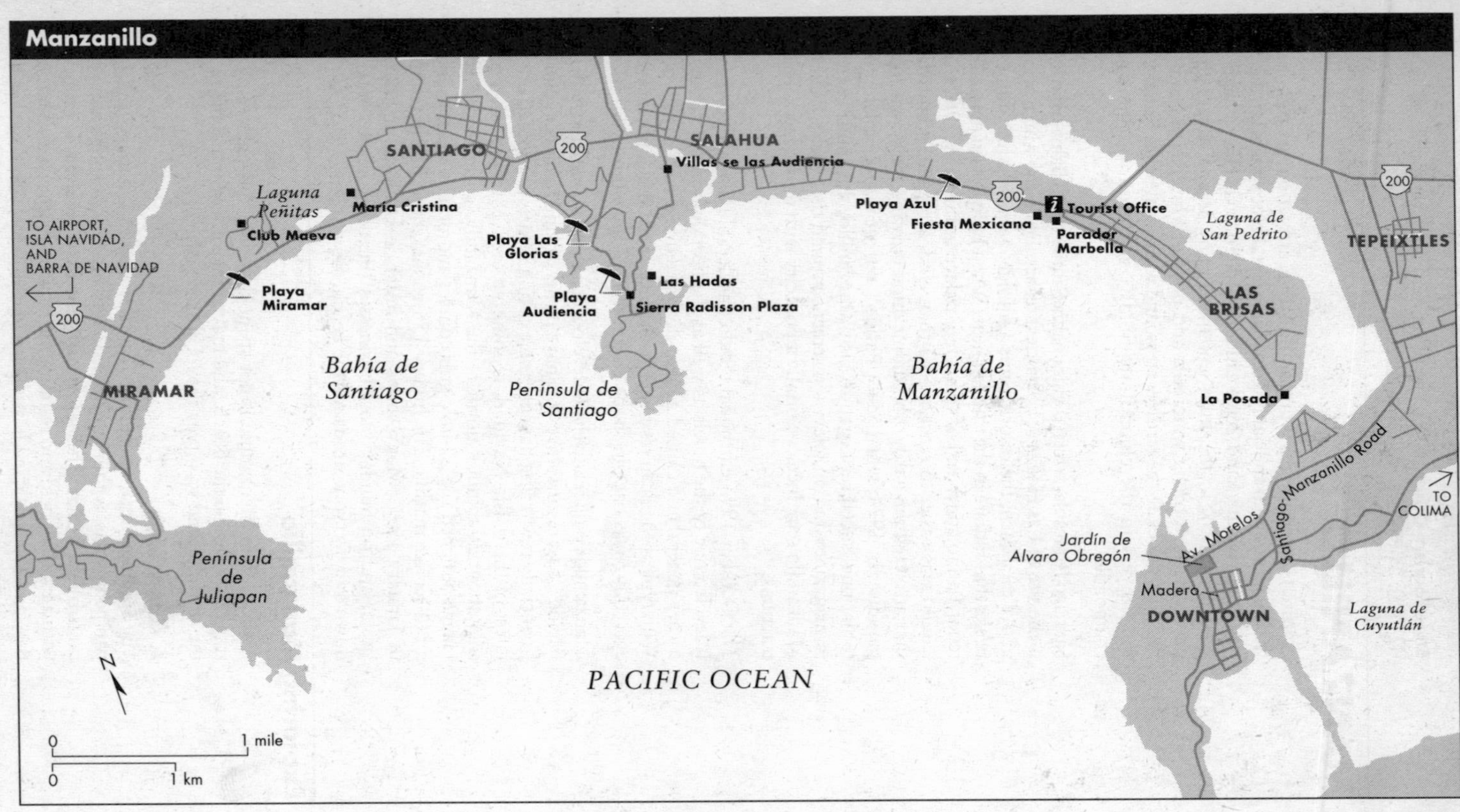
Manzanillo
SANTIAGO
200
SALAHUA
Villas se las Audiencia
Laguna Peñitas
María Cristina
Club Maeva
TO AIRPORT, ISLA NAVIDAD, AND BARRA DE NAVIDAD
Playa Miramar
Playa Las Glorias
Playa Audiencia
Las Hadas
Sierra Radisson Plaza
Playa Azul
Fiesta Mexicana
Tourist Office
Parador Marbella
Laguna de San Pedrito
TEPEIXTLES
LAS BRISAS
MIRAMAR
Bahía de Santiago
Península de Santiago
Bahía de Manzanillo
La Posada
Santiago-Manzanillo Road
TO COLIMA
Av. Morelos
Jardín de Alvaro Obregón
Madero
DOWNTOWN
Laguna de Cuyutlán
Península de Juliapan
N
PACIFIC OCEAN
0
1 mile
0
1 km

Morelos leads past the shipyards and into town. Just before you reach the port, stop at **Laguna de San Pedrito,** where graceful white herons and vivid pink flamingos assemble at sunset. The **zócalo,** or **Jardín de Obregón,** is right on the main road by the waterfront. It's a small square, quite lively in the evening.

Beaches

Manzanillo's biggest attraction is its beaches. Every day is a beach day, and Sundays are downright festive, with half the town gathered to play onshore. The volcanic sand is a mix of black, white, and brown, with the southernmost beaches the blackest. Most beaches post warning flags if the conditions are dangerous or jellyfish have been sighted.

Playa Miramar, at the north end of Santiago Bay, is populated by windsurfers and boogie-boarders. The beach in front of Club Santiago, once the favored hangout for locals, is now accessible only by walking north along the beach from the highway or by passing the guards at the club gates. The main stretch of beach is across the highway from Club Maeva. Manzanillo's best beach is probably **Playa Audiencia,** in a cove along the north side of Santiago Peninsula. The local Indians supposedly granted Cortés an audience here—thus the name. Located between two rock outcroppings, it's a good spot for snorkeling. The Sierra hotel is located in the middle of the beach, making public access limited. **Playa Azul,** also called Playa Santiago, is a long strand that runs from Santiago Peninsula along Manzanillo Bay to Playa Las Brisas. The surf gets rough along the north end; swimming is better toward Las Brisas. South of town is **Playa Cuyutlán,** a black-sand beach on the open sea. Legend has it that the great *ola verde* (green wave) rises some 30 ft each spring during the full moon. In reality, the surf is high in spring but not quite as big as the original ola verde, which took the tiny town of Cuyutlán by surprise in 1959.

Barra de Navidad and **San Patricio Melaque,** to the north, have popular beaches that are good for surfing in the fall months. Palapa restaurants along the beach serve fresh fish. In Barra there are panga trips to a small island just offshore, where unbroken seashells are abundant. When the tide is low, it is possible to walk along the beach from Barra to Melaque, a distance of about 6 km (almost 4 mi).

Dining

$$$ ★ ✕ **Legazpi.** Manzanillo's only gourmet restaurant is at Las Hadas, and it is beautiful. The service is white-glove perfection, but friendly rather than pretentious, and the food is decidedly elegant. The emphasis is on Continental cuisine with a Mexican touch, including coconut shrimp, and fish over a sauce prepared with mango and papaya. ✉ *Las Hadas,* ☎ *333/4–00–00. AE, DC, MC, V. Closed Wed., Fri., Sun. No lunch.*

$$–$$$ ✕ **El Bigotes.** Great seafood served—very leisurely—under an incredible palapa on the beach.The house specialty is the spicy *pescado sarandeado* (whole fish marinated and grilled over hot coals). The flan *napolitano* is a good choice for dessert. ✉ *Blvd. Miguel de la Madrid 3157,* ☎ *333/4–08–31;* ✉ *Puesta del Sol 3,* ☎ *333/3–12–36;* ✉ *Graciano Sánchez 8,* ☎ *333/3–24–99. DC, MC, V.*

$$–$$$ ✕ **El Vaquero.** *Vaquero* means "cowboy," so it's no surprise to find a setting reminiscent of a ranchers' saloon and a menu emphasizing beef, either marinated and seasoned as *carne asada* or grilled as good old American steaks. Some steaks are served and priced by weight to satisfy the healthiest appetite. ✉ *Crucero Las Brisas,* ☎ *333/3–16–54. MC, V.*

$$–$$$ ★ ✕ **Los Tibores.** One of Manzanillo's special-occasion spots, this place is popular with locals and visitors alike. The menu doesn't try to be inventive, offering standard international and Mexican fare. The food is well prepared and beautifully presented, and the seafood dishes are truly outstanding, especially the *parrillada de mariscos* (seafood grill), which contains an amazing variety of tasty shellfish. ⊠ *Sierra, Av. de la Audiencia 1,* ☎ *333/3–20–00. AE, DC, MC, V. No lunch.*

$$–$$$ ★ ✕ **Willy's.** Some people have been known to dine at Willy's every night of their stay in Manzanillo. The food is that good, and the owner, Jean François, is that personable and gracious. Michelle, Jean's wife, prepares delicious onion soup, a sublime bordelaise sauce, and decadent desserts. A guitarist enlivens the informal beachfront setting of wooden chairs and tables under a wooden roof. ⊠ *Crucero Las Brisas,* ☎ *333/3–17–94. MC, V. No lunch.*

$$ ✕ **Carlos 'n' Charlie's.** Can any Mexican beach destination survive without at least one member of the Anderson chain? Obviously not. And this is one of the best. The decor, as usual, is frenetic, as are the waiters, the service, and most of the clientele. The menu offers the standard selection of tasty ribs, steaks, and salads. There's a great view of the sunset, and a DJ who selects music to suit the clientele. ⊠ *Santiago–Manzanillo Rd., Km 6.5,* ☎ *333/3–11–50. AE, DC, MC, V.*

$$ ✕ **Guadalajara Grill.** This is another link in the Anderson chain. The menu is similar—ribs, fajitas, and good salads—but the atmosphere is more subdued. If you crave more action, head next door to the disco-bar. ⊠ *Av. Audiencia, in Plaza Pacífico shopping center,* ☎ *333/4–05–55. AE, MC, V.*

$ ✕ **Juanito's.** This gringo hangout is owned by an American who married a local girl and settled in Manzanillo. It specializes in great burgers, malts, and fries, American breakfasts, barbecued ribs, and fried chicken. ⊠ *Blvd. Costero M. de la Madrid, Km 14,* ☎ *333/3–13–88. Reservations not accepted. AE, MC, V.*

$ ✕ **La Posada.** Breakfast here is an integral part of any Manzanillo experience. Pancakes, French toast, fried eggs, and bacon are made to order and served in the large *sala* (living room) facing the sea. The mood is casual. Sandwiches and drinks are offered in the afternoon, but breakfast is your best bet. ⊠ *La Posada, Las Brisas,* ☎ *333/3–18–99. Reservations not accepted. MC, V.*

$ ✕ **Rosalba's.** Tasty *huevos rancheros* (fried eggs), American-style breakfasts, seafood, steaks, and tacos served under a palapa have made this place popular with residents and tourists alike. ⊠ *Blvd. Miguel de la Madrid, Km 13, next to gas station in Santiago,* ☎ *333/3–04–88. No credit cards. No dinner.*

Lodging

Lodging in Manzanillo was at one time a bargain, and although the $10 room is a thing of the past, there are still several decent places where you can lay your head for less than $40. Travelers on a tighter budget usually head to the towns of Barra de Navidad and Melaque. As with the rest of the Pacific Coast, Manzanillo is undergoing a building boom, mainly condominiums, to accommodate the growing number of people from Guadalajara buying vacation homes here. The resorts are spread out along the Santiago–Manzanillo Road.

$$$$ 🏨 **Grand Bay.** The most expensive hotel in the area (rooms start at $450 and the Presidential suite goes for $2,800 dollars a night) was inaugurated in January 1997. Located on a 1,320-acre residential-golf-tourist development on a peninsula between the Pacific and the Navidad lagoon, about 20 minutes from the Manzanillo airport, the hotel cascades down a hill to a delightful stretch of private beach. The rooms in this

traditionally Mexican-style hotel, with Spanish arches, balconies, fountains, shady patios, and lush gardens, offer mountain or sea views, deluxe amenities, and marble baths. The Governor's and Presidential suites, which are perched at the top of the hill, share a private pool. Golfers will enjoy the 27-hole Robert Von Hagge–designed golf course. ✉ *Isla Navidad, Puerto de la Navidad 28200,* ☎ *335/5–63–90 or 305/445–2493,* FAX *305/445–4255. 158 rooms, 33 suites. 3 restaurants, 3 bars, 2 pools, 27-hole golf course, 3 tennis courts, beach. AE, DC, MC, V.*

$$$$ ★ **Las Hadas.** A member of the Leading Hotels of the World, Las Hadas was for many years Manzanillo's premier resort, the kind of place where vacationers were content to check in and stay put. The setting and grounds are still beautiful, and underwent a face-lift in 1996. A major refurbishing of the rooms and furnishings was under way at press time. Although the service is not quite up to original standards, there has been a marked improvement lately, making a stay at Las Hadas a very special experience. ✉ *Santiago Peninsula off Santiago–Manzanillo Rd., 28200,* ☎ *333/4–00–00 or 800/722–6466,* FAX *333/4–13–70. 220 rooms, including 41 suites. 4 restaurants, 5 bars, 2 pools, beauty salon, massage, golf course, 8 tennis courts, beach. AE, DC, MC, V.*

$$$ **Club Maeva.** Families love the playgrounds and children's pools, small theater, tennis courts, and disco at this all-inclusive resort. The blue-and-white bungalows are spread along the road to the water. ✉ *Santiago–Manzanillo Rd. at Playa Miramar, 28200,* ☎ *333/5–05–93 or 800/466–2382,* FAX *333/5–03–95. 514 rooms. 4 restaurants, 4 pools, 12 tennis courts, beach, water slide, 2 dance clubs. AE, DC, MC, V.*

$$$ **Sierra.** This 19-story white stucco giant is popular with families (two children under 18 years of age stay free in their parents' room) and conventioneers. Most of the 350 inviting rooms and suites have private balconies and a view of the bay. A large free-form pool, four tennis courts, and several bars and restaurants round out the property. Light wood and pastel colors dominate the pleasant decor. Three buffet meals, domestic drinks, and tennis are included in the price. ✉ *Av. de la Audiencia 1, 28200,* ☎ *333/3–20–00 or 800/882–6684. 350 rooms and suites. 3 restaurants, 4 bars, pool, 4 tennis courts, beach. AE, DC, MC, V.*

$$ ★ **Fiesta Mexicana.** This bright white five-story hotel stands out on the highway. It has a lovely central courtyard with a large swimming pool. The rooms have pretty wood-frame windows and comfortable bentwood lounges; those on the ocean side are the most quiet. ✉ *Santiago–Manzanillo Rd., Playa Azul, 28260,* ☎ *333/3–21–80,* FAX *333/3–21–80. 187 rooms. 2 restaurants, bar, piano bar, dance club, travel services. AE, MC, V.*

$$ ★ **La Posada.** This "passionate pink" hotel has been a favorite for North Americans since 1957. With only 24 rooms, most guests get to know each other well, mingling in the sala, a large living-dining room with a communal coffeepot. Rooms are comfortable and simple; old iron keys work the antique locks. The room rate includes a complete breakfast. ✉ *Las Brisas, 28200,* ☎ *333/3–18–99,* FAX *333/3–18–99. 24 rooms. Bar, snack bar, pool, beach. MC, V.*

$ **María Cristina.** This super-clean two-story motel is located in the Santiago area, just a couple of blocks from the beach. All the rooms have TVs, but only two of them—they call them "suites"—are air-conditioned; they're well worth the small difference in price. ✉ *Calle 28 de Agosto 36, 28860,* ☎ *333/3–09–66,* FAX *333/4–14–30. 21 rooms. Pool. V.*

$ **Parador Marbella.** This hotel is one of the few reasonably priced places on the beach. The best rooms are on the ocean; each has a tiny balcony under the palms. The accommodations are color-coordinated and offer air-conditioning and TV. ✉ *Santiago–Manzanillo Rd., Km 9.5, 28869,* ☎ *333/3–11–03,* FAX *333/3–12–22. 94 rooms. Restaurant, bar, pool. MC, V.*

$ **Villas la Audiencia.** Well located—it's a block from the Las Hadas turnoff and about four blocks from the beach—this small white-and-red hotel and villa complex overlooks the Mantarraya golf course. Everything is spotless, and the air-conditioned rooms and villas (the villas have kitchenettes) are pleasantly decorated and quite comfortable. ✉ *Av. de la Audiencia and Las Palmas, off Santiago–Manzanillo Rd., 28200,* ☎ *333/3–08–61,* FAX *333/3–26–53. 20 rooms, 26 villas. Restaurant, pool. AE, MC, V.*

Nightlife and the Arts

For a rowdy drinking and dancing scene, head for **Carlos 'n' Charlie's** (☎ 333/3–11–50). **VOG** (✉ Km 9.2 on Santiago–Manzanillo Rd., ☎ 333/3–18–75), the disco-bar at **Guadalajara Grill** (☎ 333/4–05–55), and **Boom Boom** at Club Maeva (☎ 333/5–05–93) are popular places to boogie. The **Legazpi** (☎ 333/4–00–00) piano bar at Las Hadas is a relaxing, romantic spot for a nightcap. **Las Hadas** hosts a lively Mexican fiesta around the pool Friday, during the high season, and **El Herradero** (☎ 333/3–11–00), at the Fiesta Mexicana hotel, features Mexican fiestas year-round.

Outdoor Activities and Sports

Fishing

Sportfishing charters ($100–$500) are available at the major hotels and tour agencies.

Golf

La Mantarraya (☎ 333/4–00–00), the 18-hole golf course at Las Hadas, designed by Roy Dye, has been rated among the world's 100 best courses by *Golf Digest.* **Club Santiago** (☎ 333/5–04–10) has a nine-hole course designed by Larry Hughes. Robert Von Hagge created the 27-hole course at **Isla Navidad** (☎ 333/5–63–90).

Water Sports

Windsurfing has become quite popular on Manzanillo's beaches, and Jet Skis roar about, but there isn't much in the way of parasailing. The rocky points off Manzanillo's peninsulas and coves make good spots for snorkeling and scuba diving. Pangas can be rented on some beaches so you can reach the better spots.

Shopping

Most of the hotels offer a small selection of folk art and beachwear, but, in general, shops selling items that might interest tourists don't fare well in Manzanillo, probably because most visitors are more interested in activities involving the sun and sea. There are some fairly uninteresting shops around Manzanillo's main square, hardly worth the trip downtown, and there are some shops at Plaza Manzanillo, a shopping center at Km 7.5 of the Santiago–Manzanillo Road. Most of the shops are closed from 2 to 4; many are open Sunday from 10 to 2. **Centro Artesenal Las Primaveras** (✉ Juárez 40 in Santiago, ☎ 333/3–16–99) is about the best bet for handcrafted folk art.

Side Trip

Colima

311 km (192 mi) northeast of Manzanillo.

Colima, the state capital, is less than two hours from Manzanillo via an excellent toll road that continues on to Guadalajara. An easygoing provincial city, with well-maintained colonial buildings, Colima is most famous for the pre-Hispanic "Colima Dog" figurines, which originated in this state and which are on display, along with other archaeological pieces, at the **Museo de las Culturas del Occidente** (Museum of Western Cultures) (✉ Casa de la Cultura, Calzada Galván, and Av. Ejército Nacional, ☎ 331/2–31–55). The **Museo de Artes Populares Maria Teresa Pomar** (María Teresa Pomar Handicrafts Museum; ✉ Calle Gabino Barreda and Manuel Gallardo, ☎ 331/2–68–69) displays a large collection of pre-Hispanic and contemporary Indian costumes, masks, instruments, and other artifacts. The town of **Comala,** a 15-minute ride north of Colima, is noted for hand-painted colonial furniture and ironwork. The imposing twin peaks of Colima's volcanoes rise up from the **Volcán de Colima National Park,** about 30 km (18 mi) north of Comala.

Manzanillo A to Z

Arriving and Departing

BY BUS

Tres Estrellas de Oro and **Estrella Blanca** (☎ 333/2–01–35 for both) have first-class service (lavatory, TV, and air-conditioning) to Guadalajara, Tijuana, Acapulco, and Mexico City. Service is also available to the coastal towns. Many of the area's resorts are located 1–2 km (½–1 mi) from the bus stop on the highway.

BY CAR

The trip south from the Arizona border to Manzanillo is about 2,419 km (1,500 mi); from Guadalajara, it is 332 km (200 mi); from Puerto Vallarta, 242 km (150 mi). Highway 200 runs along the coast from Tepic, Nayarit, to Manzanillo. The road is quite narrow but well maintained. However, drivers should constantly be on the alert for an unexpected cow, burro, dog—or drunk—on the road. Detours are frequent, especially during the raining season.

BY PLANE

Airport and Airlines. Manzanillo's **Aeropuerto Internacional Playa de Oro** (☎ 333/2–25–25) is 32 km (20 mi) north of town, on the way to Barra de Navidad. Both **Aeromexico** (☎ 333/2–08–25) and **Mexicana** (☎ 333/3–23–23) have connecting service to most major cities via Guadalajara and Mexico and Mexico City. **America West** (☎ 800/235–9292, no local phone) flies in from Phoenix, with a stop in Puerto Vallarta, and **Aero California** (☎ 333/4–14–14) flies in from Los Angeles.

From the Airport. Volkswagen vans transport passengers from the airport to the major resorts; these shuttle services are less expensive than taxis.

BY TRAIN

Second-class trains run to Manzanillo from Guadalajara—an adventure for some, but for most a tedious trip, lasting a minimum of eight hours and ending at the ship and freight yards outside town.

Getting Around

A car is almost essential for exploring the area on your own. The highway from Santiago to Manzanillo is commonly called Carretera Santiago–Manzanillo, Manzanillo–Aeropuerto, Salahua–Santiago, or any number of things depending on the closest landmark. It's called the Santiago–Manzanillo Road throughout this chapter to lessen confusion. Route 200 runs north along the coast past Manzanillo and Santiago bays to Barra de Navidad and Melaque; Highway 110 goes east to Colima.

Avenida Morelos, the main drag in town, runs from Manzanillo Bay past the port and shipyards to the plaza. If you plan to explore the downtown, park along the waterfront across from the plaza and walk—all the shops and hotels are within a few blocks. Rates vary depending on where you rent your car, but rentals are fairly costly ($50 per day for a standard shift without air-conditioning, to $70 for a model with automatic transmission and air-conditioning). Most offer 200 km (120 mi) free, which should give you enough roaming for one day.

Street addresses are not often used in Manzanillo; instead, locations are designated by neighborhood—the Las Brisas area, Santiago Peninsula (also known as the Las Hadas Road), and so on. Maps with actual street names are rare (or inaccurate).

Contacts and Resources

CAR RENTAL

Avis (☎ 333/3–01–90), **Budget** (☎ 333/3–14–45), and **National** (☎ 333/3–06–11) have offices in the airport, and most big hotels have at least one company represented.

EMERGENCIES

Police (☎ 333/2–10–04), **Hospital** (☎ 333/2–00–29).

GUIDED TOURS

Manzanillo is so spread out that if you want to get the lay of the land, it's best to go on a guided tour. More appealing, though, than the city tours are the sportfishing trips, sunset cruises, horseback outings, and excursions to Colima, Comala, and the volcanoes that can be arranged through a travel agency.

TRAVEL AGENCIES

Most hotels offer at least one agency's services. Agencies include **Bahías Gemelas Agencia de Viajes** (✉ Santiago–Manzanillo Rd., Km 10, ☎ 333/3–10–00), **Aeroviajes Manzanillo** (✉ Av. México 69, ☎ 333/2–25–65), and **Viajes Héctur** (✉ Av. Costero Miguel de la Madrid 3147, ☎ 333/3–17–07).

VISITOR INFORMATION

State Tourism Office (✉ Blvd. Costero Miguel de la Madrid, Km 9.5, ☎ 333/3–22–77). The office is open weekdays 9–3 and 6–8.

IXTAPA/ZIHUATANEJO

One of the most appealing of the Pacific Coast destinations, Ixtapa/Zihuatanejo offers visitors a taste of Mexico present and past. Ixtapa (pronounced eeks-*tah*-pa), where most Americans stay—probably because they can't pronounce Zihuatanejo (see-wha-tah-*nay*-ho)—is young and glitzy. Exclusively a vacation resort, it was created in the early 1970s by Fonatur, Mexico's National Fund for Tourism Development, which also brought us Cancún. World-class hotels cluster in the hotel zone around Palmar Bay, where conditions are ideal for swimming and water sports; across the road are clusters of shopping plazas. The hotels are well spaced; there's always plenty of room on the beach, which is lighted for strolling at night; and the pace is leisurely.

Zihuatanejo, only 7 km (4 mi) down the coast (southeast) from Ixtapa, is an old fishing village on a picturesque sheltered bay. Until the advent of Ixtapa, it was hardly known even among Mexicans. But long before Columbus sailed to America, Zihuatanejo was a sanctuary for indigenous nobility. Figurines, ceramics, stone carvings, and stelae still being found in the area verify the presence of civilizations dating as far back as the Olmecs (3000 BC). The original name, Cihuatlán, means "place of women" in the Náhuatl language. Weaving was likely the dominant industry in this matriarchal society, as evidenced by pre-Hispanic figurines, bobbins, and other related artifacts found in the area.

In 1527, Spanish conquistadors launched a trade route from Zihuatanejo Bay to the Orient. Galleons returned with silks, spices, and, according to some historians, the first coconut palms to arrive in the Americas, brought from the Philippines. But the Spaniards did little colonizing here. A scout sent by Hernán Cortés reported back to the conquistador that the place was nothing great, tagging the name Cihuatlán with the demeaning Spanish suffix "nejo"—hence "Zihuatanejo."

With the advent of Ixtapa, Zihuatanejo began to grow and the little dirt streets were paved with decorative brick. The place has managed to retain its charm, but it's also the area's municipal center, and its malecón and narrow streets are lined with hotels, restaurants, and boutiques.

Exploring Ixtapa/Zihuatanejo

Ixtapa and Zihuatanejo have few sights per se, but they're both pleasant places to stroll—the former especially if you enjoy a modern beach ambience and shops, the latter if you like local color.

A Good Tour

The entire **hotel zone** in **Ixtapa** extends along a 3-km (2-mi) strip of wide sandy beach called Playa del Palmar, on the open Pacific. It's fun to walk along the beach to check out the various hotel scenes and water-sports activities. Alternatively, you can stroll the length of the zone on Boulevard Ixtapa, a nicely landscaped and immaculate thoroughfare; a series of Mexican village–style shopping malls line the boulevard across the street from the hotels. At one end of the hotel zone (when you enter from Zihuatanejo) is the 18-hole Ixtapa Golf Club, while on the other (generally described as being "up the coast," but actually lying to the northwest) you'll come to the Marina Ixtapa development, which includes a 600-slip yacht marina, a promenade with restaurants and shops, and the 18-hole Marina Golf Course. If you want to venture out of this compact resort area, take a taxi 15 minutes up the coast to **Playa Linda**; it's a 10-minute boat ride from here to **Ixtapa Island** (☞ Beaches, *below,* for both), where you can spend the day eating, sunning, and swimming.

Zihuatanejo flanks a charming enclosed bay with calm beaches. A simple way to tour the town is to take a taxi to the **municipal pier** (*muelle*), from which skiffs continually depart for the 10-minute ride to **Playa Las Gatas** (☞ Beaches, *below*), accessible only by water. The sportfishing boats depart from this pier, too, and it's the beginning of the **Paseo del Pescador** (Fisherman's Walk) or malecón, which runs along the municipal beach, the most picturesque part of town. The brick-paved seaside path, only ½ km (¼ mi) long, is lined with small restaurants and overflowing shops; you'll pass a basketball court that doubles as the town square. The malecón ends at the **Museo Arquélogico** (✉ East end of Paseo del Pescador, ☎ 753/3–25–52), where close to a thousand pre-Hispanic pieces as well as murals and maps are on permanent display; it's open Tuesday–Sunday 10–6. If you continue beyond the museum, you can take a footpath cut into the rocks to **Playa la Madera** (☞ Beaches, *below*).

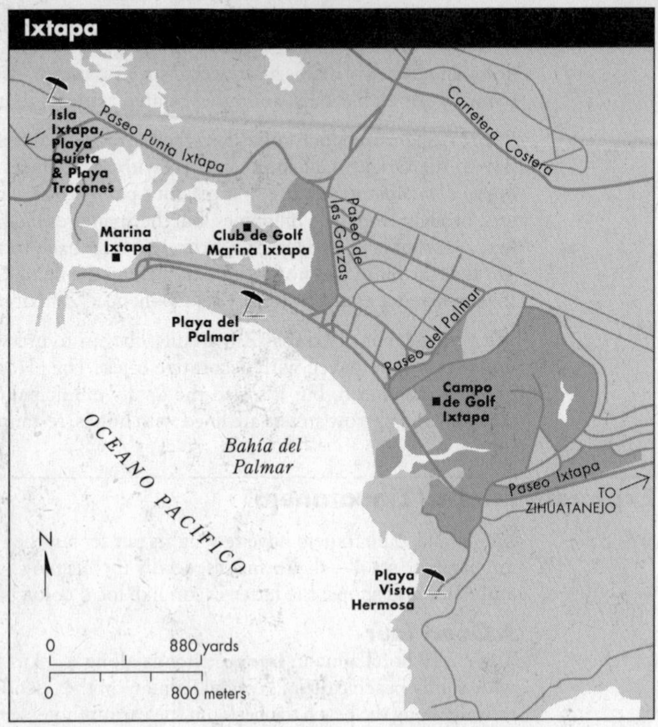

Beaches

Ixtapa

IXTAPA ISLAND

The most popular beach on Ixtapa Island is **Playa Cuachalalate,** named for a local tree whose bark has been used as a remedy for kidney ailments since ancient times. This beach is lined with good seafood eateries. A short walk across to the other side of the island takes you to the gorgeous sandy **Varadero beach,** a wonderful spot for sunset viewing. It is also lined with small restaurants, and there are water-sports facilities. Just behind the restaurants is **Playa Coral,** with crystal-clear water that's ideal for snorkeling. **Playa Carey,** toward the south end of the island, is small and isolated. Pangas run between the boat landings at both Cuachalalate and Varadero beaches and Playa Linda on the mainland.

PLAYA DEL PALMAR

Ixtapa's main beach, this 3-km-long (2-mi-long) broad sandy stretch runs along the hotel zone. Water-sports facilities are available all along the shore. Since this is essentially open sea, the surf can be quite strong.

PLAYA LINDA

About 10 minutes beyond the Ixtapa hotel zone, the long, pristine Playa Linda has a handicraft mart at its edge, as well as a rock jetty from which covered pangas take passengers on a 10-minute ride to Ixtapa Island (☞ *above*). The boats run continuously from early morning until 5 PM. A round-trip costs about $2 (hold on to your ticket stub for the return).

Zihuatanejo

PLAYA LA MADERA

Across Zihuatanejo Bay from Playa Municipal, Playa la Madera may be reached via a seaside footpath cut into the rocks. Also accessible by

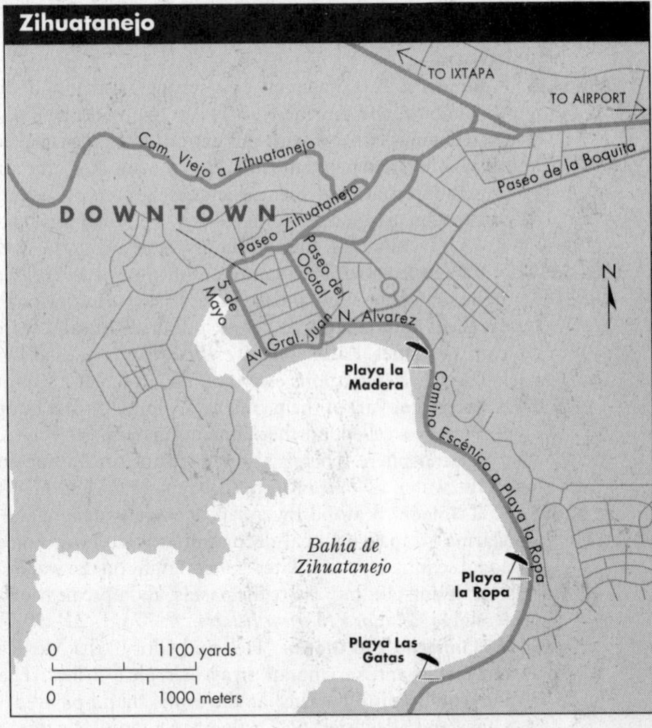

car, this pancake-flat beach has a sprinkling of small hotels and restaurants. It was named madera, or "wood," beach because it was a Spanish port for shipping oak, pine, cedar, and mahogany cut from the nearby Sierra Madre Sur.

PLAYA LA ROPA

On the other side of a rocky point, Playa la Ropa is the most beautiful beach in the area; it's a five-minute taxi ride from town. Along this 1-km (½-mi) stretch of soft sand are water-sports facilities, open-air restaurants, and a few hotels. It got its name ("clothes beach") when a Spanish galleon returning from the Orient ran aground here, strewing its cargo of silks and clothing.

PLAYA LAS GATAS

Named for the *gatas* (docile nurse sharks) that used to linger here, this beach has a mysterious long row of hewn rocks just offshore that serves as a breakwater. Legend has it that a Tarascan king built it to shelter his royal daughter's private beach. It is now lined with simple seafood eateries that also have lounge chairs for sunning. Las Gatas is accessible only by boat, and pangas run continuously to and from the municipal pier until 5 PM. Purchase your round-trip ticket (about $2) at the Cooperativa office at the beginning of the pier. Keep the ticket stub for your return trip.

PLAYA MUNICIPAL

At the edge of town, the town's picturesque main beach is rimmed by the Paseo del Pescador (fisherman's walk). Here local fishermen keep their skiffs and gear, used for nightly fishing journeys out to sea. They return here in the morning to sell their catch to the local townspeople and to restaurateurs.

Dining

Ixtapa

$$$–$$$$ ✕ **Bogart's.** Play it again: The setting is strikingly Moroccan, à la *Casablanca,* and anyone who's been to any of the links in the Krystal hotel chain is familiar with this exotic (and expensive) eatery. A Moorish fountain and piano music add to the movie-theme atmosphere. The largely international menu includes Suprema Casablanca, breaded chicken breasts stuffed with lobster. ✉ *Hotel Krystal, Blvd. Ixtapa,* ☎ *755/3-03-03. Reservations essential. AE, DC, MC, V.*

$$$–$$$$ ✕ **Villa de la Selva.** The multilevel cliff-top terraces offer romantic views of the sunset, the stars, and the night-lit surf breaking on the rocks below. Excellent international dishes include grilled steaks, seafood, and Mexican specialties. ✉ *Beyond Westin Brisas on Paseo la Roca,* ☎ *755/3-03-62. Reservations essential. AE, DC, MC, V. No lunch.*

$$$ ✕ **Beccofino.** Part of the promenade along Marina Ixtapa, this restaurant offers excellent northern Italian cuisine in a serene Mediterranean-style atmosphere. There's alfresco seating on a canopied deck that sits on the water. ✉ *Plaza Marina Ixtapa,* ☎ *755/3-17-70. AE, MC, V.*

$$$ ✕ **El Galeón.** Seafood lovers and people-watchers like to settle in at Marina Ixtapa's nautical-decor bar and outdoor terrace; there's additional seating on a simulated galleon right on the water. The fresh tuna steak is outstanding, as are the pastas, and upscale Mexican fare is also available. ✉ *Plaza Marina Ixtapa,* ☎ *755/3-21-50. AE, MC, V.*

$$ ✕ **El Infierno y la Gloria.** "Hell and Glory" is a Mexican cantina-bar and restaurant, serving an array of typical dishes. The food is good and you'll enjoy looking at the walls, hand-painted with Mexican scenes and allegories. ✉ *La Puerta Shopping Center,* ☎ *755/3-02-72. AE, MC, V.*

$$ ✕ **El Marlin.** This a great place to settle in for some lunch, swimming, and sun. Simple, wholesome, and delicious seafood dishes include (naturally) marlin: Try it steamed with vegetables in aluminum foil. El Marlin closes at 5 PM, when the last boats leave for the mainland. ✉ *Varadero Beach, Ixtapa Island, no phone. No credit cards.*

$$ ★ ✕ **La Valentina.** This recent addition to Ixtapa's dining scene is part of a relatively new—and highly successful—group of restaurants that have opened in Mexico City. The team of PR whizzes who are behind these ventures have access to some of the finest Mexican gourmet recipes, many from celebrities such as artist Martha Chapa. Truly memorable is the *pollo en mole de tamarindo* (chicken in a spicy sauce flavored with tamarind and chocolate). The decor is as Mexican as the menu. Also on the premises is a video bar and disco. ✉ *Blvd. Ixtapa, next to Doubletree hotel,* ☎ *755/3-11-90. AE, MC, V.*

$$ ✕ **Señor Frog's.** You can tell this is part of the Anderson chain of zany restaurants by the entrance signs that read, SORRY, WE'RE OPEN and MEMBERS AND NONMEMBERS ONLY. As usual the atmosphere is raucous and the food—tapas, burgers, and Mexican dishes—plentiful and good. ✉ *Opposite the Hotel Presidente,* ☎ *755/3-06-92. Reservations not accepted. AE, MC, V. No lunch.*

$ ✕ **Nueva Zelanda.** From breakfast through dinner everybody drops in to this sparkling little coffee shop–style eatery, which serves tortas and an array of fresh tropical fruit juices and fruit salads. ✉ *Los Patios Shopping Center, behind bandstand, Ixtapa,* ☎ *755/3-08-38;* ✉ *Calle Cuauhtémoc 23, Zihuatanejo,* ☎ *755/4-23-40. Reservations not accepted. No credit cards.*

$ ✕ **Pizzeria Mamma Norma.** You can dine indoors or alfresco at this casual Italian eatery, which offers the best pizzas in town as well as wholesome salads. ✉ *La Puerta Shopping Center,* ☎ *755/3-02-74. Reservations not accepted. MC, V. No lunch.*

Zihuatanejo

$$ ✕ **Casa Elvira.** Opened in 1956, this Zihuatanejo institution has a pleasant dining room and serves a wide variety of seafood and Mexican dishes. It gets crowded during high season. ✉ *Paseo del Pescador 16,* ☎ *755/4–20–61. MC, V.*

$$ ✕ **El Patio.** Seafood and authentic Mexican dishes are served in a delightful hacienda-style garden. There's live music during high season. ✉ *5 de Mayo 3,* ☎ *755/4–30–19. AE, MC, V.*

$$ ✕ **Kau-Kan.** Opened at the end of 1995, this restaurant immediately became a local favorite. Owner-chef Ricardo Rodriguez, previously the chef at the nearby Casa que Canta and, before then, at Mexico City's Champs-Elysées restaurant, serves imaginative, exquisitely prepared seafood, from fillet of sea bass to delicate manta ray in butter sauce. Although the restaurant is right on Madera beach, the service and setting are elegant. ✉ *Playa Madera,* ☎ *755/4–84–46. AE, MC, V.*

$$ ✕ **Paul's.** Swiss chef-owner Paul Karrer prepares every entrée, including escargots, sashimi, fresh quail, and shrimp in dill sauce, with loving attention to detail. The setting is far more casual than the menu. ✉ *5 de Mayo across from handicraft market,* ☎ *755/4–80–63. Reservations not accepted. MC, V.*

$–$$ ✕ **La Sirena Gorda.** Oil paintings and a bronze statue depict the namesake "fat mermaid," and a small boutique sells logo T-shirts and memorabilia. Specialties at this friendly restaurant near the pier include seafood tacos and octopus kebab. The setting is casual, with an outdoor patio. ✉ *Paseo del Pescador 20,* ☎ *755/4–26–87. Reservations not accepted. MC, V. Closed Wed.*

$–$$ ✕ **Rossy.** A local favorite for dining on the roof terrace or right on the beach, Rossy's offers an array of seafood dishes, including a tempting shrimp-and-pineapple brochette. Musicians usually serenade diners on the weekends. ✉ *South end of Playa la Ropa,* ☎ *755/4–40–04. Reservations not accepted. MC, V.*

$ ✕ **Casa Puntarenas.** Talk about homey restaurants: Casa Puntarenas is not only family-owned and -operated, but it's run out of the family residence. You'll select from a menu of seafood specialties and write your order on a piece of paper, which later becomes your check. To get here, cross the footbridge over the lagoon at the west end of the town near the pier (or take a taxi). ✉ *Noria 12,* ☎ *755/4–21–09. Reservations not accepted. No credit cards. Closed in low season.*

$ ✕ **La Mordida.** Join the throngs at this simple, very popular eatery for pizza and tasty charcoal-broiled burgers. ✉ *Paseo de la Boquita 20,* ☎ *755/4–82–16. No credit cards. No lunch.*

$ ✕ **La Perla.** Eat indoors if you want video sports-bar action, or outdoors on La Ropa beach. Among the seafood specialties, *filete "La Perla"* (baked with cheese in aluminum foil) is a favorite. ✉ *Playa la Ropa,* ☎ *755/4–27–00. AE, MC, V.*

Dining and Lodging

Zihuatanejo

$$$$ ★ ✕🏨 **La Casa Que Canta.** Resembling a thatched-roof pueblo village, "The House That Sings" is perched on a cliff-side high above Zihuatanejo Bay. The multilevel palapa-topped lobby is adorned with folk-art furnishings, including hand-painted chairs with Frida Kahlo motifs. The individually designed rooms, named for Mexican songs, also feature beautiful handcrafted pieces and offer modern amenities such as air-conditioning and hair dryers. Because of the stepped architecture, the main swimming pool seems to be airborne. Below, overlooking the sea, a saltwater pool features a therapeutic whirlpool. Seven extra-spacious suites—five of them in a wing completed in early 1996—have

their own pools. The multilevel restaurant offers fine Continental and Mexican fare as well as stupendous views (reservations required). Children under 16 are not accepted at either the restaurant or the hotel. ✉ *Camino Escénico a Playa la Ropa, 40880,* ☎ *755/4–27–22 or 800/525–4800,* FAX *755/4–20–06. 23 suites. Restaurant, 2 pools, exercise room. AE, DC, MC, V.*

$$$$ ★ ✕ **Villa del Sol.** This is the ultimate in luxurious beach living. One- and two-story suites in a series of casitas nestle amid coconut palms, lush tropical gardens, fountains, and meandering paths leading to Playa la Ropa, one of the loveliest beaches on the Pacific Coast. Guest rooms and baths are artistically designed, with canopied king-size beds, colorful folk-art furnishings, and terraces or balconies with hammocks; all offer satellite TVs, minibars, and hair dryers, and some boast private outdoor hot tubs. You can sit under a palapa on the beach and order snacks, lunch, or drinks from a casual menu. In the evening, the European and Mexican chefs prepare fine international and local dishes, using the freshest of ingredients. Even if you're not staying here, don't miss the elaborate "Mexican Fiesta" buffet on Friday nights. Children under 14 are not accepted during high season. ✉ *Playa la Ropa, Box 84, 40880,* ☎ *755/4–22–39; 888/389–2645 direct toll-free;* FAX *755/4–40–66. 36 1- and 2-bedroom suites. Restaurant, 2 pools, 2 tennis courts, beach. AE, MC, V.*

Lodging

There is a wide range of hotel accommodations in Ixtapa and in Zihuatanejo. Pricier Ixtapa has almost exclusively deluxe, beachfront properties, and almost all are located along the Zona Hoteleria, a 3-km (2-mi) stretch of Palmar Beach; they do not always match the other members of international chains whose names they bear in quality, however. Most of the budget accommodations are in Zihuatanejo, where the best hotels are on or overlooking La Madera or La Ropa beach, and the least expensive are downtown.

Elizabeth Williams (✉ Box 168, Zihuatanejo, Guerrero, ☎ 755/4–26–06, FAX 755/4–47–62) specializes in apartment, home, and villa rentals and sales.

Ixtapa

$$$–$$$$ ★ **Westin Brisas Ixtapa.** This immense, pyramid-shape architectural wonder slopes down a hillside to its own secluded cove and beach, Playa Vista Hermosa. The grounds are luxuriant with jungle vegetation; fresh flowers on the bed welcome you to your room. Every vibrantly colorful unit has a private balcony with a hammock, ocean view, and a table for room-service dining; spacious junior suites offer larger balconies with hot tubs. Guests and nonguests enjoy the hotel's excellent **Portofino** and **El Mexicano** restaurants. ✉ *Playa Vista Hermosa, Box 97, 40880,* ☎ *755/3–21–21 or 800/228–3000,* FAX *755/3–07–51. 428 rooms and suites. 4 restaurants, 2 bars, 3 pools, wading pool, 4 tennis courts. AE, DC, MC, V.*

$$$ **Dorado Pacífico.** This privately owned beachfront hotel is known for its fine food and good service. The huge pool, with two water slides, makes it a favorite with youngsters. The furnishings are fairly nondescript, but the ocean-view rooms have private balconies. Glass elevators look out on the dramatic atrium lobby and fountains. Try the beachside **Cebolla Roja** restaurant for dinner. ✉ *Blvd. Ixtapa, 40880,* ☎ *755/3–20–25 or 800/448–8355,* FAX *755/3–01–26. 285 rooms and suites. 3 restaurants, bar, pool, 2 tennis courts. AE, DC, MC, V.*

$$$ **Krystal Ixtapa.** This beachfront hotel, shaped like a boat with its bow pointing to the sea, is part of a Mexican chain. Rooms are stan-

dard contemporary style. The Club Krystalito provides recreational activities for children, and because of its meeting facilities, the hotel is often filled with conventioneers. The Krystal is home to **Christine,** Ixtapa's most popular disco, and **Bogart's** (☞ Dining, *above*). ✉ *Blvd. Ixtapa, 40880,* ☎ *755/3-03-33 or 800/231-9860,* FAX *755/3-02-16. 254 rooms and suites. 2 restaurants, coffee shop, pool, 2 tennis courts, dance club. AE, DC, MC, V.*

$$$ **Presidente Forum Resort.** This all-inclusive property is a member of the Inter-Continental Hotel chain. Rooms are attractively decorated in cool creams and whites. The room rates include all meals, 24-hour beverage service, and 17 hours of recreational activities, including snorkel and scuba-diving clinics. If you want tranquillity, request a room near the east pool, away from where the action is. ✉ *Blvd. Ixtapa, 40880,* ☎ *755/3-00-18 or 800/327-0200,* FAX *755/3-23-12. 400 rooms and suites. 3 restaurants, bar, 2 pools, wading pool, sauna, steam room, 2 tennis courts, exercise room. AE, DC, MC, V.*

$$$ **Villa del Lago.** This B&B in a modern colonial-style house is the only listed Ixtapa property that is not on the beach. It is, however, a golfer's dream, facing the sixth hole tee-off of the **Campo de Golf Ixtapa** (by Robert Trent Jones Jr.). The two-level master suite, terrace, and swimming pool offer views of the lush green course and the mountains beyond. Golf packages are available. ✉ *Retorno Alondras 244, 40880,* ☎ *755/3-14-82;* FAX *755/3-14-22 or 619/575-1766 in the U.S. 6 suites. Library. AE, DC, MC, V.*

$$ **Posada Real.** Smaller and more intimate than most of the other Ixtapa hotels, this member of the Best Western chain sits on Palmar Beach, has lots of charm, and offers good value. ✉ *Blvd. Ixtapa, 40880,* ☎ *755/3-16-85 or 800/528-1234,* FAX *755/3-18-05. 110 rooms. 2 restaurants, bar, 2 pools, wading pool. AE, DC, MC, V.*

Trocones

$$ ✕ **El Burro Borracho.** For out-of-the-way seclusion, you can venture some 30 minutes northwest up the coast to 5-km-long (3-mi-long) Troncones beach, near the tiny village of the same name. Six comfortable stone cottages and a congenial restaurant-bar sit right on the beach. The menu ranges from cheeseburgers to fresh lobster. Lie in a hammock or go beachcombing, boogie-boarding, hiking, or cave exploring. Owners Dewey and Carolyn are also known for their **Casa de la Tortuga** B&B, just up the beach. ✉ *Troncones Beach, Apdo. 277, Zihuatanejo, Guerrero 40880,* ☎ FAX *755/4-32-96. 6 bungalows. Restaurant. No credit cards.*

Zihuatanejo

$$$ **Puerto Mío.** Just inside the mouth of Zihuatanejo Bay, this small hotel, now under management of the Villa del Sol group, has a seaside level with a pool, terrace bar, dining room, guest rooms, and a marina where the Zihuatanejo Scuba Center is based. A hilltop "mansion" level features another pool and additional suites with sweeping bay views. Locals as well as guests enjoy the seafood, Continental cuisine, and romantic setting of the hotel's restaurant. Children under 14 are not accepted during the high season. ✉ *Playa del Almacen, 40880,* ☎ *755/4-27-48; 888/389-2645 direct-dial toll free;* FAX *755/4-36-24. 31 rooms and suites. Restaurant, bar, 2 pools, dive shop. AE, MC, V.*

$$–$$$ **Catalina-Sotavento.** Really two hotels in one, this multilevel oldie-but-goodie sits on a cliff overlooking the bay. Below, accessible by extensive stairs, is Playa la Ropa and the hotel's beach bar and lounge chairs. Rooms are large and well maintained, with ceiling fans and ample terraces. ✉ *Playa la Ropa, Box 2, 40880,* ☎ *755/4-20-32,* FAX *755/4-29-75. 125 units. 2 restaurants, 2 bars. AE, DC, MC, V.*

$$ **Villas Miramar.** This pleasant colonial-style hotel is in two sections (divided by a small street). The front section overlooks and has access to Madera Beach. The rooms are nicely decorated and have balconies, tiled showers, air-conditioning, and ceiling fans. ✉ *Playa la Madera, Box 211, 40880,* ☎ *755/4–21–06,* FAX *755/4–21–49. 17 rooms, 1 suite. Restaurant, bar. AE, MC, V.*

$–$$ **Avila.** In the center of town facing the beachside Paseo del Pescador, the Avila has large clean rooms (all are air-conditioned), TVs, and ceiling fans. ✉ *Calle Juan N. Alvarez 8, 40880,* ☎ *755/4–20–10,* FAX *755/4–32–99. 27 rooms. AE, MC, V.*

$–$$ **Bungalows Pacíficos.** Terraced down a cliff-side above Madera Beach, each of the spacious bungalows has its own large veranda with a sweeping view of Zihuatanejo Bay as well as a fully equipped kitchen. The owner speaks Spanish, English, and German. ✉ *Cerro de la Madera, Box 12, 40880,* ☎ FAX *755/4–21–12. 6 units. No credit cards.*

$–$$ **Las Urracas.** Each of the casita-style units has a porch in a shaded garden, a kitchen, and a stove. Located on La Ropa Beach, it is a great bargain—which lots of people know about, so reserve far in advance. ✉ *Playa la Ropa, Box 141, 40880,* ☎ *755/4–20–53. 16 bungalows. No credit cards.*

$–$$ **Solimar Inn.** Near the town center, this comfortable hotel features large, air-conditioned rooms with kitchenettes and ceiling fans. Guests tend to stay for weeks or more. ✉ *Plazas los Faroles, 40880,* ☎ FAX *755/4–36–92. 12 rooms. Bar, pool. MC, V.*

$ **Irma.** One of Zihuatanejo's originals, this simple and clean colonial-style hotel sits on a bluff overlooking Madera Beach (accessible by a stairway). ✉ *Playa la Madera, Box 4, 40880,* ☎ *755/4–21–05,* FAX *755/4–37–38. 73 rooms. Restaurant, bar, pool. AE, DC, MC, V.*

Nightlife

A good way to start an evening is a happy hour at one of Ixtapa's hotels. Sunset is an important daily event, and plans should be made accordingly. Tops for sunset viewing (with live music) is the lobby bar at the **Westin Brisas.** To follow sunset viewing by dancing to tropical music until about 2 AM, take the elevator up to the **Faro Bar** nightclub atop the 85-ft-high faux-lighthouse tower in Marina Ixtapa (☎ 755/3–20–90). **Christine,** at the Krystal in Ixtapa, is the town's liveliest high-tech disco; a spectacular runner-up is **Euforia** (✉ Alongside the Posada Real Hotel, ☎ 755/3–11–90). **Carlos 'n' Charlie's** (✉ Blvd. Ixtapa, next to the Hotel Camino Real, ☎ 755/3–10–85) has a party atmosphere, with late-night dancing on a raised platform by the beach. There's a new desert-inspired disco, complete with blue sky and cactus, at **La Valentina** restaurant–video bar–disco complex (✉ Blvd. Ixtapa, next to the Doubletree hotel, ☎ 755/3–11–90)

A number of hotels feature **Mexican Fiesta Nights** with a buffet, handicraft bazaars, and live folkloric music and dance performances. During the high season you'll find Mexican Fiesta Nights on Mondays at the Krystal and on Tuesdays at the Dorado Pacífico.

Outdoor Activities and Sports

Fishing

Bookings and information about sportfishing can be obtained through **Ixtapa Sportfishing Charters** (✉ 33 Olde Mill Run, Stroudsburg, PA 18360, ☎ 717/424–8323, FAX 717/424–1016) or in Zihuatanejo (✉ Paseo del Pescador 6, ☎ 755/4–41–62).

Golf

There are two 18-hole championship courses in Ixtapa. The **Campo de Golf Ixtapa** (☎ 755/3–10–62), designed by Robert Trent Jones Jr., is on a wildlife preserve that runs from a coconut plantation to the beach. Part of the Marina Ixtapa complex, the highly challenging **Club de Golf Marina Ixtapa** (☎ 755/3–14–10) layout was designed by Robert Von Hagge. Each has its own clubhouse with a restaurant as well as tennis courts. Green fees run approximately $60, including caddie or cart.

Horseback Riding

You can rent horses at Playa Linda just up the coast from Ixtapa, or at La Manzanillo Ranch, near Playa la Ropa in Zihuatanejo.

Scuba Diving

Some 30 dive sites in the area range from deep canyons to shallow reefs. The waters here are teeming with sea life and visibility is excellent. At the north end of Playa Cuachalalate on Ixtapa Island, **Nacho's Dive Shop** (no phone) provides rental equipment, instruction, and guided dives. The **Zihuatanejo Scuba Center** (✉ Calle Cuauhtémoc 3, ☎ FAX 755/4–27–48; ✉ At marina of Hotel Puerto Mío), owned and operated by master diver and marine biologist Juan Barnard and his partner Ed Clark, offers one- and two-tank dives as well as an intensive five-day certification course. Divers can have their underwater adventures photographed or videotaped for an additional fee. This authorized NAUI (National Association of Underwater Instructors) Pro Facility has an enthusiastic and knowledgeable staff, including some expatriate Americans.

Tennis

All major Ixtapa hotels have night-lit tennis courts, as do the **Campo de Golf Ixtapa** (☎ 755/3–10–62) and the **Club de Golf Marina Ixtapa** (☎ 755/3–14–10).

Water Sports

You'll find a variety of water sports along Playa del Palmar in Ixtapa. Parasailing costs about $20 for an eight-minute ride; waterskiing runs about $20 per half hour; banana boat rides are about $2.50 per person for a 20-minute trip. On La Ropa Beach, next to La Perla restaurant, Hobie Cats rent for $20 per hour and classes cost $25 per half hour. Windsurfers rent for $20 per hour; classes, which include six hours over four days, cost $40.

Shopping

Ixtapa

As you enter Ixtapa from the airport or from Zihuatanejo, you'll see a large handicrafts market, **Mercado de Artesanía Turístico,** on the right side of Boulevard Ixtapa. The result of a state law that banned vendors from the beach, this market hosts some 150 stands, selling handicrafts, T-shirts, folk apparel, and souvenirs.

Across the street from the hotel zone, the shopping area is loosely divided into *centros comerciales,* or malls. These clusters of pleasant colonial-style buildings feature patios containing boutiques, restaurants, cafés, and grocery minimarkets. The first one you'll come to is **Los Patios,** where La Fuente (☎ 755/3–08–12) sells locally designed clothes, art, crafts, and home furnishings. Behind Los Patios, in a terra-cotta–color building, is **Plaza Ixpamar,** host to El Amanecer (☎ 755/3–19–02) and its nice array of folk art. After Plaza Ixpamar comes **Las Fuentes,** where you'll find Polo Ralph Lauren (☎ 755/3–12–72); Bye-Bye (☎ 755/3–09–79) beach and casual wear; the ubiquitous sportswear emporium **Aca Joe** (☎ 755/3–03–02); and the handy **Supermercado Scruples** (☎ 755/3–21–28). The last mall in the hotel zone strip is **La Puerta,** which includes **Ferrioni Collection** (☎ 755/3–23–43) with colorful Scottish terrier–logo casual wear, and **Mic-Mac** (☎ 755/3–17–33) with crafts and Mexican regional art and clothing.

Zihuatanejo

Downtown Zihuatanejo has a colorful **municipal market** with a labyrinth of small stands on the east side of the town center, on Calle Benito Juárez at Antonio Nava. On the west edge of town, along Calle 5 de Mayo, is the **Mercado de Artesanía Turístico,** similar to the craft and souvenir market in Ixtapa, but larger, with 255 stands. Good purchases include local hand-painted Guerrero wooden masks and ceramics, huaraches, and silver jewelry.

Near the mercado, across from the Aeromexico office and facing the waterfront, **Casa Marina** (✉ Paseo del Pescador 9, ☎ 755/4–23–73) is a two-story building containing several boutiques, all belonging to the same family. **El Embarcadero** has an extensive selection of folk art from all over Mexico; **Manos** sells handicrafts; **La Zapoteca** features hammocks and hand-loomed rugs; and **El Jumil** has an array of Guerrero ceremonial masks. You might want to poke around here first to check prices, and then head for the market, where you'll often pay less for the same wares if you have a good eye and are willing to bargain.

There are a number of interesting shops in the tiny three-block nucleus of central Zihuatanejo. **Galeria Maya** (✉ Calle Nicolás Bravo 31, ☎ 755/4–46–06) is very browsable for its folk art and leather goods. **Nando's** (✉ Juan N. Alvarez 5, ☎ 755/4–22–38) has a selection of colorful handmade tropical-chic women's apparel from Oaxaca and Chiapas. **Alberto's** (✉ Calle Cuauhtémoc 12 and 15, ☎ 755/4–21–61) is one of the best places to find authentic Taxco silver jewelry. **Coco Cabaña** (✉ Agustín Ramírez 1, ☎ 755/4–25–18) is a fascinating folk-art shop. Over at Playa la Ropa, **Gala Art** (✉ Hotel Villa del Sol, ☎ 755/4–22–39) exhibits and sells paintings and sculptures by prominent local artists.

Ixtapa/Zihuatanejo A to Z

Arriving and Departing

BY BUS

Estrella Blanca (☎ 755/4–34–77) and **Estrella de Oro** (☎ 755/4–21–75) offer deluxe service (with air-conditioning, video, bathrooms, and soft drinks) between Acapulco and Zihuatanejo. The trip takes less than four hours and costs about $8.

BY CAR

The trip from Acapulco is a 3½-hour drive over a good two-lane road that passes through small towns and coconut groves and has some spectacular ocean views for the last third of the way.

BY PLANE

Mexicana (☎ 755/4–28–05) offers direct daily flights from Los Angeles, while **Aeromexico** (☎ 755/4-22–37) flies direct from Atlanta, Los Angeles, New York/JFK, and Houston. Both airlines operate several daily nonstops (35 mins) between Mexico City and Zihuatanejo. **Continental** (☎ 755/4–25–79) flies nonstop from Houston. **Northwest** (☎ 91–800/9–07–47) departs from Minneapolis/St. Paul and Detroit Saturdays from mid-December to April.

BY SHIP

Several cruise lines, including **Cunard, Holland American Lines, Krystal Cruises, Princess Cruises, Royal Caribbean Cruises,** and **Royal Cruise Lines,** sail to Ixtapa/Zihuatanejo from Los Angeles during the winter months.

Getting Around

Unless you plan to travel great distances or visit remote beaches, taxis and buses are by far the best way to get around. Taxis are plentiful, clean, and reliable, and fares are reasonable and fixed. The fare from the Ixtapa hotel zone to Zihuatanejo is under $4. Taxis are usually lined up in front of hotels. Two radio taxi companies are **APAAZ** (☎ 755/4–36–80) and **UTAAZ** (☎ 755/4–33–11). Minibuses run frequently between the Ixtapa hotels and between the Ixtapa hotel zone and downtown Zihuatanejo; fare is about 30¢.

Rental cars, from Jeeps to sedans with automatic transmission and air-conditioning, are available from major car-rental agencies (☞ *below*). You can also rent a gasoline-powered golf cart in Ixtapa from **Tropical Transportation** (⊠ Las Fuentes Shopping Center, ☎ 755/3–24–88). They're for local transportation only, however—don't consider taking one to Zihuatanejo—and cost from about $12 for one hour to $55 for 24 hours.

Contacts and Resources

CAR RENTAL

Hertz, Dollar, and **National** have locations at the airport and in Ixtapa and/or Zihuatanejo. A good local agency is **Quick Rent-A-Car** (⊠ Westin Las Brisas, ☎ 755/3–18–30).

EMERGENCIES

Police (☎ 755/4–38–37); **Public Safety** (Seguridad Publica; ☎ 755/4–71–71); **Red Cross** (☎ 755/4–20–09).

GUIDED TOURS

Most major hotels have lobby tour desks or travel agencies that offer a selection of sightseeing tours of Ixtapa, Zihuatanejo, and surrounding areas. Another option is a six-hour cruise on the 100-passenger trimaran *Tri-Star,* which sets sail from the Puerto Mío hotel marina in Zihuatanejo. For $60, you'll get ground transportation, an open bar (domestic drinks), and a fresh-fish lunch at Ixtapa Island. You can also book a two-hour sunset cruise of Zihuatanejo Bay or a four-hour cruise to Playa Manzanillo, just outside the mouth of the bay, for great snorkeling and swimming. For details about all of these cruises, contact **Yates del Sol** (☎ 755/4–26–94).

TRAVEL AGENCY

American Express (⊠ Arcade of Krystal Hotel, Ixtapa, ☎ 755/3–08–53, FAX 755/3–12–06).

VISITOR INFORMATION

Municipal Tourism Office (⊠ Zihuatanejo City Hall, ☎ 755/4–20–01), **Guerrero State Tourism Office** (⊠ La Puerta Shopping Center, Ixtapa, ☎ 755/3–19–68).

7 Guadalajara

The colonial architecture that dates to Guadalajara's heyday as a regional commercial center for the Spanish is among the lures of Mexico's second-largest city; Guadalajara also introduced the world to mariachis and tequila. Some of the best arts and crafts in Mexico can be found at Tlaquepaque, on the city's outskirts, and Tonalá, about 10 minutes farther away.

Updated by
Trudy Balch

TRADITIONS ARE PRESERVED and customs perpetuated in Guadalajara; it's a place where the siesta is an institution and the fiesta an art form. The city is the birthplace of *el jarabe tapatío* (the Mexican hat dance), *charreadas* (rodeos), mariachis, and tequila.

Mexico's second-largest city, and capital of the state of Jalisco, Guadalajara is engaged in a struggle to retain its provincial ambience and colonial charm as its population approaches 6 million. Émigrés from Mexico City after the devastating 1985 earthquake and staggering numbers of the rural poor seeking employment created a population explosion that continues to strain public services and the city's often outdated infrastructure. Visitors to the city can enjoy the tree-lined boulevards, parks, plazas, and stately churrigueresque architecture, but recent years have brought traffic jams and increasingly heavy pollution.

Guadalajara has always been one of the most socially traditional and politically conservative cities in Mexico. It has also been the seat of Christian fundamentalism and was one of the strategic areas of the *Cristeros,* a movement of right-wing Catholic zealots in western Mexico in the 1920s. *Tapatíos,* as the city's residents are called (the name comes from *tlapatiotl,* three units or purses of cacao or other commodities used as currency by the Indians of the area), even seem to take a certain amount of pride in their straight and narrow outlook.

Still, Tapatíos are historically accustomed to challenge and change. Within 10 years of its founding in 1531, the location of the city changed three times. In 1542 the City Council followed the advice of Doña Beatriz Hernández to build the city in the center of the Atemajac Valley, where it could expand. Thus Guadalajara was placed on a mile-high plain of the Sierra Madre, bounded on three sides by rugged cliffs and on the fourth by the spectacular Barranca de Oblatos (Oblatos Canyon). A near-perfect semitropical climate and proximity to the Pacific Ocean (240 km, or 150 mi, away) ensure warm, sunny days with just a hint of humidity and cool, clear nights.

Geographically remote from the rest of the republic during the nearly 300 years of Spanish rule, the city cultivated and maintained a political and cultural autonomy. By the end of the 16th century, money was flowing into Guadalajara from the rich farms and silver mines in the region, creating the first millionaires of what was then known as New Galicia. Under orders from Spain, much of the wealth was lavished on magnificent churches, residences, and monuments. Many of these reminders of the golden era still stand in downtown Guadalajara.

The suburbs of San Pedro Tlaquepaque (Tla-kay-*pah*-kay) and Tonalá (Toe-na-*la*) produce some of Mexico's finest and most popular traditional crafts and folk art. Lake Chapala and the nearby towns of Chapala and Ajijic have attracted retired former residents of the United States and Canada, who enjoy most of the amenities and services they were accustomed to north of the border.

Pleasures and Pastimes

Arts and Architecture

All manner of Mexican and international arts can be found in Guadalajara. You'll find everything from the traditional Ballet Folklórico at the Teatro Degollado to rock groups at the Instituto Cultural Cabañas. Galleries and museums around town also offer the best of modern and traditional creations. Numerous 16th-century colonial buildings fill the downtown area, connected by a series of large, Spanish-style plazas.

Churches

Guadalajara seems to have a church every block or two—there are 15 in the downtown area alone, all dating from the colonial era. Some have elaborately carved facades, and others conceal ornate baroque altars and priceless colonial oil paintings behind sober stone exteriors.

Dining

Guadalajara offers an impressive variety of restaurants, with choices ranging from classic Mexican dishes to continental delicacies, Argentine-style steaks, and fresh seafood. Savory regional specialties—often served in simpler establishments—include *birria,* a spicy stew prepared with goat, lamb, or pork in a light tomato broth; *pozole,* a thick pork and hominy soup; and *carne en su jugo,* consisting of steak bits in a clear spicy broth with bacon, beans, and cilantro, usually served with a side of tiny, grilled whole onions.

Lodging

Hotel choices run the gamut from older establishments in the downtown historic district—including one lovingly restored building that has been a hotel since 1610—to representatives of the large chains, most of which are on or near Avenida López Mateos Sur, a 16-km (10-mi) strip extending from the Minerva Fountain to the Plaza del Sol shopping center. In the mid-1990s several hotels have also gone up close to Expo-Guadalajara (one of Latin America's largest convention centers), which opened in 1987.

Shopping

Traditional to the area are blown glass, hand-carved wood furniture, fine leatherwork, and delicately painted pottery. Two of the most common techniques are *barro bruñido,* in which the pieces are hand-burnished to a soft sheen, and *petatillo,* featuring finely painted crosshatched patterns on red-glazed clay. Guadalajara is also home to a thriving shoe industry. At sprawling markets you can bargain for anything from embroidered shirts to huaraches, and sleek shopping malls offer full-service department stores and trendy boutiques.

Sports

Highly stylized charreadas, traditional Mexican rodeos, are presented here weekly, and there are bullfights in October and November. From late August through May, enthusiastic soccer fans crowd Jalisco Stadium.

EXPLORING GUADALAJARA

Metropolitan Guadalajara consists of the historic city center and the nearby urban districts, as well as the neighboring towns of Tlaquepaque and Tonalá and the tranquil villages on the shores of Lake Chapala.

Numbers in the text correspond to numbers in the margin and on the Downtown Guadalajara, Lake Chapala Area, Tlaquepaque, and Tonalá maps.

Great Itineraries

It's not surprising that Guadalajara has been described as *señorial y moderna* (lordly and modern). Here, you can experience the graciousness of colonial Mexico, accompanied by however much you want of the 20th century. The nearby pueblos offer an eye into traditional rural life. Ten days would allow you to fully explore the city and surrounding villages, as well as take an excursion or two to points farther afield. With five days to spend here, you'll have time to tour many city highlights and get to know Tlaquepaque, Tonalá, and the Lake Chapala area. In three days, you can take in the historic city center and make day trips to Tlaquepaque, Tonalá, and Lake Chapala.

IF YOU HAVE 3 DAYS

Spend your first day in the historic **city center** (*el centro*) ①–⑩. The next day, spend the morning in **Tlaquepaque** ㉗–㊱, have lunch there, and visit **Tonalá** ㊲–㊹ in the afternoon. On your third day, head for the **Lake Chapala** ⑳–㉖ area; stroll and shop, perhaps take a boat trip on the lake, and enjoy lunch or dinner in one of the area's fine restaurants.

IF YOU HAVE 5 DAYS

See the city center on your first day. Then consider your interests. If traditional crafts lure you, devote a day to Tlaquepaque and the following day to Tonalá. Or you can explore the two towns in one day, leaving you a day—or two—for the Lake Chapala area. During your final one or two days, you can spend part or all of a day visiting other historical or art museums in, around, and outside the city center. You might take in some additional churches, including the **Basilica of the Virgin of Zapopan** ⑯ for which you'll need several hours; and visit the Guadalajara **zoo** ⑭ and **planetarium** ⑮. Or spend a few hours strolling by the mansions built by Guadalajara's upper classes in the waning glory days before the 1910 revolution; the best area is roughly in a six-block radius around Avenida Vallarta west of Avenida Chapultepec. If you decide to tour the village of **Tequila,** allow at least half a day. If your taste runs more to naturist activities, allow a day to see the zoo and hike in the nearby **Barranca de Oblatos.**

IF YOU HAVE 10 DAYS

You will be able to cover all of el centro plus the other city sights, and Tlaquepaque, Tonalá, and the Lake Chapala area. Fill in the gaps with a visit to Tequila and a stay in the soothing thermal waters of **San Juan Cosalá** or **Rancho Río Caliente.** For an excursion to the **Sierra de Manantlán,** allow two to three days.

Guadalajara

Beginning around 1960, 20th-century architecture started to threaten the historical integrity of this provincial state capital. In the early 1980s the city declared a 30-square-block area in the heart of downtown a cultural sanctuary, and in the late 1990s private-sector groups formed a trust to continue spiffing up el centro. The 16th-century buildings here are connected by a series of large Spanish-style plazas where today's inhabitants enjoy life: Young children chase gaily colored balloons, young lovers cuddle on tree-shaded park benches, and grandparents stroll hand in hand past vendors and marble fountains. At nearby Plaza de los Mariachis, the nostalgic songs and music of sombrero-topped troubadours can be heard.

In addition to el centro, most tourist sights and large hotels are located in three other areas: near Avenida Chapultepec; near the Minerva Fountain and Los Arcos monument; and in the Plaza del Sol shopping area (several miles southwest of downtown).

A Good Walk

Begin a tour of downtown at the 17th-century **Catedral** ① on Avenida Alcalde between Avenida Hidalgo and Calle Morelos. Go out through the main doors and cross Avenida Alcalde to Plaza Guadalajara, dotted with benches beneath square-cut laurel trees. To your right (with your back toward the cathedral) across Avenida Hidalgo is the **Palacio Municipal** ②, or City Hall.

Return to Avenidas Alcalde and Hidalgo and proceed one block east to Calle Liceo, where you'll see the **Museo Regional de Guadalajara** ③. You'll pass the Rotonda de Hombres Ilustres de Jalisco, a tree-shaded square whose central colonnaded rotunda covers a mausoleum containing the remains of 17 of the state of Jalisco's favorite sons. Surrounding the square are brass sculptures representing those buried inside.

When you exit back onto Calle Liceo, you have two alternatives: Three blocks to your right is the **Casa-Museo López Portillo** ④ and beyond that, on Avenida Alcalde, the **Museo del Periodismo y de las Artes Gráficas** ⑤. Around the corner to the left of the Museo Regional, on Avenida Hidalgo, are the Palacio Legislativo, a former customs house, tobacco warehouse, and inn that today houses Jalisco's state legislature, and the Palacio de Justicia, built in 1588 as part of Guadalajara's first convent and now the state courthouse. Across Avenida Hidalgo on your right sprawls the Plaza de la Liberación, at the east end of which rises the spectacular **Teatro Degollado** ⑥. Behind it begins the Plaza Tapatía, a five-block-long pedestrian mall lined with shops, trees, and whimsical sculptures and frequented by mimes and street musicians. At the end, visit the **Instituto Cultural Cabañas** ⑦; then proceed back west to the modernistic Quetzalcóatl Fountain in the center. Turn left and walk down the stairs to the three-story **Mercado Libertad** (☞ Shopping, *below*). Turn left again when you leave the market and cross the pedestrian bridge over Avenida Javier Mina to the **Plaza de los Mariachis** ⑧.

Return to Plaza Tapatía by heading right to the intersection of Calzada Independencia Sur and Avenida Javier Mina, in front of the Iglesia de San Juan de Dios. Continue two blocks past the church and go back up the stairs. Turn left and walk west four blocks (so you can see the stores on this side of the plaza) to the **Iglesia de San Agustín** ⑨.

As you leave the church, turn left down Calle Morelos to Avenida Corona. Turn left again and walk a half block to the main entrance of the **Palacio de Gobierno** ⑩. Exit the Palacio de Gobierno back onto Avenida Corona (the way you came in) and cross the street to the Plaza de Armas, where you can rest on a wrought-iron bench, or imagine yourself a gracious *don* or *doña* as you stroll amid the trees and flower beds surrounding an ornately sculpted kiosk, a gift from France in 1910. You have now come full circle, with the cathedral to your right, on the north side of the plaza.

TIMING

You can take in most of downtown Guadalajara in a day. The other groups of sights can easily take one-half or one full day each. Most museums, the zoo, and the planetarium are closed Monday. During October, the city puts on the Fiestas de Octubre, a monthlong cultural festival that's sprinkled with top-flight international entertainment.

Sights to See

⑯ **Basílica de la Virgen de Zapopan.** This vast church, with an ornate plateresque facade and *mudéjar* (Moorish) tiled dome, was consecrated in 1730. It is known throughout Mexico as the home of La Zapopanita, Our Lady of Zapopan. The 10-inch-high statue is venerated as the source of many miracles in and around Guadalajara. Every year on October 12, more than 1 million people crowd the streets leading to Zapopan as the Virgin is returned to the basilica after a five-month absence, during which she visits every parish church in the state. In the right side of the basilica is the Museo Huichol (✉ Avs. Avila Camacho and de las Américasa), a small gallery and shop featuring exquisite beadwork and other handicrafts by the Huichol Indians of northern Jalisco and neighboring states Zacatecas and Nayarit. It's

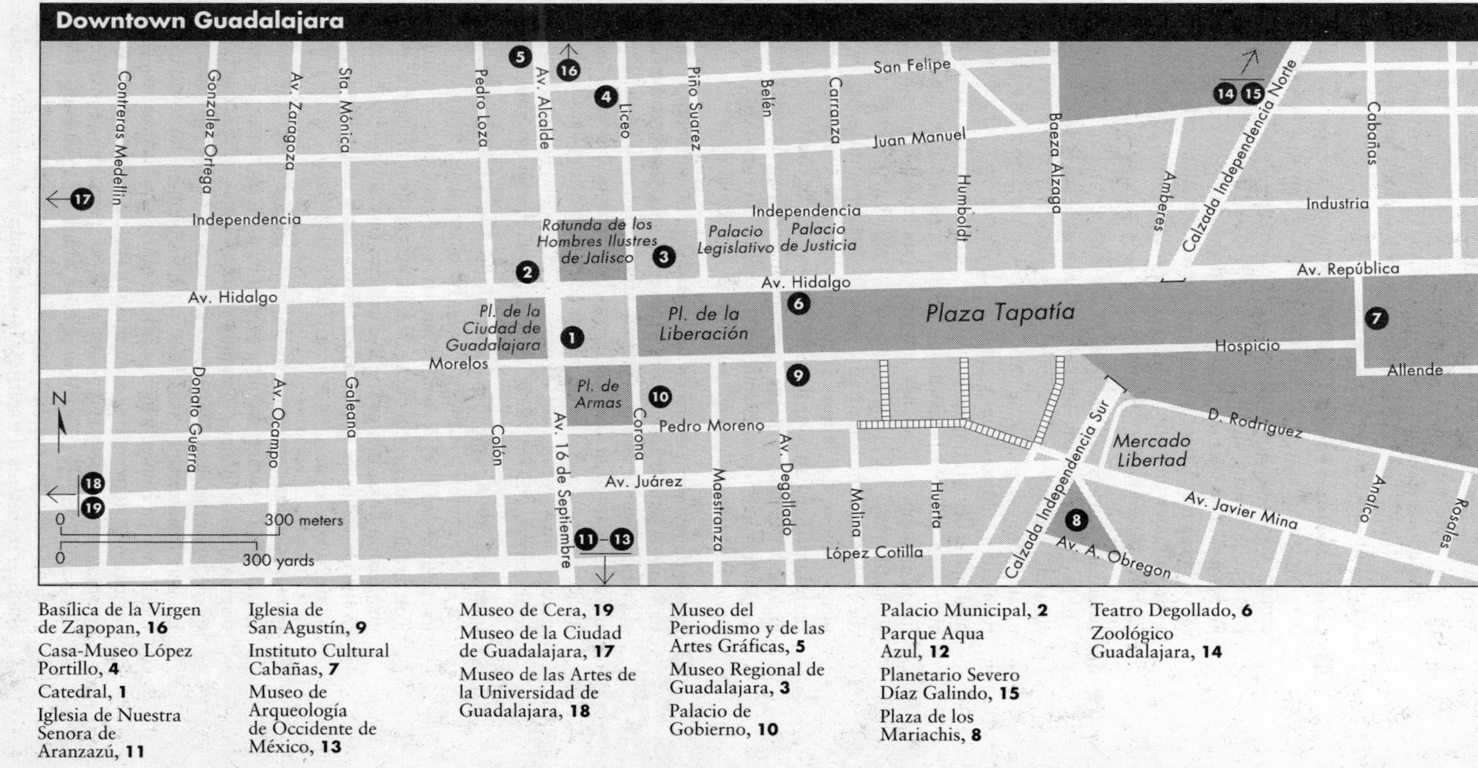
Downtown Guadalajara
Contreras Medellín
Gonzalez Ortega
Av. Zaragoza
Sta. Mónica
Pedro Loza
Av. Alcalde
Liceo
Piño Suarez
Belén
Carranza
San Felipe
Juan Manuel
Humboldt
Baeza Alzaga
Amberes
Calzada Independencia Norte
Cabañas
Industria
Independencia
Rotunda de los Hombres Ilustres de Jalisco
Palacio Legislativo
Palacio de Justicia
Av. República
Av. Hidalgo
Pl. de la Ciudad de Guadalajara
Pl. de la Liberación
Plaza Tapatía
Hospicio
Allende
Morelos
Pl. de Armas
Pedro Moreno
Corona
Donato Guerra
Av. Ocampo
Galeana
Colón
Av. 16 de Septiembre
Av. Juárez
Maestranza
Av. Degollado
Molina
Huerta
López Cotilla
Calzada Independencia Sur
Mercado Libertad
D. Rodriguez
Av. Javier Mina
Av. A. Obregon
Analco
Rosales
N
0
300 meters
0
300 yards
1
2
3
4
5
6
7
8
9
10
11–13
14
15
16
17
18
19
Basílica de la Virgen de Zapopan, 16
Casa-Museo López Portillo, 4
Catedral, 1
Iglesia de Nuestra Senora de Aranzazú, 11
Iglesia de San Agustín, 9
Instituto Cultural Cabañas, 7
Museo de Arqueología de Occidente de México, 13
Museo de Cera, 19
Museo de la Ciudad de Guadalajara, 17
Museo de las Artes de la Universidad de Guadalajara, 18
Museo del Periodismo y de las Artes Gráficas, 5
Museo Regional de Guadalajara, 3
Palacio de Gobierno, 10
Palacio Municipal, 2
Parque Aqua Azul, 12
Planetario Severo Díaz Galindo, 15
Plaza de los Mariachis, 8
Teatro Degollado, 6
Zoológico Guadalajara, 14

open weekdays 9–1 and 4–7, Saturday 9–1. The basilica is 7 km (4½ mi) west–northwest of downtown. Additional information is available from the municipal tourist office (✉ Vicente Guerrero 233, ☎ 3/636–6727 or 3/633–2412), which is a block behind the basilica and open weekdays 9–8.

❹ **Casa-Museo López Portillo.** Guadalajara's illustrious López Portillo family included prominent writers and politicians, such as an early 20th-century Jalisco governor and his Mexico City–born grandson, José López Portillo, president of Mexico from 1976 to 1982. As is typical of homes built by Mexico's 19th-century upper class, the plain stucco exterior belies the rich interior, where French Baroque–style rooms ring a spacious interior patio. ✉ *Liceo 177, at San Felipe,* ☎ *3/613–2411.* *Free.* ⏲ *Weekdays 9–8:30, Sat. 9–1.*

★ ❶ **Catedral.** Consecrated in 1618, this is the focal point of downtown. The building is an intriguing mélange of baroque, churrigueresque, neoclassical, and other architectural styles, the result of design and structural modifications during its 57 years of construction. Its emblematic twin towers replaced the original, much shorter ones, which were toppled in the devastating earthquake of 1818. Ten of the silver-and-gilt altars were gifts of King Fernando VII, in appreciation of Guadalajara's financial support of Spain during the Napoleonic Wars; the 11th, of sculpted white marble, was carved in Italy in 1863. On the walls of the cathedral hang some of the world's most beautiful *retablos* (altarpieces); above the sacristy is the priceless 17th-century painting of Bartolomé Esteban Murillo, *The Assumption of the Virgin.* In a loft high above the main entrance is a magnificent late-19th-century French organ, featured in an organ festival usually held every May. ✉ *Av. Alcalde between Av. Hidalgo and Morelos.* ⏲ *Daily 8–7.*

⓫ **Iglesia de Nuestra Señora de Aranzazú.** Don't be fooled by Our Lady of Aranzazú's drab brown stone exterior: Inside is a spectacular baroque gilt retablo whose 14 niches contain life-size statues of saints. The walls and ceilings are painted in bright shades of turquoise, rose, and rust, with intricate floral detail. The church sits at the west side of Parque San Francisco, a small green oasis that draws food vendors, families, and sedate senior citizens. ✉ *Av. 16 de Septiembre and Prisciliano Sánchez.*

❾ **Iglesia de San Agustín.** The venerable St. Augustine Church is one of the oldest churches in the city. It has been remodeled many times since its consecration in 1574, but the sacristy is preserved in its original form. The building to the left of the church, originally a cloister of the Augustinian monks, is now the **Escuela de Música,** or School of Music, of the University of Guadalajara. Free recitals and concerts are held on the school's patio. ✉ *Morelos at Av. Degollado.*

★ ❼ **Instituto Cultural Cabañas.** A Guadalajara landmark and major cultural center, this sprawling building topped by a stately, pillared dome was originally an orphanage founded by Bishop Juan Cruz Ruíz de Cabañas y Crespo in the early 19th century. It was home for 400 orphans and indigent children until the 1970s, when the orphanage moved to a new location. The rooms, which surround 23 flower-filled patios, contain permanent and revolving art exhibits. The central dome and walls of the main chapel display a series of murals painted by José Clemente Orozco in 1938–39. *The Man of Fire,* which depicts a man enveloped in flames who is ascending toward infinity and yet not consumed by the fire, represents the spirit of humankind. It is generally considered to be his finest work. There is a permanent exhibit of Orozco's paintings, cartoons, and drawings in Room 33. Ask the attendant at the front desk for an English-speaking guide. ✉ *Calle Cabañas 8, at Plaza Ta-*

patía, ☎ *3/617–4322 or 3/617–4440.* 🎫 *About $1; free Sun.* ⏲ *Tues.–Sat. 10:15–6, Sun. 10:15–3.*

13 **Museo de Arqueología de Occidente de México.** The Archaeological Museum of Western Mexico houses pottery and other artifacts used by ancient peoples of what are now the states of Colima, Jalisco, and Nayarit. It's in the street divider across from the entrance to Parque Agua Azul. ✉ *Calzada Independencia Sur and Av. del Campesino, no phone.* 🎫 *15¢.* ⏲ *Tues.–Sun. 10–2 and 4–7.*

19 **Museo de Cera.** Guadalajara's 120-figure wax museum is in an elegantly restored turn-of-the-century house. Go eye-to-eye with Madonna, Mahatma Gandhi, and beloved Mexican comic Cantinflas, as well as a host of other Mexican and international political and artistic luminaries. Finish up with the dungeonlike chamber of horrors in the basement. The museum is located three blocks south of Avenida Chapultepec, behind the U.S. Consulate. ✉ *Libertad 1872,* ☎ *3/825–8956.* 🎫 *About $2.* ⏲ *Daily 10–7.*

17 **Museo de la Ciudad de Guadalajara.** In a series of rooms surrounding the tranquil interior patio of this spacious remodeled home, you'll find artwork, artifacts, and reproductions of documents that provide extensive information about the city's development. ✉ *Av. Independencia 684, between Contreras Medellín and Mariano Bárcenas,* ☎ *3/658–2531 or 3/658–3706.* 🎫 *40¢; free Sun.* ⏲ *Wed.–Sat. 10–5:30, Sun. 10–2:30.*

18 **Museo de las Artes de la Universidad de Guadalajara.** This impressive contemporary art museum, housed in an exquisite early 20th-century building belonging to the University of Guadalajara, has a permanent collection of 20th-century drawings and paintings, as well as revolving exhibits of modern Latin American, U.S., and European works. Also in the building are the first murals painted by Orozco after he returned to Guadalajara at age 53, as well as a charming café and small gift shop. Behind the museum, you'll see the **Templo Expiatorio,** a striking Gothic-style church built at the turn of the century and modeled after the Cathedral of Orvieto in Italy. ✉ *Av. Juárez at Av. Enrique Díaz de León,* ☎ *3/826–6114 or 3/826–1959, ext. 24.* 🎫 *About 70¢; free Sun.* ⏲ *Tues.–Sat. 10–8, Sun. noon–6.*

5 **Museo del Periodismo y de las Artes Gráficas.** In 1792 Guadalajara's first printing press was set up on this site, where today you can see displays of historic newspapers, printing presses, recording equipment, and a complete television studio. The building has long been known as the Casa de los Perros because of the two wrought-iron dogs (*perros*) "guarding" the roof. ✉ *Av. Alcalde 225,* ☎ *3/613–9285.* 🎫 *About 70¢.* ⏲ *Tues.–Sat. 10–6, Sun. 11–5:30.*

★ 3 **Museo Regional de Guadalajara.** Constructed as a seminary in the late 17th century, this distinguished building has been home to the Regional Museum (also known as the State Museum) since 1918. The first-floor galleries, which surround a garden courtyard, contain artifacts and memorabilia that trace the history of western Mexico from prehistoric times through the Spanish conquest; there are also revolving arts and crafts exhibits. On the second-floor balcony are five 19th-century carriages; the galleries offer an impressive collection of paintings by European and Mexican artists, including Bartolomé Esteban Murillo, and displays about the history of Jalisco. ✉ *Liceo 60,* ☎ *3/614–9957.* 🎫 *About $1.90; free Sun.* ⏲ *Tues.–Sat. 9–6:45, Sun. 9–3.*

10 **Palacio de Gobierno.** Built in 1643, this churrigueresque and neoclassical structure houses Jalisco's state government offices and two of José

Clemente Orozco's most passionate murals. You'll see the first one in the stairwell to the right after you enter: a gigantic Father Miguel Hidalgo looming amid shadowy figures representing oppression and slavery. The second, in the former state legislature quarters on the upper level, depicts Juárez and other figures of the 1850s Reform era. ✉ *Av. Corona between Morelos and Pedro Moreno.* ⏲ *Daily 9–8:45.*

❷ **Palacio Municipal.** Guadalajara's city hall is a clever, colonial-style fake: It was built in 1952 with an arched facade and interior patio so it would fit in with neighboring buildings. Inside is a colorful mural depicting the founding of the city. ⏲ *Daily 9–8.*

⓬ **Parque Agua Azul.** Amid acres of trees and flowers, this popular park has carnival rides, tropical birds in cages, an orchid house, and a geodesic dome covering a tropical garden. Next to the park entrance, the small **Teatro Experimental** (☎ 3/619–3770) presents many Spanish-language children's plays, including English-language classics in translation. Dramas and chamber music are also performed here. A remodeled **Museo Infantil** (no phone), with lively displays focusing on geography, space, and natural history, is expected to reopen in 1998; it's located on the southeast side of the park. ✉ *Calzada Independencia Sur and Av. del Campesino,* ☎ *3/619–0328.* *55¢.* ⏲ *Tues.–Sun. 10–6.*

⓯ **Planetario Severo Díaz Galindo.** A modern facility with astronomy shows and aeronautical displays, the planetarium also has exhibits that allow children to test the forces and laws of nature. It's 6 km (nearly 4 mi) northeast of downtown. ✉ *Calzada Ricardo Flores Magón 599,* ☎ *3/674–4106 or 3/674–3978.* *Museum 20¢; astronomy show and movie 40¢.* ⏲ *Tues.–Sun. 9–7.*

★ ❽ **Plaza de los Mariachis.** Experience the most Mexican of music in this picturesque little plaza complete with cafés, where strolling mariachi groups perform. Though the action here lasts all night, it's best to visit during the day. The plaza is next to the **Iglesia de San Juan de Dios**; use the pedestrian overpass from the Mercado Libertad to avoid the heavy traffic. ✉ *Calzada Independencia Sur between Av. Javier Mina and Alvaro Obregón.* *Mariachi serenade about $4 a song.*

★ ❻ **Teatro Degollado.** Inaugurated in 1866, this magnificent theater was modeled after Milan's La Scala. Above the Corinthian columns gracing the entranceway is a relief depicting Apollo and the nine Muses. Inside, red and gold balconies ascend to a multitiered dome adorned with Gerardo Suárez's depiction of Dante's *Divine Comedy.* The theater is the permanent home for the Jalisco Philharmonic and the Ballet Folklórico of the University of Guadalajara and also hosts visiting orchestras, plays, and numerous other performances. According to tradition, Guadalajara was founded on the site of what is now the **Plaza de los Fundadores,** which flanks the east side of the theater. A sculpted frieze on the rear wall of the Teatro Degollado depicts the historic event. ✉ *Calle Belén between Av. Hidalgo and Morelos,* ☎ *3/614–4773.* ⏲ *Daily 10–1 and 4–7 and during performances.*

NEED A BREAK? A signature pink-and-white color scheme heralds the city's most popular ice-cream chain. A stop at **Helados Bing** (on the north side of Plaza Tapatía, east of the Quetzalcóatl Fountain) provides a welcome respite from an afternoon of sightseeing. Choose from more than 20 flavors of pasteurized ice cream and ices, and relax on a shaded bench.

⓮ **Zoológico Guadalajara.** Located on the edge of the jagged Barranca Huentitán, or Huentitán Canyon, the Guadalajara Zoo has more than 1,500 animals representing some 300 species. For 40¢ a train provides guided tours. The adjacent **Selva Mágica,** or Magic Jungle amusement park, has carnival rides and attractions for about $1.30. The complex is 6 km (nearly 4 mi) northeast of downtown, near the planetarium. ✉ *Paseo del Zoológico 600,* ☎ *3/674–1034.* *About $1.85.* ⏲ *Tues.–Sun. 9:30–6 (Selva Mágica 10–7).*

OFF THE BEATEN PATH

BARRANCA DE OBLATOS – A spectacular 2,000-ft-deep gorge, Oblatos Canyon also has hiking trails and the narrow **Cola de Caballo** waterfall, named for its horse-tail shape. For the best view, go to the lookout area, or Parque Mirador, at the top. ✉ *10 km (6 mi) northeast of downtown Guadalajara via Calzada Independencia Norte.*

DINING

Guadalajara restaurants continue to offer excellent value for your dollar. Most are open throughout the evening, though seafood establishments often close earlier. A number of restaurants listed below have branches elsewhere in the city; our choices are either the most colorful, original locations or those most convenient to the hotel areas. Generally, you will feel comfortable wearing casual-chic clothes at establishments in the $$ and $ categories, but Guadalajara is a big, business-oriented city, which means diners tend to dress up a bit. Still, Maximino's is the only restaurant where men are likely to feel out of place without a jacket. Some restaurants close on national holidays; call ahead to be sure.

CATEGORY	COST*
$$$	$15–$25
$$	$10–$15
$	under $10

**per person for a three-course meal, excluding drinks, service, and 15% sales tax*

$$$ ★ ✕ **Maximino's.** A favorite with the upper crust of Guadalajara, Maximino's is located in a beautiful two-story mansion in a quiet neighborhood near the U.S. Consulate. The elegantly decorated interior is dominated by a sweeping staircase, and the savory international menu has strong French influences, offering such delicacies as flamed steak fillet in Roquefort sauce; the seafood choices are extensive, including Norwegian salmon and a variety of shrimp dishes. Soft strains of a jazz trio play during most meals. ✉ *Lerdo de Tejada 2043,* ☎ *3/615–3424, 3/615–3435, or 3/825–0076. AE, MC, V.*

$$ ★ ✕ **Copenhagen.** Decorative tilework by Tonalá artisan Jorge Wilmot covers the walls here, where the signature dish is paella. Since 1952 the Copenhagen has served up the famous dish of Valencia, Spain, as well as beef and seafood entrées, pastas, and Spanish-style tortillas, which—unlike the Mexican variety—are large omelets stuffed with potato and onion. Copenhagen is also the unofficial headquarters for Guadalajara's jazz aficionados; it showcases some of the city's best jazz musicians, who entertain each afternoon and every evening but Sunday after 8. ✉ *Marcos Castellanos 136-Z,* ☎ *3/826–1787. AE, V.*

$$ ★ ✕ **El Farallón de Tepic.** Set underneath a bright blue awning, this open-air establishment is reminiscent of beach restaurants in Tepic, a popular seaside town in the nearby state of Nayarit. Order your fresh *pescado* (fish)—usually red snapper or an equally mild fish—grilled with garlic or butter, in classic tomato sauce, breaded, or stuffed with seafood and cheese. *Pescado zarandeado* is grilled to order over a wood fire and worth every second of the 30-minute wait. Try the homemade flan for dessert. ✉ *Av. Niño Obrero 560,* ☎ *3/121–2616 or 3/121–9616. MC, V.*

$$ ✕ **Guadalajara Grill.** Fun and revelry share top billing with the food at this Carlos 'n' Charlie's affiliate. The large, tri-level room is decorated with Mexican knickknacks and antique street lamps; turn-of-the-century photographs of Guadalajara are displayed in the foyer and on the back wall. The tender barbecued baby ribs are a favorite, as are the numerous shrimp dishes. There is live entertainment every evening. ✉ *Av. López Mateos Sur 3771,* ☎ *3/631–5622. MC, V.*

$$ ✕ **La Destilería.** If you can't make it to the village of Tequila, here's the next best thing: a restaurant cum "Tequila Museum" that serves nouvelle Mexican specialties and more than 100 varieties of the fiery liquor. Lining the redbrick walls are antique photos of tequila distilleries, authentic implements, and bilingual plaques explaining tequila's history. ✉ *Av. México 2916,* ☎ *3/640–7361 or 3/640–3110. MC, V.*

$$ ✕ **Parilla Argentina.** Animal hides and posters of Argentina adorn the walls of this restaurant where—as throughout Argentina—tender grilled meat reigns supreme. Choose from T-bones, ribs, flank steaks, sausages, and Argentine-style *parillada* (a mixed grill of beef, sausages, and selected organ meats). Grilled chicken is also on the menu. ✉ *Fernando Celada 176,* ☎ *3/615–7361. AE, MC, V.*

$$ ✕ **Picasso.** Replicas of the namesake artist's masterpieces crowd the walls here, and columns painted deep blue offer a contrast to the polished hardwood floors. Eclectic offerings range from a creamy version of *sopa azteca* (chicken-based soup) to panfried yellowtail snapper, egg rolls, and steak in red wine sauce with tequila butter. The restaurant is across the street from the Plaza Patria mall. ✉ *Av. de las Américas 1939,* ☎ *3/636–6141. AE, MC, V.*

$$ ★ ✕ **Pierrot.** This quiet French dining room offers mouthwatering pâtés followed by seafood, chicken, and beef entrées, among them trout almondine, osso buco, and chicken breast stuffed with pâté in tarragon sauce. Wall-mounted lamps with fringed velvet shades and fresh flowers on each table lend a gracious touch. ✉ *Justo Sierra 2355,* ☎ *3/630–2087 or 3/615–4758. AE, DC, MC, V. Closed Sun.*

$$ ✕ **Sacromonte.** Bullfight posters and photos of the old gypsy section of the city (Sacromonte) line the walls of this spacious, remodeled home, where the food centers on elegant nouvelle Mexican specialties such as vegetable crepes in creamy chili sauce, shrimp in lobster sauce with orange essence, and beef fillet grilled with chili. Dine on or around the leafy patio, accompanied by quiet chamber music. ✉ *Pedro Moreno 1398,* ☎ *3/825–5447. MC, V.*

$ ✕ **Café Madrid.** White-jacketed waiters with black bow ties offer a sharp contrast to the Formica-topped tables and bright orange booths. This downtown institution offers daily lunch specials, as well as hamburgers, sandwiches, traditional Mexican dishes, and absolutely delicious coffee. ✉ *Av. Juárez 264,* ☎ *3/614–9504. No credit cards.*

$ ✕ **Kamilo's 333.** Moments after you sit down, waiters come bearing crisp tostadas, tiny grilled onions, and small bowls of *frijoles* (beans). Now try one of the Mexican-style steaks or the local specialty carne en su jugo. Decor is solidly ranch, with cattle gear and wagon wheels on wood-paneled walls. ✉ *José Clemente Orozco 333,* ☎ *3/825–7869. AE, MC, V.*

$ ✕ **La Chata.** Sombreros, gaily striped serapes, and exquisitely painted plates adorn the white walls of this popular downtown eatery. Start off with guacamole and then savor the zesty *chiles rellenos* (stuffed chili peppers). Or try one of the spicy roasted meat dishes, such as *carne tampiqueña,* served with rice, beans, and enchiladas. Complement your meal with a cool, sweet *horchata,* a drink made from rice and brown sugar simmered in milk and then chilled. ✉ *Av. Corona 126, between López Cotilla and Av. Juárez,* ☎ *3/613–0588. AE, MC, V.*

$ ★ ✕ **La Pianola.** The entrance—through what looks like an open-air kitchen where costumed women are making tortillas—may be misleading to first-timers: In back is a large restaurant and garden with an excellent, varied Mexican menu. Specialties include pozole; *chiles en nogada,* spicy stuffed chili peppers in a walnut cream sauce; and *menudo,* a spicy tripe soup. The signature player-piano music accompanies your meal. ✉ *Av. México 3220,* ☎ *3/813–1385 or 3/813–2412. AE, V.*

$ ★ ✕ **Los Itacates.** Excellently prepared traditional Mexican dishes at more than reasonable prices are what draw diners here. Most entrée items can also be ordered in tacos, so you can try unfamiliar food in small portions. Even the ambience is solidly traditional, with carved wooden chairs and bright pottery. ✉ *Av. Chapultepec Norte 110, between Av. México and Justo Sierra,* ☎ *3/825–1106. MC, V.*

$ ✕ **Restaurant Vegetariano Zanahoria.** The name of this casual dining spot means "carrot," but that's far from the only vegetable on the all-vegetarian menu. Choose from fresh fruit juices, fruit and vegetable salads, soups, and "fish" dishes made from cheese, potatoes, and soy. ✉ *Av. de las Américas 538,* ☎ *3/616–6161. AE, DC, MC, V.*

LODGING

Guadalajara offers a fine variety of hotels in all price ranges. Call ahead if you're apprehensive about noise levels outside your hotel room. Many hotels are located on busy intersections, and you'd be well advised to consult the reservation clerk on the matter of a room away from the hubbub.

The rates given are based on the year-round or peak-season price; off-peak (summer) or promotional rates may be lower. You can expect hotels in the $$$ and $$$$ categories to have purified-water systems and English-language TV channels. Many hotels have begun to install in-room modem lines, so ask when you reserve.

CATEGORY	COST*
$$$$	over $160
$$$	$90–$160
$$	$40–$90
$	under $40

**All prices are for a standard double room, excluding 15% VAT and 2% hotel tax.*

$$$$ ★ **Quinta Real.** Stone and brick walls, colonial arches, and objets d'art highlight all public areas of this luxury hotel on the city's west side. Suites are plush and intimate, with select neocolonial furnishings, including glass-topped writing tables with carved-stone pedestals and fireplaces with marble mantelpieces. Tiled bathrooms have marble sinks and bronze fixtures; some suites have sunken tubs with hot tubs. Deluxe tower accommodations are more lavish, though removed from the lush gardens below. ✉ *Av. México 2727, at López Mateos Sur, 44680,* ☎ *3/615–0000 or 800/3–62–15; 800/445–4565 in the U.S.;* FAX *3/630–1797. 78 suites. Restaurant, piano bar, minibars, no-smoking floor, room service, pool, baby-sitting, laundry service and dry cleaning, concierge, meeting rooms, free parking. AE, DC, MC, V.*

$$$ **Camino Real.** A 15-minute cab ride from downtown will bring you to this sprawling resort located 3 km (2 mi) west of the Minerva Fountain. The rooms are in two-story wings surrounding manicured lawns and tropical gardens. All rooms are large and have placid pastel color schemes, matching bedspreads and curtains, and modern furniture. Those in the rear face busy, noisy Avenida Vallarta. ✉ *Av. Vallarta 5005, 45040,* ☎ *3/121–8000 or 800/9–01–23; 800/722–6466 in the*

U.S.; FAX 3/121–8070. 205 rooms. Restaurant, bar, coffee shop, in-room modem lines, minibars, no-smoking rooms, room service, 5 pools, beauty salon, tennis court, health club, dance club, baby-sitting, playground, laundry service and dry cleaning, concierge, concierge floor, business services, meeting rooms, travel services, free parking. AE, DC, MC, V.

$$$ **Crowne Plaza Guadalajara.** Those who come to Guadalajara for its eternally springlike climate will enjoy the expansive, shaded, well-tended gardens surrounding a large pool and sunbathing area. The rooms have marble baths, upholstered furniture, carpeting, and lots of natural light. Tower rooms offer mountain views. ✉ *Av. López Mateos Sur 2500, 45050, ☎ 3/634–1034 or 800/3–65–55; 800/227–6943 in the U.S.; FAX 3/631–9393. 291 rooms, 4 suites. Restaurant, bar, coffee shop, in-room modem lines, minibars, no-smoking floor, refrigerators, room service, pool, beauty salon, massage, miniature golf, 2 tennis courts, health club, baby-sitting, playground, laundry service and dry cleaning, concierge, concierge floor, business services, meeting rooms, travel services, airport shuttle, car rental, free parking. AE, DC, MC, V.*

$$$ ★ **Fiesta Americana.** The dramatic glass facade of this luxury high-rise faces the Minerva Fountain, on the city's west side. Four glass-enclosed elevators ascend above the 11-story atrium lobby and adjoining **Lobby Bar** to ample, pastel rooms with modern furnishings and panoramic views. The best rooms are on the upper floors, well away from the revelers down in the bar. ✉ *Aurelio Aceves 225, 44110, ☎ 3/825–3434 or 800/5–04–50; 800/343–7821 in the U.S.; FAX 3/630–3725. 391 rooms, 38 suites. Restaurant, bar, coffee shop, in-room modem lines, minibars, no-smoking floor, refrigerators, room service, pool, beauty salon, 2 tennis courts, exercise room, nightclub, baby-sitting, laundry service and dry cleaning, concierge, concierge floor, business services, meeting rooms, travel services, car rental, free parking. AE, DC, MC, V.*

$$$ **Presidente Inter-Continental.** Spacious, carpeted rooms surround the plush 12-story atrium lobby of this imposing pyramidical structure. For the best city view, request a room on an upper floor facing the Plaza del Sol shopping center. There's a Tane silver shop on the premises, and guests may use nearby golf and tennis facilities. ✉ *Av. López Mateos Sur and Moctezuma, 45050, ☎ 3/678–1234 or 800/3–63–30; 800/327–0200 in the U.S.; FAX 3/678–1222. 414 rooms, 44 suites. Restaurant, bar, coffee shop, in-room modem lines, minibars, refrigerators, room service, pool, beauty salon, massage, spa, health club, shops, baby-sitting, laundry service and dry cleaning, concierge, concierge floor, business services, meeting rooms, travel services, airport shuttle, car rental, free parking. AE, DC, MC, V.*

$$ **Carlton.** This modern 20-story tower hotel on the edge of downtown offers oversize rooms with light beige walls and ceilings and matching pale turquoise curtains and bedspreads. Ivy-draped walls surround the rear gardens and fountain. Though the hotel is convenient for tourists, it caters to the business traveler. The upper floors offer a spectacular city view and a retreat from the horrendous street noise. ✉ *Av. Niños Héroes 125, at Av. 16 de Septiembre, 44100, ☎ 3/614–7272; 800/3–62–44 in Mexico; FAX 3/613–5539. 212 rooms, 10 suites. Restaurant, 2 bars, air-conditioning, no-smoking floor, room service, pool, beauty salon, sauna, health club, dance club, laundry service and dry cleaning, concierge floor, meeting rooms, travel services, free parking. AE, DC, MC, V.*

$$ **De Mendoza.** Mature travelers and tour groups from the United States and Canada often choose this downtown hotel because of its convenient location—on a quiet side street just one block from the Teatro Degollado—and charming postcolonial architecture and ambience. Beamed ceilings, hand-sculpted wood furniture and doors, and wrought-iron railings decorate public areas and rooms. ✉ *Venustiano Car-*

ranza 16, 44100, ☎ 3/613–4646 or 800/3–61–26; 800/221–6509 in the U.S.; FAX 3/613–7310. 89 rooms, 15 suites. Restaurant, air-conditioning, in-room modem lines, no-smoking rooms, room service, pool, laundry service and dry cleaning. AE, DC, MC, V.

$$ **Diana.** Mexican and European tourists favor this six-story hotel, located two blocks from the Minerva Fountain. The white-stucco lobby adjoins a small lounge and busy restaurant. Standard-size rooms have white-on-white walls and ceilings with brightly patterned curtains and bedspreads. The quietest rooms are on the upper floors in the rear; some suites have private saunas. ✉ *Circunvalacíon Agustín Yáñez 2760, 44100, ☎ 3/615–5510 or 800/3–67–89; FAX 3/630–3685. 134 rooms, 21 suites. Restaurant, bar, coffee shop, air-conditioning, room service, pool, baby-sitting, laundry service and dry cleaning, concierge floor, business services, meeting rooms, airport shuttle, free parking. AE, DC, MC, V.*

$$ ★ **Francés.** Guadalajara's oldest hotel (1610) was declared a national monument in 1981 following extensive restoration and renovation. Stone columns and colonial arches surround a three-story enclosed atrium lobby with a polished marble fountain and cut-crystal chandeliers. Though room sizes vary, all share a colonial ambience, with white stucco walls, polished wood floors, and high-beamed ceilings. For the best city views (though there's a slight noise trade-off), ask for a room facing Calle Maestranza. ✉ *Maestranza 35, 44100, ☎ 3/613–1190 or 3/613–0917, FAX 3/658–2831. 52 rooms, 8 suites. Restaurant, bar, fans, room service, dance club, laundry service and dry cleaning, meeting room, car rental, free parking. AE, DC, MC, V.*

$$ **Plaza Del Sol.** Location and price make families, young adults, and tour groups head for this two-building hotel at the south end of the Plaza del Sol shopping center. Rooms—all modern and carpeted—and public areas are painted glossy white trimmed in aquamarine, beige, or green. Accommodations in the cylindrical tower are a bit larger and have a view of the shopping center below. ✉ *Avs. López Mateos and Mariano Otero, 45050, ☎ 3/647–8790 or 800/3–66–80; 800/882–8215 in the U.S.; FAX 3/122–9685. 357 rooms, 14 suites. Restaurant, bar, coffee shop, air-conditioning, room service, pool, beauty salon, baby-sitting, laundry service and dry cleaning, concierge floor, meeting rooms, travel services, free parking. AE, DC, MC, V.*

$$ **Posada Guadalajara.** Rooms in this colonial-style hotel open onto airy, wrought-iron railed hallways overlooking the small patio and circular pool that spouts an enormous stone fountain. Accommodations are clean and comfortable, with carved wood furniture. In addition to its loyal international patrons, the Posada welcomes visiting sports teams, so evenings here may seem either festive or raucous. The hotel is just south of Calzada Lázaro Cárdenas, about 1½ km (1 mi) northeast of Plaza del Sol. ✉ *Av. López Mateos Sur 1280, 45040, ☎ 3/121–2022, FAX 3/122–1834. 153 rooms, 27 suites. Restaurant, bar, air-conditioning, room service, pool, beauty salon, baby-sitting, laundry service and dry cleaning, concierge floor, meeting rooms, free parking. AE, DC, MC, V.*

$$ **Santiago de Compostela.** This cozy downtown hotel in a converted older building is across from the Parque San Francisco and offers modern, carpeted accommodations with a sea-green color scheme. Rooms overlooking the park—where you can watch worshipers file into the two colonial churches—have tall, narrow windows with metal grillwork; inside, all rooms open onto an atrium painted in turquoise, tan, and lavender. ✉ *Colón 272, 44100, ☎ 3/613–8880 or 800/3–65–53; FAX 3/658–1925. 100 rooms, 5 suites. Restaurant, bar, air-conditioning, room service, pool, baby-sitting, laundry service and dry cleaning, free parking. AE, MC, V.*

$ 🏨 **Posada San Pablo.** Inside a renovated white-stucco house (look for the large painting of Our Lady of Guadalupe above the door) are tidy, though slightly threadbare, rooms with private or shared bath. The friendly, eager-to-please owners have decorated the freshly painted lobby courtyard with brightly colored photographs of Guadalajara. For little over $1 per day, you can have kitchen privileges. ✉ *Madero 429, between Donato Guerra and Ocampo, 44100,* ☎ *3/614–2811. 14 rooms. Coin laundry. No credit cards.*

$ 🏨 **San Francisco.** Though located on a quiet downtown side street, you can't miss the attractive pale orange walls of this restored two-story colonial-style building. The lushly planted courtyard makes a pleasant sitting area, and brightly polished copper lamps lend a delightful sparkle to the simply furnished, earth-tone rooms. ✉ *Degollado 267, 44100,* ☎ *3/613–8954,* FAX *3/613–3257. 74 rooms, 2 suites. Restaurant, air-conditioning, room service, baby-sitting, laundry service and dry cleaning, free parking. AE, MC, V.*

Spa

$$ 🏨 **Rancho Río Caliente.** Many activities at this health resort and vegetarian, alcohol-free spa are literally in hot water—therapeutic hot mineral water. Steam away your tensions and body toxins, then dip into a mineral water–filled swimming pool. The resort offers spare but comfortable accommodations, facials, mud packs, t'ai chi instruction, hiking, horseback riding, and classes in yoga and body awareness. Rates include three meals a day and activities; treatments, trips, and horseback riding are extra. Río Caliente is off Highway 15, 30 km (19 mi) northwest of the Minerva Fountain; bookings must be prepaid to the U.S. office via personal or traveler's check. ✉ *Apdo. 5-67, Zapopan, Jal. 43042,* ☎ *3/615–7800 answering service in Guadalajara; U.S. reservations:* ✉ *Box 897, Millbrae, CA 94030,* ☎ *415/615–9543,* FAX *415/615–0601. 50 rooms. Restaurant, 4 pools, massage, spa, travel services. No credit cards.*

NIGHTLIFE AND THE ARTS

Guadalajara is an active cultural and performing arts center, offering excellent local talent and well-known artists and entertainers from abroad. The U.S. and Canadian communities have also developed a schedule of English-language cultural events. Besides the selections listed below, many cafés along Avenida Chapultepec have live music—usually singers and guitarists—in the afternoon and evening.

The Arts

Dance

Ballet Folklórico of the University of Guadalajara. The university's nationally acclaimed troupe offers traditional Mexican folkloric dances and music in the Teatro Degollado every Sunday at 10 AM. ☎ *3/614–4773 or 3/616–4991.* 🎫 *$2–$11.*

Performance Venues

Cine Cinematógrafo. Founded by two Guadalajara-area movie buffs, this theater often presents English-language films with Spanish subtitles. It's two blocks west of the Museo de las Artes de la Universidad de Guadalajara. ✉ *Av. Vallarta 1102,* ☎ *3/825–0514.*

Ex-Convento del Carmen. Music groups of all types perform on the spacious patio of the former convent of Our Lady of Mt. Carmel. There's also a café, spacious art gallery, and small bookshop. It's 6½ blocks west of Avenida 16 de Septiembre. ✉ *Av. Juárez 638,* ☎ *3/614–7184.*

Instituto Cultural Cabañas. Large-scale theater, dance, and musical performances take place on a patio within the institute. The Tolsá Chapel hosts more intimate events, and subtitled English-language films are often shown in a movie theater. ✉ *Calle Cabañas 8, at Plaza Tapatía,* ☎ *3/617–4322 or 3/617–4440.*

Plaza de Armas. The State Band of Jalisco plays here every Thursday and Sunday evening at 6:30. On Tuesday evening, the **Municipal Band of Guadalajara** performs at 6:30. ✉ *Av. Corona between Morelos and Pedro Moreno, across from Palacio de Gobierno.*

Teatro Degollado. Nationally and internationally famous artists perform here throughout the year. The refurbished velvet seats are comfortable, the acoustics are excellent, and the central air-conditioning is a treat. ✉ *Av. Degollado and Belén,* ☎ *3/614–4773.*

Symphony

Orquesta Filarmónica de Jalisco. Conducted by Maestro José Guadalupe Flores, performances take place Sunday and Friday at the Teatro Degollado (☞ *above*). ☎ *3/658–3812.*

Nightlife

Guadalajara is not known for its nightlife. The nightclubs in major hotels provide good local entertainment and, occasionally, internationally known performers. The best hotel clubs are the Fiesta Americana's sleek **Lobby Bar,** dotted with small tables and offering pop and mariachi-style music, and the **Caballo Negro** dance club, with live entertainment; **La Diligencia,** a romantic spot in the Camino Real featuring tropical and other music for dancing; and the Crowne Plaza's **Manglar,** a sort of jungle theme park (including waiters in pith helmets and hunters' garb), with game room, large-screen TV, and Latin and mariachi music for dancing.

As in the coffeehouses of the 1960s, patrons sit around a small stage at **Peña Cuicacalli** (✉ Av. Niños Héroes 1988, on the traffic circle, ☎ 3/825–4690) and listen nightly to jazz, blues, and folk, or Latin American music; call to check performance times. **La Peñita** (✉ Av. Vallarta 1110, ☎ 3/825–5853) presents similar music Tuesday through Saturday at 9 PM and Sunday at 6:30 PM in an airy patio setting, while **El Solar** (✉ Av. de la Paz 1840, ☎ 3/825–3168) offers the same fare after 8 PM daily on the patio of a turn-of-the-century house.

Dance Clubs and Discos

You can dance most of the night to live Latin music at the multilevel **Tropigala** (✉ Av. López Mateos Sur and Iztaccíhuatl, across from Plaza del Sol shopping center, ☎ 3/122–5553 or 3/122–7903) or **Co-Co & Co-Co** at the Fenix hotel downtown (✉ Av. Corona 160, ☎ 3/614–5714). The spare **Casino Veracruz** (✉ Manzano 486, ☎ 3/613–4422), also downtown, offers top-quality live music for serious Latin-style dancers; it's open Wednesday through Sunday, 9 PM–4 AM; Thursday and Sunday the music starts at 7 PM.

Two good downtown discos are **Maxim's** in the Francés (☞ Lodging, *above*) and the **Factory** in the Plaza Del Sol (☞ Lodging, *above*; ☎ 3/658–2831) and the Hotel Aranzazú (✉ Av. Revolución 110, ☎ 3/613–3232).

OUTDOOR ACTIVITIES AND SPORTS

Spectator Sports

Bullfights

Corridas (bullfights) begin at 4:30 PM at **Plaza Nuevo Progreso**; they're usually held on Sundays in October and November. You can buy tickets for either the *sol* (sunny) or *sombra* (shady) side of the bullring. Since the action begins in the late afternoon, opt for the cheaper seats on the sunny side. You can buy tickets at the bullring (about 5 km [3 mi] northeast of downtown) or at the Plaza del Sol, Plaza México, and Gran Plaza shopping centers. ✉ *Calzada Independencia Norte across from Estadio Jalisco,* ☎ *3/637–9982 or 3/651–8506.* 🎫 *About $3.35–$32.*

Charreadas

Charreadas (traditional Mexican rodeos) take place at the **Lienzo Charros de Jalisco** every Sunday at noon. The *charros* (cowboys) compete in 10 events; mariachis perform during breaks. ✉ *Av. Dr. R. Michel 577, next to Parque Agua Azul,* ☎ *3/619–0315.* 🎫 *About $2.70.*

Soccer

You can see afternoon and evening professional soccer matches at **Estadio Jalisco.** Schedules vary with the team. ✉ *Calzada Independencia Norte, across from bullring,* ☎ *3/637–0563.* 🎫 *80¢–$13.35, depending on the team.*

Participant Sports

Fitness Clubs

The **Presidente Inter-Continental** (☎ 3/678–1234) fitness club is open to nonguests for a fee. At **Nuevo Gold's Gym** (✉ Av. Xóchitl 4203, near Plaza del Sol shopping center, ☎ 3/647–0420) guest passes are available for about $3.35 per day.

Golf

Golf clubs that admit foreign travelers upon payment of a greens fee include **Atlas Golf Club** (✉ Carretera Guadalajara-Chapala, across from Montenegro Park, ☎ 3/689–2620 or 3/689–2783), **Las Cañadas Country Club** (✉ Carretera a Saltillo, Km 14.5, ☎ 3/685–0170, 3/685–0420, or 3/685–0412), the **Chula Vista Country Club** (✉ Paseo de Golf 5, near Lake Chapala, ☎ 376/5–22–81), and the **Club de Golf Santa Anita** (✉ Carretera a Morelia, Km 6.5, ☎ 3/686–0361 or 3/686–0386).

Ice-Skating

The **Iceland Pista de Hielo** (✉ Av. México 2582, ☎ 3/615–4438) offers daily one-hour public ice-skating sessions, as well as classes. There's also a restaurant and ice-cream parlor.

Tennis

The **Crowne Plaza Guadalajara** (☎ 3/634–1034) and **Camino Real** (☎ 3/121–8000) allow nonguests to use their courts for a fee. The municipal courts at **Parque Avila Camacho** (✉ Av. Avila Camacho, just south of Plaza Patria shopping mall, no phone) can be used for a nominal entrance fee.

SHOPPING

Shoppers in Guadalajara can choose from a broad variety of high-quality merchandise at low prices. Of course, you will also find low-quality products at high prices, so *caveat emptor.* Store hours are generally Monday–Saturday 9–8, Sunday 10–2; stores in shopping malls do not generally close for lunch. Street markets, or *tianguis,* are set up every day throughout the Guadalajara area; you never know what you'll find. The local newspaper *Siglo 21* lists locations daily.

The major areas for shopping in the city are outlined below; those interested in traditional arts and crafts should visit Tlaquepaque and Tonalá (☞ Side Trips, *below*).

Malls

In Guadalajara, as in all other major cities, shopping malls are springing up everywhere; the metropolitan area now has more than 30. **El Charro,** an excellent leather-goods store, has branches in La Gran Plaza and Plaza del Sol as well as downtown. **Gepetto's,** in Plaza del Sol, offers exquisite handmade wooden toys.

La Gran Plaza. A sleek three-story glass-and-steel exterior houses 334 commercial spaces and a 14-plex cinema. It's just east of the Guadalajara Chamber of Commerce and the Camino Real hotel, on the city's far west side. ✉ *Av. Vallarta 3959,* ☎ *3/122–3004.* ⏲ *Daily 10–8:30.*

Plaza del Sol. The city's largest mall sprawls like a park, with 270 commercial spaces, outdoor patios, trees and garden areas, and parking for 2,100 cars. It's across from the Presidente Inter-Continental hotel. ✉ *Avs. López Mateos Sur and Mariano Otero,* ☎ *3/121–5950.* ⏲ *Weekdays 10–8, Sat. 10–9, Sun. 10–7.*

Plaza Galería del Calzado. The 60 stores in this west-side complex all sell shoes. Guadalajara is one of Mexico's leading shoe centers, and high-quality footwear and accessories are available here, many at lower prices than in the States. ✉ *Av. México and Juan Palomar y Arias (formerly Yáquis),* ☎ *3/647–6422.* ⏲ *Mon.–Sat. 11–9, Sun. 11–8:30.*

Plaza México. There is room for 120 commercial establishments in the city's second most popular shopping mall, seven blocks west of the Plaza Galería del Calzado. ✉ *Av. México 3300,* ☎ *3/813–2488.* ⏲ *Daily 10–8.*

Markets and Handicrafts

Calle Esteban Alatorre. Several blocks of shoe stores—all reasonably priced—line this street. ✉ *East of Calzada Independencia Norte and 4 blocks north of Av. Hidalgo.*

Casa de las Artesanías de Jalisco. Run by the state government, this store offers a wide selection of the exquisite blown glass and hand-painted pottery typical of Jalisco artisans. There are also fine crafts from other parts of Mexico. Everything is sold at fixed prices. ✉ *Calzadas Independencia Sur and González Gallo, next to Parque Agua Azul,* ☎ *3/619–4664.* ⏲ *Weekdays 10–6, Sat. 11–5, Sun. 11–3.*

El Baratillo. This is one of the world's largest flea markets. Thirty city blocks are lined with stalls, tents, and blankets piled high with new, used, and antique merchandise. ✉ *On and around Calle Esteban Loera, some 15 blocks east of Mercado Libertad.* ⏲ *Sun. 7–5.*

Mercado Libertad. Also known as the Mercado San Juan de Dios, the Liberty Market is one of Latin America's largest enclosed markets. Within a three-square-block area you can browse through more than 1,000 privately owned stalls selling everything from clothing to crafts to live animals and gold watches. ✉ *Calzada Independencia Sur between Dionisio Rodríguez and Av. Javier Mina.* ⏲ *Daily 10–8.*

SIDE TRIPS

Tequila

56 km (35 mi) northwest of Guadalajara.

For a close look at how Mexico's most famous liquor is made from the spiny blue agave cacti that grow in the fields alongside the highway, spend part or all of a day in this tidy village. Centuries ago the Tiquilas, a small Nahuatl-speaking tribe, were said to have discovered that the heart of the agave produced a juice that could be fermented to make various intoxicating drinks. When distilled (an innovation introduced after the arrival of the Spanish in the 16th century), the fermented liquid turns into the now-famous heady liquor. You can tour the famous Sauza Distillery or one of the other modern tequila distilleries here. Follow the signs, and plan to arrive on a weekday between 10 AM and 1 PM. Frequent bus service is available from Guadalajara's Old Bus Station, and various Guadalajara tour companies offer guided excursions (☞ Guadalajara A to Z, *below*).

Around Lake Chapala

Perhaps it is the Mexican arts and culture, perhaps the favorable exchange rate, or perhaps the springlike climate; whatever the reason, more than 25,000 U.S. and Canadian citizens have retired in the Guadalajara area. The majority reside along the shores of Lake Chapala, Mexico's largest inland lake.

The jagged mountains that ring the lake make it seem a world away from Guadalajara. The tranquillity of the area offers a welcome contrast to bustling Guadalajara. Sunsets are spectacular, and there's just enough humidity to keep the abundant bougainvillea blooming and ensure no drastic temperature fluctuations. Unfortunately, the lake is polluted and fighting an ongoing battle with *lirio* (water hyacinth), a succulent plant that threatens to cover much of the water surface. Water levels continue to shrink to alarming lows, while demand from Guadalajara, which the lake supplies with water, remains high.

Spanish settlement in the area dates from 1538, when Franciscan friar Miguel de Bolonio arrived and began to convert the Taltica Indians to Christianity. Their chief was named Chapalac, from which the name Chapala is said to have originated. Today, Chapala is the area's largest settlement; 8 km (5 mi) to the west, the more tranquil village of Ajijic has been home to expatriate artists and writers since the 1920s. The towns and villages along the lake are linked by one highway with multiple names, such as Carretera Chapala-Ajijic or Carretera Ajijic-Jocotepec.

Chapala

45 km (28 mi) south of Guadalajara.

With Chapala's proximity to rapidly growing Guadalajara, as well as its comfortable climate, it is surprising that tourists did not frequent the area until the late 19th century. Then-president Porfirio Díaz heard that aristocrats had discovered this ideal place for weekend getaways and he began spending holidays here in 1904. Soon summer homes were built, and in 1910 the Chapala Yacht Club opened. Word of the town, with its lavish lawn parties and magnificent estates, spread quickly to the United States and Europe.

Nowadays the town of Chapala has a population of some 35,000 and attracts a less influential but equally fun-loving assortment of visitors. On weekends the streets are filled with Mexican families. Throughout the week American and Canadian retirees stroll along the lakeside promenade, play golf, and relax on the verandas of downtown restaurants.

Avenida Madero, lined with pleasant restaurants, shops, and cafés, is the town's main drag. On Madero four blocks north of the lake, the
20 **plaza,** at the corner of López Cotilla, is a relaxing spot for townspeople and tourists to sit and read the paper. Two blocks south of the plaza,
21 the **Iglesia de San Francisco** is easy to spot by the blue neon crosses on its twin steeples. The church was built in 1528 and reconstructed in 1580.
22 On weekends, the tranquil lakeside **Parque la Cristianía,** on the south side of the malecón, fills with Tapatíos taking a respite from the city and browsing the ever-present souvenir booths. At the end of the park are a small handicrafts market and a number of open-air cafés featuring *pescado blanco,* the white fish native to the lake. Because of pollution, we do not recommend that you partake of this regional delicacy, though other food is fine.

23 A visit to **Isla de los Alacranes** (Scorpion Island) is a popular excursion from the Chapala pier at the end of Avenida Madero. The view of the shore area is enchanting. From the same pier, you can also take
24 a trip to **Isla de Mezcala,** about 12 km (7½ mi) northeast of Isla de los Alacranes, and explore the ruins of a fortress that housed a band of rebels during the early 19th-century war of independence with Spain. Depending on the duration of the trip, the price ranges from about $9.35 to $60 for a launch with a capacity of eight adults.

DINING AND LODGING

$$ ✕ **Beer Garden.** Enjoy the expansive lake view while you eat one of the tasty seafood, chicken, or beef specialties. ✉ *Paseo Ramón Corona at northwest corner of Av. Madero,* ☎ *376/5–22–57. AE, MC, V.*

$ ✕ **Restaurant Cazadores.** This grandly turreted building was once the summer home of the Braniff family, owners of the now-defunct airline. Enjoy a cool liquid refreshment and watch the action along the malecón. (You can skip the main courses, which focus on meats and fish.) ✉ *Av. Madero and Paseo Ramón Corona, northeast corner,* ☎ *376/5–21–62. AE, MC, V. Closed Mon.*

$$$ ★ **Quinta Quetzalcóatl.** Behind 12-ft stone walls, the "QQ" is located on the grounds of the villa where D.H. Lawrence wrote *The Plumed Serpent* in the 1920s. Owners Dick and Barbi Henderson have restored and enlarged the property and furnished it with colorful antiques; guests also enjoy a living-dining room and lush tropical gardens. Rates include breakfast (except on Sunday); for high-season, seven-day packages, two gourmet dinners and one barbecue are also included. There's a three-night minimum, and a deposit is required by check, preferably through the U.S. office. ✉ *Zaragoza 307, 45900,* ☎ *376/5–36–53,* FAX *376/5–34–44;* ☎ *800/577–2555,* FAX *415/898–1184 in the U.S.; payments to:* ✉ *Box 27, Point Richmond, CA 94807. 8 suites. 2 bars, pool, hot tub, library, meeting room. No credit cards.*

$ **Hotel Nido.** The oldest hotel on the lake was built in the early 1900s to accommodate President Porfírio Díaz and his entourage. In the 1940s Mexican film star María Félix spent the first of her numerous honeymoons here, and the whitewashed high-ceiling lobby still feels like the scene of a melodrama waiting to happen. Photos of turn-of-the-century Chapala adorn the walls, and there's a picturesque patio and garden in the rear. However, rooms are strictly functional, and only the ones in the front have TVs. ✉ *Av. Madero 202, 45900,* ☎ *376/5–21–16. 30 rooms. Restaurant, bar, room service, pool, laundry service and dry cleaning, free parking. MC, V.*

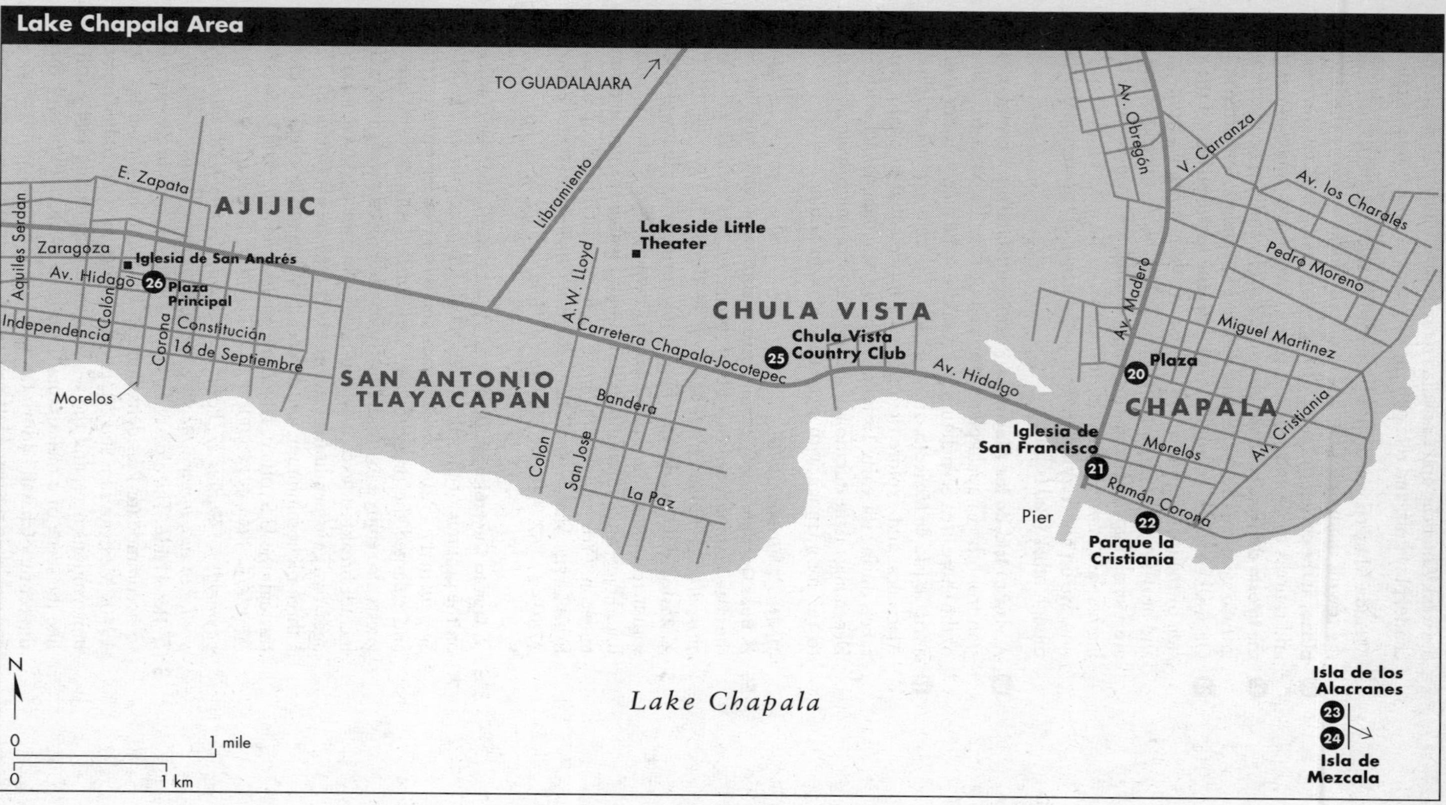
Lake Chapala Area
TO GUADALAJARA
E. Zapata
AJIJIC
Aquiles Serdan
Zaragoza
Iglesia de San Andrés
Av. Hidago
26 Plaza Principal
Colón
Corona
Independencia
Constitución
16 de Septiembre
Morelos
Libramiento
Lakeside Little Theater
A.W. Lloyd
Carretera Chapala-Jocotepec
CHULA VISTA
25 Chula Vista Country Club
SAN ANTONIO TLAYACAPAN
Bandera
Colon
San Jose
La Paz
Av. Hidalgo
Av. Obregón
V. Carranza
Av. los Charales
Pedro Moreno
Miguel Martinez
Av. Madero
20 Plaza
CHAPALA
Av. Cristiania
Iglesia de San Francisco
21
Morelos
Ramón Corona
Pier
22 Parque la Cristianía
N
0 1 mile
0 1 km
Lake Chapala
Isla de los Alacranes
23
24
Isla de Mezcala

$ **Hotel Villa Montecarlo.** Look out on spacious lawns, complete with strolling peacocks, high on a hill above the lake. The comfortable rooms, in three-story contiguous units, have carved wooden furniture and light multicolored bedspreads. The two swimming pools are filled with natural thermal water. ✉ *Hidalgo 296, about 1 km (½ mi) west of Av. Madero, 45900,* ☎ FAX *376/5–22–16, 376/5–21–20, or 376/5–20–24. 46 rooms, 1 suite. Restaurant, bar, room service, 2 pools, laundry service and dry cleaning, free parking. AE, MC, V.*

Chula Vista

3 km (2 mi) west of Chapala.

Chula Vista, the most American colony in Mexico, lies between Chapala and Ajijic. Dozens of condos dot the hillside north of the road.

25 The **Chula Vista Country Club** (✉ Paseo de Golf 5, ☎ 376/5–22–81) is a favorite of the local *norteamericano* community. The "billy-goat" golf course here—open to nonmembers who pay the greens fee—affords great vistas of the lake as well as a workout, since the rugged terrain cannot be negotiated by golf cart.

DINING

$ ✕ **Chicken Little.** As its name suggests, this place serves infinite varieties of chicken (chicken lasagna, anyone?) as well as American-style pies and cakes. You know the birds are fresh—you're right next door to Puritan Poultry. ✉ *Carretera Chapala-Ajijic 101, in Riberas del Pilar subdivision,* ☎ *376/5–43–99. No credit cards. Closed Sun.*

NIGHTLIFE AND THE ARTS

Just west of Chula Vista, above the PAL Trailer Park and next to the Oak Hill High School, is the 112-seat **Lakeside Little Theater** (☎ 376/6–09–54), which stages English-language musicals and plays throughout the year. Box office hours are 10 AM to 1 PM starting three days before performances and during the run of any show.

Ajijic

8 km (5 mi) west of Chapala.

Despite blocks of galleries and crafts shops, Ajijic's small-town ambience is still defined by its narrow cobblestone streets, whitewashed buildings, and gentle pace. Still, the foreign influence is unmistakable: English is spoken almost as widely here as Spanish, and license plates run the gamut from Alaska to Texas.

26 Most visitors park near the **Plaza Principal** (also called the Plaza de Armas or Jardín), the tree- and flower-filled central square. The **Iglesia de San Andrés** (Church of St. Andrew) sits on the Jardín's north side. In late November the plaza fills for the saint's nine-day fiesta, including fireworks, parades, music, and dancing.

Walk down Calle Morelos (the continuation of Avenida Colón) toward the lake and you'll find stores and boutiques that sell everything from designer fashions to traditional arts and crafts.

DINING AND LODGING

In addition to the establishments listed below, there are other good-quality lodgings in the area. Consult the tourist office in Chapala, the *Ojo del Lago* newspaper, or the *Guadalajara Colony Reporter.* Be aware: Restaurants in Ajijic often seem to come and go yearly.

$$ ★ ✕ **Ajijic Grill.** Savor Japanese specialties prepared table-side, grilled meats, seafood, and fresh salads (quite safe) in an airy, partially roofed patio. ✉ *Morelos 5,* ☎ *376/6–24–58. MC, V. Closed Sun.*

$ ✕ **La Mandrágora.** No magical mandrakes (*mandrágoras*) grow here, but the verdant sculpture garden still casts a delightful spell. The menu offers sandwiches, seafood, and such entrées as chicken with mango and grilled beef fillet with vegetable stuffing. ✉ *Colón 43,* ☎ *376/6–19–20. No credit cards. Closed Mon.–Thurs.*

$ ✕ **Manix.** Soft lighting, brick-and-white-plaster walls, and the quiet location lend a homey touch to your excellently prepared meal. Five daily fixed-price offerings—usually meat or poultry—include soup or salad, entrée, dessert, and coffee or tea. ✉ *Ocampo 57,* ☎ *376/6–00–61. MC, V. Closed Sun.*

$$ ★ ✕ **La Nueva Posada.** Luxuriant gardens framed in bougainvillea overlook the lake at this charming inn, run by a gracious Canadian family. The spacious, airy, and well-lit rooms have colonial furniture and original watercolors. Chef Lorraine Rousseau's eclectic menu is delicious, and there is fine entertainment most evenings, typically an American jazz trio or tropical music. ✉ *Donato Guerra 9, Apdo. 30, 45920,* ☎ *376/6–14–44,* ☎ FAX *376/6–13–44. 17 suites. Restaurant, bar, fans, room service, pool, laundry service and dry cleaning, free parking. MC, V.*

$$ **Real de Chapala.** Suites here are airy and ample, and some have small individual swimming pools. The Sunday mariachi lunch is popular with weekend visitors from Guadalajara. ✉ *Paseo del Prado 20, 45920,* ☎ *376/6–00–14, 376/6–00–21, or 376/6–00–28;* FAX *376/6–00–25; reservations in Guadalajara at the Hoteles Real (✉ La Villita 78, Colonia Chapalita, Zapopan, 45080,* ☎ *3/121–8878,* FAX *3/122–1936). 79 suites. Restaurant, bar, fans, no-smoking rooms, room service, pool, wading pool, tennis court, volleyball, baby-sitting, laundry service and dry cleaning, meeting rooms, free parking. AE, MC, V.*

$$ **Villa del Gallo Cantador.** Host Robert Hocking has furnished his sprawling hilltop home—"Villa of the Crowing Rooster"—with eye-catching antiques and carved furniture. All rooms have magnificent views, and two have private kitchens and TVs. ✉ *Av. Colón 117 (mail to Apdo. Postal 252), 45920,* ☎ FAX *376/6–03–08. 4 rooms. Pool, free parking. No credit cards.*

NIGHTLIFE AND THE ARTS

The rambling, hacienda-style **Posada Ajijic** (✉ Calle Morelos, facing the lake, ☎ 376/6–07–44 or 376/6–04–30), closed Monday, is a restaurant, bar, and popular weekend dance place with a spectacular water view. Dance clubs and nightspots come and go quickly here; ask about the latest craze at your hotel or the tourist office.

SHOPPING

Though Ajijic does not have as many boutiques and crafts shops as inhabitants, it sometimes seems that way. **Casa de la Tortuga** (✉ Marcos Castellanos 4, no phone) sells high-end crafts, beadwork, and lovely watercolors by local artists. **Casa de las Artesanías Ajijik** (✉ Carretera Chapala-Jocotepec, Km 6.5, ☎ 376/6–05–48) is a branch of the state-run Casa de las Artesanías de Jalisco crafts shop (☞ Guadalajara Shopping, *above*). Inside the bright yellow building of **La Colección Bárbara** (✉ Av. Colón 30, ☎ 376/6–10–65) are traditional crafts, antiques, and fine furniture. **La Colección Moon** (✉ Río Zula 4, just south of Ocampo, ☎ 376/6–10–00) features a selection of owner Billy Moon's lamps, wrought-iron furniture, and other decorative items, as well as an international-style restaurant (☎ 376/6–18–00), closed Monday. **Mi México** (✉ Morelos 8, ☎ 376/6–01–33) boutique sells pottery, blown glass, women's clothing, and other crafts and gifts.

SPORTS

Take a break with the kids—or pretend you're one again—and explore the **Tobolandia** water park. ✉ *Carretera Chapala-Ajijic, Km 7,* ☎ *376/6–21–20.*

San Juan Cosalá

10 km (6½ mi) west of Chapala.

San Juan Cosalá is known for its natural thermal-water spas located on the shores of Lake Chapala, with the mountains rising to the north. The **Hotel Balneario San Juan Cosalá** (☎ 376/3–03–02) welcomes both day-trippers and overnight guests to its four large swimming pools and two wading pools. The **Villas Buenaventura Cosalá** (☎ 376/1–02–22) only accepts overnight guests. Facilities here include six one-bedroom furnished suites and 11 with two bedrooms, all with kitchenettes, TVs, and thermal-water bathtubs; there are also thermal hot tubs and swimming pools. ✉ *Apdo. Postal 181, Chapala, Jalisco 45900 is reservations address for both hotels.*

Lake Chapala A to Z

ARRIVING AND DEPARTING

By Bus. There is frequent bus service to Chapala, Ajijic, and other lakeside towns from Guadalajara's **Antigua Central Camionera** (Old Bus Station) and the **Chapala bus station.**

By Car. From downtown Guadalajara take Avenida Federalismo south to Calzada Lázaro Cárdenas, turn left, and continue southeast. Follow the signs as Lázaro Cárdenas converges with the Carretera a Chapala, whose route number is both 23 and 44; the trip takes 50 minutes.

ENGLISH-LANGUAGE PUBLICATIONS

The *Ojo del Lago* monthly newspaper is available free of charge throughout town. The *Guadalajara Colony Reporter* weekly newspaper (☞ Contacts and Resources *in* Guadalajara A to Z, *below*) devotes a section to lakeside news and events. **Libros de Chapala,** across from the plaza on Avenida Madero in Chapala, has an extensive range of English-language magazines, with some newspapers and books. In Ajijic, **Portalibros** offers a wide selection of used books in English (Constitución 2A, no phone); closed Monday.

VISITOR INFORMATION

The **Jalisco state tourism office** (✉ Aquiles Serdán 26, ☎ 376/5–31–41) has a branch in Chapala; open weekdays 9–7, weekends 9–1.

In Ajijic, the nonprofit **Lake Chapala Society** (✉ Av. 16 de Septiembre, No. 16A, no phone), open Monday–Saturday 10–1, provides information about the area.

Sierra de Manantlán Biosphere Reserve

144 km (90 mi) southwest of Guadalajara.

Consider this trip if you are a confirmed nature lover. The 345,000-acre Sierra de Manantlán Biosphere Reserve is a vast nature preserve high in the Sierra Madre del Sur, near the town of Autlán de Navarro. Oak and pine forests abound, with hiking paths lined by bright-colored wildflowers. Stand at a mountain lookout and on a clear day you can see all the way to the Pacific beach resort of Manzanillo. The area was incorporated into the United Nations worldwide chain of biosphere reserves in 1987 and is administered by the University of Guadalajara, which runs a research outpost here.

Accommodations here are rustic and the food simple but filling. You must reserve space in advance, preferably with a group; unaccompanied, unannounced guests are not permitted. For more information or to apply for a three-day group tour, contact the reserve's Guadalajara office (✉ Juan Manuel 130 or Apdo. Postal 1-3933, Guadalajara, Jalisco 44100, ☎ 3/613–4938, ☎ FAX 3/613–8256). Guadalajara-area writer and guide Tony Burton (✉ Apdo. Postal 79, Jocotepec, Jalisco 45800, ☎ FAX 376/3–04–92) also arranges and leads excellent group tours. The reserve may only be visited during parts of the dry season, from late September through March; at other times, the roads are impassable. The trip to Autlán de Navarro takes several hours, after which it takes another two to three hours—in a four-wheel-drive vehicle—to get to the preserve.

Tlaquepaque and Tonalá

For inveterate shoppers, a combined visit to the crafts meccas of Tlaquepaque and Tonalá makes a perfect day trip from Guadalajara. There's at least one bed-and-breakfast in Tlaquepaque if you really want to shop until you drop, but it's easy enough to return to the wider selection of lodgings in Guadalajara.

Tlaquepaque

7 km (4½ mi) southeast of downtown Guadalajara.

Tlaquepaque is known throughout Mexico as an arts-and-crafts center; among its offerings are intricate blown-glass miniatures; exquisite hand-painted pottery; jewelry, silver, and copperware; leather and hand-carved wood furniture; and handwoven clothing. More than 300 shops line pedestrian malls and plazas in this charming town, which is also said to be the birthplace of mariachi music.

Distinctive hand-painted pottery, sold in stores throughout the town, was first fashioned by nearby Tonaltecan Indians in the mid-16th century. The small village remained virtually isolated until June 13, 1821, when local authorities met here to sign a regional proclamation of independence from Spain. Soon after, wealthy Guadalajara residents began to build palatial summer homes. Many of these magnificent buildings have been restored, and today they house shops and restaurants.

During this period, according to one legend, a growing French colony in the area was (inadvertently) responsible for naming one of Mexico's most renowned musical institutions. French aristocrats hired groups of street singers and musicians to entertain at weddings. The French word *mariage* was soon transformed into *mariachi.*

In 1870 the art of glass-blowing was introduced from Europe. As people started coming to purchase the pottery and intricate glass creations, more artisans—weavers, jewelers, and wood-carvers—arrived and built workshops. In 1973 downtown Tlaquepaque underwent a major renovation, the highlight of which was the creation of a wide pedestrian mall, Calle Independencia. More shops line Calle Juárez, a block south, as well as the many side streets. Typical store hours are Monday through Saturday 10–2 and 4–7, and Sunday 10–2; unless otherwise indicated, the stores listed here keep roughly these hours.

The following are some of the highlights you'll come across if you start walking from the west end of Calle Independencia.

27 Color seems to explode in the more than 10 rooms of **La Casa Canela,** exquisitely decorated with vivid papier-mâché flowers and delicately painted pottery. All surround a patio blooming with tropical plants. ✉ *Independencia 258,* ☎ *3/635–3717 or 3/657–1343.*

★ 28 Housed in a colonial mansion, **Museo Regional de la Cerámica,** the Regional Museum of Ceramics, offers exhibits that trace the evolution of

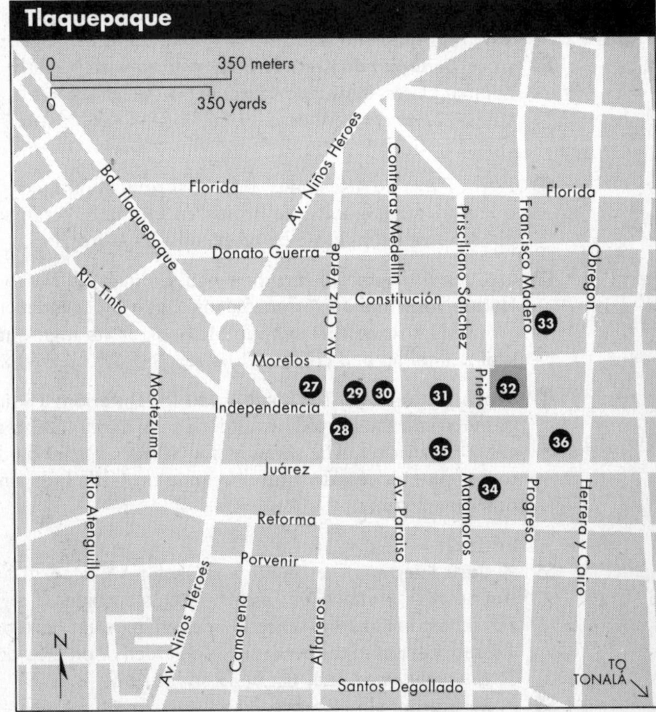

ceramics in the Atemajac Valley during the past century. ✉ *Independencia 237,* ☎ *3/635–5404.* *Free.* ⌚ *Tues.–Sat. 10–6, Sun. 10–3.*

29 Sergio Bustamante's work is found in galleries throughout the world, but you can purchase one of his whimsical sculptures or silver- and gold-plated jewelry for considerably less at **Galería Sergio Bustamante.** The flamingos under the waterfall in the rear are real. ✉ *Independencia 236,* ☎ *3/657–8354.*

30 **La Rosa de Cristal** contains a large variety of handblown glass objects and figures, including surprisingly inexpensive miniatures. Almost all the work is made in Tlaquepaque's oldest blown-glass factory, which is just around the corner. Here you can watch glassmakers shove long tubes into a white-hot fire, retrieve a bubbling glob, and create a piece similar to the ones you saw in the store. *Store:* ✉ *Independencia 232,* ☎ *3/639–7180.* ⌚ *Mon.–Sat. 9–6:30, Sun. 10–2. Factory:* ✉ *Contreras Medellín 173, corner of Donato Guerra.* ⌚ *Weekdays 8–1, Sat. 8–noon.*

31 Step through the doors of **Agustín Parra Diseño Barroco,** and you'll swear you've gone back into the 18th century. Here are exquisite baroque-style statues, wood-and-gilt altarpieces, candlesticks, and other fine ornaments. ✉ *Independencia 158,* ☎ *3/657–8530 or 3/657–0316.*

32 Franciscan friars founded the **Templo Parroquial de San Pedro** during the Spanish conquest, naming the parish church in honor of San Pedro de Analco. In line with the custom of naming a town after its principal church, in 1915 the town's name was officially changed to San Pedro Tlaquepaque. The altars of Our Lady of Guadalupe and the Sacred Heart of Jesus are intricately carved in silver and gilt. ✉ *In square at Calles Guillermo Prieto and Morelos.* ⌚ *Daily 7 AM–9 PM.*

In 1959 Ken Edwards developed a technique to transform the fragile Tonalá pottery into lustrous, hardened, lead-free, glazed stoneware. His
33 store, **Cerámica de Ken Edwards,** is filled with brightly colored, hand-painted plates, cups, and vases. Ask to see the seconds, some real bargains. ⊠ *Francisco Madero 70,* ☎ *3/635–2426.* ⊙ *Mon.–Sat. 10:30–7, Sun. 11:30–7.*

34 At the **Plaza de Artesanías,** browse through boutiques featuring high-quality leather goods, embroidered clothing, ceramics, and blown glass. Some shops close on weekends. ⊠ *Juárez 145.*

35 Striking hand-carved furniture and antiques fill the two-story **Bazar Hecht,** until mid-1996 located on Calle Independencia. The Hecht family is known throughout Mexico for its high-quality, ornately sculpted tables and chairs. ⊠ *Juárez 162,* ☎ *3/659–0205.*

36 When you're ready for lunch, head for **El Parián,** a square just north of Independencia ringed by outdoor cafés and frequented by mariachis eager to perform. The shops in the arcades here should be used only to compare prices; do your shopping on Calle Independencia or another main street.

DINING

$$ ✕ **Casa Fuerte.** Dine on such gourmet Mexican dishes as chicken stuffed with *huitlacoche* (a corn fungus considered a great delicacy) and shrimp in tamarind sauce. For dessert, try some homemade ice cream. There are tables in the verdant patio garden or on the sidewalk in front. ⊠ *Independencia 224,* ☎ *3/639–6481. AE.*

$$ ✕ **Restaurant sin Nombre.** The "Restaurant with No Name" serves Spanish nouvelle cuisine, a combination of pre-Hispanic and modern recipes. High adobe walls surround the 17th-century colonial building and extensive gardens. Daily entertainment includes *suave* jazz and traditional Mexican music. ⊠ *Francisco Madero 80,* ☎ *3/635–4520 or 3/635–9677. AE, MC, V.*

$ ✕ **Fonda la Medina.** Enjoy traditional Mexican dishes, such as stuffed lamb (a northern delicacy), chicken dishes in spicy mole sauce, and grilled fish wrapped in corn husks. Watch your meal being prepared in the open-air kitchen near the dining area, a spacious courtyard with a trickling fountain. ⊠ *Independencia 195,* ☎ *3/657–9467. AE, DC, MC, V.*

Tonalá

8 km (5 mi) east of Tlaquepaque.

Tonalá is 10 minutes away but centuries removed from its commercial neighbor, Tlaquepaque. One of Mexico's oldest pueblos, Tonalá is a quiet village with dusty, cobblestone streets and adobe houses. The village was both the pre-Hispanic capital of the Indians of the Atemajac Valley and the capital of New Spain when Captain Juan de Oñate moved Guadalajara here in 1532. Within three years, however, unfriendly Indians and a lack of water had forced the Spaniards out.

Today, municipal officials say more than 6,000 artisans live and work here; indeed, most of the ceramics and pottery sold in Tlaquepaque (and in many other parts of the world) are made in Tonalá. In small home studios, families create the lovely ceramics, cobalt-blue glassware, and playful animals with the same materials and techniques their ancestors used centuries ago. It's possible to visit many home studios (☞ Casa de los Artesanos, *below*), but it's a good idea to call first. If you don't speak Spanish, ask someone who does to call for you.

On Thursday and Sunday, much Tonalá merchandise is sold at bargain prices at one of the best tianguis in all of Mexico. Most stores in Tonalá are open Monday through Saturday 10–2 and 4–7, Sunday 10–2.

Casa de los Artesanos, **37**
Cerámica de Ken Edwards, **42**
El Bazar de Sermel, **39**
El 7, **43**
Galería José Bernabe, **40**
Museo Nacional de la Cerámica, **41**
Salvador Vásquez Carmona, **44**
Santuario, **38**

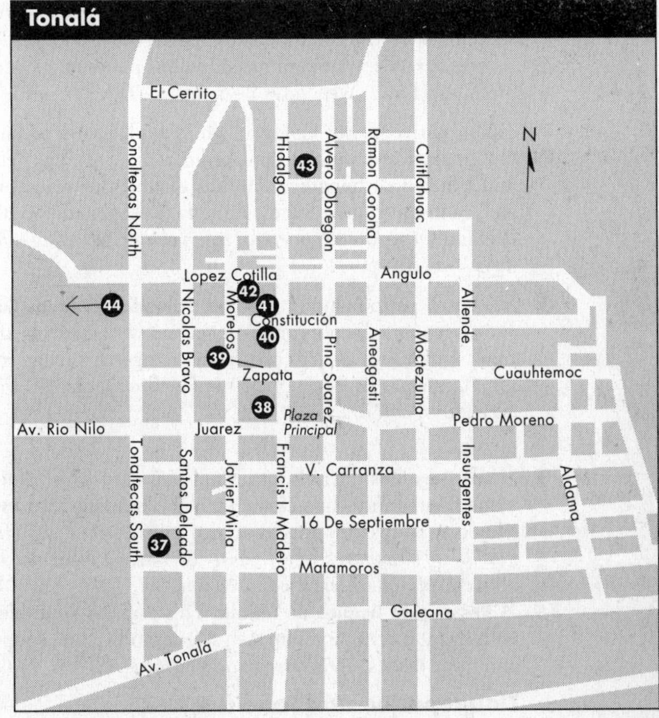

Below are some of the highlights you can visit as you walk north and generally east of Avenida de los Tonaltecas, a main drag lined with shops and cafés.

37 The showroom of the **Casa de los Artesanos** displays an excellent selection of works—mainly ceramics—by Tonalá artisans. More than 20 techniques are used in the village. The staff here can direct you to local artisans' studios. ✉ *Av. de los Tonaltecas 140,* ☎ *3/683–0590.* ⏲ *Weekdays 9–3.*

38 In the **Santuario,** or parish church, large paintings of the 14 stations of the cross fill the walls. Next door is the simple **Palacio Municipal,** or City Hall. The **Plaza Principal** is across the street.

39 A papier-máché giraffe stands over the doorway of **El Bazar de Sermel,** an airy, rambling boutique filled with brightly painted papier-mâché animals (ranging from fish to birds to nearly life-size zebras) and ornaments. ✉ *Hidalgo 67,* ☎ *3/683–0010.* ⏲ *Weekdays 9–6:30, Sat. 9–2, Sun. 10–3.*

40 The Bernabe family has made exquisitely painted petatillo ceramics for generations, as well as more simple stoneware. The sprawling workshop in back of the **Galería José Bernabe** is also open to visitors. ✉ *Hidalgo 83, between Zapata and Constitución,* ☎ *3/683–0040.* ⏲ *Weekdays 10–3 and 4–7, weekends 10–3; workshop closed weekends.*

41 Exhibits at the **Museo Nacional de la Cerámica** (National Ceramics Museum) include ceramics and pottery of several Mexican states dating from pre-Columbian times to the present. There is also a workshop and a small store. ✉ *Constitución 104,* ☎ *3/683–0494.* 🎟 *Free.* ⏲ *Tues.–Sun. 10–2 and 3–4:30, Sat. 10–3, Sun. 10–2.*

42 At the **Cerámica de Ken Edwards** workshop, you can view Edwards's trademark lead-free stoneware, which revolutionized centuries-old techniques. Meet the ceramicist himself if he's in. ✉ *Morelos 184,* ☎ *3/683–0313.* ⏲ *Weekdays 9–6, Sat. 9–1.*

Tonalá native J. Cruz Coldívar, who signs his work and named his shop
43 **El 7,** makes striking hand-painted masks, as well as decorative plates and other wall hangings. He has exhibited throughout Mexico, as well as in the United States, Canada, Europe, and South America. ✉ *Privado Obregón 28, north of town center,* ☎ *3/683–0873.* ⏲ *Weekdays 9–6, Sat. 9–1.*

44 In a small patio behind his home, **Salvador Vásquez Carmona** molds enormous ceramic pots and paints them with intricate and fanciful designs. Numerous awards certificates hang in his living room. ✉ *Av. de los Maestros 328, west of Av. de los Tonaltecas,* ☎ *3/683–2896.* ⏲ *Weekdays; call first.*

DINING

$ ✕ **Los Geranios.** Here is a tranquil pink-and-white dining room with wood booths and white-clothed tables. The menu focuses on traditional Mexican soups (try the avocado) and entrées. ✉ *Hidalgo 71,* ☎ *3/683–0010 (shares phone with El Bazar de Sermel next door* [☞ above]*). No credit cards. Closed Sat.*

$ ✕ **Restaurant Trópico de Tonalá.** This popular six-table luncheonette with counter area serves up tasty, fresh sandwiches, soups, and chicken and meat dishes. ✉ *Madero 15,* ☎ *3/683–03–98. No credit cards.*

Tlaquepaque and Tonalá A to Z

ARRIVING AND DEPARTING

By Bus. There is frequent public bus service from downtown Guadalajara and the Plaza del Sol shopping center to Tlaquepaque and Tonalá. The trips take around 30 minutes and 45 minutes, respectively.

By Car. From Guadalajara, take Avenida Revolución southeast; at the Plaza de la Bandera, jog to your right onto Boulevard General Marcelino García Barragán, which becomes Boulevard Tlaquepaque as it leads into town. When you reach the *glorieta* (traffic circle), follow the circle around to Avenida Niños Héroes. The first intersection is Calle Independencia, the pedestrian mall. From the Plaza del Sol area, take Calzada Lázaro Cárdenas southeast to the Alamo traffic circle. Fork off to the north onto Avenida Niños Héroes. Both routes take around 20 minutes.

To get from Tlaquepaque to Tonalá, take Avenida Río Nilo southeast directly into town, to the intersection of Avenida de los Tonaltecas.

By Taxi. The fare from downtown Guadalajara to Tlaquepaque is about $3.25; from downtown Guadalajara, the cab ride to Tonalá costs about $4.70. A cab from Tlaquepaque to Tonalá runs about $3.35.

VISITOR INFORMATION

The **Tlaquepaque municipal tourist office** (✉ Donato Guerra 160, ☎ 3/659–0238), open weekdays 9–7, is in the Centro Cultural el Refugio.

Tonalá's municipal tourist office (✉ Av. de los Tonaltecas 140 Sur, ☎ 3/683–1740), open weekdays 9–3 and Saturday 9–1, is next to the Casa de los Artesanos.

GUADALAJARA A TO Z

Arriving and Departing

By Bus

First-class, air-conditioned buses with rest rooms provide daily service to Guadalajara from most major cities on the border. **Greyhound** (☎ 800/231–2222) has schedule and fare information for service into Mexico, though you will have to change to a Mexican carrier at the border. Guadalajara's **Nueva Central Camionera** (New Bus Station) is located 10 km (6 mi) southeast of downtown Guadalajara on the highway to Zapotlanejo. First-class bus companies that serve Guadalajara from within Mexico include **Elite** (☎ 3/679–0404); **ETN** (☎ 3/600–0605 or 3/600–0858); **Primera Plus** (☎ 3/600–0398 or 3/600–0014); and **Omnibus de México** (☎ 3/600–0469).

Buses to and from such nearby destinations as Chapala, Ajijic, and Tequila depart from the Antigua Central Camionera (Old Bus Station), located just northeast of the Parque Agua Azul on Avenida Dr. R. Michel between Calles Los Angeles and 5 de Febrero.

By Car

Major routes include Highway 54, which leads south to Colima (220 km, or 136 mi) and north to Zacatecas (320 km, or 198 mi). Highway 15D goes southeast to Morelia (255 km, or 158 mi), continuing to Mexico City (209 km, or 130 mi). If you have a choice between a free or toll road, remember that the latter tend to be quite expensive but are usually in far better condition than their free counterparts.

By Plane

The **Libertador Miguel Hidalgo International Airport** (☎ 3/688–5248 or 3/688–5127) is 16½ km (11 mi) south of Guadalajara. A new international terminal is planned in the next decade to help meet the demands of the increased air service to the area.

Aeromexico (☎ 3/669–0202 or 800/3–62–02) has nonstop service to Guadalajara from Los Angeles; **Mexicana** (☎ 3/112–0101 or 800/5–02–20) offers direct flights from Chicago, Los Angeles, San Francisco, and San José; **Taesa** (☎ 3/679–0900 or 800/9–04–63) flies direct from Chicago and Oakland. Through Dallas, **American Airlines** (☎ 3/616–4090 or 800/3–62–70) provides service to Guadalajara from all cities in its system. **Continental Airlines** (☎ 3/647–4446 or 800/9–00–50) provides the same service through Houston. **Delta Airlines** (☎ 3/630–3530 or 800/9–02–21) flies direct from Los Angeles.

FROM THE AIRPORT

By Car. The Chapala Highway 23 (also numbered 44)—a well-paved four-lane thoroughfare—stretches north from the airport to the city. The 30-minute trip can be delayed by slow-moving caravans of trucks and weekend recreational traffic.

By Limousine. Royal Limousines (✉ Hotel Quinta Real, Av. Mexico 2727, ☎ 3/615–0000, ext. 121) offers chauffeur-driven stretch limousines to any Guadalajara location for about $25. Reserve at least 24 hours in advance.

By Taxi or Van. Autotransportes Terrestres del Aeropuerto (☎ 3/688–5890 or 3/688–5431) is a *combi* (VW minibus) and taxi service to and from anywhere in the Guadalajara area. Fares, based on distance from the airport, range from $8 to $12 for up to three people going to the same destination. At the airport, buy a ticket from the booth outside the terminal exit. Going to the airport, a regular city taxi should charge similar fares, though they are not allowed to pick up passengers at the airport.

By Train

The Mexican train system has been in a state of flux. At press time, the only rail service to Guadalajara from near the U.S. border was via *La Estrella,* a first-class train that departs from Mexicali (across from Calexico, CA) at 8 AM daily and arrives in about 38 hours; a first-class train from Guadalajara to Mexicali departs at 9:30 AM daily and also takes 38 hours. A round-trip fare is $106. The *Tapatío,* departing from Mexico City at 8:30 PM, arrives at Guadalajara at 8:30 AM; it departs Guadalajara at 9 PM, arriving in Mexico City at 9 AM. The round-trip fare to Mexicali is $106; to Mexico City, $26 first-class coach, $64 Pullman. No food is available on the trains. Some information is available from **Mexico by Train** (☎ 800/321–1699, FAX 210/725–3659). The Estación de Ferrocarriles (✉ At train station, ☎ 3/650–0826 or 3/650–1082) is at the south end of Avenida 16 de Septiembre, just past Parque Agua Azul.

Getting Around

Guadalajara's major attractions are best seen on foot. For points outside the city center, Guadalajara has an inexpensive, well-organized public transportation system.

By Bus

This is without a doubt the most economical and efficient but sometimes least comfortable means of traversing the city. Buses run every few minutes between 6 AM and 10 PM to all local attractions, including Tlaquepaque, Tonalá, and Zapopan. Fares are roughly 20¢, making buses the preferred mode of transportation for Guadalajara natives, so expect to stand during daylight hours. The Tur III buses—which run on some of the main routes through the city, including out to Tlaquepaque and Tonalá—cost 50¢ and are much less crowded.

By Car

Beware of heavy traffic and *topes* (speed bumps). Glorietas (traffic circles) are common at many busy intersections. Parking in the city center can be scarce, so take a taxi or bus if you're not staying nearby; otherwise, try the underground lots across from the Palacio Municipal (✉ Av. Hidalgo and Calle Pedro Loza) and below the Plaza de la Liberación (✉ Av. Hidalgo and Calle Belén, in front of the Teatro Degollado). If you park illegally, the police may remove your license plates (*placas*), and you'll have to go to the municipal transit office to pay a fine and retrieve them.

By Subway

Guadalajara's underground *tren ligero* (light train) system is clean, safe, and efficient. Line 1 runs along Avenida Federalismo from the Periférico (city beltway) Sur to Periférico Norte, near the Benito Juárez Auditorium. Line 2 runs east–west along Avenida Javier Mina (which becomes Avenida Juárez at the Calzada Independencia) from Tetlán in eastern Guadalajara to Avenida Federalismo. Trains run about every 15 minutes from 6 AM to 10:30 PM; a token for one trip costs about 20¢.

By Taxi

Taxis are readily available and reasonably economical. Tell the driver where you are going and agree on a fare *before* you enter the cab. Fare schedules listing prices to downtown and all major attractions are posted in the lobby of most hotels. *Sitios* (cab stands) are near all hotels and attractions.

Contacts and Resources

Car Rental

Car-rental agencies with offices at the Guadalajara airport include **Avis** (☎ 3/688–5528), **Budget** (☎ 3/688–5216; also ✉ Av. Niños Héroes 934, at Av. 16 de Septiembre, ☎ 3/613–0027), **Dollar** (☎ 3/688–5659; also ✉ Av. Federalismo Sur 540A, ☎ 3/826–7959), **Hertz** (☎ 3/688–5633; also ✉ Av. 16 de Septiembre 738-B, ☎ 3/614–6162), and **National** (☎ 3/688–5021; also ✉ Av. Niños Héroes 961-C, ☎ 3/614–7175).

Consulates

United States (✉ Progreso 175, between López Cotilla and Libertad, ☎ 3/825–2700 or 3/825–2998; 3/826–5553 after-hrs emergency); open weekdays 8–4:30. American Citizens Services office is open weekdays 8–11:30.

Canada (✉ Fiesta Americana hotel, Aurelio Aceves 225, ☎ 3/616–6226 or 3/616–5642; 800/7–06–29 after-hrs emergency), open weekdays 9–5.

For information about other consulates, including **Great Britain,** call Guadalajara's consular association (☎ 3/616–0629), open weekdays 9–3 and 5–8.

Emergencies

City police (☎ 3/617–6060); **State police** (☎ 3/617–5838 or 3/617–5538); **Highway patrol** (☎ 08); **Fire department** (☎ 3/619–5241 or 3/619–5155); **Cruz Roja** (Red Cross; ☎ 3/613–1550, 3/614–5600, or 3/614–2707); and **Cruz Verde** (municipal emergency medical service; ☎ 3/613–5389).

DOCTORS AND DENTISTS

The U.S. Consulate (☞ Consulates, *above*) maintains a list of English-speaking doctors and dentists. All major hotels have the names of doctors who are on 24-hour call.

HOSPITALS

Hospital del Carmen (✉ Tarascos 3435, near Plaza México mall, ☎ 3/813–0025 or 3/813–0042), **Hospital México-Americano** (✉ Colomos 2110, ☎ 3/641–3141 or 3/641–3319), and **Hospital Santa María Chapalita** (✉ Av. Niño Obrero 1666, in Chapalita district, ☎ 3/678–1400).

English-Language Bookstores and Publications

Sandi Bookstore (✉ Av. Tepeyac 718, in Chapalita district, ☎ 3/121–0863) sells many newspapers, magazines, and books.

The weekly *Guadalajara Colony Reporter* newspaper, sold for 70¢ at newsstands and hotels, provides news stories and excellent community and cultural listings. Distributed in hotels, the monthly *Let's Enjoy/Disfrutemos Guadalajara* offers feature articles and information on attractions. An excellent source of information on the Lake Chapala area and other excursions in the states of Jalisco, Colima, Nayarit, and Michoacán is Tony Burton's *Western Mexico: A Traveller's Treasury* (Espadaña Press, 1993).

Guided Tours

Most of the tour operators in the city offer guided city tours and excursions to Tequila, Lake Chapala, Tlaquepaque, and Tonalá.

CALANDRIAS

You can hire a horse-drawn carriage in front of the Museo Regional, the Mercado Libertad, or Parque San Francisco. The charge is about $13.50 for a 45-minute tour for up to four passengers. Few drivers speak English.

PERSONAL GUIDES

The **Sindicato de Guías de Turistas** (☏ 3/657–8376) maintains a list of licensed bilingual guides, though you may have trouble getting an answer if you phone. These guides charge about $13.50 per hour (4-hr minimum) for guided tours on foot or in their own automobiles. Most hotels have a list of guides available on short notice.

TOUR OPERATORS

Copenhagen Tours (✉ Av. J. Manuel Clouthier 152, in Colonia Prados Vallarta, ☏ 3/629–7957 or 3/629–4758). **Panoramex** (✉ Av. Federalismo Sur 944, ☏ 3/810–5109 or 3/810–5005).

Money Exchange

The most convenient places to change dollars are *casas de cambio,* generally open weekdays from 9 until 6 (though they may close between 2 and 4) and Saturday morning. There are many such establishments on Calle López Cotilla downtown and in the Plaza del Sol area. Banks tend to have more limited hours and longer waits.

Pharmacies

Farmacias Guadalajara (✉ Av. Las Americas 2, ☏ 3/615–8516; ✉ Av. Javier Mina 221, between Cabañas and Vicente Guerrero, ☏ 3/617–8555; ✉ Av. Tepeyac 646, in Chapalita district, ☏ 3/121–2581; ✉ Plaza México, ☏ 3/813–2698) has several branches that are open 24 hours.

Travel Agencies

Many of the city's more than 100 travel agencies are in the two hotel zones, el centro (downtown) and Avenida López Mateos Sur, on the city's southwest side. Near the Minerva Fountain you'll find **American Express** (✉ Av. Vallarta 2440, near Los Arcos monument, ☏ 3/615–8712 or 3/615–8910).

Visitor Information

The **Jalisco state tourist office** (✉ Calle Morelos 102, in Plaza Tapatía, ☏ 3/658–2222 or 800/3–63–22) downtown also has information about other parts of Mexico. It's open weekdays 9–8, weekends 9–1.

The city of Guadalajara has **tourist information booths** (☏ 3/616–3332, 3/616–3333, or 3/616–3335) downtown in the Plaza Guadalajara, in Los Arcos monument on Avenida Vallarta just east of the Minerva Fountain, in Parque San Francisco, in front of the Instituto Cultural Cabañas, and at the airport. They're open daily 9–6:30.

8 The Heartland of Mexico

Rich with the history of Mexico's revolution, the heartland is a treasure of colonial towns—among them Guanajuato, Zacatecas, Querétaro, Morelia, and Pátzcuaro—whose residents lead quiet, largely traditional lives. Even in San Miguel de Allende, an American art colony and home to a well-known language institute, women wash their clothes and gossip at the local lavandaría as they have for hundreds of years.

Updated by Jane Onstott

MEXICO'S HEARTLAND, so named for its central location, has neither the beaches of the west coast nor the ruins of Yucatán. Rather, this fertile farmland, along with the surrounding mountains, is known for its leading role in Mexican history, particularly during the War of Independence, and for its especially well-preserved examples of colonial architecture. The Bajío (ba-*hee*-o), as it is also called, corresponds roughly to the states of Guanajuato and parts of Querétaro and Michoacán. In the hills surrounding the cities of Guanajuato, Zacatecas, Querétaro, and San Miguel de Allende, the Spaniards found silver in the 1500s, leading them to colonize the area heavily.

Three centuries later, wealthy Creoles (Mexicans of Spanish descent) in Querétaro and San Miguel took the first audacious steps toward independence from Spain. When their clandestine efforts were discovered, two of the early insurgents, Ignacio Allende and Father Miguel Hidalgo, began in earnest the 12-year War of Independence. One of the bloodiest skirmishes was fought in the Alhóndiga de Granaditas, a mammoth grain-storage facility in Guanajuato that is now a state museum.

When Allende and Hidalgo were executed in 1811, another native son, José María Morelos, picked up the independence banner. This mestizo (mixed race) mule skinner–turned–priest–turned soldier, with his army of 9,000, came close to gaining control of the land before he was killed in 1815. Thirteen years later, the city of Valladolid was renamed Morelia in his honor.

Long after the War of Independence ended in 1821, the cities of the Bajío continued to play a prominent role in Mexico's history. Three major events took place in Querétaro alone: In 1848 the Mexican-American War ended with the signing of the Treaty of Guadalupe Hidalgo; in 1867 Austrian Maximilian of Hapsburg, crowned emperor of Mexico by Napoleon III of France, was executed in the hills north of town; and in 1917 the Mexican Constitution was signed here.

The heartland honors the events and people that helped to shape modern Mexico. In ornate cathedrals or bucolic plazas, down narrow alleyways or atop high hillsides, you will discover monuments—and remnants—of a heroic past. During numerous fiestas, you can savor the region's historic spirit. On a night filled with fireworks, off-key music, and tireless celebrants, it's hard not to be caught up in the vital expression of national pride.

Tourism is welcomed in the heartland, especially in these hard economic times, and tourists do not disrupt the normal routines of residents. Families visit parks for Sunday picnics, youngsters tussle in school courtyards, old men chat in shaded plazas, and Tarascan women in traditional garb sell their wares in crowded *mercados* (markets). Unlike areas where attractions have been specifically designed for tourism, the Bajío relies on its historic ties and the architectural integrity of its cities to appeal to travelers. Although this is an interesting area to tour by car, there is frequent inexpensive bus service from one city to the next throughout the Bajío.

Pleasures and Pastimes

Architecture

Paid for in large part by the region's fabulously wealthy silver mines, the cities of the heartland are architectural masterpieces. From the stately,

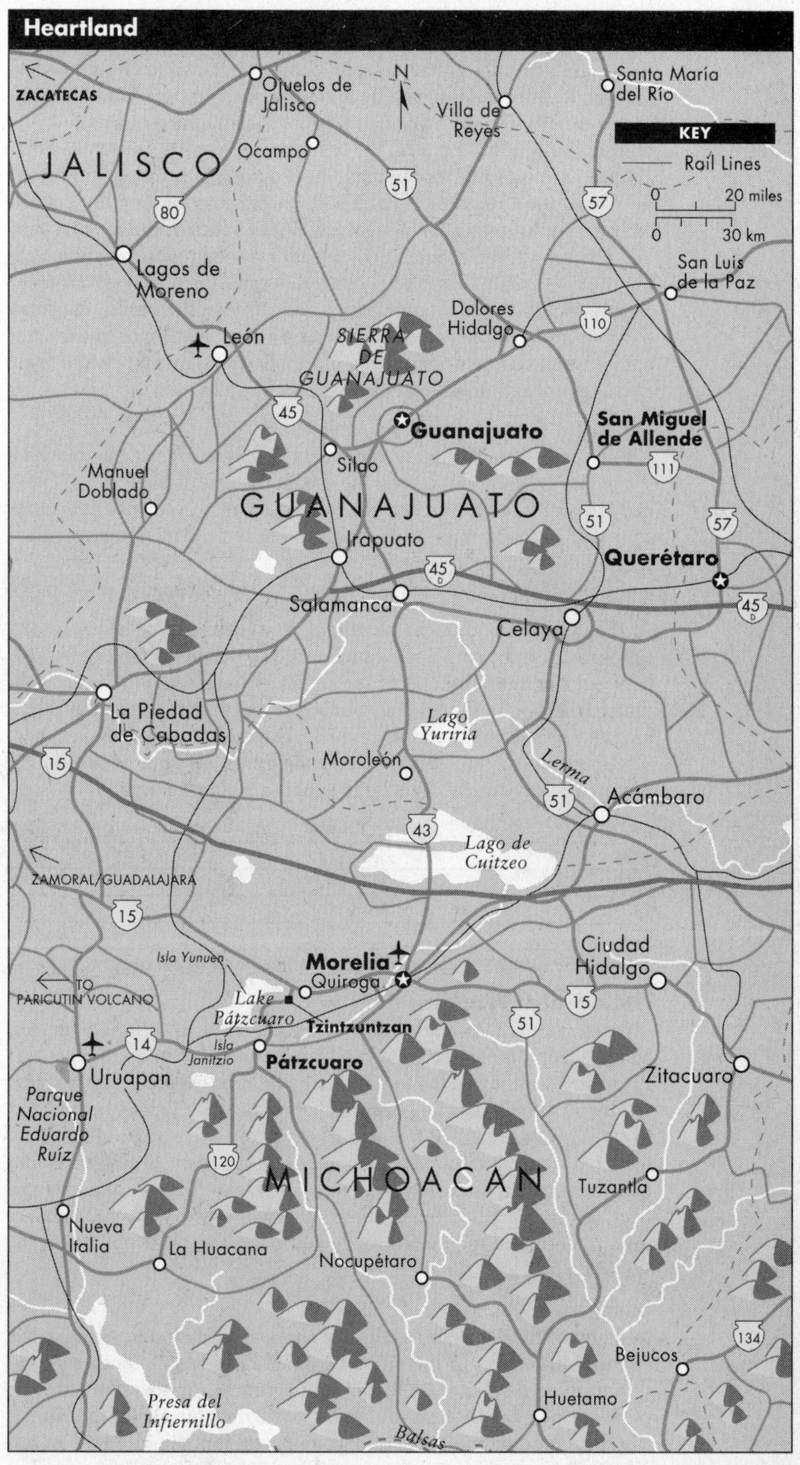
Heartland
ZACATECAS
Ojuelos de Jalisco
N
Villa de Reyes
Santa María del Río
KEY
Rail Lines
0 20 miles
0 30 km
JALISCO
Ocampo
51
57
80
Lagos de Moreno
San Luis de la Paz
Dolores Hidalgo
110
León
SIERRA DE GUANAJUATO
45
Guanajuato
San Miguel de Allende
Silao
111
Manuel Doblado
GUANAJUATO
51
57
Irapuato
45 D
Querétaro
Salamanca
Celaya
45 D
La Piedad de Cabadas
Lago Yuriria
15
Moroleón
Lerma
51
Acámbaro
43
Lago de Cuitzeo
ZAMORA/GUADALAJARA
15
Isla Yunuen
Morelia
Ciudad Hidalgo
Quiroga
TO PARICUTIN VOLCANO
Lake Pátzcuaro
Tzintzuntzan
15
51
Isla Janitzio
14
Pátzcuaro
Uruapan
Zitacuaro
Parque Nacional Eduardo Ruíz
120
MICHOACAN
Tuzantla
Nueva Italia
La Huacana
Nocupétaro
134
Bejucos
Presa del Infiernillo
Huetamo
Balsas

almost European grandeur of Morelia to the steep, labyrinthine allure of Guanajuato and the sandstone pink splendor of Zacatecas, no two towns are alike. La Parroquia, the Gothic-style parish church of San Miguel de Allende, designed by an Indian mason, puts a Gallic touch on an otherwise very Mexican skyline. Guanajuato boasts a 17th-century baroque centerpiece, the Basílica Colegiata de Nuestra Señora. Zacatecas, a national monument city, has the best example in Mexico of a baroque cathedral. The 200-ft baroque towers of the central cathedral in Morelia are among the tallest in Mexico; and in Pátzcuaro and Querétaro, the ornate 16th-century colonial mansions surrounding the city squares have been converted into hotels and government offices, making their interior patios accessible to the public. Mexican baroque architecture is characterized by a combination of human, animal, plant, and geometric motifs; alternating straight and curved lines; and an emphasis on the play between light and shadow.

Dining

It's no surprise that culinary tastes vary widely in the heartland, which spans a large area across central Mexico. In the state of Michoacán, Tarascan Indian influences predominate. The tomato-based *sopa tarasca* (a soup with cheese, cream, and tortillas) is one of the best-known regional specialties. Because of the numerous lakes and rivers in the state, several types of freshwater fish are often served in Michoacán restaurants.

At the northern end of the heartland, in Zacatecas, the hearty, meat-eating tastes of the *norteños* (northerners) rule the dinner table. Although beef is the favored dish, other specialties include *asado de boda* (wedding barbecue), pork in a spicy but semisweet sauce. The region is also known for its cheeses and fine wines. Although it doesn't have a particular specialty, San Miguel de Allende offers a wealth of fine dining opportunities because of its large expatriate community.

CATEGORY	COST*
$$$$	over $15
$$$	$10–$15
$$	$5–$10
$	under $5

**per person for a three-course meal, excluding drinks and service*

Hiking and Walking

With its rolling farmland, lofty volcanoes, lakes, and Indian villages, Michoacán is a perfect area in which to take day hikes. Trails near Pátzcuaro wind up to the top of nearby hilltops for great views across town and the surrounding countryside, while in Uruapan—just 64 km (39 mi) away yet 2,000 ft lower in elevation—you can walk along a lush, raging river valley. And of course no tour of the heartland would be complete without a few days of leisurely strolling the avenues and back streets of the colonial cities and towns—admiring the architecture, lingering in the museums, or resting in the plaza, watching the world go by.

Lodging

In many of the heartland's colonial cities, the best lodgings are in the restored haciendas of the fabulously rich residents of centuries past. Often near the center of town, sometimes facing directly onto the plaza, some of these beautiful mansions date from the 16th century. There are also deluxe modern high-rises and functional, low-cost hotels for those with different tastes or budgets. Except for five-star hotels, most properties in the region are not heated, and you may want to bring warm, comfortable clothes for indoor wear, or to inquire in advance if heating is important to you. In restored colonial properties, rooms often vary dramatically as to size and furnishings, so if you aren't satisfied with the one you are shown, ask to see another. High season, for the most part, is limited to specific dates surrounding Christmas, Easter, and regional festivals. Note that most moderate and inexpensive hotels quote prices with 15% value-added tax already included.

CATEGORY	COST*
$$$$	over $90
$$$	$50–$90
$$	$25–$50
$	under $25

**All prices are for a standard double room, including 15% tax.*

Exploring the Heartland

Many travelers barrel past the heartland to points north or west of Mexico City. But there are many reasons others make it their destination. Some stop for a few days to browse in the shops of San Miguel or Guanajuato for bargains in silver and other local crafts. Others venture to the state of Michoacán, renowned for its folklore and folk crafts, especially ceramics and lacquerware. Those who stay longer and tour the region can linger over the wealth of architectural styles that each of the colonial cities has to offer.

Numbers in the text correspond to numbers in the margin and on the San Miguel de Allende, Guanajuato, Zacatecas, Querétaro, Morelia, and Pátzcuaro maps.

Great Itineraries

Those with only a couple of days to spare can visit any of several colonial cities to catch a taste for life in the Mexican heartland, but each one has its own particular flavor. Visitors who fall under the spell of this peaceful, friendly region will want to spend a week to 10 days to allow themselves the time to sit back and drink in the atmosphere of two or three of the heartland cities.

IF YOU HAVE 3 DAYS

Head to **Guanajuato** ⑫–㉒ (432 km, or 268 mi, from Mexico City), the most architecturally dramatic of the heartland cities. Make a day trip from here to the sleepy town of **San Miguel de Allende** ①–⑪, just 90 minutes away by car or bus, to shop for arts and crafts.

Another option would be to go from Mexico City to the Michoacán capital of **Morelia** ㊵–㊾ (about four hours by car) and spend a day enjoying its stately architecture and café-lined plaza. The next day, drive 56 km (34 mi) through Quiroga to **Pátzcuaro** ㊿–(56), set among volcanoes in the center of Tarascan Indian country. Spend the morning walking through the bustling market or strolling the surrounding countryside before returning to Mexico City in the late afternoon.

IF YOU HAVE 5 DAYS

Make Guanajuato your base, and then devote an extra day to its churches and museums—even the gruesome Mummy Museum. Stop off at the town of Dolores Hidalgo, home of Mexican independence, on your way to a day of shopping in San Miguel. Overnight in San Miguel and the next morning head for **Querétaro** ㉜–㊳, 63 km (38 mi) away; this quiet colonial city is considered the capital of the Bajío. After a night in one of Querétaro's many downtown hotels, drive the three hours to Mexico City or the 2½ hours to the airport outside Guanajuato.

Visitors choosing to spend several days in Michoacán will easily fill their time exploring the state's colonial towns and enjoying the lush, mountainous countryside. After three days in Morelia and Pátzcuaro, take a day trip to explore the crater on an extinct volcano in **San Juan Parangaricútiro** or the ruins of an ancient Tarascan Indian capital, **Tzintzuntzan** (both are less than an hour from Pátzcuaro), before returning on the final day to Morelia and Mexico City.

IF YOU HAVE 7 DAYS

From your base in Guanajuato, consider adding to the first of the five-day itineraries a round-trip flight from Guanajuato airport to **Zacatecas**; that would give you a day and a half to explore this northern colonial mining city. Because it lies off the main tourist track, Zacatecas has a refreshingly unselfconscious feel to it. Another possibility for a week-long heartland tour would be to make a loop from Mexico City that includes both Morelia and Guanajuato; you'd have time for leisurely side trips to Pátzcuaro and San Miguel and a stop off in Querétaro. When in Pátzcuaro, be sure to take a boat out to the island town of **Janítzio** on nearby Lake Pátzcuaro, home of Mexico's most famous November 2 Day of the Dead festival, or to the more authentic island of Yunuen, which is not as yet besieged by tourists.

When to Tour the Heartland

One of the most pleasing aspects of the heartland is its superb climate—it rarely gets overly hot, even in the middle of summer, and although winter days can get nippy, especially in the northern city of Zacatecas, they are generally temperate. Average temperatures in the southern city of Morelia range from 20°C (68°F) in May to just under 10°C (49°F) in January. Zacatecas is more extreme, with winter temperatures as low as 0°C (32°F) and snow flurries every several years, and summer highs of 28°C–30°C (81°F–85°F). Nights are cool all year in most of the region's cities. The rainy season all across the heartland hits between April and September and is generally strongest in July and August.

A trip to the heartland can be planned around cultural festivals or religious events. The International Cervantes Festival, a two-week-long celebration of the arts, attracts actors, musicians, painters, and hundreds of thousands of visitors to Guanajuato every year in October. In San Miguel, the Jazz Festival International is beginning to attract visitors in late November. And on the island of Janítzio, local Tarascan Indians hold a spectacular November 2 festival in honor of their ancestors during Mexico's Day of the Dead.

SAN MIGUEL DE ALLENDE

San Miguel de Allende first began luring foreigners in the late 1930s when Stirling Dickinson, an American, and prominent local residents founded an art school in this mountainous settlement. The school, now called the Instituto Allende, has grown in stature over the years—as has the city's reputation as a writers' and artists' colony. Walk down any cobblestone street and you're likely to see residents of a variety of national origins. Some come to study at the Instituto Allende or the Academia Hispano-Americana, some to escape the harsh northern winters, and still others to retire.

Cultural offerings in this town of about 110,000 reflect its large American and Canadian community. There are literary readings, art shows, a lending library, psychic fairs, aerobics and past-life-regression classes, and a yearly jazz festival. International influence notwithstanding, San Miguel, declared a national monument in 1926, retains its Mexican characteristics. Wandering down streets lined with 18th-century mansions, you'll also discover fountains, monuments, and churches—all reminders of the city's illustrious, and sometimes notorious, past. The

In case you want to be welcomed there.

We're here to see that you're always welcomed at establishments everywhere. That's why millions of people carry the American Express® Card – for peace of mind, confidence, and security, around the world or just around the corner.

do more®

Cards

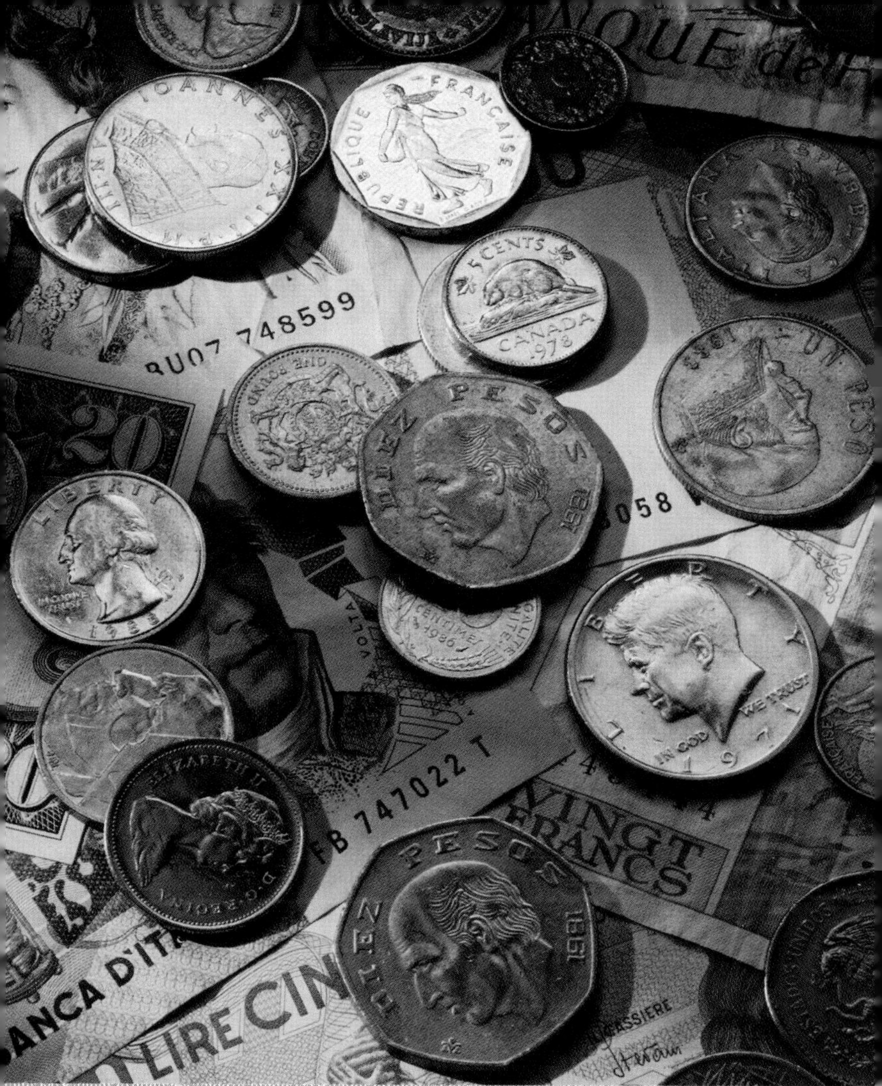
RÉPUBLIQUE FRANÇAISE
5 CENTS
CANADA 1978
PESOS
LIBERTY
ELIZABETH II
BU07 748599
FB 747022 T
VINGT FRANCS
LIRE CIN

onetime headquarters of the Spanish Inquisition in New Spain, for example, is located at the corner of Calles Hernández Macías and Pila Seca; the former Inquisition jail stands across the way. Independence day is celebrated with exceptional fervor in San Miguel, with fireworks, dances and parades on September 15 and 16, and bullfights and cultural events for the remainder of the month, including the running of the bulls, Pamplona style.

Exploring San Miguel de Allende

Most of San Miguel's sights are clustered in the downtown area and can be seen in a couple of hours.

A Good Walk

Begin at the main plaza, otherwise known as **El Jardín** ①; after you get a feel for the square, stop into **La Parroquia** ②, the sandstone church on its south side. Three blocks northeast of La Parroquia (take Calle San Francisco, on the north side of El Jardín, to Calle Juárez) is the **Iglesia de San Francisco** ③, with its fine churrigueresque facade. Take a few steps north on Calle Juárez to Calle Mesones, where the colorful **Mercado Ignacio Ramírez** (☞ Shopping, *below*) occupies a small plaza. The dome of the **Oratorio de San Felipe Neri** ④ is visible just beyond the market.

Go a block west from the church on Calle de los Insurgentes to reach **La Biblioteca Pública** ⑤, a great place to catch up on town events and replace your paperback book. From the library, continue west for two blocks to Calle Hernández Macías and then head south to the **Bellas Artes** ⑥ cultural center at No. 75 and the **Iglesia de la Concepción** ⑦ right behind it. Take Hernández Macías south for a block and turn left on Umarán to reach the **Casa de Ignacio Allende** ⑧, birthplace of the Mexican national hero. You've circled back to the southwest corner of the Jardín.

After exploring the center of town, you might want to take a leisurely stroll to sights a bit farther afield. From the south side of the plaza (where La Parroquia sits), head west four blocks on Calle Umarán until you reach Calle Zacateros. Turn south on this narrow cobblestone street to reach some of the town's most interesting crafts shops—stocked with everything from silver jewelry to Mexican ceremonial masks.

Past the shops, Calle Zacateros becomes Ancha de San Antonio. On your left at No. 20 is the renowned **Instituto Allende** ⑨, where many of San Miguel's foreign visitors come to study. From the institute, continue south on Ancha de San Antonio until you reach Callejón del Cardo on your left. Continue past St. Paul's Episcopal Church, where many foreigners worship, until you arrive at the cobblestone Calle Aldama on your left. Head downhill and walk briefly through a neighborhood of whitewashed houses before reaching the north entrance to the 5-acre Parque Benito Juárez, the largest park in town and an oasis of evergreens, palm trees, and gardens.

From the north edge of the park, follow Calle Diezmo Viejo to the imposing terra cotta–color mansion known as La Huerta Santa Elena. From here turn left and walk one block uphill to the **Lavandería** ⑩, San Miguel's outdoor laundry and a favorite gathering spot for local women. Calle de Recreo, above the Lavandería, heads north back toward the plaza: Follow Recreo until reaching Calle Correo, turn left, and walk three blocks to return to El Jardín.

Bellas Artes, **6**
Casa de Ignacio Allende, **8**
El Jardín, **1**
El Mirador, **11**
Iglesia de la Concepción, **7**
Iglesia de San Francisco, **3**
Instituto Allende, **9**
La Biblioteca Pública, **5**
La Parroquia, **2**
Lavandería, **10**
Oratorio de San Felipe Neri, **4**

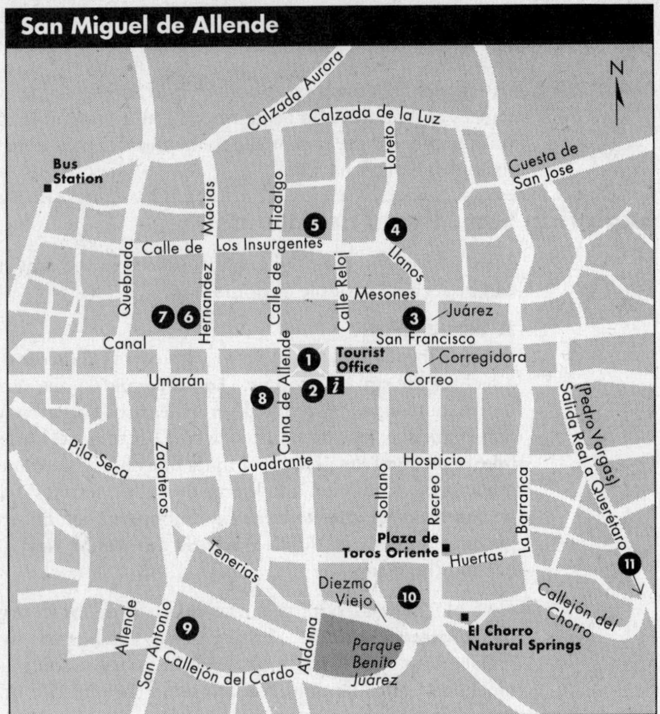

Sights to See

6 **Bellas Artes.** This impressive cloister across the street from the U.S. Consulate was once the Royal Convent of the Conception and is now an institute for the study of music, dance, and the visual arts. There are rotating art exhibits, and a cafeteria on the patio; a bulletin board at the entrance indicates upcoming cultural events. ✉ *Calle Hernández Macías 75,* ☎ *415/2-02-89.* ⏲ *Mon.–Sat. 9–8, Sun. 10–3.*

8 **Casa de Ignacio Allende.** Now housing a museum and gallery, this is the birthplace of Ignacio Allende, one of Mexico's great independence heroes. Allende was a Creole aristocrat who, along with Father Miguel Hidalgo, plotted in the early 1800s to overthrow the Spanish regime. At clandestine meetings held in San Miguel and nearby Querétaro, the two discussed strategies, organized an army, gathered weapons, and enlisted the support of clerics for the struggle ahead.

Spanish Royalists learned of their plot and began arresting conspirators in Querétaro on September 13, 1810. Allende and Hidalgo received word of these actions and hastened their plans. At dawn on September 16, they rang out the cry for independence, and the fighting began. Allende was captured and executed by the Royalists the following year. As a tribute to his brave efforts, San Miguel El Grande became San Miguel de Allende in the 20th century. ✉ *Calle Cuna de Allende 1, no phone.* 🎟 *Free.* ⏲ *Tues.–Sun. 10–3:30.*

NEED A BREAK? On the southwest corner of the main plaza is **Café del Jardín** (✉ Portal Allende 2, ☎ 415/2-50-06). This unassuming little café has excellent coffee, cappuccino, hot chocolate, and in the evening, pizza; breakfasts are tasty and inexpensive. There's friendly service and best of all—it's that American influence—free coffee refills.

1 **El Jardín.** The heart of San Miguel is the plaza commonly known as El Jardín (the Garden). Seated on one of its wrought-iron benches, you'll quickly get a feel for the town: Old men with canes exchange tales, young lovers smooch, fruit vendors hawk their wares, and bells from the nearby La Parroquia pierce the thin mountain air at each quarter hour. ⊠ *Bounded by Calle Correo on the south, Calle San Francisco on the north, Portal Allende on the west, and Portal Guadalupe on the east.*

11 **El Mirador.** For great views, consider a climb to El Mirador (the Lookout), which offers a panorama of the city, mountains, and reservoir below. The vista is most commanding at sunset, and chances are you won't be alone; locals and tourists like to join Ignacio Allende, whose bronze image commands this spot. ⊠ *1 block before town, turn right off Calle Recreo onto Calle Hospicio. Follow Hospicio 3 blocks to Calle Pedro Vargas. Turn right and head uphill to the overlook.*

7 **Iglesia de la Concepción.** Located just behind the Bellas Artes cultural center, this church touts one of the largest domes in Mexico. Its two-story roof, completed in 1891, boasts both elegant Corinthian columns and ornamental pilasters and is said to have been inspired by the dome of Les Invalides in Paris. Ceferino Gutiérrez (of La Parroquia fame) is credited with its design. ⊠ *Calle Canal between Hernández Macías and Zacateros.*

3 **Iglesia de San Francisco.** The San Francisco Church has one of the finest churrigueresque facades in the state of Guanajuato. This term refers to José Churriguera, a 17th-century Spanish architect, noted for his extravagantly decorative baroque style. Built in the late 18th century, it was financed by donations from wealthy patrons and by revenue from bullfights. Topping the elaborately carved exterior is the image of Saint Francis of Assisi; below are sculptures of Saint John and Our Lady of Sorrows, as well as a crucifix. ⊠ *Calle Juárez between San Francisco and Mesones.*

9 **Instituto Allende.** The school is set in the former country estate of the Count of Canal. Since its founding in 1951, thousands of students from around the world have come to learn Spanish and to take classes in social studies and the arts. Courses last from a couple of weeks to a month or longer. Lush with bougainvillea, rosebushes, and ivy vines, the grounds provide a quiet refuge for students and visitors alike. ⊠ *Ancha de San Antonio 20,* ☎ *415/2–01–90,* FAX *415/2–45–38.* ⊙ *Weekdays 9–6, Sat. 9–1.*

5 **La Biblioteca Pública.** Posted on the bulletin board in the entranceway to the library are many notices (mostly in English) about events such as literary readings or yoga and aerobics classes. Inside are the offices of the bilingual newspaper, *Atención San Miguel,* as well as a reading room with back issues of popular publications and English books. It's a great place to take a breather from sightseeing. On Sunday the library offers a two-hour house-and-garden tour of San Miguel that departs at noon. Tickets cost about $15, with all proceeds going to the library. ⊠ *Calle de los Insurgentes 25,* ☎ *415/2–02–93,* FAX *415/2–37–70.* ⊙ *Weekdays 10–2 and 4–7, Sat. 10–2.*

2 **La Parroquia.** This imposing pink Gothic-style parish church, made of local *cantera* sandstone, was designed in the late 19th century by self-trained Indian mason Ceferino Gutiérrez, who sketched his designs in the sand with a stick. Gutiérrez was purportedly inspired by postcards

of European Gothic cathedrals. Since the postcards gave no hint of what the back of those cathedrals looked like, the posterior of La Parroquia was done in quintessential Mexican style.

La Parroquia still functions as a house of worship, though its interior has been changed over the years. Gilded wood altars, for example, were replaced with neoclassical stone altars. The original bell, cast in 1732, still calls parishioners to Mass several times daily. ✉ *South side of El Jardín on Calle Correo.*

10 **Lavandería.** At this outdoor public laundry—a collection of cement tubs set above Juárez Park—local women gather daily to wash clothes and gossip as their predecessors have done for centuries. Though some women claim to have more efficient washing facilities at home, the lure of the spring-fed troughs—not to mention the chance to catch up on the news—brings them daily to this shaded courtyard. ✉ *Calle Jesús.*

4 **Oratorio de San Felipe Neri.** Built by local Indians in 1712, the original chapel can still be glimpsed in the eastern facade, made of pink stone and adorned with a figure of Our Lady of Solitude; the newer, southern front was built in an ornate baroque style. In 1734 the wealthy Count of Canal paid for an addition to the Oratorio. His **Templo de Santa Casa de Loreto,** dedicated to the Virgin of Loreto, is just behind the Oratorio; its main entrance, now blocked by a grille, is on the Oratorio's left rear side. Peer through the grille to see the heavily gilded altars and effigies of the count and his wife, under which they are buried. ✉ *Calles de los Insurgentes and Loreto.*

Dining

For its size, San Miguel has a surprising number of international restaurants. The recent influx of Americans and Canadians has given rise to new Tex-Mex and health-food establishments; a European influence has contributed to variations on French, Italian, and Spanish themes.

$$$ ✕ **La Antigua Restaurant y Tapa Bar.** A cheerful room with fewer than a dozen tables (each with a vase of orange carnations) and a polished wood bar that can seat up to 15 people, La Antigua puts its clientele in the mood for a large variety of tapas with its European café furniture and Spanish bolero music. Among its specialties are *queso antiguo* (baked cheese with chilies), *chisterra* (a sliced and fried Spanish-style sausage), *camarones con tocineta* (jumbo shrimp fried with bacon), and *pulpo antiguo* (squid sautéed in garlic and herbs). ✉ *Calle Canal 9,* ☎ *415/2–25–86. AE, MC, V.*

$$ ★ ✕ **Fonda Mesón de San José.** On a tree-shaded cobblestone patio inside a complex of small shops, this well-established restaurant offers German, Mexican, and vegetarian cuisines. Owner-chef Angela Merkel is enthusiastic about her roulade, potato pancakes, and German chocolate cake as well as her *chile en nogada,* a mild chili stuffed with ground meat and raisins and topped with cream sauce and pomegranate seeds. This is a great place for a sunny patio lunch, and is less popular for dinner, especially in wintertime. ✉ *Mesones 38,* ☎ *415/2–38–48. MC, V.*

$$ ✕ **Mama Mía.** Those who want a change from Mexican food will enjoy Mamá Mía's satisfying assortment of pastas and pizzas, as well as a decent fettuccine Bolognese and spaghetti Parmesana. Try the house special: fettuccine Alex (with white wine, ham, cream, and mushrooms). Folk musicians entertain on the lush outdoor patio come dusk. ✉ *Calle de Umarán 8,* ☎ *415/2–20–63. MC, V.*

$$ ✕ **Rincón Español.** The soft pink walls of this pleasant Spanish restaurant are covered with reproductions of the works of famous Spanish

artists—Joan Miró, Picasso, and Salvador Dalí—and its nickname, La Casa de la Paella, reveals the dining room's specialty. Not a little of the charm of this place derives from the evening guitar music and flamenco dancing, pleasing adjuncts to dessert. ✉ *Correo 29,* ☎ *415/2–29–84. MC, V.*

$ ✕ **Café de la Parroquia.** Stop in for either breakfast or lunch, both served either outside on the charming patio or indoors. Economical daily lunch menus include soup, main dish, beverage, dessert, and coffee. ✉ *Calle Jesús 11,* ☎ *415/2–31–61. No credit cards. Closed Mon. No dinner.*

$ ✕ **La Buena Vida.** Do not bypass this fabulous bakery and tiny coffee shop, serving mouthwatering orange scones, chocolate chip cookies, and light breakfasts, along with some of San Miguel's best coffee. If the few patio tables are full, you can eat your treats in the plaza. ✉ *Hernádez Macías 72–5,* ☎ *415/2–22–11. No credit cards. Closed Sun.*

Lodging

San Miguel has a wide selection of hotels, ranging from cozy bed-and-breakfasts to elegant all-suites properties. Rooms fill up quickly during summer and winter seasons, when northern tourists migrate here in droves. Make reservations several months in advance if you plan to visit at these times or during the September Independence Day festivities.

$$$$ ★ **Casa de Sierra Nevada.** Built in 1580 as the residence of the archbishop of Guanajuato, this elegant country-style inn still attracts ambassadors, diplomats, film stars, and other luminaries; children under 16 are not admitted, however. Its complex of six colonial buildings, located a few blocks from the main plaza, contains 32 individually decorated suites and five standard rooms. Lace curtains, handwoven rugs, and chandeliers adorn some rooms; fireplaces, cozy private terraces, and skylights enhance others. The international cuisine at the hotel's restaurant is delicately prepared and beautifully presented. Jazz enlivens the rather formal restaurant on Wednesday evenings, and classical duets play during weekend lunch. Restaurant reservations required. ✉ *Calle Hospicio 35, 37700,* ☎ *415/2–70–40, 888/441–5995 in the U.S.;* FAX *415/2–23–37. 37 suites and rooms. Restaurant, bar, pool, massage, spa, horseback riding, meeting rooms. AE, MC, V.*

$$$ **Casa Carmen.** Run by a very friendly San Miguel family, this pension is an oasis of peace in the center of town. Set in a 200-year-old house just two blocks from the Jardín, it has large, immaculate rooms, each with desk or writing table and portable gas heater, and two small patios for relaxing with a good book. The large suite on the top floor has a great view of the city for the same price, but is often booked far in advance. Breakfast and lunch are included in the room rate. ✉ *Correo 31, 37700,* ☎ *415/2–08–44. 12 rooms. No credit cards.*

$$$ **La Mansión del Bosque.** On a quiet side street across from the Parque Benito Juárez, this cozy guest house caters to long-term guests, especially in wintertime. The hotel, which operates on a Modified American Plan that includes breakfast and dinner, is attractive red stucco of many levels, resembling a Taos Indian dwelling. Rooms vary in furnishing and style: Some have motel-like furnishings and day beds, others are more pleasingly decorated. Many rooms have working fireplaces; all have private or shared plant-filled terraces. The lounge invites mingling with other guests and has books, magazines, cable TV, and a telephone for long-distance calls. ✉ *Calle Aldama 65, 37700,* ☎ FAX *415/2–02–77. 23 rooms. Restaurant, bar, lounge. No credit cards.*

$$$ **Villa Jacaranda.** Located near the Parque Benito Juárez, the Villa Jacaranda has a full range of amenities. Rooms, though unimaginatively decorated, have space heaters (not something to be taken for granted in these parts) and cable TVs. The hotel's **Cine/Bar** shows Amer-

ican movies Tuesday–Saturday at 7:30 PM and live sports events on a giant screen. The price of admission—roughly $3—includes a drink. The hotel's award-winning restaurant serves international and Mexican cuisine, and a delicious Sunday champagne brunch for about $7.50. Meals are served in the homey dining room or the stained-glass gazebo just beyond. ✉ *Calle Aldama 53, 37700,* ☎ *415/2–10–15 or 415/2–08–11; 800/310–9688 reservations from U.S.;* FAX *415/2–08–83. 16 rooms and suites. Restaurant, hot tub, cinema. AE, MC, V.*

$$$ **Villa Mirasol.** Each of this lodging's eight rooms is tastefully decorated with original prints, oil paintings, pastels, or small sculptures; most of the rooms are flooded with sunlight during the day. All have either a private or shared terrace; the ones facing Calle Pila Seca have beautiful vistas of the surrounding hills. On a quiet street no more than a 10-minute walk from the main plaza, the hotel was a private house until 1983, and its cozy and intimate atmosphere affords visitors a welcome change from larger, less personal hotels. Villa Mirasol includes in its price a rich breakfast, and offers guests who stay more than a week use of the Golf Club free of charge. ✉ *Pila Seca 35, 37700,* ☎ *415/2–15–64,* FAX *415/2–15–64. 8 rooms. MC, V.*

$$ **Posada de las Monjas.** This 19th-century structure has been operating as a hotel for more than 50 years. Rooms are furnished in a colonial style, with some furniture in the old wing looking worn enough to be authentically 17th century. The rooftop public terrace has tables and lounge chairs and offers commanding views of mountains and city. Some rooms have fireplaces, and there's a communal television in the lobby, which looks like a formal Mexican living room, with plastic flowers in vases and stiff furniture lining the walls. ✉ *Calle de Canal 37, 37700,* ☎ *415/2–01–71,* FAX *415/2–62–27. 65 rooms. Restaurant, bar, laundry service. AE, MC, V.*

$ **Quinta Loreto.** Clean, plain, comfortable rooms, pleasantly groomed and shady grounds, and excellent *comida casera* (home cooking) make this inexpensive hotel a favorite with snowbirds and other San Miguel aficionados. Each room has a gas heater, television, and telephone. There is a dilapidated tennis court and an unheated pool, which is uninvitingly dirty. The hotel is about a 10-minute walk north of the main plaza, near the market. Many nonguests take their meals in the unpretentious dining room, especially the diet-defying *comida corrida* (fixed-menu lunch) served daily. ✉ *Calle Loreto, No. 15, 37700,* ☎ *415/2–00–42,* FAX *415/2–36–16. 38 rooms. Restaurant, pool. AE, MC, V.*

Nightlife and the Arts

The Arts

San Miguel, long known as an artists' colony, continues to nurture that image today. Galleries, museums, and arty shops line the streets near El Jardín, and two government-run salons—at **Bellas Artes** and **Instituto Allende** (☞ Exploring San Miguel de Allende, *above,* for both)—showcase the work of Mexican artists. For a sampling of regional talent, visit the **Galería San Miguel** (✉ Plaza Principal 14, ☎ 415/2–04–54), **Galería Atenea** (✉ Calle Cuna de Allende 15, ☎ 415/2–07–85), and the **Kligerman Gallery** (✉ San Francisco 11, ☎ 415/2–09–51 or 415/2–15–14). The **Jazz Festival International,** now in its fourth year, takes place around the last week in November, and offers live jazz, workshops, and after-hour jam sessions. Also, coinciding with Christmas vacation in late December, San Miguel hosts the **Winter Festival,** a feast of classical music. Tickets may be purchased individually or for the series. Contact the tourist office for dates and details.

Nightlife

On most evenings in San Miguel you can readily satisfy a whim for a literary reading, an American movie, a theatrical production, or a turn on a disco dance floor. The most up-to-date listings of events can be found in the bilingual paper *Atención San Miguel,* published every Friday. The bulletin board at the public library (✉ Calle de los Insurgentes 25) is also a good source of current events.

Live music can be heard at **Pancho and Lefty's** (✉ Calle Mesones 99, ☎ 415/2–19–58) from rock, jazz, or blues bands, depending on the night. **La Fragua** (✉ Calle Cuna de Allende 3, ☎ 415/2–11–44), located just a couple of doors off the Plaza, often has traditional Mexican soloists or bands, and couples dance in the courtyard. At **Mamá Mía** (✉ Calle de Umarán 8, ☎ 415/2–20–63) you can hear everything from Peruvian folk music, classical guitar, and flamenco to salsa and rock. **San Miguelito** (✉ Calle San Francisco 1, ☎ 415/2–33–72) bills itself as "A Place for Grown-Ups" and attracts a mixed crowd of Mexicans and foreigners, who listen to piano music in the evenings as they lounge on comfortable couches under twinkling lights and organ cactuses. **Laberintos Disco** (✉ Calle Ancha de San Antonio 7, ☎ 415/2–03–62), across from the Instituto Allende outside the center of town, is often hopping until the early morning hours.

Outdoor Activities and Sports

The **Hotel Hacienda Taboada** (✉ Dolores Hidalgo Hwy., Km 8, ☎ 415/2–08–88, FAX 415/2–17–98) has a swimming pool and tennis courts open to the public for a nominal fee. The **Club de Golf Malanquin** (✉ Celaya Hwy., Km 3, ☎ 415/2–05–16) has a heated pool, steam baths, tennis courts, and nine holes of golf, all of which are open to the public.

Bicycle Rental

Bikes for exploring San Miguel and environs can be rented (or serviced) at **Bici-Burro** (✉ Calle Hospicio 1, esq. Barranca, ☎ 415/2–15–26). **Aventuras San Miguel** (✉ Calle Recreo, No. 10, ☎ FAX 415/2–64–06) rents both horses and bicycles at reasonable prices.

Horseback Riding

Adventuras San Miguel (☞ Bicycle Rental, *above*) rents horses at reasonable rates. The equestrian center of the **Casa de Sierra Nevada** (☞ Lodging, *above*) offers riding lessons, carriage rides, and horse rental at its 500-acre ranch for $20 per hour.

Spectator Sports

Visitors who want to witness the pageantry of a traditional Mexican bullfight can do so at the **Plaza de Toros Oriente** (✉ Off Calle de Recreo) several times a year. The most important contest takes place during the last week of September during *la fiesta de San Miguel.* Contact the tourist office (☞ Visitor Information *in* San Miguel de Allende A to Z, *below*) for more information.

Shopping

For centuries San Miguel's artisans have been creating a wide variety of crafts ranging from straw products to metalwork. Though some boutiques in town may be a bit pricey, you can find good buys on silver, brass, tin, woven-cotton goods, and folk art; locally crafted metal objects—such as plates and trays, chests, mirrors, and decorative animals and birds—are popular souvenirs. Opening and closing hours are erratic; a number of stores open at 9 AM, but many others don't start conducting business until 11; some shut their doors for traditional afternoon siesta (2 through 4 or 5). Closing hour tends to be around 7 or 8 PM, and most (but not all) shops are closed Sunday. Most San Miguel shops accept MasterCard and Visa.

Market

Occupying the small plaza directly in front of the Oratorio de San Felipe Neri, the **Mercado Ignacio Ramírez** spills over onto the surrounding streets (for about six blocks). It is particularly active on Sunday, when country folk come to town with pigs, chickens, and other livestock, along with succulent produce. During the week, rows of fresh fruits and vegetables are supplemented by racks of cheaply made clothing, inexpensive plastic toys, and blaring Mexican-made tapes and records.

Specialty Shops

FOLK ART

Artes de México (✉ Aurora 47 at Dolores Hidalgo exit, ☎ 415/2–07–64) has been producing and selling traditional crafts, including furniture, metalwork, and ceramics, for more than 40 years. Although the inventory at the **Casa Maxwell** (✉ Calle de Canal 14, ☎ 415/2–02–47) has slipped in quality, there is still a reasonable selection of folk art. **La Calaca** (✉ Mesones 93, no phone) also focuses on folk art from the Americas, mainly Mexico, Guatemala, and Peru. **Tonatiu Metzli** (✉ Las Flores 27, ☎ 415/2–08–69) has a colorful selection of work from Mexico, China, Africa, and elsewhere. **Veryka** (✉ Zacateros 6-A, ☎ 415/2–21–14), whose emphasis is on Latin American folk art, has a particularly fine selection of *muertos* (skeleton figurines for the Day of the Dead) from Puebla.

HOUSEWARES

Casa Canal (✉ Calle Canal 3, ☎ 415/2–04–79), set in a beautiful old hacienda, sells new furniture, though much of it is made in traditional styles. **Casa María Luisa** (✉ Calle Canal 40, ☎ 415/2–01–30) has a fantastic jumble of furniture, glassware, wall hangings, and lamps, as well as an enormous selection of collectibles made of tin, iron, wood, and glass. **Casa Vieja** (✉ Calle Mesones No. 83, ☎ 415/2–12–84) has tons of glassware and ceramics, decorative and functional housewares, picture frames, furniture, and more.

JEWELRY

Established in 1963, **Joyería David** (✉ Calle Zacateros 53, ☎ 415/2–00–56) has an extensive selection of gold, silver, copper, and brass jewelry, all made on the premises. A number of pieces contain Mexican opals, amethysts, topaz, malachite, and turquoise. The reputable **Beckmann Joyería** (✉ Calle Hernández Macías 115, ☎ 415/2–16–13) designs its own gold and silver pieces. **Platería Cerro Blanco** (✉ Calle de Canal 17, ☎ 415/2–05–02) also creates and crafts its own silver and gold jewelry and will arrange a visit to its *taller* (workshop) on request.

Side Trip

Dolores Hidalgo

50 km (30 mi) north of San Miguel via Rte. 51.

Dolores Hidalgo played an important role in the fight for independence. It was here, before dawn on September 16, 1810, that Father Miguel Hidalgo—the local priest—gave an impassioned sermon to his clergy that ended with the *grito* (cry), "Viva Ferdinand VII [king of Spain at the time]! Death to bad government!" At 11 PM on September 15, politicians throughout the land repeat a revised version of the grito—"Viva Mexico! Viva Mexico! Viva Mexico!"—signaling the start of Independence Day celebrations. On September 16 (and only on this day), the bell in Hidalgo's parish church is rung.

Casa Hidalgo, the house where Father Hidalgo lived, is now a museum. It contains copies of important letters Hidalgo sent or received, and other independence memorabilia. ✉ *Calle Morelos 1,* ☎ *418/2-01-71.* *About $2; free Sun.* *Tues.-Sat. 10-5:45, Sun. 10-4:45.*

Dolores Hidalgo is also known for its output of hand-painted ceramics, most notably tiles and tableware. The town can be reached easily by bus from San Miguel de Allende. Buses depart frequently from the Central de Autobuses; travel time is about one hour.

San Miguel de Allende A to Z

Arriving and Departing

BY BUS

Direct bus service is available daily between the Central del Norte (North Bus Station) in Mexico City and the Central de Autobuses in San Miguel. Several major lines—including **Flecha Amarilla, Herradura de Plata, Primera Plus,** and **Tres Estrellas de Oro**—offer frequent service. Travel time is about four hours.

BY CAR

Driving time from Mexico City to San Miguel is roughly four hours via Route 57 (to Querétaro) and Route 111 (Querétaro to San Miguel). Traveling on Route 45 from Mexico City, drivers can take a road connecting to Route 57, bypassing Querétero and saving a half hour.

BY PLANE

International airlines that fly into Guanajuato International Airport, which is about two hours from San Miguel, include **Aeromexico** (☎ 47/14-05-74), from Los Angeles; **American** (☎ 47/16-05-02), from Dallas–Fort Worth; **Continental** (☎ 47/14-71-10), from Houston; **Mexicana** (☎ 47/13-45-50), from Chicago; and **Taesa** (☎ 47/16-98-31), from Oakland, CA.

Taxis from the Leon/Guanajuato airport to downtown San Miguel take about 1½ hours and cost about $45.

BY TRAIN

Train travel is not recommended as it is slow and there are no sleeper cars. The train leaves Mexico City for San Miguel de Allende at 9 AM, arriving in San Miguel at 2:30 PM. The San Miguel–Mexico City train leaves at 1:15 PM and arrives at 9 PM. The first-class one-way fare is $9. The train from Monterrey to Mexico City also stops at San Miguel. For current schedules and fares, contact **Mexico by Train** (☎ FAX 210/725-3659 or ☎ 800/321-1699). The local train station (✉ Calzada de Estación s/n, ☎ 415/2-00-07) answers the phone only around departures; it's best to call 915/547-1084 or 915/547-6593 for schedule information within Mexico.

The **San Miguel train station** (☎ 415/2-00-07) is on La Calzada de Estación (Station Highway).

Getting Around

San Miguel de Allende is best negotiated on foot, keeping in mind two pieces of advice. The city is more than a mile above sea level, so visitors not accustomed to high altitudes may tire quickly during their first few days there. Streets are paved with rugged cobblestone, and some of them do not have sidewalks. Sturdy footwear, such as athletic or other rubber-soled walking shoes, is therefore highly recommended.

BY TAXI

Taxis can easily be hailed on the street or found at taxi stands such as **Sitio Allende** in the main plaza (☎ 415/2-05-50 or 415/2-01-92),

Sitio San Francisco on Calle Mesones (no phone), or **Sitio San Felipe** on Calle Juárez (no phone). Flat rates to the bus terminal, train station, and other parts of the city apply.

Contacts and Resources

BUSINESS SERVICES

La Conexión (✉ Aldama 1, ☎ FAX 415/2–16–87 or 415/2–15–99) offers 24-hour answering and fax service, a Mexico address for receiving mail, lockboxes, packing and shipping, and other services.

CAR RENTAL

Renta de Autos Gama (✉ Calle de Hidalgo 3, ☎ 415/2–08–15) has a limited selection of standard-shift compacts available.

CONSULATE

U.S. Consulate (✉ Calle Hernández Macías 72, ☎ 415/2–23–5 during office hrs, 415/2–00–68 or 415/2–00–99 emergencies); open Monday and Wednesday 9–1 and 4–7, Tuesday and Thursday 4–7.

EMERGENCIES

Police (☎ 415/2–00–22), **Emergency,** including fire, ambulance, traffic accident, police, etc. (☎ 415/2–09–11), **Red Cross** (☎ 415/2–16–16).

Hospital. The staff at **Hospital de la Fé** (✉ Libramiento a Dolores Hidalgo 43, ☎ 415/2–22–33 or 415/2–23–20) can refer you to an English-speaking doctor.

Pharmacies. San Miguel has many pharmacies, but American residents recommend **Botica Agundis** (✉ Calle de Canal 26, ☎ 415/2–11–98), where English speakers are often on hand. It's open daily 10–midnight.

ENGLISH-LANGUAGE BOOKSTORES

El Colibrí (✉ Sollano 30, ☎ FAX 415/2–07–51) has a good selection of novels, magazines, and a few art supplies. Mostly magazines are available at **Lagundi** (✉ Calle de Umarán 17, ☎ 415/2–08–30). **El Tecolote** (✉ Calle de Jesús 11, ☎ 415/2–73–95) has a great selection of books on Mexican art, history, and cooking.

MONEY EXCHANGE

A better bet for money exchange than the slow-moving bank lines is **Deal Casa de Cambio** (✉ San Francisco 4, ☎ 415/2–29–32), open weekdays 9–6, Saturday 9–2.

TOUR OPERATORS

Aventuras San Miguel (✉ Recreo 10, ☎ FAX 415/2–64–06) offers off-the-beaten track tours, including mountain-bike treks, trips to the "ghost town" of Real de Catorce, and even *lunadas* (semimonthly nighttime excursions during full moon). Recommended for local tours is the **Instituto de Viajes** (✉ Cuna de Allende 11, ☎ 415/2–00–78, FAX 415/2–01–21).

TRAVEL AGENCY

Viajes Vértiz (✉ Calle de Hidalgo 1A, ☎ 415/2–18–56 or 415/2–16–95, FAX 415/2–04–99) is the American Express representative.

VISITOR INFORMATION

Delegación de Turismo (✉ Southeast corner of Plaza Principal, ☎ 415/2–17–47); open weekdays 10–7, Saturday 10–5, Sunday 10–2.

GUANAJUATO

100 km (60 mi) west of San Miguel de Allende, 365 km (227 mi) northwest of Mexico City.

Once Mexico's most prominent silver-mining city, Guanajuato is a colonial gem, tucked into the mountains at 6,700 ft. This provincial state capital is distinguished by twisting cobblestone alleyways, pastel-wall houses, 15 shaded plazas, and a vast subterranean roadway (where a rushing river once flowed). In the center of town is **Alhóndiga de Granaditas**—an 18th-century grain-storage facility that was the site of Mexico's first major victory in its War of Independence from Spain.

The city fills to overflowing in mid-October with the **International Cervantes Festival,** a two-week celebration of the arts. Hotels and private dwellings are completely saturated with guests, and some visitors must lodge in nearby cities. During the week, however, things regain a semblance of normalcy. Students rush to class with books tucked under their arms, women eye fresh produce at the Mercado Hidalgo, and old men utter greetings from behind whitewashed doorways. On weekend nights, *estudiantinas* (student minstrels dressed as medieval troubadours) serenade the public in the city squares.

Guanajuato celebrates its annual **Hot Air Balloon Festival** for a week in late November each year. Colorful balloons fill the sky, and events such as antique car parades and student art contests are scheduled.

Exploring Guanajuato

Though Guanajuato's many plazas and labyrinthine streets may seem confusing at first, this is not a bad city in which to get lost. The center is small, and there are wonderful surprises around every corner. Remember that the top of the Alhóndiga (which can be seen from many spots in town) points north, and the spires of the Basílica Colegiata Nuestra Señora de Guanajuato, at the Plaza de la Paz, point south.

A Good Walk

The tourist office, at Plaza de la Paz 14, is a good place to begin a walking tour. Turn right and walk up Avenida Juárez to reach **Jardín Unión** ⑫, Guanajuato's central square. The ornate **Teatro Juárez** ⑬ is just past the Jardín to your right on Calle Sopeña. The hardy might want to make a detour to **El Pípila** ⑭, a monument looming over the center of the city and a steep half hour's climb. Those interested should bear right on Calle Sopeña just past the Teatro Juárez; a sign marked El Pípila will direct you onto Callejón de Calvario, which eventually leads up to the hillside memorial.

Head back into town via Calle Cantarranas, a main street that winds down the hill and around the Jardín Unión. Just before Calle Cantarranas changes its name to Calle Pocitos, you'll see the **University of Guanajuato** ⑮. A short way down from where Calle Cantarranas becomes Calle Pocitos is **El Museo Casa Diego Rivera** ⑯, birthplace of Mexico's famous muralist. Calle Pocitos weaves past more residences and eventually becomes Calle 28 de Septiembre. On the left, just past the junction with Mendizabal, looms the **Alhóndiga de Granaditas** ⑰, a former fortress converted into a state museum. Head one block south to return to Avenida Juárez and the enclosed **Mercado Hidalgo** ⑱.

Turn right on Juárez as you leave the market and continue on until the road splits near the Jardín Reforma. Bear to the left and cut down Calle Reforma, a short alleyway lined with shops. Keep left at the end of the street and you'll come to two pleasant courtyards: Plaza San Roque, which hosts outdoor performances during the Cervantes Festival, and Plaza San Fernando, a shady square where many book fairs are held. This short detour will return you to Avenida Juárez, where it's a slight climb up to Plaza de la Paz, a square built from 1895 to 1898 and surrounded by some of the city's finest colonial buildings, including the

Guanajuato

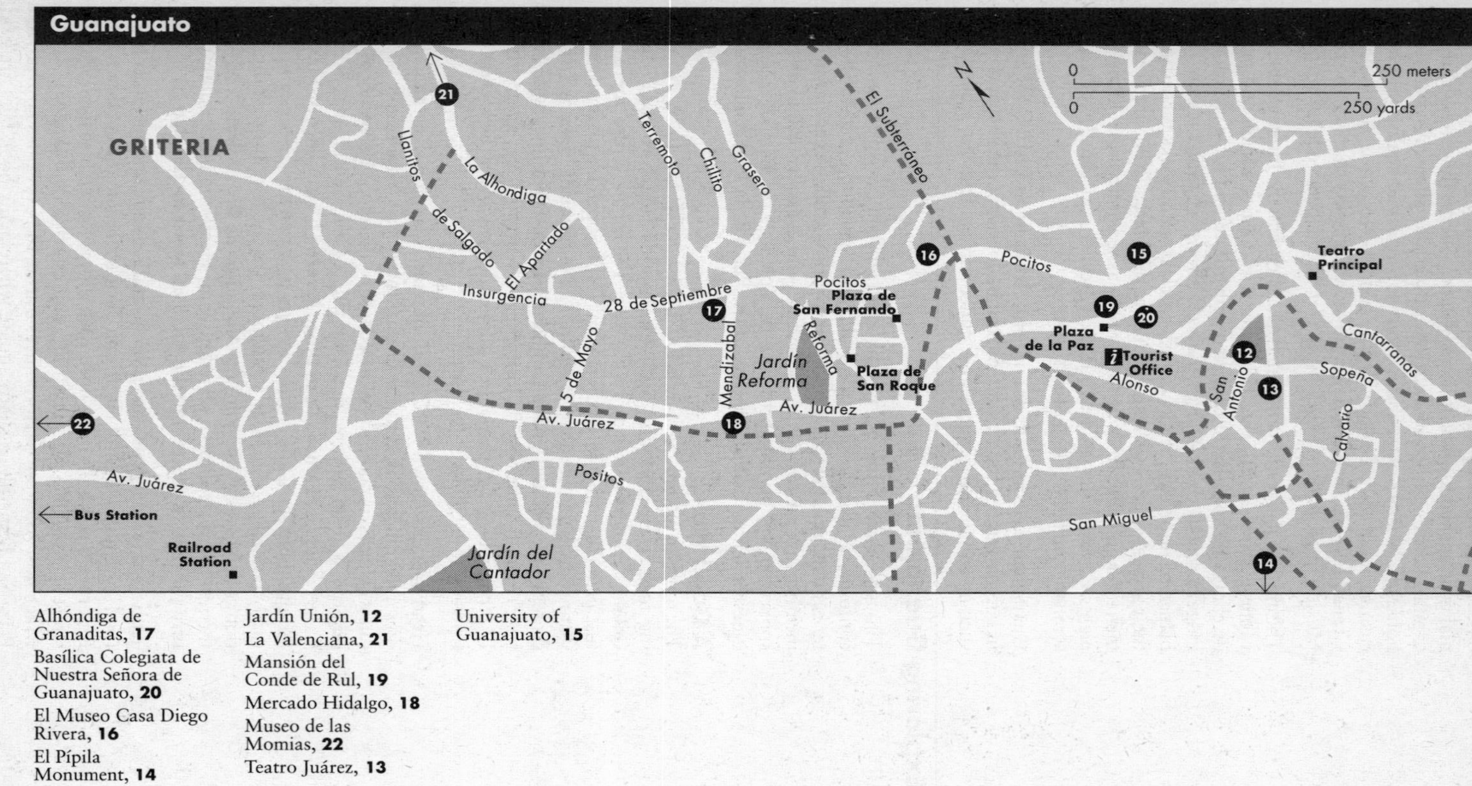

Alhóndiga de Granaditas, **17**
Basílica Colegiata de Nuestra Señora de Guanajuato, **20**
El Museo Casa Diego Rivera, **16**
El Pípila Monument, **14**
Jardín Unión, **12**
La Valenciana, **21**
Mansión del Conde de Rul, **19**
Mercado Hidalgo, **18**
Museo de las Momias, **22**
Teatro Juárez, **13**
University of Guanajuato, **15**

18th-century **Mansión del Conde de Rul** ⑲. Dominating the plaza is the imposing **Basílica Colegiata de Nuestra Señora de Guanajuato** ⑳, a bright-yellow 17th-century baroque church. If you continue up Avenida Juárez about half a block past the plaza, you'll pass the tourist office again and arrive back at the Jardín Unión.

Sights to See

17 **Alhóndiga de Granaditas.** A massive stone structure with horizontal slit windows, this 18th-century grain-storage facility served as a jail under Emperor Maximilian and a fortress during the War of Independence, where ☞ **El Pípila** committed his courageous act. It is now a state museum with exhibits on local history, archaeology, and crafts. The hooks on which the Spanish Royalists impaled the heads of Father Hidalgo, Ignacio Allende, and two other independence leaders still hang on the exterior. ✉ *Calle 28 de Septiembre 6,* ☎ *473/2–11–12.* *About $2; free Sun.* ⏲ *Tues.–Sat. 10–2 and 4–6, Sun. 10–3.*

20 **Basílica Colegiata de Nuestra Señora de Guanajuato.** A 17th-century baroque church painted a striking shade of yellow, the Basílica dominates the Plaza de la Paz. Inside is the oldest Christian statue in Mexico, a bejeweled 8th-century statue of the Virgin. The highly venerated figure was a gift from King Philip II of Spain in 1557. On the Friday preceding Good Friday, miners, accompanied by floats and mariachi bands, parade to the basilica to pay homage to the Lady of Guanajuato. ✉ *Plaza de la Paz.*

16 **El Museo Casa Diego Rivera.** This museum, birthplace of Mexico's best-known muralist, Diego Rivera, contains family portraits and furniture as well as works by the master, among them his studies for the controversial mural commissioned for New York City's Rockefeller Center. Completed in 1933, the mural contained a portrait of Lenin and had a decidedly Communist bent, which caused it to be removed immediately after it was displayed. The museum's upper galleries house revolving contemporary art exhibits. ✉ *Calle Pocitos 47,* ☎ *473/2–11–97.* *$1.30.* ⏲ *Mon.–Sat. 10–6:30, Sun. 10–2:30.*

14 **El Pípila.** A half hour's climb from downtown is the monument to Juan José de los Reyes Martínez, a young miner and hero of the War of Independence of 1810. Nicknamed El Pípila, De los Reyes crept into the **Alhóndiga de Granaditas,** where Spanish Royalists were hiding. With a stone shield strapped to his back, he set the front door ablaze. The Spanish troops were captured by Father Hidalgo's army in this early battle, giving the independence forces their first major military victory. There's a splendid panoramic view of the city from the monument. It's easiest to take a taxi or a bus (marked PÍPILA) from the Jardín. ✉ *Carretera Panorámica, on bluff above south side of Jardín Unión.*

12 **Jardín Unión.** This tree-lined, wedge-shape plaza is Guanajuato's central square. All three sides of the wedge are pedestrian walkways. On Tuesday, Thursday, and Sunday evenings, musical performances take place in the bandshell here; at other times, groups of musicians break into impromptu song along the plaza's shaded tile walkways.

NEED A BREAK? For alfresco dining at the Jardín, try the terrace at the **Hotel Museo Posada Santa Fé** (✉ Jardín Unión 12, ☎ 473/2–00–84). You can order a cappuccino and a slice of cake, or a full meal. Try the *pozole estilo Guanajuato* (hominy soup into which you spoon, or squeeze, the desired amounts of onions, radishes, lettuce, lime, and chili peppers). **El Agora** (✉ El Agora del Baratillo, ☎ 473/2–33–00), an outdoor café located down an alley off the plaza's southeast corner, has less expensive offerings. A four-course lunch—including soup, rice, entrée, and dessert—runs about $4.

21 **La Valenciana.** Officially called La Iglesia de San Cayetano, this is one of the best-known colonial churches in all of Mexico. The pink stone facade, constructed in the latter part of the 18th century, is brilliantly ornate. Inside are three altars, each hand-carved in wood and covered in gilt, in separate styles: plateresque, churrigueresque, and baroque. There are also fine examples of religious painting from the viceregal period. The silver mine near the church, also called La Valenciana, was discovered in 1760 and is still in operation today. Although you can't descend into the 1,650-ft-deep mine shaft, if the caretaker is around he'll usually let you take a peek down. La Valenciana is included in any guided tour of the city, and there are also frequent buses (marked LA VALENCIANA) from the center. ✉ *Carretera a Dolores Hidalgo, Km 2.*

19 **Mansión del Conde de Rul.** This 18th-century residence, now a government office, housed the count of Rul and Valenciana, who owned what was then the country's richest silver mine (☞ La Valenciana, *above*). The two-story structure was designed by famed Mexican architect Eduardo Tresguerras. ✉ *Plaza de la Paz at Av. Juárez and Callejón del Estudiante.* ⏲ *Weekdays 8–3.*

18 **Mercado Hidalgo.** You can't miss this 1910 cast-iron-and-glass structure, designed by Gustave Eiffel, of Eiffel Tower fame. Though the balcony stalls are filled with T-shirts and cheap plastic toys, the lower level offers authentic local wares, including fresh produce, peanuts, honey-drenched nut candies, and colorful basketry. Vendors line the sidewalk in front of the market, hawking flowers and local crafts. ✉ *Calle Juárez near Mendizabal.* ⏲ *Daily.*

22 **Museo de las Momias.** For a macabre thrill, check out this unique museum located at the municipal cemetery off Calzada del Panteón, at the west end of town. In the museum, mummified human corpses—once buried in the cemetery—are on display. Until the law was amended in 1858, if a grave site had not yet been paid for after five years, the corpse was removed to make room for new arrivals. Because of the mineral properties of the local soil, these cadavers (the oldest is more than 130 years old) were in astonishingly good condition upon exhumation. The most gruesome are exhibited in glass cases. ✉ *Panteón Municipal,* ☎ *473/2–06–39.* 🎟 *$2.* ⏲ *Daily 9–6.*

13 **Teatro Juárez.** Adorned with bronze lion sculptures and a line of large Greek muses overlooking the Jardín from the roof, the theater was inaugurated by Mexican dictator Porfirio Díaz in 1903 with a performance of *Aïda.* It now serves as the principal venue of the annual International Cervantes Festival (☞ Nightlife and the Arts, *below*). A brief tour of the Art Deco interior is available for about 50¢. ✉ *Calle de Sopeña,* ☎ *473/2–01–83.* ⏲ *Tues.–Sun. 9–1:45 and 5:15–7:45.*

15 **University of Guanajuato.** Founded in 1732, the university was formerly a Jesuit seminary. The original churrigueresque church, **La Compañía,** still stands next door. The facade of the university building, built in 1955, was designed to blend in with the town's architecture. If you do wander inside, check out the bulletin boards for notices of cultural events in town. (Also check bulletin boards along the pedestrian walkways of the Jardín.) ✉ *Calle Lascurain de Retana, ½ block north of Plaza de la Paz,* ☎ *473/2–00–06.*

Dining

Guanajuato's better restaurants are located in hotels near the Jardín Unión and on the highway to Dolores Hidalgo. For simpler fare, private establishments around town offer a good variety of Mexican and international dishes. Dress tends to be casual in this provincial university town.

$$$ ★ ✕ **El Comedor Real.** Continental cuisine served in a medieval environment defines El Comedor Real. The bright whitewashed and brick-domed restaurant in the Hotel Castillo Santa Cecilia serves such specialties as *filete pimiente* (steak with peppercorns), breaded trout with tartar sauce, and fish soup with vegetables. Troubadours perform every Friday and Saturday at 10:30 PM at **La Cava,** the bar next door. ✉ *Camino a la Valenciana s/n, Km 1,* ☎ *473/2–04–85. AE, MC, V.*

$$$ ✕ **Le Casserole.** Not far from the Parador San Javier is a pleasant French restaurant where you'll receive the personal attention of the owner, Maria Eugenia. There are fresh-cut flowers on every table, and the food is a nice change from regional cuisine. You might start off with the cold cream of avocado soup or the spinach crepes, and move on to the house specialty: grilled trout crusted in green, red, and black peppercorns. ✉ *Calle Alhóndiga 84,* ☎ *473/2–33–45. MC, V. Closed Mon. No dinner Tues.–Thurs.*

$$$ ★ ✕ **Tasca de los Santos.** This cozy restaurant, across the street from the Basílica, specializes in Spanish and international cuisines. Recommended dishes include the *sopa de mariscos* (a rich broth with shrimp, mussels, clams, and crabs, all in their shells) and *filete parrilla* (grilled beef with baked potatoes and spinach). *Huevos Reina* is a delicious light dish consisting of eggs and mushrooms baked in a cheese and wine sauce. Dine indoors or outside under white umbrellas on the plaza, with a view of the fountain. A variety of music, ranging from French to Russian, enhances the cosmopolitan mood. ✉ *Plaza de la Paz 28,* ☎ *473/2–23–20. AE, MC, V.*

$$ ✕ **El Retiro.** This traditional Mexican restaurant up the street from the Teatro Juárez is often crowded for the main midday meal; at other times you can relax with a steaming cappuccino. Though local residents swear by this restaurant's reputation, it is hardly the "retreat" that its name implies. The food is still good, but the waiters are often mesmerized by televised soccer games, and pop music sometimes replaces the classical fare that prevailed in gentler times. A full comida corrida runs less than $3; or try the *mole poblano* with chicken, broiled steak with mushroom sauce, or Spanish omelet. ✉ *Calle de Sopeña 12,* ☎ *473/2–06–22. Reservations not accepted. MC, V.*

$ ✕ **El Pingüis Cafeteria.** Cheap and plentiful food attracts the university crowd to this spartan eatery decorated with Mexican art posters. A midday meal consisting of soup, Mexican rice, a chicken or beef dish, dessert, and coffee costs about $3. The *café americano* is good, as is the *consumé de verduras* (vegetable soup). The service can be slow, but vibrant music and a lively crowd will keep you entertained. ✉ *Jardín Unión at Allende 3,* ☎ *473/2–14–14. Reservations not accepted. No credit cards.*

$ ✕ **El Unicorno Azul.** Those growing weary of heavy meat dishes might want to stop by this food counter just behind Jardín Unión: It offers fruit drinks, yogurt, and vegetarian burgers and sandwiches. The owner will cheerfully recommend other health-food establishments and yoga classes. ✉ *Plaza del Baratillo 2,* ☎ *473/2–07–00. No credit cards. Closed Sun.*

$ ★ ✕ **Truco 7.** Red tile floors, *equipale* (pigskin) chairs, and original art enliven this cozy coffeehouse and restaurant. In the morning, serious students hunch over coffee and textbooks; later in the day locals and savvy tourists pile in for the inexpensive comida corrida, sandwiches, or grilled chicken. The atmosphere is also lively at night, when Mexican wines are served by the glass. ✉ *Calle Truco 7,* ☎ *473/3-83-74. No credit cards.*

Lodging

Guanajuato's less expensive hotels are located along Avenida Juárez and Calle de la Alhóndiga. Moderately priced and upscale properties are near the Jardín Unión and on the outskirts of town. It's best to secure reservations at least six months in advance if you plan to attend the Cervantes Festival, which usually runs from mid- to late October.

$$–$$$ ★ **Parador San Javier.** This immaculately restored hacienda was converted into a hotel in 1971. In fact, a safe from the Hacienda San Javier and old wood trunks still decorate the large, plant-laden lobby. The rooms are clean and have attractive appointments: lace curtains, crisp coverlets, and blue-and-white-tiled baths. A few of the 16 colonial-style rooms reached via a stone archway have fireplaces. Newer rooms in the adjoining high rise have satellite TVs. A word of caution: Large convention groups sometimes crowd the facility. ✉ *Plaza San Javier, 36000,* ☎ *473/2-06-26,* FAX *473/2-31-14. 115 rooms. 2 restaurants, bar, café, pool, dance club, meeting rooms. AE, MC, V.*

$$ **Hostería del Frayle.** Just a half block off Jardín Unión, this quiet four-story lodging was once the Casa de Moneda, where ore was taken to be refined after it was brought out of the mines. Built in 1673 and turned into a hotel in the mid-1960s, it has whitewashed plaster and wood-beamed rooms (which nonetheless are somewhat dark), arranged around a small maze of stairways, landings, and courtyards; all have telephones and TVs (local channels only), and some afford excellent views of the Pípila, Teatro Juárez, and Jardín Unió. The staff is extremely friendly and helpful. ✉ *Calle Sopeña 3,* ☎ *473/2-11-79,* FAX *473/2-11-79, ext. 138. 37 rooms. Restaurant, bar. MC, V.*

$$ **Hotel Museo Posada Santa Fé.** This colonial-style property, located at the Jardín Unión, has been in operation since 1862. Large historic paintings by local artist Don Manuel Leal hang in the wood-paneled lobby; a sweeping carpeted stairway leads to second-floor quarters. Each room—decorated in warm, autumnal colors—has a wood minibar, cable TV, and telephone. Rooms facing the plaza can be noisy; quieter rooms face narrow alleyways. ✉ *Plaza Principal at Jardín Unión 12, 36000,* ☎ *473/2-00-84 or 473/2-02-07,* FAX *473/2-46-53. 47 rooms and suites. Restaurant, bar, outdoor hot tub, meeting rooms, airport shuttle. AE, MC, V.*

$ **Hotel Socavón.** One of Guanajuato's newer hotels, this modest five-story property was built in 1981. Don't be put off by the gloomy, tunnel-like entrance: Open-air walkways, with views of surrounding mountains, lead to guest quarters. Each small room—simply furnished with a bed, desk, and tiny television—has a wood-beamed ceiling and a modern bath. Fourth-floor corner rooms offer some good views. ✉ *Calle de la Alhóndiga 41A, 36000,* ☎ *473/2-66-66,* ☎ FAX *473/2-48-85. 37 rooms. Restaurant. AE, MC, V.*

Nightlife and the Arts

Guanajuato, on most nights a somnolent provincial capital, awakens each fall for the **International Cervantes Festival.** During two weeks in October world-renowned actors, musicians, and dance troupes (which have included the Bolshoi Ballet) perform nightly at the Teatro Juárez and at other venues in town. The Plaza San Roque, a small square near the Jardín Reforma, hosts a series of *Entremeses Cervantinos*—swashbuckling one-act farces by classical Spanish writers. Grandstand seats require advance tickets, but crowds often gather by the edge of the plaza for free. An estimated 450,000 people attended the 1996 festivities, a fact that those who abhor crowds should take into account. If you plan to be in Guanajuato for the festival, contact the Festival Internacional Cervantino office (✉ Plaza de San Francisquito 1, ☎ 473/2–57–96 or 473/2–64–87, FAX 473/2–67–75) or Ticketmaster (☎ 5/325–9000) at least six months in advance for top-billed events.

At other times of the year, nightlife in Guanajuato mostly consists of dramatic, dance, and musical performances at the **Teatro Juárez** (✉ Calle de Sopeña, ☎ 473/2–01–83). On Friday and Saturday evenings at 8 PM *callejóneadas* (mobile musical parties) begin in front of the Teatro Juárez and meander through town (don't forget to tip the musicians). The **Teatro Principal** (✉ Calle Hidalgo, ☎ 473/2–15–23) shows American movies several times a week, and some hotels, including the Parador San Javier and the Castillo Santa Cecilia, provide evening musical entertainment. There are several nightclubs located in or near the downtown area, including **Discoteque El Pequeño Juan** (✉ Panorámica Al Pípila at Callejón de Guadalupe, ☎ 473/2–23–08), whose panoramic view of the city at night is stunning, and the small but lively **Discoteque La Fragua** (✉ Calle Tepetapa 45, ☎ 473/2–27–15).

Shopping

Some jewelry and regional knicknacks can be found at the **Mercado Hidalgo** (☞ Exploring Guanajuato, *above*). Talavera ceramic ware from Dolores Hidalgo can be seen at **Artesanías Vázques** (✉ Cantarranas 8, ☎ FAX 473/2–52–31). Shops selling ceramic ware or woolen shawls and sweaters can be found around the Plaza de la Paz and Jardín Unión.

Side Trip

León

56 km (35 mi) northwest of Guanajuato.

Best known as the shoemaking capital of Mexico, León is also an important center for industry and commerce. With more than 1 million people, it is the state's most populous urban area.

If you know footwear and have the time (and patience) to browse through the downtown shops, you may find some good buys in León. First try the **Plaza del Zapato,** a mall with 70 stores located on Boulevard Adolfo López Mateos (☎ 47/17–29–08), roughly one block from the bus station. From here take a taxi west (about a 10-minute ride) to the **Zona Peatonal,** a pedestrian zone with several shoe stores. On **Calle Praxedis Guerrero** there are various artisans' stands selling leather goods.

Flecha Amarilla buses leave Guanajuato's Central Camionera every 15 minutes for León; the ride takes about 45 minutes and costs less than $1. Taxis cost about $16 one way. Pick up a map of León at the tourist office in Guanajuato.

Guanajuato A to Z

Arriving and Departing

BY BUS

Direct bus service is available between the Central del Norte (North Bus Station) in Mexico City and Guanajuato's Central Camionera (☎ 473/3–13–33); taxis to downtown from the Camionera cost $2–$3. Several lines—including **Flecha Amarilla** and **Estrella Blanca**—offer hourly service. Travel time is about five hours. Deluxe buses, including those of **ETN, Primera Plus,** and **Omnibus de México,** connect Guanajuato to Mexico City, San Miguel, and Guadalajara; there are several departures daily.

BY CAR

Guanajuato is 432 km (268 mi) northwest of Mexico City via Route 57 (to Querétaro) and Route 45 (through Celaya and Irapuato), approximately a five-hour drive.

BY PLANE

Guanajuato International Airport is 56 km (35 mi) north of Guanajuato. *See* Arriving and Departing by Plane *in* San Miguel de Allende A to Z, *above,* for international carriers that service this airport. The taxi ride from the airport to town costs about $16 and takes about 45 minutes.

Getting Around

Don't bother with a car in Guanajuato. Many of the attractions are within strolling distance of one another and located between Avenida Juárez and Calle Pocitos, the city's two major north–south arteries. The twisting subterranean roadway—El Subterráneo—also has a primarily north–south orientation.

BY TAXI

Nonmetered taxis can be hailed on the street or found at *sitios* (taxi stands) near the Jardín Unión, Plaza de la Paz, and Mercado Hidalgo.

Contacts and Resources

CAR RENTAL

Rent A Car (⊠ Blvd. López Mateos 201, ☎ 473/2–34–07, FAX 473/2–09–74) has an office at the airport, and will deliver a car to your hotel.

EMERGENCIES

Police (☎ 473/2–02–66). **Ambulance–Red Cross** (☎ 473/2–04–87). **Hospital General** (☎ 473/3–15–77 or 473/3–15–76). Note: Few people in Guanajuato have a good command of English, so in an emergency it's best to contact your hotel manager or the tourist office.

GUIDED TOURS

The following tour operators offer half and full-day tours with English-speaking guides. These tours typically include the Museum of Mummies, the church and mines of Valenciana, the monument to Pípila, the Panoramic Highway, subterranean streets, and residential neighborhoods. Night tours often begin at the Pípila Monument for a nighttime city view and end at a discothèque. Estudiantinas usually perform during the weekend tours.

SITSA (⊠ Hidalgo 6, ☎ FAX 473/2–79–90 or 473/2–90–24) can arrange walking or coach tours in addition to making travel arrangements.

Transporte Exclusivo de Turismo (⊠ Av. Juárez and Calle 5 de Mayo, ☎ 473/2–59–68) is a kiosk that offers several tours of Guanajuato and its environs.

Transporte Turísticos de Guanajuato (⊠ Plaza de la Paz s/n, by Basílica de Guanajuato, ☎ 473/2–21–34 or 473/2–28–38); also has a kiosk at the main bus terminal (☎ 473/2–37–64).

PHARMACY

A recommended pharmacy is **El Fénix** (⊠ Juárez 104, ☎ 473/2–61–40). It is open Monday–Saturday 7:45 AM–9:45 PM, Sunday 8:45 AM–9 PM.

TRAVEL AGENCIES

Viajes Georama (⊠ Plaza de la Paz 34, ☎ 473/2–59–09, 473/2–19–54, or 473/2–51–01; FAX 473/2–35–97) is the American Express representative. **Viajes Frausto** (✉ Calle González Obregón 10, ☎ 473/2–35–80) is reliable for hotel and airline reservations.

VISITOR INFORMATION

The **Guanajuato tourist office** (✉ Plaza de la Paz 14, ☎ 473/2–15–74, 473/2–00–86, or 473/2–19–82; FAX 473/2–42–510), at the back of a courtyard, is open weekdays 8–8, weekends and holidays 10–2.

There is also a **tourist information kiosk** at the Central Camionera bus station.

ZACATECAS

In colonial days Zacatecas was the largest silver-producing city in the world and sent great treasures of the precious metal to the king of Spain. Still a large silver-mining center, with factories producing silver jewelry and trade schools training apprentices in the fine art of handmade silver craft, Zacatecas is a relatively undiscovered jewel for tourists. Although it is a state capital with a population of some 300,000, it has the feel of a much smaller place; the town is kept spotlessly clean by Zacatecan pride, under a mandate by the governor of the state of Zacatecas. This destination is also famous for its historical role as the scene of one of Pancho Villa's most spectacular battles and for its 18th-century colonial architecture.

One of the town's unique charms is the *tambora,* a musical walk up and down the streets and alleyways led by a *tamborazo,* a typical local band that shatters the evening quiet with merriment. Also known as a callejóneada (*callejón* means "alley"), the tambora is a popular free-for-all, in which everyone along the way either joins in the procession or leans from balconies and doorways to cheer the group on. During the December *feria* (festival), the tamborazos play night and day as they serenade the Virgin of Zacatecas.

Exploring Zacatecas

Most of Zacatecas's colonial sights are located near the center of the city, making it an easy place to explore on foot. There is rarely much traffic in town, an added bonus. For an overview of Zacatecas, you can walk or taxi up to the mine, catch an elevator to a nearby hilltop, and take the cable car across the city, then return to your starting point below by taxi or bus.

A Good Walk

Start your tour at the Plaza de Armas, in the center of the city. Here you'll find the **Catedral de Zacatecas** ㉓ and the **Palacio del Gobierno** ㉔. Across the street from the plaza are two beautiful colonial buildings worth exploring; one is known as the **Palacio de la Mala Noche** ㉕ because of a local legend. Go to the Plaza Santo Domingo, two blocks west of the cathedral, to see the **Pedro Coronel Museum** ㉖ and the 17th-century **Templo de Santo Domingo** ㉗ right next door. To visit the museum of the other Coronel brother—both were equally fanatical art collectors—return to the cathedral, turn left on Avenida Hidalgo, and walk about 1 km (½ mi) north of the plaza to the **Rafael Coronel Museum** ㉘.

For a longer walk, head south on Avenida Hidalgo until you come to Juárez, then go right (roughly west) up the hill, passing the several-block-long Alameda park and the Social Security Hospital to arrive at the **Eden Mine** ㉙. After touring the mine, you can take an elevator up to Cerro del Grillo (Cricket Hill) and catch the **Teleférico** ㉚ cable car across the city to **Cerro de la Bufa** ㉛, site of Pancho Villa's famous battle.

Cathedral de Zacatecas, **23**
Cerro de la Bufa, **31**
Eden Mine, **29**
Palacio de la Mala Noche, **25**
Palacio del Gobierno, **24**
Pedro Coronel Museum, **26**
Rafael Coronel Museum, **28**
Teleférico, **30**
Templo de Santo Domingo, **27**

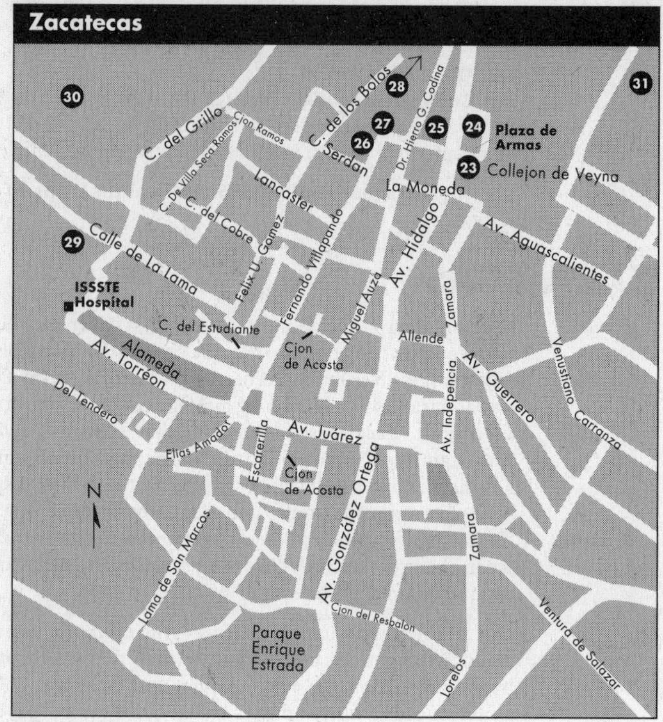

Sights to See

23 **Catedral de Zacatecas.** The ornate cathedral is considered one of the best examples of Mexican baroque style in the country. Each of the facades tells a different legend; according to one of them, an anticlerical governor of the state used the cathedral's silver cross and baptismal font to mint Zacatecas's first silver coins. ✉ *South side of Plaza de Armas on Av. Hidalgo.*

NEED A BREAK? The **Café y Nevería Acrópolis** (✉ Av. Hidalgo at Plazuela Candelario Huizar, ☎ 492/2–12–84), alongside the cathedral, is a quaint diner where locals talk shop as they drink strong Turkish coffee (under $1). There are lots of homemade pastries and cakes to choose from. Breakfast is served from 8 to 12:30.

31 **Cerro de la Bufa.** The city trademark, this rugged hill is the site of Pancho Villa's definitive battle against dictator Victoriano Huerta in June 1914. The spacious **Plaza de la Revolución,** paved with the three shades of pink Zacatecan stone, is crowned with three huge equestrian statues of Villa and two other heroes, Felipe Angeles and Panfilo Natera. Also on the site are the **Sanctuary of the Virgin of Patrocinio,** a chapel dedicated to the patron of the city, and the **Museo de la Toma de Zacatecas,** which has nine rooms filled with historic objects such as guns, newspapers, furniture, and clothing from the days of Pancho Villa. On the very tip of the hill there's a meteorological observatory; you'll need to get special permission from the Zacatecas tourist office to visit. ✉ *If driving, follow Av. Hidalgo north from town to Av. Juan de Tolosa; turn right and continue until you come to a fountain; take 1st immediate right off retorno (crossover) onto Calle Mexicapan,*

which leads to Carretera Panorámica. Turn right to signposted Carretera La Bufa, which leads to top of hill. ☎ *492/2–80–66 museum.* 🎟 *$1.* ⏲ *Tues.–Sun. 10–5.*

29 **Eden Mine.** Now a tourist attraction, La Mina Eden supplied most of Zacatecas's silver from 1586 until 1960. An open mine train runs down into the underground tunnels; there's a small gift shop at the entrance. The tour is in Spanish, but you'll have no trouble imagining what the life of the miners was like. Be sure to wear sturdy shoes. Remember that mines are dark; through much of the tour, your only light may be the guide's flashlight. Farther down the train track there is another stop at, of all places, a discotheque (☞ Nightlife and the Arts, *below*). ✉ *Entrance on Antonio Dovali off Av. Torreon beyond Alameda García de la Cadena,* ☎ *492/2–30–02.* 🎟 *$2.* ⏲ *Daily 10–6.*

25 **Palacio de la Mala Noche.** The Palace of the Bad Night is one of two beautiful 18th-century colonial buildings, both declared national monuments, right across from the downtown plaza. They are built from native pink stone and have lacy ironwork balconies. One of them now houses the Continental Plaza hotel (☞ Dining and Lodging, *below*), and the other is presently a municipal building known as El Palacio de la Mala Noche. Legend has it that this was the home of a silver-mine owner who was called upon so often to help the needy that he built a hidden door from which he could enter and leave the palace undisturbed. One night a terrible storm was raging, yet a worker had the temerity to pound on the front door. He finally gained entrance with his good news: Silver had been found in a mine considered exhausted. Up the hill along the side of the palace, you will find the so-called hidden door. ✉ *Av. Hidalgo 639.* ⏲ *Weekdays 10–2 and 4–7.*

24 **Palacio del Gobierno.** The Governor's Palace is an 18th-century mansion containing flower-filled courtyards and, on the main staircase, a powerful mural depicting the history of Zacatecas. ✉ *East side of Plaza de Armas.* ⏲ *Weekdays 9–2 and 5–8, Sat. 9–1.*

26 **Pedro Coronel Museum.** Originally a Jesuit monastery, this building was used as a jail in the 18th century. The museum is one of a kind in Mexico and Latin America, housing the work of Zacatecan artist and sculptor Pedro Coronel and his extensive collection of works by Picasso, Dali, Miró, Braque, and Chagall among others, as well as art from Africa, China, Japan, India, Greece, and Egypt. ✉ *Av. Fernando Villalpando at Plaza Santo Domingo,* ☎ *492/2–80–21.* 🎟 *About $1.50.* ⏲ *Fri.–Wed. 10–2 and 4–7.*

28 **Rafael Coronel Museum.** The museum is in the Ex-Convento de San Francisco, northeast of the town center toward Lomas del Calvario. Its 18th-century facade of mellowed pink tones conceals a rambling structure of open-arched corridors, all leading through garden patios to rooms that contain an amazing collection of some 3,700 *máscaras* (masks)—including saints and devils, wise men and fools, animals and humans—used in regional festivals all over Mexico. There is also an outstanding display of puppets. ✉ *Off Vergel Nuevo between Chaveño and Garcia Salinas,* ☎ *492/2–81–16.* 🎟 *About $1.50.* ⏲ *Mon.–Tues. and Thurs.–Sat. 10–2 and 4–7, Sun. 10–5.*

30 **Teleférico.** The only cable car in the world that crosses an entire city, the Teleferico takes passengers from **Cerro del Grillo** (Cricket Hill) above the Eden Mine to **Cerro de la Bufa** and runs from 10 to dusk daily. True, it crosses at the narrowest point, but it presents a magnificent panoramic view of the city and its many baroque church domes and spires. It's also well worth the cost (about 75¢ each way) to get the ride up to Cerro de la Bufa, which is quite a climb otherwise. ✉ *Cerro*

del Grillo station of Teleférico is just off Paseo Díaz Ordaz, a steep walk from plaza, no phone. ⏲ *Daily noon–dusk.*

27 **Templo de Santo Domingo.** Built by the Jesuits in the 18th century, this church has an ornate baroque facade and an elaborate interior, including gold-leaf religious paintings. The sacristy also contains a collection of religious art. ✉ *Av. Fernando Villalpando at Plaza Santo Domingo.*

Dining

Several of Zacatecas's better restaurants are located in hotels; another is right in El Mercado, the boutique area on Calle Hidalgo near the cathedral. Other popular restaurants can be found on Avenida Juárez, which intersects Hidalgo.

$$$ ✕ **La Cuija.** Regional food is the strength of this large restaurant, whose name means "the gecko." Start off with appetizer of three quesadillas: one each of squash blossoms, cheese, and *huitlacocha* (a corn fungus delicacy). Also recommended are the *sopa campera* (a cream soup with corn and squash blossoms), and *asado de boda* (pork in a semisweet and spicy sauce). The decor approximates a wine cellar, and in addition to fine food, the restaurant serves wine from the owner's Cachola Vineyards in Valle de las Arsinas (☞ Side Trips, *below*). A traditional Mexican trio plays Thursday–Sunday evenings. ✉ *Centro Commercial El Mercado, bottom level,* ☎ *492/2–82–75. AE, MC, V.*

$$ ✕ **Cenaduría Los Dorados.** Hidden on a small square adjacent to the Ex-Convent of San Francisco, this small, cheery restaurant is packed with memorabilia from the War of Independence. There is a no-smoking section, and the food is tasty and wholesome, if perhaps a bit toned down for tourists' palates. Dinner is the most popular meal here. ✉ *Plazuela de García 1314,* ☎ *492/2–57–22. No credit cards.*

$ ✕ **Mesón la Mina.** Hang with the local small-business men in this no-frills restaurant near the Jardín Independencia. In seeming contradiction, waiters in crisp black and white hurry attentively to your faux-grain Formica table, bringing tasty meals in extra-large portions on institution-style plastic plates. There are meats, burgers, sandwiches, and enchiladas in addition to a huge fixed-price midday meal of soup, rice, main dish, vegetable, beans, dessert, and coffee—for about $3. ✉ *Juárez 15,* ☎ *492/2–27–73. No credit cards.*

$ ✕ **Rancho Viejo.** This informal ranch-style restaurant serves dishes with a Zacatecan flavor, including *huchepos* (tamales with sour cream) and enchiladas covered with vegetables and a rich red chili sauce. ✉ *Av. Universidad 101,* ☎ *492/2–67–47. MC, V.*

Dining and Lodging

$$$ ✕🏨 **Continental Plaza.** Formerly the Radisson Paraiso Zacatecas, this beautiful old colonial building faces the Plaza de Armas and the cathedral in the heart of the city. The pink-stone facade dates from the 18th century, and the more recent additions match perfectly. Rooms are decorated in new but unexceptional furniture. Those facing the plaza are susceptible to late-night and early morning tamborazo music during festivals; on the other hand, from your small balcony you'll get a great view of the goings-on. The hotel's restaurant, **Candiles,** is popular with the local business crowd as well as guests. It has soft lighting, and the black lacquer chairs contrast with white tablecloths and crystal. The impressive menu includes both continental and regional dishes, and there is a daily breakfast buffet. ✉ *Av. Hidalgo 703, 98000,* ☎ *492/2–61–83 or 492/2–61–86,* FAX *492/2–62–45. 115 rooms and suites. Restaurant, bar, convention center. AE, MC, V.*

Lodging

Many of Zacatecas's best lodgings are in the city's treasured historic buildings, which have been preserved in all their 18th- and 19th-century beauty.

$$$$ ★ **Quinta Real.** This hotel must be one of the most unusual in the world: It is built around Mexico's oldest bullring, the second one constructed in the Western Hemisphere. The terrazzo-paved ring provides a unique view for the guest rooms, each with a balcony overlooking the *plaza de toro*. Large and bright, the rooms are decorated in pastel fabrics that complement the dark traditional furniture. The bar occupies some of the former bull pens, and an outdoor café with bright-yellow umbrella tables occupies two levels of the spectator area. Fine continental cuisine is served in the elaborate, formal restaurant, with an awesome view of the bullring with the aqueduct beyond. ✉ *Gonzales Ortega at aqueduct, 98000,* ☎ *492/4–25–33, 492/4–27–08, or 800/426–0494;* FAX *492/4–21–92. 49 rooms. Restaurant, bar, café. AE, MC, V.*

$$$ **Holiday Inn.** One of the most modern hotels in Zacatecas, this pleasant property is only three blocks from the historic town center. From the bay windows of its front rooms you can see over the rooftops of the whitewashed dome of the beautiful baroque-style Templo San José. Rooms—all with satellite TVs, individual climate control, and marble baths—are done in cool blue, green, and white; furnishings include Mexican chests painted white and lacy white ironwork headboards. ✉ *Blvd. López Matéos y Callejón del Barro, 98000,* ☎ *492/2–33–11; 800/465–4329 in the U.S.;* FAX *492/2–34–15. 111 rooms, 15 suites. 2 restaurants, bar, coffee shop, pool, sauna, shop, nightclub, playground, meeting rooms. AE, MC, V.*

$$$ **Mesón de Jobito.** This early 19th-century apartment building lasted for well over a hundred years before its recent conversion to a four-star hotel. The two levels of guest rooms are done in modern decor, with wall-to-wall carpet and striped drapes. All rooms have cable TVs and telephones. The restful atmosphere is enhanced by the Mesón's perfect location on a blissfully quiet little plaza just a few blocks from the cathedral. ✉ *Jardín Juárez 143, 98000,* ☎ FAX *492/4–17–22. 31 rooms. Restaurant, bar. AE, MC, V.*

$ **Posada de la Moneda.** Adequate for those on a budget is this very Mexican hotel in the middle of downtown. Everything is highly polished, especially the lobby's marble floor. If the room furnishings are a bit threadbare, they are clean, and the carpet is new. Each room has a telephone and TV (local channels only); the second-floor lounge has some impressive chartreuse Naugahyde furniture. ✉ *Hidalgo 413, 98000,* ☎ *492/2–08–81. 34 rooms, 2 suites. 2 restaurants, bar. No credit cards.*

Nightlife and the Arts

If only for its uniqueness, a must-visit is **El Malacate** (☎ 492/2–30–02), the discotheque in La Mina Eden, a stop on the Eden Mine train and more than 1,000 ft underground. It's best to make reservations at this popular place, which is both crowded and noisy. There is a $5 cover charge. Atop a mountain outside Zacatecas, **El Elefante Blanco** (✉ Mina La Gallega 15, ☎ 492/2–71–04), a discotheque with a panoramic view of the city, is open Thursday–Saturday nights. For some surprisingly good local blues and jazz, head to **Arcano** (✉ Hidalgo 111, downstairs, ☎ 492/2–05–38), a small lounge-bar favored by the Zacatecas art and intellectual crowd. The band plays Thursday through Saturday until 1 AM. There's live music in the lobby bar of the **Continental Plaza**

(☞ Dining and Lodging, *above*), and the **Holiday Inn** has a nightclub with live entertainment (☞ Lodging, *above*).

Shopping

Don't expect to find quality crafts in Zacatecas: souvenirs are more along the line of tacky knickknacks than handicrafts. There is some decent silver jewelry, although not as much as one would expect.

Crafts

Opposite the east end of the Plaza de Armas is **La Cazzorra** (✉ Hidalgo 713, ☎ 492/4–04–84), a collectibles shop with authentic antiques, books about Zacatecas, wood furniture, Huichol art, and ceramics. The owners—husband and wife—are a good source of information about the city.

Silver

Centro Platero Zacatecas, located downtown in **Centro Comercial El Mercado** (✉ Calle Hidalgo, next to cathedral, ☎ 492/3–10–07), sells silver jewelry with regional designs, made in its factory in nearby Guadalupe (☞ Side Trips, *below*).

Yohuatl, also located in the **Centro Comercial El Mercado** (✉ Calle Hidalgo, no phone), has a large selection of silver jewelry and accessories for women and men.

Side Trips

Valle de las Arsinas

27 km (16 mi) east of Zacatecas.

A visit to the award-winning Cachola Vineyards in Valle de las Arsinas is worth your while. The cold winters, mild springtimes, and temperate summers in the valley produced a silver medal for the vineyard's 1986 Cachola French Columbard at the VINEXPO 1991 in France. Tours of the vineyard are best arranged beforehand, especially if you would like a tasting. The most interesting time to visit is August–October, when grapes are being picked and processed. ✉ *Cruce de Carretera Panamericana, Km 634, con Carretera a San Luis Potosí, Km 161, Las Arsinas, Guadalupe,* ☎ *492/2–82–75 or 492/4–15–55.*

Guadalupe

7 km (4 mi) southeast of Zacatecas.

Those interested in colonial art and architecture should not miss seeing this small town. Its centerpiece is the **Ex-Convento de Guadalupe,** founded by Franciscan monks in 1707. It currently houses the **Museo de Arte Virreinal** (*virreinal* means "viceregal," or colonial), run by the Instituto Nacional de Antropología e Historia. The convent is itself a work of art, with its baroque-style **Templo de Guadalupe** and the **Capilla de Nápoles,** but even more impressive is the stunning collection of art under its roof. Works by Miguel Cabrera, Nicolás Rodríguez Juárez, Cristóbal de Villalpando, and Andrés López are included, among others. ✉ *Jardín Juárez s/n,* ☎ *492/3–23–86.* 🎫 *$2; free Sun.* ⏲ *Tues.–Sun. 10–5.*

Also of interest is a visit to the **Centro Platero Zacatecas** (✉ Casco de la Ex-Hacienda Bernárdez, ☎ 492/3–10–07), a school and factory for fine handmade silver jewelry and other items; it's housed in the 18th-century mansion of don Ignacio de Bernárdez. It's fascinating to watch student silversmiths master this fine tradition.

Zona Arqueológica La Quemada

50 km (30 mi) southwest of Zacatecas on Highway 54, 3 km (2 mi) off highway.

This ancient city was already a ruin before the Spaniards arrived in the 16th century. Although it was once believed that seven different Indian cultures built here, one community atop the other, this theory is currently under scrutiny. Nonetheless, the site's original name, "Chicomostoc," means "place of the seven tribes." The remaining edifices appear to be constructed of thin slabs of stone wedged into place. The principal draw is a group of rose-color ruins containing 11 large, round columns built entirely of the same small slabs of rock seen in the rest of the ruins. There is now an impressive site museum with a scale model of the ruins and some interesting artifacts. To get there, take a bus toward Villanueva, get off at the entrance to La Quemada, and walk in 3 km (1.8 mi). The bus ride takes about an hour. Alternately, take a taxi or guided tour. 🎫 *$2; free Sun.* ⏲ *Site daily 10–5, museum daily 10–4.*

Zacatecas A to Z

Arriving and Departing

BY BUS

Omnibus de México and **Primera Plus** operate several first- and second-class buses daily from Mexico City to Zacatecas. The trip takes 8–9 hours.

BY CAR

Zacatecas is 603 km (375 mi) northwest of Mexico City via Route 57 (to Querétaro and San Luis Potosí) and Route 49, approximately a 7½- to 8-hour drive.

BY PLANE

Mexicana (☎ 492/2–74–29, 492/2–74–70, or 492/2–32–48) has direct service to Zacatecas from Chicago, Denver, and Los Angeles. In Zacatecas, the Mexicana Airlines office is located at Hidalgo 406, ☎ 492/2–74–29). The airport is 29 km (18 mi) north of town; **Aerotransportes** (☎ 492/2–59–46) provides transportation for about $3; a private taxi costs about $12.

Getting Around

You can reach most of the town-center attractions by foot, although you might want to hire a taxi if you want to tour a mine or take a ride on the Teleférico (cable car) to the top of Cerro de la Bufa. The city has an excellent and inexpensive bus system.

Contacts and Resources

EMERGENCIES

Police (☎ 492/2–01–80). **Red Cross** (☎ 492/2–30–05). **Hospital** (☎ 492/3–30–04). **Emergency Service** (☎ 06). English is not generally spoken in Zacatecas, so it's best to contact your hotel manager or the tourist office in case of an emergency.

GUIDED TOURS

Viajes Mazzoco (✉ Enlace 115, ☎ 492/2–08–59, FAX 492/2–55–59), a well-established travel agency and the local American Express representative, offers a four-hour tour of the city center, the Eden Mine, the Teleférico, and La Bufa for about $11 per person. There are also tours to La Quemada ruins and environs ($15) and organized callejóneadas through the streets.

Operadora Zacatecas (☎ 492/4–00–50 or 492/4–37–17) is recommended by the tourism office, and offers much the same tours as **Viajes Mazzoco** (☞ *above*).

PHARMACY

Farmacia Isstezac (✉ Dr. Ignacio Hierro 522, ☎ 492/2–80–89) is open 24 hours a day.

VISITOR INFORMATION

The **tourist information** booth (Módulo de Información Turística) (✉ Av. Hidalgo 629, ☎ 492/4–03–93 or 492/4–05–52), open weekdays 9–8, weekends 9–7, is across the street from the town cathedral.

The state **Dirección Estatal de Turismo** (✉ Prolongación González s/n, ☎ 492/4–05–52 or 492/4–03–93, FAX 492/2–93–29) is across from the train station.

QUERÉTARO

A state capital and industrial center of nearly 1 million people, Querétaro, like other Bajío cities, has played a significant role in Mexican history. In 1810, in the home of Josefa Ortiz de Domínguez—a heroine of the independence movement known as La Corregidora—the first plans for independence were hatched. In 1848 the Mexican-American War was concluded in this city with the signing of the Treaty of Guadalupe Hidalgo. Emperor Maximilian made his last stand here in 1867 and was executed by firing squad in the *Cerro de las Campanas* (Hill of the Church Bells), north of town. A small memorial chapel, built by the Austrian government, marks the spot. A gigantic statue of Benito Juárez crowns a park on the crest of the hill just above it. In 1917 the Mexican Constitution, which still governs the land, was signed in this city.

Throughout Querétaro are markers, museums, churches, and monuments that commemorate the city's heroes and historic moments. A prevailing sense of civic pride is evident in the impeccably renovated mansions, the flower-draped cobblestone pedestrian walkways, and the hospitable plazas, which are softly lit at night. On Sunday evenings couples dance to live *danzón* music in the main plaza, or simply chat and enjoy the company of their friends. The people are among the most congenial in central Mexico and are quick to share their favorite sites and tales with travelers.

Querétaro is also renowned for opals—red, green, honey, and fire stones, as opposed to the milky Australian kind. However, visitors should beware of street vendors, who may sell opals so full of water that they crumble shortly after purchase; depend upon reputable dealers (☞ Shopping, *below*).

Exploring Querétaro

Though Querétaro's boundaries extend for some distance, the historic district is in the heart of town. A day or two can easily be spent here, visiting museums, admiring the architecture, and learning the local history.

A Good Walk

Most of the city's sights are near the **Plaza de la Independencia** ㉜. The **Palacio del Gobierno del Estado** ㉝ is on the plaza's northwest corner; if you walk around the square counterclockwise, you'll come to the Palacio de Justicia, originally built as a mansion for the wealthy Domingo Iglesia and, beside it, the **Casa de Ecala** ㉞. Just past the Casa de Ecala is Avenida Libertad Oriente, one of the city's bougainvillea-draped pedestrian walkways. Turn west here and walk two blocks to reach Calle Corregidora. Bear right again, and in the middle of a long block you'll find the entrance to the **Museo Regional de Querétaro** ㉟. Cross the street to Avenida Madero, another "pedway," this one lined with shops. The city's main square, Jardín Obregón, will be on your right.

One block past Avenida Juárez on the corner of Allende Sur and Madero you'll see the former **Casa de la Marquesa** ㊱, an old estate converted into a hotel (☞ Lodging, *below*). Across Allende, next to the Church of Santa Clara, is the neoclassical **Fountain of Neptune** ㊲. From the fountain, make a left on Calle Allende and walk almost a block to a fine example of baroque architecture, the **State Museum of Art** ㊳. Retrace your steps to Calle Corregidora. Make a left and walk one block to Calle 16 de Septiembre. Across the street is the **Jardín de la Corregidora** ㊴.

Sights to See

34 **Casa de Ecala.** Currently housing the offices of DIF, a family services organization, this Mexican baroque palace retains its original facade. As the story goes, its 18th-century owner adorned his home elaborately in order to outdo his neighbor, starting a remodeling war in which the Casa de Escala eventually triumphed. Visitors are welcome to walk around the courtyard when the offices are open. ✉ *Pasteur Sur 6, Plaza de la Independencia.* ⏲ *Weekdays 9–9, Sat. 9–1.*

36 **Casa de la Marquesa.** Today a five-star hotel, this beautifully restored 18th-century home was built by the second Marqués de la Villa del Villar del Aguila. There are many legends regarding the house's construction, most of which indicate that it was built to impress a nun with whom the marquis was terribly smitten. The marquis did not live to see the completion of the building (1756), and its first resident was his widow, who had a penchant for things Arabic: The building's interior is Mudejar style, with lovely tilework. ✉ *Madero 41.*

37 **Fountain of Neptune.** Built in 1797 by Eduardo Tresguerras, the renowned Mexican architect and a native of the Bajío, the fountain originally stood in the orchard of the Monastery of San Antonio. According to one story, when the monks faced serious economic problems, they sold part of their land and the fountain along with it. It now stands next to the Church of Santa Clara. ✉ *Calle Allende at Madero.*

39 **Jardín de la Corregidora.** This plaza is prominently marked by a statue of the War of Independence heroine after whom it is named. Behind the monument stands the **Arbol de la Amistad** (Tree of Friendship). Planted in 1977 in a mixture of soils from around the world, the tree symbolizes Querétaro's hospitality to all travelers. You may want to find a bench in the Jardín and sit for a while: This is the calmest square in town, with many choices for patio dining. ✉ *Av. Corregidora and Andador 16 de Septiembre.*

35 **Museo Regional de Querétaro.** This bright yellow, 17th-century Franciscan monastery displays the works of colonial and European artists in addition to historic memorabilia, including early copies of the Mexican Constitution and the table on which the Treaty of Guadalupe Hidalgo was signed. ✉ *Calle Corregidora at 5 de Mayo,* ☎ *42/12–20–31.* 🎟 *About $2.50.* ⏲ *Tues.–Sun. 10–4.*

33 **Palacio del Gobierno del Estado.** Also known as La Casa de la Corregidora, the Palacio houses municipal government offices, but in 1810 it was the home of Querétaro's mayor-magistrate (El Corregidor) and

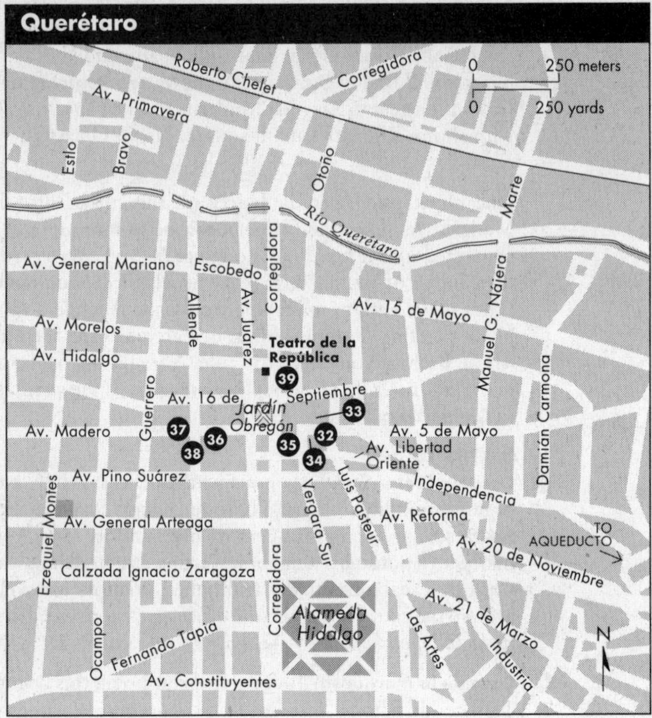

his wife, Josefa Ortiz de Domínguez (La Corregidora). On many evenings conspirators—including Ignacio Allende and Father Miguel Hidalgo—came here under the guise of participating in La Corregidora's literary salon. When the mayor-magistrate learned that they were actually plotting the course for independence, he imprisoned his wife in her room. La Corregidora managed to whisper a warning to a coconspirator, who notified Allende and Hidalgo. A few days later, on September 16, Father Hidalgo tolled the bell of his church to signal the beginning of the fight for freedom. A replica of the bell can be seen atop the building. ✉ *Northwest corner of Plaza de la Independencia.* ⏲ *Weekdays 9–9, Sat. 9–2.*

32 **Plaza de la Independencia.** Bordered by carefully restored colonial mansions, this immaculate square, also known as Plaza de Armas, is especially lovely at night, when the central fountain is lit. Built in 1842, the fountain is dedicated to the Marquis de la Villa del Villar, who constructed Querétaro's elegant aqueduct and provided the city with drinking water. The old stone aqueduct with its 74 towering arches still stands at the east end of town, though it no longer brings water into the city. ✉ *Bounded by Av. 5 de Mayo on the north, Av. Libertad on the south, Luis Pasteur on the east, and Vergara Sur on the west.*

38 **State Museum of Art.** A fine example of baroque architecture, the museum is housed in an 18th-century Augustinian monastery. Its collection focuses on European and Mexican paintings from the 17th through 19th centuries, but there are rotating exhibits of 20th-century art. Take note of the baroque patio, considered by some to be the most beautiful in the world, and ask one of the museum's curators to explain the fascination symbolism of the patio's columns and the figures in the conch

shells at the top of each arch. ✉ *Calle Allende 14 Sur,* ☎ *42/12-23-57.* 🎫 *About $1.50; free Tues.* ⏲ *Tues.–Sun. 11–7.*

Dining

Many of Querétaro's dining spots are located near the main plaza (Jardín Obregón), along Calle Corregidora, near the Teatro de la República, and particularly in the Jardín de la Corregidora. There are more upscale restaurants in hotels on the Plaza Independencia or off Route 57, north of the city.

$$$ ✕ **Fonda del Refugio.** Situated in the Jardín de la Corregidora, this restaurant offers intimate indoor and outdoor dining. Inside, fresh flowers adorn white-clothed tables; outside, comfortable leather chairs face the surrounding gardens. Seafood and beef fillets are the specialty; order the fillet of beef cooked in red wine, lemon, mustard, and peppers, or the scallops prepared in marsala. Cocktails are served on the terrace at night, when diners are often serenaded by guitar-playing trios. ✉ *Jardín de la Corregidora 26,* ☎ *42/12-07-55. AE, MC, V.*

$$$ ★ ✕ **Restaurante Josecho.** Bullfight aficionados and other sports fans frequent this highway road stop next to the bullring at the southwest end of town as much for the lively atmosphere as for the food. Wood-paneled walls are hung with hunting trophies, including geese, elk, bears, and leopards; waiters celebrate patrons' birthdays by banging on pewter plates and blasting a red siren. Though the place can be raucous, it does quiet down at night, when a classical guitarist or pianist performs. House specialties include *filete Josecho* (steak with cheese and mushrooms), *filete Chemita* (steak sautéed in butter with onions), and shrimp crepes smothered in a cheese-and-tomato sauce. ✉ *Dalia 1, next to Plaza de Toros Santa María,* ☎ *42/16-02-29 or 42/16-02-01. AE, DC, MC, V.*

$$ ✕ **El Mesón de Chucho el Roto.** Named after Querétaro's version of Robin Hood, this restaurant is located on the quiet Plaza de Armas. It has an interesting menu that highlights regional cooking, including exotic tacos of either steamed goat, shrimp with nopal cactus, or squash blossoms. The chile en nogada is a mild pepper stuffed with ground beef and dried fruits and covered in walnut sauce. You can enjoy a variety of breakfast foods here as well, either overlooking the plaza from the café tables outside, indoors, or on the back patio. ✉ *Plaza de Armas,* ☎ *42/12-42-95. AE, MC, V.*

$ ✕ **La Flor de Querétaro.** There should be something for everyone at "the flower of Querétaro": a plain but pleasant eatery in the heart of the city. Groups of the neighborhood's small-business men seem permanently ensconsed at their favorite Formica tables. There is a vintage cappuccino machine, an ancient freezer, and best of all, no television: Classical music plays unobtrusively in the background. Most of the menu is à la carte: there are good chicken enchiladas *suizas* (with a mild red sauce) and *chile rellenos* (green pepper stuffed with seasoned ground meat), and those starved for fresh veggies can order a massive side dish of sautéed carrots or other vegetable. ✉ *Av. Juarez 5, no phone. No credit cards.*

$ ✕ **La Mariposa.** Celebrating more than 50 years in business, La Mariposa is easily recognized by a wrought-iron butterfly (*mariposa*) over the entrance. This is the place for coffee and cake or a light Mexican lunch: enchiladas, tacos, tamales, and *tortas* (sandwiches). It's a favorite among locals despite its very plain, cafeteria-like appearance; some visitors describe it as "sterile." ✉ *Angela Peralta 7,* ☎ *42/12-11-66, 42/12-48-49, or 42/12-18-71. Reservations not accepted. No credit cards.*

Lodging

Several new hotels in various price ranges have opened in Querétaro in the past 10 years. Lower-priced hotels are located near the main plaza and thus tend to be noisy; restored colonial mansions are on or near the city's many plazas in the heart of town; and deluxe properties, including a Holiday Inn, are on the outskirts of town.

$$$$ ★ **Casa de la Marquesa.** This beautifully restored property, originally an 18th-century private home (☞ Exploring Querétaro, *above*), is perfectly situated in the heart of Querétaro. The central courtyard of the main building is a beautifully decorated sitting room. Each large guest room is furnished differently with antique furniture, tasteful art, parquet floors, and area rugs. Comfort is ensured with modern amenities such as air-conditioning and heat, cable TVs, deep bathtubs, and direct-dial telephones. There are two buildings; rooms in the main building are more elegant and expensive, and quieter than those in La Casa Azul. Children are not admitted. The property's award-winning restaurant, **Comedor de la Marquesa,** is elegant and a bit austere: it specializes in such regional rarities as boar, venison, and *escamole* (ant eggs) in season, as well as more traditional international cuisine. ✉ *Madero 41, 76000,* ☎ *42/12–00–92,* FAX *42/12–00–98. 25 rooms. 2 restaurants, bar, room service, shop, meeting rooms. AE, MC, V.*

$$$$ ★ **Mesón de Santa Rosa.** Located on the quiet Plaza de la Independencia, this elegant all-suites property was used almost 300 years ago as a stopover for travelers to the north. Rooms are clustered around a quiet courtyard, and lace-hung glass doors, warm autumn-colored decor and furnishings, and wood-beamed ceilings maintain the colonial charm. Amenities such as satellite TVs, minibars, and a heated pool make this lovely hotel comfortable as well. ✉ *Pasteur Sur 17, 76000,* ☎ *42/24–29–93 or 42/24–26–23,* FAX *42/12–55–22. 21 suites. Restaurant, bar, pool, meeting rooms. AE, MC, V.*

$$ **Hotel Mirabel.** A favorite among business travelers and conventioneers, this modern high-rise hums with activity. Its carpeted rooms, however, are insulated and quiet and have satellite TVs, telephones, wood desks, FM stereos, and air-conditioning. Some double rooms have views of the Alameda Hidalgo park; some singles overlook a soccer stadium. ✉ *Av. Constituyentes Oriente 2, 76000,* ☎ *42/14–30–99 or 42/14–34–44,* FAX *42/14–35–85. 171 rooms. Restaurant, bar, convention center. AE, MC, V.*

$ **Hotel Plaza.** This modest property, located on the main plaza, offers clean accommodations, lots of hot water, and a courteous staff. Rooms facing the principal square are extremely noisy—even at night. Inside rooms, particularly those on the second floor, are much quieter but dark. All rooms have telephones, TVs, and very tiny bathrooms. ✉ *Av. Juárez Norte 23, 76000,* ☎ *42/12–11–38 or 42/12–65–62. 29 rooms. MC, V.*

$ **Hotel Señorial.** Built in 1981, this sprawling four-story property has plain yet clean, large, and modern rooms with telephones and cable TVs. Rooms in front face a narrow, busy street, but traffic slows in the evening. There are purified-water dispensers in the hallways. The restaurant serves a Sunday buffet lunch. ✉ *Guerrero Norte 10-A, 76000,* ☎ *42/14–37–00,* FAX *42/14–19–45. 45 rooms. Restaurant, meeting room. MC, V.*

Nightlife and the Arts

Band concerts are held in the **Jardín Obregón,** Querétaro's main square, every Sunday evening at 6. A leaflet called *Cartelera de Eventos,* available at the tourist office or around town, provides information about current festivals, concerts, and other cultural events.

Shopping

A number of stores around town sell **opals** (not milky white, like Australian opals, but beautiful nonetheless) and other locally mined gems. If you're in the market for loose stones or opal jewelry, do some comparison shopping, as you're apt to find better prices here than in the United States. Just off Plaza Principal, **El Rubi** (✉ Av. Madero 3 Pte., ☎ 42/12–09–84) is a reputable dealer. The owner, Señora Villalon, provides information on the mining, care, and value of opals. The store is open weekdays 10–2 and 4–5, Saturday 10–2.

Side Trips

San Juan del Río and Tequisquiapan

San Juan del Río and Tequisquiapan are both within an hour's drive of Querétaro. The highway between Querétaro and San Juan del Río is paved with factories, and San Juan is a bustling manufacturing center whose only real attraction for tourists are the semiprecious gems—especially opals, topaz, and amethyst—sold there, both loose or in settings. Tequisquiapan, on the other hand, is a tranquil and pretty *pueblo* (town) drenched in sun and bougainvilleas and flowering trees, and known as a producer of wicker and other handcrafts. Once frequented by harried Mexican urbanites who came to soak in the area's thermal waters, "Tequis" (as the locals call it) now suffers a dearth of hot water.

The simplest way to reach either town is by car. Buses service both towns from Querétaro, but the trip is longer. If you plan to visit both towns, you'll probably want to do your shopping first in San Juan del Río, then head to Tequisquiapan to look around, shop a bit, and perhaps have a meal or a snack. A taxi ride between these two towns costs about $4.50.

SAN JUAN DEL RÍO

51 km (32 mi) southeast of Querétaro via Rte. 57.

Most of San Juan's gem shops are located near the main plaza downtown, and along Av. Juárez and Calle 16 de Septiembre. **Lapidaria Guerrero** (✉ Av. Juárez Poniente 4, ☎ 472/2–14–81) has an exceptionally large collection of opal, amethyst, turquoise, and topaz jewelry.

TEQUISQUIAPAN

19 km (12 mi) east of San Juan, off Rte. 120.

This town, which has been famous for centuries for its restorative thermal waters, has in recent years lost much of its thermal flow, reportedly due to the extraordinary water consumption of a new paper mill in the area. Many spas struggle on as simple swimming pools/recreation areas, but the main tourist draw has receded with the once-warm waters, and most are deserted midweek, although things liven up on hot weekends. The **tourist office** (✉ Morelos 7, ☎ 472/3–02–95), open Tuesday–Sunday 10–5, seems unaware of these geothermal changes, and will cheerfully direct you to one or more of the spas, most of which are outside of town.

After lunch or a snack, head to the shops or to the **Mercado de Artesanías** (✉ Calzado de los Misterios s/n, no phone), where woven goods, jewelry, and locally made furniture are sold. The **Templo de Santa María de la Asunción,** on the main plaza, was begun in 1874 in the neoclassical style, but not completed until the beginning of the current century. Each August the city hosts a weeklong **wine and cheese festival** that includes open-air theater, expositions, and concerts.

Querétero A to Z

Arriving and Departing

BY BUS

Direct bus service is available daily between the Central del Norte (North Bus Station) in Mexico City and Querétaro's Central de Autobuses. Major lines—including **Flecha Amarilla, Omnibus de México, Tres Estrellas de Oro,** and **Transportes del Norte**—offer frequent service; travel time is about three hours. Buses also leave several times a day for Guanajuato, San Miguel de Allende, and Morelia.

BY CAR

Querétaro is 220 km (136 mi) northwest of Mexico City, a three-hour drive via Route 57.

BY TRAIN

The *Constitucionalista* departs from Mexico City at 9 AM and arrives in Querétaro at 1 PM; the return trip leaves Querétaro at 2:40 PM and arrives in Mexico City at 6:40 PM. Tickets should be purchased one day in advance; the one-way fare is $6. For current schedule and rate information, contact **Mexico by Train** (☎ FAX 210/725–3659 or 800/321–1699) or call the local station (☎ 42/12–17–03 or 42/12–17–89). If the local station does not answer, call 915/547–1084 or 915/547–6593 in Mexico City for schedule information.

Getting Around

Most of Querétaro's historic sites are within walking distance of one another in the downtown district and can be reached by a series of walkways that are closed to automobile traffic most of the day. If you want to venture farther afield, you will find that buses and taxis run frequently along the main streets and are inexpensive.

Contacts and Resources

CAR RENTAL

Budget (✉ Av. Constituyentes Oriente 73, ☎ 42/13–44–98, FAX 42/13–44–38). **National** (✉ Calle 13 de Septiembre 34, ☎ 42/16–35–44), FAX 42/16–52–40).

EMERGENCIES

Police (☎ 42/20–83–83 or 42/20–85–03). **Ambulance–Red Cross** (☎ 42/29–05–45 or 42/29–06–65). **Fire Department** (☎ 42/16–06–27 or 42/12–39–39). **Green Angels** (☎ 42/13–84–24).

Hospital. Sanatorio Alcocer Pozo (✉ Calle Reforma 23, ☎ 42/12–01–49 or 42/12–17–87).

GUIDED TOURS

The tourist office conducts a 90-minute walking tour of the city's historic landmarks at 10:30 AM and 6PM daily. Although the morning tour is supposed to be in English, this is not always the case. To arrange a city tour, call the office (☞ Visitor Information, *below*), if possible one day in advance.

MONEY EXCHANGE

Casa de Cambio Acueducto (✉ Av. Juárez Sur 58, ☎ 42/12–93–04 or 42/14–31–89) is open weekdays 9–2 and 4–6, Saturday 9–1.

TRAVEL AGENCY

Wagons-Lits Viajes (✉ Av. Tecnologia N-2, interior 209, ☎ 42/15–04–67 or 42/15–04–79, FAX 42/15–04–39).

VISITOR INFORMATION

Dirección de Turismo del Estado (✉ Plaza de la Independencia at Pasteur 4 Norte, ☎ 42/12–14–12 or 42/12–09–07, FAX 42/12–10–94) is open weekdays 9–9, weekends 9–8.

MORELIA

With its long, wide boulevards and earth-tone colonial mansions, Morelia is the gracious capital of the state of Michoacán. Founded in 1541 as Valladolid (after the Spanish city), it changed its name in 1828 to honor José María Morelos, the town's most famous son. The legendary mule skinner–turned–priest took up the battle for independence after its early leaders were executed in 1811.

Morelos began with an ill-equipped army of 25 but soon organized a contingent of 9,000 that nearly gained control of the country. Though he was defeated and executed in 1815, he left behind a long-standing reformist legacy that called for universal suffrage, racial equality, and the demise of the hacienda system. The city today still pays tribute to Morelos: His former home has been turned into a museum, and his birthplace is now a library.

Morelianos love music, and several festivals each year are designed to indulge them. Each year in May the city celebrates the **International Organ Festival** in the cathedral, giving voice to its outstanding 4,600-pipe organ. The last two weeks in July are given to the **Festival Internacional de Música,** featuring baroque and chamber music, with orchestras participating from throughout Mexico.

In addition, Morelia has the delicious distinction of being the candy capital of Mexico. So strong, in fact, is the sweet-eating tradition that the city offers a **Mercado de Dulces**, or sweets market. Morelia is also the home of writers, artists, philosophers, and poets, as well as American retirees.

Exploring Morelia

To explore Morelia and its surrounding hillside neighborhoods thoroughly would take some time. However, if you stroll through the historic plazas and frequent the cafés (as many locals do), you will begin to feel the city's vitality. Although the vehicle and sidewalk traffic can get a little heavy at times, Morelia is a pedestrian-friendly city.

A Good Walk

Begin your walk in Morelia's tree-lined downtown **Plaza de Armas** ⑩, on the east side of which is the city's famed **Catedral** ㊶. As you leave the cathedral, cross Avenida Madero to the **Palacio de Gobierno** ㊷, a former seminary. From the palace it's four blocks east along Avenida Madero to Calle de Belisario Domínguez. Make a right and walk one block south to the Church of San Francisco. To the rear of the church, in the former convent of San Francisco, is the entrance to the **Casa de las Artesanías del Estado de Michoacán** ㊸, a virtual cornucopia of crafts from around the state.

Walk two blocks south on Calle Vasco de Quiroga, a street lined with vendors, until you come to Calle del Soto Saldaña. Head west another two blocks to Avenida Morelos Sur; the corner building on your right is the **Casa Museo de Morelos** ㊹, showcasing memorabilia of the independence leader. It's one block north from the museum to Calle Antonio Alzate and then one block west (where the street name changes to Calle Corregidora) to Calle García Obeso. On this corner stands the **Museo Casa Natal de Morelos** ㊺, Morelos's birthplace. Continue

Casa de las Artesanías del Estado de Michoacán, **43**
Casa Museo de Morelos, **44**
Catedral, **41**
Mercado de Dulces, **48**
Museo Casa Natal de Morelos, **45**
Museo de Arte Contemporáneo, **49**
Museo del Estado, **47**
Museo Michoacano, **46**
Palacio de Gobierno, **42**
Plaza de Armas, **40**

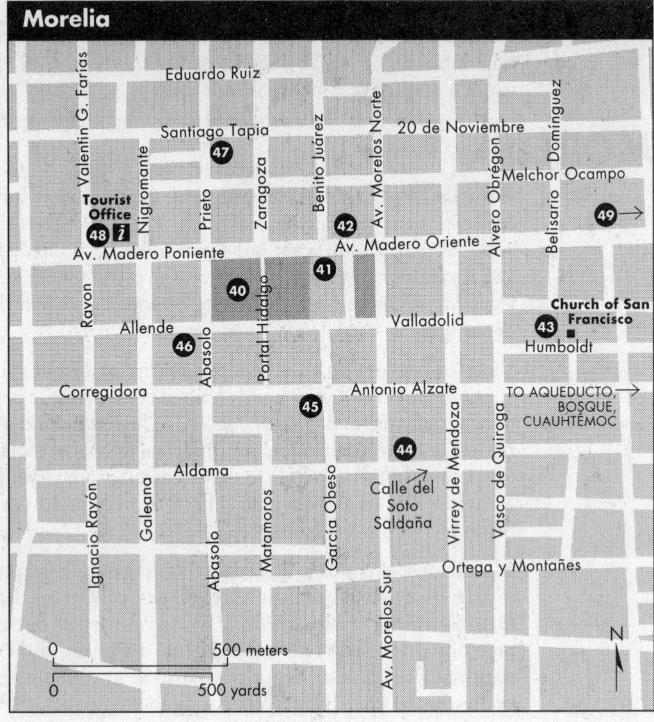

west on Calle Corregidora until you reach Calle Abasolo; on Calle Allende, one block to the north, you'll find the **Museo Regional Michoacano** ㊻.

After leaving the museum, take Calle Abasolo back to the plaza; 2½ blocks to the north, you'll see the **Museo del Estado** ㊼ on the right side of the street (which changes its name to Calle Guillermo Prieto at Avenida Madero). Return to Avenida Madero, and then go two blocks to the right to the corner of the Valentín Gómez Farias, where the **Mercado de Dulces** ㊽ is located.

Those seeking a longer stroll might take Avenida Madero east a dozen blocks or so to where it forks. Stay to the right; you'll see the **Fountain of the Tarascans** on a traffic island to your left. Just past the fountain, Morelia's mile-long **aqueduct** begins. This structure, which consists of 253 arches, was built in 1785 and was once the city's main source of drinking water. It's particularly beautiful at night when its arches—some rising to 30 ft—are lit. Two blocks farther along (Madero is now called Avenida Acueducto) is the entrance to **Bosque Cuauhtémoc,** Morelia's largest park. If you happen by during the week, you may encounter university students studying (or lounging) beneath the palms and evergreens; on weekends, especially Sunday, families on outings take over. Two blocks past the park entrance, you'll see the **Museo de Arte Contemporáneo** ㊾, also on the right side of the street.

Sights to See

㊸ **Casa de las Artesanías del Estado de Michoacán.** In the 16th century, Vasco de Quiroga, the bishop of Michoacán, helped the Tarascan Indians develop artistic specialties so they could be self-supporting. At this two-story museum and store, you can see the work the Tarascans still produce: copper goods from Santa Clara del Cobre, lacquerware from Uruapan, straw items and pottery from Pátzcuaro, guitars from Paracho, macabre ceramic figures from Ocumicho. At the **Museo Michoacana de las Artesanías** in the two main floors around the courtyard, some of these items are showcased behind glass while artists demonstrate how they are made. There is a gift shop to the right of the museum entrance. ✉ *Calle Fray Juan de San Miguel s/n,* ☎ *43/12–24–86 museum, 43/12–12–48 store.* ⏲ *Daily 9–8.*

44 **Casa Museo de Morelos.** What is now a two-story museum was acquired in 1801 by the Mexican independence leader and served as home to generations of the Morelos family until 1934. Owned by the Mexican government, it contains family portraits (including one of Morelos's mother, who, he said, "gave him constant spirit and strength"), a copy of Morelos's birth certificate, various artifacts from the independence movement (such as a camp bed used by Ignacio Allende), and the blindfold Morelos wore for his execution. The excellent free tour is in Spanish only. ✉ *Av. Morelos Sur 323,* ☎ *43/13–26–51.* 🎟 *Small fee.* ⏲ *Daily 9–7.*

41 **Catedral.** Morelia's cathedral is a majestic structure built between 1640 and 1744. It is known throughout Mexico for its 200-ft baroque towers, among the tallest in the land, and for its 4,600-pipe organ, one of the finest in the world. The organ is on the balcony at the back of the cathedral. An international organ festival is held here each May. ✉ *Av. Madero between Plaza de Armas and Av. Morelos.*

48 **Mercado de Dulces.** Those with a sweet tooth won't want to miss Morelia's famous candy market, just behind the tourist office. All sorts of local sweets are for sale, such as *ate* (a candied fruit) and various confections made from evaporated milk. ✉ *Av. Madero Poniente and Valentín Gómez Farías.* ⏲ *Daily 9–9.*

45 **Museo Casa Natal de Morelos.** Morelos's birthplace is now a library and national monument housing mostly history and literature books (as well as two murals by Alfredo Zalce). Be sure to visit the courtyard in back: It's a tranquil square, adjacent to the Church of San Agustín, with rosebushes, evergreens, and wild poinsettias; a marker and an eternal flame honor the fallen hero. ✉ *Calle Corregidora 113,* ☎ *43/12–27–93.* 🎟 *Free.* ⏲ *Weekdays 9–2 and 4–8, Sat. 9:30–2, Sun. 9–2.*

49 **Museo de Arte Contemporáneo.** The works of contemporary Mexican and international artists are on view at this well-lighted museum near the Bosque Cuauhtémoc. ✉ *Av. Acueducto 18,* ☎ *43/12–54–04.* 🎟 *Free.* ⏲ *Tues.–Sun. 10–1:45 and 4–7:45.*

47 **Museo del Estado.** Just across from a small plaza with statues of Bishop Vasco de Quiroga and Spanish writer Miguel de Cervantes, this history museum is located in a stately mansion that was once the home of the wife of Augustín de Iturbide, Mexico's only native-born emperor. ✉ *Guillermo Prieto 176,* ☎ *43/13–06–29.* 🎟 *Free.* ⏲ *Weekdays 9–2 and 4–8.*

46 **Museo Regional Michoacano.** An 18th-century former palace, the museum traces the history of Mexico from its pre-Hispanic days through the Cardenista period, which ended in 1940. President Lázaro Cárdenas, a native of Michoacán, was one of Mexico's most popular leaders because of his nationalization of the oil industry and his support of other populist reforms. The ground floor contains an art gallery, plus archaeological exhibits from Michoacán. Upstairs is an assortment of colonial objects, including furniture, weapons, and religious paint-

ings. ✉ *Calle Allende 305,* ☎ *43/12–04–07.* *About $2; free Sun.* ⏲ *Tues.–Sat. 9–7.*

NEED A BREAK?

When you've finished your tour of the Museo Michoacana, walk across the street to the *portales.* A number of popular sidewalk cafés are set among these colonial stone arcades. For a sandwich or a fruit cocktail, or a good selection of juices, coffees, and teas, try **Café Catedral** (✉ Portal Hidalgo 213, ☎ 43/12-32-89). No one will mind if you linger over a book or newspaper for the better part of an hour sipping an excellent café americano (and, in fact, you might have to wait that long just to get the bill).

42 **Palacio de Gobierno.** This former Tridentine seminary, built in 1770, has had such notable graduates as independence hero José María Morelos, social reformer Melchor Ocampo, and the first emperor of Mexico, Agustín de Iturbide. Striking murals decorate the stairway and second floor. Painted by local artist Alfredo Zalce in the early 1960s, they depict dramatic, often bloody scenes from Mexico's history. From the second floor you can catch a glimpse of the cathedral's spires across the way. ✉ *Av. Madero 63,* ☎ *43/12–78–72.* ⏲ *Daily 7 AM–10 PM.*

40 **Plaza de Armas.** During the War of Independence, several rebel priests were brutally murdered on this site, and the plaza, known as Plaza de los Mártires, is named after them. Today, however, the square belies its violent past: Sweethearts stroll along the tree-lined walks, vendors sell mounds of roasted peanuts, placards announce cultural events, and lively recorded music blasts from a silver-domed bandshell. ✉ *Bounded on the north by Av. Madero, on the south by Calle Allende, on the west by Calle Abasolo, and on the east by cathedral.*

Dining

Some of Michoacán's tastiest dishes—Lake Pátzcuaro white fish, tomato-based Tarascan soup, corn products such as huchepos and *corundas* (small, sweet cakes), and game (rabbit and quail)—are served at Morelia restaurants. Traditional chicken and beef fare are also available, as well as international dishes. As a rule, more upscale restaurants are located in hotels near the plaza and on the outskirts of town.

$$$ ★ ✕ **Fonda Las Mercedes.** This delightful restaurant's arty, modern furnishings somehow fit perfectly in the plant-filled stone patio of this restored colonial mansion. The ambience is intimate yet airy, with a lovely soft natural light during the day. The inside dining room, which is equally pleasant, may be cozier on chilly days or evenings. Offerings from the eclectic menu include lots of soups and six kinds of crepes. If you dare, try the sinfully rich pasta with pistachios and pine nuts in cream sauce. ✉ *León Guzmán 47,* ☎ *43/12–61–13. AE, MC, V.*

$$ ✕ **Boca del Río.** Large picture windows opening onto a busy intersection provide ample light for this cheerful yet cafeteria-like restaurant, which claims to have fresh fish and seafood trucked in daily from Sinaloa and Veracruz. There are light snacks such as *coctel de camarones* (shrimp cocktail) or the hands-on sopa de mariscos, along with heartier fare, such as the *jaiba rellena* (crabs stuffed with mushrooms and cheese and liberally seasoned with garlic). Beef and chicken dishes and a vegetarian sandwich are also served. After lunch you can indulge in dessert at the overwhelming *Mercado de Dulces* (sweets market), just across the street. ✉ *Valentín Gómez Farías 185,* ☎ *43/12–99–74. AE, MC, V.*

$$ ★ ✕ **Cenaduría Lupita II.** This restaurant is located outside the city center in the financial district near the Gigante supermarket and cinema.

Although the name labels it a dinner spot (*cena* means dinner), enormous buffets are served for all three meals. The lunch buffet offers unlimited access to salads, soup, meats, desserts, coffee, juices, and beer or tequila. Dinner is built around *antojitos* (appetizers), but this is still a huge amount and assortment of foods. Eating here is a great way to try different regional specialties and find your favorites. ✉ *Av. Camelinas 3100, Col. Jardines del Rincón,* ☎ *43/24–40–67. MC, V.*

$ ★ ✕ **Taquería Pioneros.** There's a reason the tables are full during lunchtime at this positively plain taco shop: They have absolutely delicious grilled meats, served Michoacán style with several different salsas and mountains of fresh, hot tortillas made right on the premises. The *pionero* (beef, ham, bacon, onions, and cheese, all grilled) is the only style served in a half portion, which is plenty for most appetites. Quesadillas, *sincronizadas* (quesadillas with ham), and beans are also served, along with beer and sodas. ✉ *A. Serdán 7 at Ocampo, no phone. No credit cards.*

Lodging

Morelia offers a number of pleasant colonial-style hotels both in the downtown and outlying areas. Generally, the cheapest properties are located near the bus station, moderately priced selections are clustered around the plaza (or on nearby side streets), and deluxe resort hotels are in or near the Santa María hills.

$$$$ ★ **Villa Montaña.** This deluxe property, owned by French count Philippe de Reiset, has all the markings of a wealthy Mexican estate. Set high above Morelia in the Santa María hills, its 5 impeccably groomed acres are dotted with a pool, tennis court, and fanciful stone sculptures. Each individually decorated unit has at least one piece of antique furniture and often a fireplace and private patio. Guests can choose either the Continental Plan (with breakfast) or Modified American Plan (with breakfast and lunch or dinner). The hotel's renowned restaurant offers North American, French, and Mexican cuisine, and huge windows afford a marvelous view of Morelia, especially at night. ✉ *Calle Patzimba s/n, 58000,* ☎ *43/14–02–31 or 43/14–01–79; 800/525–4800 in the U.S.;* FAX *43/15–14–23. 55 rooms. Restaurant, piano bar, pool, tennis court, recreation room, laundry service, convention center. AE, MC, V.*

$$ **Hotel Catedral.** Located in a restored colonial mansion, this three-story property began operating as a hotel some 30 years ago. Its modern rooms are clustered around a skylit courtyard; eight of them overlook the main plaza and cathedral on Avenida Madero. Interior quarters have less dramatic views but are less noisy. All rooms have dark wood furnishings, telephones, and cable TVs. The rather soft beds have dark blue flowered spreads; the newly stuccoed walls are devoid of decoration. ✉ *Calle Zaragoza 37, 58000,* ☎ *43/13–04–06 or 43/13–04–67,* FAX *43/13–07–83. 44 rooms. Restaurant, bar, dry cleaning. AE, MC, V.*

$$ **Hotel Mansión Acueducto.** An elaborate wood and wrought-iron staircase leads from the elegant lobby to more modest quarters upstairs. Rooms have dark, colonial-style furniture, telephones, and color cable TVs. Older rooms overlook the aqueduct and nearby park; rooms in the motel-like wing have views of the garden, pool, and surrounding city. Student groups at times book the entire property. ✉ *Av. Acueducto 25, 58000,* ☎ *43/12–33–01,* FAX *43/12–20–20. 36 rooms. Restaurant, bar, pool. AE, MC, V.*

$$ ★ **Hotel Posada de la Soledad.** Set in a restored private mansion built in the late 17th century, the Posada de la Soledad is conveniently located one block from the Plaza de Armas. Rooms vary in size, deco-

ration, amenities, and price. The rooms in the original section surround an elegant patio with a large fountain and massive bougainvilleas, where birds twitter at dusk. Rooms in a newer section are smaller and plainly furnished but are quiet and have cable TVs. Rooms on Calle Ocampo have fuzzy local TV only, and loud traffic noise from the street. If you're not impressed with the room you are shown, ask to see another. ✉ *Ignacio Zaragoza 90, 58000,* ☎ *43/12–18–88,* FAX *43/12–21–11. 58 rooms. Restaurant, bar. AE, MC, V.*

$ **Hotel Valladolid.** Located right on the plaza and a sister to the slightly more impressive Hotel Catedral, the Valladolid has plain but clean rooms with brick floors and striped bedspreads. There is no TV or telephone, but the price includes a continental breakfast in the hotel's restaurant, right across from the Plaza de Armas. ✉ *Portal Hidalgo 241,* ☎ *43/12–00–27 or 43/12–46–63. 32 rooms. Restaurant. MC, V.*

Morelia A to Z

Arriving and Departing

BY BUS

Direct bus service is available daily between the Terminal Poniente (West Terminal) in Mexico City and Morelia's **Central de Autobuses** (☎ 43/12–56–04). Several bus lines offer frequent service; the most direct trip (🎫 $12.50) takes four hours and is on Herradura de Plata. Buses leave every hour or two around the clock.

BY CAR

The drive from Mexico City to Morelia (302 km, or 187 mi) on the toll road through Toluca, Atlacamulco, Contepec, and Maravatio takes about four hours.

BY PLANE

There are daily flights between Francisco Mujica International Airport, 24 km (15 mi) north of Morelia, and Mexico City's International Airport on **Aeromexico** (☎ 43/13–58–33). Flights are subject to cancellation, and flight times change often and must be confirmed one day in advance. The 25-minute taxi ride from the airport to Morelia costs about $10.

BY TRAIN

Train travel is not recommended, as the journey is long, and there is no sleeper car. For those who insist on riding the rails, the *Purepecha* leaves Mexico City at 9 PM, arriving in Morelia at 6:30 AM; the return train leaves Morelia at 11 PM and arrives in Mexico City at 7:30 AM. A one-way, first-class ticket costs about $9. Train schedules are subject to change without notice. For current schedules and rates, contact **Mexico by Train** (☎ FAX 210/725–3659 or ☎ 800/321–1699) or the local train station (☎ 43/16–16–97). If the local train station does not answer, call 915/547–6593 or 915/547–1084 in Mexico City for schedule information.

Getting Around

As in many of the heartland cities, Morelia's principal sights are near the center of town and you can reach them on foot. Street names in Morelia change frequently, especially on either side of Avenida Madero, the city's main east–west artery. Taxis in Morelia can be hailed on the street or found near the main plaza. Buses run the length of Avenida Madero.

Contacts and Resources

CAR RENTAL

Budget has an office at Francisco Mujica International Airport (☎ 43/13–33–99).

EMERGENCIES

Police (☎ 43/12–22–22). **Ambulance-Red Cross** (Cruz Rojo, ☎ 43/14–51–51; Hospital de la Cruz Roja, ☎ 43/14–50–25). **Consumer Protection Office** (☎ 43/12–40–49). **Fire Department** (☎ 43/12–12–35). **Hospital Memorial** (☎ 43/15–10–47 or 43/15–10–99). **Green Angels** (☎ 43/12–77–77).

GUIDED TOURS

The following operators conduct tours of Morelia: **Morelia Operadores de Viajes** (✉ Gómez Farías 131, ☎ 43/12–95–91 or 43/12–87–47, FAX 43/12–87–23) and **Wagon-Lits Mexicana** (✉ Calle Madero Poniente 313, ☎ 43/12–42–95 or 43/12–77–66, FAX 42/12–76–60).

MONEY EXCHANGE

Casa Cambio Valladolid (✉ Portal Matamoros 86, ☎ 43/12–85–86) is open weekdays 9–6, Saturday 9–1:30.

TRAVEL AGENCIES

Viajes Lopsa is the American Express representative (✉ Service Las Américas, Local 27, Artilleros del 47, ☎ 43/14–19–50, FAX 43/14–77–16). **Servicios Establecidos Para el Turismo** (✉ Portal Hidalgo 229, ☎ 43/12–90–02 or 43/13–19–02) makes typical travel arrangements.

VISITOR INFORMATION

Secretaría Estatal de Turismo (✉ Palacio Clavijero, Calle Nigromante 78, ☎ 43/13–26–54 or 43/12–80–81, FAX 43/12–98–16) is open weekdays 8–8, weekends 9–4.

PÁTZCUARO

Pátzcuaro, the 16th-century capital of Michoacán, exists in a time warp. A bit more than an hour by car from Morelia, this beautiful lakeside community set at 7,250 ft in the Sierra Madre is home to the Tarascan Indians, who fish, farm, and ply their crafts as they have for centuries. Women wrapped tightly in their striped wool *rebozos* (shawls) hurry to market in the chill, smoky morning air. Men in traditional straw hats wheel overburdened carts down crooked, dusty backstreets.

The architecture, too, has remained largely unchanged throughout the years. In the 16th century, under kindly Bishop Vasco de Quiroga, Pátzcuaro underwent a building boom of sorts. After he died in 1565, the state capital was moved to Morelia, and the town became a cultural (and architectural) backwater for hundreds of years. Modern visitors will see 16th-century mansions surrounding the downtown plazas; one-story whitewashed houses with sloping tile roofs line the side streets and hills.

Despite the altitude, the weather in Pátzcuaro is temperate year-round. (Autumn and winter nights, however, are cold; sweaters and jackets are a must.) On November 1—the night preceding the Day of the Dead—the town is inundated with tourists en route to **Janitzio,** an island in Lake Pátzcuaro, where one of the most elaborate graveyard ceremonies in all of Mexico takes place. The island of **Yunuen** now has overnight accommodations, allowing visitors a more authentic glimpse of daily island life. And around the lake are numerous small towns where one can purchase handicrafts direct from the producers, and understand a bit about life in rural and small-town Mexico. These towns are just beginning to attract tourism, and many new dining and lodging venues are opening up outside of Pátzcuaro. The **Delegación de Turismo** will enthusiastically share suggestions for adventures outside Pátzcuaro.

Exploring Pátzcuaro

Most of Pátzcuaro's sights can be seen in a few hours, but the town and outlying areas deserve to be explored at a leisurely pace. There can be some traffic in the Plaza Bocanegra and on the main road coming into town, but elsewhere it is blissfully quiet.

A Good Walk

Start your stroll at the **tourist office** (Ibarra 2), where you can pick up maps and brochures. Directly across the street is the large **Plaza Vasco de Quiroga** (50). Go to the east side of the square and turn right on Calle Dr. José Marí Coss; in less than a block you'll see a long cobblestone walkway leading to **La Casa de los 11 Patios** (51), a former convent now housing a number of shops. As you leave the complex, continue up a stone walkway to Calle Lerín. To the north (past Calle Portugal) is the **Templo de la Compañía** (52), the state's first cathedral. After visiting the church, continue another half block along Calle Lerín to the **Museo de Artes Populares** (53) on your right.

Directly down Calle Lerín and across a cobblestone courtyard is **La Basílica de Nuestra Señora de la Salud** (54). Walk downhill from the basilica (take Buenavista to Libertad and turn left) to reach the **Biblioteca Pública Gertrudis Bocanegra** (55). For a nice detour from the library, continue for a half block to the large outdoor **mercado** sprawled along Calle Libertad and its side streets. At times the road is so crowded with people and their wares—fruit, vegetables, beans, rice, herbs, and other necessities of daily life—that it is difficult to walk. If you press on for about a block, you'll see an indoor market to your left, filled with more produce, large hanging slabs of meat, hot food, and a variety of cheap trinkets. When you're done with your market tour, retrace your steps down Calle Libertad. Across the street from the library, you can rest at **Plaza Bocanegra** (56), just one block north of your starting point, Plaza Vasco de Quiroga.

Sights to See

55 **Biblioteca Pública Gertrudis Bocanegra.** In the back of this library, a vast mural painted by Juan O'Gorman in 1942 depicts in great detail the history of the region and of the Tarascan people. Look at the bottom right of the mural to see Gertrudis Bocanegra, a local heroine who was shot in 1814 for refusing to divulge the revolutionaries' secrets to the Spaniards. ✉ *North side of Plaza Bocanegra.* ⏲ *Weekdays 9–7.*

54 **La Basílica de Nuestra Señora de la Salud.** The church was begun in 1554 by Vasco de Quiroga, and throughout the centuries others—undaunted by earthquakes and fires—took up the cause and constructed a church in honor of the Virgin of Health. Near the main altar is a statue of the Virgin made of derivatives of cornstalks and orchids. Several masses are still held here daily; the earliest begins shortly after dawn. Out front, Tarascan women sell hot tortillas, herbal mixtures for teas, and religious objects. You can glimpse Lake Pátzcuaro in the distance from here. ✉ *Calle Lerin s/n, near Calle Cerrato.*

51 **La Casa de los 11 Patios.** An 18th-century convent, La Casa houses a number of high-quality shops featuring Tarascan handiwork. As you meander through the shops and courtyards, you'll encounter weavers producing large bolts of cloth, artists trimming black lacquerware with gold, and seamstresses embroidering blouses. If you plan to shop

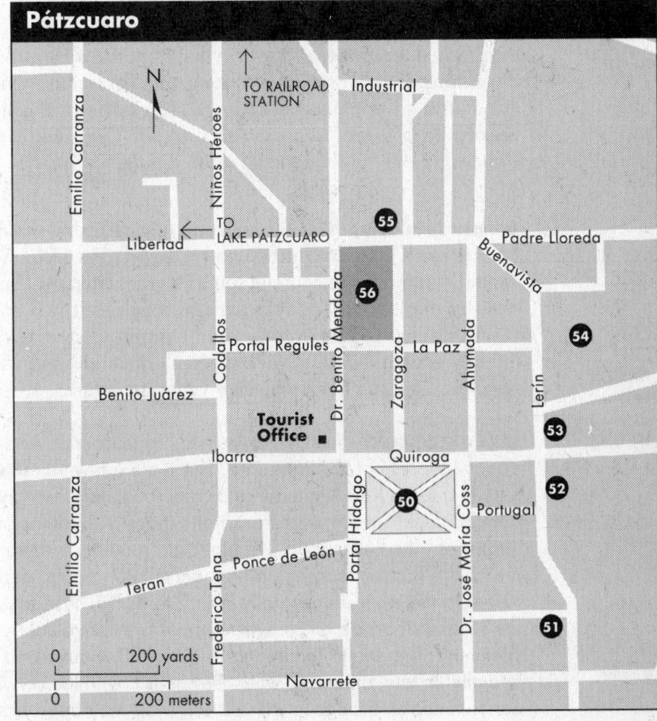

in Pátzcuaro, this is a good place to start. You can view the selection of regional goods and begin to compare prices. ✉ *Calle Madrigal de los Altos 2.* ⏲ *Daily 10–2 and 4–8.*

53 **Museo de Artes Populares.** Home to the Colegio de San Nicolás Obispo in the 16th century, the building today houses displays of colonial and contemporary crafts, such as ceramics, masks, lacquerware, paintings, and ex-votos in its many rooms. Behind this building is a *troje* (traditional Tarascan wood house) braced atop a stone platform. ☎ *434/2–10–29.* 💵 *About $2; free Sun.* ⏲ *Tues.–Sat. 9–7, Sun. 9–3.*

56 **Plaza Bocanegra.** The smaller of the city's two squares (it's also called Plaza Chica), this is the center of Pátzcuaro's commercial life. Bootblacks, pushcart vendors, and bus and taxi stands are all in this plaza, which is embellished by a statue of the local heroine. ✉ *Bounded by Av. Libertad on the north, Portal Regules on the south, Dr. Benito Mendoza on the west, and Calle Zaragoza on the east.*

NEED A BREAK?

Before heading to Lake Pátzcuaro, sit in the shady square for a moment and enjoy a rich Michoacán ice-cream or fruit bar. Then grab a taxi or the San Bartolo–Lago bus to the *embarcadero* (wharf).

50 **Plaza Vasco de Quiroga.** A tranquil courtyard surrounded by ash and pine trees and 16th-century mansions (since converted into hotels and shops), the larger of the two downtown plazas commemorates the bishop who restored dignity to the Tarascan people. During the Spanish conquest, Nuño de Guzmán, a lieutenant in Hernán Cortés's army, committed atrocities on the local population in his efforts to conquer western Mexico. He was eventually arrested by the Spanish authori-

ties, and in 1537 Vasco de Quiroga was appointed bishop of Michoacán. Attempting to regain the trust of the indigenous people, he established a number of model villages in the area and promoted the development of commerce among the Tarascans. Quiroga died in 1565, and his remains were consecrated in the ☞ **Basílica de Nuestra Señora de la Salud.** ✉ *Bounded by Calle Quiroga on the north, Av. Ponce de León on the south, Portal Hidalgo on the west, and Dr. José María Coss on the east.*

52 **Templo de la Compañía.** Michoacán's first cathedral was begun in 1540 by order of Vasco de Quiroga and completed in 1546. When the state capital was moved to Morelia some 20 years later, the church was taken over by the Jesuits. Today it remains much as it was in the 16th century. Moss has grown over the crumbling stone steps outside; the dank interior is planked with thick wood floors and lined with bare wood benches. ✉ *Calle Lerin s/n, near Calle Alcantaría.*

OFF THE BEATEN PATH

LAKE PÁTZCUARO – Just a 10-minute taxi ride from downtown are the tranquil shores of Lake Pátzcuaro. There are a few lakeside restaurants here that serve fresh whitefish and other local catches. Amble along the dock or peek into the waterfront crafts shops. A boat trip to Janitzio (the largest of Lake Pátzcuaro's five islands), or to tiny Yunuen, is recommended. Wooden launches, with room for 25 people, depart for Janitzio and the other islands daily from 9 to 6. Purchase round-trip tickets for $3 at a dockside office (where prices are controlled by the tourist department). The ride to Janitzio takes about 30 minutes and is particularly beautiful in late afternoon, when the sun is low in the sky. Once you're out on the lake, fishermen with butterfly nets may approach your boat. The nets are no longer used for fishing, but for a small donation these locals will let you take their picture.

On most days (November 2 being the exception), Janitzio is a quiet albeit touristy island inhabited by Tarascan Indians. It is crowned by a huge statue of independence hero José María Morelos, which is accessible by a cobblestone stairway. Though the road twists past many souvenir stands as it ascends, don't be discouraged. The view from the summit—of the lake, the town, and the surrounding hills—is well worth the climb. Inside the statue are some remarkable murals that spiral up from the base to the tip of the monument.

Although Janitzio has definitely succumbed to tourism, the small island of Yunuen is just beginning to attract visitors. This tranquil town has just 21 families, and provides a more accurate picture of island life than does Janitizio. You can get a boat to here from the ferry landing, or arrange to stay overnight in simple yet clean and new cabins recently opened for visitors. The office of tourism will gladly provide information.

Dining

Many restaurants in Pátzcuaro specialize in seafood. In addition to whitefish, look for *trucha* (trout) and *charales* and *boquerones* (two small, locally caught fish served as appetizers). Tarascan specialties, such as sopa tarasca, are also common. As a rule, restaurants are located around the two plazas and in hotels. Since the large meal is served at midday, many dining establishments are shuttered by 9.

$$$ ★ ✕ **El Primer Piso.** This second-floor restaurant overlooks the plaza, and on warm nights one can watch the comings and goings from a balcony table. There's plenty to look at inside, as well, for the restaurant dou-

bles as an art gallery and its walls are covered with original prints or paintings. The eclectic menu provides a break from the rather monotonous Pátzcuaro fare: Try the pear salad with goat cheese, nuts, and watercress, or the daily special. ✉ *Plaza Vasco de Quiroga 29,* ☎ *434/2–01–22. MC, V. Closed Tues.*

$$ ✕ **El Patio.** Though this low-key restaurant features mouthwatering whitefish platters (including salsa, vegetables, and french fries), it's possible to duck in at midday for just a strong cappuccino or glass of local wine. (There are several varieties of wine; waiters can help you choose one.) For a late-afternoon snack, a plate of quesadillas with a side order of guacamole is highly recommended, and the sopa tarasca is superb. ✉ *Plaza Vasco de Quiroga 19,* ☎ *434/2–04–84. DC, MC, V.*

$ ✕ **Restaurante Gran Hotel.** Though this one-room restaurant is connected to the Gran Hotel, it is independently owned and attracts a mix of locals and tourists to its midday meal. The furnishings are simple: tables covered with amber-colored cloths and set beneath wood chandeliers. The food is good and wholesome. Specialties include lightly breaded whitefish, chicken with mole sauce, and Tarascan soup. ✉ *Portal Regules 6,* ☎ *434/2–04–43. Reservations not accepted. V.*

Lodging

Though Pátzcuaro has no deluxe hotels, there are an ample number of clean, moderately priced properties. Most are located on or within a few blocks of the Plaza Vasco de Quiroga. Several more expensive hotels are situated on Avenida Lázaro Cárdenas, the road to Lake Pátzcuaro. If you're planning to be in town on or near November 2, the Mexican Day of the Dead, make hotel reservations at least six months in advance.

$$$ 🏨 **Hotel Posada de Don Vasco.** Located several minutes out of town on the road to Lake Pátzcuaro, this sprawling resort hotel offers a wide range of amenities, including satellite TV. Its 30 newer rooms are thickly carpeted and have either balconies or patios; the older quarters, which are oddly decorated with gold and brown patterned rugs and bright checkered bedspreads, are smaller and open onto a courtyard. The lovely, manicured grounds are relatively quiet despite the occasional rumbling of a passing bus or truck. The restaurant is decorated like a prosperous country estate, with a large fireplace that blazes on cold nights. At the Monday buffet lunch the regional Dance of the Old Men is performed. ✉ *Av. Las Americas 450, 61500,* ☎ *434/2–39–71 or 434/2–24–90,* FAX *434/2–02–62. 99 rooms, 4 suites. Restaurant, pool, tennis courts, badminton, bowling, billiards, meeting rooms. AE, MC, V.*

$$ 🏨 **Cabañas Yunuen.** This complex was recently built on the island of Yunuen in collaboration with the Department of Tourism to promote visits to some of the area's more authentic communities. There are six cabins in all: two each for two, four, and 16 persons; each has a kitchenette with small refrigerator, and—surprise!—satellite TV. Breakfast or dinner and round-trip transportation by boat is included in the price: about $28 for two people. Arrangements must be made through the Department of Tourism (☞ Visitor Information in Pátzcuaro A to Z, *below*). ✉ *Domicilio Conocido, Isla de Yunuen, no phone. 6 cabins. Dining room, kitchenettes. No credit cards.*

$$ 🏨 **Los Escudos.** Today a cozy hotel, this property was originally a 16th-century home. Its courtyards bloom with potted plants, and some guest rooms contain small murals of Tarascan Indian scenes. Ten rooms situated in back and shielded from street noise open onto an outdoor patio. All rooms have color TVs and telephones; five have fireplaces. The adjoining restaurant has a varied menu, ranging from club sandwiches to multicourse midday meals. Particularly tempting is the *pollo especial Los Escudos* (chicken sautéed in tomato sauce and vegetables). ✉ *Portal Hidalgo 73, 61600,* ☎ FAX *434/2–01–38 or 434/2–12–90. 30 rooms. Restaurant. MC, V.*

$$ ★ **Mansión Iturbe.** This hotel, housed in a 17th-century mansion, still retains much of its colonial charm. Both the rooms and corridors are frailly lighted, giving the impression of a true 17th-century home. Plant-filled courtyards are ringed by stone archways. Rooms, with large wood-and-glass doors, are partially carpeted and decorated with red-and-black–checked spreads and curtains. Bicycles are lent to guests for a few hours per stay, and every fourth night is free. Breakfast is included in the room rate. There are several restaurants, the most lively being **El Viejo Gaucho,** where pizzas, meats, and *empanadas* (meat-filled pastries) are served and live music is performed most nights. ✉ *Portal Morelos 59, 61600,* ☎ *434/2–03–68,* FAX *43/13–45–95 in Morelia. 12 rooms. 3 restaurants, bicycles, shop. MC, V.*

$ **Hotel Posada La Basílica.** This colonial-style inn, housed in a 17th-century building, faces the Basilica of the Virgin of Health. On some mornings strains from a post-dawn mass filter softly into the hotel. The property has comfortable, individually decorated rooms, some with fireplaces. Thick wood shutters cover floor-to-ceiling windows and walls are trimmed in hand-painted colonial designs. The restaurant has views of the mountains, the lake, and tile-roofed homes. Open for breakfast and lunch only, this dining spot offers such regional specialties as broiled trout with garlic and tamales with cheese and cream. Service can be slow, as waiters tend to hide in the kitchen. ✉ *Calle Arciga 6, 61600,* ☎ *434/2–11–08 or 434/2–11–81; 434/2–06–59 reservations. 11 rooms. Restaurant. MC, V.*

$ **Mesón del Gallo.** On a fairly quiet side street near the Casa de los 11 Patios, this two-story property is beginning to look a bit shabby. Beds have wood-and-tile headboards and magenta spreads and curtains. Suites, complete with minibars, are furnished in more subdued hues. All rooms have telephones but no TV. There is a grassy patio encircled by bougainvillea and fruit trees with a lonely umbrella table in the middle. ✉ *Calle Dr. Coss 20, 61600,* ☎ *434/2–14–74,* FAX *434/2–15–11. 20 rooms, 5 suites. Restaurant, bar. MC, V.*

Nightlife and the Arts

The **Danza de los Viejitos** (Dance of the Little Old Men), a widely known regional dance, is performed during Monday lunch at Hotel Posada de Don Vasco (☞ Lodging, *above*) for approximately $12 (includes lunch). The dance is also performed Saturday nights at 8 PM at the Hotel Los Escudos, on Plaza de Quiroga. There you can have either drinks or dinner.

Live music can be heard most nights at **El Viejo Gaucho** (✉ Iturbe 10, ☎ 434/2–03–68), which is within the Hotel Mansión Iturbe. The club's entrance is on the side street Iturbe.

Side Trips

Tzintzuntzan

17 km (10½ mi) northeast of Pátzcuaro.

When the Spanish came to colonize the region in the 16th century, some 40,000 Tarascans lived and worshiped in this lakeshore village, which they called "place of the hummingbirds." The ruins of the pyramid-shape temples, or *yacatas,* found in the ancient capital of the Tarascan kingdom still stand today and are open to the public for a small admission charge. Visitors can also find vestiges of a 16th-century Franciscan monastery where Spanish friars attempted to convert the Indians to Christianity. Though Tzintzuntzan lost some prominence when Bishop Vasco de Quiroga moved the seat of his diocese to Pátzcuaro in 1540, the village is still well known for the straw and ceramic handicrafts made by the Tarascan Indians and sold in numerous shops along the main street of town. To reach Tzintzuntzan, take the bus marked Quiroga from Pátzcuaro's Central Camionera; travel time is about 30 minutes.

Uruapan

64 km (40 mi) west of Pátzcuaro.

The subtropical town of Uruapan is distinctly different from its lakeside neighbor: Some 2,000 ft lower than Pátzcuaro, though still at an elevation of 5,300 ft, it is a populous commercial center with a warm climate and lush vegetation. The town's name is derived from the Tarascan word *urupan,* meaning "where the flowers bloom."

Uruapan can be reached from Pátzcuaro by car, bus, or train. Route 14 is the most direct route between the two cities. There is also frequent bus service on the Flecha Amarilla and other major lines; travel time is about 70 minutes. The train takes about two hours each way, passing through lovely wooded countryside.

You can see several points of interest within a few hours. The first, **La Huatápera,** is located off Uruapan's Plaza Principal. This 16th-century hospital has been converted into the **Museo Regional de Arte Popular.** It houses a collection of crafts from the state of Michoacán, including an excellent display of lacquerware made in Uruapan. ☎ *452/4-34-34.* *Free.* *Tues.–Sun. 10–6.*

The **Mercado de Antojitos,** an immense, sprawling market, begins directly in back of the museum and extends quite a distance north along Calle Constitución. Along the road, Tarascan Indians sell large mounds of produce, fresh fish, beans, homemade cheese, and a variety of cheap manufactured goods. If you travel south along Calle Constitución, you'll come to a courtyard where vendors sell hot food.

At the **Parque Nacional Eduardo Ruiz,** about six long blocks from the Plaza Principal off Calle Independencia, you can stroll through the verdant acreage to the source of the River Cupatitzio and abundant fountains, waterfalls, and springs.

Eleven kilometers (7 miles) south along the river is the magnificent waterfall at **Tzaráracua.** At this point the Cupatitzio plunges 150 ft off a sheer rock cliff into a riverbed below; a rainbow seems to hang perpetually over the site. Buses marked Tzaráracua leave sporadically from the Plaza Principal in Uruapan. You can also take a taxi for about $3, or drive there via Avenida Lázaro Cárdenas.

Farther afield, about 32 km (20 mi) north of Uruapan, lies the dormant **Paricutín volcano.** Its initial burst of lava and ashes wiped out the nearby village of San Juan Parangaricutiro in 1943. Today travelers can visit this buried site by hiring gentle mountain ponies and a Tarascan guide in the town of Angahuan. To reach Angahuan, take the Los Reyes bus from Uruapan's Central Camionera or go by car via the Uruapan–Carapan highway.

DINING

For good comida casera, try **El Rincón del Burrito** (✉ Portal Matamorros 7, ☎ 452/3-79-89) or the restaurant at **Mansión de Cupatitzio,** in the national park at the mouth of the Cupatitzio River (✉ Parque Nacional s/n, ☎ 452/3–20–70 or 452/3–21–00).

Pátzcuaro A to Z

Arriving and Departing

BY BUS

Direct bus service is available daily between the Terminal Poniente (West Terminal) in Mexico City and Pátzcuaro's Central Camionera. Several bus lines offer frequent service; the most direct trip, which takes five hours, is on **Herradura de Plata** (✉ Via Corta). Transportation coming from most of the heartland cities would be to Morelia; buses leave about every 15 minutes from there to Patzuaro and take about 45 minutes.

BY CAR

A new highway now connects Mexico City to Guadalajara, cutting driving time to Pátzcuaro to 4½ or five hours. The new highway has also cut travel time from Guadalajara to Pátzcuaro to four hours by car; it's a bit longer by direct bus. From Morelia, two roads lead to Pátzcuaro: The newer passes through Tiripetio; the older passes through Quiroga and Tzintzuntzan. Cars can be rented at locations in Mexico City or Morelia; there are no rental outlets in Pátzcuaro.

BY TRAIN

Train service between Mexico City and Pátzcuaro is available daily but not recommended. There are no sleeping cars, but train seats do recline. The 11-hour trip is scheduled to leave Mexico City at 9 PM and arrive in Pátzcuaro at 4 AM, but is often late; the return trip leaves Pátzcuaro at 9:30 PM and arrives in Mexico City at 4:30 AM. The one-way, first-class fare is $10.50. Train schedules are subject to change without notice. For current schedules and rates, contact **Mexico by Train** (☎ FAX 210/725–3659 or 800/321–1699) or the local train station (☎ 434/2–08–03). If the local station does not answer, call 915/547–1084 or 915/547–6593 in Mexico City for schedule information.

Getting Around

Many of Pátzcuaro's principal sights are located near the Plaza Vasco de Quiroga and Plaza Bocanegra in the center of town. Taxis and buses to the lake can also be found at the latter square. If you want to visit surrounding villages, taxi drivers will drive you for a reasonable rate. Be sure to agree on a fee before setting out.

Contacts and Resources

EMERGENCIES

Police (☎ 434/2–05–65 or 434/2–00–04). **Rescue** (☎ 434/2–21–65).

Clinics. Centro Médico Quirúrgico (✉ Portal Hidalgo 76, ☎ 434/2–19–98). **Hospital Civil** (☎ 434/2–02–85).

Pharmacy. Farmacia La Paz (✉ La Paz and Bocanegra in Plaza Bocanegra, ☎ 434/2–08–10).

MONEY EXCHANGE

Banca Promex (✉ Portal Regules 9, ☎ 434/2–24–66). **Banamex** (✉ Portal Juárez 32, ☎ 434/2–15–50 or 434/2–10–31). **Bancomer** (✉ Zaragoza 23, ☎ 434/2–03–34). A **Banamex Caja Permanente ATM** is located on Dr. Benito Mendoza, between the two plazas. Note: Many Pátzcuaro restaurants and hotels do not accept traveler's checks, though some will take major credit cards.

VISITOR INFORMATION

Delegación de Turismo (✉ Ibarra 2, Interior 4, off Plaza Vasco de Quiroga, ☎ 434/2–12–14) is the official tourism office and the best place to get information regarding excursions outside Pátzcuaro; open Monday–Saturday 9–2 and 4–7, Sunday 9–2.

Dirección de Orientación y Fomento al Turismo (⊠ Portal Hidalgo 1 on Plaza de Quiroga, ☎ 434/2–02–15 or 434/2–02–16, FAX 343/2–09–67) offers maps and can answer basic questions about tourist facilities in Pátzcuaro.

9 Acapulco

If Acapulco no longer tops the glitterati top-ten list, it remains both a sentimental favorite and a party-hearty resort town, with miles of beaches and some of the glitziest discos this side of the Pacific. A delightful three-hour drive from Acapulco is Taxco, a colonial treasure, where the baroque towers of Santa Prisca church overlook cobblestone streets lined with silversmiths.

Updated by Wendy Luft

FOR SUN LOVERS, beach bums, and other hedonists, Acapulco is the ideal holiday resort. Don't expect high culture, museums, or historic monuments. Anyone who ventures to this Pacific resort 433 km (260 mi) south of Mexico City does so to relax. Translate that as swimming, shopping, and enjoying the nightlife. Everything takes place against a staggeringly beautiful natural backdrop. Acapulco Bay, one of the world's best natural harbors, is the city's centerpiece. By day the water looks temptingly deep blue; at night it flashes and sparkles with the city lights.

The weather is Acapulco's major draw—warm waters, almost constant sunshine, and year-round temperatures in the 80s F. It comes as no surprise, then, that most people plan their day around laying their towel on some part of Acapulco's many kilometers of beach. Both tame and wild water sports are available—everything from waterskiing to snorkeling, diving, and parasailing. Less strenuous possibilities are motorboat rides and fishing trips. Championship golf courses, tennis courts, and the food and crafts markets also occasionally lure some visitors away from the beach, but not out of the sun.

Most people rouse themselves from their hammocks, deck chairs, or towels only when it is feeding time. Eating is one of Acapulco's great pleasures. In addition to the glitzy places, there are many good no-frills, down-home Mexican restaurants. Eating at one of these spots gives you a glimpse into the real Mexico: office workers breaking for lunch, groups of men socializing over cups of coffee.

At night Acapulco is transformed as the city rouses itself from the day's torpor and prepares for the long hours ahead. Even though Acapulco's heyday is past, its nightlife is legendary, and the constant opening of new and ever more spectacular dance clubs is proof positive that Acapulco remains the disco capital of the world. Perpetually crowded, the discos are grouped in twos and threes, so most people go to several places in one night.

Acapulco was originally an important port for the Spanish, who used it to trade with countries in the Far East. The Spanish built Fuerte de San Diego (Fort San Diego) to protect the city from pirates, and today the fort houses a historical museum. The name of the late Teddy Stauffer, an entrepreneurial Swiss, is practically synonymous with that of modern Acapulco. He hired the first cliff divers at La Quebrada in Old Acapulco and founded the Boom Boom Room, the town's first dance hall, and Tequila A Go-Go, its first discotheque. The Hotel Mirador at La Quebrada and the area stretching from Caleta to Hornos beaches, near today's Old Acapulco, were the center of activity in the 1950s, when Acapulco was a town of 20,000 with an economy based largely on fishing.

Former president Miguel Alemán Valdés bought up kilometers of the coast just before the road and the airport were built. Avenida Costera Miguel Alemán bears his name today. Since the late 1940s, Acapulco has expanded eastward so that today it is one of Mexico's largest cities, with a population of approximately 2 million. Currently under development is a 3,000-acre expanse known as Acapulco Diamante, which encompasses the areas known as Punta Diamante and Playa Diamante and some of Acapulco's most sparkling hotels and residential developments.

Pleasures and Pastimes

Beaches

The lure of sun and sand in Acapulco is legendary. Every sport is available, and you can eat in a beach restaurant, dance, and sleep in a *hamaca* (hammock) without leaving the water's edge. If you want to avoid the crowds, there are also plenty of quiet and even isolated beaches within reach.

Dining

Dining in Acapulco is more than just eating out—it is the most popular leisure activity in town. Every night the restaurants fill up, and every night the adventurous diner can sample a different cuisine: Italian, Belgian, Japanese, American, Tex-Mex, and, of course, plain old Mex. The variety of styles matches the range of cuisines: from greasy spoons that serve regional favorites to gourmet restaurants with gorgeous views of Acapulco Bay. Most restaurants fall somewhere in the middle, and on the Costera are dozens of beachside restaurants with *palapa* (palm frond) roofs, as well as wildly decorated rib and hamburger joints popular with visitors under 30—not necessarily in age, but definitely in spirit.

Another plus for Acapulco dining is that the food is garden fresh. Each morning the Mercado Municipal is abuzz with restaurant managers and locals buying up the fish, poultry, and vegetables that will appear on plates that evening. Although some top-quality beef is produced in the states of Sonora and Chihuahua, many of the more expensive restaurants claim that they import their beef from the States. In either case, the beef is excellent in most places. Establishments that cater to tourists purify their drinking water and use it to cook vegetables.

Lodging

Accommodations in Acapulco run the gamut from sprawling, big-name complexes with nonstop amenities to small, family-run inns where hot water is a luxury. Wherever you stay, however, prices will be reasonable compared with those in the United States, and service is generally good, as Acapulqueños have been catering to tourists for half a century.

Nightlife

Acapulco has always been famous for its nightlife, and justifiably so. For many visitors the discos and restaurants are just as important as the sun and the sand. The minute the sun slips over the horizon, the Costera comes alive with people milling around window-shopping, deciding where to dine, and generally biding their time till the disco hour. The legendary Acapulco discos are open 365 days a year from about 10:30 PM until they empty out, often not until 4 or 5 AM. Obviously you aren't going to find great culture here; theater efforts are few and far between, and except for an occasional benefit concert by Placido Domingo, there is no classical music. But disco-hopping is a high art in Acapulco, and for those who care to watch, there are live shows and folk-dance performances.

Shopping

The abundance of air-conditioned shopping malls and boutiques makes picking up gifts and souvenirs one of the highlights of a visit to Acapulco. The malls are filled with clothing shops, and many others are strung along the Costera. There are also a few high-fashion boutiques that carry custom-designed clothes. Malls in Acapulco range from the shopping arcades at several of the more lavish hotels to the huge completely enclosed and air-conditioned Plaza Bahía.

There are several good shops specializing in Mexican crafts, and the Mercado Municipal, whose aisles are piled high with fruits, vegetables, poultry, fish, and meats, is also is a good source of local handicrafts. Flea markets abound, carrying what seems to be an inexhaustible supply of inexpensive collectibles and souvenirs.

The State of Guerrero is especially known for hand-painted ceramics, items made from *palo de rosa* wood, primitive bark paintings depicting scenes of village life, local flora and fauna, and embroidered textiles. Silver is a real bargain in Mexico. Taxco, three hours away, is one of the silver capitals of the world.

Sports and the Outdoors

Acapulco has lots for sports lovers to enjoy. Most hotels have pools, and many have private tennis clubs as well as courts. The fitness craze has caught on, and many of the hotels have gyms, too. Acapulco's waters are teeming with sailfish, marlin, shark, and mahimahi, and although the waters aren't as clear as in the Caribbean, scuba diving is popular, as are waterskiing, windsurfing, kayaking, and bronco riding (an activity done in one-person motorboats). Parasailing looks terrifying and can be dangerous, but most people who do it love the view and go back again and again. Golfers can tee off at the nine-hole municipal course, in town, or at one of the five 18-hole championship courses (three are open to the public) in the Acapulco Diamante area.

EXPLORING

It's possible to get a feel for Acapulco during a short stay if you take in some downtown sights along with your beach activities. Those who have a longer time to spend can really soak up the ambience of the place and can enjoy excursions to some isolated beaches as well as to Taxco.

Numbers in the text correspond to numbers in the margin and on the Acapulco and Taxco Exploring maps.

Great Itineraries

IF YOU HAVE 3 DAYS

Spend the first day enjoying your favorite beach activity, be it parasailing, waterskiing, or simply sunning. That evening, to get the lay of the land, take a sunset cruise that includes a ringside view of Acapulco's daredevil *clavadistas* (divers) at **La Quebrada** ⑧. The following day, experience Acapulco at its most authentic, paying an early visit to the **Mercado Municipal** ④, the **waterfront** ⑥, and the **zócalo** (town square) ⑦. After some late afternoon shopping in the boutiques and handicrafts markets along the Costera Miguel Alemán, "shake off the dust" (as they say in Mexico) at one of the city's glitzy discos. The next day you'll want to try to land a sailfish, take in the Mexican Fiesta at the **Acapulco International Center** (drinks and show only), and bid farewell to Acapulco with a late candlelit dinner at one of the city's romantic dining spots.

IF YOU HAVE 5 DAYS

Add on to the three-day itinerary a visit to **El Fuerte de San Diego** ⑤, built in the 18th century to protect Acapulco from pirates, and today home of the Anthropology Museum. For a taste of the 1950s Acapulco of John Wayne and Johnny Weissmuller, get a taxi to take you up into the hills above Caleta and Caletilla. Head out to Pie de la Cuesta for a late lunch and boat ride or waterskiing on Coyuca Lagoon, and then cross the road and park your body under a palm-frond umbrella for a spectacular sunset on the beach. Save one morning for the thrilling **Shotover Jet** boat ride on the Papagayo river (☞ Water Sports *in* Participant Sports, *below*). Especially if you're traveling with kids, devote a few hours to **Mágico Mundo Marino** ⑨ and the glass-bottom boat trip to Roqueta Island.

IF YOU HAVE 7 DAYS

For a complete change of pace, you'll want to rent a car or arrange for a tour to **Taxco,** a glorious treasure of twisting cobblestone streets and some 1,000 silver shops, about a three-hour drive from Acapulco; plan to spend the night. For a change from shopping for silver, visit the **Santa Prisca church** ⑩, Taxco's most important landmark, on Plaza Borda, and the **Casa Humboldt** ⑫, which now houses a museum of viceregal art. Try to get a front-row seat at one of the bars or restaurants on the square and spend an hour watching the constant activity: weddings, communions, funerals, and baptisms, and vendors selling baskets and painted animals. The following day, before the return trip to Acapulco, tour the **Caves of Cacahuamilpa** ⑭, an amazing expanse of subterranean chambers.

Acapulco

Acapulco is a city that is easily understood, easily explored. During the day the focus for most visitors is the beach and the myriad activities that happen on and off it. At night the attention shifts to the restaurants and discos. The **Costera Miguel Alemán,** the wide boulevard that hugs Acapulco Bay from the Scenic Highway to Caleta Beach (about 8 km, or 5 mi), is central to both day and night diversions. All the major beaches, shopping malls, and big hotels—minus the more exclusive Acapulco Diamante properties—are off the Costera. Hence most of the shopping, dining, and clubbing takes place within a few blocks of this main drag, and many an address is listed only as "Costera Miguel Alemán." Although the Costera runs completely across Acapulco, most of the action is between the naval base, La Base, next to the Hyatt (which anchors the eastern terminus of the Costera) and Papagayo Park. Because street addresses are not often used and streets have no logical pattern, directions are usually given from a major landmark, such as CiCi (a theme park) or the zócalo.

Old Acapulco, the only area of Acapulco that can easily be visited on foot, is where the Mexicans go to run their errands: mail letters at the post office, buy supplies at the Mercado Municipal, and pay their taxes. Also known as El Centro, it's where you'll find the zócalo, the church, and Fort San Diego. Just up the hill from Old Acapulco is La Quebrada.

The peninsula south of Old Acapulco contains remnants of the first version of Acapulco. This primarily residential area was prey to dilapidation and abandonment for many years, but efforts were made to revitalize it—such as reopening the Caleta Hotel and opening the aquarium on Caleta Beach and the zoo on Roqueta Island. Although its prime is definitely past, it is now a popular area for budget travelers, especially Mexican and European. The **Plaza de Toros,** where bullfights are held on Sundays from Christmas to Easter, is in the center of the peninsula.

If you arrived by plane, you've already had a royal introduction to Acapulco Bay. **Acapulco Diamante** is the area stretching east of Acapulco proper from Las Brisas to Barra Vieja beach. You'll need a car or a taxi to explore this area, where you'll find most of Acapulco's poshest hotels—Las Brisas, the Acapulco Sheraton, Camino Real, the Princess and Pierre Marqués, and Vidafel—and residential developments, as well as several exclusive private clubs, pounding surf, and beautiful beaches.

A Good Tour

If you want to get the lay of the land, you might take a drive or taxi ride along the Costera Miguel Alemán, starting on its eastern edge at **La Base,** the Mexican naval base south of Playa Icacos. When you come to Playa Icacos, you'll see the **Casa de la Cultura** ① cultural complex on the beach side (just past the Hyatt Regency hotel); a little farther down is **CiCi** ②, a children's amusement park. About 1 km (½ mi) past CiCi, on the right side of the Costera, lies the **Acapulco International Center** (often called the Convention Center); you might return here in the evening to attend a Mexican fiesta. Continue along through the commercial heart of the Costera until you reach **Papagayo Park** ③, one of the top municipal parks in the country. When you arrive at the intersection of the Costera with Diego H. de Mendoza, detour a few blocks inland to find Old Acapulco and the sprawling **Mercado Municipal** ④. You'll want to take the bus marked "Mercado" or have your taxi drop you off; it's best to navigate this area by foot. A few blocks west and closer to the water, **El Fuerte de San Diego** ⑤ sits on the hill overlooking the harbor next to the army barracks. You'll next see the **waterfront** ⑥ (locally known as the *malecón*) with its series of docks and, adjoining it, the **zócalo** ⑦, the center of Old Acapulco. A 15-minute walk up the hill from the zócalo brings you to **La Quebrada** ⑧, where the famous cliff divers perform their daredevil stunt daily.

Sights to See

❶ **Casa de la Cultura.** This cultural complex includes a small archaeological museum, an exhibit of Mexican and international crafts, and the Ixcateopan art gallery, with changing exhibits. ✉ *Costera Miguel Alemán 4834,* ☎ *74/84–38–14.* 🎟 *Free.* ⏲ *Weekdays 9–2 and 5–8, Sat. 9–2.*

❷ **CiCi** (Centro Internacional para Convivencia Infantil). A water-oriented theme park for children, CiCi features dolphin and seal shows, a freshwater pool with wave-making apparatus, a water slide, mini-aquarium, and other attractions. ✉ *Costera Miguel Alemán, across from Hard Rock Cafe,* ☎ *74/84–82–10.* 🎟 *$5.* ⏲ *Daily 10–6.*

❺ **El Fuerte de San Diego.** An 18th-century fortress, El Fuerte de San Diego was designed to protect the city from pirates. (The original fort, destroyed in an earthquake, was built in 1616.) The fort now houses the **Museo Historico de Acapulco.** The exhibits portray the city from prehistoric times through Mexico's independence from Spain in 1821. Especially noteworthy are the displays touching on the Christian missionaries sent from Mexico to the Far East and the cultural interchange that resulted. ✉ *Calle Hornitos and Morelos,* ☎ *74/82–38–28.* 🎟 *$2; free Sun.* ⏲ *Tues.–Sun. 10–5.*

❽ **La Quebrada.** High on a hill above downtown Acapulco, La Quebrada is home to the Mirador Hotel, *the* place for tourists in the 1940s; it still retains mementos from its glory days. But these days most visitors eventually make the trip here because this is where the famous cliff divers jump from a height of 130 ft daily at 1 PM and evenings at 7:30, 8:30, 9:30, and 10:30. The dives are thrilling, so be sure to arrive early. Before they take the plunge, the brave divers say a prayer at a small shrine near the jumping-off point. Sometimes they dive in pairs; often they carry torches. The hotel's La Perla supper club is the traditional—and most comfortable—viewing spot. The divers can also be seen from a general observation deck next to the hotel (🎟 About $1.50). When you exit, some of the divers may also be waiting to greet you—and to ask for tips. (For information about viewing the divers on sunset cruises, *see* Guided Tours *in* Acapulco A to Z, *below.*)

Casa de la Cultura, **1**
CiCi, **2**
El Fuerte de San Diego, **5**
La Quebrada, **8**
Mágico Mundo Marino, **9**
Mercado Municipal, **4**
Papagayo Park, **3**
Waterfront, **6**
Zócalo, **7**

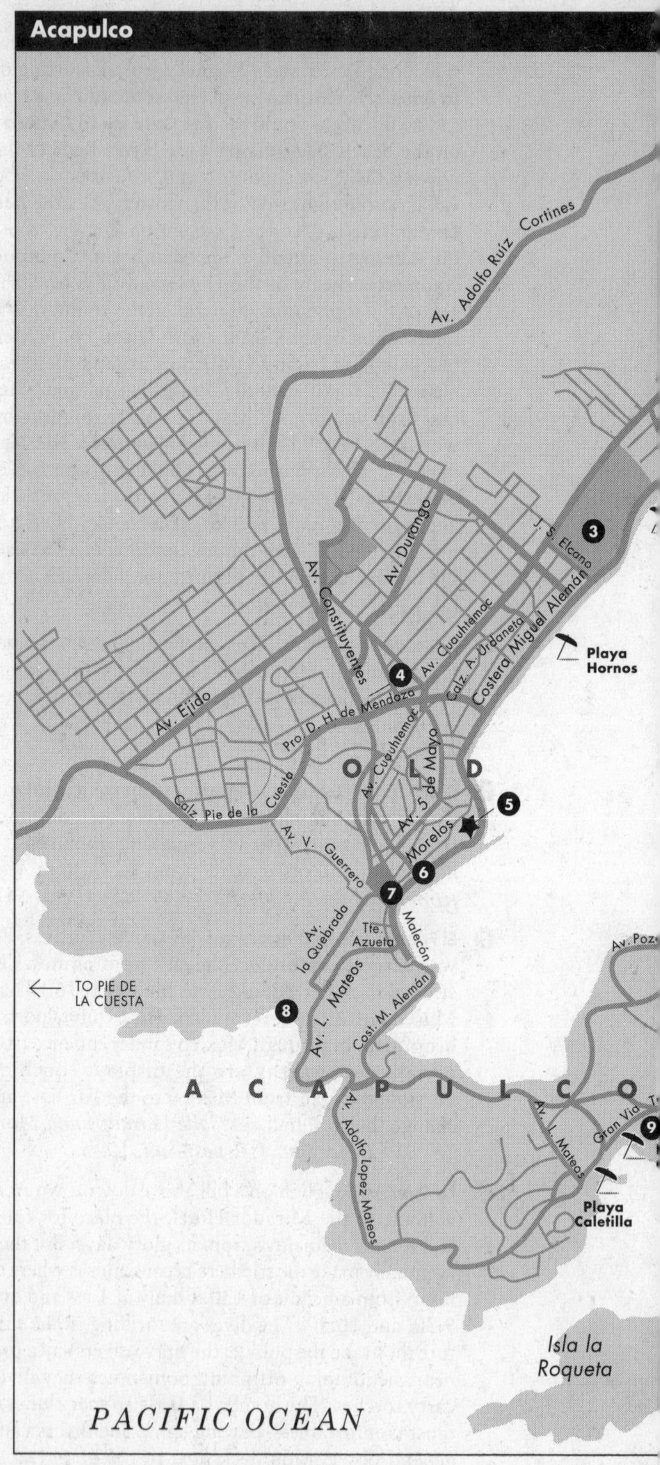

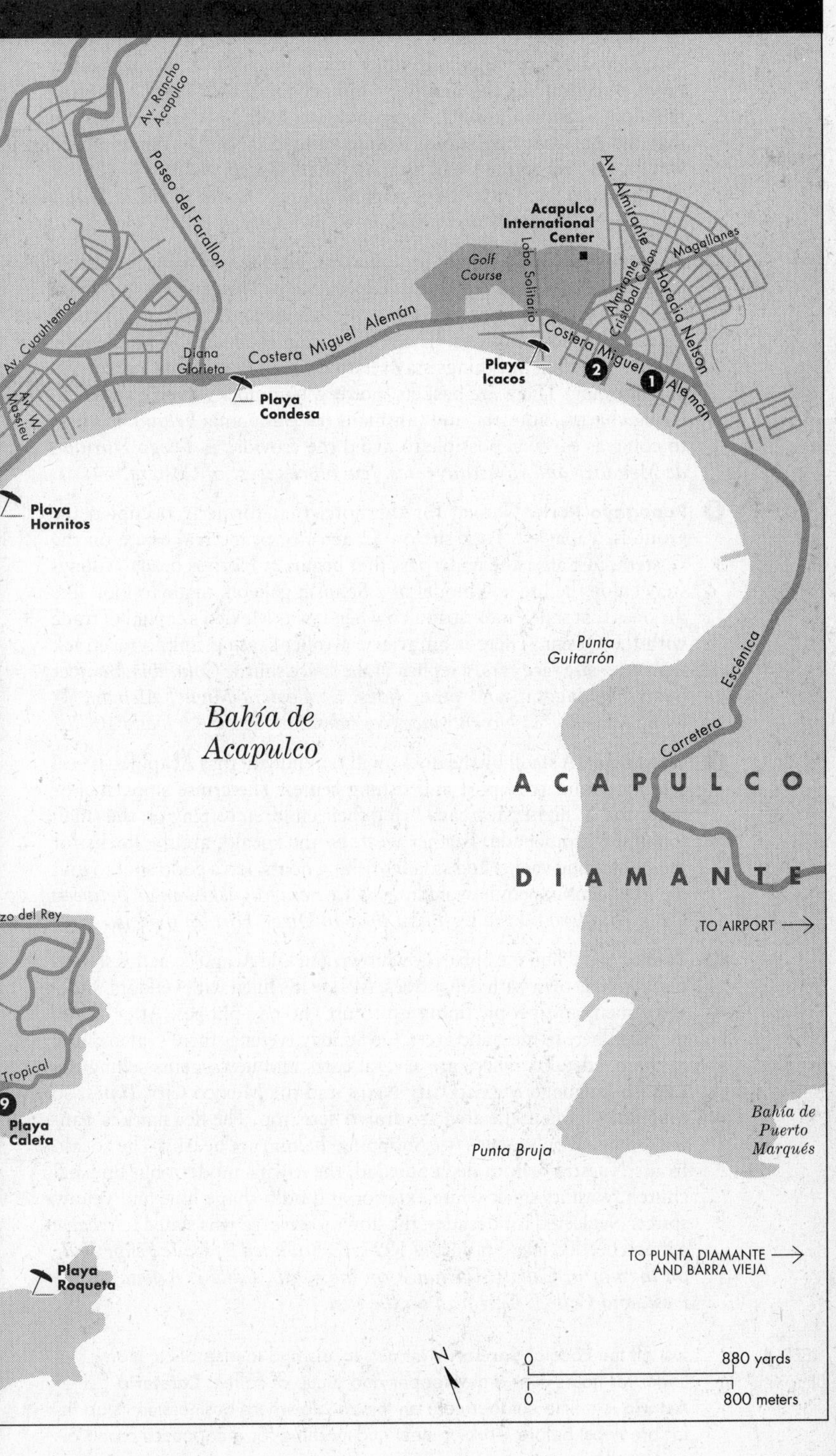
Av. Rancho Acapulco
Paseo del Farallon
Av. Cuauhtemoc
Av. W. Massieu
Diana Glorieta
Costera Miguel Alemán
Playa Condesa
Playa Hornitos
Golf Course
Lobo Solitario
Acapulco International Center
Av. Almirante
Almirante Cristobal Colon
Magallanes
Horacio Nelson
Playa Icacos
Costera Miguel Aleman
Punta Guitarrón
Bahía de Acapulco
Carretera Escénica
ACAPULCO DIAMANTE
TO AIRPORT
Tropical
Playa Caleta
Punta Bruja
Bahía de Puerto Marqués
TO PUNTA DIAMANTE AND BARRA VIEJA
Playa Roqueta
880 yards
800 meters

❾ **Mágico Mundo Marino.** In addition to an aquarium, the Magic Marine World features a sea-lion show, swimming pools, a toboggan, scuba diving, and (for rent) Jet Skis, inner tubes, bananas (inflatable rubber tubes pulled along the beach by motorboats), and kayaks—not to mention clean rest rooms. From Mágico Mundo Marino, you can take the glass-bottom boat to **Roqueta Island** (about 10 minutes each way) for a visit to the small zoo. ✉ *Caleta Beach,* ☎ *74/83–12–15.* *Aquarium $2.50; round-trip ferry service to Roqueta Island, including zoo, $3.* *Mágico Mundo daily 9–7, zoo daily 9–5.*

❹ **Mercado Municipal.** It's not for everyone, but the sprawling municipal market is Acapulco as the locals experience it. They come to purchase their everyday needs, from fresh vegetables and candles to plastic buckets and love potions. The stalls within the mercado are densely packed together, but things stay relatively cool despite the lack of air-conditioning. There are baskets, pottery, hammocks, even a stand offering charms, amulets, and talismans (☞ Shopping, *below*). It's best to come as early as possible to avoid the crowds. ✉ *Diego Hurtado de Mendoza and Constituyentes, few blocks west of Costera.*

❸ **Papagayo Park.** Named for the hotel that formerly occupied the grounds, Papagayo Park sits on 52 acres of prime real estate on the Costera, just after the underpass that begins at Hornos beach. Youngsters enjoy the life-size model of a Spanish galleon, made to look like the ones that sailed into Acapulco when it was Mexico's capital of trade with the Orient. There is an aviary, a roller-skating rink, a racetrack with mite-size race cars, a replica of the space shuttle *Columbia,* bumper boats in a lagoon, and other rides. ✉ *Costera Miguel Alemán,* ☎ *74/85–96–23.* *No entrance fee; rides 25¢–$1.50.* *Daily 10–8.*

❻ **Waterfront.** A stroll by the docks will remind you that Acapulco is still a lively commercial port and fishing center. The cruise ships anchor here, and at night Mexicans bring their children to play on the small tree-lined promenade. Farther west, by the zócalo, are the docks for the sightseeing yachts and smaller fishing boats. It's a good spot to join the Mexicans in people-watching. ✉ *Costera Miguel Alemán, between Calle Escudero on the west and the San Diego Fort on the east.*

❼ **Zócalo.** You'll find the hub of downtown and Old Acapulco at this shaded plaza, overgrown with dense trees. All day it's filled with vendors, shoeshine men, and people lining up to use the pay phones. After siesta, they drift here to meet and greet. On Sunday evenings there's often music in the bandstand. There are several cafés and newsagents selling the English-language Mexico City *News* and the Mexico City *Times,* so tourists lodging in the area are drawn here, too. The flea market, Sanborns, and Woolworth's (☞ Shopping, *below*) are nearby. The zócalo fronts **Nuestra Señora de la Soledad,** the town's modern but unusual church, with its stark-white exterior and bulb-shape blue and yellow spires. Neglected for decades, the downtown area was slated to receive a much needed face-lift during 1997. ✉ *Bounded by Calle Felipe Valle on the north, Calle J. Carranza on the south, Calle J. Azueta on the west, and Calle J. Carranza on the east.*

NEED A BREAK?

Just off the zócalo, **Sanborns** attracts locals and tourists alike; many linger for hours over a newspaper and a cup of coffee. **Cafetería Astoria** is a little outdoor café on the zócalo where businessmen stop in for breakfast before work or meet mid-morning for a cappuccino and a sweet roll.

Beaches

Some beaches, such as Revolcadero and Pie de la Cuesta, have very strong undertows and surf, so swimming is not advised. Despite an enticing appearance and claims that officials are cleaning up the bay, it remains polluted. In addition, although vending on the beach has been officially outlawed, you'll still find yourself approached by souvenir hawkers. If these things bother you, we suggest that you follow the lead of the Mexican cognoscenti and enjoy the waters at your hotel pool.

Beaches in Mexico are public, even those that seem to belong to a big hotel.

Barra Vieja

About 27 km (16 mi) east of Acapulco, between Laguna de Tres Palos and the Pacific, this long stretch of uncrowded beach is even more inviting than Pie de la Cuesta (☞ *below*) because the drive out is much more pleasant.

Caleta and Caletilla

On the peninsula in Old Acapulco, these two beaches once rivaled La Quebrada as the main tourist area in Acapulco's heyday. Now they attract families. Motorboats to Roqueta Island (☞ Mágico Mundo Marino *in* Exploring, *above*) leave from here.

Condesa

Facing the middle of Acapulco Bay, this stretch of sand has more than its share of tourists, especially singles, and the beachside restaurants are convenient for bites between parasailing flights.

Hornos and Hornitos

Running from the Plaza las Glorias Paraíso to Las Hamacas hotel, these beaches are packed shoulder to shoulder on the weekends with locals and Mexican tourists who know a good thing: Graceful palms shade the sand, and there are scads of casual eateries within walking distance.

Icacos

Stretching from the naval base to El Presidente hotel, this beach is less populated than others on the Costera, and the morning waves are especially calm.

Pie de la Cuesta

You'll need a car or cab to reach this relatively unpopulated spot, about a 25-minute drive west of Acapulco, through one of the least picturesque parts of town. A string of rustic restaurants border the wide beach, and straw palapas provide shade. What attracts people to Pie de la Cuesta, besides the long expanse of beach and spectacular sunsets, is beautiful **Coyuca Lagoon,** a favorite spot for waterskiing, freshwater fishing, and boat rides.

Puerto Marqués

Tucked below the airport highway, this strand is popular with Mexican tourists, so it tends to get crowded on weekends.

Revolcadero

A wide, sprawling beach next to the Vidafel, Pierre Marqués, and Princess hotels, its water is shallow and its waves are fairly rough. People come here to surf and ride horses.

DINING

The top restaurants in Acapulco can be fun for a splurge and provide very good value. Even at the best places in town, dinner rarely exceeds

$35 per person, and the atmosphere and views are fantastic. Ties and jackets are out of place, but so are shorts or jeans. Unless stated otherwise, all restaurants are open daily from 6:30 or 7 PM until the last diner leaves. Several restaurants have two seatings: 6:30 for the gringos and 9 for the Mexican crowd, who wisely head directly to the discos after dinner to dance off the calories.

Note: Loud music blares from many restaurants along the Costera, and proprietors will aggressively try to hustle you inside with offers of drink specials. If you're looking for a hassle-free evening, it's best either to avoid this area or decide in advance precisely where you want to dine.

CATEGORY	COST*
$$$$	over $35
$$$	$25–$35
$$	$15–$25
$	under $15

**per person for a three-course meal, excluding drinks, service, and 15% sales tax*

American

$$ ✕ **Carlos 'n' Charlie's.** An Acapulco landmark, this is still one of the most popular restaurants in town. Part of the Anderson group (with restaurants in the United States and Spain as well as Mexico), Carlos 'n' Charlie's cultivates an atmosphere of controlled craziness. Prankster waiters, a jokester menu, and eclectic decor add to the chaos. The crowd is mostly young and relaxed, seemingly oblivious to the rush-hour traffic noise that filters up to the covered balcony where people dine. The menu straddles the border, with ribs, stuffed shrimp, and oysters among the best offerings. ✉ *Costera Miguel Alemán 112,* ☎ *74/84–12–85 or 74/84–00–39. Reservations not accepted. AE, DC, MC, V.*

$$ ✕ **Hard Rock Cafe.** This link in the international Hard Rock chain is one of the most popular spots in Acapulco, and with good reason. The southern-style food—fried chicken, ribs, hamburgers—is very well prepared and the portions are more than ample. The taped rock music begins at noon, and a live group starts playing at 11 PM (except Tues.). There's always a line at the small boutique on the premises, where you can buy sports clothes and accessories bearing the Hard Rock label. ✉ *Costera Miguel Alemán 37,* ☎ *74/84–66–80. Reservations not accepted. AE, MC, V.*

Belgian

$$ ★ ✕ **La Petite Belgique.** Mexican-born Yolanda Brassart, who spent years in Europe studying the culinary arts, reigns in the kitchen of this small bistro. Guillermo, her Belgian husband, makes certain that the customers are happy. Diners are greeted by the enticing aromas of gooseliver pâté, home-baked breads, and apple strudel. The menu changes every four months but usually includes boned duck stuffed with almonds and mushrooms and served with a white wine and mushroom sauce. ✉ *Plaza Marbella,* ☎ *74/84–77–25. AE, DC, MC, V.*

French

$$ ✕ **El Olvido.** The view, the foliage, the Mediterranean decor, and the flickering candles combine to make this one of Acapulco's most romantic dining spots. A terraced dining area and huge windows provide all diners with a panoramic vista of the bay. French chef Daniel Janny blends the techniques of his native land with Mexican ingredients, which results in creations such as salmon roll with mango vinaigrette and quail in a honey, pineapple, and *pasilla* chili sauce. ✉ *Plaza Marbella,* ☎ *74/81–02–14. AE, DC, MC, V.*

Health Food

$ ✕ **100% Natural.** Six family-operated restaurants specialize in light, healthful food—yogurt shakes, fruit salads, and sandwiches made with whole-wheat bread. The service is quick and the food is a refreshing alternative to tacos, particularly on a hot day. Look for the green signs with white lettering. ✉ *Costera Miguel Alemán 200, near Acapulco Plaza (open 24 hrs),* ☎ *74/85–39–82;* ✉ *Next to Oceanic 2000,* ☎ *74/84–84–40. MC, V.*

International

$$$ ★ ✕ **Coyuca 22.** This is Acapulco's most beautiful restaurant. Diners eat on terraces that overlook the bay from the west, on a hilltop in Old Acapulco. The understated decor consists of Doric pillars and sculptures, and diners gaze down on an enormous illuminated obelisk and a small pool. It's like eating in a partially restored Greek ruin without the dust. Diners can choose from two fixed menus or order à la carte. Seafood and prime ribs are house specialties. ✉ *Av. Coyuca 22 (10-min taxi ride from zócalo),* ☎ *74/82–34–68 or 74/83–50–30. Reservations essential. AE, DC, MC, V. Closed Apr. 30–Nov. 1.*

$$–$$$ ✕ **Bella Vista.** This alfresco restaurant in the exclusive Las Brisas area has fantastic sunset views of Acapulco. Its large menu offers a wide variety of dishes that range from Asian appetizers to Italian and seafood entrées. Try the delicious (and spicy!) Thai shrimp, sautéed in sesame oil, ginger, Thai chili, and hoisin sauce; or the red snapper étouffée, cooked in chardonnay, tomato, herbs, basil, and oyster sauce. ✉ *Carretera Escéncia 5255,* ☎ *74/84–15–80, ext. 500. Reservations essential. AE, DC, MC, V.*

$$–$$$ ★ ✕ **Madeiras.** One of Acapulco's favorite dining spots, Madeiras is very difficult to get into, especially on weekends and during the Christmas and Easter holidays. The bar-reception area features startling coffee tables made of glass resting on wooden animals; the dishes and flatware were created by silversmiths in nearby Taxco; and all the tables have a view of Acapulco glittering at night. Dinner is served from a four-course, prix-fixe menu and costs about $25 without wine. Specialties include the delicious Spanish dish of red snapper in sea salt, tasty chilled soups, stuffed red snapper, and a choice of steaks and other seafood, as well as the *crepas de huitlacoche* (*huitlacoche,* or *cuitlacoche,* is a corn fungus that was a delicacy to the Aztecs). There are seatings every 30 minutes from 7 to 10:30 PM. Children under eight are not admitted. ✉ *Scenic Hwy. 33-B, just past La Vista shopping center,* ☎ *74/84–69–21. Reservations essential. AE, DC, MC, V.*

$$–$$$ ★ ✕ **Spicey.** In addition to another spectacular view of Acapulco's diamond-studded bay from the air-conditioned dining room or the terrace, this relative newcomer offers diners an innovative menu of dishes that blend international techniques and spices. The results are delicious, as well as a delight to the eye: spring rolls filled with smoked salmon, cream cheese, and vegetables served with a Chinese plum sauce, and whole red snapper flavored with star anise and rosemary, glacéed with honey. ✉ *Scenic Hwy., Fracc. Marina Las Brisas,* ☎ *74/81–13–80. Reservations essential. AE, MC, V.*

Italian

$$$ ★ ✕ **Casa Nova.** Another ultraromantic spot created by Arturo Cordova, the man behind Coyuca 22 (☞ *above*), Casa Nova is carved out of a cliff that rises up from Acapulco Bay. The views, both from the ter-

Acapulco Dining and Lodging

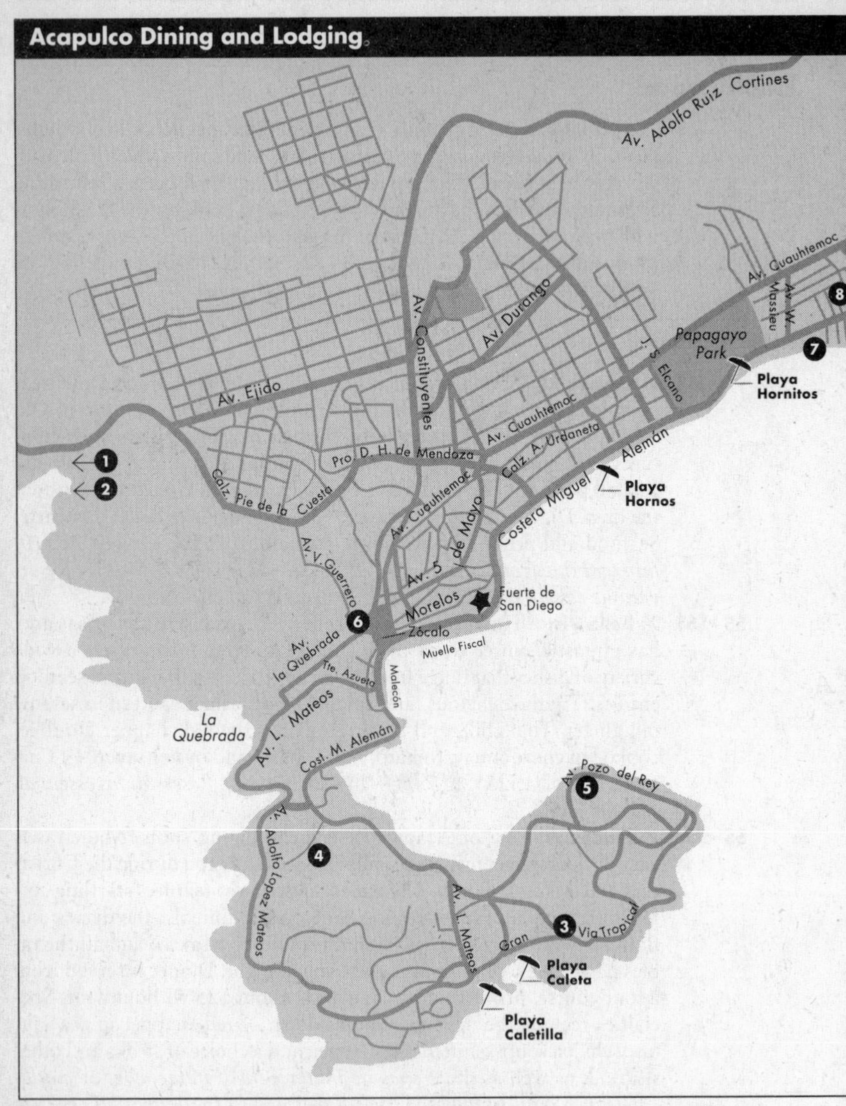

Dining
Bella Vista, **29**
Beto's, **12**
Carlos 'n' Charlie's, **14**
Casa Nova, **30**
Coyuca 22, **4**
El Cabrito, **21**
El Olvido, **22**
Hard Rock Cafe, **19**
La Petite Belgique, **23**
La Vela, **32**
Los Rancheros, **26**
Madeiras, **28**
100% Natural, **8**
Pipo's, **20**
Spicey, **31**
Suntory, **24**
Villa Fiore, **17**
Zorrito's, **7**

Lodging
Acapulco Plaza, **10**
Acapulco Princess, **34**
Camino Real Acapulco Diamante, **32**
Continental Plaza, **11**
Elcano, **18**
Fiesta Americana Condesa Acapulco, **15**
Hotel Acapulco Tortuga, **13**
Howard Johnson Moralisa, **9**
Hyatt Regency Acapulco, **25**
Majestic, **5**
Parador del Sol, **1**
Pierre Marqués, **33**
Plaza las Glorias El Mirador, **6**
Sheraton Acapulco, **27**
Suites Alba, **3**
Ukae Kim, **2**

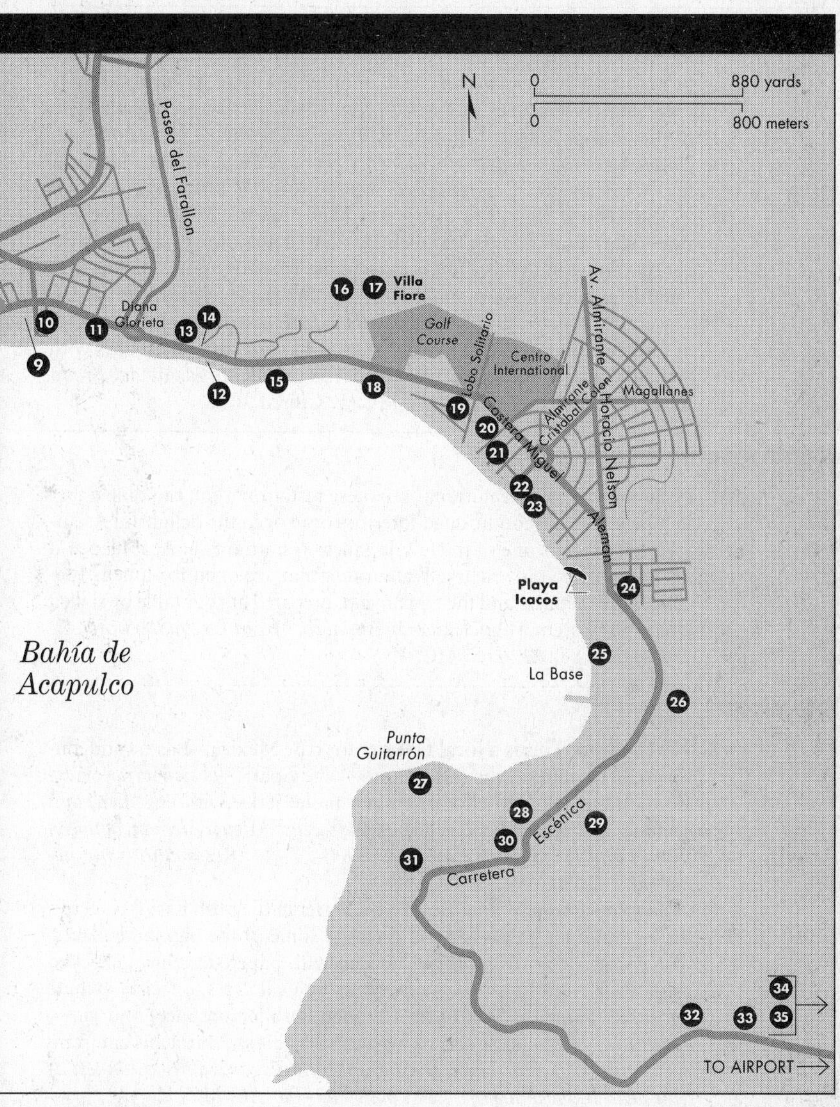
N
0
880 yards
0
800 meters
Paseo del Farallon
Diana Glorieta
Villa Fiore
Golf Course
Lobo Solitario
Centro International
Av. Almirante Horacio Nelson
Almirante Cristobal Colon
Magallanes
Costera Miguel Aleman
Playa Icacos
Bahía de Acapulco
La Base
Punta Guitarrón
Carretera Escénica
TO AIRPORT
9
10
11
12
13
14
15
16
17
18
19
20
21
22
23
24
25
26
27
28
29
30
31
32
33
34
35

race and the air-conditioned dining room, are spectacular, the service impeccable, and the Italian cuisine divine. Diners can choose the fixed-price menu (called *menu turístico*) or order à la carte. Favorites include antipasto, fresh pastas, a delightful *cotolette de vittello* (veal chops with mushrooms), lobster tail, and *linguini alle vongole* (linguine with clams, tomato, and garlic). ✉ *Scenic Hwy. 5256, just past Madeiras,* ☎ *74/84–68–19. Reservations essential. AE, DC, MC, V.*

$$ ✕ **Villa Fiore.** Here, the owners of Madeiras (☞ *above*) bring you fine Italian dining in the candlelit garden of what looks like an 18th-century Venetian villa. Diners can choose from two fixed menus that include appetizer, soup, main course (chicken, fish, meat, or pasta), dessert, and coffee. Opt for the calamari *fritti* (fried in marinara sauce) as a starter, and one of the veal dishes or fillet of stuffed sea bass with artichoke sauce for an entrée. Service is excellent. ✉ *Av. del Prado 6,* ☎ *74/84–20–40. AE, DC, MC, V. Closed Wed.*

Japanese

$$$ ✕ **Suntory.** At this traditional Japanese restaurant you can dine either in a blessedly air-conditioned interior room or in the delightful Asian-style garden. It's one of the few Japanese restaurants in Acapulco and also one of the only deluxe restaurants that are open for lunch. Specialties are the sushi and the teppanyaki, prepared at your table by skilled chefs. ✉ *Costera Miguel Alemán 36, across from La Palapa hotel,* ☎ *74/84–80–88. AE, DC, MC, V.*

Mexican

$ ✕ **El Cabrito.** This is a local favorite for true Mexican cuisine and ambience. The name of the restaurant—"The Goat"—is also its specialty. In addition, you can choose among mole; jerky with egg, fish, and seafood; and other Mexican dishes. ✉ *Costera Miguel Alemán, between Nina's and Hard Rock Cafe,* ☎ *74/84–77–11. Reservations not accepted. AE, MC, V.*

$ ✕ **Los Rancheros.** With a view of the water in the posh East Bay, here's dining at about half what you'd pay at some of the big-name places. The decor is colorful, folksy Mexican with paper streamers, checked tablecloths, and lopsided mannequins in local dress. Specials include *carne tampiqueña* (fillet of beef broiled with lemon juice) and *queso fundido* (melted cheese served with tortilla chips). Mariachis entertain weekends. ✉ *Scenic Hwy. just before Extravaganzza disco (on left as you head toward airport),* ☎ *74/84–19–08. AE, MC, V.*

$ ✕ **Zorrito's.** When Julio Iglesias is in town, this is where he heads in the wee hours of the morning, after the discos close. He's been known to sing along with the band that's on hand to play every evening, from 6 PM on. The menu features a host of steak and beef dishes, and the special, *filete tampiqueña,* comes with tacos, enchiladas, guacamole, and frijoles. ✉ *Costera Miguel Alemán and Anton de Alaminos, next to Banamex,* ☎ *74/85–37–35. Reservations not accepted. AE, MC, V. Closed 7 AM–9 AM and Tues. 7 AM–2 PM.*

Seafood

$$–$$$ ★ ✕ **La Vela.** Set on a wharf that juts out into Pichilingue Bay, this open-air dining spot is protected by a dramatic roof that simulates a huge white sail. It's very atmospheric after dark, when a stillness hangs over the bay and the lights of Puerto Marqués flicker in the distance. The menu features a variety of fish and shellfish dishes, but the specialty of the house is the red snapper *à la talla* (basted with chili and other spices and broiled over hot coals). ✉ *Camino Real Acapulco Diamante,*

Carretera Escénica, Km 14, ☎ *74/66–10–10. AE, DC, MC, V.*

$$ ✕ **Beto's.** By day you can eat right on the beach and enjoy live music; by night this palapa-roofed restaurant is transformed into a dim and romantic dining area lighted by candles and paper lanterns. Whole red snapper, lobster, and seviche are recommended. There is a second branch next door and a third at Barra Vieja Beach—where the specialty is *pescado* (fish) à la talla. Beto's Safari turns into a disco Friday and Saturday after 10:30 PM. ✉ *Beto's, Costera Miguel Alemán at Condesa Beach,* ☎ *74/84–04–73; Beto's Safari,* ✉ *Costera Miguel Alemán, next to Beto's,* ☎ *74/84–47–62; Beto's Barra Vieja,* ✉ *Barra Vieja Beach, no phone. AE, MC, V.*

$$ ★ ✕ **Pipo's.** Situated on a rather quiet part of the Costera, this family-run seafood restaurant doesn't have an especially interesting view, but diners come here for the fresh fish, good service, and reasonable prices. *Huachinango veracruzano* (red snapper prepared with tomatoes, peppers, onion, and olives) and fillet of fish in *mojo de ajo* (garlic butter) are about as sophisticated as the food preparation gets. The seviche is an Acapulco tradition, as is *vuelve à la vida,* an immense seafood cocktail that, as the name implies, is guaranteed to bring you "back to life." ✉ *Costera Miguel Alemán and Nao Victoria, across from Acapulco International Center,* ☎ *74/84–01–65;* ✉ *Almirante Bretón 3, downtown,* ☎ *74/82–22–37. Reservations not accepted. AE, MC, V.*

LODGING

Although Acapulco has been an important port since colonial times, it lacks the converted monasteries and old mansions found in Mexico City. But the Costera is chockablock with new luxury high-rises and local franchises of such major U.S. hotel chains as Hyatt and Howard Johnson. As these hotels tend to be characterless, your choice will depend on location and what facilities are available. All major hotels can make water-sports arrangements.

In Acapulco geography is price, so where you stay determines what you pay. The most exclusive area is the Acapulco Diamante, home to some of the most expensive hotels in Mexico—so lush and well equipped that most guests don't budge from the minute they arrive. The minuses: Revolcadero Beach is too rough for swimming (though great for surfing), and this area is a 15- to 25-minute (expensive) taxi ride from the heart of Acapulco. The atmosphere of Acapulco Diamante is refined and revolves around a game of golf or tennis, dining at some of Acapulco's better restaurants, and dancing at the glamorous Extravaganzza, Palladium, and Fantasy discos.

There is much more activity on Costera Miguel Alemán, where the majority of large hotels, discos, American-style restaurants, and airline offices may be found, along with Acapulco's most popular beaches. All the Costera hotels have freshwater pools and sundecks, and most have restaurants and/or bars overlooking the beach, if not on the sand itself. Hotels across the street are almost always less expensive than those directly on the beach; because there are no private beaches in Acapulco, all you have to do is cross the road to enjoy the sand.

Moving west along the Costera leads you to downtown Acapulco. The beaches and restaurants here are popular with Mexican vacationers, and the dozens of hotels attract Canadian and European bargain hunters.

You can assume that accommodations that cost above $50 (double) will be air-conditioned (though you can find air-conditioned hotels for less) and will include a telephone, TV, and a view of the bay. There is usually a range of in-house restaurants and bars, as well as a pool. Exceptions exist, such as Las Brisas, which, in the name of peace and quiet, has banned TVs from all rooms. So if such extras are important to you, be sure to ask ahead. If you can't afford air-conditioning, don't panic. Even the cheapest hotels have cooling ceiling fans.

Note: Most hotels are booked solid Christmas and Easter week, so if you plan to visit then, it's wise to make reservations months in advance.

CATEGORY	COST*
$$$$	over $200
$$$	$100–$200
$$	$50–$100
$	under $50

**All prices are for a standard double room, excluding 15% sales (called IVA) tax.*

Acapulco Diamante

$$$$ ★ 🏨 **Acapulco Princess.** This is the first hotel you'll see as you leave the airport. The Princess is one of those megahotels that are always holding at least three conventions. But more rooms equals more facilities. The Princess has seven restaurants, seven bars (several of which close during the low season—Apr. through Oct.), a video bar, tennis, golf, and shopping in a cool arcade. The pool near the reception desk is sensational—fantastic tropical ponds with little waterfalls and a slatted bridge leading into a swimming-sunning area. Rooms are light and airy, with cane furniture and rugs and curtains in colorful tropical prints. During the winter season guests can also use the facilities of the hotel's smaller sibling, the Pierre Marqués. The Modified American Plan (breakfast and dinner) is obligatory from December 15 through February. ✉ *Box 1351, Playa Revolcadero, 39300,* ☎ *74/69–10–00 or 800/223–1818,* FAX *74/69–10–16. 1,019 balconied rooms. 7 restaurants, 7 bars, 5 pools, 18-hole golf course, 11 tennis courts, basketball, exercise room. AE, DC, MC, V.*

$$$$ ★ 🏨 **Camino Real Acapulco Diamante.** Opened in 1993, Acapulco's newest hotel is set at the foot of a lush tropical hillside on exclusive Pichilingue Beach, far from the madding crowd. All rooms are done in luscious pastels, with tiled floors, balcony or terrace, luxurious baths, ceiling fans, and air-conditioning. Each has a view of peaceful Puerto Marqués bay. Rates include a buffet breakfast. ✉ *Carretera Escénica, Km 14, Calle Baja Catita, 39867,* ☎ *74/66–10–10 or 800/7–22–64–66,* FAX *74/66–11–11. 156 rooms. 2 restaurants, 2 bars, 3 pools, tennis court, exercise room. AE, DC, MC, V.*

$$$$ ★ 🏨 **Pierre Marqués.** This hotel is doubly blessed: It is closer to the beach than any of the other East Bay hotels, and guests have access to all the Princess's facilities without the crowds. In addition, it has an 18-hole golf course, three pools, and five tennis courts illuminated for nighttime play. Rooms are furnished identically to those at the Princess (no TVs here, however), but villas and duplex bungalows with private patios are available. The hotel—along with its installations—closes from April through October. From January through March accommodations include mandatory breakfast (breakfast and dinner during Christmas week). ✉ *Box 1351, Playa Revolcadero, 39907,* ☎ *74/66–10–00 or 800/223–1818,* FAX *74/66–10–46. 344 rooms. 2 restaurants, bar, 3 pools, 18-hole golf course, 5 tennis courts. AE, DC, MC, V. Open winter season only.*

$$$$ 🏨 **Sheraton Acapulco.** Perfect for those who want to enjoy the sun and the sand but don't have to be in the center of everything, this Sheraton is isolated from the hubbub of the Costera and is rather small in comparison with the chain's other Mexican properties. The spacious, attractively decorated rooms and suites—all with private balconies, and many with sweeping views of the entire bay—are distributed among 13 villas that are set on a hillside on secluded Guitarrón Beach, 10 km (6 mi) east of Acapulco proper. In order to reach your room, it's necessary to wait for a staff-operated funicular—a slow, sometimes frustrating procedure. The hotel's romantic fine-dining room, **La Bahía**, serves excellent international cuisine. ✉ *Costera Guitarrón 110, 39359,* ☎ *74/81–22–22 or 800/325–3535,* FAX *74/84–37–60. 197 rooms, 15 suites. 3 restaurants, 3 bars, 2 pools. AE, DC, MC, V.*

$$$$ **Vidafel Mayan Palace.** This all-suites resort will knock your socks off. Guests are welcomed in a 100,000-square-ft lobby that's sheltered under 75-ft palapa roofs. The rooms, on the other hand, are surprisingly subdued. Airy and spacious, they are beautifully appointed with marble floors, light-wood furniture, sand-color walls, original paintings, and luxurious baths; they range from a studio with hot tub (Crown Suite) to a one-bedroom with kitchenette and sitting areas (Acapulco Suite). Guests may ride a canoe or a paddleboat around the man-made, fish-filled canal or swim in the 850-yard pool. ✉ *Playa Revolcadero, 39000,* ☎ FAX *74/69–02–01 or 800/843–2335. 350 suites. 3 restaurants, 2 bars, 18-hole golf course, 12 tennis courts. AE, DC, MC, V.*

$$$$ ★ **Westin Las Brisas.** Set high on a hillside and across the bay from most of the other main hotels, the Las Brisas remains distinct in Acapulco for the secluded haven it provides its guests. This self-contained luxury complex covers 110 acres and has accommodations that range from one-bedroom units to deluxe private casitas, complete with private pools that are small yet swimmable. All have beautiful bay views. Attention to detail is Las Brisas's claim to fame: Fresh hibiscus blossoms are set afloat in the pools each day. There are almost three employees per guest during the winter season. Transportation is by white-and-pink Jeep. You can rent one for about $60 a day, including tax, gas, and insurance; or, if you don't mind a wait, the staff will do the driving. And transport is necessary—it is a good 15-minute walk to the beach restaurant, and all the facilities are far from the rooms. Tipping is not allowed, but a service charge of $16 a day is added to the bill. The rate includes Continental breakfast. ✉ *Carretera Escénica 5255, 39868,* ☎ *74/84–15–80 or 800/228–3000,* FAX *74/84–22–69. 300 rooms. 3 restaurants, 2 bars, 3 pools (2 saltwater), hot tub, sauna, 5 tennis courts. AE, DC, MC, V.*

The Costera

$$$ **Acapulco Plaza.** Although the Plaza is once again a single pyramid-shape tower (the other two towers are now under separate management), this Fiesta Americana resort still has more facilities than many Mexican towns: four bars and an equal number of restaurants, tennis courts, a sauna, three pools, and a location next door to the Plaza Bahía, Acapulco's largest shopping mall. The **La Jaula** bar, at the mezzanine level, is most extraordinary—a wooden hut, suspended by a cable from the roof, reached by a gangplank and overlooking a garden full of flamingos and other exotic birds. Guest rooms tell the same old story—pastels and blond wood replacing passé dark greens and browns—but guests continue to be content with the facilities and service. ✉ *Costera Miguel Alemán 123, 39670,* ☎ *74/85–90–50 or 800/343–7821,* FAX *74/85–54–93. 506 rooms. 4 restaurants, 4 bars, 3 pools, sauna, 3 tennis courts, health club. AE, DC, MC, V.*

$$$ **Continental Plaza.** Built by former president Miguel Alemán during Acapulco's heyday, this landmark hotel—right in the center of everything—is still quite popular. The 390 large and airy rooms (including

12 suites) have terraces overlooking the bay. There are several good eating spots, including a **Tony Roma's,** an excellent beach, shopping center, and meeting and banquet facilities. Most spectacular is the large and lavish pool that winds around an "island" and through lush, palm-shaded gardens. ✉ *Costera Miguel Alemán, 39580,* ☎ *74/84–28–28 or 800/882–6684,* FAX *74/84–20–81. 390 rooms. 3 restaurants, 3 bars, pool, tennis court, exercise room. AE, DC, MC, V.*

$$$ ★ **Elcano.** One of Acapulco's traditional favorites has been completely remodeled, while still (thankfully) maintaining its '50s flavor. The interior decorators get an A+: The rooms are snappily done in white and navy blue, with white tiled floors and beautiful modern bathrooms. The only exception is the lobby, which is excruciatingly blue. There's a delightful outdoor restaurant, a more elegant indoor one, and a gorgeous pool that seems to float above the bay, with whirlpools built into its corners. Maintenance is excellent throughout the hotel. ✉ *Costera Miguel Alemán 75, 39690,* ☎ *74/84–19–50,* FAX *74/84–22–30. 180 rooms. 2 restaurants, bar, pool. AE, DC, MC, V.*

$$$ **Fiesta Americana Condesa Acapulco.** Right in the thick of the main shopping-restaurant district, the Condesa, as everyone calls it, is ever popular with tour operators. Bedrooms have hot-pink lamps, pastel bedspreads, and deep-blue curtains; baths have raspberry-red shower curtains. ✉ *Costera Miguel Alemán 1220, 39690,* ☎ *74/84–28–28 or 800/343–7821,* FAX *74/84–18–28. 500 rooms. 2 restaurants, bar, 2 pools. AE, DC, MC, V.*

$$$ **Hyatt Regency Acapulco.** A megahotel that you never have to leave, this property is popular with business travelers and conventioneers. Insist on a room on the seventh to the 22nd floor, which were totally refurbished in 1996 (the rooms on the other floors are quite shabby). The new decor is striking, with strong Caribbean colors replacing the pastels. Tennis courts, four eateries (including a beachside seafood place, a popular Mexican dining spot, and a kosher restaurant), three bars, and a lavish shopping area are among the reasons for guests to stay put. The Hyatt is a little out of the way, a plus for those who seek quiet. To avoid the noise of the maneuvers at the neighboring naval base, ask for a room on the west side of the hotel. ✉ *Costera Miguel Alemán 1, 39869,* ☎ *74/69–12–34 or 800/233–1234,* FAX *74/84–30–87. 645 rooms. 3 restaurants, 3 bars, snack bar, 2 pools, massage, 5 tennis courts, shops, parking (fee). AE, DC, MC, V.*

$$ **Hotel Acapulco Tortuga.** A helpful staff and prime location make the "Turtle Hotel" an appealing choice. It is also one of the few nonbeach hotels to have a garden (handkerchief-size), a beach club (in Puerto Marqués), and a pool where most of the guests hang out. At night the activity shifts to the piano bar. The downside of this merriment is the noise factor. The best bet is a room facing west on an upper floor. All rooms have blue-green pile rugs and small tables. Breakfast is served in the lobby café; lunch and dinner can be taken in the more formal restaurant. ✉ *Costera Miguel Alemán 132, 39300,* ☎ *74/84–88–89 or 800/832–7491,* FAX *74/84–73–85. 252 rooms. 2 restaurants, coffee shop, piano bar, pool, exercise room, free parking. AE, DC, MC, V.*

$$ ★ **Howard Johnson Maralisa.** Formerly the sister hotel of the Villa Vera (☞ *below*), this hotel, located on the beach side of the Costera, is now part of the Howard Johnson chain. The rooms are light, decorated in whites and pastels. This is a small, friendly place; all rooms have TVs, some have balconies, and the price is right. ✉ *Box 721, Calle Alemania, 39670,* ☎ *74/85–66–77 or 800/446–4656,* FAX *74/85–92–28. 90 rooms. Restaurant, bar, 2 pools, beach. AE, DC, MC, V.*

$$ **Villa Vera.** A five-minute drive north of the Costera leads to what was once one of Acapulco's most exclusive hotels. Some of the villas, which were once private homes, have their own pools. Standard rooms, in pas-

tels and white, are not especially large. No matter; no one spends much time in the rooms. The main pool, with its swim-up bar, is the hotel's hub. By night guests dine at the terraced restaurant, with its stunning view of the bay. There's an exercise facility, and two championship tennis courts host the Celebrity and Veterans tennis tournaments. Children under 16 are not allowed. ✉ *Box 560, Lomas del Mar 35, 39690,* ☎ *74/84-03-33,* FAX *74/84-74-79. 74 rooms. Restaurant, piano bar, 6 pools, beauty salon, massage, sauna, 2 tennis courts. AE, MC, V.*

Old Acapulco

$$ ★ **Majestic.** This dowager hotel was totally renovated in 1995. The electric-blue postmodern exterior is somewhat shocking, but the stunning decor of the spacious rooms—tile floors, cool colors, and good lighting—is completely unexpected in a hotel in this price category. Entrance is through the seventh-floor lobby, and the rest of the hotel is terraced down a rocky cliff (in fact, seen from the Costera Miguel Alemán, the Majestic has often been described as looking like a typewriter). The rooms in the main building each have air-conditioning, cable TV, private terrace, a double bed, and two studio couches; the villa rooms are smaller. There is no beach at the hotel, but free transportation is provided to the hotel's beach club, which is located next to the Club de Yates. An all-inclusive plan is also available. ✉ *Av. Pozo del Rey 73, 39390,* ☎ *74/83-27-13,* FAX *74/84-20-32. 200 rooms. 2 restaurants, 2 bars, 2 pools, tennis court, dance club, parking. AE, DC, MC, V.*

$$ **Plaza las Glorias El Mirador.** The old El Mirador has been taken over by the Plaza las Glorias chain, which is part of the Sidek conglomerate responsible for marina and golf developments all over Mexico. Very Mexican in style—white with red tiles—the Plaza las Glorias is set high on a hill with a spectacular view of Acapulco and of the cliff divers performing at La Quebrada. ✉ *Quebrada 74, 39300,* ☎ *74/83-11-55 or 800/342-2644,* FAX *74/82-45-64. 143 rooms. 2 restaurants, 3 pools. AE, DC, MC, V.*

$$ **Suites Alba.** Situated on a quiet hillside in "Acapulco Tradicional," the Alba is a resort-style hotel that offers bargain prices. All suites are air-conditioned and have a kitchenette, private bath, and terrace. There is no extra charge for up to two children under 12 sharing a room with relatives, which makes it especially popular with families. It's a 15-minute walk to Caleta and Caletilla beaches. A cable car takes guests to the hotel's beach club, on the bay, located next door to the Club de Yates, with a 330-ft toboggan. ✉ *Grand Via Tropical 35, 39390,* ☎ *74/83-00-73,* FAX *74/83-83-78. 244 rooms. 3 restaurants, bar, grocery, 3 pools, tennis court, beach, free parking. AE, DC, MC, V.*

$ **Hotel Misión.** Two minutes from the zócalo, this attractive budget hotel is the only colonial-style hotel in Acapulco. The English-speaking family that runs the Misión lives in a traditional house built in the 19th century. A newer structure housing the guest rooms was added in the 1950s. It surrounds a greenery-rich courtyard with an outdoor dining area. The rooms are small and by no means fancy, with bare cement floors and painted brick walls. But every room has a shower, and there is even hot water. The Misión appears in several European guidebooks, so expect a Continental clientele. The best rooms are on the second and third floors; the top-floor room is large but hot in the daytime. ✉ *Calle Felipe Valle 12, 39300,* ☎ *74/82-36-43. 27 rooms, showers only. No credit cards.*

Pie de la Cuesta

$$$ ★ **Parador del Sol.** Traversing both the lagoon and the Pacific Ocean sides of the Pie de la Cuesta road, this all-inclusive property gives the impression that it was designed as a luxury resort. The 150 rooms are

distributed among pink villas that are scattered over some 1,100 square ft of gardens. Spacious, with tile floors and baths, each room is air-conditioned and equipped with color TV, phone, and a fan-cooled terrace complete with hammocks. The rate includes all meals and refreshments, domestic drinks, tennis, and nonmotorized water sports. ✉ *Carretera Pie de la Cuesta–Barra de Coyuca, Km 5, Box 1070, 39300,* ☎ *74/60–20–03,* FAX *74/60–16–49. 150 rooms. Restaurant, 2 bars, 2 pools, miniature golf, 4 tennis courts, health club, dance club. AE, DC, MC, V.*

$ **Ukae Kim.** A cluster of 21 rooms and junior suites that is especially popular with Europeans and Canadians, Ukae Kim is set among towering palms on Acapulco's famous "sunset" beach, just across the road from the tranquil Coyuca Lagoon. The charming rooms are fitted with canopied beds, sitting areas, and Mexican tiled baths, and although the furnishings are a bit worn, a fresh coat of bright paint gives the place a festive air. The rooms on the beach aren't air-conditioned, but there is generally enough of a breeze to make them comfortable. ✉ *Av. Pie de la Cuesta 358,* ☎ *74/60–21–87,* FAX *74/60–21–88. 21 rooms. Restaurant, pool. DC, MC, V.*

NIGHTLIFE AND THE ARTS

The companies listed in the Orientation Tours section of Acapulco A to Z (☞ *below*) can organize evening jaunts to most of the dance and music places listed below. And don't forget the nightly entertainment at most hotels. The big resorts have live music to accompany the early evening happy hour, and some feature big-name bands from the United States for less than you would pay at home. Many hotels sponsor theme parties—Italian Night, Beach Party Night, and similar festivities.

Cultural Shows

Acapulco International Center (✉ Costera Miguel Aleman, ☎ 74/84–32–18), also known as the Convention Center, has a Mexican fiesta Wednesday and Friday; it features mariachi bands, singers, and the "Flying Indians" from Papantla. The show with dinner and drinks costs about $25, entrance to the show alone is $10, and the performance with open bar is $14. The buffet dinner starts at 7:15, the performance at 8. On Friday at El Mexicano restaurant in **Las Brisas** hotel, the Mexican Fiesta starts off with a *tianguis* (marketplace) of handicrafts and ends with a spectacular display of fireworks.

Dance

Nina's (✉ Costera Miguel Alemán 2909, ☎ 74/84–24–00) is a combination dance hall and disco where the bands play salsa and other Latin rhythms. There's a live show weekends—mostly impersonations of famous entertainers—at 12:45.

Discos

Reservations are advisable for a big group, and late afternoon or after 9 PM are the best times to call. New Year's Eve requires advance planning.

Except for Palladium, Fantasy, and Extravaganzza, all the discos are clustered on the Costera.

Andromeda, which opened in July 1996, is the latest addition to Acapulco's disco scene, and proof that Acapulco remains the disco capital of the world. Quite spectacular, even for a city known for its splendiferous discos, this one will impress even the most jaded discoers. Entrance to the Queen of the Sea's "castle" is over a torch-lit moat; once inside, the impression is of being in a submarine, with a window to the sea. There are supposedly two dance floors, but the 18-to-25 crowd dances everywhere to the latest techno and techno-pop sounds. ⊠ *Costera Miguel Alemán 15, at Fragata Yucatán,* ☎ *74/84–88–15.*

Baby O is a private club that is known to accept a few select nonmembers. Eschewing the glitz and mirrors of Acapulco's older discos, Baby O resembles a cave in a tropical jungle. The crowd is 25 to 35, mostly well-dressed, wealthy Mexicans. When the pandemonium gets to you, retreat to the little snack bar downstairs. ⊠ *Costera Miguel Alemán 22,* ☎ *74/84–74–74.*

Discobeach is Acapulco's only alfresco disco and its most informal one. The under-30 crowd sometimes even turns up in shorts. The waiters are young and friendly—some people find them overly so. (In fact, this is one of Acapulco's legendary pickup spots.) One night they're all in togas carrying bunches of grapes; the next they're in pajamas. Every Wednesday, ladies' night, all the women receive flowers. "Sex on the Beach"—rum, vodka, Cointreau, fruit juice, and grenadine (don't say you weren't warned!)—is the house specialty, in all senses of the word. ⊠ *On Condesa Beach,* ☎ *74/84–70–64.*

★ **Extravaganzza** boasts the ultimate in light and sound. It accommodates 700 at a central bar and in comfortable booths, and a glass wall provides an unbelievably breathtaking view of Acapulco Bay. No food is served, but Los Rancheros is just a few steps away. The music (which is for all ages) starts at 10:30. ⊠ *On Scenic Hwy. to Las Brisas,* ☎ *74/84–71–64.*

★ **Fantasy** attracts a 25–50 crowd—mainly couples—and is one of the few discos where people really dress up, with the men in well-cut pants and shirts and the women in racy outfits and cocktail dresses. Singles gravitate toward the two bars in the back. Fantasy is quite snug, to put it nicely, and people tend to come here earlier than they do to other places. By midnight the dance floor is so packed that people dance on the wide windowsills that look out over the bay. At 2 AM there is a fireworks display. A glassed-in elevator provides an interesting overview of the scene and leads upstairs to a little shop that stocks T-shirts and lingerie. ⊠ *On Scenic Hwy., next to Las Brisas,* ☎ *74/84–67–27.*

Hard Rock Cafe, filled with rock memorabilia, is part bar, part restaurant, part dance hall, and part boutique (☞ Dining, *above*). **Planet Hollywood** is basically more of the same, but with Hollywood memorabilia and California-style cuisine. ⊠ *Costera Miguel Alemán 2917, next to Cici,* ☎ *74/84–42–84.*

News is enormous, with seating for 1,200 people in love seats and booths. The most popular night is Friday, when everyone is bathed in foam, with a kind of wet-T-shirt effect. From 10:30 (opening time) to 11:30, the music is slow and romantic; then the disco music and the light show begin, and they go on till dawn. ⊠ *Costera Miguel Alemán 3308, across from Hyatt Regency,* ☎ *74/84–59–02.*

Palladium, inaugurated at the end of 1993, is another spectacular production of Tony Rullán, the creator of Extravaganzza (☞ *above*). A waterfall that cascades down the hill from the dance-floor level makes this place hard to miss. As at Extravaganzza, the dance floor is nearly surrounded by 50-ft-high windows, giving dancers a spectacular view of all Acapulco. ⊠ *On Scenic Hwy. to Las Brisas,* ☎ *74/81–03–30.*

OUTDOOR ACTIVITIES AND SPORTS

Participant Sports

Fishing

Fishing trips can be arranged through your hotel, downtown at the Pesca Deportiva near the *muelle* (dock) across from the zócalo, or through travel agents. At the docks near the zócalo you can hire a boat for $30 a day (two lines). It is safer to stick with one of the reliable companies whose boats and equipment are in good condition. Boats accommodating four to 10 people cost $180–$500 a day, $45–$60 by chair. Excursions usually leave about 7 AM and return at 1 or 2 PM. You are required to get a fishing license ($7) from the Secretaría de Pesca; you'll find their representative at the dock. Don't show up during siesta, between 2 and 4 in the afternoon.

For deep-sea fishing, **Divers de México** (☞ Scuba Diving, *below*) has well-maintained boats for four to 10 passengers for $200 to $800. It also offers private yacht charters. Small boats for freshwater fishing can be rented at **Cadena's** and **Tres Marías** at Coyuca Lagoon.

Fitness and Swimming

Most of the time, Acapulco weather is like August in the warmest parts of the United States. This means that you should cut back on your workouts and maintain proper hydration by drinking plenty of water.

Acapulco Princess Hotel offers the best hotel fitness facilities, including a gym with stationary bikes, Universal machines, and free weights. Because the Princess is about 15 km (9 mi) from the city center and the pollution of Acapulco, you can even swim in the ocean here if you beware of the strong undertow.

Villa Vera Spa and Fitness Center (✉ Lomas del Mar 35, ☎ 74/84–03–33) has a modern spa and fitness center and is equipped with exercise machines (including step machines), free weights, and benches. Masseuses and cosmetologists give facials and massages inside or by the pool, as you wish. Both the beauty center and the gym are open to nonguests.

Westin Las Brisas is where you should stay if you like to swim but don't like company or competition. Individual casitas come with private or semiprivate pools; the beach club has two saltwater pools (☞ Lodging, *above*). Most of the major hotels in town along the Costera Miguel Alemán also have pools.

Golf

Two 18-hole championship golf courses are shared by the **Princess** and **Pierre Marqués** hotels. Reservations should be made in advance (☎ 74/69–10–00). Greens fees are $60 for guests and $80 for nonguests. A round at the 18-hole **Vidafel** (☎ 74/69–02–01) course is $45 for guests and $60 for nonguests. There is also a public golf course at the **Club de Golf** (☎ 74/84–07–81) on the Costera across from the Acapulco Malibú hotel. Greens fees are $25 for nine holes, $35 for 18 holes. Guests at Las Brisas can play on the links at Tres Vidas, otherwise Tres Vidas and Diamante Country Club are reserved for members and their guests.

Jogging

If you don't like beach jogging, the only real venue for running in the downtown area is along the sidewalk next to the Costera Miguel Alemán at the seafront, but you'll have to go very early, before traffic fumes set in. Away from the city center, the best area for running is out at the Acapulco Princess Hotel, on the airport road. A 2-km (1-mi) loop is laid out along a lightly traveled road, and in the early morning you can also run along the asphalt trails on the golf course.

Rollerblading

For a change of pace from sand and sea activities, **Roller Gran Prix** (✉ Brisamar, east of Costera Miguel Aleman, just before Los Rancheros restaurant, ☎ 74/84–93–13) features roller blading to disco music and formula-style go-carts. The $3 fee includes blades, and instruction is available; go-karts cost $2.50 for five minutes.

Scuba Diving

Divers de México (✉ Downtown near Fiesta and Bonanza yachts, ☎ 74/82–13–98), owned by a helpful and efficient American woman, provides English-speaking captains and comfortable American-built yachts. A three- to four-hour scuba-diving excursion—including equipment, lessons in a pool for beginners, and drinks—costs about $55 per person. If you are a certified diver, the excursion is $45.

Arnold Brothers (✉ Costera Miguel Alemán 205, ☎ 74/82–18–77) runs daily scuba-diving excursions and snorkeling trips. The scuba trips cost $25 and last for two to 2½ hours.

Tennis

Court fees range from about $5 to $15 an hour during the day and are 15% more in the evening. At the hotel courts, nonguests pay about $5 more per hour. Lessons with English-speaking instructors start at about $10 an hour; ball boys get a $2 tip.

Places in town to play tennis include **Acapulco Plaza** (☎ 74/85–90–50), three hard-surface courts, two lighted; **Acapulco Princess** (☎ 74/69–10–00), two indoor courts, nine outdoor; **Club de Tennis and Golf** (✉ Costera Miguel Alemán, across from Hotel Malibu, ☎ 74/84–07–81), four courts; **Hyatt Regency** (☎ 74/69–12–34), five lighted courts; **Pierre Marqués** (☎ 74/66–10–00), five courts; **Tiffany's Racquet Club** (✉ Av. Villa Vera 120, ☎ 74/84–79–49), five courts; **Vidafel Mayan Plaza** (☎ 74/69–02–01), 12 lighted courts; and **Villa Vera Hotel** (☎ 74/84–03–33), two outdoor lighted clay courts.

Water Sports

Waterskiing, broncos (one-person motorboats), and parasailing can all be arranged on the beach. Parasailing is an Acapulco highlight; an eight-minute trip costs $20. Waterskiing is about $25 an hour; broncos cost $15 for a half hour. Windsurfing can be arranged at Caleta and most of the beaches along the Costera but is especially good at Puerto Marqués. At Coyuca Lagoon, you can try your hand (or feet) at barefoot waterskiing. The main surfing beach is Revolcadero.

Acapulco's latest attraction, the **Shotover Jet,** is an import from Queenstown, New Zealand, that began operating here in December 1996. For $35, passengers are transported from the outfit's Acapulco offices, via air-conditioned coach, to the town of Tierra Colorado (35 mins each way). There, they board the 12-passenger craft for an exciting 30-minute boat ride on the Papagayo River, complete with a thrilling 360-degree turn (made possible by the boats' flat design) and vistas of local flora and fauna (orchids, iguanas, and armadillos). After the ride, passengers are welcome to return directly to Acapulco or take a later shuttle bus and linger at the riverside property, which features a restaurant, souvenir shop, and children's playground. ✉ *Hotel Continental Plaza, locale 3,* ☎ *74/84–11–54.*

Spectator Sports

Bullfights

The season runs from about Christmas to Easter, and *corridas* are held on Sunday at 5:30. Tickets are available through your hotel or at the **Plaza de Toros** ticket window (✉ Av. Circunvalación, across from Caleta Beach, ☎ 74/82–11–81) Monday–Saturday 10–2 and Sunday 10:30–5. Tickets in the shade (sombra)—the only way to go—cost about $15. Preceding the fight are performances of Spanish dances and music by the Chili Frito band.

Jai Alai

The **Jai Alai Acapulco Race & Sports Book** (✉ Costera Miguel Alemán 498, ☎ 74/81–16–50) has two restaurants and a bar, and a capacity for 1,500 spectators. The fast-paced games take place Thursday through Sunday at 9 PM, mid-December through August. Entrance is $6, but $2.50 to $4 is reimbursed with your first bet. In addition to bets on jai alai, wagers are taken on all major sports events—basketball, football, baseball, boxing, horse and greyhound racing—that are transmitted directly via satellite.

SHOPPING

The main shopping strip is on Costera Miguel Alemán from the Acapulco Plaza to the El Presidente Hotel. Here you can find **Guess, Peer, Aca Joe, Amarras, Polo Ralph Lauren,** and other fashionable sportswear boutiques. Downtown (Old) Acapulco doesn't have many name shops, but this is where you'll find the inexpensive tailors patronized by the Mexicans, lots of little souvenir shops, and a vast flea market with crafts. Also downtown are **Woolworth's** and **Sanborns.** Most shops are open from 10 to 7 Monday through Saturday and closed on Sunday.

Department Stores and Supermarkets

Except for the waitresses' uniforms, the food, and a good handicrafts selection, **Sanborns** is very un-Mexican. Still, it is an institution throughout Mexico. It sells English-language newspapers, magazines, and books, as well as a line of high-priced souvenirs. This is a useful place to come for postcards, cosmetics, and medicines. Sanborns' restaurants are popular for their enchiladas *suizas* (prepared with lots of cream and cheese), *molletes* (toasted rolls spread with refried beans and cheese), and their seven-fruit drink. The Estrella del Mar branch (✉ Costera Miguel Alemán 1226, ☎ 74/84–44–13) and the downtown branch (✉ Costera Miguel Alemán 209, ☎ 74/82–61–67) are both open from 7 AM to midnight during the high season and from 7:30 AM to 11 PM the rest of the year.

Branches of **Aurrerá, Gigante, Price Club, Sam's,** and **Comercial Mexicana** are all on the Costera and sell everything from liquor and fresh and frozen food to lightbulbs, clothing, garden furniture, and sports equipment.

Woolworth's (✉ Escudero 250 in Old Acapulco) is much like the five-and-dime stores found all over the United States, but with a Mexican feel.

Malls

Malls in Acapulco range from the delightful air-conditioned shopping arcade at the Princess hotel to rather gloomy collections of shops that sell cheap jewelry and embroidered dresses. Malls are listed below from east to west.

The multilevel **Marbella Mall,** at the Diana Glorieta, is home to **Martí,** a well-stocked sporting-goods store; a health center (drugstore, clinic, and lab); and **Bing's Ice Cream,** as well as several restaurants. **Aca Mall,** which is next door, is all white and marble; here you'll find **Polo Ralph Lauren, Ferrioni,** and **Aca Joe.**

Plaza Bahía, next to the Acapulco Plaza hotel, is a place for serious shopping. It is a huge, completely enclosed and air-conditioned mall where you could easily spend an entire day. Stores include **Dockers, Benetton, Nautica,** and **Ferrioni,** for chic casual wear for men and women; **Ragazza,** which carries an exquisite line of fine lingerie; **Aspasia,** which offers locally designed, glitzy evening dresses and chunky diamanté jewelry; **Bally** for shoes; a large **Martí** for sporting goods; restaurants and snack bars; and a bowling alley and video-game arcade.

Markets

In addition to fresh fruits and vegetables, meat, fowl, fish, and flowers, the **Mercado Municipal** is also stocked with serapes, piñatas, leather goods, baskets, hammocks, framed paintings done on velvet of the Virgin of Guadalupe, as well as traditional Mexican cooking utensils. There are even stands offering charms, amulets and talismans, bones, herbs, fish eyes, sharks' teeth, lotions, candles, incense, and soaps said to help one find or keep a mate, increase virility or fertility, bring peace to the home, or ward off the evil eye (☞ Exploring, *above*).

El Mercado de Artesanías El Parazal, a conglomeration of every souvenir in town, is a 15-minute walk from Sanborns. You'll find fake ceremonial masks, the ever-present onyx chessboards, $15 hand-embroidered dresses, imitation silver, hammocks, ceramics, even skin cream made from turtles (don't buy it, because turtles are endangered and you won't get it through U.S. Customs). ✉ *From Sanborns downtown head away from the Costera to Vázquez de León and turn right 1 block.* ⏲ *Daily 9–9.*

In an effort to get the itinerant vendors off the beaches and streets, the local government set up a series of **flea markets** along the Costera, mostly uninviting dark tunnels of stalls that carry what seems to be an inexhaustible supply of inexpensive collectibles and souvenirs, including serapes, ceramics, straw hats, shell sculptures, carved walking canes, and wooden toys. The selections of archaeological-artifact replicas, bamboo wind chimes, painted wooden birds (from $5 to $30 each), shell earrings, and embroidered clothes begin to look identical. Prices at the flea markets are often quite low, but it's a good idea to compare prices of items you're interested in with prices in the shops, and bargaining is essential. It's best to buy articles described as being made from semiprecious stones or silver in reputable establishments. If you don't, you may find that the beautiful jade or lapis lazuli that was such a bargain was really cleverly painted paste, or that the silver was simply a facsimile called *alpaca*.

Specialty Shops

Art

Edith Matison's Art Gallery (✉ Costera Miguel Alemán 2010, across from Club de Golf, ☎ 74/84–30–84) shows the works of renowned international and Mexican artists, including Calder, Dalí, Siquieros, and Tamayo. **Galería Rudic** (✉ Yañez Pinzón 9, across from Continental Plaza, ☎ 74/84–48–44) is one of the best galleries in town, with a good collection of top contemporary Mexican artists, including Armando Amaya, Leonardo Nierman, Gastón Cabrera, Trinidad Osorio, and Casiano García. **Pal Kepenyes** (✉ Guitarrón 140, ☎ 74/84–37–38) continues to receive good press for his sculpture and jewelry, on display in his workshop. The whimsical painted papier-mâché and giant ceramic sculptures of **Sergio Bustamente** (✉ Costera Miguel Alemán 120-9, across from Fiesta American Condesa hotel, ☎ 74/84–49–92) can be seen at his gallery.

Boutiques

KOS (✉ Costera Miguel Alemán, outside entrance to Fiesta Americana Condesa del Mar hotel, ☎ 74/81–24–34; ✉ Acapulco Plaza Hotel, ☎ 74/85–25–15) carries a sensational line of swimsuits for equally sensational bodies. **Nautica** (✉ Plaza Bahía, ☎ 74/85–75–11; smaller shop at ✉ Las Brisas hotel, ☎ 74/84–16–50) is a boutique stocked with stylish casual clothing for men. **Pasarela** (✉ Galerís Acapulco Plaza, at entrance to Acapulco Plaza hotel, ☎ 74/85–00–17) carries its own line of gauzy dresses with a Mexican flavor, as well as some interesting accessories. **Pit** (✉ Princess arcade, ☎ 74/69–10–00) offers a smashing line of beach cover-ups and hand-painted straw hats, as well as bathing suits and light dresses.

Custom-Designed Clothes

Benny (✉ Costera Miguel Alemán 98, across from Hotel El Presidente, ☎ 74/84–15–47; ✉ Downtown at Ignacio de la Llave 2, local 10, ☎ 74/82–22–28), known for years for his custom-designed resort wear for men, now caters to women as well.

Esteban's (✉ Costera Miguel Alemán 2010, across from Club de Golf, ☎ 74/84–30–84) is the most glamorous shop in Acapulco, boasting a clientele of international celebrities and many of the important local families. Estaban's made-to-order clothes are formal and fashionable; his opulent evening dresses range from $200 to $3,000, though daytime dresses average $100. The real bargains are on the second floor, where some items are marked down as much as 80%. If you scour the racks, you can find something for $10 to $15. Esteban has a back room filled with designer clothes.

Handicrafts

AFA (✉ Horacio Nelson and James Cook, near Hyatt Regency, ☎ 74/84–80–39) is a huge shop offering a vast selection of jewelry, handicrafts, clothing, and leather goods from all over Mexico. **La Placita** (✉ Plaza Bahía, no phone) comprises two shops designed to look like flea-market stalls. Top-quality merchandise is on display, including papier-mâché fruits and vegetables, Christmas ornaments, wind chimes, and brightly painted wooden animals from Oaxaca.

Silver and Jewelry

Antoinette (✉ Acapulco Princess shopping arcade, ☎ 74/69–10–00) has gold jewelry of impeccable design, set with precious and semiprecious stones, that you wouldn't be surprised to find on Fifth Avenue. Also on display is Emilia Castillo's line of brightly colored porcelain ware, inlaid with silver fish, stars, and birds. It's worth going to window-shop, even if you know you won't buy anything.

Suzette's (✉ Hyatt Regency hotel, ☎ 74/69–12–34), a tony shop that's been around for years, has a very laudable selection of gold jewelry.

Tane (✉ Hyatt Regency hotel, ☎ 74/84–63–48; ✉ Las Brisas hotel, ☎ 74/81–08–16) carries small selections of the exquisite flatware, jewelry, and objets d'art created by one of Mexico's most prestigious (and expensive) silversmiths.

SIDE TRIP

Taxco, the Silver City

275 km (165 mi) north of Acapulco.

It's a picture-postcard look—Mexico in its Sunday best: white stucco buildings nuzzling cobblestone streets, red-tile roofs, and geranium-filled window boxes bright in the sun. Taxco (pronounced *tahss*-co), a colonial treasure that the Mexican government declared a national monument in 1928, tumbles onto the hills of the Sierra Madre in the state of Guerrero. Its silver mines drew foreign mining companies here for centuries. Now its charm, mild temperatures, sunshine, flowers, and silversmiths make Taxco a popular tourist destination.

Hernán Cortés discovered Taxco's mines in 1522. The silver rush lasted until the next century, when excitement tapered off. Then in the 1700s a Frenchman, who Mexicanized his name to José de la Borda, discovered a rich lode that revitalized the town's silver industry and made him exceedingly wealthy. After Borda, however, Taxco's importance faded, until the 1930s and the arrival of William G. Spratling, a writer-architect from New Orleans. Enchanted by Taxco and convinced of its potential as a silver center, Spratling set up an apprentice shop, where his artistic talent and his fascination with pre-Columbian design combined to produce silver jewelry and other artifacts that soon earned Taxco its worldwide reputation as the Silver City. Spratling's inspiration lives on in his students and their descendants, many of whom are the city's current silversmiths.

10 The **Church of San Sebastián and Santa Prisca** has dominated Plaza Borda—one of the busiest and most colorful town squares in all Mexico—since the 18th century. Usually just called Santa Prisca, it was built by French silver magnate José de la Borda in thanks to the Almighty for his having literally stumbled upon a rich silver vein. The style of the church—sort of Spanish baroque meets rococo—is known as churrigueresque, and its pink exterior is a stunning surprise. This is one of Mexico's most beautiful colonial churches and Taxco's most important landmark. ⊠ *Southwest side of Plaza Borda.*

NEED A BREAK?

Around Plaza Borda are several *neverías* where you can treat yourself to an ice cream in exotic flavors such as tequila, corn, avocado, or coconut. **Bar Paco's,** directly across the street from Santa Prisca, is a Taxco institution; its terrace is the perfect vantage point for watching the comings and goings on the zócalo while sipping a margarita or a beer.

11 The former home of William G. Spratling houses the **Spratling Museum.** This small gallery explains the working of colonial mines and displays Spratling's collection of pre-Columbian artifacts. ⊠ *Porfírio Delgado and El Arco,* ☎ *762/2-16-60.* *Small entrance fee.* *Tues.–Sat. 10–5, Sun. 9–3.*

12 **Casa Humboldt** was named for the German adventurer Alexander von Humboldt, who stayed here in 1803. The Moorish-style 18th-century house has a finely detailed facade. It now houses a wonderful little museum of colonial art. ⊠ *Calle Juan Ruíz Alarcón 6,* ☎ *762/2-55-01.* *Small entrance fee.* *Tues.–Sat. 10–5, Sun. 10–3.*

If you want to experience a typical Mexican market, with everything
13 from peanuts to electrical appliances, the **Municipal Market** is worth a visit. On Saturday and Sunday mornings, when locals from surrounding towns come with their produce and crafts, the market spills

Casa Humboldt, **12**
Caves of Cacahuamilpa, **14**
Church of San Sebastián and Santa Prisca, **10**
Municipal Market, **13**
Spratling Museum, **11**

Taxco Exploring

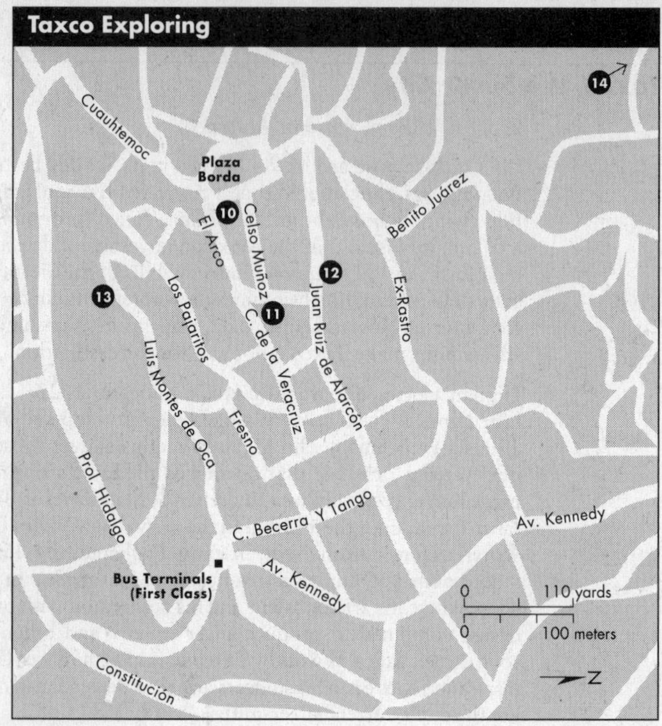

out onto the surrounding streets. You'll find it directly down the hill from Santa Prisca.

14 The largest caverns in Mexico, the **Caves of Cacahuamilpa** (Grutas de Cacahuamilpa) are about 15 minutes northeast of Taxco. These 15 large chambers comprise 12 km (8 mi) of geological formation. Only some caves are illuminated. Plans to turn the caves into a dinosaur park have, thankfully, been laid to rest. A guide can be hired at the entrance.

Dining and Lodging

Gastronomes can find everything from tagliatelle to iguana in Taxco restaurants, and meals are much less expensive than in Acapulco. Dress is casual, but less so than at the resorts. There are several categories of hotel to choose from within Taxco's two types: the small inns nestled on the hills skirting the zócalo and the larger, more modern hotels on the outskirts of town.

$$ ✕ **La Ventana de Taxco.** The Italian recipes of manager Mario Cavagna, coupled with Mexican specialties and a fantastic view, still draw an enthusiastic crowd to this restaurant, in spite of its location in what has become an unattractive neighborhood. ⊠ *Hacienda del Solar Hotel, Hwy. 95, south of town,* ☎ *762/2–05–87. Reservations essential on weekends. AE, MC, V.*

$$ ★ ✕ **Pagaduría del Rey.** This restaurant has a long-standing reputation for international fare served in comfortable surroundings. ⊠ *Calle H. Colegio Militar 8 (Col. Cerro de la Bermeja, south of town),* ☎ *762/2–34–67. MC, V.*

$$ ✕ **Toni's.** Prime rib and lobster are the specialties. There's also a great view and a romantic setting. ⊠ *Monte Taxco Hotel,* ☎ *762/2–13–00. AE, DC, MC, V.*

$ ✕ **Cielito Lindo.** This charming restaurant features a Mexican-international menu. Give the Mexican specialties a try—for example, *pollo* *en pipian verde* (chicken simmered in a mild, pumpkin seed–based sauce). ✉ *Plaza Borda 14,* ☎ *762/2–06–03. Reservations not accepted. MC, V.*

$ ★ ✕ **Hostería el Adobe.** The lack of view (there are only two window tables) is more than made up for by the original decor—for example, hanging lamps made of a cluster of masks—and the excellent food. Favorites include the garlic-and-egg soup and the *queso adobe* (fried cheese served on a bed of potato skins and covered with a green tomatillo sauce). ✉ *Plazuela de San Juan 13,* ☎ *762/2–14–16. MC, V.*

$ ★ ✕ **Pizza Pazza.** All nine varieties of pizza served here are tasty, but for a real treat order the *pozole norteño,* a spicy pork and hominy soup that comes with pork cracklings, chopped onion, lemon, and avocado. This cozy place, with scotch-plaid tablecloths and flowering plants, overlooks Plaza Borda. ✉ *Calle del Arco 1,* ☎ *762/2–55–00. Reservations not accepted. MC, V.*

$ ✕ **Santa Fe.** Mexican family-type cooking at its best is served in this simple place. Puebla-style mole, Cornish hen in garlic butter, and enchiladas in green or red chili sauce are among the tasty offerings. ✉ *Hidalgo 2,* ☎ *762/2–11–70. AE, MC, V.*

$ ✕ **Señor Costilla.** That's right. This translates as Mr. Ribs, and the whimsical name says it all. The Taxco outpost of the zany Anderson chain serves barbecued ribs and chops in a restaurant with great balcony seating. ✉ *Plaza Borda 1,* ☎ *762/2–32–15. MC, V.*

$$ 🏨 **Hacienda del Solar.** This small resort (off Hwy. 95 south of town) was once the best in town. The rooms, grounds, and restaurant are still beautiful, but the surrounding neighborhood has seen better days. Its restaurant, La Ventana de Taxco (☞ *above*), maintains many loyal patrons. ✉ *Box 96, 40200,* ☎ *762/2–03–23,* FAX *762/2–03–23. 22 rooms. Restaurant, pool, tennis court. AE, MC, V.*

$$ 🏨 **Monte Taxco.** A colonial style predominates at this hotel, which has a knockout view, a funicular, three restaurants, a disco, and nightly entertainment. ✉ *Box 84, Lomas de Taxco, 40200,* ☎ *762/2–13–00,* FAX *762/2–14–28. 156 rooms, suites, and villas. 3 restaurants, 9-hole golf course, 3 tennis courts, horseback riding, dance club. AE, DC, MC, V.*

$$ ★ 🏨 **Posada de la Misión.** Laid out like a village, this hotel is close to town. The pool area is adorned with murals by the noted Mexican artist Juan O'Gorman. ✉ *Box 88, Cerro de la Misión 32, 40230,* ☎ *762/2–00–63,* FAX *762/2–21–98. 150 rooms. Pool. AE, MC, V.*

$ 🏨 **Agua Escondida.** Popular with some regular visitors to Taxco, this small hotel has simple rooms decorated with Mexican-style furnishings. ✉ *Guillermo Spratling 4, 40200,* ☎ *762/2–07–26,* FAX *762/2–13–06. 50 rooms. Restaurant, bar, café, pool. MC, V.*

$ 🏨 **De la Borda.** Long a Taxco favorite, De la Borda is a bit worn, but the rooms are large and comfortable and the staff couldn't be more hospitable. Ask for a room overlooking town. There's a restaurant with occasional entertainment, and many bus tours en route from Mexico City to Acapulco stay here overnight. ✉ *Box 6, Cerro del Pedregal 2, 40200,* ☎ *762/2–00–25,* FAX *762/2–06–17. 95 rooms. Restaurant, pool. AE, MC, V.*

$ 🏨 **Los Arcos.** For those seeking lodgings in central Taxco, Los Arcos offers basic accommodations around a pleasant patio. ✉ *Calle Juan Ruíz de Alarcón 12, 40200,* ☎ *762/2–18–36,* FAX *762/2–32–11. 21 rooms. MC, V.*

$ 🏨 **Posada de los Castillo.** This in-town inn is straightforward, clean, and good for the price. The Emilia Castillo silver shop is off the lobby. ✉ *Juan Ruíz de Alarcón 7, 40200,* ☎ *762/2–13–96. 15 rooms. DC, MC, V.*

$ ★ **Posada de San Javier.** This sprawling, very private establishment is set somewhat haphazardly around a charming garden with a pool and a wishing well. In addition to the rooms, there are seven one-bedroom apartments with living rooms and kitchenettes (generally monopolized by wholesale silver buyers). ✉ *Estacas 32 or Exrastro 6, 40200,* ☎ *762/2–31–77,* FAX *762/2–23–51. 18 rooms. Pool. MC, V.*

$ **Rancho Taxco-Victoria.** This in-town hotel, in two buildings connected by a bridge over the road, is under the same management as the De la Borda (☞ *above*). Like the De la Borda, it is past its prime but exudes a certain charm. The rooms have been freshly painted, and the Mexican decor is simple but attractive. There's also the requisite splendid view. ✉ *Box 83, Carlos J. Nibbi 5, 40200,* ☎ *762/2–02–10,* FAX *762/2–00–10. 64 rooms. Restaurant, bar, pool. AE, MC, V.*

$ **Santa Prisca.** The patio with fountains is a plus at this colonial-style hotel. ✉ *Cena Obscuras 1, 40200,* ☎ FAX *762/2–00–80,* FAX *762/2–29–38. 40 rooms. Restaurant, bar. AE, MC, V.*

Nightlife and the Arts

FESTIVALS

Except for the Jornadas Alarconas—which honors one of Mexico's greatest dramatists with theater, dance, and concerts (dates change every year)—Taxco has no abundance of cultural events. But it *is* noted for its festivals, an integral part of the town's character. These fiestas provide an opportunity to honor almost every saint in heaven with music, dancing, marvelous fireworks (Taxco is Mexico's fireworks capital), and lots of fun. The people of Taxco demonstrate their pyrotechnical skills with set pieces—wondrous blazing "castles" made of bamboo. (Note: Expect high occupancy at local hotels and inns during fiestas.)

January 18, the feast of Santa Prisca and San Sebastián, the town's patron saints, is celebrated with music and fireworks.

Holy Week, from Palm Sunday to Easter Sunday, brings processions and events that blend Christian and Indian traditions; the dramas involve hundreds of participants, images of Christ, and, for one particular procession, black-hooded penitents. Most events are centered on Plaza Borda and the Santa Prisca Church.

September 29, Saint Michael's Day (Dia de San Miguel), is celebrated with regional dances and pilgrimages to the Chapel of Saint Michael the Archangel.

In **early November,** on the Monday following the Day of the Dead celebrations on November 1 and 2, the entire town takes off to a nearby hill for the Fiesta de los Jumi. The *jumil* is a crawling insect that is said to taste strongly of iodine and is considered a great delicacy. Purists eat them alive, but others prefer them stewed, fried, or combined with chili in a hot sauce.

In **late November or early December,** the National Silver Fair (Feria Nacional de la Plata) draws hundreds of artisans from around the world for a variety of displays, concerts, exhibitions, and contests held around the city.

NIGHTLIFE

You should satisfy your appetite for fun after dark in Acapulco. Taxco has a few discos, open only on weekends, a couple of piano bars, and some entertainment, but the range is limited.

Still, you might enjoy spending an evening perched on a chair on a balcony or in one of the cafés surrounding the Plaza Borda. Two traditional favorites are the **Bar Paco** (✉ Plaza Borda 12, ☎ 762/2–00–64) and **Bertha's** (✉ Plaza Borda 9, ☎ 762/2–01–72), where a tequila, lime, and club-soda concoction called a Bertha is the house specialty. In addition, some of the town's best restaurants have music on weekends.

Or immerse yourself in the thick of things, especially on Sunday evening, by settling in on a wrought-iron bench on the zócalo to watch children, lovers, and fellow people-watchers.

Most of Taxco's nighttime activity is at the Monte Taxco hotel, either at the **Bongolé** discotheque, on weekends, or at **Tony's Bar,** where the Papantla fliers ($6) perform nightly, except Sunday. On Saturday night, the hotel offers a buffet, a terrific fireworks display, and a show put on by the hotel's employees.

Outdoor Activities and Sports

You can play golf or tennis, swim, and ride horses at a few hotels around Taxco. Call to see if the facilities are open to nonguests. Bullfights are occasionally held in the small town of Acmixtla, 6 km (4 mi) from Taxco. Ask at your hotel about the schedule.

Shopping

CRAFTS

Lacquered gourds and boxes from the town of Olinalá, masks, bowls, straw baskets, bark paintings, and many other handcrafted items native to the state of Guerrero are available from strolling vendors and are displayed on the cobblestones at "sidewalk boutiques."

Arnoldo (⊠ Palma 2, ☎ 762/2–12–72) has an interesting collection of ceremonial masks; originals come with a certificate of authenticity as well as a written description of origin and use.

Elsa Ruíz de Figueroa (⊠ Plazuela de San Juan 13, ☎ 762/2–16–83) offers a selection of native-inspired clothing for women, and a wide and well-chosen selection of arts and handicrafts.

Sunday is market day, which means that artisans from surrounding villages descend on the town, as do visitors from Mexico City. It can get crowded, but if you find a seat on a bench in **Plaza Borda,** you're set to watch the show and peruse the merchandise that will inevitably be brought to you.

SILVER

Most of the people who visit Taxco come with silver in mind. Many of the more than 1,000 silver shops carry almost identical merchandise, although a few are noted for their creativity. Three types are available: sterling, which is always stamped .925 (925 parts in 1,000) and is the most expensive (and desirable); plated silver; and the inexpensive alpaca, which is also known as German silver or nickel silver. Sterling pieces are usually priced by weight according to world silver prices; of course, fine workmanship will add to the cost. Work is also done with semiprecious stones; you'll find garnets, topazes, amethysts, and opals.

Bangles start at $2, and bracelets range from $10 to $250. William Spratling, Andrés Mejía, and Emilia Castillo are some of the more famous design names. Designs range from traditional bulky necklaces (often inlaid with turquoise) to streamlined bangles and chunky earrings.

Alvaro Cuevas (⊠ Plaza Borda 1, ☎ 762/2–18–78) has fine workmanship to match its fine designs.

The stunning pieces at **Galería de Arte en Plata Andrés** (⊠ Av. John F. Kennedy 28, ☎ 762/2–37–78) are created by the talented Andrés Mejía.

Emilia Castillo (✉ Juan Ruíz de Alarcón 7, ☎ 762/2–34–71) is the most famous and decidedly one of the most exciting silver shops; it's especially renowned for innovative designs and for combining silver with porcelain.

Joyería San Agustín (✉ Cuauhtémoc 4, ☎ 762/2–34–16) carries a large collection of well-crafted silver jewelry and serving pieces. There's a branch at Talleres de los Ballesteros (✉ Florida 14, ☎ 762/2–10–76).

Spratling Ranch (✉ South of town on Hwy. 95, ☎ 762/2–61–08) is where the heirs of William Spratling turn out designs using his original molds.

Taxco A to Z

ARRIVING AND DEPARTING

By Bus. First-class **Estrella de Oro** buses leave Acapulco several times a day from the Terminal Central de Autobuses de Primera Clase (✉ Av. Cuauhtémoc 158, ☎ 74/85–87–05). The cost for the approximately 5½-hour ride is about $10 one way for deluxe service. The Taxco terminal is at Avenida John F. Kennedy 126 (☎ 762/2–06–48). First-class **Flecha Roja** buses depart Acapulco several times a day from the Terminal de Autobuses (✉ Ejido 47, ☎ 74/69–20–29). The one-way ticket is about $8 for first-class service. The Taxco terminal for this line is at Avenida John F. Kennedy 104 (☎ 762/2–01–31).

By Car. There are several ways to travel to Taxco from Acapulco, and all involve ground transport. It takes about three hours to make the drive, using the expensive (about $18) toll road. It is common practice to take an overnight tour. Check with your hotel for references and prices.

GETTING AROUND

Unless you're used to byways, alleys, and tiny streets, maneuvering anything bigger than your two feet through Taxco will be difficult. Fortunately, almost everything of interest is within walking distance of the zócalo. Minibuses travel along preset routes and charge only a few cents, and Volkswagen "bugs" provide inexpensive (average $1) taxi transportation. Remember that Taxco's altitude is 5,800 ft. Wear sensible shoes for negotiating the hilly streets, and if you have come from sea level, take it easy on your first day.

CONTACTS AND RESOURCES

Visitor Information. Tourism Office (✉ Av. de los Plateros 1, ☎ 762/2–15–25), open weekdays 9–2 and 4–7.

ACAPULCO A TO Z

Arriving and Departing

By Bus

Bus service from Mexico City to Acapulco is excellent. First-class buses, which leave every hour on the hour from the Tasqueña station, are comfortable and in good condition. The trip takes 5½ hours, and a one-way ticket costs about $15. There is also deluxe service, called *Servicio Diamante,* with airplanelike reclining seats, refreshments, rest rooms, air-conditioning, movies, and hostess service. The deluxe buses leave four times a day, also from the Tasqueña station, and cost about $19. *Futura* service (regular reclining seats, air-conditioning, and a rest room) costs $17.

By Car

The trip to Acapulco from Mexico City on the old road takes about six hours. A privately built and run four-lane toll road connecting Mexico City with Acapulco is expensive (about $35 one-way) but well maintained, and it cuts driving time between the two cities from six hours to 3½ hours. Many people opt for going via Taxco, which can be reached from either road.

By Plane

The **Juan N. Alvarez International Airport** (☎ 74/66–94–34) is located about 20 minutes east of the city. From the United States, **American** (☎ 74/81–01–61) has nonstop flights from Dallas, with connecting service from Chicago and New York. **Continental** (☎ 74/66–90–34) offers nonstop service from Houston. **Delta**'s (☎ 74/66–90–32) direct flights are from Los Angeles. **Mexicana's** (☎ 74/84–12–15) flights from Chicago and Los Angeles stop in Mexico City before continuing on to Acapulco. **Aeromexico's** (☎ 74/85–16–00) flight from New York to Acapulco stops in Mexico City. The carrier also offers one-stop or connecting service from Atlanta, Chicago, Houston, Los Angeles, New York, Miami, and Orlando.

From New York via Dallas, flying time is 4½ hours; from Chicago, 4¼ hours; from Los Angeles, 3½ hours.

BETWEEN THE AIRPORT AND CITY CENTER

Private taxis are not permitted to carry passengers from the airport to town, so most people rely on **Transportes Aeropuerto** (☎ 74/66–99–88), a special airport taxi service. The system looks confusing, but there are dozens of helpful English-speaking staff to help you figure out which taxi to take.

Look for the name of your hotel and the number of its zone on the overhead sign on the walkway in front of the terminal. Then go to the desk designated with that zone number and buy a ticket for an airport taxi. The ride from the airport to the hotel zone on the trip costs about $3.50 per person for the *colectivo* and starts at $17 for a nonshared cab, depending on your destination. The drivers are usually helpful and will often take you to hotels that aren't on their list. Tips are optional. The journey into town takes 20 to 30 minutes.

By Ship

Many cruises include Acapulco as part of their itinerary. Most originate from Los Angeles. Cruise operators include **Celebrity Cruises** (☎ 800/437–3111), **Crystal P&O** (☎ 310/785–9300), **Cunard Line** (☎ 800/528–6273), **Krystal Cruises** (☎ 800/446–6640), **Princess Cruises** (☎ 800/421–0522), and **Royal Caribbean Cruises** (☎ 800/327–6700). Bookings are generally handled through a travel agent.

By Train

There is no train service to Acapulco from anywhere in the United States or Canada, nor is there service from Mexico City.

Getting Around

Getting around in Acapulco is quite simple. You can walk to many places, and the bus costs less than 20¢. Taxis cost less than they do in the United States, so most tourists quickly become avid taxi takers.

By Bus

The buses tourists use the most are those that go from Puerto Marqués to Caleta and stop at the fairly conspicuous metal bus stops along the way. If you want to go from the zócalo to the Costera, catch the bus that says "La Base" (the naval base near the Hyatt Regency). This bus detours through Old Acapulco and returns to the Costera just east of the Ritz Hotel. If you want to follow the Costera for the entire route, take the bus marked "Hornos." Buses to Pie de la Cuesta or Puerto

Marqués say so on the front. The Puerto Marqués bus runs about every 10 minutes and is always crowded. If you are headed anywhere along the Costera Miguel Alemán, it's best to go by the Aca Tur bus. For 30¢ you can ride in deluxe, air-conditioned vehicles that travel up and down the main drag from the Hyatt to the Caleta hotels every 10 minutes.

By Car

If you plan to visit some of the more remote beaches or decide to visit Taxco on your own, renting a car is convenient but fairly expensive. Prices start at about $45 a day for a Volkswagen sedan without air-conditioning. Don't expect a full tank; your car will have just about enough gas to get you to the nearest Pemex station.

By Horse and Carriage

Buggy rides up and down the Costera are available evenings. There are two routes: from Papagayo Park to the zócalo and from Condesa Beach to the Naval base. Each costs about $10 (be sure to agree on the price beforehand).

By Taxi

How much you pay depends on what type of taxi you get. The most expensive are hotel taxis. A price list that all drivers adhere to is posted in hotel lobbies. Fares in town are usually about $1.50 to $5; to go from downtown to the Princess Hotel is about $10; to go from the Hotel Zone to Caleta Beach is about $5. Hotel taxis are by far the roomiest and are kept in the best condition.

Cabs that cruise the streets usually charge by zone. There is a minimum charge of $1; the fare should still be less than it would be at a hotel. Some taxis that cruise have hotel or restaurant names stenciled on the side but are not affiliated with an establishment. Before you go anywhere by cab, find out what the price should be and agree with the driver on a price.

A normal—i.e., Mexican-priced—fare is about $1.50 to go from the zócalo to the International Center. Rates are about 50% higher at night, and though tipping is not expected, Mexicans usually leave small change.

You can also hire a taxi by the hour or the day. Prices vary from about $10 an hour for a hotel taxi to $8 an hour for a street taxi. Never let a taxi driver decide where you should eat or shop, since many get kickbacks from some of the smaller stores and restaurants.

Contacts and Resources

Car Rental

Local car-rental agencies include **Hertz** (☎ 74/85–49–47), **Avis** (☎ 74/62–00–85), **Dollar** (☎ 74/66–94–93), **Quick** (☎ 74/86–34–20), and **Saad** (☎ 74/84–34–45). All have offices at the airport.

Consulates

United States (✉ Club del Sol Hotel, ☎ 74/85–72–07); **Canada** (✉ Club del Sol Hotel, ☎ 74/85–66–21).

Doctors and Dentists

Your hotel can locate an English-speaking doctor, but they don't come cheap—house calls are about $100. The U.S. consular representative has a list of doctors and dentists, but it's against their policy to recommend anyone in particular.

Emergencies

Police (☎ 74/85–06–50). **Red Cross** (☎ 74/85–41–00). Two reliable hospitals are **Hospital Privado Magallanes** (✉ Wilfrido Massiue 2, ☎

74/85–65–44) and **Hospital Centro Médico** (✉ J. Arevalo 620, ☎ 74/86–36–08).

English-Language Bookstores

English-language books and periodicals can be found at **Sanborns,** a reputable American-style department-store chain, and at the newsstands in some of the larger hotels. Many small newsstands and the Super-Super carry the Mexico City *News* and the Mexico City *Times*. *Acapulco Heat,* also in English, is a good source of information about local events and gossip.

Guided Tours

ORIENTATION TOURS

There are organized tours everywhere in Acapulco, from the red-light district to the lagoon. Tours to Mexican fiestas in the evenings or the markets in the daytime are easy to arrange. Tour operators have offices around town and desks in many of the large hotels. If your hotel can't arrange a tour, contact **Consejeros de Viajes** at the Torre de Acapulco (✉ Costera Miguel Alemán 1252, ☎ 74/84–74–00) or **Turismo Caleta** (✉ Andrea Doria 2, in Costa Azul, ☎ 74/84–65–70).

SUNSET CRUISES

The famous cliff divers at La Quebrada (☞ Exploring, *above*) give one performance in the afternoon and four performances every night. For about $30, **Divers de México** organizes sunset champagne cruises that provide a fantastic view of the spectacle from the water. For reservations, call 74/82–13–98 or stop by the office downtown near the *Fiesta* and *Bonanza* yachts. The *Fiesta* (☎ 74/82–49–47) runs cruises at 7:30 PM on Tuesday, Thursday, and Saturday for about $38. The *Bonanza*'s (☎ 74/82–49–47) sunset cruise, with open bar (domestic drinks) and live and disco music, costs about $10. All boats leave from downtown near the zócalo. Many hotels and shops sell tickets, as do the ticket sellers on the waterfront.

Travel Agencies

American Express (✉ La Gran Plaza shopping center, Costera Miguel Alemán 1628, Suites 7, 8, and 9, ☎ 74/69–11–20 to 25); **Viajes Wagon-Lits** (✉ Las Brisas Hotel, Scenic Hwy. 5255, ☎ 74/84–16–50, ext. 392).

Visitor Information

State of Guerrero Department of Tourism (SEFOTUR; ✉ Costera Miguel Alemán 187, across from Bodegas Aurrerá, ☎ 74/86–91–64 or 74/86–91–71), open weekdays 9–2 and 4–7.

10 Oaxaca

The geographic, ethnic, and culinary diversity of Oaxaca has made the state a favorite of Mexico aficionados. The majority of residents are descendants of the Zapotec and Mixtec Indians, who built the Monte Albán and Mitla complexes near Oaxaca City; their handicrafts and festivals are extremely colorful. Though less exotic than Oaxaca City, the state's coastal developments of Puerto Escondido and Bahías de Huatulco are beloved by surfers and beach bums.

Updated by Jane Onstott

THE CITY OF OAXACA (Wah-*hah*-kah), one of Mexico's colonial treasures, sits on the vast, fertile, 1½-km- (¾-mi-) high plateau of the Oaxaca Valley, encircled by the majestic Sierra Madre del Sur mountain range. It is at the geographic center of the state of Oaxaca, of which it is the capital.

The state, Mexico's fifth largest, is situated in the southeast, bordered by the states of Chiapas to the east, Veracruz and Puebla to the north, and Guerrero (whose touristic claims to fame are Acapulco and Ixtapa) to the west. The south of Oaxaca State spans 509 km (316 mi) of lush tropical Pacific coastline with magnificent beaches. Until recently, these beaches had been relatively unknown and unexploited, except for the long-established small fishing town and seaside hideaway of Puerto Escondido and the even smaller town of Puerto Angel. But now Bahías de Huatulco, 125 km (75 mi) west of Puerto Escondido, is beginning to appear on maps as the government works to turn it into a world-class resort.

Oaxaca is endowed with a vast geographic and ethnic diversity. Together with neighboring Chiapas, Oaxaca has one of the largest Indian populations in the country, which explains its richness and variety in handicrafts, folklore, culture, and gastronomy. Most are descendants of the Zapotec or Mixtec Indians, whose villages dot the valleys, mountainsides, and coastal lowlands. Today two out of every three Oaxaqueños are Indians and come from one of 16 distinct linguistic groups within the Mixtecs and Zapotecs. They speak 52 dialects—each very different from the other. If they speak Spanish—which many now do—it is a second language to them.

The Zapotecs and Mixtecs flourished in the area thousands of years ago. The archaeological ruins of Monte Albán, Mitla, and Yagul are among the vivid reminders of their splendid legacies. Located within a 40-km (25-mi) radius of the city of Oaxaca, the ruins bear witness to highly religious, creative, advanced civilizations that were knowledgeable in geometry and engineering.

Their civilizations were conquered by the Aztecs, who in the 15th century gave Oaxaca its name: *Huaxyaca.* In the Náhuatl language it probably means "by the acacia grove," referring to the location of the Aztec military base. Then came the Spanish conquest in 1528. The Spanish monarch Charles V gave Cortés the title of *Marqués del Valle de Oaxaca* as a reward for his conquest of Mexico. Cortés preferred to live elsewhere, so an estate was never built on the lands conferred with the title, but Cortés's descendants kept the property until Mexico's bloody 1910 Revolution.

Oaxaca's legacy to Mexican politics was two presidents: Benito Juárez, the first full-blooded Indian to become chief of state, and Porfirio Díaz, a military dictator who declared himself President-for-Life. Juárez, a Zapotec, was a sheepherder from San Pablo Gelatao, a settlement about 64 km (40 mi) north of Oaxaca. As a child he spoke only his native Zapotec tongue. Often referred to as Mexico's Abraham Lincoln, Juárez was trained for the clergy but later studied law and entered politics. He was elected governor of the state (1847), chief justice of the Supreme Court of Mexico (1857), and then president (1858–72), defeating efforts to convert the country into a monarchy under Maximilian. Porfirio Díaz, one of Juárez's generals, seized the presidency by coup in 1877 and held office until overthrown in 1911.

Pleasures and Pastimes

Dining

One of the highlights of visiting Oaxaca is the opportunity to enjoy its traditional cuisine, one of the finest and most elaborate in all Mexico. Oaxaca is known as "the land of seven moles" because of its seven distinct kinds of multispiced mole sauces. Only one of them, *mole negro*, is made with chocolate, and it rivals that of Puebla in thickness and flavor because of the outstanding quality of the local chocolate. Tamales, either sweet or stuffed with chicken, are another treat. The home- and factory-produced mezcal, made from a cactus, differs in flavor with its maker and can be as high as 80 proof, so be careful when you imbibe. The cream variety, thicker and sweeter, is flavored with orange, lime, or other fruits or nuts; others are sold in festive ceramic jugs.

Unfortunately, Oaxacan cuisine—the cheeses, mole sauces, and meats that make dining in the capital memorable—is in short supply along the coast, where seafood is your best bet. Huatulco's restaurants are getting better, and some of the places in Puerto Escondido are very good. With a few exceptions, the cooking in Puerto Angel is mediocre. Dress is casual at all restaurants except where noted, and reservations are not necessary unless noted. Prices tend to be slightly cheaper in the coastal dining establishments except in Huatulco.

CATEGORY	COST*
$$$$	over $15
$$$	$10–$15
$$	$5–$10
$	under $5

**per person for a three-course meal, excluding drinks and tip*

Lodging

Oaxaca City has no luxury resorts, but it does have some magnificently restored properties including a 16th-century convent and dozens of smaller, moderately priced accommodations, most in downtown locations. These smaller hotels are very popular around December and January and require six months to a year advance booking. The Day of the Dead (November 1 and 2 nationwide) and Holy Week are also times of high occupancy, so make plans accordingly.

Hotel rates vary considerably in the coastal area. In Puerto Escondido and Puerto Angel, most of the accommodations fall into the $$ or $ price range. Those in Huatulco, where you'll find luxury compounds, are considerably pricier, with the Omni Zaashila topping the scale. The high season along the coast runs from mid-December through Holy Week; rates increase by 20% during this time. Budget accommodations are scarce in Huatulco, although more moderately priced rooms are becoming available, especially in La Crucecita.

CATEGORY	COST*
$$$$	over $120
$$$	$70–$120
$$	$30–$70
$	under $30

**All prices are for a standard double room, including 15% tax.*

Shopping

Oaxaca City is a magnet for both mestizos and indigenous people who live in the valley and nearby mountains. They come to town to buy and sell, especially on Saturday. Although the market is no longer as colorful as it was in D. H. Lawrence's day (read his *Mornings in Mexico*), it remains an authentic exotic spectacle. El Central de Abastos is the largest Indian market in all Mexico, and only Michoacán and Chiapas can rival Oaxaca in the variety and quality of crafts. Expect hectic activity and bright colors. (It might come as a surprise not to hear much Spanish spoken at the markets but rather the singsong Zapotec and Mixtec languages, in which changes in the pitch of the voice change the meaning of the word.) In town, galleries exhibit the pottery, textiles, and fanciful wooden animals, called *alebrijes*, that have drawn international attention to Oaxaca's artisans.

Surfing

Oaxaca's Puerto Escondido is a household name for serious surfers who migrate to this sunny port for top-of-the-line surfing championships each year. These challenging waves have been attracting surfers from all parts of the globe since the 1960s, when the word first got out.

Exploring Oaxaca

Oaxaca has two main regions favored by tourists—Oaxaca City, the state capital, spread over a valley in the Sierra Madre mountains, and the coastal area on the rim of the Pacific Ocean due south of the capital.

Numbers in the text correspond to numbers in the margin and on the Oaxaca City and Oaxaca Coast maps.

Great Itineraries

If you only have three days to spend in the state, choose between Oaxaca City and the coast. Outdoor buffs seeking unspoiled beaches and wildlife should gravitate toward Puerto Escondido or Puerto Angel, while those looking for a chic, upscale ambience will like the million-dollar resort hotels of Huatulco. Oaxaca City is food for the soul for history and folk-art aficionados, with its magnificent colonial buildings, world-famous handicrafts, and ancient temples just outside the city. If you want a culture-beach combination, a minimum of seven days is advisable—Oaxaca City and the coastal resorts deserve at least three days apiece.

IF YOU HAVE 3 DAYS IN OAXACA CITY

Explore downtown to see the stunning colonial monuments that have been declared World Heritage structures by the United Nations. The first day, take in the **Catedral Metropolitana** ④, the **Museo de Arte Contemporáneo** ⑤, the **Iglesia de Santo Domingo** ⑦, and the adjoining **Museo Regional** ⑧. Day 2, catch a tour or bus for the ruins at **Monte Alban** right after breakfast to beat some of the crowds. After returning to the city and a late lunch, you can enjoy coffee at the 16th-century **Ex-Convento de Santa Catalina** ⑥, now the Camino Real hotel, and view the pretty patio garden with the stone tub where the nuns washed clothes. Day 3, visit the **Museo Rufino Tamayo** ⑩, then shop for regional arts and crafts at the **Mercado Benito Juárez** and the **Mercado de Artesanías** (☞ Shopping, *below*). Watch the sun set over Oaxaca from the terrace bar of the **Hotel Victoria** (☞ Lodging, *below*), just above the city proper.

IF YOU HAVE 5 DAYS IN OAXACA CITY

Follow the three-day itinerary and, on Day 4, add a visit to the Mixtec ruins at **Mitla,** stopping on the way or back to see the 2,000-year-old *ahuehuete* cypress in Tule (or, on a Sunday, to experience a country market day in **Tlacolula**); then spend the rest of the afternoon back in Oaxaca City people-watching and dining at the **zócalo** ①. Day 5, take a trip to one or more of the villages near Oaxaca City, where beautiful handicrafts are made before your eyes. Back again in Oaxaca City, visit the **Soledad Basilica** ⑪ and the boutiques full of high-quality crafts on **Calle Macedonio Acalá.**

IF YOU HAVE 3 DAYS IN THE COASTAL BEACH RESORTS

Using **Bahías de Huatulco** ⑭–⑯ as your base, take a boat tour of the bays on the first day, followed by a spell at the beach for a blazing sunset finale. Day 2, tour the small beaches and hidden bays of picturesque **Puerto Angel** ⑬ and **Puerto Escondido** ⑫. On Day 3, laze on the beach and, in late afternoon, taxi to **La Crucecita** ⑯ for some strolling, followed by dining at one of the small restaurants on the main square.

IF YOU HAVE 5 DAYS IN THE COASTAL BEACH RESORTS

Sign up for bird-watching with an ornithologist on the **Manialtepec Lagoon** on Day 4. Day 5, book the **Museum of the Sea Turtle tour.**

If you choose the laid-back Puerto Escondido as your base, you might spend Day 4 touring the **Lagoon of Chacahua,** and Day 5 riding horses on the beach in the morning, and relaxing with a soothing Temescal steam bath (a pre-Hispanic–style sauna) and massage in the afternoon.

IF YOU HAVE 7 DAYS OR MORE

You can immerse yourself in the cultural treasures of **Oaxaca City** ①–⑪ and then kick back with some sea and sun. Days 1 to 4 might be spent visiting the sights outlined in the first four days of the city itinerary. On Day 5, fly to **Bahías de Huatulco** and, on arrival, sign up for a boat tour of the bays. Days 6 and 7 can be spent beaching, bird-watching, and exploring **La Crucecita.** Those staying longer should not miss the Museum of the Sea Turtle tour.

When to Tour Oaxaca

Oaxaca celebrates Mexican holidays and its own state's fiestas with an intensity of color, tradition, and talent that attracts visitors in hordes. *El día de Muertos* (Day of the Dead) begins with graveyard celebrations in the nearby villages of Xoxo and Atzompa on October 31 and ends in the cemeteries on November 2, when families partake of the favorite food of those they are honoring; in between, the city, and especially the zócalo, are abuzz with activity. On December 23, the *Noche de Rábanos* (Night of the Radishes), the zócalo is packed with growers and artists displaying their hybrid radishes carved and arranged in tableaux that depict everything from Nativity scenes to space travel. Prizes are awarded for the biggest and the best, and the competition is fierce. Other arrangements are made with *flores immortales* (small dried flowers) or *totomoxtl* (corn husks). Bring plenty of film.

Oaxaca's other major celebration is the *Guelaguetza* (Zapotec for "offering" or "gift"), usually held on the last two Mondays in July. Dancers from all the various mountain and coastal communities converge on the city bearing tropical fruits, baskets, weavings, and pottery. They perform elaborate dances in authentic costumes from early morning until late at night at the Guelaguetza Auditorium, an open-air amphitheater in the hills just northwest of the city's center.

Keep in mind, of course, that if you plan to come for these celebrations, you'll need to book far in advance; don't expect to come to town and find a hotel room.

OAXACA CITY

Oaxaca City—officially, Oaxaca de Juárez—is still the state's major attraction, with a population of about 800,000 and more than a million visitors a year. The city is traditionally Indian, but cosmopolitan touches are everywhere. Women and children peddle everything from gardenias to grasshoppers seasoned with salt and chili, men and boys offer shoe shines around the city's many parks, and families play accordions along the city streets in the hopes of acquiring spare change.

Exploring Oaxaca City

The colonial heart of Oaxaca is laid out in a simple grid, with all major attractions within walking distance of one another. Many of the streets in the city's core change names once they pass the zóalo.

A Good Walk

Begin your exploration of Oaxaca at the shady **zócalo** ①, the heart of the city and its pedestrian-only main square. On the south side of the square visit the **Palacio de Gobierno** ②—you can go inside and check out the mural stretching from the first to second floor. Upon leaving the government palace, go to the northwest corner of the zócalo and you will reach **El Alameda** ③, a second square that abuts the zócalo. On the east side of the Alameda, you can't miss the **Catedral Metropolitana de Oaxaca** ④. After visiting the cathedral, turn right on Avenida Independencia and left at the next corner. This puts you on the pedestrian mall on Calle Macedonio Alcalá, where you'll see restored colonial mansions in a palate of pastels, and some of Oaxaca's best galleries, shops, museums, and restaurants. It is also lively and well lit at night, and there are frequent outdoor arts-and-crafts exhibits. After a short 1½ blocks you'll see the **Museo de Arte Contemporáneo de Oaxaca** ⑤ on your right. Continue north on Alcalá, turn right on Calle Murguía, and left on the first street, Avenida 5 de Mayo. Taking up the entire block on the east side of the street is the **Ex-Convento de Santa Catalina** ⑥, now the Hotel Camino Real. Catecorner from the Camino Real is Parque Labastida, where young artists sell their wares, and musicians sometimes entertain. Continue north until Avenida 5 de Mayo dead-ends at Calle Gurrión and the fabulous **Iglesia y Ex-Convento de Santo Domingo** ⑦. You can enter the church from its southern entrance, and leave via the front door onto Calle Alcalá. Adjacent to the church is the **Museo Regional de Oaxaca** ⑧, which contains priceless artifacts taken from Tomb 7 of Monte Albán, as well as an interesting ethnographic exhibit.

Continue north on Calle Alcalá a half block and walk up the steps of La Plazuela del Carmen Alto, where Triquis women in colorful red, beribboned *huipiles* sell embroidered blouses, dresses, and other handicrafts. Take a right on Calle García Vigil, and just half a block up, on the left side of the street, you'll find the **Museo Casa de Benito Juárez** ⑨, a museum honoring Oaxaca's most revered statesman. Upon leaving, return south on García Vigil 4½ blocks and turn right on Avenida Morelos. One and a half blocks up on the right, in a beautifully restored colonial mansion, is the **Museo de Arte Prehispánico "Rufino Tamayo"** ⑩. After seeing the museum, continue west on Morelos 2½ blocks. Go down the steps and across the large plaza, past the vendors of interesting religious trinkets, to the massive **Basílica de Nuestra Señora de la Soledad** ⑪. On the left side of the church is a small museum housing items related to Oaxaca's patron saint. Go east on Avenida Independencia past the telegraph office and you'll be back at El Alameda, where you can rest on a park bench.

Sights to See

⓫ **Basílica de Nuestra Señora de la Soledad.** The baroque basilica houses the statue of Our Lady of Solitude, Oaxaca's patron saint. According to legend, this statue was found in the pack of a mule that had mysteriously joined a mule train bound for Guatemala; when the mule perished at the site of the present church and the statue was discovered, the event was construed as a miracle, and the church was built in 1682

Basílica de Nuestra Señora de la Soledad, **11**
Catedral Metropolitana de Oaxaca, **4**
El Alameda, **3**
Ex-Convento de Santa Catalina, **6**
Iglesia y Ex-Convento de Santo Domingo, **7**
Museo Casa de Benito Juárez, **9**
Museo de Arte Contemporáneo de Oaxaca, **5**
Museo de Arte Prehispánico "Rufino Tamayo," **10**
Museo Regional de Oaxaca, **8**
Palacio de Gobierno, **2**
Zócalo, **1**

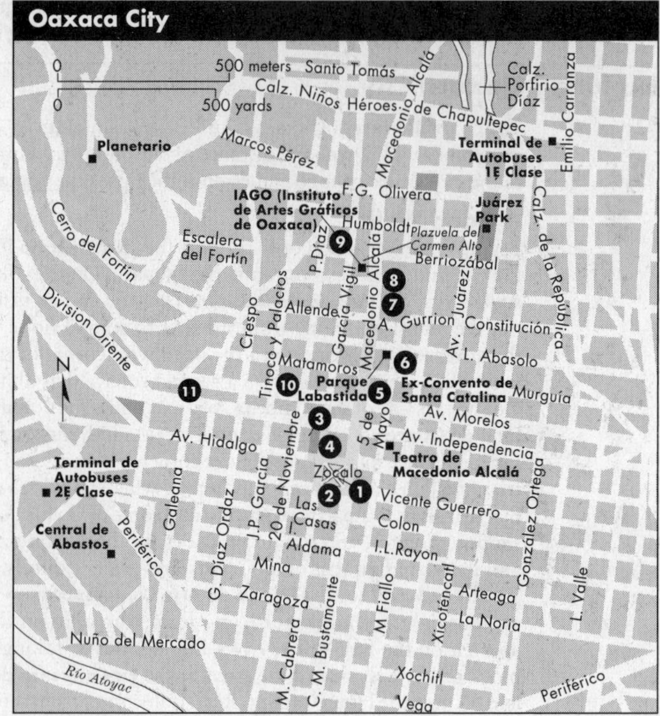

to commemorate it. The Virgin, who is believed to have supernatural healing powers and remains the object of fervent piety for the devout populace, now stands in a gilded shrine and wears a magnificent robe of jewel-studded black velvet. A small museum at the side of the church displays devotional items left by the faithful over the years. ✉ *Av. Independencia 107 at Galeana,* ☎ *951/4-01-69.* 🎫 *Donation.* ⏲ *Daily 6 AM–8 PM.*

❹ **Catedral Metropolitana de Oaxaca.** Begun in 1544, the cathedral was destroyed by earthquakes and not finished until 1733. The facade is baroque, with a wood-cogged clock presented to the city by the king of Spain. ✉ *Av. Independencia 700,* ☎ *951/6-44-01.* ⏲ *Daily 7 AM–9 PM.*

❸ **El Alameda.** This shady square is home to the cathedral and the post office. Vendors here sell Che Guevara T-shirts, huge elongated balloons, cassette tapes, snacks, and, during festivals, a myriad of souvenirs and handicrafts.

❻ **Ex-Convento de Santa Catalina.** This building is now the Hotel Camino Real and a national monument. It's worthwhile to explore the hotel's three courtyards; a large stone basin where the nuns did the convent's laundry 400 years ago can still be seen in the center of one of the patios. ✉ *Cinco de Mayo 300.*

❼ **Iglesia y Ex-Convento de Santo Domingo.** One of the most brilliantly decorated of the city's many churches, the 16th-century monastery has an ornate carved facade between two high bell towers. The interior is a profusion of white and gold—yes, that's real gold leaf—typical of the energy with which Mexico seized on the baroque style and made of it something unique. The entire complex of the Ex-Convento de Santo Domingo is being renovated; slated for completion by mid-1998 are botanical gardens, a café, and an art school. ✉ *Calle Macedonio Alcalá and Av. Gurrión,* ☎ *951/6–37–20.* ⏲ *Daily 7 AM–8 PM.*

NEED A BREAK? **El IAGO** (Instituto de Artes Gráficos de Oaxaca), just across the street and north of the Ex-Convent of Santo Domingo, has a pretty outdoor café in its back patio. You can relax under the massive bougainvillea over coffee or ice cream, or enjoy a light snack or full lunch. ✉ *Macedonio Alcalá 507,* ☎ *951/46–69–80. No credit cards. Closed Tues.*

9 **Museo Casa de Benito Juárez.** Benito Juárez lived in this house as a servant during his youth. Basically, this museum re-creates a typical 19th-century house; none of the furnishings or memorabilia belonged to Juárez or his employer/benefactor. ✉ *Calle García Vigil 609,* ☎ *951/6–18–60.* 🎟 *About $2; free Sun.* ⏲ *Tues.–Fri. 10–6, weekends 10–5.*

5 **Museo de Arte Contemporáneo de Oaxaca.** This museum, also known as the MACO, is housed in a former colonial residence. Exhibits feature contemporary artwork in a variety of media—often by one or more of Oaxaca's native sons, including Rufino Tamayo, Rodolfo Morales, and Francisco Toledo. Be sure to check out what remains of the frescoes in the second-floor gallery at the front of the building. There is a cafeteria in the shady back patio, and free art films are often shown Friday–Sunday at 6 PM. ✉ *Calle Macedonio Alcalá 202,* ☎ *951/4–71–10.* 🎟 *About $1.50.* ⏲ *Wed.–Mon. 10:30–8.*

10 **Museo de Arte Prehispánico "Rufino Tamayo."** This carefully restored colonial mansion contains a small but excellent collection of pre-Hispanic pottery and sculpture. It was originally the private collection of the late painter-muralist Rufino Tamayo, who presented it to his hometown in 1979. There are exhibits from all over the country, arranged geographically and chronologically. ✉ *Av. Morelos 503,* ☎ *951/6–47–50.* 🎟 *About $1.50.* ⏲ *Mon. and Wed.–Sat. 10–2 and 4–7, Sun. 10–3.*

8 **Museo Regional de Oaxaca.** Currently undergoing reconstruction but still open to the public, the museum is laid out in a series of galleries around the **Ex-Convento de Santo Domingo**'s cloister. The centerpiece of this ethnological collection, which focuses on the various Indian groups within Oaxaca, is the treasure taken from the tombs at Monte Albán (☞ Side Trips, *below*), just outside the city; the stunning gold jewelry from Tomb 7 was one of the greatest archaeological finds of all times. There is also a large collection of costumes from the different tribes of the valley; some of the Indian women who come into town for the market still wear traditional costumes, and with a bit of study here at the museum, you will be able to identify their home villages. ✉ *Plaza Santa Domingo,* ☎ *951/6–29–91.* 🎟 *$2; free Sun. and national holidays.* ⏲ *Tues.–Fri. 10–6, weekends 10–5.*

2 **Palacio de Gobierno.** The splendid state capitol building constructed in the 19th century in neoclassical style, sits on the south side of the zócalo. The fascinating murals inside depict the history and cultures of Oaxaca. ☎ *951/4–40–16.* ⏲ *Daily 8 AM–10 PM.*

1 **Zócalo.** During the day, locals and visitors are drawn to Oaxaca's shady main plaza, with its many green wrought-iron benches and matching bandstand. At night, mariachi and marimba bands play under colonial archways or in the bandstand, filling the air with music. ✉ *Bounded by Portal de Claverí on the north, Portal del Palacio on the south, Portal e Flores on the west, and Portal de Mercaderes on the east.*

Dining

The open-air cafés surrounding the zócalo are good for drinks, snacks, and people-watching, with the scene changing from peaceful serenity over early-morning coffee to pulsating frenzy on holiday evenings. Some offer *comida corrida*—the set menu served at midday—which is an economical choice. But you won't be very much out of pocket wherever you choose to dine: The devaluation of the peso has put even most higher-quality restaurants into the $$ price range.

$$$ ★ ✕ **El Asador Vasco.** Basque (*vasco*) cuisine is served in this prizewinning restaurant, along with an outstanding Oaxacan version of mole sauce—sweet and mildly spicy, and marvelous on chicken or turkey—and a sumptuous gratiné of oysters in *chipotle* chili sauce. The tables overlooking the zócalo are in great demand. Live serenading by the *tuna* student minstrels evokes medieval Spain. ✉ *On west side of zócalo, upstairs, Portal de Flores 11,* ☎ *951/4–47–55. AE, DC, MC, V.*

$$ ✕ **Catedral.** This local favorite calls itself the House of Fillets. It offers six meat fillet entrées, as well as regional dishes, hamburgers, sandwiches (try the Monte Cristo, called *sandwich especial*), and a variety of soups. You can pig out at the large daily lunch buffet after 2 PM, ending up with some of the Catedral's great strong coffee. ✉ *1 block north of cathedral, Calle García Vigil and Av. Morelos,* ☎ *951/6–32–85. MC, V.*

$$ ✕ **El Laurel.** Owner and chef Lina Fernandez creates a hospitable atmosphere in her tiny restaurant, which serves traditional dishes from throughout Mexico. Tasty meals are built around organic vegetables and skillfully applied seasonings. Lunch begins with a tiny glass of local sherry, and might end with a homemade coconut or *guayaba* (guava) flan and Italian coffee. The daily specials are not on the menu: Be sure to ask. ✉ *M. Bravo 210, esq. Porfirio Diaz, at back of Plaza San Cristóbal,* ☎ *951/5–78–00. AE, V. Closed Sun. No dinner.*

$$ ✕ **Neptuno.** Don't miss the delicious seafood at one of the most dependably good fish restaurants in town. Each meal starts with a thimbleful of mezcal (there are about 15 flavors, all homemade), an appetizer, and a delicious small seafood soup—all complimentary and designed to "open" your appetite. Main dishes are served with rice and veggies. Order a jar of *agua fresca* (fresh fruit water) to accompany your meal. Although this restaurant is a bit out of town, it's worth the trip. ✉ *Carretera a San Agustín Yatareni, Km 1,* ☎ *951/5–68–70. AE.*

$$ ★ ✕ **Nuu-Luu.** The name in Mixtec, "picturesque place," couldn't be more appropriate. Located in a pretty suburb in the northern part of town (just eight minutes from the zócalo), this delightful open-air restaurant overlooks a large country garden lush with exotic fruit trees. Renowned chef-owner Guadalupe Salinas prepares a changing array of Oaxacan specialties, including a spectacular mole made with seven kinds of chilies; it's served with turkey, chicken, or pork. Private transportation is provided for groups of four or more. ✉ *Iturbide 100, San Felipe del Agua,* ☎ *951/5–31–87. AE.*

$$ ✕ **Pizza Nostrana.** If you tire of Mexican food, try the delicious pizzas and pastas in this cozy restaurant directly across from Santo Domingo church. Vegetarians as well as carnivores will find something that pleases, as each pasta dish comes with a choice of fresh and cooked sauces. Among the favorites is *boscaiola* sauce (with garlic, mushrooms, parsley, peas, and cream). Spanish, Chilean, and Italian wines are offered along with Mexican vintages. ✉ *Allende esq. M. Alcalá,* ☎ *951/4–07–78. AE.*

$$ ✕ **Terranova.** Although the food at most of the restaurants on the zócalo is more or less the same, this restaurant—on the east side of the plaza—has attentive service, and musicians play most nights. The mole tamales

are good, as is the *caldo tlalpeño* (chicken-based soup with rice, avocado, chili, and tomato). The daily touristic menu, served after 2 PM, and other full meals are also available. ✉ *Portal B. Juárez 116,* ☎ *951/4-05-33. MC, V.*

$ ✕ **El Biche Pobre "2."** This place is a bit of a hike from the city center, but your bill for the fine *botana surtida* (sampler plate)—with tamales, *sopas* (soups), *chiles rellenos* (stuffed peppers), croquettes, and other treats—will be astonishingly low. You can walk the meal off afterward in nearby Juárez Park. ✉ *Calzada de la República 600, at Calle Hidalgo,* ☎ *951/3-46-36. MC, V.*

$ ★ ✕ **El Mesón.** The inviting, inexpensive buffet draws locals and visitors to this casual restaurant right off the zócalo. Stop by for a snack or full meal from the long paper menu, where you check off your items of choice. The tortillas are made fresh on site, and there are 13 types of tacos, as well as *pozole* (hominy soup), *cochinita pibil* (spicy Yucatecan-style pork), and other Mexican dishes. For an intense sugar fix, have a cup of rich Oaxacan chocolate and a slice of nut or cheese pie. ✉ *Av. Hidalgo 805, at Valdivieso,* ☎ *951/6-27-29. MC, V.*

Coffeehouses

✕ **Coffee Beans.** This is a great place for coffee, and there is a small selection of cakes and quiches. Different types and roasts of Mexican coffee beans are also on sale. ✉ *Calle 5 de Mayo 400, no phone. No credit cards.*

✕ **El Gecko.** The mustard-color courtyard of this tranquil coffeehouse is drenched in purple flowering vines. There is a variety of coffee drinks (including a fabulous iced cappuccino), as well as light food and snacks. ✉ *Calle 5 de Mayo 412, in Plaza Gonzalo Lucero,* ☎ *951/4-80-24. No credit cards. Closed Sun.*

Lodging

$$$$ ★ **Hotel Camino Real Oaxaca.** A monastic air lingers in the breezy patios and enclosed gardens of this beautifully restored former convent (1576), and Gregorian chants float softly through the hotel in the morning hours. Although the rooms themselves are far from austere, the nicest thing about the hotel is its divine atmosphere. **El Refectorio** restaurant is open for breakfast, lunch, and dinner, but the most popular meals are the massive buffets: the Saturday-night spread, accompanied by mariachi music; the magnificent Sunday *comida* (late lunch); and the daily breakfast buffet. ✉ *Cinco de Mayo 300, Oaxaca, Oax. 68000* ☎ *951/6-06-11 or 800/722-6466,* FAX *951/6-07-32. 91 rooms. Restaurant, 2 bars, pool, travel services. AE, DC, MC, V.*

$$$ ★ **Hotel Victoria.** Surrounded by terraced grounds and well-kept gardens, this sprawling salmon-color complex is perched on a hill overlooking the city. Draw back your curtains at dawn and catch your breath at the view: Oaxaca awakening under the Sierra Madre. The hotel has a good restaurant, tennis court, and heated pool. Rooms, bungalows, and suites are available; be sure to request one with a view. Buses shuttle guests on the half hour to the city center, 10 minutes away. **El Tule,** the veranda dining room, which serves international fare in addition to such Oaxacan specialties as chicken in mole and *queso asadero* (baked cheese), overlooks the hotel gardens and the valley below. ✉ *Lomas del Fortin 1, Oaxaca, Oax. 68070,* ☎ *951/5-26-33,* FAX *951/5-24-11. 150 units. Restaurant, bar, pool, tennis court, shop, meeting rooms, travel services. AE, MC, V.*

$$ **Fortín Plaza.** This modern six-story hotel just downhill from the Victoria makes lavish use of marble, wood, glass, and stone. Front balconied rooms offer the best views, but if you're looking for a good night's

sleep, choose the quieter rear rooms. The hotel has a pool, but it's small and is sandwiched between the highway and the building. Only the rooms on the top two floors have cable TV; those below get local channels. There are ceiling fans but no air-conditioning. ✉ *Av. Venus 118, Oaxaca, Oax. 68040,* ☎ *951/5–77–77,* FAX *951/5–13–28. 93 rooms. Restaurant, bar, room service, pool, meeting rooms, travel services. AE, DC, MC, V.*

$$ **Misión de los Angeles.** Though this resort-style hotel is a long way from the zócalo, its peaceful gardens and relaxed ambience make it a good choice. The hotel is near Plaza Juárez, a central park and plaza frequented more by locals than by tourists, and the commodious dining room is popular with tour groups. ✉ *Calzada Porfirio Díaz 102, Oaxaca, Oax. 68000,* ☎ *951/5–15–00,* FAX *951/5–16–80. 173 rooms. 2 restaurants, 2 bars, pool, tennis court, jogging, recreation room, meeting room. AE, MC, V.*

$ **Hotel Las Rosas.** This small second-floor hotel half a block off the zócalo offers clean, basic rooms—some of which have TVs—around a central courtyard at a price that's hard to beat. The owners are pleasant, and there are pretty mountain views from the little roof garden. ✉ *Trujano 112, Oaxaca, Oax. 68000,* ☎ *951/4–22–17. 19 rooms. No credit cards.*

$ **Hotel Mesón de Angel.** This large hotel, located southwest of the zócalo near the markets, is a favorite with Mexican families, groups, and traveling salesmen. There is a huge pool in the hotel garden. The attractively remodeled rooms have wide terraces, orthopedic mattresses, desk fans, telephones, and TVs (channels in Spanish only). Tourist buses to Monte Albán leave from here on the half hour until 3:30 PM. ✉ *F. J. Mina 518, Oaxaca, Oax. 68000,* ☎ *951/6–66–66,* FAX *951/4–54–05. 62 rooms. Restaurant, room service, pool, travel services. No credit cards.*

$ **Hotel Señorial.** This is a good choice for those who want an inexpensive hotel right on the zócalo; the seven rooms that overlook the square have tiny balconies. Uncarpeted rooms have TVs and telephones, and the beds are fairly comfortable, although far from firm. The clean bathrooms are tiled in cheerful light blue tiles. ✉ *Portal de Flores 6, Oaxaca, Oax. 68000,* ☎ *951/6–39–33,* FAX *951/6–36–68. 128 rooms. Restaurant, café, pool. No credit cards.*

$ ★ **Las Golondrinas.** This intimate hotel is tastefully ablaze with color, both from the flowering plants growing everywhere to the walls—painted pink, blue, mustard, and rust. Guests read books or lounge in the property's blissfully tranquil patios. Plain but cheerful rooms have red-tile floors and comfortable beds; none has TV or telephone, but there is a TV in the common sitting room. ✉ *Tinoco y Palacios 411, Oaxaca, Oax. 68000,* ☎ *951/4–32–98,* FAX *951/4–21–26. 24 rooms. No credit cards.*

$ **Villa María.** Popular with foreigners, this compound of one-, two-, and three-bedroom furnished apartments overlooks a spacious patio. Friendly, bilingual hostess María García makes her guests feel at home. Linens and dishes come with the units (which have suitable touches of Mexican decor), but phones, cable TVs, and maid service are extra. It's a small hike to the main square from here, but taxis and buses run frequently. Rentals are by the week or month, with rates starting at $400 a month for a one-bedroom unit; advance reservations and deposits—up to a year prior to arrival depending on the season—are required. ✉ *Arteaga 410, Oaxaca, Oax. 68000,* ☎ *951/6–50–56,* FAX *951/4–25–62. 14 apartments. No credit cards.*

Nightlife and the Arts

Oaxaca has plenty to entertain in evening hours. On almost any night you'll find live marimba, Andean music, or nouveau flamenco in the open-air cafés surrounding the zócalo. There are plenty of discotheques playing salsa or Western music, and Sunday at 1 PM the **Oaxaca State Band** sets up under the Indian laurel trees in the main square. For symphony buffs, the **Teatro Macedonio Alcalá** has orchestral performances sporadically throughout the year: See the monthly *Guía Cultural* (on sale in bookstores for about 70¢) for information on these and other events.

El Sol y La Luna is the place to listen to live music, often jazz or jazzy Mexican and American ballads. You can sit over drinks or order dinner on the covered outside patio or inside this residence-turned-restaurant. A $2 cover is charged when the music begins at 9 PM. ✉ *Calle M. Bravo 209,* ☎ *951/4–81–05.*

Candela hums with live salsa, *cumbia* (a Latin dance of Cuban origin), and styles of Latin music as foreigners and locals crowd the tiny dance floor. ✉ *Calle Allende 211,* ☎ *951/4–12–54.* *$3 cover.*

Every Wednesday and Friday night at 7 PM the Hotel Camino Real hosts the **Guelaguetza,** a smaller version of the pre-Hispanic Oaxacan dance fête displaying regional dances from throughout the state. The $25 price includes buffet dinner, open bar, and show in the former convent's 16th-century chapel. For reservations call 951/6–06–11.

Shopping

Prospective folk-art buyers in Oaxaca City and surrounding villages should heed one major caveat, or risk being saddled with more than they expected. It is not too difficult to ship your purchases home from many of the city's shops and shipping services, provided you have a receipt showing that you paid the 15% sales tax on all items purchased. Many of the artisans have begun giving out official government tax receipts, but if you buy from one who does not, you may have a hard time finding someone to ship your wares for you, and when you do, it will be very expensive. Ask for receipts and for referrals to shipping agents. Also, check out the displays at the shops in town and learn about quality and design before you start spending lots of pesos.

Markets

The Saturday market is held at the **Central de Abastos** (Supply Center) on the southern edge of the town center. Late Friday and early Saturday, Indians stream to this site, spreading their wares through an enormous central warehouse. By noon on Saturday, the market is swarming with thousands of sellers and shoppers, and the experience can be quite overwhelming. Don't burden yourself with a lot of camera equipment or purses and bags; you'll have a hard enough time keeping track of companions in the jostling, bumping crowd. If you see something you really want, purchase it on the spot—you'll never find your way back. The market is active during the rest of the week, too; if you go then, you can check out the mounds of multicolored chilies and herbs, the piles of tropical fruit, and the aisles of baskets, rugs, and jewelry. But it's on Saturday that you see the best handicrafts: huipiles (embroidered blouses) that vary with the village of origin; *rebozos* (shawls) of cotton and silk; distinctive pottery from many villages; colorful woven baskets; wooden and tin toys; machetes with leather sheaths. Bargaining is expected.

Several other markets in Oaxaca are active daily. **Mercado Benito Juárez** is south of the zócalo between Calles 20 de Noviembre and Miguel Cabrera at Colón. Here there are handicrafts as well as cheese, mole, chocolate, fruits, and much more. **Mercado 20 de Noviembre** is directly south of the Juarez market; here locals, budget travelers, and other adventurers eat prepared food at tiny stalls. Two blocks farther south is **Mercado de Artesanías,** at the corner of Calles J.P. García and Ignacio Zaragoza, which sells mostly textiles. While they tend their stands, Trique Indian women and children weave wall hangings with simple back-strap looms.

Each neighborhood has its own market day in a nearby square or structure, although these do not generally sell handicrafts. If you're interested in seeing neighborhood markets, check out **Mercado de Conzatti** on Friday until 4 PM (Calle Reforma at Humboldt STK) or the **Mercado de Merced** (Calzada de la República at Morelos) on Sunday.

For information on the colorful markets in the Indian villages outside Oaxaca, *see* Side Trips, *below.*

Shops and Galleries

Besides having a mother lode of markets, Oaxaca has some spectacular shops and galleries—some are closed Sunday and others close at midday—so plan your shopping days accordingly.

FINE ARTS

La Mano Mágica (✉ Macedonio Alcalá 203, ☎ 951/6–42–75) is an upscale crafts and fine arts gallery with a large inventory and a high price tag. **Galería Quetzalli** (✉ Constitución 104, ☎ 951/4–26–06) features both established and the up-and-coming Oaxacan artists—prices are not cheap, but the work is excellent. **Galería Arte Mexicano** (✉ Plaza Santo Domingo, M. Alcalá 407–15, ☎ 951/4–38–15) displays the work of local artists, and in a second store next door, original folk art and antiques.

HANDICRAFTS

ARIPO (✉ García Vigil 809, ☎ 951/4–40–30) is a government-run artist cooperative offering competitive prices and a large selection of exclusively Oaxacan art. The **FONART** store (✉ M. Bravo 116 at García Vigil, ☎ 951/6–57–64) has a representative selection of quality arts and crafts from elsewhere in Mexico. You can support the woman-artists' co-op by shopping at the huge warren of shops that make up **Mujeres Artesanas de las Regiones de Oaxaca** (✉ Av. 5 de Mayo 204, ☎ 951/6–06–70): Each room has crafts from a different town or region of Oaxaca. **Artesanías Chimalli** (✉ García Vigil 513–A, ☎ 951/4–21–01) has an excellent selection of alebrijes—brightly painted copal-wood animals with comical expressions and fantasy shapes. There is also a large assortment of quality crafts from throughout Mexico. Chimalli will cheerfully ship what you buy there as well as elsewhere. **Artesanías del Patrón** (✉ Macedonio Alcalá 104, ☎ 951/6–21–08) specializes in tableware from Michoacán, woven goods, Nativities, and elegant stylized statues that reinvent black pottery from San Bartolo Coyotepec. The two-story **Corazón del Pueblo** (✉ M. Alcalá 307–9, ☎ 951/3–05–47) has beaded Huichol (tribal) masks and wool "paintings" from Nayarit, *papel picado* (colorful cutout paper flags), and a good selection of English-language books on Mexican art and history; the furniture is also for sale.

JEWELRY

Oro de Monte Albán (✉ Macedonio Alcalá 307, ☎ 951/6–18–12) is one of several branches of this store selling gold and silver reproductions of pre-Columbian jewelry found in the tombs of royalty at the

Monte Albán archaeological site. There are many other fine jewelry shops selling jewelry in both traditional and modern motifs; many of these are found along the length of M. Alcalá and adjacent streets as well as the streets west of the 20 de Noviembre market.

Side Trips

A trip to the colonial city of Oaxaca sees its natural complement in an exploration of the area's more ancient past. The dramatic settings of the Zapotec ruins of Monte Albán, Mitla, and Yagul enhance the interest of these ruins. Similarly, it's fascinating to see the wares sold in the Oaxaca City market being produced in nearby villages that have changed little over the centuries. All of the destinations are easily reached by public transportation, taxi, or tour. Recently, SEDETUR, the state tourism board, has developed a project called Tourist Yu'u, which provides comfortable and clean if spartan accommodations in small artisan villages, where tourists can get a real feel for life outside the city. Contact the tourism department (☞ Visitor Information, *below*) for details and reservations.

Monte Albán

9 km (5½ mi) southwest of Oaxaca.

The onetime holy city of more than 40,000 Zapotecs, Monte Albán is among the most interesting and well-preserved archaeological ruins in the country. Experts estimate that a mere 10% of the site is uncovered; excavations are constantly taking place to unearth more knowledge about the fascinating Zapotec culture.

Monte Albán overlooks the Oaxaca Valley from a flattened mountaintop 1,300 ft high. The Zapotecs leveled the area in about 600 BC. They arranged the buildings along a perfect north–south axis, with the exception of one structure thought to have been an observatory, which is more closely aligned with the stars than with the earth's poles. The oldest of the four temples is the **Temple of the Dancers,** so named because of the elaborately carved stone figures that once covered the building. The figures are nude and, because of their distorted positions, have since come to be thought of not as dancers but as prisoners of war on their way to be sacrificed.

Another major point of interest is the **ball court,** site of a complicated game—part basketball, part soccer. The players' objective was to navigate the ball into a lowered area in the opponents' court with only their hips and elbows. There is some speculation that the captain of the losing team was sacrificed, but this is dubious.

About 1,000 years ago, the Zapotecs were conquered by the Mixtecs. The Mixtecs never lived in Monte Albán but used it as a city of the dead, a massive cemetery of lavish tombs. More than 160 have been discovered, and in 1932 **Tomb 7** yielded a treasure unequaled in North America. Inside were more than 500 priceless Mixtec objects, including gold breastplates; jade, pearl, ivory, and gold jewelry; and fans, masks, and belt buckles of precious stones and metals. Some of these treasures are now on view at the Museo Regional de Oaxaca (☞ Exploring Oaxaca City, *above*).

There are special tourist buses to Monte Albán from the Mesón del Angel hotel running every half hour from 8:30 to 3:30; the last bus back is at 5:30. The fare is about $1.50 round-trip. A taxi from the zócalo should run $4 or $5. 🎫 *$2.50; free Sun. and holidays.* 🕒 *Daily 8–5.*

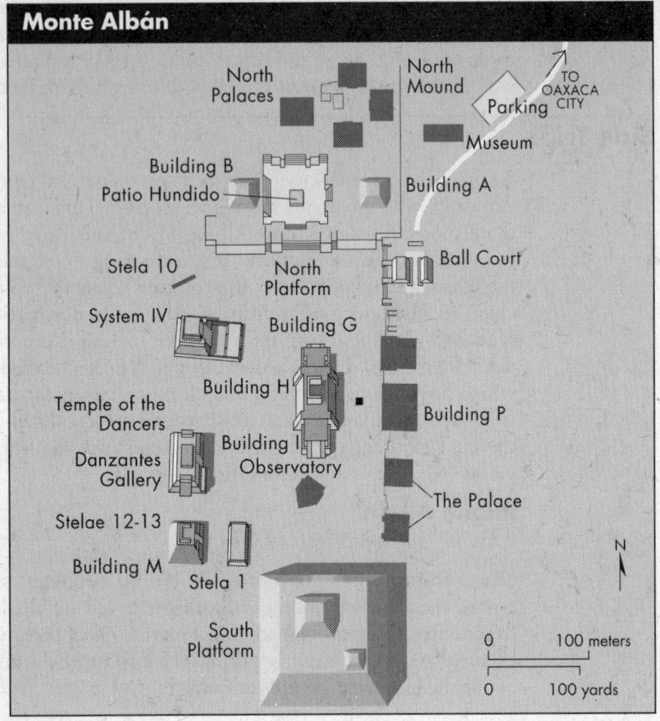

Mitla

40 km (25 mi) southeast of Oaxaca.

Mitla, like Monte Albán, is a complex of ceremonial structures started by the Zapotecs but taken over and heavily influenced by the Mixtecs. However, the architecture here is totally different from that of any of the other ruins in the area. The stone walls are inlaid with smaller stones cut into geometric patterns, forming a mosaic that is sometimes almost Grecian in appearance. Unlike other ancient buildings in North America, there are no human figures or mythological events represented—only abstract designs. The name, from the Aztec word *mictlan,* means "place of the dead." *$2; free Sun. and holidays. Archaeological zone daily 8:30–6.*

Yagul

36 km (22 mi) southeast of Oaxaca.

Although the ruins at Yagul are not nearly as elaborate as those at Monte Albán or Mitla, they are set in a lovely spot on top of a hill, and are certainly interesting enough to make it worth the trip, especially for archaeology enthusiasts. This city was predominantly a fortress set slightly above a group of palaces and temples; it includes a ball court and more than 30 uncovered underground tombs. *$1; free Sun. and holidays. Archaeological zone daily 8–5.*

Indian Villages

Many of the dozen or more villages surrounding Oaxaca City are known for the skills of their artisans, who use both ancient and modern techniques to create their folk-art pieces; they often live among generations of families who have their own special designs for pottery, woven rugs, and wood carvings.

A west-to-south counterclockwise route from the city takes in **Atzompa,** where Dolores Porras, the descendants of Teodora Blanco, and most others in town create fanciful clay pots and sculptures; other potters make the region's traditional green-glazed plates, bowls, and cups—all in array on Tuesday market day. In **Arrazola,** artists carve alebrijes. On Thursday, **Zaachila** has the most authentic livestock and food market in the area, while **Etla**'s Wednesday market is famous for its cheeses, mole, and chocolate. The southern route goes to **San Bartolo Coyotepec,** the center for glossy black pottery sold in people's yards and from a multistalled building on the side of the road. In **Santo Tomás Jalietza,** women work on small, back-strap looms in the center of town, weaving elaborate belts and table runners from pastel cotton. San Marín Tilcajete, south of Santo Tomás Jalietza on the same road, also has a town full of alebrijes. Friday's market in **Ocotlán** is known for its handicrafts, especially woven baskets, and for its handcrafted machetes and knives, famous throughout Mexico. Some of the impressive knives are inscribed with colorful local sayings.

An eastward route includes **Teotitlán del Valle,** where giant rug looms sit in the front rooms of many houses; one of the town's most respected rug makers is Isaac Vásquez. The Museo Comunitario (closed Mon.) on the main square focuses on the anthropology, crafts, and culture of the area. In **Santa Ana del Valle,** Lucio Aquino is the most famous rug maker. In **Tlacolula,** the Sunday market spreads for blocks around a baroque 16th-century chapel. On Sunday it seems that all of Oaxaca takes this route, starting at the Tule Tree (☞ *below*), moving to the ruins of Mitla, and then on to the crafts centers and market. The markets on other routes are held on special days throughout the week, and you can easily fill a week with tours and never see the same sight twice. If you have to budget your time, use tour guides for these trips so you don't miss out on the fascinating details.

The Tule Tree

14 km (8 mi) east of Oaxaca.

In the town of Santa María del Tule stands a huge ahuehuete cypress estimated to be more than 2,000 years old. One of the largest in the world, it is some 140 ft high, with roots buried more than 60 ft in the earth; it takes 35 adults with their arms outstretched to embrace it. The tree is the traditional center of the town of Santa María and is larger than the church behind it.

OAXACA CITY A TO Z

Arriving and Departing

By Bus

There are nonstop deluxe bus trips from Mexico City to Oaxaca; the trip takes about five hours and costs about $16. The first-class bus terminal (called the ADO) is at Calzada Niños Héroes de Chapultepec at Emilio Carranza (☏ 951/6–22–70). **ADO** (☏ 951/5–17–03) and **Cristóbal Colón** (☏ 951/5–12–14) both provide first-class service. The second-class bus station is on the Periférico at Las Casas (☏ 951/4–57–00 or 951/6–22–70). Several other bus lines serve the surrounding states and have desks at one or both terminals.

By Car

From Mexico City, you can take Mexico 190 (Pan American Highway) south and east through Puebla and Izúcar de Matamoros to Oaxaca City—a distance of 546 km (338 mi) along a rather curvy road. This route takes about six hours. Better is the toll road, which connects Mexico City to Oaxaca City via Tehuacan; it cuts down on curves and on driving time by about an hour and a half.

By Plane

Mexicana (☎ 951/6–84–14 or 951/6–73–52) offers service from various U.S. cities (including Chicago, Los Angeles, San Francisco, Miami, and New York) to Oaxaca City with a stop in Mexico City. Otherwise, flights from the United States require travelers to change planes in Mexico City for either an **Aeromexico** (☎ 951/6–10–66) or **Mexicana** nonstop to Oaxaca City's **Benito Juárez Airport,** about 8 km (5 mi) south of town. There is also service for triangle flight itineraries, including the Oaxacan coastal resorts of Bahís de Huatulco or Puerto Escondido. Local domestic airlines serving Oaxaca are **Aviacsa** (☎ 951/3–18–09) from Tuxtla Gutiérrez; **Aero Vega** (☎ 951/6–27–77), which operates as a chartered air taxi from Puerto Escondido; and **Aeromorelos** (☎ 951/1–51–00) from Puerto Escondido and Huatulco. **Aerocaribe** (☎ 951/6–02–66) flies Oaxaca City–Acapulco and Oaxaca City–Huatulco.

Getting Around

By Car

It's not necessary to have a car in Oaxaca City, which is very compact; most visitors opt to take taxis or tours to the outlying sights.

By Taxi

Taxis are clearly marked, plentiful, and reasonably priced; you can usually find them at any hour of the day cruising on downtown streets. It's a good idea to check with your hotel for going rates to sights you want to visit, as cabs are not metered.

Transportation from your hotel to the airport costs just $1.50 through **Transportes Aeropuerto** (✉ Alameda de León, ☎ 951/4–43–50), a few steps from the post office.

Contacts and Resources

Car Rental

Cars are for rent at the airport, in town, and through travel agencies at various hotels. **Hertz** is conveniently located on the zócalo in the Hotel Marqués del Valle (✉ Portal de Clavería s/n, Local 7, ☎ 951/6–24–34). They also have a booth at the airport (☎ 951/1–54–78).

Consulate

U.S. Consulate (✉ Macedonio Alcalá 201, int. 204, ☎ FAX 951/4–30–54), open weekdays 10–5.

Emergencies

Dial 06 locally for all emergencies, including police and hospital. **Police** (☎ 951/6–04–55 or 951/4–45–25). **Hospital–Red Cross** (☎ 951/6–48–09 or 951/6–48–03).

Guided Tours

Unless you're on a strict budget, take advantage of the many tour companies that offer guided trips to the archaeological sites, colonial churches and monasteries, outlying towns (some of which have weekly market days), and folk-art centers; prices start at $10. Licensed guides are available as well through the tourism office and travel agencies for up to $5 per hour for a minimum of three persons. **Viajes Turísticos Mitla** (✉ F. J. Mina 518, in the Hotel Mesón de Angel, ☎ FAX 951/6–61–75 or 951/4–31–52), and **Agencia Marqués del Valle** (✉ Portal de Clavería s/n, ☎ 951/4–69–70 or 951/4–69–62, FAX 951/6–99–61) are among the most established agencies.

Visitor Information

Tourist office (✉ Cinco de Mayo 200 at Morelos, ☎ 951/6–48–28), open daily 9–8. There is also a small branch at Independencia and García Vigil (☎ 951/4–77–33), open daily 9–3 and 4–8.

THE OAXACA COAST

Oaxaca's 520-km (322-mi) coastline is mainland Mexico's last Pacific frontier. Huatulco is the newest project of Fonatur, the Mexican government's tourism developers, although it was launched more than 10 years ago. Bahías de Huatulco, as the entire area is being called, covers 51,900 acres of mountain lowlands and coastal stretches, the vast majority of which have never been developed. The focal point of the master-planned development is a string of nine sheltered bays (*bahías*) swathed in golden sand beaches that stretch across 33½ km (23 mi) of the Pacific coastline.

Today Huatulco's beauty can best be seen from a boat (☞ Guided Tours *in* Oaxaca Coast A to Z, *below*), even though six of the bays are accessible by road now. Tangolunda Bay is the site of the area's major hotels. The towns of Santa Cruz and La Crucecita are being developed as well. (The town of Santa María Huatulco, for which the tourism destination is named, is 18 km, or 11 mi, inland from the bays and is largely ignored by developers.)

Puerto Escondido has long been prime territory for international surfers. The town has the coast's first airport (not international) and has grown up to tourism in a much more natural, and to some minds, pleasant, way than Huatulco. Although the four-block pedestrian walkway—crowded with open-air seafood restaurants, shops, and café bars—is lively, the "real" town above the strip, with its busy market and stores, provides a look at local life and a dazzling view of the coast. Puerto Angel, midway between the two airports, is a tiny port town that barely acknowledges the lure of tourism. It has a limited selection of hotels and bungalows spread into the hills overlooking the bay and, incongruously, a military installation smack in its center.

Puerto Escondido

12 *310 km (192 mi) from Oaxaca City.*

A coffee-shipping port in the 1920s, Puerto Escondido is the first touristic coastal town in Oaxaca state southeast of Acapulco on Highway 200. The airport is on the northern edge of town, as are the hotels favored by charter groups. **Playa Bacocho,** just south of the airport, is an upscale housing-and-hotel development; some inviting bars, discos, and restaurants have opened in this area, although most of the action still centers around the tourist zone to the south.

The main intersection in Puerto Escondido is at Highway 200 (also called the *carretera costera,* or coast highway) and Avenida Alfonso Pérez Gasga, which meanders south into the tourist zone. On the north side of the highway this street is called Avenida Oaxaca. Traveling down a steep hill, Avenue Gasga passes many of the tourist hotels; at the bottom, traffic is prohibited and the street becomes a four-block-long pedestrian mall lined with shops, restaurants, and lodgings that spread to the sands of the main beach. The town market, **Mercado Benito Juárez,** is a long walk (but a short cab or bus ride) from most of the tourist hotels, but it's worth checking out, especially on market days: Satur-

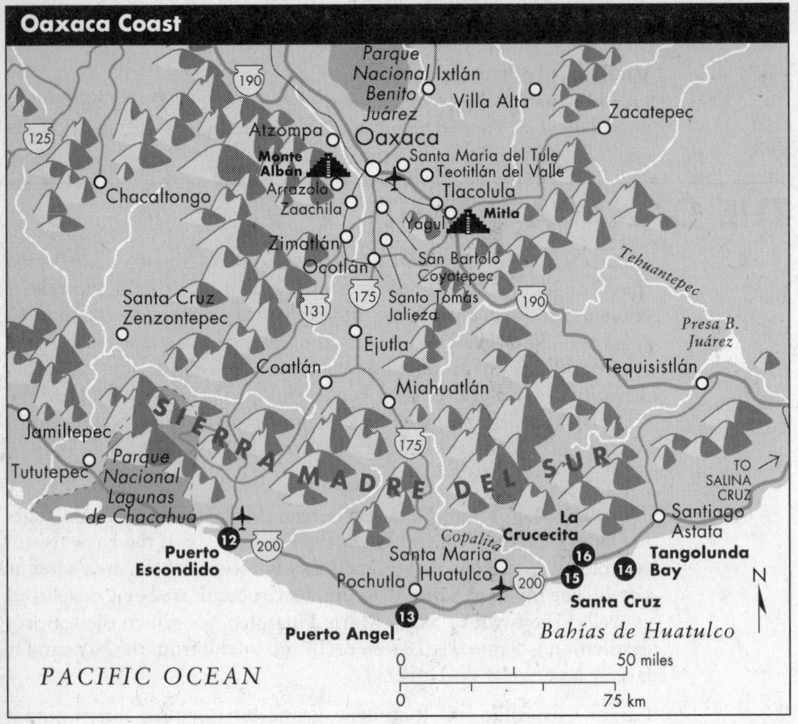

day and Wednesday. Those who want a bit of pampering can cleanse both body and soul according to ancient traditions at the **Temazcalli** (✉ Av. Infraganti, esq. Calle Temascalli, ☎ 958/2–10–23), which "combines the energy of wood, fire, rock and medicinal herbs." Massages are also offered, and afterward you can watch the sunset from the cliffs above the ocean. The *panga* (small boat) fleet, at the north end of the main beach, can be hired for bay tours or fishing excursions. **Laguna Agua Dulce** is at the south end of the tourist strip, followed by **Marinero Beach,** then a sharp outcropping of rocks, and, finally, the most famous beach of all, ☞ **Zicatela.**

Beaches

One of the top 10 surfing beaches in the world, **Zicatela** is a long stretch of cream-color sand battered by the Mexican Pipeline, as this stretch of mighty surf is called. In August and November international surfing championships are held here, and the town fills with sun-bleached blonds of both sexes intent on serious surfing and hard partying. Do not swim in these waters unless you can withstand deadly undertows and rip currents. Instead, watch the surfers at sunset from the *palapa* (thatched-roof) restaurant at the Arco Iris Hotel.

The safest swimming and snorkeling beaches in Puerto Escondido are **Puerto Angelito** and **Carrizalillo**; both can be reached on foot, but more easily by cab or by boat from the town beach. Transportation is available from the many fishermen who park their pangas on the sand near town and use them as water taxis. The ride should cost a few dollars.

Dining and Lodging

Understandably, coastal cuisine centers around fresh seafood dishes, although some savvy townspeople are introducing Italian and even California cuisine for variety. For such a small town, Puerto Escondido has more than its share of good restaurants, most in the inexpensive or moderate categories.

Just 20 years ago, the surfers who made the long journey to Puerto Escondido made do with palm-frond shacks with packed-dirt floors. Today, Puerto Escondido has comfortable hotels with hot water, fluffy towels, and ceiling fans or air-conditioning. Significant discounts may be obtained during low season: Try bargaining for a reduced rate September–early November.

$$ ✕ **La Galería.** In this cheerful eatery, diners can gaze as they eat at the roomful of excellent albeit expensive paintings done by Italian owner Aldo Ciardiello. The pizza and tortellini are first-rate, as are the salads and the fresh rounds of toasted rye bread that accompany them. Upbeat contemporary music further compels one to enter this small establishment at the west end of the tourist esplanade. ✉ *Av. La Gasga s/n, no phone. No credit cards.*

$$ ✕ **La Perla.** Because it's in the "real" town uphill from the tourist zone, this excellent seafood restaurant has some of the best prices in town. *Pulpo* (octopus) is wonderfully tender; the excellent seviche comes in a spicy cocktail sauce. It's a bit of a walk but a short, cheap cab ride. ✉ *Av. Rafael Ortega Velarde s/n,* ☎ *958/2–04–61. No credit cards.*

$$ ✕ **Mario's Pizzaland.** The proprietor is a courtly, generous Italian who produces in short order pizzas with all sorts of exotic toppings, including seafood. Also on the abbreviated menu are vegetarian and standard lasagna, enormous salads, and *bistec alla pizzaiola* (steak smothered in melted cheese and pizza sauce). ✉ *Av. Gasga just east of tourist zone,* ☎ *958/2–05–70. No credit cards.*

$$ ✕ **Perla Flameante.** The fresh dorado, shark, tuna, and pompano come with teriyaki, Cajun, or garlic seasonings at this second-story bamboo restaurant overlooking the beach. The deep-fried onion rings and zucchini are terrific. The restaurant is open for breakfast. ✉ *Av. Gasga near end of tourist strip,* ☎ *958/2–01–67. MC, V.*

$ ✕ **Art 'n' Harry's.** This surfer hangout overlooking the Pipeline is the place to relax with a drink and watch videos or zone out on heavy-metal CDs. The menu offers all types of stir-fries, salad, spaghetti dishes, and seafood. ✉ *South end of Zicatela Beach, no phone. No credit cards.*

$ ★ ✕ **Brunos.** The former head chef of the Esalen Institute cooking school in Big Sur brings California cuisine to Puerto Escondido in this laid-back restaurant, frequented by an often shirtless and shoeless (but not clueless) surfer clientele. Foxy waitresses of various nationalities serve mouthwatering shrimp brochettes with peanut sauce and steamed veggies, or the special pepper-crusted tuna with wasabi and mango sauce as dogs wander among the white plastic tables and chairs. There are a variety of simple breakfast and lunch items, including the "starving surfer": rice, beans, salsa, guacamole, chips, and tortillas for less than $2. The second-floor balcony has a great view of the sea. ✉ *Calle del Morro s/n, no phone. No credit cards.*

$ ★ ✕ **Carmen's Bakery** (a.k.a. La Patisserie). This is a tiny green oasis of soothing classical music and great coffee and pastries along the hot dusty road to Playa Marinero. A breakfast of fruit salad with yogurt and granola is sublime. The same owner runs **Cafecito,** a popular surfers' hangout at Zicatela beach. ✉ *Entrada Playa Marinero s/n,* ☎ *958/2–08–60. No credit cards. No dinner.*

$ ✕ **La Gota de Vida.** This small vegetarian café and health-food store on the bottom of the Gasga hill has all sorts of delicious salads; tofu and tempeh dishes; *licuados* (milk shakes) made with yogurt, papaya, and mango; vegetable soups; and fresh carrot juice—at very reasonable prices. There is a second store and cafe at Zicatela Beach. ✉ *Av. Gasga, no phone. No credit cards.*

$$ ★ ✗🏨 **Flor de María.** Hand-painted birds, flowers, and tropical scenes illuminate this bright, attractive hotel half a block up from Playa Marinero. Crisp sheets cover firm beds, and rooms are bright and immaculate—with powerful ceiling fans, but no TV or telephone. On the roof, guests swing in a row of hammocks or cool off in the small pool and, in high season, mingle at the bar around the satellite-dish TV. Unfortunately, the hotel is a short but very dark walk from the tourist esplanade. In the outstanding restaurant, efficient, Italian-born owner Maria combines New World ingredients with old-world recipes to create delicious pastas, chicken, and steaks in addition to Mexican specialties. Each day a different homemade dessert is featured. *Entrance Playa Marinero s/n,* ☎ FAX *958/2–05–36. 24 rooms. Restaurant, bar, pool, laundry service. AE, MC. V.*

$$ ★ ✗🏨 **Hotel Santa Fe.** This pretty hotel, framed by exuberant tropical plants at the north end of Zicatela beach, has colonial furnishings and curtains and spreads of woven Mexican cloth in soothing lavenders and blues. Rooms have air-conditioning, ceiling fans, TVs, and phones. Some rooms have balconies overlooking the pool or the beach. The hotel also manages the eight one-bedroom **Bungalows Santa Cruz** next door, which have well-stocked kitchenettes, cozy furnishings, and wide verandas. By all means treat yourself to at least one meal at the hotel restaurant—whether or not you are a guest. The menu is divided between seafood, vegetarian, and traditional Mexican dishes. The tables overlooking the surf are wonderful at dawn and sunset. ✉ *Calle del Morro s/n, Col. Marinero,* ☎ *958/2–01–70,* FAX *958/2–02–60. 51 rooms, 8 bungalows. Restaurant, bar, air-conditioning, pool, shop, laundry service. MC, V.*

$$$ 🏨 **Hotel Aldea del Bazar.** This new, sparkling white hotel sits on a bluff overlooking the beach at Playa Bacocho, just south of the airport. The restaurant and some of the rooms have a view of the beach below, which can be reached by way of a ramp—a long walk back up the hill. All the tastefully decorated rooms have small separate living rooms and color TVs. One of the hotel's best features is the pre-Hispanic–style eucalyptus sauna, and mediocre mud, soap, or oil massages can be arranged. ✉ *Av. Benito Juarez s/n, Fracc. Bacocho, Puerto Escondido, Oax. 71980,* ☎ FAX *958/2–05–08. 47 rooms. Restaurant, bar, pool, massage, spa, dance club, meeting rooms, travel services. MC, V.*

$$ 🏨 **Paraíso Escondido.** Hidden halfway up the steps of Calle Union, this colonial-style hotel has the charm of the house of a wealthy, eccentric, and somewhat dotty relative. No two rooms are alike, and all are furnished with a folkloric mixture of wood dressers, tin mirrors, and brightly colored curtains and spreads. The only negative is the curmudgeonly owner himself, who appears reluctant to have tourists invading his space. ✉ *Calle Union 10, Puerto Escondido, Oax. 71980,* ☎ *958/2–04–44. 20 rooms. Restaurant, bar, pool. No credit cards.*

$$ 🏨 **Studios Tabachín del Puerto.** Special touches such as clocks, vases, and bookshelves with books give these wonderfully furnished studio apartments a homey feel. Especially wonderful is the fourth-floor "penthouse," with its awesome view of the coast. Each of the six studios, behind the Hotel Santa Fe near Zicatela beach, has a kitchenette stocked with necessities. The owner also manages a small country inn, **Posada Nopala,** about two hours north of town, which operates from October 31 to April 30. It sits in the pine forests of the Oaxaca mountains, amid coffee plantations and crystal-clear rivers. This comfortable yet rustic lodge is perfect for self-sufficient guests who want to

experience life in rural Mexico. The helpful staff will teach them to roast coffee beans and make Mexican hot chocolate and regional dishes. ✉ *Calle de Morro by Zicatela Beach, Apdo. 210, Puerto Escondido, Oax. 71890,* ☎ FAX *958/2–11–79. 6 apartments. Restaurant, air-conditioning. MC, V.*

$ **Casas de Playa Acali.** A variety of sizes and styles of accommodations are available at this cluster of cabañas and bungalows on Zicatela beach. Guests mingle around the large central pool. The least expensive rooms are in small, rustic cabañas without air-conditioning; the most expensive, though still a bargain, are five bungalows with terraces, kitchens, air-conditioning, and dining areas. This is a good choice for groups of four or six surfers who want to share expenses and prepare their own meals. ✉ *Calle del Morro s/n, 71980 Puerto Escondido, Oax.,* ☎ *958/2–07–54. 9 cabañas and 5 bungalows. Kitchenettes, pool. No credit cards.*

$ **Castillo de Reyes.** Manager don Fernando runs an amiable show in his small, clean, and economical establishment. It has no pool or restaurant, so clients tend to congregate around the front desk, drinking their own sodas and beer. The simple rooms have white walls and powerful showers with plenty of hot water. ✉ *Av. Gasga 105, Puerto Escondido, Oax. 71980,* ☎ *958/2–04–42. 26 rooms. No credit cards.*

$ **Hotel Arco Iris.** This sprawling, three-story hotel on Zicatela beach resembles a gracefully aging, old-fashioned guest house. The rooms are simple yet clean, with firm beds and worn but comfortable furnishings. Some rooms have kitchenettes; all have wide verandas, some of which overlook the surfing beach just beyond. There is a large pool, and the small third-story salon has cable TV and videos and a wonderful ocean breeze. ✉ *Calle del Morro s/n, Col. Marinero, Box 105, Puerto Escondido, Oax. 71980,* ☎ FAX *958/2–04–32 or 958/2–14–94. 26 rooms. Restaurant, bar, snack bar, pool. MC, V.*

Outdoor Activities and Sports

RIVER TRIPS

Next door to Bruno's restaurant on Calle del Morro at Zicatela Beach, **Big Jim's River Trips** (no phone) organizes 2½-hour trips down the Colotepec River. A half-hour truck ride takes clients to the drop-off point, and a kayak-paddling guide will accompany your downriver as you float idyllically in a truck inner tube. A minimum of two clients is required, and life jackets are provided. Excursions usually depart at 9:30 AM and 2:30 PM and cost about $10.

WATER SPORTS

Boogieboards and surf boards can be rented at **Las Olas** (✉ Calle del Morro s/n, no phone) for about $6.50 per day. You must pay a deposit of about $80, which will be refunded at the end of the day unless the equipment is damaged.

Puerto Angel

13 *81 km (50 mi) southeast of Puerto Escondido.*

The leading seaport of the state 100 years ago, Puerto Angel today is a dusty village on a beautiful bay that, sadly, shows signs of pollution. The central town beach has been taken over by the navy, and the most popular swimming-and-sunning territory is at **Playa Panteón,** just past the oceanfront cemetery (*panteón* means "cemetery"). Other good (and less populated) swimming and snorkeling beaches are nearby. Six kilometers (4 miles) west of town is **Zipolite,** a bay known for its nude sunbathing; it's a favorite with surfers, aging hippies, and travelers who are content with a hammock on the beach and little else in the way of creature comforts. The undertow is extremely dangerous here—*zipo-*

lite means killer, and several dozen foolish swimmers die in these waters every year.

The **Museum of the Sea Turtle** in Mazunte makes an interesting side trip from Puerto Angel. The popularity of turtle hunting once put the sea creatures, who come to this coastal area to lay eggs each year, in danger of extinction; Mazunte even had its own slaughterhouse for their meat. The carnage stopped with the 1990 government ban on turtle hunting, and now Mazunte is devoted to protecting the species. A dozen aquariums are filled with turtle specimens that once again flourish in the nearby ocean. To get here from Puerto Angel, take Highway 200 toward San Pedro Pochutla; about 15 km (9 mi) past the town, follow the turnoff marked SAN AGUSTÍN. A few kilometers down the road, you'll come to a sign for PLAYA MAZUNTE; ask for directions to the "museo," which is on the beach. ✉ *Playa Mazunte,* ☎ *958/4–30–55,* FAX *959/4–30–63.* 🎫 *$1.25.* ⏲ *Tues.–Sun. 9–4.*

Dining and Lodging

$ ✕🏨 **La Buena Vista.** This pretty hotel offers clean, simple accommodations—some with balconies, some with hammocks just outside, but none with hot water. Although the view from the third-floor restaurant is now somewhat blocked by exuberant foliage, this is one of the most dependable kitchens in town, and rooms at the top level of the hotel still have a great view as well as the best breeze. There are a lot of steps to negotiate here, and no elevator. ✉ *Apdo. 48, Puerto Angel, Oax. 70902,* ☎ FAX *958/4–31–04. 18 rooms. No credit cards.*

$ ✕🏨 **Posada Cañon Devata.** California comes to Puerto Angel in this ecological hideaway carved into a forested canyon. Simple bungalows on the hill offer private quarters; at the top is **El Cielo** (Heaven), where guests gather at the bar to take in the sunset. Windows have screens, and the only drawback to this tranquil space are the incredibly scratchy sheets. Boat trips and occasional hatha yoga retreats are offered. The cool, palapa-covered restaurant below, open to nonguests (you must reserve before 2 PM for the large dinner, about $5), is a find for vegetarians. Meals are healthy and creative, and portions are very generous. ✉ *Past the cemetery, off Blvd. Virgilio Uribe, Apdo. 10, Puerto Angel, Oax. 70902,* ☎ FAX *958/4–30–48. 10 inn rooms, 6 bungalows. Restaurant, bar. No credit cards. Closed May–June.*

$ 🏨 **La Cabaña de Puerto Angel.** This plain but adequate hotel is located just across from Playa Panteón. The accommodating proprietors keep a big pot of coffee at the front desk for early risers, along with a library of paperback novels and maps of Mexico. The rooms have louvered windows with screens and ceiling fans; some have small, shadeless balconies. It's worth the extra $4 per night to rent the one triple room, which has a fantastic ocean view. ✉ *Across from Playa Panteón at Calle Pedro Sainz de Barranda s/n, Puerto Angel, Oax. 70902,* ☎ *958/4–31–05 or 958/4–00–26. 23 rooms. No credit cards.*

$ 🏨 **Posada Rancho Cerro Largo.** Feeling adventurous? Take a cab from town, or a bus to Zipolite and a cab from there, to this simple inn with a spectacular view. You can take the path down to the beach, or just relax in a hammock while the proprietor, Mario Corella, whips up an excellent lunch of local fish or, if you're vegetarian, produce. If you *really* want to get away from it all, you can rent one of his four pretty palapa cabins overlooking the water (no plumbing, but jugs of clean, fresh water) and let him cook three meals a day for you. ✉ *Above Playa Aragon, off the highway west of Zipolite and before San Agustínillo and Mazunte,* ☎ *958/4–30–55 (leave message). No credit cards.*

Bahías de Huatulco

237 km (147 mi) from Oaxaca City, 111 km (70 mi) from Puerto Escondido, 48 km (30 mi) from Puerto Angel.

Bahías de Huatulco, the Fonatur development, is still suffering growing pains. Investors suffered major setbacks because of the peso devaluation in 1994, and Huatulco has an unfinished look about it, unbecoming to a major resort destination. But the setting is undeniably tropical, hot, and beautiful: There are a total of 36 beaches contained by Huatulco's pristine bays. Because of its lack of polish, this area is less expensive than similar beach destinations such as Cancun. If you have a car at your disposal, you can drive to several bays that, so far, have not been subject to any development, and play Robinson Crusoe to your heart's content.

Another popular option is to tour the bays by boat. The venture takes four to eight hours (depending on how many you visit) with stops at Bahía San Agustín or El Maguey (where fishermen grill their catch over open fires) and at one of several secluded beaches for swimming and snorkeling.

14 The Huatulco of the future is most evident at **Tangolunda Bay,** where the major hotels are in full swing, and parasailers glide over fleets of sightseeing boats. The site was chosen by developers because of its five beautiful beaches. A small shopping-restaurant center is located across from the entrance to the Sheraton, but most of the shopping and dining takes place in the towns of Santa Cruz and La Crucecita, each about 10 minutes from the hotels by taxi, or, for the economy-minded, by buses or cooperative taxis that connect these two towns with Tangolunda.

15 **Santa Cruz** is on the bay of the same name. Glass-bottom boats, sightseeing tours, and fishing trips can be arranged here. A central zócalo with a wrought-iron gazebo has been built nearby, and tourists and locals alike mingle in the little plaza.

16 **La Crucecita,** just off Highway 200, is the only place in Huatulco that resembles a real Mexican town, with a central plaza and a recently constructed church covered inside with frescoes. Modern buildings with arches and balconies are going up along the streets by the park, and this is becoming *the* place for hanging out at sidewalk cafés and shopping in boutiques. The bus station, tourism office, Bing's ice-cream shop, and long-distance telephone office are here, along with a smattering of smaller, cheaper, and more intimate hotels.

Dining and Lodging

$$ ✕ **½ Carlos 'n' Charlie's.** The odd name refers to the size of this closet-like addition to the Carlos 'n' Charlie's chain, with all the trappings of the famous franchise packed in meager space. ½ has dependable food—barbecued ribs, tortilla soup, fries, and platters of fresh oysters—and fun for those who like downing shots of tequila and beer. ✉ *Av. Flamboyan and Calle Carrizal, La Crucecita,* ☎ *958/7–00–05. AE, MC, V.*

$$ ★ ✕ **Restaurant de doña Celia.** Although the official name of this long-time favorite beachfront restaurant is **Avalos,** everyone knows it by the owner's name: doña Celia. Even Presidente Zedillo stopped by in 1996 for a seafood feast. Make your selection from the large menu, and prepare for large portions as well. Tables face the sand and sea at Santa Cruz Bay, just beyond the marina. ✉ *Bahía Santa Cruz,* ☎ *958/7–01–28. MC, V.*

$$ ✕ **Restaurante María Sabina.** Strangely named for an Oaxaca medicine woman immortalized for her use of "magic" (hallucinogenic) mush-

rooms, this is a great place from which to watch locals and tourists mingle in La Crucecita's pretty plaza. Grill orders are prepared on the outdoor *parrilla,* and served with grilled onion, baked potato, and sour cream. A favorite plate is *Reboso María Sabina* (steak with melted cheese, guacamole, and fresh salsa); there are also nine spaghetti dishes offered. ✉ *Calle Flamboyant (west side of plaza), La Crucecita,* ☎ *958/7-10-39. D, DC, MC, V.*

$$$–$$$$ ✕🏨 **Sheraton.** Now offering all-inclusive as well as standard room tariffs, the Sheraton is the most user-friendly of the upscale hotels on Tangolunda Bay, with boutiques, a travel agency, and a selection of restaurants. The rooms have bathtubs—a real luxury in these parts. Water sports and equipment—including kayaks, windsurfers, sailboats, and catamarans—are considered top notch, and dive masters are on hand with dive equipment (☞ Outdoor Activities and Sports, *below*). The **Casa Real** restaurant still offers the most glamorous dining in Huatulco. The menu emphasizes northern Italian dishes and the ambience is decidedly upscale, with elaborate floral arrangements and flickering candles at night. Restaurant is closed in low season. ✉ *Tangolunda Bay, Blvd. Benito Juárez, Bahías de Huatulco, Oax. 70989,* ☎ *958/1-00-55; 800/325-3535 reservations in the U.S.;* FAX *958/1-01-13. 347 rooms. 3 restaurants, 3 bars, 2 pools, massage, sauna, steam room, 4 tennis courts, exercise room, beach, boating, shops, travel services. AE, DC, MC, V.*

$$$$ 🏨 **Caribbean Village.** This all-suites hotel, formerly the Holiday Inn, has changed hands and gone all-inclusive. It consists of 10 buildings built in a series of tiers separated by banks of steps. It is set on 2½ acres of landscaped gardens. Rooms are large, with private terraces, and have regional furnishings complemented by bright Mexican color schemes. All rooms have minibars, and the 32 master suites have whirlpool baths. Although the hotel is not on the water, it offers free transportation to its beach club next to the Sheraton. ✉ *Tangolunda Bay, Blvd. Benito Juárez 8, Bahías de Huatulco, Oax. 70989,* ☎ *958/1-00-44,* FAX *958/1-02-21. 135 suites. 3 restaurants, 3 bars, 3 pools, steam room, 18-hole golf course, tennis court, exercise room. AE, DC, MC, V.*

$$$$ 🏨 **Club Med.** This club's 500 rooms cut a lavender-and-peach swath on a hillside overlooking Tangolunda Bay. There are three beaches, and an endless list of amenities. Weeklong fitness programs are particularly popular. Although some guests are content to never leave the grounds, coastal excursions and tours to Oaxaca City are offered. Packages with airfare included are usually available. Advance booking is mandatory. ✉ *Tangolunda Bay, 70900; reservations:* ✉ *40 W. 57th St., New York, NY 10019,* ☎ *958/1-00-33; 800/258-2633 reservations;* FAX *958/1-01-01 or 958/1-01-56. 500 rooms. 5 restaurants, 3 pools, 12 tennis courts, exercise room, 3 beaches. AE, MC, V.*

$$$$ ★ 🏨 **Omni Zaashila.** This contemporary stucco Mexican-cum-Mediterranean palace overlooks a secluded lagoon with its own private beach. The resort has 27 landscaped acres of gardens, fountains, and waterfalls. There are 32 luxurious suites, each with its own private pool. The rates are high, and unlike those at most of the other high-end properties, they aren't all-inclusive. ✉ *Playa Rincón Sabroso s/n, Tangolunda Bay, Bahías de Huatulco, Oax. 70989,* ☎ FAX *958/1-04-60; 800/223-5652 in the U.S.;* FAX *958/1-04-61. 128 rooms and suites. 3 restaurants, bar, pool, tennis court, travel services. AE, MC, V.*

$$$$ 🏨 **Royal Maeva.** This all-inclusive resort caters to charter groups and Mexican families as well as lone travelers. The emphasis is on fun, fun, fun—and if you're not a fan of loud music, stay in a room that's away from the pool area. The rooms are spacious, colorful, and adorned with heavy blue-and-peach fabric and light-wood furniture. Considering that the price per person includes all food, drinks, and access to most water and gym sports, this is a good deal for those who want to do more than just work on their tans. ✉ *Tangolunda Bay, Blvd. Benito Juárez 227, Bahías de Huatulco, Oax. 70989,* ☎ *958/1–00–00; 800/466–2382 in the U.S.;* FAX *958/1–02–20. 290 rooms. 3 restaurants, 5 bars, pool, 3 tennis courts, exercise room, beach. AE, DC, MC, V.*

$$$ **Marina Resort Huatulco.** Overlooking the marina on Santa Cruz Bay is this five-star resort offering lots of amenities and a proximity to rental boats and the marina. Each comfortable suite's ample living area contains a sofa bed, small dining table, satellite TV, and kitchenette. The upper-floor rooms have the best bay views; all rooms have bathtubs. Soon slated for inauguration is the beach club, with water sports and a disco. ✉ *Calle Tehunatepec 112, Santa Cruz Bay, Huatulco, Oax. 70989,* ☎ *958/7–09–63,* FAX *958/7–08–30. 47 suites. Bar, 2 pools, coffee shop, grocery, room service, kitchenette, aerobics, shop. MC, V.*

$$ **Posada Flamboyant.** This is the classiest option for those who want to stay in the town of La Crucecita, about a five-minute cab ride from Tangolunda Bay. The ivy-covered, four-story edifice has a vaguely European feel, and the reasonable price includes Continental breakfast. All rooms have firm beds, TVs, and telephones, and both the pool and surrounding area are large and inviting. Four comfortable two-bedroom, two-bath suites with well-furnished living rooms and kitchens are available for about $135 for up to eight people. ✉ *Calle Gardenia esq. Tamarindo, Bahías de Huatulco, Oax. 70989,* ☎ *958/7-01-13,* FAX *958/7-01-21. 66 rooms. Restaurant, bar, air-conditioning, pool, shop, travel services. AE, D, MC, V.*

$ **Hotel Begonias.** Located catercorner from the plaza in La Crucecita, this sweet, simple hotel (formerly called Hotel Bugambilia) has colonial-style furnishings, ceiling fans, comfortable beds, and color TVs. The enthusiastic owner also runs sportfishing tours. ✉ *Calle Bugambilia 503, La Crucecita, Oax. 70989,* ☎ *958/7-00-18,* FAX *959/7–13–90. 13 rooms. Fishing. Reservations not accepted for high season. AE, MC, V.*

$ **Hotel Las Palmas.** Plain but acceptable furnishings and rock-bottom prices (for Huatulco) are offered at this small second-story hotel just a block from the plaza in La Crucecita. The small rooms have TVs, hot water, and air-conditioning. ✉ *Calle Guamuchil 206, La Crucecita, Oax. 70989,* ☎ *958/7–00–60. 11 rooms. Restaurant, bar, air-conditioning. Reservations not accepted for high season. AE, V.*

Outdoor Activities and Sports

BICYCLING

Mountain bikes can be rented from **Jeep Safaris Huatulco** (☞ Guided Tours *in* Oaxaca Coast A to Z, *below*) or from **Rent-a-Bike** (✉ In Oasis Restaurant in La Crucecita, Calle Flamboyant esq. Bugambilias, ☎ 958/7–06–69) for guided or unguided tours. Since the bike rental owner, Erasto, is in and out, it's best to telephone first before making the trip to La Crucecita.

FISHING

Sportfishing for sailfish, tuna, dorado, and other fish can be arranged through **Sociedad Cooperative Tangolunda,** the boat-owners cooperative at the marina on Santa Cruz Bay (☎ 958/7–00–81), **Hotel Begonias** (☞ Dining and Lodging, *above*), or **Servicios Turísticos del Sur,** the travel agency at the Sheraton Hotel (☎ FAX 958/1–02–00).

WATER SPORTS

The dive masters and dive equipment based at the Sheraton Hotel are among the most reliable in Huatulco. Four-day certification courses are also offered, as are dive trips: $40 for one tank, $60 for two. ✉

Paseo Benito Juárez s/n, at Sheraton Hotel, ☎ 958/1–00–55, ext. 842, FAX 958/1–01–13.

Shopping

Although Huatulco isn't exactly a shopper's paradise, there are several places worth mentioning. In La Crucecita, **Paradise** boutique (✉ Calle Gardenia esq. Guarumbo, no phone), open seven days a week, has an excellent selection of casual yet stylish beach and resort wear, much of which comes from Bali and India. The batik and hand-painted T-shirts make great gifts, as do the Mexican crafts, including silver jewelry, coconut masks from Guerrero, and black Oaxacan pottery.

The **Museo de Artesanías Oaxaqueñas** (✉ Calle Flamboyant 216, La Crucecita, ☎ 958/7–15–13) is really a store, not a museum, but the artisans who make the fanciful wooden alebrijes, the woven tablecloths, typical pottery, painted tinware, and rugs from Teotitlán del Valle are on hand to demonstrate how their traditional crafts are made. It's open every day; avoid going at lunchtime, when the artisans take a break. Another fun place to shop is La Crucecita's **Mercado Municipal,** or municipal market (✉ Calle Guanacaste con Bugambilias, no phone), where in addition to leather sandals, postcards, and other tourist items, you'll see the mountains of fresh fruits and vegetables Oaxaca State is famous for.

OAXACA COAST A TO Z

Arriving and Departing

By Bus

Cristóbal Colón has three first-class buses per day leaving from Oaxaca's first-class bus terminal, frequently referred to as the ADO (✉ Calzada Niños Héroes 1036, ☎ 951/5–12–14), to Huatulco (7½ hours; $14). The same bus continues on to Puerto Escondido (9 hours; $15.50). There are several first-class buses each day to Pochutla (6½ hours; $15), where a connection can be made to Puerto Angel, but none is direct. Cristóbal Colón also has a booking office near the zócalo (✉ Calle 20 de Noviembre 204A, ☎ 951/4–66–55). Buses return to Oaxaca City from Huatulco's bus station (✉ Calle Gardenias esq. Ocotillo, La Crucecita, ☎ 958/7–02–61) and Puerto Escondido (✉ Calle Primera Norte 201, ☎ 958/2–10–73).

Estrella del Valle's first-class buses run at night; daytime ordinario (u-l) buses make many stops and are not recommended. Buses leave from the second-class station (✉ Corner of Trujano and the Periférico, ☎ 951/4–57–00 or 951/6–22–70) for Huatulco ($9) and Puerto Escondido ($9.75). The Huatulco station is in Crucecita (✉ Calle Jazmin s/n, behind Corona beer warehouse, ☎ 958/7–01–93); in Puerto Escondido, buses depart from Av. Hidalgo (✉ Calle 3a Oriente, ☎ 958/2–00–50 or 958/2–09–53).

Direct service between Oaxaca City and Puerto Escondido is available on **Autotransportes Turísticos.** Buses leave from Oaxaca City (✉ Calle Armenta y López 721, ☎ 951/4–08–06) and Puerto Escondido (✉ Av. Hidalgo between 16 de Septiembre and 4a Norte, ☎ 958/2–09–53 or 958/2–00–50) twice a day.

By Car

The drive from Oaxaca City to the coast on Highway 175 or 190 is challenging: The mountain scenery is superb, and it's not a bad drive, but there are lots of curves and hairpin turns. Do not attempt this drive at night. Plan on taking eight hours or so, and leave early enough to be at your destination before dark. The new Highway 131 was 90% complete, and completely passable, at press time. Once at the coast, Highway 200 links Huatulco, Puerto Angel, and Puerto Escondido, in that order from east to west. If you want to tool around the various beaches, a car is useful here.

By Plane

Puerto Escondido has a national airport (☎ 958/2–04–92 or 958/2–04–91) with daily service from Oaxaca's International Airport on **Aeromorelos** (☎ 958/2–06–53) and **Aero Vega** (☎ 958/2–01–51). **Mexicana** (☎ 958/2–04–14 or 958/2–00–98) flies to Puerto Escondido daily from Mexico City and also from Los Angeles and other U.S. cities (via Mexico City). **Mexicana** (☎ 958/7–02–23 or 958/7–02–43) flies to **Huatulco** from Mexico City, Guadalajara, Monterrey, and several other Mexican and U.S. gateways. **Aeromorelos** (☎ 958/1–04–44) connects Huatulco with Oaxaca City and other destinations. **Continental** (☎ 958/1–90–28) has service from Houston to Huatulco three times weekly during the high winter season. A regional air carrier, **Aerocaribe** (☎ 958/7–12–20), connects Oaxaca City and Acapulco to Huatulco.

Aeropuerto Bahías de Huatulco (☎ 958/1–90–04 or 958/1–90–05) is about 16 km (10 mi) from town on Highway 200.

Getting Around

By Bus

Frequent, inexpensive second-class buses connect Puerto Escondido, Puerto Angel, and Huatulco but you must stop at Pochutla, just off the highway near Puerto Angel. These buses roar down the highway every 15 minutes or so, and each costs about $1. If you are going to Huatulco, be sure to specify that your final destination is the bus terminal in La Crucecita, which is closest to the bays.

By Car

The drive on Highway 200 from Puerto Escondido to Huatulco should be relatively hassle-free, and having a car allows you to turn off the main road onto unmarked dirt roads leading to secluded beaches.

Contacts and Resources

Car Rental

Cars can be rented at the Huatulco airport, in Puerto Escondido, and in the Huatulco Bays area. International firms include **Budget** (☎ 958/7–00–34 in La Crucecita; 958/1–00–36 at the airport; 958/2–03–12 in Puerto Escondido) and **Dollar** (☎ 958/1–00–55, ext. 787, in Huatulco, at the Sheraton Hotel). Rental cars are expensive, starting at $45 per day for a Volkswagen Beetle, for example, and there is an additional drop-off fee if you don't return the car where you picked it up. Nonaffiliated local firms often quote lower rates, but their vehicles may be in questionable condition.

Emergencies

For all emergencies including police and hospital, dial 06 locally.

Guided Tours

In **Puerto Escondido** the most exciting tours are run by ornithologist Michael Malone, who offers dawn and sunset excursions (Dec.–Apr.) into the Manialtepec Lagoon, a prime bird-watching area. Tours are about $40 per person and can be arranged through your hotel or through **Turismo Rodimar** (✉ Av. Gasga 905–B, ☎ FAX 958/2–07–37 downtown; 958/2–15–15 at Hotel Aldea del Bazar, the most reliable and comprehensive agency in town. The agency also has a day tour to Puerto Angel, which includes the Museum of the Sea Turtle.

Bahías Plus, with offices in the Royal Maeva hotel (☎ 958/1–00–00) and in Santa Cruz at the Posada Binniguenda (☎ 958/7–09–32, FAX 958/7–02–16), is one of the most comprehensive travel agencies in **Huatulco** and has suburban van or bus tours to Puerto Angel and Puerto Escondido (van tours start at a bit less than $20 per person in a group of six), as well as plane tours to Oaxaca ($337 per person). Most of the major hotels also have travel agencies.

Daylong tours into the Sierra Madre are available with the bilingual guides of **Jeep Safaris Huatulco.** One of their tours includes a visit to a working coffee plantation, with elaborate lunch. This agency also does horse, four-wheel drive, and mountain-bike treks. ✉ *Paseo B. Juarez, in small commercial plaza across from Sheraton Hotel,* ☎ *958/1–03–23.*

Bay cruises are available through **Servicios Turísticos del Sur,** at the Sheraton Hotel (☎ FAX 958/1–02–00) for $10–$20 a person, excluding food. You can arrange the same trip through the **Sociedad Cooperative Tangolunda,** a boat-owners cooperative at the marina on Santa Cruz Bay (☎ 958/7–00–81), with substantial discounts for groups, which they will put together.

Visitor Information

Puerto Escondido tourism office (✉ Blvd. Benito Juárez, about a block from Aldea del Bazar Hotel at Playa Bacocho development, ☎ 958/2–01–75), open weekdays 9–3 and 6–8; Saturday 10–1. The small information desk (no phone) at the north end of the pedestrian walkway is even more helpful than the main tourism office.

Huatulco municipal tourist office (✉ La Crucecita, Blvd. Chahue near the post office building, ☎ 958/7–00–95 or 958/7–01–96), open weekdays 9–3 and 6–9, Saturday 9–3.

Tangolunda Bay tourist office (✉ In small commercial plaza across from Sheraton Hotel, Paseo B. Juarez s/n, ☎ 958/7–01–77), open weekdays 9–3 and 6–9, Saturday 9–3.

11 Chiapas and Tabasco

The state of Chiapas has always been an off-the-beaten-path destination, best known for the colonial town of San Cristóbal and the jungle-covered ruins of Palenque, considered by many to be the most fascinating in Mexico. But a number of those who plan just to pass through here on the way to Guatemala find themselves lingering on.

Updated by Patricia Alisau

KNOWN TO MOST foreigners only as gateways to Guatemala and home to the ruins of Palenque and the colonial town of San Cristóbal de Las Casas, Chiapas and Tabasco were never prime destinations for first-time visitors to Mexico. World attention was drawn to Chiapas in early 1994 as the site of an indigenous uprising, but as peace negotiations progress, it's been almost forgotten again. If you're looking for an outstanding travel experience, a well-planned trip to this area can be very satisfying, particularly if you arrange for your visit to coincide with a local festival. Unlike beach resorts such as Cancún and Acapulco, this area is not one that visitors can jet to in a few hours from major U.S. gateways. Substantial ground transportation, either by bus or car, is absolutely necessary. People working in the tourist industry often don't speak English, but they are becoming more professional in dealing with tourists. Tourist information can be more difficult to obtain in Tabasco than in Chiapas.

A bloody past of exploitation by and fierce confrontation with outsiders remains vividly present, as already impoverished indigenous communities in Chiapas are forced to compete for their lands with developers and new settlers. Because of its isolation, Chiapas has been at the margin of the nation's development. It is one of the poorest states in Mexico, with appallingly high rates of alcoholism, violence, illiteracy, and death due to unhygienic conditions. Land distribution, too, is skewed: 1% of the landowners hold 15% of the territory (about 50% of the arable land), keeping the colonial system nearly intact, and repression is rampant. It was the indifference of the Mexican government to their plight that helped bring the anger of the indigenous people to a boil in early 1994, leading to an armed uprising by a group calling themselves the Zapatista National Liberation Army. The willingness of the government to negotiate with the rebels—and international interest in their plight—bodes well for the possibility of change in the region. The pipe-smoking Zapatista spokesman, Subcomandante Marcos, has become a cult figure in Mexico, his ski-masked image appearing on everything from magazine covers to children's toys, and he puts his poetic communiqués on the Internet for worldwide consumption.

Although it was nominally made rich half a century ago with the discovery of oil in the Gulf of Mexico on its northern border, Tabasco also has a bloody past. During the 1920s and 1930s, Tomás Garrido Canabal, a vehemently anticlerical governor, outlawed priests and had all the churches either torn down or converted to other uses. Riots, deportations, and property confiscations were common. When British writer Graham Greene visited Tabasco in 1938, he called it "the Godless state"; his novel *The Power and the Glory* grew out of his experience. Yet to the visitor, Tabasco's turbulent past is barely evident today; a wholly different spirit prevails here than in Chiapas.

Although the Mexican economic crisis will delay some plans for building more tourism infrastructure, Chiapas is getting an extra boost from a government promotion program. It is an important segment of the Mundo Maya travel circuit created by the Mexican government in the early 1990s to showcase its splendid Maya ruins and colonial cities in the name of regional development and preservation. Development in the past has been a two-edged sword. The Lacandon jungle is already disappearing, its Maya inhabitants being driven to live in a smaller portion of their ancestral lands. Massive erosion and deforestation are taking their toll as the new settlers burn the forest and exhaust the soil by raising cattle.

For the present, however, travelers threading their way along tortuous mountain roads—full of dramatic hairpin turns along the edges of desolate ravines—will come upon remote clusters of huts and cornfields planted on near-vertical hillsides. They will pass Indian women wrapped in deep blue shawls and coarsely woven wool skirts, and Indian children selling fruit and flowers by the roadside. Chiapas has nine separate Indian groups, primarily the highland-dwelling Maya Tzeltals and Tzotzils, many of whom do not speak Spanish.

Tabasco is of interest primarily as a gateway to the Maya ruins at Palenque in Chiapas and to ecologically minded tourists, lured by lakes, lagoons, and caves and by the wild rivers surging through the jungle. Travelers will find Villahermosa's museum of pre-Columbian archaeology at the CICOM research complex and the collection of Olmec heads at Parque Museo La Venta a good introduction to the Indian heritage of Tabasco, so evident also in Chiapas.

Note: As of March 1997, travel to Chiapas was considered safe. If you are in doubt, however, contact any of the Mexican Government Tourist Offices in the United States for any change in status, or the U.S. State Department for any traveler's advisories at the time you are planning to visit.

Pleasures and Pastimes

Archaeological Sites

Ruins of Maya cities in mysterious, overgrown jungles are a big draw in this area. Unparalleled Palenque attracts the most visitors, but inveterate archaeology buffs are also attracted to more obscure sites such as Bonampak and Yaxchilán.

Dining

Chiapas has regional specialties but borrows heavily from Yucatán and Oaxaca. Adventurous palates should try *atole* (cornmeal drink), tamales, locally smoked ham, candied fruit, and any dishes that contain the tasty herbs *chipilín* and *yerba santa* (or *mumu,* as the locals call it). San Cristóbal's restaurants offer an ample choice of Mexican and international cuisines, and lately most of them have added vegetarian dishes to their menus. Although they can be rated the best in the state, they're not outstanding compared to those in other regions of Mexico. Prices, however, are quite reasonable: A filling dinner (helped out by tortillas in one of their myriad forms) with beer rarely costs more than $10 per person. There is no dress code to speak of in this part of Mexico, and no reservations are necessary. San Cristóbal closes down early, so unlike in other parts of Mexico, it is a fairly common practice to eat dinner before 8.

Tabasco saves some of its export beef for the Villahermosa restaurants, which also serve lots of fresh fish from the Gulf coast. Local specialties, or oddities, if you wish, include *pejelagarto,* a fish that resembles a small, ugly alligator but that, nonetheless, is succulent. Fried plantain chips, dried bananas, banana liquor, chocolate, and a special white cheese are some local food products you can enjoy.

Generally speaking, the food served in Palenque town is modest in both quality and price. On the other hand, most of the restaurants are open-air, which is where you want to be in this humid, hot part of Mexico (except when it rains, and then the thatched roofs are welcome).

CATEGORY	COST*
$$	$8–$15
$	under $8

**per person for a three-course meal, excluding drinks, service, and 15% sales tax*

Lodging

Almost all the hotels in **San Cristóbal** are within walking distance of the major attractions. Most of those listed are colonial—historically and architecturally—in keeping with the rest of the town. All rooms, unless otherwise stated, have showers; air-conditioning is not necessary at this high altitude and, in fact, fireplaces are welcome.

Tuxtla Gutiérrez lodgings tend to be more functional than frilly because the town is the no-nonsense business and transportation hub of the state. An exception to the rule is the Camino Real, opened in 1994 and resembling a small palace perched on a hilltop.

Villahermosa hotels are relatively expensive, especially when compared with those in San Cristóbal. New, American-style hotels tend to be away from the city center, near Tabasco 2000 and Parque La Venta, while the older and more modest hotels are downtown.

Palenque is no longer the jungle outpost that it used to be, fit only for souls who considered rustic amenities colorful or liked "going native." Instead, it has metamorphosed into a pretty little tropical town with modern, comfortable hotels. The best and newest are strung along the highway that goes to the Palenque ruins just outside town. Geared for groups as well as individuals, these hotels have lush gardens, inviting pools, air-conditioning or ceiling fans, and private baths. There's a clutch of simple, older remodeled hostels downtown.

CATEGORY	COST*
$$$$	over $90
$$$	$60–$90
$$	$25–$60
$	under $25

**All prices are for a standard double room, excluding 15% tax.*

Shopping

The artisans of San Cristóbal and Chiapas produce some of the most striking indigenous folk art of Mexico. Best are the blouses, tunics, bedspreads, and tablecloths finely embroidered with native designs; brightly colored *fajas* (sashes); and leather goods, such as belts and purses. Lacandon bows and arrows and the beribboned hats worn by local men also make good souvenirs. Chiapas is also one of the few spots in the world that have amber mines, so finely crafted jewelry made from this prehistoric resin is easy to find in San Cristóbal. San Cristóbal is also known for its quality wrought-iron crosses (which are hard to find, however).

Tuxtla Gutiérrez and Palenque, although not known for handicrafts, have a few shops selling quality crafts from other parts of the state.

Exploring Chiapas and Tabasco

Tabasco is lush, green, and flat, the abode of the ancient Olmecs, who gave Mexico its mother culture, whereas Chiapas is sinuous, mountainous, and filled with Maya ruins and villages where time stands still. The colonial city of San Cristóbal de las Casas once dominated both regions when the Spanish conquistadores held sway over the country. Modern Villahermosa now is the dominant economic force in the two regions because of the petroleum industry.

The highlights of a trip to Chiapas or Tabasco are still the ruins of Palenque and the colonial town of San Cristóbal de las Casas. These and all other major attractions are accessible by road from either Tuxtla Gutiérrez or Villahermosa, the only cities with international airports. Palenque's airport went into operation in mid-1996 but only receives small-bodied jets. Charter service to the ruins on bush planes is also available from the two internationally connected cities as well as from San Cristóbal and Comitán, and there's bus service to the ruins from the major towns. If you're a first-time visitor, and especially if you don't speak Spanish, it's faster, more efficient, and more comfortable to take tours to the area's major attractions. But if you prefer to rent a car, road directions are included in the listing of the sights.

Numbers in the text correspond to numbers in the margin and on the Chiapas and Tabasco and San Cristóbal de las Casas maps.

Great Itineraries

The farther you wander into the region, the more you'll be fascinated with its natural diversity and its remnants of Maya and Spanish colonial cultures. A three-day trip gives only a fairly superficial glance at what the region has to offer, but it will afford you the opportunity to visit Palenque and San Cristóbal de las Casas, two of Mexico's outstanding attractions. Stays of 5, 8, or 10 days will allow you to cover greater distances in an area where the major cities are at least two hours by road from one another.

IF YOU HAVE 3 DAYS

Spend the first day and night at the Maya ruins at **Palenque** ㉓, with a side visit to the lovely jungle waterfalls at **Misol-Há** ㉒ and **Agua Azul** ㉑. The next day drive south to colonial **San Cristóbal de las Casas** ①–⑨, the oldest city in Chiapas; spend at least two hours on a walking tour of town, starting at the centuries-old *zócalo*. Overnight at San Cristóbal and, on the third day, visit the Indian villages of **San Juan Chamula** ⑮, known for its Christian church with pre-Hispanic rituals, and **Zinacantán** ⑯, famous for its handwoven tunics and pink shawls. Return to San Cristóbal to visit the market and shop for Indian handicrafts, and overnight there again.

IF YOU HAVE 5 DAYS

Spend the first day and night in **Villahermosa** ㉗, exploring the giant Olmec heads, the river walkway, and the anthropology museum. Day 2, visit Palenque, Misol-Há, and Agua Azul, and overnight in Palenque. Day 3, drive to San Cristóbal de Las Casas, stopping off at the small Maya site of **Toniná** ⑳ along the way; overnight in San Cristóbal. Day 4, see San Juan Chamula and Zinacantán in the morning and then return to San Cristóbal to shop for native crafts and spend the night. On Day 5, start early for the drive south on Highway 190 to the **Lagunas de Montebello** ⑭; en route, visit **Amatenango del Valle** ⑪ and the small Maya ruins at **Chincultik** ⑬.

IF YOU HAVE 8 DAYS

Spend the first day and night in Villahermosa. Next day, drive north of the city to visit the unusual Maya temples at **Comalcalco** ㉘; return to Villahermosa for a dinner cruise on the *Capítan Buelo* along the Grijalva River and overnight here again. Spend the next four days as you would were you following the five-day itinerary, above. On Day 7, drive to **Tuxtla Gutiérrez** ⑱, stopping off at colonial **Chiapa de Corzo** ⑰ along the way; overnight in Tuxtla. On Day 8, tour the impressive **Sumidero Canyon** ⑲ by boat, and then head for Tuxtla's zoo; overnight in Tuxtla again.

Chiapas and Tabasco

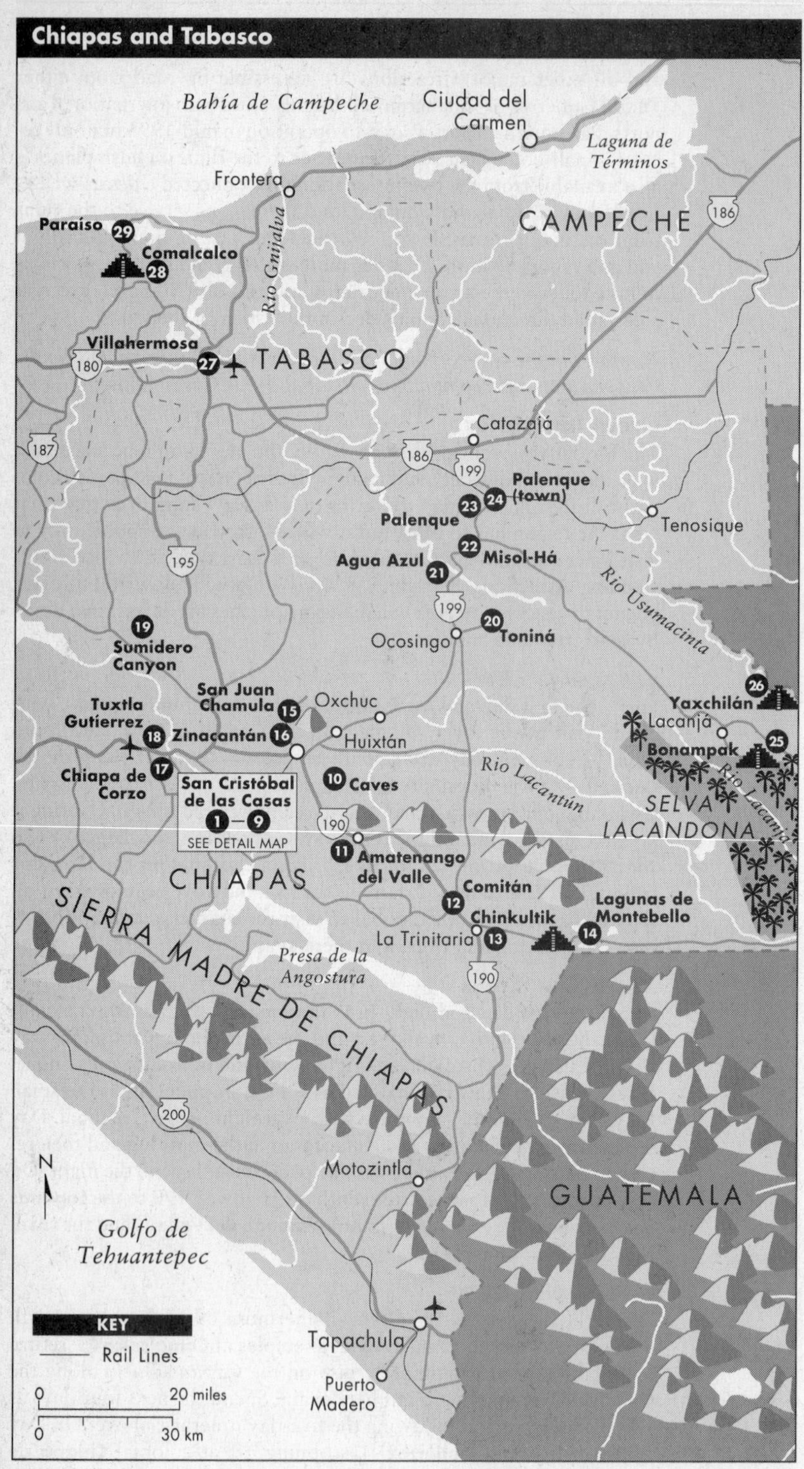

IF YOU HAVE 10 DAYS

Add an excursion to the Maya ruins of **Bonampak** ㉕ on one day and **Yaxchilán** ㉖ on another; although they look close to each other on the map, there's impenetrable jungle between them and there's quite a lot to take in during a tour, so they should be visited on separate days. You can fly to each from Palenque, San Cristóbal, or Tuxtla Gutiérrez. Extend your exploration of the Montebello Lakes with an overnight stay in **Comitán** ⑫.

When to Tour

Try to schedule your visit to coincide with one of the local festivals. Major festival dates in the area (check with the tourist office for a broader sampling) are January 20–22, San Sebastian festival in Zinacantán; Carnival and Easter Week in San Juan Chamula, Zinacantán, and other villages; every Friday during Lent in Zinacantán; June 22–24, San Juan festival in Chamula; July 24–25, festival of the patron saint of San Cristóbal; August 9–10, celebration of San Lorenzo in Zinacantán; December 12, feast of the Virgin of Guadalupe (celebrated for a week in Tuxtla Gutiérrez); and December 31 in several indigenous highland villages, celebrations to install the new civil officials.

SAN CRISTÓBAL DE LAS CASAS

San Cristóbal, the chief city of the Chiapas highlands, is a pretty town of about 120,000 situated in a valley of pine forests and orchards and has an altitude of 6,888 ft above sea level. Native Indian women are as common a sight as hardy backpackers, who come because the place is inexpensive and the perfect hub for exploring off-the-beaten-track places. More Europeans than Americans visit San Cristóbal. Small enough to be seen on foot in the course of a day, the town is also captivating enough to invite a stay of three days, a week, or even a month. In addition to viewing the monuments from the colonial era, visitors usually plan an early-morning visit to see the Indians gather at the *mercado* (market), browse for local handicrafts, or explore one of the indigenous villages in the vicinity. Just soaking up the ambience in one of San Cristóbal's little cafés or unpretentious restaurants is a pleasure.

San Cristóbal is among the finest colonial towns in Mexico: It has churches, red-tile roofs, elegant Spanish mansions, and cobblestone streets. The haunting atmosphere of the place is intensified by the remarkable quality of the early-morning and late-afternoon light.

In 1524, the Spaniards under Diego de Mazariegos decisively defeated the Chiapan Indians at a battle outside town. Mazariegos founded the city, which was called Villareal de Chiapa de los Españoles, in 1528. For most of the viceroyalty, or colonial era, Chiapas, with its capital at San Cristóbal, was a province of Guatemala. Lacking the gold and silver of the north, it was of greater strategic than economic importance to the Spaniards. Under Spanish rule the state's agricultural resources became entrenched in the *encomienda* system, tantamount to slavery. "In this life all men suffer," lamented a Spanish friar in 1691, "but the Indians suffer most of all."

The situation improved only slightly through the efforts of Bartolomé de las Casas, the bishop of San Cristóbal who in the mid-1500s protested the colonials' torture and massacre of the Indians. The Indians protested in another way, murdering priests and other *ladinos* (whites) in infamous uprisings.

Mexico, Guatemala, and the rest of New Spain declared independence in 1821. For just two years, Chiapas remained part of Guatemala, electing by plebescite to join Mexico on September 14, 1824, the *día de la mexicanidad* of Chiapas (the day is still celebrated in San Cristóbal and all over Chiapas). In 1892, because of San Cristóbal's allegiance to the Royalists during the War of Independence, the capital was moved to Tuxtla Gutiérrez; with it went all hope that the town would keep pace with the rest of Mexico. It was not until the 1950s that the roads into town were paved and the first automobiles arrived. Modern times came late to San Cristóbal, for which most visitors are thankful.

It gets quite cool, even cold at night and in the first hours of dawn, so pack a light sweater or jacket before you travel to San Cristóbal. The cobblestone streets are also best suited to wearing tennis shoes, hiking boots, or other flat-heeled sports shoes.

Exploring San Cristóbal de las Casas

San Cristóbal is laid out in a grid pattern and centered on the **zócalo,** with street names changing on either side of the square. For example, Francisco Madero to the east of the square becomes Calle Diego de Mazariegos to the west.

The town is divided into several **barrios** (neighborhoods) that are within easy walking range. The barrios originated in colonial times, when the Indian allies of the triumphant Spaniards were moved onto lands on the outskirts of the nascent city. Each barrio was dedicated to a different occupation. There were Mexican weavers, Tlaxcala fireworks manufacturers, and pig butchers from Cuxtitali. Although these divisions no longer exist, other customs have been kept alive. For example, each Saturday certain houses downtown will put out red lamps to indicate that fresh homemade tamales are for sale. The San Cristóbal tourist office can provide details and arrange trips to the barrios.

A Good Walk

Head for the heart of old downtown or **zócalo** ① and take in the colonial buildings around the square, many of them homes of the Spanish conquistadores. Note the 16th-century **Casa de Diego de Mazariegos** ② on its southeast corner. Continue in a northwesterly direction around the square to the **Palacio Municipal** ③, with its numerous archways covering a city block. The ocher **La Catedral** ④ or cathedral is a heavier-looking building on the north side of the zócalo. Walk a block north of the cathedral to the **Museo del Ambar** ⑤. If you wish to add the **Museo Sergio Castro** ⑥ to your walk, you must call ahead for an appointment. Continue north three blocks along Av. Gen. Utrilla to the 16th-century **Templo de Santo Domingo** ⑦ and its ornamental baroque facade; walk around the complex to its museum and famous handicrafts shop amid the Indian women selling goods on the small cobblestone patios. Head for Av. Gen. Utrilla again and walk north three blocks to the **mercado** ⑧ and visit the stalls filled with indigenous wares. Walk to Av. Gen. Utrilla again and south three blocks to Comitán; turn left and walk 10 blocks to the **Centro de Estudios Científicos Na-Bolom** ⑨.

Sights to See

❷ **Casa de Diego de Mazariegos.** This is one of the most exquisite specimens of colonial architecture in Mexico; the Casa is now the Hotel Santa Clara. The stone mermaid and lions outside it are typical of the period's plateresque style, as ornate and busy as the work of a silversmith. ✉ *Insurgentes 14.*

Casa de Diego de Mazariegos, **2**
Centro de Estudios Científicos Na-Bolom, **9**
La Catedral, **4**
Mercado, **8**
Museo del Ambar, **5**
Museo Sergio Castro, **6**
Palacio Municipal, **3**
Templo de Santo Domingo, **7**
Zócalo, **1**

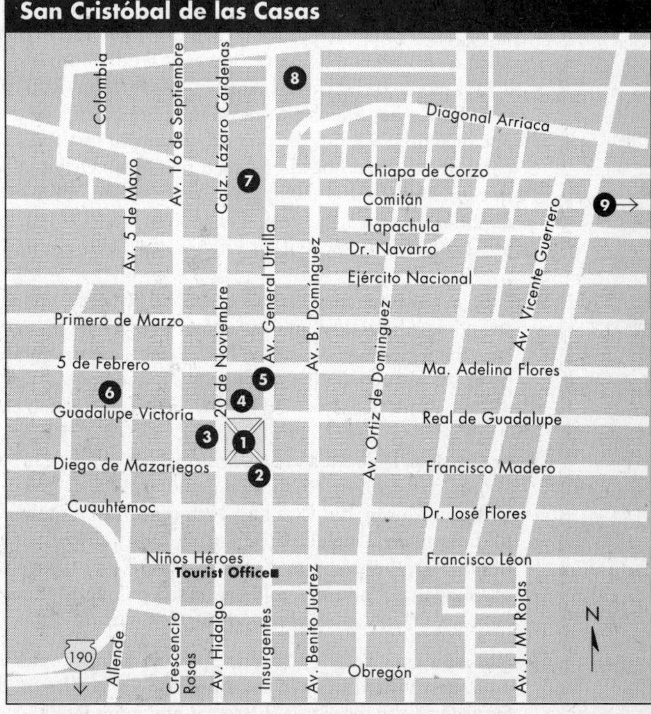

NEED A BREAK?

The cozy and relaxing **Los Amorosos** (The Lovers) **Cafe** (✉ Calle Dr. José Flores 12A, corner of Av. Belisario Domínguez, ☏ 967/8–49–28), in the Jaime Sabines cultural center, is the favorite haunt of local intellectuals and poets who dine on Mexican specialties or drink their way through seven different kinds of cappuccino until midnight.

❾ **Centro de Estudios Científicos Na-Bolom.** Visitors who are interested in the culture and history of the Indians, particularly the Lacandons, should set aside an afternoon to tour this institute, a handsome 22-room colonial building built as a Christian seminary in 1891. Na-Bolom (House of the Jaguar), as it is now called, was donated by Franz and Gertrude "Trudi" Blom in 1950 for the purpose of founding an institute dedicated to ethnological and ecological research; this work is still carried on today. Trudi was a social activist born in the Swiss Alps and Franz was a Danish archaeologist.

Na-Bolom showcases the Bloms' collection of religious treasures that had been hoarded in attics during the anticlerical 1920s and 1930s. A museum houses Franz Blom's findings from the classic Maya site of Moxviquil (mosh-vee-*keel*), found in the outskirts of San Cristóbal, and his personal effects, like his Remington typewriter, eyeglasses, and bottle of mescal liquor. Trudi's bedroom, which is like a minimuseum, has been opened to the public and contains a case full of silver jewelry, along with her shawls, canes, collection of indigenous handicrafts, and wondrous wardrobe of 95 embroidered dresses. Also on the premises is a room full of objects from the daily life of the Lacandons, a tribe descended from the ancient Maya; the Bloms documented their traditions and helped ensure their survival. A library holds more than 5,000 volumes on Chiapas and the Maya. Na-Bolom is also a guest house, and revenues from guests, tours, and the bookshop go to support the work of the institute (☞ Lodging, *below*). Arrange for a meal at Na-Bolom, even if you are not staying there (☞ Dining, *below*).

Na-Bolom is dedicated to reforestation of the surrounding area, planting 35,000 trees each year. Its own extensive garden is filled with firs, fruit trees, vegetables, and flowers. Trudi Blom, who was born in 1901, received the United Nations' 500 Global Roll of Honor award in 1991 for her lifelong work on the preservation of the environment. She died in 1993, but the private, nonprofit institute is being run by a carefully selected board of directors. ✉ *Av. Vicente Guerrero 31, between Comitán and Chiapa de Corzo,* ☎ *967/8–14–18.* 🎫 *Library donation expected.* ⏲ *Mon.–Thurs. 9–3; Fri. 9–11* AM*; tours Tues.–Sun. at 11:30 in Spanish, 4:30 in English.* 🎫 *Tours about $2.*

NEED A BREAK? Drop into **Na-Bolom** in the late afternoon (4–6) for high tea (or coffee) served with flaky pastries—baked according to instructions gleaned from the recipe box of the late Trudi Blom—in an intimate, tree-shaded patio. Also on the institute's agenda is a Sunday Mexican buffet (1:30–4), sometimes accompanied by folk dances or a piano concert.

4 **La Catedral.** Dedicated to San Cristóbal Martir (St. Christopher the martyr), it was built in 1528, then demolished and rebuilt in 1693, with additions during the 18th and 19th centuries. Noteworthy attractions in the cathedral include the painting *Our Lady of Sorrows,* to the left of the altar; the gold-plated *retablo de los Reyes* (altarpiece); the Chapel of Guadalupe; and the gold-encrusted pulpit. ✉ *Guadalupe Victoria between 20 de Noviembre and Av. Gen. Utrilla.* ⏲ *Daily 10:30–8.*

8 **Mercado** (market). This municipal market occupies an eight-block area. Best visited early in the morning—especially on the busiest day, Saturday—the market is the social and commercial center for the Indians from surrounding villages. Stalls overflow with local produce, such as turkeys, medicinal herbs, flowers, firewood, and wool, as well as huaraches (sandals), grinding stones, and candied fruit. Be discreet about taking photographs. ✉ *Between Gral. Utrilla, Nicaragua, Honduras, and Belisario Domínguez.*

5 **Museo del Ambar** (Amber Museum). This is a must for those intrigued by this prehistoric resin, which produces some of the most beautiful ornamental jewelry around. José Luis Coria and his wife, Guadalupe, are the proud owners of this immense collection of pieces carved by local artisans. Many items contain fossilized insects and plant life and others are shaped into pre-Hispanic figures, which are absolutely fascinating. ✉ *Av. Gen. Utrilla 10,* ☎ *967/8–35–07.* 🎫 *Free.* ⏲ *Sun.–Fri. 10–8.*

6 **Museo Sergio Castro.** Those interested in regional ethnic apparel might consider a visit to this private gallery. Sergio Castro has spent more than 20 years working with the Indians; many of the ceremonial costumes are collector's items. You must call ahead for an appointment. ✉ *Calle Guadalupe Victoria 47,* ☎ *967/8–42–89.* 🎫 *Free; donation expected.*

3 **Palacio Municipal.** Perhaps the most famous mansion in San Cristóbal is this building, with wide colonial arches and tiled patio, which was the seat of the state government until 1892, when Tuxtla Gutiérrez became the capital. ✉ *Av. Hidalgo between Diego de Mazariegos and Guadalupe Victoria.* 🎫 *Free.* ⏲ *8* AM*–9* PM*.*

7 **Templo de Santo Domingo.** This three-block-long complex houses a church, former convent, regional history museum, and **Templo de la Caridad.** A two-headed eagle—emblem of the Hapsburg dynasty that once ruled Spain and its American dominions—broods over the pediment of the church, which was built between 1547 and 1569. The pink

stone facade (which needs a good cleaning) is carved in an intensely ornamental style known as Baroque Solomonic: Saints' figures, angels, and grooved columns overlaid with vegetation motifs abound. The interior is dominated by lavish altarpieces; an exquisitely fashioned pulpit; a sculpture of the Holy Trinity; and wall panels of carved cedar, one of the precious woods of Chiapas that centuries later lured the woodsmen of Tabasco to the obscure highlands surrounding San Cristóbal.

At the southeast corner of the church park lies the tiny **Templo de la Caridad,** built in 1711 to honor the Immaculate Conception. Its highlight is the finely carved altarpiece. The Ex-Convento de Santo Domingo, immediately adjacent to the Santo Domingo church, now houses **San Jolobil,** an Indian cooperative selling rather expensive local weavings and a good selection of colorful postcards. The handicrafts shop is open daily 9–2 and 4–7; the small regional history museum, also part of the complex, is open Tuesday–Sunday 9–6. ✉ *Calzada Lazaro Cardenas 42.*

❶ **Zócalo.** This main square around which the colonial city is built has in its center the gazebo used by musicians on festive occasions. Surrounding the square are a number of 16th-century buildings, many former mansions of the conquistadores. Tile roofs and wood-beamed ceilings adorn corridors flanking central patios, which are surrounded by arched columns and filled with huge potted plants. (Don't be afraid to go into buildings whose doors are open.) ✉ *Between Gral. Utrilla, Diego de Mazariegos, 16 de Septiembre, and Guadalupe Victoria.*

Surrounding San Cristóbal are many small and seldom-visited Indian villages that are celebrated for the exquisite colors and embroidery work of their inhabitants' costumes. Huixtán (Hwees-*tan*) and Oxchuc (Os-*chuc*) are about 28 and 43 km (17 and 26 mi), respectively, on the road to Ocosingo; Chenalhó lies 32 km (20 mi) along the paved road beyond Chamula. The Sunday market and weaver's cooperative in Tenejapa (27 km, or 17 mi, northeast of San Cristóbal) are worth seeing. Tenejapa has a small pension.

Dining

$ ★ ✕ **Casa del Pan Cantante.** Organically grown fruits, vegetables, and coffee get top billing at this hip vegetarian restaurant, which even attracts meat-lovers. Owner "Kippy" Crocker Blake from Denver just added sandwiches to the menu, such as baguette stuffed with Italian eggplant. Other offerings include tasty *tamales Chiapanecos* with a spicy cheese filling, hot bean soup, and the best salads in town. Top it off with chocolate brownies or cheese-fruit pie. The four-course special of the day, which includes other variations on traditional Mexican cooking, really shines. A small bakery sells homemade breads, bagels, coffee, cookies, and fruit preserves—as well as Celtic flute music cassettes and Kippy's new cookbook. Musical groups with repertoires from jazz to pop perform 8–10 PM weekends. ✉ *Av. Belisario Domínguez and Dr. Navarro,* ☎ *967/8-04-68. MC, V. Closed Mon.*

$ ★ ✕ **Eden.** Local ex-pats rave about the steaks at this small, charming chalet-style restaurant run, naturally, by a Swiss national. It has sturdy sienna-brown walls trimmed in blue, eight cozy dining tables, piped-in classical music, and pleasant service; the margaritas are the biggest in San Cristóbal. Swiss delights include classic raclette—melted cheese and potato—and beef fondue for two. Homemade lime or raspberry pie is the perfect finish to a meal. The wine list has an appropriate selection of Italian, Spanish, Chilean, and Mexican labels. ✉ *Av. 5 de Febrero 19,* ☎ *967/8-00-85. AE, DC, MC, V.*

$ ✕ La Galeria. This Italian restaurant in a two-story colonial home with huge inner patio is San Cristóbal's oldest informal social center as well as a dance club come Thursday night. The food consists of 11 different kinds of pizzas plus Neopolitan dishes such as lasagna with eggplant and minestrone, with Mexican *pozole* (boiled corn dish) thrown in for good measure. Art expositions, a permanent billiards table, and occasional U.S. movie showings are appealing extras. ✉ *Hidalgo 3,* ☎ *967/8–15–47. MC, V.*

$ ✕ La Langosta. This simply furnished restaurant with bright tablecloths is San Cristóbal's best-kept secret for authentic colonial cuisine. Some samples? Try *chalupa coleta,* a deep-fried tortilla covered with refried beans, chopped vegetables, cheese, pork chunks, and salsa Mexicana; tamales stuffed with either pork or chicken, chopped prunes, almonds, mole, and bits of *chili morron*; *tascalate,* a cold corn-meal drink made with sugar and mild *achiote* spice; and several dishes using smoked and pressed ham made in San Cristóbal. Although La Langosta means lobster, only one lobster dish is served here. ✉ *Madero 9,* ☎ *967/8–22–38. MC, V.*

$ ✕ La Selva Café. Mexico's answer to Starbucks, this coffee shop has 27 different kinds of organic javas and assorted concoctions plus coffee cookies, coffee sorbet, chocolate-covered coffee beans, and mocha ice cream. For a real caffeine jag, try the Jungle coffee. The coffee is the homegrown Chiapas variety harvested by a Maya Indian cooperative and good enough to export; it's sold under the Aztec Harvest label in the United States. All this is served in the nostalgic atmosphere of a simulated Havana coffeehouse of the 1950s complete with beamed ceilings and rattan furniture. The house also offers codfish pie, chopped meat pie, Chiapas tamales, and much more on the big menu. There's a shop selling fresh-ground blends ranging from smooth to Cuban espresso. ✉ *Cresencio Rosas 9, at corner of Cuauhtémoc,* ☎ *967/8–72–44. No credit cards.*

$ ✕ Na-Bolom. Doña Bety, the late Trudi Blom's adopted daughter, heads up the kitchen at this famous ethnological/ecological institute. Good, old-fashioned home-cooked meals served at a communal dining table are the norm here with, perhaps, roast chicken, coleslaw, avocado strips, and Mexican *chayote* (green squashlike vegetable). Guests share the meal with international volunteers, Lacandon Indians, resident scholars, and artists in a congenial setting where the conversation is lively and light. Nonguests can dine here with at least two hours advance notice. ✉ *Av. Vicente Guerrero 33,* ☎ *967/8–14–18. No credit cards.*

$ ✕ Restaurante el Teatro. Decorated with both European and local artwork, this popular French-Italian restaurant across from the Hotel Flamboyant Español specializes in chateaubriand, crepes, fresh pasta dishes, and chocolate mousse. The French owner keeps the atmosphere unhurried. ✉ *Av. 1 de Marzo 8,* ☎ *967/8–31–49. AE, MC, V.*

Lodging

$$$$ 🏨 El Jaracandal. The four guest rooms in this beautiful private estate overlooking town are the most expensive in San Cristóbal but the perfect choice if you want a special experience. American owners Nancy and Percy Wood, who restored the 19th-century mansion and gardens to their original magnificence, offer guests the run of the house, which includes the libraries, sitting rooms, terraces, and garden nooks; it's like one big house party. All rooms have folk-art furnishings made by local artisans as well as bathtubs. The Woods lead horseback and other excursions at no extra charge. Meals are included; the kitchen is headed by Doña Fedela, a former chef at a leading Mexico City hotel, who turns her expertise to such dishes as deboned chicken stuffed with cheese, ham, and *acelgas* (spinachlike vegetable) and simmered in sour orange juice; crepes stuffed with large seta mushrooms and cheese; and, for dessert, guava or mango mousse. Nonguests can dine here with 24 hours notice. Transportation to and from the Tuxtla Gutiérrez airport available at extra cost. ✉ *Comitán 7, 29220,* ☎ *967/8–10–65. 4 rooms. Dining room. No credit cards.*

$$ 🏨 **Hotel Casa Mexicana.** This beautifully designed hotel in a restored colonial mansion is colorful, clean, bright, and friendly. Large rooms, good beds, beamed ceilings, a lovely garden, attractive artwork, and a Mexican chef in the hotel restaurant concocting such dishes as chicken in pistachio sauce all help make this an outstanding hostelry. All the accommodations have telephones and TVs, and the two junior suites offer hot tubs. ✉ *28 de Agosto 1, 29200,* ☎ *967/8–06–98, 967/8–06–83, or 967/8–13–41;* FAX *967/8–26–27. 29 rooms, 2 junior suites. Restaurant, bar, room service, massage, sauna, exercise room, babysitting, free parking. AE, DC, MC, V.*

$$ ★ 🏨 **Hotel Casavieja.** Three blocks east of the zócalo and close to many of the town's attractions, this spectacular hotel is built around a centuries-old house and replicates the colonial architecture of that structure. Each spacious, comfortable room has large windows looking out onto one of the three interior courtyards and is charmingly decorated in Mexican furnishings; in addition to the telephones and TVs with English channels found in all the rooms, the suites have hot tubs. The Espinosa family, who run and own the hotel, are extremely warm and knowledgeable hosts. ✉ *Ma. Adelina Flores 27, 29230,* ☎ *967/8–03–85,* FAX *967/8–52–23. 36 rooms, 3 suites. Restaurant, bar, car rental, free parking. MC, V.*

$$ 🏨 **La Catedral.** Reconstructed from a colonial inn and movie house, this luxury hotel, opened in December 1995, uses church nomenclature for its public areas: The bar is called **El Confesionario** (the confessional) and the pool is **El Pila** (baptismal fount). Beamed ceilings, terrazzo floors, and replicas of handmade wood furniture from the 16th and 17th centuries add to the colonial atmosphere, but the hotel also boasts a San Cristóbal first—solar energy for heating the bathwater and the swimming pool. The guest rooms surround a three-story atrium topped with a stained-glass image of San Cristóbal's cathedral. All have tiled baths with phones, piped-in music, and color satellite TVs; 10 rooms offer hot tubs. ✉ *Guadalupe Victoria 21, in Historic Center, 29200,* ☎ FAX *967/8–13–63. 85 rooms, including 10 suites. Restaurant, bar, pool, business services, meeting rooms, free parking. AE, MC, V.*

$$ 🏨 **Posada Diego de Mazariegos.** This elegant hotel, adapted from two colonial mansions that face one another across a busy thoroughfare, has the largest number of rooms in town. Rooms have charming wrought-iron window frames, oak balustrades, red-tile floors, and wood-beamed ceilings; most rooms contain fireplaces, and all have views of five flower-filled garden patios. The older section of the hotel is covered with a giant fiberglass dome; here are the bar, coffee shop, guest library with English and French tomes, and a new wing with 43 rooms added in 1997. ✉ *5 de Febrero 1, 29200,* ☎ *967/8–06–21 or 967/8–07–28,* FAX *967/8–08–27. 120 rooms. Restaurant, bar, coffee shop, meeting rooms, travel services, car rental. AE, DC, V.*

$ 🏨 **Hotel Posada El Paraíso.** This charming colonial home has 13 guest rooms with beamed ceilings: Some have lofts and carpeting, but there are no TVs; eight rooms have phones. Comfortable leatherback chairs in the guest lounge overlook a sunny patio with tables for breakfasting. The bar-restaurant, **Eden,** offers the personal attention of owners Daniel Suter and his Mexican wife, Teresa, who met as students in

Switzerland. Choose a room away from the street and lounge for more solitude. ✉ *Av. 5 de Febrero 19, 29200,* ☎ *967/8–00–85,* FAX *967/8–51–68. 13 rooms. Restaurant, bar. AE, DC, MC, V.*

$ **Hotel Santa Clara.** In the historic Casa de Diego Mazariegos on the zócalo, this rambling 16th-century mansion has an oil painting of St. Clara over the front desk, a friendly Siamese cat named Menini, and three brilliantly colored guacamaya birds that entertain guests in the lovely indoor patio. The appealing hotel, convenient to all town-center attractions, has an air of past grandeur about it with beamed ceilings, antique furnishings, and time-worn hardwood floors. Five of the 10 extra-roomy units with balconies overlook the pretty main square. Folk dancers entertain in the **Bar Cocodrilo** from time to time. ✉ *Insurgentes 1, 29200,* ☎ *967/8–08–71 or 967/8–11–40,* FAX *967/8–10–41. 40 rooms. Restaurant, bar, coffee shop, pool, travel services. MC, V accepted but with 10% charge.*

$ **Mansión del Valle.** A few blocks from the zócalo, this 19th-century property has been converted into a hotel with tasteful Spanish colonial design details, such as wrought-iron banisters, terrazzo floors, and a large inner atrium filled with greenery. Rooms are spacious; seven have patios overlooking a park. ✉ *Calle Diego de Mazariegos 39, 29240,* ☎ *967/8–25–82 or 967/8–25–83,* FAX *967/8–25–81. 45 rooms. Restaurant, bar, coffee shop, meeting room, free parking. AE, MC, V.*

$ ★ **Na-Bolom.** Each of the rustic but cozy rooms available at this center for the study and preservation of the Lacandon Indians and the rain forest is decorated with the accoutrements of a specific indigenous community—crafts, photographs, and books—and contains what might be the only bathtubs in San Cristóbal hostelries. Guests staying at Na-Bolom receive a free tour of the house, free entrance to a documentary presentation, access to the library, and information about the area. Book well in advance; ask for a garden view. Guests share the dining room with staff and volunteers at a separate charge (☞ Dining, *above*). ✉ *Av. Vicente Guerrero 33, 29200,* ☎ *967/8–14–18. 14 rooms. Restaurant. MC, V.*

$ **Posada Córtes.** This snug little 10-room inn, which opened at the end of 1995 on a tranquil plaza in a residential neighborhood, is probably the best deal and best-kept secret in town. Good-size rooms—two overlooking the plaza—have two double beds each and tiled-floor bathrooms; there's no phone or TV but for under $10 a room, you can't beat the price. It's two blocks from the mercado and four blocks from the zócalo. There's a restaurant a block away. ✉ *Plazuela Mexicanos off 16 de Septiembre, 29240,* ☎ *967/8–74–86. 10 rooms. No credit cards.*

$ **Posada Jovel.** Students as well as professionals on a budget choose this converted three-story home, four blocks from the main square, for its simple but clean rooms and free breakfasts. Nine rooms have private baths and nine share baths. ✉ *Flavio A. Paniagua 28, 29240,* ☎ *967/8–17–34. 18 rooms. No credit cards.*

$ **Rincón del Arco.** Near Na-Bolom, this hotel has charming touches, especially each room's fireplace (some are shaped like bulls or jaguars) and bedspreads. The best room is number 11; it's secluded and has a pretty view of the garden. The dining room has two fireplaces, wrought-iron wagon-wheel chandeliers, and other regional touches. Service can be slow. ✉ *Calle Ejército Nacional 66, 29200,* ☎ *967/8–13–13,* FAX *967/8–15–68. 36 rooms. Restaurant, bar. AE, MC, V.*

Nightlife and the Arts

San Cristóbal is acquiring more cultural events than before. Ask at the tourist office and bookshops about upcoming lectures on ecology, regional ethnography, the Selva Lacandona, or concerts. The elegant **Teatro de la Ciudad** (✉ Hnos. Domínguez 7, ☎ 967/8–36–37) reopened in 1996 after an extensive remodeling; it features such programs as the National Ballet of Cuba. **Na-Bolom** occasionally sponsors talks and audiovisual presentations. **La Galeria** (☞ Shopping, *below*) and **La Puente** (✉ Real de Guadalupe 55, ☎ 967/8–37–23) have art expositions and movie nights.

Although San Cristóbal has one disco—frequented mostly by young locals—nightlife is not one of the city's main draws. Plan to catch up on your reading.

Outdoor Activities and Sports

A horseback ride into the neighboring indigenous villages can exercise the mind as well as the body. Most hotels can arrange for rentals of horses. Guides working through the tourist office and travel agencies can also hire horses and will accompany tourists. Allow a minimum of six hours for a satisfying trip. Mountain biking is offered by a new outfit called **Los Pinguinos** (✉ 5 de Maya 5B, no phone).

Shopping

There are no department stores in San Cristóbal. The market, although picturesque, sells more produce than handicrafts. The side streets leading to the market are flooded with goods from Guatemala and not always those of the highest quality. Always ask if an item comes from Guatemala. If the answer is yes—you'll be lucky to encounter such honesty—bargain fiercely: Guatemalan goods are priced several times higher in San Cristóbal than they would be if purchased in Guatemala. Guatemalan cloth is easily recognizable: Most of it is rough, dark blue cotton with multicolor cotton needlepoint or trim.

Shops in town are generally open 9–2 and 4–8. Indian women and children often accost visitors on the streets with their wares, mostly textiles, but their selections are not as varied as those in the shops, and prices will not necessarily be any better. You can be assured, though, that the proceeds go directly to the craftspersons themselves.

Among its excellent selection of wares, **San Jolobil** (✉ Ex-Convento de Santo Domingo, 20 de Noviembre, ☎ 967/8–26–46), the regional crafts cooperative, sells hand-dyed woolen sweaters and men's tunics, embroidered pillow covers, and pre-Hispanic design wall hangings. **La Galeria** (✉ Hidalgo 3, ☎ 967/8–15–47) offers exclusive designs by Kiki Oberstenfeld, who imbues her dolls, posters, woodcuts, and children's books with primitive and folk-art motifs. The store also carries hand-painted tiles and winsome weavings from Teneapa and appealing items from other regions of Mexico. Among the smart shops clustered along Real de Guadalupe is **El Arbor de la Vida** (formerly Citlali) (✉ Real de Guadalupe 27, ☎ 967/8–40–85), which specializes in attractive designer amber jewelry mixed with silver and gold. Although the prices are higher than those in other shops, the designs are more sophisticated. The government-run **Casa de las Artesanías** (✉ Calle Niños Héroes and Av. Hidalgo, ☎ 967/8–18–80) has wooden toys, ceramic jugs, embroidered blouses, bags, and handwoven textiles for sale by the yard, and a tiny ethnographic museum with indigenous costumes in back. **Arte Sandia** (✉ Calle 28 de Agosto, No. 2-C, in front of Casa Mexicana Hotel, ☎ 967/8–42–40), which means "Watermelon Art," is a whimsical little boutique with handicrafts sporting—you guessed it—watermelon motifs; in addition to the coffee mugs, swizzle sticks, rugs, and T-shirts there are nonwatermelon articles, such as embroidered designer dresses and hard-to-find gold filigree jewelry. **Textiles Soriano** (✉ Rincón del Arco Hotel, Calle Ejercito Nacional 66, ☎ 967/8–13–13) specializes in handwoven bedspreads.

An unusual shop in an old colonial home, **Taller Leñateros** (✉ Flavio A. Paniagua 54, ☎ 967/8–51–74) carries handmade books, boxes, postcards, and writing paper fashioned on the premises out of recycled flower petals, plants, and bark. Owner Amber Past from Minneapolis conducts free tours of the workshop, which employs about two dozen Maya.

SOUTH AND EAST OF SAN CRISTÓBAL

Southeast of San Cristóbal lies one of the least explored and most exotic regions of Chiapas: the **Selva Lacandona,** said to be the second-largest rain forest in the western hemisphere. Incursions of developers, land-hungry settlers, and refugees from neighboring Guatemala are transforming Mexico's last frontier, which for centuries has been the homeland of the Lacandons, a small tribe descended from the ancient Maya who still live in huts, wear long tunics, and maintain their ancient customs. However, their custom of not marrying outside the tribe is causing serious problems and their numbers have been reduced to a mere 350. The beautiful **Lakes of Montebello** are within this region. En route to the lakes, you can visit the fabulous **Caves of San Cristóbal.**

The Caves of San Cristóbal

❿ *11 km (7 mi) southeast of San Cristobal off Route 190.*

The spectacular limestone stalactites and stalagmites are illuminated for an entire kilometer (more than ½ mi) inside these labyrinthine caves, which were discovered in 1960 and were fully explored only a few years ago. The park surrounding the caves has a picnic area. A Spanish-speaking guide is usually available for a small fee. Horses can be rented on weekends. The caves are in the **San Cristóbal Recreational Park,** in the midst of a pine forest. *No phone.* 🎫 *40¢.* ⏲ *Check with San Cristóbal tourist office to see if caves are open; when open, hrs are 9–4.*

Amatenango del Valle

⓫ *35 km (22 mi) south of San Cristóbal.*

Amatenango del Valle is a small village known for the handsome, primitive pottery made by the women of the town. By the side of the road, they sell ocher, black, and brown clay flowerpots and animal figurines that have been fired on open kilns.

En Route The rugged foothills and pine groves surrounding San Cristóbal subside into a low plain along the next stretch of the road; the mountains appear to have been sliced in two, revealing their rust-red innards, sad artifacts of the erosion caused by the clearing of the forests.

Comitán

⓬ *50 km (31 mi) southeast of Amatenango del Valle.*

Comitán is halfway between San Cristóbal and the Lagunas de Montebello, and though the city has few attractions, it is one of the few places on the way to Guatemala that offer lodgings and restaurants.

Many of the Mexicans who work at the few remaining Guatemalan refugee camps in Chiapas live in Comitán. Beginning in 1981, some 46,000 Guatemalan peasants fled a wave of political repression by crossing the border into ramshackle camps, only to be hunted down by the Guatemalan army. However, most of these refugees headed home under an amnesty program put into effect in 1993. Comitán, whose original Maya name was Balún-Canán, or "Nine Stars," flourished early on as a major center linking the lowland temperate plains to the edge of the Maya empire on the Pacific. Even today, it serves as the principal trading point for the Tzeltal Indians and such Guatemalan goods as sugarcane liquor and orchids. The present city was built by the Spaniards, but few traces of the colonial era remain. Notable exceptions are two churches, **Santo Domingo de Guzmán** and **San Sebastián,** in which part of Chiapas's struggle for independence from Spain took place. From the zócalo there are fine views of the hills.

The **Casa-Museo Dr. Belisario Domínguez,** former home of a martyr of the revolution, opened as a museum in 1985 and re-creates that turbulent era with an array of documents and photographs. ✉ *Av. Dr. Belisario Domínguez Sur 17.* *About 25¢.* ⏲ *Tues.–Sun. 9–4.*

On the outskirts of town, small **Maya sites** that have been unearthed include **Tenan Puente** and **Junchavin,** ceremonial centers built around the same time as Chincultik (☞ *below*). Restoration work has begun on Tenan Puente and a royal tomb was discovered in 1996; both sites are open to the public.

Chincultik

13 *49 km (30 mi) southeast of Comitán.*

The small, late-classic Maya site of Chincultik will interest only hardcore archaeology buffs, although it has a lovely forest location, a view of the Montebello Lakes, and a large *cenote* (sacred well). The **ruins,** which are only partially restored, include a ball court, pyramid, cenote, and stelae. *About $1.50.* ⏲ *Daily 8–4.*

To get to Chincultik from Comitán, continue south 15 km (9 mi) on Route 190 until you see a very small turnoff for the lakes (marked only by a green-and-white sign depicting a tree) outside of La Tinitaria; after 39 km (24 mi), there's a dirt road on the left leading to the ruins, which are 5 km (3 mi) off the highway; a 10-minute hike is then required.

Dining and Lodging

$$ **Museo Parador Santa Maria.** Built around the remains of an old hacienda, this lodging has a restaurant and seven well-appointed rooms decorated with period antiques. ✉ *22 km (13½ mi) from Chincultik,* ☎ *963/2–33–46 or 963/2–51–16. No credit cards.*

Lagunas de Montebello

14 *9 km (5 mi) east of Chincultik, 155 km (96 mi) southeast of San Cristóbal.*

The 60-odd lakes and surrounding selva (rain forest) of Lagunas de Montebello (Montebello Lakes) constitute a 2,437-acre national park that is shared with Guatemala. A different color permeates each lake, whose waters glow with vivid emerald, turquoise, amethyst, azure, and steel-gray tints, caused by various oxides. The setting is serene and majestic, with clusters of oak, pine, and sweet gum. Practically the only denizens of the more accessible part of the forest are the clamorous goldfinch, mockingbirds, and the rare quetzal bird. To the east, wild animals roam: pumas and jaguars, deer and bears.

At the park entrance, the road forks. The left leads to the **Lagunas Coloradas** (Colored Lakes). At **Laguna Bosque Azul,** the last lake along that road, there are picnic tables, rest rooms, and, at the end of the road, a shabby but serviceable café. The right fork at the park entrance continues along dirt roads for 14 km (9 mi) before dwindling to a footpath. If you walk down the right fork, you will see some of the more beautiful lakes. The largest, **Tziscao,** forms the border between Mexico and Guatemala and is the site of the Tziscao Lodge and the Albergue Quinta Cielo hostelries, both of which are dirt cheap and very basic (no hot water) but offer food service, horses, boats, and excellent fishing. Buses leave infrequently from Comitán (✉ 2 Av. Poniente Sur 17–B, ☎ 963/2–08–75) to Laguna Bosque Azul and Tziscao.

NORTH AND WEST OF SAN CRISTÓBAL

San Juan Chamula and Zinacantán are traditional villages in the scenic western outskirts of San Cristóbal. The small colonial town of Chiapa de Corzo will be the first major town you come to when you drive west from San Cristóbal along Route 190. Tuxtla Gutiérrez, the modern state capital, is a short distance away. From Tuxtla, the Sumidero Canyon can be easily reached.

San Juan Chamula

⓯ *12 km (7½ mi) northwest of San Cristóbal de las Casas.*

The spiritual and administrative center of the Chamula Indians is justly celebrated, as much for its rich past as for its turbulent present. The Chamula are a Tzotzil-speaking Maya group of nearly 52,000 individuals (out of a total of 300,000 Tzotzils) who live in hamlets scattered throughout the highlands; there are several thousand of them in San Juan Chamula.

The Chamula are fiercely religious, a trait that has played an important role in their history. The Chamula uprising of 1869 started when some tribesmen were imprisoned for crucifying a boy in the belief that they should have their own Christ. Some 13,000 Chamula then rose up to demand their leaders' release and massacred scores of ladino villagers in the process. More recently, the infiltration of Protestant evangelists into the community led to the expulsion of the Indian converts by Chamula authorities. In the last 20 years, more than 30,000 have been forced to abandon their ancestral lands and now live on the outskirts of San Cristóbal de las Casas, dressing in conventional clothing and usually found selling handicrafts in San Cristóbal's street markets. The Human Rights Commission is trying to mediate their return to the Chamula community.

Physically and spiritually, life in San Juan Chamula revolves around the church, a white-stucco building with red, blue, and yellow trim. To get permission to enter the church, go first to the tourist office on the main square. Admission to the church is about 40¢. Extreme discretion must be exercised once you are inside. Taking photographs is absolutely prohibited.

There are no pews in the church, the floor of which is strewn with fragrant pine needles. The Indians sit chanting while facing colorfully attired saints' statues. For the most part, worshipers appear oblivious to intruders, continuing with their rituals: They burn candles of various colors, drink Coca-Cola, and may have a live chicken or eggs with them for healing the sick. They "pass" the illness to the chicken or egg, which then gets disposed of outside the church. The church is named after Saint John the Baptist, the main god of the universe, according to Chamulan belief—which also relegates Jesus Christ to the position of a minor saint.

Outside the church there is no taboo against photography, but adults prefer not to be photographed. Flocks of children will pester you to buy small trinkets and will allow you to photograph them in exchange for a small fee (about 30¢ a shot). The best time to visit San Juan Chamula is on Sunday, when the market is in full swing and more formal religious rites are performed.

To get to San Juan Chamula from San Cristóbal, head west on Guadalupe Victoria, which forks to the right onto Ramón Larrainzar. Continue 4 km (2½ mi) until you reach the entrance to the village. Most of these roads are paved, and they are far more interesting than the alternate route, which is to take the main road to Tuxtla 8 km (5 mi) and then turn right when you see signs.

Zinacantán

16 *4 km (2½ mi) west of San Juan Chamula.*

The village of Zinacantán (Place of the Bats) is even smaller than San Juan Chamula (☞ *above*) and is reached by taking a paved road west just outside San Juan Chamula (from San Cristóbal, take the Tuxtla road about 8 km [5 mi] and look for the signed turnoff on your right). Here photography is totally forbidden, except for the row of village weavers on view along the main street. It is the scenery en route to Zinacantán—terraced hillsides with cornfields and orchards—that draws visitors. There isn't much to see in the village except on Sundays, when people gather from the surrounding parishes, or during religious festivals. The men wear bright pink tunics; the women cover themselves with bright pink *rebozos* (shawls). Watch for the plethora of crosses around the springs and mountains on the way to Zinacantán: They mark a Chamula cemetery of Christian origin.

The **Museo Ik'al Ojov** shows off Zinacatán costumes down through the ages. ✉ *Main street, no phone.* 🎫 *Free.* ⏲ *Tues.–Sun. 8–5.*

Chiapa de Corzo

17 *70 km (44 mi) northwest of San Cristóbal.*

Chiapa de Corzo was founded in 1528 by Diego de Mazariegos, who one month later fled the mosquitoes and transported all the settlers to San Cristóbal (then called Chiapa de los Españoles, to distinguish it from Chiapa de los Indios, as Chiapa de Corzo was originally known). The mosquitos are still here.

Life in this small, dusty town on the banks of the Grijalva revolves, inevitably, around the **zócalo,** lorded over by a bizarre 16th-century Mozarabic fountain modeled after Isabella's crown. The interior is decorated with stories of the Indians. Several handicraft shops line the square, selling huaraches, ceramics, lacquerware, the famous Parachico masks, and regional costumes.

Chiapa's **lacquerware museum,** facing the plaza, contains a modest collection of delicately carved and painted *jícaras* (gourds). ("The sky is no more than an immense blue jícara, the beloved firmament in the form of a cosmic jícara," explains the *Popul Vuh,* a 16th-century chronicle of the Quiché Maya.) The lacquerware on display is both local and imported, coming from Michoacán, Guerrero, Chiapas, and Asia. A workshop behind the museum is open during the week and generally keeps the same hours as the museum. *No phone.* 🎫 *Free.* ⏲ *Tues.–Sat. 9–2 and 4–6, Sun. 9–1.*

Just outside of town, behind the Nestlé plant, are some nearly unnoticeable Maya-Olmec ruins dating from 1450 BC.

Dining

On the opposite side of the square from the museum, the **Jardines de Chiapa** (Portal Oriente s/n) serves an excellent and inexpensive variety of regional cuisines in a lovely patio setting. Try the *tasajo* (sun-dried beef served with pumpkin-seed sauce) and the *chipilín con bolita* soup, made with balls of ground corn paste cooked in a creamy herbal sauce and topped with Chiapas's famous cheese.

Tuxtla Gutiérrez

18 *289 km (180 mi) southwest of Villahermosa, 15 km (9 mi) northwest of Chiapa de Corzo, 85 km (54 mi) northwest of San Cristóbal.*

Tuxtla Gutiérrez is the thriving capital city of the state of Chiapas. In 1939 Graham Greene characterized it as "not a place for foreigners—the new ugly capital of Chiapas, without attractions. . . . It is like an unnecessary postscript to Chiapas, which should be all wild mountain and old churches and swallowed ruins and the Indians plodding by." That bleak description is slowly changing, as new luxury buildings like the Camino Real Hotel (opened in 1994) add sparkle to the city. Nonetheless, Tuxtla Gutiérrez is a city through which most visitors to Chiapas will pass, and it is of vital economic and political importance. It is the state's transportation hub, and it has what is probably the most exciting zoo in Latin America, along with a comprehensive archaeology museum. It is also convenient for its proximity to Chiapa de Corzo and the Sumidero Canyon, which have few accommodations.

Tuxtla's first name derives from the Nahuatl word *tochtlan,* meaning "abundance of rabbits." Its second name, Gutiérrez, honors Joaquín Miguel Gutiérrez, who fought for the state's independence and incorporation into Mexico.

The highway into town is endless. Tuxtla (population 525,000), the state capital since 1892, does not have many conveniences for tourists, but you can get your bearings best by staying on the main drag, which will run you smack into the zócalo, known locally as the **parque central,** which is fronted by huge government buildings.

Only the most obstinate animal-hater would fail to be captivated by the free-roaming inmates of the **Tuxtla Zoomat,** all native Chiapans. The 100-plus species on display include black widows, jaguars, marsupials, iguanas, quetzal birds, boa constrictors, tapirs, eagles, and monkeys. ✉ *Southeast of town off Libramiento Sur.* *Free but donation appreciated.* ⏲ *Tues.–Sun. 8:30–5.*

Amateur archaeologists and botanists should head for **Parque Madero,** which includes the **Botanical Garden,** the **Orchid House,** and the **Regional Museum of Chiapas.** One of the largest collections of Maya artifacts worldwide is on the ground floor of the museum, an innovative structure of glass, brick, and marble. On the upper floor are displays of colonial pieces and regional handicrafts and costumes. ✉ *Northeast of downtown, between Av. Norte 5a and Calle Oriente 11a.* *Free.* ⏲ *Garden Tues.–Sun. 8–6, Orchid House Tues.–Sun. 10–1, museum Tues.–Sun. 9–4.*

A fine small museum of indigenous Indian cultures throughout Chiapas opened in 1993 at the government-run **Casa de Las Artesanías,** which also has a good selection of regional handicrafts for sale. Amber from Chiapas fashioned into necklaces, earrings, and pendants, as well as hand-embroidered and brocaded table mats and leather bags, gold filigree jewelry, and lacquerware, are among the local specialties. ✉ *Blvd. Dr. Belisario Domínguez Km 1083,* ☎ *961/2–22–75.* *Free.* *Daily 9–2 and 5–8.*

As its name suggests, **Parque de Las Marimbas** (✉ Centro and 8 Pte.) hosts marimba bands, which play old-fashioned dancing music—you can grab a partner and join in—Thursday through Sunday at 7 PM.

Dining and Lodging

$$$ ✕ **Montebello.** Lobster and prime rib headline the menu at this classy specialty restaurant at the Camino Real Hotel. This intimate (16 tables) place is most romantic at night, when the city lights shimmer into view. The elegance of the earth-tone decor is set off by an unusual white mural of the Sumidero cliffs sculpted into a wall. Soft piano music accompanies diners from 3 PM until closing. ✉ *Blvd. Dr. Belisario Domínguez 1195,* ☎ *961/7–77–77. AE, DC, MC, V. Closed Sun.*

$$ ✕ **La Selva.** Specialties from Chiapas such as a mixed *Chiapaneco* platter with mole, rice, beans, and grilled beef top a menu that satisfies multiple tastes with a broad sampling of international dishes. A tropical atmosphere sizzles with marimba music. It's open from 8 AM to midnight. ✉ *Blvd. Dr. Belisario Domínguez 1360,* ☎ *961/5–07–18. MC, V.*

$ ★ ✕ **Las Pichanchas.** This restaurant, open for breakfast, lunch, and dinner, offers an outstanding variety of regional dishes, as well as live marimba music and nightly folkloric dances. ✉ *Central Oriente 837,* ☎ *961/2–53–51. AE, MC, V.*

$$$ ★ **Camino Real.** A new star appeared on the hotel horizon in 1994 with the opening of this hilltop oasis of luxury and comfort. It has already been dubbed "the Chiapanecan Dream" by locals who have never seen anything so fairy-tale beautiful in the state capital. Rooms surround a huge open-air pool and bar area with exotic vegetation. A concierge floor, business center with computer rentals, and meeting facilities draw many business travelers, who entertain clients in the **Azulejos** restaurant, enclosed in a sky-blue glass dome (there's a champagne brunch on Sundays), or at the upscale **Montebello** (☞ Dining and Lodging, *above*). All rooms have a view of the mountains, remote-control satellite color TVs, room safes, minibars, phones, and full bathroom amenities. ✉ *Blvd. Dr. Belisario Domínguez 1195, 29060,* ☎ *961/7–77–77 or 800/722–6466,* FAX *961/7–77–71. 210 rooms and suites. 2 restaurants, bar, pool, 2 tennis courts, health club, travel services, car rental. AE, DC, MC, V.*

$$ **Bonampak.** This hotel has small rooms and a pool set in lush gardens, which have been whittled down to make way for a shopping mall next door. The cafeteria and restaurant have a well-deserved reputation for good regional cooking, steaks, and soups. ✉ *Blvd. Dr. Belisario Domínguez 180, 29030,* ☎ *961/3–20–50,* FAX *961/2–77–37. 70 rooms. Restaurant, bar, cafeteria, pool, tennis court, travel services, car rental. AE, MC, V.*

$$ **Hotel Flamboyant.** If you want something with Moorish touches and a restful atmosphere, try one of the guest rooms in this luxury hotel. Accommodations are set off long hallways with wide archways; all are air-conditioned and have TVs with some channels in English. Twenty-four rooms face the large garden, while a dozen are located off a smaller and extremely tranquil inner garden. Capacious is the byword: The pool is huge, and so are the public areas. The restaurant is light and airy, but the bar is dark and tacky. A disadvantage is the location—a 10-minute drive west of town—but there's a pretty shopping mall next door. ✉ *Blvd. Dr. Belisario Domínguez Km 1081, 29000,* ☎ *961/5–08–88 or 961/5–09–99,* FAX *961/5–00–87. 118 rooms. Restaurant, bar, meeting rooms, travel services. AE, MC, V.*

$ **Gran Hotel Humberto.** Close to the main square, this hotel has small but air-conditioned rooms, all with TVs (local stations only). The elevators in this eight-story property are old and the hallways are dismal, but proximity to downtown is an advantage. ✉ *Central Poniente 180, 29030,* ☎ *961/2–20–80 or 961/2–20–44,* FAX *961/2–97–71. 112 rooms. Restaurant. AE, MC, V.*

Sumidero Canyon

19 *18 km (11 mi) northeast of Tuxtla.*

The gaping, almost vertical walls of Sumidero Canyon descend 4,000 ft for some 15 km (9 mi). The gorge lends itself to comparison with the Grand Canyon; it was formed about 12 million years ago, and the Grijalva River slices through it, erupting in waterfalls and coursing through caves. Ducks, pelicans, herons, raccoons, iguanas, and butterflies live at the base, which can be viewed from five lookout points off the highway; the two-hour trip via *colectivo* (shared van or minibus) costs $4 per person for a minimum of 12 persons. As you visit the canyon, think about the fate of the Chiapa Indians, who jumped into it rather than face slavery at the hands of the Spaniards. Boat trips to the hydroelectric dam in Chicoasen and back depart daily between 7 AM and 4 PM from the tiny island of Cahuaré and the dock at Chiapa de Corzo; they take approximately two hours and cost about $6 per person (there's a four-person minimum). You can rent your own boat for about $40.

THE ROAD TO PALENQUE AND BEYOND

The road from San Cristóbal to Palenque veers slightly east on Highway 199 upon leaving town, then links up to Highway 190, which heads north to Palenque. You'll pass Ococingo and the turnoff to Toniná along the first half of the journey, then Agua Azul and Misol-Há before reaching the ruins. It's hilly sierra country most of the way, and the climate will get progressively hotter the closer you get to Palenque. The vegetation will also change from mountain pine to thick, green tropical foliage. To get to Villahermosa from Palenque, head north for a short stretch on Highway 190, and then turn left onto Highway 186 at Catazajá for a leisurely drive on a fairly straight road.

Toniná

20 *98 km (60 mi) northeast of San Cristóbal.*

Between San Cristóbal and Palenque, on a dirt road running along the Jatate River in the midst of the steamy jungle, is the archaeological site of Toniná. Currently under exploration, this site is closely linked to Palenque. Excavations indicate that the vanquished rulers of Palenque and Yaxchilán were brought here as prisoners for execution. To date, several ball courts and the main pyramid platform, taller than those of Tikal and Teotihuacán, have been uncovered, and an on-site museum was scheduled to open in 1997. As one of the last major ceremonial centers to flourish before the Maya decline in this area, Toniná, with its monumental architecture and noteworthy sculptures, is rapidly adding to our knowledge of Maya civilization. The site can be reached by following the dirt road from Ocosingo, off Route 199. *$2.* ⏲ *9–4.*

Lodging

$$ **Rancho Esmeralda.** This new rustic hotel on a macadamia nut farm has wooden cabins, no electricity or phones, and is a 10-minute walk from the ruins. There's a common bathhouse and outhouses; meals are

available at extra cost. The place is run by a couple of ex-pats who can arrange air excursions to the ruins of Bonampak and Yaxchilán. ✉ *Apartado 68, Ococsingo, Chiapas,* ☎FAX *967/3–07–11. Turnoff ½ mi before reaching Toniná along the dirt road. 5 cabins. No credit cards.*

Agua Azul

㉑ *68 km (42 mi) northwest of Toniná.*

The series of waterfalls at Agua Azul are breathtaking to behold as they surge and foam in and out of small gorges during their slow descent to earth. Unfortunately, since a road to the falls was cleared in the 1980s, the place has been littered with food shacks; the government is currently cleaning it up. Swimming is permitted. The cataracts are surrounded by giant palm fronds and tropical flowers; monkeys and toucans frolic in the vicinity.

Misol-Há

㉒ *42 km (26 mi) northeast of Agua Azul, 18 km (11 mi) southwest of Palenque.*

Smaller than the falls at Agua Azul (☞ *above*), the cascades at Misol-Há are also less littered with vendors and trash. Swimming is permitted in the pool formed by the 100-ft cascade, surrounded by oversize tropical vegetation. Rustic rest rooms, restaurants, and campgrounds are available here.

Palenque

㉓ *177 km (110 mi) northeast of San Cristóbal de las Casas, 150 km (95 mi) southeast of Villahermosa.*

The ruins of Palenque are to many people the most beautiful in all Mexico. Chichén Itzá may be more expansive, and Teotihuácan more monumental, but Palenque possesses a mesmerizing quality, perhaps because of its intimacy. It is, after all, just a cluster of white buildings intermingled with grassy mounds and tall palm groves set in a rain forest. But in the early morning or late afternoon, sunlight illuminates the structures in a hazy, iridescent glow; birds call shrilly and eerily, and the local Indians, descendants of the Maya, wander about collecting banana leaves, oranges, and avocados. Whether or not visitors are archaeology fans, they cannot fail to be moved by the sanctity of Palenque.

Antonio de Solis, a Spanish priest, accidently dug into a buried wall of Palenque in 1740 while he was trying to plant crops; in 1805 a royal Spanish expedition made its way to Palenque to follow up on the discovery. In 1832 an eccentric German count, Jean-Frederic Maximilien de Waldeck, set up house with his mistress for a year in a building known today as the **Templo del Conde** (Temple of the Count). American explorers John Lloyd Stephens and Frederick Catherwood lived briefly in the palace during their 1840 expedition. In 1923 serious excavations began under the direction of Franz Blom, cofounder of Na-Bolom in San Cristóbal. Work continued intermittently until 1952, when Alberto Ruz Lhuillier, a Mexican archaeologist, uncovered the tomb of the 7th-century ruler Pacal beneath the Temple of the Inscriptions.

Seeing Palenque, one can understand why archaeologist Sylvanus Morley honored the Maya as the "Greeks of the New World." The most important buildings of the site date from the mid- to late-classic period (6th–9th centuries), although it was inhabited as early as 1500 BC. At its zenith, Palenque dominated the greater part of Tabasco and Chiapas. The site was abandoned around AD 800 for reasons still hotly

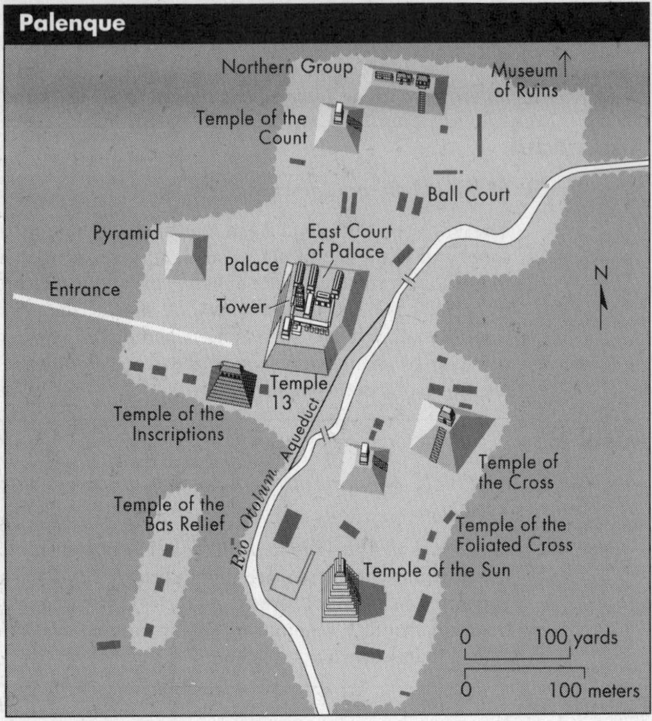

disputed, making it one of the earliest Maya sites to be deserted in a west-to-east extinction pattern.

Palenque marks the architectural apogee of the western Maya empire, with its mastery of the ability to model stucco, ceramic, and stone into ornate but ethereal-looking designs. The rulers of Palenque had no interest in freestanding sculpture, so you will find no stelae here. Artificial terraces were built to support the temples, which surrounded plazas, a ball court, altars, and burial grounds. The temples themselves had a complex array of corridors, narrow subterranean stairways, and galleries; they served as fortresses in time of war.

Since the early 1970s, groundbreaking work has been done on the Maya by archaeologists, linguists, and astronomers. The ruling priest-kings communicated life at Palenque in elaborate glyphs and reliefs on the temples. The deciphering of a good portion of Palenque's hieroglyphics in 1988 has revolutionized scholars' understanding of both the Maya and the bloody history of Palenque. Only 800 out of thousands of glyphs have been deciphered so far, but they have already revealed the complex history of the Palenque dynasties.

In its heyday, Palenque encompassed more than 128 square km (50 square mi); only about 25% of the site has been excavated. Since late 1994, a huge portion of the ruins around the Temple of the Inscriptions has been reconstructed and can be visited. In addition, explanations in Spanish, English, and Tzotzil have been placed at all major buildings.

The first temple you see on your right as you enter the site is the reconstructed **Temple of the Skull,** which was once painted red and blue. A skull-shape stucco relief, presumed to be that of a rabbit, was found at the small entrance to the temple and can be reached by climbing the stairway.

At the left of this temple, past Temple 13, is a 75-ft pyramid, the **Temple of the Inscriptions.** Reaching the tomb inside involves a relatively easy, if slow, climb. The pyramid is dedicated to Pacal, the "Mesoamerican Charlemagne," who took Palenque to its most glorious heights during his 28- to 38-year reign, which ended circa AD 692. (Pacal became ruler at the age of 12 and died between the ages of 40 and 50.)

Once at the summit, take a good, long look around you, particularly at the imposing palace to your right, which fills the field of vision. This is the best view of Palenque, and it provides an excellent orientation to the other buildings. Atop this temple and the smaller surrounding temples are vestiges of roof combs—delicate vertical extensions that resemble ornamental hair combs worn by Spanish women—one of the most distinctive architectural features of the southern Mayas. Then descend 80 ft down a steep, damp flight of stairs into the tomb, one of the first crypts ever found inside a Mexican pyramid. (This is not for claustrophobes.) Pacal's remains along with his diadem and majestic jade, shell, and obsidian mask are in Mexico City's Museum of Anthropology. The intricately carved sarcophagus lid, weighing some 5 tons and measuring 10 by 7 ft, however, remains. A "psychoduct," or hollow stone tube in the shape of a snake through which Pacal's soul was thought to have passed to the netherworld, leads up to the temple. It can be difficult to make out the carvings on the slab, but they depict Pacal, prostrate beneath a sacred ceiba tree. The lords of the nine underworlds are carved into stucco reliefs on the walls around him. ⏲ *Tomb daily 10:30–4.*

In 1994, the small and unassuming **Temple 13** attached to the Temple of the Inscriptions revealed a royal tomb hidden in its depths. The tomb, which probably belonged to Pacal's mother or grandmother, is under investigation on site and will return public view in the future.

Built at different times, the **Palace** is a complex of patios, galleries, and other buildings set on a 30-ft-high platform. Stucco work adorns the pillars of the galleries and the inner courtyards. There are numerous friezes and masks inside, most of them depicting Pacal and his dynasty. Steam baths in the Southwestern Patio suggest that priests once dwelled in the adjoining cellars. One building called the Tower was built on three levels, representing the three levels of the universe as well as the movement of the stars.

To the right of the Palace you'll cross the tiny Otulum River, which in ancient times was roofed over to form a 9-ft-high vaulted causeway, or aqueduct. It leads to the reconstructed **Plaza of the Cross,** which contains the Temple of the Exfoliated Cross, Temple of the Sun, Temple 14, and the Temple of the Cross, the largest of the group. Inside Temple 14, there's an underworld scene in stucco relief, done 260 days after Pacal died. The most exquisite roof combs are found on these buildings, which are now, thankfully, open to the public.

To reach the cluster called the **Northern Group,** walk north along the river, passing the palace and then the unexcavated ball court on your left. This group includes five buildings in varying states of disrepair, of which the largest and best preserved is the Temple of the Count.

A short hike northwest of the Northern Group lies **Grupo C,** an area containing remains of the homes of Maya nobles and a few small temples completely shrouded in jungle. In order to maintain the natural setting in which the ruins were found, minimal restoration is being done. Human burials, funeral offerings of Jaina figurines, ceramics, and kitchen utensils have been found here as well as in **Grupo B,** near a small waterfall called El Baño de la Reina (The Queen's Bath). Early explorers cut pathways through the area, which can still be followed down through two meandering creeks with footbridges.

A **museum,** which opened in 1994, has a remarkable collection of finely preserved heads of Maya deities in elaborate zoomorphic headdresses, discovered in front of the Temple of the Foliated Cross; the group includes 13 different figures of the sun god Kinich Ahau. Also noteworthy are the handsome stucco faces of Maya men; their realistic style can be compared to that of ancient Greek sculpture. The displays are labeled in English, Spanish, and Tzotzil. In addition, there's a snack bar and a very good handicrafts store. Sponsored by the Mexican Family Institute (DIF), it has weavings, hand-embroidered fabrics, leather, ceramics, amber jewelry, hand-painted wooden crosses, and children's toys. The museum, about a kilometer (½ mile) before the parking lot entrance to the ruins along the highway, is open Tuesday–Sunday 9–4:15. You can visit before entering the ruins or get there by walking through the Grupo C and B sections of the ruins, which end at the highway. The museum is about 100 yards away. Entrance is free with your purchased ticket to the ruins area; otherwise it's around $2.

The ruins are open daily 9–5, and there is an admission charge of about $2. You can hire one of Palenque's multilingual guides at the ticket booth.

Palenque Town

㉔ *8 km (5 mi) east of the ruins.*

Whereas cool highlander San Cristóbal presents a polite but reserved exterior to the visitor, tropical Palenque town is all hugs and kisses. Still, its days as a sleepy little cattle town are far behind, as more tourists interested in visiting the ruins discover it. In only the last few years, Palenque Town has turned into a sparkling little tourist center with upgraded services like cellular phones, signage identifying major attractions in town, public long-distance telephone booths, satellite color TV in hotel rooms, a money-exchange house, and, on the highway to Palenque, its first ATM machine. Shops on the main street look less tacky than before and are selling higher-quality regional crafts.

The principal landmark in Palenque town is the "cabeza Maya," a giant sculpture of the head of a Maya chieftain that graces the town's one traffic circle.

Dining and Lodging

$$ ✕ **La Selva.** This spacious palapa-roof restaurant wrapped in jungle gardens serves good local cuisine. ✉ *Carr. Ruinas Km 5,* ☎ *934/5–03–63. No credit cards.*

$ ★ ✕ **The Maya.** The most famous restaurant in Palenque, if not the whole state, the Maya is a plain-looking eatery where service can be slow. The place exudes such local ambience, however, that it's always packed. Try *huevos chiapanecos* (eggs scrambled in fried tortilla chips) for breakfast, or the *pollo Palenque* (chicken cooked in beer) for lunch or dinner. ✉ *Corner of Hidalgo and Independencia, in front of town park,* ☎ *934/5–00–42. No credit cards.*

$$$ ★ **Misión Palenque.** A lovely resort property, surrounded by several acres of tropical gardens and resembling a private estate from the outside, Misión Palenque is the only luxury hotel in town. The lobby is a sweeping affair set off with elegant dark-wood paneling, and the terraced restaurant glows with candlelight at night. Located on the north side of town off Route 199, it offers a free shuttle bus to the ruins. All rooms are air-conditioned and have a terrace, minibar, and phone. ✉ *Rancho San Martín de Porres, 29960,* ☎ *934/5–03–00 or 934/5–04–*

44; 800/221–6509 in the U.S.; FAX 934/5–04–55. 144 rooms. Restaurant, bar, pool, tennis court, travel services. AE, DC, MC, V.

$$ ★ **Chan Kah.** Four kilometers (2½ miles) from the ruins in a paradisiacal jungle setting that is also a forest reserve, Chan Kah has a stone-lined, lagoon-style pool, a resident spider monkey, fox, and raccoon, aromatic jasmine bushes, and a stream flowing around the back. The restaurant is overpriced, and meals are accompanied by Muzak and movie sound tracks, but the 14 bungalows have mahogany furnishings and all but three have ceiling fans (not helpful in combatting the humidity); bungalows 6 through 10 offer views of both the pool and the stream. ✉ *Carr. Ruinas Km 3.5, 29960, ☎ 934/5–11–00, 934/5–07–62, 934/5–08–26, or 934/5–09–74; FAX 934/5–08–20. 38 units. Restaurant, bar, pool. MC, V.*

$$ **Nututún Calinda Viva Palenque.** This property, a member of the Choice Hotels International chain, was in need of an upgrading at press time. Although it has light-filled, air-conditioned rooms with color satellite TVs, phones, and simple wooden furnishings, the air-conditioning leaks and the furniture looks worn out. The real draw is the natural pool, which forms from a river running through the grounds. The restaurant is worth trying, even if you're not staying here. ✉ *Apdo. 74, Carr. Ruinas Km 3.5, 29960, ☎ 934/5–01–00 or 934/5–01–61; 800/221–2222 in the U.S.; FAX 934/5–06–33. 60 rooms. Restaurant, bar, pool. AE, DC, MC, V.*

$$ **Plaza Palenque Best Western.** This pleasant, low-slung hotel, opened in 1992 on the outskirts of town, was custom-built for tropical Palenque: A large, airy marble lobby leads to an inviting pool for cooling off in the heat of the day, and the place is decorated in equally cool pastels. In 1996 a gymnasium was added. Turn-of-the century *National Geographic* photos of the ruins of Palenque are hung in the restaurant. Rooms, which open onto the garden, all have air-conditioning, color TVs, and two double beds; two suites have minibars. ✉ *Carr. Ruinas Km 27, 29960, ☎ 934/5–05–55; 800/334–7234 in the U.S.; FAX 934/5–03–95. 100 rooms. Restaurant, bar, pool, shop, meeting rooms. AE, MC, V.*

$ **Tulija.** You can't beat the price or location of this cheerful little hotel, about a 10-minute walk from downtown. Part of the Days Inn chain since late 1995, it has a fresh open-air lobby, a warm, efficient staff, and the basics for a comfortable stay: Color satellite TVs, air-conditioning, and phones in the smallish rooms, some of which face the garden. ✉ *Apdo. 57, Carr. Ruinas Km 27.5, 29960, ☎ 934/5–01–04 or 934/5–01–65; 800/325–2525 in the U.S.; FAX 934/5–01–63. 48 rooms. Restaurant, bar, pool. MC, V.*

Bonampak

25 *183 km (114 mi) southeast of Palenque.*

Because access is difficult, only the most devoted fans of the Maya will attempt the trip to the ruins of Bonampak and Yaxchilán (☞ *below*). Both sites can be reached by making arrangements for a small chartered plane in Palenque, Tuxtla Gutiérrez, or San Cristóbal. A road that will connect Bonampak with Yaxchilán was not yet complete at press time. Whether you go on a tour or travel independently, wear sturdy shoes, carry insect repellent, good sunglasses, and a hat to protect yourself from mosquitoes, ticks, sand flies, undergrowth, and the jungle sun.

Bonampak is renowned for its vivid murals of ancient Maya life, though some segments of them are sadly deteriorated. The murals are under constant restoration because the high humidity in the area eats away at the colors, and thick white deposits of calcium from dripping water have covered some of them over completely. In 1984, Mexican experts devised a technique for cleaning and restoring the murals, and with the help of the National Geographic Society, using digital amplification with computers, remarkable details and color have come to light. (Still, the reproductions at the archaeological museums in Mexico City and Villahermosa are better than the on-site specimens.)

Bonampak was built on the banks of the Lacanjá River during the 7th and 8th centuries and remained undiscovered until 1946. Explorer Jacques Soustelle called it "a pictorial encyclopedia of a Mayan city." Indeed, the scenes portrayed in the three rooms of the **Templo de las Pinturas** graphically recall subjects such as life at court and the prelude and aftermath of battle. *$2. Daily 9–5.*

Yaxchilán

26 *50 km (32 mi) northeast of Bonampak.*

Excavations at Yaxchilán (Ya-she-*lan*), bordering the Usumicinta River, have uncovered captivating temples and carvings in a superb jungle setting. Yaxchilán, which means "place of green stones," is a contemporary of Bonampak. It is dominated by two acropolises containing a palace, temples with finely carved lintels, and great staircases. Until very recently, the Lacandon, who live in the vicinity, made pilgrimages to this site in the heart of the jungle, leaving behind "god pots" (incense-filled ceramic bowls) in honor of ancient deities. They were particularly awed by the headless sculpture of Xachtun (Washa-*tun*) at the entrance to the temple (called structure 33) and believe that the world will end when its head is replaced on its torso.

Yaxchilán was situated on the trade route between Palenque and Tikal, and the existence of a 600-ft bridge crossing the Usumacinta River to connect Yaxchilán to Guatemalan territory was discovered. The engineering know-how of the people of Yaxchilán is still being deciphered by modern-day engineers. The site has been threatened with destruction by a huge dam to be built by Mexico and Guatemala. The plans have been put on hold due to lack of funds, though they may yet come to fruition. *$2. Daily 9–5.*

VILLAHERMOSA AND TABASCO

Graham Greene's succinct summation of Tabasco as a "tropical state of river and swamp and banana grove" captures its essence. Though the state played an important role in the early history of Mexico, its past is rarely on view; instead, it is Tabasco's modern-day status as a supplier of oil that defines it. Set on a humid coastal plain and crisscrossed by 1,930 km (1,200 mi) of rivers, low hills, and unexplored jungles, the land is still rich in banana and cacao plantations but occasionally marred by shantytowns and refineries reeking of sulfur. The capital city of Villahermosa epitomizes the mercurial development of Tabasco (the airplane was here before the automobile). Thanks to oil and urban renewal, the cramped and ugly neighborhoods in the mosquito-ridden town of the 1970s have been replaced by spacious boulevards, lush green parks, cultural centers, and beautiful buildings.

This is not to say that the rest of Tabasco has nothing to offer the visitor. There are beaches, lagoons, caves, and nature reserves, but the tourist infrastructure is minimal. The fired-brick Maya ruins of Comalcalco attest to the influence of Palenque. Probably the most interesting region is the one to the south and east of Villahermosa, where rivers and canyons are home to jaguars, deer, and alligators; this was where the English pirate Sir Francis Drake hid from the Spaniards.

Tabasco—specifically the mouth of the River Grijalva—lay along the route of the Spanish explorations of Mexico in 1518–19. At that time, the state's rivers and waterways, along which the Olmecs and the Maya lived, served as a trade route between the peoples of the north and those of the south. When the Spaniards came to Tabasco, they had to bridge 50 rivers and contend with swarms of mosquitoes, beetles, and ants, as well as with almost unbearable heat, but the region was so lush that one early chronicler termed it a Garden of Eden.

The Spanish conquest was made easier by the state of almost constant tribal warfare between the Tabascans and their Aztec overlords. Among the 20 slave women turned over to the victors was a Chiapan named Malintzín, who was singled out by the Spaniards for her ability to speak both the Maya and the Nahuatl languages. Called Marina by the Spaniards, she learned Spanish and became not only Cortés's mistress and the mother of his illegitimate son but also the willing interpreter of Indian customs. Marina's cooperation helped the conquistador trounce both Moctezuma and Cuauhtémoc, the last Aztec rulers.

Until the early 20th century Tabasco slumbered; it did not become a state until 1924. After the American Civil War, traders from the southern United States began operating in the region and on its rivers, hauling the precious mahogany trees upstream from Chiapas and shipping them north from the small port of Frontera. This was Tabasco's most prosperous era until the discovery of oil 50 years ago and the oil boom of the 1980s. Although PEMEX (the government-run oil monopoly) was plagued with workers' strikes throughout 1995 in Villahermosa, the oil company plans to relocate its research offices there.

Villahermosa

27 *821 km (503 mi) southeast of Mexico City, 632 km (398 mi) southwest of Mérida.*

There are a good many ways to spend your time in Tabasco's capital. Downtown Villahermosa contains a pedestrian street with beautifully restored colonial buildings, a museum of popular culture, and a folk-art shop, but the **Carlos Pellicer Camera Museo de Antropologia** (Museum of Anthropology) should be seen first. Named after the man who donated many of the artifacts and whom the locals call the "poet laureate of Latin America," the museum is on the right bank of the Grijalva and is part of the huge CICOM cultural complex dedicated to research on the Olmec and Maya (which is what the Spanish acronym CICOM stands for). It provides one of the last tranquil vistas of Villahermosa as it might have looked 50 years ago. Although all the explanations are in Spanish, that should not detract from the visual pleasure of the displays.

The entire ground floor is devoted to Tabasco and the Olmec, or "inhabitants of the land of rubber," who flourished in Tabasco as early as 1200 to 1300 BC and disappeared about 800 years later. The Olmecs have long been honored as inventors of the numerical and calendrical systems that spread throughout the region; the pyramid is also attributed to them. Some of the most interesting artifacts of the Olmec, other than the giant stone heads on view at Parque Museo La Venta (☞ *below*), are the remnants of their jaguar cult displayed here. The jaguar symbolized the earth fertilized by rain, and many Olmec sculptures portray werejaguars (half-human, half-jaguar, similar to werewolves) or jaguar babies. Other sculptures portray human heads emerging from the mouth of a jaguar, bat gods, bird-headed humans, and female fertility figurines. The collection of burial urns, found in the Tapijulapa caves west of Palenque, is outstanding.

All of Mexico's ancient cultures are represented on the upper two floors, from the red-clay dogs of Colima and the nose rings of the Huichol Indians of Nayarit to the huge burial urns of the Chontal Maya, who built Comalcalco. The CICOM building complex also houses a theater, restaurant, and handicrafts shop. ✉ *Carlos Pellicer 511, an extension of the malecón,* ☎ *93/12–95–21.* 🎟 *About 40¢.* ⏲ *Daily 9–8.*

The giant stone heads carved by the Olmec and salvaged from the oil fields of La Venta, on the western edge of Tabasco near the state of Veracruz, are on display in **Parque Museo La Venta,** situated west of CICOM in a tropical garden on the beautiful Lago de las Ilusiones (Lake of Illusions) founded also by Carlos Pellicer. These 6-ft-tall, African-featured heads, wearing helmets and weighing upwards of 20 tons, have sparked endless scholarly debate. It has been theorized that they depict ancient Phoenician slaves who wound up on the coasts of Mexico, that they were meant to represent space invaders, and that because of the obesity and short limbs of the figures, they are proof of endocrine deficiencies among the ancient Olmec. The latest theory is that the faces on the sculptures—very similar to today's Tabasco Maya—represent actual rulers of the Olmec. La Venta contains 33 sculptures, not all of them heads. There are also jaguars, priests, monsters, stelae, and stone altars oddly reminiscent of ancient Mesopotamian art. The park also has a tiny **zoo** with creatures such as Tabascan river crocodiles, deer, coatimundi, monkeys, and wild parrots.

A small natural history museum, the **Museo del Historia Natural,** is located just outside the entrance to the park, to the left of the admission booths. It's filled with attractive displays of Tabasco's native plants and animal species, which are now under government protection. ✉ *Blvd. Ruíz Cortines near Paseo Tabasco,* ☎ *93/15–22–28.* 🎟 *Museum, zoo, and park about $1.50; park only 90¢.* ⏲ *Tues.–Sun. 9–5, Mon. 8–4.*

One of Villahermosa's newest attractions is **Yumka',** a nature reserve spread over 250 acres of jungle, savannah, and wetlands; guided tours picked up at the entrance to the reserve will take you over a hanging bridge and past free-roaming endangered or threatened species like spider monkeys, red macaws, toucans, crocodiles, turtles, and native tepezcuintles, a variety of giant rodent; boat tours glide past birds wading or taking flight. ✉ *16 km (10 mi) from downtown past the airport at Poblado Dos Montes,* ☎ *93/56–01–07.* 🎟 *$5.* ⏲ *Daily 9–5.*

Dining and Lodging

$$ ✕ **El Mesón del Duende.** This restaurant, which translates as the House of the Elf, adds a regional accent to standard meat and fish dishes. Try the house favorites, *filete en salsa de espinaca y queso* (beef fillet in a cheese and spinach sauce) and *la posta de robalo* (snook grilled in butter). The modest decor is in keeping with the family-style atmosphere. ✉ *Gregorio Méndez 1703,* ☎ *93/15–13–24. AE, MC, V. Closed Wed.*

$$ ★ ✕ **Los Tulipanes.** Next door to the CICOM Museum, the spacious Los Tulipanes specializes in steaks and seafood and has a tranquil view of the river. Try the stuffed crab, shrimp, or the Tabasco specialty, pejelagarto, a succulent treat. ✉ *Carlos Pellicer 511,* ☎ *93/12–92–09 or 93/12–92–17. AE, MC, V.*

$ ✕ **Leo.** This popular spot for tasty beef and pork tacos, with a large menu and a spacious dining area, is frequented by local artists and students. ✉ *Paseo Tabasco 429,* ☎ *93/12–44–63. MC, V.*

$$$ **Holiday Inn.** Situated across from La Choca Park, this inviting nine-story resort property offers air-conditioned rooms with cable TV, minibars, and room service. The rambling lobby, with attractive niches and corners and rattan furniture, eventually leads to the Tabasco 2000 shopping mall, which has the largest number of upscale stores in Villahermosa. A restaurant below the hotel lobby has floor-to-ceiling windows shaded by bamboo curtains and a lovely garden view. There's live entertainment in the lobby lounge nightly except Sunday. At press time, a badly needed remodeling of the hotel was scheduled to be completed by fall 1997. ✉ *Paseo Tabasco 1407, 86030,* ☎ *93/16–44–00 or 800/465–4329,* FAX *93/16–45–69. 190 rooms. Restaurant, bar, coffee shop, pool, exercise room, meeting rooms, travel services, car rental. AE, DC, MC, V.*

$$$ **Hyatt Regency Villahermosa.** This American-style luxury hotel built in 1983 offers the amenities of the worldwide Hyatt chain: air-conditioned rooms with cable TV, voice mail, and minibars, plus two executive floors with concierge service. Marble floors are replacing the rugs in all rooms. The coffee shop has pleasing tropical decor, and the popular **El Plataforma** video bar in the lobby is decked out like the inside of an offshore oil platform with photos of oilmen at work. The lobby bar has live music nightly at 8. ✉ *Av. Juárez 106, Zona Hotelera, 86050,* ☎ *93/13–44–44, 93/15–12–34, or 800/228–9000;* FAX *93/15–58–08 or 93/15–12–35. 211 rooms. 2 restaurants, 3 bars, pool, 2 tennis courts, travel services, car rental. AE, DC, MC, V.*

$$ **Calinda Viva Villahermosa.** This member of the Choice Hotels International chain has an attractive whitewashed exterior reminiscent of a hacienda and a spacious lobby decorated in earth tones that has an Old Mexico feel. The hotel's restaurant, in fact, is named **La Hacienda** and serves many regional dishes, like tamales with chipílin herb and cream of *chaya* (a spinachlike plant) soup. The staff is helpful. All rooms have air-conditioning, FM stereos, color TVs, and phones; many have balconies. ✉ *Paseo Tabasco 1201, 86050,* ☎ *93/15–00–00 or 800/221–2222,* FAX *93/15–30–73. 241 rooms. Restaurant, 2 bars, coffee shop, pool, dance club. AE, DC, MC, V.*

$$ **Cencali.** This colonial-style hotel in the hotel zone is situated in a park and surrounded by lakes and lush greenery; it has the best view in town. All the cheerfully decorated rooms have lots of light and vistas of either the lakes or the lagoon; 30 of the best also have balconies looking out over coconut palm, guava, and almond trees. All the accommodations are air-conditioned. ✉ *Av. Juárez and Paseo Tabasco, 86040,* ☎ *93/15–19–94 through 93/15–19–99,* FAX *93/15–66–00. 116 rooms, 3 suites. Restaurant, bar, pool. AE, DC, MC, V.*

$$ **Maya Tabasco Best Western.** The Maya Tabasco offers rooms with air-conditioning, TVs, and phones; a rather plain lobby; a gift shop; and an energetic staff. This is the best hotel in the neighborhood near the crowded downtown area and will do if all other hotels listed are full. ✉ *Ruíz Cortines 907, 86000,* ☎ *93/14–44–66, 93/14–03–60, or 800/528–1234;* FAX *93/12–10–97. 156 rooms. 2 restaurants, bar, pool, dance club, meeting rooms. AE, DC, MC, V.*

$ **Don Carlos.** Formerly the Manzur, this downtown hotel has always been popular for its unpretentious atmosphere and good service. TVs and phones are available in every room, and all the suites have minibars. ✉ *Av. Madero 422, 86000,* ☎ *93/12–24–99,* FAX *93/12–46–22. 80 rooms, 14 suites. Restaurant, bar, lounge. AE, MC, V.*

Comalcalco

28 *60 km (37 mi) northwest of Villahermosa off Route 187.*

Comalcalco, which means "place of the clay griddles (bricks)" in Nahuatl, is the most important Maya site in Tabasco. The abundant cacao trees in the region provided food and livelihood for a booming population during the late classic period (AD 600–900), when Comalcalco was built; the site marks the westernmost reach of the Maya. Descendants of the Chontal Maya, who constructed Comalcalco, still live in the vicinity. This site is unique among Maya cities for its use of fired brick (made of sand, seashells, and clay), as the Tabasco swamplands lacked the stone for building that was found elsewhere in the Maya empire. The bricks were inscribed and painted with figures of reptiles, birds, geometric figures, and drawings of hands and feet before being covered with stucco. The major pyramid, **Temple IV,** on the Great Eastern Acropolis, is decorated with large stucco masks of the sun god Kinich Ahau and carvings, and the **museum** houses many of the artifacts that were uncovered there. *About $2. Daily 9–4:30.*

Paraíso

29 *19 km (12 mi) north of Comacalco.*

If not seeing the Gulf of Mexico will leave you feeling deprived, you can continue on from Comalco to the coast and Paraíso, where you'll get a glimpse of small town life and a pretty coast. Take a boat ride through channels lined with mangroves or climb nearby **Teodomiro Hill** for a spectacular view of Las Flores lagoon and coconut plantations. Small seafood restaurants and several small hotels dot the shore here; others are a few kilometers inland, in town.

CHIAPAS AND TABASCO A TO Z

Arriving and Departing

By Bus

PALENQUE

First- and second-class service is available from Villahermosa (1½ hrs), San Cristóbal (5 hrs), Mexico City (14 hrs), Mérida (8 hrs), Campeche (6 hrs), and Tuxtla Gutiérrez (9 hrs). In Palenque, the **ADO** and **Cristóbal Colón** buses leave from the terminal at Cinco de Mayo and Juárez (☎ 934/5–00–00).

SAN CRISTÓBAL

The **Cristóbal Colón** terminal in San Cristóbal is at Avenida Insurgentes and Pan American Highway (Hwy. 190, ☎ 967/8–02–91). Second-class service on **Transportes Tuxtla Express Plus** (☎ 967/8–48–69) to Tuxtla, Palenque, and Guatemala departs from the terminal at Allende and Pan American Highway.

TUXTLA GUTIÉRREZ

Omnibus Cristóbal Colón (✉ Av. 2 Norte Pte., ☎ 961/2–16–39 or 961/2–26–24) offers deluxe and first- and second-class bus service between Tuxtla and Oaxaca, Palenque, Villahermosa, Tapachula, Mérida, Mexico City, and San Cristóbal.

VILLAHERMOSA

There is frequent second-class service to Campeche, Chetumal, Mérida, Mexico City, Palenque, San Cristóbal, Tapachula, Tuxtla Gutiérrez, Veracruz, and elsewhere. Buses arrive and depart from **Central Camionera de 2nd Clase** (✉ Av. Ruíz Cortines s/n, ☎ 93/12–41–84 or 93/12–

16–89). Deluxe and first-class service is available to the above cities at the **ADO** bus terminal (✉ Calle F.J. Mina 297), which is serviced by **ADO** (☎ 93/12–76–27 or 93/12–14–46), **UNO** (☎ 93/14–58–18), **G.L.** (☎ 93/12–76–27), and **Cristóbal Colón** (☎ 93/12–89–00).

By Car

From Tuxtla Gutiérrez, Highway 190 goes east through Chiapa de Corzo to San Cristóbal before continuing southeast to Comitán and the Guatemalan border. Highway 199 to Highway 186 (the turnoff is at Catazajá) is the preferred route from San Cristóbal to Villahermosa; it'll take you via Toniná, Agua Azul, and Palenque. The drive from San Cristóbal to Palenque takes about five hours along a winding paved road, and it's another 90 minutes from Palenque to Villahermosa along a fairly straight road. On the map, Highway 195 may look like the most direct way to travel between San Cristóbal and Villahermosa, but it entails hours upon hours of hairpin curves; it's only for the stalwart and absolutely not to be traveled at night because of seasonal fog as well as a lack of reflectors, illumination, and other cars to help in case of emergency. To get to Villahermosa from Coatzacoalcos and Veracruz, take Highway 180. In all cases, exercise caution during the rainy season (June through October), when the roads are slick. Though expensive, car rentals are available at the Tuxtla and Villahermosa airports as well as in San Cristóbal (☞ Car Rentals, *below*).

By Plane

BONAMPAK AND YAXCHILÁN

For charter flights to the ruins of Bonampak and Yaxchilán, contact **Montes Azules** (☎ 961/3–22–56 or 961/3–22–93), an air charter company in Tuxtla Gutiérrez, or **Servicios Aereos Cristóbal** (☎ 967/8–42–23), in Comitán, an hour by road from San Cristóbal de las Casas.

PALENQUE

Chartered flights are available through travel agencies in Tuxtla Gutiérrez, San Cristóbal, and Villahermosa. **Aerocaribe** (☎ 934/5–06–18) has nonstop or connecting flights to and from Acapulco, Cancún, Merida, Vellahermosa, Huatulco, and Chetumal.

SAN CRISTÓBAL

The closest major airport is in Tuxtla Gutiérrez (☞ *below*), 85 km (53 mi) to the west. San Cristóbal's intended airport has been indefinitely postponed. The easiest way to get from Tuxtla to San Cristóbal is by taxi. The two-hour ride costs about $13 for one to four persons. Many travel agencies in both cities provide private taxi service. By car, follow Route 190. First-class bus service on Cristóbal Colon costs under $4. You can also catch a colectivo to San Cristóbal at either of the two airports in Tuxtla Gutiérrez: From the Mexicana airport, it costs about $5 per person; from the Aviasca airport, $3 per person.

TUXTLA GUTIÉRREZ

Mexicana (☎ 961/2–00–20 or 961/2–20–53, FAX 961/1–14–90; ☎ 961/3–49–21 at airport) flies nonstop from Mexico City to the Tuxtla airport, which is in the town of Ocozocoautla, 22 km (14 mi) west. **Aviacsa** (☎ 961/2–80–81, FAX 961/3–50–29 in Tuxtla; ☎ FAX 961/5–10–11 at airport) also operates daily flights from Mexico City. Note: Mexicana uses the Tuxtla airport, which is frequently fogged in; Aviacsa flies into Aeropuerto Fco. Sarabia, which is not. In 1994, Mexicana got permission to use Aviacsa's airport in foggy weather.

VILLAHERMOSA

Aeromexico (☎ 93/12–15–28 or 93/12–95–54) has daily nonstop service from Mexico City. **Mexicana** (☎ 93/16–31–32 or 93/16–31–33) has three daily nonstop flights from Mexico City, and both airlines offer connecting flights to other Mexican cities. **Aerocaribe** (☎ 93/16–50–46) flies here with nonstop or connecting flights (☞ Palenque, *above*).

By Train

PALENQUE

Daily trains from Mexico City take at least 24 hours and are very uncomfortable. First-class service from Mérida takes 11 hours; second-class service makes more stops and takes 16 hours. The train station is 10 km (6 mi) from town.

Getting Around

Palenque

Visitors with a car or those taking a tour through a local travel agency will have the easiest time reaching both Palenque and its surrounding attractions; inexpensive colectivo service to the ruins is also available from town at the corner of Hidalgo and Allende. The local *sitio* (taxi stand) is at the town park (☎ 934/5–01–12). The town itself is small enough to traverse on foot.

San Cristóbal

As with many other colonial towns, the most enjoyable and thorough way to explore San Cristóbal is on foot. Trying to maneuver a car on its narrow, cobblestone streets filled with pedestrians is a needless test of patience. If you do come to town with a car, leave it in the hotel garage until you're ready to take an excursion outside San Cristóbal. Taxis cruise the streets and can also be found at the sitio next to the cathedral (☎ 967/8–03–96); there is colectivo service to outlying villages, departing from and returning to the market.

Villahermosa

Villahermosa is surrounded by three rivers but oriented toward the River Grijalva to the east, which is bordered by the *malecón* (boardwalk). The city is huge, and driving can be tricky. The main road through town is almost a highway; exit ramps are about 1 km (½ mi) apart, and tourist destinations are not clearly marked. Most taxi service is collective and runs along fixed routes, but if an empty one comes along, the driver will gladly take you to where you want to go. Hotels can also call a private cab. Information about city buses can be difficult to find.

Contacts and Resources

Car Rental

SAN CRISTÓBAL

Budget (✉ Calle Diego de Mazariegos 36, ☎ 967/8–18–71 or 967/8–31–00).

TUXTLA GUTIÉRREZ

Budget (☎ 961/5–13–82 or 961/5–76–72) and **Dollar** (☎ 961/2–52–61 or 961/2–89–32) are both represented at the Tuxtla airport.

VILLAHERMOSA

Avis, Budget, Hertz, and **National** have offices in town and at the airport. Reliable local companies include **Tabasco Auto Rent** (✉ Blvd. Ruíz Cortines 1201, ☎ 93/2–80–03 or 93/12–34–69) and **Rentauto Usumacinta** (✉ Hotel Cencali, ☎ 93/15–18–21 or 93/12–7756; also at airport).

Emergencies

Throughout the region, dial **06** for fire, theft, and medical emergencies.

PALENQUE

Contact the office of the local **tourism delegate** (✉ Jiménez and Cinco de Mayo, ☎ 934/5-03-56), open 9-3 and 6-9 weekdays; for missing persons or cars, call **LOCATEL** (☎ 934/5-01-46 or 934/5-02-39), available 24 hours.

SAN CRISTÓBAL

Municipal police (☎ 967/8-05-54); **Federal Highway Police** (☎ 967/8-64-66); **Cruz Roja** (Red Cross; ✉ Prolongación Ignacio Allende, ☎ 967/8-07-72); **Hospital Regional** (✉ Insurgentes 26, ☎ 967/8-07-70); **Social Security Clinic** (✉ Calle Tabasco and Diagonal Centenario, outside of town, ☎ 967/8-07-68); **24-hour pharmacy** (☎ 967/8-02-41); **LOCATEL,** for missing persons and cars (☎ 967/8-32-32).

TUXTLA GUTIÉRREZ

Fire (☎ 961/2-11-15); **Police** (☎ 961/2-16-76); **Red Cross Hospital** (☎ 961/2-00-96). **24-Hour Pharmacy: Farmacia del Ahorra** (✉ Calle Central and 8 Poniente, ☎ 961/2-26-54; ✉ 9 Sur and 2 Poniente, no phone).

VILLAHERMOSA

Cruz Roja (✉ Paseo Usumacinta and Ayuntamiento, ☎ 93/13-35-93 or 93/13-34-39); **Fire and Police Department** (✉ Av. 16 de Septiembre and the Periférico, ☎ 93/13-91-42).

English-Language Bookstores

In San Cristóbal, **Chilam Balam,** the best bookstore in Mexico's southeast (✉ 3 locations at Casa Utrilla, Av. Gen. Utrilla and Dr. Navarro; Insurgentes 18; Real de Guadalupe 20) has the latest editions of travel, archeology, and art books along with posters and maps of Mexico; **La Pared** (✉ Hidalgo 2) has more than 1,500 novels and nonfiction books that you can buy, trade, or rent. Local children sell Mexico City English-language newspapers plus the *New York Times* and *London Guardian* around the main plaza at around 4 PM each afternoon. **La Mercantil** (✉ Diego Mazariegos 21) also sells these periodicals.

Guided Tours

PALENQUE

From the town of Palenque you can book day trips to the ruins of Palenque, Toniná, and waterfalls at Misol-Há and Agua Azul. Longer trips to San Cristóbal and the Sumidero Canyon are also available. Contact **Viajes Shivalva** (✉ Calle Merle Green 1A or Apdo. 237, ☎ 934/5-04-11, FAX 934/5-03-92) or **Viajes Yax-Ha** (✉ Av. Juárez 123, ☎ 934/5-07-67) for trips to Bonampak and Yaxchilán; these take five hours and cost about $300. Some trips add the Lacandon village of Lacanjá. **Ceiba Adventures** (✉ Box 2274, Flagstaff, AZ 86003, ☎ 602/527-0171, FAX 602/527-8127) offers guided adventure tours from Palenque to Bonampak and Yaxchilán, including cave explorations plus river rafting along several Chiapan waterways sunk deep in the jungle.

SAN CRISTÓBAL

Orientation Tours. Full-day city bus tours also cover the village of San Juan Chamula and the San Cristóbal Caves. Five-hour horseback tours to the caves or San Juan Chamula can also be arranged.

Personal Guides. Check with the head of the state tourism or municipal tourist offices (☞ Visitor Information, *below*) for names of licensed, bilingual guides who lead tours to San Juan Chamula, Zinacantán, and area ruins.

Regional Tours. A.T.C. (✉ Av. 5 de Febrero 15, ☎ 967/8-25-50, 967/8-25-57, 967/8-18-75, or 967/8-25-88), **Viajes Pakal** (✉ Calle Cuauhtémoc, No. 6A, ☎ 967/8-28-18 or 967/8-42-93, FAX 967/

8–28–19), **Lacantún** (✉ Calle Madero 18–21, ☎ 967/8–25–87 or 967/8–25–88), and **Viajes Pedrero** (✉ Calle Insurgentes Sur, N1 on main square, ☎ 967/8–11–40) all organize tours to Bonampak, Yaxchilán, Palenque, Agua Azul, Lagunas de Montebello, Amatenango, Chincultik, Comitán, Sumidero Canyon, and Tuxtla Gutiérrez; trips to Guatemala, the Yucatán, and Belize are also offered by the first three. The six-hour round-trip tour to Bonampak and Yaxchilán costs about $300 (possibly less, with a minimum of four people) and includes lunch. Special-interest tours and treks—Lacandon Indians, bird-watching, flora and fauna, river trips, rain-forest excursions—are also available through **Pronatura** (✉ Av. Juárez 9, ☎ 967/8–50–00); 10% of the profits go to Chiapas conservation programs. Most tour operators transport passengers in minibuses and can arrange hotel pickup. Nonprofit **Dana** (✉ Dr. Navarro 10, ☎ 967/8–04–68, FAX 967/8–43–07) offers low impact four-day guided tours to Laguna Miramar in the Lacandon rain forest with lakeside camping, swimming, snorkeling, fishing, hiking, and visits to small area ruins.

TUXTLA GUTIÉRREZ

Viajes Miramar (✉ 1A Oriente Norte 310, ☎ 961/2–39–83 or 961/2–39–30; ✉ Hotel Camino Real, local 2, ☎ 961/7–77–77, ext. 7230, FAX 961/5–59–25), run by the Fernandez sisters, offers city tours of Tuxtla Gutiérrez, plus excursions to Chiapa de Corzo and Sumidero Canyon.

VILLAHERMOSA

Agencia de Viajes Tabasco (✉ Madero 718, ☎ 93/12–53–18 or 93/12–50–96, FAX 93/14–27–80; ✉ Galeria Tabasco 2000, ☎ 93/16–40–88, FAX 93/16–43–37) and **Turismo Grijalva** (✉ Zaragoza 911, ☎ 93/14–42–04 or 93/14–42–05, FAX 93/12–25–96) both offer city tours as well as trips to Comalcalco, Palenque, and San Cristóbal.

Visitor Information

The state of Chiapas has a toll-free tourist information number, which can be dialed from anywhere in Mexico (☎ 91–800/2–80–35).

COMITÁN

Tourist office (✉ Ground floor of Municipal Palace, facing zócalo, ☎ 963/2–40–47), open Monday–Saturday 9–8:30, Sunday 9–2.

PALENQUE

Tourist information (✉ Av. Juárez and Abasolo at the Plaza de las Artesanias, ☎ 934/5–07–60), open Monday–Saturday 8:30–8:30, Sunday 9–1.

SAN CRISTÓBAL

Municipal tourist office (✉ Palacio Municipal [City Hall], ground floor, on zócalo, ☎ 967/8–06–65 or 967/8–01–35) and **State tourist office** (✉ Miguel Hidalgo 3, ½ block from zócalo, ☎ FAX 967/8–65–70), both open weekdays 9–9, Saturday 9–8, Sunday 9–2.

TUXTLA GUTIÉRREZ

Tourist office (✉ Edificio Plaza de las Instituciones, ground floor, Blvd. Dr. Belisario Domínguez 950, ☎ 961/3–93–96), open weekdays 9–3 and 6–9.

VILLAHERMOSA

Tourist Office (✉ Paseo Tabasco 1504, Tabasco 2000 complex, ☎ 93/16–28–90 or 93/16–28–89), open weekdays 9–3 and 6–8. Auxiliary office at Parque Museo La Venta open daily 9–4.

12 Northeastern Mexico and Veracruz

Many Texans get their first taste of Mexico in the northeastern border towns of Nuevo Laredo, Reynosa, and Matamoros; those who venture farther down to Monterrey are rewarded with the far more sophisticated dining, shopping, and cultural attractions of the country's third-largest city. The little-explored pyramids of El Tajín and the raffish charm of Veracruz, the first European city established on the North American mainland, are among the many reasons to continue south.

Updated by Patricia Alisau

IF THE NORTHEASTERNMOST Mexican states of Nuevo Leon and Tamalipaus are not, for the most part, the Mexico touted in glossy color brochures, they are by no means bereft of attractions. A hybrid of Mexican and U.S. culture, the three border cities of Nuevo Laredo, Reynosa, and Matamoros are good places to pick up handicrafts and sample authentic Mexican dishes at relatively low prices. Improved roads have also led more people to take advantage of the opportunity to visit Monterrey, Mexico's third-largest city and the region's highlight, offering cultural attractions, five-star hotels and restaurants, and, of course, shops. In Monterrey, you can arrange horseback rides, mountain biking excursions, and treks into the pine forests of the nearby Sierra Madre mountains. And in southern Tamaulipas state, the port of Tampico prides itself on its fine river fishing.

If you venture down into the state of Veracruz you'll be well rewarded for your efforts. The area is rich in culture and history: You can explore El Tajín, one of Mexico's most fascinating and least visited archaeological sites; wander the venerable port of Veracruz, where the Spanish first landed in 1519; witness the fascinating ritual of the *voladores* (fliers) of Papantla; and enjoy an archaeological museum second only to the one in Mexico City. You can also stroll the plazas of quaint mountain villages, laze on sandy beaches, and dine on some of the best seafood in Mexico, prepared in the famous Veracruz style.

Pleasures and Pastimes

Dining

Although northeastern Mexico isn't especially renowned for its cuisine, a nice variety of dishes from around the country is available here. Among the regional specialties are *cabrito* (roast kid), *carne asada* (grilled fillet of beef), and *café de olla* (a delicious blend of coffee, cinnamon, and brown sugar brewed in a clay pot). The state of Veracruz is famous for its signature dish, known as *pescado à la veracruzana* (red snapper covered in tomatoes, onions, olives, and herbs). Leaving Veracruz without sampling this would be both a shame and a bit of a feat, as every chef has his own special version, which he will insist you try.

In **Veracruz,** as befits a hot, breezy port town, the emphasis is on simple, fresh food, mostly *pescado* (fish) and *mariscos* (shellfish). Whether at night or during the day, a stop at one of the town's cafés is de rigueur; the 18th-century Café de la Portal is known internationally for its atmosphere and its fantastic coffee. **Jalapa** probably has the best restaurants in the state; the cookery is just as creative as the town's arts and music scene. It's not uncommon to hear the pat-pat of tortillas being hand-formed as you eat, and beans, rice and cheese, and occasionally chilies (this is, after all, the hometown of the jalapeño) are cleverly integrated into main dishes of meat and river fish such as trout. You can eat cheaply and heartily in **Papantla,** but with little variation. Just as **Tuxpán**'s best attractions are its pretty river and nearby beaches, some of the best places to eat here are the small, family-run seafood *palapas* (thatch-roofed huts) lining the beach as well as the river as it makes its way to the Gulf at Playa Tuxpán. If you ask for the *platillo del día* (daily dish), most likely you'll be treated to a cold shrimp, calamari, or crab cocktail, or a plate of fried fish or shrimp with Mexican rice and tortillas.

Very little in northeastern Mexico or the state of Veracruz is truly formal. Even in the cities of Monterrey and Veracruz, reservations are almost never necessary, and a jacket and tie would look out of place almost anywhere (unless we note otherwise). In a town like Papantla, to say that dress is casual would be an understatement: Shorts and a T-shirt won't get you a second glance even in the town's fanciest dining room.

CATEGORY	COST*
$$$$	over $20
$$$	$15–20
$$	$8–$15
$	under $8

**per person for a three-course meal, excluding drinks, service, and tax*

Fishing

Northeastern Mexico is a popular place for American anglers. **Lake Vicente Guerrero,** near Ciudad Victoria, has some of the best bass fishing in Mexico. As its name (meaning "the fish") suggests, you're likely to hook something at **La Pesca,** on the Tamaulipas coast between Matamoros and Tampico east of Ciudad Victoria and Soto La Marina.

Lodging

Catering mostly to business travelers and short-term tourists, the hotels in the **border towns** are what you'd expect—not luxurious but reasonably priced and mostly well kept. **Monterrey** affords more choices in all price ranges, and new hotels keep popping up to keep pace with the increase in corporate travelers. The posh Quinta Real, opened in late 1995, typifies the new breed of lodgings.

Veracruz's tourist industry is less well developed than one might expect. The state is just starting to get world-class hotels like the superdeluxe Fiesta Americana, which opened in the **port of Veracruz** at the beginning of 1996. The port city also offers a number of inexpensive hotels with plenty of atmosphere, and the moderately priced and more expensive places offer good value for your money, especially in comparison with their counterparts in areas that see more foreign tourism.

Although there are plenty of clean, comfortable, and inexpensive options in downtown **Jalapa,** more upscale choices are limited. The two nicest hotels, the Fiesta Inn and Posada de Coatepec, are a bit out of town, which can be inconvenient if you don't have a car, because local bus service is infrequent and Jalapa's many cultural offerings are concentrated in the *zona centro*. Many people choose to see Tajín as a day trip from the more developed city of Tuxpán, only briefly passing through Papantla. If you decide to spend a night or two here, your options are limited. **Papantla** has few hotels, and none are exceptional, though the Premier is well equipped. Fortunately, they are concentrated in a five-block radius and almost never fill up, so you can simply walk around town once you arrive and decide which suits you best. **Tuxpán** opened its first five-star hotel, a fancy (for Tuxpán) establishment called Hotel May Palace, in 1995 on Parque Reforma. Otherwise, there are plenty of safe and comfortable budget rooms in town. The town sees very little foreign tourism, and aside from during Semana Santa (Easter week) and July and August, when middle-class Mexicans head en masse for the beach, its hotels are usually empty.

CATEGORY	COST*
$$$$	over $110
$$$	$70–$110
$$	$40–$70
$	under $40

**All prices are for a standard double room, excluding tax.*

Exploring Northeastern Mexico and Veracruz

This area has two basic regions. The first comprises a string of border towns next to the United States as well as the city of Monterrey and some surrounding natural attractions. The second takes in the adjoining lush coastal state of Veracruz and its lively port, of vital importance in the history of the Spanish conquest of Mexico.

Numbers in the text correspond to numbers in the margin and on the Northeastern Mexico, Monterrey, Veracruz and East Central Mexico, and Veracruz maps.

Great Itineraries

Although the border towns are worth a visit to sample Mexican cuisine and buy handicrafts at cheaper prices than in the United States, their charm is limited. You might want to linger longer in Monterrey, a major city with some worthwhile restaurants and attractions. The real prize in this part of Mexico, however, is Veracruz, a region rich in archaeological ruins, colonial history, and newly established adventure-tourism routes.

IF YOU HAVE 3 DAYS

If you are driving down from Texas and have limited time, you could simply explore the area around **Monterrey** ④–⑪, the cultural and industrial giant of northeastern Mexico, to get a flavor of Mexico. Spend the first day walking around the Gran Plaza area, where the modern art and history museums are outstanding, and then drive to the Cuauhtémoc brewery on the outskirts of town. Devote the next two days to enjoying some of the region's natural attractions, including the **Barranca de la Huasteca** ⑫, an impressive gorge; the ancient **Grutas de García** ⑭ (Garcia Caves); and the **Parque Nacional Cumbres de Monterrey** ⑮, with its spectacular waterfall. For some colonial color, visit the downtown of **Saltillo** ⑬, where Mexican tiles are made; if you get hooked on its charm, spend one night here instead of driving back to Monterrey.

If you are flying, head straight for the port of **Veracruz** ⑱–㉒, the most Caribbean of the Gulf of Mexico cities. You'll have no problem occupying two days here: In addition to the excellent aquarium or the museums showcasing the city's colonial past, the city offers some of the best cafés, music, and seafood restaurants in the country. The last day, take a day trip to the state capital, **Jalapa** ㉕, and its magnificent Museum of Anthropology; stop on the way at **Antigua,** where the ruins of the house of Cortés stand, and at the archaeological site of **Cempoala** ㉔, a major Totonac religious and military city.

IF YOU HAVE 5 DAYS

If you leave early enough, you can make the drive down from the border town of Matamoros to **Tampico** ⑰, on the Gulf of Mexico, by nightfall. After spending the first night in Tampico, head south to the splendid **El Tajín** ㉗ archaeological ruins and overnight in the nearby town of **Papantla de Olarte** ㉖. Leave early in the morning on Day 3 and continue south to the port of **Veracruz,** stopping on the way at **Antigua** and **Cempoala.** On Day 4, tour the attractions in the city of Veracruz, and on the last day visit the renowned Museum of Anthropology in the city of **Jalapa.**

If you fly into Veracruz, add the visit to El Tajín and a side trip to the cool hill towns of **Los Tuxtlas** ㉓, where you can consult a *curandero* (healer) for whatever ails you.

IF YOU HAVE 7 DAYS

Follow the five-day itinerary above, but extend the trip to **Jalapa** by overnighting in the picturesque colonial town of Coatepec, only about 10 km (6 mi) away. The next day, go river rafting on the Río Pescados southeast of Jalapa. Drivers can add on the visit to **Los Tuxtlas,** whereas those who flew to Veracruz might want to spend a leisurely extra day enjoying the beaches and seafood restaurants of **Boca del Río,** a small fishing village that is turning into a suburb of Veracruz, or visiting more of the attractions you missed in the port's downtown.

When to Tour

The hottest months in northeastern Mexico are April through June. The cooling rains arrive in July and last through August. There are never any crowds at the border towns or in Monterrey except during major U.S. holidays, when Americans head south for a day or weekend.

In Veracruz, the weather is balmy between November and April. The famous *nortes*—gusty, chilly winds that blow in off the Gulf of Mexico—usually appear between October and February, and especially in December. Pack a sweater and light coat or jacket if you plan to travel during these months. In summer, both the temperature and humidity soar, but the frequent rains afford a respite from the heat.

The best time for many to visit Veracruz is the week before Ash Wednesday, when *Carnaval,* Mexico's version of Mardi Gras, takes place. It's wild and merry but has a small-town ambience that makes it saner and safer than the better-known celebrations in Río or New Orleans. The biggest problem at such times is finding a room, but the local tourist office can usually come up with acceptable accommodations. The same is true during Christmas and Easter week, when all of Mexico goes on vacation and heads for the beach.

NORTHEASTERN MEXICO

Few travelers go out of their way to visit northeastern Mexico, an arid area that's becoming increasingly industrial as more and more multinational companies establish *maquiladoras* (foreign-owned factories in duty-free zones) along the border and create more and more air pollution. But day- and weekend-trippers from Texas enjoy the foreign color and cuisine of border towns like Nuevo Laredo, Matamoros, and Reynosa. And only about three hours from the border is Monterrey, a fast-paced city that's home to Mexico's major brewery, some good museums, and one of Latin America's finest universities.

Nature lovers can enjoy the **Parque Nacional Cumbres de Monterrey,** northwest of the city, with its impressive Cola de Caballo (Horsetail Falls). Also near Monterrey are the dramatic **Barranca de la Huasteca** (Huasteca Canyon) and **Grutas de García,** caves with an underground lake and a stalactite and stalagmite forest. Many sports enthusiasts are lured farther down into the area by the magnificent hunting and fishing at **Lake Vincente Guerrero,** not far from Ciudad Victoria. Those seeking saltwater attractions will find plenty by the sea near **Tampico,** which also boasts many interesting architectural sights.

Nuevo Laredo

❶ *1½ km (1 mi) south of Laredo, Texas.*

Of all the eastern border towns, Nuevo Laredo receives the largest onslaught of American souvenir seekers. Shopping is the primary pursuit here, and you'll find a warren of stalls and shops plus a large handicrafts market concentrated on Avenida Guerrero in a seven-block stretch that extends from the International Bridge to the main plaza. In addition to the standard border-town schlock, Nuevo Laredo shops stock a good selection of high-quality handicrafts from all over Mex-

Northeastern Mexico

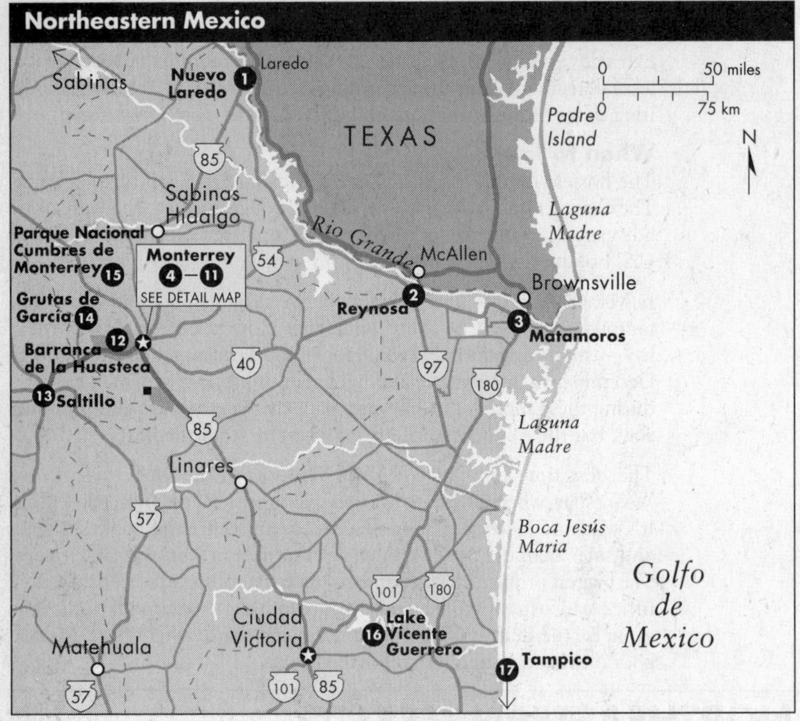

ico, at somewhat inflated prices. Wander a few blocks off the main drag in any direction for better prices and smaller crowds.

Nuevo Laredo was founded after the Treaty of Guadalupe Hidalgo in 1848, which ended the Mexican-American War. The treaty established the Río Bravo (or Rio Grande) as the border between the two countries and forced Mexico to give up a substantial amount of territory. Many of Laredo's Mexican residents, who suddenly found themselves living in the United States, crossed the river and founded Nuevo Laredo on what had been the outskirts of town. Today, Nuevo Laredo's economy depends greatly on gringos who head south for a few days of drunken revelry, returning home with a bottle of tequila, suitcases full of souvenirs, and a mean hangover.

Dining and Lodging

$$$ ★ ✕ **Winery (La Vinteria).** This Mexican version of a Continental wine bar serves such regional specialties as *carne tampiqueña* (grilled steak) and *queso fundido* (melted cheese), often served in a bowl with chorizo (spicy sausage) to be spread on tortillas. It has the best selection of Mexican wines in town. ✉ *Matamoros 308 at Victoria,* ☎ *87/12–08–95. Reservations not accepted. AE, DC, MC, V.*

$$ ✕ **El Dorado.** Dating from the Prohibition era, this spot is a favorite with the Texas crowd—a hangout better known for its atmosphere than for its cuisine. Try the combination plate of grilled meat, which includes two selections of either goat, quail, or frogs' legs. ✉ *Ocampo at Belden,* ☎ *87/12–00–15. Reservations not accepted. AE, MC, V.*

$$ ✕ **Mexico Tipico.** This establishment, gaily decorated in bright Mexican colors, offers both indoor and outdoor patio dining, with mariachis coming in from the street to entertain patrons. The patio, partially covered, features a waterfall. Specialties are carne asada and cabrito. True to its name, Mexico Tipico serves the typical Mexican plate of

beef or chicken enchiladas with rice and refried beans. ✉ *Guerrero 934,* ☎ *87/12-15-25. Reservations not accepted. MC, V.*

$ El Río. A modern white structure spread out on large landscaped grounds, this motel has a spacious lobby and large guest rooms. Forty-six rooms in Section 200 have been redecorated; other rooms still have dark Spanish colonial furniture. All units include shower, satellite color TV, and telephone. ✉ *5 km (3 mi) south on Hwy. 85, Nuevo Laredo, Tamps. 88000,* ☎ *87/14-36-66. 149 rooms. Restaurant, bar, 2 pools, free parking. AE, MC, V.*

$ Hotel Posada Mina. This is a good bet for those who are seeking budget accommodations, not luxury, in a quiet location. A remodeled old yellow-brick building about six blocks west of the bridge, the Mina has very small rooms, but they are clean with good beds, individual air-conditioning and heat, color TVs, and private baths. ✉ *Mina 35, Nuevo Laredo, Tamps. 88000,* ☎ *87/13-14-73. 5 rooms. Coffee shop. MC, V.*

$ Hotel Reforma. An older hotel just a half block south of Plaza Hidalgo, Reforma has a restaurant, remodeled marble lobby, and secure parking a block away. Rooms in the older section, although somewhat small and rather nondescript, are comfortable; junior suites in the newer section are slightly bigger and have fresh carpets and curtains, although the hallways smell musty. All units come with shower, TV, and telephone. ✉ *Guerrero 822, Nuevo Laredo, Tamps. 88000,* ☎ *87/12-62-50,* FAX *87/12-67-14. 38 rooms. Restaurant, bar. MC, V.*

Nightlife and the Arts

Victoria's, three blocks from Bridge 1, is a noisy favorite; the **Winery** and **El Dorado** are somewhat more sedate; and **Quintana Rock** and the new **Plaza San Miguel** are the local discos. All of the above are located on Avenida Guerrero in the heart of the shopping district.

Shopping

On the stretch where International Bridge 1 leads into Avenida Guerrero you'll find most of Nuevo Laredo's shops—classy and junky alike. **Granada** (✉ Guerrero 504, ☎ 87/12-86-44) has better-quality items than many of the other vendors, including lead crystal and serapes. Artisan shops selling lots of leather goods and ceramics are in the **Nuevo Mercado de la Reforma** market, three blocks south of the bridge at Avenida Guerrero and Calle Belden. The **Ma Cristina** mall, one-half block north of the square at Avenida Guerrero 631, houses about three dozen curio outlets. Most stores remain open until 8 PM.

Reynosa

❷ *16 km (10 mi) south of McAllen, Texas.*

Because of its manageable size and mellow attitude, Reynosa is one of the most pleasant points of entry into Mexico and a convenient starting point if you're bound for Mexico City, Monterrey, or Veracruz. That said, Reynosa is still an industrial border town of limited charm, driven economically by the petrochemical industry, agriculture, and the ever-present tourist trade. As you enter town, you'll see the **Zona Rosa** (Pink Zone) tourist district, with a few curio shops and a couple of bars and restaurants. The heart of the city, around **Plaza Principal,** is about five blocks from the International Bridge. It's being made even more presentable with an urban renewal project started in 1996 that is enlarging sidewalks and putting in cobblestone streets, new street signs, and park benches. After leaving downtown, the rest of Reynosa is a jumble of tacky border-town urban sprawl.

Plaza Principal is in many ways a typical Mexican town center, but its original colonial church has been joined like a Siamese twin to an ultra-modern newer addition with arches and stained-glass windows. **Hidalgo Street,** a colorful pedestrian mall of shops and street vendors, leads off from the plaza. Many Texans save money by having their teeth fixed south of the Rio Grande—which explains the many dental offices you'll see in this area.

Dining and Lodging

$$ ✕ **La Majada.** Like all good cabrito restaurants, this one is simple and to the point: Roast kid, guacamole, and quesadillas are pretty much what you'll find. Don't come for the atmosphere but for the local specialty at its best. ⊠ *Av. Miguel Aleman (½ block from bridge), no phone. Reservations not accepted. MC, V.*

$$ ✕ **Sam's.** Wild game like quail and dove served in season (November–January) and seafood are the specialties here. Desserts, however, are limited to flan (caramel custard) and cheesecake. In winter, Sam's is frequented by Americans from the Rio Grande Valley and snowbirds from Minnesota. ⊠ *Allende 990,* ☎ *89/22–00–34 or 89/22–34–34. Reservations not accepted. MC, V.*

$$ 🏨 **Hacienda.** Located along the highway to Monterrey about 16 km (10 mi) from the U.S. border, this sparkling new hotel is luxurious by Reynosa standards. Its pretty tiled lobby is decorated with lots of colonial style furniture and handicrafts, which carry over into the light-filled, cheerful rooms; all have color cable TVs, air-conditioning, and direct-dial phones. ⊠ *Blvd. Hidalgo 2013, Reynosa, Tamps. 88500,* ☎ *89/24–60–10 or 89/24–61–01,* FAX *89/23–59–62. 34 rooms and suites. Restaurant, bar, meeting room, travel services, car rental, free parking. AE, MC, V.*

$ 🏨 **Astromundo.** Downtown and handy to the market and the few good local restaurants, this popular hotel gets a lot of traffic from weekending Texans. ⊠ *Juárez at Guerrero, Reynosa, Tamps. 88500,* ☎ FAX *89/22–56–25. 94 rooms. Restaurant, bar, free parking. AE, MC, V.*

$ 🏨 **San Carlos.** This five-story hotel on the square has air-conditioned rooms with colonial-style furniture and satellite TVs. Business travelers and tourists appreciate its central location, close to the square and shopping center, and the friendly staff, which aims to please. ⊠ *Hidalgo 970, Reynosa, Tamps. 88500,* ☎ *89/22–12–80,* FAX *89/22–26–20. 65 rooms. Restaurant. AE, MC, V.*

Nightlife and the Arts

The **Imperial** offers quiet, slow-dance music with a combo or strolling trio, depending on the night; the older clientele is well dressed. The Zona Rosa has several discos and **Trevino's** (⊠ Av. Virreyes 1075, ☎ 89/22–14–44), with a piano bar.

Shopping

Trevino's (☞ *above*) has a good selection of Mexican arts and crafts, sculpture, papier-mâché, perfumes, liquors, and clothing, with a cocktail lounge in the rear.

Matamoros

❸ *1 km (about ½ mi) south of Brownsville, Texas.*

Matamoros, across from Brownsville, Texas (the southernmost point in the continental United States), is the most historic of the border towns, dating from the 18th century. It is named H. Matamoros, or Heroic Matamoros, for one of the many rebellious priests who were executed by the Spaniards during the War of Independence (1810–21). The first major battle of the Mexican-American War was fought here when guns in Matamoros began shelling Fort Brown on the north side of the Rio Grande. Shortly afterward, troops of Zachary Taylor occupied Matamoros and began their march south.

Today Matamoros is the commercial center of a rich agricultural area and a manufacturing center for Mexico's in-bond industry. Some 20 years ago, **Avenida Alvaro Obregón,** which leads from the main bridge, was spruced up to "dignify" the Mexican side of the border, and today it's the prettiest entryway into Mexico of the three border towns. This is where you'll find the town's best shops, restaurants, and accommodations. Also of interest is the **Casa Mata Museum** in the remains of Fort Mata, built in 1845 to defend the city against American invasion. The fortress wasn't completed in time, and Zachary Taylor's troops were able to capture Matamoros easily. Casa Mata now displays photos and artifacts, mostly from the Mexican Revolution. ✉ *Guatemala and Santos Degollado,* ☎ *88/13–59–29.* *Free.* *Tues.–Sun. 9:30–5:30.*

Beach

About 30 km (18 mi) from downtown Matamoros is **Playa Bagdad,** worth a visit only if you hanker for the Gulf of Mexico. It's the site of the Confederacy's only open harbor during the U.S. Civil War. Freighters skirting the Union naval blockade unloaded their war supplies and loaded up with Confederate cotton destined for Europe. Today, there's an air of decrepit charm about the place: About 100 palapas are lined up in neat rows along the gritty shore waiting for visitors, accompanied by a couple of seafood restaurants that seem to be barely surviving. On the weekends, hordes of Mexican middle-class families pour into the place. The entrance fee is $1.25 per vehicle.

Dining and Lodging

$$ ✕ **Drive Inn.** In spite of the name, this is a formal restaurant with crystal chandeliers, linen tablecloths, and a dance floor. Expect a romantic evening, and stick with steak and seafood specialties. ✉ *Av. Hidalgo at Calle 6a,* ☎ *88/12–00–22. Reservations not accepted. MC, V.*

$$ ★ ✕ **Garcia's.** Rebuilt and redecorated over its own parking garage, this is a romantic place for dancing and dining on lobster or steak and your choice of a dozen fine tequilas. An elevator from the garage leads up to a gift shop with wares from all over Mexico as well as to the restaurant and a bar. ✉ *Calle Alvaro Obregón,* ☎ *88/12–39–29 or 88/13–18–33. Reservations not accepted. AE, DC, MC, V.*

$ ✕ **Los Nortenos.** A goat slow-roasting over hot coals in the window is the not-so-subtle advertisement for the best cabrito in town. A dozen plain tables with plastic tablecloths are the setting for an equally spare menu—goat, guacamole, and quesadillas. ✉ *Calle 9a and Abosolo across from market, no phone. Reservations not accepted. No credit cards.*

$$ ★ **Gran Hotel Residencial.** The best hotel in the city, this pleasant low rise built along Spanish colonial lines is the center of activity for much of Matamoros. All rooms were remodeled in 1995 and have a terrace, two queen-size beds, air-conditioning, heat, and color cable TVs. There's also a large pool and a play area for children in the lush garden. ✉ *Alvaro Obregón at Amapolas, 6 blocks from bridge, Matamoros, Tamps. 87330,* ☎ *88/3–94–40. 120 rooms. Restaurant, bar, pool. AE, MC, V.*

Nightlife and the Arts

Garcia's and the **Gran Hotel Residencial** (☞ Dining and Lodging, *above*) are where the action is in Matamoros.

Shopping

The most appealing shops are on Calle Alvaro Obregón, the street that leads from the border bridge to the center of town. The salmon-color building that hosts **Garcia's** restaurant (☞ Dining and Lodging, *above*) also contains a huge gift shop, where you can buy everything from tacky souvenirs and big sombreros to quality tequila, silver, Oaxaca wedding dresses, and leather jackets. Across from Garcia's, the shacklike **Bob's Azteca Gift Shop** (☒ Alvaro Obregón 77, ☎ 88/12–88–19) offers run-of-the-mill woolen rugs and crafts at discount prices. **Barbara** (☒ Alvaro Obregón 37, ☎ 88/16–54–56) has an attractive assortment of quality handicrafts, carved wood, home furnishings, and even good costume jewelry and imported cosmetics. **Matamoros Market,** a block-long covered affair downtown, is the place to haggle for bargains; you get what you pay for.

Monterrey

235 km (146 mi) southwest of Nuevo Laredo, 225 km (140 mi) west of Reynosa, 325 km (200 mi) west of Matamoros.

Mexico's third-largest city and the capital of the state of Nuevo León, Monterrey celebrated the 400th anniversary of its founding in 1996. This industrial center is a brewer of beer and forger of steel, with nothing in the way of a laid-back lifestyle. This is where some of the country's most powerful captains of industry hold sway—a fact that earned the city its nickname, the Sultan of the North. Monterrey also has the country's most sophisticated convention complex—a high-tech facility called Cintermex—and is building a gigantic sports arena to host international events; the Dallas Cowboys and San Diego Padres have started playing exhibition games in the summer. Still, it is a favorite with weekenders and "winter Texans" from the Rio Grande valley who find Monterrey so near—a three-hour drive from the border or a short flight from Dallas, Houston, or San Antonio—and yet so foreign. The top hotels are clustered close together downtown in an area called the Zona Rosa (Pink Zone) or Barrio Antiguo (Old Quarter), and several streets, including Avenida Morelos—the main drag—are now pedestrian malls.

The impressive **Gran Plaza**—at 100 acres one of the country's largest squares—was completed in 1985 as part of an urban renewal project that also includes the first stages of a San Antonio–style riverwalk with cafés and shops; it's within walking distance of the downtown hotels. Better known as Macroplaza, it extends from the modernistic Palacio Municipal (City Hall) several blocks past the newly painted cathedral, the old City Hall, and the Legislative Palace to the Palacio de Gobierno (State House).

4 Towering above the neoclassical **Palacio de Gobierno** is a concrete slab topped by the Lighthouse of Commerce, a laser beam that flashes from 8 to 11 nightly. It was designed by Luis Barragán to commemorate the 100th anniversary of the founding of the city's Chamber of Commerce. Handsome Saddle Mountain and the craggy Sierra Madre provide a majestic backdrop to this austere postmodern monument. ☒ *Between Av. Constitución, Av. Cuauhtémoc, Calz. Francisco Madero, and Av. Felix Gomez.*

5 The opulent **Museo de Arte Contemporaneo (MARCO)** (Museum of Contemporary Art), which opened in the early 1990s, is the crown jewel of the Gran Plaza. Designed in the style of a Moorish palace by renowned Mexican architect Ricardo Legorretta, it features 14 galleries that display the cutting-edge art of Mexico and Latin America and, at times, of other parts of the world. There's an outstanding collection of art books

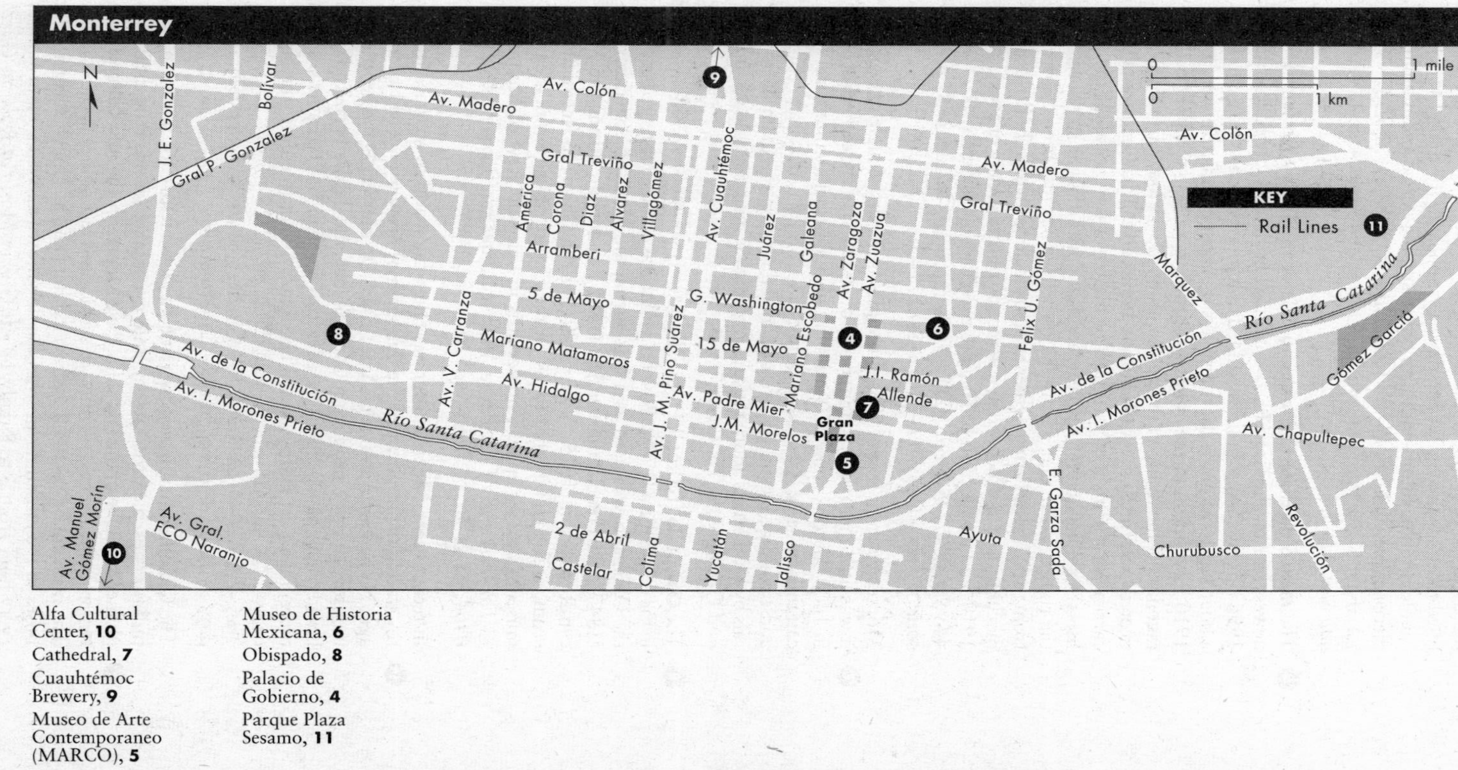

Alfa Cultural Center, **10**
Cathedral, **7**
Cuauhtémoc Brewery, **9**
Museo de Arte Contemporaneo (MARCO), **5**
Museo de Historia Mexicana, **6**
Obispado, **8**
Palacio de Gobierno, **4**
Parque Plaza Sesamo, **11**

for sale at the gift shop. You can listen to live music on a beautiful water-filled marble patio on Wednesday afternoons (4:30–8) and watch the candlelit tables fill up with arts types, sipping coffee and nibbling on pieces of pie. ⊠ *Gran Plaza at Zuazua and Ocampo,* ☎ *8/342–4820.* 🎟 *About $1.50; free Wed. and Sat.* 🕓 *Tues. and Thurs.–Sat. 11–7, Wed. and Sun. 11–9.*

6 The **Museo de Historia Mexicana** (Mexican History Museum) is the newest star on the Gran Plaza's cultural horizon. Opened in 1995, in 1996 this two-story building added a mini–river walk with cafés and a boat ride to its grounds. It displays the most complete history of the 1910 Revolution in the country. Battles, marches, and political protagonists come to life in the newsreels of the period, part of a sophisticated multimedia show held inside a railroad car that served as a troop carrier for the insurgents. Life-size plaster-of-paris casts of the "Villistas" (soldiers under the command of Pancho Villa) sit shotgun on the roof of a car that we are led to believe has just been "liberated" from the Mexican army. Other exhibits include the first bottle-capping machine used by Coca-Cola; a depiction of café society in Mexico circa 1910; and a collection of Huastec pre-Hispanic artifacts. ⊠ *Dr. Coss 445 Sur,* ☎ *8/345–9898.* 🎟 *$1.50; guided tours in English $1 per person.* 🕓 *Tues.–Thurs. 11–7, Fri.–Sun. 11–8.*

Monterrey dates from 1596, although for the first couple of centuries
7 it was little more than an outpost. Construction of the **cathedral** began in 1600 but took some 250 years to finish. Distinct architectural styles can thus be seen: A baroque facade is set off by neoclassical columns and two huge ornate plateresque medallions on the main door. Murals by local artists adorn the area framing the main altar. ⊠ *Gran Plaza and Ocampo and Dr. Coss.*

8 The **Obispado** (Bishop's House) is the only landmark to be completed in the colonial era (1788). Built on a hilltop as a home for retired prelates, the Obispado was used as a fort during the Mexican-American War (1847), the French Intervention (1862), and again during the Mexican Revolution (1915). Today it houses the **Obispado Regional Museum,** with exhibits that focus on the history of the entire area. The museum's major appeal, however, is its splendid view of Monterrey. ⊠ *Far west end of Av. Padre Mier at Rafael José Berger,* ☎ *8/346–0404.* 🎟 *$1.50.* 🕓 *Tues.–Sun. 10–4.*

In recent years, Mexican beer has taken the world by storm. Monter-
9 rey started the trend when the **Cuauhtémoc Brewery** opened a century ago. Named after a famous Aztec chief, the brewery is the heart of an industrial empire producing Carta Blanca and Tecate beer. Today the brewery complex includes the Mexican Baseball Hall of Fame, a sports museum, an art gallery, and a beer garden with free beer (the biggest draw). ⊠ *Av. Alfonso Reyes 2202,* ☎ *8/328–5746.* 🎟 *Free.* 🕓 *Tues.–Fri. 9:30–5, weekends 10–6. Brewery tours by request only, weekdays 9–1 and 3–6; call 8/375–2200 to book.*

The Cuauhtémoc Brewery spawned a glass factory for bottles, a steel mill for caps, a carton factory, and, eventually, several industrial con-
10 glomerates. One of the last, Alfa, gave Monterrey the **Alfa Cultural Center,** probably the best museum of science and technology in the country. The museum has many hands-on exhibits and an IMAX theater. Free buses to the museum run from the downtown *alameda* (main square) every hour from 3 to 8 daily. ⊠ *Av. Gómez Morín at Roberto Garza Sada,* ☎ *8/356–5696.* 🎟 *About $3.* 🕓 *Tues.–Sun. 3–9:30.*

The newest recreational/educational play area for children is the cleverly designed **Parque Plaza Sesamo** (Sesame Plaza Park), a sprawling theme park built on the grounds of Parque Fundidora that also houses the city's Cintermex convention complex. Tots and adults alike can wander through three areas offering a world of water sports with 17 water toboggans, pint-size pools, interactive games, and minirivers; a second area has a computer center where kids can plug into the Internet and play nonviolent video games; the last section is taken up by restaurants and theaters where the park's own personalities put on musical shows. You can easily spend an entire day here. ✉ *Calle Agricola 3700–1 Oriente, Col. Agricola in Parque Fundidora,* ☎ *8/354–5400.* *$9.* *Tues.–Fri. 3–9, weekends 3–10.*

11

Dining and Lodging

$$ ★ ✕ **Luisiana.** Perhaps the most elegant dining room downtown, this is a taste of how New Orleans is imagined in Mexico. There are no Cajun specialties on the menu, but the deepwater crawfish are divine. Wonderfully prepared steak and seafood dishes make this one of the best restaurants in the country. The waiters wear tuxedos, and there's always soft piano music playing at dinnertime. ✉ *Hidalgo Ote. 530,* ☎ *8/340–2185 or 8/343–1561. AE, DC, MC, V.*

$$ ★ ✕ **Residence.** A clubby meeting place for Monterrey's high-power industrialists and executives, Residence has a menu featuring both Mexican specialties and Continental dishes like prime rib cooked slowly in its juice. ✉ *Degollado and Matamoros,* ☎ *8/342–7230, 8/345–5040, or 8/345–5478. Jacket and tie. AE, DC, MC, V.*

$ ✕ **El Rey de Cabrito.** The restaurant's name ("King of Cabrito") is no lie: This is *the* place to try the regional specialty dish, probably the best roast kid you'll ever eat. (The owner keeps his own goat herds.) The pastel-color restaurant covers half a city block and has become so well known that it's constantly filling out-of-town orders. Steaks and ribs can be ordered as well as the famous cabrito. ✉ *817 Constitución,* ☎ *8/343–5560. Reservations not accepted. MC, V.*

$ ✕ **Sanborns.** Part of a national chain that is a Mexican institution, this is the place for hamburgers and malts as well as tacos and enchiladas. ✉ *Escobedo 920 off Plaza Hidalgo,* ☎ *8/343–1834. Reservations not accepted. AE, MC, V.*

$$$$ ★ **Ambassador Camino Real.** One of the best hotels in this part of Mexico, this downtown landmark was restored several years ago and is now operated by the Camino Real chain. It offers spacious rooms and a newly remodeled executive floor that has rooms with computer ports, a work area with desk, and fresh juice and coffee with your wake-up call; there's also a concierge with secretarial and fax service. A health club with tanning beds, a French restaurant, and a piano bar with an old-fashioned stained-glass ceiling are among the Ambassador's many amenities. ✉ *Hidalgo at Emilio Carranza, 64000,* ☎ *8/340–6390 or 8/342–2040; 800/722–6466 in the U.S.;* FAX *8/342–1904. 241 rooms and suites. 2 restaurants, 3 lounges, pool, 2 tennis courts, racquetball, travel services, free parking. AE, DC, MC, V.*

$$$$ ★ **Gran Ancira Radisson Plaza Hotel Monterrey.** Built in 1912, this hotel is reminiscent of the grand hotels of Europe: An elegant spiral staircase dominates an expansive Art Deco lobby accented by a black-and-white tile floor and crystal chandeliers. Legend has it that Pancho Villa, taken with the place, settled in and stabled his horse in the lobby. Rooms are conservatively decorated with tasteful pastel walls and matching furnishings; all have minibars, satellite TVs, and large marble baths. The Plaza Club business-floor suites offer exercise bicycles and impeccable concierge service. Rooms were refreshed with new rugs,

curtains, and electronic card keys in 1996. ✉ *Hidalgo at Escobedo, 64000,* ☎ *8/345–7575 or 800/333–3333,* FAX *8/344–5226. 240 rooms and suites. Restaurant, 2 bars, coffee shop, pool, business services, travel services, car rental, free parking. AE, DC, MC, V.*

$$$$ **Holiday Inn Crowne Plaza.** Well-heeled travelers take to this sleek, modern high-rise that's like a small city unto itself, with every conceivable service under the sun, just minutes from the city's top tourist attractions. It has amenities like executive floors with concierge service, rooms with computer ports and work desks, multiple meeting rooms (including the largest in town for 1,200), and a well-staffed business center. The hotel has a spectacular atrium lobby filled with marble, glass, and gleaming brass; four see-through elevators whisk guests to their destination. Recreational areas include a huge solarium with streams of hanging plants and indoor pool, tennis courts, and billiards and Ping-Pong. A top-rated steak house with cuts from north of the border and lively bar with evening shows provide after-hours relaxation. ✉ *Av. Constitución 300 Oriente, 64000,* ☎ *8/319–6000 or 800/227–6963,* FAX *8/344–3007. 403 rooms. 2 restaurants, bar, pool, exercise room, business services, meeting rooms, travel services, car rental, free parking. AE, DC, MC, V.*

$$$$ ★ **Quinta Real.** This elegant, new all-suites business hotel built by a prestigious Mexican chain holds sway in Monterrey's financial district and exudes the aura of a prosperous hacienda of bygone days. This is carried out in its ocher-color facade, arched porticos, high ceilings, marble staircases, and beautiful replicas of colonial paintings. The high-domed lobby is set with French furnishings in soothing colors, huge bowls of fresh flowers, and carvings of classic Mexican handicrafts, many of them one-of-a-kind art pieces. A collection of finely executed indigenous weavings and embroideries lines the long lobby corridors. The suites, which are decorated in earth tones and rich floral prints, come in 16 different varieties; they have either two double or one king-size bed, room safes, robes, minibars, color TVs, bathtub/showers, and a full range of luxury bathroom soaps and lotions. Four conference rooms accommodate up to 350 persons. The hotel's restaurant, which serves excellent gourmet Mexican cuisine, has already built up quite a local following. ✉ *Av. Diego Rivera 500, Fracc. Valle Oriente, 64000,* ☎ *8/368–1000 or 800/445–4565,* FAX *8/368–1080. 125 suites. Restaurant, bar, exercise room, business services, meeting rooms, travel services, car rental, free parking. AE, DC, MC, V.*

$$$ ★ **Chipinque.** This hilltop resort overlooking the city on 700 acres of forest land is an ideal choice if you have a car. The view from the restaurant is extraordinary, especially at night. All rooms were remodeled in 1995 and offer fireplaces, queen-size beds, cable TVs, and phones. There's also a small zoo on the premises. ✉ *Meseta de Chipinque, Monterrey, NL 66297,* ☎ *8/378–1100,* FAX *8/378–1338. 43 rooms. Restaurant, bar, pool, tennis court. AE, MC, V.*

$$ **Hampton Inn Monterrey Airport.** This snug new 90-room lodge is the city's first airport hotel and a boon to travelers who wish to be close to the international terminal or away from the congestion of downtown. Units have two double beds, sitting/work area with a sofa, coffee table and desk, satellite TVs, and beige-and-blue color scheme; half the rooms are no-smoking. Although there's no restaurant, complimentary breakfast rolls, juice, and coffee are included in the price of the room along with free local calls. Airport transfers can be arranged with prior reservation. ✉ *Carretera Miguel Aleman Km 23.7, Apodaca, NL 66600,* ☎ *8/386–3800 or 800/426–7866,* FAX *8/386–4335. 90 rooms. Pool, exercise room, meeting rooms, free parking. AE, DC, MC, V.*

$$ **Howard Johnson Hotel Plaza Suites.** In the center of the Zona Rosa is a spiffy-looking pink sandstone building with a striking atrium lobby. Opened in 1994, it's been abuzz with business travelers ever since. The light-filled units (all of them two-room suites) include an office with a hookup for a personal computer and fax; they're tastefully decorated in light colors. The high-ceiling restaurant offers a big picture window facing a garden. ✉ *Av. Corrigidora Ote. 519, Zona Rosa, 64000,* ☎ *8/319–0900 or 91–800/5–0549; 800/654–2000 in the U.S.;* FAX *8/319–0909. 155 suites. Restaurant, 2 bars, pool, exercise room, business center, meeting rooms, free parking. AE, DC, MC, V.*

$ **Colonial.** This no-frills hotel—the oldest in Monterrey—is ideal because of its central downtown location and budget-price rooms. The small lobby, furnished in colonial style, has one of the last remaining manually operated elevators in the city (it's more than 100 years old). Rooms have color TVs, bathroom tiles, carpeting, and air-conditioning units have been installed. There's no restaurant or bar and the noisy disco next door has gone out of business, so guests can get a peaceful night's rest. ✉ *Hidalgo 475, 64000,* ☎ *8/343–6791,* ☎ FAX *8/342–1169. 100 rooms. MC, V.*

$ **Royalty.** You get your money's worth at this downtown hotel, where prices are lower than usual for this expensive city. In 1995 the Royalty got new cable TVs, and air-conditioning units. The interior, including the lobby and terrace restaurant, is dominated by a cheerful pink-and-white color scheme. Extras include a tiny outdoor pool, video bar, massage services, happy hour every afternoon between 4 and 6, and a complimentary American-style breakfast Monday–Saturday. ✉ *Hidalgo Oriente 402, 64000,* ☎ *8/340–2800,* FAX *8/340–5812. 66 rooms. Restaurant, bar, pool, exercise room. MC, V.*

Nightlife and the Arts

Fashionable folk, residents, and visitors alike flock to the downtown hotels for after-dark action. **Scaramouche** (☎ 8/319–6000) at the Crowne Plaza lobby bar delights the young-at-heart crowd. At the **Ambassador** (☎ 8/342–2040), the pianist is more reserved. **El Cid,** in the Hotel Monterrey (✉ Morelos and Zaragoza, ☎ 8/319–6000), packs them into an off-track betting parlor, and **Bar 1900** at the Gran Ancira Radisson Plaza (☎ 8/345–7575), a classic but upscale Mexican cantina, has flamenco dancers every Thursday night. **Baccarat** (✉ Río Grijalva and Mississippi, no phone) is a top disco, reachable by taxi. The new **Far West Rodeo** (✉ Av. Los Angeles and Universidad, no phone) features line dancing to Tex-Mex country music Thursday to Sunday.

Shopping

Top-quality shops center on Plaza Hidalgo, near the major hotels, with leather and cowboy boots as the local specialties. Owner Porfirio Sosa has handpicked every item he sells at the upscale **Carapan** (✉ Hidalgo 305, Monterrey Ote., ☎ 8/345–4422) and loves to tell you about them. His array of Mexican antiques, hand-loomed rugs, shawls, clay figures from Michoacán, metal sculptures, and hand-blown glassware rivals that of stores anywhere in the country. **Sanborns** (✉ Escobedo 920, off Plaza Hidalgo, ☎ 8/342–1441 or 8/343–1824) offers a standard selection of silver, onyx, and other Mexican craft items. The **Mercado Indio** (✉ Bolivar Nte. 1150), a typical Mexican market with dozens of stalls, is a favorite with souvenir hunters, although the selections are a little monotonous.

Sports

GOLF

Hotels can arrange temporary memberships in one of **Monterrey**'s three golf courses.

Barranca de la Huasteca

12 *43 km (27 mi) southeast of Monterrey.*

The Barranca de la Huasteca (Huasteca Canyon), with its 1,000-ft-deep gorge, is spectacular for the striated grooves etched into its walls, making it resemble a giant piece of Lalique glassware. A play area for children includes a miniature train ride, two pools, and rest rooms. ✉ *From Monterrey, 20 km (12 mi) east on Hwy. 40 to Santa Catarina, then 3 km (2 mi) south on marked road to canyon.* *Small admission fee.* ⏲ *Daily 9–6.*

Saltillo

13 *40 km (25 mi) southwest of Monterrey.*

Saltillo is perhaps best known these days for the unglazed terra-cotta tiles it produces; knockoffs of these plain but attractive tiles line patios and floors throughout Mexico and the southwest United States. But the city, founded in 1577 by Spanish captain Alberto de Canto, was a crucial colonial outpost in its heydey because it occupied a strategic position along the Camino Real, the main artery from Mexico City north into what is now Texas. In fact, it served as the capital of the Texas territory from 1835 to 1847, when Mexico lost it to the United States. Although Saltillo is a prosperous city with a great deal of industrial sprawl, the city fathers have preserved the historical **main plaza,** which is surrounded by buildings dating back to the colonial period. Much smaller than Monterrey, Saltillo nonetheless has its own convention center and some outstanding hotels and restaurants.

Grutas de García

14 *49 km (30 mi) southwest of Monterrey.*

The **Grutas García** (Garcia Caves) are an estimated 50 to 60 million years old and at one time were submerged by an ocean; petrified sea animals can be seen in some of its walls. You can hike the 1 km (½ mi) from the entrance to the caves or hop on a swaying funicular where guides lead the way through a mile of underground grottoes through 16 caverns. This site is far less commercialized than are similar attractions north of the border. ✉ *From Monterrey, Hwy. 40 west for 40 km (25 mi) to Saltillo, then 9 km (6 mi) on marked road to caves.* *$2 without funicular, $3.50 to ride funicular.* ⏲ *Daily 9–5.*

Parque Nacional Cumbres de Monterrey

15 *90 km (56 mi) northwest of Monterrey.*

One of the highlights of a trip to the Parque Nacional Cumbres de Monterrey, tucked into the Sierra Madre mountains, is a view of **La Cascada Cola de Caballo** (Horsetail Falls), a dramatic 75-ft-high waterfall that tumbles down from the pine-forested heights. The waterfall is about 1 km (½ mi) from the park's entrance, up a cobblestone road; you can rent a docile horse or burro for about $2.25 per hour from the local kids who hang out by the ticket booth, or hop on a horse-pulled carriage for $2. ✉ *From Monterrey, Hwy. 85 145 km (90 mi) northwest to falls, no phone.* *$1.50.* ⏲ *Daily 9–6.*

Lake Vicente Guerrero

16 *316 km (192 mi) southwest of Matamoros, 304 km (191 mi) southeast of Monterrey.*

The man-made Lake Vicente Guerrero is a favorite with American bass fishermen year-round and, during the winter months, an excellent place to hunt duck and white-wing dove. Several camps in the area, such as El Tejon and El Sargento lodges, cater to American sports enthusiasts. For information on the most popular sports in the area, contact **Sunbelt Hunting and Fishing** (✉ Box 3009, Brownsville, TX 78520, ☎ 210/546–9101 or 800/876–4868, FAX 210/544–4731). ✉ *From Monterrey, 288 km (181 mi) south on Hwy. 85 to Ciudad Victoria, then 16 km (10 mi) northeast on Hwy. 101 to lake.*

Tampico

17 *504 km (320 mi) south of Matamoros, 583 km (330 mi) southeast of Monterrey.*

Tampico is a picturesque port adjoining Ciudad Madero, an oil-refining center. Usually a low-profile place, Tampico made big news in 1995 when it was discovered to be the hometown of the elusive subcomandante Marcos, spokesman of the Zapatista rebels in Chiapas.

Shortly after the Spanish conquest, the Franciscans established a mission in the area near a Huastec fishing village, but the settlement was constantly battered by hurricanes and pirate attacks. In 1828 the Spaniards attempted to reconquer then-independent Mexico by landing troops at Tampico, but they were soundly defeated. With later invasions by the Americans and then the French, the port languished until oil was discovered in the region at the turn of the 20th century. The British and Americans developed the industry until it was nationalized in 1938. Petroleum helped Tampico prosper but didn't enhance tourism in the area. Río Pánuco is so polluted that it no longer attracts tarpon fishermen, although the big ocean freighters are an impressive sight.

Still, because of its relative proximity to the border, Tampico gets a smattering of U.S. visitors and is a fascinating place in which to wander around for a spell; the old part has a bit of the feel of a run-down New Orleans French Quarter. **Plaza Libertad,** near the harbor, is shaggy and unkempt—very much the tropical waterfront. A block away is the regal **Plaza de Armas,** with its majestic City Hall guarded by towering palms. The **cathedral** here, started in 1823, was completed with funds donated by Edward L. Doheny, an oil magnate implicated in the Teapot Dome scandal of the 1920s.

Beaches

Playa Miramar, about 5 km (3 mi) from town, is a favorite with locals. Lounge chairs, towels, and showers are available for rent from the hotels and restaurants along the beach. Public transportation is available from Tampico for about 35¢.

Dining and Lodging

$$ ✕ **Diligencias.** The crowd pleaser here is a dish called Pancho Lopez—grilled fillet of fish crowned with a sauce of octopus, shrimp, and onions. If that doesn't grab you, there's always stuffed crabs, another specialty at this well-known seafood café. It's easy to find: The facade is covered with a colorful mural depicting denizens of the deep. ✉ *Ayuntamiento 2702,* ☎ *12/13–76–42. AE, MC, V.*

$ ✕ **Café y Nevería Elite.** This is a popular gathering spot for breakfast, coffee, and ice-cream treats. Don't be put off by the noise and the rather worn Formica tables; it's all part of the local color. ✉ *Av. Díaz Mirón 211 Ote.,* ☎ *12/12–03–64. No credit cards.*

$$ 🏨 **Camino Real.** Attractively decorated, this low-rise property 20 minutes from the city center is a resort hotel and the best you'll find in

Tampico (in spite of the name, it's not part of the Camino Real chain). Its rooms and bungalows surround a huge garden filled to overflowing with tropical trees and flowers. Rooms contain Chippendale-style furniture, minibars, satellite color TVs, and direct-dial telephones. Fishing excursions can be booked through the hotel's travel agency. ✉ *Hidalgo 2000, Tampico, Tamps. 89140,* ☎ *12/13–88–11,* FAX *12/13–92–26. 102 rooms. Restaurant, bar, pool, golf course, tennis court, travel service, car rental. AE, DC, MC, V.*

$ **Howard Johnson Tampico.** This hotel, the former Colonial, became a Howard Johnson franchise in 1996 after meeting the U.S. chain's standards; it charges only $28 for a double room. A new paint job, new rugs, curtains, beds, carpets, and added services now are being touted. White walls make the rather small rooms seem larger. ✉ *Madera 210 Ote., Tampico, Tamps. 89000,* ☎ *12/12–76–76 or 800/654–2000,* FAX *12/12–06–53. 138 rooms. Restaurant, bar, beauty salon, travel services, free parking. AE, MC, V.*

$ **Plaza.** This centrally located budget hotel is clean and comfortable, if a little drab. Rooms are small but air-conditioned, and all have phones and TVs. ✉ *Madero 204, Tampico, Tamps. 89000,* ☎ *12/14–16–78 or 12/14–17–84. 40 rooms. Restaurant. MC, V.*

Nightlife and the Arts

Eclipse (✉ Universidad 2004, ☎ 12/13–14–95) has dancing on Thursday only; the rest of the week, it's a video bar. **Byblos** (✉ Byblos 1, ☎ 12/13–08–27) is another popular disco. The bar at the **Camino Real Hotel** (✉ Hidalgo 2000, ☎ 12/13–88–11) offers music and dancing Thursday to Saturday evenings.

Outdoor Activities and Sports

FISHING

Although the river is polluted, tarpon and snapper fishing is still popular at **Chairel Lagoon,** with boats and equipment available for rent (just don't plan to eat what you hook). You can also arrange for a boat, guide, and equipment through the Camino Real Hotel in Tampico.

GOLF

Lagunas de Miralta Country Club (☎ 12/23–87–27) sells day passes at Centro Commercial Tres Arcos on Hidalgo for its golf course at Km 26.1 on the Carretera Tampico–Altamira. Ask at your hotel about passes or special discounts at other local clubs.

NORTHEASTERN MEXICO A TO Z

Arriving and Departing

By Car

With unleaded gasoline now more widely available, an increasing number of American motorists are exploring Mexican highways. A car trip is not without its red tape, however.

For details about driving into Mexico, *see* Driving *in* the Gold Guide. It's essential to have all your documents in order. **Sanborn's Mexican Insurance** (✉ 2009 S. 10th St., McAllen, TX, ☎ 800/222–0158, FAX 210/686–0732) can help you complete the paperwork in advance—for free if you buy insurance there, otherwise for a fee.

Distances are deceiving in this part of Mexico because of mountainous driving in the Sierra Madre Oriente. It generally takes three hours to drive from the border to Monterrey; from Monterrey to Ciudad Victoria, it's another four hours.

BORDER TOWNS

Downtown Nuevo Laredo is reached by two bridges: International Bridge 1 in town, and the Columbia–Laredo Bridge (42 km, or 26 mi, northwest of Laredo). Both have facilities for clearing people and vehicles for travel to the interior of Mexico. (Be extra careful when parking your vehicle in Nuevo Laredo; use only parking lots with attendants on duty as there have been a number of reports of theft of luggage and car stereos.)

The New Bridge is the best route from downtown Brownsville to downtown Matamoros. U.S. 281 leads down to Hidalgo, Texas, and the bridge crossing into Reynosa. For brief excursions across the border, consider leaving your car in Texas and walking over. This eliminates the long wait—often a half hour or more—to bring a car back into the United States.

From Matamoros, Mexico 180 runs down the Gulf coast to Tampico, Veracruz, and beyond. A turnoff on Mexico 101 leads to the hunting and fishing camps at Lake Vicente Guerrero. Mexico 97 leads from Reynosa into Mexico 101/180, which meet up for a bit. From Reynosa, you can drive the free routes Mexico 40 to Mexico 35 to Linares; here Mexico 58 will lead you across to San Roberto (and Mexico 57) via a spectacular road with a most unusual mural by Frederico Cantu chiseled out of the side of a mountain.

MONTERREY

From Laredo, the old Pan-American Highway, Mexico 85 Libre (free), and the four-lane Mexico 85 Cuota (toll) both lead to Monterrey, some 242 km (150 mi) south; the latter road, which ends in Monterrey, is a much better one, although the toll is expensive (about $15). It's around the same price to take the toll road Mexico 40 to Monterrey from Reynosa; although the Laredo route is more scenic, traversing some nice mountains, Laredo itself is more congested to get through than Reynosa. The Reynosa road, although flat and dull, is more convenient to downtown Monterrey.

TAMPICO

The port is roughly a seven-hour drive from Matamoros on Mexico 180, or eight hours from Monterrey via Mexico 85, which connects with Mexico 80.

By Plane

BORDER CITIES

From Mexico City, **Aeromexico** has service to Matamoros (☎ 89/7–79–45) and Reynosa (☎ 89/22–1115); **Mexicana** flies to Nuevo Laredo (☎ 87/12–20–52).

MONTERREY

Mexicana (☎ 8/380–7300) has flights from Chicago and San Antonio to Monterrey. **Aeromexico** (☎ 8/343–5560) offers service from Houston, New York, and Los Angeles via Mexico City. **Continental** (☎ 8/333–2622) flies from Chicago, Las Vegas, Los Angeles, Miami, and New York, via Houston. **American** (☎ 8/340–3031) has five flights a day to Monterrey from Dallas. **Aerolitoral** (☎ 8/386–2070) has service from McAllen and San Antonio, Texas. **Taesa** (☎ 8/343–3077) flies from Mexico City.

Monterrey's **Aeropuerto Internacional Mariano Escobedo** (☎ 8/345–4432), equipped with luggage storage ($4 per day) and a money-exchange booth, is 6 km (4 mi) northeast of downtown. The only way to get here is by taxi, which will cost about $8.

TAMPICO

Aerolitoral (☎ 12/28–05–55) has nonstop flights to Tampico from Mexico City. Both **Aeromexico** (☎ 12/17–08–88) and **Mexicana** ☎ 12/28–21–95) offer flights between Tampico and Mexico City.

By Train

Currently, there is no first-class train service from the border to Monterrey or Tampico, although the first-class ***El Regiomontano,*** with seats and sleeping berths, runs from Monterrey to Saltillo and Mexico City. For up-to-date information about schedules and prices, contact **Mexico by Train** in Laredo (☎ FAX 210/725–3659 or 800/321–1699).

Getting Around

By Bus

Northeastern Mexico is well connected by buses, which are becoming downright luxurious while fares remain low. Information on Mexican bus service is available from terminals in Laredo (Valley Transit, ☎ 210/723–4324), McAllen (Valley Transit, ☎ 210/686–5479), and Brownsville (Valley Transit, ☎ 210/546–7171). **Transportes del Norte** (☎ 8/372–4965), in conjunction with **Greyhound,** goes from San Antonio, Dallas, and Houston to Monterrey.

By Subway

The Monterrey metro, which runs along elevated tracks across the city, is modern and efficient. There are only two lines. Magnetic cards are used to enter the station; buy them from station vending machines in units of one, three, or five rides; each ride costs less than 30¢. The metro runs every day from 6 AM to midnight.

By Taxi

Taxis are pretty scarce in border towns but plentiful in Monterrey and Veracruz. They usually cruise the streets on a 24-hour basis.

Contacts and Resources

Consulates

MATAMOROS

United States (✉ Calle 1, 2002 and Azaleas, ☎ 88/12–44–02).

MONTERREY

Canada (✉ Edificio Kalos, Calle Mariano Escobedo and Av. Constitución, Suite 108, ☎ 8/344–3200 or 8/344–2753). **United States** (✉ Av. Constitución 411 Poniente, ☎ 8/343–0650 or 8/345–2120).

Emergencies

MATAMOROS

Police (✉ González and Calle Venteuno, ☎ 88/17–88–83). **Cruz Roja (Red Cross) Hospital** (✉ García and L. Caballero, ☎ 88/12–00–44).

MONTERREY

Police (✉ Gonzalitos and Lincoln, ☎ 8/370–0048). **Cruz Roja Hospital** (✉ Universidad and Camelo, ☎ 8/342–1212).

NUEVO LAREDO

Police (✉ Maclovio Herréra and Ocampo, ☎ 87/12–21–46 or 87/12–30–25). **Cruz Roja** (✉ Independencia 1619 and San Antonio, ☎ 87/12–09–49 or 87/12–09–89).

REYNOSA

Police (✉ Morales between Veracruz and Nayarit, ☎ 89/22–00–08 or 89/22–09–02). **Hospital Santander** (✉ Alvaro Obregón 101, ☎ 89/22–96–22).

TAMPICO

Police (✉ Sor Juana Ines de la Cruz and Tamaulipas, ☎ 12/12–10–32. **Cruz Roja Hospital** (✉ Tamaulipas and Colegio Militar, Zona Centro, ☎ 12/12–13–33).

English-Language Bookstore

In Monterrey, the **American Bookstore** (✉ Garza Sada 2404-A near Pemex station, ☎ 8/387–0838) has a great selection of books in English.

Guided Tours

Several U.S. tour operators, including **Sanborn's Viva Tours** (✉ 2015 S. 10th St., McAllen, TX, ☎ 210/682–9872 or 800/395–8482), run shopping and sightseeing tours to the border towns and coach excursions into the interior, including to El Tajín (☞ The State of Veracruz, *below*). **Osetur Tours** (✉ Calles San Francisco and Loma Larga, ☎ 8/347–1599 or 8/347–1614) in Monterrey provides sightseeing excursions in the areas.

Visitor Information

The best information about this part of Mexico is found in Texas border towns, especially at places that sell the (mandatory) Mexican automobile insurance. These include **Sanborn's Viva Tours** (✉ 2015 S. 10th St., McAllen, TX, ☎ 210/682–9872 or 800/395–8482), **Sanborn's Mexican Insurance** (✉ 2009 S. 10th St., McAllen, TX, ☎ 800/222–0158, FAX 210/686–0732), **Bravo Insurance** (✉ 2212 Santa Ursula, Laredo, TX, ☎ 210/723–3657, FAX 210/723–0000), and **Johnny Ginn's Travel** (✉ 1845 Expressway 77, Brownsville, TX, ☎ 210/542–5457, FAX 210/504–2919). The **Brownsville Chamber of Commerce** (✉ 1600 E. Elizabeth, 1 block from International Bridge into Matamoros, ☎ 210/542–4341) is open daily 9–5.

Matamoros Tours-Transport (✉ Tamaulipas and Alvaro Obregón, few blocks from International Bridge, ☎ 88/12–21–18) is open daily 8–6. **Nuevo Laredo** (✉ Guerrero near Puente Internacional, ☎ 87/12–01–04) is open daily 8:30–8. **Reynosa** (✉ Puente Internacional, ☎ 89/2–11–89 or 89/2–24–49) is open weekdays 7:30 AM–8 PM. **Monterrey Infotour** (✉ Calle Padre Mier and Dr. Coss near the Macro Plaza, ☎ 8/345–0870, 8/345–0902, or 91–800/83–222; 800/235–2438 in the U.S.) is open Tuesday–Sunday 10–5. **Tampico** (✉ Olmos 101 at Carranza, ☎ 12/12–26–78) is open weekdays 9–7.

THE STATE OF VERACRUZ

A long, skinny crescent of land bordering the Gulf of Mexico, the state of Veracruz is often ignored by travelers, many of whom do no more than glimpse the state through the window of a bus barreling toward the Yucatán Peninsula. Although Veracruz's ruins and beaches can't compare with those on the Yucatán, the state is popular with vacationing Mexicans, drawn to the cool hill towns of the Sierra de Los Tuxtlas and the liveliness of Veracruz city.

Descending from the volcanic Sierra, the Veracruz coast consists of flat lowlands characterized by terrible heat and swamps and pockmarked by noisome oil refineries. As you head inland a ways—Veracruz is only 140 km (87 mi) across at its widest point—the land rises to meet the Sierra Madre Oriental range, with its 5,610-meter Pico de Orizaba (also called Citlaltépetl), Mexico's highest mountain. In the foothills of this range, you'll find the university town and state capital of Jalapa, where students share the colonial streets with local farmers who have come to town to market their crops. The state does have some good beaches along the coast, particularly around the northern city of Tuxpán, but the real reasons to come are the atmosphere, the history, and the people. All these are to be found at their best in the city of Veracruz, a working port with so many marimba bands in the *zócalo* (main square) on weekend evenings that they must compete to be heard.

Olmec civilization thrived in Veracruz long before the rise of the Maya. The state's best-preserved ruins, at El Tajín near Papantla, are thought to have been the work of yet another civilization, which had its heyday later, between AD 550 and AD 1100. By the time Hernán Cortés landed in Veracruz in 1519, the Aztecs held sway, but within a very short time the Indian population was decimated by disease and war.

The state of Veracruz played a pivotal role in Cortés's march to Tenochchitlan. Foreign tourism is expected to be boosted through a circuit sponsored by the Mexican government called the *Ruta de Cortés* (Route of Cortés), which traces the Spanish conquistador's footsteps, beginning with his Veracruz landing through to his arrival in Mexico City, where he defeated the Aztec rulers. It's a mélange of soft adventure excursions like river rafting combined with visits to colonial cities, old haciendas, and archaeological zones that were instrumental in the Spanish Conquest.

In modern times, the discovery of oil in Veracruz caused a population explosion that saw the number of Veracruzanos go from about 1 million at the beginning of the century to more than 7 million today. For most foreign travelers, the occasional sulfurous stench of a coastal oil refinery is an unpleasant intrusion on their tropical reverie, but for many of the state's residents, it's their lifeblood.

Veracruz

502 km (320 mi) south of Tampico, 345 km (211 mi) west of Mexico City.

Veracruz was Mexico's premier seaside resort and the port of entry for most foreign visitors until a few decades ago; travelers arrived by ship, then boarded a train to Mexico City, often looking wistfully back. Today relatively few foreigners find their way to Veracruz's beaches, but domestic vacationers are lured into the fun-loving town by prices far lower than those found in Acapulco, Puerto Vallarta, or Cancún.

Veracruz was the first European city to be established on the North American mainland and the major gateway for Spanish settlement of Mexico, although the spot where Cortés landed in 1519 lies about 50 km (30 mi) to the northwest in a tiny slip of a place called Antigua. To meet their labor needs, the Spanish brought a large number of Africans to Veracruz as slaves. Later, the port was flooded with Cuban immigrants. This mix has created an open-minded city, where tourists of all cultural extractions are generously welcomed.

But perhaps the most profound influence of Veracruz's mixed population can be seen in its music and dance. Veracruz is the hometown of La Bamba, a song that dates back to the 17th century. In addition to its most famous song, the city has a special brand of music, played by lively trios outfitted in white and slapping away at tiny guitars and portable harps. In the evening, mariachis entertain outside the sidewalk cafés around the main plaza. Whether at night or during the day, a stop at one of these coffeehouses is de rigueur.

The *danzón,* a langorous two-person dance with lots of hip movement, was brought to the city by penniless refugees fleeing Cuba in 1879 following its War of Independence. Most ended up living outside the city walls (only Veracruz aristocrats were allowed to live inside), but the sons of the elite, who sneaked into the poor neighborhoods at night,

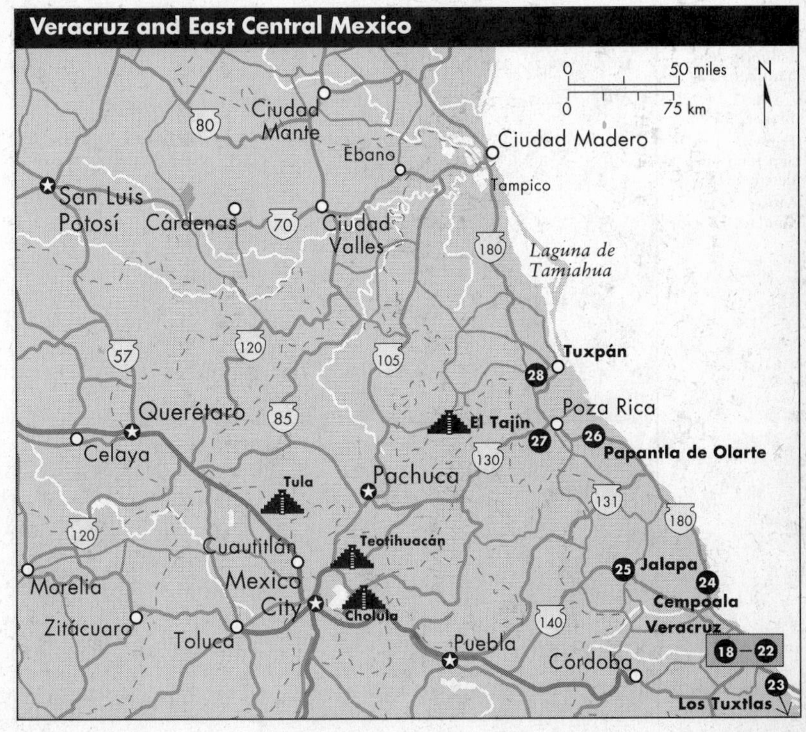

eventually introduced the danzón to high society. Sensuous compared to the stiff and formal dance that had been the norm until this time, the danzón was at first considered scandalous, but it soon won the hearts of even its detractors and became the most popular dance in the city. It later spread throughout the country.

If this is your first visit to the port of Veracruz, a good place to get ori-
18 ented is the **Museo de la Ciudad.** The region's history is narrated through artifacts and displays, and scale models of the city help you get the lay of the land. Also exhibited are copies of pre-Columbian statues and contemporary indigenous art. A $1 donation pays for a guided tour by a bilingual student. ✉ *Zaragoza at Morelos, no phone.* *Free.* ⏲ *Mon.–Sat. 9–4.*

During the Viceregal era, Veracruz was the only east-coast port permitted to operate in New Spain. As a result, it was frequently attacked
19 by pirates. The great **Fort of San Juan de Ulúa,** built shortly after the conquest and the last territory in Mexico to be held by the Spanish Royalists, is a monument to that swashbuckling era. A miniature city in itself, the island fort is a maze of moats, ramparts, and drawbridges smack in the middle of the busy port area (it's now connected to the mainland by a causeway). Fortification of the island began in 1535 under the direction of Antonio de Mendoza, the first viceroy of New Spain. Ground coral, sand, and oyster shells were used for the original walls. A few centuries later, the fort was used as a prison, housing such figures as Benito Juárez, who was held prisoner here by conservative dictator Santa Anna before being exiled to Louisiana in 1853. After Independence, it was used in unsuccessful attempts to fight off first the invading French, the Americans, then the French again and, in 1914, the Americans again. ✉ *Reached via causeway from downtown Veracruz, no phone.* *$2; free Sun.* ⏲ *Tues.–Sun. 9–4.*

Acuario de Veracruz, **21**
Baluarte de Santiago, **20**
Casita Blanca, **22**
Fort of San Juan de Ulúa, **19**
Museo de la Ciudad, **18**

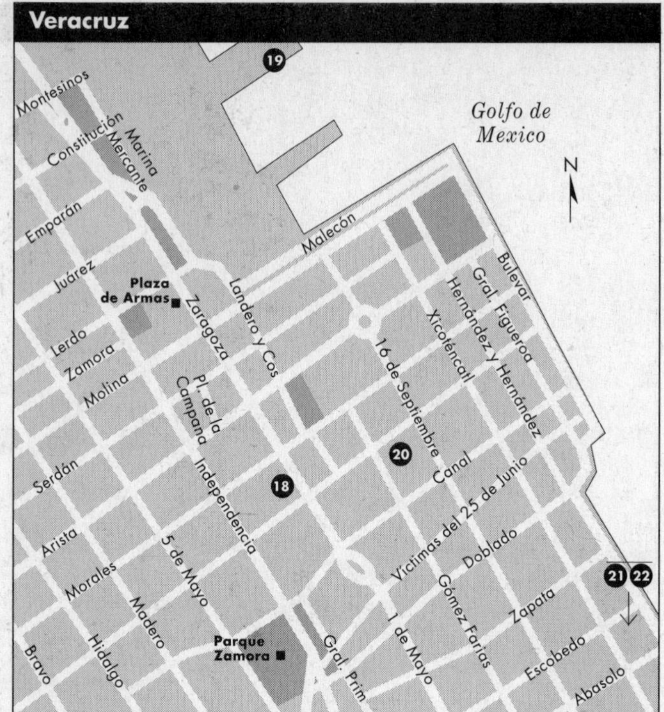

20 The **Baluarte de Santiago,** a fortress and museum, is all that's left of the old city walls; like the Fort of San Juan de Ulúa, the colonial bulwark was built as a defense against pirates (but some 100 years later, in 1635). The structure is impressively solid from the outside and romantically lit at night. Inside is a small museum that has an exquisite permanent exhibit of gold pre-Columbian jewelry—definitely Spanish plunder—which was accidently discovered by a fisherman 25 years ago and has been on display since 1991. ✉ *Canal at 16 de Septiembre, no phone.* 🎫 *$1.75; free Sun.* ⏲ *Tues.–Sun. 10–4:30.*

Since 1993, Veracruz has been the home of one of the three most im-
21 portant aquariums in the world, the state-of-the-art **Acuario de Veracruz.** In addition to its public displays, this impressive complex also houses a marine research center. Among the main exhibits are a tank containing 3,000 different species of marine life native to the Gulf of Mexico, including nurse sharks, manta rays, barracudas, sea turtles, and the pre-Hispanic *pejelagartos,* which look like a combination of crocodile and fish. Smaller display cases host swimming sea horses and the lethal but beautiful scorpion fish, with its long, porcupine-like quills. Check out the 18-ft-long outline on the far wall, above the caption "This is the actual size of a great white shark caught off the coast of Tuxpán, Veracruz." ✉ *Plaza Acuario in Malecón del Puerto de Veracruz,* ☎ *29/34–79–84.* 🎫 *$3.* ⏲ *Mon.–Thurs. 10–7, Fri.–Sun. 10–7:30.*

22 Don't miss the **Casita Blanca** (White House), the museum-home of Agustín Lara, one of Mexico's most beloved songwriters and singers. Lara's occupations included playing the piano in a house of ill repute and being a bullfighter; he is also famous for marrying seven women, including Mexican screen goddess Maria Felíx. He died in 1970 at the age of 73 after spending the last years of his life writing and recording music at La Casita Blanca. Among his most famous songs, piped

in via cassette, are "Maria Bonita," which he dedicated to Felíx, and "Granada." Newspaper clippings, caricatures, and a replica of the radio station where Lara went on the air nightly with "La Hora Azul" (The Blue Hour) help plunge you into a life that was constantly in the public eye. ✉ *Blvd. Adolpho Ruíz Cortines s/n, Boca del Río, no phone.* 🎫 *$2.* 🕑 *Tues.–Sun. 10–2 and 4–8.*

OFF THE BEATEN PATH

ANTIGUA – This town, which was given its name by the Spaniards after they abandoned it, was the site of the first European landing in the New World and the conquistadors' capital for 75 years. Cortés's home, which once had 22 rooms surrounding a huge courtyard, lies abandoned on the northern edge of the village; it's worth seeing if only for its crumbling, roofless masonry, taken over by clinging vines and massive tree roots. Antigua also hosts the first church of New Spain, a little white stucco structure in remarkably good condition. Here, where Cortés and his soldiers prayed and the first converted Indian was baptized, masses are still said today.

Beaches

Veracruz City's beaches are much less inviting than you might expect: Most are somewhat dirty, and the water is polluted. The beach begins on the southern edge of the city at **Villa del Mar** but is at its best down toward **Mocambo,** about 7 km (4 mi) from downtown Veracruz. Better beaches are farther from town: About 4 km (2½ mi) south of Playa Mocambo is **Boca del Río,** a small fishing village at the mouth of the Río Jamapa that is quickly getting sucked into Veracruz.

Dining and Lodging

In addition to the restaurants in Veracruz, you'll want to try one in the fishing village of **Boca del Río,** where the little Jamapa river meets the sea about 10 km (6 mi) south of downtown. Many of them—they seem to turn up between every other house—are modest but serve some of the finest seafood in Mexico. (Boca del Río holds a spot in *The Guinness Book of Records* for the largest fish fillet stuffed with shellfish—it was prepared at Pardiño's restaurant.) The area fronting the water south of downtown toward Boca del Río, and especially along Playa Mocambo, is where you will find the better beaches, as well as most of the fancier hotels and resorts.

$$$ ✕ **La Mansion.** This elegant restaurant is part of a nationwide chain specializing in grilled meats. The Veracruz branch, on the boulevard east of downtown in Boca del Río, has attractive southwestern decor in subdued greens and peach, as well as brisk and efficient service. A few soups and salads are served, but the menu is dominated by thick cuts of steak. The extensive wine selection consists almost exclusively of domestic, Spanish, and French reds. A jacket and tie would not be out of place here. ✉ *Blvd. Adolpho Ruíz Cortines s/n next to Agustín Lara Museum, Boca del Río,* ☎ *29/37–13–38. AE, MC, V.*

$$$ ★ ✕ **Mariscos Villa Rica.** This casual, seafront palapa restaurant is worth the small effort to find it. Hidden on a small street that runs parallel to Playa Mocambo, the Villa Rica is a favorite with locals in the know but sees almost no casual tourists. The menu consists entirely of seafood. Specialties include sea bass, snapper, prawns, and lobster, prepared as you wish. However, the restaurant keeps a few meat dishes in the kitchen for carnivores. There is a small, reasonably priced wine list, but the beverage of choice among loyal patrons is cold Corona with lime. Live music is performed Thursday–Sunday from 2:30 PM on. ✉ *Calle Mocambo s/n, Boca del Río,* ☎ *29/37–76–80. MC, V.*

$$ ✕ **La Fragata.** Those who are not staying in the old-fashioned Hotel Mocambo can visit its restaurant for an evening meal and see the place at its best—when the breezes off the water blow at night and the terraced gardens are illuminated. For the full effect, request an outdoor table. Dinner offerings range from filet mignon to *huachinango* (sea bass) stuffed with shrimp and calamari, but there's nothing in the way of lighter fare beyond a few disappointing salads. The restaurant is rarely crowded, and service is casual and very friendly. ✉ *Ruíz Cortines s/n on Playa Mocambo, Boca del Río,* ☎ *29/22–05–05. AE, MC, V.*

$$ ★ ✕ **Pardiño's.** This modest eatery is a star among Boca del Río's many seafood restaurants and a favorite of the port's residents. Its fame has even spread abroad; it's not unusual for the chef to be invited to gastronomic festivals in France. Plain tables in a storefront on the village's main square belie the elegant preparation of such dishes as crabs *salpicón* (finely chopped with cilantro, onion, and lime), grilled sea bass, and, of course, *huachinango à la veracruzana,* here served with *plátanos fritos* (fried plantains). Also delicious are the simple, fresh appetizers, such as shrimp cocktail with generous chunks of ripe avocado. Owner Rafael Pardiño, who comes from many generations of restaurateurs, just spruced up the menu with his own creations—coconut stuffed with succulent seafood plus mouthwatering breaded crab claws. Pardiño's has another, much smaller, location in downtown Veracruz in a restored colonial building. The Boca del Río restaurant is the only one in the area with air-conditioning. ✉ *Zamora 40, Boca del Río,* ☎ *29/86–01–35;* ✉ *Landero y Coss 146 at malecón, Veracruz,* ☎ *29/31–48–81. MC, V.*

$$ ✕ **Restaurant Albatros.** This unlikely establishment, tucked away in a residential neighborhood a few blocks from the waterfront, has the feel of a semi-exclusive men's club, an effect enhanced by the dark-wood furnishings. The menu includes some new unusual dishes, such as *filete de res Banderas* (steak with three different sauces—tomato, creamy mushroom and avocado—representing the red, green, and white colors of the Mexican flag). The real attraction, however, is the fresh seafood, which the accommodating chef will prepare to your specifications. ✉ *16 de Septiembre 1480, at Azueta,* ☎ *29/31–25–85. MC, V.*

$ ✕ **Gran Café de la Parroquia.** Don't be confused if someone tells you this is the wrong Gran Café de la Parroquia: The coffeehouse that long held that name is now called Gran Café del Portal (☞ *below*); while this malecón eatery is run by a black-sheep faction of the Fernandez family, kicked out of Del Portal in 1995 after the settlement of a 20-year lawsuit. The story makes for a good soap opera. The menu and music are practically the same at both places and both tend to draw lots of local families. ✉ *Insurgentes Veracruzanos 340,* ☎ *29/32–25–84. No credit cards.*

$ ✕ **Gran Café del Portal.** Opened by a Spanish immigrant in 1835 in a former monastery, this most famous of Veracruz's sidewalk cafés eventually grew to cover an entire city block. For a long time it was called the Gran Café de la Parroquia, but following a family feud that ousted the cousins who had been running the place, it resumed its original name, Gran Café del Portal, in 1995. An indispensable stop for a *café lechero* (coffee with hot milk)—every Mexican president since Benito Juárez has been here—it's lively from dawn to dusk with the animated babble of customers, the tapping of spoons against glasses to summon waiters, and live marimba music played by the best musicians in town. The menu has a wide selection of egg dishes, as well as soups, sandwiches, a traditional version of huachinango à la veracruzana, and hearty steak and chicken entrées, but the coffee—the formula for which is a well-guarded family secret—is the real draw. ✉ *Independencia 105 across from cathedral,* ☎ *29/31–27–59. No credit cards.*

$ ✕ **La Bamba.** This casual eatery sits just off the malecón, suspended on stilts above the water. Seats on the terrace enjoy a cooling sea breeze and Mexican ballads play over the sound system. The management prides itself on its innovative seafood dishes; these include *pámpano Bamba* (the house special sea bass), which comes smothered in shrimp, calamari, and shellfish, all sautéed in garlic. The menu also features not-too-expensive lobster, as well as a number of beef and poultry dishes. A modest selection of wines, most of them Mexican, and cocktails complement the food. ✉ *Avila Camacho at Zapata,* ☎ *29/32–53–55. MC, V. Closed Mon.*

$ ✕ **Tortas Koy Koy.** This unpretentious sandwich joint, set right on the verdant Parque Zamora, is a favorite date spot for young *jarochos* (as natives of Veracruz are called). It specializes in excellent sandwiches of house-roasted chicken, pork, or beef served with beans, cheese, tomato, and avocado and accompanied by a plate of spicy pickled vegetables. Burgers and fries are also on the menu, along with traditional Mexican offerings such as tacos and tamales. ✉ *Manuel Doblado s/n,* ☎ *1–50–49. No credit cards.*

$$$ 🏨 **Continental Plaza Veracruz.** Opened in early 1994 between Veracruz and Boca del Río, this Mexican chain hotel was built atop a 3,000-capacity convention facility. It has a complete business center staffed by bilingual secretaries. The amply furnished rooms, decorated in a bright, tropical motif, have climate control, satellite TVs, minibars, and taps spouting potable water. One- or two-bedroom suites, some with hot tubs, are also available, and accommodations on an executive floor entitle guests to concierge service and complimentary Continental breakfast. ✉ *Av. Adolpho Ruíz Cortines 3501, Boca del Río, 94260,* ☎ *29/85–05–05 or 91–800/2–99–00; 800/882–6684 in the U.S.;* FAX *29/85–05–01. 212 rooms, 23 suites. Restaurant, bar, indoor pool, exercise room, baby-sitting, travel services, car rental. AE, MC, V.*

$$$ 🏨 **Fiesta Americana.** This splashy hotel on Playa Costa de Oro, inaugurated by the Mexican president in January 1996, has the best business facilities in the state of Veracruz. It has six floors and miles of marble corridors, all of which seem to lead to the giant serpentine pool and lush gardens facing the ocean. There are three hot tubs, one with a waterfall. Rooms are done in soft creams and beiges, and their amenities include terraces, voice mail, closet safes, and hair dryers. The swank Fiesta Club floors offer a business center, concierge service, and a bilingual staff. Guests have access to a nine-hole golf course, 20 minutes away. No-smoking rooms and wheelchair-accessible units are available. ✉ *Blvd. Manuel Avila Camacho at Bacalao, Fraccionamiento Costa de Oro, Veracruz 94299,* ☎ *29/22–22—28 or 29/22–22–30; 800/343–7821 in the U.S. 233 rooms and suites. 2 restaurants, 3 bars, room service, 2 pools, barbershop, beauty salon, 3 hot tubs, exercise room, baby-sitting, business services, meeting rooms, travel services, car rental. AE, DC, MC, V.*

$$$ 🏨 **Torremar.** This deluxe high-rise resort on Playa Mocambo underwent a complete refurbishing in 1994, when 50 new rooms and a pool were added. The accommodations, somewhat excessively decorated in pastels, contain all the amenities, including minibars. Suites have small balconies with fantastic views of the Gulf of Mexico. An executive floor, with special concierge service and complimentary breakfast, is also available. Kids will like the cascading poolside fountain and the organized activities in the children's play area. ✉ *Av. Adolpho Ruíz Cortines 4300, Boca del Río 94260,* ☎ *29/21–34–35, 29/21–34–43, 29/21–34–75, or 91–800/2–99–00,* FAX *29/21–02–91. 232 rooms. 2 restaurants, 2 bars, 2 pools, beauty salon, exercise room, children's programs, business services, travel services, car rental. AE, MC, V.*

$$ ★ 🏨 **Emporio.** This large, business-oriented hotel, well situated on the malecón, was turned into an elegant hostelry by a top-to-bottom makeover in 1995. The lobby is a dramatic sweep of marble and rattan furniture, and the guest rooms are bright and cheery. Some have

sea views, and all have marbled bathrooms with bathtubs (those in the suites are hot tubs), satellite color TVs, and air-conditioning. Dine in the popular restaurant, redecorated in neoclassic French style, or in the shade of an umbrella at any of the hotel's three pools (one is equipped with a waterfall, slides, and a miniature ship for children). Business travelers have a small business center and meeting rooms at their disposal. ✉ *Insurgentes Veracruzanos 210, Veracruz 91700,* ☎ *29/32–00–20 or 91–800/2–95–20,* FAX *29/31–22–61. 202 rooms, 40 suites. Restaurant, bar, coffee shop, 3 pools, exercise room, children's programs, business center, travel services, free parking. AE, MC, V.*

$$ **Hotel Mocambo.** When the Mocambo was built in 1934, it was Mexico's only Gulf Coast resort. However, what used to be the loveliest and most romantic hotel in the Veracruz area is becoming a bit threadbare. The spacious guest rooms offer cable TVs, direct-dial telephones, and air-conditioning. The hotel's sprawling, terraced gardens lead down toward the palm-lined Playa Mocambo, but it's a five-level trek down to the beach and pools. Dark-wood fixtures and art-deco touches (such as a set of flowerlike pillars around the indoor pool and stained-glass windows in the lobby) all add to the feeling that the Mocambo belongs in another, more decorous age. ✉ *Av. Adolpho Ruíz Cortines s/n on Playa Mocambo, Boca del Río 94260,* ☎ *29/22–02–05 or 91–800/2–90–01,* FAX *29/22–02–12. 123 rooms. Restaurant, bar, coffee shop, 2 pools, exercise room, free parking. AE, MC, V.*

$$ **Villa del Mar.** This unassuming hotel, just across from one of the nicer sections of the downtown beach, is an ideal place to bring kids. The standard, motel-style rooms are spacious and comfortable and surround a large, pretty garden with a tennis court, pool, and small playground. All the accommodations have color TVs, telephones, and air-conditioning. The staff is very helpful, and some English is spoken at the reception desk. A number of bungalows (accommodating up to five people) are also available: These are a bit gloomy, but some have kitchenettes. ✉ *Avila Camacho s/n at Bartolomé de las Casas, Veracruz 91700,* ☎ *29/31–15–90 or 29/31–33–66,* FAX *29/32–71–35. 90 rooms, 15 bungalows. Restaurant, bar, pool, hot tub, tennis court, playground, free parking. AE, MC, V.*

$–$$ **Hotel Imperial.** This hotel, built in 1750, is not only a national monument but also the best place to sleep on the zócalo. Emperor Maximilian and President Alvaro Obregón are said to have stayed here. Reopened in 1994 after a massive renovation, the hotel has a dazzling lobby with a stained-glass ceiling, cage elevator, grand staircase, and antique furniture. However, most of the rooms are nondescript. At present they have air-conditioning but no phones or TVs (although these are promised for the future), and are reached by way of an unattractive cement staircase off a carpeted corridor. If you can afford it, stay in one of the split-level junior suites, which have attractive colonial furnishings and claw-foot tubs. ✉ *Miguel Lerdo 153, Veracruz 91700,* ☎ *29/31–17–41, 29/31–18–66, or 29/31–65–65. 76 rooms, 16 suites. Restaurant, bar. MC, V.*

$ **Hotel Concha Dorada.** The basically characterless Concha Dorada has the cheapest accommodations on the zócalo. Rooms are cramped but clean, and some have color TVs (local stations only), telephones, and air-conditioning. The downstairs restaurant–sidewalk café serves simple fare and is especially popular (noisy) at lunchtime and on weekend nights. ✉ *Miguel Lerdo 77 near Zaragoza, Veracruz 91700,* ☎ *29/31–29–96,* FAX *29/31–31–21. 36 rooms. MC, V.*

$ ★ **Hotel Hawaii.** This little jewel of a hotel with a prime location on the malecón is one of the best deals in town, offering comfort, class, and personalized service at a reasonable price. All the impeccably maintained rooms come with a pair of queen-size beds, air-conditioning, phone, color cable TV, purified water, and marble bathroom. The staff is eager to please, and there's always a bowl of fresh flowers at the check-in desk. Guests can have all the free coffee they want at the snug ground-floor coffee shop, and maps are available for the asking. The management also sees to it that each guest gets a bag of fine Veracruz coffee to take home. ✉ *Insurgentes Veracruzanos 458, Veracruz 91700,* ☎ *29/38–00–00 or 29/31–04–27,* FAX *29/32–55–24. 32 rooms. Coffee shop, room service, laundry service, free parking. MC, V.*

$ **Hotel Ruiz Milan.** This multistory waterfront hotel is a good value for the price. Guest rooms, though on the small side, are clean, comfortable, and modern. All have color cable TVs, telephones, balconies, ample closet space, and sizable bathrooms; about half the rooms have air-conditioning. The pleasantly cool pink-and-marble lobby is always crowded with Mexican businesspeople, and the hotel itself has all the amenities of a much more expensive establishment, including an indoor pool with a bar, a lobby bar, a comfortable restaurant, and free covered parking. ✉ *Paseo del Malecón 432, Veracruz 91700,* ☎ *29/32–27–72,* FAX *29/32–37–77, ext. 106. 88 rooms. Restaurant, 2 bars, pool, room service. MC, V.*

$ **Hotel Villa Florencia.** This comfortable, quiet hotel is tucked away on an affluent residential street paralleling one of the prettier stretches of Playa Mocambo. Large, standard motel-style rooms are brightened by splashes of tilework; all have two beds, TVs, and sliding-glass doors that open onto patios overlooking the attractive pool area. None of the rooms, however, has a phone. ✉ *Calzada Mocambo 207, Boca del Río 94260,* ☎ *29/21–02–44. 27 rooms. Free parking. MC, V.*

Nightlife and the Arts

Every Tuesday, Friday, and Saturday night after 8, at the **Plaza de Armas** (zócalo), a local troupe dressed in white performs danzón on stage and then goes into the street to join the townsfolk in this traditional Veracruz dance, accompanied by live marimba music. Sunday nights, the dancing is to salsa as well as danzón and moves to **Parque Zamora.** The **Instituto Veracruzo de Cultura** (Veracruz Cultural Institute) (✉ Calles Rayon and Gomez Farias, ☎ 29/22–45–03) offers danzón classes for a minimal fee three times a week.

For authentic Cuban music, head for the unpretentious **El Rincón de la Trova** (✉ Callejon de Lagunilla 59, no phone), where people of all ages gather to dance to a famous tropical band until the wee hours; the floors are cement and the ambience is fun and strictly local.

Discos and video bars are plentiful along the malecón. Both **Ocean** (✉ Av. Adolpho Ruíz Cortines 8, at Ávila Camacho, ☎ 29/37–63–27), a flashy, modern discotheque, and **Blue Ocean** (✉ Ávila Camacho 9, ☎ 29/22–03–66), a video bar with a light show, are packed on Friday and Saturday nights with a young, largely local crowd.

Outdoor Activities and Sports

Deep-sea fishing is popular in Veracruz, and you'll find places to windsurf in the coastal areas a few miles beyond Boca del Río. An annual regatta from the Port of Galveston in Texas to the Port of Veracruz takes place at the end of May. Check with the Mexican Government Tourist Office in Houston for details (☎ 713/629–1611, ext. 27).

Shopping

Stands lining the **malecón** sell a variety of ocean-related items: seashells and beauty creams and powders derived from them; black coral jewelry; ships-in-a-bottle; key rings with miniature sea-life inside; and more. You'll also find flasks of the famous vanilla from Papantla, T-shirts, and tacky stuffed frogs, iguanas, and armadillos. The **Playa Artesanía** market on the malecón purveys higher-quality goods, including leather and jewelry, with higher prices to match. You can bargain at the waterfront stands but not at the Playa.

One of the most unusual shops in town is in the aquarium: **Fiora** (✉ Plaza Aquario, ☎ 29/31–90–29) sells unique and beautiful jewelry designed from miniature flowers grown in Veracruz.

Los Tuxtlas

23 *140 km (84 mi) south of Veracruz.*

A small volcanic mountain range, the Sierra de Los Tuxtlas, meets the sea at Las Tuxtlas; this area has lakes, waterfalls, rivers, mineral springs, and access to beaches, making it a popular stopover for travelers heading east from Mexico City to the Yucatán. The region's three principal towns—**Santiago Tuxtla, San Andrés Tuxtla,** and **Catemaco**—are carved into the mountainsides more than 600 ft above sea level, lending them a coolness even in summer that's the envy of the perspiring masses on the coastal plain. The Tuxtlas gain an air of mystery from the cool, gray fog that slips over the mountains and lakes and the whisperings among the townspeople about the *brujos* (witches), also called curanderos (healers), who read tarot cards, prescribe herbal remedies, and cast spells here. Today, the economic life of Los Tuxtlas depends on cigar manufacturing (the town of San Andrés Tuxtla is famous for its hand-rolled variety, which comes in several sizes) and tourism.

Although much of the architecture here is of the 1960s school of looming cement, all three towns are laid out in the colonial style around a main plaza and a church, and all have a certain amount of charm; Santiago Tuxtla has managed to retain more of its colonial character than the other two Tuxtla towns. The region was also a center of Olmec culture, and Olmec artifacts and small ruins abound. A huge stone Olmec head dominates the zócalo at Santiago Tuxtla, and 21 km (13 mi) east are the ruins of **Tres Zapotes,** now decidedly unspectacular but once an important Olmec ceremonial center believed to have been occupied as early as AD 100. The town also has an informative museum, where you can learn about the region's indigenous heritage and contemporary local cultures.

The largest of the three towns is San Andrés, which is also the local transport hub. With plenty of hotels, it serves as a good base from which to explore the entire region. **Catemaco** is popular among Mexicans as a summer and Christmas resort and is also the place to go for a *consulta* (consultation) with a brujo or curandero, should you have any problems or questions that require some spiritual clarity or supernatural intervention. Tours of Lake Catemaco, which was formed from the crater of a volcano and which harbors a colorful colony of fish-eating baboons, can be arranged through most local hotels.

Cempoala

24 *42 km (26 mi) north of Veracruz.*

Cempoala (often spelled Zempoala) was the capital of the Totonac nation, whose influence spread throughout Veracruz in pre-Hispanic times; the name means "Place of 20 Waters" after the sophisticated irrigation system employed by the Totonacs. The site gains its role in history as the place where, in 1519, conquistador Hernán Cortés formed his first alliance with a native chief; at the time, the population of Cempoala was estimated at around 20,000. The alliance with the Totonacs enlarged Cortés's paltry army of 200 men and encouraged the Spaniard to push on to Mexico City and fight the Aztecs. In his turn, the leader of the Totonacs—dubbed "Fat Chief" by his own people because of his enormous girth—was an avowed enemy of the powerful Aztecs, who forced his people to perform human sacrifices to their war god and put military garrisons on Totonac land.

Cempoala was discovered by Francisco del Paso y Troncoso in 1891. Seven out of the 60 to 90 structures at Cempoala have been excavated and can be visited; all are built of river stones, shells, sand, and "glue" made from the whites of turtle and bird eggs. As the story goes, when Cortés first sighted Cempoala at night, the buildings glowed white under a full moon and the avaricious Spaniard thought he had discovered a city of silver.

Upon entering the ruins, one comes upon **Circulo de los Gladiadores,** a small circle of waist-high walls to the right of center. This was the site of contests between captured prisoners of war and Totonac warriers: each prisoner was required to fight two armed warriors. One such prisoner, the son of a king from Tlaxcala, won the unfair match and became a national hero. His statue stands in a place of honor in Tlaxcala. Another small structure to the left of the circle marks the spot where an eternal flame was kept lit during the sacred 52-year cycle of the Totonacs.

The **Templo Mayor,** the main pyramid, is the largest structure on the site; follow the dirt path that lies straight when you enter. Cortés, after gaining the allegiance of the Fat Chief, placed a Christian cross atop this temple—the first gesture of this sort in New Spain—and had Mass said by a Spanish priest in his company.

At the smaller **Templo de la Luna** (Temple of the Moon), to the far left of Templo Mayor, outstanding warriors were honored with the title "Eagle Knight" or "Tiger Knight" and awarded an obsidian nose ring to wear as a mark of their status. Just to the left of the Moon Temple is the **Templo del Sol** (Temple of the Sun), where the hearts and blood of sacrificial victims were placed.

Back toward the dirt road and across from it is the **Templo de la Diosa de la Muerte** (Temple of the Goddess of Death), where a statue of the pre-Hispanic deity was found along with 1,700 small idols.

A small on-site **museum** opened in 1997. The voladores of Papantla usually give a performance on weekends. Well-trained guides are available but tours are mainly in Spanish. *No phone.* *$1.25; free Sun.* *Daily 10–5.*

Jalapa

25 *90 km (56 mi) northwest of Veracruz.*

Jalapa, which was a Totonac ceremonial center when Cortés arrived, is perched on the side of a mountain, between the coastal lowlands of Veracruz and the high central plateau. More than 4,000 ft above sea level, the city has a bizarre climate—sun, rain, and fog are all likely to show themselves in the course of a day. However, for perspiration-soaked escapees from the coast, it's an enviable change. The capital and cultural hub of the state of Veracruz, Jalapa is a university town with a diverse population; you are as likely to see longhaired young people sitting around in cafés as you are wizened campesinos walking to work. The town is also home to a symphony orchestra, a ballet company, and a state theater that attracts big-name performers. Jalapa is filled with pretty parks and lakes, and since the grit has been removed from their surfaces, the government buildings downtown are showing off their stateliness once more. The hills here pose intriguing engineering problems—in some places you'll find the twisting, cobblestone streets bordered by 6-ft-high sidewalks built to compensate for sudden, sharp inclines. (Note: You'll often see the name of the city spelled Xalapa; Jalapa is the Hispanicized version of the latter, a Nahuatl word.)

The town's prime cultural attraction is the **Museo de Antropología de Jalapa.** With 3,000 out of 29,000 pieces on display, it is second only to Mexico City's archaeological museum and is a treasure trove of artifacts from the three main pre-Hispanic cultures of Veracruz: Huastec, Totonac, and, most important, Olmec. Its three sections are filled with magnificent stone Olmec heads; carved stelae and offering bowls; terracotta jaguars and cross-eyed gods; cremation urns in the forms of bats and monkeys; lovely Totonac murals; and, most touching of all, life-size sculptures of women who died in childbirth (the ancients elevated them to the status of goddesses). At a burial site, you can see ancient bones, ritually deformed skulls, and ceremonial figurines. Guided tours by English-speaking students are available Tuesday–Sunday 11 AM–4 PM, but you may want to call in advance and make an appointment, as the tour schedule is unpredictable. ✉ *Av. Jalapa s/n,* ☎ *28/15–49–52.* 🎫 *$2.* ⏲ *Daily 10–5.*

Dining and Lodging

$$ ★ ✕ **La Casa de Mama.** This extremely popular restaurant is on a busy thoroughfare just east of the center of town. The dark, antique furnishings and lazy ceiling fan almost succeed in giving this place the feel of a northern Mexican hacienda, but the incessant street noise reminds you that you're in a busy capital city. Never mind; you'll be focusing on the generous portions of charcoal-broiled steaks and the succulent shrimp and fish dishes, served with *charro* beans (black beans cooked in a spicy sauce) or Mexican rice. The place is especially well known for its desserts, which include smooth lemon tarts, bananas flambéed in brandy, and vanilla ice cream topped with Kahlua. ✉ *Ávila Camacho 113,* ☎ *28/17–31–44 or 28/17–62–32. AE, MC, V. No dinner Mon.*

$$ ★ ✕ **La Estancia de los Tecajetes.** For fine regional dishes with a dash of creativity, try this rustic, lodgelike restaurant overlooking beautiful Juárez Park. It's cozy and relaxing, always buzzing with diners feasting on *cecina* (paper-thin fillet of beef) with enchiladas, beans, and avocado; *pollo à la Ribera* (deboned chicken breast, grilled and bathed in salsa and mushrooms); or *crepa consentida* (crepes filled with chicken and smothered in poblano chilies and local cheese). Corn tortillas are made on the premises, and the walls are filled with charming sepia-tone photos of Jalapa past. ✉ *Avila Camacho 90–12, Plaza Tecajetes,* ☎ *28/18–07–32. AE, MC, V.*

$$ ✕ **La Pérgola.** Designed in the early 1960s by Enrique Murillo, the attractive Pérgola is a relaxing place for an afternoon or evening meal. The menu concentrates on steaks and shrimp, painstakingly prepared and imaginatively presented. For dessert, try the *plátanos flameados con brandy* (bananas flambéed in brandy) or an order of crepes suzette. Umbrella-shaded tables on the patio offer a view of the leafy entrance to the Universidad Veracruzana and its enormous sports stadium. ✉ *Av. Universidad at Calle Pérgola, Lomas del Estadio,* ☎ *28/17–47–14. AE, MC, V. No dinner Sun.*

$ ✕ **El Balcón de la Agora.** This small café, part of the Agora de la Ciudad cultural center in Parque Juárez, is popular with students who come to study over a strong cup of coffee or an inexpensive sandwich. Open-air balcony seating provides an excellent view of the green city below and, in the distance, the Pico de Orizaba mountain. Order at the cash register as you enter, and then present your receipt at the counter as you repeat your order. ✉ *Bajos del Parque Juárez,* ☎ *28/18–57–30. No credit cards.*

$ ✕ **La Fonda.** The entrance to this charming, traditional restaurant is hidden on a small pedestrian walkway off the busy Calle Enríquez, a block from Parque Juárez. Brightly colored streamers, baskets, flowers, and murals adorn the walls and ceiling, and the warm corn tortillas served with every meal are made before your eyes. The food is hearty northern Veracruzan fare: Beef or chicken and beans, *nopales* (cactus strips), and/or chili are essential elements of almost every dish. ✉ *Antonio M. de Rivera 1 (also known as Callejon del Diamante) at Enríquez,* ☎ *28/18–45–20. AE, MC, V. Closed Sun.*

$ ✕ **La Sopa.** Modest as it may look, this 20-table restaurant draws food connoisseurs from all ranks of society—local politicians, students, and blue-collar workers—who make a beeline for the bargain *comida corrida* (fixed price) lunch. One of the best-kept secrets in town, La Sopa's four-course attraction might include carrot-and-potato soup, chicken with rice accompanied by fresh corn tortillas, and vanilla pudding served with coffee or tea. The menu features light Mexican *antojitos* (appetizers) in the evening, including *chiles rellenos* (green chili peppers stuffed with meat or cheese and fried in egg batter), and tamales. Live music fills the air every Wednesday (danzón), Thursday (Huastec folk music), Friday and Saturday (harpist), from 1 in the afternoon until 11:30 at night. ✉ *Antonio M. de Rivera 3-A (also known as Callejon del Diamante),* ☎ *28/17–80–69. No credit cards. Closed Sun.*

$ ✕ **1-2-3.** This midsize restaurant, located on a busy thoroughfare in the northern part of the city, looks unpromising from the street, but the interior is a pleasant surprise. Painted in muted, contrasting shades of green and purple, the dining-room walls are lined with the work of local artists, and modern sculpture is scattered about the room. The food, a combination of Mexican and international dishes, is more than reasonably priced. Mexican entrées include sirloin tips with chipotle chilies and *crepas de huitlacoche* (crepes filled with a delicacy corn fungus and bathed in cream sauce). International choices such as Waldorf salad, curried chicken, and steak tartare are knowledgeably prepared. Adjoining the dining rooms is a quiet, casual bar that opens onto the restaurant's simple courtyard. ✉ *Av. Adolpho Ruíz Cortines 857,* ☎ *28/14–71–22. AE, MC, V. No dinner Sun.*

$$ **Fiesta Inn Xalapa.** This pretty chain hotel, which opened in 1993, has the fresh look of a beach property in tropical climes—perhaps to offset the rather gloomy weather typical of Jalapa—and although it's the most expensive hotel in the area, it has the most upscale amenities. It's a bit out of the way—in a primarily residential neighborhood, some 10 minutes by car from the center of town—but a good bet for those who have wheels and are looking for a comfortable, quiet, secure, and well-equipped base. The modern guest rooms in the two-story, colonial-style structure are decorated in cool blues and grays and have satellite-programmed color TVs, telephones, air-conditioning, bathtubs, and plenty of morning sunlight. Airport transfers from the port of Veracruz are available at an extra charge. ✉ *Km 2.5 Carretera Xalapa–Veracruz, Fracc. Las Animas, 91000,* ☎ *28/12–79–20 or 800/343–7821,* FAX *28/12–79–46. 116 rooms, 4 suites. Restaurant, bar, coffee shop, pool, exercise room, business services, free parking. AE, MC, V.*

$$ ★ **Posada Coatepec.** When actor Harrison Ford was filming *Clear and Present Danger* in this area, he stayed at this member of the prestigious Small Grand Hotels of Mexico group, a 15-minute drive from Jalapa. Specializing in fine food (but slow service) and catering to French and German travel groups, the Posada is the former villa of a coffee baron. It now comprises beautifully decorated one- and two-room suites,

each with color satellite TV and minibar; some units have heaters for Coatepec's chilly, rainy winters. Ask for one away from the murmur of street noise. The lobby and inner courtyard are splendidly decorated with a fine collection of antiques; a bar framed by lead crystal windows is cozy and clubby. The hotel offers tours to nearby coffee plantations. ✉ *Hidalgo 9, Coatepec 91501,* ☎ *28/16–05–44,* FAX *28/16–00–40. 24 suites. Restaurant, bar, pool. AE, MC, V.*

$ Hotel Salmones. Once a high-class establishment, the Hotel Salmones has seen better days, but a hotel-wide remodeling started in 1996. Vestiges of its lost glory remain—the high ceilings, sweeping staircases, dark-wood fixtures, and big, beautiful windows are untouched by time. The very clean rooms (which start at $13) lack air-conditioning but are tastefully and simply decorated. All have televisions (local stations only) and telephones; some offer small balconies. ✉ *Zaragoza 24, 91000,* ☎ *28/17–54–31. 60 rooms. Restaurant, bar. MC, V.*

$ Hotel Xalapa. The Hotel Xalapa is the best-equipped downtown hotel, with all the amenities of a much more expensive establishment: air-conditioning, telephones, color TV, bathtubs, and minibars in some rooms; free, covered parking for guests; and a disco. The building itself—another 1960s-style institutional behemoth—is not particularly attractive, but the rooms are large, sunny, and very quiet. ✉ *Esq. Victoria y Bustamante, Zona Centro 91000,* ☎ *28/18–22–22 or 28/17–70–64,* FAX *28/18–94–24. 170 rooms, 30 suites. Restaurant, bar, dance club, free parking. AE, MC, V.*

Nightlife and the Arts

The **Ágora** (✉ Parque Juárez, ☎ 28/18–57–30) cultural center stages art exhibits and the occasional folk-music performance and shows classic and avant-garde films in its cinema club. Stop by during the day to see what's planned. The **Teatro del Estado** (✉ Ignacio de la Llave s/n, ☎ 28/17–41–77, ext. 38) is the big, modern, state theater of Veracruz. The Orquesta Sinfónica de Jalapa performs here, often giving free concerts during the off-season (early June–mid-August). Check *El Diario de Jalapa* (the Jalapa city newspaper in Spanish, available at newsstands) for dates and times of performances, or stop by the Ágora. You may find someone who speaks English here if you are lucky.

Such other nightlife as there is in this student town is generally youth oriented. **La 7a Estacion** (✉ 20 de Noviembre near Central Camionera) is packed with salsa dancers on Wednesday nights; Thursday–Saturday, rock and alternative music are performed. The **Bar Lovento** (✉ 20 de Noviembre Ote. 641) heats up with a salsa beat for dancing Wednesday–Saturday nights. The **Tacotaro** (✉ Calle Avila Camacho and Tecajetes) is a popular video bar. **La Mulada** (✉ Across the street from bus station at Calzada de Tejas) is a disco for dancing.

Outdoor Activities and Sports

RIVER RAFTING

River rafting along the Río Pescados is gaining in popularity. Most of the operators who run these trips are trained in Canada and are highly professional. Base camps with tents, rafting equipment, and dining facilities are located near the river at Jalcomulco, 42 km (26 mi) southeast of Jalapa. (☞ Guided Tours *in* Veracruz A to Z, *below.*)

Shopping

Mexico's finest export coffee is grown in this region, specifically in the highlands around the picturesque colonial towns of Coatepec and Xico, less than 10 km (6 mi) from Jalapa. Shops selling the prized *café de altura* abound in the main squares of both places, and you can get the beans ground to your specifications.

Papantla de Olarte

26 *250 km (150 mi) northwest of Veracruz.*

Papantla de Olarte sits amid tropical hills, the center of a vanilla-producing region. A distinctive mix of Spanish colonial and indigenous influence can be seen here: Totonac men in flowing white pants lead their donkeys through the crowded streets, and palm trees shade the traditional, tiled zócalo. The town is best known for its voladores, who twirl off an 82-ft pole next to Papantla's ornate cathedral. This ritual was originally performed as a tribute to the god of sun and rain. The four fliers begin the dance on a platform at the top of the ceremonial pole, each facing one of the cardinal directions. They start their descent from the side of the platform facing east—where the sun rises and the world awakes—twisting left for 13 full rotations each. Between them, the four fliers circle the pole 52 times, representing the sacred 52-year cycle of the Totonacs. A fifth man, the prayer giver, sits atop the pole, playing a small flute while keeping rhythm on a drum as the fliers descend. Originally, the ceremony was held on the vernal equinox, but now the voladores fly for the crowds every Saturday and Sunday at 12:45 PM and give special performances during Corpus Christi.

El Tajín

27 *13 km (8 mi) west of Papantla.*

The extensive ruins of El Tajín (a Totonac word meaning "thunder") express the highest degree of artistry of any ancient city in the coastal area. The city remained hidden until 1785, when it was discovered by a Spanish engineer. Early theories attributed the complex—believed to be a religious center—to a settlement of Maya-related Huastecs, one of the most important cultures of the Veracruz area. Because of its immense size and unique architecture, however, scholars now believe it may have been built by a distinct El Tajín cultural group related to the Maya. Although much of the site has been restored, many structures are still hidden under thick jungle growth; some archaeologists speculate that hundreds of buildings remain to be excavated.

El Tajín is thought to have reached its peak from about AD 600 to 1200. During this time, hundreds of structures of native sandstone were built here, including temples, double-storied palaces, ball courts, large retaining walls, and hundreds of houses. But El Tajín was already an important religious and administrative center during the first three centuries AD. Its influence is in part attributed to the fact that it had large reserves of cacao beans, used as money in pre-Hispanic times.

Evidence suggests that the southern half of the uncovered ruins—the area around the lower plaza—was reserved for ceremonial purposes. Its centerpiece is the 60-ft-high **Pyramid of the Niches,** an impressive seven-level structure with 365 indentations—one for each day of the solar year. The reliefs on the pyramid depict the ruler, 13-Rabbit—all the rulers' names were associated with sacred animals—and allude also to El Tajín's main god, the benign Quetzalcóatl. One panel on the pyramid tells the tale of heroic human sacrifice and of the soul's imminent descent to the underworld, where it is rewarded with the gift of sacred *pulque* (a milky alcoholic beverage made from cactus) from the gods.

Just south of the pyramid, a series of 10 I-shape **ball courts** were the site of a sacred ball game; the crosslike glyphs on the facades are related to the planet Venus. This game, played throughout Mesoamerica, is similar in some ways to soccer—players used a hard rubber ball that could not be touched with the hands, and suited up in knee pads and body protectors—but far more deadly: Intricate carvings at this and other complexes indicate that the games ended with human sacrifice. It's still a subject of debate whether the sacrificial victim was the winner or loser of the match. It is surmised that the players may have even been high-standing members of the priest or warrior classes.

El Tajín Chico, to the north, is thought to have been the secular part of the city, administrative and residential; it was likely the location of the elite's living quarters. Floors and roofing were made out of a pre-Colombian cement of volcanic rock and limestone. The most important structure here is the Complejo de los Columnos (Complex of the Columns). The columns once held up the cement ceilings, but early settlers in Papantla removed the ceiling stones to construct houses.

Guided tours of the El Tajín are not available: The plaque at the entrance tells some of what little is known about the site in Spanish, English, and French, but the rest is up to your imagination. The entrance is lined with *fondas* (covered stalls) that sell inexpensive meals and mountains of tacky souvenirs, and there's a large, cafeteria-style restaurant at the site. If you're prepared to work your way through the thick jungle, you can see some more recent finds along the dirt paths that lead over the nearby ridges. *$2.50; free Sun. Tues.–Sun. 9–6.*

Note: In early 1994, the most important archaeological find in the Veracruz area in more than 200 years was announced. Another ancient site was discovered some 64 km (40 mi) from El Tajín, near the coastal village of El Pital. Covered by jungle, this seaport, which likely thrived between AD 100 and 600, extended more than 100 square km (40 square mi) and was occupied by thousands of people. Research is still at very preliminary stages and excavation has barely begun, but it is believed that El Pital may shed much light on the history of pre-Hispanic culture and perhaps even provide a missing link between the Olmec and Maya civilizations.

Dining and Lodging

$ ★ ✕ **Restaurante Sorrento.** The Sorrento is the most popular restaurant in Papantla, crowded at mealtimes with locals who come to enjoy the cheap regional seafood and to catch a few minutes of the *telenovela* (soap opera) on the corner set. The dining room is painted lavender and lined with colorful tilework. ✉ *Enríquez 104, no phone. No credit cards.*

$ ✕ **Restaurant Tajín.** The Hotel Tajín's sunny restaurant is comparatively elegant and hardly more expensive than the storefront eateries near the second-class bus station. House specialties include a fillet of fish stuffed with shellfish, *jaibas rellenas* (stuffed crab), rabbit marinated in chili, and Yucatecan *pollo píbil* (chicken in a mild orange *achiote* sauce). Don't be alarmed by the misleading bilingual menu—the *tasajo cerdo* is not, in fact, "steak porpoise" but marinated pork. ✉ *Hotel Tajín, Nuñez y Domínguez 104,* ☎ *784/2–06–44. MC, V.*

$ **Hotel Premier.** Right on Papantla's pretty, lively zócalo, the Premier is the town's swankiest hotel and a real bargain at its tariff of $30 for a double. The lobby is lined with mirrors and furnished with small purple chairs that were once dedicated to the no-longer-functional bar. The rooms themselves are spotless and good-size and have tiny balconies overlooking the square. Amenities include tiled bathrooms, air-conditioning, telephones, and color satellite TVs. However, if you want to dine or drink, you'll have to frequent one of the restaurants or bars around the square.

✉ *Enríquez 103, 93400,* ☎ *784/2–00–80,* FAX *784/2–10–62. 20 rooms. MC, V.*

$ **Hotel Tajín.** Under the same management as the Hotel Premier, the Tajín is less expensive than its slightly more central cousin and has more amenities. Some of the televisions are black and white, some rooms have ceiling fans instead of air-conditioning, and the telephones don't always work, but all in all, the Tajín isn't a bad deal. Its hillside perch makes for nice views, and the rooms, although fairly small, are spotless and comfortable. Hotel services are located in an annex adjoining the main building; there's usually an English-speaking staff member at the reception desk. With one week's notice, the hotel can arrange horseback-riding tours for groups of five to 10 persons for $23 per person to the ruins at El Tajín. ✉ *Nuñez y Domínguez 104, 93400,* ☎ *784/2–06–44 or 784/2–16–23,* FAX *784/2–01–21 or 784/2–10–62. 59 rooms. Restaurant, bar, beauty salon, free parking. MC, V.*

$ **Hotel Totonacapan.** This slightly gloomy hotel is located a few blocks from the center, near the second-class bus station. It's acceptable but should be an option only if you don't want to pay for the Premier and the Tajín is full. The rooms are big and bare, with large windows that don't quite dispel a sense of claustrophobia. Still, the staff is extremely friendly and the rooms have air-conditioning, color TVs (local stations only), and telephones. Coolers in the hall dispense purified water, and a diner-style restaurant downstairs serves standard breakfast. ✉ *20 de Noviembre at Olivo, 93400,* ☎ *784/2–12–16. 36 rooms and suites. No credit cards.*

Tuxpán

28 *193 km (125 mi) south of Tampico, 309 km (192 mi) north of Veracruz, 133 km (84 mi) northeast of Papantla.*

Tuxpán is a peaceful riverside town—the Río Tuxpán is even clean enough to swim in—with graceful winding streets. **Juárez,** the main street, running parallel to the river, is lined with diners, hotels, and shops. The **Parque Reforma** is the center of social activity in town, with more than a hundred tables set around a hub of cafés and fruit stands. It hosts a memorial to Fausto Vega Santander, a member of the 201st squadron of the Mexican Air Force and the first Mexican to be killed in combat during World War II. *Lanchas* (flat-bottom boats) shuttle passengers across the river to the **Casa de Fidel Castro,** where Castro lived for a time while planning the overthrow of Fulgencio Batista. A replica of the *Granma,* the ship that carried Fidel's men from Tuxpán to Cuba, molders outside. Inside, the casa is bare save some black-and-white photos of Fidel and Mexican president Lázaro Cárdenas.

Beaches

Tuxpán's main draw is the untouristed miles of beaches that begin just 7 km (4 mi) east of the town. The first, and most accessible, is **Playa Tuxpán.** The surf here isn't huge, but there's enough action to warrant breaking out your surf- or boogieboard. Of the palapas on Playa Tuxpán, the most established is **Restaurant Miramar,** which has an extensive menu and also provides umbrellaed beach chairs for customers. Farther down, try **El Tigre Costeño,** run by a friendly family whose male members moonlight weaving palm-frond hats to sell on the beach.

Dining and Lodging

$$ ✕ **Antonio's.** Next to the Hotel Reforma on Juárez and serving as its restaurant, Antonio's is a quiet, comparatively elegant eatery with a varied menu. The *cazuela de mariscos* (shellfish stew) is excellent, as are the prawns, served grilled or in garlic sauce. A number of beef dishes and sandwiches are also available, as well as cocktails from the full bar. ✉ *Av. Juárez s/n at Garizurieta,* ☎ *783/4–16–02. MC, V.*

$$ ✕ **Charlôt.** For anything other than seafood or tacos, the best place in Tuxpán is undoubtedly Charlôt. This French and international restaurant is a favorite of local businesspeople, and it's not uncommon to find an entire corner of the restaurant taken over by an expansive lunch meeting. The pretty dining room is decorated with ceramics and other artesanía. The house specialty is medallions of beef in mushroom sauce, but simple steaks as well as some fish dishes and pizzas are also featured. Service is good and there's a full bar. ✉ *Reyes Heroles 35, at Zozimo Pérez,* ☎ *783/4–40–28. MC, V. Closed Mon.*

$$ ✕ **El Volador.** The restaurant in the Hotel Tajín, across the river from central Tuxpán, is bright and airy, with a semicircular wall of windows overlooking the Río Tuxpán. Corn chips and fresh salsa with plenty of cilantro arrive at your table as soon as you order. Dishes run the gamut from local favorites such as *camarones al mojo de ajo* (shrimp in garlic sauce) and pescado à la veracruzana to American-style offerings such as T-bone steaks and hamburgers. It's nothing to make a special trip for, but come if you happen to be on this side of the river visiting the Casa de Fidel Castro (still a taxi ride away from here, however) or just want an excuse to make the pleasant skiff crossing. ✉ *Hotel Tajín, Km 2.5 Carretera a Cobos,* ☎ *783/4–22–60. MC, V.*

$ ★ **Hotel Florida.** Don't be deceived by the dark lobby or the cramped elevator: The Hotel Florida is the best hotel deal in downtown Tuxpán. The rooms are decorated in bright pastels and offer ample light and space, as well as large, immaculate bathrooms. Basic rooms have telephones and vigorous ceiling fans; slightly more expensive rooms add TVs (local stations only) and air-conditioning. Terraces on each floor enjoy views of the cathedral and waterfront. ✉ *Av. Juárez 23, across from cathedral, 92801,* ☎ *783/4–02–22 or 783/4–06–02. 78 rooms. Restaurant, bar, coffee shop. MC, V.*

$ **Hotel May Palace.** The most luxurious lodgings in Tuxpán can be secured at this five-star hotel in the center of town. Opened in early 1995, the modern five-story property is geared to a business clientele. The rooms are swathed in pastels and set off by cool-looking rattan furniture custom designed for the hotel; all the units offer phones, satellite-reception TVs, and air-conditioning. Guest services include a small video bar, a restaurant specializing in seafood and regional dishes, a rooftop pool, and meeting salons. ✉ *Av. Juárez 44, facing Parque Reforma, 92800,* ☎ FAX *783/4–88–82 or 783/4–44–61. 70 rooms. Restaurant, bar, room service, free parking. MC, V.*

$ **Hotel Reforma.** The Reforma is a lovely building located a block from the waterfront in the heart of downtown. It lacks a lobby but has a central courtyard with a number of skylights, a fountain, and a few wrought-iron tables where guests often congregate in the afternoon. The hotel was remodeled in 1995, and rooms were spruced up with new air-conditioning units, beds, bureaus, carpets, and a coat of paint; there are phones, color satellite TVs, and good-size bathrooms in all of them. Street noise can be a problem on the first floor. ✉ *Av. Juárez 25, 92801,* ☎ *783/4–02–10 or 783/4–04–60,* FAX *783/4–06–25. 98 rooms. Restaurant, bar, room service, free parking. MC, V.*

$ **Hotel Tajín.** This place looks like a first-class resort from the outside, but once you enter, you'll be reminded of nothing so much as a college dorm: Long beige hallways with faded blue carpets lead past scores of identical, bland rooms with almost no decorative touches. However, the Tajín's location on the banks of the river, a bit east of and across from the center, means that almost every room overlooks the water and the green city of Tuxpán. It also means that the traffic noise of downtown is replaced by the sounds of river birds at night. The hotel is easy to reach by car (just cross the bridge and drive east for about five minutes), but there is no bus service. Pedestrians must either take a longish taxi ride from the center or catch a beach-bound bus to the Paso de Esquifes La Peñita, where a small motorboat will shuttle them across the river. From the skiff landing, the hotel is a three-minute (if often muddy) walk away. ✉ *Km 2.5 Carretera a Cobos, 92801,* ☏ *783/4–22–60 or 783/4–25–72,* FAX *783/4–51–84. 140 rooms. Restaurant, bar, pool, dock, dance club. AE, MC, V.*

Outdoor Activities and Sports

WATER SPORTS

There are some nice places to submerge in the Tuxpán area. For scuba diving, head to **Tamiaula,** a small village just north of Tuxpán, where you can hire a fishing boat for the 45-minute journey to the prime diving around **Isla Lobos** (Wolf Island), a protected eco reserve that shares its space with a military outpost and a lighthouse. In the shallow water offshore you'll find a few shipwrecks and colorful reefs that are home to a large variety of sea life, including puffer fish, parrot fish, damselfish, and barracuda. **Aquasport** (☏ 783/7–02–59), just before Playa Tuxpán, arranges scuba-diving trips to Isla Lobos and also offers deep-sea fishing excursions. Other outfits run trips to the island that include permits, scuba gear, lunch, and transportation.

VERACRUZ A TO Z

Arriving and Departing

By Car

The city of Veracruz can be reached within about eight hours by traveling south from Tampico via Mexico 180, or within six hours from Mexico City via Mexico 150. The roads throughout the state, paved and kept up with oil money, are generally very good.

By Plane

Both **Mexicana** (☏ 29/32–22–42 or 29/32–86–99) and **Aeromexico** (☏ 29/34–70–76 or 29/34–34–28) provide nonstop service from Mexico City to the port of Veracruz. **Aerocaribe** (☏ 29/37–02–60 or 29/35–05–68), a regional airline, has flights from Cancún to Veracruz. No city bus serves the airport, and a cab to the city center costs $7. An air-conditioned minivan ($9) runs between the airport and the downtown office of **Transportación Terrestre Aeropuerto** (✉ Hidalgo 826 between Canal and Morales, ☏ 29/32–32–50).

Getting Around

By Bus

Veracruz's main bus terminal (✉ Díaz Mirón 1698, ☏ 29/37–57–44) is about 4 km (2½ mi) south of the zócalo. The main bus company is **Autobuses del Oriente (ADO)** (☏ 29/37–57–88), with daily service to Jalapa every 20 minutes from 6 AM to midnight and round-the-clock departures for Mexico City. ADO also offers first- and second-class service to Reynosa, on the Texas border. For those headed north and east, the deluxe bus line **UNO** (☏ 29/35–03–17) goes to Jalapa, Puebla, and Mexico City; **Cuenca** (☏ 29/35–54–05) goes south to Oaxaca and Chiapas. **Cristóbal Colón** (☏ 29/37–57–44) operates from another station on the same block and offers frequent first- and second-class service to Los Tuxtlas.

Contacts and Resources

Car Rental

JALAPA

Viajes Herlu (✉ Av. Orizaba 125, ☎ 28/15–51–81, FAX 28/15–45–53) can arrange car rentals.

VERACRUZ

Avis (✉ Airport, ☎ 29/31–15–80), **Dollar** (✉ Víctimas del 5 y 6 de Julio 883, ☎ 28/35–52–31), **Hertz** (✉ Aquiles Serdan 14, downtown, ☎ 29/32–40–21), **National** (✉ Díaz Mirón 1036, ☎ 28/31–75–56).

Consulate

VERACRUZ

United States Consulate (✉ Víctimas del 25 del Julio 384, between Gómez Farias and 16 de Septiembre, ☎ 29/31–58–21).

Currency Exchange

JALAPA

One block from Parque Juárez, **Casa de Cambio Jalapa** (✉ Zamora 36, ☎ 28/18–68–60) offers good rates; it's open 9–1:30 and 4–6 weekdays. You can also change money in the mornings at several banks on Parque Juárez.

PAPANTLA

Banamex (✉ Enríquez 102 past Andy's Cadillac Bar) changes both cash and traveler's checks weekdays 9–noon and has an ATM that accepts Cirrus, Plus, Visa, and MasterCard.

TUXPÁN

Bancomer (✉ Av. Juárez at Escuela Médico Militar, ☎ 783/4–00–09) changes cash and traveler's checks weekdays 8:30–1:30.

VERACRUZ

The best rates in town are available at **Bancomer** (✉ Av. Juárez at Independencia), but money-changing hours are limited to weekdays 9 AM–11:30 AM, so you'll have to arrive early to make it through the lines. For later hours, try **Casa de Cambio Puebla** (✉ Av. Juárez 112, ☎ 29/31–24–50), open weekdays 9–6, or use the ATM at **Banamex** (✉ Av. Juárez at Independencia) that accepts Cirrus, Plus, Visa and MasterCard.

Emergencies

JALAPA

Police (☎ 28/17–63–10); for an ambulance, call the **Cruz Roja** (Red Cross) (☎ 28/14–45–00).

PAPANTLA

Police (☎ 784/2–01–93), **Cruz Roja** (☎ 784/2–01–01).

TUXPÁN

Police (☎ 783/4–02–52), **Cruz Roja** (☎ 783/4–01–58).

VERACRUZ

Dial **06** for medical, fire, and theft emergencies. **Oficinas Para La Seguridad del Turista** (☎ 91–800/9–03–92) operates a 24-hour toll-free hot line to provide legal and medical help for tourists in Veracruz. **Police** (✉ Playa Linda 222, ☎ 29/38–06–64 or 29/38–06–93); **Hospital Regional de Veracruz** (✉ 20 de Noviembre s/n, ☎ 29/32–27–05 or 29/32–36–90); **Cruz Roja** (☎ 29/37–55–00).

Pharmacies

JALAPA

Calle Enríquez is lined with pharmacies. For 24-hour service, the **Farmacia Plus** (✉ Revolución 171 at Sagayo, ☎ 28/18–09–35) is your best option.

PAPANTLA

Farmacia Médico (✉ Gutierrez Zamora 3, ☎ 784/2–19–41), open daily 7:30 AM–10 PM, is the largest pharmacy in town.

VERACRUZ

Benavides (✉ Independencia 1291, at Serdán ☎ 29/31–89–29) is a big, convenient drugstore downtown, but it closes at 10 PM daily. For 24-hour service, try **Farmacia Mercado Bravo** (✉ Independencia 1197, ☎ 29/31–08–83).

Guided Tours

JALAPA

Expediciones Mexico Verde (✉ José M. Vigil 2406, Colonia Italia Providencia, Guadalajara, Jal. 44610, ☎ 3/641–09–93, 3/641–55–98, or 91–800/36–288) offers river rafting for individuals or groups along the Río Pescados near Jalapa; one-day or overnight excursions are available. All equipment, including life jackets, helmets, and oars, is provided. English is spoken.

VERACRUZ

An ecotourism outfit called **Campamento Jamapa** (✉ Cotaxtla Sur 16, Colonia Petrolero, Boca del Río, ☎ FAX 29/21–15–50), with an all-female staff, offers river rafting, diving, kayaking, sportfishing, windsurfing, and mountain-biking excursions in the state of Veracruz. The company's private camp along the Jamapa River, 11 km (7 mi) from Boca del Río, provides large tents, a dining room, bar, and hammocks. Night dives, diving instruction, and rental equipment are also available at the camp. Most of the staff speaks English.

Boat tours of the bay depart from the malecón daily 7–7. Boats leave whenever they're full, and the $2.50 half-hour ride includes a (Spanish-language) talk on Veracruz history. Longer trips to nearby **Isla Verde** (Green Island) and **Isla de Enmedio** (Middle Island) leave daily from the shack marked PASEO EN LANCHITA near the Plaza Acuario. Again, boats wait until they're full to set off, so it's best to be in a group. The cost should be about $3–$5 per person, but feel free to bargain.

Operadora Terrestre de Veracruz (✉ Pedro de Alvarado 223, Fracc. Reforma, ☎ 29/37–66–19 or 29/37–06–61) offers city tours as well as tours of Tajín and Papantla, Los Tuxtlas, and Jalapa. Diving and fishing trips are available, too. There are also travel desks at the Torremar, Emporio, Continental Plaza, and Fiesta Americana hotels.

Intercontinental Adventures (✉ Georgia 120, Suite 9A, Colonia Napoles, Mexico, D.F. 03810, ☎ 5/536–3700; 800/382–3249 in the U.S.; FAX 5/69–0086) is the exclusive operator for the 7- or 10-day Cortés Route tour, which includes Veracruz City, Antigua, Cempoala, Jalapa, and Coatepec in the state of Veracruz and continues on to conquistador-related sites in the states of Tlaxcala, Puebla, and Mexico. The company also runs river-rafting excursions to the Río Pescados near Jalapa.

Visitor Information

The **Jalapa tourist office** (✉ Blvd. Cristóbal Colón 5, Jardines de las Animas on main square, ☎ 28/12–85–00, ext. 126 or 127) is open weekdays 9–9.

The **Papantla tourist office** (✉ Palacio Municipal on zócalo, ☎ 784/2-01-77) is open weekdays 9-3, Saturday 9-1.

The **Tuxpán tourist office** (✉ Av. Juárez 65, ☎ 783/4-01-77) is open daily 10-3 and 5-7.

The **Veracruz Dirección Municipal de Turismo** (✉ Palacio Municipal on zócalo, ☎ 29/32-19-99) is open Monday-Saturday 9-9, Sunday 10-1.

13 The Yucatán Peninsula

Mexico's most visited region, the Yucatán has something for everyone: the high-profile sparkle of Cancún; the spectacular snorkeling of Cozumel; the laid-back beachcombing of Isla Mujeres; the fascinating Spanish-Maya mix of Mérida; and the evocative Maya ruins of Tulum, Chichén Itzá, and Uxmal. The region is an ecotourist's dream, too, from the huge Sian Ka'an Biosphere Reserve on the Caribbean Coast to Río Lagartos National Park on the Gulf of Mexico, migration ground for thousands of flamingos and other birds.

WHEN ASKED what attracts them to Mexico, most visitors will mention beaches and ruins—and some of the best of each are found on the Yucatán Peninsula. Yucatán contains Mexico's most popular tourist destination, Cancún, and some of the country's most celebrated ruins, the pre-Columbian cities of the Maya. Although much of the peninsula is vast, scrubby desert with a smattering of jungles and hills, its eastern coastline on the clear, turquoise waters of the Caribbean has superb natural endowments. In addition to a semitropical climate, the Caribbean coast offers unbroken stretches of beach and the world's fifth-longest barrier reef, which lies just off the island of Cozumel. Also part of the Yucatán is the diminutive Isla Mujeres (Isle of Women) and, on the west side of the peninsula, Mérida, a city that deserves more tourists than it gets. Mérida was one of the first cities built by the Spaniards, and it retains its colonial ambience and charm.

Updated by Patricia Alisau and Dan Millington

The peninsula's spectrum of attractions is matched by an equal range of accommodations, from the never-leave-the-site resorts of Cancún to more modest properties near the ruins and humble but adequate beach shacks. Yucatán therefore appeals to travelers of all budgets and inclinations, from package tour–takers to backpackers and travelers who prefer to rent a car. It offers bird-watching, water sports, archaeology, handicrafts, and the savory Yucatecan cuisine. Above all, however, there are the *Yucatecos* themselves: Veteran travelers to Mexico often remark on the openness and friendliness of these people, who, like their Maya ancestors, are short and swarthy, with prominent cheekbones and aquiline noses.

The peninsula encompasses the states of Yucatán, Campeche, Quintana Roo (until 1974 a Mexican territory), Belize, and a part of Guatemala and covers 113,000 square km (43,630 square mi). International airports at Cancún and Cozumel provide nonstop service from several North American cities; the Mérida airport handles primarily domestic flights. Cruise ships call at Cozumel and Playa del Carmen, and other harbor facilities are being developed at Progreso on the north coast off the Gulf of Mexico.

Pleasures and Pastimes

Beaches

Cancún and the rest of Yucatán offer a wonderful variety of beaches: Those who thrive on the resort atmosphere will probably enjoy Playa Chac Mool and Playa Tortugas on the bay side of Cancún, which is calmer, if less beautiful than, the windward side. On the north end of Isla Mujeres, Playa Cocoteros and Playa Norte offer handsome sunset vistas. Beaches on the relatively sheltered leeward side of Cozumel are wide and sandy. The Caribbean Coast abounds with hidden and not-so-hidden beaches (at Xcaret, Paamul, Chemuyil, Xcacel, and Punta Bete, south of Tulum, and along the Boca Paila peninsula). There are also long stretches of white sand, usually filled with sunbathers, at Puerto Morelos, Playa del Carmen, and especially Akumal. Travelers to Campeche and Progreso will find the waters of the Gulf of Mexico deep green, shallow, and tranquil.

Bird-Watching

The Yucatán Peninsula is one of the finest areas for birding in Mexico. Habitats range from wildlife and bird sanctuaries to unmarked lagoons, estuaries, and mangrove swamps. Frigates, tanagers, warblers, and macaws inhabit Isla Contoy (off Isla Mujeres) and the Laguna

Colombia on Cozumel; an even greater variety of species are to be found in the Sian Ka'an Biosphere Reserve on the Boca Paila peninsula south of Tulum. Along the north and west coasts of Yucatán—at Río Lagartos, Laguna Rosada, and Celestún—flamingos, herons, ibis, cormorants, pelicans, and peregrine falcons thrive.

Dining

The mystique of Yucatecan cooking has a lot to do with the generous doses of local spices and herbs, although generally the food tends not to be too spicy. Among the specialties are *cochinita píbil* and *pollo píbil* (succulent pork or chicken baked in banana leaves with a spicy, pumpkin-seed-and-chili sauce); *poc chuc* (Yucatecan pork marinated in the same sour-orange sauce with pickled onions); *tikinchic* (fried fish prepared with sour orange); *panuchos* (fried tortillas filled with black beans and topped with turkey, chicken, or pork, pickled onions, and avocado); *papadzules* (tortillas piled high with hard-boiled eggs and drenched in a sauce of pumpkin seed and fried tomato); and *codzitos* (rolled tortillas in pumpkin-seed sauce). *Achiote* (annatto), cilantro (coriander), and the fiery *chile habanero* are heavily favored condiments.

The following price categories apply everywhere outside of Cancún and Cozumel, which are more expensive than the rest of the destinations in the Yucatán and for which we have included separate price charts in the relevant sections of this chapter.

CATEGORY	COST*
$$$$	over $20
$$$	$15–$20
$$	$8–$15
$	under $8

**per person for a three-course meal, excluding drinks and service*

Fishing

Sportfishing is popular in Cozumel and throughout the Caribbean Coast. The rich waters of the Caribbean and the Gulf of Mexico support hundreds of species of tropical fish, making the Yucatán coastline and the outlying islands a paradise for deep-sea fishing, fly-fishing, and bonefishing. Particularly between the months of April and July, the waters off Cancún, Cozumel, and Isla Mujeres teem with sailfish, marlin, red snapper, tuna, barracuda, and wahoo, among other denizens of the deep. Bill fishing is so rich around Cozumel and Puerto Aventuras that each holds an annual tournament.

Farther south, along the Boca Paila peninsula, banana fish, bonefish, mojarra, shad, permit, and sea bass provide great sport for flat fishing and fly-fishing, while oysters, shrimp, and conch lie on the bottom of the Gulf of Mexico near Campeche and Isla del Carmen. At Progreso, on the north coast, sportfishing for grouper, dogfish, and pompano is quite popular.

Lodging

Accommodations in the Yucatán range from the ultraglitzy megaresorts of Cancún to the charming colonial mansions in Mérida and the rustic but characterful lodgings near the ruins. The following price categories apply everywhere outside of Cancún and Cozumel, which are more expensive than the rest of the destinations in the Yucatán and for which we have included separate price charts.

CATEGORY	COST*
$$$$	over $90
$$$	$60–$90
$$	$25–$60
$	under $25

**All prices are for a standard double room in the high season, excluding service charges and tax.*

Ruins

Amateur archaeologists will find heaven in the Yucatán, where the ancient Maya most abundantly left their mark. Pick your period and your preference, whether for well-excavated sites or overgrown, out-of-the-way ruins barely touched by a scholar's shovel. The major Maya sites are Cobá and Tulum on the Caribbean Coast and Chichén Itzá and Uxmal in the state of Yucatán, but smaller ruins scattered throughout the peninsula are often equally fascinating.

Scuba Diving and Snorkeling

Underwater enthusiasts come to Cozumel, Akumal, Xcalak, Xel-Há, and other parts of Mexico's Caribbean Coast for the clear turquoise waters, the colorful and assorted tropical fish, and the exquisite coral formations along the Belize reef system. Currents allow for drift diving, and both reefs and offshore wrecks lend themselves to dives, many of which are safe enough for neophytes. The peninsula's cenotes, or natural sinkholes, provide an unusual dive experience.

Water Sports

All manner of water sports—jet skiing, catamaran sailing, sailboarding, waterskiing, sailing, and parasailing—are practiced in Cancún, Cozumel, and along the Caribbean Coast, where you'll find well-equipped water-sports centers.

Exploring the Yucatán Peninsula

Numbers in the text correspond to numbers in the margin and on the Cancún, Isla Mujeres, Cozumel, Caribbean Coast, Campeche City, Mérida, and State of Yucatán maps.

Great Itineraries

Most people who travel to the major beach-resort destinations of Cancún and Cozumel tend to settle in for their entire stay, perhaps taking side trips to the ruins of Tulum or Chichén Itzá and to Xcaret, a man-made theme park that re-creates the Yucatecan landscape. Those who want to try two distinct types of beach experiences might divide their time between the higher-profile (and more expensive) Cancún and the laid-back Isla Mujeres. The following itineraries are designed for those who want to keep on the move and have based themselves either in one of the Caribbean Coast towns or in Mérida. The former is ideal for the water-sports oriented, the latter for lovers of the ancient Maya civilization.

IF YOU HAVE 3 DAYS

If you want to base yourself on the Caribbean Coast, get a room in **Playa del Carmen** ㉒, and start out by visiting **Tulum** ㉝ to view the cliff-side Castillo temple; afterward, climb down to the small beach alongside it for a dip in the ocean. Day 2, head out to the cenote at **Xel-Há** ㉛, where you can snorkel, swim, or sunbathe. Follow this with a visit to the CEDAM museum at **Puerto Aventuras** ㉕, full of displays salvaged from old shipwrecks. Day 3, head for **Akumal** ㉗ for a diving or deep-sea fishing excursion, snorkeling, or swimming; later in the day visit the tiny lagoons of **Xpuhá** ㉖ and **Yalkú** ㉘, which were around during the time of the Maya traders.

An alternative is to spend two days in **Mérida** ⑭–⑳, savoring the city's unique character as you make your way among the historic churches and mansions and enjoy the parks and restaurants. You can easily devote a full day to exploring the heart of downtown, including the **zócalo** ⑭ and its surrounding buildings, the **Casa de Montejo** ⑮, **Palacio Municipal** ⑯, and the **catedral** ⑱. Take a second, more leisurely day to visit the Museum of Anthropology and History in the **Palacio Cantón** ⑱ and, perhaps, the **Museo de Arte Popular** ⑲ or the **El Centenario Zoo.** On the third day, drive or take a tour to one of Yucatán's most famous Maya ruins—either **Chichén Itzá** ⑫ or **Uxmal** ⑰. Each is within about two hours of Mérida, making for an ideal day trip.

IF YOU HAVE 7 DAYS

Again basing yourself in Playa del Carmen, visit Tulum on the first day, and then spend Day 2 touring **Xcaret** ㉓, an ecological theme park where you can swim with dolphins, snorkel in a cenote, and take in a Mexican rodeo show. Day 3, start the morning at the archaeological ruins of **Cobá** ㉞ and spend the afternoon at Xel-Há cooling off in the water. Day 4, head for Akumal and its water sports. Day 5, sign up for a tour of the **Sian Ka'an Biosphere Reserve.** On Day 6, explore the southern Caribbean coast: Drive to the enormous **Bacalar Lagoon** to marvel at its transparent layers of turquoise, green, and blue waters (it should take about three hours if you drive straight through); visit the colonial San Felipe Fortress in the village of **Bacalar**; and overnight in **Chetumal.** On Day 7, head out early for **Kohunlich,** which has a huge stucco mask of the Maya sun god surrounded by jungle ruins. Then head back up the coast to Playa del Carmen, stopping at the **Cenote Azul,** the largest sinkhole in Mexico; at the town of **Felipe Carrillo Puerto,** where you can get a taste of old Maya culture; and finally at **Muyil,** with its pretty Maya temple.

Those with a week in the Mérida area should first explore the sights of the city and then take two separate overnight excursions. Spend the night at one of the archaeological hotels near Uxmal, and the next day explore the Ruta Puuc, the series of lost cities south of Uxmal that includes **Kabah, Sayil,** and **Labná,** as well as the fascinating **Loltún Caves.** On the second excursion, to Chichén Itzá, allow as much as a full day en route to explore some of the present-day Maya villages along the way, especially **Izamal** ⑪. After visiting Chichén Itzá, you may wish to beat the afternoon heat by exploring the **Cave of Balankinchén** ⑭ or swimming in one of the cool subterranean cenotes nearby; you might also head north from **Valladolid** ⑮ to see to see the flamingo nesting grounds at **Río Lagartos National Park** ⑯.

IF YOU HAVE 10 DAYS

Those who have a longer time to spend in this area might want to continue on from Mérida to **Campeche City** ㊱–㊳. After spending a day exploring the city's sights—almost all those of interest to visitors are located within the compact historical district—head inland the next morning to visit **Edzná,** a magnificently restored ceremonial center an hour's drive from the city. Return to your Campeche City hotel—accommodations are crude or nonexistent in the area—and set out the next day to the **Hopelchén** region, beyond Edzná, where you can explore the little-known Maya temples at **Hochob** and **Dzibilnocac,** as well as **Bolonchén de Rejón,** one of the large cave systems on the peninsula.

When to Tour the Yucatán Peninsula

Thousands of visitors swarm to Chichén Itzá for the vernal equinox (the first day of spring) to witness the astronomical phenomenon that makes a shadow resembling a snake—which represented the plumed serpent god Kukulcán—appear on the side of the main pyramid. The phenomenon also occurs on the first day of fall, but the rainy weather typical at that time of year tends to discourage visitors. Both the capital and outlying villages of Campeche state, with their predominantly Maya population, celebrate the Day of the Dead (November 1 and 2) with special fervor because it corresponds to a similar observance in ancient Maya tradition.

High season in the states of Yucátan and Campeche generally corresponds to high season in the rest of Mexico: the Christmas period, Easter week, and the month of August. Rainfall is heaviest between May and October, bringing with it an uncomfortable humidity. On the Caribbean Coast, including Cancún, Cozumel, and Isla Mujeres, the peak tourist times are mid-December–late March. In the less visited towns, levels of service differ drastically between the high and low seasons (when staff and activities may be cut back), so you should be prepared for a trade-off.

CANCÚN

The jewel of Mexico's Caribbean Coast, Cancún is for those who want dazzle for their dollar: The hotel zone is lined with high-rise lodgings, glitzy discos, air-conditioned malls, and gorgeous beaches. For a glimpse of the real Mexico, go downtown, where Yucatecan specialties are served at casual eateries.

Flying into Cancún, Mexico's most popular destination, you see nothing but green treetops for kilometers. It's clear from the air that this resort was literally carved out of the jungle. When development began here in 1974, the beaches were deserted except for their iguana inhabitants. Now, luxury hotels line the oceanfront, and nearly 2 million visitors a year come for the white-sand beaches and crystalline Caribbean waters. They also come for the sizzling nightlife and, in some cases, for proximity to the Yucatán ruins. Although the resort is too glitzy and tourist oriented for many, it draws thousands of repeat visitors.

Cancún City is on the mainland, but the hotel zone is on a 22½-km (14-mi) barrier island off the Yucatán peninsula. The resort is designed to please American tastes; most people speak English, and devotees of cable TV and Pizza Hut will not be disappointed. Beach lovers can bask in Cancún's year-round tropical warmth and sunny skies. The sun shines an average of 240 days a year, reputedly more than at almost any other Caribbean spot. Temperatures linger appealingly at about 80°F. You can sample Yucatecan foods and watch folkloric dance demonstrations as well as knock back tequila slammers at the myriad nightspots.

But there can be more to the resort than plopping down under a *palapa* (thatched roof). For divers and snorkelers, the reefs off Cancún, nearby Cozumel, and Isla Mujeres are among the best in the world. Cancún also provides a relaxing home base for visiting the stupendous ruins of Chichén Itzá, Tulum, and Cobá on the mainland—remnants of the area's rich Maya heritage—as well as the Yucatán coast and its lagoons.

The most important buildings in Cancún, however, are modern hotels. The resort has gone through the life cycle typical of any tourist destination. At its inception, the resort drew the jet set; lately, it has attracted increasing numbers of less affluent tourists, primarily package-tour takers and college students, particularly during spring break when hordes of flawless, tanned young bodies people the beaches and restaurants.

As for the island's history, not much was written about it before its birth as a resort. The island does not appear on the early navigators' maps, and little is known about the Maya who lived here; apparently Cancún's marshy terrain discouraged development. It is recorded that Maya settled the area during the pre-classical era, in about AD 200, and remained until about the 14th or 15th century. In the mid-19th century minor Maya ruins were sighted; however, they were not studied by archaeologists until the 1950s. In 1970 then-president Luis Echeverría first visited the site that had been chosen to retrieve the state of Quintana Roo from obscurity and abject poverty.

Cancún's natural environment has paid a price. Its lagoons and mangrove swamps have become polluted, and a number of species, like conch and lobster, are dwindling. Although the beaches still appear pristine for the most part, an increased effort will have to be made in order to preserve the physical beauty that is the resort's prime appeal.

Exploring

Cancún is divided into two zones: the hotel zone, which is shaped roughly like the numeral 7, and Cancún City or downtown Cancún, known as *el centro,* 4 km (2½ mi) west of the hotel zone on the mainland.

Paseo Kukulcán is the main drag in the hotel zone, and because most of the 7 is less than 1 km (½ mi) wide, both the Caribbean and the lagoons can be seen from either side of it. The hotel zone consists entirely of hotels, restaurants and shopping complexes, marinas, and time-share condominiums; there are no residential areas as such. The lagoon side of the boulevard consists of scrubby stretches of land, many of them covered with construction cranes, alternating with marinas, shopping centers, and restaurants.

A Good Tour

Cancún's scenery consists mostly of its beautiful beaches and crystal-clear waters, but there are also a few intriguing historical sites tucked away among the modern hotels. In addition to the attractions listed below, two modest vestiges of the ancient Maya civilization are worth a visit only for dedicated archaeology buffs. Neither is identified by name. On the 12th hole of Pok-Ta-Pok golf course (✉ Paseo Kukulcán, between Km 6 and Km 7), whose Maya name means "ball game," stands a ruin consisting of two platforms and the remains of other buildings. And the ruin of a tiny Maya shrine is cleverly incorporated into the architecture of the Hotel Camino Real (on the beach at Punta Cancún).

You don't need a car in Cancún, but if you've rented one to make extended trips, it might be worth starting in the southern hotel zone at **Ruinas del Rey** ① and **San Miguelito** ②, driving north to **Yamil Lu'um** ③, and then stopping in at the **convention center** ④ before heading west to **downtown** ⑤.

Sights to See

❹ **Cancún Convention Center.** This strikingly modern venue for cultural events is the jumping-off point for a 1-km-long (½-mi-long) string of shopping malls that extend west to the Hotel Presidente. In the convention center complex itself, **Inter Plaza** contains 15 restaurants, 21 boutiques, a bank, and several airline offices. ✉ *Paseo Kukulcán, Km 9,* ☎ *98/830199.*

The **National Institute of Anthropology and History,** the small museum on the ground floor of the convention center, traces Maya culture by showcasing a fascinating collection of 1,000- to 1,500-year-old artifacts collected throughout Quintana Roo. ☎ *98/830305.* 🎫 *About $3; free Sun.* ⏲ *Tues.–Sun. 9–7. Guided tours available in English, French, German, and Spanish.*

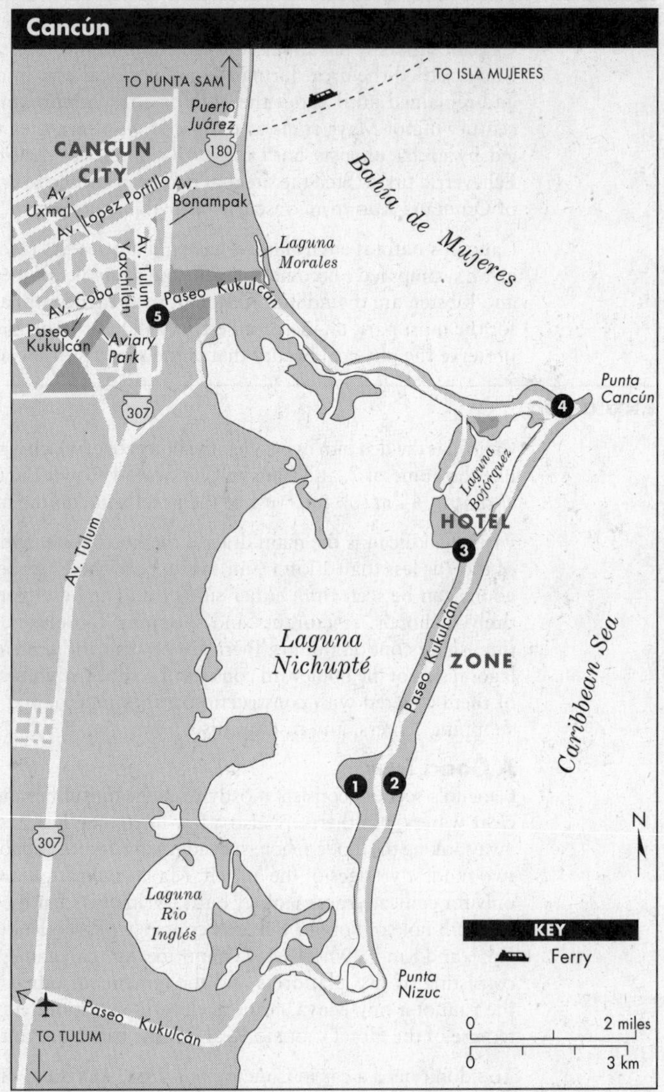

5 **Downtown Cancún.** The main thoroughfare is Avenida Tulum, which begins at the spot where Paseo Kukulcán turns into Avenida Cobá. Many restaurants and shops are located along here, as is Ki Huic, the largest crafts market in Cancún. Life-size reproductions of ancient Mexican art, including the Aztec calendar stone, a giant Olmec head, the Atlantids of Tula, and the Maya chac mool (reclining rain god), line the grassy strip dividing Tulum's northbound and southbound lanes. Visitors looking for shopping bargains, however, generally find better prices if they stick to the parallel Avenida Yaxchilán.

1 **Ruinas del Rey.** Located on the lagoon side at Cancún Island, roughly opposite El Pueblito and Playa de Oro, these small ruins have been incorporated into the Caesar Park Resort complex; large signs point out the site. Del Rey may not be particularly impressive when compared to major archaeological sites such as Tulum or Chichén Itzá, but it is the largest ruin in Cancún and definitely worth a look. Skeletons found buried both at the apex and at the base indicate that the site may have been a royal burial ground. ✉ *Paseo Kukulcán, Km 17, no phone.* 🎫 *About $3; free Sun.* ⏲ *Daily 8–5.*

❷ **San Miguelito.** On the east side of Paseo Kukulcán is a very small stone building (about the size of a shack) with a number of columns about 4 ft high. At press time, this modest Maya site was fenced off and not accessible to the public, but this may change after archaeologists have fully examined the ruins. ✉ *Paseo Kukulcán, Km 16.5, no phone.*

❸ **Yamil Lu'um.** A small sign at the Sheraton will direct you to the dirt path leading to this site, which stands on the highest point of Cancún adjoining the hotel—the words "Yamil Lu'um" mean hilly land. Although it comprises two structures—one probably a temple, the other probably a lighthouse—this is the smallest of Cancún's ruins. Discovered in 1842 by John Lloyd Stephens, the remains date from the late-13th or early 14th century. ✉ *Paseo Kukulcán, Km 12, no phone.*

Dining

At last count, there were more than 1,200 restaurants in Cancún, but—according to one successful restaurateur—only about 100 are worth their salt, so to speak. Finding the right restaurant in Cancún is not easy. The downtown restaurants that line the noisy Avenida Tulum often have tables spilling onto pedestrian-laden sidewalks; however, gas fumes and gawking tourists tend to detract from the romantic outdoor-café ambience. Many of the hotel-zone restaurants, on the other hand, cater to what they assume is a tourist preference for bland, not-too-foreign-tasting food.

One key to good dining in Cancún is to find the haunts—mostly in the downtown area—where locals go for Yucatán-style food prepared by the experts. A cheap and filling trend in Cancún's dining scene is the sumptuous buffet breakfasts offered by an increasing number of restaurants and hotels on the island. Another hint: Many $$$$ and $$$ restaurants have floor shows during peak months—mid-December–late March. Usually there are two seatings nightly, each including entertainment and dinner; reservations are advised, since the shows draw crowds.

Generally speaking, dress is casual here, but many restaurants will not admit diners with bare feet, short shorts, or no shirts.

CATEGORY	COST*
$$$$	over $35
$$$	$25–$35
$$	$15–$25
$	under $15

**per person for a three-course meal, excluding drinks and service*

Hotel Zone

Hotel-zone restaurants are located on the Cancún Hotel Zone Dining and Lodging map.

$$$$ ✕ **Bogart's.** Whether you consider it amusingly elaborate or merely pretentious, it's hard to be neutral about Bogart's, probably the most expensive and talked-about restaurant in town. Taking off from the film *Casablanca,* the place is decorated with Persian rugs, fans, velvet-cushioned banquettes, and fountains. A menu as eclectic as the patrons of Rick's Cafe lists many seafood and Mediterranean dishes. The food is okay, but don't expect large portions; servings are nouvelle style. Seatings are at 6:30 and 9:30. ✉ *Paseo Kukulcán, Hotel Krystal,* ☎ *98/831133. Reservations essential. AE, DC, MC, V. No lunch.*

$$$$ ★ ✕ **Club Grill.** Another prime choice for that romantic, special-occasion dinner, the Ritz-Carlton's fine dining room is divided into intimate cham-

Dining
Bogart's, **10**
Captain's Cove, **2, 19**
Carlos 'n Charlie's, **3**
Casa Rolandi, **7**
Club Grill, **14**
El Mexicano, **6**
Hacienda El Mortero, **10**
La Dolce Vita, **16**
Lorenzillos, **11**
100% Natural, **5, 12**
Splash, **12**

Lodging
Caesar Park Beach & Golf Resort, **20**
Calinda Viva Cancún, **4**
Casa Turquesa, **13**
Club Las Velas, **1**
El Pueblito Beach Hotel, **21**
Fiesta Americana Condesa, **18**
Fiesta Americana Coral Beach Cancún, **8**
Hyatt Regency Cancún, **9**
Marriott Casa Magna, **15**
Meliá Cancún, **17**
Ritz-Carlton Cancún, **14**
Westin Regina Resort Cancún, **22**

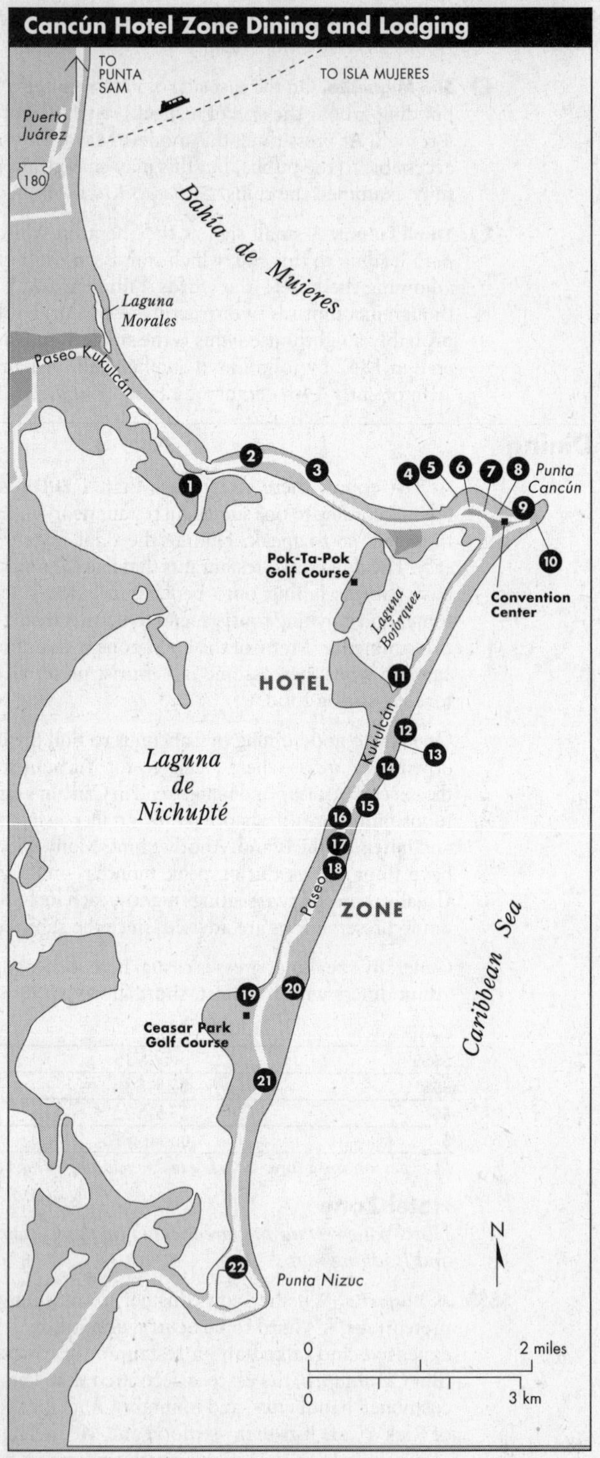

bers; one of them has a dance floor and a small stage for live music in the evening. Tall windows look out onto a bubbling courtyard fountain and the Caribbean beyond. European grill is the house specialty; rich sauces and decorative touches give a distinctly Mexican spin to the grilled chops, steaks, chicken, and seafood. Try the *chipotle* (a smoked pepper) duck in honey tequila sauce. Service is attentive and discreet. ✉ *Paseo Kukulcán (Retorno del Rey 36),* ☎ *98/850808. AE, DC, MC, V.*

$$$ ✕ **Hacienda El Mortero.** Pampering waiters, strolling mariachis, lush hanging plants, fig trees, and candlelight make this reproduction plantation home a popular spot to dine. The menu offers a selection of country cooking, and the chicken fajitas and rib steaks are first class. Seatings are at 6:30 and 9:30. ✉ *Paseo Kukulcán, Hotel Krystal,* ☎ *98/831133. Reservations essential. AE, DC, MC, V. No lunch.*

$$$ ★ ✕ **La Dolce Vita.** Over the past decade, this appealing restaurant developed a strong and well-deserved local following at its original downtown location on Avenida Cobá. In its new (1996) incarnation in the hotel zone, across from the Marriott CasaMagna and overlooking Laguna Nichupté, La Dolce Vita has maintained its romantic atmosphere, while almost doubling its space. Favorites from the excellent Northern Italian and Continental menu include seafood antipasto, *boquinete dolce vita* (a local white fish stuffed with shrimp and mushrooms and baked in puff pastry), and creamy tiramisu. ✉ *Paseo Kukulcán, Km 14.5,* ☎ *98/850150 or 98/850161. AE, MC, V. No weekend lunch.*

$$$ ✕ **Lorenzillos.** Perched on its own peninsula in the lagoon, this nautical spot provides a pleasant place to watch the sun set, sip a drink on the outdoor patio, or sample excellent seafood. Specialties include grilled or broiled lobster (you can pick out your own) and whole fish Veracruz-style. The seafaring theme extends to the names of both the dishes (like Jean Lafitte beef) and the restaurant itself (Lorenzillo was a 17th-century pirate). ✉ *Paseo Kukulcán, Km 10.5,* ☎ *98/831254. AE, MC, V.*

$$ ✕ **Captain's Cove.** Both waterfront locations have popular breakfast buffets served under palapa roofs. The decor is decidedly nautical, with rigging draped on the walls and chandeliers in the shape of ships' steering wheels. The restaurant near the Casa Maya Hotel overlooks the Caribbean Sea toward Isla Mujeres; the other is situated beside the Nichupté Lagoon. Both present lunch and dinner menus filled with seafood dishes and charbroiled steak and chicken. Parents appreciate the lower-priced children's menu, an unusual feature in Cancún. ✉ *Paseo Kukulcán, Km 16.5, lagoon-side across from Royal Mayan Hotel,* ☎ *98/850016;* ☎ *98/830669 beachside next to Casa Maya Hotel. Reservations not accepted. AE, MC, V.*

$$ ✕ **Carlos 'n' Charlie's.** A lively atmosphere, a terrific view of the lagoon, and good food make this newly remodeled restaurant—part of the popular Anderson chain—Cancún's best-known hot spot. You'll never run out of bric-a-brac to look at: Sombreros, birdcages, and wooden birds and animals hang from the ceilings. Try the barbecued ribs sizzling on the open grill, or one of the steak or seafood specials. After your meal, dance off the calories under the stars at the restaurant's Pier Dance Club. ✉ *Paseo Kukulcán, Km 5.5,* ☎ *98/830846. Reservations not accepted. AE, MC, V.*

$$ ★ ✕ **Casa Rolandi.** Authentic northern Italian and Swiss dishes are skillfully prepared by the Italian owner-chef, who grew up near the Swiss border. If it's on the menu, start with the lobster-stuffed black ravioli, and go on to grilled seafood garnished with a zesty olive oil. Alternatively, try the homemade lasagna, baked in the large stucco oven; accompanied by a lavish antipasto bar, it makes for a satisfying dinner. Service is friendly and efficient, and prices surprisingly reasonable for this level of quality cuisine. The decor is appropriately Mediterranean

and the back room offers a view of the beach. ✉ *Plaza Caracol,* ☎ *98/831817. AE, MC, V.*

$$ ✕ **El Mexicano.** This 300-seat restaurant hosts a dinner show in a room resembling a hacienda's patio. Folkloric ballet performances are held at 8 PM. Elaborately hand-carved chairs created by Indians from central Mexico and regional Mexican dishes convey a feeling of authenticity. Be forewarned, however: Though indisputably popular, this is a touristy spot, and the dancing-girl show is not a window into Yucatecan culture. Try the *empanxonostle* (steamed lobster, shrimp, fish, and herbs); it's as extravagant as El Mexicano's surroundings. ✉ *La Mansión–Costa Blanca mall,* ☎ *98/832220 or 98/832220. AE, MC, V.*

$$ ★ ✕ **Splash.** Good-quality Art Deco furnishings, lots of purple and aqua, and neon lights add to the sleek atmosphere of this restaurant. During high season, the outside terrace with its peekaboo view of the lagoon is usually full. Never mind—the inside bar area and dining room are cooler. The downstairs area offers the most intimate dining experience. You can't go wrong with any of the homemade pastas or the charcoal-grilled grouper Bora Bora–style (in a rich sauce of peaches and clarified butter). Splash has great happy-hour specials and all-you-can-eat breakfast, lunch, and dinner deals. ✉ *Paseo Kukulcán at Kukulcán Plaza,* ☎ *98/853011. Reservations not accepted. AE, MC, V.*

$ ✕ **100% Natural.** Looking for something light? Head to one of the three locations of this cheery open-air eatery. Identical menus at all of them appeal to vegetarians, with a broad array of soups, salads, and fresh fruit drinks. Egg dishes, sandwiches, grilled chicken and fish, and Mexican and Italian fare are available as well. ✉ *Paseo Kukulcán at Kukulcán Plaza,* ☎ *98/852904;* ✉ *Plaza Terramar,* ☎ *98/831180;* ✉ *Av. Sunyaxche 62,* ☎ *98/843617. Reservations not accepted. AE, MC, V.*

Downtown

Downtown restaurants are located on the Downtown Cancún Dining and Lodging map.

$$$ ✕ **Bucanero.** Quiet dining in a candlelit marine atmosphere is the drawing card for this seafood restaurant, built to resemble the interior of a Spanish galleon, and the seafood—particularly the lobster specialties—is tops. Heaping servings are enough to feed two (which puts this in the $$ price range if you don't mind sharing your meal). Piano music played throughout the evening and waiters dressed as pirates add character to the place. ✉ *Av. Cobá 88,* ☎ *98/842280. AE, MC, V. No lunch.*

$$$ ★ ✕ **La Habichuela.** This charmer—once an elegant home—is perfect for hand-holding romantics or anyone looking for a relaxed, private atmosphere. The candlelit garden, with white, wrought-iron chairs, pebbled ground, and thick, tropical greenery, exudes peacefulness. Try the *cocobichuela*—lobster and shrimp in a light Indian sauce served on a bed of rice inside a coconut—a specialty of the house. ✉ *Margaritas 25,* ☎ *98/843158. AE, MC, V. No lunch during low season.*

$$ ★ ✕ **El Pescador.** It's first-come, first-served, with long lines, especially during high season. But people still flood into this rustic Mexican-style restaurant with nautical touches; the open-air patio is particularly popular. Heavy hitters on the menu include red snapper broiled with garlic and freshly caught lobster specials. La Mesa Del Pescador, a newer offshoot in Plaza Kukulcán (☎ 98/850505), is not usually as crowded as this place. ✉ *Tulipanes 28,* ☎ *98/842673. Reservations not accepted. AE, MC, V.*

$$ ✕ **La Parrilla.** If you're looking for the place where local Mexicans—young and old—hang out, you've found it in this popular downtown spot, an old classic by Cancún standards (it opened in 1975). Everything from the food to the bougainvillea and palapa roof is authentic.

Dining
Bucanero, **1**
Carillo's, **5**
El Pescador, **7**
El Tacolote, **2**
La Habichuela, **10**
La Parrilla, **11**
Perico's, **8**
Rosa Mexicano, **3**

Lodging
Antillano, **4**
Holiday Inn Centro Cancún, **12**
Plaza Carrillo's, **6**
Tropical Inn, **9**

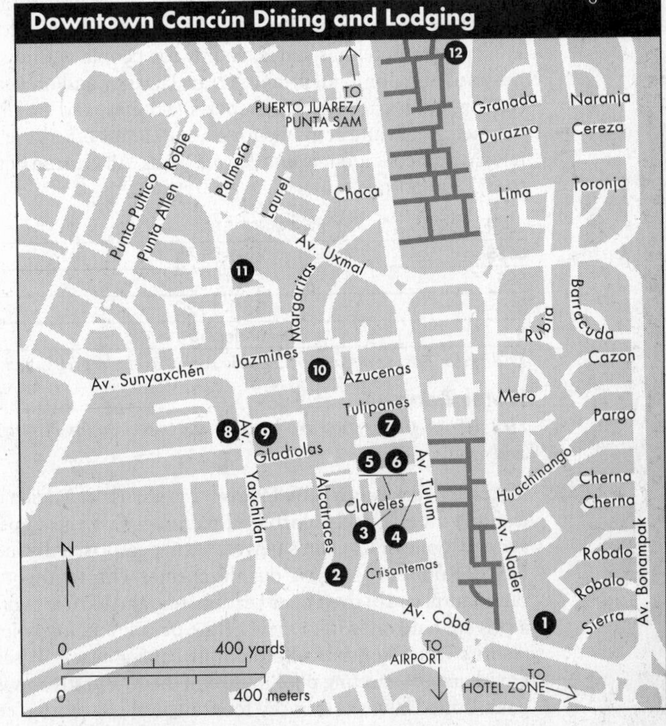

Downtown Cancún Dining and Lodging

Popular dishes include the grilled beef with garlic sauce and the *tacos al pastor* (tacos with pork, pineapple, coriander, onion, and salsa). ✉ *Av. Yaxchilán 51,* ☏ *98/845398. Reservations not accepted. AE, MC, V. No lunch.*

$$ ✕ **Perico's.** Find the antique car perched atop the palapa roof and you've located this zany, eclectic restaurant and bar. Saddles top bar stools, and caricature busts of political figures from Castro to Queen Elizabeth line the walls. The Mexican menu, including "Pancho Villa" (grilled beef with Mexican side dishes), is reliable, but the real reason to come here is the party atmosphere that begins nightly at 7 when the mariachi and marimba bands play. ✉ *Av. Yaxchilán 61,* ☏ *98/843152. Reservations essential for 8 or more. AE, MC, V.*

$$ ★ ✕ **Rosa Mexicano.** One of Cancún's prettiest Mexican colonial–style restaurants presents waiters dressed as *charros* (Mexican cowboys), embroidered wall hangings, and floor tiles with floral designs. For extra romance, make a reservation for the candlelit patio. Specialties include *filete Rosa* (beef and onions in a tequila-orange sauce) and *camarones al ajillo* (shrimp sautéed in olive oil and garlic, with chili peppers). ✉ *Calle Claveles 4,* ☏ *98/846313. AE, MC, V. No lunch.*

$ ✕ **El Tacolote.** A lively neighborhood *taquería,* El Tacolote has successfully expanded on its original tacos offerings and now serves fajitas, grilled kebabs, and other traditional Mexican favorites. ✉ *Av. Cobá 19,* ☏ *98/873045. Reservations not accepted. MC, V.*

Lodging

Cancún has a bewildering variety of hotels to choose from. For the most part, those in the downtown area don't offer anything close to the luxury or amenities of the hotel-zone properties. They do, however, afford visitors the opportunity to stay in a popular resort without paying resort prices, and many offer free shuttle service to the beach. Expect minibars, satellite TV, laundry and room service, private safes, and bathroom hair dryers in hotels in the $$$$ category; in addition, almost every major hotel has suites, rooms for people with disabilities, and no-smoking rooms, an in-house travel agency and/or a car-rental concession, guest parking, water-sports facilities, and a daily schedule of planned games and activities for guests. Unless otherwise noted, all hotels have air-conditioning and private baths. All Cancún hotels are within the 77500 postal code.

CATEGORY	COST*
$$$$	over $175
$$$	$120–$175
$$	$50–$120
$	under $50

**All prices are for a standard double room, excluding 10% tax.*

Hotel Zone

Hotel-zone properties are located on the Cancún Hotel Zone Dining and Lodging map.

$$$$ **Caesar Park Beach & Golf Resort.** Liberal use of Mérida marble, Mexican tile murals, and colorful oil paintings give this appealing Westin property, one of Cancún's newest luxury resorts, a distinctly Mexican flavor. Rooms, too, carry out the theme, with terra-cotta tile floors, rattan furniture, woven fiber headboards, and local artwork; some have a private balcony with a view of the ocean, and a few let you see the resort's championship 18-hole golf course across Paseo Kukulcán. Lavish interconnecting pools (*seven* of them) and streams wind through palm-dotted lawns; a terraced fountain in the cavernous central atrium brings the dancing water into the hotel's interior. ✉ *Paseo Kukulcán, Km 17 (Box 1810),* ☎ *98/818000 or 800/228–3000,* FAX *98/818080. 426 rooms. 3 restaurants, 3 bars, lobby lounge, 7 pools, beauty salon, 2 hot tubs, 2 saunas, 18-hole golf course, 2 tennis courts, aerobics, exercise room, shops, children's programs. AE, DC, MC, V.*

$$$$ ★ **Casa Turquesa.** The tranquil atmosphere of this small, elegant retreat belies its central location next to the bustling Plaza Kukulcán. The public rooms are palatial, with high ceilings, stone bas-reliefs, and marble floors. The 31 spacious suites are decorated individually in pastel tones, with modern furnishings; all have ocean-view private balconies with hot tubs. The privacy and discreet service afforded at this intimate retreat have made it the choice for celebrities such as Ivana Trump and the Planet Hollywood crew. They also enjoy frequenting the aptly named **Celebrity** restaurant, a subtly lit, romantic spot with a wonderfully creative menu that highlights local seafood. ✉ *Paseo Kukulcán, Km 13.5,* ☎ *98/852924,* FAX *98/852922. 31 suites. 2 restaurants, 2 bars, pool, beauty salon, sauna, tennis court, exercise room. AE, MC, V.*

$$$$ **Fiesta Americana Condesa.** This sprawling, friendly hotel offers the same casual elegance and luxurious amenities as its older sister, the Fiesta Americana Cancún. Situated toward the southern end of the hotel zone, the Condesa has a Mediterranean-style facade featuring balconies, rounded arches, and alternating ocher, salmon, and sand-color walls. But it's the huge palapa fronting the structure that makes it hard to miss. An attractive and spacious lobby bar has Tiffany-style stained-glass awnings, tall palms, and ceiling fans. Three seven-story towers overlook a tranquil inner courtyard with hanging plants and falling water. The rooms, highlighted by dusty-pink stucco walls and Mexican tile floors, offer the same tranquillity. Balconies are shared by three standard rooms; the costlier accommodations have their own. Oceanfront suites have a private hot tub on the terrace. ✉ *Paseo*

Kukulcán, Km 16.5 (Box 5478), ☎ *98/851000 or 800/343–7821,* FAX *98/851650. 502 rooms. 5 restaurants, 2 bars, pool, beauty salon, 3 tennis courts, health club, shops. AE, DC, MC, V.*

$$$$ **Fiesta Americana Coral Beach Cancún.** The newest of the Cancún Fiesta properties, this all-suites hotel lies just in front of the convention center and shopping malls. All rooms in the large salmon-color structure are ample in size, with oceanfront balconies and marble floors; slate-blue, lavender, and beige tones create a soothing, pleasant mood. The hotel's **La Joya** restaurant, serving nouvelle-style Mexican fare, is a fine spot for dinner. As for outdoor activities, choose between the 1,000-ft beach and the 660-ft pool. This is Cancún's largest convention hotel; expect the clientele and occasional slow service to match. ✉ *Paseo Kukulcán, Lote 6 (Box 14),* ☎ *98/832900 or 800/343–7821,* FAX *98/833173. 602 suites. 3 restaurants, 3 bars, pool, 3 tennis courts, health club, shops. AE, DC, MC, V.*

$$$$ **Marriott CasaMagna.** The six-story Marriott is rather eclectically designed: In the lobby modern furnishings are set in an atrium with Mediterranean-style arches, crystal chandeliers, and hanging vines. The rooms, decorated in contemporary Mexican style, have tile floors and ceiling fans and follow a soft rose, mauve, and earth-tone color scheme. You can learn to prepare Mexican dishes if you attend cooking lessons (one of many guest activities), or you can sit back and watch the chef do the work at **Mikado,** the hotel's fine Japanese steak house. ✉ *Paseo Kukulcán (Retorno Chac L-41),* ☎ *98/852000 or 800/228–9290,* FAX *98/851385. 450 rooms, including 36 suites. 3 restaurants, bar, beauty salon, 2 hot tubs, sauna, 2 tennis courts, health club, shops. AE, DC, MC, V.*

$$$$ **Meliá Cancún.** The Meliá Cancún is a boldly modern version of a Maya temple, fronted by a sheer black marble wall and a sleek waterfall. Public spaces exude elegance; the boutiques could not be more chic. Ivory, dusty-pink, and light-blue hues softly brighten rooms (all with private balcony or terrace); ivory-lacquered furniture and wall-to-wall carpeting create a luxurious ambience. An upscale spa, with modern equipment and an array of body treatments, was added in 1995. The Meliá Turquesa, a 408-room sister property across the street from Flamingo Plaza, is not as glitzy but has a more intimate, friendlier atmosphere. ✉ *Paseo Kukulcán, Km 16,* ☎ *98/851160 or 800/336–3542,* FAX *98/851263. 450 rooms. 5 restaurants, 3 bars, 2 pools, spa, 18-hole golf course, 3 tennis courts, health club, shops. AE, DC, MC, V.*

$$$$ ★ **Ritz-Carlton Cancún.** This ultraposh, peach-color property set new standards for luxury and service in Cancún when it opened in 1993. The air-conditioned lobby and public areas are richly appointed with fine European and American antiques, thick carpets, and marble floors. Stylish rooms, done in comfortable shades of blue, beige, and peach, offer all the amenities—wall-to-wall carpeting, travertine marble bathrooms with telephones, separate tub and shower, plush terry robes, and large balconies overlooking the Caribbean. The hotel's elegant restaurants, especially the **Club Grill** (☞ Dining, *above*) and the newer **Fantino** (serving northern Italian dinner fare), are standouts. ✉ *Paseo Kukulcán, Retorno del Rey 36,* ☎ *98/850808 or 800/241–3333,* FAX *98/851015. 370 rooms, including suites. 3 restaurants, 2 bars, 3 pools, beauty salon, hot tub, 2 saunas, 2 spas, 2 steam rooms, 3 tennis courts, health club, pro shop, shops. AE, DC, MC, V.*

$$$$ **Westin Regina Resort Cancún.** This luxury property at the southern end of the island, on Punta Nizuc, is one of the few hotels with direct access to both a 1,600-ft beach and Laguna Nichupté. The low-rise, postmodern-style hotel was designed and decorated by one of Latin America's leading architects. From the lobby, you can look down on a stylish restaurant with stunning ocean views. In the spacious guest rooms, handsome rustic furnishings and colorful Mexican folk art stand out against white walls and pale marble floors. Concierge tower rooms are available. ✉ *Paseo Kukulcán, Km 20 (Box 1808),* ☎ *98/850086, 98/850537, or 800/228–3000;* FAX *98/850074. 385 rooms. 4 restaurants, 3 bars, 5 pools, hot tub, 5 outdoor hot tubs, 2 tennis courts, exercise room, children's programs. AE, DC, MC, V.*

$$$ ★ **Club Las Velas.** Once you go past the wrought-iron gates of this all-inclusive property, you'll be in a delightfully private enclave. The complex is a replica of a Mexican village, complete with central plaza and lush gardens. Nonmotorized water sports, children's programs, and a water taxi to a nearby ocean beach are part of the package. Rooms are light and airy, with white stucco walls, tropical print bedspreads, and rattan furniture, and the duplex villas are especially suited to families. The food—served buffet style at breakfast, and buffet style or à la carte at dinner—is plentiful and good. Nightly theme parties with live entertainment fill the plaza after dinner. ✉ *Paseo Kukulcán y Galeon,* ☎ *98/832222 or 800/707–8815,* FAX *98/832118. 285 rooms, including 59 villas. 2 restaurants, 2 bars, snack bar, 2 pools, 2 tennis courts, aerobics, exercise room, shops, children's programs. AE, MC, V.*

$$$ **Hyatt Regency Cancún.** A cylindrical 14-story tower with the Hyatt trademark atrium affords a 360° view of the sea and the lagoon. Soothing blue, green, and beige tones prevail in the rooms, which also feature contemporary Mexican furniture and striking green or rose-color marble vanities. This hotel, much larger and livelier than its sister property, boasts an enormous two-level pool with a waterfall. **Cilantro,** the hotel's pretty waterfront dining room, has a good breakfast buffet. The hotel is convenient to the convention center and several shopping malls. ✉ *Paseo Kukulcán (Box 1201),* ☎ *98/830966, 98/831234, or 800/233–1234;* FAX *98/831438. 300 rooms. 2 restaurants, 3 bars, pool, health club, recreation room. AE, MC, V.*

$$ **Calinda Viva Cancún.** This beige stucco eight-story building—part of the Quality hotel chain—is not one of the most attractive in town, but it makes a reliable standby and is in a good location, on the north beach near many malls. The functional, moderate-size rooms have marble floors and contemporary pastel decor; half have private balconies and ocean views. The property also features a small garden, a beach, and a Mexican restaurant. ✉ *Paseo Kukulcán, Km 8.5 (Box 673),* ☎ *98/830800 or 800/221-2222. 216 rooms. Restaurant, bar, pool, 2 tennis courts, boating, shop. AE, DC, MC, V.*

$$ ★ **El Pueblito Beach Hotel.** El Pueblito, meaning "little town," is an apt name for this all-inclusive property, which consists of clusters of guest rooms in tri-level units that invoke Old Mexico. Interconnecting pathways lined with tropical foliage lead to terrace pools with waterfalls and stone archways; there's even a long water slide for kids. Rooms, which are large for the price, have marble floors and simple rattan furnishings; a few have kitchenettes. ✉ *Paseo Kukulcán, Km 17.5,* ☎ *98/850422,* FAX *98/850731. 239 rooms. 3 restaurants, bar, 5 pools, tennis court, shop, travel services. AE, MC, V.*

Downtown

Downtown properties are located on the Downtown Cancún Dining and Lodging map.

$$$ ★ **Holiday Inn Centro Cancún.** The place to stay if you want to be downtown and have all the amenities, the upscale Holiday Inn is less expensive than similar properties in the hotel zone and provides free transportation to the beach of the Crown Princess Club. The attractive pink four-story structure, with a Spanish tile roof, affords easy access to restaurants and shops. Although rooms are somewhat generic motel modern, with mauve and blue color schemes, they have appealing

Mexican touches. ✉ *Av. Nader 1, SM 2,* ☎ *98/84455 or 800/465–4329,* FAX *98/847954. 246 rooms. 2 restaurants, 2 bars, pool, beauty salon, tennis court, exercise room, nightclub, coin laundry, travel services, car rental. AE, DC, MC, V.*

$$ ★ **Antillano.** This old but prettily appointed property features wood furnishings, a cozy little lobby bar, and a tiny pool. Extras such as tiled bathroom sinks and air-conditioning in the halls and rooms make this hotel stand out a bit from the others in its league. ✉ *Av. Tulum at Calle Claveles,* ☎ *98/841532 or 98/841132,* FAX *98/841878. 48 rooms. Pool, shop. AE, DC, MC, V.*

$$ ★ **Plaza Carrillo's.** One of the first hotels to be built in Cancún City, this one is conveniently located in the heart of the downtown area next to the Plaza Carrillo shopping arcade and Carrillo's restaurant, which are under the same ownership. The hotel corridors are exceptionally clean and well maintained. Rooms are bright, with simple functional decor. ✉ *Calle Claveles 35,* ☎ *98/841227,* FAX *98/842371. 43 rooms. Restaurant, pool. AE, MC, V.*

$$ **Tropical Inn.** This three-story Spanish colonial–style hotel, a block south of the Margarita Cancún, reopened in 1995 after a floor-to-ceiling renovation. Long popular with students, Europeans, and Canadians, it has rooms done in tasteful tones of brown. A pretty courtyard entrance leads to the reception desk. ✉ *Av. Yaxchilán 31,* ☎ *98/843078 or 98/843–3690,* FAX *98/849209. 81 rooms. Restaurant, bar, pool. AE, DC, MC, V.*

Nightlife and the Arts

The multi-story **Party Center** (✉ Paseo Kukulcán, Km 9, ☎ 98/830351), next to the convention center, is an entertainment complex that hosts several clubs, a sports bar, and two discos (**Tequila Rock** and **Baja Beach Club**), as well as numerous restaurants, specialty boutiques, and a money exchange. Live folkloric bands perform nightly in the central courtyard, which provides access to the clubs, bars, discos, and restaurants. You can also lobby bar-hop at the big resorts, sampling the happy hours and diverse selection of live music.

Dinner Cruises

A dinner cruise on board the 62-ft vessel ***Columbus*** (☎ 98/831488 or 98/833268) includes a full lobster or steak spread, open bar, and dancing for $70; the boat departs the Royal Mayan Yacht Club Monday–Saturday and sails at 4 and 7:30. The ***Cancún Queen*** (☎ 98/852288), a paddle wheeler departing from the AquaWorld Marina (✉ Paseo Kukulcán, Km 15.2), runs a similar excursion for $65. **Aqua Tours Adventures** (✉ Paseo Kukulcán, Km 6.25, ☎ 98/830400) offers a pleasantly romantic lobster dinner and sunset cruise to Isla Mujeres that includes dancing under the stars and an open bar. Departures are at 6 PM on Monday, Tuesday, Thursday, and Saturday. **Asterix Party Fishing** (✉ Paseo Kukulcán, Km 5.5 at Carlos 'n' Charlie's, ☎ 98/864847) offers evening cruises where you catch the fish and the crew prepares it for you. The bar is open, and the price is $50, fishing gear included. Cruises are Monday–Friday, departing at 6 PM and returning at midnight. **Pirates Night,** departing from Playa Langosta Dock (✉ Paseo Kukulcán, ☎ 98/831488), offers a three-course buffet dinner with trips to Treasure Island. Kids under 12 are half price and those under 5 are free. Cruises are Tuesday and Thursday, leaving at 6:30 PM and returning at 11:30. It's wise to be at the dock 30 minutes before departure time.

Discos

Cancún wouldn't be Cancún without its glittering discos, which generally start jumping about 10:30. **Azucar** (✉ Camino Real Hotel, ☎

98/830100) sizzles to a salsa beat nightly; the beautiful people don't turn up here until *really* late. **Dady'O** (✉ Paseo Kukulcán, Km 9.5, ☎ 98/833333) has been around for a while but is still a very "in" place, especially with the younger set. The **Dady Rock** (✉ Paseo Kukulcán, Km 9.5, ☎ 98/831626) bar and grill, next door to Dady'O, opens at 6 PM and draws a high-energy clientele with live music, a giant screen, contests, and food specials. **Christine** (✉ Krystal Cancún hotel, ☎ 98/831133) attracts a slightly older, elegantly attired crowd and features an incredible light show. **La Boom** (✉ Paseo Kukulcán, Km 3.5, ☎ 98/831152) includes a video bar with a light show and is not always crowded, although it can squeeze in 1,200 people.

Festivals

Cancún's **Jazz Festival** premiered in 1991 and featured Wynton Marsalis and Gato Barbieri. It's an annual event that takes place in late May; the Cancún Hotel Association (✉ Av. Ign. García de la Torre, SM 1, Lote 6, Cancún, QR 77500, ☎ 98/842853) can provide information.

Music

Batacha (✉ Hotel Miramar Misión, ☎ 98/831755), a small Caribbean nightclub, is a low-key spot to enjoy some Latin sounds. Visit the **Hard Rock Cafe** (✉ Plaza Lagunas, Paseo Kukulcán, ☎ 98/832024) for live rock bands (generally six nights a week) and music nostalgia. You can hear Caribbean-beat dance music (marimba, mariachi, reggae, etc.) at **Jalapeños** (✉ Paseo Kukulcán, Km 7, ☎ 98/832896) nightly from 8. The place to go for hot live reggae is **Mango Tango** (✉ Paseo Kukulcán, Km 14.2, ☎ 98/850303), which sits lagoonside across the street from the Ritz-Carlton. **Planet Hollywood** (✉ Flamingo Plaza, Paseo Kukulcán, Km 11.5, ☎ 98/850723) is currently the top ticket in town; crowds push their way in for the Hollywood memorabilia—and hope to catch a glimpse of such stars as Demi Moore and Arnold Schwarzenegger, who occasionally check in on their investment.

Performances

The most elaborate ballet folklórico dinner show is held at the **Hotel Continental Villas Plaza** (✉ Paseo Kukulcán, Km 11, ☎ 98/831095); it consists of stylized performances of regional Mexican dances including the hat dance and *la bamba*. The **Convention Center** hosts another popular ballet folklórico dinner show nightly (✉ Paseo Kukulcán, Km 9, ☎ 98/830199). **El Mexicano** (✉ La Mansión–Costa Blanca mall, ☎ 98/832220 or 98/832220), one of Cancún's largest restaurants, seats 300 for a folkloric dinner show every evening. For all of the above, expect large buffet spreads and at least one drink to be included in the admission charge; call ahead for dates, prices, and reservations.

A Mexican ***charreada,*** or rodeo show (✉ El Corral de JF, Km 6, Prolongación Av. Lopez Portillo, no phone), is performed Monday–Saturday at 7 PM. In addition to the show you get dinner and domestic drinks. You can book reservations through your hotel.

Outdoor Activities and Sports

Bullfighting

The Cancún **bullring,** a block south of the Pemex station, hosts year-round bullfights. A matador, charros, a mariachi band, and flamenco dancers entertain during the hour preceding the bullfight (from 2:30 PM). ✉ *Paseo Kukulcán at Av. Bonampak,* ☎ *98/845465 or 98/848248.* 🎫 *About $40.* ⏲ *Fights Wed. at 3:30.*

Golf

The main course is at **Pok-Ta-Pok** (✉ Paseo Kukulcán between Km 6 and Km 7, ☎ 98/830871), a club with fine views of both sea and lagoon, whose 18 holes were designed by Robert Trent Jones, Sr. The **Caesar Park Cancún** (✉ Paseo Kukulcán, Km 17, ☎ 98/818000) has an 18-hole championship course. The 18-hole executive course (par 53) at the **Hotel Melia Cancún** (✉ Paseo Kukulcán, Km 12, ☎ 98/851160) circles half the property and shares its beautiful ocean views. Greens fees are about $20.

Water Sports

There are myriad ways you can get your adrenalin going while getting wet in Cancún. The most popular ones are detailed below. In addition, you'll also be able to find places to go parasailing (about $35 for eight minutes); waterskiing ($70 per hour); or jet skiing ($70 per hour, or $60 for Wave Runners, double-seated Jet Skis). Paddle boats, kayaks, catamarans, and banana boats are also readily available. **Aqua Tours** (✉ Paseo Kukulcán, Km 6.25, ☎ 98/830400, FAX 98/830403) and **AquaWorld** (✉ Paseo Kukulcán, Km 15.2, ☎ 98/852288, FAX 98/852299) maintain large fleets of water toys.

FISHING

Some 500 species of tropical fish, including sailfish, bluefin, marlin, barracuda, and red snapper, live in the waters adjacent to Cancún. Deep-sea fishing boats and other gear may be chartered from outfitters for about $350 for four hours, $450 for six hours, and $550 for eight hours. Charters generally include a captain, a first mate, gear, bait, and beverages. **Aqua Tours, AquaWorld,** and the **Royal Yacht Club** (✉ Paseo Kukulcán, Km 16.5, ☎ 98/852930) are just a few of the companies that operate large fishing fleets. **Pelican Pier Fishing Excursions** (✉ Paseo Kukulcán, Km 5.5, across from Casa Maya Hotel, ☎ 98/830315) offers six hours on their six-person charter boats for $99 per person. Price includes soft drinks, bait, and fishing gear. Also available are deep-sea charters starting at $318 for four hours.

SAILBOARDING

Although some people sailboard on the ocean side in the summer, activity is limited primarily to the bay between Cancún and Isla Mujeres. If you visit the island in July, don't miss the National Windsurfing Tournament (☎ 98/843212), in which athletes test their mettle. The **International Windsurfer Sailing School** (☎ 98/842023), at Playa Tortugas, rents equipment and gives lessons; the **Windsurf Association of Quintana Roo** (☎ 98/871771) can provide information about the tournament. Sailboards are available for about $50 an hour; classes go for about $35 an hour.

SNORKELING AND SCUBA DIVING

Snorkeling is best at Punta Nizuc, Punta Cancún, and Playa Tortugas, although you should be especially careful of the strong currents at the last; gear can be rented for $10 per day. Some charter-fishing companies offer a two-tank scuba dive for about $100. As the name implies, **Scuba Cancún** (☎ 98/831011) specializes in diving trips and offers NAUI, CMAS, and PADI instruction. **Aqua Tours Adventures** (☎ 98/830400 or 98/830227) offers scuba tours and a resort course, as well as snorkeling trips. **AquaWorld Adventures** (☎ 98/852288) runs 2½-hour daily jungle tours through dense mangroves. A guide leads the way as you drive your own Aqua Ray on Laguna Nichupté. The $40 price includes snorkeling and light refreshments. If you've brought your own snorkeling gear and want to save money, just take a city bus down to Club Med and walk along the resort's beach for about 1½ km (1 mi) until you get to Punta Nizuc. **Blue Peace Diving** (✉ Paseo Kukulcán, Km 16.2, ☎ 98/851447) offers two-tank dives for $85 with NAUI, SSI, and PADI instruction. The areas explored are Cozumel, Akumal, Xpu-ha, and Isla Mujeres. Extended three-day diving trips are available for about $280.

Shopping

Resortwear and handicrafts are the most popular purchases in Cancún, but the prices are high and the selection standard; if you're traveling elsewhere in Mexico, it's best to postpone your shopping spree until you reach another town. Bargaining is expected in Cancún, but mostly in the market. If you can do without plastic, you may get the 12% sales tax lopped off at shops that don't want to pay high commissions to credit-card companies.

Shopping hours are generally weekdays 10–1 and 4–7, although more and more stores are staying open throughout the day rather than closing for siesta between 1 and 4 PM. Many shops keep Saturday morning hours, and some are now open on Sunday until 1 PM. Shops in the malls tend to be open weekdays from 9 or 10 AM to 8 or 10 PM.

Downtown

The wide variety of shops downtown along Avenida Tulum between Av. Cobá and Uxmal includes **Fama** (✉ Av. Tulum 105, ☎ 98/846586), a department store offering clothing, English reading matter, sports gear, toiletries, liquor, and *latería* (crafts made of tin). Also on Tulum is the oldest and largest of Cancún's crafts markets, **Ki Huic** (✉ Av. Tulum 17, between Bancomer and Banco Atlantico, ☎ 98/843347), which is open daily from 9 AM to 10 PM and houses about 100 vendors.

Hotel Zone

Fully air-conditioned malls (known as *centros comerciales*), as streamlined and well kept as any in the United States or Canada, sell everything from fashion clothing, beachwear, and sportswear to jewelry, household items, video games, and leather goods.

The newest mall on the scene is **Kukulcán Plaza** (✉ Paseo Kukulcán, Km 13), with around 130 shops (including Izod, Benetton, and Harley Davidson boutiques), 12 restaurants, a bar, a liquor store, a bank, a cinema, bowling lanes, and a video arcade.

Flamingo Plaza (✉ Paseo Kukulcán, Km 11.5, across from Hotel Flamingo) includes an exchange booth, some designer emporiums and duty-free stores, several sportswear shops, two boutiques selling Guatemalan imports, a pharmacy, and a Planet Hollywood boutique. At the food court, in addition to the usual McDonald's, Domino's Pizza, and fried-chicken concessions, you'll find **Checandole**, offering what might be the only fast-food mole enchiladas around.

Just across from the convention center site, **Plaza Caracol** (✉ Paseo Kukulcán, Km 8.5) is the largest and most contemporary mall in Cancún, with about 200 shops and boutiques, including two pharmacies, art galleries, a currency exchange, and folk art and jewelry shops, as well as cafés and restaurants. Fashion boutiques include Benetton, Bally, Gucci, and Ralph Lauren; in all these stores, prices are lower than in their U.S. counterparts.

To the back of—and virtually indistinguishable from—Plaza Caracol are two outdoor shopping complexes. The pink stucco **La Mansion–Costa Blanca** specializes in designer clothing and has several restaurants, art galleries, a bank, and a liquor store. **Plaza Lagunas** is the home of the Hard Rock Cafe; some fast-food places (KFC, Subway, Dunkin' Donuts); sportswear shops, such as Ellesse; and a number of souvenir stands. Also near Plaza Caracol, **Plaza Terramar** (opposite the Hotel

Fiesta Americana) sells beachwear, souvenirs, and folk art and has a restaurant and a pharmacy.

Plaza Nautilus (✉ Paseo Kukulcán, Km 3.5, lagoon side), the mall closest to downtown, has lost most of its pizzazz and shops, with just a small restaurant, a Super Deli and liquor shop, and a car-rental office among the few survivors.

Specialty Shops

Orbe (✉ Plaza Caracol, ☎ 98/831571) specializes in sculptures and paintings by contemporary Mexican artists. **Mordo's** (✉ La Mansíon–Costa Blanca mall, ☎ 98/830838) is the local outlet for a small Mexico City chain that sells handcrafted leather jackets, belts, and boots, and can customize your purchase with decorative patches, needlework, or metallic trim. **Mayart** (✉ La Mansíon–Costa Blanca mall, ☎ 98/841272 or 98/841569) displays replicas of Maya art, temple rubbings, and contemporary painting and sculpture. Those interested in contemporary art should stop by the **Xamanek Gallery** (✉ Plaza Caracol, no phone) to see the work of Sergio Bustamante, one of the most popular Mexican artists today.

Cancún A to Z

Arriving and Departing

BY BUS

The bus terminal (✉ Avs. Tulum and Uxmal, ☎ 98/841378 or 98/843948) downtown serves first-class buses making the trip from Mexico City and first- and second-class buses arriving in Cancún from Puerto Morelos, Playa del Carmen, Tulum, Chetumal, Cobá, Valladolid, Chichén Itzá, and Mérida. Public buses (Rte. 8) make the trip out to Puerto Juárez and Punta Sam for the ferries to Isla Mujeres, and taxis will take you from the bus station to Puerto Júarez for about $2.

BY CAR

Cancún is at the end of Route 180, which goes from Matamoros on the Texas border to Campeche, Mérida, and Valladolid. The road trip from Texas to Cancún can take up to three days. Cancún can also be reached from the south via Route 307, which passes through Chetumal and Belize. There are few gas stations on these roads, so try to keep your tank filled. Route 307 has a Pemex station between Cancún and Playa Del Carmen. Construction is ongoing to increase the two lanes to four.

BY PLANE

Cancún International Airport is 16 km (9 mi) southwest of the heart of Cancún City, 10 km (6 mi) from the southernmost point of the hotel zone. **Aeromexico** (☎ 98/841097 or 98/843571) flies nonstop from Houston, Miami, and New York. **American** (☎ 98/860086) has nonstop service from Dallas and Miami. **Continental** (☎ 98/860040) offers daily direct service from Houston. **Mexicana** (☎ 98/874444 or 98/860120) nonstops depart from Los Angeles, Miami, and New York. In Cancún, Mexicana subsidiaries **Aerocaribe** (☎ 98/842000 downtown, 98/860083 airport) and **Aerocozumel** (☎ 98/842000 downtown, 98/860162 airport) offer flights to Cozumel, the ruins at Chichén Itzá, Mérida, and other Mexican destinations.

Between the Airport and Hotels. A counter at the airport exit sells tickets for vans (called *colectivos*) and for taxis. Vans, which cost about $8, are air-conditioned and sell soft drinks and beer on board but may be slow if they're carrying a lot of passengers and need to stop at many hotels. Approximate taxi fares: from the airport to the hotel zone, about $23; from the hotel zone to the airport, about $10.

Getting Around

Motorized transportation of some sort is necessary, since the island is somewhat spread out. Public bus service is good, and taxis are relatively inexpensive.

BY BUS

Public buses operate between the hotel zone and downtown from 6 AM to midnight; the cost is about 3 pesos. There are designated bus stops, but drivers can also be flagged down along Paseo Kukulcán. The service is a bit erratic, but buses run frequently and can save you considerable money on taxis, especially if you're staying at the southern end of the hotel zone.

BY CAR AND MOPED

Renting a car for your stay in Cancún is probably an unnecessary expense, entailing tips for valet parking, as well as gasoline and rather costly rental rates (on a par with those in any major resort area around the world). What's more, driving here can be harrowing when you don't know your way around. Downtown streets, being cobblestoned to give the area an "Old Mexico" look, are frequently clogged with traffic. However, if you plan to do some exploring, using Cancún as a base, the roads are excellent within a 100-km (62-mi) radius.

BY SHIP

Boats leave Puerto Juárez and Punta Sam—both north of Cancún City—for Isla Mujeres every half hour or so (☞ Isla Mujeres A to Z, *below*).

BY TAXI

Taxis to the ferries at Punta Sam or Puerto Juárez cost $15–$20 or more; between the hotel zone and downtown, $8 and up; and within the hotel zone, $5–$7. All prices depend on the distance, your negotiating skills, and whether you pick up the taxi in front of the hotel or go onto the avenue to hail a green city cab (the latter will be cheaper). Most hotels list rates at the door; confirm the price with your driver before you set out. If you lose something in a taxi or have questions or a complaint, call the **Sindicato de Taxistas** (☎ 98/886985).

Contacts and Resources

CAR AND MOPED RENTAL

Rental cars are available at the airport or from any of a dozen agencies in town, and most are standard-shift subcompacts and Jeeps; air-conditioned cars with automatic transmissions should be reserved in advance. Rental agencies include **Avis** (☎ 98/860222 airport; 98/830800 Hotel Calinda Viva; 98/830803 Mayfair Plaza); **Budget** (☎ 98/860026 airport; 98/840204 Av. Tulum 231); **Econo-Rent** (☎ 98/876487 airport; 98/860171 Av. Bonampak); **National** (☎ 98/860153 airport); and **Hertz** (☎ 98/860150 airport; 98/876644 Reno 35). The **Car Rental Association** (☎ 98/842039) can help you arrange a rental as well. Rates average around $45 per day.

Mopeds and scooters are also available throughout the island. Although fun, they are risky, and there is no insurance available for the driver or the vehicle. The accident rate is high, especially downtown, which is considered too congested for novice moped users. Rates start at around $25 per day.

CONSULATES

U.S. Consulate (✉ Av. Nader 40, SM 2A, Edificio Marruecos 31, ☎ 98/830272) is open weekdays 9–1.

Canadian Consulate (✉ Plaza Mexico Local 312, upper floor, ☎ 98/846716) is open daily 11 AM–1 PM. For emergencies outside office hours, call the Canadian Embassy in Mexico City (☎ 5/254–3288).

DOCTORS AND DENTISTS

Hospital Americano (✉ Calle Viento 15, ☎ 98/846133) and **Total Assist** (✉ Claveles 5, ☎ 98/841092 or 98/848116), both with English-speakers on staff, provide emergency medical care.

EMERGENCIES

Police (☎ 98/841913). **Red Cross** (✉ Av. Xcaret and Labná, SM 21, ☎ 98/841616). **Highway Patrol** (☎ 98/841107).

GUIDED TOURS

Air Tours. Aerolatino (✉ Plaza México, Av. Tulum 200, ☎ 98/871353 or 98/843938), a small Guatemalan carrier, flies between Cancún and Guatemala City, continuing on to Flores and the ruins at Tikal, for $290 round-trip.

Trans Caribe (☎ 98/871599 or 98/871692) sea planes offer panoramic tours of Cancún that depart daily from Laguna Nichupté. Prices vary according to the length of the ride, starting at about $35 for 20 minutes. Trans Caribe also will take you island-hopping to Isla Mujeres or Cozumel for diving, and sightseeing to the archaeological sites at Tulum and Chichén Itzá.

Day Cruises. Day cruises to Isla Mujeres are popular; they include snorkeling in El Garrafón, time for shopping downtown, as well as Continental breakfast, open-bar buffet lunch, and music. **Aqua Tours Adventures** (✉ Paseo Kukulcán, Km 6.25, ☎ 98/830400) books the "Isla Mujeres Adventure," which is particularly popular with locals; it departs at 10 AM from the pier in front of Fat Tuesday's, returns at 5 PM, and costs about $55. The **Tropical Cruiser** (✉ Playa Langosta, ☎ 98/831488) runs an excursion cruise to Isla Mujeres Monday through Saturday, departing from Playa Langosta.

Submarine Cruises. ***Nautibus*** (☎ 98/833552 or 98/832119), or the "floating submarine," has a 1½-hour Caribbean-reef cruise that departs the Playa Linda marina four times daily. The $30 price includes music and drinks. Tours aboard one of the **Sub See Explorer** (☎ 98/852288) "yellow submarines" depart from AquaWorld in the central hotel zone and can be combined with snorkeling for a full day's outing; the cost with snorkeling is about $40, $35 without. Latest to join the underwater ranks is ***Atlantis*** (☎ 98/833021), Cancún's first true submarine (the others float on the surface and have window seats below). Tours, available every hour from 10 to 3, include an hour-long cruise from Playa Linda to and from the submarine site, and 50 minutes dive time in the sub. The basic price is $80; add $10 and more time if you want to include lunch.

LATE-NIGHT PHARMACIES

Farmacia Turística (✉ Plaza Caracol, ☎ 98/831894) and **Farmacia Extra** (✉ Plaza Caracol, ☎ 98/832827) deliver to hotels 9 AM–10 PM, and **Farmacia Paris** (✉ Av. Yaxchilán, in the Marrufo Bldg., ☎ 98/840164) also fills prescriptions.

TRAVEL AGENCIES AND TOUR OPERATORS

American Express (✉ Av. Tulum at Agua, ☎ 98/841999); **Intermar Caribe** (✉ Av. Bonampak at Calle Careza, ☎ 98/844266); **Turismo Aviomar** (✉ Calle Venado 30, ☎ 98/846433).

VISITOR INFORMATION

Cancún Tips (✉ Av. Tulum 29, Suites 1–5, ☎ 98/841458), open daily 9–9.

State tourist office (✉ Av. Tulum 26, next to Multibanco Comerex, ☎ 98/848073), open daily 9–9.

ISLA MUJERES

Updated by Dan Millington

A tiny fish-shape island 8 km (5 mi) off Cancún, Isla Mujeres (*ees*-lah moo-*hair*-ayce) is a tranquil alternative to its bustling western neighbor. Only about 8 km (5 mi) long by 1 km (½ mi) wide, Isla has flat, sandy beaches on its northern end and steep, rocky bluffs to the south. Because of its proximity to Cancún, it has turned into a small-scale tourist destination, but it is still a peaceful island retreat with a rich history and culture centered on the sea. That legacy is evident in the names, features, and language of today's inhabitants, descendants of the ancient Maya.

The Spanish conquistadors arrived on the island by accident: After setting sail from Cuba in 1517, Hernández de Córdoba's ship blew here in a storm. Credited with "discovering" the island, he and his crew dubbed their find Isle of Women. One explanation of the name's origins is that Córdoba and company came upon wooden idols of Maya goddesses. Another theory claims the Spaniards found only women when they arrived—the men were out fishing.

For the next several centuries, Isla, like many Caribbean islands, became a haven for pirates and smugglers, then settled into life as a quiet fishing village. In this century, it started out as a vacation destination for Mexicans; the '60s witnessed a hippie influx; and since the late '70s, day-trippers from Cancún increasingly disembark here, bringing Isla's hotel, restaurant, and shop owners more business than ever.

The laid-back life here attracts a crowd that prefers beach pleasures to nightlife; *isleños* (islanders) themselves are working to preserve the island's ecology and tranquillity so that first-time visitors will still find an unusually peaceful, authentically Mexican retreat. As part of this effort, plans are currently afoot to have the Mexican government declare Isla Mujeres a national park.

Exploring

For orientation purposes, think of Isla Mujeres as an elongated fish: The southern tip is the head and the northern prong the tail. The island's only town, known simply as *el pueblo*, extends the full width of Isla's northern tail. The village is sandwiched between sand and sea to the north, south, and east; no high-rises block the view.

A Good Tour

Start out in the island's little town and walk north on Avenida Lopez Mateos to reach Isla's historical **cemetery** ⑥. To explore the rest of the island, you'll need to take a moped or taxi south along Avenida Rueda Medina, which leads out of town. The first landmark you'll pass after the piers is the Mexican naval base. It's off-limits to tourists, but from the road you can see the modest flag-raising and -lowering ceremonies at sunrise and sunset (no photo-taking permitted). Continue south and you'll see the **Laguna Makax** ⑦ on your right.

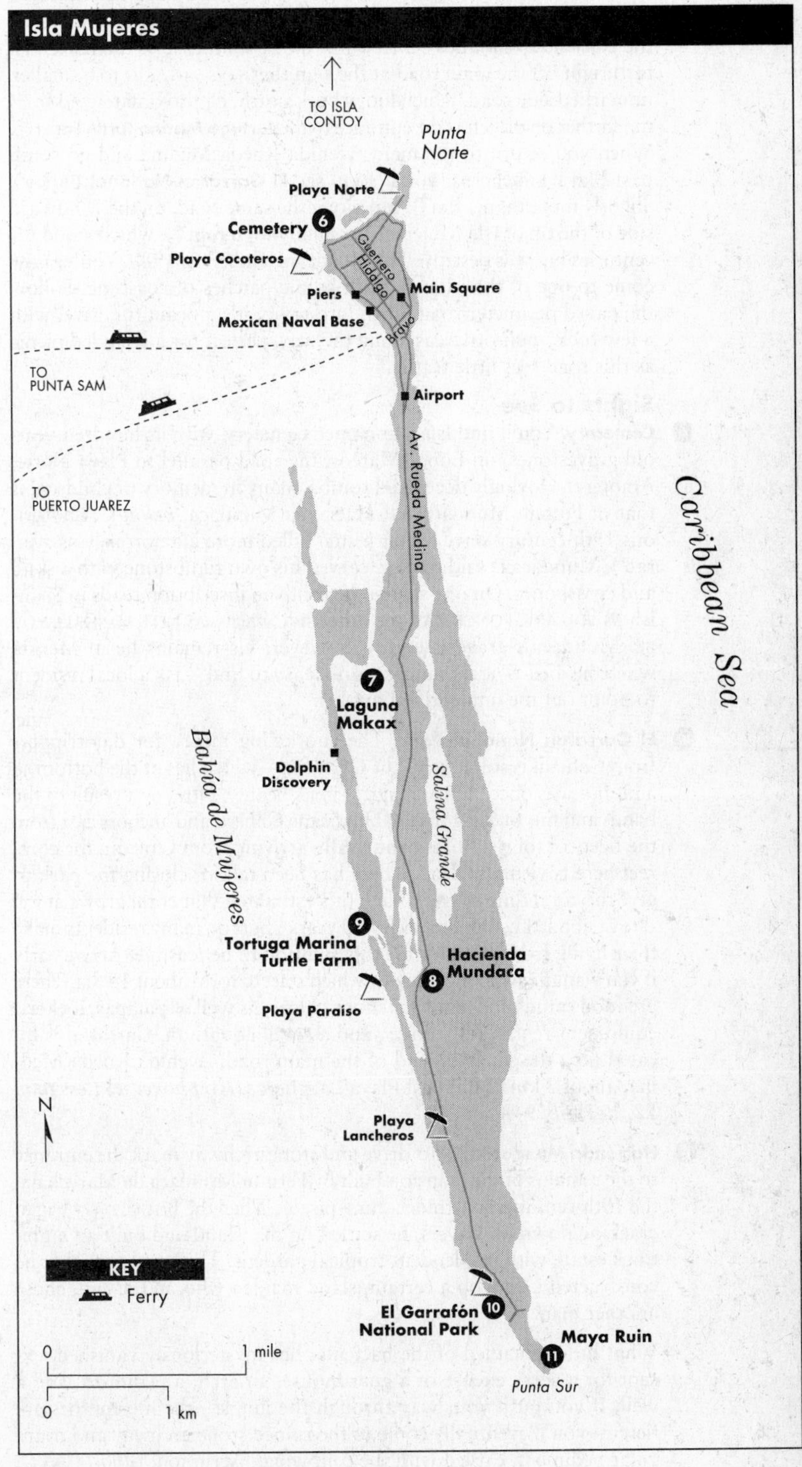
Isla Mujeres
TO ISLA CONTOY
Punta Norte
Playa Norte
Cemetery 6
Playa Cocoteros
Guerrero
Hidalgo
Main Square
Piers
Mexican Naval Base
Bravo
TO PUNTA SAM
Airport
TO PUERTO JUAREZ
Av. Rueda Medina
Caribbean Sea
7 Laguna Makax
Bahía de Mujeres
Dolphin Discovery
Salina Grande
9 Tortuga Marina Turtle Farm
8 Hacienda Mundaca
Playa Paraíso
Playa Lancheros
KEY
Ferry
El Garrafón National Park 10
Maya Ruin 11
Punta Sur
0
1 mile
0
1 km

At the end of the lagoon, a dirt road to the left leads to the remains of the **Hacienda Mundaca** ⑧. About a block southeast of the hacienda, turn right off the main road at the sign that says SAC BAJO to a smaller, unmarked side road, which loops back north. Approximately ½ km (¼ mi) farther on the left is the entrance to the **Tortuga Marina Turtle Farm** ⑨. When you return to the main Avenida Rueda Medina and go south past Playa Lancheros, you'll soon see **El Garrafón National Park** ⑩. Slightly more than 1 km (½ mi) along the same road, on the windward side of the tip of Isla Mujeres, is a small **Maya ruin** ⑪, which stood for centuries but was destroyed by Hurricane Gilbert in 1988. You've now come to one of the island's most scenic patches of coastline. Follow the paved perimeter road north into town; it's a beautiful drive, with a few rocky pull-off areas along the way, perfect for a secluded picnic as this road sees little traffic.

Sights to See

6 **Cemetery.** You'll find Isla's unnamed cemetery, with its hundred-year-old gravestones, on Lopez Mateos, the road parallel to Playa Norte. Among the lovingly decorated tombs, many in memory of children, is that of Fermín Mundaca (☞ Hacienda Mundaca, *below*). A notorious 19th-century slave trader (often billed more glamorously as a pirate), Mundaca is said to have carved his own tombstone with a skull and crossbones. On one side of the tomb an inscription reads in Spanish AS YOU ARE, I ONCE WAS; the other side warns, AS I AM, SO SHALL YOU BE. Mundaca's grave is empty, however; his remains lie in Mérida where he died. The monument is not easy to find—ask a local resident to point out the unidentified marker.

10 **El Garrafón National Park.** The snorkeling mecca for day-trippers from Cancún is still lovely, but Garrafón—which lies at the bottom of a bluff—was once almost magical in its beauty. Now, as a result of the hands and fins of eager divers, Hurricane Gilbert, and anchors cast from the fleets of tourist boats continually arriving from Cancún, the coral reef here is virtually dead. There has been talk of closing the park to give the coral time to grow back (it's estimated that coral grows at the rate of about 1 centimeter every 40 years), but too many residents make their living from the park for this solution to be feasible. Arrive early if you want to avoid the crowds, which start to form about 10 AM. There are food stands and souvenir shops galore, as well as palapas, lockers, equipment rental, rest rooms, and a small aquarium. Garrafón is located near the southern end of the main road, Avenida Rueda Medina, about 3 km (2 mi) past Playa Lancheros. *No phone.* *Less than $2.* *Daily 9–4.*

8 **Hacienda Mundaca.** A dirt drive and stone archway mark the entrance to the remains of the mansion built by Fermín Mundaca de Marechaja, the 19th-century slave trader–cum–pirate. When the British navy began cracking down on slavers, he settled on the island and built an ambitious estate with resplendent tropical gardens. The story goes that he constructed it to woo a certain island maiden who, in the end, chose another man.

What little remained of the hacienda has mysteriously vanished, except for a sorry excuse of a guardhouse, an arch, a pediment, and a well. If you push your way through the jungle—the mosquitoes are fierce—you'll eventually come to the ruined stone archway and triangular pediment, carved with the following inscription: *HUERTA DE LA HACIENDA DE VISTA ALEGRE MDCCCLXXVI* (Orchard of the Happy View Hacienda, 1876). To get here, continue south from town along the main road until you come to the "S" curve at the end of Laguna Makax (☞ *below*). You'll see the dirt road to your left. *No phone.* *Free.*

7 **Laguna Makax.** Heading south from town along Avenida Rueda Medina, you'll pass a Mexican naval base and see some *salinas* (salt marshes) on your left; across the road is this lagoon, where pirates are said to have anchored their ships as they lay in wait for the hapless vessels plying the Spanish Main (the geographical area in which Spanish treasure ships trafficked).

11 **Maya Ruin.** The sad vestiges of a temple once dedicated to Ixchel, the goddess of fertility, are about 1 km (½ mi) below El Garrafón National Park, at the southern tip of Isla. Though Hurricane Gilbert walloped the ruin and succeeded in blowing most of it away, restoration efforts are under way. The adjacent **lighthouse** still stands, and the keeper sometimes allows visitors to ascend it.

9 **Tortuga Marina Turtle Farm.** Run by an outfit called Eco Caribe, this facility is devoted to the study and preservation of sea turtles. During working hours, visitors can examine tanks that contain hundreds of hatchlings and young turtles of various species. The farm's budget is small, but because the turtle population of the Mexican Caribbean continues to dwindle toward extinction, these dedicated ecologists have devoted themselves to care for the hatchlings until they are large enough to be let out to sea; they release about 6,000 infant turtles each month during the hatching season (May through September). Within the confines of the turtle farm are various fenced-in beachfront areas where turtles can be viewed swimming and feeding in the ocean. To get here, follow the main road until, about a block southeast of Hacienda Mundaca, it forks. Follow the right-hand fork, the smaller road that loops back north. About ½ km (¼ mi) to the left you'll see the entrance to the turtle farm. *No phone.* 🎫 *$2.* ⏲ *Daily 9–5.*

NEED A BREAK? Walk north from the Turtle Farm along the lovely beach past the Cristalmar Hotel to reach **Hacienda Gomar** (☎ 987/70541), a good Mexican restaurant featuring a buffet lunch and marimba music. If you'd rather not put your shoes back on, try the excellent barbecued grouper, snapper, or barracuda at **Blacky's** (✉ Playa Paraíso, no phone) open grill on the beach. Also in the area you'll find handicraft and souvenir shops, a beach bar, and small palapas for shade.

Beaches

The island's finest and most popular beach is on the northwest part of the island: Follow any of the north–south streets in town to **Playa Norte** (sometimes called Playa Cocoteros, or Cocos). You can sit at congenial palapa bars for drinks and snacks; recommended are **Rutilio's y Chimbo's,** twin palapa restaurant-bars right on the beach. There are lots of stands on the beach where you can rent snorkel gear, Jet Skis, floats, sailboards, and sometimes parasails. At the northernmost end of Playa Norte, you'll find **Punta Norte** and an abandoned hotel on its own private islet. The other building you'll see jutting out on a rocky point is a private home.

On the western side of Isla Mujeres lie **Playa Paraíso** and **Playa Lancheros,** tranquil spots where you can have lunch or shop for handicrafts, souvenirs, and T-shirts at the small stands. Also housed at Playa Lancheros, in a sea pen, are some pet sea turtles and harmless *tiburóns gatos* (nurse sharks). On the ocean side live the carnivorous *tintoreras* (female sharks), which have seven rows of teeth and weigh as much as 1,100 pounds.

Dining

$$$ ✕ **Maria's Kan Kin.** Near El Garrafón, at the southern end of the island, this appealing beach restaurant has a choice location and attractive decor. Choose a live lobster or try one of the specialties, which tend to be prepared with a French twist, like lobster bisque and coconut mousse. It's the perfect spot for a long lunch that extends to sunset. ✉ *On main road to Garrafón,* ☎ *987/70015. AE, MC, V.*

$$$ ★ ✕ **Zazil-Ha.** This fine restaurant, on the grounds of the Na-Balam hotel (☞ Lodging, *below*) at Playa Norte, offers well-prepared regional specialties as well as interesting vegetarian dishes. The service is friendly and the setting is relaxing; you can eat indoors in the cozy palapa dining room or outdoors on a shady terrace. Try the shrimp seviche for the first course, followed by the seafood special of the day. At breakfast, the restaurant features homemade bread, tropical fruits, and good coffee, plus a full array of egg dishes. ✉ *Na-Balam hotel,* ☎ *987/70279. AE, MC, V.*

$$ ★ ✕ **Pizza Rolandi.** Red tables, yellow director's chairs, and green walls and window trim set an upbeat tone at this very "in" chain restaurant. Select from a broad variety of Italian food: lobster pizzas, calzones, and pastas. Grilled fresh fish and shrimp are highly recommended, and salads are excellent. Or just stop in for a drink at one of the outside tables; the margaritas, cappuccino, and espresso are the best in town. ✉ *Av. Hidalgo between Avs. Madero and Abasolo,* ☎ *987/70430. Reservations not accepted. AE, MC, V.*

$ ★ ✕ **Lonchería La Lomita.** With a bright aqua interior and plastic tablecloths, this simple, home-style diner isn't much to look at, but you'll find hearty servings of chicken, steak, and seafood cooked to order (grilled, fried, or sautéed) here. Amazingly low-priced lunch and dinner set menus include beans, rice, and tortillas or bread; breakfast is also available. On Avenida Juárez between Avenidas Madero and Morelos is **La Lomita II,** like its sister establishment a no-frills eatery that offers daily specials featuring generous servings and good value. ✉ *Av. Juárez 25-B (past Av. Allende), no phone. Reservations not accepted. No credit cards.*

$ ✕ **Mirtita's** and **Villa del Mar.** Next to each other on Avenida Rueda Medina across from the ferry dock, these are favorite local hangouts. Both serve fresh seafood and Yucatecan specialties. ✉ *Av. Rueda Medina, no phone. No credit cards.*

$ ✕ **Red Eye Café.** A bright red awning marks this open-air café where Gus and Inga serve hearty American-style breakfasts with German flair. Fresh German sausage, made by a German sausage maker in Cancún, accompanies the egg dishes. ✉ *Av. Hidalgo, no phone. No credit cards. Closed Tues.*

Lodging

The approximately 25 hotels (about 600 rooms) on Isla Mujeres generally fall into one of two categories: The older, more modest places are right in town, and the newer, more costly properties tend to have beachfront locations around Punta Norte and, increasingly, on the peninsula near the lagoon. Most hotels have ceiling fans; some have air-conditioning, but few offer TVs or phones. Luxurious, self-contained time-share condominiums are another option, which you can learn more about from the tourist office (☎ 987/70316). All hotels share the 77400 postal code.

$$$ ★ 🏨 **Na-Balam.** This intimate, informal hostelry set on Playa Norte will fulfill all your tropical-paradise fantasies. Three corner suites with balconies affording outstanding views of sea and sand are well worth

$85. The simple, attractive rooms have turquoise-tiled floors, carved wood furniture, dining areas, and patios facing the beach. Breakfast at the hotel's Zazil-Ha restaurant (☞ Dining, *above*) is a delightful way to kick off the day. ✉ *Calle Zazil Ha 118,* ☎ *987/70279,* FAX *987/70446. 31 rooms. Restaurant, bar, pool, beach. AE, MC, V.*

$$$ 🏨 **Perla del Caribe.** On the eastern edge of town facing the sea wall and promenade, the three-story Perla has rooms that look out either on the open sea or town, priced accordingly. All rooms have balconies and are comfortable and functional but not palatial. You can listen to music in the restaurant-bar most evenings. ✉ *Av. Madero 2,* ☎ *987/70444 or 800/258–6454,* FAX *987/70011. 91 rooms. Restaurant, bar, pool. AE, MC, V.*

$$ 🏨 **Belmar.** Right in the heart of town, above Pizza Rolandi, this small hotel shares a charming plant-filled inner courtyard with the restaurant, which means it can occasionally be noisy here until 11 PM. Standard rooms are pretty, with tiled baths and light-wood furniture. One enormous suite has a private hot tub on a patio, a tiled kitchenette, and a sitting area. All rooms have phones, satellite TV, and air-conditioning. ✉ *Av. Hidalgo 110, between Avs. Madero and Abasolo,* ☎ *987/70430,* FAX *987/70429. 11 rooms. AE, MC, V.*

$$ ★ 🏨 **Cabañas María del Mar.** A rather mind-boggling assortment of rooms is available in this friendly beachfront hotel, but all have a great deal of Mexican character. Some of the rooms are rather spare, but those in the slightly more expensive "castle" section have hand-carved wood furnishings by local artisans in a combination of Spanish and Maya styles. The hotel has a prime location on Playa Norte, next to Na-Balam, and its reasonable room rates include Continental breakfast. ✉ *Av. Carlos Lazos 1,* ☎ *987/70179,* FAX *987/70213. 55 rooms, including 14 cabanas. Restaurant, bar, pool, motorbikes, travel services. MC, V.*

$$ 🏨 **Posada del Mar.** This hotel's assets include its prime location between town and Playa Norte and its reasonable prices. Rooms have balconies overlooking a main road and beyond to the waterfront. The simple wood furnishings appear somewhat worse for wear, although baths are clean, with cheerful colored tiles. Private bungalows in the $ price category are also available. The pool bar is as popular as the street-front palapa-roof restaurant. ✉ *Av. Rueda Medina 15A,* ☎ *987/70300 or 987/70044,* FAX *987/70266. 40 rooms. Restaurant, bar, pool. AE, MC, V.*

Nightlife and the Arts

Nightlife

Most restaurant bars hold a happy hour, offering two drinks for the price of one, from 5 to 7; the palapa bars at Playa Norte are an excellent place to watch the sun set. The current hot spot is **YaYa's** (✉ Av. Rueda Medina 42, near lighthouse and Playa Norte, no phone), run by some good ol' boys from Dallas who serve up huge Texas steaks, chili dogs, and shrimp étouffée along with live jazz, rock, and reggae jam sessions until 2 or 3 AM. The bar at the **Posada del Mar** (☞ Lodging, *above*) can be subdued or hopping, depending on what's going on in town. **Buho's,** the bar-restaurant at Cabañas María del Mar (✉ Av. Carlos Lazo 1, ☎ 987/70179), serves food and is a good choice for a relaxing drink at sunset or later at night. **Restaurante La Peña** (✉ Av. Guerrero 5, ☎ 987/70309) has music and dancing on its open-air terrace overlooking the sea. **Palapa Disco** (✉ Playa Norte off Av. Rueda Medina, no phone) has music and dancing from midnight until 4 AM.

The Arts

Festivals and cultural events are held on many weekends, with live entertainment on the outdoor stage in the main square (la placita, or la parque). The whole island celebrates the spring regattas and the Caribbean music festivals. **Casa de la Cultura,** near the youth hostel, offers folkloric dance classes year-round. The center also operates a small public library and book exchange. ✉ *Av. Guerrero,* ☎ *987/70639.* ⏲ *Mon.–Sat. 9–1 and 4–8.*

Outdoor Activities and Sports

For any water sport, beaches on the north and west sides are the calmest.

Fishing

Bahía Dive Shop (✉ Av. Rueda Medina 166, across from pier, ☎ FAX 987/70340) charges $250 for a day of deep-sea fishing, $200 a day for cast fishing (tarpon, snook, and bonefish), and $20 an hour for offshore fishing (barracuda, snapper, and smaller fish).

Snorkeling and Scuba Diving

Bahía Dive Shop (☞ Fishing, *above*) rents snorkeling and scuba equipment and runs three-hour boat and dive trips to the reefs and the Cave of the Sleeping Sharks. Snorkel gear goes for $5 a day; tanks, $45–$60, depending on the length of the dive. **Mexico Divers** (✉ Avs. Rueda Medina and Medaro, 1 block from ferry, ☎ 987/70131), also called **Buzos de México,** runs three-hour snorkeling tours for $15; two-tank scuba trips start at $55 for a reef dive and $75 for the shark cave dive. Rental gear is available. Dive master Carlos Gutiérrez also gives a resort course for $80 and open-water PADI certification for $350 (his prices are generally negotiable).

Swimming with Dolphins

If you're fascinated by Flipper and his ilk, **Dolphin Discovery** (☎ 987/70742) will give you the chance to sport in the water with them in a small, supervised group. There are four swims daily, at 9 and 11 AM and 1 and 3 PM. Each session is one hour, consisting first of a half hour instruction video, and then 30 minutes in the water; the cost is $79.

Shopping

Casa del Arte Mexica (✉ Av. Hidalgo 6, ☎ 987/70459) has a good selection of clay reproductions, silver jewelry, batiks, rubbings, wood carvings, leather, and hammocks. **La Sirena** (✉ Av. Morelos, 1 block from ferry dock through pine arch marking the way to the island's shopping area, ☎ 987/70223) is distinguished by its extensive array of handcrafted goods. The owners of this small store have collected masks, textiles, and other fine Mexican crafts—including unusual clothing, pottery, and jewelry. Although the prices are not low, they are fair for the quality of items offered. **Van Cleef & Arpels** (✉ Avs. Juárez and Morelos, ☎ 987/70299) has an impressive jewelry selection in a large corner shop. **Tienda Paulita** (✉ Avs. Morelos and Hidalgo, ☎ 987/70014) stocks a standard selection of folk art and handmade clothing.

Isla Mujeres A to Z

Arriving and Departing

BY BOAT

To Isla Mujeres. The ***Caribbean Express*** and the ***Caribbean Miss*** (☎ 987/70254 or 987/70253), both air-conditioned cruisers with bar service, make several 30-minute crossings daily. They leave Puerto Juárez on the mainland for the main ferry dock in Isla Mujeres from 6:30 AM to 8 PM at approximately 20-minute intervals; the fare is under $3 per person.

Three slower **passenger ferries** run on the hour; the schedule varies depending on the season—check the times posted at the dock. The one-way fare is only about $1.50 and the trip takes 45 minutes, but delays and crowding are frequent.

A convenient, more expensive service, the **Shuttle** (✉ Cancún, ☏ 98/83448), runs directly from the Playa Tortugas dock in Cancún's hotel zone at least four times a day and costs about $15 round-trip. Cars are unnecessary on Isla, but **municipal ferries** that accommodate vehicles as well as passengers leave from Punta Sam and take about 45 minutes. Check departure times posted at the pier, but you can count on the schedule running from about 7 AM to 9 PM. The fare is under $2 per person and $10 per vehicle.

From Isla Mujeres. The ***Caribbean Express*** and the ***Caribbean Miss*** (☏ 987/70254 or 987/70253) make the trip from Isla Mujeres to Puerto Juárez between 7 AM and 8 PM at approximately 30-minute intervals; the fare is under $3 per person. The slower **passenger ferry** departs from the main dock at Isla Mujeres to Puerto Juárez at approximately one-hour intervals. The first **car ferry** from Isla Mujeres to Punta Sam leaves at about 6 AM and the last departs at about 7:15 PM. Again, schedules vary, so you should call ahead or check the boat schedule posted at the pier.

Getting Around

BY BICYCLE

Bicycles are available for hardy cyclists, but don't underestimate the hot sun and the tricky road conditions. Watch for the many speed bumps, which can give you an unexpected jolt, and avoid riding at night; some roads have no streetlights. **Rent Me Sport Bike** (✉ Avs. Juárez and Morelos, 1 block from main pier, no phone) offers five-speed cycles starting at less than $2 for an hour; a full day costs about $5.

BY CAR

There is little reason for tourists to bring cars to Isla Mujeres, because there are plenty of other forms of transportation that cost far less than renting and transporting a private vehicle. Moreover, though the main road is paved, speed bumps abound and some areas are poorly lighted.

BY GOLF CART

The newest way for tourists to explore Isla is by golf cart. **P'pe's Rentadora** (✉ Av. Hidalgo 19, ☏ 987/70019) and almost all of the moped rental shops listed below, as well as some hotels, rent them for about $10 an hour.

BY MOPED

The island is full of moped-rental shops. **Motorent Kankin** (✉ Av. Abasolo 15, no phone) will provide a two-seat, three-speed Honda for about $5 per hour or $20 per day ($40 for 24 hours); a $20 deposit—or a credit card or passport left behind—is required. **P'pes** (✉ Av. Hidalgo 19, ☏ 987/70019) offers two-seat, fully automatic Honda Aeros, starting at $5 per hour, for a minimum of two hours; it's under $35 for 24 hours.

BY TAXI

If your time is limited you can hire a **taxi** (✉ Av. Rueda Medina, ☏ 987/70066) for a private island tour at about $15 an hour. Fares run $1–$2 from the ferry or downtown to the hotels on the north end, at Playa Norte. Taxis line up right by the ferry dock around the clock.

Contacts and Resources

EMERGENCIES

Medical Service (☎ 987/70195 or 987/70607). **Hospital** (☎ 987/70017). **Police** (☎ 987/70082). **Red Cross** (☎ 987/70282).

GUIDED TOURS

Boat Tours. Cooperativa Lanchera (✉ Waterfront near dock, no phone) offers four-hour launch trips to the Virgin, the lighthouse, the turtles at Playa Lancheros, the coral reefs at Los Manchones, and El Garrafón, for about $25 including lunch. **Cooperativa Isla Mujeres** (✉ Av. Rueda Medina, ☎ 987/70274), next to Mexico Divers, rents out boats at $120 for a maximum of four hours and six people, and $15 per person for an island tour with lunch (minimum six people). At least two of Isla Mujeres's boating cooperatives sell day tours to Isla Contoy, a national wildlife park and bird sanctuary. **Sociedad Cooperativa "Isla Mujeres"** (☎ 987/70274 pier) and **La Isleña** (✉ ½ block from pier, corner of Avs. Morelos and Juárez, ☎ 987/70036) launch boats daily at 8:30 AM; they return at 4 PM. The trip takes about 45 minutes, depending on the size of the boat, and runs about $30 to $40.

LATE-NIGHT PHARMACIES

Farmacia Isla Mujeres (✉ Av. Juárez, next to Caribbean Tropic Boutique, ☎ 987/70178) and **Farmacia Lily** (✉ Avs. Madero and Hidalgo, ☎ 987/70164) are open Monday–Saturday 8:30 AM–9:30 PM and Sunday 8:30–3.

VISITOR INFORMATION

Tourist office (✉ Plaza Isla Mujeres at north end of main shopping street, ☎ 987/70316), open weekdays 9–2 and 7–9.

COZUMEL

Updated by Dan Millington

Cozumel provides a balance between Cancún and Isla Mujeres: Though attuned to North American tourism, the island has managed to keep development to a minimum. Its expansive beaches, superb coral reefs, and copious wildlife—in the sea, on the land, and in the air—attract an active, athletic crowd. Rated one of the top destinations in the world among underwater enthusiasts, Cozumel is encircled by a garland of reefs entrancing divers and snorkelers alike. Despite the inevitable effects of docking cruise ships, the island's earthy charm and tranquillity remain intact. The relaxing atmosphere here is typically Mexican—friendly and unpretentious. Cozumel's rich Maya heritage is reflected in the faces of 60,000 or so isleños; you'll see people who look like ancient statues come to life, and occasionally hear the Maya language spoken.

A 490-square-km (189-square-mi) island 19 km (12 mi) to the east of Yucatán, Cozumel is mostly flat, its interior covered by parched scrub, dense jungle, and marshy lagoons. White sandy beaches with calm waters line the island's leeward (western) side, which is fringed by a spectacular reef system, while the powerful surf and rocky strands on the windward (eastern) side, facing the Caribbean, are broken up here and there by calm bays and hidden coves. Most of Cozumel is undeveloped, with a good deal of the land and the shores set aside as national parks; the island once capitalized on the chicle its zapote trees produced, which the chewing-gum industry prized before the advent of synthetic chewing gum. A few Maya ruins provide what limited sightseeing there is aside from the island's glorious natural attractions. San Miguel is the only established town.

Exploring

Cozumel is about 53 km (33 mi) long and 15 km (9 mi) wide, but only a small percentage of its roads—primarily those in the southern half—are paved. Dirt roads can be explored, with care, in a four-wheel-drive vehicle. Aside from the 3% of the island that has been developed, Cozumel is made up of expanses of sandy or rocky beaches, quiet little coves, palm groves, scrubby jungles, lagoons and swamps, and a few low hills (the maximum elevation is 45 ft).

A Good Tour

It's worth renting a Jeep to explore Cozumel, which has more sights than either Cancún or Isla Mujeres. If you go south from Cozumel's principal town, **San Miguel** ⑫, in about 10 minutes you'll come to **Chankanaab Nature Park** ⑬. Continue past Chankanaab and past Playa Corona, Playa San Francisco, and Playa del Sol; at Km 17.5 a turnoff leads about 3 km (2 mi) inland to the village and ruins of **El Cedral** ⑭ (take this detour only if you have a four-wheel-drive vehicle). Backtrack to the coast and go south past Playa de Palancar (the famous reef lies offshore) to the island's southern tip, where you'll find a dirt trail to **Laguna Colombia** ⑮.

If you head east on the paved road, you'll come to the eastern Caribbean coast. Make a right turn onto a dirt road and follow it for 4 km (2½ mi) south to get to the **Punta Celerain Lighthouse** ⑯. When you return to the paved road and head north, you will first pass the Tumba del Caracol, another Maya ruin that may have served as a lighthouse; a bit farther on are the minuscule ruins of El Mirador and the Throne. Beyond Punta Chiqueros, Playa Bonita, Playa Chen Río, and Punta Morena you'll see Playa Oriente, where the cross-island road meets the east coast; you can take the cross-island road west toward town or continue north. If you choose the latter route, you'll need a four-wheel-drive vehicle to travel on a rough dirt road that dead-ends past Punta Molas; eventually you'll have to turn around. A sign at this junction warns that drivers proceed at their own risk. This pothole-ridden road is the preferred sunbathing spot of boa constrictors, crocodiles, and other jungle denizens.

If you're going toward town, it's worth making a detour inland to view the ruins of **San Gervasio** ⑰; take the cross-island road west to the army airfield and turn right; follow this road north for 7 km (4½ mi). The road to the ruins is a good one, but a nearly unmaneuverable dirt road leads northeast of San Gervasio back to the unpaved coast road. At the junction is a marvelously deserted beach where you can camp. Heading north along this beach, you'll come to **Castillo Real** ⑱, another Maya site. A number of other minor ruins are spread across the northern tip of Cozumel, which terminates at the **Punta Molas Lighthouse** ⑲.

Sights to See

18 **Castillo Real.** A Maya site on the eastern coast, near the northern tip of the island, the castillo (castle) comprises a lookout tower, the base of a pyramid, and a temple with two chambers capped by a false arch. The waters here harbor several shipwrecks, remnants from the days when buccaneers lay in wait for richly cargoed galleons en route to Europe. It's a fine spot for snorkeling because there are few visitors to disturb the fish.

13 **Chankanaab Nature Park.** Chankanaab (the name means "small sea"), a 10-minute drive south of San Miguel, is a lovely saltwater lagoon that the government has made into a wildlife sanctuary, botanical garden, and archaeological park. The treasures from the Cozumel Ar-

Cozumel

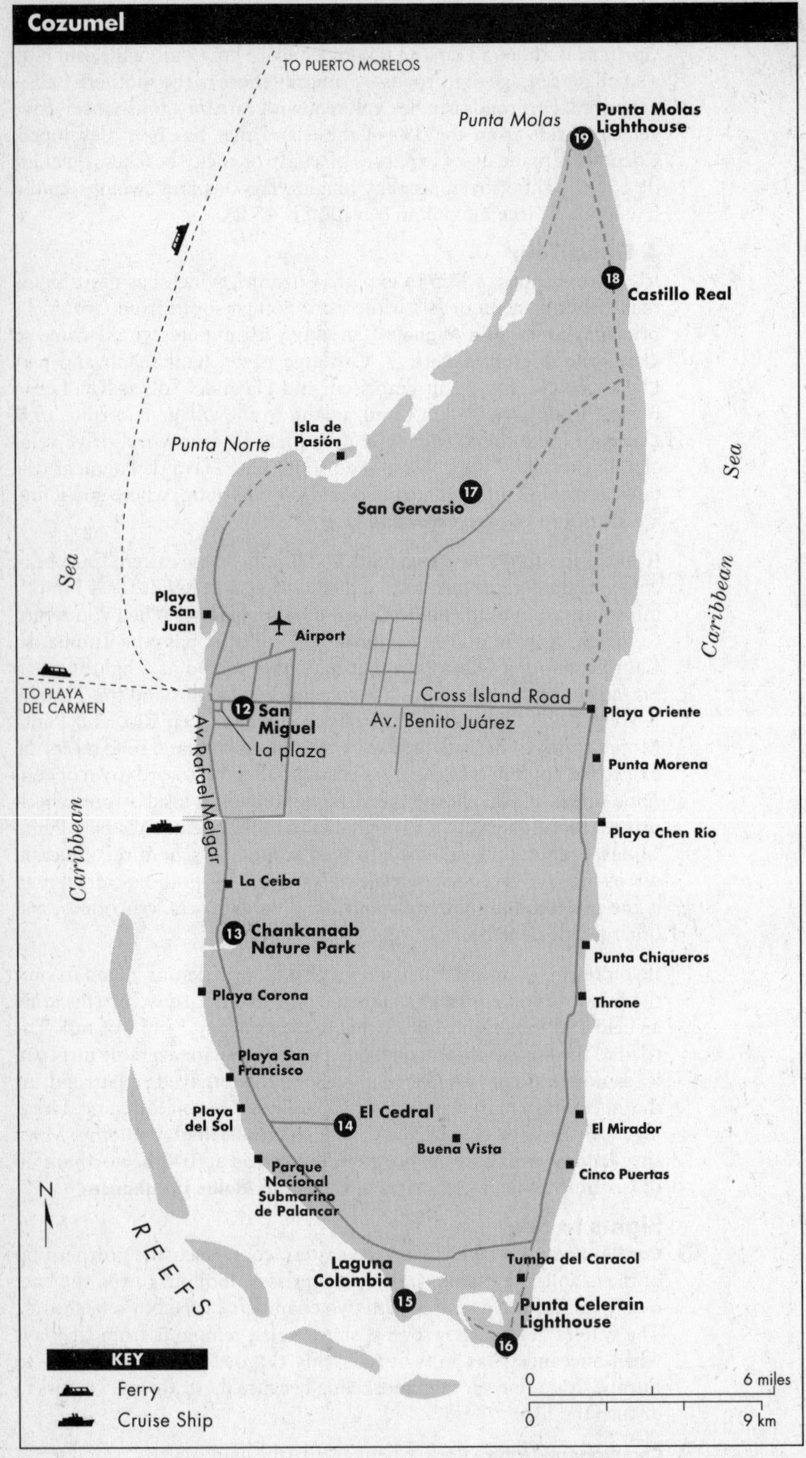
TO PUERTO MORELOS
Punta Molas
Punta Molas Lighthouse
19
18
Castillo Real
Isla de Pasión
Punta Norte
17
San Gervasio
Sea
Caribbean
Sea
Playa San Juan
Airport
TO PLAYA DEL CARMEN
12 San Miguel
La plaza
Cross Island Road
Av. Benito Juárez
Av. Rafael Melgar
Playa Oriente
Punta Morena
Playa Chen Río
Caribbean
La Ceiba
13 Chankanaab Nature Park
Punta Chiqueros
Playa Corona
Throne
Playa San Francisco
Playa del Sol
14 El Cedral
Buena Vista
El Mirador
Cinco Puertas
Parque Nacional Submarino de Palancar
N
REEFS
Tumba del Caracol
Laguna Colombia
15
Punta Celerain Lighthouse
16
KEY
Ferry
Cruise Ship
0
6 miles
0
9 km

chaeological Park, full-size replicas of Toltec, Mexican, and Maya statues and stone carvings—have recently found a new home here. Underwater caves, offshore reefs, a protected bay—which hides crusty old cannons and anchors as well as statues of Jesus Christ and Chac Mool—and a sunken ship attract droves of snorkelers and scuba divers. An interactive educational museum, four dive shops, two restaurants, two gift shops, a snack stand, and a dressing room with lockers and showers are on the premises. ✉ *Carretera Sur, Km 9, no phone.* 🎫 *$7.* ⏲ *Daily 6–5:30.*

14 **El Cedral.** Once the tiny village and ruins composed the largest Maya site on Cozumel; this was the temple sighted by the original Spanish explorers in 1518, and the first Mass in Mexico was reportedly celebrated here. These days, there's little archaeological evidence of El Cedral's past glory. All that remains is a small structure capped by jungle growth; its Maya arch, best viewed from inside, is covered by faint traces of paint and stucco. After exploring the ruins, you can take a rest nearby in a small green-and-white cinder-block church, typical of rural Mexico. ✉ *Turnoff at Km 17.5 of main island road, then 3 km (2 mi) inland to site, no phone.*

Isla de Pasión. Beyond Punta Norte, in the middle of Abrigo Bay, this tiny island is now part of a state reserve. Fishing is permitted and the beaches are secluded, but there are no facilities on the island, and since so few people go, there are no scheduled tours. You'll have to bargain with a local boat owner for transportation if you want to visit.

15 **Laguna Colombia.** A prime site for jungle aficionados, this lagoon lies at the island's southern tip and is most commonly reached by boat, although there is a trail. Fish migrate here to lay their eggs, and barracuda, baby fish, and birds show up in great numbers in season. Popular diving and snorkeling spots can be found offshore in the reefs of Tunich, Colombia, and Maracaibo.

16 **Punta Celerain Lighthouse.** Located on the southernmost tip of the island, the lighthouse is surrounded by sand dunes at the narrowest point of land. Alligators were once hunted nearby; nowadays you may spot a soldier or two from the adjacent army post catching an iguana. The point comes to life at midday when the lighthouse keeper serves fried fish and beer and locals and tourists gather to chat; Sundays are particularly popular. The lighthouse is at the end of a 4-km-long (2½-mi-long) dirt road—a four-wheel-drive vehicle is strongly recommended if you plan to visit.

Punta Molas. If you are going to attempt to reach the northernmost tip of the island, be sure you have plenty of time and a reliable four-wheel-drive vehicle: The pothole-ridden road is the preferred sunbathing spot of boa constrictors, crocodiles, and other jungle denizens.

19 **Punta Molas Lighthouse** is an excellent spot for sunbathing, birding, and camping. Although this entire area is accessible only by four-wheel-drive vehicles or by boat, the jagged shoreline and the open sea offer magnificent views, making it well worth the trip.

17 **San Gervasio.** The largest existing Maya and Toltec site on Cozumel, San Gervasio was once the island's capital and probably its ceremonial center, dedicated to the fertility goddess Ixchel. The classical- and postclassical-style site was continuously occupied from AD 300 to AD 1500. Typical architectural features from the era include limestone plazas and masonry superstructures atop stepped platforms, as well as stelae, bas-reliefs, and frescoes. What remains today are several small mounds scattered around a plaza and several broken columns and lin-

tels that were once part of the main building or observatory. There are a snack bar and some gift shops at the entrance. To get here, take the cross-island road (Avenida Juárez) to the San Gervasio access road; follow this road north for 7 km (4½ mi). *$1 access to road, $3.50 access to ruins. Daily 8–5.*

12 **San Miguel.** Cozumel's only town retains the laid-back tenor of a Mexican village, although its streets are dotted with an interesting variety of shops and restaurants. Avenida Rafael Melgar, San Miguel's waterfront boulevard, has a wide cement walkway, called the *malecón,* separating Avenida Melgar from the town's narrow sandy beach. As in most Mexican towns, the main square, here called the **Plaza del Sol,** is where townspeople and visitors hang out, particularly on Sunday nights, when mariachi bands join the nightly assortment of food and souvenir vendors.

Museo de la Isla de Cozumel is housed on two floors of what was once the island's first luxury hotel. Four permanent exhibit halls of dioramas, sculptures, and charts explain the island's history and ecosystem. Well laid-out and labeled displays cover pre-Hispanic, colonial, and modern times and detail the local geology, flora, and fauna. A charming reproduction of a Maya house is a highlight. The museum also presents temporary exhibits, guided tours, and workshops. ✉ *Av. Rafael Melgar between Calles 4 and 6 N,* ☎ *987/21475. $3. Daily 10–6.*

NEED A BREAK? On the terrace off the second floor of the Cozumel museum, the **Restaurante del Museo** (☎ 987/20838) offers breakfast, drinks, or a full meal of fajitas or grilled red snapper, all enhanced by a great waterfront view.

Beaches

Cozumel's beaches vary from long, treeless, sandy stretches to isolated coves and rocky shores. Virtually all development remains on the leeward (western) side, where the coast is relatively sheltered by the proximity of the mainland 19 km (12 mi) to the west. Reaching beaches on the windward (eastern) side is more difficult and requires transportation, but you'll be rewarded if you are looking for solitude.

Dining

Dining options on Cozumel reflect the nature of the place, with some harmless pretension at times but mainly the insouciant, natural style of the tropical island. More than 80 restaurants in the downtown area alone offer a broad choice, from air-conditioned fast-food outlets and Americanized places serving Continental fare and seafood in semiformal "nautical" settings to simple outdoor eateries that specialize in fish. Resort hotels offering buffet breakfasts and dinners are good values for bottomless appetites.

CATEGORY	COST*
$$$	$25–$35
$$	$15–$25
$	under $15

**per person for a three-course meal, excluding drinks and service*

$$$ ★ ✕ **Arrecife.** A well-trained staff and impeccably prepared seafood and Mediterranean fare put this hotel restaurant in a class by itself. Tall windows and excellent views of the sea complement the stylish decor—potted palms, white wicker furniture, pink walls—while musicians, who play regularly, further enhance the romantic mood. ✉ *Hotel Presidente*

Inter-Continental Cozumel, ☎ 987/20322. AE, DC, MC, V. Closed Sept.–Oct.

$$$ ✕ **La Cabaña del Pescador.** To get to this rustic palapa-covered hut, you've got to cross a gangplank, but it's worth it if you're looking for well-prepared fresh lobster. The crustaceans are sold by weight, and the rest—including a delicious eggnog-type drink served at the end of the meal—is on the house. Seashells and nets hang from the walls of this small, dimly lit room; geese stroll outside. ✉ *Carretera San Juan, Km 4, across from Playa Azul Hotel north of town, no phone. No credit cards. No lunch.*

$$ ✕ **El Capi Navegante.** Locals say you'll find the best seafood in town here: The captain's motto is: "The fish we serve today slept in the sea last night." Specialties like whole red snapper and stuffed squid are skillfully prepared and sometimes flambéed at your table. Highly recommended dishes include conch seviche and deep-fried whole snapper. Nautical blue-and-white decor, accented by the life preservers on the walls, adds personality to this place. ✉ *Av. 10a S 312, at Calle 3, ☎ 987/21730. MC, V.*

$$ ★ ✕ **La Choza.** Home-cooked Mexican food—primarily from the capital and among the best in town—is the order of the day at this family-run establishment. Dona Elisa Espinosa's specialties include chicken mole, red snapper in sweet mustard sauce, and grilled lobster. For dessert, try the refreshing frozen avocado pie. The informal palapa-covered patio is furnished with simple wood tables and chairs and hand-painted pottery dishes. ✉ *Calle Rosada Salas 198, at Av. 10a S, ☎ 987/20958. AE, MC, V.*

$$ ★ ✕ **Pancho's Backyard.** A jungle of greenery, trickling fountains, ceiling fans, and leather chairs set the tone at this inviting restaurant, located on the cool patio of Los Cincos Soles shopping center. The menu highlights local standards such as black bean soup, *camarones al carbon* (grilled prawns), and fajitas. Round out your meal with coconut ice cream in Kahlúa. ✉ *Av. Rafael Melgar N 27, at Calle 8 N, ☎ 987/22141. AE, MC, V. Closed Sun. No lunch Sat.*

$$ ✕ **Tony Rome's.** Finger-licking, Texas-style barbecued ribs and Las Vegas–style crooning (courtesy of owner Tony Rome) are the drawing cards of this open-air eatery wrapped around a palapa-covered dance floor. In addition to the ribs and the live entertainment, you'll find chicken, lobster, Kansas City steaks, and great happy-hour specials. ✉ *Av. 5 S 21, between Av. Rosado Salas and Calle 3 S, ☎ 987/20131. MC, V.*

$ ✕ **Diamond Café.** This airy retreat in the back of the elegant Diamond Creations is artfully decorated like a typical Mexican patio, with a central fountain and terraced seating at wrought-iron tables. The café specializes in home-baked pastries to accompany the espresso and cappuccino brewed on the premises and served all day long. ✉ *Av. Rafael Melgar 131, ☎ 987/23869. No credit cards. Closed Sun.*

$ ✕ **El Foco.** A taquería serving soft tacos stuffed with pork, chorizo (spicy Mexican sausage), and cheese, this eatery also does ribs and steak. Graffitied walls and plain wood tables make it a casual, fun spot to grab a bite and a *cerveza* (beer). ✉ *Av. 5 S 13-B, between Calle Rosado Salas and Calle 3, no phone. No credit cards.*

$ ✕ **El Moro.** This family-run restaurant on the eastern edge of town specializes in low-priced local cuisine—seafood, chicken, and meat. Inside, the decor follows the regional theme, beginning with Yucatecan baskets hanging on the walls. Divers flock to this place, so you know portions are hearty and the food is delicious. Take a taxi; El Moro is too far to walk to and difficult to find. ✉ *Calle 75 N 124, between Calles 2 and 4, ☎ 987/23029. MC, V. Closed Thurs.*

$ ✕ **Prima Pasta & Prima Deli.** You'll find hearty, inexpensive pizzas, calzones, sandwiches, pastas, whole king crab, and catch-of-the-day seafood dishes at this northern Italian diner just off the plaza. The breezy dining area on the second-floor terrace above the kitchen has a charming Mediterranean mural painted on two walls. Business has been so good that the owner branched out in 1994, opening Prima Deli, a tiny sandwich shop, just a few doors down (at Calle Rosado Salas 113). ✉ *Calle Rosado Salas 109,* ☎ *987/24242. MC, V.*

Lodging

Cozumel's hotels are located in three main areas, all on the island's western, or leeward, side: in town, and north and south of town. Because of the proximity of the reefs, divers and snorkelers tend to congregate at the southern properties. Sailors and anglers, on the other hand, prefer the hotels to the north, where the beaches are better. Most budget hotels are in town. All hotels have air-conditioning unless otherwise noted, and all share the 77600 postal code.

CATEGORY	COST*
$$$$	over $160
$$$	$90–$160
$$	$40–$90
$	under $40

**All prices are for a standard double room in the high season, excluding service charges and tax.*

$$$$ 🏨 **Meliá Mayan Peradisus.** Lush tropical foliage and spectacular sunsets over the beach combine with modern architecture and amenities to make this property north of town a memorable place to stay. Standard rooms, some with small patios opening out onto the lawn, are attractively decorated with tropical print bedspreads and light-wood furniture; superior rooms are larger and have balconies overlooking the water. This resort turned all-inclusive in late 1994, bringing on an international staff of entertainers and activity coordinators to keep guests busy. ✉ *Box 9, Carretera a Sta. Pilar 6,* ☎ *987/20411 or 800/336–3542,* FAX *987/21599. 200 rooms. 3 restaurants, 5 bars, 2 pools, hot tub, steam room, miniature golf, 2 tennis courts, health club, horseback riding, dive shop, bicycles, shops, children's program, playground. AE, DC, MC, V.*

$$$$ ★ 🏨 **Presidente Inter-Continental Cozumel.** This hotel exudes luxury, from the courteous, prompt, and efficient service to the tastefully decorated interior. The Presidente is famed not only for possessing one of the best restaurants on the island, Arrecife (☞ Dining, *above*), but also for its professional water-sports center. Located on its own broad, white beach south of the town of San Miguel, the property ranks among the best on the island for snorkeling. All rooms are done in bright, contemporary colors with white cedar furnishings; deluxe rooms, with their own private terraces fronting the beach or gardens, are huge. ✉ *Carretera a Chankanaab, Km 6.5,* ☎ *987/20322 or 800/327–0200,* FAX *987/21360. 253 rooms. 2 restaurants, 3 bars, coffee shop, pool, hot tub, 2 tennis courts, dive shop, motorbikes, shops, children's program, car rental. AE, DC, MC, V.*

$$$ 🏨 **Fiesta Americana Cozumel Reef.** Reasonable prices and a good location have made the Fiesta Americana one of the most popular hotels on the island. The hotel's beach—reachable via a walkway from the property—offers easy access to spectacular underwater scenery. Standard rooms are large, with sea-green headboards and well-made light-wood furnishings; all have balconies looking out on the ocean, as well as hair dryers and direct-dial phones. Fifty-six rooms form a semicir-

cular cluster of villas facing the hotel's main entrance. ✉ *Carretera a Chankanaab, Km 7.5,* ☎ *987/22622 or 800/343–7821,* FAX *987/22666. 228 rooms. 3 restaurants, 3 bars, 2 pools, 2 tennis courts, dive shop, motorbikes, travel services, car rentals. AE, MC, V.*

$$$ **Galápago Inn.** This pretty white stucco hotel just south of town primarily accommodates divers; the simply furnished, brightly tiled rooms are not sold by the night but exclusively as part of dive packages—booked via the 800 number or your travel agent—that take full advantage of the hotel's expert diving staff and advanced certification diving school. The central garden, with tiled benches and a small fountain, contributes to the inn's Mediterranean feel. The staff here are cheerful and accommodating. ✉ *Carretera a Chankanaab, Km 1.5,* ☎ *987/20663 or 800/847–5708. 58 rooms. 2 restaurants, bar, pool. MC, V.*

$$ ★ **Casa del Mar.** Located south of town near several boutiques, sports shops, and restaurants, this three-story hotel is frequented by divers. An unpretentious but tasteful lobby overlooks a small garden. Cheerful rooms feature yellow-tiled headboards, nightstands, and sinks; Mexican artwork; and small balconies with views of the pool just outside or the sea across the road. The bi-level cabanas, which sleep three or four, are a very good buy at $115. ✉ *Box 129, Carretera a Chankanaab, Km 4,* ☎ *987/21944 or 800/877–4383,* FAX *987/21855. 98 rooms, 8 cabanas. 2 restaurants, 2 bars, pool, hot tub, dive shop, travel services, car rental. AE, MC, V.*

$$ ★ **Villas Las Anclas.** Conveniently located parallel to the malecón, these villas are actually furnished apartments for rent by the day, week, or month. The duplexes include a downstairs sitting room, dining area, and kitchenette; a spiral staircase leads up to a small bedroom with a large desk (but no phone or TV). Rooms are extremely attractive, with tastefully bright patterns set off against white walls; they all overlook a quiet courtyard garden. Each apartment is stocked with fresh coffee and a coffeemaker. ✉ *Box 25, Av. 5a S 325, between Calles 3 and 5 S,* ☎ *987/21403,* FAX *987/21955. 7 units. Kitchenettes. No credit cards.*

$ **Bazar Colonial.** This attractive, modern three-story hotel, located over a small cluster of shops, has pretty red tile floors and bougainvillea, which add splashes of color. Natural wood furniture, TVs, kitchenettes, bookshelves, sofa beds, and an elevator make up for the lack of other amenities, such as a restaurant and a pool. ✉ *Av. 5a S 9, near Calle 3 S,* ☎ *987/20506,* FAX *987/20542 or 987/20211. 28 rooms. Kitchenettes, shops. AE, MC, V.*

$ **Bed & Breakfast Caribo.** This recent (1994) Cozumel arrival was formerly a doctor's residence, renovated by a family from Michigan. The nine air-conditioned rooms are spacious and well furnished, featuring white wicker, blue floral upholstered chairs, and matching serape bedspreads. There's cable TV for guests in the first-floor sitting room. A full (meatless) breakfast buffet is included in the price. Weekly and monthly rates are available. Ask for a room in the back, away from busy Avenida Juárez. ✉ *Av. Juárez 799,* ☎ *987/23195 or 800/830–5558. 9 rooms, including 2 kitchenette apartments. MC, V.*

$ ★ **Mesón San Miguel.** Situated right on the square, this hotel sees a lot of action because of the accessibility of its large public bar and outdoor café, which are often filled with locals. The remodeled rooms are clean and functional, with air-conditioning, satellite TV, phones, and balconies—amenities unusual in a budget hotel, making this a good bet for your money. ✉ *Av. Juárez 2 Bis,* ☎ *987/20323 or 987/20233,* FAX *987/21820. 60 rooms. Bar, café, pool, recreation room. AE, MC, V.*

Nightlife and the Arts

Fiesta Mexicana nights are offered at the **Fiesta Americana Hotel** (☎ 987/22622) Thursday and Sunday 6–9 PM during high season; they feature folkloric dancers, mariachis, a cockfight, an open-bar buffet dinner, and tequila shots; the cost is about $70.

Bars

For a quiet drink and good people-watching, try **Video Bar Aladino** at the Mesón San Miguel, at the northern end of the plaza. Serious bar-hoppers like **Carlos 'n' Charlie's** (✉ Av. Rafael Melgar 11, between Calles 2 and 4 N, ☎ 987/20191) for hang-off-the-rafters, raucous fun; don't come here if you're the retiring type. Folks are always spilling out over the outdoor patio (sometimes literally) at **Sharkey's** (✉ Av. Rafael Melgar near Av. Benito Juárez, ☎ 987/21832), where a papier-mâché Marilyn Monroe in a *Some Like It Hot* pose surveys a rowdy crowd. The **Hard Rock Cafe** (✉ Av. Rafael Melgar 2A, near Av. Benito Juárez, ☎ 987/25271) includes all the nostalgic music memorabilia that characterizes the international chain. You and your friends provide the entertainment at the sing-along **Laser-Karaoke Bar** (✉ Fiesta Inn, ☎ 987/22811). The Terminator and Rambo have done it again with a new **Planet Hollywood** (✉ Rafael Melgar 161, ☎ 987/25795). Jock types can play video games or check football scores at the **Sports Page Video Bar and Restaurant** (✉ Av. 5 N and Calle 2 N, ☎ 987/21199).

Live Music

Sunday evenings bring locals to the **zócalo** to hear mariachis and island musicians playing tropical tunes. The piano bar in **La Gaviota** (✉ Sol Caribe Cozumel Hotel, ☎ 987/20700, ext. 251) is well attended, and trios and mariachis perform nightly in the lobby bar from 5 to 11 during high season. For romantic piano or guitar serenades, try the dining room of **Arrecife** (✉ Hotel Presidente Inter-Continental Cozumel, ☎ 987/20322 high season only). If Frank Sinatra–style entertainment turns you on, check out **Tony Rome's** (✉ Av. 5 S 21, between Av. Rosado Salas and Calle 3 S, ☎ 987/20131), where the owner holds forth at the microphone. In addition to tasty lobster dishes, **Joe's Lobster House** (✉ Av. 10 S 229, between Calle Rosada Salas and Calle 3 S, ☎ 987/23275) serves up lively reggae and salsa every night around 9 PM; this is *the* hot spot for live entertainment.

Outdoor Activities and Sports

Most people come to Cozumel to take advantage of the island's water-related sports—scuba diving, snorkeling, and fishing are particularly big, but jet skiing, sailboarding, waterskiing, and sailing remain popular as well. You will find services and rentals throughout the island, especially through major hotels and water-sports centers such as **Del Mar Aquatics** (✉ Carretera a Chankanaab, Km 4, ☎ 987/21665 or 800/877–4383, FAX 987/21833) and **Aqua Safari** (✉ Av. Rafael Melgar 429, between Calles 5 and 10 S, ☎ 987/20101).

Fishing

The annual **International Billfish Tournament,** held the last week in April or the first week in May, draws anglers from around the world to Cozumel; for more information, contact the International Billfish Tournament (✉ Box 442, Cozumel 77600, ☎ 800/253–2701, FAX 987/20999).

High-speed fishing boats can be chartered for $300 for a half day or $350 for a full day, for a maximum of six people, from the **Club Naútico de Cozumel** (✉ Puerto de Abrigo, Av. Rafael Melgar, Box 341, ☎ 987/20118 or 800/253–2701, FAX 987/21135), the island's headquarters for game fishing. Daily charters are easily arranged from the dock or at your hotel, but you might also try **Aquarius Fishing and Tours** (⊠ Calle 3 S, ☎ 987/21092) or **Dive Cozumel** (⊠ Av. Rosado Salas 85, between Av. Rafael Melgar and Av. 5 S, ☎ 987/24110, ☎ FAX 987/21842). All rates vary with the season.

Scuba Diving

With more than 30 charted reefs whose average depths range from 50 to 80 ft and a water temperature that hits about 75°F–80°F during peak diving season (June–August, when the hotel rates are coincidentally at their lowest), Cozumel is far and away Mexico's number one diving destination. The diversity of options for divers in Cozumel includes deep dives, drift dives, shore dives, wall dives, and night dives, as well as theme dives focusing on ecology, archaeology, sunken ships, and photography. Make sure your instructor has PADI certification (or FMAS, the Mexican equivalent) and is affiliated with the **SSS recompression chamber** (⊠ Calle 5 S 21B, between Av. Rafael Melgar and Av. 5a S, next to Discover Cozumel, ☎ 987/22387 or 987/21848) or the recompression chamber at the **Hospital Civil** (⊠ Av. 11 S, between Calles 10 and 15, ☎ 987/20140 or 987/20525).

DIVE SHOPS AND TOUR OPERATORS

You can choose from a variety of two-tank boat trips and specialty dives ranging from $45 to $60; two-hour resort courses cost about $50–$60, and 1½-hour night dives, $30–$35. Basic certification courses, such as PADI's Discover Scuba or NAUI's introductory course, are available for about $350, while advanced certification courses cost as much as $700. Equipment rental is relatively inexpensive, ranging from $6 for tanks or a lamp to about $8–$10 for a regulator and B.C. vest; underwater camera rentals can cost as much as $35, video-camera rentals run about $75, and professionally shot and edited videos of your own dive are priced at about $160.

In addition to the dive shops in town, many hotels have their own operations and offer dive and hotel packages starting at about $350 for three nights, double occupancy, and two days of diving. You can also pick up a copy of the *Chart of the Reefs of Cozumel* in any dive shop. Before choosing a shop, check credentials, look over the boats and equipment, and consult experienced divers who are familiar with the operators here. Here's a list to get you started on your search: **Aqua Safari** (⊠ Av. Rafael Melgar 429, between Calles 5 and 10 S, ☎ 987/20101); **Blue Angel** (⊠ Av. Rafael Melgar, next to Hotel Villablanca, ☎ 987/21631), for PADI certification; **Blue Bubble** (⊠ Av. 5a S at Calle 3 S, ☎ 987/21865), for PADI instruction; **Dive Paradise** (⊠ Av. Rafael Melgar 601, ☎ FAX 987/21007); **Michelle's Dive Shop** (⊠ Av. 5 S 201 at Calle Adolfo Rosado Salas, ☎ 987/20947); **Ramone Zapata Divers** (⊠ Chankanaab Nature Park, ☎ 987/20502); **Scuba Du** (⊠ Hotel Presidente Inter-Continental Cozumel, ☎ 987/20322 or 987/21379, FAX 987/24130); **Studio Blue** (⊠ Calle Rosado Salas 121, between Calles 5 and 10, ☎ FAX 987/24330); **Tico's Dive Center** (⊠ Av. 5 N 121, between Calles 2 and 4, ☎ FAX 987/20276); **Chino's Scuba** (⊠ Av. Adolfo Rosado Salas 16A, ☎ 987/24487); **Dive Cozumel** (⊠ Av. Rosado Salas 72 and Av. 5 S, ☎ 987/24110, ☎ FAX 987/21842).

Snorkeling

Snorkeling equipment is available at the Hotel Presidente Inter-Continental, La Ceiba, Chankanaab Bay, Playa San Francisco, Club Cozumel Caribe, and directly off the beach near the Fiesta Americana Cozumel Reef and Playa Corona for less than $10 a day.

Snorkeling tours run from $25 to $50, depending on the length, and take in the shallow reefs off Palancar, Colombia, and Yucab. Contact **Apple Vacations** (✉ Calle 11 and Av. 30 598, ☎ 987/24311 or 987/20725) for snorkeling, sunset cruises, or tours around the island, or **Caribe Tours** (✉ Av. Rafael Melgar at Calle 5 S, ☎ FAX 987/23100 or 987/23154) for information and reservations. **Fiesta Cozumel** (✉ Calle 11 S 598, between Avs. 25 and 30, ☎ 987/20725, FAX 987/21389) runs snorkeling tours from the 45-ft catamaran *El Zorro*. The *Zorro* and the 60-ft catamaran *Fury* are also used for sunset cruises, both of which can be booked through Caribe Tours.

Shopping

Cozumel has three main shopping areas: **downtown** along the waterfront, on Avenida Rafael Melgar, and on some of the side streets around the plaza (there are more than 150 shops in this area alone); at the **crafts market** (✉ Calle 1 S, behind plaza) in town, which sells a respectable assortment of Mexican wares; and at the cruise-ship **passenger terminal** south of town, near the Casa Del Mar, La Ceiba, and Sol Caribe hotels. There are also small clusters of shops at **Plaza del Sol** (on the east side of the main plaza), **Villa Mar** (on the north side of the main plaza), the **Plaza Confetti** (on the south side of the main plaza), and **Plaza Maya** (across from the Sol Caribe). As a general rule, the newer, trendier shops line the waterfront, while the area around Avenida 5a houses the better crafts shops. The **town market** (✉ Calle Rosada Salas between Avs. 20a and 25a) sells fresh produce and other essentials.

Department Stores

Relatively small and more like U.S. variety stores than department stores, the following nevertheless carry a relatively wide array of goods, from the useful to the frivolous. **Chachy Plaza** (✉ Av. Benito Juárez 5, near church at back of plaza, ☎ 987/20130) sells everything from liquor and perfume to snorkeling gear and snack food. **Duty Free Mexico** (✉ Av. Rafael Melgar at Calle 3 S, ☎ 987/20796) puts a strong emphasis on top-line fragrances. **Pama** (✉ Av. Rafael Melgar S 9, ☎ 987/20090), near the pier, features imported food, luggage, snorkeling gear, jewelry, and crystal. **Prococo** (✉ Av. Rafael Melgar N 99, ☎ 987/21875 or 987/21964) offers a good selection of liquor, jewelry, and gift items.

Specialty Stores

CLOTHING

Several trendy sportswear stores line Avenida Rafael Melgar between Calles 2 and 6): **Miro** (✉ Av. Rafael Melgar, 1 block from town pier, ☎ 987/20260) has a wide variety of Mexican resortwear with the latest designs and styles. **Explora** (✉ Av. Rafael Melgar 49, ☎ 987/20316) offers a casual line of modish cotton sports clothing. **La Fiesta Cozumel** (✉ Av. Rafael Melgar N 164-B, ☎ 987/22032), a large store catering to the cruise ships, sells a variety of T-shirts as well as souvenirs.

JEWELRY

Jewelry on Cozumel is pricey, but it tends to be of higher quality than the jewelry you'll find in many of the other Yucatán towns. **Casablanca** (✉ Av. Rafael Melgar N 33, ☎ 987/21177) specializes in gold, silver, and gemstones, as well as expensive crafts. The elegant **Diamond Creations** (✉ Av. Rafael Melgar Sur 131, ☎ 987/25330 or 800/322–6476, FAX 987/25334) lets you custom design a piece of jewelry from an extensive collection of loose diamonds—or emeralds, rubies, sapphires, or tanzanite. Nothing but fine silver, gold, and coral jewelry—particularly silver bracelets and earrings—is sold at **Joyería Palancar** (✉ Av.

Rafael Melgar N 15, ☎ 987/21468). Quality gemstones and striking designs are the strong point at **Rachat & Romero** (✉ Av. Rafael Melgar 101, ☎ 987/20571). The tony **Van Cleef & Arpels** (✉ Av. Rafael Melgar N 54, ☎ 987/21143) offers a superlative collection of high-end silver and gold jewelry.

MEXICAN CRAFTS

Los Cinco Soles (✉ Av. Rafael Melgar N 27, ☎ 987/20132 or 987/22040) is your best bet for one-stop shopping. The nearly block-long store features an excellent variety of well-priced, well-displayed items, including blue-rim glassware, brass and tin animals from Jalisco, and silver jewelry. **Talavera** (✉ Av. 5a S 349, ☎ 987/20171) carries beautiful ceramics from all over Mexico—including tiles from the Yucatán—as well as masks from Guerrero, brightly painted wooden animals from Oaxaca, and carved chests from Guadalajara.

Cozumel A to Z

Arriving and Departing

BY CRUISE SHIP

At least a dozen cruise lines call at Cozumel and/or Playa del Carmen, including, from Fort Lauderdale, **Chandris/Celebrity** (☎ 800/437-3111), **Cunard/Crown** (☎ 800/221–4770), and **Princess** (☎ 800/568–3262); from Miami, **Carnival** (☎ 800/327–9501), **Costa** (☎ 800/327–2537), **Dolphin/Majesty** (☎ 800/222–1003), **Norwegian** (☎ 800/327–7030), and **Royal Caribbean** (☎ 800/327–6700); from New Orleans, **Commodore** (☎ 800/327–5617); and from Tampa, **Holland America** (☎ 800/426–0327).

BY FERRY

Passenger-only ferries depart from the dock at **Playa del Carmen** (no phone) for the 40-minute trip to the main pier in Cozumel. They leave approximately every hour between 5:15 AM and 8:45 PM and cost about $5 one way, $7 round-trip. Return service to Playa operates from roughly 4 AM to 7:45 PM. Verify the regularly changing schedule. The car ferry from **Puerto Morelos** (☎ 987/21722), on the mainland to the north of Playa del Carmen, is not recommended unless you *must* bring your car.

BY JETFOIL

A water-jet catamaran and two large speed boats make the trip between Cozumel (downtown pier, at the zócalo) and Playa del Carmen. This service, operated by **Aviomar** (✉ Av. 5a between Calles 2 and 4, ☎ 987/20588 or 987/20477), costs the same as the ferry and takes almost as much time, but the vessel is considerably more comfortable and offers onboard videos and refreshments. The boats make at least 10 crossings a day, leaving Playa del Carmen approximately every one to two hours between 5:15 AM and 8:45 PM and returning from Cozumel between 4 AM and 8 PM. Tickets are sold at the piers in both ports one hour before departure; call to confirm the schedule as it tends to be erratic.

BY PLANE

The **Cozumel Airport** (☎ 987/20928) is 3 km (2 mi) north of town. **Continental** (☎ 987/20487) provides nonstop service from Houston. **Mexicana** (☎ 987/20157) flies nonstop from Miami and San Francisco; **Aerocaribe** (☎ 987/20503) and **Aerocozumel** (☎ 987/20928), both Mexicana subsidiaries, fly to Cancún and other destinations in Mexico, including Chichén Itzá, Mérida, and Playa del Carmen.

Between the Airport and Hotels. Because of an agreement between the taxi drivers' and the bus drivers' unions, there is no taxi service from the airport; taxi service is available *to* the airport, however. Arriving passengers reach their hotels via the colectivo, a van with a maximum capacity of eight. Buy a ticket at the airport exit: The charge is $5 per passenger to the hotel zones, a little under $3 into town. If you want to get to your hotel without waiting for the van to fill and for other passengers to be dropped off, you can hire an *especial*—an individual van costing a little under $20 to the hotel zones, about $8 to the city. Taxis to the airport cost about $8 from the hotel zones and approximately $5 from downtown. Most car-rental agencies (☞ Contacts and Resources, *below*) maintain offices in the terminal.

Getting Around

BY BICYCLE, MOPED, AND MOTORCYCLE

Mopeds and motorcycles are very popular here but also extremely dangerous because of heavy traffic, potholes, and hidden stop signs; accidents happen all too frequently. Mexican law now requires all passengers to wear helmets; it's a $25 fine if you don't. For mopeds, go to **Auto Rent** (✉ Carretera Costera S, ☎ 987/20844, ext. 712), **Rentadora Caribe** (✉ Calle Rosada Salas 3, ☎ 987/20955 or 987/20961), or **Rentadora Cozumel** (✉ Calle Rosada Salas 3 B, ☎ 987/21503; ✉ Av. 10a S at Calle 1, ☎ 987/21120). Mopeds go for about $25 per day; insurance is included.

BY BUS

Local bus service runs mainly within the town of San Miguel, although there is a route from town to the airport. Service is irregular but inexpensive (under 20¢).

BY CAR

Open-air Jeeps and other rental cars, especially those with four-wheel drive, are a good way of getting down dirt roads leading to secluded beaches and small Maya ruins (although the rental insurance policy may not always cover these jaunts). The only gas station on Cozumel, at the corner of Avenida Juárez and Avenida 30a, is open daily 7 AM–midnight.

BY TAXI

Taxi service is available 24 hours a day, with a 25% surcharge between midnight and 6 AM, at the main location (✉ Calle 2 N, ☎ 987/20041 or 987/20236) or at the malecón at the main pier in town. You can also hail taxis on the street, and there are taxis waiting at all the major hotels. Fixed rates of about $3 are charged to go between town and either hotel zone, about $8 from most hotels to the airport, and about $6–$12 from the northern hotels or town to Chankanaab park or San Francisco beach.

Contacts and Resources

CAR RENTAL

Following is a list of rental firms that handle two- and four-wheel-drive vehicles (all the major hotels have rental offices): **Budget** (✉ Av. 5a at Calle 2 N, ☎ 987/20903; 987/21732 cruise-ship terminal; 987/21742 airport), **Hertz** (☎ 987/23888 airport), **National Interrent** (✉ Av. Juárez, Lote 10, near Calle 10, ☎ 987/23263 or 987/24101), and **Rentadora Aguilla** (✉ Av. Rafael Melgar 685, ☎ 987/20729). Rental rates start at $50 a day.

DOCTORS AND DENTISTS

The **Centro de Salud clinic** (✉ Av. 20 at Calle 11, ☎ 987/20140) provides 24-hour emergency care, and the **Medical Specialties Center** (✉ Av. 20 N 425, ☎ 987/21419 or 987/22919) offers 24-hour air ambulance service and a 24-hour pharmacy. **Cozumel Chiropractic** (✉ Av. 5

Sur 24-A, between Calles 3 and 5, ☎ 987/25099) offers bargain-priced therapeutic massage.

EMERGENCIES

Police (✉ Anexo del Palacio Municipal, ☎ 987/20092). **Red Cross** (✉ Av. Rosada Salas at Av. 20a S, ☎ 987/21058). **Air Ambulance** (☎ 987/24070). **Recompression Chamber** (✉ Calle 5 S 21-B, between Av. Rafael Melgar and Av. 5a S, ☎ 987/21430).

GUIDED TOURS

See Travel Agencies and Tour Operators, *below,* for addresses and telephone numbers of the companies mentioned here.

Air Tours. Caribe Tours offers a plane trip to **Chichén Itzá**; the price of $145 includes the flight, transfers to the ruins, buffet lunch, and a guide. The company also flies to the **Sian Ka'an Ecological Biosphere**; in addition to lunch, this $160 plane trip includes a boat ride through the biosphere's mangroves for a closer look at the flora and fauna of the region.

Horseback Tours. Rancho Buenavista (☎ 987/21537) runs four-hour guided horseback tours that visit three Maya ruins tucked away in Cozumel's tropical forest. The tour departs from Restaurant Acuario (✉ Av. Rafael Melgar at Calle 11), weekdays at noon and Saturday at 11.

Orientation Tours. Tours of the island's sights cost about $35 and can be arranged through a travel agency such as Fiesta Cozumel. Caribe Tours focuses on the botanical gardens, archaeological replicas, and reef snorkeling at Chankanaab; the cost is about $40 and includes an open-bar lunch. Private taxi tours range from $30 to $50 per day depending on which parts of the island you wish to visit.

Specialty Tours. Glass-bottom-boat trips are provided by Turismo Aviomar. The air-conditioned semisubmarine *Mermaid* glides over a number of reefs that host a dazzling array of fish; the daily tour, which costs about $30, lasts one hour and 45 minutes and includes soft drinks. A similar trip aboard the *Nautilus IV* is available through Fiesta Cozumel.

Off-island tours to **Tulum** and **Xel-Há,** run by Turismo Aviomar and Caribe Tours, cost about $75 and include the 30-minute ferry trip to Playa del Carmen, the 45-minute bus ride to Tulum, 1½–2 hours at the ruins, entrance fees, guides, lunch, and a stop for snorkeling at Xel-Há lagoon.

Day trips to the eco-archaeological theme park of **Xcaret,** about halfway between Playa del Carmen and Tulum, are offered by Fiesta Cozumel. The $50 price includes round-trip ferry to Playa del Carmen, entrance to the park, and a bilingual guide.

LATE-NIGHT PHARMACY

Farmacia Joaquín (✉ Main Plaza, north side, ☎ 987/22520) is open Monday–Saturday 8 AM–10 PM and Sunday 9–1 and 5–9.

TRAVEL AGENCIES AND TOUR OPERATORS

Caribe Tours (✉ Av. Rafael Melgar at Calle 5 S, ☎ FAX 987/23100 or 987/23154); **Fiesta Cozumel Holidays/American Express** (in all major hotel lobbies; ✉ Calle 11 S 598, between Avs. 25 and 30, ☎ 987/20725); **Turismo Aviomar** (in several hotel lobbies, including El Presidente; ✉ Av. 5 N 8, between Calles 2 and 4, ☎ 987/20588); **Apple Vacations** (✉ Calle 11 and Av. 30th 598, ☎ 987/24311 or 987/20725).

VISITOR INFORMATION

State tourism office (✉ Upstairs in Plaza del Sol mall, at east end of main square, ☎ 987/20218) is open weekdays 9–2:30. A good source of information on lodgings (and many other things) is the **Cozumel Island Hotel Association** (✉ Calle 2 N at 15a, ☎ 987/23132, FAX 987/22809), open weekdays 8–2 and 4–7.

THE NORTH CARIBBEAN COAST

Updated by Patricia Alisau

Above all else, beaches are what define the eastern coast of the Yucatán peninsula. White, sandy strands with offshore coral reefs, oversize tropical foliage and jungle, Maya ruins, and abundant wildlife make the coastline of Quintana Roo a marvelous destination for lovers of the outdoors. The scrubby limestone terrain is mostly flat and dry, punctuated only by sinkholes, while the shores are broken up by freshwater lagoons, underwater caves, and cliffs.

The various destinations on the coast cater to different preferences. The once laid-back town of Playa del Carmen is now host to resorts as glitzy as those found in Cancún and Cozumel, though still not quite as expensive, while the lazy fishing village of Puerto Morelos so far has been only slightly altered to accommodate foreign tourists. Rustic fishing and scuba diving lodges on the even more secluded Boca Paila peninsula are gaining a well-deserved reputation for bone fishing and superb diving on virgin reefs. The beaches, from Punta Bete to Sian Ka'an, south of Tulum, are beloved of scuba divers, snorkelers, birders, and beachcombers and offer accommodations to suit every budget, from campsites and bungalows to condos and luxury hotels. Ecotourism is on the rise, with special programs designed to involve visitors in preserving the threatened sea-turtle population. Then, too, there are the Maya ruins at Tulum, superbly situated on a bluff overlooking the Caribbean, and, a short distance inland, at Cobá, whose towering jungle-shrouded pyramids evoke its importance as a leading center of commerce in the Maya world. The waters up and down the coast, littered with shipwrecks and relics from the heyday of piracy, are dotted with mangrove swamps and minuscule islands where only the birds hold sway.

Exploring

The coast is basically divided into two areas: Puerto Morelos to Tulum, which has the most sites and places to lodge; and Tulum to Chetumal, where civilization thins out quite a bit. We detail only the first part of the coast. If you want to venture farther, you'll be rewarded by alluringly beautiful and remote beaches, coves, inlets, lagoons, and tropical landscapes. The southern Caribbean area includes Xcalak, a fishing village near the tip of the Xcalak peninsula; the spectacularly vast and beautiful Laguna de Bacalar, the second largest lake in Mexico; and Chetumal, the last Mexican town on the southern Caribbean. Chetumal feels more Central American than Mexican—not surprising, given its proximity to Belize. The many Middle Eastern inhabitants have influenced the cuisine, which represents an exotic blend of Yucatecan, Mexican, and Lebanese.

Puerto Morelos

20 *36 km (22 mi) south of Cancún.*

Puerto Morelos has been left remarkably free of the large-scale development so common farther south, though each year more and more tourists stop here to take in its easygoing pace, cheap accommodations,

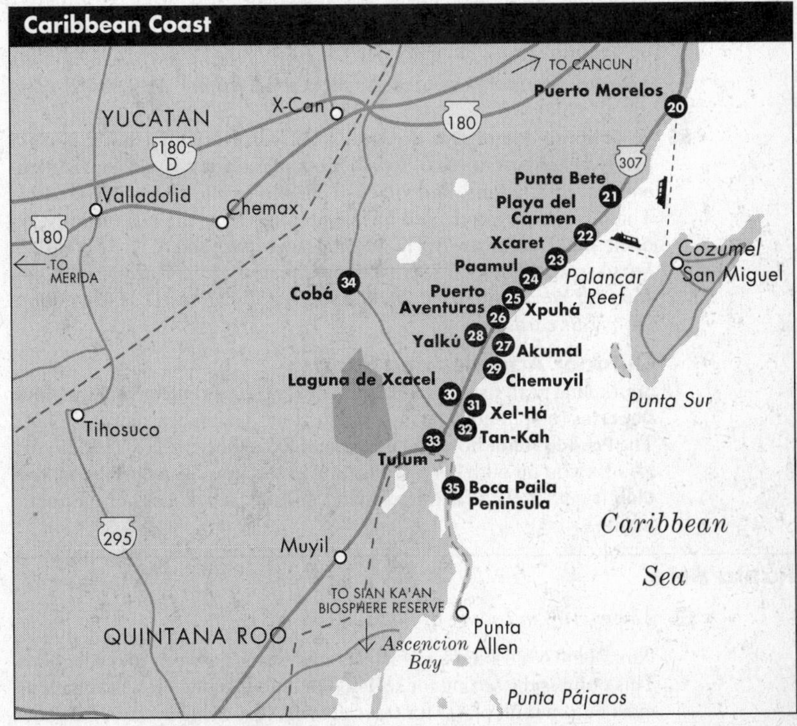

and convenient seaside location near a superb offshore coral reef. The reef at Morelos is about 1,800 ft offshore. The caves of the sleeping sharks of documentary movie fame are also 8 km (5 mi) east of the town.

Once a point of departure for Maya women making pilgrimages by canoe to Cozumel, the sacred isle of the fertility goddess, Ixchel, Morelos today is not very different from many small towns in the Spanish-speaking Caribbean. There is not much to it beyond a gas station, a central square, and auto repair shops. The town square is much prettier now after having been remodeled at the beginning of 1997. Most of the action is centered on the long pier south of the square, where vehicles line up for hours waiting for the ferry to depart for Cozumel. Three lighthouses from different eras break up the long stretch of beach, and boats to take out to the surrounding reefs can be rented on the beach.

Dining and Lodging

$ ✕ **Los Pelícanos.** If you're looking for good fresh fish, stop by this thatched-roof restaurant on the beach, where you can spend hours feasting on the catch of the day and watching the boats go by. ✉ *On oceanfront near main plaza,* ☎ *987/10014. MC, V.*

$$$$ ★ ✕🏨 **Caribbean Reef Club at Villa Marina.** This rather functional-looking white condo complex is one of the newest hideaways along the coast. The colonial-style suites have marble floors, air-conditioning, ceiling fans, blue-tile kitchenettes, floral pastel linens, and arched windows. Sliding glass doors lead to balconies outside, where you can slip in an afternoon nap on your own private hammock. The adjacent restaurant is easily the most picturesque in town, with a balcony overlooking the sea, hand-painted tile tables, and candlelight at night. A Cuban chef pre-

pares superb coconut shrimp, seafood gumbo, jerk chicken, and other Caribbean specialties. ✉ *South of ferry dock. For reservations:* ☎ *98/834999 in Cancún,* ☎ *987/10191 or 800/322–6286,* FAX *987/10190. 21 suites. Restaurant, bar, pool, snorkeling, fishing. MC, V.*

$$ **Cabañas Playa Ojo de Agua.** This dive-oriented hotel is on a lovely beach just north of town. Most of the guest rooms have kitchenettes, ceiling fans, and views of the sea or the courtyard gardens. There is a freshwater pool on the premises, but the restaurant stays open only December–April. ✉ *1 block north of town,* ☎ *987/10027. For reservations:* ☎ *98/834999 in Cancún; or* ✉ *Calle 12, No. 96, Mérida, Yucatán 97050,* ☎ *99/250292. 30 rooms. Pool, dive shop. No credit cards.*

Outdoor Activities and Sports

Snorkeling gear, fishing tackle, and boats can be rented from the **Aqua Deportes** (no phone) dive shop on the town's main beach, by the plaza. The **Posada Amor** hotel (✉ Av. Xavier Rojo Góez, ☎ 987/10033) can also fix you up with deep-sea fishing excursions. The **Caribbean Reef Club** (☞ *above*) can arrange diving, fishing, snorkeling, or mountain biking.

Punta Bete

21 *22 km (16½ mi) south of Puerto Morelos.*

Punta Bete is a 6-km (4-mi) white-sand beach between rocky lagoons. This point is the setting for several bungalow-style hotels that have almost become cult places for travelers who love being in or on the water. All the properties are set off from Route 307 at the end of a 3-km (2-mi) paved road; many of them are still recovering from the damage that Hurricane Roxanne caused in late 1995.

Lodging

$$$$ ★ **Posada del Capitán Lafitte.** Set on an invitingly long stretch of beach just 10 km (6 mi) north of Playa del Carmen at Punta Bete, this lodging is known for its genuinely chummy, unpretentious atmosphere. It's a simple cluster of two-unit cabañas, each with its own private bath and ceiling fan. Fourteen units have air-conditioning. A duplex at the south end of the property has four two-bedroom, two-bath units, ideal for families. Breakfast, dinner, tax, and tips are included in the room rate. Group activities include snorkeling trips, scuba certification and dives, horseback riding, fishing, and birding. All reservations must be prepaid. ✉ *On dirt road (follow signs) about 3 km (2 mi) off Rte. 307 at Km 62,* ☎ *987/30214,* FAX *987/45226. For reservations:* ✉ *Turquoise Reef Group, Box 2664, Evergreen, CO 80439,* ☎ *303/674–9615 or 800/538–6802,* FAX *303/674–8735. 47 rooms. Restaurant, bar, pool, beach, dive shop, car rental, Cancún airport transfers. AE, MC, V.*

Outdoor Activities and Sports

Posada de Capitan Lafitte (☎ 987/30214 or 800/538–6802), off Route 307 just north of Playa del Carmen, has an excellent, full-service dive shop called Buccaneer's Landing. Services include diving and snorkeling excursions, and scuba resort courses.

Playa del Carmen

22 *10 km (6 mi) south of Punta Bete, 68 km (41 mi) south of Cancún.*

Only a few decades ago, Playa del Carmen was a deserted beach where Indian families raised coconut palms to produce copra. Nowadays its alabaster-white beach and small offshore reefs attract swimmers, snorkelers, and turtle watchers, and the town has become the preferred destination of travelers who want easy access to gorgeous beaches and the archaeological sites of Yucatán. Playa is no longer a budget destination, but you still get more for your money here than in Cancún or Cozumel. Playa now has 35 hotels, about 60% more than a few years ago.

The busiest parts of Playa are down by the **ferry pier,** around the **main plaza,** and along the pedestrian walkway. Take a stroll north from the pier along the beach and you'll see the essence of the town: simple restaurants roofed with palm fronds, where people sit around drinking beer for hours; a few campgrounds; and lots of hammocks. On the south side of the pier is the **Continental Plaza Playacar,** a first-class, lavish hotel that brought a sense of luxury and style to Playa del Carmen in 1991. If you walk away from the beach, you'll come upon the affluent section: several condominium projects and well-tended gardens and lawns that can be seen from the street. From here, only the sandy streets, the small vestiges of Maya structures, and the stunning turquoise sea on the horizon suggest you're in the tropics. The streets at both ends of town peter out into the jungle.

Dining and Lodging

$$ ★ ✕ **Da Gabi.** There are two Da Gabi restaurants on the planet—one in Playa and the other in Boulder, Colorado—and both are successful. Residents flock here at night to dine under a romantic candlelit palapa on remarkable Italian cuisine. Enjoy the Maya chef's homemade pastas or oven-baked pizza. You can't go wrong with the daily specials either. Service is especially cordial here, and owner John Lackey is always around to keep things running smoothly. ✉ *Av. 1 and Calle 12 in Da Gabi Hotel,* ☎ *987/30048. No credit cards. No lunch.*

$$ ✕ **La Parrilla.** The far end of the pedestrian walkway gained a social center when La Parrilla opened in 1994 at the Rincón del Sol plaza. A branch of an enduringly popular Cancún chain, the open-air restaurant sits a few feet above the street, and it's hard to resist stopping in for a beer, a platter of chicken fajitas, or lobster. This is one of the most animated places in town on weekends, with tables spilling out onto the street and a heavy noise level until the wee hours of the morning. ✉ *Av. 5 at Calle 8, no phone. MC, V.*

$$ ✕ **La Placita.** This attractive restaurant is about as authentic as they come in Playa. A narrow table-filled entranceway opens up into a delightful patio in back where northern Mexican dishes such as *cabrito* (roasted kid), grilled fillets of meat and fish, and bone-marrow soup get top billing. Save room for dessert and a flambéed café Maya made of Kahlúa, *Xtabetum* (honey liqueur), and vanilla ice cream. The Mexican handicrafts—piñatas and colored-paper cutouts—used to decorate the place are so attractive that tourists often buy them right off the wall. There's live music nightly. ✉ *Av. 5 between Calles 4 and 6,* ☎ *987/31067. AE, MC, V.*

$$ ✕ **Limones.** A romantic little spot right off Avenida 5, this restaurant offers dining by candlelight, either alfresco in a courtyard or under the shelter of a palapa indoors. Wine bottles hanging from the ceiling and soft guitar music add to the amorous atmosphere. House favorites include copious entrées such as fettuccine, lasagna, and lemon-sautéed beef scallopini. The daily dinner special is the best bargain in town. ✉ *Av. 5 at Calle 6, no phone. MC, V.*

$$ ★ ✕ **Máscaras.** The wood-burning brick oven here produces exceptionally good thin-crusted pizzas and breads; the homemade pastas are also excellent. Be sure to try the calamari in garlic and oil. Masks from throughout the world cover the walls; live music including salsa bands starts nightly at 7. Máscaras is a central gathering spot with a view of

the goings-on at the zócalo (main plaza). ✉ *Av. Juárez across from plaza,* ☎ *987/30153. MC, V.*

$ ✕ **El Tacolote.** Opened in 1992, this fanciful, colorful, open-air restaurant continues expanding, overtaking less popular eateries. Mariachis play on most evenings in front of the sidewalk tables, where diners feast on platters of grilled meats, fajitas, or tacos with all sorts of fillings. You can eat cheaply or splurge on a multicourse feast while watching the action on the plaza from an outdoor table. ✉ *Av. Juárez across from plaza,* ☎ *987/30066. MC, V.*

$$$$ **Continental Plaza Playacar.** The centerpiece of an 880-acre master-planned resort, this pastel, blush-colored palace faces the sea on the south side of the ferry pier. The tropical-style rooms have ocean views and balconies or patios. The beach is one of the nicest in Playa del Carmen and far less crowded than those to the north. The breakfast buffet is excellent. A shopping-dining-banking complex links the hotel with downtown Playa del Carmen via a pleasant pedestrian mall. There's a full-scale scuba and water-sports facility and an 18-hole championship golf course; ask about golf packages. ✉ *Fraccionamiento Playacar, Playa del Carmen, Quintana Roo 77710,* ☎ *987/30100 or 800/882–6684. 188 rooms, 16 suites. 2 restaurants, bar, pool, 18-hole golf course, dive shop, shop, travel services, car rental. AE, MC, V.*

$$$$ **Diamond Resort.** Part of the Playacar development, Diamond is an all-inclusive resort that sprawls down a sloping hill to the sea. The guest rooms are spread out in thatched-roof villas along winding paths. Unlike that of many other all-inclusive resorts, Diamond's design allows peace and privacy. Buffet-style meals are plentiful and imaginatively prepared; there are also two à la carte restaurants. Playa del Carmen is a 20-minute walk or a $4 cab ride north. ✉ *In Playacar development,* ☎ *987/30039,* FAX *987/30346. For reservations:* ✉ *901 Ponce de Leon Blvd., Suite 400, Coral Gables, FL 33134,* ☎ *800/858–2258,* FAX *305/444–4848. 296 rooms. 3 restaurants, bar, 2 pools, 4 tennis courts, dive shop, shop, children's program (ages 5–10), car rental. AE, MC, V.*

$$$$ ★ **Mayan Paradise.** This new hotel located at the northern end of Playa has truly beautiful old Maya architecture; the rooms are set in two-story bungalows with thatched roofs, terraces, and dark hardwood siding, and they surround a pretty pool and jungle palms. Local hardwood lines the walls of the guest rooms, which have all the amenities of a luxury hotel at reasonable prices (low end of $$$$). Each has a small kitchenette, color satellite TV, two double beds, room safe, air-conditioning, and furnishings in rich fabrics; suites have whirlpool baths. The restaurant and bar are under a palapa and meals are served at a fixed time each day. Although not on the ocean, the hotel has its own private beach club and complimentary shuttle service for guests. ✉ *Av. 10 between Calles 12 and Bis,* ☎ FAX *987/30933. 44 rooms and suites. Restaurant, bar, pool, travel services, free parking. MC, V.*

$$$$ **Royal Maeva Playacar.** This all-inclusive Mexican club opened in 1996 in the Playacar development south of the ferry pier, and already draws plenty of Italian and German vacationers. The complex looks like a small, salmon-color Mexican village sprinkled liberally with red-tile roofs and colonial arches. Several pools surround a thatched pavilion restaurant in the middle of the tropical garden, beyond which is a powder-sand beach that stretches several kilometers north to town. ✉ *In Playacar development,* ☎ *213/935–6089 and 800/466–2382,* FAX *213/935–6197. 300 rooms. 2 restaurants, 4 bars, 4 pools, 4 tennis courts, basketball, exercise room, volleyball, snorkeling, fishing, dance club, theater, children's program, meeting rooms, travel services, car rental, free parking. AE, DC, MC, V.*

$$$ **Albatros Royale.** The nicest complex right on the beach, the Royale opened in 1991 but still looks brand new. Two-story palapa-covered buildings face each other along a pathway to the sand, resembling a small village. Sea breezes and ceiling fans cool the small rooms, simply decorated with white walls and tile floors; five have a view of the ocean. Guests can have a breakfast buffet, included in the price of the room, across the street at the sister Pelicano Inn hotel. The Royale fills up quickly; advance reservations are advised. ✉ *Calle 8 between beach and Av. 5,* ☎ *987/30001,* FAX *987/30002. For reservations:* ✉ *Turquoise Reef Group, Box 2664, Evergreen, CO 80439,* ☎ *303/674–9615 or 800/538–6802,* FAX *303/674–8735. 31 rooms. Restaurant, in-room safes, dive shop, travel services. MC, V.*

$$$ ★ **El Tucan Condotel.** This lodging in the residential north end of town looks like a very exclusive and expensive hotel but actually is the best deal for your money in Playa. Catering to lots of German tour groups, it is set around a huge jungle garden with a pool and offers the ultimate in tranquillity well away from the noise of downtown Avenida 5; however, it's a mere 10-minute walk to get there. All rooms and apartments in the slate-color buildings are fairly well separated from one another and have burnished brown tile floors and hand-painted flower tile sinks in the bathrooms. Each has a private terrace, overhead fan, and tiny kitchenette; groceries can be purchased at a small shopping center nearby. A Continental breakfast is included. ✉ *Av. 5 between Calles 14 and 16, Quintana Roo 77710,* ☎ *987/30417,* FAX *987/30668. 32 rooms, 24 apartments. Restaurant, bar, grocery, pool, hot tub, gift shop. MC, V.*

$$$ ★ **Las Palapas.** At this ideal get-away-from-it-all destination resort, white cabañas are cheerfully trimmed in blue, and duplexes have balconies or porches, palapas, and hammocks. The beach and pool are complemented by a shuffleboard area, clubhouse, beach bar, palapa bar, and attractive palapa restaurant (the buffets can be elaborate, but we've had reports that the food was disappointing in low season). Room rates include breakfast and dinner. Reserve early; a three-night minimum stay is required. ✉ *Km 292 on Rte. 307, Box 116, Playa del Carmen, Quintana Roo 77710,* ☎ *987/30582 or 800/433–0885,* FAX *987/30458. 55 cabanas. Restaurant, 2 bars, in-room safes, pool, beach. MC, V.*

$$$ **Pelicano Inn.** Formerly Cabañas Albatros, this rather austere-looking hotel has been completely restructured into one- to three-story beach villas. It reopened in November 1995 and is the sister hotel to the Albatros Royale. The entrance is an odd tunnel painted with scenes from the deep. Six rooms face the ocean directly; the other 32 have peekaboo views of the sea. All are fairly spacious and offer ceiling fans, private bathrooms, and double beds. Breakfast is included in the price of the room. ✉ *On beach at Calle 8,* ☎ *987/30001,* FAX *987/30002. For reservations:* ✉ *Turquoise Reef Group, Box 2664, Evergreen, CO 80439,* ☎ *303/674–9615 or 800/538–6802,* FAX *303/674–8735. 38 rooms. Restaurant. MC, V.*

$$ **Alejari.** This two-story complex set amid lush gardens is one of the most pleasant accommodations on Playa's north beach. Some rooms have kitchenettes and fans or air-conditioning. Breakfast comes with the room. ✉ *Calle 6N. For reservations:* ✉ *Box 166, Playa del Carmen, Quintana Roo 77710,* ☎ *987/30374,* FAX *987/30005. 29 rooms. Restaurant, bar, kitchenettes. MC, V.*

$$ **Maya-Bric.** Larger than most beachfront hotels in Playa, the Maya-Bric has a pretty landscaped courtyard and pool area, which affords a pleasant escape from the hot sandy beach; the staff, however, could benefit from charm school. The rooms have fans and are comfortable and basic, with few frills. Try to avoid the rooms overlooking the park-

ing lot as they get all the street noise at night. The gates are locked at night, making this one of the most private places around. The on-site dive shop runs snorkeling, diving, and sightseeing trips to the nearby reefs. ✉ *Av. Norte 5a, between Calles 8 and 10, Playa del Carmen, Quintana Roo 77710,* ☎ FAX *987/30011. 29 rooms. Breakfast room, pool, dive shop. No credit cards.*

$ **Elefante.** Three blocks from the beach, this two-story, family-run hotel is well kept and the best deal around for price; the only sore spot is the unkempt field you pass on the way to the rooms. All bare-bones units overlook a small plant-filled walkway and have tile floors and bathrooms, two double beds, and fans; some have kitchenettes. There's a restaurant down the street. ✉ *Av. 12 and Calle 10,* ☎ *987/91987. 38 rooms. No credit cards.*

Outdoor Activities and Sports

The oldest dive shop in town, **Tank Ha** (✉ Maya-Bric hotel, ☎ FAX 987/30011), with PADI-certified teachers, arranges diving and snorkeling trips to the reefs and caverns. **Wet Dreams** (✉ Albatros Royale hotel, ☎ 987/30001) also has certified, bilingual instructors.

Shopping

Avenida 5 between Calles 4 and 10 is definitely the best place to shop in Playa if not along the whole coast. Pretty shops and boutiques have sophisticated offerings from all of Mexico and hand-painted batiks from Indonesia. Even the ubiquitous T-shirts sold here have exotically creative designs. All shops close in the afternoon between 1 and 5 following a long-established tradition of the coast, and then stay open until 9 at night.

Xop (✉ Rincón del Sol, Av. 5 at Calle 8, no phone) is one of the best places on the coast for handcrafted wooden masks and statues and incredibly carved amber pendants, along with earrings, necklaces, and bracelets set with silver and semiprecious stones. **El Vuelo de los Niños Pajaros** (✉ Rincón del Sol, Av. 5 at Calle 8, ☎ 987/30445) has a great selection of regional music on CD and tape, along with handcrafted paper, cards, incense, and beaded baskets. **Museum Shop** (✉ Av. 5 between Calles 4 and 6, ☎ 987/30446) has simple but elegantly crafted amber jewelry by a German designer who also keeps a shop in Chiapas near the mines that provide the raw material. **La Calaca** (✉ Av. 5 between Calles 6 and 8 and Av. 5 and Calle 4, ☎ 987/30177 for both locations) probably has the biggest selection of playful wooden devils and angels in Playa.

Off Av. 5, try **Gaitan** (✉ On west side of main plaza, no phone), a branch of a respected Mexico City leather shop that sells vests, boots, belts, purses, and wallets. **Promoshow** (✉ Calle 6 between Avs. 5 and 10, ☎ 987/31202) sells pre-Hispanic music instruments such as tambors, flutes, ocarinas, rain sticks, and a "tepozazki" made from an armadillo shell; it also stocks famous handmade guitars from Paracho, Michoacan. **Artesanías Margarita** (✉ Calle 2 and Av. 5, no phone) has exquisite hand-painted sun hats and wind chimes designed by Luis de Ocampo. **El Dorado** (✉ Calle 1 between Av. 5 and ferry pier in Las Molcas Hotel shopping arcade, no phone) has replicas of pre-Hispanic Inca and Maya jewelry fashioned in silver dipped in gold.

Xcaret

23 *6 km (4 mi) south of Playa del Carmen, 72 km (50 mi) south of Cancún.*

This sacred Maya city and port has been developed into a 250-acre ecological theme park on a gorgeous stretch of coastline. Maya ruins are scattered over the lushly landscaped property. Attractions include an underground river ride through a series of caves and the opportunity to swim with dolphins ($60); only 36 people are allowed in the water with them each day, so arrive early to sign up for your slot. An artificially created beach, breakwater, and lagoons are perfect for snorkeling and swimming; instruction and water-sports equipment rentals are available. Xcaret also includes a botanical garden, a museum with reproductions of the Yucatán peninsula's main archaeological sites, a tropical aquarium, a wild-bird sanctuary, stables with riding demonstrations, a dive shop, and several restaurants. The highlight of the dinner show (presented daily at 6 PM) is an exhibition by the famed Flying Indians of Papantla. Tickets can be purchased in advance from travel agencies and major hotels at Playa del Carmen or Cancún. ☎ *98/830632 or 98/830765.* *$30, includes show ($25 on Sun., no show).* *May–Oct., daily 8:30–5; Nov.–Apr., daily 8:30–8:30.*

Dining

$ ✕ **Restaurant Xcaret.** This small palapa restaurant, its walls lined with photos from diving expeditions, serves conch seviche, lobster, poc chuc, and french fries at prices far lower than those inside the Xcaret theme park. ✉ *Hwy. 307 at Xcaret turnoff, no phone. No credit cards.*

Paamul

24 *10 km (6 mi) south of Xcaret.*

Beachcombers and snorkelers are fond of Paamul, a crescent-shape lagoon with clear, placid waters sheltered by the coral reef at the lagoon's mouth. Shells, sand dollars, and even glass beads—some from the sunken pirate ship at Akumal—wash onto the sandy parts of the beach. Trailer camps, cabañas, and tent camps are scattered along the shore; a restaurant sells cold beer and fresh fish; and in the summer visitors may view one of Paamul's chief attractions: sea turtle hatchlings on the beach. A jungle path to the north leads to a lagoon four times the size of Paamul and even more private.

Dining and Lodging

$$ **Cabañas Paamul.** This small hostelry on a perfect white-sand beach combines seclusion and comfort. The seven white sea-facing bungalows all have two double beds, ceiling fans, and hot-water showers. The hotel turns Mexican holidays into fiestas for the guests, and there are activities galore. The property includes 190 camping sites for motor homes and tents, and a full-service dive shop. ✉ *Km 85, Hwy. 307. For reservations:* ✉ *Box 83, Playa del Carmen, Quintana Roo 77710,* ☎ *99/259422,* FAX *987/256913. 7 rooms. Restaurant, dive shop. No credit cards.*

Puerto Aventuras

25 *12 km (7 mi) south of Paamul.*

Puerto Aventuras is a 900-acre self-contained resort, which will eventually include a 250-slip marina, tennis club, beach club, 18-hole golf course, shopping mall, movie theater, and five deluxe hotels with a total of 2,000 rooms. Facilities in operation include several restaurants and shops, nine holes of the golf course, an excellent dive shop, and a 95-slip marina. In addition, the **underwater archaeology museum,** founded by Mexican diver-businessman Pablo Bush Romero, displays models of old ships as well as coins, cannons, sewing needles, and nautical devices recovered from Mexican waters by CEDAM (Mexican Underwater Explorers Club) members; it's open daily 10–1 and 2–6. Also in operation are three hotels and several condo and time-share units.

Currently, the entire complex is losing money, and some of the services are not up to par.

Dining and Lodging

$$ ✕ **Carlos 'n' Charlie's.** Having a branch of this popular restaurant chain in town is a sign of true resort status. Carlos Anderson's restaurants are known for being wacky, wild, and rowdy and for serving ample portions of well-prepared barbecued ribs and chicken, enchiladas, *carne asada* (grilled meat), and other Mexican dishes, and powerful tequila drinks. ✉ *In commercial center, no phone. MC, V.*

$$$$ **Club de Playa.** This 30-room hotel underwent extensive renovations in 1995 and has become part of the Colony Resorts chain. The spacious rooms have stunning views of the Caribbean, and the swimming pool seems to flow right into the sea. One of the coast's best dive shops is on the property. Guests can also enjoy the facilities (including nine holes of golf) and restaurants at the all-inclusive Club Oasis hotel on the other side of the marina. ✉ *On beach near marina,* ☎ FAX *987/35100 reservations. 30 rooms. Restaurant, pool, exercise room, dive shop, boating. AE, MC, V.*

$$$$ **Continental Plaza Puerto Aventuras.** Situated on the marina a short distance from the beach, the Continental Plaza has a variety of rooms, many with kitchenettes. Most guest quarters are decorated in soft shades of blue and peach and feature French doors opening onto balconies overlooking the pool. The hotel has a shuttle service to the beach; restaurants, shops, and water-sports services are within walking distance. ✉ *At marina, Puerto Aventuras, Quintana Roo 77710,* ☎ *987/35133 or 800/882–6684,* FAX *987/35134. 56 rooms. Restaurant, bar, pool, bicycles, car rental. AE, MC, V.*

Outdoor Activities and Sports

Mike Madden's CEDAM Dive Centers (✉ Club de Playa Hotel, ☎ 987/35147 or 987/35129, FAX 987/41339) is a full-service dive shop with certification courses; cave and cenote diving is a specialty.

Xpuhá

26 *9 km (5½ mi) south of Puerto Aventuras.*

The little fishing village of Xpuhá, where residents weave hammocks and harvest coconuts, is down a sandy road off Route 307. Some small, overgrown pre-Hispanic ruins in the area still bear traces of paint on the inside walls. A cluster of pastel-color hotel buildings sit on the beach; inexpensive rooms are available on a first-come, first-served basis, although the smaller properties close for September and October. Hammocks are for sale along the main highway.

Akumal

27 *37 km (22 mi) south of Playa del Carmen, 102 km (59 mi) south of Cancún.*

The name Akumal, meaning "Place of the Turtle," recalls ancient Maya times, when the beach was the nesting ground for thousands of turtles. The place first attracted international attention in 1926, when explorers discovered the *Mantanceros,* a Spanish galleon that sank in 1741. Three decades later, Akumal became headquarters for the Mexican Underwater Explorers Club (CEDAM). Akumal continues to be famous for its diving. Area dive shops sponsor resort courses and certification courses, and luxury hotels and condominiums offer year-round packages comprising airfare, accommodations, and diving. Deep-sea fishing for giant marlin, bonito, and sailfish is also popular. Hotel rooms are at a premium during the high season, December 15–April 30, and reservations should be made well in advance.

Akumal consists of three distinct areas. Half Moon Bay to the north is lined with private homes and condominiums and has some of the prettiest beaches and best snorkeling in the area. Akumal proper consists of a large resort and small Maya community with a market, grocery stores, laundry facilities, and pharmacy. There's also an Ecology Center next to the Dive Shop with a staff of ecologists. More condos and homes and an all-inclusive resort are at Akumal Aventuras to the south. People come here to walk on the deliciously long beaches filled with shells, crabs, and migrant birds.

28 Devoted snorkelers may want to walk to **Yalkú**, a practically unvisited lagoon just north of Akumal along an unmarked dirt road. Wending its way out to the sea, Yalkú hosts throngs of parrot fish in superbly clear water with visibility to 160 ft, but it has no facilities.

Dining and Lodging

$$ ✕ **La Lunita.** Locals and enterprising tourists congregate at the indoor and patio tables of this converted one-bedroom condo at Half Moon Bay for good conversation and innovative cuisine. Regulars swear by the fresh fish served with a lime and cilantro sauce or smothered in tomatoes and onions. You'll need a car, a cab, or strong legs to reach this place, but it's worth it. ✉ *Hacienda de la Tortuga; go through entranceway at Club Akumal Caribe, then turn left (north) at dirt road to Half Moon Bay,* ☎ *987/22421 for condo office. No credit cards.*

$$$ ✕🏨 **Club Akumal Caribe & Villas Maya.** Accommodations at this resort, situated on the edge of a cove overlooking a small harbor, range from rustic but comfortable bungalows with red-tile roofs and garden views (Villas Maya) to beachfront rooms in a modern three-story hotel building. All have air-conditioning, ceiling fans, and refrigerators. Also available are the more secluded one-, two-, and three-bedroom condominiums called the Villas Flamingo, on Half Moon Bay and a kilometer from the beach. The bungalows and hotel rooms are cheerfully furnished in rattan and dark wood, with attractive tile floors; the high-domed, Mediterranean-style condominium units have kitchens and balconies or terraces overlooking the pool and beach. A vast array of diving options are available, as are other water sports. The best of the three restaurants is **Lol Ha**: The grilled steak and seafood dinner entrées are bountiful. An optional meal plan includes breakfast and dinner. ✉ *Km 104, Hwy. 307,* ☎ *987/22532. For reservations:* ✉ *Akutrame, Box 13326, El Paso, TX 79913,* ☎ *915/584–3552 or 800/351–1622; 800/343–1440 in Canada. 40 bungalows, 21 rooms, 4 villas, 5 condos. 3 restaurants, bar, grocery, ice-cream parlor, pizzeria, snack bar, pool, beach, 2 dive shops, shop. AE, MC, V.*

$$$$ 🏨 **Club Oasis Akumal.** An all-inclusive luxury hotel, this sprawling property started as the private preserve of millionaire Pablo Bush Romero, a friend of Jacques Cousteau. Today the beautiful beach—protected by an offshore reef—and the pier are used as the starting point for canoeing, snorkeling, diving, fishing, and windsurfing jaunts. The U-shape building, with nautical decor, features handsome mahogany furniture and sunken blue-tile showers between Moorish arches (no doors!). All rooms have balconies (you can choose a sea view or a garden view) and air-conditioning or ceiling fans (same price). ✉ *For reservations: 3520 Piedmont Rd. NE, Suite 325, Atlanta, GA 30305,* ☎ *987/22828 or 800/446–2747,* FAX *987/35051 or 404/240–5500. 120 rooms.*

Restaurant, 2 bars, 2 pools, tennis court, beach, dive shop, shops, recreation room, travel services, car rental. AE, MC, V.

Outdoor Activities and Sports

Akumal Dive Center rents equipment, runs dive trips, and has certification programs. For dive packages, including accommodations, contact Akutrame Inc. (✉ Box 13326, El Paso, TX 79913, ☎ 915/584–3552 or 800/351–1622; 800/343–1440 in Canada). **Mike Madden dive shop** is at the Aventuras Akumal (☎ 987/22828).

Chemuyil

29 *7 km (4½ mi) south of Akumal.*

You can lunch on fresh seafood here at a modest eatery on the beach and swim at the little cove at Chemuyil. The crescent-shape beach, which has been declared an official sea-turtle reserve, is popular with tour groups and campers who pitch their tents under the few remaining palms (most were destroyed by disease and have not been replaced).

Laguna de Xcacel

30 *8 km (5 mi) south of Chemuyil.*

The Laguna de Xcacel sits on a sandy ridge overlooking yet another long white beach. The calm waters provide excellent swimming, snorkeling, diving, and fishing; birders and beachcombers like to stroll in the early morning. Camping is permitted, and there's a restaurant (closed Sunday) on the site. Tour buses full of cruise-ship passengers stop here for lunch, and the showers and dressing rooms get crowded at dusk.

Xel-Há

31 *2 km (about 1 mi) south of Laguna de Xcacel.*

Now managed by the same people that run Xcaret, Xel-Há (pronounced zhel-hah) is a natural aquarium cut out of the limestone shoreline. The national park consists of several interconnected lagoons where countless species of tropical fish breed; the rocky coastline curves into bays and coves in which enormous parrot fish cluster around an underwater Maya shrine. Several low wooden bridges over the lagoons have benches at regular points, so you can take in the sights at leisure. The waters are remarkably clear. Lockers and dressing rooms are available, and you can buy snorkel gear (it is not available for rent) and underwater cameras (the $18 price includes a roll of film). Other park attractions include several small Maya ruins, a huge but overpriced souvenir shop, food stands, and a small museum. Plan to arrive in the early morning before all the tour-bus traffic hits. For a pleasant breakfast or lunch, any of the five restaurants serve reasonably good seviche, fresh fish, and drinks. ☎ *98/833280.* 🎫 *$10.* 🕓 *Daily 8–5.*

Tan-Kah

32 *10 km (6 mi) south of Xel-Há.*

In the depths of the jungle stands a small grouping of pre-Hispanic structures that cover 10 square km (4 square mi) and once composed a satellite city of Tulum. They have not yet been fully explored. In the 1930s an airstrip was built here; Charles Lindbergh, who was making an aerial survey of the coast, was one of the first to land on it.

Tulum

33 *2 km (about 1 mi) south of Tan-kah, 130 km (80 mi) south of Cancún.*

One of the Caribbean coast's biggest attractions, and the Yucatán peninsula's most visited Maya ruin, Tulum is the largest Maya city built on the coast and the only Maya city known to have been inhabited when the conquistadores arrived. The spectacle of those gray limestone temples against the blue-green Caribbean waters is nothing less than riveting. Visitors are no longer allowed to climb or enter Tulum's most impressive buildings (only three, described below, really merit close inspection), so you can see the ruins in two hours. You may, however, wish to allow extra time for a swim or a stroll on the beach, where it's likely that the ancient Maya beached their canoes.

The first significant structure you'll see is the two-story **Temple of the Frescoes,** to the left of the entryway. The temple's vaulted roof and corbeled arch are examples of classical Maya architecture. Faint traces of blue-green frescoes outlined in black on the inner and outer walls refer to ancient Maya beliefs.

The largest and most famous building, the **Castillo** (castle), looms at the edge of a 40-ft limestone cliff just past the Temple of the Frescoes. Atop the castle, at the end of a broad stairway, sits a temple with stucco ornamentation on the outside and traces of fine frescoes inside the two chambers. The regal structure overlooks the rest of Tulum and an expanse of dense jungle to the west; the blue Caribbean blocks access from the east. Researchers think the Castillo may have functioned as a watchtower to monitor enemy approaches by sea. To the left of the Castillo is the **Temple of the Descending God**—so called for the carving of a winged god plummeting to earth over the doorway.

Tourist services are clustered at the old turnoff from Route 307 to the ruins, marked by restaurants and two hotels. The new road is a few yards farther south and is clearly marked with overhead signs. Still farther south is the turnoff for the Boca Paila Peninsula, the Sian Ka'an preserve, and several small waterfront hotels. The fourth turnoff you'll come to, about 4 km (2½ mi) south of the ruins, is for the present-day village of Tulum. This small community is becoming rather unsightly and congested as its prosperity increases: Markets, auto-repair shops, and other businesses continue to spring up along the road, which has been widened to four lanes.

Dining and Lodging

$$ ★ ✕ **Casa Cenote.** Don't miss this outstanding restaurant beside a large cenote—this one's a minipool of fresh- and saltwater full of tropical fish, perfect for a pre-meal swim. The restaurant's beef, chicken, and cheese are imported from the United States, and the burgers, chicken fajitas, and nachos are superb. On Sunday afternoon the expats living along the coast gather at Casa Cenote for a lavish barbecue featuring ribs, chicken, beef brisket, or lobster kebabs. The restaurant operates without electricity or a generator (perishables are packed in ice coolers) and closes at dark. ✉ *On dirt road off Rte. 307, between Xel-Há and Tulum, no phone. Reservations not accepted. No credit cards.*

$$$ ★ **Cabañas Ana y José.** Several two-story buildings face the beach at this small, well-loved hotel south of the ruins owned by a Mexican couple who left the big city to build this retreat at the edge of the Sian Ka'an biosphere. All rooms have fans, tile floors, hot-water showers, and hammock hooks; those on the second floor are cooler, thanks to the sea breezes. A new suite was added to this floor in 1995. The restaurant ($) is one of the best along this road, and management is more than

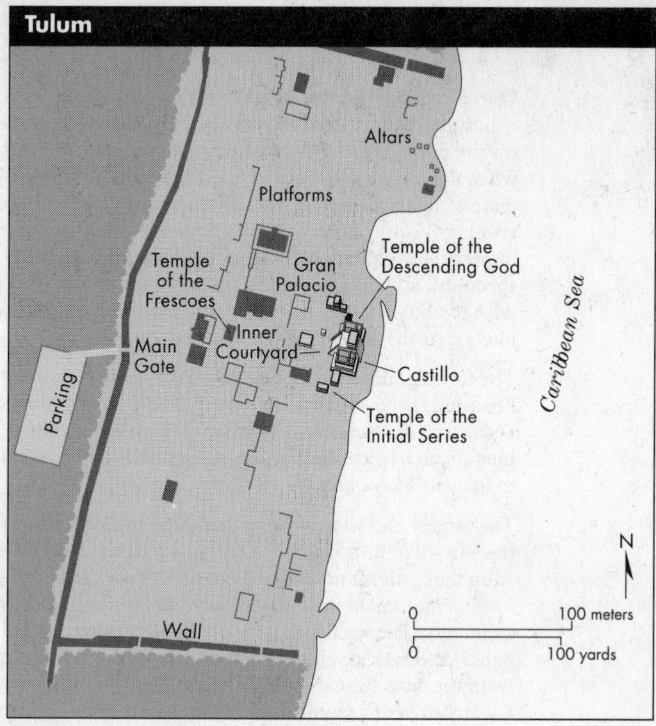

helpful. Mountain bikes are available for rent, making it easy for those without cars to visit the ruins and secluded beaches in the area. The electricity goes on only five hours a day between 5 in the afternoon and 10 at night. ✉ *On dirt road off Rte. 307 between ruins entrance and Tulum pueblo, 6 km (4 mi) south of ruins; Box 15, Tulum, Quintana Roo 77780,* ☎ *98/806022,* FAX *98/806021. 16 rooms. Restaurant. No credit cards.*

$ **Cabañas Tulum.** This property, idyllically situated in a coconut grove on a beach, is 7 km (4½ mi) south of the Tulum ruins on the dirt road leading to Boca Paila. Eighteen palapa bungalows with private bathrooms (but without fans) and an indoor-outdoor restaurant, bar, and game room make a good package. ✉ *Box 10, Tulum, Quintana Roo 77780,* ☎ *98/258295. 18 cabanas. Restaurant, bar, recreation room. No credit cards.*

Shopping

The **Mercado de los Artesanías** at the Tulum ruins contains at least 50 stalls displaying woven rugs, clay reproductions of Maya gods, and a wide array of tacky souvenirs.

Cobá

34 *37 km (22½ mi) northwest of Tulum, 167 km (109 mi) southwest of Cancún.*

Beautiful but barely explored, Cobá was once one of the most important city-states in the entire Maya domain. It now stands in solitude; the spell this remoteness casts is intensified by the silence at the ruins, broken occasionally by the shriek of a spider monkey or the call of a bird. Archaeologists estimate the presence of some 6,500 structures in the Cobá area, but only 5% have been uncovered, and it will take decades before the work is completed. The site is not inaccessible, however. Cobá is a 35-minute drive northwest of Tulum down a well-marked and well-paved road that leads straight through the jungle. Two tiny pueblos, **Macario Gómez** and **Balché,** with their clusters of thatch-roof white huts, are the only signs of habitation en route.

The city flourished from AD 400 to 1100, probably boasting a population of as many as 40,000 inhabitants. Situated on five lakes between coastal watchtowers and inland cities, its temple-pyramids towered over a vast jungle plain; one of them is 138 ft tall, the largest and highest in northern Yucatán. Cobá (meaning "ruffled waters") exercised economic control over the region through a network of at least 16 *sacbeob* (white stone roads), one of which, measuring 100 km (62 mi), is the longest in the Maya world. Cobá's massive, soaring structures and sheer size—the city once covered 210 square km (81 square mi)—made it a noteworthy sister nation to Tikal in northern Guatemala, to which it apparently had close cultural and commercial ties.

The first major grouping, off a path to your right as you enter the ruins, is the **Cobá Group,** whose pyramids are built around a sunken patio. At the near end of the group, facing a large plaza, you'll see the 79-ft-high Iglesia (church), where some Indians still place offerings and light candles in hopes of improving their harvests. Farther along the main path to your left is the **Chumuc Mul Group,** little of which has been excavated. The principal pyramid here is covered with the stucco remains of vibrantly painted motifs (*chumuc mul* means "stucco pyramid"). A kilometer past this site is the **Nohoch Mul** (Large Hill) **Group,** the highlight of which is the pyramid of the same name, the tallest at Cobá. The pyramid, which has 120 steps—equivalent to 12 stories—shares a plaza with Temple 10. The Descending God (also seen at Tulum) is depicted on a facade of the temple atop Nohoch Mul, from which the view is excellent. The unrestored **Crossroad Pyramid** opposite Nohoch Mul was the meeting point for three sacbeob.

Beyond the Nohoch Mul Group is the **Castillo;** its nine chambers are reached by a stairway. To the south are the remains of a ball court, including the stone ring through which the ball was hurled. From the main route follow the sign to **Las Pinturas Group,** named for the still discernible polychromatic friezes on the inner and outer walls of its large, patioed pyramid. Take the minor path for a kilometer to the **Macanxoc Group,** not far from the lake of the same name. The main pyramid at Macanxoc is accessible by a stairway. Many of the stelae here are intricately carved with dates and other symbols of the history of Cobá.

Cobá can be comfortably visited in a half day, but if you want to spend the night, opt for the Villa Arqueológica Cobá (☞ Dining and Lodging, *below*), operated by Club Med and only a 10-minute walk from the site along the shores of Lake Cobá. Spending the night is highly advised—the nighttime jungle sounds will lull you to sleep, and you'll be able to visit the ruins in solitude when they open at 8 AM. Even on a day trip, consider taking time out for lunch and a swim at the Villa—an oasis of French civilization—after the intense heat and mosquito-ridden humidity of the ruins. *Buses depart Cobá for Playa del Carmen and Valladolid twice daily. Check with your hotel and clerk at the ruins for times, which may not be exact.* 🎫 *$6.50; free Sun.* ⏲ *Daily 8–5.*

Dining and Lodging

$$ ★ ✕🏨 **Villa Arqueológica Cobá.** This Club Med property overlooks one of the region's vast lakes, where turtles swim to the hotel's dock for a breakfast of bread and rolls. Tastefully done in white stucco, with museum pieces throughout the property, the hotel has a clean, airy feel.

The air-conditioned rooms are small but they feel cozy, not claustrophobic. A handsome library features a large VCR and a pool table. Dining choices near the isolated Cobá ruins are quite limited, so the good restaurant here is an attractive option (food is not included in the room rates as at most other Club Med properties). ☎ *800/258–2633 for reservations,* ☎ FAX *987/42087. 40 rooms. Restaurant, bar, pool, tennis court, shop. AE, MC, V.*

$ ✕🏨 **El Bocadito.** Though nowhere near as lavish as the Villa Arqueológica (☞ *above*), El Bocadito is a friendly, satisfactory budget alternative and only a five-minute walk from the ruins. The simple, tiled rooms fill up quickly—if you're thinking of spending the night, stop here first before visiting the ruins. There is no hot water, and only fans to combat the heat, but the camaraderie of the clientele and staff makes up for the discomforts. The restaurant is decent, clean, and popular with tour groups. ✉ *On road to ruins, Apdo. 56, Valladolid, Yucatán, Mexico 97780, no phone. 8 rooms. Restaurant. No credit cards.*

Sian Ka'an and the Boca Paila Peninsula

35 *15 km (9½ mi) south of Tulum to Boca Paila turnoff, located within Sian Ka'an; 137 km (84 mi) south of Cancún.*

Sian Ka'an, meaning "where the sky is born," was first settled by the Xiu tribe from Central America in the 5th century BC. In 1987 the 1.3-million-acre Sian Ka'an Biosphere Reserve became one of UNESCO's internationally protected areas. Assisted by scientists, the local population makes a living through fishing, lobster harvests, and small farming and receives support from the low-impact tourism, biological research, and sustainable development programs under way. The program has started to meet with modest success.

The reserve, expanded in 1996 by 200,000 acres, constitutes 10% of the land in Quintana Roo and covers 100 km (62 mi) of coast; its approximately 27 sites of ruins scattered about are linked by a unique canal system—the only one of its kind in the Maya world in Mexico.

Many species of the once-flourishing wildlife have fallen into the endangered category, but the waters here still teem with rooster fish, bonefish, mojarra, snapper, shad, permit, sea bass, and crocodiles. Fly-fishing and fishing the flats for bonefish are especially popular, and the peninsula's few lodges run deep-sea fishing trips. Birders take launches out to Culebra (Rattlesnake Cay) or to Isla de Pájaros to view the pelicans, frigate birds, woodpeckers, sparrow hawks, and some 15 species of heron and egret. The more adventuresome travelers can explore some of the waterways' myriad caves or trek out to the tiny ruins of Muyil.

The best way to explore on your own is to enter via the Punta Allen turnoff, south of Cancún on the coastal road; you'll be on a secluded 35-km (22-mi) coastal strip of land that is part of the reserve.

The narrow, rough dirt road down the peninsula is dotted with campgrounds, fishing lodges, and deserted palapas and copra farms. It ends at **Punta Allen**, a fishing village whose main catch is the spiny lobster; it hosts several small guest houses. The road is filled with potholes; in the rainy season it may be completely impassable. Most fishing lodges along the way close for the rainy season in August and September, and accommodations are hard to come by. If you haven't booked ahead, start out early in the morning so you can get back to civilization before dark.

Dining and Lodging

$$$$ ★ ✕🏨 **Caphé-Ha.** Built as a private home by an American architect, this small guest house—between a lagoon and the ocean—is a perfect place to stay if you're interested in bonefishing or bird-watching. A two-bedroom house with a kitchen, bath, and living room, and a two-unit bungalow (with shared baths) are your choices; though neither has fans or electricity, all the windows have screens and catch the ocean breeze. A caretaker-chef from Mérida cooks meals that are served in the solar-powered community palapa. The room rates include breakfast and dinner; advance reservations must be accompanied by a 50% deposit, and a three-day or longer stay is required during high season. ✉ *30 km (19 mi) south of Tulum, on road to Sian Ka'an, 5 km (3 mi) past bridge at Boca Paila and around next rocky point,* ☎ *610/912–9392 for reservations. 1 villa, 1 bungalow. Restaurant, fishing. No credit cards.*

$$$$ ✕🏨 **Casa Blanca Lodge.** Punta Pájaros, to which this remote fishing resort provides unique access, is reputed to be one of the best places in the world for light-tackle saltwater fishing. The American-managed, all-inclusive lodge—just 100 ft from the ocean—is set on a rocky outcrop covered with palm trees. The lodge's nine large, modern guest rooms provide a pleasant tropical respite at dusk. The lodge is closed September through December but will open during that time for groups of four or more. Prepayment is required. To get here, you must take a charter flight from Cancún to the Punta Pájaros airstrip, or rent a car in Cancún and drive to Punta Allen (three hours). From there, it's a one-hour boat trip across the bay. ✉ *For reservations: Frontiers, Box 959, Wexford, PA 15090,* ☎ *412/935–1577 or 800/245–1950,* FAX *412/935–5388. 1-wk reservation required during high season with 50% prepayment. 9 rooms. Restaurant, bar, fishing. No credit cards.*

The North Caribbean Coast A to Z

Arriving and Departing

BY BUS

There is first-class and deluxe service on the **ADO** line (✉ Av. Juárez at Av. 5, ☎ 987/30109) between Playa del Carmen and Cancún, Valladolid, Chichén Itzá, Chetumal, Tulum, Xel-Há, Mexico City, and Mérida daily. **Autotransportes del Caribe** (✉ Av. Juárez, no phone) runs second-class buses to the above destinations, and deluxe express buses to Chetumal. **Autotransportes Oriente** (✉ Av. Juárez, no phone) has express service to Mérida eight times daily, and one bus daily to Cobá. **ATS** (✉ Av. Juárez at Av. 5, no phone) offers first-class service about every 20 minutes to Cancún.

BY FERRY

Ferries and jet foils—which can be picked up at the dock—run between Playa del Carmen and Cozumel about every two hours (more frequently in the early morning and evening); trips on the old ferry take about 40 minutes, those on the two enclosed hydrofoils 30 minutes. The fee varies depending on which boat you choose, but the one-way trip costs approximately between $4 and $6.

BY PLANE

Almost everyone who arrives by air into this region flies into Cancún (☞ Cancún A to Z, *above*).

Getting Around

BY CAR

The entire coast, from Punta Sam near Cancún to the main border crossing to Belize at Chetumal, is traversable on Route 307.This straight road is entirely paved and has been widened into four lanes to Playa del Carmen; eventually, it will be widened as far south as Chetumal (but be careful—many motorists see the road's straightness as an opportunity to speed). Gas stations are becoming more prevalent, but it's still a good idea to fill the tank whenever you can; there are gas stations in Cancún, Puerto Juárez, Puerto Morelos, Playa del Carmen, Tulum, Felipe Carrillo Puerto, and Chetumal.

BY PLANE

In **Chetumal,** the airport is on the southwestern edge of town, along Avenida Alvaro Obregón where it turns into Route 186. **Bonanza** (☏ 983/28306) has daily flights from Chetumal to Cancún. **Aerocaribe** (☏ 983/26675) has flights to Cancún four times a week.

BY TAXI

Taxis can be hired in Cancún to go as far as Playa del Carmen, Tulum, or Akumal, but the price is steep unless you have many passengers. Fares run about $55 or more to Playa alone; between Playa and Tulum or Akumal, expect to pay at least $25. It's much cheaper from Playa to Cancún, with taxi fare running about $30; negotiate before you hop into the cab. There's a taxi stand at the entrance to Akumal.

Contacts and Resources

CAR RENTAL

In **Playa del Carmen,** car-rental agencies include **National** (✉ Hotel Molcas, ☏ 987/30360; 987/59000 Akumal), **Hertz** (✉ Plaza Marina Playacar 40, ☏ 987/30703), and **Budget** (✉ Hotel Continental Plaza Playacar, ☏ 987/30100). If you want air-conditioning, reserve your car in advance.

EMERGENCIES

Playa del Carmen. Police (✉ Av. Juárez, between Avs. 15a and 20a, next to post office, ☏ 987/30021). **Red Cross** (✉ Av. Héroes de Chapultapec at Independencia, ☏ 987/30045).

GUIDED TOURS

Although some guided tours are available in this area, the roads are quite good for the most part, so renting a car is an efficient and enjoyable alternative: Most of the sights you'll see along this stretch are natural, and you can hire a guide at the ruins sites.

Ecotourism. Naviera Asterix (☏ 98/864847 or 99/864270 in Cancún) offers guided yacht tours to Contoy Island. **Ecolomex Tours** (☏ 98/843805 or 98/871776 in Cancún) does off-the-beaten-path trips to little-known areas along the coast. **Ava Tours** (☏ 98/848676 or 98/848696 in Cancún) specializes in aerial tours of the coast. All will pick up at hotels along the coast from Puerto Morelos to Playa del Carmen.

An excellent tour of Sian Ka'an Reserve and a Maya temple can be arranged through the private, nonprofit **Amigos de Sian Ka'an** (✉ Plaza América, Av. Cobá, No. 5, Suites 48–50, Cancún, QR 77500, ☏ 98/849583, FAX 98/873080).

Maya Ruins. Mayaland Gray Line Tours (✉ Hotel America, Av. Tulum at Calle Brisa, ☏ 98/872450 or 800/235–4079, FAX 98/872438 in Cancún; ✉ Las Molcas Hotel, Calle 1 Sur between Av. 5 and the ferry pier, ☏ 987/31106 or 800/235–4079 in Playa del Carmen), one of the Yucatán's leading tour companies, is now running tours to Chichén Itzá from hotels around Punta Bete, Playa del Carmen, and Akumal.

MEDICAL CLINICS

Chetumal: Hospital General (✉ Av. Andres Quintana Roo, ☏ 983/21932). **Playa del Carmen:** Centro de Salud (✉ Av. Juárez at

Avenida 15a, ☎ 987/21230, ext. 147); or **Dr. Victor Macias,** a bilingual physician (⊠ Av. 35 between Calles 21 and 4, ☎ 987/30493).

TRAVEL AGENCIES

There are more major travel agencies and tour operators up and down the coast than before, and first-class hotels in Playa del Carmen, Puerto Aventuras, and Akumal usually have their own in-house travel services.

VISITOR INFORMATION

Both the **tourist office** (⊠ Palacio del Gobierno, 2nd floor, ☎ 983/20266, FAX 983/20855) and **tourist information booth** (⊠ Av. Héroes, opposite Av. Efraín Aguilar, ☎ 983/23663) in **Chetumal** are open weekdays 9–2:30 and 4–7.

The **tourist information booth** (⊠ 1 block from beach on Av. 5, no phone) in Playa del Carmen has very sporadic hours. The **Playa del Carmen Hotel Association** has a new information service (⊠ Av. 30 and Calle 6 Sur, ☎ 987/30646), open weekdays 9–1 and 3:30–5:30 and Saturday 9–2. In the United States, call 800/467–5292.

THE STATE OF CAMPECHE

Updated by Patricia Alisau

Campeche, the least-visited part of the Yucatán, is not for everybody, but the adventuresome visitor will discover both charm and mystery here. Three-hundred-year-old cannons point across the Gulf of Mexico from fortress battlements, recalling pirate days and lending an air of romance to the walled capital city of Campeche. Beyond the city, ancient pyramids and ornate temple facades from the area's Maya past lie hidden deep in tropical forests.

Most of the State of Campeche is flat—never higher than 1,000 ft above sea level—but more than 60% of its territory is covered by jungle, where precious mahogany and cedar abound. Campeche's economy is based on agriculture, fishing, logging, salt, tourism, and—since the 1970s—hydrocarbons, of which it is the largest producer in Mexico. But most of the oil industry is concentrated at the southern end of the state, near Ciudad del Carmen.

Campeche City

The city of Campeche has a time-weathered and lovely feel to it: No self-conscious, ultramodern tourist glitz here, just a friendly city by the sea (population 270,000), proud of its heritage and welcoming all to share in it. That good-humored, open-minded attitude is enshrined in the Spanish adjective *campechano,* meaning hearty and jovial.

Because it has been walled since 1686, most of the historic downtown is neatly contained in an area measuring just five blocks by nine blocks. The old city, or "Viejo Campeche," looks fresh with newly painted and remodeled buildings and new signs guiding tourists to attractions along the streets. *Baluartes* (bastions) in various stages of disrepair or reconstruction stand on seven corners. These were once connected by a 3-km (2-mi) wall in a hexagonal fortification that was built to safeguard the city against the pirates who kept ransacking it. However, it was not until 1771, when Fuerte San Miguel was built on a hilltop on the outskirts of town, that pirates finally ceased their attacks. Only short stretches of the wall exist, and two stone archways—one facing the sea, the other the land—are all that remain of the four gates that provided the only means of access to Campeche.

Avenida Ruíz Cortines is Campeche's waterfront boulevard with a broad
36 pedestrian walkway called the **malecón.** The sidewalk runs the length

of the waterfront, from the Ramada Inn south to the outskirts of town, and is popular with joggers and strollers enjoying the cool sea breezes and view at sunset.

37 A modernistic building resembling a flying saucer houses the **Congreso del Estado,** the State Congress building, where government activities take place. One block inland from the malecón, on Avenida 16 de Septiembre, the Congreso del Estado shares a broad plaza with the
38 much taller **Palacio de Gobierno,** dubbed El Tocadiscos (The Jukebox) by locals because of its outlandish facade.

39 The **Baluarte San Carlos,** the bastion where Avenida 16 de Septiembre curves around and becomes Circuito Baluartes, houses the Sala de las Fortificaciones (Chamber of the Fortifications), containing scale models of the original defense system and the Museo Grafico de la Ciudad, or City Museum, with photographs of the city as it developed. Don't miss the dungeon inside the bastion, where captured pirates were jailed.

40 The **Ex-Templo de San José,** built by the Jesuits in 1756, occupies the full city block between Calles 10 and 12 and Calles 63 and 65. Its immense portal is completely covered with blue Talavera tiles and crowned by seven narrow, stone finials that resemble the roof combs on many Maya temples. Campeche's first lighthouse, built in 1864, sits atop a brick pillar next to the church. *Tues.–Fri. 9–2 and 5–10.*

41 The **Iglesia de San Román** sits just outside the intramural boundary in the barrio of the same name at Calles 10 and Bravo. The church became central to the lives of the Indians when an ebony image of Christ, the "Black Christ," was brought in about 1565. The legend goes that a ship that refused to carry the statue was wrecked, whereas the ship that did take it on board reached Campeche in record time. To this day, the Feast of San Román—when the icon is carried through the streets as part of a procession—is the biggest such celebration in Campeche.

42 On **Calle 59,** between Calles 8 and 18, once stood some of Campeche's finest homes. Geometric motifs decorate the cornices, and the windows are gaily adorned with iron latticework. The richest inhabitants built as close to the sea as possible, in case escape became necessary. Just
43 east of Calle 12, the architecture and ambience of the tiny **Iglesia de San Francisquito** do justice to historic Calle 59's old-fashioned beauty.

44 Old Campeche ends at the **Puerta de Tierra,** the only one of the four city gates that still stands with its basic structure intact. *Calle 18 at Calle 59. $12. Sound-and-light shows weekdays 8:30 PM with a translation in English.*

To take in the heart of a true Mexican inner city, stroll through the
45 **Mercado Municipal,** where locals congregate en masse to shop for seafood, produce, and housewares. The market is open daily from dawn to dusk.

46 The centerpiece of the old city is **Parque Principal** or **Plaza de la Independencia** (Bounded by Calle 10 on the east, Calle 8 on the west, and Calle 55 on the north), the southern side of which—Calle 57—is lined with several agreeable cafés and hotels. Concerts are held here on Sunday evenings.

47 On the south side of Parque Principal, the **Baluarte de la Soledad** houses the Museo de los Estela Dr. Roman Pina Chan in a separate section. The largest of the bastions, this one has comparatively complete parapets and embrasures that offer a sweeping view of the cathedral, the

Baluarte de la Soledad, **47**
Baluarte San Carlos, **39**
Baluarte Santiago, **50**
Calle 59, **42**
Catedral, **48**
Congreso del Estado, **37**
Ex-Templo de San José, **40**
Fuerte de San Miguel, **53**
Fuerte San José, **52**
Iglesia de San Francisco, **51**
Iglesia de San Franciscquito, **43**
Iglesia de San Román, **41**
Malecón, **36**
Mansión Carvajal, **49**
Mercado Municipal, **45**
Palacio del Gobierno, **38**
Parque Principal, **46**
Puerta de Tierra, **44**

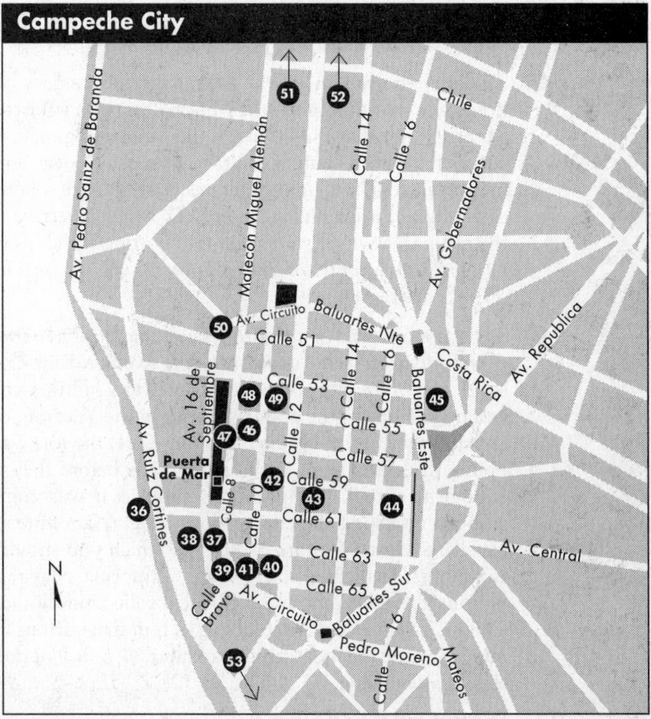

municipal buildings, and the Gulf of Mexico. Artifacts are housed inside and around the outside of the museum—the museum includes 20 beautiful and well-proportioned Maya stelae and other pieces from various periods. This museum is not to be missed. ✉ *Calle 8 at Calle 57, no phone.* 🎫 *50¢.* ⏲ *Tues.–Sat. 8–8, Sun. 8–1.*

48 An exception to the generally somber architecture rule of colonial Campeche, the **catedral** took two centuries (from 1650 to 1850) to build and incorporates neoclassical and Renaissance elements. The present cathedral occupies the site of Montejo's original church, which was built in 1540 on what is now Calle 55, between Calles 8 and 10. Inside, the pièce de résistance is the magnificent ebony Holy Sepulcher.

49 Built in the early 20th century by one of the wealthiest plantation owners in Yucatán, the opulent, eclectic **Mansión Carvajal** did time as the Hotel Señorial before arriving at its present role as an office for the Family Institute run by the state governor's wife and her staff. ✉ *Calle 10 s/n, between Calles 53 and 55, no phone.* 🎫 *Free.* ⏲ *Mon.–Sat. 8–2:30 and 5–8:30.*

50 The **Baluarte Santiago,** the last of the bastions to be built (1704), has been transformed into a botanical garden. The original bastion was demolished at the turn of the century, but it was rebuilt in the 1950s. ✉ *Calle 8 at Calle 49,* ☎ *981/66829.* 🎫 *Free.* ⏲ *Tues.–Sat. 9–1 and 4:30–8, Sun. 9–1.*

51 Away from the city center, in a residential neighborhood, stands the beautifully restored **Iglesia de San Francisco** (✉ Av. Gustavo Díaz Ordaz at Av. Francisco I. Madero) (1546), the oldest church site in Campeche. Some contend it marks the spot where the first Mass on the North American continent was said, in 1517 (the same claim has

been made for Veracruz and Cozumel). One of Cortés's grandsons was baptized here, and the baptismal font still stands.

52 The lofty **Fuerte San José** at the northern boundary of the old city is home to a new museum—the **Museo de Armas y Barcos,** which is half of the exhibit that used to be in the Museo Regional. The display focuses on the 18th-century military weapons of siege and defense in the many wars fought against the pirates. Scale ships-in-a-bottle, manuscripts, and religious art can also be seen. The view is terrific from the top of the ramparts, which were used for spotting the ships of the invaders. ⊠ *North of downtown on Av. Francisco Morazon s/n, no phone.* *50¢.* ⏲ *Tues.–Sun. 8–8.*

53 At the opposite end of town from Fuerte San José is **Fuerte de San Miguel.** A well-marked scenic drive turns off Avenida Ruíz Cortines near the south end of the city and winds its way to a hilltop, where the fortress commands one of the grandest views in the Yucatán, overlooking the city and the Gulf of Mexico. Built in 1771, the fort was positioned to bombard enemy ships with cannonballs before they could get close enough to attack Campeche; as soon as it was completed, pirates stopped attacking the city without a fight. The fort now houses the excellent **Museo Cultura Maya,** for which you should allow at least two hours. Dedicated solely to the Campeche Maya and with explanations in English, the archaeological collection should not be missed. The six exquisite jade funeral masks found at various tombs at Calakmul comprise the most striking exhibit. ⊠ *South of downtown on Av. Resurgimiento s/n, no phone.* *50¢.* ⏲ *Tues.–Sat. 8–8, Sun. 8–1.*

Dining and Lodging

$$ ★ ✕ **La Pigua.** A favorite with local professionals lingering over long lunches, La Pigua is perhaps the best seafood restaurant in town, with the most pleasant ambience. The long, glass-walled dining room is surrounded by trees and plants. ⊠ *Av. Miguel Alemán 197-A,* ☎ *981/13365. MC, V. No dinner.*

$ ★ ✕ **Marganzo.** This rustically furnished restaurant, a half block south of the plaza, is a popular tourist spot—which is not to its detriment. It's impeccably clean, with a colorful decor, and the seafood dishes served at lunch and dinner are very characteristic of the cuisine for which this region is known. ⊠ *Calle 8, No. 267,* ☎ *981/13898. AE, MC, V.*

$ ✕ **Miramar.** This restaurant across from Hotel Castelmar offers fabulous *huevos motuleños* (fried eggs smothered in refried beans and garnished with peas, chopped ham, shredded cheese, and tomato sauce), red snapper, shellfish, soups, and meat dishes. The heavy wooden tables and chairs and the paintings of coats-of-arms give Miramar a colonial feel. ⊠ *Calle 8, No. 293 A,* ☎ *981/62883. MC, V.*

$$ ★ **Ramada Inn.** At the luxurious Ramada, fairly large rooms, with all the necessary amenities, are decorated in shades of blue and have rattan furnishings; balconies overlook the pool or the bay. The lobby restaurant, El Poquito, is extremely popular with locals at breakfast and at night before the disco Atlantis opens. ⊠ *Av. Ruíz Cortines 51, along waterfront,* ☎ *981/62233 or 800/228–9898,* FAX *981/11618. 149 rooms. Restaurant, coffee shop, pool, exercise room, shop, dance club, travel services. AE, MC, V.*

$ **Alhambra.** A great choice away from the bustle of the city, the Alhambra is a modern hotel facing the waterfront near the university. A wide-screen TV plays softly in the lobby; TVs in the rooms get U.S. stations, sometimes including CNN. Rooms are carpeted and clean, with king- and double-size beds. ⊠ *Av. Resurgimiento 85, between Avs.*

Universidad and Augusto Melgar, ☎ *981/66822,* FAX *981/66132. 98 rooms. Restaurant, bar, pool, tennis court. MC, V.*

$ ★ **Colonial.** This building—the former home of a high-ranking army lieutenant—dates back to 1850 but was made over as a hotel in the 1940s, when its wonderful tiles were added. As befits a colonial mansion, all rooms are delightfully different in structure but are basically pastel-colored and spacious with ceiling fans or air-conditioning, cool cotton bedding, good mattresses, tile bathrooms, window screens, and phones. In addition, Rooms 16, 18, 27, and 28 have lots of windows with ambient light and wonderful views of the cathedral and city at night. The well-kept public areas include two foliated patios, a small sun roof for sunning, and a sitting room on the second floor for reading. Guests breakfast at a small eatery down the street. ✉ *Calle 14, No. 122, between Calles 55 and 57,* ☎ *981/62222 or 981/62630. 30 rooms. No credit cards.*

$ **Debliz.** Those traveling by car may wish to stay outside town at this modern hotel in a residential area north of the city. Room amenities at the four-story, elevator-equipped property, renovated in 1994, include color TV, reading lamps, and double beds. The Debliz can seem deserted and lonely—until the tour buses that frequent the place pull into the parking lot. ✉ *Av. Las Palmas 55, off Av. Pedro Sainz de Baranda, near baseball stadium,* ☎ *981/52222,* FAX *981/52277. 120 rooms. Restaurant, bar, coffee shop, pool, free parking. AE, MC, V.*

$ **Del Paseo.** Located in the quiet San Román neighborhood, a block from the ocean, this hotel is cheerful and well lit. Rooms, painted in a soft rose with tasteful rattan furniture, have balconies, cable TV, and air-conditioning. A glass-roofed atrium next to the lobby is lovely, with park benches and plants. ✉ *Calle 8, No. 215,* ☎ *981/10084 or 981/10100,* FAX *981/10097. 40 rooms. Restaurant, bar, shop. MC, V.*

$ **El Regis.** This seven-room hotel two blocks from the plaza has to be the best bargain in town with prices at the low end of the $ category. Opened in March 1996, the Regis is a lovely two-story colonial home with a humongous wooden front door, wrought-iron staircase, high ceilings, balconies, and an airy inner atrium. All rooms are spic-and-span with new black-and-white tile floors, two double beds, a cupboard closet, shower in the bathroom, and cream-color walls. Four rooms come with air-conditioning and a TV with Spanish channels. The rest have overhead fans. The front doors close at 11 PM but there's a night watchman who opens up for guests who come in later. ✉ *Calle 12, No. 148, between Calles 55 and 57,* ☎ *981/53175. 7 rooms. No credit cards.*

$ **Lopez.** Cheerful pink, yellow, and white walls and an open, airy ambience make this little two-story hotel a pleasant place to stay. Standard rooms include colonial-style desks and armoires, luggage stands, and easy chairs. Although the restaurant (closed Sunday) serves basic Continental fare, it's a convenient enough stop for breakfast, lunch, or dinner. ✉ *Calle 12, No. 189, between Calles 61 and 63,* ☎ *981/63344,* FAX *981/62488. 39 rooms. Restaurant. No credit cards.*

Nightlife and the Arts

If you're in the mood to dance, try Campeche's two discos, **Atlantis** (✉ Ramada Inn, ☎ 981/62233), the only chic club in town, where politicians go to party, or the student-oriented **El Dragon** (✉ Sajuge complex on Av. Resurgimiento, ½ block from Alhambra Hotel, ☎ 981/11810 or 981/64289). Both are open Thursday through Saturday nights only. Two of Campeche's most conveniently located movie theaters, **Cine Estelar** (✉ Av. Miguel Alemán and Calle 49-B) and **Cine Alhambra** (✉ At shopping center at Hotel Alhambra, Av. Resurgimiento 85), show

American films, with Spanish subtitles; they're only open on weekend nights.

Outdoor Activities and Sports

Hunting, fishing, and birding are popular throughout the State of Campeche. Contact Don José Sansores at his office in the Hotel Castelmar (✉ Calle 61, No. 2, ☎ 981/62356, FAX 981/10624) in Campeche, or his office at the Snook Inn hotel in Champotón (☎ 982/80018, FAX 981/10624) for bookings and for information regarding the regulations and best areas for each sport.

Shopping

Folk art in Campeche is a little different from the rest of Yucatán's handicrafts as it's a seaport. Black coral and mother-of-pearl jewelry, seashells, and ships-in-a-bottle are everywhere. You can also find basketry, leather goods, embroidered cloth, and clay trinkets. With a few exceptions, listed below, most of the shops sell cheap-looking trinkets.

Visit the **municipal market** (✉ Circuito Baluartes at Calle 53), at the eastern end of the city, for crafts and food. The brand-new **Casa de Artesanía** (✉ Calle 55, No. 25, no phone), is operated by the government-run Family Institute; you'll find well-made embroidered dresses and blouses, regional dress for men and women, hammocks, hats, lawn chairs, stucco reproductions of Maya motifs, and much more. **Veleros** (✉ Ah-Kin-Pech shopping center, ☎ 981/12446), formerly called Aresanía Boutique, is owned by craftsman David Pérez and stocks his miniature ships, coral jewelry, furniture with nautical motifs, and, new to the market, jewelry fashioned from sanded and polished bull's horns.

Campeche City and Route 261 toward Mérida

This is by far the longer—and more interesting—way to reach the Yucatán capital. The highway takes you through green hills covered by low scrub with occasional stands of tall, dark forest. In the valleys, cornfields and citrus orchards surround the occasional thatched-roof hut.

Edzná

55 km (34 mi) southeast of Campeche City.

Archaeologists consider Edzná one of the peninsula's most important ruins because of the crucial transitional role it played among several architectural styles. Occupied from 300 BC to AD 900, the site was not discovered until 1927 and although restoration work is going ahead now, there was little funding for it after its initial excavation in 1943. A tourist facility with a cafeteria, rest rooms, and bookshop opened in 1996 here as well as at the rest of Campeche's major ruin sites. The 6-square-km (2-square-mi) expanse of savanna is situated in a broad valley prone to flooding. Surrounding the site are vast networks of irrigation canals, the remnants of a highly sophisticated hydraulic system that channeled rainwater and water from the Champotón River into human-made *chultunes,* or wells. Commanding center stage in the **Gran Acrópolis,** or Great Acropolis complex, is the **Pirámide de los Cinco Pisos** (Five-Story Pyramid), which rises 102 ft. The temple was so constructed that, during certain dates of the year, the setting sun would illuminate the mask of the sun god, Itzamná, located inside one of the pyramid's rooms. Carved into Building 414 of the Great Acropolis are some grotesque masks of the sun god with huge and sinister protruding eye sockets. Local lore holds that Edzná, which means the House of the Gestures, or Grimaces, may have been named for these images.

If you're not driving, consider taking one of the inexpensive day trips offered by most travel agencies in Campeche; this is far easier than trying to get to Edzná by bus. If you do go by bus, be forewarned that you must walk about 1 km (½ mi) from the main road to the ruins. Check and double check with the driver about return buses—they are few and far between, and many tourists have been stranded until the next day. ✉ *From Campeche City, take Rte. 261 east for 44 km (27 mi) to Cayal, then Rte. 188 southeast for 18 km (11 mi).* 🎫 *$2.* ⏲ *Daily 8–5.*

Hopelchén

41 km (25 mi) north of the Edzná turnoff on Rte. 261.

Hopelchén—the name means Place of the Five Wells—is a traditional Maya town noted for the lovely Franciscan church built in honor of St. Francis of Padua in 1667. Corn, beans, tobacco, fruit, and henequen are cultivated in this rich agricultural center.

Bolonchén de Rejón

34 km (21 mi) north of Hopelchén.

Just short of the state line, Bolonchén de Rejón is named for the adjacent Cave of the Nine Wells, where legend says a distressed Maya girl took refuge from the vagaries of love. In ancient times, cenotes deep in the extensive cave system provided an emergency water source during droughts. Visitors can admire the delicate limestone formations in the upper part of the cave on an easy two-hour guided tour booked through a travel agency in the city of Campeche city; there are no guides at the site. 🎫 *$2.* ⏲ *Daily 8–5.*

Hochob

41 km (25 mi) south of Hopelchén.

The small Maya ruin of Hochob is an excellent example of the Chenes architectural style, which flowered in the classical period from about AD 200 to 900. Found throughout central and southern Campeche, Chenes-style temples are easily recognized by their elaborate stucco facades forming giant masks of jaguars, birds, or other creatures, with doorways representing the beasts' open jaws. Since work began at Hochob in the early 1980s, eight temples and palaces have been excavated at the site, including two that have been restored to their original grandeur. ✉ *South of Hopelchén on Dzibalchén–Chenko road, no phone.* 🎫 *Free.* ⏲ *Daily 8–5.*

Dzilibnocac

25 km (16 mi) east of Hochob.

Dzilibnocac, reached by a good but unpaved road, was a fair-size ceremonial center between AD 250 and 900. Although at least seven temple pyramids have been located here, the only one that has been excavated is the Palacio Principal, an unusual rounded pyramid resembling a smaller version of the one at Uxmal and combining elements of the Puuc and Chenes architectural styles. ✉ *East of Hochob on Iturbide road, no phone.* 🎫 *Free.* ⏲ *Daily 8–5.*

The State of Campeche A to Z

Arriving and Departing

BY BUS

ADO (✉ Av. Gobernadores 289 at Calle 45, along Rte. 261 to Mérida, ☎ 981/62802), a first-class line, runs buses to Campeche from Ciudad del Carmen and Mérida every half hour. The deluxe **Expreso del Caribe** (☎ 981/13973) travels between Campeche, Mérida, Villahermosa, and Cancún. Buses depart from the Plaza Ah-Kim-Pech on Avenida Pedro Sainz de Baranda, No. 120. There is less desirable second-class service on **Autobuses del Sur** (☎ 981/63445) from Chetumal, Ciudad del Carmen, Escárcega, Mérida, Palenque, Tuxtla Gutiérrez, Villahermosa, and intermediate points throughout the Yucatán Peninsula.

BY CAR

Campeche can be reached from Mérida in about 1½ hours along the 160-km (99-mi) *via corta* (short way, Route 180). The alternative route, the 250-km (155-mi) *via larga* (long way, Route 261), takes at least three hours but crosses the major Maya ruins of Uxmal, Kabah, and Sayil.

BY PLANE

Aeromexico (☎ 981/65678) has one flight daily from Mexico City to Campeche City.

Getting Around

BY BUS

The municipal bus system covers all of Campeche City, but you can easily visit the major sights on foot. Public buses run along Avenida Ruíz Cortines and cost under $1.

BY TAXI

Taxis can be hailed on the street in Campeche City, or—more reliably—commissioned from the main taxi stand (✉ Calle 8 between Calles 55 and 53, ☎ 981/62366 or 981/65230) or at stands by the bus stations and market. Because of the scarcity of taxis, it's quite common to share them with other people headed in the same direction as you. Don't be surprised to see one already occupied slow down to where you are standing if the cab driver thinks he can pick up another fare.

Contacts and Resources

CAR RENTAL

There is a **Hertz** representative at the Torres de Crital building in Campeche City (✉ Av. Ruíz Cortines 112, ☎ 981/12106) and the airport (☎ 981/68848).

EMERGENCIES

Throughout the state, call **06** locally in case of emergency.

Campeche City. Police (✉ Av. Resurgimiento s/n, ½ block from Hotel Alhambra, ☎ 981/62329). **Red Cross** (✉ Av. Resurgimiento s/n, ☎ 981/52411).

MEDICAL CLINICS

In Campeche City, **Hospital General** (✉ Av. Central at Circuito Baluartes, ☎ 981/60920 or 981/64233) and **Social Security Clinic** (✉ Av. Lopez Mateos s/n, ☎ 981/65202) are both open 24 hours for emergencies.

TRAVEL AGENCIES AND TOUR OPERATORS

Campeche City. American Express/VIPs (✉ Prolongación Calle 59, Edificio Belmar, Depto. 5, ☎ 981/11010 or 981/11000, FAX 981/68333); **Viajes Campeche** (✉ Calle 10, No. 339, ☎ 981/65233, FAX 981/62844);

and **Destinos Maya** (✉ Av. Miguel Aleman no. 162, locale 106, ☎ 981/13726; 713/440-0291 or 713/440-0253 in the U.S.; FAX 981/10934).

VISITOR INFORMATION

Campeche City. The **Tourist Office** (✉ Av. Ruiz Cortines s/n, across the street from the Palacio de Gobierno, ☎ 981/65593 or 981/66829) has moved to a new location, open daily 9–3 and 5–8; there's an information booth at the Baluarte de Santiago at the Botanical Gardens.

Ciudad del Carmen. Tourist office (✉ Palacio Municipal on the main plaza, ☎ 938/20311 or 938/21137) is open weekdays 9–3 and 6–9.

THE STATE OF YUCATÁN

Updated by Patricia Alisau

Almost five centuries after the conquest, Yucatán state remains one of the last great strongholds of Mexico's indigenous population. To this day, in fact, many Maya do not even speak Spanish, primarily because of the peninsula's geographic and, hence, cultural isolation from the rest of the country.

Physically, too, Yucatán differs from the rest of the country. Its geography and wildlife have more in common with Florida and Cuba—with which it was probably once connected—than with the central Mexican plateau and mountains. A mostly flat limestone slab possessing almost no bodies of water, it is rife with underground cenotes, caves with stalactites, small hills, and intense jungle.

It is, of course, the celebrated Maya ruins, Chichén Itzá and Uxmal especially, that bring most tourists to Yucatán, but small towns such as Valladolid, while bereft of star-quality sightseeing, charm visitors with their very unpretentiousness. Mérida, the capital, has excellent restaurants and markets and a unique mix of Maya, Spanish, and French architectural styles.

Mérida

There is a marvelous eccentricity about Mérida. Fully urban, with maddeningly slow-moving traffic, it has a self-sufficient, self-contented air that would suggest a small town more than a state capital of some 600,000 inhabitants (locals say there are about 1 million). Gaily pretentious turn-of-the-century buildings have an Iberian-Moorish flair for the ornate, but most of the architecture is low-lying, and although the city sprawls, it is not imposing. Grandiose colonial facades adorned with iron grillwork, carved wooden doors, and archways conceal marble tiles and lush gardens; horse-drawn carriages hark back to the city's heyday as the wealthiest capital in Mexico.

Mérida is a city of subtle contrasts, from its opulent yet faded facades to its residents, very European yet very Maya. The Indian presence is unmistakable: People are short and dark-skinned, with sculpted bones and almond eyes; women pad about in *huipiles* (hand-embroidered, sacklike white dresses), and craftsmen and vendors from the outlying villages come to town in their huaraches.

Mérida is the cultural and intellectual center of the peninsula, with museums, schools, and attractions that greatly enhance the traveler's insights into the history and character of Yucatán. Consider making it one of the first stops in your travels, and make sure your visit includes a Sunday, when traffic is light and the city seems to revert to a more gracious era. Sunday is also the day when admission to archaeological sites is free.

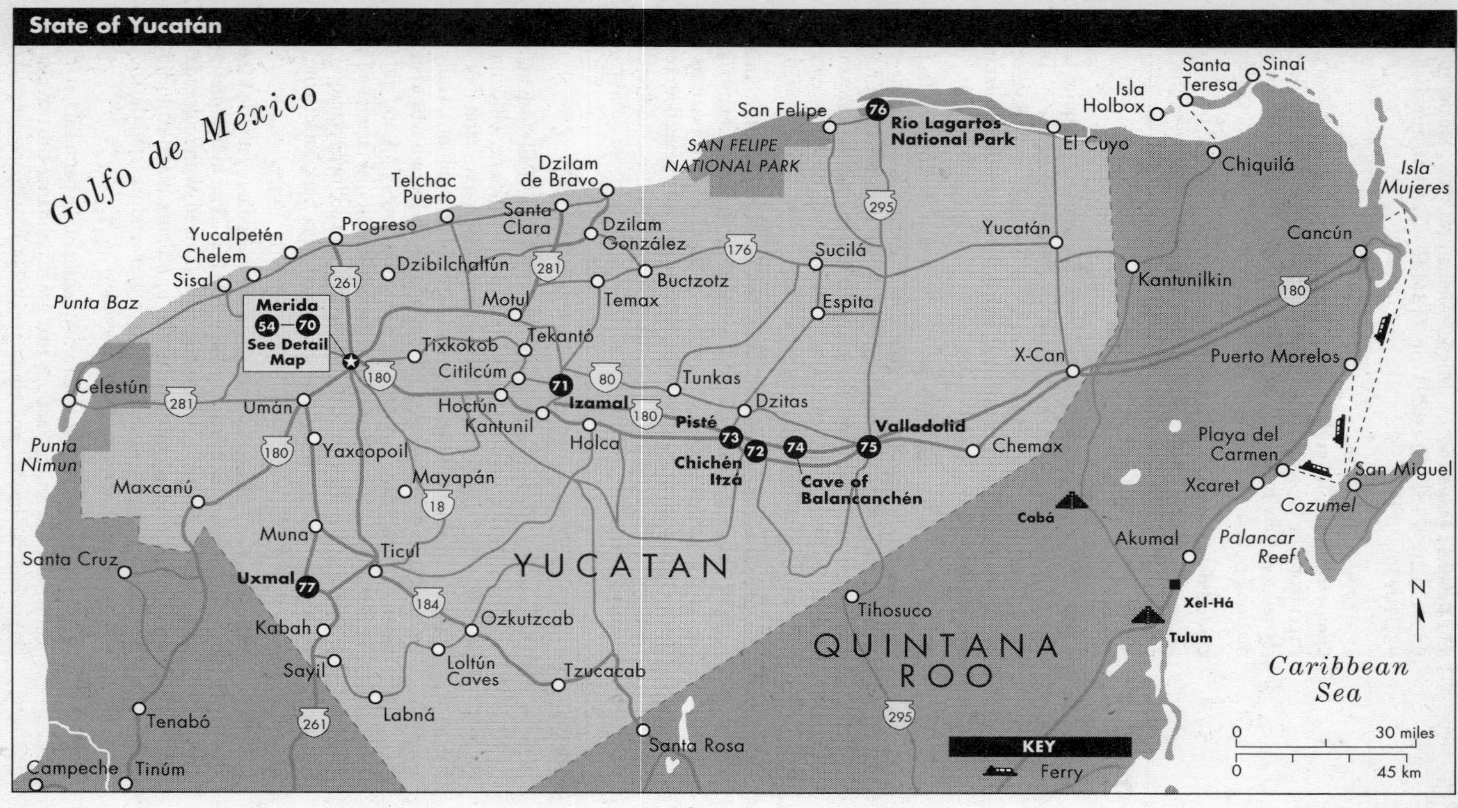
State of Yucatán
Golfo de México
Caribbean Sea
YUCATAN
QUINTANA ROO
KEY
Ferry
0 30 miles
0 45 km
N
Isla Mujeres
Sinaí
Santa Teresa
Chiquilá
Isla Holbox
El Cuyo
Cancún
Kantunilkin
Puerto Morelos
San Miguel
Cozumel
Playa del Carmen
Xcaret
Palancar Reef
Akumal
Xel-Há
Tulum
Cobá
X-Can
Chemax
Yucatán
Río Lagartos National Park
Valladolid
Cave of Balancanchén
San Felipe
SAN FELIPE NATIONAL PARK
Sucilá
Espita
Dzitas
Tunkas
Pisté
Chichén Itzá
Tihosuco
Santa Rosa
Buctzotz
Dzilam González
Temax
Dzilam de Bravo
Izamal
Holca
Santa Clara
Tekantó
Kantunil
Motul
Citilcúm
Hoctún
Tixkokob
Dzibilchaltún
Telchac Puerto
Progreso
Mayapán
Tzucacab
Ozkutzcab
Loltún Caves
Ticul
Labná
Yaxcopoil
Merida
54—70
See Detail Map
Umán
Muna
Uxmal
Kabah
Sayil
Yucalpetén
Chelem
Sisal
Punta Baz
Celestún
Punta Nimun
Maxcanú
Santa Cruz
Tenabó
Tinúm
Campeche
180
295
176
80
281
261
18
184
71
72
73
74
75
76
77

54 The **zócalo** (main square), which the Méridanos also call by its traditional names—the **Plaza Principal** and **Plaza de la Independencia**—was laid out in 1542 on the ruins of T'hó, the Maya city demolished to make way for Mérida, and is still the focal point around which the most important public buildings cluster. The plaza is bordered to the east and west by Calles 60 and 62 and to the north and south by Calles 61 and 63.

55 The **Casa de Montejo** sits on the south side of the plaza, on Calle 63. Montejo—father and son—conquered the peninsula and founded Mérida in 1542; they built this stately palace 10 years later. The property remained with the family until the late 1970s, when it was restored and converted into a bank. Built in the French style during Mérida's heyday as the world's henequen capital, it now represents the city's finest—and oldest—example of colonial Plateresque architecture, which typically features elaborate ornamentation. Step into the building weekdays between 9 and 5 to glimpse the lushly foliated inner patio.

56 The west side of the main square is occupied by the 17th-century **Palacio Municipal** (⊠ Calle 62 between Calles 61 and 63)—the city hall—which is painted yellow and trimmed with white arcades, balustrades, and the national coat of arms.

57 Occupying the northeast corner of the main square is the **Palacio del Gobierno,** or Governor's Palace (⊠ Calle 61 between Calles 60 and 62), built in 1885 on the site of the Casa Real (Royal House). The upper floor of the Governor's Palace contains Fernando Castro Pacheco's murals of the history of Yucatán, painted in 1978.

58 The oldest **catedral** on the North American mainland stands catercorner from the Palacio del Gobierno. Begun in 1561, it took several hundred Maya laborers, working with stones from the pyramids of the ravaged Maya city, 36 years to complete. Its somber Renaissance-style facade is stark and unadorned. Inside, the black **Cristo de las Ampollas** (Christ of the Blisters), on a side altar to the left of the main one, is a replica of the original, which was destroyed during the Revolution. According to legend, the Christ figure was carved from a tree that had burned all night yet appeared the next morning unscathed.

59 At the somewhat sterile **Mercado de Artesanías "García Rejón"** (⊠ Calles 60 and 65) you'll find local handicrafts and souvenirs. Shops selling dry goods, straw hats, and hammocks occupy both sides of Calle 65.

On Calle 65, between Calles 56 and 58, stand two picturesque 19th-century edifices housing the main post office and telegraph buildings.
60 Behind them sprawls the pungent, labyrinthine **Mercado Municipal,** filled with local color, where almost every patch of ground is occupied by Indian women selling chilies, herbs, and fruit. On the second floor of the main building is the **Bazar de Artesanías Municipales,** the principal handicrafts market, where you can buy jewelry (gold or gold-dipped filigree earrings), pottery, embroidered clothes, hammocks, and straw bags.

61 History lovers should stop in at the small but informative **Museo de la Ciudad.** Once a hospital chapel for the only convent in the entire bishopric, it now houses prints, drawings, photographs, and other displays that recount the history of Mérida. ⊠ *Calle 61 at Calle 58, no phone.* *Free.* *Tues.–Sun. 8–8.*

62 Only half a block north of the main plaza is the small, cozy **Parque Hidalgo,** or Cepeda Peraza, as it is officially known. Renovated mansions turned hotels and sidewalk cafés stand at two corners of the park, which comes alive at night with marimba bands and street vendors.

Casa de Montejo, **55**
Catedral, **58**
Ermita de Santa Isabel, **70**
Iglesia de Jesús, **63**
Mercado de Artesanías Garcia Rejón, **59**
Mercado Municipal, **60**
Museo de Arte Popular, **69**
Museo de la Ciudad, **61**
Palacio Cantón, **68**
Palacio del Gobierno, **57**
Palacio Municipal, **56**
Parque Hidalgo, **62**
Parque de Santa Lucía, **66**
Paseo de Montejo, **67**
Teatro Peón Contreras, **64**
Universidad Autonoma de Yucatán, **65**
Zócalo, **54**

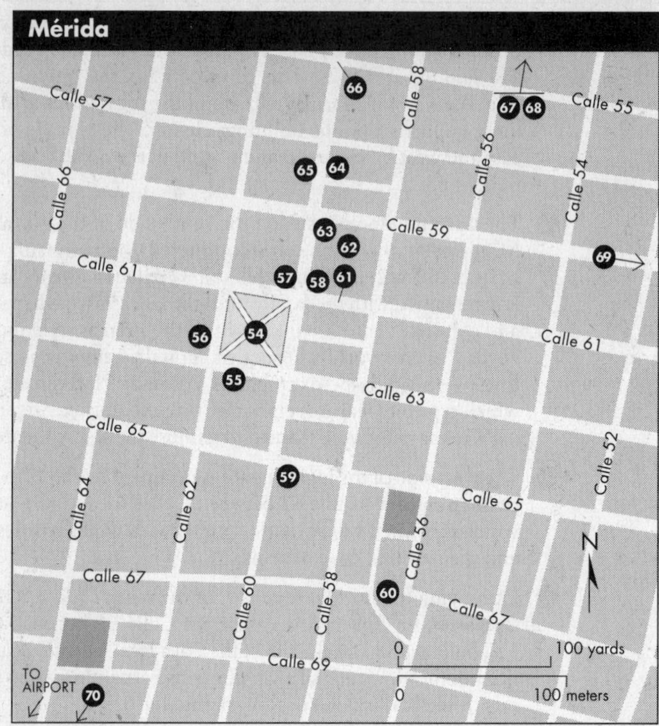

63 The **Iglesia de Jesús,** facing Parque Hidalgo on the north side, is one of Mérida's oldest buildings and the first Jesuit church in the Yucatán. The church was built in 1618 of limestone from a Maya temple that had previously stood on the site. The former convent rooms in the rear of the building now host a pair of small art museums—the **Juan Gamboa Guzmán Painting Museum** and the adjoining **Gottdeiner Museum.** You might pass on the former, which contains oil paintings of past governors and other public figures but rarely identifies them. The latter, on the other hand, displays striking bronze sculptures of the Yucatán's indigenous people by its most celebrated 20th-century sculptor, Enrique Gottdiener. The museums' hours are sporadic, and they often do not keep to their published schedule. ✉ *Calle 59 between Calles 60 and 58, no phone.* 🎫 *Free.* ⏲ *Tues.–Sun. 8–8.*

64 The Italianate **Teatro Peón Contreras,** north of Parque Hidalgo on Calle 60, was designed in 1908 along the lines of the grand European turn-of-the-century theaters and opera houses. Today, in addition to performing arts, the theater also houses temporary art exhibits and the main **Centro de Información Turistica** (☎ 99/249122), which is to the right of the lobby. A café spills out to a patio from inside the theater to the right of the information center.

65 The arabesque **Universidad Autonoma de Yucatán** plays a major role in the city's cultural and intellectual life. The folkloric ballet performs on the patio of the main building. The building, dating from 1711, features Moorish-style crownlike upper reaches and uncloistered archways. It's on Calle 60 just opposite the Teatro Peón Contreras.

66 The rather plain **Parque de Santa Lucía,** at Calles 60 and 55, draws crowds to its Thursday-night serenades, performed by local musicians and folk dancers. The small church opposite the park dates from 1575

and was built as a place of worship for the African and Caribbean slaves who lived here; the churchyard functioned as the cemetery until 1821.

67 North of downtown, the 10-block-long street known as the **Paseo de Montejo** exemplifies the Parisian airs the city took on in the late 19th century, when wealthy plantation owners were building opulent, impressive mansions. The broad boulevard, lined with tamarinds and laurels, is sometimes wistfully referred to as Mérida's Champs Elysées. Although the once-stunning mansions fell into disrepair a few years ago, their stateliness is being restored by a citywide beautification program. This part of town is also where the posh new hotels are opening.

The most compelling of the mansions on Paseo de Montejo, the pale
68 peach **Palacio Cantón** presently houses the **Museum of Anthropology and History,** dedicated to the culture and history of the Maya; although it's not that impressive compared to its counterparts in other Mexican cities, it serves as an opener to visiting nearby Maya sites. Bilingual legends accompany the displays, but lengthier explanations are in Spanish only; private guides are available for hire. There's also a bookstore. ⊠ *Calle 43 at Paseo de Montejo,* ☎ *99/230557.* *$2.* *Tues.–Sat. 9–6, Sun. 9–2; bookstore weekdays 9–3.*

69 Several blocks east of the main plaza is the **Museo de Arte Popular,** housed in a fine old mansion. The ground floor is devoted to Yucatecan arts and crafts, while the second floor focuses on the popular arts of the rest of Mexico. ⊠ *Calle 59 at Calle 52, no phone.* *Free.* *Tues.–Sat. 8–8.*

At the far south of the city, about nine blocks south of the square at
70 Calles 66 and 77, stands the **Ermita de Santa Isabel** (circa 1748), part of a Jesuit monastery also known as the Hermitage of the Good Trip. A resting place in colonial days for travelers heading to Campeche, the restored chapel is an enchanting spot to visit at sunset. Next door is a huge garden with a waterfall and footpaths bordered with bricks and colored stones. The church hours are irregular, but the garden is almost always open during the day.

El Centenario Zoological Park, Mérida's great children's attraction, is a large, somewhat tacky amusement complex consisting of playgrounds; rides (including ponies and a small train); a roller skating rink; snack bars; and cages with more than 300 marvelous native monkeys, birds, reptiles, and other animals. There are also pleasant wooded paths, picnic areas, and a small lake where you can rent rowboats. ⊠ *Av. Itzaes between Calles 59 and 65 (entrances on Calles 59 and 65).* *Free.* *Daily 9–6.*

Dining and Lodging

$$ ★ ✕ **Alberto's Continental Patio.** The setting—an early 18th-century building adorned with mosaic floors from Cuba—is romantic; an inner patio surrounded by rubber trees is ideal for starlit dining. Most of the guests are tourists, but that need not detract from the surroundings or the excellent cuisine. If you order Lebanese food, your plate will be heaped with servings of shish kebab, fried kibbe, cabbage rolls, hummus, eggplant, and tabbouleh. Black bean soup, enchiladas, fried bananas, and caramel custard make up the Mexican dinner; there are also a Yucatecan dinner, an Italian dinner, and à la carte appetizers and entrées. ⊠ *Calle 64, No. 482, at Calle 57,* ☎ *99/285367. AE, MC, V.*

$$ ✕ **Amaro.** Amaro is no longer strictly vegetarian, but its menu is heavy on health drinks, made mostly with local vegetables, fruit, and herbs (all washed with purified water). Recommended dishes include eggplant curry and soup made with *chaya,* a local vegetable that looks like spinach. The terrace of this old historic home provides a quiet din-

ing atmosphere beneath a big tree. ✉ *Calle 59, No. 507, between Calles 60 and 62,* ☎ *99/282451. No credit cards. Closed Sun.*

$$ ★ ✕ **La Bella Epoca.** For a truly special dinner, nothing matches the elegance and style of the second-story dining room, the former ballroom of an old mansion that has been restored well beyond its original grandeur. An ambitious menu includes French, Mexican, Middle Eastern, Yucatecan, vegetarian, and unusual Maya dishes—try the succulent *pollo píbil* (chicken baked in banana leaves). Arrive for dinner before 8 PM to claim one of the small balcony tables overlooking Parque Hidalgo. The ground floor is outfitted more casually with plain wooden tables and chairs but has windows overlooking the street and the same fine menu. ✉ *Hotel del Parque, Calle 60 between Calles 57 and 59,* ☎ *99/281928. AE, MC, V.*

$$ ✕ **La Casona.** This pretty mansion turned restaurant near Parque de Santa Ana has an inner patio, arcade, and swirling ceiling fans; a bar features live romantic music nightly. The accent is Yucatecan, with poc chuc, pollo píbil, and *huachinango* (sea bass baked in banana leaf) among the recommended dishes. Some Italian offerings include homemade pasta. ✉ *Calle 60, No. 434, between Calles 47 and 49,* ☎ *99/239996. AE, MC, V.*

$$ ✕ **Los Almendros.** A Mérida classic, this restaurant credits itself with the invention of poc chuc. The restaurant provides a good introduction to the variety of Yucatecan cuisine, including papadzules and *pollo ticuleño* (boneless, breaded chicken in tomato sauce filled with fried beans, peas, red peppers, ham, and cheese). All dishes are described in English with pictures on the paper menus. ✉ *Calle 50-A, No. 493, between Calles 57 and 59,* ☎ *99/238135 or 99/285459. AE, DC, MC, V.*

$$ ★ ✕ **Pórtico del Peregrino.** A red-tile floor, iron grillwork, and lots of plants set the tone in both the indoor and outdoor patio sections of this colonial-style restaurant with only 12 tables. The menu features lime soup, baked eggplant with chicken, mole enchiladas, and seafood stew. For dessert, try the coconut ice cream with Kahlúa. ✉ *Calle 57, No. 501, between Calles 60 and 62,* ☎ *99/286163. MC, V.*

$ ★ ✕ **Cafetería Pop.** Across the street from the university and a favorite with the student crowd, this place always seems to be crowded. The busiest time is 8 AM–noon, but for late risers the breakfast menu can be ordered à la carte all day, and the noteworthy coffee is freshly brewed around the clock. In addition, sandwiches, hamburgers, spaghetti, chicken, fish, beef, and tacos are available. Beer, sangria, and wine are served only with food orders. ✉ *Calle 57, No. 501, between Calles 60 and 62,* ☎ *99/286163. MC, V.*

$ ✕ **Nicte-Ha.** Located under an arcade on the main square, this modest eatery is a fine place for people-watching. A good selection of Yucatecan fare is offered at budget prices. Afterward, stop in at the *sorbetería* next door for a sherbet. ✉ *Calle 61, No. 500, at Calle 60,* ☎ *99/230784. No credit cards.*

$ ★ ✕ **Santa Lucía.** Locals crowd this small dining room, a few steps below the sidewalk, at lunch time, when the bountiful *comida corrida* (fixed-price meal) is served. The bargain three-course lunch usually includes such Yucatecan specialties as *sopa de lima* (lime soup) and pollo píbil. Service is friendly and efficient. There's a live band Thursday through Sunday nights. ✉ *Calle 60, No. 481, next to Parque de Santa Lucía,* ☎ *99/285957. MC, V.*

$$$$ ★ ✕🏨 **Hacienda Katanchel.** This rambling 17th-century henequen hacienda on 220 acres has been lovingly restored to its former splendor by Anibal Gonzalez and his wife Monica Hernandez. The couple is also restoring endangered Maya plants, trees, and medicinal herbs along with a small ruin they found on the estate. The guest rooms are set in small pavilions

built along a garden walkway; the floors are made of local hardwoods, the roofs of red Marseille tile, and there are overhead fans, hammocks, and double beds that look like pieces of modern sculpture. The bathrooms stock the hacienda's own homemade soaps and talc. The chef, a devotee of French cooking master Paul Boucuse, prepares contemporary Mexican cuisine such as vol-au-vent puff pastry stuffed with huitlacoche (mushrooms that grow on ripe corn) and tarragon sauce or cold avocado cream soup with prawns and goat cheese. ✉ *25 km (15 mi) east of Mérida on Hwy. 180, on road toward Izamal,* ☎ *99/200997 in Mérida; 800/223–6510 in the U.S.;* FAX *99/200995. 34 rooms. Restaurant, bar, pool, mineral baths, airport shuttle. AE, MC, V.*

$$$$ ★ **Fiesta Americana Mérida.** Opened in early 1995 across the street from the Hyatt Regency, this posh hotel caters to business travelers, groups, and conventions, but also attracts the locals who come to see and be seen. Its lovely pink facade mirrors the architecture of Paseo de Montejo mansions on an epic scale. The echoes of classic grandeur carry into the spacious upper lobby with its massive columns, gleaming marble and brass work, and 300-ft-high glass-roof atrium. Rich floral prints, dark wood furnishings, and slightly larger-than-life proportions maintain the theme of bygone elegance in the guest rooms, but the units are carpeted and have all the modern conveniences, including modems. They all offer L-shape conversation areas, separate dressing rooms, and remote-control TVs concealed in armoires. ✉ *Paseo de Montejo and Av. Colón,* ☎ *99/202194 or 800/343–7821,* FAX *99/202198. 350 rooms and suites. Restaurant, bar, health club, shop, business services, meeting rooms, travel services. AE, DC, MC, V.*

$$$$ **Hyatt Regency Mérida.** The first of the deluxe hotels to open on Paseo de Montejo (in 1994), the 17-story Hyatt brought a new level of hotel service to Mérida. The rooms are regally decorated with russet-hued bed quilts and rugs set off by modern blond-wood furniture and cream-color walls. Satellite TV, direct-dial long-distance phone service, and minibars have been artfully integrated into each unit. Amenities not commonly found in Mérida include 24-hour room service and a state-of-the-art business center, plus the city's only tapas bar. ✉ *Calle 60, No. 344, at Av. Colón,* ☎ *99/420202 or 800/228–9000,* FAX *99/257002. 299 rooms and suites. 2 restaurants, 2 bars, pool, tennis court, exercise room, shop, travel services, car rental. AE, DC, MC, V.*

$$$ ★ **Casa del Balam.** This very pleasant hotel on well-heeled Calle 60 has a lovely, peaceful courtyard ornamented with a fountain, arcades, ironwork, and a black-and-white tile floor; cocktails and light meals are served here. The rooms are capacious and well maintained, featuring painted sinks, wrought-iron accessories, and minibars. The suites are especially agreeable, with large bathrooms and tiny balconies. ✉ *Calle 60, No. 488, Box 988,* ☎ *99/248844, 99/242150, or 800/223–4084;* FAX *99/245011. 54 rooms. Restaurant, 2 bars, pool, shop, travel services, car rental. AE, MC, V.*

$$$ **Mérida Misión Park Inn Plaza.** Part of the city's landscape for decades (in its earlier incarnation it was the Hotel Mérida), the Misión has two major assets: an excellent location in the heart of downtown and a genuine colonial ambience, with chandeliers, wood beams, archways, patios, and fountains in public areas. A modern addition offers fine views from the upper floors. Forty-five units in the old colonial section are set around a pretty courtyard. All rooms were remodeled in 1996. ✉ *Calle 60, No. 491,* ☎ *99/237665 or 800/221–6509,* FAX *99/239500. 145 rooms. Restaurant, bar, snack bar, pool, shop, meeting rooms, travel services, car rental, free parking. AE, DC, MC, V.*

$$ **Caribe.** An old Mérida standard, the Caribe is done in typical colonial style, including tile floors, dark-wood furniture, and a large inner courtyard with arcades. It is on Parque Hidalgo, but most of its rooms (38 of them with air-conditioning) overlook the inner courtyard and restaurant, as do the open balconies, which are lined with comfortable chairs. The rooftop sundeck and swimming pool have a great view of the plaza and downtown. The hotel's outdoor café, **El Mesón,** is one of the better restaurants in Parque Hidalgo. ✉ *Calle 60, No. 500,* ☎ *99/249022 or 800/826–6842,* FAX *99/248733. 56 rooms. Restaurant, café, pool, travel services, free parking. AE, DC, MC, V.*

$$ **Casa Mexilio.** This choice bed-and-breakfast has a wonderfully eclectic decor, including Middle Eastern wall hangings, French tapestries, colorful tile floors, tile sinks, and folk-art furniture. Casa Mexilio lacks the amenities of the larger hotels (only three rooms have air-conditioning), but if you enjoy a casual ambience and the feeling of staying in a private home, you'll be happy here. Reservations are required between December 15 and the end of April. ✉ *Calle 68, No. 495, between Calles 57 and 59,* ☎ FAX *99/282505; 303/674–9615 or 800/538–6802 reservations;* FAX *303/674–8735. 8 rooms. Pool. AE, MC, V all accepted only with prior payment in the U.S.*

$$ ★ **Gran Hotel.** Cozily situated on Parque Hidalgo, this legendary 1901 hotel is the oldest in the city. The three-story neoclassical building exudes charm; its centerpiece is an art nouveau courtyard. High-ceilinged rooms are furnished in antique cedar. Thirteen units have balconies—most of the others have no windows at all—and 24 have air-conditioning. The rooms on the second floor in the back are the quietest. Porfirio Díaz and Fidel Castro stayed in sumptuous room 17 (not together). ✉ *Calle 60, No. 496,* ☎ *99/236963 or 99/247632,* FAX *99/247622. 31 rooms. Restaurant. MC, V.*

$ **Hotel Mucuy.** The Mucuy is one of the best bargains around. The delightful owners make you feel like part of the family and are eager to share information about the city. The rooms, which are always immaculate, have good screens on the windows and face a tranquil, flower-filled garden. ✉ *Calle 57, No. 481, between Calles 56 and 58,* ☎ *99/285193,* FAX *99/237801. 22 rooms. No credit cards.*

Nightlife and the Arts

Mérida enjoys an unusually active and diverse cultural life, including free government-sponsored music and dance performances nightly plus sidewalk art shows in four local parks. For information on these and other performances, consult the tourist office, the local newspapers, or the billboards and posters at the Teatro Peón Contreras (✉ Calle 60 at Calle 57) or Café Pop (✉ Calle 57 between Calles 60 and 62).

DANCING

If you want pop music mixed with salsa, try **Saudaje** (✉ Prolongación Montejo, No. 477, ☎ 99/264330 or 99/292310). A number of restaurants feature live music and dancing, including **El Tucho** (✉ Calle 60, No. 482, between Calles 55 and 57, ☎ 99/242323), **Xtabay** (✉ Above El Tucho, ☎ 99/280961), and **Pancho's** (✉ Calle 59 between Calles 60 and 62, ☎ 99/230942).

FOLKLORIC SHOWS

The **Hyatt Regency Hotel** (✉ Calle 60, No. 344, at Av. Colon, ☎ 99/420202) stages folkloric dances Tuesday nights beginning at 8 at the La Peregrina restaurant along with a buffet dinner. Among a variety of performances presented at the **Teatro Peón Contreras** is "The Roots of Today's Yucatán," a combination of music, dance, and theater presented by the Folkloric Ballet of the University of Yucatán on Tuesday at 9 PM.

Outdoor Activities and Sports

BULLFIGHTS

Bullfights are most often held from November through January, or during other holiday periods at the **bullring** (✉ Paseo de la Reforma near Av. Colón, ☎ 99/257996). Contact the travel desk at your hotel or one of the tourist information centers.

GOLF

There is an 18-hole championship golf course (and restaurant, bar, and clubhouse) at **Club de Golf de Yucatán** (✉ Carr. Mérida-Progreso, Km 14.5, ☎ 99/220053 or 99/220071), 16 km (10 mi) north of Mérida on the road to Progreso.

Shopping

On the second floor of the **Mercado Municipal** (✉ Between Calles 65 and 56 and Calles 54 and 59) you'll find crafts, food, flowers, and live birds, among other items. If you're interested solely in handicrafts, visit the **Mercado de Artesanías "García Rejón"** (✉ Calles 65 and 62), which has neat rows of indoor stalls with leather items, palm hats, and handmade guitars, among other things. On Sunday in Mérida, you will find an array of wares at the **Handicraft Bazaar** (✉ In front of Municipal Palace across from main square), filled with huipiles, hats, and costume jewelry, and the **Popular Art Bazaar** (✉ Parque Santa Lucía, Calles 60 and 55), a very small flea market offering paintings, engravings, and woodcuts by local artists.

SPECIALTY STORES

Clothing. Tastefully designed batik dresses and pillow covers with Maya motifs, along with a nice selection of silver jewelry, can be found at **El Paso** (✉ Calle 60, No. 501, at Calle 61, ☎ 99/285452). You might not wear a guayabera to a business meeting as some men in Mexico do, but the shirts are cool, comfortable, and attractive; for a good selection, try **Camisería Canul** (✉ Calle 62, No. 484, between Calles 57 and 59, ☎ 99/230158). Pick up a jipi at **Tejidos Y Cordeles Nacionales** (✉ Calle 56, No. 516-B, ☎ 99/285561), a hat emporium with styles for men and ladies in casual as well as dressy designs.

Crafts. The best place for hammocks is **Hamacas El Aguacate** (✉ Calle 58, No. 604, at Calle 73, ☎ 99/286429), a family-run establishment selling a wide variety of sizes and designs. **Casa de Artesanías** (✉ Calle 63, No. 503, between Calles 64 and 66, ☎ 99/235392) purveys folk art from throughout Mexico, such as hand-painted, wooden mythical animals from Oaxaca, handmade beeswax candles, and leather bags from Mérida, and hand-embroidered vests, shawls, blouses, and place mats from Chiapas. The streets north of the main square, especially **Calle 60,** are lined with crafts and jewelry stores.

Galleries. The **Teatro Daniel Ayala** (✉ Calle 60, between Calles 59 and 61, ☎ 99/214391) showcases contemporary paintings and photography. **Galería Manolo Rivero** (✉ Hotel Galería Trinidad, Calle 60 at Calle 61, ☎ 99/232463) displays paintings and sculptures by young, new-wave contemporary artists from all over the world.

Jewelry. La Perla Maya (✉ Calle 60, Nos. 485–487, between Calles 50 and 61, ☎ 99/285886) is one of the few jewelry shops selling difficult-to-find old-fashioned Yucatecan filigree earrings and bracelets—in silver dipped in gold. The store also stocks quality silver jewelry in modern designs. **Tane** at the Hyatt Regency Hotel (✉ Calle 60, No. 344, and Av. Colon, ☎ 99/420202) is an outlet for exquisite quality (and expensive) silver earrings, necklaces, and bracelets, some with ancient Maya designs.

Mérida and the Scenic Route to Chichén Itzá

Although it's possible to reach Chichén Itzá (120 km, or 75 mi, east of Mérida) along the shorter Route 180, it's far more scenic to follow Route 80 until it ends at Tekantó, then head south to Citilcúm, east to Dzitas, and south again to Pisté. These roads have no signs but are the only paved roads going in these directions. Ask directions frequently.

Izamal

71 *68 km (42 mi) southeast of Mérida.*

Izamal is nicknamed Ciudad Amarillo (Yellow City) because its buildings are painted earth-tone yellow. In the center of town stands the enormous 16th-century **Monastery of St. Anthony de Padua,** perched on—and built from—the remains of a pyramid devoted to Itamná, god of the heavens, day and night. The monastery's church, which was visited by Pope John Paul II in 1993, boasts a gigantic atrium (supposedly second only to that of the Vatican in size) and newly discovered frescoes of saints. The Virgin of the Immaculate Conception, to whom the church is dedicated, is the patron saint of the Yucatán; miracles are ascribed to her, and a yearly pilgrimage takes place in her honor. Another pyramid, called **Kinich Kakmó,** is all that remains of a royal Maya city that flourished here hundreds of years ago.

Chichén Itzá

72 *116 km (72 mi) from Mérida.*

Probably the best-known Maya ruin, Chichén Itzá was the most important city in Yucatán from the 10th to the 12th century. An architectural mélange, Chichén was altered by each successive wave of inhabitants. The site is believed to have been first settled in AD 432, abandoned for an unknown period of time, then rediscovered in 964 by the Maya-speaking Itzás, believed to have come from the Petén rain forest around Tikal, in what is now northern Guatemala; *Chichén Itzá* means "the mouth of the well of the Itzás." The Itzás also abandoned the site, and later in the 10th century it was rediscovered by the central-Mexican Toltecs, who abandoned the site forever in 1224.

The majesty and enormity of this site are unforgettable. Chichén Itzá encompasses approximately 6 square km (2 square mi), though only 20 to 30 buildings of the several hundred at the site have been fully explored. It's divided into two parts, called Old and New, although architectural motifs from the classical period are found in both sections. A more convenient distinction is topographical, since there are two major complexes of buildings separated by a dirt path.

The martial, imperial architecture of the Toltecs and the more cerebral architectural genius and astronomical expertise of the Maya are married in the 98-ft-tall pyramid called **El Castillo** (the castle), which dominates the site. Atop the castle is a temple dedicated to Kukulcán (the Maya name for Quetzalcóatl), the legendary priest-king from Tula in the Valley of Mexico who was incarnated by the plumed serpent. An excellent sound-and-light show in the evening highlights the architectural details in the Castillo and other buildings with a clarity the eye doesn't see in daylight. A more ancient temple inside the Castillo is open to the public for only a few hours in the morning and again in the afternoon. Claustrophobes should think twice before entering: The stairs are narrow, dark, and winding.

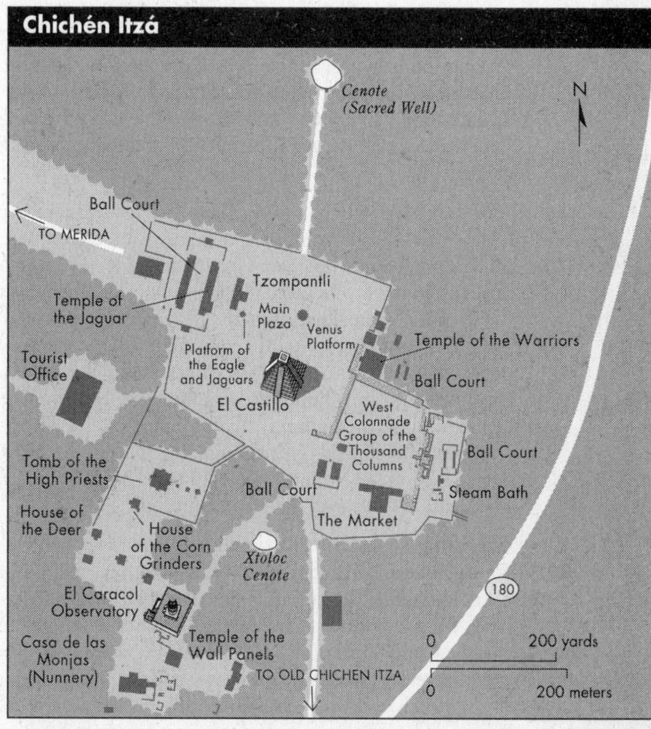

The temple rests on a massive trapezoidal square, on the west side of which is Chichén Itzá's largest **ball court,** one of seven on the site. The game played here was something like soccer (no hands were used), but it had a strictly religious significance. Bas-relief carvings at the court depict a player being decapitated, the blood spurting from his severed neck fertilizing the earth.

Between the ball court and El Castillo stands a **Tzompantli,** or stone platform, carved with rows of human skulls. In ancient times it was actually covered with stakes on which the heads of enemies were impaled. In the **Sacred Well,** a cenote 65 yards in diameter that sits 1 km (½ mi) north of El Castillo at the end of a 900-ft-long sacbe ("white road" in Maya), skeletons of about 50 people were found. Thousands of artifacts made of gold, jade, and other precious materials, most of them not of local provenance, have been recovered from the brackish depths of the cenote. The well's excavation launched the field of underwater archaeology, later honed by Jacques Cousteau.

Returning to the causeway, you will see on your left the **Group of the Thousand Columns** with the famous **Temple of the Warriors,** a masterful example of the Toltec influence at Chichén Itzá. Murals of everyday village life and scenes of war can be viewed here, and an artistic representation of the defeat of the Maya can be found on the interior murals of the adjacent **Temple of the Jaguar.**

To get to the less visited cluster of structures at "New" Chichén Itzá—often confused with "Old" Chichén Itzá—take the main road south from the Temple of the Jaguar past El Castillo and turn right onto a small path opposite the ball court on your left. Archaeologists are currently restoring several buildings, including the **Tomb of the High Priest,** where several tombs with skeletons and jade offerings were found. The most impressive structure within this area is the astronomical observatory, called **El Caracol.** The name, meaning "snail," refers to the spiral staircase at the building's core. Although definitely used for observing the heavens, it also served a religious function. After leaving El Caracol, continue south several hundred yards to the beautiful **Casa de las Monjas** (Nunnery) and its annex, which have long panels carved with flowers and animals, latticework, hieroglyph-covered lintels, and masks.

At Old Chichén Itzá, "pure Maya" style—with playful latticework, Chaac masks, and gargoyle-like serpents on the cornices—dominates. Highlights include the **Date Group** (so named because of the complete series of hieroglyphic date inscriptions), the **House of the Phalli,** and the **Temple of the Three Lintels.** Maya guides will lead you down the path by an old narrow-gauge railroad track to even more ruins, barely unearthed, if you ask. A fairly good restaurant and great ice-cream stand are in the entrance building, and there are refreshment stands by the cenote and on the pathway near El Caracol. *Site and museum $4, free Sun.; sound-and-light show $1 in Spanish, $5 in English; parking $1; use of video camera $8.* ⏲ *Daily 8–5. Sound-and-light show (Spanish) at 7 PM and (English) at 9 PM.*

Lodging

$$$ ★ **Mayaland.** This charming 1920s lodging, on a 100-acre site, is the hotel closest to the ruins. Colonial-style rooms in the main building have decorative tiles, ceiling fans, air-conditioning (except for five rooms), and TVs. Eighteen bungalows were added in 1996; 13 of them have TVs and air-conditioning. Tour buses fill the road in front of the hotel, so choose a room at the back. Light meals served poolside and at tables overlooking the garden are a far better choice than the fixed-price meals served in the dining room. ✉ *Carretera Mérida–Cancún, Km 120,* ☎ *985/10129. For reservations:* ✉ *Mayaland Tours, Av. Colón 502, Mérida, Yucatán 97000,* ☎ *99/236851 or 800/235–4079,* FAX *99/642335. 83 rooms. Restaurant, bar, pool. AE, DC, MC, V.*

$$ ★ **Hacienda Chichén.** A converted 17th-century hacienda, this hotel once served as the home of U.S. Consul General Edward S. Thompson and later as the headquarters for the Carnegie expedition. The rustic cottages have been modernized, and all rooms, which are simply furnished in colonial Yucatecan style, have private baths, verandas, and air-conditioning, but no phones or TVs; there's a color satellite TV in the lobby area. Four rooms were added in 1997. An enormous old pool sits in the midst of the landscaped gardens. Fairly good meals are served on the patio overlooking the grounds; stick with the Yucatecan specialties. ✉ *Carretera Mérida–Puerto Juarez, Km 120, Yucatán 97000,* ☎ *985/10045, 99/248844, 99/242150, or 800/223–4084;* FAX *99/245011. 22 rooms. Restaurant, bar, pool, free parking. No credit cards.*

Pisté

73 *1 km (½ mi) west of Chichén Itzá on Rte. 180.*

The town of Pisté serves mainly as a base camp for travelers to Chichén Itzá, and its hotels, campgrounds, and handicrafts shops tend to be cheaper than south of the ruins. At the west end of town are a Pemex station and a bank. On the outskirts of Pisté, a short walk from the ruins, **Pueblo Maya,** a pseudo-Maya village, provides a shopping and dining center for tour groups. The restaurant serves a bountiful buffet at lunch ($10). Most other restaurants in town are only fair, and overpriced. Try one of the palapa-covered cafés along the main road or the small markets and produce stands, which can provide the makings for a modest picnic.

Lodging

$ **Dolores Alba.** The best low-budget choice near the ruins is this family-run hotel, a longtime favorite in the country south of Pisté. The rooms are simple, clean, and comfortable; some have air-conditioning. Hammocks hang by the small pool, and breakfast and dinner are served family-style in the main building. Free transportation to the ruins is provided. ✉ *Carretera Pisté–Cancún, 2½ km (1½ mi) south of Chichén Itzá. For reservations:* ✉ *Calle 63, No. 464, Mérida,* ☎ *99/285650,* FAX *99/283163. 28 rooms. Dining room, pool. MC, V.*

$ **Pirámide Inn Resort.** The rooms in this American-owned two-story motel are being completely refurbished; ask for one that is finished. All have air-conditioning. The garden contains a small Maya pyramid, a swimming pool, and a tennis court, and the restaurant is one of the best in Pisté. ✉ *For reservations: Box 433, Mérida,* ☎ *985/10115. 44 rooms. Restaurant, pool, tennis court, travel services. MC, V.*

Cave of Balancanchén

74 *5 km (3 mi) northeast of Chichén Itzá.*

The Cave of Balancanché, a shrine whose Maya name translates as "hidden throne," remained virtually undisturbed from the time of the Conquest until its discovery in 1959. Inside is a large collection of artifacts—mostly vases, jars, and incense burners. An underground lake is filled with blindfish (small fish with functionless eyes), and an altar to the rain god rises above it. In order to explore the shrine you must take one of the guided tours, which depart almost hourly, but it's necessary to be in fairly good shape, because some crawling is required. Also offered at the site is a sound-and-light show that fancifully recounts Maya history. You can catch a bus or taxi to the caves from Chichén Itzá. *Caves (including tour) $7, free Sun.; show $3. Daily 9–5. Tours in English at 11 AM, 1, and 3; in Spanish at 9 AM and noon; in French at 10 AM.*

Valladolid

75 *44½ km (23 mi) east of Chichén Itzá.*

The second-largest city in the State of Yucatán, Valladolid is enjoying growing popularity among travelers en route to or from Chichén Itzá or Río Lagartos. Montejo founded Valladolid in 1543 on the site of the Maya town of Sisal. The city suffered during the Caste War, when virtually the entire Spanish population was killed by the rebellious Maya, and again during the Mexican Revolution.

Today, however, placidity reigns in this agricultural market town (population 70,000). The center is mostly colonial, although it has many 19th-century structures. The main sights are the colonial churches, principally the large **cathedral** on the central square and the 16th-century **San Bernardino Church and Convent** three blocks southwest. A briny, muddy **cenote** in the center of town draws only the most resolute swimmers; instead, visit the adjacent **ethnographic museum.** Outside town, for $4, you can swim in **Cenote Dzitnup,** located in a cave lit by a small natural skylight.

Valladolid is renowned for its cuisine, particularly its sausages; try one of the restaurants within a block of the square. You can find good buys on sandals, baskets, and the local liqueur, Xtabentún, flavored with honey and anise.

Lodging

$$ **El Mesón del Marqués.** This building, on the north side of the main square, is a well-preserved, very old hacienda built around a lovely courtyard. Rooms in the modern addition at the back of the hotel have air-conditioning and are attractively furnished with rustic and colonial touches; rooms in the older section have ceiling fans. Unusually large bathrooms boast bathtubs—a rarity in Mexican hotels. El Mesón also features a pool, a crafts shop, and a restaurant that serves local specialties. ✉ *Plaza Principal, Calle 39, No. 203, 97780,* ☎ *985/62073,* FAX *985/62280. 26 rooms, 12 suites. Restaurant, bar, pool, shop. MC, V.*

$ **María del Luz.** Another choice by the main plaza, this hotel is built around a small swimming pool and courtyard. The rooms have tiled bathrooms, air-conditioning, and color TVs (local channels only). The attractive street-side restaurant offers predictable and inexpensive Mexican dishes. ✉ *Plaza Principal, Calle 2, No. 195, 97780,* ☎ *985/62071. 33 rooms. Restaurant, bar, pool. No credit cards.*

Río Lagartos National Park

76 *101 km (63 mi) north of Valladolid.*

If you're a flamingo fan (flamingo season runs from June through March), don't miss Río Lagartos National Park. Actually encompassing a long estuary, not a river, the park was developed with ecotourism in mind, though the alligators for which it and the village were named have long since been hunted into extinction. In addition to sighting flamingos, birders can spot egrets, herons, ibis, cormorants, pelicans, and even peregrine falcons flying over these murky waters; fishing is good, too, and hawksbill and green turtles lay their eggs on the beach at night. **Hotel Nefertiti,** one of five hotels in town, offers boat tours, or you can hire a boat from the docks near the hotel.

Uxmal and the Puuc Route

As soon as they pass through the large Maya town of Uman on Mérida's southern outskirts, travelers find themselves in one of the least populated areas of the Yucatán. The highway to Uxmal and Kabah is a fairly traffic-free route through uncultivated woodlands. The forest seems to become more dense beyond Uxmal, which was connected to a number of smaller ceremonial centers in ancient times. Several of these satellite sites, including **Kabah, Sayil,** and **Labná,** are open to the public along a side road known as the Ruta Puuc, which winds its way eastward and eventually joins busy Route 184, a major highway. Along this route you'll also find the **Loltún Caves,** the largest known cave system in the Yucatán, containing wall paintings and stone artifacts from Maya and pre-Maya times. In the little town of **Ticul,** which produces much of the pottery you'll see around the peninsula, is **Los Almendros,** considered by many the best regional restaurant in the Yucatán.

Uxmal

77 *78 km (48 mi) south of Mérida on Rte. 261.*

If Chichén Itzá is the most impressive Maya ruin in Yucatán, Uxmal is arguably the most beautiful. Where the former has a Toltec grandeur, the latter seems more understated and elegant—pure Maya. The architecture reflects the late classical renaissance of the 7th to 9th centuries and is contemporary with that of Palenque and Tikal, among other great Maya metropolises of the southern highlands.

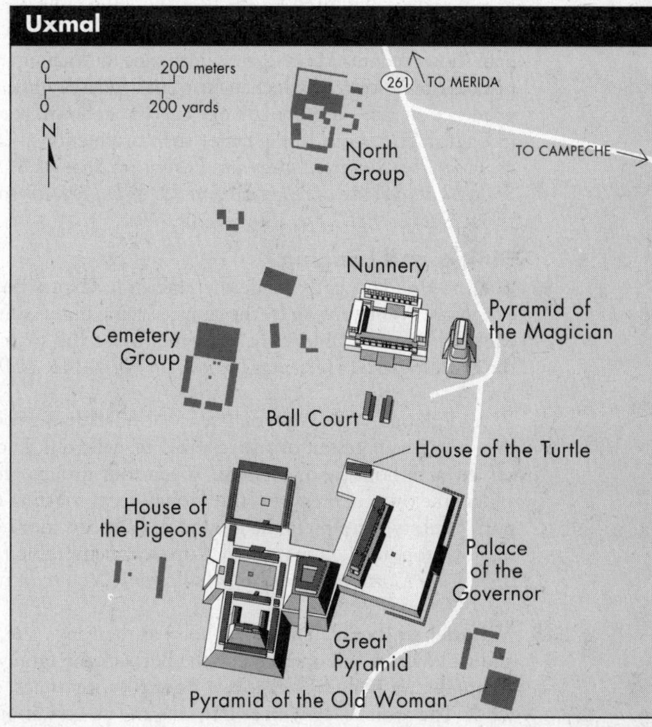

The site is considered the finest and largest example of Puuc architecture, which embraces such details as ornate stone mosaics and friezes on the upper walls, intricate cornices with curled noses, rows of columns, and soaring vaulted arches. Lines are clean and uncluttered, with the horizontal—especially the parallelogram—preferred to the vertical.

Although most of Uxmal remains unrestored, three buildings in particular merit attention. The most prominent, the **Pyramid of the Magician,** is, at 125 ft high, the tallest structure at the site. Unlike most other Maya pyramids, which are stepped and angular, it has a strangely elliptical design. Built five times, each time over the previous structure, the pyramid has a stairway on its western side that leads through a giant mask of Chaac with its mouth wide open to two temples at the summit.

West of the pyramid lies the **Nunnery,** or Quadrangle of the Nuns, considered by some to be the architectural jewel of Uxmal. You may enter the four buildings; each comprises a series of low, gracefully repetitive chambers that look onto a central patio. Elaborate decoration blankets the upper facades.

Continue walking south; you'll pass the ball court before reaching the **Palace of the Governor,** which archaeologist Victor von Hagen considered the most magnificent building ever erected in the Americas. Interestingly, the palace faces east while the rest of Uxmal faces west. Archaeologists believe this is because the palace was used to sight the planet Venus. Covering 5 acres and rising over an immense acropolis, the palace lies at the heart of what must have been Uxmal's administrative center. Decorating the uppermost section of the facade are intricate friezes that required more than 20,000 individually cut stones.

First excavated in 1929 by the Danish explorer Franz Blom, the site served in 1841 as home to John Lloyd Stephens. Today a sound-and-light show recounts Maya legends, including the kidnapping of an Uxmal princess by a king of Chichén Itzá, and focuses on the people's dependence on rain—thus the cult of Chaac. The show is performed nightly in English and is one of the better such productions. *Site and museum $4, free Sun.; sound-and-light show in Spanish $1.50, in English $5; parking $1; use of video camera $8. Daily 8–5; sound-and-light show (Spanish) at 7 PM, (English) at 9 PM.*

Dining and Lodging

$$ **Nicte-Ha.** This café beside the Hacienda Uxmal hotel is the least expensive dining option by the ruins, serving pizzas, sandwiches, and Mexican snacks. Diners are welcome to use the swimming pool by the restaurant. *Hacienda Uxmal, on Hwy. 261, FAX 99/494754. MC, V.*

$ **Las Palapas.** A great alternative to the hotel dining rooms at Uxmal, this family-run restaurant specializes in delicious Yucatecan dishes served with homemade tortillas. When tour groups request it in advance, the owners prepare a traditional feast, roasting the chicken or pork píbil style in a pit in the ground. If you see a tour bus in the parking lot, stop in—you may chance upon a memorable fiesta. *Hwy. 261, 5 km (3 mi) north of ruins, no phone. No credit cards.*

$$$ **Hacienda Uxmal.** The oldest hotel at the Maya site, built in 1955 and still owned and operated by the Barbachano family, this pleasant colonial-style building has lovely floor tiles, ceramics, and iron grillwork. The rooms—all with ceiling fans and air-conditioning—are tiled and decorated with worn but comfortable furniture. Ask about packages that include free or low-cost car rentals for the nights you spend at Uxmal and at the Mayaland hotel in Chichén Itzá. *Within walking distance of ruins, FAX 99/494754; Mayaland Tours, Av. Colón 502, Mérida, 99/462331 or 800/235–4079, FAX 99/462335. 80 rooms. Restaurant, bar, pool, shop. AE, DC, MC, V.*

$$ **Villa Arqueológica Uxmal.** The hotel closest to the ruins is this two-story Club Med property built around a large Mediterranean-style pool. The functional rooms have cozy niches for the beds, tiled bathrooms, and powerful air conditioners. Maya women in traditional dress serve well-prepared French cuisine in the restaurant. For a fee, day-trippers can use the pool, then dine in the restaurant. *Carrerera Uxmal, Km 76, Yucatán 97000, within walking distance of ruins, 99/247053; 800/258–2633 for reservations in the U.S. 44 rooms. Restaurant, bar, pool, tennis court, shop. AE, MC, V.*

The State of Yucatán A to Z

Arriving and Departing

BY BUS

The **main bus station** (Calle 69, No. 544, between Calles 68 and 70, 99/247868) in Mérida offers frequent first- and second-class service to Akumal, Cancún, Chichén Itzá, Playa del Carmen, Tulum, Uxmal, Valladolid, and Xel-Há. The **ADO bus terminal,** nearby at Calle 70, between Calles 69 and 71, can also be reached by phone (99/247868). Several lines, such as Expreso del Oriente (99/232287) and Super Expreso (99/248391) now offer deluxe service with air-conditioning, refreshments, and movies shown en route. **Autotransportes del Sureste** (99/281595) has the best coverage for out-of-the-way destinations, with daily service to the Guatemalan border, Palenque, and San Cristóbal de las Casas, and four buses daily to Uxmal.

BY CAR

Route 180, the main road along the Gulf coast from the Texas border to Cancún, runs into Mérida. Mexico City lies 1,550 km (960 mi) to the west; Cancún, 320 km (200 mi) due east. The *autopista,* a four-lane toll highway between Cancún and Mérida, runs somewhat parallel to Route 180 and cuts driving time between Cancún and Mérida—formerly around 4½ hours—by about one hour.

BY PLANE

The Mérida airport is 7 km (4½ mi) west of the city's central square, about a 20-minute ride. The following airlines serve Mérida: **Aeromexico** (☎ 99/279000) flies direct from Miami with a stop (but no plane change) in Cancún; **Mexicana** (☎ 99/286790 or 99/281817) has a connecting flight from Newark via Cancún, and a number of connecting flights from the United States via Mexico City; **Aerocaribe** (☎ 99/286786 or 99/286790), a subsidiary of Mexicana, has flights from Cancún, Chetumal, Cozumel, Oaxaca, Tuxtla Gutiérrez, and Villahermosa; **Aviateca** (☎ 99/258062 or 99/258059), a Guatemalan carrier, flies from Houston and Guatemala City; and **Taesa** (☎ 99/202077) flies from Mexico City.

Between the Airport and City Center. A private taxi costs about $7; collective service (usually a Volkswagen minibus), about $3. For both, pay the taxi-ticket vendor at the airport, not the driver. The inexpensive but irregular Bus 79 goes from the airport to downtown.

Getting Around

BY BUS

Mérida's municipal buses run daily from 5 AM to midnight, but service is somewhat confusing until you master the system. In the downtown area, buses go east on Calle 59 and west on Calle 61, north on Calle 60 and south on Calle 62. You can catch a bus heading north to Progreso on Calle 56. Unfortunately, there is no bus service from the hotels around the plaza to the long-distance bus station.

BY CAR

Driving in Mérida can be frustrating because of the one-way streets (many of which end up being one-lane because of the parked cars) and because traffic is dense. But having your own wheels is the best way to take excursions from the city. Prices are sometimes lower if you arrange your rental in advance through one of the large international companies.

BY CARRIAGE

Horse-drawn *calesas* (carriages) that drive along the streets of Mérida can be hailed along Calle 60. A ride to the Paseo de Montejo and back will cost about $7 to $9, and you can bargain.

BY TAXI

Taxis don't cruise the streets for passengers; instead, they are available at 13 taxi stands around the city, or from the main taxi office (☎ 99/285324); taxis wait in front of the larger hotels, but they're often more expensive. Individual cabs cost $3 minimum.

Contacts and Resources

CAR RENTAL

There are almost 20 car-rental agencies in town, including **Budget** (⊠ Hyatt Regency, Calle 60, No. 344, at Av. Colon, ☎ 99/421226; ⊠ Holiday Inn next to Hyatt, ☎ 99/255453; ⊠ Airport, ☎ 99/461380), **Dollar** (⊠ Hotel Mérida Misión, ☎ 99/286759; 99/461323 airport), **National** (⊠ Fiesta Americana ☎ 99/421111, ext. 6737; 99/461791 airport), and **Thrifty** (✉ Calle 60 between Calles 49 and 51, ☎ 99/232440; 99/462515 airport).

CONSULATES

United States (✉ Paseo de Montejo 453, ☎ 99/255011, 99/258677, or 99/255409). **United Kingdom** (✉ Calle 58, No. 450, at Calle 53, ☎ 99/286152).

EMERGENCIES

Mérida. Police (☎ 99/252555). **Red Cross** (Calle 68, No. 583, at Calle 65, ☎ 99/249813). **Fire** (☎ 99/249242); **general emergency** (☎ 06).

Hospital. Hospital O'Horan (✉ Avs. Internacional and Itzaes, ☎ 99/244111, 99/242911, or 99/244800).

GUIDED TOURS

There are more than 50 tour operators in Mérida, and they generally offer the same destinations. What differs is how you go—in a private car, a van, or a bus—and whether the vehicle is air-conditioned. A two- to three-hour city tour will cost between $7 and $20; or you can pick up an open-air sightseeing bus at Parque de Santa Lucía for $5; departure times Monday–Saturday are 10, 1, 4, and 7; Sunday 12:30 and 5. A day trip to Chichén Itzá, with guide, entrance fee, and lunch, runs approximately $40. For about the same price you can see the ruins of Uxmal and Kabah in the Puuc region, and for a few more dollars you can add on the neighboring sites of Sayil, Labná, and the Loltún Caves. Afternoon departures to Uxmal allow you to take in the sound-and-light show at the ruins and return by 11 PM, for $40–$50 (including dinner). There is also the option of a tour of Chichén Itzá followed by a drop-off in Cancún for about $50. Most tour operators take credit cards.

Special-Interest Tours. Several of the tour operators in Mérida run overnight excursions to archaeological sites farther afield, notably Cobá, Tulum, Edzná, and Palenque. Tours of the Ruta Maya including sites in Mexico, Guatemala, and Belize are offered by **VN Travel** (✉ Calle 58, No. 488, ☎ 99/239061 or 99/245996) and **Mayaland Tours** (✉ Holiday Inn, Av. Colón, No. 502, ☎ 99/236851 or 800/235–4079, FAX 99/462335), which also offers self-guided tours with economical rental-car rates. **Ecoturismo Yucatán** (✉ Calle 3, No. 235, at Col. Pensiones, ☎ 99/252187, FAX 99/259047) specializes in nature tours, including bird-watching, natural history, anthropology, and the Mundo Maya. **Emerald Planet** (✉ 4076 Crystal Court, Boulder, CO 80304, ☎ 303/541–9688, FAX 303/449–7805) and **Siteseer Journeys** (✉ 27210 SW 166th Ave., Homestead, FL 33031, ☎ 800/615–4035, FAX 305/242–9009) offer bird-watching tours and other trips into wildlife reserves in the state of Yucatán.

TRAVEL AGENCIES AND TOUR OPERATORS

Mérida's local agencies and operators include **American Express** (✉ Calle 56-A, No. 494, ☎ 99/284222, FAX 99/284373), **Buvisa** (✉ Paseo de Montejo, No. 475, ☎ 99/277933, FAX 99/277414), **Ceiba Tours** (✉ Calle 60, No. 495, ☎ 99/244477 or 99/244499, FAX 99/244588), **Intermar Caribe** (✉ Prolongación Paseo de Montejo 74 at Calle 30, ☎ 99/445249 or 99/445222, FAX 99/445259), **Mayaland Tours** (✉ Av. Colón, No. 502, ☎ 99/462331 or 800/235–4079, FAX 99/462335; ✉ Casa del Balam hotel, Calle 60, No. 488, ☎ 99/244919), **Turismo Aviomar** (✉ Calle 58A, 500-C, ☎ 99/200444 or 99/200443, FAX 99/246887), **Viajes Novedosos** (✉ Calle 58, No. 488, ☎ 99/245996, FAX 99/239061), and **Yucatán Trails** (✉ Calle 62, No. 482, ☎ 99/241928 or 99/282582, FAX 99/244919 or 99/285913).

24-HOUR PHARMACIES

Farmacia Yza Aviación (✉ Calle 71 at Av. Aviación, ☎ 99/238116), **Farmacia Yza Tanlum** (✉ Glorieta Tanlum, ☎ 99/251646), and **Farmacia Canto** (✉ Calle 60, No. 514, at Calle 63, ☎ 99/248265).

VISITOR INFORMATION

Mérida. Tourist Information Center (✉ Teatro Peón Contreras, Calle 59 between Calles 62 and 64, ☎ 99/249290), open daily 8–8. **Information kiosks:** At the airport (☎ 99/246764), open daily 8–8; and at Calles 59 and 62 (no phone), open weekdays 8–8 and weekends 9–7.

14 Portrait of Mexico

MEXICO AT A GLANCE: A CHRONOLOGY

Pre-Columbian Mexico

ca. 50,000 BC Asian nomads cross land bridge over the Bering Strait to North America, gradually migrating south

ca. 5000–2000 BC Archaic period, which marked the beginnings of agriculture and village life

ca. 2000–200 BC Formative or pre-Classic period: development of pottery, incipient political structures

ca. 1500–900 BC The powerful and sophisticated Olmec civilization develops along the Gulf of Mexico in the present-day states of Veracruz and Tabasco. Olmec culture, the "mother culture" of Mexico, flourishes along gulf coast

ca. 200 BC–AD 900 Classic period: height of pre-Columbian culture. Three centers at Teotihuacan (near Mexico City), Monte Albán (Oaxaca), and Maya civilization in the far south. Peaceful, priest-run city-states produce impressive art and architecture

650–900 Decline of Classic cultures: fall of Teotihuacan ca. 650 leads to competition among other city-states, exacerbated by migrations of northern tribes

ca. 900–1521 Post-Classic period: rule passes to military; war and war gods gain prominence

ca. 900–1150 Toltecs, a northern tribe, establish a flourishing culture at their capital of Tula under the legendary monarch Topiltzin-Quetzalcoatl

ca. 1200 Rise of Mixtec culture at Zapotec sites of Monte Albán and Mitla; notable for production of picture codices, which include historical narratives

ca. 1000–1450 Maya culture, declining in south, emerges in the Yucatán; under Toltec rule, Chichén Itzá dominates the peninsula

1111 Aztecs migrate to mainland from island home off the Nayarit coast. Vulgar and partial to human sacrifice, they are not welcomed by the peoples of central Mexico

1150–1350 Following the fall of Tula, first the Chichimecs, then the Tepanecs assert hegemony over central Mexico. The Tepanec tyrant Tezozómoc (1320–1426), like his contemporaries in Renaissance Italy, establishes his power with murder and treachery

1376 Tezozómoc grants autonomy to the Aztec city of Tenochtitlán, built in the middle of Lake Texcoco

1420–1500 Aztecs extend their rule to much of central and southern Mexico. A warrior society, they build a great city at Tenochtitlán

1502 Moctezuma II assumes throne at the height of Aztec culture and political power

1517 Spanish expedition under Francisco Hernandez de Córdoba lands on Yucatán coast

1519 Hernán Cortés lands in Cozumel, founds Veracruz, determines to conquer. Steel weapons, horses, and smallpox, combined with a belief that Cortés was the resurrected Topiltzin-Quetzalcoatl, minimize

Aztec resistance. Cortés enters Tenochtitlán and captures Moctezuma

The Colonial Period

1520–21 Moctezuma is killed; Tenochtitlán falls to Cortés. The last Aztec emperor, Cuauhtemoc, is executed

1528 Juan de Zumarraga arrives as bishop of Mexico City, gains title "Protector of the Indians"; native conversion to Catholicism begun

1535 First Spanish viceroy arrives in Mexico

1537 Pope Paul III issues a bull declaring that native Mexicans are indeed human and not beasts. First printing press arrives in Mexico City

1546–48 Silver deposits discovered at Zacatecas

1547 Spanish conquest of Aztec Empire—now known as "New Spain"—completed, at enormous cost to native peoples

1553 Royal and Pontifical University of Mexico, first university in the New World, opens

1571 The Spanish Inquisition established in New Spain; it is not abolished until 1820

1609 Northern capital of New Spain established at Santa Fe (New Mexico)

1651 Birth of Sor (Sister) Juana Inés de la Cruz, greatest poet of colonial Mexico (d. 1695)

1718 Franciscan missionaries settle in Texas, which becomes part of New Spain

1765 Charles III of Spain sends José de Galvez to tour New Spain and propose reforms

1769 Franciscan Junipero Serra establishes missions in California, extending Spanish hegemony

1788 Death of Charles III; his reforms improve administration, but also raise social and political expectations among the colonial population, which are not fulfilled

1808 Napoléon invades Spain, leaving a power vacuum in New Spain

The War of Independence

1810 September 16: Father Miguel Hidalgo y Costilla preaches his *Grito de Dolores,* sparking rebellion

1811 Hidalgo is captured and executed; leadership of the movement passes to Father José Maria Morelos

1813 Morelos calls a congress at Chilpancingo, which drafts a Declaration of Independence

1815 Morelos is captured and executed

The Early National Period

1821 Vicente Guerrero, a rebel leader, and Agustín de Iturbide, a Spanish colonel converted to the rebel cause, rejuvenate the Independence movement. Spain recognizes Mexican independence with the Treaty of Córdoba

1822 Iturbide is named Emperor of Mexico, which stretches from California through Central America

1823 After 10 months in office, Emperor Agustín is turned out

1824 A new constitution creates a federal republic, the Estados Unidos Mexicanos; modeled on the U.S. Constitution, the Mexican version retains the privileges of the Catholic Church and gives the president extraordinary "emergency" powers

1829 President Vicente Guerrero abolishes slavery. A Spanish attempt at reconquest is halted by General Antonio López de Santa Anna, already a hero for his role in the overthrow of Emperor Agustín

1833 Santa Anna is elected president by a huge majority; he holds the office for 11 of its 36 changes of hands by 1855

1836 Although voted in as a liberal, Santa Anna abolishes the 1824 constitution. Already dismayed at the abolition of slavery, Texas—whose population is largely American—declares its independence. Santa Anna successfully besieges the Texans at the Alamo. But a month later he is captured by Sam Houston following the Battle of San Jacinto. Texas gains its independence as the Lone Star Republic

1846 The U.S. decision to annex Texas leads to war

1848 The treaty of Guadalupe Hidalgo reduces Mexico's territory by half, ceding Texas, New Mexico, and California to the United States

1853 Santa Anna agrees to the Gadsden Purchase, ceding a further 48,000 square km (30,000 square mi) to the United States

The Reform and French Intervention

1855 The Revolution of Ayutla topples Santa Anna and leads to the period of The Reform

1857 The liberal Constitution of 1857 disestablishes the Catholic Church among other measures

1858–61 The civil War of the Reform ends in liberal victory. Benito Juárez is elected president. France, Spain, and Britain agree jointly to occupy the customs house at Veracruz to force payment of Mexico's huge foreign debt

1862 Spain and Britain withdraw their forces; the French, seeking empire, march inland. On May 5, General Porfirio Díaz repulses the French at Puebla

1863 Strengthened with reinforcements, the French occupy Mexico City. Napoléon III of France appoints Archduke Ferdinand Maximilian of Austria as Emperor of Mexico

1864 Maximilian and his empress Charlotte, known as Carlota, land at Veracruz

1867 With U.S. assistance, Juárez overthrows Mexico's second empire. Maximilian is executed; Carlota, pleading his case in France, goes mad

1872 Juárez dies in office. The Mexico City–Veracruz railway is completed, symbol of the new progressivist mood

The Porfiriato

1876 Porfirio Díaz comes to power in the Revolution of Tuxtepec; he holds office nearly continuously until 1911. With his advisers, the *cientificos,* he forces modernization and balances the budget for the first time in Mexican history. But the social cost is high

1890 José Schneider, who is of German ancestry, founds the Cerveceria Cuauhtemoc, brewer of Carta Blanca

1900 Jesús, Enrique, and Ricardo Flores Magón publish the anti-Díaz newspaper *La Regeneración.* Suppressed, the brothers move their campaign to the United States, first to San Antonio, then to St. Louis

1906 The Flores Magón group publish their Liberal Plan, a proposal for reform. Industrial unrest spreads

The Second Revolution

1910 On the centennial of the Revolution, Díaz wins yet another rigged election. Revolt breaks out

1911 Rebels under Pascual Orozco and Francisco (Pancho) Villa capture Ciudad Juárez; Díaz resigns. Francisco Madero is elected president; calling for land reform, Emiliano Zapata rejects the new regime. Violence continues

1913 Military coup: Madero is deposed and murdered. In one day Mexico has three presidents, the last being General Victoriano Huerta. Civil war rages

1914 American intervention leads to dictator Huerta's overthrow. Villa and Zapata briefly join forces at the Convention of Aguascalientes, but the Revolution goes on

1916 Villa's border raids lead to an American punitive expedition under Pershing. Villa eludes capture

1917 Under a new constitution, Venuziano Carranza, head of the Constitutionalist Army, is elected president. Zapata continues his rebellion, which is brutally suppressed

1918 CROM, the national labor union, is founded

1919 On order of Carranza, Zapata is assassinated

1920 Carranza is assassinated; Alvaro Obregón is elected president, beginning a period of reform and reconstruction. Schools are built and land is redistributed. In the next two decades, revolutionary culture finds expression in the art of Diego Rivera and José Clemente Orozco, the novels of Martin Luis Guzmán and Gregorio Lopez y Fuentes, and the music of Carlos Chavez

1923 Pancho Villa is assassinated. The United States finally recognizes the Obregón regime

1926–28 Catholics react to government anticlericalism in the Cristero Rebellion

1934–40 The presidency of Lázaro Cárdenas leads to the fullest implementation of revolutionary reforms

1938 Cárdenas nationalizes the oil companies, removing them from foreign control

Post-Revolutionary Mexico

1951 Mexico's segment of the Pan-American Highway is completed, confirming the industrial growth and prosperity of post-war Mexico. Culture is increasingly Americanized; writers such as Octavio Paz and Carlos Fuentes express disillusionment with the post-revolution world

1968 The Summer Olympics in Mexico City showcase Mexican prosperity, but massive demonstrations indicate underlying social unrest

1981–82 Recession and a drop in oil prices severely damage Mexico's economy. The peso is devalued

1985 Thousands die in the Mexico City earthquake

1988 American-educated economist Carlos Salinas de Gortari is elected president; for the first time since 1940, support for the PRI, the national political party, seems to be slipping

1993 North American Free Trade Agreement (NAFTA) is signed with United States and Canada

1994 Uprising by the indigenous peoples of Chiapas, led by the Zapatistas and their charismatic ski-masked leader, Subcomandante Marcos; election reforms promised as a result

Popular PRI presidential candidate Luis Donaldo Colosio assassinated while campaigning in Tijuana. Ernesto Zedillo, generally thought to be more of a technocrat and "old boy"–style PRI politician, replaces him and wins the election

Zedillo, blaming the economic policies of his predecessor, devalues the peso in December

1995 Recession sets in as a result of the peso devaluation. The former administration is rocked by scandals surrounding the assassinations of Colosio and another high-ranking government official; ex-President Carlos Salinas de Gortari moves to the United States

1996 Mexico's economy, bolstered by a $28 billion bailout program led by the United States, turns upward, but the recovery is fragile. The opposition National Action Party (PAN), which is committed to conservative economic policies, gains strength. New details of scandals of the former administration continue to emerge.

1997 Mexico's top anti-drug official is arrested on bribery charges. Nonetheless, the United States recertifies Mexico as a partner in the war on drugs. The Zedillo administration faces midterm party elections.

FURTHER READING

The best nonfiction on Mexico blends history, culture, commentary, and travel description. Some may be out of print and available only in libraries.

Pre-Columbian and Colonial History

Good general reference works that can deepen your understanding of Mexico's indigenous peoples (and enrich your trips to the many marvelous archaeological sites in Mexico) include *The Conquest of the Yucatán* by celebrated ethnographer and champion of indigenous cultural survival Frans Blom; *A Rain of Darts: The Mexica Aztecs,* by Burr Cartwright Brundage; *In the Land of the Aztec* and *The Maya and Mexico,* by Michael D. Coe; *The Toltec Heritage,* by Nigel Davies; *The Last Lords of Palenque: The Lacandon Mayas of the Mexican Rain Forest,* by Victor Perera and Robert D. Bruce; and *The Blood of Kings: Dynasty & Ritual in Maya Art,* by Linda Schele and Mary Ellen Miller. Mary Miller has also collaborated with Karl Taube to produce a useful glossary-style handbook called *The Gods and Symbols of Ancient Mexico and the Maya.*

A number of fascinating first-hand accounts of the colonial period by some of its most important figures have been translated and published. Of these, the most compelling may be *Letters from Mexico,* by conquistador Hernán Cortés, and *Tears of the Indians,* an unsparing account of Spanish brutality toward the native population by the outspoken Catholic priest Bartolomé de las Casas.

For decades, the standard texts written by scholars for popular audiences have been *A History of Mexico,* by Henry B. Parkes; *Many Mexicos,* by Lesley Byrd Simpson; and *A Compact History of Mexico,* an anthology published by the Colegio de México. Michael C. Meyer and William L. Sherman's *The Course of Mexican History* and Eric Wolf's *Sons of the Shaking Earth* are also good survey works.

Contemporary Mexico

Jorge Castañeda's 1995 *The Mexican Shock* is an important study of the financial and political crisis in Mexico and its ramifications for United States–Mexico relations. His previous works, *Utopia Unarmed* and, with American political scientist Robert A. Pastor, *Limits to Friendship: The United States and Mexico,* are also excellent resources. A number of journalists have made important contributions to the literature on historical and contemporary Mexico: Alan Riding's *Distant Neighbors: A Portrait of the Mexicans* and Jonathan Kandell's *La Capital: The Biography of Mexico City* are both notable. Elena Poniatowska, better known in the English-speaking world for her fiction, is one of Mexico's most highly respected journalists. *Massacre in Mexico,* her account of government repression of a demonstration in Mexico City in 1968, is an enlightening and disturbing work. More academic works on Mexico's modern history include Hector Aguila Camín's *In the Shadow of the Mexican Revolution,* Roderic A. Camp's *Politics in Mexico,* and Merilee Grindle's *Bureaucrats, Politicians and Peasants in Mexico.*

Culture/Ethnography

Excellent ethnographies include Oscar Lewis's classic works on the culture of poverty, *The Children of Sanchez* and *Five Families*; *Juan the Chamula,* by Ricardo Pozas, about a small village in Chiapas; *Mexico South: The Isthmus of Tehuantepec,* by Miguel Covarrubias, which discusses Indian life in the early 20th century; Gertrude Blom's *Bearing Witness,* on the Lacandones of Chiapas; and *Maria Sabina: Her Life and Chants,* an autobiography of a shaman in the state of Oaxaca.

Food

Perhaps one of the most unusual and delightful books published on Mexican cookery in recent years is *Recipe of Memory: Five Generations of Mexican Cuisine* (New Press, 1995). Written by Pulitzer Prize–winning food journalist Victor Valle and his wife, Mary Lau Valle, this book reproduces recipes the couple found in an antique chest passed down through the Valle family and in the process weaves an intriguing family and social history. Two lushly photographed cookbooks capturing the culinary history and culture of Mexico are Patricia Quintana's *The Taste of Mexico* (Stewart, Tabori & Chang, 1993) and *Mexico the Beautiful Cookbook* (HarperCollins, 1991). Diane Kennedy's culinary works are also popular; one is *The Art of Mexican Cooking* (Bantam, 1989).

Travelogues

Two of the more straightforward accounts from the early 19th century are the letters of Frances Calderón de la Barca, *Life in Mexico,* and John Lloyd Stephens's *Incidents of Travel in Central America, Chiapas and Yucatán.* Foreign journalists have described life in Mexico during and after the revolution: John Reed, *Insurgent Mexico*; John Kenneth Turner, *Barbarous Mexico*; Aldous Huxley, *Beyond the Mexique Bay*; and Graham Greene, *The Lawless Roads,* a superbly written narrative about Tabasco and Chiapas, which served as the basis for *The Power and the Glory.* In much the same vein, but more contemporary, are works by Patrick Marnham (*So Far from God*), about Central America and Mexico, and Hugh Fleetwood, whose *A Dangerous Place* is informative despite its cantankerousness. Alice Adams's 1991 *Mexico: Some Travels and Some Travelers There,* which includes an introduction by Jan Morris, is available in paperback; James A. Michener's 1992 novel, *Mexico,* captures the history of the land and the personality of the people. Probably the finest travelogue-cum-guidebook is Kate Simon's *Mexico: Places and Pleasures.*

Modern Literature in Translation

Poet-philosopher Octavio Paz is the reigning dean of Mexican intellectuals. His best works are *Labyrinth of Solitude,* a thoughtful, far-reaching dissection of Mexican culture, and the biography of Sor Juana Inés de la Cruz, a 17th-century nun and poet. For more on Sor Juana, including her own writings, see Alan Trueblood's *A Sor Juana Anthology.* Other top authors include Carlos Fuentes (*The Death of Artemio Cruz* and *The Old Gringo* are some of his most popular novels), Juan Rulfo (his classic is *Pedro Páramo*), Jorge Ibarguengoitia, Elena Poniatowska (*Dear Diego* and *Fleur de Lis,* among others), Rosario Castellanos (*The Nine Guardians* and *City of Kings*), Elena Garros (*Recollections of Things to Come*), Gregorio López y Fuentes (*El Indio*), Angeles Mastretta (*Mexican Bolero*), and José Emilio Pacheco (*Battles in the Desert and Other Stories*). Recent biographies of the artist couple Frida Kahlo and Diego Rivera (by Hayden Herrera and Bertram D. Wolfe, respectively) provide glimpses into the Mexican intellectual and political life of the '20s and '30s. Laura Esquivel's novel-cum-cookbook, *Like Water for Chocolate,* captures the passions and palates of Mexico during the revolution.

Foreign Literature

D. H. Lawrence's *The Plumed Serpent* is probably the best-known foreign novel about Mexico, although its noble savage theme is considered slightly offensive today. Lawrence recorded his travels in Oaxaca in *Mornings in Mexico.* A far greater piece of literature is Malcolm Lowry's *Under the Volcano.* The mysterious recluse B. Traven, whose fame rests largely on his *Treasure of the Sierra Madre,* wrote brilliantly and passionately about Mexico in *Rebellion of the Hanged* and *The Bridge in the Jungle.* Also noteworthy is John Steinbeck's *The Sea of Cortez.*

SPANISH VOCABULARY

Note: *Mexican Spanish differs from Castilian Spanish.*

Words and Phrases

Basics

English	*Spanish*	*Pronunciation*
Yes/no	Sí/no	see/no
Please	Por favor	pore fah-*vore*
May I?	¿Me permite?	may pair-*mee*-tay
Thank you (very much)	(Muchas) gracias	(*moo*-chas) *grah*-see-as
You're welcome	De nada	day *nah*-dah
Excuse me	Con permiso	con pair-*mee*-so
Pardon me/what did you say?	¿Como?/Mánde?	ko-mo/mahn-dey
Could you tell me?	¿Podría decirme?	po-*dree*-ah deh-*seer*-meh
I'm sorry	Lo siento	lo see-*en*-toe
Good morning!	¡Buenos días!	*bway*-nohs *dee*-ahs
Good afternoon!	¡Buenas tardes!	*bway*-nahs *tar*-dess
Good evening!	¡Buenas noches!	*bway*-nahs *no*-chess
Goodbye!	¡Adiós!/¡Hasta luego!	ah-dee-*ohss*/*ah*-stah -*lwe*-go
Mr./Mrs.	Señor/Señora	sen-*yor*/sen-*yore*-ah
Miss	Señorita	sen-yo-*ree*-tah
Pleased to meet you	Mucho gusto	*moo*-cho *goose*-to
How are you?	¿Cómo está usted?	*ko*-mo es-*tah* oo-*sted*
Very well, thank you.	Muy bien, gracias.	*moo*-ee bee-*en*, grah-see-as
And you?	¿Y usted?	ee oos-*ted*
Hello (on the telephone)	Bueno	*bwen*-oh

Numbers

1	un, uno	oon, *oo*-no
2	dos	dos
3	tres	trace
4	cuatro	*kwah*-tro
5	cinco	*sink*-oh
6	seis	sace
7	siete	see-*et*-ey
8	ocho	*o*-cho
9	nueve	new-*ev*-ay
10	diez	dee-*es*
11	once	*own*-sey
12	doce	*doe*-sey
13	trece	*tray*-sey
14	catorce	kah-*tor*-sey
15	quince	*keen*-sey
16	dieciséis	dee-es-ee-*sace*
17	diecisiete	dee-*es*-ee-see-*et*-ay
18	dieciocho	dee-*es*-ee-*o*-cho
19	diecinueve	*dee-es*-ee-new-*ev*-ay
20	veinte	*bain*-tay
21	veinte y uno/veintiuno	*bain*-te-oo-no

30	treinta	*train*-tah
32	treinta y dos	train-tay-*dose*
40	cuarenta	kwah-*ren*-tah
43	cuarenta y tres	kwah-*ren*-tay-*trace*
50	cincuenta	seen-*kwen*-tah
54	cincuenta y cuatro	seen-*kwen*-tay *kwah*-tro
60	sesenta	sess-*en*-tah
65	sesenta y cinco	sess-*en*-tay *seen*-ko
70	setenta	set-*en*-tah
76	setenta y seis	set-*en*-tay *sace*
80	ochenta	oh-*chen*-tah
87	ochenta y siete	oh-*chen*-tay see-*yet*-ay
90	noventa	no-*ven*-tah
98	noventa y ocho	no-*ven*-tah *o*-cho
100	cien	see-*en*
101	ciento uno	see-en-toe *oo*-no
200	doscientos	doe-see-*en*-tohss
500	quinientos	keen-*yen*-tohss
700	setecientos	set-eh-see-*en*-tohss
900	novecientos	no-veh-see-*en*-tohss
1,000	mil	meel
2,000	dos mil	dose meel
1,000,000	un millón	oon meel-*yohn*

Colors

black	negro	*neh*-grow
blue	azul	ah-*sool*
brown	café	kah-*feh*
green	verde	*vair*-day
pink	rosa	*ro*-sah
purple	morado	mo-*rah*-doe
orange	naranja	na-*rahn*-hah
red	rojo	*roe*-hoe
white	blanco	*blahn*-koh
yellow	amarillo	ah-mah-*ree*-yoh

Days of the Week

Sunday	domingo	doe-*meen*-goh
Monday	lunes	*loo*-ness
Tuesday	martes	*mahr*-tess
Wednesday	miércoles	me-*air*-koh-less
Thursday	jueves	who-*ev*-ess
Friday	viernes	vee-*air*-ness
Saturday	sábado	*sah*-bah-doe

Months

January	enero	eh-*neh*-ro
February	febrero	feh-*brair*-oh
March	marzo	*mahr*-so
April	abril	ah-*breel*
May	mayo	*my*-oh
June	junio	*hoo*-nee-oh
July	julio	*who*-lee-yoh
August	agosto	ah-*ghost*-toe
September	septiembre	sep-tee-*em*-breh
October	octubre	oak-*too*-breh
November	noviembre	no-vee-*em*-breh
December	diciembre	dee-see-*em*-breh

Useful Phrases

Do you speak English?	¿Habla usted inglés?	*ah*-blah oos-*ted* in-*glehs*
I don't speak Spanish	No hablo español	no *ah*-blow es-pahn-*yol*
I don't understand (you)	No entiendo	no en-tee-*en*-doe
I understand (you)	Entiendo	en-tee-*en*-doe
I don't know	No sé	no *say*
I am American/ British	Soy americano(a)/ inglés(a)	soy ah-meh-ree-*kah*-no(ah)/ in-*glace*(ah)
What's your name?	¿Cómo se llama usted?	*koh*-mo say *yah*-mah oos-*ted*
My name is . . .	Me llamo . . .	may *yah*-moh
What time is it?	¿Qué hora es?	keh *o*-rah es
It is one, two, three . . . o'clock.	Es la una; son las dos, tres	es la *oo*-nah/sone lahs dose, trace
Yes, please/No, thank you	Sí, por favor/No, gracias	*see* pore fah-*vor*/no *grah*-see-us
How?	¿Cómo?	*koh*-mo
When?	¿Cuándo?	*kwahn*-doe
This/Next week	Esta semana/ la semana que entra	*es*-tah seh-*mah*-nah/lah say-*mah*-nah keh *en*-trah
This/Next month	Este mes/el próximo mes	*es*-tay mehs/el *proke*-see-mo mehs
This/Next year	Este año/el año que viene	*es*-tay *ahn*-yo/el *ahn*-yo keh vee-*yen*-ay
Yesterday/today/ tomorrow	Ayer/hoy/mañana	ah-*yair*/oy/mahn-*yah*-nah
This morning/ afternoon	Esta mañana/tarde	*es*-tah mahn-*yah*-nah/*tar*-day
Tonight	Esta noche	*es*-tah *no*-cheh
What?	¿Qué?	keh
What is it?	¿Qué es esto?	keh es *es*-toe
Why?	¿Por qué?	pore *keh*
Who?	¿Quién?	kee-*yen*
Where is . . . ?	¿Dónde está . . . ?	*dohn*-day es-*tah*
the train station?	la estación del tren?	la es-tah-see-*on* del *train*
the subway station?	la estación del Metro?	la es-ta-see-*on* del *meh*-tro
the bus stop?	la parada del autobús?	la pah-*rah*-dah del oh-toe-*boos*
the post office?	la oficina de correos?	la oh-fee-*see*-nah day koh-*reh*-os
the bank?	el banco?	el *bahn*-koh
the . . . hotel?	el hotel . . . ?	el oh-*tel*
the store?	la tienda . . . ?	la tee-*en*-dah

the cashier? the . . . museum? the hospital? the elevator? the bathroom?	la caja? el museo . . . ? el hospital? el ascensor? el baño?	la *kah*-hah el moo-*seh*-oh el ohss-pea-*tal* el ah-*sen*-sore el *bahn*-yoh
Here/there	Aquí/allá	ah-*key*/ah-*yah*
Open/closed	Abierto/cerrado	ah-be-*er*-toe/ ser-*ah*-doe
Left/right	Izquierda/derecha	iss-key-*er*-dah/ dare-*eh*-chah
Straight ahead	Derecho	der-*eh*-choh
Is it near/far?	¿Está cerca/lejos?	es-*tah sair*-kah/ *leh*-hoss
I'd like . . . a room the key a newspaper a stamp	Quisiera . . . un cuarto/una habitación la llave un periódico un timbre de correo	kee-see-air-ah oon *kwahr*-toe/ *oo*-nah ah-bee- tah-see-*on* lah *yah*-vay oon pear-ee-*oh*- dee-koh oon *team*-bray day koh-*reh*-oh
I'd like to buy . . . cigarettes matches a dictionary soap a map a magazine paper envelopes a postcard	Quisiera comprar . . . cigarrillo cerillos un diccionario jabón un mapa una revista papel sobres una tarjeta postal	kee-see-*air*-ah kohm-*prahr* ce-gar-*reel*-oh ser-*ee*-ohs oon deek-see-oh- *nah*-ree-oh hah-*bone* oon *mah*-pah *oon*-ah reh-*veess*-tah pah-*pel* *so*-brace *oon*-ah tar-*het*-ah post-*ahl*
How much is it?	¿Cuánto cuesta?	*kwahn*-toe *kwes*-tah
It's expensive/ cheap	Está caro/barato	es-*tah kah*-roh/ bah-*rah*-toe
A little/a lot	Un poquito/ mucho . . .	oon poh-*kee*-toe/ *moo*-choh
More/less	Más/menos	mahss/*men*-ohss
Enough/too much/too little	Suficiente/de- masiado/muy poco	soo-fee-see-*en*-tay/ day-mah-see-*ah*- doe/*moo*-ee *poh*-koh
Telephone	Teléfono	tel-*ef*-oh-no
Telegram	Telegrama	teh-leh-*grah*-mah
I am ill/sick	Estoy enfermo(a)	es-*toy* en-*fair*-moh(ah)
Please call a doctor	Por favor llame un médico	pore fa-*vor ya*-may oon *med*-ee-koh
Help!	¡Auxilio! ¡Ayuda!	owk-*see*-lee-oh/ ah-*yoo*-dah

Fire!	¡Encendio!	en-*sen*-dee-oo
Caution!/Look out!	¡Cuidado!	kwee-*dah*-doh

On the Road

Highway	Carretera	car-ray-*ter*-ah
Causeway, paved highway	Calzada	cal-*za*-dah
Route	Ruta	*roo*-tah
Road	Camino	cah-*mee*-no
Street	Calle	*cah*-yeh
Avenue	Avenida	ah-ven-*ee*-dah
Broad, tree-lined boulevard	Paseo	pah-*seh*-oh
Waterfront promenade	Malecón	mal-lay-*cone*
Wharf	Embarcadero	em-bar-cah-*day*-ro

In Town

Church	Templo/Iglesia	*tem*-plo/e-*gles*-se-*ah*
Cathedral	Catedral	cah-tay-*dral*
Neighborhood	Barrio	*bar*-re-o
Foreign exchange shop	Casa de cambio	*cas*-sah day *cam*-be-o
City hall	Ayuntamiento	ah-yoon-tah-mee *en*-toe
Main square	Zócalo	*zo*-cal-o
Traffic circle	Glorieta	glor-e-*ay*-tah
Market	Mercado (Spanish)/ Tianguis (Indian)	mer-*cah*-doe/ tee-*an*-geese
Inn	Posada	pos-*sah*-dah
Group taxi	Colectivo	co-lec-*tee*-vo
Group taxi along fixed route	Pesero	pi-*seh*-ro

Items of Clothing

Embroidered white smock	Huipil	whee-*peel*
Pleated man's shirt worn outside the pants	Guayabera	gwah-ya-*beh*-ra
Leather sandals	Huaraches	wah-*ra*-chays
Shawl	Rebozo	ray-*bozh*-o
Pancho or blanket	Serape	seh-*ra*-peh

Dining Out

A bottle of . . .	Una botella de . . .	*oo*-nah bo-*tay*-yah deh
A cup of . . .	Una taza de . . .	*oo*-nah *tah*-sah deh

A glass of . . .	Un vaso de . . .	oon *vah*-so deh
Ashtray	Un cenicero	oon sen-ee-*seh*-roh
Bill/check	La cuenta	lah *kwen*-tah
Bread	El pan	el pahn
Breakfast	El desayuno	el day-sigh-*oon*-oh
Butter	La mantequilla	lah mahn-tay-*key*-yah
Cheers!	¡Salud!	sah-*lood*
Cocktail	Un aperitivo	oon ah-pair-ee-*tee*-voh
Dinner	La cena	lah *seh*-nah
Dish	Un plato	oon *plah*-toe
Dish of the day	El platillo de hoy	el plah-*tee*-yo day oy
Enjoy!	¡Buen provecho!	bwen pro-*veh*-cho
Fixed-price menu	La comida corrida	lah koh-*me*-dah co-*ree*-dah
Fork	El tenedor	el ten-eh-*door*
Is the tip included?	¿Está incluida la propina?	es-*tah* in-clue-*ee*-dah lah pro-*pea*-nah
Knife	El cuchillo	el koo-*chee*-yo
Lunch	La comida	lah koh-*me*-dah
Menu	La carta	lah *cart*-ah
Napkin	La servilleta	lah sair-vee-*yet*-uh
Pepper	La pimienta	lah pea-me-*en*-tah
Please give me	Por favor déme	pore fah-*vor day*-may
Salt	La sal	lah sahl
Spoon	Una cuchara	*oo*-nah koo-*chah*-rah
Sugar	El azúcar	el ah-*sue*-car
Waiter!/Waitress!	¡Por favor Señor/Señorita!	pore fah-*vor* sen-*yor*/sen-yor-*ee*-tah

INDEX

✕ = restaurant, 🏨 = hotel